Lecture Notes in Computer Science 6199

Commenced Publication in 1973
Founding and Former Series Editors:
Gerhard Goos, Juris Hartmanis, and Jan van Leeuw

Advanced Research in Computing and Software Science

Subline of Lectures Notes in Computer Science

Samson Abramsky
Cyril Gavoille
Claude Kirchner
Friedhelm Meyer auf der Heide
Paul G. Spirakis (Eds.)

Automata, Languages and Programming

37th International Colloquium, ICALP 2010
Bordeaux, France, July 6-10, 2010
Proceedings, Part II

Springer

Volume Editors

Samson Abramsky
Oxford University Computing Laboratory
Wolfson Building, Parks Road, Oxford OX1 3QD, UK
E-mail: samson.abramsky@comlab.ox.ac.uk

Cyril Gavoille
Université de Bordeaux (LaBRI) & INRIA
351, cours de la Libération, 33405 Talence Cedex, France
E-mail: gavoille@labri.fr

Claude Kirchner
INRIA, Centre de Recherche Bordeaux – Sud-Ouest
351 cours de la Libération, 33405 Talence Cedex, France
E-mail: claude.kirchner@inria.fr

Friedhelm Meyer auf der Heide
Heinz Nixdorf Institute, University of Paderborn
Fürstenallee 11, 33102 Paderborn, Germany
E-mail: fmadh@upb.de

Paul G. Spirakis
University of Patras and RACTI
26500 Patras, Greece
E-mail: spirakis@cti.gr

Library of Congress Control Number: 2010929577

CR Subject Classification (1998): C.2, F.2, D.2, H.4, F.1, E.1

LNCS Sublibrary: SL 1 – Theoretical Computer Science and General Issues

ISSN 0302-9743
ISBN-10 3-642-14161-7 Springer Berlin Heidelberg New York
ISBN-13 978-3-642-14161-4 Springer Berlin Heidelberg New York

springer.com

Printed in Germany

Typesetting: Camera-ready by author, data conversion by Scientific Publishing Services, Chennai, India
Printed on acid-free paper 06/3180

Preface

ICALP 2010, the 37th edition of the International Colloquium on Automata, Languages and Programming was held July 6-10, 2010 in Bordeaux, France. ICALP is a series of annual conference of the European Association for Theoretical Computer Science (EATCS) which first took place in 1972, organized by Maurice Nivat and his colleagues in Paris. This year, the program consisted of the established track A, focusing on Algorithms, Complexity and Games, chaired by Paul G. Spirakis; Track B, focusing on Logic, Semantics, Automata and Theory of Programming, chaired by Samson Abramsky; Track C focusing this year on Foundations of Networked Computation: Models, Algorithms and Information Management, chaired by Friedhelm Meyer auf der Heide.

The three Program Committees received a total of 389 submissions: 222 for Track A, 114 for Track B and 53 for Track C, written by authors from 45 different countries. Of these, 60, 30 and 16, respectively, were selected for inclusion in the scientific program. Each paper got on average 3.5 referee reports.

The Program also included six invited talks by Pierre Fraigniaud (CNRS and Univ. Paris Diderot), Jean Goubault-Larrecq (ENS Cachan and LSV), Burkhard Monien (Univ. Paderborn), Joel Ouaknine (Oxford Univ. Computing Lab.), Roger Wattenhofer (ETH Zurich), and Emo Welzl (ETH Zurich).

These 112 contributed and invited papers are presented in two proceedings volumes. The first contains the contributed papers of Track A and the invited talks of Burkhard Monien and Emo Welzl. The second volume contains the contributed papers of Tracks B and C as well as the invited talks of Pierre Fraigniaud, Jean Goubault-Larrecq, Joel Ouaknine and Roger Wattenhofer.

The day before the main conference, five satellite workshops were held:

- AlgoGT : Workshop on Algorithmic Game Theory: Dynamics and Convergence in Distributed Systems
- DYNAS 2010: International Workshop on DYnamic Networks: Algorithms and Security
- ALGOSENSORS 2010: International Workshop on Algorithmic Aspects of Wireless Sensor Networks
- SDKB 2010: Semantics in Data and Knowledge Bases
- TERA-NET: Towards Evolutive Routing Algorithms for Scale-Free/Internet-Like Networks.

We wish to thank all the authors of submitted papers, all the members of the three Program Committees for their scholarly effort and all 737 referees who assisted the Program Committees in the evaluation process.

We are very pleased to thank INRIA for organizing the conference, LaBRI for their collaboration, and the sponsors (Conseil Rgional d'Aquitaine, Communauté Urbaine de Bordeaux, CEA, CNRS via the GDR IM, Total) for their strong support. We are also very grateful to Ralf Klasing for chairing the workshop organization and to all the members of the Organizing Committee: Laëtitia Grimaldi, Alice Rivière, Nicolas Bonichon, Pierre Casteran, Lionel Eyraud-Dubois and Frédéric Mazoit.

It is also our great pleasure to acknowledge the use of the EasyChair conference management system, which was of tremendous help in handling the submission and refereeing processes as well as in intelligently assisting us in the design of the final proceedings.

May 2010

Samson Abramsky
Cyril Gavoille
Claude Kirchner
Friedhelm Meyer auf der Heide
Paul G. Spirakis

Organization

Conference Chairs

Cyril Gavoille	University of Bordeaux (LaBRI) and INRIA, Bordeaux, France
Claude Kirchner	INRIA, Bordeaux, France

Programme Chairs

Samson Abramsky	Oxford University, UK
Friedhelm Meyer auf der Heide	University of Paderborn, Germany
Paul G. Spirakis	University of Patras and RACTI, Greece

Workshops Chair

Ralf Klasing	CNRS, University of Bordeaux (LaBRI) and INRIA, France

Program Committee

Track A

Dimitris Achlioptas	University of Santa Cruz, USA
Kwstis Daskalakis	MIT, USA
Anuj Dawar	Cambridge University, UK
Xiaotie Deng	City University of Hong Kong, China SAR
Philippe Flajolet	INRIA, France
Michele Flammini	University of L'Aquila, Italy
Oscar Ibarra	UCSB (Santa Barbara), USA
Giuseppe Italiano	University of Rome 2, Italy
Kazuo Iwama	University of Kyoto, Japan
Klaus Jansen	University of Kiel, Germany
Elias Koutsoupias	University of Athens, Greece
Ludek Kucera	Charles University, Czech Republic
Daniel Marx	Budapest University, Hungary
Burkhard Monien	University of Paderborn, Germany
Amin Coja Oghlan	University of Edinburgh, UK
Tonyann Pitassi	University of Toronto, Canada
John Reif	Duke University, USA
Jose Rolim	University of Geneva, Switzerland

Paul G. Spirakis	University of Patras and RACTI, Greece, (Chair)
Leslie Valiant	Harvard University, USA
Emo Welzl	ETH, Switzerland
Gerhard Woeginger	University of Eindhoven, The Netherlands

Track B

Samson Abramsky	Oxford University, UK, (Chair)
Luca Aceto	University of Rejkjavik, Iceland
Lars Birkedal	IT University of Copenhagen, Denmark
Mikolaj Bojanczyk	University of Warsaw, Poland
Patricia Bouyer	CNRS, LSV Cachan, France
Josée Desharnais	University of Laval, Canada
Gilles Dowek	Ecole Polytechnique and INRIA, France
Manfred Droste	University of Leipzig, Germany
Peter Dybjer	University Chalmers, Sweden
Jose Felix Costa	University of Lisbon, Portugal
Phokion Kolaitis	IBM Almaden, USA
Ugo Dal Lago	University of Bologna, Italy
Daniel Leivant	University of Indiana, USA
Andrzej Murawski	Oxford University, UK
Filip Murlak	University of Warsaw, Poland
Flemming Nielsen	University of Copenhagen, Denmark
Dominique Perrin	University of Paris Est, France
Alex Rabinovich	University of Tel Aviv, Israel
Lutz Schröder	DFKI Bremen, Germany
Ian Stark	University of Edinburgh, UK

Track C

Debora Donato	Yahoo! Research Barcelona, Spain
Faith Ellen	University of Toronto, Canada
Phil Gibbons	Intel Research Pittsburgh, USA
Rob van Glabbeek	Stanford University and National ICT Australia
Monika Henzinger	EPFL Lausanne, Switzerland
Christos Kaklamanis	University of Patras, Greece
Fabian Kuhn	MIT, USA
Miroslaw Kutylowski	Wroclaw University of Technology, Poland
Christian Lengauer	University of Passau, Germany
Stefano Leonardi	Sapienza University of Rome, Italy
Friedhelm Meyer auf der Heide	University of Paderborn, Germany, (Chair)
Dusko Pavlovic	Oxford University and Kestrel Institute, UK
Andrzej Pelc	Université du Qubec en Outaouais, Canada
Giuseppe Persiano	University of Salerno, Italy

Organizing Committee

Sponsoring Institutions

CEA (Commissariat à l'énergie atomique et aux énergies alternatives)
Communauté Urbaine de Bordeaux
Conseil Régional d'Aquitaine
GDR Informatique Mathmatique (CNRS)
INRIA
Total

Referees for Tracks B and C

Olivier Carton
Didier Caucal
Karlis Cerans
Krishnendu Chatterjee
Ioannis Chatzigiannakis
Panagiotis Cheilaris
Yijia Chen
Flavio Chierichetti
Jacek Cichon
Miroslav Ciric
Pierre Clairambault
Barry Cooper
Pierluigi Crescenzi
Paolo D'Arco
Ellie D'Hondt
Thao Dang
Varacca Daniele
Anupam Datta
Xiao David
Søren Debois
Stephane Demri
Yuxin Deng
Nachum Dershowitz
Cinzia Di Giusto
Alessandra Di Pierro
Martin Dietzfelbinger
Lucas Dixon
Benjamin Doerr
Laurent Doyen
Marcin Dziubinski
Jeff Egger
Uli Fahrenberg
Alexander Fanghänel
Carlo Fantozzi
Ansgar Fehnker
Amos Fiat
Piotr Filipiuk
Michael Fischer
Tamas Fleiner
Paola Flocchini
Vojtech Forejt
Pierre Fraigniaud
Jonas Frey
Sigurour Freyr Hafstein
Oliver Friedmann
Fabio Gadducci
Stefan Galler
Richard Garner
Paul Gastin
Archis Ghate
Giorgio Ghelli
Hugo Gimbert
Aristides Gionis
Arne Glenstrup
Jens Chr. Godskesen
Sergey Goncharov
Valentin Goranko
Roberto Gorrieri
Fabrizio Grandoni
Serge Grigorieff
Marcus Groesser
Martin Grohe
Helia Guerra
Peter Habermehl
Serge Haddad
Matthew Hague
Bjarni Halldorsson
Sariel Har-Peled
Sariel Har-Peled
Tero Harju
Russ Harmer
Nicholas Harvey
Ichiro Hasuo
Keijo Heljanko
Alejandro Hernandez
Peter Hertling
Peter Hines
Martin Hoefer
Markus Holzer
Richard Holzer
Florian Horn
Marieke Huisman
Dieter Hutter
Tomasz Idziaszek
Jan Jürjens
Aaron D. Jaggard
Emmanuel Jeandel
Mark Jerrum
Aaron Johnson
Steffen Joost
Line Juhl
Marcin Jurdzinski
Tomasz Jurdzinski
Lukasz Kaiser
Florian Kammueller
Panagiotis Kanellopoulos
Christos Kapoutsis
Frank Kargl
Lila Kari
Elham Kashefi
Shiva Kasiviswanathan
Mark Kattenbelt
Tomasz Kazana
Thomas Kesselheim
Marcin Kik
Daniel Kirsten
Felix Klaedtke
Robert Kleinberg
Bartek Klin
Marek Klonowski
Sebastian Kniesburges
Barbara Koenig
Phokion Kolaitis
Leszek Kolodziejczyk
Charalampos Konstantopoulos
Eryk Kopczynski
Dariusz Kowalski
Lukasz Krzywiecki
Manfred Kufleitner
Michal Kunc
Dietrich Kuske
Christof Löding
Salvatore La Torre
Ivan Lanese
Jerome Lang
Slawomir Lasota
Christoph Lath
Axel Legay
Rasmus Lerchedahl Petersen
Jerome Leroux
Lin Liu
Kamal Lodaya

Hugo A. Lopez
Tzvi Lotker
Tomasz Luczak
Rasmus Møgelberg
Christian Maeder
Stephen Magill
Jean Mairesse
Krzysztof Majcher
Rupak Majumdar
Pasquale Malacaria
Andreas Maletti
Adam Malinowski
Sebastian Maneth
Yishai Mansour
Yishai Mansour
Giulio Manzonetto
Maurice Margenstern
Nicolas Markey
Simone Martini
Francisco Martins
Andrea Masini
Paulo Mateus
Marios Mavronicolas
Richard Mayr
Greg McColm
James McDonald
Ingmar Meinecke
Ida Mele
Massimo Merro
Antoine Meyer
Henryk Michalewski
Jakub Michaliszyn
Avery Miller
Alan Mislove
Michael Mitzenmacher
Remi Morin
Christophe Morvan
Larry Moss
Madhavan Mukund
Toby Murray
Sebastian Nanz
Mark-Jan Nederhof
Martin Neuhauaer
Frank Neven
Joachim Niehren
Ulrik Nyman
Jan Obdrzalek
Marcel Ochel
Jose Oliveira
Luke Ong
Joel Ouaknine
Luca Padovani
Catuscia Palamidessi
Jens Palsberg
Prakash Panangaden
Evi Papaioannou
Joachim Parrow
Madhusudan Parthasarathy
Francesco Pasquale
Dirk Pattinson
Parys Pawel
Mikkel Larsen Pedersen
Paolo Penna
Enoch Peserico
Eudes Petonnet
Ion Petre
Laure Petrucci
Alberto Pettarin
Seth Pettie
Andrea Pietracaprina
Henrik Pilegaard
Jean-Eric Pin
Nir Piterman
Cinzia Pizzi
Thomas Place
Wojciech Plandowski
Christina Poepper
Randy Pollack
Christian W Probst
Gabriele Puppis
Sergio Rajsbaum
Steven Ramsay
Joao Rasga
António Ravara
Laurent Regnier
Rogério Reis
Juan Reutter
Mark Reynolds
Hanne Riis Nielson
Giuseppina Rindone
Markus Roggenbach
Bill Roscoe
Gianluca Rossi
Eric Ruppert
Jan Rutten
Wojciech Rytter
Amin Saberi
Joshua Sack
Kai Salomaa
Arnaud Sangnier
Zdenek Sawa
Henning Schnoor
Ulrich Schoepp
Florian Schoppmann
Robert Schweller
Michele Scquizzato
Michael Segal
Michael Segal
Peter Selinger
Geraud Senizergues
Olivier Serre
Peter Sestoft
Aneesh Sharma
Pedro V. Silva
Jakob Grue Simonsen
Alexander Skopalik
Nataliya Skrypnyuk
Geoffrey Smith
Michael Smith
Pawel Sobocinski
Ana Sokolova
Mariya Soskova
Jiri Srba
Mike Stannett
Sam Staton
Benjamin Steinberg
Darren Strash
Howard Straubing
Lutz Struengmann
Kohei Suenaga
Eijiro Sumii
Tony Tan
Qiang Tang
Eva Tardos

Nadia Tawbi
Balder ten Cate
Jacob Thamsborg
Mikkel Thorup
Srikanta Tirthapura
Stefano Tonetta
Szymon Toruńczyk
Ashutosh Trivedi
Angelo Troina
Mirek Truszczynski
Tobias Tscheuschner
Nikos Tzevelekos
Frank Valencia
Benoit Valiron
Franck van Breugel
Benno van den Berg
Vasco T. Vasconcelos
Carmine Ventre
Stephane Vialette
Ignacio Viglizzo
Ivan Visconti
Andrea Vitaletti
Heiko Vogler
Tomas Vojnar
Bogdan Warinschi
Andrzej Wasowski
Ingmar Weber
Pascal Weil
Rafael Wisniewski
James Worrell
Francesco Zappa Nardelli
Marcin Zawada
Konrad Zdanowski
Szymon Zeberski
Fuyuan Zhang
Lijun Zhang
Pawel Zielinski

Table of Contents – Part II

Invited Talks

Session 1-Track B. Automata

Session 1-Track C. Communication in Networks

Session 2-Track B. Formal Languages

Session 4-Track B. Semantics

Session 4-Track C. Fault Tolerance, Ranking

Session 5-Track B. Graphs, Categories and Quantum Information

Session 6-Track B. Best Paper Award

Session 6-Track C. Best Paper Award

Session 7-Track B. Logic

Session 7-Track C. Privacy, Selfishness

Session 8-Track B. Concurrency

Session 8-Track C. Mobile Agents

Session 9-Track B. Probabilistic Computation

Session 10-Track B. Automata

Table of Contents – Part I

Invited Talks

Session 1-Track A. Combinatorial Optimization

Session 2-Track A1. Game Theory

Session 2-Track A2. Security

Session 3-Track A1. Data Structures

Session 3-Track A2. Sorting & Hashing

Session 4-Track A. Graphs, Nets and Optimization

Session 5-Track A1. Scheduling

Session 5-Track A2. Graphs & Hypergraphs

Session 6-Track A. Best Paper Award

Session 7-Track A. Algebraic Problems

Session 8-Track A. Networks & Communication Complexity

Session 9-Track A1. Complexity & Automata

Session 9-Track A2. Finding & Testing

Session 10-Track A1. Approximations

Session 10-Track A2. Streaming & Preprocessing

Session 11-Track A1. Adaptive, Knowledge & Optimality

Session 11-Track A2. Covering, Graphs & Independence

Informative Labeling Schemes

Pierre Fraigniaud

CNRS and University Paris Diderot
France
Pierre.Fraigniaud@liafa.jussieu.fr

Abstract. Network representations play an important role in many domains of computer science, ranging from data structures and graph algorithms, to parallel and distributed computing, and communication networks. Traditional network representations are usually global in nature. That is, in order to retrieve useful information, one must access a global data structure representing the entire network, even if the desired information is solely local, pertaining to only a few nodes. In contrast, the notion of informative labeling schemes suggests the use of a local representation of the network. The principle is to associate a label with each node, selected in a way that enables to infer information about any two nodes directly from their labels, without using any additional sources of information. Hence in essence, this method bases the entire representation on the set of labels alone. Obviously, labels of unrestricted size can be used to encode any desired information, including in particular the entire graph structure. The focus is thus on informative labeling schemes which use labels as short as possible. This talk will introduce the notion of informative labeling scheme to the audience, and will survey some of the important results achieved in this context. In particular, we will focus on the design of compact adjacency-, ancestry-, routing-, and distance-labeling schemes for trees. These schemes find applications in various contexts, including the design of small universal graphs, and the design of small universal posets.

S. Abramsky et al. (Eds.): ICALP 2010, Part II, LNCS 6199, p. 1, 2010.

Noetherian Spaces in Verification

Jean Goubault-Larrecq

Preuves, Programmes et Systèmes, UMR 7126, CNRS and University Paris Diderot
LSV, ENS Cachan, CNRS, INRIA

Abstract. Noetherian spaces are a topological concept that generalizes well quasi-orderings. We explore applications to infinite-state verification problems, and show how this stimulated the search for infinite procedures à la Karp-Miller.

1 Introduction

The purpose of this paper is to given a gentle introduction to the theory of Noetherian spaces, in the context of verification of infinite-state systems.

Now such a statement can be intimidating, all the more so as Noetherian spaces originate in algebraic geometry [20, chapitre 0]. Their use there lies in the fact that the Zariski topology of a Noetherian ring is Noetherian.

My purpose is to stress the fact that Noetherian spaces are merely a topological generalization of the well-known concept of *well quasi-orderings*, a remark that I made in [19] for the first time. Until now, this led me into two avenues of research.

The first avenue consists in adapting, in the most straightforward way, the theory of *well-structured transition systems* (WSTS) [1,4,16,21] to more general spaces. WSTS include such important examples as Petri nets and extensions, and lossy channel systems. After some technical preliminaries in Section 2, I will describe the basic theory of Noetherian spaces in Section 3. This leads to a natural generalization of WSTS called *topological WSTS*, which I will describe in Section 4.

In [19], I described a few constructions that preserve Noetherianness. We shall give a more complete catalog in Section 3: $\mathbb{N}^k$, Σ^* and in general every well-quasi-ordered set, but several others as well, including some that *do not* arise from well-quasi-orders.

We apply this to the verification of two kinds of systems that are *not* WSTS. We do not mean these to be any more than toy applications, where decidability occurs as a natural byproduct of our constructions. I certainly do not mean to prove any new, sophisticated decidability result for some realistic application in verification, for which we should probably exert some more effort. I only hope to convince the reader that the theory of Noetherian spaces shows some potential.

The first application, *oblivious stack systems*, are k-stack pushdown automata in which one cannot remember which letter was popped from a stack: see Section 5. The second one, *polynomial games*, is an extension of Müller-Olm and Seidl's static analysis of so-called polynomial programs [29] to games played between two players that can compute on real and complex numbers using addition, subtraction, multiplication, and (dis)equality tests: see Section 6, where we also consider the case of lossy *concurrent* polynomial games, i.e., networks of machines running polynomial programs and which communicate through lossy signaling channels.

S. Abramsky et al. (Eds.): ICALP 2010, Part II, LNCS 6199, pp. 2–21, 2010.

The second avenue of research has led Alain Finkel and myself to make significant progress in designing extensions of the Karp-Miller coverability algorithm to other WSTS than just Petri nets or even counter machines. I will say a bit more in Section 7. This line of research stemmed from the remarkable relationship between the concepts of Noetherianness and of sobriety, which I will explain. It is fair to say that the results obtained with A. Finkel could be proved without any recourse to Noetherian spaces. But the decisive ideas come from topology, and in particular from the important role played by *irreducible* closed sets in Noetherian spaces.

2 Technical Preliminaries

A well quasi-ordering (*wqo*) is a quasi-ordering (a reflexive and transitive relation) that is not only well-founded, i.e., has no infinite descending chain, but also has no infinite antichain (a set of incomparable elements). An alternative definition is: $\leq$ is a wqo on X iff every sequence $(x_n)_{n\in\mathbb{N}}$ in X contains a pair of elements such that $x_i \leq x_j$, $i < j$. Yet another equivalent definition is: $\leq$ is wqo iff every sequence $(x_n)_{n\in\mathbb{N}}$ has a non-decreasing subsequence $x_{i_0} \leq x_{i_1} \leq \ldots \leq x_{i_k} \leq \ldots$, $i_0 < i_1 < \ldots < i_k < \ldots$

WSTS. One use of well quasi-orderings is in verifying *well-structured transition systems*, a.k.a. *WSTS* [1,4,16,21]. These are transition systems, usually infinite-state, with two ingredients. (For simplicity, we shall consider *strongly monotonic* well-structured transition systems only.)

First, there is a *well* quasi-ordering $\leq$ on the set X of states. Second, the transition relation δ commutes with $\leq$, i.e., if $x \;\delta\; y$ and $x \leq x'$, then there is a state y' such that $x' \;\delta\; y'$ and $y \leq y'$:

$$\begin{array}{ccc} x & \xrightarrow{\leq} & x' \\ \delta\downarrow & & \downarrow\delta \\ y & \xrightarrow{\leq} & y' \end{array} \qquad (1)$$

Examples include Petri nets [34] and their extensions, reset/transfer Petri nets for example, in general all affine counter systems [15], the close concept of VASS [23], BVASS [37,11], lossy channel systems [3], datanets [26], certain process algebras [7]; and some problems, such as those related to timed Petri nets [5] admit elegant solutions by reduction to an underlying WSTS.

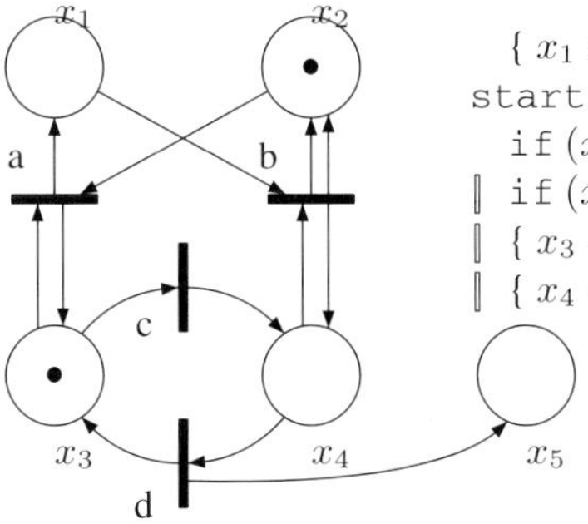


```
  { x1 = x4 = x5 = 0; x2 = x3 = 1; };                    // init
start:
  if (x3 >= 1) { x2 --; x1 ++; goto start; }             // a
[] if (x4 >= 1) { x1 --; x2 += 2; goto start; }          // b
[] { x3 --; x4 ++; goto start; }                         // c
[] { x4 --; x3 ++; x5 ++; goto start; }                  // d
```

Fig. 1. A Petri Net

We illustrate the concept using Petri nets. I won't define what Petri nets are exactly. Look at Figure 1, left, for an example. This is a net with 5 *places* x_1, …, x_5, each containing a certain number of *tokens* (shown as bullets): the initial state is shown, with one token in places x_2 and x_3, and none anywhere else. Petri nets run by firing *transitions*, shown as black bars |. Doing so means, for each incoming arrow ○→|, remove one token from the source place ○, and for each outgoing arrow |→○, add one token to the target place. This can only be done provided there are enough tokens in the source places. E.g., transition a can only fire provided there is at least one token in x_2 and at least one token in x_3 (which is the case in the initial state shown in the figure), will remove one from x_2 and one from x_3, then put back one into x_3 and put one into x_1. The net effect of transition a is therefore to *move* one token from x_2 to x_1, *provided* there is at least one token in x_3. If we agree to use a variable x_i to hold the current number of tokens in place x_i, a C-like notation for this is `if` $(x_3 \geq 1)$ { $x_2 - -;\ x_1 + +;$ }, as we have shown on the right-hand side of the figure.

In general, Petri nets are just another way of writing *counter machines without zero test*, i.e., programs that operate on finitely many variables $x_1, \ldots, x_k$ containing natural numbers; the allowed operations are adding and subtracting constants from them, as well as testing whether $x_i \geq c$ for some constants c. The general counter machines also offer the possibility of testing whether x_i equals 0. Crucially, Petri nets do not allow for such zero tests. This makes a difference, as reachability and coverability (see later) is undecidable for general counter machines [28], but decidable for Petri nets [34].

Let us check that Petri nets define WSTS. Consider a Petri net with k places x_1, …, x_k. The states, also called *markings*, are tuples $\boldsymbol{n} = (n_1, \ldots, n_k) \in \mathbb{N}^k$, where n_i counts the number of tokens in place x_i. The state space is $\mathbb{N}^k$. Order this by the canonical, pointwise ordering: $(n_1, \ldots, n_k) \leq (n'_1, \ldots, n_k)$ iff $n_1 \leq n'_1$ and … and $n_k \leq n'_k$. This is wqo by *Dickson's Lemma*, whose proof can be safely left to the reader (reason componentwise, observing that $\mathbb{N}$ is itself well-quasi-ordered).

The transitions are each given by a pair of constant vectors $\boldsymbol{a}, \boldsymbol{b} \in \mathbb{N}^k$: we have $\boldsymbol{n}\ \delta\ \boldsymbol{n}'$ iff $\boldsymbol{a} \leq \boldsymbol{n}$ and $\boldsymbol{n}' = \boldsymbol{n} - \boldsymbol{a} + \boldsymbol{b}$ for one of the transitions. For example, transition a in Figure 1 can be specified by taking $\boldsymbol{a} = (0, 1, 1, 0, 0)$ and $\boldsymbol{b} = (1, 0, 1, 0, 0)$. It is easy to see that Diagram (1) holds. Indeed, if some transition is firable from $\boldsymbol{n}$, then it will remain firable even if we add some tokens to some places, and triggering it will produce a new state with more tokens as well.

The standard backward algorithm for WSTS [4,16]. The *coverability* problem is: given two states x, y, can we reach some state z from x such that $y \leq z$? This is a form of reachability, where we require, not to reach x exactly, but some state in the upward closure $\uparrow x$ of x.

For any subset A of X, let $\mathrm{Pre}^{\exists}\delta(A)$ be the preimage $\{x \in X \mid \exists y \in A \cdot x\ \delta\ y\}$. The commutation property (1) of strongly monotonic systems ensures that the preimage $\mathrm{Pre}^{\exists}\delta(V)$ of any upward closed subset V is again upward closed (V is upward closed iff whenever $x \in V$ and $x \leq x'$, then $x' \in V$). One can then compute $\mathrm{Pre}^{\exists *}\delta(V)$, the set of states in X from which we can reach some state in V in finitely many steps, assuming that upward closed subsets are representable and $\mathrm{Pre}^{\exists}(A)$ is computable from any upward closed subset A: Compute the set V_i of states from which we can reach some state in V in at most i steps, backwards, by $V_0 = V$, $V_{i+1} = V_i \cup \mathrm{Pre}^{\exists}\delta(V_i)$: this stabilizes at some stage i, where $V_i = \mathrm{Pre}^{\exists *}\delta(V)$.

To decide coverability, then, compute $\mathrm{Pre}^{\exists *}\delta(\uparrow y)$, and check whether x is in it.

This is a very simple algorithm. The only subtle point has to do with termination. One notices indeed that $V_0 \subseteq V_1 \subseteq \ldots \subseteq V_i \subseteq \ldots$, and that if the sequence ever stabilizes at stage i, we can detect it by testing whether $V_{i+1} \subseteq V_i$. Now it must stabilize, *because* $\leq$ *is wqo*. Indeed, in a wqo every upward closed subset U must be the upward closure $\uparrow E = \{x \in X \mid \exists y \in E \cdot y \leq x\}$ of some finite set E. (Proof: any element $x \in U$ is above a minimal element in U: start from x and go down until you cannot go further—which must eventually happen since $\leq$ is well-founded. The set E of all minimal elements of U must then be finite since there is no infinite antichain.) In particular, $V_\omega = \bigcup_{i \in \mathbb{N}} V_i$ can be written $\uparrow\{x_1, \ldots, x_n\}$. Each x_j, $1 \leq j \leq n$, must be in some V_{i_j}, so they are all in V_i, where $i = \max(i_1, \ldots, i_n)$: it follows that $V_\omega = V_i$, and we are done.

Noetherian spaces. The idea of [19] lies in replacing order theory by topology, noticing that the role of wqos will be played by Noetherian spaces.

Indeed, topology *generalizes* order theory. (To do so, we shall require topological spaces that are definitely non-Hausdorff, even non-T_1, hence very far from metric spaces or other topological spaces commonly used in mathematics.) Any topological space X indeed carries a quasi-ordering $\leq$ called the *specialization quasi-ordering* of X: $x \leq y$ iff every open neighborhood U of x also contains y. It is fruitful, from a computer science perspective, to understand opens U as *tests*; then $x \leq y$ iff y *simulates* x, i.e., passes all the tests that x passes.

Note that in particular every open U is upward closed in $\leq$, and every closed subset F is downward closed. Similarly, continuous map $f : X \to Y$ are in particular monotonic (the converse fails).

In the opposite direction, there are several topologies on X with a given specialization quasi-ordering $\leq$. The finest one (with the most opens) is the *Alexandroff topology*: its opens are all the upward closed subsets. The coarsest one (with the fewest opens) is the *upper topology*: its closed subsets are all unions of subsets of the form $\downarrow E$ (the downward closure of E), E finite. In between, there are other interesting topologies such as the Scott topology, of great use in domain theory [6].

3 The Basic Theory of Noetherian Spaces

A topological space X is *Noetherian* iff every open subset of X is compact. (I.e., one can extract a finite subcover from any open cover.) Equivalently:

Definition 1. *X is Noetherian iff there is no infinite ascending chain $U_0 \subsetneq U_1 \subsetneq \ldots \subsetneq U_n \subsetneq \ldots$ of opens in X.*

The key fact, showing how Noetherian spaces generalize wqos, is the following [19, Proposition 3.1]: $\leq$ is wqo on the set X iff X, equipped with the Alexandroff topology of $\leq$, is Noetherian. This provides plenty of Noetherian spaces.

It turns out that there are also Noetherian spaces that do not arise from wqos, thus Noetherian spaces provide a strict generalization of wqos. The prime example is $\mathbb{P}(X)$, the infinite powerset of X, with the *lower Vietoris topology*, defined as the coarsest that makes $\Diamond U = \{\{A \in \mathbb{P}(X)$ resp., $\in \mathbb{P}^*(X) \mid A \cap U \neq \emptyset\}$ open for every open subset U of X. When X is a poset, $\mathbb{P}(X)$ is quasi-ordered by the *Hoare quasi-ordering* $\leq^\flat$: $A \leq^\flat B$ iff for every $a \in A$, there is a $b \in B$ such that $a \leq b$. Assuming X wqo, $\mathbb{P}(X)$ is not wqo in general, however it *is* Noetherian in the lower Vietoris topology—which turns out to be the upper topology of $\leq^\flat$ [19, Corollary 7.4]. A related example, in fact almost the same one, is the *Hoare powerdomain* $\mathcal{H}(X)$ of a space X: this is the space of all non-empty (even infinite) closed subsets F of X, with the lower Vietoris topology, namely the upper topology of $\subseteq$. This is one of the powerdomains used in domain theory, and is a model of the so-called *angelic* variant of non-deterministic choice [6]. Then $\mathcal{H}(X)$ is Noetherian as soon as X is [19, Theorem 7.2].

We don't have any practical applications of $\mathbb{P}(X)$ or $\mathcal{H}(X)$ in verification today. We shall give an application of Noetherian spaces in Section 6, where the underlying space is Noetherian, but is not the Alexandroff topology of a wqo. A simpler example is given by Σ^*, the space of all finite words over a finite alphabet Σ, with the upper topology of the prefix ordering $\leq^{\text{pref}}$. We shall see below why this is Noetherian, and shall use it in Section 5. Note that $\leq^{\text{pref}}$ is certainly *not* wqo, as soon as Σ contains at least two letters a and b: b, ab, aab, ..., $a^n b$, ..., is an infinite antichain.

The key insight in the theory of Noetherian spaces is how Noetherianness interacts with *sobriety*. A topological space X is *sober* if and only if every irreducible closed subset C is the closure $\downarrow x$ of a unique point $x \in X$. The closure of a point x is always the downward closure $\downarrow x$ with respect to the specialization quasi-ordering. A closed subset C is *irreducible* iff $C \neq \emptyset$, and whenever C is included in the union of two closed subset, then C must be contained in one of them. For every $x \in X$, it is clear that $\downarrow x$ is irreducible. A sober space has no other irreducible closed subset.

Sober spaces are important in topology and domain theory [6], and are the cornerstone of Stone duality. We refer the reader to [6, Section 7] or to [18, Chapter V] for further information. We shall be content with the following intuitions, which show that sobriety is a form of *completeness*. A space is T_0 iff its specialization quasi-ordering $\leq$ is an ordering, i.e., any two distinct points x, y, can be separated by some open U (think of it as a test that one point passes but not the other one). So a space is T_0 if it has *enough opens* to separate points. A sober space is a T_0 space that also has *enough points*, in the sense that any closed set C that looks like the closure of a point (in the sense that it is irreducible) really is so: $C = \downarrow x$, where necessarily $x = \max C$. Another indication is that, if X is sober, then X is a *dcpo* [6, Proposition 7.2.13]: for every directed family $(x_i)_{i \in I}$, in particular for every chain, the *limit* $\sup_{i \in I} x_i$ exists. So a sober space is complete also in this sense.

Any topological space X can be completed to obtain a sober space $\mathcal{S}(X)$, the *sobrification* of X, which has the same lattice of open subsets (up to isomorphism), and possibly more points. In a sense, we add all missing limits $\sup_{i \in I} x_i$ to X. $\mathcal{S}(X)$ is defined as the collection of all irreducible closed subsets C of X, with the upper topology of $\subseteq$. X is then embedded in $\mathcal{S}(X)$, by equating each point $x \in X$ with $\downarrow x \in \mathcal{S}(X)$.

The first key point about the interaction between sobriety and Noetherianness is that for any space X, X is Noetherian iff $\mathcal{S}(X)$ is Noetherian [19, Proposition 6.2]. This is obvious: X and $\mathcal{S}(X)$ have isomorphic lattices of open sets. Thus, to show that X

is Noetherian, it is enough to show that $\mathcal{S}(X)$ is. The following is the cornerstone of the whole theory, and allows one to check that a sober space is Noetherian by checking simple properties of its specialization quasi-ordering [19, Theorem 6.11]:

Theorem 1 (Fundamental Theorem of Sober Noetherian Spaces). *The sober Noetherian spaces are exactly the spaces whose topology is the upper topology of a well-founded partial order $\leq$ that has properties W and T.*

We say that X has *property W* iff, for every $x, y \in X$, there is a finite subset E of maximal lower bounds of x and y, such that every lower bound of x and y is less than or equal to some element of E; i.e., $\downarrow x \cap \downarrow y = \downarrow E$. Similarly, it has *property T* iff the space X itself is of the form $\downarrow E$, E finite.

This allows us to prove that the product of two Noetherian spaces X, Y is again Noetherian [19, Theorem 6.13]. The specialization quasi-ordering on $\mathcal{S}(X \times Y) \cong \mathcal{S}(X) \times \mathcal{S}(Y)$ is the product ordering, and it is easy to see that the product of two well-founded orderings is again well-founded, and similarly for properties T and W.

Since every wqo is Noetherian, classical spaces such as $\mathbb{N}^k$, or Σ^* with the (Alexandroff topology of the) divisibility ordering (Higman's Lemma [22]), or the set of all ground first-order terms $\mathcal{T}(X)$ (a.k.a., vertex-labeled, finite rooted trees) with tree embedding (Kruskal's Theorem [25]), are Noetherian.

It is natural to ask ourselves whether there are topological version of Higman's Lemma and Kruskal's Theorem. There are indeed, and at least the former case was alluded to in [13, Theorem 5.3]. Let X be a topological space, X^* the space of all finite words on the alphabet X with the *subword topology*, defined as the coarsest one such that $X^*U_1X^*U_2X^* \dots X^*U_nX^*$ is open for every sequence of open subsets U_1, U_2, $\dots$, U_n of X. The specialization quasi-ordering of X^* is the embedding quasi-ordering $\leq^*$, where $w \leq^* w'$ iff one obtains w' from w by increasing some letters and inserting some others, and:

Theorem 2 (Topological Higman Lemma). *If X is Noetherian, then so is X^*.*

One also observes that if X is Alexandroff, then so is X^*. One therefore obtains Higman's Lemma, that $\leq^*$ is wqo as soon as $\leq$ is wqo on X, as a consequence. Thinking of opens as tests, a word passes the test $X^*U_1X^*U_2X^* \dots X^*U_nX^*$ iff it has a length n subword whose letters pass the tests $U_1, \dots, U_n$.

As a corollary, the space $X^{\circledast}$ of all *multisets* of elements of X, with the *sub-multiset* topology, is Noetherian whenever X is. This is the coarsest one that makes open the subsets $X^{\circledast} \odot U_1 \odot U_2 \odot \dots \odot U_n$ of all multisets containing at least one element from U_1, one from U_2, $\dots$, one from U_n, where $U_1, U_2, \dots, U_n$ are open in X. This follows from Theorem 2 because $X^{\circledast}$ is the image of X^* by the *Parikh mapping* $\Psi : X^* \to X^{\circledast}$ that sends each word to its multiset of letters, and because of the easy result that the continuous image of any Noetherian space is again Noetherian.

The way I initially proved Theorem 2 [13, full version, available on the Web, Theorem E.20] is interesting. One first characterizes the irreducible closed subsets of X^* as certain regular expressions, the *word-products* $P = e_1e_2 \dots e_n$, where each e_i is an *atomic expression*, either of the form F^* with F non-empty and closed in X, or $C^?$ (denoting sequences of at most one letter taken from C), where C is irreducible closed in X. Note how close this is from the definition of products and SREs [2]. In fact, the latter are the special case one obtains when considering X finite, in which case irreducible closed sets C are single letters a, and non-empty closed sets F are just non-empty subsets of X.

Properties T and W are easy, and one realizes that there is no infinite descending chain of word-products $P_0 \supsetneq P_1 \supsetneq \ldots \supsetneq P_k \supsetneq \ldots$, as soon as X is Noetherian. This may seem surprising, however one can characterize inclusion of word-products in an algorithmic way (see [13, Definition 5.1]), and from this definition it is clear that if $P \supsetneq P'$, where $P = e_1 e_2 \ldots e_m$ and $P' = e'_1 e'_2 \ldots e'_n$, then the multiset $\{\!|e_1, e_2, \ldots, e_m|\!\}$ is strictly larger than $\{\!|e'_1, e'_2, \ldots, e'_n|\!\}$ in the multiset extension $\sqsupset^{mul}$ of $\sqsupset$, defined by: $C'^? \sqsupset C^?$ iff $C' \supsetneq C$; $F'^* \sqsupset F^*$ iff $F' \supsetneq F$; $F'^* \sqsupset C^?$ iff $F' \supseteq C$; and $C'^? \not\sqsupset F^*$. When X is Noetherian, $\supsetneq$ is well-founded, and we conclude by Theorem 1. (This has some similarities to Murthy and Russell's argument [30], by the way.)

Using a similar line of proof, we obtain an analogous result on finite trees. We equate finite trees on X with ground, unranked first-order terms with function symbols taken from X, which we simply call *terms* on X. Let X be a topological space, $\mathcal{T}(X)$ be the set of all terms on X, defined by the grammar $s, t, \ldots ::= f(t_1, \ldots, t_n)$ ($f \in X$, $n \in \mathbb{N}$). Write $\boldsymbol{t}$ for the sequence $t_1 \ldots t_n$. Define the *simple tree expressions* by the grammar $\pi ::= \Diamond U(\pi_1 \mid \ldots \mid \pi_n)$ (U open in X, $n \in \mathbb{N}$), and let $\Diamond U(\pi_1 \mid \ldots \mid \pi_n)$ denote the collection of all terms that have a subterm $f(\boldsymbol{t})$ with $\boldsymbol{t}$ in the word-product $\mathcal{T}(X)^* \pi_1 \mathcal{T}(X)^* \ldots \mathcal{T}(X)^* \pi_n \mathcal{T}(X)^*$. We equip $\mathcal{T}(X)$ with the *tree topology*, defined as the coarsest one that makes every simple tree expression open in $\mathcal{T}(X)$. The specialization quasi-ordering of $\mathcal{T}(X)$ is the usual *tree embedding* quasi-ordering $\preceq_\leq$, defined inductively by $s = f(\boldsymbol{s}) \preceq_\leq t = g(\boldsymbol{t})$ iff either $s \preceq_\leq t_j$ for some j, $1 \leq j \leq n$ (where $\boldsymbol{t} = t_1 t_2 \ldots t_n$), or $f \leq g$ and $\boldsymbol{s} \preceq_\leq^* \boldsymbol{t}$. And:

Theorem 3 (Topological Kruskal Theorem). *If X is Noetherian, then so is $\mathcal{T}(X)$.*

Simple tree expressions are best explained as tests. A simple tree expression $\pi ::= \Diamond U(\pi_1 \mid \ldots \mid \pi_n)$ is, syntactically, just a finite tree whose root is labeled U and with subtrees $\pi_1, \ldots, \pi_n$. Then a term t passes the test π iff it has an embedded term of the same shape as π and whose symbol functions f are all in the opens U labeling the corresponding nodes of π. E.g., whenever $f \in U$, $a \in V$, $b \in W$, $t = g(h(f(g(a, c, c), b), h(g(c))))$ is in $\Diamond U(\Diamond V() \mid \Diamond W())$, because it embeds the term $f(a, b)$, and $f \in U$, $a \in V$, $b \in W$.

We have already dealt with trees, in the special case of *ranked* terms on a *finite* space X in [13, Definition 4.3, Theorem 4.4]. However, these were flawed: the tree-products defined there are irreducible, but not closed. The characterization of irreducible closed subsets of $\mathcal{T}(X)$ is in fact significantly more complicated than for words, although they are still a form of regular expression. This will be published elsewhere.

By the way, I am, at the time I write this, discontent with the above proofs of Theorem 2 and Theorem 3, as they are arguably long and complex. I have found much simpler proofs, which escape the need for characterizing the irreducible closed subsets, and are in fact closer to Nash-Williams celebrated minimal bad sequence argument [31]. This, too, will be published elsewhere.

We have already mentioned that some Noetherian spaces did not arise from wqos. Theorem 1 makes it easy to show that Σ^* with the upper topology of the prefix ordering (where Σ is finite, with the discrete topology) is Noetherian. Consider indeed $\Sigma^* \cup \{\top\}$, where $\top$ is a new elements, and posit that $w \leq^{\text{pref}} \top$ for every $w \in \Sigma^*$. Equip $\Sigma^* \cup \{\top\}$ with the upper topology of $\leq^{\text{pref}}$. The purpose of adding $\top$ is to enforce property T. Property W is obvious, as well as well-foundedness. So $\Sigma^* \cup \{\top\}$ is sober Noetherian. One now concludes using the easy result that any subspace of a Noetherian space is Noetherian.

One can generalize this to cases where we replace Σ by an arbitrary Noetherian space X, defining an adequate *prefix topology* on X^*. We omit this here. We write $X^{*,\text{pref}}$ the resulting space. We return to $\Sigma^{*,\text{pref}}$ in Section 5.

Let us summarize these results by the grammar of Figure 2: every space D shown there is Noetherian. We have not yet dealt with the case of polynomials; we shall touch upon them in Section 6. The constructions marked with a star are those that have no equivalent in the theory of well-quasi-orderings.

$D ::= A$	(finite, Alexandroff topology of some quasi-ordering $\leq$)	
$\mid \mathbb{N}$	(Alexandroff topology of the natural ordering $\leq$)	
$\mid \mathbb{C}^k$	(with the Zariski topology, see Section 6)	*
$\mid \text{Spec}(R)$	(with the Zariski topology, R a Noetherian ring, Section 6)	*
$\mid D_1 \times D_2 \times \ldots \times D_n$	(with the product topology)	
$\mid D_1 + D_2 + \ldots + D_n$	(disjoint union)	
$\mid D^*$	(with the subword topology, Theorem 2)	
$\mid D^{\circledast}$	(with the submultiset topology)	
$\mid \mathcal{T}(D)$	(with the tree topology, Theorem 3)	
$\mid D^{*,\text{pref}}$	(with the prefix topology)	*
$\mid \mathcal{H}(D)$	(with the upper topology of $\subseteq$)	*
$\mid \mathbb{P}(D)$	(with the lower Vietoris topology)	*
$\mid \mathcal{S}(D)$	(with the lower Vietoris topology)	*

Fig. 2. An algebra of Noetherian datatypes

4 Effective TopWSTS

It is easy to extend the notion of WSTS to the topological case. Say that a *topological WSTS* (topWSTS) is a pair (X, δ), where X, the *state space*, is Noetherian, and δ, the *transition relation*, is lower semi-continuous. The former is the topological analogue of a wqo, and the latter generalizes strong monotonicity (1). Formally, δ is *lower semi-continuous* iff $\text{Pre}^{\exists}\delta(V) = \{x \in X \mid \exists y \in V \cdot x \; \delta \; y\}$ is open whenever V is.

Modulo a few assumptions on effectiveness, one can then compute $\text{Pre}^{\exists *}\delta(V)$ for any open V: since X is Noetherian, the sequence of opens $V_0 = V$, $V_{i+1} = V_i \cup \text{Pre}^{\exists}\delta(V_i)$ eventually stabilizes. So we can decide, given V and $x \in X$, whether some element in V is reachable from the state x: just test whether $x \in \text{Pre}^{\exists *}\delta(V)$. This is a general form of the standard backward algorithm for WSTS.

Let us make the effectiveness assumptions explicit. We need codes for opens, and ways of computing $\text{Pre}^{\exists}\delta$. The following definition is inspired from Smyth [35] and Taylor [36, Definition 1.15], taking into account simplifications due to Noetherianness.

Definition 2 (Computably Noetherian Basis). *Let X be a Noetherian space. A* computably Noetherian basis *(resp.,* subbasis*) on X is a tuple $(N, \mathcal{O}[\![\_]\!], 0, 1, +, \prec\!\!\!\prec)$ (resp., $(N, \mathcal{O}[\![\_]\!], 0, 1, +, \star, \prec\!\!\!\prec)$) where:*

- *N is a recursively enumerable set of so-called* codes,
- *$\mathcal{O}[\![\_]\!] : N \to \mathcal{O}(X)$ is a surjective map, $\mathcal{O}[\![0]\!] = \emptyset$, $\mathcal{O}[\![1]\!] = X$, $\mathcal{O}[\![u+v]\!] = \mathcal{O}[\![u]\!] \cup \mathcal{O}[\![v]\!]$ (and $\mathcal{O}[\![u \star v]\!] = \mathcal{O}[\![u]\!] \cap \mathcal{O}[\![v]\!]$ in the case of subbases);*
- *finally, $\prec\!\!\!\prec$ is a decidable relation satisfying: if $u \prec\!\!\!\prec v$ then $\mathcal{O}[\![u]\!] \subseteq \mathcal{O}[\![v]\!]$ (*soundness*), and for any family $(v_i)_{i \in I}$ of codes, there are finitely many elements $i_1, \ldots, i_k \in I$ such that $v_i \prec\!\!\!\prec v_{i_1} + \ldots + v_{i_k}$ for all $i \in I$ (*syntactic compactness*).*

If in addition $u \prec\!\!\!\prec v$ iff $\mathcal{O}[\![u]\!] \subseteq \mathcal{O}[\![v]\!]$ for all codes $u, v \in N$, then we say that $(N, \mathcal{O}[\![\_]\!], 0, 1, +, \prec\!\!\!\prec)$ is a strongly computably Noetherian *basis.*

It is important to notice that such bases describe codes for open subsets, but that we don't care to even represent points, i.e., states, themselves.

The condition $u \prec\!\!\!\prec v$ iff $\mathcal{O}[\![u]\!] \subseteq \mathcal{O}[\![v]\!]$ for all codes $u, v \in N$ trivially entails both soundness and syntactic compactness. The latter follows from the fact that the open $\bigcup_{i \in I} \mathcal{O}[\![v_i]\!]$ is compact, since X is Noetherian. It is an easy exercise to show that *all* the spaces of Figure 2 have a strongly computably Noetherian basis. E.g., for $\mathbb{N}$, the codes are $\underline{n}$, $n \in \mathbb{N}$, plus 0; we take $1 = \underline{0}$, $\mathcal{O}[\![\underline{n}]\!] = \uparrow n$. If $(N_i, \mathcal{O}[\![\_]\!]_i, 0_i, 1_i, +_i, \star_i, \prec\!\!\!\prec_i)$ are strongly computably Noetherian bases of X_i, $1 \le i \le n$, then $(N', \mathcal{O}'[\![\_]\!], 0', 1', +', (\star',) \prec\!\!\!\prec')$ defines one again for $X_1 \times \ldots \times X_n$, where $N' = \mathbb{P}_{\text{fin}}(N_1 \times \ldots \times N_n)$ and $\mathcal{O}'[\![u]\!] = \bigcup_{(u_1,\ldots,u_n) \in u} \mathcal{O}[\![u_1]\!] \times \ldots \times \mathcal{O}[\![u_n]\!]$. If $(N, \mathcal{O}[\![\_]\!], 0, 1, +, \star, \prec\!\!\!\prec)$ is a strongly computably Noetherian basis for X, where $N' = \mathbb{P}_{\text{fin}}(N^*)$ and for every $u' \in N'$, $\mathcal{O}'[\![u']\!]$ is the union, over each word $w = u_1 u_2 \ldots u_n$ in u', of the basic open set $\mathcal{O}'[\![w]\!] = X^* \mathcal{O}[\![u_1]\!] X^* \mathcal{O}[\![u_2]\!] X^* \ldots X^* \mathcal{O}[\![u_n]\!] X^*$.

This also works for infinite constructions such as $\mathbb{P}(X)$ or $\mathcal{H}(X)$: if $(N, \mathcal{O}[\![\_]\!], 0, 1, +, \prec\!\!\!\prec)$ is a strongly computably Noetherian basis for X, then $(N', \mathcal{O}'[\![\_]\!], 0', 1', +', \star', \prec\!\!\!\prec')$ is a strongly computably Noetherian subbasis for $\mathbb{P}(X)$, where $N' = \mathbb{P}_{\text{fin}}(N)$, and for every $u \in N'$, $\mathcal{O}'[\![u]\!] = \bigcap_{a \in u} \Diamond \mathcal{O}[\![a]\!]$ (this is X' itself when $u = \emptyset$).

One sometimes also needs a *representation of points*, which we define as some subset P of some r.e. set, with a map $X[\![\_]\!] : P \to X$, and a decidable relation ε on $P \times N$ such that $p \;\varepsilon\; u$ iff $X[\![p]\!] \in \mathcal{O}[\![u]\!]$. If X is T_0, there is always a surjective, canonical representation of points derived from a strongly computable Noetherian subbasis $(N, \mathcal{O}[\![\_]\!], 0, 1, +, \prec\!\!\!\prec)$: take P to be the subset of all codes $u \in N$ such that $\mathcal{O}[\![u]\!]$ is the complement of some set of the form $\downarrow x$, then let $X[\![u]\!] = x$. So we don't formally need another structure to represent points: any computably Noetherian basis already cares for that. But some other representations of points may come in handy in specific cases.

Definition 3 (Effective TopWSTS). *An* effective topWSTS *is a tuple $(X, \delta, N, \mathcal{O}[\![\_]\!], 0, 1, +, \prec\!\!\!\prec, R_\exists)$, where (X, δ) is a topWSTS, $(N, \mathcal{O}[\![\_]\!], 0, 1, +, \prec\!\!\!\prec)$ is an effective basis on X, $R_\exists : N \to N$ is computable, and* $\text{Pre}^\exists\delta(\mathcal{O}[\![u]\!]) = \mathcal{O}[\![R_\exists(u)]\!]$ *for every $u \in N$.*

In other words, one may compute a code of $\text{Pre}^\exists\delta(U)$, given any code u of U, as $R_\exists(u)$. The following is then clear.

Proposition 1. *Let* $(X, \delta, N, \mathcal{O}\,[\![\_]\!]\,, 0, 1, +, \prec\!\!\!\prec, R_\exists)$ *be an effective topWSTS. One can effectively compute a code of* $\mathrm{Pre}^{\exists *}\delta(U)$ *from any given code* u *of the open subset* U.

Assume additionally a representation $(P, X\,[\![\_]\!]\,, \varepsilon)$ *of points. Given any code* p *for a point* $x \in X$*, and any code* u *for an open subset* U *of* X*, one can decide whether there is a trace* $x = x_0\ \delta\ x_1\ \delta \ldots \delta\ x_k$ *such that* $x_k \in U$.

One can in fact go further and model-check some infinite two-player games. We consider a *may player*, who will play along lower semi-continuous transition relations, and a *must player*, who will play along upper semi-continuous transition relations: δ is *upper semi-continuous* iff $\mathrm{Pre}^{\forall}\delta(F)$ is *closed* whenever F is.

Formally, one posits a finite set $L = L_{\text{must}} \cup L_{\text{may}}$ of *transition labels*, taken as the (not necessarily disjoint) union of two subsets of *must labels* and *may labels*, and calls a *topological Kripke structure* any tuple $I = (X, (\delta_\ell)_{\ell \in L}, (U_A)_{A \in \mathcal{A}})$, where X is a topological space, δ_ℓ is a binary relation on X, which is lower semi-continuous when $\ell \in L_{\text{may}}$ and upper semi-continuous when $\ell \in L_{\text{must}}$, and U_A is an open of X for every atomic formula A. An *environment* ρ maps variables ξ to opens of X, and serves to interpret formulae in some modal logic. In [19, Section 3], we defined the logic L_μ as follows. The formulae F are inductively defined as atomic formulae A, variables ξ, true $\top$, conjunction $F \wedge F'$, false $\bot$, disjunction $F \vee F'$, must-modal formulae $[\ell]F$, may-modal formulae $\langle\ell\rangle F$, and least fixed points $\mu\xi \cdot F$. The semantics of L_μ is standard: the set $I\,[\![F]\!]_\delta\,\rho$ of states $x \in X$ such that x satisfies F is in particular defined so that $I\,[\![\langle\ell\rangle F]\!]_\delta\,\rho = \mathrm{Pre}^{\exists}\delta_\ell(I\,[\![F]\!]_\delta\,\rho)$, $I\,[\![[\ell]F]\!]_\delta\,\rho = \mathrm{Pre}^{\forall}\delta_\ell(I\,[\![F]\!]_\delta\,\rho)$ (where, if F is the complement of V, $\mathrm{Pre}^{\forall}(V)$ is the complement of $\mathrm{Pre}^{\exists}(F)$), and $I\,[\![\mu\xi \cdot F]\!]_\delta\,\rho = \bigcup_{i=0}^{+\infty} U_i$, where $U_0 = \emptyset$ and $U_{i+1} = I\,[\![F]\!]_\delta\,(\rho[\xi := U_i])$. When X is Noetherian, the latter will in fact arise as a *finite* union $\bigcup_{i=0}^{n} U_i$. We define effective topological Kripke structures in the obvious way, imitating Definition 3: just require computable maps $R_\ell^{\exists} : N \to N$ representing δ_ℓ for each $\ell \in L_{\text{may}}$, $R_\ell^{\forall} : N \to N$ representing δ_ℓ for each $\ell \in L_{\text{must}}$, and codes u_A of U_A for each atomic formula A. Computing (a code for) $I\,[\![F]\!]_\delta\,\rho$ by recursion on F yields the following decision result.

Proposition 2. *Given an effective topological Kripke structure, any formula* F *of* L_μ*, and any sequence of codes* v_ξ*, one for each variable* ξ*, one can effectively compute a code of* $I\,[\![F]\!]_\delta\,\rho$*, where* ρ *is the environment mapping each* ξ *to* $\mathcal{O}\,[\![v_\xi]\!]$.

Given any representation of points, and any code for a point $x \in X$*, one can decide whether* x *satisfies* F.

5 Oblivious Stack Systems

Let Σ be a finite alphabet. Reachability and coverability in k-stack pushdown automata are undecidable as soon as $k \geq 2$: encode each half of the tape of a Turing machine by a stack. Here is relaxation of this model that will enjoy a decidable form of coverability.

Define *oblivious* k-stack systems just as pushdown automata, except they cannot check what letter is popped from any stack. Formally, they are automata on a finite set Q of control states, and where transitions are labeled with k-tuples $(\alpha_1, \ldots, \alpha_k)$ of actions. Each action α_i is of the form $\mathtt{push}_a$, for each $a \in \Sigma$ (push a onto stack number i) pop (pop the top letter from stack i, if any, else block), and `skip` (leave stack i unchanged), and all actions are performed in parallel.

This defines an effective topWSTS on the state space $Q \times (\Sigma^{*,\mathrm{pref}})^k$. As we have seen, the latter is Noetherian, although its specialization ordering is certainly not wqo. So the theory of WSTS, as is, does not bring much in solving oblivious k-stack systems. However, Proposition 1 applies: one can decide whether we can reach a given open set V from any state. One observes that one can specify an open set by a finite set $\{p_1, \ldots, p_n\}$ of *forbidden patterns*. A forbidden pattern p is a tuple $(q, w_1, \ldots, w_n)$ where $q \in Q$, and each w_i is either a word in Σ^* or the special symbol $\top$. Such a pattern is *violated* in exactly those states $(q, w'_1, \ldots, w'_n)$ such that for each i such that $w_i \neq \top$, w'_i is a prefix of w_i. It is *satisfied* otherwise. Then $\{p_1, \ldots, p_n\}$ denotes the open subset of all states that satisfy every p_i, $1 \leq i \leq n$. It follows:

Theorem 4. *Given an oblivious k-stack system, any initial configuration and any finite set of forbidden patterns, one can decide whether there is a configuration that is reachable from the initial configuration and satisfies all forbidden patterns.*

In particular, *control-state reachability*, which asks whether one can reach some state $(q, w_1, \ldots, w_n)$, for some fixed q, and arbitrary $w_1, \ldots, w_n$, is decidable for oblivious k-stack systems: take all forbidden patterns of the form $(q', \top, \ldots, \top)$, $q' \in Q \setminus \{q\}$. This much, however, was decidable by WSTS techniques: as S. Schmitz rightly observed, one can reduce this to Petri net control-state reachability by keeping only the lengths of stacks. Theorem 4 is more general, as it allows one to test the contents of the stacks, and comes for free from the theory of topWSTS.

The reader may see a similarity between k-stack pushdown automata and the concurrent pushdown systems of Qadeer and Rehof [32]. However, the latter must push and pop on one stack at a time only. Pushdown automata may require one to *synchronize* push transitions taken on two or more stacks. I.e., if the only transitions available from control state q are labeled ($\mathtt{push}_a$, $\mathtt{push}_a$, `skip`, ..., `skip`) and ($\mathtt{push}_b$, $\mathtt{push}_b$, `skip`, ..., `skip`), then this forces one to push the same letter, a or b, onto the first two stacks when exiting q.

6 Polynomial Games

Let $\mathbb{C}$ be the field of complex numbers, and $k \in \mathbb{N}$. Let R be the ring $\mathbb{Q}[X_1, \ldots, X_k]$ of all polynomials on k variables with coefficients in $\mathbb{Q}$. The *Zariski topology* on $\mathbb{C}^k$ is the one whose opens are $O_I = \{\boldsymbol{x} \in \mathbb{C}^k \mid P(\boldsymbol{x}) \neq 0 \text{ for some } P \in I\}$, where I ranges over the ideals of R. I.e., its closed subsets are the *algebraic varieties* $F_I = \{\boldsymbol{x} \in \mathbb{C}^k \mid P(\boldsymbol{x}) = 0 \text{ for every } P \in I\}$. This is a much coarser topology that the usual metric topology on $\mathbb{C}^k$, and is always Noetherian.

There is an obvious computably Noetherian subbasis (*not* strongly so) from computable algebraic geometry. The set N of codes is the collection of *Gröbner bases* [9, Section 11], which are finite sets of polynomials $u = \{P_1, \ldots, P_n\}$ over $\mathbb{Q}$, normalized with respect to a form of completion procedure due to Buchberger. Given a so-called admissible ordering of monomials, i.e., a total well-founded ordering $\geq$ on monomials such that $m_1 \geq m_2$ implies that $mm_1 \geq mm_2$ for all monomials m, every non-zero polynomial P can be written as $am + P'$, where $a \in K$, m is the largest monomial of P in $\geq$, and P' only involves smaller monomials. P can then be interpreted as a rewrite rule $m \to -\frac{1}{a}P'$ on polynomials, E.g., if $P = X^2Y - 4X + Y^2$, with X^2Y as leading monomial, one can rewrite X^5Y^2 $(= X^2Y.X^3Y)$ to $4X^4Y - X^3Y^3$; the latter $(= X^2Y.(4X^2) - X^3Y^3)$ again rewrites, using P, to $-X^3Y^3 + 16X^3 - 4X^2Y^2$, then to $-4X^2Y^2 + XY^4 + 16X^3 - 4X^2Y^2 = 16X^3 - 8X^2Y^2 + XY^4$, and finally to $16X^3 - 32XY + XY^4 + 8Y^3$. Notice that, evaluated on any zero of P, all the polynomials in the rewrite sequence have the same value; e.g., 0 when $X = Y = 0$, or $\frac{9-\sqrt{17}}{2}$ when $X = 1, Y = \frac{-1+\sqrt{17}}{2}$.

A Gröbner basis for an ideal I is a finite family w of polynomials such that $I = (w)$ and that is confluent (and necessarily terminating) when interpreted as a rewrite system. Buchberger's algorithm converts any finite set v of polynomials to a Gröbner basis w of (v).

Let then $\mathcal{O}\,[\![u]\!] = O_{(u)}$, where $(u) = (P_1, \ldots, P_n)$ is the ideal of all linear combinations of $P_1, \ldots, P_n$ with coefficients in R. One can always compute a Gröbner base for an ideal $I = (P_1, \ldots, P_n)$, given $P_1, \ldots, P_n$, by Buchberger's algorithm. The code 0 is then $\{0\}$, 1 is defined as $\{1\}$, $u + v$ is a Gröbner base for $u \cup v$. One can also define $u \star v$ to be a code for $\mathcal{O}\,[\![u]\!] \cap \mathcal{O}\,[\![v]\!]$, and compute it in at least two ways [27, Section 4.3]. The simplest algorithm [8, Proposition 4.3.9] consists in computing a Gröbner basis of $I = (YP_1, YP_2, \ldots, YP_m, (1-Y)Q_1, (1-Y)Q_2, \ldots, (1-Y)Q_n)$, where $u = \{P_1, P_2, \ldots, P_m\}$ and $v = \{Q_1, Q_2, \ldots, Q_n\}$ and Y is a fresh variable, and to define $u \star v$ as a Gröbner basis for the *elimination ideal* $\exists Y \cdot I$, defined as those polynomials in I where Y does not occur [8, Theorem 4.3.6]. Given any polynomial P and any Gröbner basis u, one can test whether $P \in (u)$ by a process akin to rewriting: each polynomial in u works as a rewrite rule, and $P \in (u)$ iff the (unique) normal form of P with respect to this rewrite system is 0. One can then test whether $u \lll v$ by checking whether, for each $P \in u$, P is in (v). It turns out that $u \lll v$ is *not* equivalent to $\mathcal{O}\,[\![u]\!] \subseteq \mathcal{O}\,[\![v]\!]$: take $u = \{X\}$, $v = \{X^2\}$, then $u \notin (v)$, although $\mathcal{O}\,[\![u]\!] = \mathcal{O}\,[\![v]\!]$. But soundness is obvious, and syntactic compactness (Definition 2) follows since R is a Noetherian ring. We mention in passing that there is also a *strongly* computably Noetherian subbasis, where $u \lll v$ iff (u) is included in the radical of (v), and this can be decided using the *Rabinowitch trick* [33].

As a representation of points, we take those u such that (u) is a prime ideal. This is in fact the canonical representation. It contains at least all rational points $(q_1, \ldots, q_k) \in \mathbb{Q}^k$, represented as the Gröbner basis $(X_1 - q_1, \ldots, X_k - q_k)$, but also many more.

One gets natural topWSTS from *polynomial programs*. These are finite automata, on some finite set Q of control states, where transitions are labeled with guards and assignments on k complex-valued variables. The guards g are finite sets $\{P_1, \ldots, P_m\}$ of polynomials in R, interpreted as disjunctions of disequalities $P_1 \neq 0 \vee \ldots \vee P_m \neq 0$. If the guard is satisfied, then the transition can be taken, and the action is triggered. The allowed actions a are parallel assignments $\boldsymbol{x} := P_1(\boldsymbol{x}), \ldots, P_k(\boldsymbol{x})$, where $\boldsymbol{x}$ is the vector of all k variables, and with the obvious semantics. Each P_i is either a polynomial in R, or the special symbol ?, meaning any element of $\mathbb{C}$.

This defines a transition relation δ on $Q \times \mathbb{C}^k$, which happens to be lower semi-continuous, and in fact computably so. As set N' of codes for opens of the state space $Q \times \mathbb{C}^k$, we use $\mathbb{P}_{\mathsf{fin}}(Q \times N)$, and define $\mathcal{O}' [\![u']\!] = \bigcup_{(q,u) \in N'} \{q\} \times \mathcal{O} [\![u]\!]$. Then, $\mathrm{Pre}^{\exists}\delta(\mathcal{O}' [\![u']\!]) = \bigcup_{(q',u) \in u', q \xrightarrow{g,a} q'} \{q\} \times \mathcal{O} [\![g \star \{P[X_i{:=}P_i]_{i \in I_{act}} \mid P \in \forall X_{i_1}, \ldots, X_{i_m} \cdot u\}]\!]$, where a is $\boldsymbol{x} := P_1(\boldsymbol{x}), \ldots, P_k(\boldsymbol{x})$, and $i_1, \ldots, i_m$ are those indices i where P_i is ?, and I_{act} are the others. $P[X_i := P_i]_{i \in I_{act}}$ is parallel substitution of P_i for X_i in P for all $i \in I_{act}$. The $\forall$ operator is defined, and shown to be computable, in [29, Lemma 4].

The polynomial programs above are exactly those of Müller-Olm and Seidl [29]. Proposition 1 then immediately applies. In particular, one can decide whether one can reach some configuration $(q', \boldsymbol{x})$ such that $P_1(\boldsymbol{x}) \neq 0$ or ... or $P_m(\boldsymbol{x}) \neq 0$ for some state q' and polynomials $P_1, \ldots, P_m$, from a given configuration, in a given polynomial program. This is a bit more than the polynomial constants problem of [29]. For example, we may want to check whether at q' we always have $Y = X^2 + 2$ and $X^2 + Y^2 = Z^2$, and for this we let $P_1 = Y - X^2 - 2$, $P_2 = Z^2 - X^2 - Y^2$, $m = 2$. Figure 3 is a rendition of an example by Müller-Olm and Seidl, in C-like syntax. The conditions (shown as '?') at lines 1 and 3 are abstracted away: `if` and `while` statements are to be read as non-deterministic choices. One may check that it is always the case that `x` is 0 at line 4. This is a polynomial program with control states 1 through 4, the variables are $X_1 =$ `x`, $X_2 =$ `y`, all the guards are trivial (i.e., the empty set of polynomials), and the actions should be clear; e.g., the only action from state 2 to state 3 is the pair of polynomials $(X_1 X_2 - 6, 0)$.

```
1.  if (?) { x = 2; y = 3; } else { x = 3; y = 2; }
2.  x = x * y − 6; y = 0;
3.  while (?) { x = x + 1; y = y − 1; };
3'. x = x^2 + x * y;
4.  return;
```

Fig. 3. Müller-Olm and Seidl's example

Polynomial Games. We can again go further. Define *polynomial games* as a topological Kripke structure where, for each may transition $\ell \in L_{\mathsf{may}}$, δ_ℓ is specified by guards and actions as above. For each must transition $\ell \in L_{\mathsf{must}}$, we specify δ_ℓ by giving ourselves a finite set A_ℓ of triples $(q, q', \alpha) \in Q \times Q \times \mathbb{Q}[X_1, \ldots, X_k, X'_1, \ldots, X'_k]$, and defining $(q, \boldsymbol{x})\, \delta_\ell (q', \boldsymbol{x}')$ iff there is a triple $(q, q', \alpha) \in A_\ell$ such that $\alpha(\boldsymbol{x}, \boldsymbol{x}') = 0$. So the must player can, in particular, compute polynomial expressions of $\boldsymbol{x}$, test polynomials against 0, and solve polynomial equations. It is easy to see that δ_ℓ is then upper semi-continuous, as $\mathrm{Pre}^{\exists}\delta_\ell(\{q'\} \times F_{(u)}) = \bigcup_{(q,q',\alpha) \in A_\ell} \{q\} \times F_{\exists X'_1 \cdot \ldots \cdot \exists X'_k \cdot (\alpha \cup \{P[X_i := X'_i]_{i=1}^k \mid P \in u\})}$. By Proposition 2:

Theorem 5. *The model-checking problem for $\mathcal{L}_\mu$ formulas on polynomial games is decidable.*

We do not know whether the added expressive power of polynomial games, compared to the simpler polynomial programs, will be of any use in verification, however the theorem stands.

Lossy Concurrent Polynomial Programs. All the above can be done without any recourse to topology, and requires one only to work with polynomial ideals. However, the topological approach is modular. If one should someday need to decide games that would involve state spaces such as $\mathbb{N}^m \times \mathbb{C}^k$, or $\mathbb{P}(\mathbb{C}^k)$, the theory of Noetherian spaces would apply right out of the box. Here is a trivial case.

Consider a network of polynomial programs communicating through specific FIFO channels. We shall call such networks *concurrent polynomial programs*. We shall assume these channels to be *lossy*, i.e., messages may disappear from the channels, non-deterministically, at any time. We shall also assume that the messages are taken from some fixed finite set Σ, i.e., the channels are only used for signaling, not for transmitting any actual value. This imitates the behavior of lossy channel systems [3], which are a special case (with no variable from $\mathbb{C}$) of our lossy concurrent polynomial programs. Lossiness is interesting, if only because the non-lossy variants are undecidable [10].

For simplicity, we shall only consider two programs A and B communicating through one FIFO channel from A to B. Dealing with more programs and more channels presents no difficulty, other than notational.

The messages sent over the channel are control signals from Σ. So the data type of the possible contents of the channel is Σ^*, with the subword topology (alternatively, the Alexandroff topology of the usual embedding quasi-ordering $\leq^*$, where $\leq$ is equality on Σ). Let Q_A be the finite set of control states of A, Q_B that of B. Let $\boldsymbol{X} = X_1, \ldots, X_m$ be the vector of the numerical variables of A, $\boldsymbol{Y} = Y_1, \ldots, Y_n$ those of B. The configurations are tuples $(q_A, \boldsymbol{X}, q_B, \boldsymbol{Y}, w)$, where $(q_A, \boldsymbol{X})$ is a configuration of the polynomial program A, $(q_B, \boldsymbol{Y})$ is a configuration of B, and $w \in \Sigma^*$ is the contents of the channel. Compared to the non-concurrent case, the guards and the actions of A (resp., B) can only deal with variables from $\boldsymbol{X}$ (resp., $\boldsymbol{Y}$), except for two new families of actions $\texttt{recv}_a$ (for B) and $\texttt{send}_a$ (for A), where a is a constant in Σ.

Formally, given any A-transition from q_A to q'_A with guard g and action $\texttt{send}_a$, $a \in \Sigma + \mathbb{C}^k$, we define δ so that $(q_A, \boldsymbol{X}, q_B, \boldsymbol{Y}, w)\ \delta\ (q'_A, \boldsymbol{X}, q_B, \boldsymbol{Y}, aw)$ provided g is satisfied (add a in front of w), while the semantics of a $\texttt{recv}_a$ action, $a \in \Sigma$, from q_B to q'_B with guard g, is given by $(q_A, \boldsymbol{X}, q_B, \boldsymbol{Y}, w_1 a w)\ \delta\ (q_A, \boldsymbol{X}, q'_B, \boldsymbol{Y}, w)$ if g is satisfied (i.e., drop enough letters from the FIFO channel until we reach an a, and pop it). It is an easy exercise to show that this is lower semi-continuous, and computably so. (We could also add transitions that drop letters from the channel, as in lossy channel systems, but this is not needed for the rest of our treatment.)

The opens are finite unions of sets of the form $\{(q_A, \boldsymbol{x}, q_B, \boldsymbol{x}, w) \mid (\boldsymbol{x}, \boldsymbol{y}) \in O_I, w \in \Sigma^* a_1 \Sigma^* \ldots \Sigma^* a_q \Sigma^*\}$, where q_A, q_B are fixed control states, $I = (p_1, \ldots, p_\ell)$ is a fixed polynomial ideal over $\mathbb{Q}[\boldsymbol{X}, \boldsymbol{Y}]$, and $a_1, \ldots, a_q$ are fixed letters from Σ. In other words, such an open subset is specified by a *forbidden pattern*: a state satisfies the forbidden pattern iff its A is in control state q_A, B is in control state q_B, $p_i(\boldsymbol{x}, \boldsymbol{y}) \neq 0$ for some i, $1 \leq i \leq \ell$, and $a_1 a_2 \ldots a_q$ is a subword of the contents w of the channel.

Theorem 6. *Given a lossy concurrent polynomial program, an initial configuration where the values of the variables are given as rational numbers, and a finite set of forbidden patterns, one can decide whether there is a configuration reachable from the initial configuration and that satisfies all forbidden patterns.*

In particular, control-state reachability (can one reach a configuration where A would be in state q_A and B in state q_B?) is decidable.

Algebraic geometry. To end this section, we only mention that $\mathbb{C}^k$ is considered as a special case in algebraic geometry. It turns out that the sobrification $\mathcal{S}(\mathbb{C}^k)$ coincides with $\mathrm{Spec}(\mathbb{Q}[X_1, X_2, \ldots, X_k])$, the *spectrum* of the (Noetherian) ring $\mathbb{Q}[X_1, X_2, \ldots, X_k]$. The spectrum $\mathrm{Spec}(R)$ of a ring R is the set of all prime ideals of R, and comes with the Zariski topology, whose closed subsets are $F_I = \{p \in \mathrm{Spec}(R) \mid I \subseteq p\}$, where I ranges over the ideals of R. It is well-known that $\mathrm{Spec}(R)$ is a Noetherian space whenever R is a Noetherian ring, see [20, chapitre premier, Section 1.1]. This provides yet another construction of Noetherian spaces, although we currently have no application in computer science that would require the added generality.

7 Completions, and Complete WSTS

The algorithm of Proposition 1 works backwards, by computing iterated sets of predecessors. The Karp-Miller algorithm [24] works *forwards* instead, but only applies to Petri nets. Forward procedures are useful, e.g., to decide boundedness, see [14].

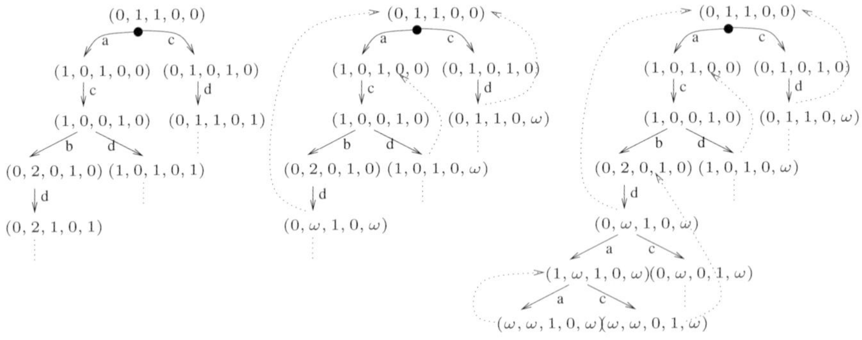

(a) Unfolding (beginning) (b) Taking some shortcuts (c) Finishing some branches

Fig. 4. Running the Karp-Miller procedure on Figure 1

Consider for example the Petri net of Figure 1, and consider it as a transition system over $\mathbb{N}^5$. The initial state is $(0, 1, 1, 0, 0)$, and there are four transitions a, b, c, and d. One can then unfold all possible runs of the net in a tree (see Figure 4, (a)). Here, from the initial state, one can trigger transitions a or c, leading to states $(1, 0, 1, 0, 0)$ and $(0, 1, 0, 1, 0)$ respectively. From the latter we can only trigger d, leading to $(0, 1, 1, 0, 1)$, and so on. Doing so would yield an infinite tree.

The Karp-Miller construction builds a finite tree by taking some shortcuts, and abstracting away the values of components of the states that may become unbounded. E.g., in Figure 1, we realize that firing c then d leads to a state $(0, 1, 1, 0, 1)$ where the first four components are the same as in the initial state $(0, 1, 1, 0, 0)$, but the fifth is larger. Iterating this c-d sequence would lead to a state $(0, 1, 1, 0, N)$ with N arbitrary large, and we abstract this away by *replacing* the state $(0, 1, 1, 0, 1)$ by $(0, 1, 1, 0, \omega)$, where ω denotes any, arbitrarily large, number. This also happens along the other two branches shown in Figure 4, (a). The dotted arrows going up in Figure 4, (b), indicate which state we can go back to in order to perform such iterations.

One can see a tuple in $\mathbb{N}_\omega^5$ (where $\mathbb{N}_\omega = \mathbb{N} \uplus \{\omega\}$) such as $(0, 1, 1, 0, \omega)$ as meaning, in particular, that there are infinitely many tokens in place x_5. While this is not quite correct, it certainly gives some further intuitions. In particular, one can continue to simulate the execution of the Petri net from such extended states. The result, apart from some irrelevant parts, is shown in Figure 4, (c). This is the *coverability tree* of the Petri net. (The dotted arrows are not part of this—the coverability *graph* would include them. We also glossed over a few details, notably that the Karp-Miller construction does not proceed to simulate the execution of the Petri net from an extended state that is identical to a state further up the same branch.)

The reason why the resulting tree is finite is twofold. First, $\mathbb{N}_\omega^k$ is wqo. This implies that, along any infinite branch, we must eventually find an extended state that is componentwise larger than another one higher in the tree, giving us an opportunity to take a shortcut. We call this a *progress* property: in any infinite run, we will eventually take a shortcut, subsuming infinitely many iterations.

Second, taking a shortcut adds an ω component to a tuple, and ω components never disappear further down the branch: so any branch must in fact be finite. It follows from König's Lemma that the tree itself is finite, and is built in finite time.

The Karp-Miller construction gives more information about the Petri net than the standard backward algorithm. Letting $A \subseteq \mathbb{N}_\omega^k$ be the set of all extended states labeling the nodes of the tree, one sees that $\mathbb{N}^k \cap \downarrow A$ is exactly the *cover* of the Petri net, i.e., the downward closure $\downarrow \mathrm{Post}^* \delta(x)$ of the set $\mathrm{Post}^* \delta(x)$ of states y that are reachable from the initial state x by the transition relation δ. In particular, one can decide coverability, by checking whether $y \in \downarrow \mathrm{Post}^* \delta(x)$. One can also decide *boundedness*, i.e., test whether $\mathrm{Post}^* \delta(x)$? is finite (check whether any ω component occurs anywhere in the coverability tree), and *place-boundedness*, i.e., test whether there is a bound on the number of tokens that can be in any given place. In the example above, and after simplification, the cover is $\mathbb{N}^5 \cap \downarrow\{(\omega, \omega, 0, 1, \omega), (\omega, \omega, 1, 0, \omega)\}$: the bounded places are x_3 and x_4.

The Karp-Miller construction is fine, but only works on Petri nets. There cannot be any similar, terminating procedure for general WSTS, since this would decide boundedness again. But boundedness is already undecidable on lossy channel systems [10] and on reset Petri nets [12].

Even if we drop the requirement for termination, finding a procedure that would compute the cover of a general WSTS (when it terminates) remained elusive for some time. Some important special cases could be handled in the literature, e.g., a large class of affine counter systems generalizing reset/transfer Petri nets [15], or lossy channel systems [2], but a general theory of covers, and of forward procedures à la Karp-Miller for general WSTS was missing. This is what we solved, with A. Finkel, in two recent papers [13,14].

This involved two tasks: (i) first, much as we needed extended states in $\mathbb{N}_\omega^k$ in the Karp-Miller procedure, we should work in an adequate *completion* $\widehat{X}$ of the state space X; (ii) then, we should understand what a Karp-Miller-like procedure actually computes. We actually cheated here, since we have already given an answer to (ii): the Karp-Miller procedure computes (among other things) the cover of the Petri net.

Completions. In (i), by *adequate* we mean that X should embed into $\widehat{X}$, in such a way that every closed subset D of X should be representable by a *finite* subset of $\widehat{X}$. (In [13], we required this for every downward closed, not just closed, D. However, if X has the Alexandroff topology of a wqo, this is the same thing.) Formally, D should be the set of those points in X that are below finitely many points in $\widehat{X}$: $D = X \cap \downarrow_{\widehat{X}} E$, E finite. We write $\downarrow_{\widehat{X}}$ to stress the fact that the downward closure is to be taken in $\widehat{X}$, i.e., E is a subset of $\widehat{X}$, not X. Typically, if $X = \mathbb{N}^k$, then $\widehat{X}$ should be $\mathbb{N}_\omega^k$, and for example, $D = \{(m,n,p) \in \mathbb{N}^3 \mid m + n \leq 3\}$ is representable as $\mathbb{N}^3 \cap \downarrow_{\widehat{\mathbb{N}^3}} \{(0,3,\omega), (1,2,\omega), (2,1,\omega), (3,0,\omega)\}$. It turns out that the sobrification $\mathcal{S}(X)$ is exactly what we need here, as advocated in [13, Proposition 4.2]:

Proposition 3. *Let X be a Noetherian space. Every closed subset F of X is a finite union of irreducible closed subsets $C_1, \ldots, C_m$.*

So let the completion $\widehat{X}$ be $\mathcal{S}(X)$. Proposition 3 states that, modulo the canonical identification of $x \in X$ with $\downarrow x \in \mathcal{S}(X)$, F is $X \cap \downarrow_{\widehat{X}} \{C_1, \ldots, C_m\}$. We have stressed the subcase where X was wqo (and equipped with its Alexandroff topology) in [13], and this handles 7 of the 13 constructions in Figure 2. We would like to note that Noetherian spaces X allow us to consider more kinds of state spaces, while ensuring that each closed subset of X is finitely representable, in a canonical way. Moreover, these representations are effective, too.

One might wonder whether there would be other adequate completions $\widehat{X}$. There are, indeed, however $\mathcal{S}(X)$ is canonical in a sense. Adapting Geeraerts *et al.* slightly [17], call *weak adequate domain of limits*, or *WADL*, over the Noetherian space X any space $\widehat{X}$ in which X embeds, and such that the closed (downward closed when X is wqo) subsets of X are exactly the subsets representable as $X \cap \downarrow_{\widehat{X}} E$ for some finite subset E of $\widehat{X}$. It is an easy consequence of Theorem 1 that $\mathcal{S}(X)$ is the *smallest* WADL, and $\mathcal{H}(X)$ is the *largest* WADL: up to isomorphism, any WADL $\widehat{X}$ must be such that $\mathcal{S}(X) \subseteq \widehat{X} \subseteq \mathcal{H}(X)$.

It is then natural to ask whether $\widehat{X} = \mathcal{S}(X)$ is effectively presented, in the sense that we have codes for all elements of $\mathcal{S}(X)$ and that the ordering (i.e., $\subseteq$) on $\mathcal{S}(X)$ is decidable. It turns out that the answer is positive for *all* the datatypes of Figure 2. E.g., given codes for elements of $\widehat{X_1}$, $\widehat{X_2}$, the codes for elements of $\widehat{X_1 \times X_2}$ are just pairs of codes (x_1, x_2) for elements of $\widehat{X_1}$, $\widehat{X_2}$. Given codes for elements of $\widehat{X}$, the codes for elements of $\widehat{X^*}$ are the word-products we mentioned in Section 3. It might seem surprising that we could do this even for the infinite powerset $\mathbb{P}(X)$. Notice that $\widehat{\mathbb{P}(X)} = \mathcal{H}(X)$, up to isomorphism, and that every element of $\mathcal{H}(X)$ can be written as $C_1 \cup \ldots \cup C_n$ for finitely many elements $C_1, \ldots, C_n$ of $\widehat{X}$ by Proposition 3. So take as codes for elements of $\widehat{\mathbb{P}(X)}$ the *finite* sets E of codes of elements $C_1, \ldots, C_n$ of $\widehat{X}$.

Clovers. Point (ii) was clarified, among other things, in [14]: Karp-Miller-like procedures compute the *clover* of a state $x \in X$ in a WSTS $\mathfrak{X}$, and this is a finite representative $\{C_1, \ldots, C_m\}$, as defined above, of the topological *closure* (in $\widehat{X}$) of the set of points reachable from x. The clover *always* exists, by Proposition 3. It may fail to be computable: if it were, it would allow us to decide boundedness for reset Petri nets or for lossy channel systems, which are undecidable.

While we investigated this for WSTS, it actually works for any *topological* WSTS. We only need to extend the transition relation $\delta \subseteq X \times X$ to one, $\mathcal{S}\delta$, on $\widehat{X} \times \widehat{X}$. The canonical candidate is such that $C \ \mathcal{S}\delta \ C'$ iff C' is included in the closure of $\mathrm{Post}\delta(C) = \{y \in X \mid \exists x \in C \cdot x \ \delta \ y\}$; and this is representable as a *finitely branching* (because of Proposition 3 again) relation $\widehat{\delta}$. E.g., the minimal such relation is such that $C \ \widehat{\delta} \ C'$ iff C' is maximal such that $C \ \mathcal{S}\delta \ C'$. We then get a completed topWSTS $\widehat{\mathfrak{X}}$.

To do anything with this, we must assume that $\widehat{\delta}$ is effective, and a bit more. We explored this in [14], in the case where $\widehat{X}$ is wqo, and $\widehat{\mathfrak{X}}$ is functional (i.e., $C \ \widehat{\delta} \ C'$ iff $C' = g_i(C)$ for some i, $1 \leq i \leq n$, where $g_1, \ldots, g_n$ is a fixed collection of partial continuous maps from $\widehat{X}$ to $\widehat{X}$) and ∞-effective (see below), and obtained a simple procedure **Clover** that computes the clover of any state $C \in \widehat{X}$ (in particular, any $x \in X$) whenever it terminates.

The role of the completion $\widehat{X}$ is again manifest in that **Clover** needs to *lub-accelerate* some infinite sequences of states obtained in a regular fashion as $C_0 < g(C_0) \leq g^2(C_0) \leq \ldots \leq g^n(C_0) \leq \ldots$ by applying one functional transition $g : \widehat{X} \to \widehat{X}$, replacing the sequence by its least upper bound $g^\infty(C_0)$ (which exists: recall that every sober space is a dcpo in its specialization quasi-ordering). This is what we called taking shortcuts until now. If $C_0 \not< g(C_0)$, then define $g^\infty(C_0)$ as just $g(C_0)$. $\widehat{\mathfrak{X}}$ is *∞-effective* iff g^∞ is computable.

Here is the procedure. $\mathrm{Max}\, A$ denotes the set of all maximal elements of $A \in \mathbb{P}_{\mathrm{fin}}(\widehat{X})$. The procedure takes an initial extended state $s_0 \in \widehat{X}$, and, if it terminates, returns a finite set $\mathrm{Max}\, A$ (the *clover* of s_0) such that $\downarrow_{\widehat{X}} \mathrm{Max}\, A$ is the closure of the cover of the WSTS.

Procedure Clover(s_0) :
1. $A \leftarrow \{s_0\}$;
2. **while** $\mathrm{Post}(\mathcal{S}\delta)(A) \not\leq^\flat A$ **do**
   (a) Choose fairly $(g, C) \in \{g_1, \ldots, g_n\}^* \times A$ such that $C \in \mathrm{dom}\, g$;
   (b) $A \leftarrow A \cup \{g^\infty(a)\}$;
3. **return** $\mathrm{Max}\, A$;

The elements g chosen at line (a) are chosen from $\{g_1, \ldots, g_n\}^*$, the set of compositions $g_{i_1} \circ g_{i_2} \circ \ldots \circ g_{i_k}$ of functions from $\{g_1, \ldots, g_n\}$. A typical implementation of **Clover** would build a tree, as in the Karp-Miller construction. In fact, a tree is a simple way to ensure that the choice of (g, C) at line (a) is *fair*, i.e., no pair is ignored infinitely long on any infinite branch. Concretely, we would build a tree extending downwards. At each step, A is given by the set of extended states written at the nodes of the current tree. One picks (g, C) as in line (a) by picking a transition g_i to apply from a yet unexplored state C' (at a leaf), and considering all states C higher in the branch (the path from C to C' being given by transitions, say, $g_{i_k}, g_{i_{k-1}}, \ldots, g_{i_2}$), letting $g = g_i \circ g_{i_2} \circ \ldots \circ g_{i_k}$.

The **Clover** procedure extends straightforwardly to topWSTS, provided they are functional (here, each g_i needs to be continuous). It is however unclear how to dispense with the requirement that it be functional. Moreover, the nice characterization that **Clover** terminates exactly on those systems that are *clover-flattable* [14, Theorem 3] seems to require the fact that X is ω^2-wqo, not even just wqo, for deep reasons.

Conclusion. Noetherian spaces open up some new avenues for verifying infinite-state systems, whether backward or forward, à la Karp-Miller. Mostly, I hope I have convinced the reader that Noetherian spaces enjoyed a rich mathematical theory, which is probably still largely unexplored today.

References

1. Abdulla, P.A., Čerāns, K., Jonsson, B., Yih-Kuen, T.: Algorithmic analysis of programs with well quasi-ordered domains. Information and Computation 160(1/2), 109–127 (2000)
2. Abdulla, P.A., Collomb-Annichini, A., Bouajjani, A., Jonsson, B.: Using forward reachability analysis for verification of lossy channel systems. Formal Methods in System Design 25(1), 39–65 (2004)
3. Abdulla, P.A., Jonsson, B.: Verifying programs with unreliable channels. In: Proc. 8th IEEE Int. Symp. Logic in Computer Science (LICS 1993), pp. 160–170 (1993)
4. Abdulla, P.A., Jonsson, B.: Ensuring completeness of symbolic verification methods for infinite-state systems. Theoretical Computer Science 256(1-2), 145–167 (2001)
5. Abdulla, P.A., Nylén, A.: Timed Petri nets and bqos. In: Colom, J.-M., Koutny, M. (eds.) ICATPN 2001. LNCS, vol. 2075, pp. 53–70. Springer, Heidelberg (2001)
6. Abramsky, S., Jung, A.: Domain theory. In: Abramsky, S., Gabbay, D.M., Maibaum, T.S.E. (eds.) Handbook of Logic in Computer Science, vol. 3, pp. 1–168. Oxford University Press, Oxford (1994)
7. Acciai, L., Boreale, M.: Deciding safety properties in infinite-state pi-calculus via behavioural types. In: Albers, S., Marchetti-Spaccamela, A., Matias, Y., Nikoletseas, S.E., Thomas, W. (eds.) ICALP 2009. LNCS, vol. 5556, pp. 31–42. Springer, Heidelberg (2009)
8. Adams, W.W., Loustaunau, P.: An introduction to Gröbner bases. Graduate Studies in Mathematics, vol. 3, 289 pages. American Mathematical Society, Providence (1994)
9. Buchberger, B., Loos, R.: Algebraic simplification. In: Buchberger, B., Collins, G.E., Loos, R., Albrecht, R. (eds.) Computer Algebra, Symbolic and Algebraic Computation. Springer, Heidelberg (1982-1983)
10. Cécé, G., Finkel, A., Purushothaman Iyer, S.: Unreliable channels are easier to verify than perfect channels. Information and Computation 124(1), 20–31 (1996)
11. de Groote, P., Guillaume, B., Salvati, S.: Vector addition tree automata. In: Proc. 19th IEEE Int. Symp. Logics in Computer Science, pp. 64–73 (2004)
12. Dufourd, C., Finkel, A., Schnoebelen, P.: Reset nets between decidability and undecidability. In: Larsen, K.G., Skyum, S., Winskel, G. (eds.) ICALP 1998. LNCS, vol. 1443, pp. 103–115. Springer, Heidelberg (1998)
13. Finkel, A., Goubault-Larrecq, J.: Forward analysis for WSTS, part I: Completions. In: Albers, S., Marion, J.-Y. (eds.) Proc. STACS 2009, Freiburg, Germany, pp. 433–444 (2009)
14. Finkel, A., Goubault-Larrecq, J.: Forward analysis for WSTS, part II: Complete WSTS. In: Albers, S., Marchetti-Spaccamela, A., Matias, Y., Thomas, W. (eds.) ICALP 2009. LNCS, vol. 5556, pp. 188–199. Springer, Heidelberg (2009)
15. Finkel, A., McKenzie, P., Picaronny, C.: A well-structured framework for analysing Petri net extensions. Information and Computation 195(1-2), 1–29 (2004)
16. Finkel, A., Schnoebelen, P.: Well-structured transition systems everywhere! Theoretical Computer Science 256(1-2), 63–92 (2001)

17. Geeraerts, G., Raskin, J.-F., Van Begin, L.: Expand, enlarge and check: New algorithms for the coverability problem of WSTS. J. Comp. Sys. Sciences 72(1), 180–203 (2006)
18. Gierz, G., Hofmann, K.H., Keimel, K., Lawson, J.D., Mislove, M., Scott, D.S.: Continuous lattices and domains. In: Encyclopedia of Mathematics and its Applications, vol. 93, Cambridge University Press, Cambridge (2003)
19. Goubault-Larrecq, J.: On Noetherian spaces. In: Proc. 22nd IEEE Int. Symp. Logic in Computer Science (LICS 2007), Wrocław, Poland, pp. 453–462 (2007)
20. Grothendieck, A.: Éléments de géométrie algébrique (rédigés avec la collaboration de Jean Dieudonné): I. Le langage des schémas, vol. 4, pp. 5–228. Publications mathématiques de l'I.H.É.S (1960)
21. Henzinger, T.A., Majumdar, R., Raskin, J.-F.: A classification of symbolic transition systems. ACM Trans. Computational Logic 6(1), 1–32 (2005)
22. Higman, G.: Ordering by divisibility in abstract algebras. Proceedings of the London Mathematical Society 2(7), 326–336 (1952)
23. Hopcroft, J., Pansiot, J.J.: On the reachability problem for 5-dimensional vector addition systems. Theoretical Computer Science 8, 135–159 (1979)
24. Karp, R.M., Miller, R.E.: Parallel program schemata. Journal of Computer and System Sciences 3(2), 147–195 (1969)
25. Kruskal, J.B.: Well-quasi-ordering, the tree theorem, and Vazsonyi's conjecture. Transactions of the American Mathematical Society 95(2), 210–225 (1960)
26. Lazič, R., Newcomb, T., Ouaknine, J., Roscoe, A.W., Worrell, J.: Nets with tokens which carry data. Fundamenta Informaticae 88(3), 251–274 (2008)
27. Lombardi, H., Perdry, H.: The Buchberger algorithm as a tool for ideal theory of polynomial rings in constructive mathematics. In: Gröbner Bases and Applications (Proc. of the Conference 33 Years of Gröbner Bases). London Mathematical Society Lecture Notes, vol. 251, pp. 393–407. Cambridge University Press, Cambridge (1998)
28. Minsky, M.L.: Recursive unsolvability of Post's problem of "tag" and other topics in the theory of Turing machines. Annals of Mathematics, Second Series 74(3), 437–455 (1961)
29. Müller-Olm, M., Seidl, H.: Polynomial constants are decidable. In: Hermenegildo, M.V., Puebla, G. (eds.) SAS 2002. LNCS, vol. 2477, pp. 4–19. Springer, Heidelberg (2002)
30. Murthy, C.R., Russell, J.R.: A constructive proof of Higman's lemma. In: Proc. 5th IEEE Symposium on Logic in Computer Science (LICS 1990), pp. 257–267 (1990)
31. Nash-Williams, C.S.-J.A.: On better-quasi-ordering transfinite sequences. In: Proc. Cambridge Philosophical Society, vol. 64, pp. 273–290 (1968)
32. Qadeer, S., Rehof, J.: Context-bounded model checking of concurrent software. In: Halbwachs, N., Zuck, L.D. (eds.) TACAS 2005. LNCS, vol. 3440, pp. 93–107. Springer, Heidelberg (2005)
33. Rabinowitch, S.: Zum Hilbertschen Nullstellensatz. Mathematische Annalen 102, 520 (1929)
34. Reutenauer, C.: Aspects Mathématiques des Réseaux de Petri. Masson (1993)
35. Smyth, M.: Effectively given domains. Theoretical Computer Science 5, 257–274 (1977)
36. Taylor, P.: Computably based locally compact spaces. Logical Methods in Computer Science 2(1) (2006)
37. Verma, K.N., Goubault-Larrecq, J.: Karp-Miller trees for a branching extension of VASS. Discrete Mathematics & Theoretical Computer Science 7(1), 217–230 (2005)

Towards a Theory of Time-Bounded Verification

Joël Ouaknine and James Worrell

Oxford University Computing Laboratory, UK
{joel,jbw}@comlab.ox.ac.uk

Abstract. We propose a theory of *time-bounded* verification for real-time systems, in which verification queries are phrased over time intervals of fixed, bounded duration. We argue that this theory is both ***pertinent***, in that it is fully adequate to handle a large proportion of 'real-world' real-time systems and specifications; and ***effective***, in that the restriction to bounded time domains reclaims as decidable several of the key decision problems of unbounded real-time verification. Finally, we discuss several directions of ongoing and future work.

1 Introduction

In an influential invited address at the 10th Annual IEEE Symposium on Logic in Computer Science (LICS 95), Boris Trakhtenbrot urged the research community to *"lift the 'classical' Trinity to real-time systems"* [51]. Trakhtenbrot's 'Trinity' consisted of Logic, Nets, and Automata, viewed as the pillars of the 'classical' theory of verification. The genesis of this theory in fact go back some five decades to the seminal work of Büchi, Elgot, and Trakhtenbrot himself relating the monadic second-order logic of order ($\mathsf{MSO}(<)$) and automata; see [53] for a detailed historical perspective on the subject.

Underlying the increasingly successful applications of verification technology to the design and validation of hardware and software systems has been the long-running and sustained elaboration of a rich body of theoretical work. One of the major accomplishments of this theory is the discovery and formulation of the robust and far-reaching correspondence among the eclectic concepts of *automata*, *temporal logic*, *monadic predicate logic*, and *regular expressions*. Each of these comes in various flavours, yet the adequation is maintained, in particular, whether the discourse is over the finite or the infinite, or (in the language of predicate logic) first or second order. A key result in this area is Kamp's theorem, which asserts the expressive equivalence of the monadic first-order logic of order ($\mathsf{FO}(<)$) and Linear Temporal Logic (LTL) [29, 19]. This influential result has largely contributed to the emergence of LTL as the canonical linear-time specification formalism in the classical theory.

On a pragmatic level, the close relationship between automata and logic has enabled the design of *model-checking* algorithms for a wide variety of specification formalisms rooted in temporal or predicate logic. While initially little more than pure decidability results, these procedures have over the last few decades been progressively honed into powerful industrial-strength tools.

S. Abramsky et al. (Eds.): ICALP 2010, Part II, LNCS 6199, pp. 22–37, 2010.

Real-time verification, by contrast, is a much younger field. Its origins date back approximately twenty-five years, when various researchers from such diverse communities as process algebra, Petri nets, automata theory, and software engineering began investigating extensions of existing formalisms to adequately handle timing considerations. By far the most prominent modelling paradigm to have emerged is Alur and Dill's notion of *timed automaton* [2], which at the time of writing has accrued nearly 4000 citations according to Google Scholar.

One of the central results concerning timed automata is the PSPACE decidability of the *language emptiness* (or *reachability*) *problem* [1]. Unfortunately, the *language inclusion problem*—given two timed automata $\mathcal{A}$ and $\mathcal{B}$, is every timed word accepted by $\mathcal{A}$ also accepted by $\mathcal{B}$?—is known to be undecidable [2]. A closely related phenomenon is the fact that timed automata are not closed under complement. For example, the automaton in Fig. 1 accepts every timed word in which there are two a-events separated by exactly one time unit.

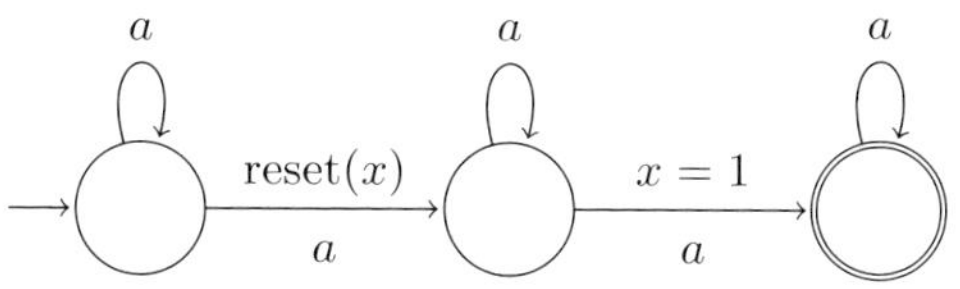

Fig. 1. An uncomplementable timed automaton

The complement language consists of all timed words in which no two a-events are separated by precisely one time unit. Intuitively, this language is not expressible by a timed automaton, since such an automaton would need an unbounded number of clocks to keep track of the time delay from each a-event. (We refer the reader to [25] for a rigorous treatment of these considerations.)

The undecidability of language inclusion severely restricts the algorithmic analysis of timed automata, both from a practical and theoretical perspective, as many interesting questions can be phrased in terms of language inclusion. Over the past two decades, several researchers have therefore attempted to circumvent this obstacle by investigating language inclusion, or closely related concepts, under various assumptions and restrictions. Among others, we note the use of (i) topological restrictions and digitisation techniques: [22, 14, 42, 39]; (ii) fuzzy semantics: [20, 23, 41, 8]; (iii) determinisable subclasses of timed automata: [4, 47]; (iv) timed simulation relations and homomorphisms: [50, 37, 31]; and (v) restrictions on the number of clocks: [43, 18]. See also Henzinger *et al.*'s paper on *fully decidable* formalisms [24].

In a strictly formal sense, the non-closure under complementation is easy to remedy—one can simply generalise the transition mode to allow both conjunctive and disjunctive transitions, an idea borrowed from the theory of untimed automata that dates back thirty years [15]. Such untimed *alternating automata* have played key roles in algorithms for complementing Büchi automata (see, e.g., [33]), temporal logic verification [52, 36], and analysis of parity games [17]. In the timed world, the resulting *alternating timed automata* [34, 44, 35, 46, 16] subsume ordinary timed automata and can be shown to be closed under all Boolean operations. They have been used, among others, to provide model-checking algorithms for various fragments of Metric Temporal Logic (MTL); see, e.g., [44, 45, 12]. Unfortunately, the price to pay for the increase in expressiveness is the undecidability of language emptiness!

Turning to temporal logic, one finds a considerable body of work in the literature concerned with adapting classical linear temporal formalisms to the real-time setting; see, e.g., [32, 38, 7, 3, 54, 48]. One of the earliest proposals, Koyman's *Metric Temporal Logic* (MTL) [32], extends LTL by constraining the temporal operators by (bounded or unbounded) intervals of the reals. For example, the formula $\Diamond_{[3,4]} \varphi$ requires φ to hold within 3 to 4 time units from the present time. MTL has since become one of the most successful and popular specification formalisms for timed systems.

Unfortunately, the *satisfiability* and *model-checking problems* for MTL are undecidable [21]. This has led researchers to consider various restrictions on MTL to recover decidability. One of the most important such proposals is *Metric Interval Temporal Logic* (MITL), a fragment of MTL in which the temporal operators may only be constrained by *non-singular* intervals. Alur *et al.* showed that the satisfiability and model-checking problems for MITL are EXPSPACE-complete [3]. A significant extension of this result, based on the notion of *flatness*, was later obtained in [13]. Another interesting approach is that of Wilke, who considered MTL over a dense-time semantics with *bounded variability*, i.e., parameterised by a fixed bound on the number of events per unit time interval [54]. Wilke showed that the satisfiability problem is decidable in this semantics and that MTL with existential quantification over propositions is precisely as expressive as Alur-Dill timed automata.

Work on real-time extensions of monadic first- and second-order logic of order has been considerably scarcer. Hirshfeld and Rabinovich examine the *monadic first-order metric logic of order* ($\mathsf{FO}(<, +1)$) and show that unfortunately, it is—in a precise technical sense—strictly more expressive over the reals than any 'reasonable' timed temporal logic, and in particular than MTL [27]; see also [11]. This sweeping inequivalence seriously dampens the hope of discovering a 'canonical' timed temporal logic over the reals with a natural predicate-logical counterpart, after the manner of LTL and $\mathsf{FO}(<)$ in the classical theory.

There has also been comparatively little research on finding suitable timed analogues of the notion of regular expression. An interesting proposal is that of Asarin *et al.* [9], who define a class of *timed regular expressions* with expressive power precisely that of Alur-Dill timed automata, mirroring Kleene's theorem in the classical theory. Unfortunately, many natural questions, such as whether two timed regular expressions are equivalent, remain undecidable.

In our view, the overall emerging picture of the present-day theory of real-time verification is one of an amalgam of constructs and results—some deep and striking—yet fundamentally constrained by a phalanx of inescapable undecidability barriers. The elegance, uniformity, and canonicity of the classical theory are lacking, and Trakhtenbrot's challenge to a large extent remains unmet.

In an attempt to address these issues, we would like to propose here a ***time-bounded theory of real-time verification***. By 'time-bounded' we mean to restrict the modelling and verification efforts to some bounded interval of time, which itself can be taken as a parameter. A proximate motivation for our proposal is the analogy with *bounded model checking*, which aims to circumvent an intractable verification task by performing instead a more restricted—but less costly—analysis. A related paradigm, originating from economics, is that of *discounting the future*, whereby the later a potential error may occur, the lesser of a concern it is.

Note that while bounded model checking restricts the total number of allowable events (or discrete steps), time-bounded verification restricts the total duration under consideration, but *not* the number of events, which can still be unboundedly large owing to the density of time. We argue that this restriction on total duration is a very natural one as regards real-time systems. For example, a run of a communication protocol might normally be expected to have an *a priori* time bound, even if the total number of messages exchanged is potentially unbounded. In fact, many real-time systems, such as the flight control software on board an aircraft, are normally rebooted and reset at regular intervals (for example, presumably, on completion of a successful flight). In such cases, a time-bounded analysis seems entirely pertinent. We note that several researchers have in fact already considered instances of time-bounded verification in the context of real-time systems [49, 10, 30].

Aside from these practical considerations, we anticipate more favourable complexity-theoretic properties from a time-bounded theory than from its unbounded counterpart. In recent work [40, 28], we have already amassed considerable evidence to this effect, which we survey below and detail at greater length in the main body of this paper.

The undecidability of language inclusion for timed automata, first established in [2], uses in a crucial way the unboundedness of the time domain. Roughly speaking, this allows one to encode arbitrarily long computations of a Turing machine. In [40], we turned to the *time-bounded* version of the language inclusion problem: given two timed automata $\mathcal{A}$ and $\mathcal{B}$, together with a time bound N, are all finite timed words of duration at most N that are accepted by $\mathcal{A}$ also accepted by $\mathcal{B}$? One of our main results is that this problem is decidable and in fact 2EXPSPACE-complete. It is worth noting that the time-boundedness restriction does not alter the fact that timed automata are not closed under complement, so that classical techniques for language inclusion do not trivially apply.

In subsequent work, we examined the substantially more sophisticated problem of time-bounded emptiness (or equivalently, language inclusion) for alternating timed automata [28]. We also succeeded in establishing decidability, but in contrast to ordinary timed automata, showed that this problem has non-elementary complexity.

A third line of investigation concerns the relative expressiveness of temporal and predicate metric logics over bounded intervals of the reals, in analogy with the classical equivalence of LTL and $\mathsf{FO}(<)$. Somewhat surprisingly, we discovered that MTL has precisely the same expressive power as FO$(<, +1)$ over any bounded time domain [40]. This is in sharp contrast to the situation over unbounded time, where neither MTL nor any 'reasonable' temporal extension of it can match the full expressiveness of FO$(<, +1)$ [27].

Finally, we devoted a significant fraction of our efforts to time-bounded model-checking and satisfiability questions for timed automata and metric logics. In addition to MTL and FO$(<, +1)$, we consider the *monadic second-order metric logic of order*, MSO$(<, +1)$. In [40], we showed that the time-bounded model-checking and satisfiability problems for monadic first- and second-order metric logics all have non-elementary complexity, whereas these problems are EXPSPACE-complete in the case of MTL (and this in spite of the expressive equivalence of MTL and FO$(<, +1)$ over bounded time domains). It is worth recalling, in contrast, that these problems are all undecidable over unbounded time.

We believe that this small but significant body of results constitutes a clear indication that the restriction to time-boundedness may lead to a substantially better-behaved theory of real-time verification, mirroring the classical theory and enabling one to lift classical results to the timed world.

It is perhaps worth stressing that we do not envisage time-bounded verification to replace its unbounded counterpart entirely; one can always imagine instances genuinely requiring unbounded real-time analysis. What we do assert, however, is that for a large proportion of hard real-time systems, a time-bounded approach should prove not only algorithmically advantageous, but will also be entirely adequate theoretically.

The remainder of the paper is organised as follows. We recall standard real-time definitions and conventions in Sec. 2. Sections 3, 4, and 5 respectively introduce ordinary timed automata, metric logics, and alternating timed automata. In Sec. 6, we turn to the relative expressiveness of MTL and FO$(<, +1)$ over bounded time domains. Section 7 then examines our various time-bounded decision problems: emptiness, language inclusion, model checking, and satisfiability. Finally, we briefly discuss some of the multiple possible future research directions in Sec. 8.

Our treatment is fairly spare; in particular, we do not present proofs, but instead offer pointers to the relevant literature. Our aim is mainly to motivate and illustrate, and we have occasionally opted to sacrifice precision for insight.

2 Real-Time Preliminaries

We fix some of the real-time notation and modelling conventions that we use throughout this paper. While there are a wealth of alternatives and variants that can be considered—many of which appear in some form or other in the literature—our aim here is not to be encyclopedic, but rather to lay a simple background in which to phrase some of the key motivating results in the area.

Two of the basic formalisms discussed in this paper are timed automata (both ordinary and alternating) and metric logics. Timed automata are most commonly given a semantics in terms of *timed words*, i.e., sequences of instantaneous, real-valued timestamped events, whereas metric logics are more naturally predicated on piecewise-continuous *flows* or *signals*. Accordingly, these are the semantics we adopt here; this does not prevent us from specifying timed-automaton behaviours using metric logics, as timed words can naturally be viewed as particular kinds of flows.

In this paper, we are largely concerned with behaviours over time domains of the form $[0, N)$, where $N \in \mathbb{N}$ is some fixed positive integer. Let us therefore in general write $\mathbb{T}$ to denote either $[0, N)$ or $\mathbb{R}_{\geq 0}$.

Let Σ denote a finite set (or *alphabet*) or *events*. Typical elements of Σ are written a, b, c, a_1, etc. A ***timed word*** is a pair (σ, τ), where $\sigma = \langle a_1 a_2 \ldots a_n \rangle \in \Sigma^*$ is a finite word and $\tau = \langle t_1 t_2 \ldots t_n \rangle \in \mathbb{T}^*$ is a strictly increasing sequence of real-valued *timestamps* of the same length.[1] Note that while we are restricting ourselves to finite timed words, there is no *a priori* bound on the number of events.

Let **MP** be a set of *monadic predicates*, denoted P, Q, R, etc. Monadic predicates will alternately be viewed as second-order variables over $\mathbb{T}$, i.e., ranging over sets of non-negative real numbers, and as atomic propositions holding at various points in time. Given $\mathbf{P} \subseteq \mathbf{MP}$ a finite set of monadic predicates, a ***flow*** (or *signal*) over $\mathbf{P}$ is a function $f : \mathbb{T} \to \mathcal{P}(\mathbf{P})$ that is *finitely variable*. Finite variability is the requirement that the restriction of f to any finite subinterval of $\mathbb{T}$ have only finitely many discontinuities.[2]

A flow $f : \mathbb{T} \to \mathcal{P}(\mathbf{P})$ corresponds to an interpretation of the monadic predicates in $\mathbf{P}$: for any $P \in \mathbf{P}$, the interpretation of P as a subset of $\mathbb{T}$ is simply $\{t \in \mathbb{T} \mid P \in f(t)\}$. Conversely, any (finitely-variable) interpretation of all the predicates in $\mathbf{P}$ defines a unique flow $f : \mathbb{T} \to \mathcal{P}(\mathbf{P})$.

Finally, note that a timed word $(\langle a_1 \ldots a_n \rangle, \langle t_1 \ldots t_n \rangle)$ over alphabet Σ can be viewed as a (particular type of) flow, as follows. Let $\mathbf{P} = \Sigma$, and set $f(t_i) = \{a_i\}$, for $1 \leq i \leq n$, and $f(t) = \emptyset$ for all other values of $t \in \mathbb{T}$.

3 Timed Automata

As discussed in the Introduction, we treat Alur-Dill timed automata, interpreted over finite timed words, as the central theoretical implementation formalism in this work.

Let X be a finite set of clocks, denoted x, y, z, etc. We define the set Φ_X of clock constraints over X via the following grammar, where $k \in \mathbb{N}$ stands for any non-negative integer, and $\bowtie \in \{=, \neq, <, >, \leq, \geq\}$ is a comparison operator:

$$\phi ::= \mathbf{true} \mid \mathbf{false} \mid x \bowtie k \mid x - y \bowtie k \mid \phi_1 \wedge \phi_2 \mid \phi_1 \vee \phi_2 \,.$$

[1] This gives rise to the so-called *strongly monotonic* semantics; in contrast, the *weakly monotonic* semantics allows multiple events to happen 'simultaneously' (or, more precisely, with null-duration delays between them).

[2] It is commonly argued that infinitely-variable flows do not correspond to 'feasible' computations, hence the above restriction. It is however important to stress that we do not place any *a priori* bound on the variability (unlike, for example, [54]), other than requiring that it be finite.

A ***timed automaton*** $\mathcal{A}$ is a six-tuple $(\Sigma, S, S_I, S_F, X, \delta)$, where:

- Σ is a finite set of events,
- S is a finite set of states,
- $S_I \subseteq S$ is a set of initial states,
- $S_F \subseteq S$ is a set of accepting states,
- X is a finite set of clocks, and
- $\delta : S \times \Sigma \times \Phi_X \to \mathcal{P}(S \times \mathcal{P}(X))$ is the transition function: if $(s', R) \in \delta(s, a, \phi)$, then $\mathcal{A}$ allows a jump from state s to state s', consuming event a in the process, provided the constraint ϕ on clocks is met. Afterwards, the clocks in R are reset to zero, while all other clocks remain unchanged. We require that δ be finite, in the sense of having only finitely many inputs not mapping to $\emptyset$.

Given a timed automaton $\mathcal{A}$ as above, a *clock valuation* is a function $\nu : X \to \mathbb{R}_{\geq 0}$. If $t \in \mathbb{R}_{\geq 0}$, we let $\nu + t$ be the clock valuation such that $(\nu + t)(x) = \nu(x) + t$ for all $x \in X$.

A *configuration* of $\mathcal{A}$ is a pair (s, ν), where $s \in S$ is a state and ν is a clock valuation.

An *accepting run* of $\mathcal{A}$ is a finite alternating sequence of configurations and delayed transitions $\pi = (s_0, \nu_0) \stackrel{d_1, a_1}{\longrightarrow} (s_1, \nu_1) \stackrel{d_2, a_2}{\longrightarrow} \ldots \stackrel{d_n, a_n}{\longrightarrow} (s_n, \nu_n)$, with each $d_i \in \mathbb{R}_{>0}$ and $a_i \in \Sigma$, subject to the following conditions:

1. $s_0 \in S_I$, and for all $x \in X$, $\nu_0(x) = 0$,
2. for each $1 \leq i \leq n$, there are some $R_i \subseteq X$ and $\phi_i \in \Phi_X$ such that: (i) $\nu_{i-1} + d_i$ satisfies ϕ_i, (ii) $(s_i, R_i) \in \delta(s_{i-1}, a_i, \phi_i)$, and (iii) $\nu_i(x) = \nu_{i-1}(x) + d_i$ for all $x \in X \setminus R_i$, and $\nu_i(x) = 0$ for all $x \in R_i$, and
3. $s_n \in S_F$.

Each d_i is interpreted as the (strictly positive) time delay between the firing of transitions, and each configuration (s_i, ν_i), for $i \geq 1$, records the data immediately following the ith transition.

A timed word $(\langle a_1 a_2 \ldots a_n \rangle, \langle t_1 t_2 \ldots t_n \rangle)$ is *accepted* by $\mathcal{A}$ if $\mathcal{A}$ has some accepting run of the form $\pi = (s_0, \nu_0) \stackrel{d_1, a_1}{\longrightarrow} (s_1, \nu_1) \stackrel{d_2, a_2}{\longrightarrow} \ldots \stackrel{d_n, a_n}{\longrightarrow} (s_n, \nu_n)$ where, for each $1 \leq i \leq n$, $t_i = d_1 + d_2 + \ldots + d_i$.

Finally, given time domain $\mathbb{T}$, we write $L_{\mathbb{T}}(\mathcal{A})$ to denote the language of $\mathcal{A}$ over $\mathbb{T}$, i.e., the set of timed words accepted by $\mathcal{A}$ all of whose timestamps belong to $\mathbb{T}$.

An example of a timed automaton is provided in Fig. 1, along with a description of its accepted language in the surrounding text.

4 Metric Logics

We introduce *metric* (or *quantitative*) logics to reason about and specify real-time behaviours. We consider both predicate and temporal formalisms, and investigate their relative expressiveness in Sec. 6.

Let **Var** be a set of *first-order variables*, denoted x, y, z, etc., ranging over $\mathbb{T}$. *Second-order monadic formulas* are obtained from the following grammar:

$$\varphi ::= \mathbf{true} \mid x < y \mid +1(x, y) \mid P(x) \mid \varphi_1 \wedge \varphi_2 \mid \varphi_1 \vee \varphi_2 \mid \neg\varphi \mid \forall x\, \varphi \mid \forall P\, \varphi\,,$$

where $P \in \mathbf{MP}$ is a monadic predicate (viewed here as a second-order variable over $\mathbb{T}$), and $+1$ is a binary relation symbol, with the intuitive interpretation of $+1(x, y)$ as '$x + 1 = y$'.[3] We refer to $\forall x$ and $\forall P$ as *first-order* and *second-order* quantifiers respectively. Existential quantifiers $\exists x$ and $\exists P$ are definable via standard dualities.

The ***monadic second-order metric logic of order***, written $\mathsf{MSO}(<, +1)$, comprises all second-order monadic formulas. Its first-order fragment, the ***(monadic) first-order metric logic of order***, written $\mathsf{FO}(<, +1)$, comprises all $\mathsf{MSO}(<, +1)$ formulas that do not contain any second-order quantifier; note that these formulas are however allowed free monadic predicates.

We also define two further purely order-theoretic sublogics, which are peripheral to our main concerns but necessary to express some key related results. The *monadic second-order logic of order*, $\mathsf{MSO}(<)$, comprises all second-order monadic formulas that do not make use of the $+1$ relation. Likewise, the *(monadic) first-order logic of order*, $\mathsf{FO}(<)$, comprises those $\mathsf{MSO}(<)$ formulas that do not figure second-order quantification.

Metric Temporal Logic, abbreviated MTL, comprises the following *temporal formulas*:

$$\theta ::= \mathbf{true} \mid P \mid \theta_1 \wedge \theta_2 \mid \theta_1 \vee \theta_2 \mid \neg\theta \mid \Diamond_I \theta \mid \Box_I \theta \mid \theta_1 \, \mathcal{U}_I \, \theta_2\,,$$

where $P \in \mathbf{MP}$ is a monadic predicate (viewed here as an atomic proposition), and $I \subseteq \mathbb{R}_{\geq 0}$ is an open, closed, or half-open interval with endpoints in $\mathbb{N} \cup \{\infty\}$. If $I = [0, \infty)$, then we omit the annotation I in the corresponding temporal operator.

Finally, *Linear Temporal Logic*, written LTL, consists of those MTL formulas in which every indexing interval I on temporal operators is $[0, \infty)$ (and hence omitted).

Figure 2 pictorially summarises the syntactic inclusions and relative expressive powers of these various logics.

We now ascribe a semantics to these various logics in terms of flows over $\mathbb{T}$. Given a formula φ of $\mathsf{MSO}(<, +1)$ or one of its sublogics, let $\mathbf{P}$ and $\{x_1, \ldots, x_n\}$ respectively be the sets of free monadic predicates and free first-order variables appearing in φ. For any flow $f : \mathbb{T} \to \mathcal{P}(\mathbf{P})$ and real numbers $a_1, \ldots, a_n \in \mathbb{T}$, the satisfaction relation $(f, a_1, \ldots, a_n) \models \varphi$ is defined inductively on the structure of φ in the standard way. For example:

[3] The usual approach is of course to define $+1$ as a unary function symbol; this however necessitates an awkward treatment over bounded domains, as considered in this paper. We shall nonetheless abuse notation later on and invoke $+1$ as if it were a function, in the interest of clarity.

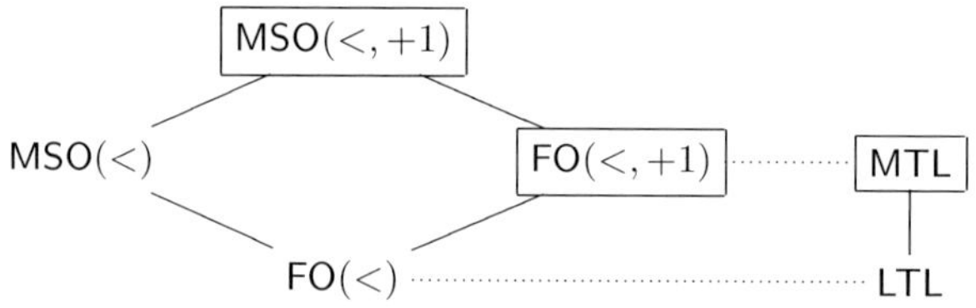

Fig. 2. Relative expressiveness among the various logics. Metric logics are enclosed in boxes. Straight lines denote syntactical inclusion, whereas dotted lines indicate expressive equivalence over bounded time domains (cf. Sec. 6).

- $(f, a) \models P(x)$ iff $P \in f(a)$.
- $(f, a_1, \ldots, a_n) \models \forall P\, \varphi$ iff for all flows $g : \mathbb{T} \to \mathcal{P}(\mathbf{P} \cup \{P\})$ extending f (i.e., such that $g\restriction_{\mathbf{P}} = f$), we have $(g, a_1, \ldots, a_n) \models \varphi$.
(Here $\mathbf{P}$ is the set of free monadic predicates appearing in $\forall P\, \varphi$, and therefore does not contain P.)

And so on.

We shall particularly be interested in the special case in which φ is a *sentence*, i.e., a formula with no free first-order variable. In such instances, we simply write the satisfaction relation as $f \models \varphi$.

For θ an MTL or LTL formula, let $\mathbf{P}$ be the set of monadic predicates appearing in θ. Given a flow $f : \mathbb{T} \to \mathcal{P}(\mathbf{P})$ and $t \in \mathbb{T}$, the satisfaction relation $(f, t) \models \theta$ is defined inductively on the structure of θ, as follows:

- $(f, t) \models \mathbf{true}$.
- $(f, t) \models P$ iff $P \in f(t)$.
- $(f, t) \models \theta_1 \wedge \theta_2$ iff $(f, t) \models \theta_1$ and $(f, t) \models \theta_2$.
- $(f, t) \models \theta_1 \vee \theta_2$ iff $(f, t) \models \theta_1$ or $(f, t) \models \theta_2$.
- $(f, t) \models \neg\theta$ iff $(f, t) \not\models \theta$.
- $(f, t) \models \Diamond_I \theta$ iff there exists $u \in \mathbb{T}$ with $u > t$, $u - t \in I$, and $(f, u) \models \theta$.
- $(f, t) \models \Box_I \theta$ iff for all $u \in \mathbb{T}$ with $u > t$ and $u - t \in I$, $(f, u) \models \theta$.
- $(f, t) \models \theta_1\, \mathcal{U}_I\, \theta_2$ iff there exists $u \in \mathbb{T}$ with $u > t$, $u - t \in I$, $(f, u) \models \theta_2$, and for all $v \in (t, u)$, $(f, v) \models \theta_1$.

Finally, we write $f \models \theta$ iff $(f, 0) \models \theta$. This is sometimes referred to as the *initial semantics*.

Note that we have adopted a *strict* semantics, in which the present time t has no influence on the truth values of future temporal subformulas.

An important point concerning our semantics is that it is *continuous*, rather than *pointwise*: more precisely, the temporal operators quantify over all time points of the domain, as opposed to merely those time points at which discontinuities occur. Positive decidability results for satisfiability and model checking of MTL over unbounded time intervals have been obtained in the pointwise semantics [44, 45, 46]; it is worth noting that none of these results hold in the continuous semantics.

5 Alternating Timed Automata

We introduce alternating timed automata as a generalisation of ordinary timed automata in which, in addition to *disjunctive* (or nondeterministic) transitions, one also allows *conjunctive* transitions. Our notation closely follows that of Sec. 3.

For *Prop* a set of propositional variables, the collection $\mathcal{B}_+(Prop)$ of positive Boolean formulas over *Prop* is given by the following grammar:

$$\psi ::= \mathbf{true} \mid \mathbf{false} \mid p \mid \psi_1 \vee \psi_2 \mid \psi_1 \wedge \psi_2 \,,$$

where $p \in Prop$. A subset $M \subseteq Prop$ *satisfies* $\psi \in \mathcal{B}_+(Prop)$ if the truth assignment that ascribes **true** to elements of M and **false** to elements of $Prop \setminus M$ satisfies ψ.

An ***alternating timed automaton*** is a six-tuple $\mathcal{A} = (\Sigma, S, S_I, S_F, X, \delta)$, where

- Σ is a finite set of events,
- S is a finite set of states,
- $S_I \subseteq S$ is a set of initial states,
- $S_F \subseteq S$ is a set of accepting states,
- X is a finite set of clocks, and
- $\delta : S \times \Sigma \times \Phi_X \to \mathcal{B}_+(S \times \mathcal{P}(X))$ is the transition function. We require that δ be finite, in the sense of having only finitely many inputs not mapping to **false**.

Intuitively, the transition function of an alternating timed automaton is interpreted as follows: in state (s, ν), if ν satisfies the clock constraint ϕ and $\{(s_1, R_1), \ldots, (s_k, R_k)\}$ satisfies $\delta(s, a, \phi)$, then we think of the automaton as having a *conjunctive transition* $(s, \nu) \xrightarrow{a} \{(s_1, \nu_1), \ldots, (s_k, \nu_k)\}$, where each clock valuation ν_i is the same as ν except for the clocks in R_i which are all reset to zero.

As an example, let us define an automaton $\mathcal{A}$ over alphabet $\Sigma = \{a\}$ that accepts those words such that for every timed event (a, t) with $t < 1$ there is an event $(a, t+1)$ exactly one time unit later. $\mathcal{A}$ has a single clock x and set of locations $\{s, u\}$, with s initial and accepting, and u non-accepting. The transition function is defined by:

$$\delta(s, a, x < 1) = (s, \emptyset) \wedge (u, \{x\}) \qquad \delta(s, a, x \geq 1) = (s, \emptyset)$$
$$\delta(u, a, x \neq 1) = (u, \emptyset) \qquad \delta(u, a, x = 1) = \mathbf{true}$$

The automaton is illustrated in Fig. 3 in which we represent the conjunctive transition by connecting two arrows with an arc.

A run of $\mathcal{A}$ starts in location s. Every time an a occurs in the first time unit, the automaton makes a simultaneous transition to both s and u, thus opening up a new thread of computation equipped with a fresh copy of the clock x. The automaton must eventually leave location u, which is non-accepting, and it can only do so exactly one time unit after first entering the location.

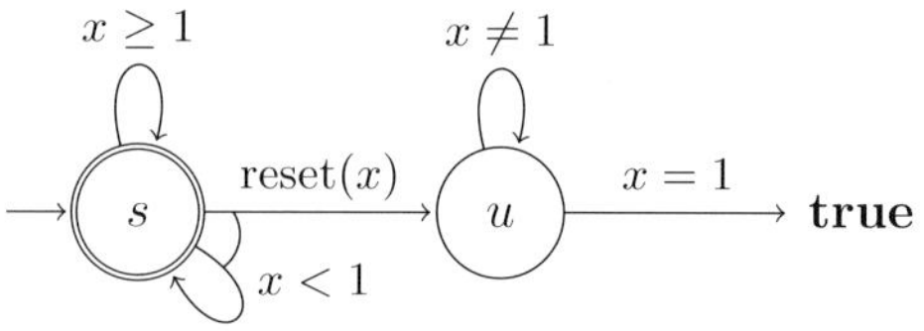

Fig. 3. Alternating timed automaton $\mathcal{A}$

We now formally define the language accepted by an alternating timed automaton $\mathcal{A} = (\Sigma, S, S_I, S_F, X, \delta)$. A run of $\mathcal{A}$ over a timed word $(\langle a_1 a_2 \ldots a_n \rangle, \langle t_1 t_2 \ldots t_n \rangle)$ is a finite dag satisfying the following conditions: (i) each vertex is a triple (i, s, ν), with $0 \leq i \leq n$, $s \in S$ a location, and ν a clock valuation; (ii) there is a vertex $(0, s_0, \nu_0)$, where $s_0 \in S_I$ and $\nu_0(x) = 0$ for all $x \in X$; (iii) each vertex (i, s, ν), $i \leq n-1$, has a (possibly empty) set of children of the form $\{(i+1, s_1, \nu_1), \ldots, (i+1, s_k, \nu_k)\}$ where, writing $\nu' = \nu + t_{i+1} - t_i$ (and adopting the convention that $t_0 = 0$), there is a conjunctive transition $(s, \nu') \xrightarrow{a_i} \{(s_1, \nu_1), \ldots, (s_k, \nu_k)\}$.

The run is *accepting* if for each vertex (n, s, ν), s is an accepting location; in this case we say that the timed word $(\langle a_1 a_2 \ldots a_n \rangle, \langle t_1 t_2 \ldots t_n \rangle)$ is *accepted* by $\mathcal{A}$. The language $L_{\mathbb{T}}(\mathcal{A})$ of $\mathcal{A}$ over $\mathbb{T}$ is the set of timed words accepted by $\mathcal{A}$ all of whose timestamps belong to $\mathbb{T}$.

One of the motivations for introducing alternating timed automata is that they enjoy better closure properties than ordinary timed automata:

Proposition 1. *For any time domain $\mathbb{T}$, alternating timed automata are effectively closed under union, intersection, and complement [35, 46].*

6 Expressiveness

Fix a time domain $\mathbb{T}$, and let $\mathcal{L}$ and $\mathcal{J}$ be two logics. We say that $\mathcal{L}$ is ***at least as expressive as*** $\mathcal{J}$ if, for any sentence θ of $\mathcal{J}$, there exists a sentence φ of $\mathcal{L}$ such that θ and φ are satisfied by precisely the same set of flows over $\mathbb{T}$.

Two logics are then said to be ***equally expressive*** if each is at least as expressive as the other.

The following result can be viewed as an extension of Kamp's celebrated theorem, asserting the expressive equivalence of $\mathsf{FO}(<)$ and LTL [29,19], to metric logics over bounded time domains:

Theorem 1. *For any fixed bounded time domain of the form $[0, N)$, with $N \in \mathbb{N}$, the metric logics $\mathsf{FO}(<, +1)$ and MTL are equally expressive. Moreover, this equivalence is effective [40].*

Note that expressiveness here is relative to a *single* structure $\mathbb{T}$, rather than to a *class* of structures. In particular, although $\mathsf{FO}(<, +1)$ and MTL are equally expressive over any bounded time domain of the form $[0, N)$, the correspondence and witnessing formulas may very well vary according to the time domain.

It is interesting to note that $\mathsf{FO}(<,+1)$ is strictly more expressive than MTL over $\mathbb{R}_{\geq 0}$ [27, 11]. For example, MTL is incapable of expressing the following formula (in slightly abusive but readable notation)

$$\exists x\, \exists y\, \exists z\, (x < y < z < x + 1 \wedge P(x) \wedge P(y) \wedge P(z))$$

over the non-negative reals. This formula asserts that, sometime in the future, P will hold at three distinct time points within a single time unit.

It is also worth noting that $\mathsf{MSO}(<,+1)$ is strictly more expressive than $\mathsf{FO}(<,+1)$—and hence MTL—over any time domain.

7 Decision Problems

We now turn to various decision problems concerning timed automata and metric logics over bounded time domains. Recall that the latter are real intervals of the form $[0, N)$, with $N \in \mathbb{N}$ considered part of the input (written in binary). We also contrast our results with their known counterparts over the non-negative reals $\mathbb{R}_{\geq 0}$.

The most fundamental verification question is undoubtedly the ***emptiness*** (or *reachability*) ***problem***: does a given timed automaton accept some timed word? It is well known that the problem is PSPACE-complete over $\mathbb{R}_{\geq 0}$ [1], and the proof is easily seen to carry over to bounded time domains:

Theorem 2. *The time-bounded emptiness problem for timed automata is PSPACE-complete (following [1]).*

The ***language-inclusion problem*** takes as inputs two timed automata, $\mathcal{A}$ and $\mathcal{B}$, sharing a common alphabet, and asks whether every timed word accepted by $\mathcal{A}$ is also accepted by $\mathcal{B}$. Unfortunately, language inclusion is undecidable over $\mathbb{R}_{\geq 0}$ [2]. However:

Theorem 3. *The time-bounded language-inclusion problem for timed automata is decidable and 2EXPSPACE-complete [40].*

For a fixed metric logic $\mathcal{L}$, the ***satisfiability problem*** asks, given a sentence φ of $\mathcal{L}$ over a set $\mathbf{P}$ of free monadic predicates, whether there exists a flow over $\mathbf{P}$ satisfying φ. The ***model-checking problem*** for $\mathcal{L}$ takes as inputs a timed automaton $\mathcal{A}$ over alphabet Σ, together with a sentence φ of $\mathcal{L}$ with set of free monadic predicates $\mathbf{P} = \Sigma$, and asks whether every timed word (viewed as a flow) accepted by $\mathcal{A}$ satisfies φ.

The canonical time domain for interpreting the metric logics $\mathsf{MSO}(<,+1)$, $\mathsf{FO}(<,+1)$, and MTL is the non-negative real line $\mathbb{R}_{\geq 0}$. Unfortunately, none of these logics are decidable over $\mathbb{R}_{\geq 0}$ [5, 6, 26]. The situation however differs over bounded time domains, as the following result indicates:

Theorem 4. *The time-bounded satisfiability and model-checking problems for the metric logics* $\mathsf{MSO}(<,+1)$, $\mathsf{FO}(<,+1)$, *and* MTL *are all decidable, with the following complexities [40]:*

MSO($<, +1$)	Non-elementary
FO($<, +1$)	Non-elementary
MTL	EXPSPACE-complete

Finally, we turn our attention to alternating timed automata. The ***emptiness*** and ***language-inclusion problems*** are of course defined in the same way as for ordinary timed automata. One may also wish to model check a timed automaton $\mathcal{A}$ (*qua* implementation) against an alternating timed automaton $\mathcal{B}$ (*qua* specification). Note that since alternating timed automata are closed under all Boolean operations (in linear time), these problems are all polynomial-time equivalent to the emptiness problem.

Unfortunately, emptiness is undecidable for alternating timed automata over $\mathbb{R}_{\geq 0}$, by immediate reduction from the undecidability of language inclusion for ordinary timed automata. Thankfully, the situation over bounded time domains is more favourable:

Theorem 5. *The time-bounded emptiness and language-inclusion problems for alternating timed automata are decidable, but with non-elementary complexity [28].*

8 Discussion and Future Directions

In this work, we have attempted to promote a theory of time-bounded verification to answer, at least in part, Trakhtenbrot's 15-year-old challenge to 'lift the classical theory to the real-time world'. We have argued that this theory is both ***pertinent***, in that it is fully adequate to handle a large proportion of 'real-world' real-time systems and specifications; and ***effective***, in that the restriction to bounded time domains reclaims as decidable several of the key decision problems of real-time verification.

In terms of future work, we list below a sample of possible research avenues, roughly divided along four main axes:

I. Extensions to further real-time formalisms. In this paper, we have entirely focussed on *linear-time* semantics. Of course, a great deal of classical and real-time verification work has been carried out in *branching-time* settings, and it would be interesting to investigate whether the time-bounded approach can be usefully combined with branching-time paradigms. Several researchers have also considered various extensions of timed automata, such as *weighted timed automata* and *hybrid automata*, and assorted verification problems; again, reformulating relevant questions in a time-bounded context may prove fruitful. Another direction is that of *timed games* and related topics such as *timed controller synthesis*.

II. Algorithmic and complexity issues. The complexity bounds presented in this paper are fairly coarse-grained. In many instances, a finer 'parameterised' analysis (in which one or more of the inputs, such as the time domain, are considered fixed) would undoubtedly yield valuable additional insight. Another promising direction is to investigate combining existing algorithmic techniques, such as those exploiting *flatness* in MTL formulas [13], with the algorithms specific to time-bounded verification.

III. Expressiveness. Many important questions regarding expressiveness are left entirely unanswered. Do metric logics have equivalent alternating timed automata counterparts, and vice-versa? Can one develop an attractive theory of *timed regular expressions* over bounded time domains? Is there a good notion of *robustness* for time-bounded languages, in the sense of being impervious to sufficiently small perturbations in the timestamps?

IV. Implementation and case studies. The history of verification has been marked by a mutually beneficial interaction of theory and practice. We believe it would be highly desirable, in conjunction with the study of the theoretical concerns discussed here, to evaluate the *practical* effectiveness of time-bounded verification on real-world examples. This will no doubt require the development of appropriate abstraction schemes, data structures, symbolic techniques, algorithmic heuristics, etc. Ultimately, however, a time-bounded theory of verification can only gain widespread acceptance if its usefulness is adequately demonstrated.

References

[1] Alur, R., Courcoubetis, C., Dill, D.: Model-checking for real-time systems. In: Proceedings of LICS. IEEE Computer Society Press, Los Alamitos (1990)
[2] Alur, R., Dill, D.: A theory of timed automata. Theor. Comput. Sci. 126 (1994)
[3] Alur, R., Feder, T., Henzinger, T.A.: The benefits of relaxing punctuality. J. ACM 43(1) (1996)
[4] Alur, R., Fix, L., Henzinger, T.A.: Event-clock automata: A determinizable class of timed automata. Theor. Comput. Sci. 211 (1999)
[5] Alur, R., Henzinger, T.A.: Logics and models of real time: A survey. In: Huizing, C., de Bakker, J.W., Rozenberg, G., de Roever, W.-P. (eds.) REX 1991. LNCS, vol. 600, Springer, Heidelberg (1991)
[6] Alur, R., Henzinger, T.A.: Real-time logics: Complexity and expressiveness. Inf. Comput. 104(1) (1993)
[7] Alur, R., Henzinger, T.A.: A really temporal logic. J. ACM 41(1) (1994)
[8] Alur, R., La Torre, S., Madhusudan, P.: Perturbed timed automata. In: Morari, M., Thiele, L. (eds.) HSCC 2005. LNCS, vol. 3414, pp. 70–85. Springer, Heidelberg (2005)
[9] Asarin, E., Caspi, P., Maler, O.: Timed regular expressions. J. ACM 49(2) (2002)
[10] Baier, C., Hermanns, H., Katoen, J.-P., Haverkort, B.R.: Efficient computation of time-bounded reachability probabilities in uniform continuous-time Markov decision processes. Theor. Comput. Sci. 345(1) (2005)
[11] Bouyer, P., Chevalier, F., Markey, N.: On the expressiveness of TPTL and MTL. In: Sarukkai, S., Sen, S. (eds.) FSTTCS 2005. LNCS, vol. 3821, pp. 432–443. Springer, Heidelberg (2005)

[12] Bouyer, P., Markey, N., Ouaknine, J., Worrell, J.: The cost of punctuality. In: Proceedings of LICS. IEEE Computer Society Press, Los Alamitos (2007)
[13] Bouyer, P., Markey, N., Ouaknine, J., Worrell, J.: On expressiveness and complexity in real-time model checking. In: Aceto, L., Damgård, I., Goldberg, L.A., Halldórsson, M.M., Ingólfsdóttir, A., Walukiewicz, I. (eds.) ICALP 2008, Part II. LNCS, vol. 5126, pp. 124–135. Springer, Heidelberg (2008)
[14] Bošnački, D.: Digitization of timed automata. In: Proceedings of FMICS (1999)
[15] Chandra, A.K., Kozen, D., Stockmeyer, L.J.: Alternation. J. ACM 28(1) (1981)
[16] Dickhöfer, M., Wilke, T.: Timed alternating tree automata: The automata-theoretic solution to the TCTL model checking problem. In: Wiedermann, J., Van Emde Boas, P., Nielsen, M. (eds.) ICALP 1999. LNCS, vol. 1644, Springer, Heidelberg (1999)
[17] Emerson, E.A., Jutla, C.S.: Tree automata, mu-calculus and determinacy (extended abstract). In: Proceedings of FOCS. IEEE Computer Society Press, Los Alamitos (1991)
[18] Emmi, M., Majumdar, R.: Decision problems for the verification of real-time software. In: Hespanha, J.P., Tiwari, A. (eds.) HSCC 2006. LNCS, vol. 3927, Springer, Heidelberg (2006)
[19] Gabbay, D.M., Pnueli, A., Shelah, S., Stavi, J.: On the temporal basis of fairness. In: Proceedings of POPL. ACM Press, New York (1980)
[20] Gupta, V., Henzinger, T.A., Jagadeesan, R.: Robust timed automata. In: Maler, O. (ed.) HART 1997. LNCS, vol. 1201. Springer, Heidelberg (1997)
[21] Henzinger, T.A.: The Temporal Specification and Verification of Real-Time Systems. PhD thesis, Stanford University, Technical Report STAN-CS-91-1380 (1991)
[22] Henzinger, T.A., Manna, Z., Pnueli, A.: What good are digital clocks? In: Kuich, W. (ed.) ICALP 1992. LNCS, vol. 623. Springer, Heidelberg (1992)
[23] Henzinger, T.A., Raskin, J.-F.: Robust undecidability of timed and hybrid systems. In: Lynch, N.A., Krogh, B.H. (eds.) HSCC 2000. LNCS, vol. 1790, p. 145. Springer, Heidelberg (2000)
[24] Henzinger, T.A., Raskin, J.-F., Schobbens, P.-Y.: The regular real-time languages. In: Larsen, K.G., Skyum, S., Winskel, G. (eds.) ICALP 1998. LNCS, vol. 1443, p. 580. Springer, Heidelberg (1998)
[25] Herrmann, P.: Timed automata and recognizability. Inf. Process. Lett. 65 (1998)
[26] Hirshfeld, Y., Rabinovich, A.: Logics for real time: Decidability and complexity. Fundam. Inform. 62(1) (2004)
[27] Hirshfeld, Y., Rabinovich, A.: Expressiveness of metric modalities for continuous time. Logical Methods in Computer Science 3(1) (2007)
[28] Jenkins, M., Ouaknine, J., Rabinovich, A., Worrell, J.: Alternating timed automata over bounded time. In: Proceedings of LICS. IEEE Computer Society Press, Los Alamitos (2010)
[29] Kamp, H.: Tense Logic and the Theory of Linear Order. PhD thesis, University of California (1968)
[30] Katoen, J.-P., Zapreev, I.S.: Safe on-the-fly steady-state detection for time-bounded reachability. In: Proceedings of QEST. IEEE Computer Society Press, Los Alamitos (2006)
[31] Kaynar, D.K., Lynch, N., Segala, R., Vaandrager, F.: Timed I/O Automata: A mathematical framework for modeling and analyzing real-time systems. In: Proceedings of RTSS. IEEE Computer Society Press, Los Alamitos (2003)
[32] Koymans, R.: Specifying real-time properties with metric temporal logic. Real-Time Systems 2(4) (1990)
[33] Kupferman, O., Vardi, M.Y.: Weak alternating automata are not that weak. ACM Trans. Comput. Log. 2(3) (2001)

[34] Lasota, S., Walukiewicz, I.: Alternating timed automata. In: Sassone, V. (ed.) FOSSACS 2005. LNCS, vol. 3441, pp. 250–265. Springer, Heidelberg (2005)

[35] Lasota, S., Walukiewicz, I.: Alternating timed automata. ACM Trans. Comput. Log. 9(2) (2008)

[36] Löding, C., Thomas, W.: Alternating automata and logics over infinite words. In: Watanabe, O., Hagiya, M., Ito, T., van Leeuwen, J., Mosses, P.D. (eds.) TCS 2000. LNCS, vol. 1872, p. 521. Springer, Heidelberg (2000)

[37] Lynch, N.A., Attiya, H.: Using mappings to prove timing properties. Distributed Computing 6(2) (1992)

[38] Ostroff, J.: Temporal Logic of Real-Time Systems. Research Studies Press (1990)

[39] Ouaknine, J.: Digitisation and full abstraction for dense-time model checking. In: Katoen, J.-P., Stevens, P. (eds.) TACAS 2002. LNCS, vol. 2280, p. 37. Springer, Heidelberg (2002)

[40] Ouaknine, J., Rabinovich, A., Worrell, J.: Time-bounded verification. In: Bravetti, M., Zavattaro, G. (eds.) CONCUR 2009 - Concurrency Theory. LNCS, vol. 5710, Springer, Heidelberg (2009)

[41] Ouaknine, J., Worrell, J.: Revisiting digitization, robustness, and decidability for timed automata. In: Proceedings of LICS. IEEE Computer Society Press, Los Alamitos (2003)

[42] Ouaknine, J., Worrell, J.: Universality and language inclusion for open and closed timed automata. In: Maler, O., Pnueli, A. (eds.) HSCC 2003. LNCS, vol. 2623, pp. 375–388. Springer, Heidelberg (2003)

[43] Ouaknine, J., Worrell, J.: On the language inclusion problem for timed automata: Closing a decidability gap. In: Proceedings of LICS. IEEE Computer Society Press, Los Alamitos (2004)

[44] Ouaknine, J., Worrell, J.: On the decidability of Metric Temporal Logic. In: Proceedings of LICS. IEEE Computer Society Press, Los Alamitos (2005)

[45] Ouaknine, J., Worrell, J.: Safety Metric Temporal Logic is fully decidable. In: Hermanns, H., Palsberg, J. (eds.) TACAS 2006. LNCS, vol. 3920, pp. 411–425. Springer, Heidelberg (2006)

[46] Ouaknine, J., Worrell, J.: On the decidability and complexity of Metric Temporal Logic over finite words. Logical Methods in Computer Science 3(1) (2007)

[47] Raskin, J.-F.: Logics, Automata and Classical Theories for Deciding Real Time. PhD thesis, University of Namur (1999)

[48] Raskin, J.-F., Schobbens, P.-Y.: State-clock logic: A decidable real-time logic. In: Maler, O. (ed.) HART 1997. LNCS, vol. 1201, Springer, Heidelberg (1997)

[49] Roux, O., Rusu, V.: Verifying time-bounded properties for ELECTRE reactive programs with stopwatch automata. In: Antsaklis, P.J., Kohn, W., Nerode, A., Sastry, S.S. (eds.) HS 1994. LNCS, vol. 999, Springer, Heidelberg (1994)

[50] Taşiran, S., Alur, R., Kurshan, R.P., Brayton, R.K.: Verifying abstractions of timed systems. In: Sassone, V., Montanari, U. (eds.) CONCUR 1996. LNCS, vol. 1119. Springer, Heidelberg (1996)

[51] Trakhtenbrot, B.A.: Origins and metamorphoses of the trinity: Logic, nets, automata. In: Proceedings of LICS. IEEE Computer Society Press, Los Alamitos (1995)

[52] Vardi, M.Y.: Alternating automata and program verification. In: van Leeuwen, J. (ed.) Computer Science Today. LNCS, vol. 1000. Springer, Heidelberg (1995)

[53] Vardi, M.Y.: From philosophical to industrial logics. In: Ramanujam, R., Sarukkai, S. (eds.) ICLA 2009. LNCS (LNAI), vol. 5378, pp. 89–115. Springer, Heidelberg (2009)

[54] Wilke, T.: Specifying timed state sequences in powerful decidable logics and timed automata. In: Langmaack, H., de Roever, W.-P., Vytopil, J. (eds.) FTRTFT 1994 and ProCoS 1994. LNCS, vol. 863. Springer, Heidelberg (1994)

Physical Algorithms

Roger Wattenhofer

Computer Engineering and Networks Laboratory TIK
ETH Zurich, 8092 Zurich, Switzerland
{wattenhofer}@tik.ee.ethz.ch

Abstract. This is the accompanying paper to an ICALP 2010 invited talk, intending to encourage research in *physical algorithms*. The area of physical algorithms deals with *networked systems of active agents*. These agents have access to limited information for varying reasons; examples are communication constraints, evolving topologies, various types of faults and dynamics. The networked systems we envision include traditional computer networks, but also more generally networked systems, such as social networks, highly dynamic and mobile networks, or even networks of entities such as cars or ants. In other words, the world is becoming algorithmic, and we need the means to analyze this world!

1 Introduction

Computer science is about to undergo major changes because of the ongoing multi-core revolution.[1] These changes will happen on several levels, quite obviously with respect to hardware, but probably multi-cores will affect software and applications as well. We believe that this is a moment of opportunity to do some soul searching, and to reconsider the foundations of computer science. In particular, we suggest to widen the base of computer science, towards parallelism and distributed systems, and as we will explain below, more generally towards physical sciences.

1.1 Algorithms

Studying and analyzing algorithms has been a research success story. Turing machines, along with other machines models, gave way to analyze the efficiency of computing problems, eventually resulting in a beautiful theory with long standing open problems such as "P vs. NP".

The key to this success was essentially abstraction. Even though there is no generally accepted definition of the term "algorithm", when it comes to the analysis of algorithms there clearly is a mainstream, namely that an algorithm

[1] Looking at microprocessor clock speed charts, one may conclude that traditional sequential algorithms had an expiration date around 2005. Since 2005 computers are mostly getting faster because of multiple cores, and hence increased parallelism.

S. Abramsky et al. (Eds.): ICALP 2010, Part II, LNCS 6199, pp. 38–51, 2010.

is a recipe that computes an output as a function of an input. Usually, one is interested in minimizing the number of machine operations.[2]

Algorithm analysis is somewhere between engineering and mathematics. Indeed, algorithm analysis seems to have added an extra dimension to mathematics – *efficiency*. Until recently, mathematics mostly cared whether or not a problem had a solution. Now the efficiency dimension adds shades of grey, as one may wonder how difficult it is to find a solution of a problem.

Computational complexity has been a veritable success story in computer science, and subsequently in mathematics, too. The practical impact of the theoretical results is a dense net of problems whose complexity in terms of the input size is known, thus permitting to estimate the required amount of resources to solve a given task. In the end, it allows to decide whether it is *economically* feasible (rather than just theoretically possible) to realize a certain solution to a problem. The success of this approach primarily comes from the simplicity and generality of the underlying input/output computational model. As such, results are comparable and robust against model changes.

In summary, computational complexity is a strong tool to analyze input/output algorithms, applied by computer science as well as other science disciplines. Not only is it a beautiful theory, it also has major practical relevance as computers are by and large equivalent to the theoretical machine models such as random access or Turing machines. Alas, ...

1.2 The King Is Dead

... as we speak, computers are changing! Physical constraints prevent sequential systems from getting faster. The speed of light limits processor *clock speeds* depending on the size of the CPU, while in turn transistors cannot be miniaturized arbitrarily due to quantum effects. Instead, hardware designers have turned to *multi-core* architectures, in which multiple processing cores are included on each chip. Today, two or four cores are standard, but soon enough the standard will be eight and more. This switch to multi-core architectures promises increased parallelism, but not increased single-thread performance. Software developers are expected to handle this increased parallelism, i.e., they are expected to write software that exploits the multi-core architecture by consisting of several components that can run in parallel without introducing substantial overhead. This is a notoriously difficult job.

Consequently, it is questionable whether the success story of sequential complexity analysis will continue. Multi-core machines are not the same as random access machines, with an exponentially growing number of cores less and less so. More generally, computing systems become more and more distributed in the sense that information is *local*. Be it the Internet or a system-on-a-chip, no

[2] There are other measures of complexity, e.g. how much space or randomness is used, however, step complexity is generally considered the most important measure. Also, typically only asymptotics are considered, i.e., how much longer the computation takes if the input gets larger.

single part of the system has access to the global state as a whole, fundamentally changing what can—or rather cannot—be done.

Essentially, the question we want to raise is whether the beauty of computational complexity continues to reflect the complexity of our physical world, or whether it will be diminished to a concept of pure theory and math.

1.3 Long Live the King

We claim that algorithm analysis needs to be adapted, to meet the requirements of current and future computer systems. Indeed, we believe that the time is right to ask this question in a more general context. It seems that more and more other sciences are dealing with systems that are distributed in one way or another. In this paper, we survey a few examples; in lack of a better name we call the area *physical algorithms.* The idea is to take techniques from algorithm analysis and computation complexity, and transform these into tools applicable also in settings which do not match the original input/output model.

2 Physical Algorithms

The area of *physical algorithms* deals with networked systems of active agents. These agents are limited in various ways; examples are communication constraints, computational or memory constraints, evolving topologies, various types of faults and dynamics. The networked systems we envision include traditional computer networks such as the Internet or clusters, but also more generally networked systems, such as social networks, or even highly dynamic and mobile "networks" of entities such as cars or ants. Often, parts of the system can be designed or influenced, but others cannot.

Our definition of physical algorithms includes, but is not limited to, the area of distributed algorithms. For instance, we may not be able to specify the protocol of any of the agents at all, instead examining the effect of changing the amount or reliability of information available to the agents. We emphasize dynamics, i.e., algorithms should (if possible) adapt to dynamic changes. In general, we attempt not to presume a potentially unrealistic amount of control of system properties.

Moreover, networks that are large (on their respective scale), suffer from the unreliability of information. Parts of the system may fail, or even behave maliciously in order to corrupt the available data. Information becomes outdated because of changing topology or inputs, or more subtle variations such as differing communication delays. Widening the scope, many systems comprise intelligent agents that act on their own behalf, not necessarily seeking to support the community. Agents may compete for resources selfishly, and cannot be expected to adhere to a specific protocol unless it maximizes their individual profit.

Physical algorithms cover e.g. distributed algorithmic game theory, networks and locality, self-organization, dynamic systems, social networks, control theory, wireless networks, multi-core systems, and – getting more ambitious – the human brain as a network of neurons [KPSS10], social insects, biological systems in general [Cha09], or also financial and political systems [ABBG10]. Figure 1 provides a "map" of what we consider physical algorithms. The general aim is to find connections between these topics, and to find a general theory that includes central aspects.

In the following, we first give a refined picture of the two axes of Figure 1. We also give a few concrete application areas of physical algorithms, to render the definition more lucid. Some of these areas are well-established already, some are developing rapidly right now.

2.1 Agents

The agents themselves can be limited in different ways. They may be constrained in computational power, in the sense that they can only compute restricted functions, or they may not be able to store (large amounts of) information. Such limitations may be particularly interesting in areas such as social insects.

Fault Tolerance: Moreover, agents may not be reliable. Agents may crash at any point in time, because of lacking energy for instance. Likewise, agents may crash and later regenerate. Also, agents may experience some kind of omission failure, e.g. failing to receive a message, or transient commission failures, e.g. a local state corruption.

Sometimes however, agents will misbehave in more awkward ways, for instance by starting to behave in erratic ways, e.g. by sending random messages. Indeed, the pioneers in fault-tolerance observed machine behavior that was essentially inexplicable. They decided that the only reasonable way to model such behavior was to consider the machines being "malicious". Following their early papers we call such behavior *Byzantine* today [SPL80, LSP82].

When a Byzantine failure has occurred, the system may respond in any unpredictable way, unless it is designed to have Byzantine fault tolerance. In a Byzantine fault tolerant algorithm, agents must take counter-measures that deal with Byzantine behavior. Essentially, in many problems, the fraction of Byzantine agents must be strictly less than a third [LSP82].

More recently, different kinds of agent (mis)behavior are getting into the spotlight, in particular selfishness.

Game Theory: Algorithmic research has often dealt with models and problems that do not follow the orthodox input/output format. Indeed, these studies are probably as old as computer science itself. One of the very fathers of computer science itself, John von Neumann, is among the pioneers of a conceptually significantly different approach.

Before writing one of the earliest articles on computer science [vN93] in 1945, von Neumann (together with Oscar Morgenstern) published *Games and Economic Behavior* [vNM47]. Today, algorithms and game theory are converging

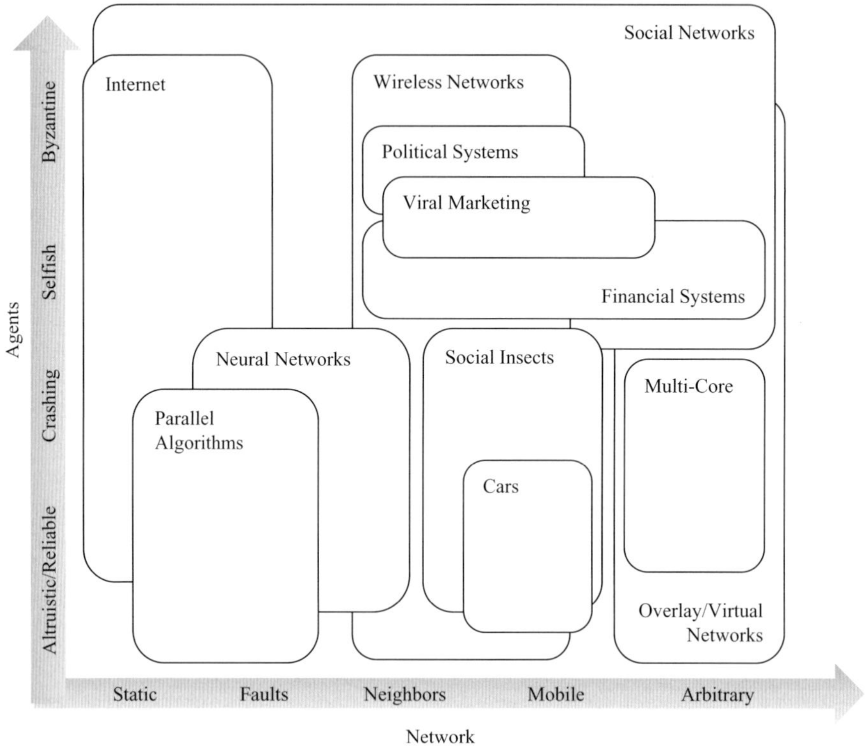

Fig. 1. A representation of the playing field of physical algorithms. On the vertical axis, we see some typical models for the agents that make up networks. In the simplest case, all agents are benevolent and reliable. In many systems, however, agents will be faulty, and for instance crash. In other systems, agents will be selfish in a game-theoretic way, i.e. they will be strategic in order to maximize their benefit. Finally, agents may be malicious (Byzantine), even to a degree that they want to harm the system. Clearly there is no total ordering between these agent models, in some systems faulty agents may be more difficult to deal with than selfish agents. Also, mixed forms of agents may be considered, i.e. some selfish, others malicious. The horizontal axis represents the dynamics of the network. Also here the variants are by no means complete, they should just give some intuition of what is possible. The simplest form of dynamics are no dynamics at all, i.e. fixed networks. In most systems, networks are not static, but allow for at least some slow form of dynamics, for instance, if once in a while—very rarely—a link will fail because of a hardware failure. Further to the right, the frequency of topology changes increases to a point where the network is continuously transforming. The level of dynamics depends on this frequency, but also how these topology changes are restricted. Maybe only local neighborhoods are changing? Maybe the agents themselves are mobile, forming edges whenever two agents are in vicinity of each other? Finally, we may consider completely virtual networks just modeling some physical process, with rather arbitrary forms of dynamics. The figure exemplarily shows typical application areas of physical algorithms. Depending on the application and the considered time frame, we allow for many forms of network dynamics.

again, as researchers are starting to view the Internet and other computer science phenomena in the light of game theory.[3]

One of the cornerstones of game theory is the so-called equilibrium,[4] which describes a state of a system where no participant of the system has an incentive to change its strategy. As a perfect example of mathematicians mostly being interested in the question whether something can be done or not, pure game theorists are generally not interested in how such an equilibrium can be reached, or how long it takes to reach the equilibrium. Computer scientists on the other hand have been interested early on how to reach such an equilibrium [DGP06]. Clearly, this is an interesting playground for physical algorithms, as the participants of the systems cannot be modeled well by an input/output algorithm.

Today, game theory is a well-accepted subject in algorithms, probably the only one that does not follow the input/output paradigm that is well represented at theoretical computer science conferences.

Recently, research is starting to combine fault-tolerance with game theory [AAC+05].[5] In [MSW06], for instance, it is shown that the presence of Byzantine players may even contribute to the social welfare of a system.

2.2 Networks

Less known, the very same John von Neumann was also seminal in the development of the horizontal axis in our map of physical algorithms. Networks exist in many variants today, apart from the predominant Internet there are also niche areas such as sensor or peer-to-peer networks. More generally (and daring), one may even consider networks beyond computing, e.g. the human society or the brain.

Locality: All networks have in common that they are composed of a multiplicity of individual entities, so-called *nodes*; e.g. human beings in society, hosts in the Internet, or neurons in the brain. Each individual node can directly communicate only to a small number of neighboring nodes. On the other hand, in spite of each node being inherently "near-sighted", i.e., restricted to *local* communication, the entirety of the system is supposed to work towards some kind of *global* goal, solution, or equilibrium.

It is at the core of really understanding networks to know the possibilities and limitations of this *local computation*, i.e., to what degree local information is sufficient to solve global tasks [Lin92, Pel00, KMW04, Suo09]. Many tasks are inherently local, for instance, how many friends of friends one has. Many other tasks are inherently global, for instance, counting all the nodes of the system, or

---

[3] Algorithmic game theory is a perfect example of the differences between the approach of computer science and mathematics/physics. In computer science, researchers try to understand the Internet by modeling the participants of the Internet as active (selfish) agents. Mathematicians and physicists take a more holistic approach and try to find random graphs that model all possible layers of the Internet (web pages, autonomous service providers, routers), or simply postulate that the bandwidth demands in the Internet are self-similar.

[4] Several different types of equilibria exist, e.g. Nash equilibria in games, or price equilibria in markets.

[5] One may argue that Byzantine agents are just selfish agents with a different goal.

figuring out the diameter of the system. To solve such global problems, there is at least some information that must traverse long distances.

It is natural to ask whether there are tasks that are in the middle of these two extremes; tasks that are neither completely local nor inherently global. Indeed, this is the case. Assume for example that the nodes want to organize themselves, some nodes should be "masters", the others will be "slaves". The rules are that no two masters shall be direct neighbors, but every slave must have at least one master as direct neighbor. In graph theory, this problem is known as the *maximal independent set* (MIS) problem. Intuitively, this problem seems local since the rules are completely local. Consequently it might be expected that every node can communicate with its neighbors a few times, and together they can decide who will become master and who will become slave. However, this intuition is misleading. Even though the problem seems local, it cannot be solved using local information only! No matter how the system tackles the problem, no matter what protocol or algorithm the nodes use, non-local information is vital to solve the task. On the other hand, the problem is also not global: Mid-range information is enough to solve the problem. As such the MIS problem establishes an example that is neither local nor global, but in-between these extremes. Since at first sight it looks local, let us call it *pseudo-local.* Using *locality-preserving reductions* one can show that there exists a whole class of pseudo-local problems, similar to the class of NP-complete problems [KMW04].

This class of pseudo-local problems also includes many combinatorial optimization problems, such as minimum vertex cover, minimum dominating set, or maximum matching. In such problems, each node must base its decision (for example whether or not to join the dominating set) only on information about its pseudo-local neighborhood, and yet, the goal is to collectively achieve a good approximation to the globally optimal solution. Studying such local approximation algorithms is particularly interesting because it sheds light on the trade-off between the *amount of available local information* and the *resulting global optimality.* Specifically, it characterizes the amount of information needed in distributed decision making: what can be done with the information that is available within some fixed-size neighborhood of a node. Positive and negative results for local algorithms can thus be interpreted as information-theoretic upper and lower bounds; they give insight into the value of information [KMW06].

We believe that studying the fundamental possibilities and limitations of local computation is of interest to theoreticians in approximation theory, distributed computing, and graph theory. Furthermore, these results may be of interest for a wide range of scientific areas, for instance dynamic systems that change over time. The theory shows that small changes in a dynamic system may cause an intermediate (or pseudo-local) "butterfly effect," and it gives non-trivial bounds for self-healing or self-organizing systems, such as self-assembling robots. It also establishes bounds for further application areas, initially in engineering and computing, possibly extending to other areas studying large-scale networks, essentially *physical algorithms.*

Studying locality and networks is at the heart of physical algorithms, as it is one of the few examples that have established some form of theory that uses concepts of complexity theory outside the input/output model.

Self-Organization and Dynamic Systems: Looking at the wider picture, one may argue that the idea of local algorithms as discussed in the last paragraph goes back to the early 1970s when Dijkstra introduced the concept of *self-stabilization* [Dij73]. A self-stabilizing system must survive arbitrary failures, including for instance a total wipe out of volatile memory at all nodes. The system must self-heal and eventually converge to a correct state from any arbitrary starting state, provided that no further faults occur.

It seems that the world of self-stabilization (which is asynchronous, long-lived, and full of malicious failures) has nothing in common with the world of local algorithms (which is synchronous, one-shot, and free of failures). However, as shown 20 years ago, this perception is incorrect [AS88], and the two areas are related. Intuitively, this is because (i) asynchronous systems can be made synchronous, (ii) self-stabilization concentrates on the case after the last failure, when all parts of the system are correct again, and (iii) one-shot algorithms can just be executed in an infinite loop. Thus, efficient self-stabilization essentially boils down to local algorithms and hence, local algorithms are the key to understanding fault-tolerance [LSW09].

Likewise, local algorithms help to understand *dynamic networks*, in which the topology of the system is constantly changing, either because of churn (nodes constantly joining or leaving as in peer-to-peer systems), mobility (edge changes because of mobile nodes in mobile networks), changing environmental conditions (edge changes in wireless networks), or algorithmic dynamics (edge changes because of algorithmic decisions in virtual or overlay networks). In dynamic networks, no node in the network is capable of keeping up-to-date global information on the network. Instead, nodes have to perform their intended (global) task based on local information only. In other words, all computation in these systems is inherently local! By using local algorithms, it is guaranteed that dynamics only affect a restricted neighborhood. Indeed, to the best of our knowledge, local algorithms always give the best solutions when it comes to dynamics. Dynamics also play a natural role in the area of self-assembly (DNA computing, self-assembling robots, shape-shifting systems, or claytronics), and as such it is not surprising that local algorithms are being considered a key to understanding self-assembling systems [Ste09, GCM05].

Social Networks: As already mentioned, there are numerous types of networks, including for instance the human society or the network of all the web pages in the world. Indeed, so-called *social networks* such as Facebook just merge the two concepts.

A decade ago Jon Kleinberg [Kle00] gave a first algorithmic explanation to a phenomenon studied almost a century ago. Back in the 1929, Frigyes Karinthy published a volume of short stories that postulated that the world was "shrinking" because human beings were connected more and more. Some claim that he was inspired by radio network pioneer Guglielmo Marconi's 1909 Nobel Prize speech, to make the century complete. Despite physical distance, the growing density of human "networks" made the actual social distance smaller and smaller. As a result, any two individuals could be connected through at most five acquaintances, i.e. within six hops.

This idea has been followed ardently in the 1960s by several sociologists, first by Michael Gurevich, later by Stanley Milgram. Milgram wanted to know the average path length between two "random" humans, by using various experiments, generally using individuals from the US Midwest as starting points and from Boston as end points. The starting points were asked to send a letter to a well-described target person in Boston, however not directly, but only through an intermediate friend, hopefully "closer" to the target person. Shortly after starting the experiment, letters have been received. Often enough of course letters were lost during the process, but if they arrived, the average path length was about 5.5.

Statisticians tried to explain Milgram's experiments, by essentially giving network models that allowed for short diameters, i.e. each node is connected to each other node by only a few hops. Until today there is a thriving research community in statistical physics that tries to understand network properties that allow for "small world" effects. One of the keywords in this area are power-law graphs, networks were node degrees are distributed according to a power-law function.

This is interesting, but not enough to really understand what is going on. For Milgram's experiments to work, it is not sufficient to connect the nodes in a certain way. In addition, the nodes *themselves* need to know how to forward a message to one of their neighbors, even though they cannot know whether that neighbor is really closer to the target. In other words, nodes are not just following physical laws, but they make decisions themselves. In contrast to those mathematicians that worked on the problem earlier, Kleinberg [Kle00] understood that Milgram's experiment essentially shows that social networks are "navigable", and that one can only explain it in terms of a *greedy routing*.

In particular, Kleinberg set up an artificial network with nodes on a grid topology, plus one additional random link per node. In a quantitative study he showed that the random links need a specific distance distribution to allow for efficient greedy routing. This distribution marks the sweet spot for any navigable network. As such it is a great example for physical *algorithms*, because physical methods alone cannot find such a sweet spot, as statistical physicists hardly argue about algorithmic properties.

The are many applications for research in social networking, for instance viral marketing [KOW08], or spreading of biological viruses.

Physical Objects: A science fiction favorite are automatic cars equipped with distance sensors, following each other at high speed and minimal distance. This is a typical instance of physical objects organizing themselves. Unlike planets these cars are not just following the laws of physics, but they will run algorithms that, depending on the values delivered by the distance sensors or other additional information (for instance wireless communication between cars), may speed up or slow down. Having studied control theory (or having been in a read-end collision accident) one knows that high speed lines of cars are not without problems. No matter what, the control loop will experience some delay. So if some car will need to break slightly, the next car might need to break a bit more already, and a few cars down the road we might have a terrible crash, because some car cannot break hard enough anymore.

There are several examples like this, e.g. coordination of helicopters or, more generally, any kind of swarm trying to maintain a certain formation based only on local distance information. In all these cases the agents may slowly drift from their desired (relative) position, because they are not able or willing to control their speeds perfectly. Furthermore, information on neighbors' positions could be outdated and/or inaccurate. Another example is clock synchronization in computer networks: Each node is equipped with a hardware clock which is not completely accurate, and nodes communicate local clock values by exchanging messages of varying delay with their neighbors.

All these examples have in common that they are algorithmic, in the sense that nodes have countless possibilities how to react to changes in the system. In a recent article [LLW10], tight bounds for some clock synchronization problem have been proved. These results are surprising in various ways. Even if all hardware clocks are accurate up to a few ticks per million ticks, it was shown that no matter what algorithm one uses, the error will depend on the size of the network. There is a simple algorithm that matches the lower bound using local information only, however, unfortunately, this algorithm is not intuitive. Indeed, it was shown that a number of canonical approaches are exponentially worse than the lower bound [LW06].

Real-time control of physical objects is of course beyond the input/output paradigm, still these problems usually have an algorithmic component which is worth studying. The range is large, from simple questions like how to organize a group of robot vacuum cleaners in order to clean a floor most efficiently, to the question of bird flocking [Cha09].

Wireless Communication: Network dynamics go well beyond mobility and failures. In some networks, communication is not graph- but geometry-based, in the sense that nodes can communicate with nearby nodes, only if not too many other nearby nodes transmit at the same time.

In the past, a large fraction of analytic research on wireless networks has focused on models where the network is represented by a graph. The wireless devices are nodes, any two nodes within communication (or interference) range are connected by an (annotated) edge. Such graph-based models are particularly popular among higher-layer protocol designers, hence they are also known as protocol models. Unfortunately, protocol models are often too simplistic. Consider for instance a case of three wireless communication pairs, every two of which can be transmitting concurrently without a conflict. In a protocol model one will conclude that all three senders may transmit concurrently. Instead, in reality, wireless signals accumulate, and it may be that any two transmissions together generate too much interference, hindering the third receiver from correctly receiving the signal of its sender.

This many-to-many relationship makes understanding wireless transmissions difficult; a model where interference accumulates seems paramount to fully comprehend wireless communication. Similarly, protocol models oversimplify wireless attenuation. In protocol models the signal is usually binary, as if there was an invisible wall at which the signal immediately drops. Not surprisingly, in reality the signal decreases gracefully with distance. Because of these shortcomings, results for protocol models are often not applicable in reality. In contrast to the algorithmic ("computer science") community which focuses on protocol models, researchers in information, communication, or network theory ("electrical engineering") are working with wireless models that add up interference and take attenuation into account. A standard model is the *physical* model.

In the *physical model* the energy of a signal fades with distance. If the signal strength received by a device divided by the interfering strength of competitor transmitters (plus the noise) is above some threshold, the receiver can decode the message, otherwise it cannot. The physical model is reflecting the physical reality more precisely, hence its name. Unfortunately, most work in this model does not focus on algorithms with provable performance guarantees. Instead heuristics are usually proposed and evaluated by simulation. Analytical work is done for special cases only, e.g. networks with a grid structure, or random traffic. However, these special cases do neither give insights into the complexity of the problem, nor do they give algorithmic results that may ultimately lead to new distributed protocols. If one is interested in the capacity of an arbitrary wireless network, and how this capacity can be achieved, the community is not able to provide an answer.

However, this is about to change. Starting with [MW06], more and more algorithms work is adopting the physical model, thus combining the best of both worlds, by giving algorithms and limits for arbitrary wireless networks (not random node distributions), using the physical model (not the protocol model). We believe that bridging the gap between protocol designers and communication theorists is a fundamental challenge of the coming years, a hot topic for the wireless network community with implications for both theory and practice, and again a nice example of physical algorithms.

Multi-Core: Let us finish with what we started, multi-core systems. The switch to multi-core architectures promises increased parallelism, but not increased single-thread performance. Software developers are expected to handle this increased parallelism.

Today, the main tool for dealing with parallelism are *locks*; locks are software constructs that allow access to shared memory cells in a mutually exclusive way. However, there seems to be a general consensus in the computer science research community that locks are not the optimal programming paradigm to deal with concurrency and synchronization. Nobody really knows how to build large systems depending on locks. The currently most promising solution is *transactional memory* [HM93]. Similarly to the database world, the programmer should encapsulate sequences of instructions within a transaction. Either the whole transaction is executed, or nothing at all. Other threads will see a transaction as one indivisible operation.

To some degree, the core of a transactional memory system is the *contention manager*. In case of a conflict between two transactions (e.g., both trying to store a value into the same memory cell), the contention manager decides which transaction must wait, or has to be aborted. The contention management policy of a transactional memory implementation can have a profound effect on its performance, and even correctness. Putting it simply, the contention manager inherits the role of the scheduler in a single core operating system.

In general, we believe that the key to understanding multi-core computing is through understanding networks. Transactions may for example be modeled as nodes in a *dependency graph* with edges between them in case of a conflict. Resolving conflicts based on local knowledge in this graph, solutions will scale canonically with multi-core systems growing. Thus, the problem naturally falls in the field of physical algorithms. A coloring of the graph yields a possible schedule for the transactions by executing all transactions of the same color in parallel.

An additional issue arises from the concurrent nature of programs in multi-core architecture. As concurrent processes interact and interfere with each other, processes also *compete* for some shared resources. If we keep in mind that in many cases, programmers who write code for a multi-core system are hardly interested in the performance of other processes, but merely on their own program's performance, we cannot desist from analyzing multi-core systems under the assumption that processes compete selfishly for system resources. To link back to our first example, game theory offers a great set of tools for this setting. We want to figure out whether existing multi-core systems are cheating-proof, i.e., incentive compatible in the sense that programmers have no interest to deviate from a behavior which is best for the overall performance of the system [EW09].

It is necessary to shed more light on the theoretical foundations of multi-core systems, with a special focus on transactional memory and its contention manager [SW09]. What one needs are refined models of efficiency and new contention managers that provably optimize the efficiency of transactional memory systems.

Acknowledgements. Thanks to Christoph Lenzen, for discussing the topic, and for reading the manuscript.

References

[AAC+05] Aiyer, A.S., Alvisi, L., Clement, A., Dahlin, M., Martin, J.-P., Porth, C.: Bar fault tolerance for cooperative services. In: SOSP, pp. 45–58 (2005)

[ABBG10] Arora, S., Barak, B., Brunnermeier, M., Ge, R.: Computational complexity and informational asymmetry in financial products (Unpublished manuscript) (2010)

[AS88] Awerbuch, B., Sipser, M.: Dynamic networks are as fast as static networks (preliminary version). In: FOCS, pp. 206–220. IEEE, Los Alamitos (1988)

[Cha09] Chazelle, B.: Natural algorithms. In: Proc. of the 20th ACM-SIAM Symposium on Discrete Algorithms, SODA (2009)

[DGP06] Daskalakis, C., Goldberg, P.W., Papadimitriou, C.H.: The complexity of computing a nash equilibrium. In: Proceedings of the thirty-eighth annual ACM symposium on Theory of computing (STOC), pp. 71–78. ACM, New York (2006)

[Dij73] Dijkstra, E.W.: Self-stabilization in spite of distributed control. EWD391 (October 1973) (manuscript)

[EW09] Eidenbenz, R., Wattenhofer, R.: Good Programming in Transactional Memory: Game Theory Meets Multicore Architecture. In: Dong, Y., Du, D.-Z., Ibarra, O. (eds.) ISAAC 2009. LNCS, vol. 5878. Springer, Heidelberg (2009)

[FLP83] Michael, J., Fischer, N.A.: Lynch, and Mike Paterson. Impossibility of distributed consensus with one faulty process. In: PODS, pp. 1–7 (1983)

[GCM05] Goldstein, S.C., Campbell, J.D., Mowry, T.C.: Programmable matter. Computer 38(6), 99–101 (2005)

[HM93] Herlihy, M., Moss, J.E.B.: Transactional memory: Architectural support for lock-free data structures. In: ISCA, pp. 289–300 (1993)

[Kle00] Kleinberg, J.M.: The small-world phenomenon: an algorithm perspective. In: STOC, pp. 163–170 (2000)

[KMW04] Kuhn, F., Moscibroda, T., Wattenhofer, R.: What Cannot be Computed Locally!. In: Proc. of the 23rd ACM Symposium on the Principles of Distributed Computing (PODC), pp. 300–309 (2004)

[KMW06] Kuhn, F., Moscibroda, T., Wattenhofer, R.: The Price of Being Near-Sighted. In: Proc. of the 17th ACM-SIAM Symposium on Discrete Algorithms, SODA (2006)

[KOW08] Kostka, J., Oswald, Y.A., Wattenhofer, R.: Word of Mouth: Rumor Dissemination in Social Networks. In: Shvartsman, A.A., Felber, P. (eds.) SIROCCO 2008. LNCS, vol. 5058, pp. 185–196. Springer, Heidelberg (2008)

[KPSS10] Kuhn, F., Panagiotou, K., Spencer, J., Steger, A.: Synchrony and asynchrony in neural networks. In: Proc. of the 21st ACM-SIAM Symposium on Discrete Algorithms, SODA (2010)

[Lin92] Linial, N.: Locality in Distributed Graph Algorithms. SIAM Journal on Computing 21(1), 193–201 (1992)

[LLW10] Lenzen, C., Locher, T., Wattenhofer, R.: Tight Bounds for Clock Synchronization. J. ACM 57(2) (2010)

[LSP82] Lamport, L., Shostak, R., Pease, M.: The Byzantine Generals Problem. ACM Trans. Program. Lang. Syst. 4(3), 382–401 (1982)

[LSW09] Lenzen, C., Suomela, J., Wattenhofer, R.: Local Algorithms: Self-Stabilization on Speed. In: 11th International Symposium on Stabilization, Safety, and Security of Distributed Systems (SSS), Lyon, France (November 2009)

[LW06] Locher, T., Wattenhofer, R.: Oblivious Gradient Clock Synchronization. In: 20th International Symposium on Distributed Computing (DISC), Stockholm, Sweden (September 2006)

[MSW06] Moscibroda, T., Schmid, S., Wattenhofer, R.: When Selfish Meets Evil: Byzantine Players in a Virus Inoculation Game. In: 25th Annual Symposium on Principles of Distributed Computing (PODC), Denver, Colorado, USA (July 2006)

[MW06] Moscibroda, T., Wattenhofer, R.: The Complexity of Connectivity in Wireless Networks. In: 25th Annual Joint Conference of the IEEE Computer and Communications Societies (INFOCOM), Barcelona, Spain (April 2006)

[Pel00] Peleg, D.: Distributed Computing: A Locality-Sensitive Approach. SIAM Monographs on Discrete Mathematics and Applications (2000)

[SPL80] Shostak, R., Pease, M., Lamport, L.: Reaching Agreement in the Presence of Faults. J. of the ACM 27(2), 228–234 (1980)

[Ste09] Sterling, A.: Memory consistency conditions for self-assembly programming. CoRR, abs/0909.2704 (2009)

[Suo09] Suomela, J.: Survey of local algorithms (2009) (manuscript)

[SW09] Schneider, J., Wattenhofer, R.: Bounds On Contention Management Algorithms. In: 20th International Symposium on Algorithms and Computation (ISAAC), Honolulu, USA (December 2009)

[vN93] von Neumann, J.: First Draft of a Report on the EDVAC. IEEE Ann. Hist. Comput. 15(4), 27–75 (1993)

[vNM47] von Neumann, J., Morgenstern, O.: Theory of games and economic behavior. Princeton University Press, Princeton (1947)

Optimal Zielonka-Type Construction of Deterministic Asynchronous Automata

Blaise Genest[1,2], Hugo Gimbert[3], Anca Muscholl[3], and Igor Walukiewicz[3]

[1] CNRS, IPAL UMI, joint with I2R-A*STAR-NUS, Singapore
[2] CNRS, IRISA UMR, joint with Université Rennes I, France
[3] LaBRI, CNRS/Université Bordeaux, France

Abstract. Asynchronous automata are parallel compositions of finite-state processes synchronizing over shared variables. A deep theorem due to Zielonka says that every regular trace language can be represented by a deterministic asynchronous automaton. In this paper we improve the construction, in that the size of the obtained asynchronous automaton is polynomial in the size of a given DFA and simply exponential in the number of processes. We show that our construction is optimal within the class of automata produced by Zielonka-type constructions. In particular, we provide the first non trivial lower bound on the size of asynchronous automata.

1 Introduction

Zielonka's asynchronous automata [15] is probably one of the simplest, and yet rich, models of distributed computation. This model has a solid theoretical foundation based on the theory of Mazurkiewicz traces [9,4]. The key property of asynchronous automata, known as Zielonka's theorem, is that every regular trace language can be represented by a deterministic asynchronous automaton [15]. This result is one of the central results on distributed systems and has been applied in many contexts. Its complex proof has been revisited on numerous occasions (see e.g. [2,3,12,13,6] for a selection of such papers). In particular some significant complexity gains have been achieved since the original construction. This paper provides yet another such improvement, and moreover it shows that the presented construction is in some sense optimal.

The asynchronous automata model is basically a parallel composition of finite-state processes synchronizing over shared (state) variables. Zielonka's theorem has many interpretations, here we would like to consider it as a result about distributed synthesis: it gives a method to construct a deterministic asynchronous automaton from a given sequential one and a distribution of the actions over the set of processes. We remark that in this context it is essential that the construction gives a deterministic asynchronous automaton: for a controller it is the behaviour and not language acceptance that is important. The result has applications beyond the asynchronous automata model, for example it can be used to synthesize communicating automata with bounded communication channels [11,7] or existentially-bounded channels [5]. Despite these achievements, from

S. Abramsky et al. (Eds.): ICALP 2010, Part II, LNCS 6199, pp. 52–63, 2010.

the point of view of applications, the biggest problem of constructions of asynchronous automata is considered to be their high complexity. The best constructions give either automata of size doubly exponential in the number of processes, or exponential in the size of the sequential automaton.

This paper proposes an improved construction of deterministic asynchronous automata. It offers the first algorithm that gives an automaton of size *polynomial* in the size of the sequential automaton and exponential only in the number of processes. We show that this is optimal for Zielonka-type constructions, namely constructions where each component has complete information about its history. For this we introduce the notion of *locally rejecting* asynchronous automaton and remark that all Zielonka-type constructions produce this kind of automata. To be locally rejecting means that a process should reject as soon as its history tells him that there is no accepting extension. We believe that a locally rejecting behavior is quite desirable for applications, such as monitoring or control. We show that when transforming a deterministic word automaton to a deterministic locally rejecting automaton, the exponential blow-up in the number of components is unavoidable. Thus, to improve our construction one would need to produce automata that are not locally rejecting.

For the upper bound we start from a *deterministic* (I-diamond) word automaton. We think that this is the best point of departure for a study of the complexity of constructing asynchronous automata: considering non deterministic automata would introduce costs related to determinization. The size of the deterministic asynchronous automaton obtained is measured as the sum of the sizes of the local states sets. It means that we do not take global accepting states into account. This is reasonable in our opinion, as it is hardly practical to list these states explicitly. From a deterministic I-diamond automaton $\mathcal{A}$ and a distributed alphabet with process set $\mathcal{P}$, we construct a deterministic asynchronous automaton of size $4^{|\mathcal{P}|^4} \cdot |\mathcal{A}|^{|\mathcal{P}|^2}$. We believe that this complexity, although exponential in the number of processes, is interesting in practice: an implementation of such a device needs only memory of size logarithmic in $|\mathcal{A}|$ and polynomial in $|\mathcal{P}|$. We also show that computing the next state on-the-fly can be done in time polynomial in both $|\mathcal{A}|$ and $|\mathcal{P}|$.

Related work. Besides general constructions of Zielonka type, there are a couple of different constructions, however they either apply to subclasses of regular trace languages, or they produce non deterministic automata (or both). The first category includes [10,3], that provide deterministic asynchronous cellular automata from a given trace homomorphism in case that the dependence alphabet is acyclic and chordal, respectively. These constructions are quite simple and only polynomial in the size of the monoid (thus still exponential in the size of a DFA). In the second category we find [16], who gives an inductive construction for non deterministic, deadlock-free asynchronous cellular automata. (A deadlock-free variant of Zielonka's construction was proposed in [14]). The paper [1] proposes a construction of asynchronous automata of size exponential only in the number of processes (and polynomial in $|\mathcal{A}|$) as our construction, but it yields non deterministic asynchronous automata (inappropriate for monitoring or control). Notice that while asynchronous automata can be determinized, there are cases where the blow-up is doubly exponential in the number of processes [8].

2 Preliminaries

We fix a finite set $\mathcal{P}$ of processes and a finite alphabet Σ. Each letter $a \in \Sigma$ is an action associated with the set of processes $\mathrm{dom}(a) \subseteq \mathcal{P}$ involved in its execution. A pair (Σ, dom) is called *distributed alphabet*. A deterministic automaton over the alphabet Σ is a tuple $\mathcal{A} = \langle Q, \Sigma, \Delta, q^0, F\rangle$ with a finite set of states Q, a set of final states F, an initial state q^0 and a transition function $\Delta : Q \times \Sigma \to Q$. As usual we extend Δ to words in Σ^*. The automaton accepts $w \in \Sigma^*$ if $\Delta(q^0, w) \in F$. We use $\mathcal{L}(\mathcal{A})$ to denote the language accepted by $\mathcal{A}$. The size $|\mathcal{A}|$ of $\mathcal{A}$ is the number of its states.

Concurrent executions of systems with shared actions given by a distributed alphabet (Σ, dom), are readily modeled by Mazurkiewicz traces [9]. The idea is that the distribution of the alphabet defines an independence relation among actions $I \subseteq \Sigma \times \Sigma$, by setting $(a, b) \in I$ if and only if $\mathrm{dom}(a) \cap \mathrm{dom}(b) = \emptyset$. We call (Σ, I) an *independence alphabet*. The independence relation induces a congruence $\sim$ on Σ^* by setting $u \sim v$ if there exist words $u_1, \ldots, u_n \in \Sigma^*$ with $u_1 = u$, $u_n = v$ and such that for every $i < n$ we have $u_i = xaby$, $u_{i+1} = xbay$ for some $x, y \in \Sigma^*$ and $(a, b) \in I$. An $\sim$-equivalence class is simply called a *(Mazurkiewicz) trace*. We denote by $[u]$ the trace associated with the word $u \in \Sigma^*$ (for simplicity we do not refer to I, neither in $\sim$ nor in $[u]$, as the independence alphabet is fixed). Trace prefixes and trace factors are defined as usual, with $[p]$ a trace prefix (trace factor, resp.) of $[u]$ if p is a word prefix (word factor, resp.) of some $v \sim u$. As usual, we write $\leq$ for the prefix order. For two prefixes T_1, T_2 of T, we let $T_1 \cup T_2$ denote the smallest prefix T' of T such that $T_i \leq T'$ for $i = 1, 2$.

For several purposes it is convenient to represent traces by (labeled) pomsets. Formally, a trace $T = [a_1 \cdots a_n]$ ($a_i \in \Sigma$ for all i) corresponds to a labeled pomset $\langle E, \lambda, \leq\rangle$ defined as follows: $E = \{e_1, \ldots, e_n\}$ is a set of events (or nodes), one for each position in T. Event e_i is labeled by $\lambda(e_i) = a_i$, for each i. The relation $\leq$ is the least partial order on E with $e_i \leq e_j$ whenever $(a_i, a_j) \notin I$ and $i \leq j$. In Figure 1 we give an example for the pomset of a trace T, depicted by its Hasse diagram. The labeling of a total order on E that is compatible with $\leq$ is called a *linearization* of T.

An automaton $\mathcal{A}$ is called *I-diamond* if for all $(a, b) \in I$, and s a state of $\mathcal{A}$: $\Delta(s, ab) = \Delta(s, ba)$. Note that the I-diamond property implies that the language of $\mathcal{A}$ is *I-closed*: that is, $u \in \mathcal{L}(\mathcal{A})$ if and only if $v \in \mathcal{L}(\mathcal{A})$ for every $u \sim v$. This permits us to write $\Delta(s, T)$ where T is a trace, to denote the state reached by $\mathcal{A}$ from s on some linearization of T. Languages of I-diamond automata are called *regular trace languages*.

Definition 1. *A deterministic asynchronous automaton over the distributed alphabet* (Σ, dom) *is a tuple* $\mathcal{B} = \langle (S_p)_{p\in\mathcal{P}}, (\delta_a)_{a\in\Sigma}, s^0, Acc\rangle$ *where:*

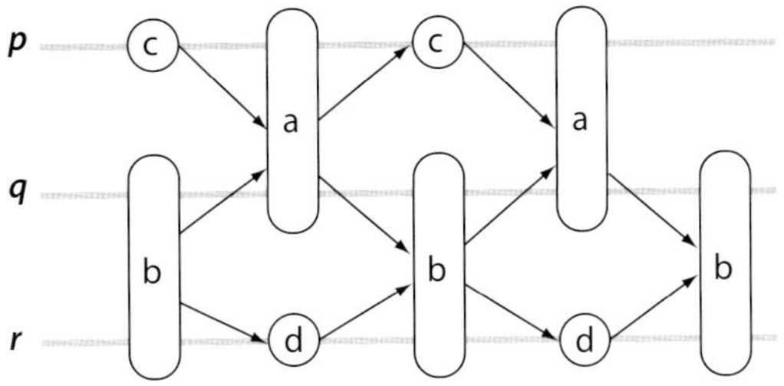

Fig. 1. The pomset associated with the trace $T = [c\,b\,a\,d\,c\,b\,a\,d\,b]$, with $\mathrm{dom}(a) = \{p, q\}$, $\mathrm{dom}(b) = \{q, r\}$, $\mathrm{dom}(c) = \{p\}$, $\mathrm{dom}(d) = \{r\}$

- S_p *is the finite set of local states of a process* $p \in \mathcal{P}$,
- $\delta_a : \prod_{p\in dom(a)} S_p \to \prod_{p\in dom(a)} S_p$ *is the local transition function associated with an action* $a \in \Sigma$,
- $s^0 \in \prod_{p\in\mathcal{P}} S_p$ *is the global initial state,*
- $Acc \subseteq \prod_{p\in\mathcal{P}} S_p$ *is a set of global accepting states.*

We call $\prod_{p\in\mathcal{P}} S_p$ the set of *global states* (whereas S_p is the set of p-local states). In this paper the size of an asynchronous automaton $\mathcal{B}$ is the total number of *local states* $\sum_{p\in\mathcal{P}} |S_p|$. This definition is very conservative, as one may want to count also Acc or the transition functions (that can be exponential in $|\mathcal{B}|$). We will see that our construction allows to compute both Acc and the transition functions in polynomial time.

With the asynchronous automaton $\mathcal{B}$ one can associate a *global automaton* $\mathcal{A}_\mathcal{B} = \langle Q, \Sigma, \Delta, q^0, Acc\rangle$ where:

- The set of states is the set of global states $Q = \prod_{p\in\mathcal{P}} S_p$ of $\mathcal{B}$, the initial and the accepting states are as in $\mathcal{B}$.
- The transition function $\Delta : Q\times\Sigma \to Q$ is defined by $\Delta((s_p)_{p\in\mathcal{P}}, a) = (s'_p)_{p\in\mathcal{P}}$ with $(s'_p)_{p\in\mathrm{dom}(a)} = \delta_a((s_p)_{p\in\mathrm{dom}(a)})$ and $s'_p = s_p$, for every $p \notin \mathrm{dom}(a)$.

Clearly $\mathcal{A}_\mathcal{B}$ is a finite deterministic automaton with the I-diamond property.

Definition 2. *The language of an asynchronous automaton* $\mathcal{B}$ *is the language of the associated global automaton* $\mathcal{A}_\mathcal{B}$.

We conclude this section by introducing some basic notations on traces. For a trace T, we denote by $\mathrm{dom}(T) = \bigcup_{e\in E} \mathrm{dom}(\lambda(e))$ the set of processes occurring in T. For a process $p \in \mathcal{P}$, we denote by $\mathrm{pref}_p(T)$ the minimal trace prefix of T containing all events of T on process p. Hence, $\mathrm{pref}_p(T)$ has a unique maximal event that is the last (most recent) event of T on process p. This maximal event is denoted as $\mathrm{last}_p(T)$. Intuitively, $\mathrm{pref}_p(T)$ corresponds to the history of process p after executing T. We extend this notation to a set of processes $P \subseteq \mathcal{P}$ and denote by $\mathrm{pref}_P(T)$ the minimal trace prefix containing all events of T on processes from P. By $\mathrm{last}(T)$ we denote the set of events $\{\mathrm{last}_p(T) \mid p \in \mathcal{P}\}$. For example, in Figure 1 we have $\mathrm{pref}_p(T) = [cbadcba]$ and $\mathrm{last}_p(T)$ is the second a of the pomset. The set $\mathrm{last}(T)$ contains the second a and the third b.

3 Zielonka-Type Constructions: State of the Art

All general constructions of deterministic asynchronous automata basically follow the main ideas of the original construction of Zielonka [15]. These constructions start with a regular, I-closed word language, that is given either by a homomorphism to a finite monoid, or by an I-diamond automaton. In most applications we are interested in the second case, where we start with a (possibly non deterministic) automaton. The general constructions yield either asynchronous automata as defined in the previous section, or asynchronous *cellular* automata, that correspond to a concurrent-read-owner-write model.

Theorem 1. *[15] Let $\mathcal{A}$ be an I-diamond automaton over the independence alphabet (Σ, I). A deterministic asynchronous automaton $\mathcal{B}$ can be effectively constructed with $\mathcal{L}(\mathcal{A}) = \mathcal{L}(\mathcal{B})$.*

We now review the constructions of [2,12,6] and recall their complexities. It is well known that determinization of word automata requires an exponential blow-up, hence the complexity of going from a non deterministic I-diamond automaton $\mathcal{A}$ to a deterministic asynchronous automaton is at least exponential in $|\mathcal{A}|$. In that case, [6] gives an optimal construction as it is simply exponential in both parameters $|\mathcal{A}|$ and $|\mathcal{P}|$. Since determinization has little to do with concurrency, we assume from now on that $\mathcal{A}$ is a deterministic automaton.

- [2] introduces asynchronous mappings and constructs asynchronous cellular automata of size $|\Sigma|^{|\Sigma|^2} \cdot |\mathcal{A}|^{2^{|\Sigma|}}$.
- [12] constructs asynchronous automata of size $|\mathcal{P}|^{|\mathcal{P}|^2} \cdot |\mathcal{A}|^{|\mathcal{A}| \cdot 2^{|\mathcal{P}|}}$.
- [6] introduces zone decompositions and constructs asynchronous automata of size $2^{3|\mathcal{P}|^3} \cdot |\mathcal{A}|^{|\mathcal{A}| \cdot |\mathcal{P}|^2}$.

Comparing our present construction with previous ones, we obtain asynchronous automata of size $4^{|\mathcal{P}|^4} \cdot |\mathcal{A}|^{|\mathcal{P}|^2}$. In all these constructions, the obtained automata are such that every process knows the state reached by $\mathcal{A}$ on its history. We abstract this property below, and show in the following section that our construction is optimal in this case.

Definition 3. *A deterministic asynchronous automaton $\mathcal{B}$ is called* locally rejecting *if for every process p, there is a set of states $R_p \subseteq S_p$ such that for every trace T:*

$$pref_p(T) \notin pref(\mathcal{L}(\mathcal{B})) \text{ iff the } p\text{-local state reached by } \mathcal{B} \text{ on } T \text{ is in } R_p.$$

Notice that R_p is a trap: if $\mathcal{B}$ reaches R_p on trace T, then so it does on every extension T' of T. Obviously, no reachable accepting global state of $\mathcal{B}$ has a component in R_p. For these reasons we call states of R_p rejecting.

Our interest in locally rejecting automata is motivated by observing that all general constructions [15,2,3,13,12,6] of deterministic asynchronous automata produce such automata. Suppose that $\mathcal{A}$ is a (possibly non deterministic) I-diamond automaton, and $\mathcal{B}$ a deterministic asynchronous automaton produced by one of the constructions in [15,13,12,6] (a similar statement applies to the asynchronous cellular automata in [2,3]). Then the local p-state s_p reached by $\mathcal{B}$ after processing the trace T determines the set of states reached by $\mathcal{A}$ on $\mathrm{pref}_p(T)$, for every process p. Thus, if no state in this set can reach a final state of $\mathcal{A}$, then we put s_p in R_p. This makes $\mathcal{B}$ locally rejecting.

4 An Exponential Lower Bound

In this section we present our lower bound result. We show that transforming an I-diamond deterministic automaton into a locally rejecting asynchronous automaton may induce an exponential blow-up in the number of processes. For this we define a family of languages Path_n, such that the minimal sequential automaton for Path_n has size $\mathcal{O}(n^2)$ but every locally rejecting asynchronous automaton recognizing Path_n is of size at least $2^{n/4}$.

Let $\mathcal{P} = \{1, \ldots, n\}$ be the set of processes. The letters of our alphabet are pairs of processes, two letters are dependent if they have a process in common. Formally, the distributed alphabet is $\Sigma = \binom{\mathcal{P}}{2}$ with $\mathrm{dom}(\{p,q\}) = \{p,q\}$.

The language Path_n is the set of traces $[x_1 \cdots x_k]$ such that every two consecutive letters have a process in common: $x_i \cap x_{i+1} \neq \emptyset$ for $i = 1, \ldots, k-1$. Observe that a deterministic sequential automaton recognizing this language simply needs to remember the last letter it has read. So it has less than $|\mathcal{P}|^2$ states.

Theorem 2. *Every locally rejecting asynchronous automaton recognizing Path_n is of size at least $2^{n/4}$.*

Proof. Take a locally rejecting automaton recognizing Path_n. Without loss of generality we suppose that $n = 4k$. To get a contradiction we suppose that process n of this automaton has less than 2^k (local) states.

We define for every integer $0 \leq m < k$ two traces: $a_m = \{4m, 4m+1\}\{4m+1, 4m+2\}\{4m+2, 4m+4\}$ and $b_m = \{4m, 4m+1\}\{4m, 4m+3\}\{4m+3, 4m+4\}$. To get some intuition, the reader may depict traces a_0 and b_0 and see that both a_0 and b_0 form a path from process 0 to process 4, the difference is that trace a_0 goes through process 2 while trace b_0 goes through process 3.

Consider the language L defined by the regular expression $(a_0 + b_0)(a_1 + b_1) \cdots (a_{k-1} + b_{k-1})$. Clearly, language L is included in Path_n and contains $2^k = 2^{n/4}$ different traces. As we have assumed that process n has less than 2^k states, there are two different traces t_1, t_2 from L such that process n is in the same state after t_1 and t_2. For simplicity of presentation we assume that t_1 and t_2 differ on the first factor: t_1 starts with a_0, and t_2 with b_0.

We can remark that processes 0 and n are in the same state after reading $t_1\{0,3\}$ and t_2. For process 0 it is clear as in both cases it sees the same trace $\{0,1\}\{0,3\}$. By our hypothesis, process n is in the same local state after traces t_1 and t_2, therefore also after traces $t_1\{0,3\}$ and t_2.

Consider now the state s_n reached by n after reading $t_2\{0,n\}$. Since $t_2\{0,n\} \in \mathrm{Path}_n$, the state s_n is not in R_n. By the above, the same state s_n is also reached after reading $t_1\{0,3\}\{0,n\}$. Trace t_1 starts with $a_0 = \{0,1\}\{1,2\}\{2,4\}$ and continues with processes whose numbers are greater than 4, so $\{0,3\}$ commutes with all letters of t_1 except $\{0,1\}$. Hence $t_1\{0,3\} \notin \text{pref}(\text{Path}_n)$. Since trace t_1 ends with an action of process n, we have $\text{pref}_n(t_1\{0,3\}\{0,n\}) = t_1\{0,3\}\{0,n\} \notin \text{pref}(\text{Path}_n)$. Since we have assumed that the automaton is locally rejecting, we should have $s_n \in R_n$. A contradiction. □

5 A Matching Upper Bound

Our goal is to modify the construction from [6] in order to make it polynomial with respect to the size of the sequential automaton. We give an overview of the new construction, first describing the objects the asynchronous automaton manipulates. Some details of the mechanics of the automaton will follow. Overall, although described in a different way, the present construction follows closely [6]. The main difference is the *state information* computed on the zone decomposition of a trace. This state information becomes polynomial (instead of exponential), but its update is much more involved than in [6].

We fix a set of processes $\mathcal{P}$ and a distributed alphabet (Σ, dom). Let $\mathcal{A} = \langle Q, \Sigma, \Delta, q^0, F\rangle$ be a deterministic I-diamond automaton. A candidate for an equivalent asynchronous automaton $\mathcal{B} = \langle (S_p)_{p\in\mathcal{P}}, (\delta_a)_{a\in\Sigma}, s^0, Acc\rangle$ has a set of states for each process and a local transition function. The goal is to make $\mathcal{B}$ calculate the state reached by $\mathcal{A}$ after reading a linearization of a trace T. Let us examine how $\mathcal{B}$ can accomplish this task. After reading a trace T the local state of a component p of $\mathcal{B}$ depends only on $\text{pref}_p(T)$. Hence, $\mathcal{B}$ can try to calculate the state reached by $\mathcal{A}$ after reading (some linearization of) $\text{pref}_p(T)$. When a next action, say a, is executed, processes in $\text{dom}(a)$ can see each others' states and make the changes accordingly. Intuitively, this means that these processes can now compose their information in order to calculate the state reached by $\mathcal{A}$ on $\text{pref}_{\text{dom}(a)}(T)\,a$. To do so they will need some information about the structure of the trace.

As usual, the tricky part of this process is to reconstruct the common view of $\text{pref}_{\text{dom}(a)}(T)$ from separate views of each process: $\text{pref}_p(T)$ for $p \in \text{dom}(a)$. For the sake of example suppose that $\text{dom}(a) = \{p,q,r\}$, and we know the states s_p, s_q and s_r, reached by $\mathcal{A}$ after reading $\text{pref}_p(T)$, $\text{pref}_q(T)$ and $\text{pref}_r(T)$, resp. We would like to know the state of $\mathcal{A}$ after reading $\text{pref}_{\{p,q,r\}}(T)$. This is possible if we can compute the contributions of $\text{pref}_q(T)\setminus\text{pref}_p(T)$ and $\text{pref}_r(T)\setminus \text{pref}_{\{p,q\}}(T)$. The automaton $\mathcal{B}$ should be able to do this by looking at s_p, s_q, and s_r, only. This remark points out the challenge of the construction: find the type information that allows to deduce the behaviour of $\mathcal{A}$, and that at the same time is updatable by an asynchronous automaton.

5.1 General Structure

Before introducing formal definitions it may be worth to say what is the general structure of the states of the automaton $\mathcal{B}$. Every local state will be a triple $(ts, ZO, \overline{\Delta})$, where

- ts will be a time stamping information as in all general constructions of asynchronous automata;
- ZO will be a zone order, a bounded size partial order on a partition of the trace;
- $\overline{\Delta}$ will be state information, recording the behavior of $\mathcal{A}$ on the partition given by ZO.

Roughly, we will use time stamping to compute zone orders, and zone orders to compute state information. The latter provides all the necessary information about the behaviour of $\mathcal{A}$ on (a linearization of) the trace.

Time stamping: The goal of the *time stamping function* [15] is to determine for a set of processes P and a process q the set $\text{last}(\text{pref}_P(T)) \cap \text{last}(\text{pref}_q(T))$. This set uniquely determines the intersection of $\text{pref}_P(T)$ and $\text{pref}_q(T)$ (for details see e.g. [13]). Computing such intersections is essential when composing information about $\text{pref}_p(T)$ for every $p \in \text{dom}(a)$ into information about $\text{pref}_{\text{dom}(a)}(T)$. The main point is that there exists a deterministic asynchronous automaton that can accomplish this task:

Theorem 3. *[13] There exists a deterministic asynchronous automaton $\mathcal{A}_{TS} = \langle (S_p)_{p\in\mathcal{P}}, (\Delta_a)_{a\in\Sigma}, s^0\rangle$ such that for every trace T and state $s = \Delta(s^0, T)$ reached by $\mathcal{A}_{TS}$ after reading T:*

> *for every $P \subseteq \mathcal{P}$ and $q, r, r' \in \mathcal{P}$, the set of local states $\{s_p \mid p \in P \cup \{q\}\}$ allows to determine if $\text{last}_r(\text{pref}_P(T)) = \text{last}_{r'}(\text{pref}_q(T))$.*

Moreover, such an automaton can be effectively computed and its local states can be described using $\mathcal{O}(|\mathcal{P}|^2 \log(|\mathcal{P}|))$ bits.

For instance, if a new b is executed after $T = [cbadcbad]$ in Figure 2, process r and processes p, q can determine that the intersection of their last-sets consists of the second b. Indeed, $\text{last}(\text{pref}_{p,q}(T))$ is made of the second a (for $\text{last}_p = \text{last}_q$) and the second b (for last_r). Also, $\text{last}(\text{pref}_r(T))$ is made of the second d (for last_r), the second b (for last_q) and the first a (for last_p).

Zone orders: Recall that one of our objectives is to calculate, for every $p \in \mathcal{P}$, the state reached by $\mathcal{A}$ on $\text{pref}_p(T)$. As the discussion on page 58 pointed out, for this we may need to recover the transition function of $\mathcal{A}$ associated with $\text{pref}_q(T) \setminus \text{pref}_P(T)$ for a process q and a set of processes P. Hence we need to store information about the behaviour of $\mathcal{A}$ on some relevant factors of T that are not prefixes. Zones are such relevant factors. They are defined in such a way that there is a bound on the number of zones in a trace. The other crucial property of zones is that for every extension T' of T and every $P \subseteq \mathcal{P}, q \in \mathcal{P}$, if a zone of T intersects $\text{pref}_q(T') \setminus \text{pref}_P(T')$ then it is entirely in this set. A zone order is an abstract representation of the decomposition of a trace into zones.

Definition 4. *[6] Let $T = \langle E, \leq, \lambda\rangle$ be a trace. For an event $e \in E$ we define the set of events $L(e) = \{f \in \text{last}(T) \mid e \leq f\}$. We say that two events e, e' are equivalent (denoted as $e \equiv e'$) if $L(e) = L(e')$. The equivalence classes of $\equiv$ are called* zones. *We denote by $dom(Z)$ the set of processes active in a zone Z.*

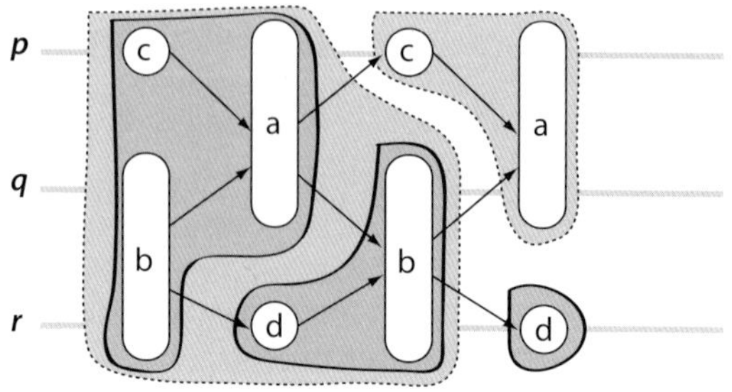

Fig. 2. The three zones of $\text{pref}_r(T)$ (darker) are marked with solid lines. The two zones of $\text{pref}_{\{p,q\}}(T)$ (lighter) are represented by dotted lines.

There is a useful partial order on zones that we define now. Let Z, Z' be two zones of some trace T. We write $Z \lessdot Z'$ if $Z \neq Z'$ and $e < e'$ for some events $e \in Z$, $e' \in Z'$. It is easy to see that $Z \lessdot Z'$ implies that $L(Z') \subsetneq L(Z)$. Thanks to this property we can define the *order on zones*, denoted $Z \leq Z'$, as the smallest partial order containing the $\lessdot$ relation.

Lemma 1. *A trace is partitioned in at most $|\mathcal{P}|^2$ zones.*

The lemma above gives a slightly better bound than [6]. Moreover, it can be shown that its bound is asymptotically optimal. Figure 2 depicts the trace $T = [cbadcbad]$. Recall that $\text{last}(\text{pref}_r(T))$ consists of the first a, the second b and the second d. There are three zones in $\text{pref}_r(T)$: Z_1 contains the first a, b and c, Z_2 the first d and the second b, and Z_3 the second d. We have $Z_1 < Z_2 < Z_3$.

Definition 5. *A* zone order *is a labeled partial order $ZO = \langle V, \leq, \xi : V \to 2^{\mathcal{P}} \rangle$, where every element is labeled by a set of processes. We require that every two elements whose labels have non empty intersection are comparable: $\xi(v) \cap \xi(v') \neq \emptyset \Rightarrow (v \leq v' \vee v' \leq v)$. We say that such a zone order is the* zone order of a trace T, *if there is a bijection μ from V to zones of T preserving the order and satisfying $\xi(v) = dom(\mu(v))$.*

Lemma 2. *The zone order of a trace can be stored in $|\mathcal{P}|^2(|\mathcal{P}|^2 + |\mathcal{P}|)$ space. So there are at most $2^{\mathcal{O}(|\mathcal{P}|^4)}$ zone orders.*

State information: We describe now the state information for each zone of the trace. Let $ZO = \langle V, \leq, \xi : V \to 2^{\mathcal{P}} \rangle$ be the zone order of some trace T, via a bijection μ. For an element $v \in V$ we denote by T_v the factor of T consisting of zones up to $\mu(v)$: that is, the factor covering $\mu(v')$ for all $v' \leq v$. Observe that T_v is a prefix of T. For instance, in Figure 2 the zone order of $\text{pref}_r(T)$ contains three vertices $v_1 < v_2 < v_3$, and T_{v_2} is the trace $[bcadb]$.

Definition 6. *We say that a function $\overline{\Delta} : V \to Q$ is* state information *for the zone order ZO of a trace T if for every v we have $\overline{\Delta}(v) = \Delta(q^0, T_v)$, namely the state of $\mathcal{A}$ reached on a linearization of T_v.*

Observe that a zone order for a trace of the form $\text{pref}_p(T)$ has one maximal element v_p: it corresponds to the last action of p. If $\overline{\Delta}$ is the state information for T, then the state reached by $\mathcal{A}$ on reading a linearization of $\text{pref}_p(T)$ is $\overline{\Delta}(v_p)$.

5.2 The Construction of the Asynchronous Automaton

Let us come back to the description of the asynchronous automaton $\mathcal{B}$. For every $p \in \mathcal{P}$, a local state in S_p will have the form $(ts_p, ZO_p, \overline{\Delta}_p)$. The automaton will be defined in such a way that after reading a trace T the state s_p reached at the component p will satisfy:

- ts_p is the time stamping information;
- ZO_p is the zone order of $\text{pref}_p(T)$;
- $\overline{\Delta}_p$ is the state information for ZO_p.

By [13] we know that $\mathcal{B}$ can update the ts_p component. The proposition below says that $\mathcal{B}$ can update the ZO_p and $\overline{\Delta}_p$ components.

Proposition 1. *Let T be a trace and $a \in \Sigma$ an action. Suppose that for every $p \in dom(a)$ we have the time stamping information ts_p and the zone order with state information $(ZO_p, \overline{\Delta}_p)$ of $pref_p(T)$. We can then calculate the zone order and the state information of $pref_p(Ta)$, for every $p \in dom(a)$.*

We also need to define the sets of rejecting states R_p and the global accepting states Acc of $\mathcal{B}$. Observe that by Proposition 1, from the local state s_p we can calculate $\Delta(q^0, \text{pref}_p(T))$, namely the state of $\mathcal{A}$ reached after reading a linearization of $\text{pref}_p(T)$. This state is exactly the state associated to the unique maximal element of the zone order in s_p. Hence, $\mathcal{B}$ can be made locally rejecting by letting $s_p \in R_p$ if $\Delta(q^0, \text{pref}_p(T))$ is not productive in $\mathcal{A}$, i.e., no final state can be reached from it.

To define accepting tuples of states of $\mathcal{B}$ we use the following proposition:

Proposition 2. *Let T be a trace. Given for every $p \in \mathcal{P}$ the time stamping ts_p, and the zone order ZO_p with state information $\overline{\Delta}_p$ of $pref_p(T)$, we can calculate $\Delta(q^0, T)$, the state reached by $\mathcal{A}$ on a linearization of T.*

In the light of Proposition 2, a tuple of states of $\mathcal{B}$ is accepting if the state $\Delta(q^0, T)$ of $\mathcal{A}$ is accepting. The two propositions give us:

Theorem 4. *Let $\mathcal{A}$ be a deterministic I-diamond automaton over the distributed alphabet (Σ, dom). We can construct an equivalent deterministic, locally rejecting asynchronous automaton $\mathcal{B}$ with at most $4^{|\mathcal{P}|^4} \cdot |\mathcal{A}|^{|\mathcal{P}|^2}$ states.*

We now describe informally the main ingredients of the proof of Proposition 1 (Proposition 2 is proved along similar lines). The zone order ZO of $\text{pref}_{P \cup \{q\}}(T)$ is built in two steps from ZO_P and ZO_q: first we construct a so-called pre-zone order ZO' by adding to ZO_P the zones from $\text{pref}_q(T) \setminus \text{pref}_P(T)$ [6]. Then we quotient ZO' in order to obtain ZO. The quotient operation amounts to merge zones. The difficulty compared to [6] is posed by the update of the state information. Since the state information for the pre-zone ZO' is inconsistent due to the merge, the crucial step is to compute this information on downward closed sets of zones:

Lemma 3. *Let $ZO = \langle V, \leq, \xi \rangle$, $\overline{\Delta}$ be the zone order and state information for a trace T (via the bijection μ). For every downward closed $B \subseteq V$ we can compute the state reached by $\mathcal{A}$ on a linearization of $T_B = \bigcup\{T_v \mid v \in B\}$, using only ZO and $\overline{\Delta}$.*

The proof of the lemma above is based on a nice observation about I-diamond automata $\mathcal{A}$, taken from [2]. It says that for every three traces T_0, T_1, T_2 with $\text{dom}(T_1) \cap \text{dom}(T_2) = \emptyset$, the state reached by $\mathcal{A}$ on a linearization of $T_0 T_1 T_2$ can be computed from $\text{dom}(T_1)$ and the states reached on (linearizations of) T_0, $T_0 T_1$, $T_0 T_2$, respectively.

We now sketch the proof of the lemma. We first choose some linearization $v_1, \ldots, v_n$ of B. For each i, k with $i \leq k$, let $B_{i,k} = \{v_1, \ldots, v_i\} \cup \{v_j \mid j > i, v_j \leq v_k\}$. For instance, if there are four zones v_1, v_2, v_3, v_4 with $v_1 < v_2 < v_4$, $v_1 < v_3 < v_4$, and $\xi(v_2) \cap \xi(v_3) = \emptyset$, then $B_{1,2} = \{v_1, v_2\}$, $B_{1,3} = \{v_1, v_3\}$, and $B_{2,3} = \{v_1, v_2, v_3\}$.

We show now how to compute inductively $\Delta(q^0, T_{B_{i,k}})$. Notice that the base case is trivial, as $B_{0,k} = \overline{\Delta}(v_k)$ for all k. Let $i \leq n$. Suppose that for all $k \geq i-1$, we know $\Delta(q^0, T_{B_{i-1,k}})$. In particular, note that the states q^{i-1}, q^i reached on $\mu(v_1 \cdots v_{i-1})$ and $\mu(v_1 \cdots v_i)$, respectively, are known (cases $k = i-1$ and $k = i$). We compute now $\Delta(q^0, T_{B_{i,k}})$, for all $k > i$. Two cases arise. If $v_i \not< v_k$ then we apply the observation of [2] to $q^{i-1}, q^i, \Delta(q^0, T_{B_{i-1,k}}), \xi(v_i)$, which yields $\Delta(q^0, T_{B_{i,k}})$. If $v_i < v_k$, then $B_{i-1,k} = B_{i,k}$ and the state $\Delta(q^0, T_{B_{i,k}})$ is already known. At the end of this polynomial time procedure, we have computed $\Delta(q^0, T_B) = \Delta(q^0, T_{B_{n,n}})$.

Remark 1. The automaton $\mathcal{B}$ of Theorem 4 can be constructed on-the-fly, i.e., given the action $a \in \Sigma$ and the local states s_p of $\mathcal{B}$, $p \in \text{dom}(a)$, one can compute the successor states $\delta_a((s_p)_{p \in \text{dom}(a)})$. The question is now how much time we need for this computation. The update of the time stamping and the update of zone orders take time polynomial in $|\mathcal{P}|$. The update of state information can be done in time polynomial in $|\mathcal{P}|$ and linear in the number of transitions of $|\mathcal{A}|$. So overall, we can compute transitions on-the-fly in polynomial time. Similarly, we can decide whether a global state is accepting in polynomial time.

6 Conclusion

In this paper we have presented an improved construction of asynchronous automata. Starting from a zone construction of [6], we have shown how to keep just one state per zone instead of a transition table. This allows to obtain the first construction that is polynomial in the size of the sequential automaton and exponential only in the number of processes.

It is tempting to conjecture that our construction is optimal. Unfortunately, it is very difficult to provide lower bounds on sizes of asynchronous automata. We have given a matching lower bound for the subclass of locally rejecting automata. It is worth to recall that all general constructions in the literature produce automata of this kind. Moreover the concept of locally rejecting automaton is interesting on its own from the point of view of applications.

We conjecture that the translation from deterministic word automata to asynchronous automata must be exponential in the number of processes (where the size means the total number of local states).

References

1. Baudru, N.: Distributed Asynchronous Automata. In: Bravetti, M., Zavattaro, G. (eds.) CONCUR 2009 - Concurrency Theory. LNCS, vol. 5710, pp. 115–130. Springer, Heidelberg (2009)
2. Cori, R., Métivier, Y., Zielonka, W.: Asynchronous mappings and asynchronous cellular automata. Information and Computation 106, 159–202 (1993)
3. Diekert, V., Muscholl, A.: Construction of asynchronous automata. In: Diekert, Rozenberg (eds.) [4], pp. 249–267
4. Diekert, V., Rozenberg, G. (eds.): The Book of Traces. World Scientific, Singapore (1995)
5. Genest, B., Kuske, D., Muscholl, A.: A Kleene theorem and model checking algorithms for existentially bounded communicating automata. Inf. Comput. 204(6), 920–956 (2006)
6. Genest, B., Muscholl, A.: Constructing Exponential-Size Deterministic Zielonka Automata. In: Bugliesi, M., Preneel, B., Sassone, V., Wegener, I. (eds.) ICALP 2006. LNCS, vol. 4052, pp. 565–576. Springer, Heidelberg (2006)
7. Henriksen, J.G., Mukund, M., Kumar, K.N., Sohoni, M., Thiagarajan, P.S.: A Theory of Regular MSC Languages. Inf. Comput. 202(1), 1–38 (2005)
8. Klarlund, N., Mukund, M., Sohoni, M.: Determinizing Asynchronous Automata. In: Shamir, E., Abiteboul, S. (eds.) ICALP 1994. LNCS, vol. 820, pp. 130–141. Springer, Heidelberg (1994)
9. Mazurkiewicz, A.: Concurrent Program Schemes and their Interpretations. DAIMI Rep. PB 78, Aarhus University, Aarhus (1977)
10. Métivier, Y.: An algorithm for computing asynchronous automata in the case of acyclic non-commutation graph. In: Ottmann, T. (ed.) ICALP 1987. LNCS, vol. 267, pp. 226–236. Springer, Heidelberg (1987)
11. Mukund, M., Kumar, K.N., Sohoni, M.: Synthesizing distributed finite-state systems from MSCs. In: Palamidessi, C. (ed.) CONCUR 2000. LNCS, vol. 1877, pp. 521–535. Springer, Heidelberg (2000)
12. Mukund, M., Sohoni, M.: Gossiping, Asynchronous Automata and Zielonka's Theorem. Report TCS-94-2, School of Mathematics, SPIC Science Foundation, Madras, India (1994)
13. Mukund, M., Sohoni, M.A.: Keeping Track of the Latest Gossip in a Distributed System. Distributed Computing 10(3), 137–148 (1997)
14. Stefanescu, A.: Automatic synthesis of distributed transition systems. PhD thesis, Universität Stuttgart (2006)
15. Zielonka, W.: Notes on finite asynchronous automata. RAIRO–Theoretical Informatics and Applications 21, 99–135 (1987)
16. Zielonka, W.: Safe executions of recognizable trace languages by asynchronous automata. In: Meyer, A.R., Taitslin, M.A. (eds.) Logic at Botik 1989. LNCS, vol. 363, pp. 278–289. Springer, Heidelberg (1989)

Pumping and Counting on the Regular Post Embedding Problem*

Pierre Chambart and Philippe Schnoebelen

LSV, ENS Cachan, CNRS
61, av. Pdt. Wilson, F-94230 Cachan, France
{chambart,phs}@lsv.ens-cachan.fr

Abstract. The Regular Post Embedding Problem is a variant of Post's Correspondence Problem where one compares strings with the subword relation and imposes additional regular constraints on admissible solutions. It is known that this problem is decidable, albeit with very high complexity.

We consider and solve variant problems where the set of solutions is compared to regular constraint sets and where one counts the number of solutions. Our positive results rely on two non-trivial pumping lemmas for Post-embedding languages and their complements.

1 Introduction

Post's Correspondence Problem, or shortly PCP, is the question whether two morphisms $u,v:\Sigma^*\to\Gamma^*$ agree non-trivially on some input, i.e., whether $u(\sigma)=v(\sigma)$ for some non-empty $\sigma\in\Sigma^+$. Post's *Embedding* Problem, shortly PEP, is a variant of PCP where one asks whether $u(\sigma)$ is a (scattered) subword of $v(\sigma)$ for some σ. The subword relation, also called embedding, is denoted "$\sqsubseteq$": $x\sqsubseteq y \overset{\text{def}}{\Leftrightarrow} x$ can be obtained from y by erasing some letters, possibly all of them, possibly none. The *Regular* Post Embedding Problem, or $\mathsf{PEP}^{\text{reg}}$, is an extension of PEP where one adds the requirement that only solutions σ belonging to a given regular language $R\subseteq\Sigma^*$ are admitted. PEP and $\mathsf{PEP}^{\text{reg}}$ were introduced, and shown decidable, in [2,3].

Regular constraints and the set of PEP-*solutions.* The decidability of $\mathsf{PEP}^{\text{reg}}$ can be restated under the following form: it is decidable, given two morphisms $u,v:\Sigma^*\to\Gamma^*$ and a regular language $R\subseteq\Sigma^*$, whether the following holds:

$$\exists x\in R: u(x)\sqsubseteq v(x). \qquad \text{(Existence)}$$

In other words, and letting $PE(u,v)\overset{\text{def}}{=}\{x\in\Sigma^*\mid u(x)\sqsubseteq v(x)\}$, one can decide whether $R\cap PE(u,v)\neq\varnothing$. However, this problem has very high complexity. Here the regular language R, acting as a constraint on the form of solutions, plays a key role. Indeed, in the special case where $R=\Sigma^+$, the problem becomes trivial (if there are solutions, in particular length-one solutions exist) which probably explains why PEP and $\mathsf{PEP}^{\text{reg}}$ had not been investigated earlier.

---

* Work supported by the Agence Nationale de la Recherche, grant ANR-06-SETIN-001.

S. Abramsky et al. (Eds.): ICALP 2010, Part II, LNCS 6199, pp. 64–75, 2010.

In this paper, we prove the decidability of the following questions:

$$\forall x \in R : u(x) \sqsubseteq v(x), \tag{Universality}$$
$$\exists^\infty x \in R : u(x) \sqsubseteq v(x), \tag{Infinity}$$
$$\neg\exists^\infty x \in R : u(x) \not\sqsubseteq v(x). \tag{Cofiniteness}$$

"Universality" asks whether all words in R are solutions. "Infinity" asks whether R contains infinitely many solutions x, while dually "Cofiniteness" asks whether all but finitely many $x \in R$ are solutions. Equivalently, these questions ask whether $R \subseteq PE(u,v)$, whether $R \cap PE(u,v) =_a \varnothing$, and whether $R \smallsetminus PE(u,v) =_a \varnothing$, writing $S =_a S'$ to denote the "quasi-equality" of two sets, i.e., equality up to a finite subset. As a consequence of these decidability results we can compute the number of words in R that are (respectively, that are not) solutions.

These results are obtained with the help of two pumping lemmas, one for sets of solutions and one for sets of "antisolutions", i.e., words x such that $u(x) \not\sqsubseteq v(x)$. These pumping lemmas are the more technically involved developments of this paper. Proving them relies on two kinds of techniques: (1) combinatorics of words in presence of the subword relation and associated operations, and (2) a miniaturisation of Higman's Lemma that gives effective bounds on the length of bad sequences.

Related work. The Regular Post Embedding Problem was introduced in [2,3] where its decidability was proved. These papers also showed that $\mathsf{PEP}^{\mathrm{reg}}$ is expressive enough to encode problems on lossy channel systems, or LCS's. In fact, encoding in both directions exist, hence $\mathsf{PEP}^{\mathrm{reg}}$ is exactly at level $\mathcal{F}_{\omega^\omega}$ in the Fast Growing Hierarchy. Thus, although it is decidable, $\mathsf{PEP}^{\mathrm{reg}}$ is not primitive-recursive, and not even multiply-recursive (see [4] and the references therein).

A consequence of the above encodings is that $\mathsf{PEP}^{\mathrm{reg}}$ is an abstract problem that is inter-reducible with a growing list of decision problems that have the same $\mathcal{F}_{\omega^\omega}$ complexity: metric temporal logic [14], products of modal logics [8], leftist grammars [9,6], data nets [11], alternating one-clock timed automata [1,10], etc.

On complexity. Aiming at simplicity, our main decidability proofs do not come with explicit statements regarding the computational complexity of the associated problems. The decidability proofs can be turned into deterministic algorithms with complexity in $\mathcal{F}_{\omega^\omega}$, providing the same upper bound that already applies to $\mathsf{PEP}^{\mathrm{reg}}$. Regarding lower bounds, it is clear that "Infinity" is at least as hard as $\mathsf{PEP}^{\mathrm{reg}}$. We do not know if the same lower bound holds for "Universality" and "Cofiniteness".

Outline of the paper. Section 2 recalls the necessary definitions and notations. Section 3 deals with combinatorics on words with subwords. Section 4 proves the decidability of comparisons with regular sets. Then our pumping lemma is stated in Section 5 and used in Section 6 for deciding finiteness, counting, and quasi-regular questions. Sections 7 and 8 prove the two halves of the pumping lemma. Proofs omitted in the main text can be found in the full version of this extended abstract.

2 Notations and Definitions

Words and morphisms. We write $x, y, z, t, \sigma, \rho, \alpha, \beta, \ldots$ for words, i.e., finite sequences of letters such as $a, b, c, i, j, \ldots$ from alphabets $\Sigma, \Gamma, \ldots$, and denote with $x.y$, or xy, the concatenation of x and y. We let ε denote the empty word. The *length* of x is written $|x|$. A *morphism* from Σ^* to Γ^* is a map $u : \Sigma^* \to \Gamma^*$ that respects the monoidal structure, i.e., with $u(\varepsilon) = \varepsilon$ and $u(x.y) = u(x).u(y)$. A morphism u is completely defined by its image $u(a)$, $u(b)$, ..., on $\Sigma = \{a, b, \ldots\}$. We often simply write $u_a, u_b, \ldots$, and u_x, instead of $u(a), u(b), \ldots$, and $u(x)$. Finally, for a morphism $u : \Sigma^* \to \Gamma^*$, we let $K_u = \max_{a \in \Sigma} |u_a|$ denote the *expansion factor* of u, thus called because clearly $|u_x| \leq K_u \times |x|$.

The *mirror image* of a word x is denoted $\widetilde{x}$, e.g., $\widetilde{abc} = cba$. The mirror image of a language L is $\widetilde{L} \stackrel{\text{def}}{=} \{\widetilde{x} \mid x \in L\}$. It is well-known that the mirror image of a regular language is regular. For a morphism $h : \Sigma^* \to \Gamma^*$, the mirror morphism $\widetilde{h}$ is defined by $\widetilde{h}(x) \stackrel{\text{def}}{=} \widetilde{h(\widetilde{x})}$, ensuring $\widetilde{h}(\widetilde{x}) = \widetilde{h(x)}$.

Syntactic congruence. For a language L, we let $\sim_L$ denote the syntactic congruence induced by L: $x \sim_L y \stackrel{\text{def}}{\Leftrightarrow} \forall w, w' (wxw' \in L \Leftrightarrow wyw' \in L)$. The Myhill-Nerode Theorem states that $\sim_L$ has finite index iff L is a regular language. For a regular L, we let n_L denote the number of equivalence classes w.r.t. $\sim_L$.[1]

Subwords and Higman's Lemma. Given two words x and y, we write $x \sqsubseteq y$ when x is a *subword* of y, i.e., when x can be obtained by erasing some letters (possibly none) from y. For example, $abba \sqsubseteq \underline{ab}racada\underline{b}r\underline{a}$. The subword relation, aka *embedding*, is a partial ordering on words. It is compatible with the monoidal structure:

$$\varepsilon \sqsubseteq x, \qquad\qquad (x \sqsubseteq y \wedge x' \sqsubseteq y') \Rightarrow xx' \sqsubseteq yy'.$$

It is well-known (Higman's Lemma) that the subword relation is a well-quasi-ordering when we consider words over a fixed finite alphabet. This means that any set of words has a finite number of minimal elements (minimal w.r.t. $\sqsubseteq$).

We say that a sequence $x_1, \ldots, x_l, \ldots$ of words in Σ^* is n-good if there exists indexes $i_1 < i_2 < \ldots < i_n$ such that $x_{i_1} \sqsubseteq x_{i_2} \sqsubseteq \ldots \sqsubseteq x_{i_n}$, i.e., if the sequence contains a subsequence of length n that is increasing w.r.t. embedding. It is n-bad otherwise. Higman's Lemma states that every infinite sequence is 2-good, and even n-good for any $n \in \mathbb{N}$. Hence n-bad sequences are finite.

Higman's Lemma is often described as being "non-effective" in that it does not give any information on the length of bad sequences. Indeed, arbitrarily long bad sequences exist. However, upper bounds on the length of bad sequences can certainly be given when one restricts to "simple" sequences. Such finitary versions of well-quasi-ordering properties are called "miniaturisations" in proof-theoretical circles.

In this paper we consider a very simple miniaturisation that applies to "controlled" sequences [7]. Formally, and given $k \in \mathbb{N}$, we say that a sequence $x_1, \ldots, x_l$ of words in Σ^* is *k-controlled* if $|x_i| \leq i \times k$ for all $i = 1, \ldots, l$. We shall use the following result:[2]

[1] If the minimal complete DFA that accepts L has q states, then n_L can be bounded by q^q.

[2] For a proof, see [7] or the long version of this paper.

Lemma 2.1. *There exists a* bounding function $H : \mathbb{N}^3 \to \mathbb{N}$ *such that, for any* $n,k \in \mathbb{N}$ *and* $l \geq H(n,k,|\Sigma|)$, *any k-controlled sequence of l words in* Σ^* *is n-good.*

The lemma states that if a k-controlled sequence is long enough, it is n-good. Equivalently, n-bad sequences are shorter that $H(n,k,|\Sigma|)$ or are not k-controlled.

3 Composing, Decomposing, and Iterating Words and Subwords

This section is devoted to the subword ordering and the way it interacts with concatenations and factorizations. It proves a few basic results, e.g., Lemma 3.7, that we have been unable to find in the technical literature [12,13].

3.1 Available Suffixes

When $x \sqsubseteq y$, we decompose y as a concatenation $y = y_1 y_2$ such that y_1 is the *shortest* prefix of y with $x \sqsubseteq y_1$. We call y_1 the "*used prefix*" and y_2 the "*available suffix*". We use $y \oslash x$ to denote the available suffix. For example, $a\underline{b}c\underline{a}bc \oslash \underline{ba} = bc$. Note that $y \oslash x$ is only defined when $x \sqsubseteq y$.

Lemma 3.1. $x \sqsubseteq y$ *and* $x' \sqsubseteq (y \oslash x)y'$ *imply* $xx' \sqsubseteq yy'$.

Corollary 3.2. $x \sqsubseteq y$ *implies* $x(y \oslash x) \sqsubseteq y$.

Lemma 3.3. $x \sqsubseteq y$ *and* $xx' \sqsubseteq yy'$ *imply* $x' \sqsubseteq (y \oslash x)y'$.

3.2 Unmatched Suffixes

When $x \not\sqsubseteq y$, we decompose x as a concatenation $x = x_1 x_2$ such that x_1 is the *longest* prefix of x with $x_1 \sqsubseteq y$. We call x_1 the "*matched prefix*" and x_2 the "*unmatched suffix*". We use $x \ominus y$ to denote the unmatched suffix. For example $\underline{a}abc\underline{a}bc \ominus b\underline{a}c\underline{a} = bcabc$. Note that $x \ominus y$ is only defined when $x \not\sqsubseteq y$ (hence $x \ominus y \neq \varepsilon$).

Lemma 3.4. $x \not\sqsubseteq y$ *and* $xx' \not\sqsubseteq yy'$ *imply* $[(x \ominus y)x'] \ominus y' = xx' \ominus yy'$.

Corollary 3.5. $x \not\sqsubseteq y$ *and* $xx' \not\sqsubseteq yy'$ *imply* $(x \ominus y)x' \not\sqsubseteq y'$.

Lemma 3.6. $x \not\sqsubseteq y$ *and* $xx' \sqsubseteq yy'$ *imply* $(x \ominus y)x' \sqsubseteq y'$.

3.3 Iterating Factors

Lemma 3.7. $xy \sqsubseteq yz$ *if, and only if,* $x^k y \sqsubseteq yz^k$ *for all* $k \in \mathbb{N}$.

Proof. We only need to prove the "$\Rightarrow$" direction. This is done by induction on the length of y. The cases where $y = \varepsilon$ or $x = \varepsilon$ or $k = 0$ are obvious, so we assume that $|y|$, $|x|$ and k are strictly positive. There are now two cases:

1. If $x \sqsubseteq y$, we consider a factorization $y = y_1 y_2$ (e.g., $y_2 = y \oslash x$ is convenient) with $x \sqsubseteq y_1$ (hence $x^k \sqsubseteq y_1^k$) and $y \sqsubseteq y_2 z$. Since $|y_2| < |y|$ (because $x \neq \varepsilon$ and hence $y_1 \neq \varepsilon$), the induction hypothesis applies and from $y_1 y_2 = y \sqsubseteq y_2 z$ one gets $y_1^k y_2 \sqsubseteq y_2 z^k$. Now $x^k y \sqsubseteq y_1^k y = y_1 y_1^k y_2 \sqsubseteq y_1 y_2 z^k = yz^k$.
2. If $x \not\sqsubseteq y$, we write $x = x_1 x_2$ with $x_2 = x \ominus y$. Thus $x_1 \sqsubseteq y$ and $x_2 y \sqsubseteq z$. Thus there exists a factorization $z = z_1 z_2$ s.t. $x_2 \sqsubseteq z_1$ (entailing $x \sqsubseteq yz_1$) and $y \sqsubseteq z_2$. Now $x^k y \sqsubseteq (yz_1)^k z_2 = yz_1(yz_1)^{k-1} z_2 \sqsubseteq yz_1(z_2 z_1)^{k-1} z_2 = yz^k$. □

Lemma 3.8. *Assume $x \not\sqsubseteq y$, $xz \not\sqsubseteq yt$, and $x \ominus y \sqsubseteq xz \ominus yt$. Then for all $k \in \mathbb{N}$:*

$$xz^k \not\sqsubseteq yt^k. \tag{Z_k}$$

Furthermore, if we let $r_k \stackrel{def}{=} xz^k \ominus yt^k$, then for all $k \in \mathbb{N}$:

$$r_0 \sqsubseteq r_k \sqsubseteq r_{k+1}. \tag{R_k}$$

Proof. The hypothesis for the Lemma are that (Z_0), (Z_1) and (R_0) hold. We prove, by induction on k, that (Z_k) and (R_{k-1}) imply (Z_{k+1}) and (R_k).

Proof of (Z_{k+1}): applying Coro. 3.5 on (Z_0) and (Z_1) yields $r_0 z \not\sqsubseteq t$, hence a fortiori $r_k z \not\sqsubseteq t$ using (R_{k-1}). Combining with (Z_k) and applying Lemma 3.6 contrapositively entails $xz^k z \not\sqsubseteq yt^k t$, i.e., ($Z_{k+1}$).

Proof of (R_k): r_{k+1} is $xz^{k+1} \ominus yt^{k+1}$. By Lemma 3.4, this is $[(xz^k \ominus yt^k)z] \ominus t$, i.e., $r_k z \ominus t$. From (R_{k-1}) we get $r_{k-1} z \ominus t \sqsubseteq r_k z \ominus t$. However $r_{k-1} z \ominus t = r_k$ (Lemma 3.4). Finally $r_k \sqsubseteq r_{k+1}$. □

4 Regular Properties of Sets of PEP Solutions

Given two morphisms $u, v : \Sigma^* \to \Gamma^*$, a word $x \in \Sigma^*$ is called a "*solution*" (of Post's Embedding Problem) when $u_x \sqsubseteq v_x$. Otherwise it is an "*antisolution*". We let $PE(u,v)$ denote the set of solutions (for given u and v). Note that ε is always a solution.

We consider questions where we are given a PEP instance u, v with $u, v : \Sigma^* \to \Gamma^*$ and a regular language $R \subseteq \Sigma^*$. The considered problems are
PEP_Inclusion: does $PE(u,v) \subseteq R$?
PEP_Containment: does $PE(u,v) \supseteq R$?
PEP_Equality: does $PE(u,v) = R$?

It is tempting to compare $PE(u,v)$ with another Post-embedding set, however:

Theorem 4.1. *The questions "does $PE(u,v) \cap PE(u',v') = \{\varepsilon\}$?" and "does $PE(u,v) \subseteq PE(u',v')$?" are Π^0_1-complete.*

Proof. Π^0_1-hardness can be shown directly by reduction from PCP. For the first question, simply let $u' = v$ and $v' = u$. Then a common solution has $u_x \sqsubseteq v_x = u'_x \sqsubseteq v'_x = u_x$, i.e., $u_x = v_x$.

For the second question we use a more subtle encoding: assume w.l.o.g. that Γ contains two distinct symbols a, b and that $u_x \neq \varepsilon$ when $x \neq \varepsilon$. Let now $u'_x \stackrel{\text{def}}{=} (ab)^{|u_x|}$ and $v'_x \stackrel{\text{def}}{=} (ba)^{|v_x|}$. Thus $u'_x \sqsubseteq v'_x$ if, and only if, $x = \varepsilon$ or $|u_x| < |v_x|$. Finally, $PE(u,v) \setminus PE(u',v')$ contains the non-trivial PCP solutions. □

Theorem 4.2. PEP_Inclusion, PEP_Containment *and* PEP_Equality *are decidable.*

Note that, while comparisons with a regular language are decidable, regularity itself is undecidable, at least in the more general form stated here:

Proposition 4.3 (Regularity is undecidable [5]). *The question "is $R \cap PE(u,v)$ a regular language?" is Σ^0_1-complete.*

The remainder of this section proves Theorem 4.2.

We first observe that PEP_Inclusion and PEP^{reg} are inter-reducible since (u, v, R) is a positive instance for PEP_Inclusion if, and only if, $(u, v, \Sigma^* \setminus R)$ is a negative instance for PEP^{reg}. Hence the decidability of PEP_Inclusion follows from the decidability of PEP^{reg}, proved in [2,3].

For the decidability of PEP_Containment (and then of PEP_Equality), we fix an instance (u, v, R).

For a word $x \in \Sigma^*$, we say that x is *good* if $u_x \sqsubseteq v_x$ and then we let $w_x \stackrel{\text{def}}{=} v_x \oslash u_x$, otherwise it is *bad* and then we let $r_x \stackrel{\text{def}}{=} u_x \ominus v_x$. We say that x is *alive* if $xy \in R$ for some y, otherwise it is *dead*. Finally, we write $|R|$ for the number of states of a FSA for R, and let $L \stackrel{\text{def}}{=} K_v \times |R|$ be a *size threshold* (more details in the proof of Lemma 4.5).

A word x is a *cut-off* if, and only if, one of the following conditions holds:

dead cut-off: x is dead;
subsumption cut-off: there exists a strict prefix x' of x such that $x' \sim_R x$, and either
1. both x and x' are good, with $w_{x'} \sqsubseteq w_x$,
2. or both x and x' are bad, with $r_x \sqsubseteq r_{x'}$;

big cut-off: x is alive, bad and $|r_x| > L$.

Let $T \subseteq \Sigma^*$ be the set of all words that do not have a cut-off as a (strict) prefix. T is prefix-closed and can be seen as a tree.

Lemma 4.4. *T is finite.*

Proof. We show that T, seen as a tree, has no infinite branch. Hence, and since it is finitely branching, it is finite (Kőnig's Lemma).

Assume, by way of contradiction, that T has an infinite branch labeled by some $x_0, x_1, x_2, \ldots$ (and recall that every x_i is a prefix of all the x_{i+k}'s). We show that one of the x_i must be a cut-off, which contradicts the assumption.

Since the syntactic congruence $\sim_R$ has finite index, there exists an infinite subsequence $x_0, x_1, x_2, \ldots$ (renumbered for convenience) of $\sim_R$-equivalent x_i's. If infinitely many of the x_i's are good, one of them must be a subsumption cut-off since, by Higman's Lemma, the infinite sequence of the w_{x_i}'s (for good x_i's) must have some $w_{x'} \sqsubseteq w_x$. If only finitely many of the x_i's are good, then infinitely many of them are bad and either some r_{x_i} has size larger than L (hence x_i is a big cut-off), or all r_{x_i}'s have size at most L, hence belong to a finite set $\Gamma^{\leq L}$, and two of them must be equal (hence there must be a subsumption cut-off). □

With the next two lemmas, we show that T contains enough information to decide whether $R \subseteq PE(u, v)$.

Lemma 4.5. *If T contains a big cut-off, then $R \not\subseteq PE(u, v)$.*

Proof. Assume x is a big cut-off (i.e., is alive, bad, and with $|r_x| > L$) in T. It is alive so $xy \in R$ for some y. We pick the smallest such y, ensuring that $|y| < |R|$ (the number of states of an FSA for R). Since x is bad, we know that $u_x \not\sqsubseteq v_x$. Note that $|v_y| \leq K_v \times |y| \leq K_v \times |R| \leq L$ so that $|v_y| < |r_x|$ and, consequently, $r_x \not\sqsubseteq v_y$. Thus, and since $r_x = u_x \ominus v_x$, applying Lemma 3.6 contrapositively gives $u_x \not\sqsubseteq v_x v_y$ and, *a fortiori*, $u_{xy} \not\sqsubseteq v_{xy}$. Finally $xy \notin PE(u, v)$. Since $xy \in R$, we conclude $R \not\subseteq PE(u, v)$. □

There is a reciprocal.

Lemma 4.6. *Assume that T has no big cut-offs and that $(R \cap T) \subseteq PE(u,v)$. Then $R \subseteq PE(u,v)$.*

Proof. Consider some $x \in R$: we show that $u_x \sqsubseteq v_x$ by induction on the size of x. If $x \in T$ then $x \in (R \cap T) \subseteq PE(u,v)$ and we are done. If $x \notin T$, then a prefix of x is a cut-off. This cannot be a big cut-off (we assumed T has none) or a dead cut-off (the prefix is alive since $x \in R$). Hence this is a subsumption cut-off, caused by one of its prefixes. Finally, x can be written under the form $x = x_1x_2x_3$ with x_1x_2 the subsumption cut-off, and x_1 the prefix justifying the subsumption. We know $x_2 \neq \varepsilon$ (x_1 is a strict prefix of the cut-off) and $x_1 \sim_R x_1x_2$. Hence $x_1x_3 \in R$ (since $x_1x_2x_3 \in R$) and $u_{x_1x_3} \sqsubseteq v_{x_1x_3}$ by induction hypothesis.

There are now two cases, depending on what kind of subsumption is at hand.

1. If x_1 is good then $u_{x_1} \sqsubseteq v_{x_1}$. Combining with $u_{x_1x_3} \sqsubseteq v_{x_1x_3}$ entails $u_{x_3} \sqsubseteq w_{x_1}v_{x_3}$ (Lemma 3.3). From $w_{x_1} \sqsubseteq w_{x_1x_2}$ (condition for subsumption) we deduce $u_{x_3} \sqsubseteq w_{x_1x_2}v_{x_3}$. Combining with $u_{x_1x_2} \sqsubseteq v_{x_1x_2}$ (x_1x_2 too is good), Lemma 3.1 yields $u_{x_1x_2}u_{x_3} \sqsubseteq v_{x_1x_2}v_{x_3}$.
2. If x_1 is bad, then $u_{x_1x_3} \sqsubseteq v_{x_1x_3}$ and $u_{x_1} \not\sqsubseteq v_{x_1}$ entail $r_{x_1}u_{x_3} \sqsubseteq v_{x_3}$ (Lemma 3.6). From $r_{x_1x_2} \sqsubseteq r_{x_1}$ (condition for subsumption) we deduce $r_{x_1x_2}u_{x_3} \sqsubseteq v_{x_3}$. Combined with $u_{x_1x_2} \not\sqsubseteq v_{x_1x_2}$ (x_1x_2 too is bad), applying Coro. 3.5 contrapositively yields $u_{x_1x_2}u_{x_3} \sqsubseteq v_{x_1x_2}v_{x_3}$.

In both cases we proved that $x_1x_2x_3 \in PE(u,v)$ as requested. □

We can now prove the decidability of PEP_Containment: the tree T can be built effectively starting from the root since it is easy to see whether a word is a cut-off. The construction terminates thanks to Lemma 4.4. Once T is at hand, Lemmas 4.5 and 4.6 gives an effective criterion for deciding whether $R \subseteq PE(u,v)$: it is enough to check that T has no big cut-off and that all the words $x \in T$ satisfy $u_x \sqsubseteq v_x$ or do not belong to R.

5 Pumpable Solutions and Antisolutions

Let $u,v : \Sigma^* \to \Gamma^*$ be a given PEP instance.

Definition 5.1. *A triple of words $(x,y,z) \in \Sigma^*$ with $y \neq \varepsilon$ is a* pumpable solution *if $xy^kz \in PE(u,v)$ for all $k \in \mathbb{N}$.*

It is a pumpable antisolution *if $xy^kz \notin PE(u,v)$ for all $k \in \mathbb{N}$.*

In other words, a pumpable solution denotes an infinite subset of $PE(u,v)$ of the form xy^*z, while a pumpable antisolution denotes an infinite subset of its complement. Our interest in pumpable solutions and antisolutions is that they provide simple witnesses proving that $PE(u,v)$ (or its complement) is infinite.

We observe that these witnesses are effective:

Proposition 5.2 (Decidability of pumpability). *It is decidable whether (x,y,z) is a pumpable solution, and also whether it is a pumpable antisolution.*

Proof. Checking that (x,y,z) is a pumpable solution reduces to the PEP_Containment problem, while checking that it is not a pumpable antisolution reduces to the $\mathsf{PEP}^{\mathsf{reg}}$ problem (or, equivalently, PEP_Inclusion). □

We can now state our main technical result. Here (and below) we speak loosely of "a pumpable solution", when we mean "*the language denoted by* a pumpable solution".

Lemma 5.3 (Pumping Lemma). *Let $R \subseteq \Sigma^*$ be a regular language.*
1. If $R \cap PE(u,v)$ is infinite, it contains a pumpable solution.
2. If $R \setminus PE(u,v)$ is infinite, it contains a pumpable antisolution.

Section 7 is devoted to a proof of the Pumping Lemma for solutions, while Section 8 proves the Pumping Lemma for antisolutions. Without waiting for that, we list the main consequences on our questions.

6 Quasi-Regular Properties and Counting Properties

For two languages L, L, we say that L is *quasi-included* in L', written $L \subseteq_a L'$, when $L \setminus L'$ is finite, and that they are *quasi-equal*, written $L =_a L'$, when $L \subseteq_a L'$ and $L' \subseteq_a L$.

We consider the following questions, where we are given a PEP instance u, v and a regular $R \subseteq \Sigma^*$:
PEP_Quasi_Inclusion: does $PE(u,v) \subseteq_a R$?
PEP_Quasi_Containment: does $PE(u,v) \supseteq_a R$?
PEP_Quasi_Equality: does $PE(u,v) =_a R$?

Theorem 6.1. PEP_Quasi_Inclusion, PEP_Quasi_Containment *and* PEP_Quasi_-Equality *are decidable.*

Proof. We start with PEP_Quasi_Inclusion. This problem is co-r.e. since when $PE(u,v) \setminus R$ is infinite, there is a pumpable solution in $\Sigma^* \setminus R$ (Pumping Lemma) that can be guessed and checked (Prop. 5.2). It is also r.e. since $PE(u,v) \subseteq_a R$ iff there is a finite language $F \subseteq \Sigma^*$ s.t. $PE(u,v) \subseteq R \cup F$, which can be checked (Theo. 4.2) since $R \cup F$ is a regular language. Thus PEP_Quasi_Inclusion, being r.e. and co-r.e., is decidable.

We use the same reasoning to show that PEP_Quasi_Containment is decidable. Then PEP_Quasi_Equality is obviously decidable as well. □

We also consider counting questions where the answer is a number in $\mathbb{N} \cup \{\omega\}$:
PEP_NbSol: what is the cardinality of $R \cap PE(u,v)$?
PEP_NbAntisol: what is the cardinality $R \setminus PE(u,v)$?

Theorem 6.2. PEP_NbSol *and* PEP_NbAntisol *are decidable (more precisely, the associated counting functions are recursive).*

Proof. We start with PEP_NbSol. We can first check whether the cardinality of $R \cap PE(u,v)$ is finite by deciding whether $PE(u,v) \subseteq_a (\Sigma^* \setminus R)$ (using the decidability of PEP_Quasi_Inclusion). If we find that the cardinality is infinite, we are done. Otherwise we can enumerate all words in R and check whether they are solutions. At any given stage during this enumeration, we can check whether the current set F of already found solutions is complete by deciding whether $PE(u,v) \cap (R \setminus F) = \varnothing$ (using the decidability of PEP_Inclusion). We are bound to eventually find a complete set since we only started enumerating solutions in R knowing there are finitely many of them.

The same method works for PEP_NbAntisol, this times using the decidability of PEP_Containment and PEP_Quasi_Containment. □

7 Pumping in Long Solutions

We start with a sufficient condition for pumpability of solutions.

Definition 7.1. *A triple $x,y,z \in \Sigma^*$ with $y \neq \varepsilon$ is* positive *if the following four conditions are satisfied:*

$$u_x \sqsubseteq v_x, \quad \text{(C1)} \qquad u_x u_y \sqsubseteq v_x v_y, \quad \text{(C2)}$$

$$u_x u_y u_z \sqsubseteq v_x v_y v_z, \quad \text{(C3)} \qquad (v_x \oslash u_x) \sqsubseteq (v_x v_y \oslash u_x u_y). \quad \text{(C4)}$$

Lemma 7.2. *If (x,y,z) is positive then (x,y,yz) is a pumpable solution.*

Proof. Assume that (x,y,z) is positive, so that (C1–4) hold. Write shortly w for $v_x \oslash u_x$ and w' for $v_{xy} \oslash u_{xy}$. From (C1) and the definition of w, Coro. 3.2 yields:

$$u_x w \sqsubseteq v_x. \qquad \text{(C5)}$$

From (C2), it further yields $u_x u_y w' \sqsubseteq v_x v_y$, from which (C4) entails:

$$u_x u_y w \sqsubseteq v_x v_y. \qquad \text{(C6)}$$

Applying Lemma 3.3 on (C1) and (C3) (respectively on (C1) and (C6)) yields:

$$u_y u_z \sqsubseteq w v_y v_z, \quad \text{(C7)} \qquad u_y w \sqsubseteq w v_y. \quad \text{(C7}')$$

Applying Lemma 3.7 on (C7') gives

$$u_{y^k} w = (u_y)^k w \sqsubseteq w (v_y)^k = w v_{y^k} \text{ for all } k \in \mathbb{N}. \qquad \text{(C8)}$$

With (C5) and (C8), Lemma 3.1 entails

$$u_x u_{y^k} w \sqsubseteq v_x v_{y^k} \text{ for all } k \in \mathbb{N}. \qquad \text{(C9)}$$

With (C7) and (C9), it then entails

$$u_x u_{y^k} u_{yz} \sqsubseteq v_x v_{y^k} v_{yz} \text{ for all } k \in \mathbb{N}, \qquad \text{(C10)}$$

which just states that (x,y,yz) is a pumpable solution. □

We now let n_R denote the number of equivalence classes induced by $\sim_R$ (Section 2). Finally, we let H_u and H_v denote, respectively, $H(n_R+1, K_u, |\Gamma|)$ and $H(n_R+1, K_v, |\Gamma|)$. Recall that, by definition of the H function (Lemma 2.1), any K_u-controlled sequence of at least H_u Γ-words is (n_R+1)-good.

Lemma 7.3. *If R contains a solution $\sigma \in PE(u,v)$ of length $|\sigma| \geq 2H_v$ then it contains a pumpable solution.*

(Observe that this will entail, as a corollary, the first half of the Pumping Lemma since, if $R \cap PE(u,v)$ is infinite, it contains solutions σ of arbitrarily large length.)

Proof. Let $\sigma \in PE(u,v)$ be a solution of length L: σ has $L+1$ prefixes $x_0, x_1, \ldots, x_L$. We consider the subsequence $x_{i_1}, x_{i_2}, \ldots x_{i_l}$ of all prefixes of σ that satisfy $u_{x_{i_j}} \sqsubseteq v_{x_{i_j}}$ (called *good prefixes*) and split the proof in three main steps.

1. We show, by induction over j, that the sequence $\left(v_{x_{i_j}} \oslash u_{x_{i_j}}\right)_{j=1,..,l}$ is K_v-controlled, i.e., writing w_j for $v_{x_{i_j}} \oslash u_{x_{i_j}}$, that $|w_j| \leq j \times K_v$ for all $j = 1, \ldots, l$. The base case is obvious since $i_1 = 0$ and $w_1 = \varepsilon$. For the inductive case, we consider $j > 0$ so that $x_{i_j} = x_{i_j - 1}.a$ for some $a \in \Sigma$ (the i_j-th letter in σ). If $u_{x_{i_j-1}} \sqsubseteq v_{x_{i_j-1}}$ (hence $i_{(j-1)} = (i_j) - 1$) then $w_j = v_{x_{i_j}} \oslash u_{x_{i_j}}$ is $(v_{x_{i_j-1}}.v_a) \oslash (u_{x_{i_j-1}}.u_a)$ which cannot be longer than $(v_{x_{i_j-1}}.v_a) \oslash u_{x_{i_j-1}}$, itself not longer than $(v_{x_{i_j-1}} \oslash u_{x_{i_j-1}}).v_a$. Thus $|w_j| \leq |w_{j-1}| + K_v$ and we conclude with the induction hypothesis. If on the other hand $u_{x_{i_j-1}} \not\sqsubseteq v_{x_{i_j-1}}$, then w_j is a suffix of v_a hence $|w_j| \leq K_v$.

2a. Assume now that $l \geq H_v$. Then, using Lemma 2.1, we conclude that there is a further subsequence $(x_{i_{j_r}})_{r=0,\ldots,n_R}$ of $n_R + 1$ prefixes of σ such that $w_{j_0} \sqsubseteq w_{j_1} \sqsubseteq \cdots \sqsubseteq w_{j_{n_R}}$. Since n_R is the index of $\sim_R$, we deduce that there exists two such prefixes $x_{i_{j_p}}$ (shortly, x) and $x_{i_{j_{p'}}}$ (shortly, x') with $x \sim_R x'$. If we write x' under the form xy (NB: $y \neq \varepsilon$) and σ under the form xyz, we have found a positive triple (x,y,z). Then Lemma 7.2 applies and shows that xy^*yz is a pumpable solution. Finally, since $x \sim_R xy$, we know that xy^*yz is a subset of R.

2b. Observe that if a prefix x_i of $\sigma = x_i.y_i$ is not good, then $\widetilde{y_i}$ is a good prefix of the solution $\widetilde{\sigma} \in PE(\widetilde{u}, \widetilde{v})$ of the mirror PEP problem. Hence if σ has $l < H_v$ good prefixes, $\widetilde{\sigma}$ has $l' \geq 2H_v - l > H_v$ good ones. Then the mirror problem falls in case 2a above (we note that $\sim_R$, n_R, and K_v do not have to be adjusted when mirroring). We deduce that there is a pumpable solution in $\widetilde{R} \cap PE(\widetilde{u}, \widetilde{v})$, whose mirror is a pumpable solution in $R \cap PE(u,v)$. □

8 Pumping in Long Antisolutions

As with pumpable solutions, there is a sufficient condition for pumpability of antisolutions.

Definition 8.1. *A triple $x, y, z \in \Sigma^*$ with $y \neq \varepsilon$ is* negative *if the following four conditions are satisfied:*

$$u_x \not\sqsubseteq v_x, \quad \text{(D1)} \qquad u_x u_y \not\sqsubseteq v_x v_y, \quad \text{(D2)}$$
$$u_x u_z \not\sqsubseteq v_x v_z \quad \text{(D3)} \qquad u_x \ominus v_x \sqsubseteq u_{xy} \ominus v_{xy} \quad \text{(D4)}$$

Lemma 8.2. *If (x,y,z) is negative then (x,y,z) is a pumpable antisolution.*

Proof. Assume that (x,y,z) is negative, so that (D1–4) hold. Write shortly r for $u_x \ominus v_x$ and r' for $u_{xy} \ominus v_{xy}$. With (D1), (D2) and (D4), Lemma 3.8 applies and yields

$$u_{xy^k} \not\sqsubseteq v_{xy^k} \text{ for all } k \in \mathbb{N}, \quad \text{(D5)}$$

with furthermore

$$u_{xy^k} \ominus v_{xy^k} \sqsubseteq u_{xy^{k+1}} \ominus v_{xy^{k+1}}. \tag{D6}$$

On the other hand, (D1) and (D3) entail $ru_z \not\sqsubseteq v_z$ by Coro. 3.5, hence $(u_{xy^k} \ominus v_{xy^k})u_z \not\sqsubseteq v_z$ by (D6). We deduce that $u_{xy^kz} \not\sqsubseteq v_{xy^kz}$. □

Lemma 8.3. *If R contains an antisolution $\sigma \notin PE(u,v)$ of length $|\sigma| \geq 2H_u$ then it contains a pumpable antisolution.*

(As a corollary, we obtain the second half of the Pumping Lemma.)

Proof (Sketch). We proceed as with Lemma 7.3. Write L for $|\sigma|$, and $x_0, x_1, \ldots, x_L$ for the prefixes of σ. Consider the subsequence $x_{i_1}, x_{i_2}, \ldots x_{i_l}$ of all *bad prefixes* of σ, i.e., such that $u_{x_{i_j}} \not\sqsubseteq v_{x_{i_j}}$ and define $r_j = u_{x_{i_j}} \ominus v_{x_{i_j}}$. The sequence $(r_j)_{j=1,\ldots,l}$ is K_u-controlled.

If $l \geq H_u$, we find two positions $1 \leq p < p' \leq l$ such that $x_{i_{j_p}} \sim_R x_{i_{j_{p'}}}$ and $r_{j_p} \sqsubseteq r_{j_{p'}}$, so that, writing x for $x_{i_{j_p}}$, x' for $x_{i_{j_{p'}}}$, writing x' under the form xy, and σ under the form xyz, we can apply Lemma 8.2 and deduce that (x,y,z) is a pumpable antisolution. Furthermore xy^*z is a subset of R since $xyz = \sigma \in R$ and $xy \sim_R x$.

Observe that if a prefix x_i is not bad, then, writing σ under the form x_iy_i, $\widetilde{y_i}$ is a bad prefix of the antisolution $\widetilde{\sigma} \notin PE(\widetilde{u}, \widetilde{v})$ of the mirror problem. Thus, if $l < H_u$, then $\widetilde{\sigma}$ has $\geq H_u$ bad prefixes in the mirror problem. Hence $\widetilde{R} \smallsetminus PE(\widetilde{u}.\widetilde{v})$ contains a pumpable antisolution, whose mirror is a pumpable antisolution in $R \cap PE(u,v)$. □

Remark 8.4. Lemmas 7.3 and 8.3 show that one can strengthen the statement of the Pumping Lemma. Rather than assuming that $R \cap PE(u,v)$ (respectively, $R \smallsetminus PE(u,v)$) is infinite, we only need to assume that they contain a large enough element. □

9 Concluding Remarks

The decidability of the Regular Post Embedding Problem means that one can find out whether the inequation $u(x) \sqsubseteq v(x)$ has a solution in a given regular R. In this paper, we investigated more general questions pertaining to the set of solutions $PE(u,v)$. We developed new techniques showing how one can decide regular questions (does $PE(u,v)$ contain, or is it included in, a given R?), finiteness and quasi-regular questions (does $PE(u,v)$ satisfy a regular constraint except perhaps for finitely many elements?), and counting questions (how many elements in some R are — or are not — solutions?).

It is not clear how to go beyond these positive results. One avenue we have started to explore [5] is to consider Post-embedding questions with two variables, e.g.,

$$\exists x \in R_1 \, \forall y \in R_2 : u(xy) \sqsubseteq v(xy).$$

Another direction is suggested by the pumpings lemmas we developed here. These lemmas have applications beyond the finiteness problems we considered. For example, they are useful in the study of the expressive power of PEP^{reg}-languages, i.e., languages of the form $R \cap PE(u,v)$ for some R, u, v. For example, using the pumping lemma we can show that $L_0 \stackrel{\text{def}}{=} \{a^n b^n \mid n \in \mathbb{N}\}$ is not a PEP^{reg}-language. Now, and since $L_1 \stackrel{\text{def}}{=} \{a^n b^{n+m} \mid n,m \in \mathbb{N}\}$ and $L_2 \stackrel{\text{def}}{=} \{a^{n+m} b^n \mid n,m \in \mathbb{N}\}$ clearly are PEP^{reg}-languages, we conclude that PEP^{reg}-languages are not closed under intersection!

References

1. Abdulla, P.A., Deneux, J., Ouaknine, J., Quaas, K., Worrell, J.: Universality analysis for one-clock timed automata. Fundamenta Informaticae 89(4), 419–450 (2008)
2. Chambart, P., Schnoebelen, P.: Post embedding problem is not primitive recursive, with applications to channel systems. In: Arvind, V., Prasad, S. (eds.) FSTTCS 2007. LNCS, vol. 4855, pp. 265–276. Springer, Heidelberg (2007)
3. Chambart, P., Schnoebelen, P.: The ω-regular Post embedding problem. In: Amadio, R.M. (ed.) FOSSACS 2008. LNCS, vol. 4962, pp. 97–111. Springer, Heidelberg (2008)
4. Chambart, P., Schnoebelen, P.: The ordinal recursive complexity of lossy channel systems. In: Proc. LICS 2008, pp. 205–216. IEEE Comp. Soc. Press, Los Alamitos (2008)
5. Chambart, P., Schnoebelen, P.: Computing blocker sets for the Regular Post Embedding Problem. In: Proc. DLT 2010. LNCS. Springer, Heidelberg (2010) (to appear)
6. Chambart, P., Schnoebelen, P.: Toward a compositional theory of leftist grammars and transformations. In: Ong, L. (ed.) FOSSACS 2010. LNCS, vol. 6014, pp. 237–251. Springer, Heidelberg (2010)
7. Cichon, E.A., Tahhan Bittar, E.: Ordinal recursive bounds for Higman's theorem. Theoretical Computer Science 201(1-2), 63–84 (1998)
8. Gabelaia, D., Kurucz, A., Wolter, F., Zakharyaschev, M.: Non-primitive recursive decidability of products of modal logics with expanding domains. Annals of Pure and Applied Logic 142(1-3), 245–268 (2006)
9. Jurdziński, T.: Leftist grammars are nonprimitive recursive. In: Aceto, L., Damgård, I., Goldberg, L.A., Halldórsson, M.M., Ingólfsdóttir, A., Walukiewicz, I. (eds.) ICALP 2008, Part II. LNCS, vol. 5126, pp. 51–62. Springer, Heidelberg (2008)
10. Lasota, S., Walukiewicz, I.: Alternating timed automata. ACM Trans. Computational Logic 9(2) (2008)
11. Lazić, R., Newcomb, T., Ouaknine, J., Roscoe, A.W., Worrell, J.: Nets with tokens which carry data. Fundamenta Informaticae 88(3), 251–274 (2008)
12. Lothaire, M. (ed.): Combinatorics on words. Encyclopedia of Mathematics and Its Applications, vol. 17. Cambridge Univ. Press, Cambridge (1983)
13. Lothaire, M. (ed.): Algebraic combinatorics on words. Encyclopedia of Mathematics and Its Applications, vol. 90. Cambridge Univ. Press, Cambridge (2002)
14. Ouaknine, J., Worrell, J.: On the decidability and complexity of Metric Temporal Logic over finite words. Logical Methods in Comp. Science 3(1), 1–27 (2007)

Alternation Removal in Büchi Automata

Udi Boker, Orna Kupferman, and Adin Rosenberg

School of Computer Science and Engineering, Hebrew University, Israel

Abstract. Alternating automata play a key role in the automata-theoretic approach to specification, verification, and synthesis of reactive systems. Many algorithms on alternating automata, and in particular, their nonemptiness test, involve removal of alternation: a translation of the alternating automaton to an equivalent nondeterministic one. For alternating Büchi automata, the best known translation uses the "breakpoint construction" and involves an $O(3^n)$ state blow-up. The translation was described by Miyano and Hayashi in 1984, and is widely used since, in both theory and practice. Yet, the best known lower bound is only 2^n.

In this paper we develop and present a complete picture of the problem of alternation removal in alternating Büchi automata. In the lower bound front, we show that the breakpoint construction captures the accurate essence of alternation removal, and provide a matching $\Omega(3^n)$ lower bound. Our lower bound holds already for universal (rather than alternating) automata with an alphabet of a constant size. In the upper-bound front, we point to a class of alternating Büchi automata for which the breakpoint construction can be replaced by a simpler $n2^n$ construction. Our class, of ordered alternating Büchi automata, strictly contains the class of very-weak alternating automata, for which an $n2^n$ construction is known.

1 Introduction

The automata-theoretic approach to formal verification uses automata on infinite words and trees in order to model systems and their specifications. By translating specifications to automata, we can reduce problems like satisfiability and model checking to the nonemptiness and containment problems of automata. The complexity of the automata-based algorithms is induced by both the blow-up involved in the translation of specifications to automata, and the complexity of the nonemptiness and containment problems for them. The automata-theoretic approach has proven to be extremely useful and popular in practice [1,22].

Early translations of temporal-logic formulas to automata use nondeterministic automata. The transition function of a nondeterministic word automaton suggests several successor states to each state and letter, and an input word is accepted by the automaton if some run on it is accepting. The translation of LTL to nondeterministic Büchi automata (NBW, for short) is exponential [14,23]. Since the nonemptiness problem for NBWs can be solved in NLOGSPACE, the translation suggested a PSPACE upper bound for the model-checking and satisfiability problems of LTL [14,23].

In the early 90s, researchers started to base the automata-theoretic approach on *alternating automata* [19,20]. In an alternating automaton, the transition function maps a

S. Abramsky et al. (Eds.): ICALP 2010, Part II, LNCS 6199, pp. 76–87, 2010.

state and a letter to a formula over the set of states, indicating by which states the suffix of the word should be accepted. For example, if $\delta(q_0, a) = q_1 \wedge (q_2 \vee q_3)$, then when the automaton is in state q_0 and reads the letter a, then the suffix of the word should be accepted both from the state q_1 and from either q_2 or q_3. Thus, several copies of the automaton run on the input word. As shown in [4,13], the translation of temporal logic to alternating automata is simple and involves no blow-up. Accordingly, the complexity is shifted to the nonemptiness problem, which is harder for alternating automata, and involves removal of alternation; that is, a translation to an equivalent nondeterministic automaton. For alternating Büchi automata (ABWs, for short), such a translation involves an exponential blow-up [16], leading to a PSPACE nonemptiness algorithm, which is tight.

It turns out that the use of intermediate alternating automata has many advantages. In some cases, such as branching-time model checking, one can reason about the alternating automaton without removing alternation [13]. In LTL, the use of intermediate alternating automata enables further optimizations on the translation of LTL to NBW [8,9,21], and has led to improved minimization algorithms for NBWs [5,6]. In addition, postponing the removal of alternation to later stages of the algorithms has led to simplified decision and synthesis procedures [7,12].

Consider an alternating automaton $\mathcal{A}$ with state space Q, transition function δ, and set α of accepting states. Removal of alternation in $\mathcal{A}$ has the flavor of removal of nondeterminism in nondeterministic automata. As there, the constructed automaton follows the subset construction applied to $\mathcal{A}$. Here, however, when the constructed automaton is in a state associated with a subset $S \subseteq Q$, the input word should be accepted from all the states in S, and there may be several successors to the state associated with S. For example, if $\delta(q_0, a) = q_1 \wedge (q_2 \vee q_3)$, then in an equivalent nondeterministic automaton, the transition function would map a state associated with the set $\{q_0\}$ and the letter a to a nondeterministic choice between the two states associated with $\{q_1, q_2\}$ or $\{q_1, q_3\}$. In the case of finite words, it is easy to see that defining the set α' of accepting states to be these associated with sets contained in α results in an equivalent nondeterministic automaton.

The case of infinite words is more difficult. Defining α' as above does not work, as it forces the different copies of $\mathcal{A}$ to visit α simultaneously. Also, it is not clear whether a "round-robin" examination of the copies (as done in the case of NBW intersection) is possible, as the number of copies is not bounded. A procedure for alternation removal in ABWs was suggested in 1984 by Miyano and Hayashi [16]. The idea behind the procedure, known as the *breakpoint construction*, is that the states of the equivalent NBW maintain, in addition to the set S associated with the subset construction, also a set $O \subseteq S \setminus \alpha$ of states along runs that "owe" a visit to the set of accepting states. [1] Thus, starting with an ABW with n states, the breakpoint construction ends up in an NBW with at most 3^n states. While the construction is only exponential (one could have expected a $2^{O(n \log n)}$ blow-up, as is the case of complementation or determinization of NBWs [15]), it is conceptually different from the simple subset construction. In particular, it is annoying that the construction does not make use of the fact that the

[1] The direct translations of LTL to NBW, which do not go via ABWs, implement a similar breakpoint construction, by means of an "eventuality automaton" [23].

Büchi condition is memoryless, which suggests that we do not have to run more than n copies. In addition, from a practical point of view, the need to maintain two subsets makes the state space exponentially bigger and makes the implementation of the breakpoint construction difficult and complex [2,5,10,17].

These drawbacks of the breakpoint construction, and its performance in practice for some natural specifications have led Gastin and Oddoux to develop an alternative translation of LTL to NBW [10]. The new translation is based on the fact that the ABWs that correspond to LTL formulas are *very weak*, in the sense that all the cycles in them are of size one (in other words, the only cycles are self-loops). It is shown in [10] that for very weak ABWs, one can replace the breakpoint construction by a simpler construction, with only an $n2^n$ blow-up.

In this paper we develop and present a complete picture of the problem of alternation removal in ABWs. In the lower bound front, we show that the breakpoint construction of [16] and its $\Omega(3^n)$ blow-up cannot be avoided. In the upper-bound front, we point to a class of ABWs that is strictly more expressive than very-weak ABW and for which the breakpoint construction can be replaced by a simpler $n2^n$ construction. Below we elaborate on the two contributions.

First, we show that the concept of the breakpoint construction captures the accurate essence of alternation removal in ABWs. Thus, there is a need to associate the states of the equivalent NBW with two sets, and the $\Omega(3^n)$ blow-up cannot be avoided. Technically, we describe a family of languages L_n such that L_n can be recognized by an alternating (in fact, a universal) Büchi automaton with n states, whereas an equivalent NBW requires at least $\frac{1}{6} \cdot 3^n$ states.[2] This solves negatively the long-standing open problem of improving the breakpoint construction to one with an $O(2^n)$ blow-up. As in [24], our lower-bound proof starts with automata with an exponential alphabet, which we then encode using a fixed-size alphabet. We show that the $\Omega(3^n)$ lower bound applies also to the determinization of nondeterministic co-Büchi word automata and for alternation removal in alternating Büchi tree automata [18].

Second, we introduce *ordered automata* and show that alternation removal in ordered ABWs can avoid the breakpoint construction and involves only an $n2^n$ blow-up. Essentially, an automaton is ordered if the only rejecting cycles induced by its transition function are self loops. Note that all very weak ABWs are ordered, but not vice versa. Indeed, in ordered automata we have no restrictions on cycles that contain accepting states. Ordered automata are strictly more expressive than very weak ABWs. For example, the specifications "p holds in all even positions" and "whenever there is *request*, then *try* and *ack* alternate until *grant* is valid" can be specified by an ordered ABW but not by a very weak ABW. As the above specifications demonstrate, ordered ABWs can handle regular specifications, which are strictly more expressive than LTL and are indeed very popular in modern specification formalisms [3]. Thus, our results extend the fragment of automata for which the breakpoint construction can be avoided. The order condition enables the equivalent NBW to examine the states of the ABW that are not in α in a round-robin fashion: whenever the NBW is in a state associated with a set S of states, it examines a single state $p \in S \setminus \alpha$ and makes sure that no path in the run of

[2] The $\frac{1}{6}$ constant can be reduced and probably also eliminated by some more technical work, which we do not find interesting enough.

the ABW gets trapped in p: as long as p is a successor of itself, it keeps examining p. Only when a chain of p's ends, the NBW changes the examined state. The acceptance condition then makes sure that the NBW does not get trapped in a rejecting state.

We study the expressive power of ordered automata and argue that the order condition defines a fragment of automata for which the breakpoint construction can be avoided. We also show that the $n2^n$ upper bound for the translation of ordered ABWs to NBWs is tight, thus even for ordered automata one needs to augment the subset construction with additional information. Finally, we show that for ordered universal Büchi automata, we can replace the examined state by a subset of letters that are examined, resulting in an alternative construction with blow-up 2^{n+m}, where m is the size of the alphabet. This is in contrast with many translations in automata-theory (c.f. [24], as well as our lower bound proof here), where moving to an alphabet of a constant size does not change the state blow-up.

2 Preliminaries

Given an alphabet Σ, an *infinite word over* Σ is an infinite sequence $w{=}\sigma_0{\cdot}\sigma_1 \cdots \sigma_2 \cdots$ of letters in Σ. For a word w and two indices $t_1, t_2 \geq 0$, we denote by $w[t_1, t_2]$ its subword $\sigma_{t_1} \cdot \sigma_{t_1+1} \cdots \sigma_{t_2}$. In particular, $w[0, t_1]$ is the prefix $\sigma_0 \cdot \sigma_1 \cdots \sigma_{t_1}$ of w, and $w[t_2, \infty]$ is its suffix $\sigma_{t_2} \cdot \sigma_{t_2+1} \cdots$.

For a given set X, let $\mathcal{B}^+(X)$ be the set of positive Boolean formulas over X (i.e., Boolean formulas built from elements in X using $\wedge$ and $\vee$), where we also allow the formulas **true** and **false**. For $Y \subseteq X$, we say that Y *satisfies* a formula $\theta \in \mathcal{B}^+(X)$ iff the truth assignment that assigns *true* to the members of Y and assigns *false* to the members of $X \setminus Y$ satisfies θ. An *alternating Büchi automaton on infinite words* is a tuple $\mathcal{A} = \langle \Sigma, Q, q_{in}, \delta, \alpha \rangle$, where Σ is the input alphabet, Q is a finite set of states, $q_{in} \in Q$ is an initial state, $\delta : Q \times \Sigma \to \mathcal{B}^+(Q)$ is a transition function, and $\alpha \subseteq Q$ is a set of accepting states. We define runs of $\mathcal{A}$ by means of infinite DAGs (directed acyclic graphs).[3] A run of $\mathcal{A}$ on a word $w = \sigma_0 \cdot \sigma_1 \cdots$ is an infinite DAG $\mathcal{G} = \langle V, E \rangle$ satisfying the following (note that there may be several runs of $\mathcal{A}$ on w).

- $V \subseteq Q \times \mathbb{N}$ is as follows. Let $Q_l \subseteq Q$ denote all states in level l. Thus, $Q_l = \{q : \langle q, l \rangle \in V\}$. Then, $Q_0 = \{q_{in}\}$, and Q_{l+1} satisfies $\bigwedge_{q \in Q_l} \delta(q, \sigma_l)$.
- $E \subseteq \bigcup_{l \geq 0}(Q_l \times \{l\}) \times (Q_{l+1} \times \{l+1\})$ is such that $E(\langle q, l \rangle, \langle q', l+1 \rangle)$ iff $Q_{l+1} \setminus \{q'\}$ does not satisfy $\delta(q, \sigma_l)$.

Thus, the root of the DAG contains the initial state of the automaton, and the states associated with nodes in level $l + 1$ satisfy the transitions from states corresponding to nodes in level l. For a set $S \subseteq Q$, a node $\langle q, i \rangle \in V$ is an S-node if $q \in S$. The run $\mathcal{G}$ accepts the word w if all its infinite paths satisfy the acceptance condition α. Thus, in the case of Büchi automata, all the infinite paths have infinitely many α-nodes. We sometimes refer also to co-Büchi automata, where a run is accepting iff all its paths have only finitely many α-nodes. A word w is accepted by $\mathcal{A}$ if there a run that accepts it. The language of $\mathcal{A}$, denoted $L(\mathcal{A})$, is the set of infinite words that $\mathcal{A}$ accepts.

[3] In general, runs of alternating automata are defined by means of infinite trees. Since we are going to deal only with acceptance conditions that have memoryless runs, we can work instead with DAGs [4,11].

We sometimes refer to automata in which the acceptance condition is defined with respect to the transitions. Thus, such an automaton is a tuple $\mathcal{A} = \langle \Sigma, Q, q_{in}, \delta \rangle$, where the transition function is $\delta : Q \times \Sigma \to \mathcal{B}^+(Q \times \{\bot, \top\})$, and a run is accepting if all its paths contain infinitely many transitions with $\top$.

When the formulas in the transition function of $\mathcal{A}$ contain only conjunctions, then $\mathcal{A}$ is universal. When they contain only disjunctions, then $\mathcal{A}$ is nondeterministic, and its runs are DAGs of width 1, where at each level there is a single node. Accordingly, we sometimes refer to the transition function of a nondeterministic automaton as $\delta : Q \times \Sigma \to 2^Q$, and refer to its runs as sequences $r = q_0, q_1, \ldots$ of states. We extend δ to sets of states, by letting $\delta(S, a) = \bigcup_{q \in S} \delta(q, a)$, and recursively to words in Σ^*, by letting $\delta(S, \epsilon) = S$, and $\delta(S, w \cdot \sigma) = \delta(\delta(S, w), \sigma)$, for every $w \in \Sigma^*$ and $\sigma \in \Sigma$. As with words, we denote the subrun of r between positions t_1 and t_2 by $r[t_1, t_2]$. The set of states that a run or a subrun r visits is denoted by $states(r)$.

Finally, we denote the different classes of automata by three letter acronyms in $\{\text{D}, \text{N}, \text{U}, \text{A}\} \times \{\text{B}, \text{C}\} \times \{\text{W}\}$. The first letter stands for the branching mode of the automaton (deterministic, nondeterministic, universal or alternating); the second letter stands for the acceptance-condition type (Büchi or co-Büchi); and the third letter indicates that the automaton runs on words. We add the prefix TR to denote automata with acceptance on transitions. For example, TR-UBW stands for a universal Büchi word automaton with acceptance on transitions.

3 The Lower Bound

In this section we show that the breakpoint construction is accurate, in the sense that it keeps the exact data required for translating an ABW to an NBW. Starting with an ABW with state space Q and acceptance set α (in fact, we even start with a UBW), the NBW generated by the breakpoint construction has a state for each pair $\langle S, O \rangle$, where $S \subseteq Q$ and $O \subseteq S \setminus \alpha$. We show that the construction is optimal, as an equivalent NBW must, essentially, have a different state corresponding to each pair $\langle S, O \rangle$. Our proof basically shows that the NBW must have a state corresponding to every two such pairs, while for simplicity reasons we ignore some cases, getting a constant factor. Formally, we prove the following.

Theorem 1. *There is a family of UBWs $\mathcal{U}_4, \mathcal{U}_5, \ldots$ over an alphabet of 8 letters, such that for every $n \geq 4$, the UBW $\mathcal{U}_n$ has n states, and every NBW equivalent to $\mathcal{U}_n$ has at least $\frac{1}{6}3^n$ states.*

In [24], Yan presents the "full automata approach", suggesting to seek for lower bounds on automata with unbounded alphabets, allowing every possible transition. Only then, should one try to implement the required rich transitions via finite words over a fixed alphabet. We adopt this approach, and further extend it. Not only do we assume an alphabet letter for every possible transition, but we also choose whether the transition visits the accepting states. For that reason, we start with TR-UBWs $\mathcal{A}_n$, having the acceptance condition on transitions rather than on states. Afterwards, we transform $\mathcal{A}_n$ to the required UBW $\mathcal{U}_n$, which is over a fixed alphabet and has acceptance on states.

The family of TR-UBWs. For every $n \geq 4$, we define the TR-UBW $\mathcal{A}_n = \langle \Gamma, Q, \delta, q_{in} \rangle$, where $Q = \{q_1, q_2, \ldots, q_n\}$, $q_{in} = q_1$, and $\Gamma = \{reach(S), award(S, O), unify(S)$ and $connect(S, O, O')$: $S \subseteq Q$ and $\emptyset \neq O, O' \subsetneq S\}$ is an alphabet consisting of four types of letters. The transition function $\delta : Q \times \Gamma \to 2^{Q \times \{\top, \bot\}}$ is defined as follows (see Figure 1):

- $reach(S)$: reaching a subset $S \subseteq Q$ from q_1, without a visit in an accepting transition. Formally,

$$\delta(q, reach(S)) = \begin{cases} S \times \{\bot\} & \text{if } q = q_1 \\ \emptyset & \text{otherwise.} \end{cases}$$

- $award(S, O)$: continuing the paths currently in S and awarding those in O with a visit in an accepting transition. Formally,

$$\delta(q, award(S, O)) = \begin{cases} \langle q, \top \rangle & \text{if } q \in O \\ \langle q, \bot \rangle & \text{if } q \in S \setminus O \\ \emptyset & \text{otherwise.} \end{cases}$$

  We also refer to $award(S, \emptyset)$, defined in the same way.
- $unify(S)$: connecting, without a visit in an accepting transition, all states in S to all states in S. Formally,

$$\delta(q, unify(S)) = \begin{cases} S \times \{\bot\} & \text{if } q \in S \\ \emptyset & \text{otherwise.} \end{cases}$$

- $connect(S, O, O')$: connecting, without a visit in an accepting transition, all states in O to all states in O' and all states in $S \setminus O$ to all states in S. Formally,

$$\delta(q, connect(S, O, O')) = \begin{cases} O' \times \{\bot\} & \text{if } q \in O \\ S \times \{\bot\} & \text{if } q \in S \setminus O \\ \emptyset & \text{otherwise.} \end{cases}$$

Consider an NBW $\mathcal{B}_n$ with state space U and acceptance set β equivalent to $\mathcal{A}_n$. For showing the correspondence between the states of $\mathcal{B}_n$ and all possible pairs $\langle S, O \rangle$, we present a set of words in $L(\mathcal{A}_n)$ that will be shown to fully utilize the required state space of $\mathcal{B}_n$.

The words. For every $n \geq 4$, consider the TR-UBW $\mathcal{A}_n$ defined above. We say that a triple $\langle S, O, O' \rangle \in 2^Q \times 2^Q \times 2^Q$ is *relevant* if $\emptyset \neq O, O' \subsetneq S$. For every relevant triple $\langle S, O, O' \rangle$, we define the infinite word $w_{S,O,O'} = reach(S) \cdot reward(S, O, O')^\omega$, where $reward(S, O, O') = unify(S) \cdot award(S, S \setminus O) \cdot connect(S, O, O') \cdot award(S, O')$.

Lemma 1. *For all relevant triples $\langle S, O, O' \rangle$, the word $w_{S,O,O'}$ is in $L(\mathcal{A}_n)$.*

Since the words are in $L(\mathcal{A}_n)$, each has an accepting run $r_{S,O,O'}$ of the equivalent NBW $\mathcal{B}_n$ on it. We first show that these runs are distinct for different Ss.

Lemma 2. *Let r_1 and r_2 be accepting runs of $\mathcal{B}_n$ on $w_1 = w_{S_1,O_1,O'_1}$ and $w_2 = w_{S_2,O_2,O'_2}$, respectively. If $S_1 \neq S_2$, then $states(r_1[1, \infty]) \cap states(r_2[1, \infty]) = \emptyset$.*

Replacing a letter $connect(S, O, O')$ in the word $w_{S,O,O'}$ with a letter $connect(S, P, P')$ (of another tuple) may result in a word out of $L(\mathcal{A}_n)$. We say

pairs of states in X_S. Therefore, there are at least $\frac{2^{|S|-2}}{\sqrt{2}} \geq \frac{2^{|S|}}{2}$ states in X_S. [5] Hence, there are at least $\Sigma_{S \subseteq Q' \setminus \{q_{acc}\}} |X_S| = \Sigma_{S \subseteq Q' \setminus \{q_{acc}\}} \frac{2^{|S|}}{2} = \frac{1}{2} 3^n$ states in $\mathcal{B}_n$. Starting with a UBW with $n+1$ states, we get a state blow-up of $\frac{1}{2} 3^{n-1} = \frac{1}{6} 3^n$.

Combined with the breakpoint construction, we have a tight bound for the translation of an ABW to an equivalent NBW. Applying the construction in [16] to UBW, one ends up with a DBW. Since we described the lower bound using UBWs, we also get a tight bound for alternation removal of UBW, and, dually, to determinization of nondeterministic co-Büchi automata. Formally, we have the following.

Theorem 2. *The tight bound for translating ABWs or UBWs to NBWs and for determinization of NCWs is* $\Theta(3^n)$.

4 Ordered Automata

In Section 3 we showed that, in general, a blow-up of $\Omega(3^n)$ cannot be avoided when translating an ABW to an NBW. In this section we introduce and explore a subclass of ABWs that can be translated to an equivalent NBW with a blow-up of only $n2^n$.

Definition 1. *An automaton* $\mathcal{A} = \langle \Sigma, Q, \delta, q_{in}, \alpha \rangle$ *is* ordered *if there exists a partial order* $\leq_{\mathcal{A}}$ *on* $Q \setminus \alpha$*, such that for every* $q, q' \in Q \setminus \alpha$ *and* $\sigma \in \Sigma$*, if* $q' \in \delta(q, \sigma)$*, then* $q' \leq_{\mathcal{A}} q$.

Note that, equivalently, $\mathcal{A}$ is ordered if the only cycles consisting solely of states not in α are self loops.

The order property is less restrictive than the very-weak condition of [10]. To demonstrate this extra strength, we describe below the ordered ABW for the property "whenever there is *request*, then *try* and *ack* alternate until *grant* is valid" over the alphabet $\Sigma = 2^{AP}$, where $AP = \{try, ack, req, grant\}$. Since the ABW has a single rejecting state, it is obviously ordered. Note that this property cannot be specified in LTL or in a very weak ABW. Note also how the ordered ABW uses universal branches in order to allow the *try-ack* cycle to be accepting. Indeed, fulfilling the eventuality is taken care by a different copy of the ABW.

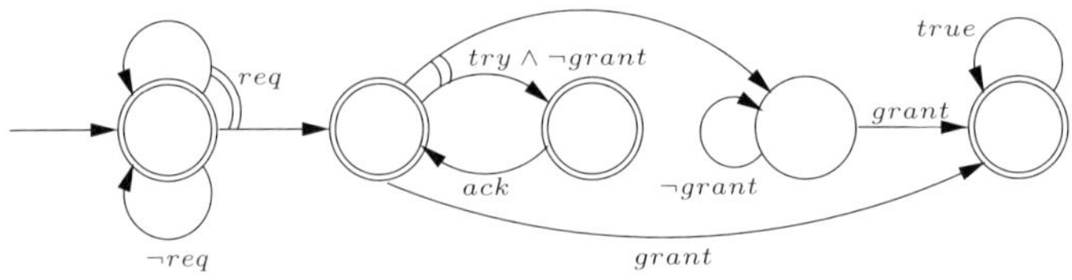

Fig. 2. An ordered ABW specifying "whenever there is *request*, then *try* and *ack* alternate until *grant* is valid". For a propositional assertion θ over AP, a transition labeled θ stands for a transition with all the letters $\sigma \in 2^{AP}$ that satisfy θ.

The automata used in the lower-bound proof have the property that every two states not in α are reachable from each other without an intermediate visit to α. In a sense, this property is an antipode of the order property presented in Definition 1. We argue

[5] This $\geq$ is not correct for a very small subset S, but since we accumulate over all the subsets, the total sum does satisfy it.

that violating the order property is what forces an equivalent NBW to associate its states with two subsets of states of the ABW. Indeed, as we show below, an ABW that has the order property can be translated to an equivalent NBW with an $n2^n$ blow-up. Still, even for ordered automata, the NBW needs to maintain information beyond the subset construction, thus the $n2^n$ translation is tight.

Theorem 3. *The tight bound for translating an ordered ABW to an NBW is* $\Theta(n2^n)$.

Proof. We start with the upper bound. Let $\mathcal{A} = \langle \Sigma, Q, \delta, q_{in}, \alpha \rangle$ be an ordered ABW, and let $\leq_{\mathcal{A}}$ be an extension of the partial order on $Q \setminus \alpha$ to a total order on Q. Let $|Q| = n$. The order $\leq_{\mathcal{A}}$ allows us to identify Q with $\{1, 2, \ldots, n\}$ while preserving the natural order. We define the equivalent NBW $\mathcal{A}' = \langle \Sigma, Q', \delta', q'_{in}, \alpha' \rangle$ as follows.

- $Q' \subseteq 2^Q \times (Q \setminus \alpha \cup \{0\})$ is such that $\langle S, p \rangle \in Q'$ iff $p \in (S \setminus \alpha) \cup \{0\}$. Intuitively, the set S follows the subset construction applied to $\mathcal{A}$: when $\mathcal{A}$ is in a state in $S \times \{0, \ldots, n\}$, the word in the input should be accepted from all the states in S. Note that since $\mathcal{A}$ is alternating, there may be several sets S' that are possible successors of a set S. Since the input word should be accepted from all the states in S, all the paths that start in states in S should not get trapped in a state not in α. To ensure this, $\mathcal{A}'$ examines the states not in α in a round-robin fashion: at each moment it examines a single state $p \in S \setminus \alpha$ and makes sure that no path in the run of $\mathcal{A}$ gets trapped in p: as long as p is a successor of itself, it keeps examining p. Only when a chain of p's ends (either because p is not in S' or because p is in S' but is not a successor of itself), $\mathcal{A}'$ changes the examined state, to the maximal state in S' that is smaller than p. If no such state exists, $\mathcal{A}'$ sets p to 0. As would be made clear below, this earns $\mathcal{A}'$ a visit in the set of accepting states, and causes it to start a new round of checks.
- $q'_{in} = \langle \{q_{in}\}, 0 \rangle$.
- In order to define the transition function, we first define a function $next : 2^Q \times 2^Q \times \{0, \ldots, n\} \times \Sigma \to \{0, \ldots, n\}$, which returns the next state that should be examined by $\mathcal{A}'$. Formally, $next(S, S', p, \sigma)$ is (we fix $\max(\emptyset) = 0$):

$$\begin{bmatrix} p & \text{if } p \neq 0 \text{ and } S' \setminus \{p\} \not\models \delta(p, \sigma) \\ \max(\{q \mid q \in S' \setminus (\alpha \cup \{p\}) \wedge q \leq p\}) & \text{if } p \neq 0 \text{ and } S' \setminus \{p\} \models \delta(p, \sigma) \\ \max(S' \setminus \alpha) & \text{if } p = 0 \end{bmatrix}$$

  Now, $\delta'(\langle S, p \rangle, \sigma) = \{\langle S', next(S, S', p, \sigma) \rangle \mid S' \models \delta(S, \sigma)\}$.
  Thus, each transition guesses the next set S' and updates the examined new state accordingly.
- $\alpha' = 2^Q \times \{0\}$.

We now turn to the lower bound. The lower bound of Theorem 1 does not hold for ordered UBWs as the UBWs $\mathcal{U}_n$ used there are, obviously, not ordered. In order to prove an $\Omega(n2^n)$ lower bound, we argue that the actions $reach()$ and $award()$ can be simulated by an ordered UBW over an alphabet whose size is linear in n, and that using them we can point to words that force the NBW to have at least $\Omega(n2^n)$ states.

For every $n \geq 4$, consider the TR-UBW $\mathcal{A}_n$ defined in Section 3. Using the actions $reach()$ and $award()$, one can define for every set $S \subseteq Q \setminus \{q_{acc}\}$ the word $w_s = reach(S) \cdot reward(S)^\omega$, where $reward(S) = \bullet_{q \in S}\, award(S, \{q\})$. These words belong to $L(\mathcal{A}_n)$, entailing for every S a distinct loop of states in an equivalent NBW. We show that the restriction of $\mathcal{A}_n$, having only the *reach*() and *award*() actions, can be simulated by an ordered UBW $\mathcal{O}_n$ over an alphabet whose size is linear in n, and that each such loop of big states in an NBW equivalent to $\mathcal{O}_n$ has at least $|S|$ states, providing the required lower bound of $\Sigma_{S \subseteq Q}|S| = \Omega(n2^n)$.

4.1 Fixed Alphabet

Usually, the alphabet size does not influence the state blow-up involved in automata translation. This is also the case with the translation of ABWs to NBWs, as shown in Section 3. Yet, ordered UBWs provide an interesting example of a case in which the alphabet size does matter. While Theorem 3 provides an $\Omega(n2^n)$ lower bound for the translation of an ordered UBW to an equivalent NBW, we show below that the translation can be done with only $O(2^n)$ state blow-up over a fixed alphabet.

Theorem 4. *An ordered UBW with n states over an alphabet with m letters has an equivalent DBW with 2^{m+n} states.*

Proof. Let $\mathcal{A} = \langle \Sigma, Q, \delta, q_{in}, \alpha \rangle$. We define $\mathcal{A}' = \langle \Sigma, Q', \delta', q'_{in}, \alpha' \rangle$, where

- $Q' = 2^Q \times 2^\Sigma$. Intuitively, the 2^Q component is a simple subset construction. The 2^Σ component has the task of maintaining a set of letters recently read from the input word, with the property that all suffixes consisting entirely of letters from this set are rejected by $\mathcal{A}$.
- For a state $\langle S, P \rangle$, we say that P *detains* S if there is a state $q \in S \setminus \alpha$ such that for every letter $\sigma \in P$, we have $q \in \delta(q, \sigma)$. Now, for all states $\langle S, P \rangle \in Q'$ and $\sigma \in \Sigma$, we define

$$\delta'(\langle S, P \rangle, \sigma) = \begin{bmatrix} \langle \delta(S, \sigma), P \cup \{\sigma\} \rangle & \text{if } P \cup \{\sigma\} \text{ detains } S. \\ \langle \delta(S, \sigma), \emptyset \rangle & \text{otherwise.} \end{bmatrix}$$

  That is, the 2^Q component follows the subset construction, while the current letter is added to the 2^Σ component as long as the required property (which is equivalent to $P \cup \{\sigma\}$ detaining S) is retained. So a path in a run of $\mathcal{A}$ gets trapped in some state q iff the 2^Σ component manages to avoid the empty set thanks to q.
- $q'_{in} = \langle \{q_{in}\}, \emptyset \rangle$.
- $\alpha' = 2^Q \times \{\emptyset\}$.

Remark 1. It is shown in [18] that the breakpoint construction is valid when applied to alternating Büchi tree automata. Our lower bound proof clearly holds also for alternation removal in tree automata. As for the upper bound, it is not hard to see that the definition of ordered automata can be extended to the setting of tree automata, and that both translations in Theorems 3 and 4 stay valid in this setting.

References

1. Accellera. Accellera organization inc. (2006), http://www.accellera.org
2. Daniele, N., Guinchiglia, F., Vardi, M.Y.: Improved automata generation for linear temporal logic. In: Halbwachs, N., Peled, D.A. (eds.) CAV 1999. LNCS, vol. 1633, pp. 249–260. Springer, Heidelberg (1999)

3. Eisner, C., Fisman, D.: A Practical Introduction to PSL. Springer, Heidelberg (2006)
4. Emerson, E.A., Jutla, C.: Tree automata, μ-calculus and determinacy. In: Proc. 32nd FOCS, pp. 368–377 (1991)
5. Etessami, K., Holzmann, G.J.: Optimizing Büchi automata. In: Palamidessi, C. (ed.) CONCUR 2000. LNCS, vol. 1877, pp. 153–167. Springer, Heidelberg (2000)
6. Etessami, K., Wilke, T., Schuller, R.A.: Fair simulation relations, parity games, and state space reduction for Büchi automata. Siam J. Comput. 34(5), 1159–1175 (2005)
7. Filiot, E., Jin, N., Raskin, J.-F.: An antichain algorithm for LTL realizability. In: Bouajjani, A., Maler, O. (eds.) Computer Aided Verification. LNCS, vol. 5643, pp. 263–277. Springer, Heidelberg (2009)
8. Fritz, C.: Constructing Büchi automata from linear temporal logic using simulation relations for alternating Büchi automata. In: Ibarra, O.H., Dang, Z. (eds.) CIAA 2003. LNCS, vol. 2759, pp. 35–48. Springer, Heidelberg (2003)
9. Fritz, C., Wilke, T.: State space reductions for alternating Büchi automata: Quotienting by simulation equivalences. In: Agrawal, M., Seth, A.K. (eds.) FSTTCS 2002. LNCS, vol. 2556, pp. 157–169. Springer, Heidelberg (2002)
10. Gastin, P., Oddoux, D.: Fast LTL to Büchi automata translation. In: Berry, G., Comon, H., Finkel, A. (eds.) CAV 2001. LNCS, vol. 2102, pp. 53–65. Springer, Heidelberg (2001)
11. Kupferman, O., Vardi, M.Y.: Model checking of safety properties. Formal Methods in System Design 19(3), 291–314 (2001)
12. Kupferman, O., Vardi, M.Y.: Complementation constructions for nondeterministic automata on infinite words. In: Halbwachs, N., Zuck, L.D. (eds.) TACAS 2005. LNCS, vol. 3440, pp. 206–221. Springer, Heidelberg (2005)
13. Kupferman, O., Vardi, M.Y., Wolper, P.: An automata-theoretic approach to branching-time model checking. Journal of the ACM 47(2), 312–360 (2000)
14. Lichtenstein, O., Pnueli, A.: Checking that finite state concurrent programs satisfy their linear specification. In: Proc. 12th POPL, pp. 97–107 (1985)
15. Löding, C.: Optimal bounds for transformations of ω-automata. In: Pandu Rangan, C., Raman, V., Sarukkai, S. (eds.) FST TCS 1999. LNCS, vol. 1738, pp. 97–109. Springer, Heidelberg (1999)
16. Miyano, S., Hayashi, T.: Alternating finite automata on ω-words. Theoretical Computer Science 32, 321–330 (1984)
17. Morgenstern, A., Schneider, K.: From LTL to symbolically represented deterministic automata. In: Logozzo, F., Peled, D.A., Zuck, L.D. (eds.) VMCAI 2008. LNCS, vol. 4905, pp. 279–293. Springer, Heidelberg (2008)
18. Mostowski, A.W.: Regular expressions for infinite trees and a standard form of automata. In: Skowron, A. (ed.) SCT 1984. LNCS, vol. 208, pp. 157–168. Springer, Heidelberg (1985)
19. Muller, D.E., Saoudi, A., Schupp, P.E.: Alternating automata, the weak monadic theory of the tree and its complexity. In: Kott, L. (ed.) ICALP 1986. LNCS, vol. 226, pp. 275–283. Springer, Heidelberg (1986)
20. Muller, D.E., Schupp, P.E.: Alternating automata on infinite trees. Theoretical Computer Science 54, 267–276 (1987)
21. Somenzi, F., Bloem, R.: Efficient Büchi automata from LTL formulae. In: Emerson, E.A., Sistla, A.P. (eds.) CAV 2000. LNCS, vol. 1855, pp. 248–263. Springer, Heidelberg (2000)
22. Vardi, M.Y.: Nontraditional applications of automata theory. In: Hagiya, M., Mitchell, J.C. (eds.) TACS 1994. LNCS, vol. 789, pp. 575–597. Springer, Heidelberg (1994)
23. Vardi, M.Y., Wolper, P.: Reasoning about infinite computations. Information and Computation 115(1), 1–37 (1994)
24. Yan, Q.: Lower bounds for complementation of ω-automata via the full automata technique. In: Bugliesi, M., Preneel, B., Sassone, V., Wegener, I. (eds.) ICALP 2006. LNCS, vol. 4052, pp. 589–600. Springer, Heidelberg (2006)

Linear Orders in the Pushdown Hierarchy

Laurent Braud and Arnaud Carayol

LIGM, Université Paris-Est & CNRS
{braud,carayol}@univ-mlv.fr

Abstract. We investigate the linear orders belonging to the pushdown hierarchy. Our results are based on the characterization of the pushdown hierarchy by graph transformations due to Caucal and do not make any use of higher-order pushdown automata machinery.

Our main results show that ordinals belonging to the n-th level are exactly those strictly smaller than the tower of ω of height $n+1$. More generally the Hausdorff rank of scattered linear orders on the n-th level is strictly smaller than the tower of ω of height n. As a corollary the Cantor-Bendixson rank of the tree solutions of safe recursion schemes of order n is smaller than the tower of ω of height n.

As a spin-off result, we show that the ω-words belonging to the second level of the pushdown hierarchy are exactly the morphic words.

1 Introduction

The pushdown hierarchy (also known as the Caucal hierarchy) is a hierarchy of families of infinite graphs having decidable monadic second-order (MSO) theory. This hierarchy has several equivalent definitions and has received a lot of attention in the last ten years (see [Tho03, Ong07] for surveys).

At the first level of this hierarchy are the transition graphs of the pushdown automata which coincide with the prefix-recognizable graphs [Cau96]. Every level can in a similar fashion be characterized as the transitions graphs of an extension of pushdown automata called an higher-order pushdown automata [Mas76]. The rewriting approach of [Cau96] was also extended to all levels in [Car05]. The deterministic trees at level n correspond to the (trees solutions of) safe recursion schemes of order $(n-1)$ [Cau02, KNU02].

An alternative characterization due to Caucal [Cau02, CW03] consists in constructing these graphs by applying MSO-interpretations and graph unfoldings starting from finite trees. The level of a graph in this approach is given by the number of times the unfolding operation has been applied.

Despite these various characterizations, one of the main question concerning this hierarchy is to characterize the graphs inhabiting each level and in particular to provide tools for showing that a structure does not belong to a certain level. For instance, to the authors knowledge, the only proof of the strictness of the pushdown hierarchy relies on the strictness of the hierarchy of languages accepted by higher-order pushdown automata obtained in [Eng91]. A partial answer is given in [Blu08] which provides a pumping lemma for these automata. However

S. Abramsky et al. (Eds.): ICALP 2010, Part II, LNCS 6199, pp. 88–99, 2010.

the bounds provided in the latter article are not tight and hence do not allow to derive the strictness level by level.

This article subscribes to this line of research and characterizes linear orders in the pushdown hierarchy.

Linear orders in this hierarchy have first been studied via recursion schemes. A natural way to define a linear order starting from an ordered tree is to consider its frontier *i.e.* its set of leaves ordered lexicographically. This approach was initiated by Courcelle in [Cou78]. Two families of linear orders are of particular interest : the well-orders (or ordinals) and the scattered orders.

At the first level of the hierarchy, the scattered frontiers of the regular deterministic tree (order-0 schemes) have an Hausdorff rank strictly less than ω [Hei80] and the ordinals are known to be those strictly smaller than ω^{ω}.

At the second level, the frontiers of order-1 recursion schemes are also called *algebraic linear orders*. Is was shown in [BÉ07, BÉ10] that algebraic ordinals are precisely the ordinals strictly smaller than $\omega^{\omega^{\omega}}$. In [BÉ09], it is shown that any scattered algebraic linear order has a Hausdorff rank strictly smaller than ω^{ω}. They conjecture that similar bounds can be obtained for recursion schemes of arbitrary orders. The results presented in this article prove this conjecture in the case of safe recursion schemes. Our main tool is the characterization of the pushdown hierarchy in terms of graph transformations.

In Section 3, we show that any linear order at level n is isomorphic to the frontier of some order-$(n-1)$ safe recursion scheme. We use this result to show that the ω-words on the second level are exactly the morphic words. In Section 4, we show that ordinals at level n are exactly the ordinals below $\omega \uparrow\uparrow (n+1)$ (which stands for the tower of ω of height $n+1$). The fact that all these ordinals are in at level n was shown in [Bra09]. This result provides a self-contained proof of the strictness of the pushdown hierarchy level by level. In Section 5, we show that the Hausdorff rank of scattered orders on level n is strictly smaller than $\omega \uparrow\uparrow n$. As a corollary we obtain that the Cantor-Bendixson rank of the tree solutions of safe recursion schemes of order n is smaller than $\omega \uparrow\uparrow n$.

2 Preliminaries

2.1 Linear Orders and Trees

A *linear order* $L = (D, <)$ is given by a set D together with a total order $<$ on D. We write L^* for the linear order $(D, <^*)$ where $x <^* y$ iff $y < x$. For a detailed presentation of linear orderings, we refer to [Ros82]. $L_1 = (D_1, <_1)$ is a *subordering* of $L_2 = (D_2, <_2)$, written $L_1 \preceq L_2$, if $D_1 \subseteq D_2$ and $<_1$ is equal to $<_2$ restricted to D_1. The order type of L is the class of all linear orders isomorphic to L. We denote by **0**,**1**, ω and ζ the order type of the order with 0 and 1 element, $(\mathbb{N}, <)$ and $(\mathbb{Z}, <)$ respectively.

A *colored linear order* is a mapping from a linear order to a finite set of symbols called colors.

A *well-order* is a linear order for which every non-empty subordering has a smallest element. The order type of a well-order is called an *ordinal*. We note

ε_0 the smallest ordinal such that $\varepsilon_0 = \omega^{\varepsilon_0}$. For all $n \geq 0$, we define $\omega \uparrow\uparrow n$ by taking $\omega \uparrow\uparrow 0 = 1$ and $\omega \uparrow\uparrow (n+1) = \omega^{(\omega \uparrow\uparrow n)}$ for $n \geq 0$. In particular $\varepsilon_0 = \sup \{\omega \uparrow\uparrow n \mid n \geq 0\}$. An *$\omega$-word* is a colored linear order of order type ω.

Let $(\Sigma, <)$ be a finite ordered alphabet. We write Σ^* the set of words over Σ. We write $u \sqsubseteq v$ if u is a prefix of v and $u \bot v$ if $u \not\sqsubseteq v$ and $v \not\sqsubseteq u$. We denote by $u \wedge v$ the greatest common prefix of u and v. The lexicographic order on Σ^* is defined by: $u <_{\text{lex}} v$ iff $u \sqsubseteq v$ or $u = waw'$ and $v = wbw''$ with $a < b \in \Sigma$.

A *deterministic tree* t over an ordered alphabet Σ is a prefix-closed subset of Σ^*. If $u \sqsubseteq v$, we say that u is an ancestor of v or equivalently that v is a descendant of u. Elements of t are called nodes and nodes without proper descendant are called *leaves.* A *colored deterministic tree* t is a mapping from a deterministic tree t to a finite set of symbols called colors.

A deterministic tree is *pruned* if it is binary (i.e. $\Sigma = \{0, 1\}$ with the usual order), *full* (i.e. every node is either a leaf or has two sons) and below every node there is at least one leaf.

The *frontier* of a deterministic tree t, denoted $\mathbf{Fr}(t)$, is the linear order obtained by considering the leaves of t with the lexicographic order. The *colored frontier* of a deterministic tree t colored by Γ is the mapping from $\mathbf{Fr}(t)$ to Γ associating to each leaf of t its color in t. In the following, whenever we talk about a deterministic tree we always assume that the alphabet is ordered.

2.2 Graphs and Monadic Second-Order Logic

Let Σ and Γ be two finite sets of arc and vertex labels respectively. Vertex labels are also called colors. A (labeled) graph G is a subset of $V \times \Sigma \times V \cup \Gamma \times V$ where V is a finite or countable arbitrary set. An element (s, a, t) of $V \times \Sigma \times V$ is an *arc* of *source* s, *target* t and *label* a, and is written $s \xrightarrow{a} t$ if G is understood. An element $(c, s) \in \Gamma \times V$ intuitively means that s is colored by c.

The set of all vertices appearing in G is its *support* V_G. A sequence of arcs $s_1 \xrightarrow{a_1} t_1, \ldots, s_k \xrightarrow{a_k} t_k$ with $\forall i \in [2, k]$, $s_i = t_{i-1}$ is a *path* starting from s_1. We write $s_1 \xrightarrow{u} t_k$ where $u = a_1 \ldots a_k$.

A graph is *deterministic* if there are no arcs with the same label that share the same source but not the same target (*i.e.*, for all $a \in \Sigma$, if $s \xrightarrow[G]{a} t$ and $s \xrightarrow[G]{a} t'$ then $t = t'$). A graph G is a *tree* if there exists a vertex r called the *root* such that for any vertex in the graph there exists a unique path from the root r to this vertex.

Linear orders and deterministic trees and their respective colored versions can be represented by graphs in a natural way. A linear order $(L, <)$ is represented by the graph $\{(u, <, v) \mid u, v \in L \text{ and } u < v\}$. A deterministic tree t over Σ is represented by the graph $\{(u, a, ua) \mid u, ua \in t \text{ and } a \in \Sigma\}$. In the following, we will not distinguish between these objects and their graph representations.

We consider *monadic second-order (MSO) logic* over graphs with the standard syntax and semantics (see e.g. [EF95] for a detailed presentation). We write $\varphi(X_1, \ldots, X_n, y_1, \ldots, y_m)$ to denote that the free variables of the formula

φ are among $X_1, \ldots, X_n$ (monadic second-order) and $y_1, \ldots, y_m$ (first-order). A formula without free variables is called a *sentence*.

For a graph G and a sentence φ, we write $G \models \varphi$ if $\mathcal{G}$ *satisfies* the formula φ. The *MSO-theory* of G is the set of sentences satisfied by G. For all formula $\varphi(X_1, \ldots, X_n, y_1, \ldots, y_m)$, all sets $U_1, \ldots, U_n$ of nodes of G and all nodes $v_1, \ldots, v_m$ of G, we write $G \models \varphi[U_1, \ldots, U_n, v_1, \ldots, v_m]$ to express that φ holds in G when X_i is interpreted as U_i for all $i \in [1, n]$ and y_j is interpreted as v_j for all $j \in [1, m]$.

2.3 Graph Transformations

The *unfolding* $\mathrm{Unf}(G, r)$ of a graph G from a vertex $r \in V_G$ is the tree T s.t. for all $a \in \Sigma$, $\pi \xrightarrow{a} \pi' \in T$ if and only if π and π' are two paths in G starting from r and $\pi' = \pi \cdot (s \xrightarrow{a} t)$. Moreover for any color $c \in \Gamma$, $(c, \pi) \in T$ if and only if π is a path in G starting with r and ending in t with $(c, t) \in G$.

An *MSO-interpretation* is given by a family $\mathcal{I} = (\varphi_a(x, y))_{a \in \Sigma} \cup (\varphi_c(x))_{c \in \Gamma}$ of MSO-formulas. Applying such an MSO-interpretation to a graph G we obtain the graph $\mathcal{I}(G)$ labeled by Σ and colored by Γ and s.t. for all $a \in \Sigma$, $(u, a, v) \in \mathcal{I}(G)$ iff $G \models \varphi_a(u, v)$ and for all $c \in \Gamma$, $(c, u) \in \mathcal{I}(G)$ iff $G \models \varphi_c(u)$.

An *MSO-coloring* is a particular MSO-interpretation that only affects colors and leaves the arcs unchanged (*i.e.*, for all $a \in \Sigma$, $\varphi_a(x, y) = x \xrightarrow{a} y$).

Interpretations cannot increase the size of a structure. To overcome this weakness the notion of a transduction was introduced [Cou94]. Let $K = \{k_1, \ldots, k_m\}$ be a finite set disjoint from Σ. A *K-copying operation* applied to G adds, to every vertex of G, m out-going arcs labeled resp. by $k_1, \ldots, k_n$ all going to fresh vertices. An *MSO-transduction* $\mathcal{T}$ is a K-copying operation followed by an MSO-interpretation $\mathcal{I}$.

2.4 MSO on Deterministic Trees

A *non-deterministic tree-walking automaton* (TWA) working on deterministic trees over Σ colored by Γ is a tuple $W = (Q, q_0, F, \Delta)$ where Q is the finite set of states, $q_0 \in Q$ is the initial state, F is the set of final states and Δ is the set of transitions. A transition is a tuple (p, c, q, a) with $p \in Q$ and $c \in \Gamma$ – corresponding respectively to the current state and the color of the current node – $q \in Q$ and $a \in (\{\uparrow, \varepsilon\} \cup \Sigma)$ – q being the new state and a the action to perform. Intuitively ε corresponds to "stay in the current node", $\uparrow$ to "go to the parent node" and $d \in \Sigma$ corresponds to "go to the d-son". We say that W accepts a pair of nodes (u, v) if it can reach v in a final state starting from u in the initial state.

Proposition 1 ([Car06, Prop. 3.2.1]). *For any deterministic tree t and any MSO-formula $\varphi(x, y)$, there exists an MSO-coloring $\mathcal{M}$ and a TWA $\mathcal{A}$ such that $t \models \varphi[u, v]$ iff $\mathcal{A}$ accepts (u, v) on $\mathcal{M}(t)$.*

2.5 The Pushdown Hierarchy

Following [Cau02], we define the pushdown hierarchy by iterating MSO-interpretations and unfoldings starting from finite graphs.

$$\begin{aligned}\mathrm{Tree}_0 &= \text{the class of finite trees}\\ \mathrm{Graph}_n &= \text{the class of graphs MSO-interpretable in a tree of } \mathrm{Tree}_n\\ \mathrm{Tree}_{n+1} &= \text{the class of the unfoldings of graphs in } \mathrm{Graph}_n.\end{aligned}$$

All the graphs in Graph_n have a decidable MSO-theory. Furthermore the hierarchy is unchanged if we require that any graph in Graph_n is MSO-interpreted in a **deterministic** tree in Tree_n [CW03]. We only recall the two properties that will be used in this article. For a more detailed presentation, we refer the reader to [Tho03].

Proposition 2 ([CW03]). *For all n, the deterministic trees of* Tree_n *are closed under MSO-coloring and* Graph_n *is closed under MSO-transduction.*

Proposition 3 ([Fra05, Car06]). *Take t a deterministic tree in* Tree_n*, $\varphi(X)$ a MSO-formula and \$ a fresh color symbol. If $t \models \exists X \varphi(X)$ then there exists $U \subseteq t$ s.t. $t \models \varphi[U]$ and $t \cup \{(\$, u) \mid u \in U\}$ also belongs to* Tree_n.

3 Frontiers of Trees in the Pushdown Hierarchy

In this section, we show that every (colored) linear order in Graph_n is the (colored) frontier of a pruned tree in Tree_n. Remark that as the lexicographic order on a deterministic tree is definable in MSO logic, the frontiers of the deterministic trees in Tree_n belongs to Graph_n. The following theorem establishes the converse inclusion.

Theorem 1. *Each colored linear order in* Graph_n *is the frontier of a colored pruned tree in* Tree_n.

Proof (Sketch). To simplify the presentation, we focus on the uncolored case. Let $L = (D, <_L)$ be a linear order in Graph_n for some $n \geq 0$.

Using the definition of Graph_n and Prop. 1 and 2, we have that there exists a colored deterministic tree $t \in \mathrm{Tree}_n$ and a TWA $\mathcal{A}$ such that D is a set of nodes of t and for all $u, v \in D$, $u <_L v$ iff $\mathcal{A}$ accepts (u, v). We can w.l.o.g. assume that D is the set of leaves of t. For instance, it is enough to add a new leaf below every node of D and to modify $\mathcal{A}$ accordingly.

The following construction rearranges the leaves of t into a new deterministic tree $s(t) \in \mathrm{Tree}_n$ so that lexicographic order on the leaves of $s(t)$ matches $<_L$ on the leaves of t. It is easy to adapt the definition of $s(t)$ to obtain a pruned tree (while remaining in Tree_n).

For all leaf $u \in D$ and for all $v \sqsubset u \in D$, we define $s(u, v)$ as the maximal length of a decreasing sequence $u_0 >_L u_1 >_L \dots >_L u_k$ of leaves starting with $u_0 = u$ and such that for $i \in [0, k-1]$, $u_i \wedge u_{i+1} = v$. Using a pumping argument on $\mathcal{A}$, we can show that there exists $n_0 \geq 1$ such that for every leaf $u \in D$ and all nodes $v \sqsubset u$, $s(u, v) \leq n_0$.

To every leaf $u = u_1 \cdots u_n$, we associate the finite sequence $\boldsymbol{s}(u)$ in $[1, n_0]^n$ defined by $\boldsymbol{s}(u) = (s(u, \varepsilon), s(u, u_1), \ldots, s(u, u_1 \cdots u_{n-1}))$. The key property of this sequence is that comparing two leaves u and v with $<_L$ is equivalent to comparing $\boldsymbol{s}(u)$ and $\boldsymbol{s}(v)$ using the lexicographic order, *i.e.* $u <_L v$ iff $\boldsymbol{s}(u) <_{\text{lex}} \boldsymbol{s}(v)$.

Consider the tree $s(t)$ over the finite alphabet $[1, n_0]$ obtained by taking the prefix-closure of $\{\boldsymbol{s}(u) \mid u \text{ leaf of } t)\}$. The frontier of $s(t)$ is isomorphic to $(D, <_L)$. These definitions are illustrated on the finite example below; t is on the left and $s(t)$ is on the right; for each leaf x, we give its order for $<_L$ and the sequence $\boldsymbol{s}(x)$.

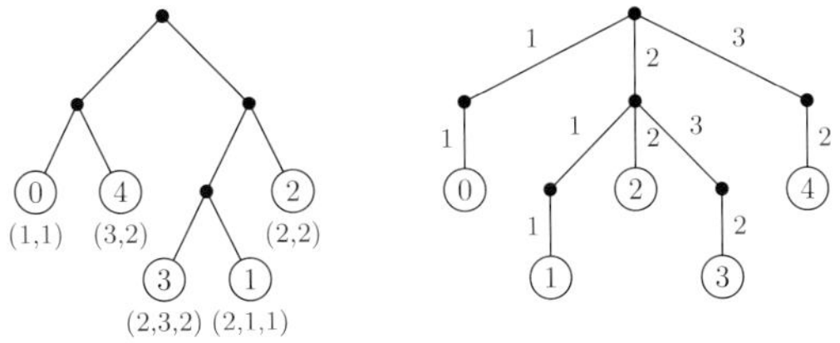

The last step of the proof is to show that $s(t)$ also belongs to Tree_n. □

We know from [Cau02] that the infinite terms in Tree_n are the terms solutions of safe recursive schemes of order $(n-1)$ (we refer the reader to [KNU02] for a formal definition of safe recursion schemes). Hence the previous theorem can be restated as follows.

Corollary 1. *A linear order colored by Γ is in* Graph_n *if and only if it is the colored frontier of some tree solution of a safe recursion scheme of order* $(n-1)$ *with one terminal f of arity* 2 *and terminal of arity* 0 *for each $c \in \Gamma$.*

As a first application of this result, we show that ω-words in Graph_2 are precisely the morphic words. A *morphic word* over a finite alphabet Γ is given by a letter $\Delta \in \Gamma$ and two morphisms τ and $\sigma : \Gamma \mapsto \Gamma^*$ such that $\tau(\Delta) = \Delta.u$ with $u \in \Gamma^*$. The associated ω-word is $\sigma(\tau^\omega(\Delta))$. For instance, the morphic word $abaab\ldots a^{2^i}b\ldots$ is given by the morphisms τ and σ defined by: $\tau(\Delta) = \Delta baa$, $\tau(a) = aa$, $\tau(b) = b$ and $\sigma(\Delta) = a$, $\sigma(a) = a$, $\sigma(b) = b$.

A direct consequence of [Cau02, Prop. 3.2] is that the morphic words belong to Graph_2. For the other direction, by Corollary 1 we only need to consider the frontier of trees solutions of order-1 schemes. As their frontier are of order type ω, these trees have at most one infinite branch which is also their right-most branch. This constraint leads to a strong normal form for the associated schemes which easily allows to show that their colored frontiers are morphic words.

Theorem 2. *The ω-words of* Graph_2 *are the morphic words.*

4 Ordinals

In this section, we characterize the ordinals in the pushdown hierarchy. In [Bra09], ordinals below $\omega \uparrow\uparrow (n+1)$ are shown to be in Graph_n. We show that they are the only ordinals in Graph_n.

By Theorem 1, we only need to consider frontiers of pruned trees. Pruned trees with a well-ordered frontier are easily characterized.

Definition 1. *A pruned tree is* well-ordered *if it does not have any infinite branch containing infinitely many 0's.*

The frontier of a pruned tree t is an ordinal if and only if t is a well-ordered tree.

Theorem 3. *For all $n \geq 0$ and ordinal α, $\alpha \in \text{Graph}_n$ if and only if $\alpha < \omega \uparrow\uparrow (n+1)$.*

Proof (Sketch). As previously mentioned, we only need to show that for all $n \geq 0$, for any well-ordered tree $t \in \text{Tree}_n$, $\mathbf{Fr}(t) < \omega \uparrow\uparrow (n+1)$.

We proceed by induction on the level n. The case $n = 0$ is obvious. Let t be a well-ordered tree in Tree_{n+1}. By definition of Tree_{n+1}, there exists a graph $G \in \text{Graph}_n$ and a vertex $r \in V_G$ such that $t = \text{Unf}(G, r)$. Furthermore, we can assume w.l.o.g. that every vertex of G is reachable from r.

We are going to consider a particular spanning tree T of G rooted at r such that T is MSO-interpretable in G.

For every node $s \in V_G$, let $\ell(s)$ be the minimal $w \in \{0,1\}^*$ (for the lexicographic order) such that $r \xrightarrow[G]{w} s$. The existence of $\ell(s)$ is ensured by the fact that G unfolds from r into a well-ordered tree. The spanning tree T is defined as the set of arcs $\{s \xrightarrow{a} t \mid \ell(t) = \ell(s) \cdot a\}$.

For technical reasons, we consider the pruned tree $\overline{T}$ obtained by adding dummy leaves below some nodes of T in such a way that their out-degree in $\overline{T}$ is equal to their out-degree in G. As any infinite branch of $\overline{T}$ is also an infinite branch of t, $\overline{T}$ is a well-ordered.

As $\overline{T}$ can be MSO-transducted in G, it belongs to Graph_n together with its frontier. Hence by induction hypothesis, $\mathbf{Fr}(\overline{T}) < \omega \uparrow\uparrow (n+1)$.

The key property that allows us to conclude is that $\mathbf{Fr}(t) \leq \omega^{\mathbf{Fr}(\overline{T})}$. To establish this inequality, recall that $\omega^{\mathbf{Fr}(\overline{T})}$ is isomorphic to the set of (non-strictly) decreasing sequences of ordinals below $\mathbf{Fr}(\overline{T})$ with the lexicographic order. Hence it is enough to show that there exists an injective mapping Φ from the leaves of t to the finite decreasing sequences of leaves of $\overline{T}$ s.t. Φ preserves the lexicographic order. Recall that a leaf u of t corresponds to a path π_u in G starting from r. Intuitively Φ associates to a leaf u of t the sequence of leaves of $\overline{T}$ corresponding to the sequence of arcs in $G \setminus T$ along the path π_u.

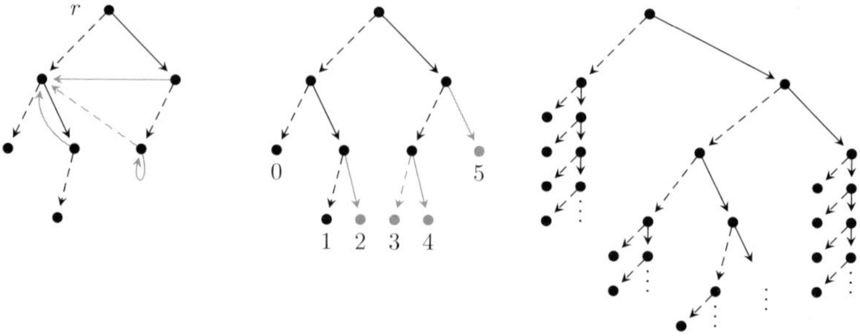

The above example shows from left to right G where dark arcs belong to T, then $\overline{T}$ and finally $\mathrm{Unf}(G, r)$. Here, $\mathbf{Fr}(\mathrm{Unf}(G, r)) = \omega^2 + \omega$. □

This result gives an alternative proof of the strictness of the pushdown hierarchy and shows that ε_0 does not belong to this hierarchy.

5 Scattered Linear Orders

In this section, we consider the scattered linear orders in the pushdown hierarchy. A linear order is *scattered* if it does not contain any dense subordering. Ordinals are a particular case of scattered linear orders. However, scattered orders are not necessarily well-orderings; consider for instance ζ or $\omega + \omega^*$. For a detailed presentation, we refer the reader to [Ros82].

For countable scattered orders, a more constructive characterization is provided by Hausdorff Theorem which also gives a measure of the *complexity* of such orders. From now on, we only consider countable scattered orders.

Theorem 4 (Hausdorff [Hau08]). *A countable linear order is scattered iff it belongs to* $\mathcal{S} = \bigcup_\alpha V_\alpha$ *where* $V_0 = \{\mathbf{0}, \mathbf{1}\}$ *and* $V_\beta = \left\{\sum_{i \in \zeta} L_i \mid \forall i, L_i \in \bigcup_{\alpha < \beta} V_\alpha\right\}$.

The Hausdorff rank[1] of a scattered order L, written $r_H(L)$, is the smallest α such that L can be expressed as a finite sum of elements of V_α. For instance, we have $r_H(\zeta) = r_H(\omega) = r_H(\omega + \omega^*) = 1$.

The Hausdorff rank of the ordinal ω^α is equal to α. In particular if α is written $\sum_{i=1}^{k} \omega^{\alpha_i}$ with $\alpha_1 \geq \ldots \geq \alpha_k$ in Cantor's normal form then $r_H(\alpha) = \alpha_1$.

5.1 Trees with Scattered Frontiers

An alternative characterization of countable scattered orders can be obtained by considering trees having these orders as frontier. The countable scattered orders are those which are frontiers of trees with only countably many infinite branches also called *tame trees.* The following proposition is part of the folklore.

Proposition 4. *Let t be a pruned tree, the following propositions are equivalent:*

1. *$\mathbf{Fr}(t)$ is a scattered linear order,*
2. *t has countably many infinite branches,*
3. *t does not contain any branching subset (i.e. a non-empty subset $U \subseteq t$ such that for all $u \in U$, $u0\{0,1\}^* \cap U \neq \emptyset$ and $u1\{0,1\}^* \cap U \neq \emptyset$).*

The Cantor-Bendixson rank of a tree is an ordinal assessing *the branching complexity* of a tree. We used a definition taken from [KRS05] which is an adaptation of the standard notion [Kec94, Exercise 6.17][2].

[1] The standard definition consider the smallest α such that L belongs to V_α. It is easy to see that this two ranks can only differ by at most one.

[2] See [KRS05, Rem. 7.2] for a comparison of the two notions.

For $X \subseteq t$, we write $d(X)$ for the set of nodes $x \in X$ with at least two infinite branches going through x in X. It is easy to see that if X is prefix closed then so is $d(X)$. Hence the operation can be iterated as follows:

$$d^0(X) = X, \quad d^{\alpha+1}(X) = d(d^\alpha(X)), \quad d^\lambda(X) = \bigcap_{\alpha<\lambda} d^\alpha(X) \text{ for limit } \lambda.$$

The Cantor-Bendixson rank (CB-rank) of t, noted $r_{CB}(t)$, is the least ordinal α such that $d^\alpha(t) = d^{\alpha+1}(t)$. The tree t is tame if and only if there exists α s.t. $d^\alpha = \emptyset$. For tame trees t, we adopt a slightly modified version of the CB-rank, denoted $\tilde{r}_{CB}(t)$, which is the smallest ordinal α such that $d^\alpha(t)$ is finite. We have $\tilde{r}_{CB}(t) \leq r_{CB}(t) \leq \tilde{r}_{CB}(t) + 1$. For pruned tame trees, the CB-rank of the tree and the Hausdorff rank of their frontier are tightly linked.

Proposition 5. *For every pruned tame tree t,*

$$\begin{cases} \tilde{r}_{CB}(t) = r_H(\mathbf{Fr}(t)) & \text{if } \tilde{r}_{CB}(t) < \omega, \\ \tilde{r}_{CB}(t) = r_H(\mathbf{Fr}(t)) + 1 & \text{otherwise.} \end{cases}$$

As the definition of the CB-rank does not use the relative order between the sons of a node, the CB-rank only depends on the underlying unordered tree. Given two deterministic trees t and t', we denote by $t \equiv t'$ the fact that t and t' are isomorphic when viewed as unordered trees. Formally, $t \equiv t'$ if there exists a bijection from t to t' preserving the ancestor relation (i.e. for all $u, v \in t$, $u \sqsubseteq v$ iff $h(u) \sqsubseteq h(v)$).

Proposition 6. *For any two pruned tame trees t and t', if $t \equiv t'$ then $\tilde{r}_{CB}(t) = \tilde{r}_{CB}(t')$ and $r_H(\mathbf{Fr}(t)) = r_H(\mathbf{Fr}(t'))$.*

5.2 Hausdorff Rank of Scattered Orders in Graph_n

From Thm. 3, we know that the pushdown hierarchy is inhabited by scattered orders with a Hausdorff rank α for every $\alpha < \varepsilon_0$. This result can be strengthened, by considering the successive powers of $\mathbb{Z}$ defined as follows:

$$\mathbb{Z}^0 = 1 \qquad \mathbb{Z}^{\beta+1} = \mathbb{Z}^\beta \cdot \omega^* + \mathbb{Z}^\beta + \mathbb{Z}^\beta \cdot \omega$$

$$\mathbb{Z}^\lambda = \left(\sum_{\alpha<\lambda} \mathbb{Z}^\alpha.\omega\right)^* + 1 + \sum_{\alpha<\lambda} \mathbb{Z}^\alpha.\omega \qquad \text{for } \lambda \text{ limit.}$$

From [Ros82, Thm. 5.37], the Hausdorff-rank of $\mathbb{Z}^\alpha$ is α. Furthermore, $\mathbb{Z}^\alpha$ is complete among the scattered orders of Hausdorff-rank α in the following sense: a scattered order L has Hausdorff-rank less than α if and only if it is a subordering of $\mathbb{Z}^\alpha$.

Proposition 7. *For all $n > 0$ and any ordinal $\alpha < \omega \uparrow\uparrow n$, $\mathbb{Z}^\alpha$ is in* Graph_n.

For instance, the following deterministic graph is in Graph_1. Its unfolding by the leftmost vertex is in Tree_2 and its frontier is $\mathbb{Z}^\omega$. Dashed arcs stand for arcs labeled by 0, plain arcs stand for for arcs labeled by 1.

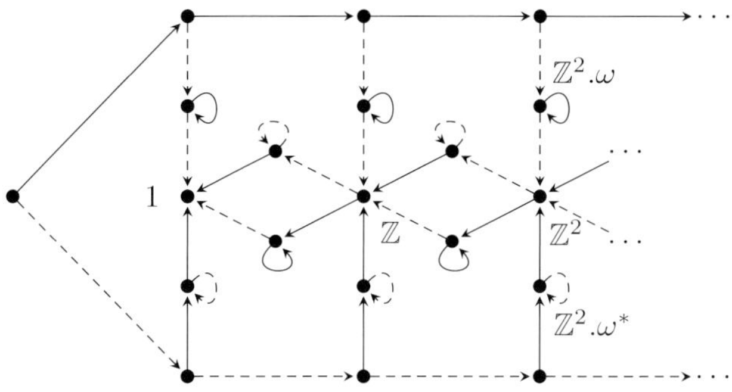

As hinted by the previous proposition, we can show that the Hausdorff rank of any scattered order in Graph_n is strictly less than $\omega \uparrow\uparrow n$. This bound is obtained by reduction to the ordinal case using the following key proposition.

Proposition 8. *For any pruned tame tree t, there exists a well-ordered tree t' such that $t \equiv t'$. Furthermore, if t belongs to* Tree_n *then t' can also be chosen in* Tree_n.

Proof (Sketch). Consider the following game played by two players Cantor and Hausdorff by moving a token on t. The two players play in turn starting with Cantor. Cantor moves the token to a node anywhere below the current position. Hausdorff can only move the token to a son of the current position. Cantor loses the game if the token reaches a leaf.

It is clear that Cantor wins the game if and only if t contains a branching subset. As t is tame (and hence does not contain any branching subset), Cantor loses the game.

From the point of view of Hausdorff this game is a reachability game. Hence Hausdorff has a positional winning strategy: there exists a mapping $\varphi : t \mapsto \{0, 1\}$ such that in any play where Hausdorff chooses his moves according to φ (i.e. at node u, Hausdorff picks the $\varphi(u)$-son) is won by him.

Consider the tree t_φ obtained from t by swapping the two sons of any node u such that $\varphi(u) = 1$. It can be shown that t_φ is a well-ordered tree : otherwise, from an infinite branch in t_φ containing infinitely many 0's, we could construct an infinite play in t (i.e. won by Cantor) following φ.

It remains to prove that t_φ can be chosen in Tree_n if t is in Tree_n. A positional winning strategy φ can be coded by two sets of vertices U_0, U_1 respectively corresponding to set of nodes u s.t. $\varphi(u) = 0$ and $\varphi(u) = 1$. Consider an MSO-formula $\psi(X_0, X_1)$ such that $t \models \psi[U_0, U_1]$ if and only if U_0 and U_1 encode a positional winning strategy for Hausdorff . Let c_0 and c_1 be two color symbols that do not appear in t. By Prop. 3, there exist V_0 and V_1 such that $t \models \psi[V_0, V_1]$ and such that $\bar{t} = t \cup \{(c_0, v) \mid v \in V_0\} \cup \{(c_1, v) \mid v \in V_1\}$ belongs to Tree_n.

The well-ordered tree t_{φ_0} corresponding to the strategy φ_0 encoded by V_0 and V_1 belongs to Tree_n. As $\bar{t}$ belongs to Tree_n, there exists a graph G in Graph_{n-1} and a vertex r of G such that $\bar{t}$ is isomorphic to $\text{Unf}(G, r)$. Consider the MSO-interpretation $\mathcal{I}$ which exchanges the out-going arcs of any vertex colored by c_1 and erases the colors c_0 and c_1. It is easy to check that $\text{Unf}(\mathcal{I}(G), r)$ is isomorphic to t_{φ_0}. □

Theorem 5. *For all $n \geq 0$, every scattered linear order in* Graph_n *has a Hausdorff rank strictly less than* $\omega \uparrow\uparrow n$.

Proof (Sketch). Let L be a scattered linear order in Graph_n. By Thm. 1 and Prop. 4, there exists a pruned tree $t \in \text{Tree}_n$ such that $L \equiv \mathbf{Fr}(t)$. By Prop. 8 there exists a well-ordered tree $t' \in \text{Tree}_n$ such that $t \equiv t'$.

By Prop. 6, we have that $r_H(\mathbf{Fr}(t)) = r_H(\mathbf{Fr}(t'))$. As t' is a well-ordered tree in Tree_n, its frontier is an ordinal in Graph_n. Hence by Thm. 3, $\mathbf{Fr}(t') < \omega \uparrow\uparrow n+1$ and hence $r_H(\mathbf{Fr}(t')) < \omega \uparrow\uparrow n$. □

Remark 1. Obviously the converse to this theorem is not true; there are uncountably many scattered orders of Hausdorff rank less than $\omega \uparrow\uparrow n$ but there are only countably many linear orderings in Graph_n. Consider for instance a non-recursive sequence $(a_i)_{i \in \mathbb{N}}$ in $\{1, 2\}^\omega$. The scattered order $a_0 + \zeta + a_1 + \zeta + a_2 + \ldots$ has Hausdorff rank 2. But as it has an undecidable MSO-theory, it does not belong to the pushdown hierarchy.

5.3 Cantor-Bendixson Rank of Deterministic Trees

By Prop. 5, Thm. 5 can by directly translated on the CB-rank of pruned tame trees in Tree_n. This leads to the following upper bound for all deterministic trees in Tree_n.

Theorem 6. *For every deterministic tree $t \in \text{Tree}_n$, $r_{CB}(t) \leq \omega \uparrow\uparrow n$.*

Proof (Sketch). For every deterministic tree $t \in \text{Tree}_n$, there exists a pruned tree $t' \in \text{Tree}_n$ with the same CB-rank. The CB-rank of t' is bounded by the supremum of the CB-ranks of the tame subtrees of t'. As every subtree of t' also belongs to Tree_n, $r_{CB}(t) = r_{CB}(t') \leq \omega \uparrow\uparrow n$. □

Acknowledgment. The authors would like to thank the anonymous referees for their helpful comments.

References

[BÉ07] Bloom, S., Ésik, Z.: Regular and algebraic words and ordinals. In: Mossakowski, T., Montanari, U., Haveraaen, M. (eds.) CALCO 2007. LNCS, vol. 4624, pp. 1–15. Springer, Heidelberg (2007)

[BÉ09] Bloom, S., Ésik, Z.: Scattered algebraic linear orderings. In: Proc. of FICS 2009, pp. 25–30 (2009)

[BÉ10] Bloom, S., Ésik, Z.: Algebraic ordinals. Fundamenta Informaticae (2010) (to appear)

[Blu08] Blumensath, A.: On the structure of graphs in the Caucal hierarchy. TCS 400(1-3), 19–45 (2008)

[Bra09] Braud, L.: Covering of ordinals. In: Proc. FSTTCS 2009, pp. 97–108 (2009)

[Car05] Carayol, A.: Regular sets of higher-order pushdown stacks. In: Jedrzejowicz, J., Szepietowski, A. (eds.) MFCS 2005. LNCS, vol. 3618, pp. 168–179. Springer, Heidelberg (2005)

[Car06] Carayol, A.: Automates infinis, logiques et langages. PhD thesis, Université de Rennes 1 (2006)

[Cau96] Caucal, D.: On infinite transition graphs having a decidable monadic theory. In: Meyer auf der Heide, F., Monien, B. (eds.) ICALP 1996. LNCS, vol. 1099, pp. 194–205. Springer, Heidelberg (1996)

[Cau02] Caucal, D.: On infinite terms having a decidable monadic theory. In: Diks, K., Rytter, W. (eds.) MFCS 2002. LNCS, vol. 2420, pp. 165–176. Springer, Heidelberg (2002)

[Cou78] Courcelle, B.: Frontiers of infinite trees. RAIRO 12, 319–337 (1978)

[Cou94] Courcelle, B.: Monadic second-order definable graph transductions: A survey. TCS 126, 53–75 (1994)

[CW03] Carayol, A., Wöhrle, S.: The Caucal hierarchy of infinite graphs in terms of logic and higher-order pushdown automata. In: Pandya, P.K., Radhakrishnan, J. (eds.) FSTTCS 2003. LNCS, vol. 2914, pp. 112–123. Springer, Heidelberg (2003)

[EF95] Ebbinghaus, H.D., Flum, J.: Finite Model Theory. Springer, Heidelberg (1995)

[Eng91] Engelfriet, J.: Iterated stack automata and complexity classes. Inf. Comp. 95(1), 21–75 (1991)

[Fra05] Fratani, S.: Automates à piles de piles.. de piles. PhD thesis, Université Bordeaux 1 (2005)

[Hau08] Hausdorff, F.: Grundzüge einer theorie der geordnete mengen. Math. Ann. 65, 435–505 (1908)

[Hei80] Heilbrunner, S.: An algorithm for the solution of fixed-point equations for infinite words. ITA 14(2), 131–141 (1980)

[Kec94] Kechris, A.: Classical Descriptive Set Theory. Springer, Heidelberg (1994)

[KNU02] Knapik, T., Niwinski, D., Urzyczyn, P.: Higher-order pushdown trees are easy. In: Nielsen, M., Engberg, U. (eds.) FOSSACS 2002. LNCS, vol. 2303, pp. 205–222. Springer, Heidelberg (2002)

[KRS05] Khoussainov, B., Rubin, S., Stephan, F.: Automatic linear orders and trees. ACM Trans. Comput. Log. 6(4), 675–700 (2005)

[Mas76] Maslov, A.N.: Multi-level stack automata. Problems Information Transmission 12, 38–43 (1976)

[Ong07] Ong, L.: Hierarchies of infinite structures generated by pushdown automata and recursion schemes. In: Kučera, L., Kučera, A. (eds.) MFCS 2007. LNCS, vol. 4708, pp. 15–21. Springer, Heidelberg (2007)

[Ros82] Rosenstein, J.: Linear orderings. Academic Press Inc., London (1982)

[Tho03] Thomas, W.: Constructing infinite graphs with a decidable MSO-theory. In: Rovan, B., Vojtáš, P. (eds.) MFCS 2003. LNCS, vol. 2747, pp. 113–124. Springer, Heidelberg (2003)

The Serializability of Network Codes

Anna Blasiak* and Robert Kleinberg**

Department of Computer Science, Cornell University, Ithaca NY 14853
ablasiak@cs.cornell.edu
rdk@cs.cornell.edu

Abstract. Network coding theory is the most general study of transmission of information in networks whose vertices may perform nontrivial encoding and decoding operations on data as it passes through the network. A solution to a network coding problem is a specification of a coding function on each edge of the network. This specification is subject to constraints that ensure the existence of a protocol by which the messages on each vertex's outgoing edges can be computed from the data it received on its incoming edges. In directed acyclic graphs it is clear how to verify these causality constraints, but in graphs with cycles this becomes more subtle because of the possibility of cyclic dependencies among the coding functions. Sometimes the system of coding functions is *serializable* — meaning that the cyclic dependencies (if any) can be "unraveled" by a protocol in which a vertex sends a few bits of its outgoing messages, waits to receive more information, then send a few more bits, and so on — but in other cases, there is no way to eliminate a cyclic dependency by an appropriate sequencing of partial messages. How can we decide whether a given system of coding functions is serializable? When it is not serializable, how much extra information must be transmitted in order to permit a serialization? Our work addresses both of these questions. We show that the first one is decidable in polynomial time, whereas the second one is NP-hard, and in fact it is logarithmically inapproximable.

1 Introduction

Network coding theory is the most general study of transmission of information in networks whose vertices may perform nontrivial encoding and decoding operations on data as it passes through the network. More specifically, a network code consists of a network with specified sender and receiver edges and coding functions on each edge. The classic definition of a network code requires that each vertex can compute the message on every outgoing edge from the messages received on its incoming edges, and that each receiver is sent the message it

* Supported by an NDSEG Graduate Fellowship, an AT&T Labs Graduate Fellowship, and an NSF Graduate Fellowship.
** Supported by NSF grant CCF-0729102, a Microsoft Research New Faculty Fellowship, and an Alfred P. Sloan Foundation Fellowship.

S. Abramsky et al. (Eds.): ICALP 2010, Part II, LNCS 6199, pp. 100–114, 2010.

requires. In directed acyclic graphs, a network code that satisfies these requirements specifies a valid communication protocol. However, in graphs with cycles this need not be the case; the definition does not preclude the possibility of cyclic dependencies among coding functions. Therefore, in graphs with cycles we also require that a network code is *serializable*, meaning it correctly summarizes a communication protocol in which symbols are transmitted on edges over time, and each symbol transmitted by a vertex is computed without knowledge of information it will receive in the future. The present paper is devoted to the study of characterizing the constraint of serializability.

Motivation. The central question in the area of network coding is to determine the amount by which coding can increase the rate of information flow as compared to transmitting information without coding. One of the most important open problems in network coding, the *undirected k-pairs conjecture*, states that in undirected graphs with k sender-receiver pairs, coding cannot increase the maximum rate of information flow; that is, the network coding rate is the same as the multicommodity flow rate. Apart from its intrinsic interest, the conjecture also has important complexity-theoretic implications: for example, if true, it implies an affirmative answer to a 20-year-old conjecture regarding the I/O complexity of matrix transposition [1]. In order to answer this question in the affirmative we need to find upper bounds on the network coding rate. On graphs with cycles, we must understand how the condition of serializability restricts the set of feasible codes in order to find tight upper bounds.

Almost all efforts to produce upper bounds on the network coding rate have focused on the following construction. We regard each edge of the network as defining a random variable on a probability space and then associate each set of edges with the Shannon entropy of the joint distribution of their random variables. This gives us a vector of non-negative numbers, one for each edge set, called the *entropic vector* of the network code. The closure of the set of entropic vectors of network codes forms a convex set, and network coding problems can be expressed as optimization problems over this set [10]. In much previous work, tight upper bounds have been constructed by combining the constraints that define this convex set. Thus, one might hope that the serializability of a network code is equivalent to a set of constraints on its entropic vector. In this paper we show that this is not the case, and we explore alternative characterizations of serializability and their implications.

Our contributions. Our work is the first systematic study of criteria for serializability of network codes. We find that serializability cannot be detected solely from the entropic vector of the network code; a counter-example is given in Section 3. Nevertheless, in Section 4 we give a polynomial-time algorithm to decide the serializability of a network code. Associated to this decision problem is a natural optimization problem: given a set of coding functions, what is the minimum number of extra bits of information that must be sent in order to make the given coding functions serializable? We call this parameter the *serializability deficit*, and in Section 5 we prove that computing it is NP-hard, and moreover, that the serializability deficit is logarithmically inapproximable. We also prove a surprising subadditivity phenomenon involving the serializability deficit: the serializability deficit for p parallel executions of a network code may be much less than p times as great as the serializability deficit of the original code. In fact, for any $\delta > 0$ there exists a network code whose p-fold parallel repetition has a serializability deficit less than δp times the serializability deficit of the original code.

Beyond providing an algorithm for deciding if a network code is serializable, our work provides important insights into the property of serializability. In Section 4 we define a certificate that we call a *non-trivial information vortex* whose existence is a necessary and sufficient condition for non-serializability. For linear network codes, an information vortex consists of linear subspaces of the dual of the message space. For general network codes, it consists of Boolean subalgebras of the power set of the message set. We prove a number of theorems about information vortices that suggest their role in the theory of network coding may be similar to the role of fractional cuts in network flow theory. In particular, we prove a type of min-max relation between serializable codes and information vortices: under a suitable definition of *serializable restriction* it holds that every network code has a unique maximal serializable restriction, a unique minimal information vortex, and these two objects coincide. Information vortices also play a key role in our theorems about serializability deficits. For example, in Section 5 we show that information vortices allow us to prove limits on the severity of the subadditivity phenomenon noted above: for every non-serializable linear code Φ, the serializability deficit of p parallel executions of Φ grows as $\Omega(p)$, where the constant inside the $\Omega(\cdot)$ depends on Φ.

As mentioned earlier, one of the motivations for our work is the objective of characterizing the information inequalities (i.e., constraints on the entropic vector) implied by serializability. While our algorithm for deciding serializability does not lead directly to such a characterization, we are able to provide one for the special case in which the underlying network is a 2-cycle. In Section 6, we present four inequalities and show that any entropic vector satisfying those inequalities as well as Shannon's inequalities can be realized by a serializable network code. (Though structurally simple, the 2-cycle graph has been an important source of inspiration for information inequalities in prior work, including the crypto inequality [6], the informational dominance bound [4], and the Chicken and Egg inequality [5].) Extending this characterization beyond the 2-cycle to general graphs is the most important open question left by our work.

Related work. For a general introduction to network coding we refer the reader to [9,11]. Definitions of network coding in graphs with cycles were considered in [1,3,4,5,7,9]. To make our exposition self-contained, we present an equivalent definition in Section 2. In its essence it is the same as the "graph over time" definition given in [9] but requires less cumbersome notation.

Although our work is the first to give precise necessary and sufficient conditions for serializability, several prior papers gave necessary conditions based on information inequalities. Large classes of such inequalities in graphs with cycles were discovered independently by Jain et al. [6], Kramer and Savari [8], and Harvey et al. [4]. These go by the names *crypto inequality*, *PdE bound*, and *informational dominance bound*, respectively. In various forms, all of them describe a situation in which the information on one set of edges completely determines the information on another set of edges. A more general necessary condition for serializability was presented in a recent paper by Harvey et al. [5]; we will henceforth refer to this information inequality as the *Chicken and Egg* inequality; see Theorem 6. As far as we are aware, our work is the first to consider the question of whether this set of inequalities (or any set of information inequalities) provides a complete characterization of serializability.

2 Definitions

We define a network code to operate on a directed multigraph we call a *sourced graph*, denoted $G = (V, E, S)$.[1] S is a set of special edges, called *sources* or *source edges*, that have a head but no tail. We denote a source with head s by an ordered pair $(\bullet, s)$. Elements of $E \cup S$ are called *edges* and elements of E are called *ordinary edges*. For a vertex v, we let $\mathsf{In}(v) = \{(u, v) \in E\}$ be the set of edges whose head is v. For an edge $e = (u, v) \in E$, we also use $\mathsf{In}(e) = \mathsf{In}(u)$ to denote the set of *incoming edges* to e.

A network code in a sourced graph specifies a protocol for communicating symbols on error-free channels corresponding to the graph's ordinary edges, given the tuple of messages that originate at the source edges.

Definition 1. *A* network code *is specified by a 4-tuple* $\Phi = (G, \mathfrak{M}, \{\Sigma_e\}_{e \in E \cup S}, \{f_e\}_{e \in E \cup S})$ *where* $G = (V, E, S)$ *is a sourced graph,* $\mathfrak{M}$ *is a set whose elements are called* message-tuples, *and for all edges* $e \in E \cup S$, Σ_e *is a set called the* alphabet *of* e *and* $f_e : \mathfrak{M} \to \Sigma_e$ *is a function called the* coding function *of* e. *If* e *is an edge and* $e_1, \ldots, e_k$ *are the elements of* $\mathsf{In}(e)$ *then the value of the coding function* f_e *must be completely determined by the values of* $f_{e_1}, \ldots, f_{e_k}$. *In other words, there must exist a function* $g_e : \prod_{i=1}^{k} \Sigma_{e_i} \to \Sigma_e$ *such that for all* $m \in \mathfrak{M}$, $f_e(m) = g_e(f_{e_1}(m), \ldots, f_{e_k}(m))$.

In graphs with cycles a code can have cyclic dependencies so Definition 1 does not suffice to characterize the notion of a valid network code. We must impose a further constraint that we call *serializability*, which requires that the network code summarizes a complete execution of a communication protocol in which every bit transmitted by a vertex depends only on bits that it has already received.

Below we define serializability formally using a definition implicit in [5].

Definition 2. *A network code* Φ *is serializable if for all* $e \in E$ *there exists a set of alphabets* $\Sigma_e^{(1\ldots k)} = \left\{\Sigma_e^{(1)}, \Sigma_e^{(2)}, \ldots, \Sigma_e^{(k)}\right\}$ *and a set of functions* $f_e^{(1\ldots k)} = \left\{f_e^{(1)}, f_e^{(2)}, \ldots, f_e^{(k)}\right\}$ *such that*

[1] In prior work it is customary for the underlying network to also have a special set of receiving edges. Specifying a special set of receivers is irrelevant in our work, so we omit them for convenience, but everything we do can be easily extended to include receivers.

1. $f_e^{(i)} : \mathfrak{M} \to \Sigma_e^{(i)}$,
2. $\forall\, m_1, m_2 \in \mathfrak{M}$, *if* $f_e(m_1) = f_e(m_2)$, *then* $\forall i,\ f_e^{(i)}(m_1) = f_e^{(i)}(m_2)$,
3. $\forall\, m_1, m_2 \in \mathfrak{M}$, *if* $f_e(m_1) \neq f_e(m_2)$, *then* $\exists i,\ f_e^{(i)}(m_1) \neq f_e^{(i)}(m_2)$, *and*
4. $\forall\ m \in \mathfrak{M},\ e \in E,\ j \in \{1 \ldots k\}$ *there exists* $h_e^{(j)}$ *such that* $f_e^{(j)}(m) = h_e^{(j)}\left(\prod_{\hat{e} \in \mathsf{In}(e)} f_{\hat{e}}^{(1..j-1)}\right)$.[2]

We call such a $\Sigma_e^{(1\ldots k)}, f_e^{(1\ldots k)}$ a serialization *of* Φ.

The function $f_e^{(i)}$ describes the information sent on edge e at time step i. Item 2 requires that together the functions $f_e^{(1..k)}$ send no more information than f_e and Item 3 requires that $f_e^{(1..k)}$ sends at least as much information as f_e. Item 4 requires that we can compute $f_e^{(j)}$ given the information sent on all of e's incoming edges at previous time steps.

In working with network codes, we will occasionally want to compare two network codes Φ, Φ' such that Φ' "transmits all the information that is transmitted by Φ." In this case, we say that Φ' is an extension of Φ, and Φ is a restriction of Φ'.

Definition 3. *Suppose that* $\Phi = (G, \mathfrak{M}, \{\Sigma_e\}, \{f_e\})$ *and* $\Phi' = (G, \mathfrak{M}, \{\Sigma'_e\}, \{f'_e\})$ *are two network codes with the same sourced graph* G *and the same message set* $\mathfrak{M}$. *We say that* Φ *is a restriction of* Φ', *and* Φ' *is an extension of* Φ, *if it is the case that for every* $m \in \mathfrak{M}$ *and* $e \in E$, *the value of* $f'_e(m)$ *completely determines the value of* $f_e(m)$; *in other words,* $f_e = g_e \circ f'_e$ *for some function* $g_e : \Sigma'_e \to \Sigma_e$.

The entropic vector of a network code gives a non-negative value for each subset of a network code. The value of an edge set F is the Shannon entropy of the joint distribution of the random variables associated with each element of F, as is formalized in the following definition.

Definition 4. *Given a network code* $\Phi = (G, \mathfrak{M}, \{\Sigma_e\}, \{f_e\}), G = (V, E, S)$, *the* entropic vector *of* Φ *has coordinates* $H(F)$ *defined for each edge set* $F = \{e_1, \ldots, e_j\} \subseteq E \cup S$ *by:*

$$H(F) = H(e_1 e_2 \ldots e_j) = \sum_{x_1 \in \Sigma_{e_1}, x_2 \in \Sigma_{e_2}, \ldots, x_j \in \Sigma_{e_j}} -p(x_1, x_2, \ldots, x_j) \log(p(x_1, x_2, \ldots, x_j)),$$

where the probabilities are computed assuming a uniform distribution over $\mathfrak{M}$.

3 Serializability and Entropy Inequalities

Constraints imposed on the entropic vector alone suffice to characterize serializability for DAGs, but, the addition of one cycle causes the entopic vector to be an insufficient characterization. We show that the entropic vector is not enough to determine serializability even on the 2-cycle by giving a serializable and non-serializable code with the same entropic vector.

---

[2] Throughout this paper, when the operator $\prod$ is applied to functions rather then sets we mean it to denote the operation of forming an ordered tuple from an indexed list of elements.

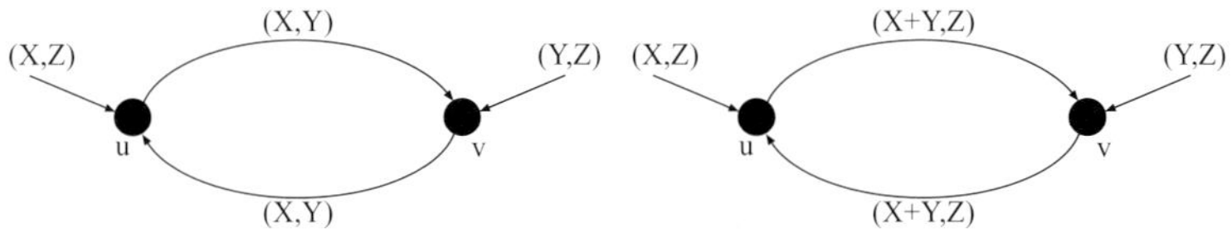

(a) Serializable (b) Not Serializable

Fig. 1. Two network codes with the same entropy function

The two codes illustrated in Figure 1 apply to the message tuple (X, Y, Z), where X, Y, Z are uniformly distributed random variable over $\mathbb{F}_2$. It is easy to check that the entropy of every subset of corresponding source and edge functions is the same, and thus the codes have the same entropic vector. The code in Figure 1(a) is clearly serializable: at time step one we send X on (u, v) and Y on (v, u); then Y on (u, v) and X on (v, u). On the other hand, the code in Figure 1(b) is not serializable because, informally, to send $X + Y$ on the top edge requires that we already sent $X + Y$ on the bottom edge, and vice versa. A formal proof that the code in Figure 2(b) is not serializable can be obtained by applying the characterization of serializability in Theorem 3.

4 A Characterization of Serializability

4.1 Linear Codes

A characterization of serializability for linear network codes is simpler than the general case because it relies on more standard algebraic tools. Accordingly, we treat this case first before moving on to the general case. Throughout this section we use $\mathfrak{M}^*$ to denote the dual of the message space over a field $\mathbb{F}$. Additionally, we use $T_e \subseteq \mathfrak{M}^*$ to denote the row space of the matrix representing the linear transformation f_e. (It makes sense to talk about such a matrix because we can pick a basis for $\mathfrak{M}$ and each Σ_e.)

Though it is impossible to characterize the serializability of a network code in terms of its entropic vector, computationally there is a straightforward solution. In polynomial time we can either determine a serialization for a code or show that no serialization exists using the obvious algorithm: try to serialize the code by "sending new information when possible." When we can no longer send any new information along any edge we terminate. If we have sent all the information required along each edge, then the greedy algorithm finds a serialization; otherwise, we show that no serialization exists by presenting a succinct certificate of non-serializability. Though our algorithm is straightforward, we believe that the change in mindset from characterizing codes in terms of the entropic vector is an important one, and that our certificate of non-serializability (see Definition 5) furnishes an effective tool for addressing other questions about serializability, as we shall see in later sections.

Before giving a more formal description of the algorithm, we would like to remark on one potential source of confusion due to the manner in which we write examples in this paper. In the examples, the coding function on an edge is not written as an abtract function f_e, but rather, we take an f_e, pick a basis, and multiply the matrix representing f_e by the message vector and write the resulting code. Given the simple greedy algorithm stated above, and such a picture representation, it is easy to think that the algorithm translates to "in each step check to see if one of the symbols written on an edge can be sent." However, this is not what we want to do. Our choice of the matrix used to represent f_e was arbitrary, so if X, Y is written on an edge, it is equally valid to write $X, X+Y$ or $Y, X+Y$, and we need the greedy algorithm to reflect that. Thus, our greedy algorithm needs to look at linear subspaces to determine if it is possible to send new information along any edge.

Given a network code $\Phi = (G, \mathfrak{M}, \{\Sigma_e\}, \{f_e\})$, with coding functions over the field $\mathbb{F}$, our greedy algorithm (denoted henceforth by **LinSerialize**) constructs a set of edge functions $f_e^{(1..k)}$ and alphabets $\Sigma_e^{(1..k)}$ for each edge. These objects are constructed iteratively, defining the edge alphabets $\Sigma_e^{(i)}$ and coding functions $f_e^{(i)}$ in the ith iteration. Throughout this process, we maintain a pair of linear subspaces A_e, $B_e \subseteq \mathfrak{M}^*$ for each edge $e = (u, v)$ of G. A_e is the linear span[3] of all the messages transmitted on e so far, and B_e is intersection of T_e with the linear span of all the messages transmitted to u so far. (In other words, B_e spans all the messages that could currently be sent on e without receiving any additional messages at u.) In the ith iteration, if there exists an edge e' such that $B_{e'}$ contains a dual vector $x_{e'}$ that does not belong to $A_{e'}$, then we create coding function $f_e^{(i)}$ for all e. The coding function of $f_{e'}^{(i)}$ is set to be $x_{e'}$ and its alphabet is set to be $\mathbb{F}$. For all other edges we set $f_e^{(i)} = 0$, and update the A_e's accordingly. This process continues until $B_e = A_e$ for every e. At that point, we report that the code is serializable if and only if $A_e = T_e$ for all e. At the end, the algorithm returns the functions $f_e^{(1..k)}$ and the alphabets $\Sigma_e^{(1..k)}$, where k is the number of iterations of the algorithm, as well as the subspaces $\{A_e\}$. If the code was not serializable, then $\{A_e\}$ is interpreted as a certificate of non-serializability (a "non-trivial information vortex") as explained below.

LinSerialize(Φ) runs in time polynomial in the size of the coding functions of Φ. In every iteration we increase the dimension of some A_e by one. A_e is initialized with dimension zero and can have dimension at most $\dim(T_e)$. Therefore, the algorithm goes through at most $\sum_{e \in E} \dim(T_e)$ iterations of the while loop. Additionally, each iteration of the while loop, aside from constant time assignments, computes only intersections and spans of vector spaces, all of which can be done in polynomial time.

To prove the algorithm's correctness, we define the following certificate of non-serializability.

[3] If $\{V_i : i \in \mathcal{I}\}$ is a collection of linear subspaces of a vector space V, their linear span is the minimal linear subspace containing the union $\bigcup_{i \in \mathcal{I}} V_i$. We denote the linear span by $+_{i \in \mathcal{I}} V_i$.

Definition 5. *An* information vortex (IV) *of a network code consists of a linear subspace $W_e \subseteq \mathfrak{M}^*$ for each edge e, such that:*

1. *For a source edge s, $W_s = T_s$.*
2. *For every other edge e, $W_e = T_e \cap \left(+_{e' \in \mathsf{In}(e)} W_{e'}\right)$.*

An information vortex is nontrivial *if $W_e \neq T_e$ for some edge e.*

We think of W_e as the information that we can send over e given that its incoming edges, $e' \in In(e)$, can send $W_{e'}$. In our analysis of the greedy algorithm, we show that the messages the greedy algorithm succeeds in sending (i.e., the linear subspaces $\{A_e\}$) form an IV and it is non-trivial if and only if the code isn't serializable.

In Section 5 we will see that information vortices provide a concise way for proving the non-serializability of a network code.

The following theorem shows the relationship between IVs, serialization, and the greedy algorithm.

Theorem 1. *For a network code $\Phi = (G, \mathfrak{M}, \{\Sigma_e\}, \{f_e\})$, the following are equivalent:*

1. *Φ is not serializable*
2. ***LinSerialize**(Φ) returns $\{A_e\}$ s.t. $\exists\, e, A_e \neq T_e$*
3. *Φ has a non-trivial information vortex*

Proof. $\neg$**2** $\Rightarrow$ $\neg$**1** If **LinSerialize**(Φ) returns $\{A_e\}$ s.t. $\forall e$, $A_e = T_e$ then Φ is serializable:
We show that the $f_e^{(1..k)}, \Sigma_e^{(1..k)}$ created by **LinSerialize**(Φ) satisfy the conditions in Definition 2:

1. $f_e^{(i)} : \mathfrak{M} \to \Sigma_e^{(i)}$ by construction.
2. The non-zero functions $f_e^{(i)}$ form a basis for T_e. Because linear maps are indifferent to the choice of basis, if $f_e(m_1) = f_e(m_2)$ then in any basis, each coordinate of $f_e(m_1)$ equals the corresponding coordinate of $f_e(m_2)$, and thus $f_e^{(i)}(m_1) = f_e^{(i)}(m_2)$ for all i.
3. If $f_e(m_1) \neq f_e(m_2)$ then for any basis we choose to represent f_e, the values $f_e(m_1), f_e(m_2)$ will differ in at least one coordinate, and thus $\exists i$, $f_e^{(i)}(m_2) \neq f_e^{(i)}(m_2)$.
4. When we assign a function $f_e^{(i)} = x_e$ we have that x_e is in B_e which guarantees it is computable from information already sent to the tail of e.

2 $\Rightarrow$ **3** If **LinSerialize**(Φ) returns $\{A_e\}$ s.t. $\exists\, e\ A_e \neq T_e$ then Φ has a non-trivial IV.

We claim the the vector spaces $\{A_e\}$ returned by **LinSerialize**(Φ) form a non-trivial IV. $\{A_e\}$ is non-trivial by hypothesis, so it remains to show it is an IV.
$\{A_e\}$ satisfies property (1): For each $S \in S$, $A_S = T_S$ by construction
$\{A_e\}$ satisfies property (2): By induction on our algorithm, B_e is exactly $T_e \cap \left(+_{e' \in \mathsf{In}(e)} A_{e'}\right)$. At termination, $B_e = A_e$ for all $e \in E$. So, we have that $A_e = T_e \cap \left(+_{e' \in \mathsf{In}(e)} A_{e'}\right)$.

3 ⇒ 1 If Φ has a non-trivial IV then it isn't serializable.

Suppose for contradiction that $\Phi = (G, \mathfrak{M}, \{\Sigma_e\}, \{f_e\}), G = (V, E, S)$ is serializable. Let $f_e^{(1..k)}$ and $\Sigma_e^{(1..k)}$ satisfy the conditions of definition 2. Let $\{W_e\}$ be a non-trivial IV for Φ.

We say that a function $f_e^{(j)}$ has property P if there $\exists\, m_1, m_2 \in \mathfrak{M}$ such that $f_e^{(j)}(m_1) \neq f_e^{(j)}(m_2)$ and $m_1, m_2 \in W_e^{\perp}$. There must be such a function since our IV is non-trivial and $\Sigma_e^{(1..k)}, f_e^{(1..k)}$ is a serialization of Φ. Let i^* be the smallest i such that any function satisfies property P and suppose $f_{e^*}^{(i^*)}$ satisfies P with messages m_1^*, m_2^*.

By definition, $W_{e^*} = T_{e^*} \cap \left(+_{e' \in \mathsf{In}(e^*)} W_{e'}\right)$, so $m_1^*, m_2^* \in W_{e^*}^{\perp}$ implies that for all $e' \in \mathsf{In}(e^*)$, $m_1^*, m_2^* \in W_{e'}^{\perp}$. But, $f_{e^*}^{(i^*)}$ can distinguish between m_1^*, m_2^* so at least one of $e' \in \mathsf{In}(e^*)$ must also be able to distinguish between m_1^*, m_2^* at a time *before* i^*. Therefore, there exists some $f_{e'}^{(i')}$, $i' < i^*$ that satisfies property P, a contradiction to the fact that i^* was the smallest such i.

4.2 General Codes

Our characterization theorem extends to the case of general network codes, provided that we generalize the greedy algorithm and the definition of information vortex appropriately. The message space $\mathfrak{M}$ is no longer a vector space, so instead of defining information vortices using the vector space $\mathfrak{M}^*$ of all linear functions on $\mathfrak{M}$, we use the Boolean algebra $2^{\mathfrak{M}}$ of all binary-valued functions on $\mathfrak{M}$. We begin by recalling some notions from the theory of Boolean algebras.

Definition 6. *Let S be a set. The Boolean algebra 2^S is the algebra consisting of all $\{0,1\}$-valued functions on S, under* AND $(\wedge)$, OR $(\vee)$, *and* NOT $(\neg)$. *If $f : S \to T$ is a function, then the* Boolean algebra generated by f, *denoted by $\langle f \rangle$, is the subalgebra of 2^S consisting of all functions $b \circ f$, where b is a $\{0,1\}$-valued function on T. If A_1, A_2 are subalgebras of a Boolean algebra A, their intersection $A_1 \cap A_2$ is a subalgebra as well. Their union is not, but it generates a subalgebra that we will denote by $A_1 + A_2$.*

If S is a finite set and $A \subseteq 2^S$ is a Boolean subalgebra, then there is an equivalence relation on S defined by setting $x \sim y$ if and only if $b(x) = b(y)$ for all $b \in A$. The equivalence classes of this relation are called the atoms of A, *and we denote the set of atoms by* $\mathrm{At}(A)$. *There is a canonical function $f_A : S \to \mathrm{At}(A)$ that maps each element to its equivalence class. Note that $A = \langle f_A \rangle$.*

The relevance of Boolean subalgebras to network coding is as follows. A subalgebra $A \subseteq 2^{\mathfrak{M}}$ is a set of binary-valued functions, and can be interpreted as describing the complete state of knowledge of a party that knows the value of each of these functions but no others. In particular, if a sender knows the value of $f(m)$ for some function $f : \mathfrak{M} \to T$, then the binary-valued messages this sender can transmit given its current state of knowledge correspond precisely to the elements of $\langle f \rangle$. This observation supplies the raw materials for our definition of the greedy algorithm for general network codes, which we denote by **GenSerialize**(Φ).

As before, the edge alphabets and coding functions are constructed iteratively, with $\Sigma_e^{(i)}$ and $f_e^{(i)}$ defined in the ith iteration of the main loop. Throughout this process, we maintain a pair of Boolean subalgebras A_e, $B_e \subseteq 2^{\mathfrak{M}}$ for each edge $e = (u, v)$ of G. A_e is generated by all the messages transmitted on e so far, and B_e is intersection of $\langle f_e \rangle$ with the subalgebra generated by all messages transmitted to u so far. (In other words, B_e spans all the binary-valued messages that could currently be sent on e without receiving any additional messages at u.) In the ith iteration, if there exists an edge e' such that $B_{e'}$ contains a binary function $x_{e'} \notin A_{e'}$, then we create a binary-valued coding function $f_e^{(i)}$ for all e, which is set to be $x_{e'}$ if $e = e'$ and the constant function 0 if $e \neq e'$. This process continues until $B_e = A_e$ for every e. At that point, we report that the code is serializable if and only if $A_e = \langle f_e \rangle$ for all e. At the end, the algorithm returns the functions $f_e^{(1..k)}$ and the alphabets $\Sigma_e^{(1..k)}$, where k is the number of iterations of the algorithm, as well as the subspaces $\{A_e\}$. The pseudocode for this algorithm **GenSerialize**(Φ) is presented in the full version of this paper [2].

If Φ has finite alphabets, then **GenSerialize**(Φ) must terminate because the total number of atoms in all the Boolean algebras A_e ($e \in E$) is strictly increasing in each iteration of the main loop, so $\sum_{e \in E} |\Sigma_e|$ is an upper bound on the total number of loop iterations. In implementing the algorithm, each of the Boolean algebras can be represented as a partition of $\mathfrak{M}$ into atoms, and all of the operations the algorithm performs on Boolean algebras can be implemented in polynomial time in this representation. Thus, the running time of **GenSerialize**(Φ) is polynomial in $\sum_{e \in E} |\Sigma_e|$. In light of the algorithm's termination condition, the following definition is natural.

Definition 7. *If $G = (V, E, S)$ is a sourced graph, a* generalized information vortex (GIV) *in a network code $\Phi = (G, \mathfrak{M}, \{\Sigma_e\}, \{f_e\})$ is an assignment of Boolean subalgebras $A_e \subseteq 2^{\mathfrak{M}}$ to every $e \in E \cup S$, satisfying:*

1. *$A_s = \langle f_s \rangle$ for all $s \in S$;*
2. *$A_e = \left(+_{\hat{e} \in \mathsf{In}(u)} A_{\hat{e}}\right) \cap \langle f_e \rangle$ for all $e = (u, v) \in E$.*

A GIV is nontrivial *if $A_e \neq \langle f_e \rangle$ for some $e \in E$. A tuple of Boolean subalgebras $\Gamma = (A_e)_{e \in E \cup S}$ is a* semi-vortex *if it satisfies (1) but only satisfies one-sided containment in (2), i.e.,*

3. *$A_e \subseteq \left(+_{\hat{e} \in \mathsf{In}(u)} A_{\hat{e}}\right) \cap \langle f_e \rangle$ for all $e = (u, v) \in E$.*

If $\Gamma = (A_e)$ and $\Upsilon = (A'_e)$ are semi-vortices, we say that Γ is contained in Υ if $A_e \subseteq A'_e$ for all e.

In full version of this paper [2] we prove a series of statements showing that:

- Semi-vortices are in one-to-one correspondence with restrictions of Φ. The correspondence maps a semi-vortex $(A_e)_{e \in E \cup S}$ to the network code with edge alphabets $\mathrm{At}(A_e)$ and coding functions given by the canonical maps $\mathfrak{M} \to \mathrm{At}(A_e)$ defined in Definition 6.
- There is a set of semi-vortices corresponding to serializable restrictions of Φ under this correspondence. They can be thought of as representing *partial serializations* of Φ.

- There is a set of semi-vortices corresponding to GIV's of Φ. These can be thought of as *certificates of infeasibility* for serializing Φ.
- **GenSerialize**(Φ) computes a semi-vortex Γ which is both a GIV and a partial serialization.

The statements combine to yield a "min-max theorem" showing that the every network code has a maximal serializable restriction that coincides with its minimal GIV, as well as an analogue of Theorem 1; proofs of both theorems are in full version of this paper [2].

Theorem 2. *In the ordering of semi-vortices by containment, the ones corresponding to partial serializations have a maximal element and the GIV's have a minimal element. These maximal and minimal elements coincide, and they are both equal to the semi-vortex $\Gamma = (A_e)_{e \in E \cup S}$ computed by* ***GenSerialize(Φ)****.*

Theorem 3. *For a network code Φ with finite alphabets, the following are equivalent:*

1. *Φ is serializable.*
2. ***GenSerialize(Φ)*** *outputs $\{A_e\}_{e \in E}$ s.t. $\forall\, e, A_e = \langle f_e \rangle$.*
3. *Φ has no nontrivial GIV.*

5 The Serializability Deficit of Linear Network Codes

The min-max relationship between serializable restrictions and information vortices (Theorem 2) is reminiscent of classical results like the max-flow min-cut theorem. However, there is an important difference: one can use the minimum cut in a network to detect *how far* a network flow problem is from feasibility, i.e. the minimum amount by which edge capacities would need to increase in order to make the problem feasible. In this section, we will see that determining how far a network code is from serializability is more subtle: two network codes can be quite similar-looking, with similar-looking minimal information vortices, yet one of them can be serialized by sending only one extra bit while the other requires many more bits to be sent.

We begin with an example to illustrate this point. The codes in Figure 2 apply to the message tuple $(X_1, \ldots, X_n, Y_1, \ldots, Y_n)$ where X_i, Y_i are independent, uniformly distributed random variables over $\mathbb{F}_2$. The codes in Figures 2(a) and 2(b) are almost identical; the only difference is that the code in Figure 2(a) has one extra bit along the top edge. The code in Figure 2(a) is serializable: transmit X_1 along (u, v), then $X_1 + Y_1$ on edge (v, u), then $X_2 + Y_1$ on (u, v), ... ,$X_n + Y_n$ on (v, u), and finally $X_1 + Y_n$ on (u, v). On the other hand, the code in Figure 2(b) is not serializable, which can be seen by applying our greedy algorithm.

Thus, the code in Figure 2(b) is very close to serializable because we can consider an extension of the code in which we add one bit[4] to the edge (u, v) to obtain the code in Figure 2(a) that is serializable. On the other hand, there are

[4] In this section, for simplicity, we refer to one scalar-valued linear function on an $\mathbb{F}$-vector space as a "bit" even if $|\mathbb{F}| > 2$.

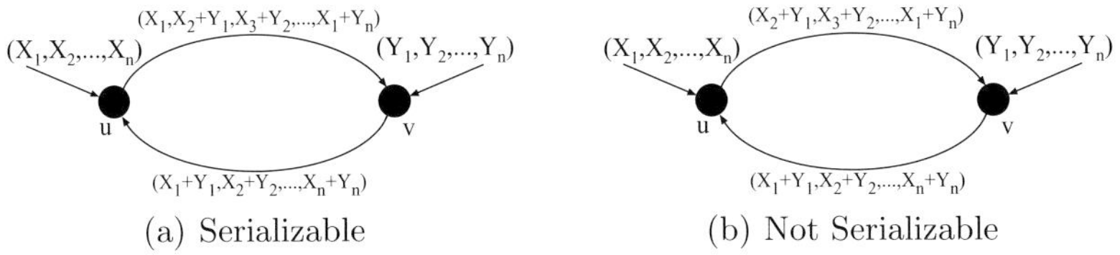

Fig. 2. Two almost identical network codes

similar codes that are very far from being serializable. If we consider the code with the same sources and $f_{(u,v)} = f_{(v,u)} = \prod_{i=1}^{n} X_i + Y_i$, its edge alphabets have the same size and its minimal information vortex is identical, yet any serializable extension requires adding n bits. To completely characterize serializability we would like to be able to separate codes that are close to serializable from those that are far. This motivates the following definition.

Definition 8. *For a network code $\Phi = (G, \mathfrak{M}, \{\Sigma_e\}, \{f_e\})$ and an extension $\Phi' = (G', \mathfrak{M}, \{\Sigma_e'\}, \{f_e'\})$, the* gap *of Φ', defined by $\gamma(\Phi') = \sum_{e \in E} \log_2 |\Sigma_e'| - \log_2 |\Sigma_e|$, represents the combined number of extra bits transmitted on all edges in Φ' as compared to Φ. The* serializability deficit *of Φ, denoted by $\mathsf{SD}(\Phi)$, is defined to be the minimum of $\gamma(\Phi')$ over all serializable extensions Φ' of Φ. The* linear serializability deficit *of a linear code Φ, denoted $\mathsf{LSD}(\Phi)$, is the minimum of $\gamma(\Phi')$ over all linear serializable extensions Φ'.*

Unfortunately, determining the serialization deficit is much more difficult than simply determining serializability.

Theorem 4. *Given a linear network code Φ, it is NP-hard to approximate the size of the minimal linear serializable extension of Φ. Moreover, there is a linear network code Φ and a positive integer n such that $\mathsf{LSD}(\Phi^n)/(n\mathsf{LSD}(\Phi)) < \mathcal{O}(\frac{1}{\log_2(n)})$.*

Both statements in the theorem follow directly from the following lemma, whose proof appears in the full version of this paper [2].

Lemma 1. *Given a hitting set instance (N, S) with universe N, $|N| = n$, subsets $S \subseteq 2^N$, an optimal integral solution k, and an optimal fractional solution $\frac{z_1}{q}, \frac{z_2}{q}, .., \frac{z_n}{q}$, with $\sum_{i=1}^{n} \frac{z_i}{q} = \frac{p}{q}$, in polynomial time we can construct a linear network code such that $\mathsf{LSD}(\Phi) = k$, but $\mathsf{LSD}(\Phi^q) \leq p$.*

The preceding results showed both that there are non-serializable codes with large edge alphabets that become serializable by adding only one bit (example in Figure 2) and that the serialization deficit can behave sub-additively when we take the n-fold cartesian product of Φ (Theorem 4). This prompts the investigation of whether there exists a code that isn't serializable, but the n-fold parallel repetition of the code can be serialized by extending it by only a constant number of bits, and thus it is essentially indistinguishable from serializable. We formalize this idea with the following definition.

Definition 9. *A network code Φ is* asymptotically serializable *if* $\lim_{n\to\infty} \frac{1}{n}\mathsf{LSD}(\Phi^n)/\mathsf{LSD}(\Phi) = 0$ *where Φ^n is n-fold cartesian product of Φ with cartesian product define in the obvious way.*

If one is using a network code to transmit infinite streams of data by chopping each stream up into a sequence of finite blocks and applying the specified coding functions to each block, then an asymptotically serializable network code is almost as good as a serializable one, since it can be serialized by adding a side channel of arbitrarily small bit-rate to each edge of the network.

We show that any non-serializable linear code is not asymptotically serializable via the following theorem.

Theorem 5. *For a linear network code $\Phi = (G, \mathfrak{M}, \{\Sigma_e\}, \{f_e\})$ over a field $\mathbb{F}$, then $\mathsf{LSD}(\Phi^n) \geq cn$ where c is a constant dependent on Φ.*

The proof of the theorem considers the alphabets of the n-fold product of Φ as elements of a tensor product space. Using this machinery, we show that information vortices in the graph are preserved if we don't increase the amount of information we send down some edge by order n bits. More specifically, if $\{W_e\}$ is a non-trivial information vortex in Φ, and e is an edge such that $\dim(W_e) < \dim(T_e) = m$, then if we add some edge function f to every edge in the graph, the information vortex remains non-trivial as long as the dimension of f is less than mn. A complete proof is provided in full version of this paper [2].

6 A Characterization Theorem for the 2-Cycle

In order to use entropy inequalities to give tight upper bounds on network coding rates, we need an enumeration of the complete set of entropy inequalities implied by serializability, i.e. a list of necessary and sufficient conditions for a vector V to be the entropic vector of a serializable code. (Note that it need not be the case that every code whose entropic vector is V must be serializable.) For the 2-cycle we can enumerate the complete set of inequalities. In particular, we give four inequalities that must hold for any serializable code on the 2-cycle: two are a result of *downstreamness* which is a condition that must hold for all graphs (it says that the entropy of the incoming edges of a vertex must be at least as much as the entropy of the incoming and outgoing edges together), the third is the *Chicken and Egg* inequality due to [5], and the fourth is a new inequality that we call the *greedy* inequality. It is equivalent to being able to complete the first iteration of our greedy algorithm in Section 4. We show that these four inequalities together with Shannon's inequalities are the only inequalities implied by serializability, in the following sense:

Theorem 6. *Given a rational-valued entropic vector, V, of a 2-cycle on nodes u, v, with source x into node u, source y into node v, and edges $a = (u, v)$ and $b = (v, u)$, there exists a serializable code that realizes cV, for some constant c, if and only if V satisfies Shannon's inequalities, downstreamness ($H(abx) = H(bx)$, $H(aby) = H(ay)$), the Chicken and Egg inequality ($H(ab) \geq H(abx) - H(x) + H(aby) - H(y)$), and the greedy inequality ($H(a) + H(b) > H(ax) - H(x) + H(by) - H(y)$ when $H(a) + H(b) \neq 0$).*

Multiplication of the vector by a constant c is a natural relaxation because the theorem becomes oblivious to the base of the logarithm we use to compute the Shannon entropy.

The proof of Theorem 6 involves considering four cases corresponding to the relationship between $H(a)$ and $H(ax), H(ay), H(x), H(y)$ and between $H(b)$ and $H(bx), H(by)H(x), H(y)$. Each case requires a distinctly different coding function to realize the entropic vector. All the coding functions are relatively simple, involving only sending uncoded bits, and the XOR of two bits. Most of the work is limiting the values of coordinates of the entropic vector based on the inequalities that the entropic vector satisfies. The proof of Theorem 6 is provided in full version of this paper [2].

The big open question left from this work is whether we can find a complete set of constraints on the entropic vector implied by the serializability of codes on arbitrary graphs. We currently do not know of any procedure for producing such a list of inequalities. Even if we had a conjecture for such a list, showing that it is complete is likely to be quite hard. If we have more than three sources, just determining the possible dependencies between sources is difficult because they are subject to non-Shannon information inequalities.

References

1. Adler, M., Harvey, N.J.A., Jain, K., Kleinberg, R., Lehman, A.R.: On the capacity of information networks. In: Proc. of the 17th ACM-SIAM Symposium on Discrete Algorithms (SODA), pp. 241–250 (2005)
2. Blasiak, A., Kleinberg, R.: The serializability of network codes. CoRR, abs/1001.1373 (2010)
3. Erez, E., Feder, M.: Efficient network codes for cyclic networks. In: Proc. 2005 International Symposium on Information Theory (ISIT), pp. 1982–1986 (2005)
4. Harvey, N.J.A., Kleinberg, R., Lehman, A.R.: On the capacity of information networks. IEEE Transactions on Information Theory 52(6), 2345–2364 (2006)
5. Harvey, N.J.A., Kleinberg, R., Nair, C., Wu, Y.: A "chicken & egg" network coding problem. In: Proc. 2007 IEEE International Symposium on Information Theory (ISIT), pp. 131–135 (2007)
6. Jain, K., Vazirani, V., Yeung, R.W., Yuval, G.: On the capacity of multiple unicast sessions in undirected graphs. In: Proc. 2005 IEEE International Symposium on Information Theory, ISIT (2005)
7. Koetter, R., Medard, M.: An algebraic approach to network coding. IEEE/ACM Transactions on Networking 11(5), 782–795 (2003)

8. Kramer, G., Savari, S.: Edge-cut bounds on network coding rates. Journal of Network and Systems Management 14(1), 49–67 (2006)
9. Lehman, A.R.: Network Coding. PhD thesis, MIT (2005)
10. Yeung, R.W.: A First Course in Information Theory. Springer, Heidelberg (2002)
11. Yeung, R.W., Li, S.-Y.R., Cai, N., Zhang, Z.: Network Coding Theory. Now Publishers (2006)

How Efficient Can Gossip Be? (On the Cost of Resilient Information Exchange)

Dan Alistarh[1], Seth Gilbert[1], Rachid Guerraoui[1], and Morteza Zadimoghaddam[1,2]

[1] Ecole Polytechnique Fédérale de Lausanne, Lausanne, Switzerland
[2] Massachusetts Institute of Technology, Cambridge, USA

Abstract. Gossip, also known as epidemic dissemination, is becoming an increasingly popular technique in distributed systems. Yet, it has remained a partially open question: how robust are such protocols? We consider a natural extension of the *random phone-call* model (introduced by Karp et al. [1]), and we analyze two different notions of robustness: the ability to tolerate *adaptive* failures, and the ability to tolerate *oblivious* failures.

For adaptive failures, we present a new gossip protocol, TrickleGossip, which achieves near-optimal $O(n \log^3 n)$ message complexity. To the best of our knowledge, this is the first epidemic-style protocol that can tolerate adaptive failures. We also show a direct relation between resilience and message complexity, demonstrating that gossip protocols which tolerate a large number of adaptive failures need to use a super-linear number of messages with high probability.

For oblivious failures, we present a new gossip protocol, CoordinatedGossip, that achieves optimal $O(n)$ message complexity. This protocol makes novel use of the *universe reduction* technique to limit the message complexity.

1 Introduction

Consider a distributed system consisting of n processes $\{p_1, \ldots, p_n\}$, each connected by a pairwise communication channel to every other process. Processes have unique identifiers, but a process does not know the identifiers of the other processes until it has exchanged information with them.

The problem of disseminating information efficiently and robustly can, roughly, be described as follows. Each process p_i begins with a *rumor* r_i; eventually, each process should learn as many rumors as possible. Moreover, this exchange of information should be *fault-tolerant*: it should succeed even if some of the processes fail (i.e., crash), and any non-failed process should succeed in disseminating its rumor to every other non-failed process. This problem is a basic building block in many distributed settings, such as distributed databases [2], group multicast [3,4], group membership [5], resource location [6], and, recently, update dissemination for mobile nodes [7].

In this paper, we investigate the relationship between *fault tolerance* and *efficiency*. We consider a natural extension of the *random phone-call* model, introduced by Karp et al. [1], and develop protocols for both *adaptive* and *oblivious* failures:

1. Adaptive failures. Our first main result is a gossip protocol, TrickleGossip, that achieves $O(n \log^3 n)$ message complexity, with high probability, when failures are

S. Abramsky et al. (Eds.): ICALP 2010, Part II, LNCS 6199, pp. 115–126, 2010.

adaptive, i.e., when failures may depend on the history of the ongoing execution. The protocol tolerates $t < n/3$ failures, and terminates in $O(\log^2 n)$ rounds. The time complexity is near-optimal–a simple modification of the result in [8] yields a lower bound of $\Omega(\log n/\log\log n)$ rounds for the problem.

The challenge, when failures are adaptive, is that the "adversary," which is dictating the failures, may select which processes to crash, and therefore can target specific rumors and prevent them from being disseminated. For example, the adversary may decide to "single out" a process p_i, failing every process that p_i sends a message to. Unless process p_i sends a large number of messages, the adversary can always prevent p_i's rumor from reaching any other process. Our algorithm introduces a scheme for processes to monitor the spread of their rumors, allowing isolated processes to send more and more messages, while preventing too many processes from sending too many messages. Thus the protocol alternates *spreading* rounds that attempt to disseminate rumors, *collection* rounds that attempt to discover new rumors, and *sampling* rounds that attempt to gauge how far rumors have spread.

We also show a trade-off between robustness and message complexity in the presence of *adaptive* faults. More precisely, any protocol that tolerates $n(1-\epsilon)$ process crashes, where $1 \geq \epsilon > 0$ is a function of n, has message complexity $\Omega(n \log(1/\epsilon))$, with high probability. Of note, for small ϵ, e.g. $\epsilon < 1/\log\log n$, this results in a super-linear lower bound on message complexity, the first such bound for gossip protocols in the presence of adaptive faults.

2. Oblivious failures. Our second main result is a gossip protocol, CoordinatedGossip, that achieves optimal $O(n)$ message complexity, with high probability, when failures are oblivious, i.e., independent of the actual execution (and hence independent of random choices made by the processes). This implies that, asymptotically, we can achieve the same level of efficiency in a crash-prone network as in a fault-free network.

The key idea underlying this algorithm is *universe reduction*: we randomly select a small set of coordinators and use them to collect and then disseminate the rumors. The main challenge here is the need for coordinators to work efficiently together; specifically, they must avoid duplicating work (i.e., messages). However, the coordinators do not initially know the identities of the other coordinators, nor how to reach them. The protocol builds simple, yet robust, overlay structures that allow coordinators to communicate amongst themselves, and allow processes to communicate with coordinators.

This result is perhaps surprising due to the $\Omega(n \log\log n)$ lower bound in [1] on the message complexity of single-source gossip, in which a single process attempts to distribute its message to all others. In [1], they consider a model in which, in each round, each process can: (i) contact a random process and (ii) either *push* information to the random process or *pull* information from it. By contrast, in this paper, we allow a process to send more than one message per round, and to reply to processes that communicate with it at later rounds. The capacity to maintain a connection over multiple rounds allows us to circumvent the lower bound and obtain significant improvements.

Discussion. While we assume, for simplicity, that processes have unique identifiers, this assumption is not needed for any of the results in this paper. A process may simply choose an identifier at random from a suitably large namespace (e.g., $\{1, \ldots, \Theta(n^2)\}$), such that, with high probability, every process selects a unique identifier. All the results in this paper continue to hold.

As a result, a process may not, *a priori*, know the identity of other processes in the system. In such a model, any deterministic protocol requires $\Omega(n^2)$ messages; the lack of knowledge about the world precludes protocols based on specially crafted overlays, such as expander graphs, as used previously in, e.g., [9]. Thus there is a significant difference in the efficiency of deterministic and randomized protocols when the adversary is adaptive.

Another interesting aspect is the gap between the TrickleGossip protocol, which requires $n-t \geq 2n/3$ correct processes, and the lower bound, which requires $n-t = o(n)$ to yield a super-linear bound on message complexity. We conjecture that this gap can be closed by making TrickleGossip more robust, i.e. requiring only $o(n)$ correct processes, while maintaining sub-quadratic message complexity.

Finally, the analysis in this paper focuses on the message complexity, while ignoring the size of messages. The protocols have very low communication overhead, as messages contain only a small number of "control bits." Thus, it seems likely that in the context of using gossip to aggregate data (e.g., calculate the maximum initial rumor), it would be possible, in addition, to achieve small message size.

2 Distributed System Model

We consider a synchronous distributed system consisting of n processes $\{p_1, \ldots, p_n\}$. An execution proceeds in synchronous rounds in which each process sends a set of messages, receives a set of messages, and updates its state. Every pair of processes is connected by a pairwise communication channel.

Faults. Up to $t < n/3$ processes may *fail* by crashing. When a process p_i crashes in some round r, any arbitrary subset of its round r messages may be delivered; process p_i then takes no further steps in any round $> r$. A process that does not fail is *correct*. We think of the failures as dictated by an *adversary*.

Communication. Each process has a unique identifier. When the execution begins, a process does not know the identity of any other process in the system[1]. The first time that a process p_i receives a message from another process p_j, it learns the identity of p_j, and hence it learns on which channel it can send messages to p_j. Formally, each process p_i has access to an unordered set of n channels S_i (including a channel connecting p_i to itself). In each round, each process can send a message on any subset of the available channels, and, in addition, it can reply to any message received in a previous round (using the channel on which that message was delivered).

Oblivious and Adaptive Failures. We distinguish two types of failures. When failures are independent of the actual execution (and hence independent of the random choices

[1] Often distributed algorithms assume that processes know the identity of their neighbors, since learning this information requires only a single exchange of messages on each channel. However, this neighbor-discovery process requires $\Theta(n^2)$ messages, and so we do not assume that a process knows the identities of any other process *a priori*.

made by the processes), we say that they are *oblivious* (i.e., the *adversary* is *oblivious*). By contrast, when failures may depend on the ongoing execution, we say that they are *adaptive* (i.e., the *adversary* is *adaptive*). Formally, when failures are *oblivious*, we assume that the adversary fixes, prior to the execution, a *failure pattern* that specifies in which round each faulty process fails, and which of its messages are delivered in that round. When failures are *adaptive*, we assume that failures in round r are determined by a *failure function* which takes as input the entire history of rounds $1, \ldots, r-1$, including the results of the random coin flips.

When we say that a protocol has message complexity M with probability p, this means that for every failure pattern/function, the probability that more than M messages are sent in an execution is no greater than p. The term *with high probability* (w.h.p.) means with probability at least $1 - O(n^{-\gamma})$, for any constant $\gamma > 0$.

3 Related Work

The idea of randomized rumor distribution dates back to Frieze and Grimmett [10], and later, Pittel [11] and Feige [12], who showed that one can distribute a single rumor in a complete graph with n vertices in time $\log n + \ln n + o(1)$, as well as in other types of random graphs. Demers et al. [2] showed that rumor spreading can be used for efficient distributed database maintenance.

In a landmark paper, Karp, Schindelhauer, Shenker and Vöcking [1] considered the problem in the *random phone-call model*. They show how to distribute a rumor (in the presence of an oblivious adversary) using $O(\log n)$ rounds and $O(n \log\log n)$ messages, which is optimal in the absence of addresses. Moreover, they show that, even using addresses, no algorithm is simultaneously time and message optimal.

The results of [1] inspired a significant amount of research. Elsässer et al. [13, 14, 15, 16] study extensions of the random phone-call model for various types of random graphs. In [17, 18], Doerr et al. consider *quasirandom* rumor spreading, in which each process has a list of its neighbors through which it is allowed to cycle when sending the rumor. Surprisingly, the time bounds of [10] and [12] are still optimal in this augmented model. In [19], the robustness of the quasirandom model is analyzed when there are probabilistic transmission failures. All these papers consider an *oblivious* adversary.

The model in this paper can be seen as an enrichment of the random phone-call model of Karp et al. [1]. Of note, this allows us to achieve $O(n)$ message complexity for oblivious failures, and it allows us to develop protocols for a stronger, adaptive adversary. Compared to the original model of [1], and the later variations in [13,15,17], our model is stronger in that it allows processes to send an arbitrary number of messages per round, and it allows processes to reply in later rounds to messages received in earlier rounds. Note that we consider *gossip* (i.e., n rumors to be spread), rather than broadcast.

There has also been much work on gossip when addresses are available, i.e., when processes know in advance the identities of all the other processes in the system. Kowalski et al. (e.g. [8, 9]) present deterministic algorithms (based on expander-graph constructions) that ensure the dissemination of rumors within time $O(\text{polylog } n)$ using $O(n \text{ polylog } n)$ total messages. These algorithms cannot be used when a process does not know the addresses of the other processes, or more generally, when the names are not derived from a fixed namespace. Earlier research [20] determined time and cost trade-offs for gossip, when only one neighbor is contacted per round. Georgiou et al. [21] provided upper and lower bounds for the complexity of gossip in an asynchronous environment. A survey of prior work on gossip can be found in [22].

A key aspect of the CoordinatedGossip algorithm, presented in Section 6, is the technique of *universe reduction*, which has been an important tool in developing distributed algorithms. Of particular note are recent algorithms by Ben-Or et al. [23], Kapron et al. [24], King et al. [25, 26] that use universe reduction to solve Byzantine agreement.

In a recent paper [27], Gilbert and Kowalski use the universe reduction technique to develop a crash-tolerant consensus protocol that has optimal communication complexity: it uses only $O(n)$ bits of communication. In the same paper, they discuss how these techniques can be used to solve gossip using $O(n)$ messages. The model in that paper, however, assumes that processes know the identities of their neighbors; as discussed in Section 2, this assumption adds a hidden implicit $\Omega(n^2)$ message cost which we avoid in this paper. Thus, we cannot take advantage of the *work sharing* techniques discussed in [27]; instead a more careful scheme is needed to avoid sending too many messages.

4 Gossip against an Adaptive Adversary

In this section, we present a gossip algorithm, TrickleGossip, that tolerates adaptive failures. The algorithm ensures, with high probability, that each correct process receives the rumors of other correct processes. It uses $O(n \log^3 n)$ messages, with high probability, and terminates in $O(\log^2 n)$ communication rounds. Previous work [8] implies that the round complexity is optimal, up to logarithmic factors.

4.1 Algorithm Description

The execution of the algorithm is divided into two epochs: the *dissemination* epoch and the *confirmation* epoch. We proceed to describe the structure of each epoch. Let β be a large integer constant, and let $\alpha = 7/12$.

The Dissemination Epoch. The dissemination epoch consists of $\log n$ phases, where each phase is $3 \log n + 1$ rounds, yielding a round complexity for the epoch of $O(\log^2 n)$.

In the first round of each phase, each process sends its own rumor to other processes. Each process is initially *unmarked*. In the first round of phase i, each unmarked process sends its rumor to a set of $2^i \log n$ randomly chosen processes. (If $2^i \log n \geq n$, then all n processes are chosen). Each process then gathers all the distinct rumors it has received thus far into a *packet*. In each of the following $\log n$ rounds of phase i, each process, whether marked or unmarked, sends its packet to $\log n$ randomly chosen neighbors.

Finally, during the remaining $2 \log n$ rounds of phase i, unmarked processes perform a *testing* process. In each *odd* testing round, each unmarked process sends a *query* to a random set of $2^i \beta \log n$ processes (or all n processes, if $2^i \beta \log n \geq n$). In the *even* testing rounds, each process that received a query sends a reply with the list of rumors it has received. An *unmarked* process changes its state to *marked* if at least $\min(\alpha 2^i \beta \log n, n - t)$ of the processes that were contacted during the previous (even) round had received its rumor. Once a process is marked, it stops sending queries, but continues replying to queries from other processes. (However, it continues to send a packet during rounds $2, \ldots, \log n + 1$ in the first part of each phase.) Once a process is marked, it remains marked for the rest of the dissemination epoch.

The algorithm guarantees that, during the dissemination epoch, the number of unmarked processes is roughly halved in every phase–we say that information "trickles" down to the last uninformed processes.

The Confirmation Epoch. This epoch also consists of $\log n$ phases, each of which consists of $2 \log n$ rounds. At the beginning of the epoch, all processes are again designated *unmarked*. In each odd round of phase i, each unmarked process sends a query to a random set of $2^i \beta \log n$ processes (or all n processes, if $2^i \beta \log n \geq n$). In even rounds, each process that received a query sends a reply with the list of rumors it has received. An unmarked process changes its state to marked if it receives at least $\min(\alpha 2^i \beta \log n, n - t)$ responses. At the end of the epoch, each process delivers all the rumors it has received at any point.

4.2 Analysis

We first show that every process delivers every rumor belonging to a correct process, w.h.p. Second, we show that the algorithm sends $O(n \log^3 n)$ messages, w.h.p. The bound on round complexity follows trivially from the structure of the algorithm. Due to space restrictions, we defer the complete proofs to the the full version of the paper [28].

To simplify the analysis, we will consider executions of the algorithm where $t < n/\kappa$, where κ is a (large) constant. We can "boost" the resiliency from $t < n/\kappa$ failures to $t < n/3$ failures, without affecting its asymptotic complexity, by re-running the protocol κ times; during at least one of these κ executions, by the pigeonhole principle, there are no more than n/κ new failures. (Failures during a previous execution of the protocol have no affect on a later execution.)

We first show that by the end of the first epoch, every rumor belonging to a non-crashed process is spread to $> n/2$ processes w.h.p. This follows since a process p_j is marked only when a large fraction of the randomly sampled query respond that they have already received p_j's rumor; this implies that at least a majority of all processes have received p_j's rumor, w.h.p. Finally, every process is eventually marked, since in the last phase an unmarked process sends its rumor directly to all n other processes.

Lemma 1 (Spreading). *For every correct process, there is a majority of correct processes that have received its rumor during the dissemination epoch, w.h.p.*

During the second epoch, w.h.p., every rumor belonging to a correct process is delivered to every other correct process by the majority that holds it at the end of the first epoch.

Lemma 2 (Delivery). *By the end of the confirmation epoch, every correct process has received every rumor initiated by a correct processes, with high probability.*

We now examine the message complexity of TrickleGossip, showing that the algorithm sends $O(n \log^3 n)$ messages, w.h.p. The argument is based on the observation that, in every phase of an epoch, the number of processes that remain unmarked is roughly halved. This implies that the number of messages sent in a phase is always bounded by $O(n \log^2 n)$, w.h.p. Finally, since there are $O(\log n)$ phases in an execution, we obtain that the total number of messages sent is $O(n \log^3 n)$, w.h.p.

In the following analysis, we consider, without loss of generality, that the adversary makes its choices of which process to fail at each round r precisely at the beginning of round r by inspecting the local state and the randomly chosen destinations for each process that has not yet been crashed (by the beginning of the previous round $r-1$). This simplifies the exposition, without decreasing the power of the adversary.

The first lemma shows that during the dissemination epoch, the number of unmarked processes is halved in each phase, w.h.p. This lemma is the main technical contribution in this section. We refer the interested reader to the full version of the paper [28] for a complete proof.

Lemma 3 (Dissemination Epoch). *At the beginning of phase number i of the first epoch, the number of unmarked processes is at most $n/2^{i-1}$, w.h.p.*

Proof. (Sketch) We proceed by induction on the phase number i. The case $i = 1$ is trivial. For the induction step, we assume that, at the beginning of phase number i, there are at most $n/2^{i-1}$ unmarked processes.

Let U_i be the set of processes that are unmarked at the beginning of phase i. We analyze the spread of rumors in U_i during the phase. Recall that, in the first round of the phase, each unmarked process sends its rumor to $2^i \log n$ randomly chosen processes. We say that a rumor from a process in U_i is *fast* in round r_1 if it is held by at least $2^{i-3} \log n$ processes that have not crashed before the beginning of the second round of the phase. We first observe that, by failing f_1 processes during the first round of the phase, the adversary may prevent at most $\Theta(f_1/2^i)$ processes from being *fast*. We denote the set of *fast* rumors for round r_1 by M_i.

Fix some sufficiently small $\delta < 1$ and $\epsilon < 1$. In the second step of the analysis, we argue that in the subsequent rounds $2, \ldots, \log n + 1$, if the adversary fails f_2 processes, then it can stop at most $\Theta(f_2)$ packets from each spreading to at least $n(\alpha + 2\epsilon)$ processes, w.h.p. We say that a packet is *fast* in round r of this part, if it is sent by at least $\min[(\delta \log n)^r, n(\alpha + 2\epsilon)]$ processes that do not crash before round $r+1$. By a counting argument, we see that by crashing f_r processes in a round r, the adversary may stop at most $\Theta(f_r)$ rumors from being *fast* in round r. Therefore, for each rumor that is *fast* throughout this part of the phase, we are analyzing an epidemic process with a growth rate of $\Theta(\log n)$. Thus, by round $\log n + 1$, each fast rumor has reached at least $(\alpha + 2\epsilon)n$ processes. On the other hand, the adversary may stop the growth for individual rumors, by failing processes at every round. A careful analysis of this procedure shows that, by failing f_2 processes during rounds $2, \ldots, \log n + 1$, the adversary can stop at most a total of $\Theta(f)$ packets from being spread to at least $n(\alpha + \epsilon)$ processes.

We now combine the previous two steps: since each rumor in M_i is distributed into at least $2^{i-3} \log n$ packets at the end of the first round in this phase, the adversary has to stop *all* packets containing the rumor from being *fast* in order to prevent the rumor from being spread to a large fraction of processes. On the other hand, since the destinations in the first round of the phase are chosen at random, a packet contains at most $\Theta(\log n)$ rumors from M_i, w.h.p. (by a Chernoff bound). Therefore, by failing f processes, and hence delaying $O(f)$ rumors in round 1 and $O(f)$ packets in rounds $2, \ldots, \log n+1$, the adversary can prevent at most $\Theta(f \log n/(2^{i-3} \log n)) \leq \Theta(f/2^i)$ rumors from being spread to at least $n(\alpha + \epsilon)$ processes each, w.h.p. Finally, we conclude that, there are at most $n/2^{i+1}$ rumors started by processes in U_i that are not spread to at least $n(\alpha + \epsilon)$ processes. So at least $|U_i| - n/2^{i+1}$ rumors are spread to at least $n(\alpha + \epsilon)$ processes.

The third and final step shows that there are at most $n/2^{i+1}$ processes associated to these $|U_i| - n/2^{i+1}$ rumors that are not marked during the testing part of the phase, with high probability. This concludes the proof of the induction step, and of the lemma.

The final lemma in the proof of the message complexity upper bound proves that the number of non-marked processes is halved in each phase of the confirmation epoch as well. The proof is similar to that of Lemma 3.

Lemma 4 (Confirmation Epoch). *At the beginning of phase i of the second epoch, the number of unmarked processes is not more than $n/2^{i-1}$, with high probability.*

5 Relating Fault-Tolerance to Message Complexity

In this section, we prove a lower bound on the message complexity of any gossip algorithm that tolerates $t < n(1 - \epsilon)$ process crashes. We assume that ϵ is a function of n, with $1 > \epsilon(n) \geq 0$. For the rest of this section, we omit the argument of the $\epsilon(n)$ function, and simply write ϵ. Theorem 1 focuses on the problem of gossip; the argument can be adapted to yield a similar result in the case of *reliable broadcast* in which a rumor delivered by a correct process has to be delivered to every correct process.

Theorem 1 (Message Complexity Lower Bound). *Any algorithm that tolerates $t < n(1 - \epsilon)$ process crashes, and guarantees gossip with constant positive probability, needs to send $\Omega(n \log(1/\epsilon))$ messages, w.h.p.*

Proof. (Sketch) We consider an algorithm $\mathcal{A}$ that solves gossip with constant positive probability, tolerating $n(1-\epsilon)$ failures, and show that there exists an adversarial strategy which forces the algorithm to generate $\Omega(n \log(1/\epsilon))$ messages w.h.p. The adversary constructs an execution as follows: it crashes any process that receives a new rumor, and it crashes every process immediately after it generates $n/4$ messages. We split the execution into phases, with the property that, in each phase, the adversary crashes exactly half of the processes that were not crashed at the end of the previous phase. Our main claim is that, w.h.p., the algorithm sends $\Theta(n)$ messages in each phase. The main difficulty in proving the claim is that the random variables corresponding to messages sent are not independent; however, we are able to show that they are *negatively associated*, in the sense of [29], which allows the use of tail bounds. Finally, we show that, in order to achieve gossip with constant probability, the algorithm needs to make the system progress for $\Omega(\log(1/\epsilon))$ phases, w.h.p.

6 Gossip and Oblivious Failures

In this section, we present the CoordinatedGossip protocol which sends only $O(n)$ messages, w.h.p. The key underlying idea is to elect a small set of $\Theta(\log n)$ *coordinators*, who then collect and disseminate the rumors. There are two main challenges:

1. Intra-coordinator communication: Since the coordinators are selected independently, they do not initially know how to contact the other coordinators. Therefore the coordinators select a set of $O(\sqrt{n}\log^2 n)$ *intermediaries* that form an overlay connecting all the coordinators.
2. Coordinator discovery: In order to collect and disseminate the rumors, the coordinators need to efficiently contact all the processes in the system. Each coordinator sending a message to each process would be too expensive, requiring $\Theta(n \log n)$ messages. Instead, each coordinator selects $\Theta(n/\log n)$ *relays*, leading to $\Theta(n)$ relays in total. To collect the rumors, each process forwards its rumor to a relay, which can then forward it to a coordinator. To disseminate rumors, the process is reversed.

We first present the protocol in Section 6.1. We then analyze the message complexity in Section 6.2. All omitted proofs can be found in the full version of this paper.

6.1 CoordinatedGossip

We split the presentation of the CoordinatedGossip protocol in three parts. First, we describe a set of initial steps in which we select three special sets of processes: *coordinators*, *intermediaries*, and *relays*. We then describe how the rumors are collected, and finally how rumors are disseminated.

Selecting processes. In the first round, each process decides whether to be a *coordinator*, an *intermediary*, a *relay*, or none of the above. (Note that a process can play more than one role.) *A. Coordinators:* Each process decides to be a coordinator with probability $\Theta(\log n/n)$. *B. Intermediaries:* Each coordinator chooses $\Theta(\sqrt{n}\log n)$ processes at random, and sends each an *intermediary-election* message; each process that receives such a message decides to be an intermediary. We say that a process is a *correct intermediary* if it receives an intermediary-election message and does not fail. For a given intermediary, we define the intermediary's *neighbors* to be the set of processes from which it received intermediary-election messages. *C. Relays:* Each coordinator participates in c relay elections, for some constant c. That is, for every $\ell \in \{1, \ldots, c\}$, each coordinator chooses $\Theta(n/\log n)$ processes at random,and sends each a *relay-election-ℓ* message. If, for any $\ell \in \{1, \ldots, c\}$, a process receives *exactly one* relay-election-ℓ message, then it decides to be an ℓ-relay. We define the *ℓ-parent* of a relay to be the coordinator that sent it a unique relay-election-ℓ message. We say that a process is a *good relay* for ℓ if: (i) it receives exactly one relay-election-ℓ message, for some ℓ; (ii) it is correct; and (iii) its ℓ-parent is correct.

We will argue that there are $\Theta(\log n)$ correct coordinators, that every pair of coordinators shares a correct intermediary, and that there are $\Theta(n)$ good relays.

Collecting rumors. After choosing coordinators, intermediaries, and relays, there is an collection phase. The goal of the collection phase is to ensure that every rumor from a correct process is known to every correct coordinator. Each process attempts to send its rumor to a relay; the relay forwards it to its parent, a coordinator; the coordinators then exchange rumors via the intermediaries. We proceed to describe this process in more detail. Specifically, the collection phase consists of $\Theta(\log n)$ iterations of the following seven rounds:

a. Each process that has not *succeeded* in a previous iteration sends its rumor to one randomly selected process.
b. Each relay sends any messages received in round (a) to its parents, for each $\ell \in \{1, \ldots, c\}$.
c. Each coordinator forwards all the rumors it has received to the set of intermediaries to which it previously sent intermediary-election messages.
d. Each intermediary forwards every rumor received to its neighbors.
e. Each coordinator sends a response to every relay from which it received a message in round (b).
f. Each relay that received a response in Round (e) sends a response to every process from which it receives a message in step (a).
g. Each process that receives a response in Round (f) has *succeeded* and remains silent thereafter.

We will argue that the collection phase uses $O(n)$ messages, with high probability, and that, by the end, every rumor from a non-failed process has been received by every non-failed coordinator, with high probability.

Disseminating rumors. After the collection phase, there is a dissemination phase. In the first round of the dissemination phase, each coordinator sends all the rumors it has learned to the set of relays that it previously sent relay-election messages to. The remainder of the dissemination phase proceeds much like the collection phase, except in reverse. As before, the dissemination phase consists of $\Theta(\log n)$ iterations of the following rounds:

a. Each process that has not *succeeded* in a prior iteration sends its message to a random process.
b. Each relay sends a response to every message received in round (a); the response includes all the rumors previously received from the coordinators.
c. Each process that receives a response in round (b) has *succeeded* and remains silent thereafter.

We will argue that the dissemination phase uses $O(n)$ messages, with high probability, and that every non-failed process learns every rumor that was previously collected by the coordinators.

6.2 Analysis

We begin by bounding the number of coordinators, which follows immediately from the fact that each process elects itself coordinator with probability $\Theta(\log n/n)$:

Lemma 5 (Coordinator-Set Size). *There are $\Theta(\log n)$ coordinators, w.h.p.*

Next, we argue that for every pair of coordinators, there is some correct intermediary that has both coordinators as neighbors. This follows from a "birthday-paradox" style argument that randomly chosen sets of size $\sqrt{n}$ intersect with constant probability:

Lemma 6 (Good Intermediaries). *For every pair of non-failed coordinators p_i, p_j, there exists some intermediary p_k such that both p_i and p_j are neighbors of p_k, w.h.p.*

Next, we argue that a constant fraction of the processes are good relays. This is perhaps the key fact that leads to good performance: the coordinators can efficiently contact a constant fraction of the world (i.e., the relays); and there are enough relays that the processes can easily find a relay, and hence a path to a coordinator. The lemma follows from a balls-and-bins style analysis.

Lemma 7 (Good Relays). *There exists some $\ell \in \{1, \ldots, c\}$ such that at least $n/18$ processes are good relays for ℓ, w.h.p.*

Next, we argue that every process succeeds during the collection and dissemination phases, resulting in every correct process learning the entire set of rumors that were initiated at correct processes. This follows from showing that during one of the $\Theta(\log n)$ iterations of collection/dissemination, each process finds a good relay.

Lemma 8 (Gossip Success). *W.h.p.: (a) By the end of the collection phase, every process has succeeded. (b) By the end of the dissemination phase, every process has succeeded. (c) When the protocol terminates, every rumor from a correct process has been received by every correct process.*

Finally, we analyze the message complexity of the collection and dissemination phases. The key part of this analysis is showing that finding relays is *efficient*. This fact follows from the following analogy: the attempts by processes to find relays is equivalent to flipping a coin until we get n heads; this requires only $O(n)$ flips, w.h.p.

Lemma 9 (Message Complexity). *The collection and dissemination phases have message complexity $O(n)$, w.h.p.*

We conclude with the main theorem:

Theorem 2. *The* CoordinatedGossip *protocol is correct, runs in $O(\log n)$ rounds, and has message complexity $O(n)$, w.h.p.*

Proof. By Lemma 8, we see that every rumor is disseminated w.h.p., and by observation, it runs for $O(\log n)$ rounds. In terms of message complexity, when Lemma 5 holds, i.e., w.h.p.: the selection of coordinators requires at most $O(\sqrt{n} \log^2 n)$ messages; the selection of relays requires at most $O(n)$ messages. Lemma 9 states that collection and dissemination have message complexity $O(n)$, w.h.p. Thus, overall, the message complexity is $O(n)$, w.h.p.

Acknowledgements. We would like to thank Prof. Hagit Attiya and the anonymous reviewers for their useful comments on earlier drafts of this paper.

References

1. Karp, R., Schindelhauer, C., Shenker, S., Vöcking, B.: Randomized rumor spreading. In: FOCS (2000)
2. Demers, A., Greene, D., Hauser, C., Irish, W., Larson, J., Shenker, S., Sturgis, H., Swinehart, D., Terry, D.: Epidemic algorithms for replicated database maintenance. In: PODC (1987)
3. Birman, K., Hayden, M., Ozkasap, O., Xiao, Z., Budiu, M., Minsky, Y.: Bimodal multicast. ACM Trans. on Comp. Sys. 17, 41–86 (1999)
4. Eugster, P., Guerraoui, R., Handurukande, S., Kermarrec, A.-M., Kouznetsov, P.: Lightweight probabilistic broadcast. ACM Trans. on Comp. Sys. 21(4) (2003)
5. Kermarrec, A., Massoulie, L., Ganesh, A.: Probabilistic reliable multicast in ad hoc networks. IEEE Trans. on Parallel and Distr. Syst. 14 (2003)

6. Kempe, D., Kleinberg, J., Demers, A.: Spatial gossip and resource location protocols. Journal of ACM, 943–967 (2004)
7. Chaintreau, A., Le Boudec, J.-Y., Ristanovic, N.: The age of gossip: spatial mean field regime. In: SIGMETRICS (2009)
8. Chlebus, B.S., Kowalski, D.R.: Robust gossiping with an application to consensus. J. Comput. Syst. Sci. 72(8), 1262–1281 (2006)
9. Chlebus, B.S., Kowalski, D.R.: Time and communication efficient consensus for crash failures (2006)
10. Frieze, A.M., Grimmett, G.: The shortest-path problem for graphs with random arc-lengths. Discrete Applied Mathematics (10), 55–77 (1985)
11. Pittel, B.: On spreading a rumor. SIAM J. Appl. Math. 47(1), 213–223 (1987)
12. Feige, U., Peleg, D., Raghavan, P., Upfal, E.: Randomized broadcast in networks. In: Asano, T., Imai, H., Ibaraki, T., Nishizeki, T. (eds.) SIGAL 1990. LNCS, vol. 450, pp. 128–137. Springer, Heidelberg (1990)
13. Elsässer, R.: On the communication complexity of randomized broadcasting in random-like graphs. In: SPAA (2006)
14. Berenbrink, P., Elsaesser, R., Friedetzky, T.: Efficient randomised broadcasting in random regular networks with applications in peer-to-peer systems. In: PODC (2008)
15. Elsässer, R., Sauerwald, T.: The power of memory in randomized broadcasting. In: SODA (2008)
16. Elsässer, R., Sauerwald, T.: On the runtime and robustness of randomized broadcasting. Theor. Comput. Sci. 410(36), 3414–3427 (2009)
17. Doerr, B., Friedrich, T., Sauerwald, T.: Quasirandom rumor spreading. In: SODA (2008)
18. Doerr, B., Friedrich, T., Sauerwald, T.: Quasirandom rumor spreading: Expanders, push vs. pull, and robustness. In: Albers, S., Marchetti-Spaccamela, A., Matias, Y., Nikoletseas, S., Thomas, W. (eds.) ICALP 2009. LNCS, vol. 5555, pp. 366–377. Springer, Heidelberg (2009)
19. Doerr, B., Huber, A., Levavi, A.: Strong robustness of randomized rumor spreading protocols. In: Dong, Y., Du, D.-Z., Ibarra, O. (eds.) ISAAC 2009. LNCS, vol. 5878. Springer, Heidelberg (2009)
20. Czumaj, A., Gasieniec, L., Pelc, A.: Time and cost trade-offs in gossiping. SIAM Journal on Discrete Mathematics 11, 400–413 (1998)
21. Georgiou, C., Gilbert, S., Guerraoui, R., Kowalski, D.R.: On the complexity of asynchronous gossip. In: PODC (2008)
22. Hromkovic, J., Klasing, R., Pelc, A., Ruzika, P., Unger, W.: Dissemination of information in Communication Networks: Broadcasting, Gossiping, Leader Election, and Fault-Tolerance. Springer, Heidelberg (2005)
23. Ben-Or, M., Pavlov, E., Vaikuntanathan, V.: Byzantine agreement in the full-information model in O(log n) rounds. In: STOC (2006)
24. Kapron, B.M., Kempe, D., King, V., Saia, J., Sanwalani, V.: Fast asynchronous byzantine agreement and leader election with full information. In: SODA, pp. 1038–1047 (2008)
25. King, V., Saia, J., Sanwalani, V., Vee, E.: Scalable leader election. In: SODA, pp. 990–999 (2006)
26. King, V., Saia, J.: Fast, scalable byzantine agreement in the full information model with a nonadaptive adversary. In: Keidar, I. (ed.) DISC 2009. LNCS, vol. 5805. Springer, Heidelberg (2009)
27. Gilbert, S., Kowalski, D.: Distributed agreement with optimal communication complexity. In: SODA (2010)
28. Alistarh, D., Gilbert, S., Guerraoui, R., Zadimoghaddam, M.: How efficient can gossip be? (technical report), `https://infoscience.epfl.ch/record/148544`
29. Dubhashi, D., Ranjan, D.: Balls and bins: A study in negative dependence. Random Structures and Algorithms 13, 99–124 (1996)

Efficient Information Exchange in the Random Phone-Call Model*

Petra Berenbrink[1], Jurek Czyzowicz[2], Robert Elsässer[3], and Leszek Gąsieniec[4]

[1] School of Computing Science, Simon Fraser University,
petra@cs.sfu.ca

[2] Department of Computer Science, University of Quebec in Hull,
jurek@uqo.ca

[3] Institute for Computer Science, University of Freiburg,
elsa@informatik.uni-freiburg.de

[4] Department of Computer Science, University of Liverpool,
L.A.Gasieniec@liverpool.ac.uk

Abstract. We consider the *gossiping* problem in the classical *random phone-call model* introduced by Demers et. al. ([6]). We are given a complete graph, in which every node has an initial message to be disseminated to all other nodes. In each step every node is allowed to establish a communication channel with a randomly chosen neighbour. Karp et al. [15] proved that it is possible to design a randomized procedure performing $O(n \log \log n)$ transmissions that accomplishes broadcasting in time $O(\log n)$, with probability $1 - n^{-1}$.

In this paper we provide a lower bound argument that proves $\Omega(n \log n)$ message complexity for any $O(\log n)$-time randomized gossiping algorithm, with probability $1-o(1)$. This should be seen as a separation result between broadcasting and gossiping in the random phone-call model.

We study gossiping at the two opposite points of the time and message complexity trade-off. We show that one can perform gossiping based on exchange of $O(n \cdot \log n / \log \log n)$ messages in time $O(\log^2 n / \log \log n)$, and based on exchange of $O(n \log \log n)$ messages with the time complexity $O(\sqrt{n})$. Both results hold wit probability $1 - n^{-1}$.

Finally, we consider a model in which each node is allowed to store a small set of neighbours participating in its earlier transmissions. We show that in this model randomized gossiping based on exchange of $O(n \log \log n)$ messages can be obtained in time $O(\log n)$, with probability $1 - n^{-1}$.

1 Introduction

The two most fundamental problems in information dissemination are *broadcasting* also known as *one-to-all communication* and *gossiping* very often referred to as *total information exchange*. In broadcasting, the goal is to distribute a portion

---

* The third author was partially supported by the German Research Foundation under contract EL 399/2-1.

S. Abramsky et al. (Eds.): ICALP 2010, Part II, LNCS 6199, pp. 127–138, 2010.

of information – *the broadcast message* – from a distinguished source node to all other nodes in the network. The gossiping task, however, is more complex. Each node is expected to send its message to every other node in the network. Efficient gossiping methods are applied in routing, spreading updates in networked databases and multicasting, see, e.g., [13,14]. Moreover, communication methods developed for gossiping provide valid solutions to other central problems in distributed computing including *leader election* and *consensus*.

In this paper we consider gossiping in the random phone-call model for complete graphs. Our goal is to develop time efficient algorithms characterized by small communication complexity. We assume that the messages received by a node (and its initial message) can be combined together and subsequently transmitted as a single message. This assumption is one of the two fundamental standards adopted in numerous gossiping algorithms designed for specific networks when the main emphasis was on the time complexity of the solution, see, e.g., [14] (the other standard assumes counting the number of initial, atomic messages transmitted). Once this *cumulative* message is transmitted through an edge, it is only counted once. Then, the number of message transmissions in one step is usually bounded by the number of used channels, and thus, we also have to reduce the number of these channels to save on communication.

The *random phone-call model* was introduced in the seminal paper [6] and later popularised in [15]. The network nodes work in synchronized steps, and during each step, every node v can establish a communication channel between itself and a randomly chosen neighbour w. This channel can be used for bi-directional communication, meaning that v can send a message to w and vice versa. In the case of push transmissions [6] the nodes establishing communication channels upload their messages to their respective neighbours. In the case of pull transmissions, nodes establishing communication channels download messages from their neighbours. The nodes are allowed to transmit over several incoming channels simultaneously. The major obstacle in the random phone-call model is that nodes do not remember with which other nodes they established communication channels in the past.

1.1 Previous Work

Broadcast versus gossiping in the deterministic phone-call model. In [5] Czumaj *et al.* study trade-offs between the time of gossiping and the number of transmissions in the telephone model. They also analyze dependence of the gossiping time on the total number of communication channels used by the algorithm. In particular they point out the difference between broadcasting and gossiping in the considered model. Note that Grigni and Peleg showed in [12] that if n is a power of 2 the optimal $\log n-$time broadcasting forces use of at least $\Omega(n \log n)$ communication channels. In contrast, if $\log n + 1$ rounds are available there exists an efficient solution based on the use of $O(n)$ communication channels. In case of gossiping, however, Czumaj et al. [5] proved that, for arbitrary constant c, any gossiping procedure with the time complexity $\log n + c$ must open a super-linear number of communication channels.

Broadcast in the random phone-call model. The phone-call model was introduced in [6]. The authors present a push algorithm that uses $\Theta(\log n)$ time and $\Theta(n \log n)$ message transmissions. For complete graphs of size n, Frieze and Grimmett [11] presented an algorithm that broadcasts in time $\log_2(n) + \ln(n) + o(\log n)$ with a probability of $1 - o(1)$. Later, Pittel [16] showed that (with probability $1 - o(1)$) it is possible to broadcast a message in time $\log_2(n) + \ln(n) + f(n)$ [16], where $f(n)$ can be any slow growing function. In [10], Feige et al. determine asymptotically optimal upper bounds for the running time of the push algorithm in $G(n, p)$ graphs (the traditional Erdös-Rényi random graphs, bounded degree graphs, and Hypercubes.

Karp et al. [15] present a push and pull algorithm which reduces the total number of transmissions to $O(n \log \log n)$, with probability $1 - n^{-1}$, and show that this result is asymptotically optimal. For sparser graphs it is not possible to stay within $O(n \log \log n)$ message transmissions together with a broadcast time of $O(\log n)$ in this phone-call model, not even for random graphs [9]. However, if each node is allowed to remember a small number of neighbors to which it has communicated in some previous steps, then the number of message transmissions can be reduced to $O(n \log \log n)$, with probability $1 - n^{-1}$ [2,8].

Gossiping in the random phone-call model. In [3] Chen and Pandurangan consider gossip-based algorithms to aggregate information. For their lower bound in the random phone-call model, they assume a scenario which is more restricted than ours, i.e., all nodes have to follow exactly the same rules in each step. The decision if a node sends a message to its communication partner does not depend on the partner's address nor on the knowledge acquired in the previous rounds. Consequently, the distribution of messages in the network is random in each step in the sense that the probability of having one of k copies of a message is the same for all nodes, and the distribution of different messages is uncorrelated. For this model, the authors of [3] show a lower bound of $\Omega(n \log n)$ on the message complexity of any gossiping algorithm, and this bound holds regardless of the running time of the algorithm. Note that in our model there is an easy $O(n)$ time gossiping algorithm that produces $O(n \log \log n)$ message transmissions.

Another recent study of randomized gossiping can be found in the context of resilient information exchange in [1]. They propose an algorithm with the optimal $O(n)$ message complexity that tolerates oblivious faults. In the case of adaptive failures they present another gossiping procedure with the message complexity $O(n \log^3 n)$. Note, however, that the model of communication adopted in [1] assumes that every process involved in exchanging information is allowed to contact multiple processes at any round as well as to maintain open connections over multiple rounds.

1.2 The Model

In this paper we use a complete graph with n nodes as underlying communication model (cf. [15]). We adopt the random phone-call model from [15] to our scenario in which we assume that every node has an estimation of n which is accurate to within a constant factor. We also assume that all nodes have access to a global clock, and that they work synchronously. In every step each node is allowed to open a channel to a randomly chosen neighbour. If node v opened a channel to node w both nodes can use the channel for a transmission. The channel is called *incoming* channel for w and *outgoing* channel for v. In the last part of the paper, in order to obtain more efficient gossiping we equip nodes with extra constant size mmemory to allow them to reuse the channels opened in previous steps. We assume that the node has to close a channel from a previous round if it decides to open a new channel. Hence, every node has at most one channel opened by itself at a time. If v sends a message to w the transmission is called *push* transmission, otherwise, when w sends a message to v, it is called *pull transmission*.

We assume that in the beginning node v stores message $m_v(0)$. These messages are called original messages. A node that received some messages in step $t-1$ combines these messages and calculates $m_v(t) = \bigcup_{i=0}^{t-1} m_v(i)$, representing the knowledge of node v at time t. To make it clear, by $m_v(t)$ we mean the message that consists of $m_v(0)$ and all messages that were received by node v during the first $t-1$ steps. Unless stated otherwise, this is the message the node will use for any transmission in step t. If it is clear from the context we will omit the time step parameter and use m_v to denote the message of v. In the following we say that the *size* of $m_v(t)$ is the number of nodes whose initial messages are included in $m_v(t)$.

Due to lack of space most of the proofs are not present in this version of the paper.

2 Broadcasting versus Gossiping (Separation Result)

We show our lower bound in a less restricted version of the phone-call model. We assume the algorithm that has global knowledge about the message distribution in the network, i.e. it knows exactly what is the message content of all nodes at each time step. The algorithm is allowed to choose the nodes which open communication channels by using this global information. However, the choice of the nodes to which channels are opened cannot be influenced by the algorithm, i.e., every node is only allowed to choose a neighbour uniformly at random, as required by the random phone-call model. We assume that, whenever a channel is opened between two nodes v_i and v_j, each of these nodes sends all its gossiping messages it knows over the link. For our lower bound we assume that v_i and v_j contain different messages. First we make the following observation.

Theorem 1. *On a complete graph of size n, any gossiping algorithm with running time $O(\log n)$ in the phone-call model requires at least $\Omega(n \log n)$ message transmissions, with probability $1 - o(1)$.*

Proof. (sketch) We assume that there exists a gossiping algorithm with a running time $c' \log n$, where c' is a constant, and that this algorithm produces at most $n \log n / f(n)$ message transmissions, where $f(n)$ is a slow growing function with $\lim_{n\to\infty} f(n) = \infty$. In a first step we conclude that this his algorithm can be transformed into another gossiping algorithm with a running time $c \log n$, where $c > c'$ is a constant, which produces excatly $n/f(n)$ message transmissions in each step.

Let $t \le c \log n$ be an arbitrary time step. We define $\ell_v(t) = |m_v(t)|$ as the *load* of node v in step t. We order our nodes decreasingly using their load at the end of the step i.e. $\ell_{v_1}(t) \le \ell_{v_2}(t) \le \ell_{v_n}(t)$. $B_{[i,j]}(t)$ is defined as the set $\{v_i, v_{i+1}, \cdots v_j\}$. We assume that, whenever a channel is opened between two nodes v_i and v_j in step t, v_i adds $\ell_j(t)$ to $\ell_i(t)$ and vice-versa. Hence, we assume that both nodes store different messages. The sum $\ell(t) = \sum_{i=1}^{n} \ell_i(t)$ is called the *total load* of the graph at time t. At the end of gossiping the total load has to be n^2.

To analyze the transformed algorithm we show the following two invariants by induction. With a probability of $1 - O(\log^{-2} n)$ we have for all $1 \le t \le c \log n$

1. $\ell(t+1) \le (1 + \epsilon + o(1)) \cdot \ell(t)$.
2. $\sum_{v_i \in B_{[1,n/(2^\phi f(n))]}} \ell_i(t+1) \le (\frac{1+\delta}{2})^\phi \cdot \epsilon \cdot \ell(t+1)$ for any integer ϕ with $0 \le \phi \le \log(n/f(n))$ and $\delta < \epsilon^2$.

This holds regardless of which nodes open these $n/f(n)$ channels. Here, ϵ is a small constant such that $(1 + \epsilon + o(1))^{c \log n} \le \sqrt[8]{n}$. The proof of the invariants is deferred to the full version of this paper.

3 Memoryless Gossiping

We present two efficient gossiping algorithms with either (close to) optimal time complexity $O(\log n)$ or algorithms whose communication complexity is $O(n \log \log n)$.

3.1 Fast Gossiping

The first algorithm consists of four phases where each phase is split into several *rounds*. The algorithm uses the following operations: `open` activates a channel to a randomly chosen neighbour; `push` (M) sends M over the open outgoing channel; `pull` (M) sends message M over all incoming channels; and `close` closes all open channels. We assume that all channels are closed at the end of every round. In the first part of Phase 2 of the algorithm below, a node v stores all incoming messages in a queue q_v. It merges incoming messages and computes m_v as described above. For push transmissions v uses the first message from q_v and deletes it from the queue. To shorten the description of the algorithm we assume that `push` (m_v) opens a channel to a randomly chosen neighbour and uses this channel for a push transmission with m_v. When we say that a node opens a new channel we implicitly assume that the node closes the channel that (possibly) remains open from a former step.

ALGORITHM I

Phase 1

for round $t = 1$ to $5 \log \log n$ **do**
  `open`
  Every node v performs the `push` $(m_v(t))$ operation
  `close`

Phase 2

1: **for** round $r = 1$ to $\log n / \log\log n$ **do**
2: Every node v flips a coin. With a probability of $\ell / \log n$, where ℓ is a large constant, v starts a random walk by performing an `open` and then a `push` $(m_v(t))$ and finally a `close` operation.
3: **for** round $r = 1$ to $6\ell \log n$ **do**
4: At every node v, for each incoming message m', if the message made less than $\log n$ random walk steps it calculates $m'_v = m' \cup m_v$ and stores m'_v at the end of q_v.
5: Every node v calculates its current m_v as usual, incorporating *all* incoming messages.
6: Every node v with a non-empty q_v takes the first message m'_v of q_v and performs an `open`, then a `push` (m'_v) and finally `close` operation.
7: Every node v that contains the end of a random walk becomes active for c steps. All other nodes are inactive.
8: **for** round $r = 1$ to $\ell \log\log n$ **do**
9: Every active node v performs an `open` and then a `push` $(m_v(t))$ and `close` operation.
10: Every node that received a message during the last c steps sets its status to active. Otherwise its status is set to inactive.

Phase 3

1: Every node starts a Broadcast using the algorithm from [15] with $10 \log\log n$ `push` steps and $5 \log\log n$ `pull` steps .

One can show, see Lemma 1, that after the first phase every message $m_v(0)$ is stored in at least $(\log n)^4$ nodes. The second phase alternates between a random walk part (steps 3-7) and a distribution part (steps 8-10). In the random walk part approximately $\ell n / \log n$ random walks of length $\log n$ are initiated. The purpose of these random walks is to collect as many original messages as possible. The random walks end in approximately $\ell n / \log n$ different nodes, and these nodes know a factor of $\log n$ messages more then they did at the beginning of the random walk. Then the distribution part of the phase is used to disseminate these "large" messages so that a constant fraction of the nodes contain one of these messages, see Lemma 3. In Phase 3 we send these messages to all nodes using the broadcast algorithm from [15]. This algorithm can be generalized to an algorithm with the running time $O(\log n \cdot T / \log T)$ and message complexity $O(n \log n / \log T)$, where $T < \log n$.

Analysis of the algorithm. In the following we say that a node stores a *copy* of message $m_v(0)$ at time t if this node received the message from v in an earlier round. A node that initiates a random walk is called *active*. A message that is stored by an active node in step t is called *active* in step t. In the first step of Phase 2 a subset of nodes start random walks by sending their currently held messages to randomly chosen neighbours. In fact random walks can be uniquely identified by those messages. Over the time each random walk will collect and combine more and more messages $m_v(0)$ that are stored in the nodes it passes through. In further stages random walks are identified by combined messages. The proof of the following lemma is deferred to the full version of the paper.

Lemma 1. *At the end of the Phase 1 every original message* $m_v(0)$ *is available in at least* $(\log n)^4$ *copies with a probability of* $1 - n^{-k}/3$*, where* $k \geq 3$ *is a constant* $<< l$.

Phase 2 consists of a **for** loop iterated $c \log n / \log\log n$ times. In the following we will call a single iteration of the loop a *round*. The goal is to have $n/\log n$ copies of each original message at the end of Phase 2. The next lemma shows that with high probability every random walk performs at least $\log n$ steps in lines 3 to 5 of Phase 2. Lemma 3 shows that the number of nodes having a copy of a message increases by a factor of $\log n$ in every round.

Lemma 2. *Assume* $\ell >> k$ *for some constant* k*. Then, with a probability of* $1 - n^{-k+1}$ *all random walks initiated in line 2 of Phase 2 perform* $\log n$ *steps.*

Proof. To show the result we fix a round r $(1 \leq r \leq c \log n / \log\log n)$ and an arbitrary set P of $\log n$ nodes of G, and calculate the number of random walks that will traverse through any node of P.

First we upper bound the number of random walks that are initialized in line 2 of round r. Let $Y_i = 1$ $(1 \leq i \leq n)$ if the i-th node starts a random walk and $Y_i = 0$ otherwise. Then $Y + Y_1 + Y_2 + \cdots + Y_n$ is the expected number of random walks started in round r and $\mathbf{E}[Y] = \ell \cdot n/\log n$. Using standard Chernoff bounds (see [4]) we get

$$\mathbf{Pr}[Y \geq 1.5 \cdot \ell \cdot n/\log n] \leq e^{-0.25/3 \cdot (\ell n)/\log n} \leq \frac{3n^{-k+1}}{2}.$$

To upper bound the number of random walks passing through P we assign a number to the nodes in P. We define random variables $X^t_{i,j}$ with $1 \leq i \leq 1.5 \cdot \ell \cdot n/\log n$, $1 \leq j \leq \log n$ and $1 \leq t \leq \log n$. $X^t_{i,j} = 1$ if the t-th step of the i-th random walk is at the j-th node of P and $X^t_{i,j} = 0$ otherwise. We define

$$X = \sum_{i=1}^{1.5 \cdot \ell \cdot n/\log n} \sum_{j=1}^{\log n} \sum_{t=1}^{\log n} X^t_{i,j}$$

which is the number of random walk steps passing through nodes in P. Then, $\mathbf{Pr}\left[X^t_{i,j} = 1\right] = 1/n$ and

$$\mathbf{E}[X] = \frac{1.5\ell \cdot n}{\log n} \cdot \log n \cdot \log n \cdot \frac{1}{n} = 1.5\ell \cdot \log n.$$

The random variables $X^t_{i,j}$ and $X^t_{i'j'}$ (with $j \neq j'$) are not independent from each other since only one of them can be equal to one. However, they are negatively associated, see [7], and we can still apply Chernoff bounds ([4]). This gives us for $\ell \geq (k+2)/3$

$$\mathbf{Pr}[X \geq 5\ell \log n] \leq \left(\frac{e}{4}\right)^{5\ell \log n} \leq \left(\frac{1}{2}\right)^{3\ell \log n} \leq n^{-(k+2)}.$$

Now we assume that P is the set of nodes that a random walk visits. Since every random walk meets over his whole lifespan with probability $1 - n^{-k-2}$ at most $5\ell \log n - 1$ messages, each walk will be able to perform $\log n$ random walk steps in $6\ell \log n$ many time steps with a probability of $1 - n^{-(k+2)}$. Since we have at most n random walks, this will hold with a probability of $1 - n^{-(k+1)}$ for all random walks initiated in round r.

Lemma 3. *Assume $\ell >> k \geq 8$ for some constant k. At the end of round r $(1 \leq r \leq \log n/\log\log n)$ of Phase 2 every message is contained in at least $\min\{(\log n)^{4+r}, n/\log^3 n\}$ many nodes with a probability of $1 - n^{-k}/3$.*

Proof. (sketch) We prove this result by induction. Fix a message $m_v(0)$. Assume that for $r \geq 1$ every message is available in at least $(\log n)^{(r-1)+4}$ copies at the beginning of round r. (For $r = 1$ this follows directly from Lemma 1). In the following we count how many random walks performed in round r will collect a copy of $m_v(0)$.

We say random walk W *contains* $m_v(0)$ in step t if $m_v(0)$ is contained in the message represented by W. Similar to the proof of Lemma 2 we can show that we have at least $(\ell n)/(2\log n)$ random walks in that round. Every random walk performs at least $\log n$ steps with a probability of $n^{-(k+1)}$ (see Lemma 2). This gives at least $\ell n/2$ random walk steps.

Then, we can show by induction that at the end of line 6 of round r every original message is contained in at least $(\log n)^{(r-1)+4}$ many nodes which are the endpoints of a random walk. Let s be the number of random walks initialized in round r. Let us call these messages $w_1, w_2, \ldots w_s$. In the following we show that every message w_i containing $m_v(0)$ is copied at least $\log n$ times with a probability of n^{-k+1}. Thus we have $\log n \cdot (\log n)^{(r-1)+4} = (\log n)^{r+4}$ copies of $m_v(0)$ at the end of round r.

To show that every message w_i $(1 \leq i \leq s)$ is copied at least $\log n$ times we use that the node v_i containing w_i can be regarded as the root of the tree T_{v_i} with the degree c and the depth $\log\log n$. Consider the sequence of trees $T_{v_1}, T_{v_2}, ...T_{v_s}$. For T_{v_i}, we scan the tree in breadth first search order and count all nodes that did not appear in $T_{v_1}, \ldots T_{v_{i-1}}$ or earlier in T_{v_i}. Then, we can show that, with a probability of n^{-k+2}, we have at least $\log n$ such nodes in every tree. Using the union bound we can show that all original messages will get a factor of $\log n$ additional messages with a probability of $1 - n^{-(k+1)}$.

Combining all arguments, all random walks in round r perform $\log n$ steps with a probability of $1 - n^{k+1}$. With the same probability we can assume that we initiate at least $\ell n/(2\log n)$ random walks. With probability $1 - n^{-(k+1)}$ the random walk part together with the distribution part result in an additional factor of $\log n$ extra messages. Hence, the probability that round r works correctly is $1 - 4n^{-(k+1)}$, and the lemma follows.

Lemma 4. *At the end of Phase 3 of* Algorithm I *all nodes store a copy of every message with a probability of $1 - n^{-2}$.*

Proof. Using Lemma 1 and Lemma 3 we can argue that with a probability of $1 - 2n^{-k}/3$ at the beginning of Phase 3 there are $n/\log^3 n$ copies of every message. From [15] it follows that after $10 \log\log n$ push steps every message is contained in $n/2$ nodes, and it takes $5 \log\log n$ pull steps after which every message is contained in each node, with probability $1 - n^{-2}$.

Theorem 2. *For ℓ large enough,* ALGORITHM I *performs gossiping in time $O(\log^2 n/\log\log n)$ with a probability of $1 - n^{-1}$. Moreover, the algorithm sends $O(n \log n/\log\log n)$ messages.*

Proof. The correctness follows directly from Lemma 4. Phase 1 and Phase 2 both have a running time of $O(\log\log n)$. Phase 2 consists of $O(\log n/\log\log n)$ rounds and each round has the running time $O(\log n)$. Phase 1 uses $O(n \log\log n)$ message transmissions. Phase 2 uses $O(n)$ message transmissions per round and produces in total $O(n \log n/(\log\log n)^2)$ message transmissions. Phase 3 uses $O(n \cdot \log\log n)$ message transmissions.

3.2 Gossiping with Bounded Communication

In this section we note that a modification of ALGORITHM I allows to perform gossiping on the basis of exchange of $O(n \log\log n)$ messages. Unfortunately the time complexity of the algorithm is much higher.

ALGORITHM II

Phase 1

for round $t = 1$ to $5 \log\log n$ **do**
  `open`
  Every node v performs the `push` $(m_v(t))$ operation
  `close`

Phase 2

Every node v flips a coin. With a probability of $1/\sqrt{n}$ it starts a random walk by performing an `open`, then a `push` $(m_v(t))$ and `close` operation.
for round $s = 1$ to $2\sqrt{n}$ **do**
  Every node v does the following for each incoming message m'. If the message made less than $\sqrt{n}$ random walk steps, it calculates $m'_v = m' \cup m_v(t-1)$ and stores m'_v at the end of q_v.
  Every node V calculates its actual m_v as usual, incorporating *all* incoming messages
  Every node v with a non-empty q_v takes the first message m'_v out of q_v and performs an `open`, then a `push` (m'_v), and `close` operation.

Phase 3

Every node that receives a message in the last step of Phase 2 becomes active.
for round $t = 1$ to $\log(\sqrt{n})$ **do**
  Every active node v performs an `open`, then a `push` $(m_v(t))$, and `close` operation.
  Every node that receives a message becomes active.

Phase 4

1: We perform a leader election. The leader starts a random walk and performs an `open` and then a `push` $(m_v(t))$ and `close` operation.
2: **for** round $s = 1$ to $\sqrt{n}$ **do**
3: The node v that received a message during the last round performs an `open` and then a `push` $(m_v(t))$ and `close` operation.

Phase 5

1: The node that corresponds to the end of the random walk starts the broadcast process from [15] (with $\log n + 10 \log\log n$ push steps and $5 \log\log n$ pull steps).

Theorem 3. *Algorithm II performs gossiping in time $O(\sqrt{n})$ with a probability of $1 - n^{-2}$. Moreover, the algorithm sends $O(n \cdot \log\log n)$ messages.*

Proof. (sketch) The proof of this theorem is deferred to the full version of the paper. At the end of Phase 1 every message is contained in $\Theta(\log^4 n)$ nodes and the message size is $\Theta(\log^4 n)$. At the end of Phase 2 every message is collected by at least $(\log n)^4$ random walks. Phase 3 creates at least $\sqrt{n} \log n$ copies of each message $m_v(0)$. Phase 4 initiates one long random walk, which collects a copy of each $m_v(0)$, and broadcasts them in Phase 5 to all nodes of the network.

4 Gossiping with Extra Storage

Here we present an algorithm in the generalized model with extra memory. The algorithm first selects a leader. We assume that leader election can be done with probability $1 - n^{-2}$ in $O(\log n)$ time using $O(n \log\log n)$ message transmissions (the corresponding algorithm is deferred to the full version of the paper). Then, the algorithm constructs a communication tree, rooted in the leader, that contains all nodes. Each node passes its initial message to its parent in the tree and the leader collects all incoming messages. The leader then bundles the received messages and broadcasts them to all nodes of the tree. For simplicity we assume in the following that this algorithm is started at time 0.

The idea of the algorithm below is as follows. In Phase 1, steps 2-7, a node which receives $m_v(0)$ transmits $m_v(0)$ to 3 randomly chosen nodes. The algorithm calculates a *communication tree*. The leader v is the root of the tree. The nodes u_1, u_2 and u_3 that got the messages in rounds 0-2 are the nodes on Level 1 of the tree. The nodes which got the message from u_1, u_2, and u_3 are on Level 2 of the tree, and so on. At the end of the sub-phase the communication tree has depth $\log n + 2 \log\log n$. Note that nodes can appear only on one level of the tree since they only become active if they got the message for the first time. The tree nodes store all edges to their children in the tree.

In Phase 1, steps 8-11, the nodes which are not in the tree try to connect themselves to tree nodes. They will open channels to randomly chosen neighbours and all nodes knowing $m_v(0)$ answer all incoming `pull` requests. Each node which gets the message for the first time will store the corresponding neighbour in the list ℓ_{pl}. The edge leading to this neighbour is now regarded as part of the communication tree and the neighbour is regarded as its predecessor in the tree. In Phase 2 of the algorithm the communication tree is used to forward all original messages to the root.

ALGORITHM III

Phase 1

Perform Leader Election
for round $t = 0$ to 2 **do**
  The leader performs an `open` and then a `push` $(m_v(0))$ and `close` operation.
for round $t = 3$ to $3(\log n + 2\log\log n)$ **do**
  Every node v that received $m_v(0)$ in round i *for the first time* (with $i = 3j + k$ and $k \in \{0, 1, 2\}$) becomes active in round $3(j+1), 3(j+1)+1$ and $3(j+1)+2$.
  Every active node v performs an `open`, then a `push` $(m_v(0))$, and `close` operation.
  Every active node v stores the time steps $3(j+1), 3(j+1)+1$ and $3(j+1)+2$ together with the neighbours it used for the `push` operations in the list ℓ_{ph}.
for round $t = 3(\log n + 2\log\log n) + 1$ to $3\log n + (6+\ell)\log\log n$ **do**
  Every node v that knows $m_v(0)$ performs `pull` $(m_v(0))$ and `close` operation.
  Every node v that does not know $m_v(0)$ performs an `open`, receives eventually $(m_v(0))$, and then performs a `close` operation.
  Every node v that receives $m_v(0)$ for the first time in round t remembers the chosen neighbour together with t in the list ℓ_{pl}.

Phase 2

$t' = 3\log n + (6+\ell)\log\log n$
for round $t = 1$ to $\ell \log\log n$ **do**
  Every node v which received the message in step $t'-t+1$ (for the first time) opens a channel to the corresponding neighbour in ℓ_{pl} and performs a `push` operation with all original messages it has.
$t' = 3\log n + (6+\ell)\log\log n$
for round $t = 1$ to $3\log n + 6\log\log n$ **do**
  Every node v which stores a neighbour with time step $t'-t+1$ in its list ℓ_{ph} opens a channel to that neighbour in ℓ_{ph} and receives the message from that neighbour. The node at the other side performs a `pull` operation with all original messages it has.

Phase 3

The leader broadcasts all original messages using the algorithm of [15].

Theorem 4. *Algorithm III performs gossiping with the running time $O(\log n)$ and produces $O(n \cdot \log\log n)$ message transmissions, with probability $1 - n^{-2}$.*

5 Conclusion and Open Problems

In this paper we considered the gossiping problem in the random phone-call model. First, we provided a lower bound argument that admits $\Omega(n \log n)$ message complexity for any $O(\log n)$-time gossiping algorithm. Further, we studied gossiping at the two points of the time and message complexity trade-off. Finally, we considered a model in which each node is allowed to store a small sequence of its earlier transmissions, and showed that in this model randomized gossiping based on exchange of $O(n \log \log n)$ messages can be obtained in the optimal time $O(\log n)$. These results should be viewed as an important step in better understanding of gossiping in the random phone-call model. The problem, however, remains unexplored in more complex topologies.

References

1. Alistarh, D., Gilbert, S., Guerraoui, R., Zadimoghaddam, M.: How Efficient is Gossip? (On the Message Complexity of Resilient Information Exchange). In: Proc. 37th International Colloquium on Automata, Languages and Programming, ICALP 2010 (2010)
2. Berenbrink, P., Elsässer, R., Friedetzky, T.: Efficient randomised broadcasting in random regular networks with applications in peer-to-peer systems. In: Proc. 27th ACM Symposium on Principles of Distributed Computing, PODC 2008, pp. 155–164 (2008)
3. Chen, J., Pandurangan, G.: Optimal Gossip-Based Aggregate Computation. In: Proc. of 22nd ACM Symposium on Parallel Algorithms and Architectures, SPAA 2010 (2010)
4. Chernoff, H.: Measure of asymptotic efficiency for tests of a hypothesis based on the sum of observations. Ann. Math. Statist. 23, 493–507 (1952)
5. Czumaj, A., Gąsieniec, L., Pelc, A.: L Gąsieniec, and A. Pelc. Time and cost trade-offs in gossiping. SIAM J. Discrete Mathematics 11(3), 400–413 (1998)
6. Demers, A., Greene, D., Hauser, C., Irish, W., Larson, J., Shenker, S., Sturgis, H., Swinehart, D., Terry, D.: Epidemic Algorithms for Replicated Database Maintenance. In: Proc. 6th ACM Symposium on Principles of Distributed Computing, PODC '87, pp. 1–12 (1987)
7. Dubhashi, D., Ranjan, D.: Balls and Bins: A Study in Negative Dependence. Random Structures and Algorithms 13(2), 99–124 (1998)
8. Elsässer, R., Sauerwald, T.: The power of memory in randomized broadcasting. In: Proc. 19th ACM-SIAM Symposium on Discrete Algorithms, SODA 2008, pp. 290–227 (2008)
9. Elsässer, R.: On the communication complexity of randomized broadcasting in random-like graphs. In: Proc. 18th ACM Symposium on Parallel Algorithms and Architectures, SPAA 2006, pp. 148–157 (2006)
10. Feige, U., Peleg, D., Raghavan, P., Upfal, E.: Randomized broadcast in networks. Random Structures and Algorithms 1(4), 447–460 (1990)
11. Frieze, A., Grimmett, G.: The shortest-path problem for graphs with random arc-lengths. Discrete Applied Mathematics 10, 57–77 (1985)
12. Grigni, M., Peleg, D.: Tight Bounds on Minimum Broadcast Networks. SIAM J. on Discrete Mathematics 4(2), 207–222 (1991)
13. Hedetniemi, S.M., Hedetniemi, S.T., Liestman, A.L.: A survey of gossiping and broadcasting in communication networks. Networks 18(4), 319–349 (1988)
14. Hromkovic, J., Klasing, R., Pelc, A., Ruzicka, P., Unger, W.: Dissemination of Information in Communication Networks - Broadcasting. Gossiping, Leader Election, and Fault-Tolerance. Springer, Heidelberg (2005)
15. Karp, R., Schindelhauer, C., Shenker, S., Vöcking, B.: Randomized rumor spreading. In: Proc. 41st Annual Symposium on Foundations of Computer Science, FOCS 2000, pp. 565–574 (2000)
16. Pittel, B.: Linear Probing: The Probable Largest Search Time Grows Logarithmically with the Number of Records. J. Algorithms 8(2), 236–249 (1987)

An $O(\log n)$-Competitive Online Centralized Randomized Packet-Routing Algorithm for Lines

Guy Even[1] and Moti Medina[1]

School of Electrical Engineering, Tel-Aviv Univ., Tel-Aviv 69978, Israel
{guy,medinamo}@eng.tau.ac.il

Abstract. We study the problem of online packet routing in dynamic store-and-forward directed line networks. We present a centralized randomized online algorithm that achieves a throughput that is $O(\log n)$-competitive, where n denotes the number of nodes. Our algorithm is applicable to all values of buffer sizes and communication link capacities. In particular, it holds also for unit buffers.

This algorithm improves the best previous $O(\log^2 n)$-competitive ratio of [6] and considers links with unit capacities.

1 Introduction

Large scale communication networks partition the messages into packets so that high bandwidth links can support multiple sessions simultaneously. Packet routing is used by the Internet as well as telephony networks and cellular networks. Thus, the development of algorithms that can route packets between different pairs of nodes is a fundamental problem in networks. In a typical setting, requests for routing packets arrive over time, thus calling for the development of online packet routing algorithms. The holy grail of packet routing is to develop online distributed algorithms whose performance is competitive with respect to multiple criteria, such as: throughput (i.e., deliver as many packets as possible), delay (i.e., guarantee arrival of packets on time), stability (e.g., constant rate, avoid buffer overflow) , fairness (i.e., fair sharing of resources among users), etc. From a theoretical point of view, there is still a huge gap between known lower bounds and upper bounds for packet routing even over very simple graphs (e.g, directed paths) with respect to centralized algorithms.

We follow the Competitive Network Throughput Model introduced by [2] for dynamic store-and-forward packet networks. Nodes in packet networks are switches with local memories, called buffers. An incoming packet is either forwarded to a neighbor switch or stored in the buffer. The resources of a packet network are specified by two parameters: the capacity of links and the size of buffers. The capacity of a link is an upper bound on the number of packets that can be transmitted in a time step along the link. The buffer size is the maximum number of packets that the switch can store between time steps.

Previous Work. Algorithms for packet routing in dynamic store-and-forward networks have been studied extensively both in theory and in practice. Our work is based on a line of research initiated by [2]. In [2], a lower bound of $\Omega(\sqrt{n})$ was proved for the greedy algorithm on directed lines if the buffer size B is at least two. For the case

S. Abramsky et al. (Eds.): ICALP 2010, Part II, LNCS 6199, pp. 139–150, 2010.

$B = 1$ (in a slightly different model), an $\Omega(n)$ lower bound for any deterministic algorithm was proved by [6,3]. Both [6] and [3] developed, among other things, online randomized centralized algorithms for directed paths with $B > 1$. In [3] an $O(\log^3 n)$-competitive algorithm was presented if the buffer size B is at least 2. For the case $B = 1$, they presented a randomized $\tilde{O}(\sqrt{n})$-competitive distributed algorithm. In [6], an $O(\log^2 n)$-competitive algorithm was presented for the case $B \geq 2$. This algorithm may work also with a FIFO policy for managing the buffers.

Our result. In this paper we present a centralized online randomized packet routing algorithm for maximizing throughput in directed paths (or lines). Our algorithm is non-preemptive; rejection is determined upon arrival of a packet. We consider two parameters: B - the buffer size, and c - the capacity of the links between nodes. Our algorithm is centralized and randomized and achieves an $O(\log n)$-competitive ratio. This algorithm improves over previous algorithms in three ways: (I) The competitive ratio is $O(\log n)$ compared to the best previous competitive ratio of $O(\log^2 n)$. (II) Our algorithm works also for buffers of size $B = 1$. (III) We consider also the parameter c of the capacity of the links ([6,3] considered only the case $c = 1$). Due to space limitations all proofs are omitted and can be found in the full version.

Techniques. Following [5,1,6,11], we apply a space-time transformation to reduce the problem of packet routing to path packing problem. Unlike [6], we do not consider fractional online multi-commodity flows. Instead, we apply the primal-dual framework of [8] to obtain an integral packing of paths. This allows us to avoid the issue of rounding a fractional packing as done in [6].

A second technique we use is an infinite tiling of the plane. This tiling serves multiple purposes. We employ tiling to define a simple classification of packet requests based on locality. Namely, packets that can be routed within a tile and packets that cannot. Since the tiles are disjoint and small, routing packets within tiles is straightforward with a $O(\log n)$-competitive ratio. Packet requests across tiles are handled differently. Tiling induces a sketch graph over the tiles and one can limit routing to linear paths in the sketch graph.

A third technique is the online translation of paths in the sketch graph to paths in the space-time graph. Tiles are defined so that edges in the sketch graph have $\Omega(\log n)$ capacity. The online translation of sketch paths to network paths works as long as the sketch edges are lightly loaded (i.e., the load is a constant fraction of the capacity). Loads of sketch graph edges are made light, w.h.p., by tossing a biased coin.

2 Problem Definition

2.1 Store-and-Forward Packet Networks

We consider a synchronous store-and-forward packet network [2,3,6]. The network is a directed graph $G = (V, E)$. Each edge has a capacity $c(e)$ that specifies the number of packets that can be transmitted along the edge in one time step. Each node has a local buffer of size B that can store at most B packets. Each node has a local input through which multiple packets may be input in each time step. In the general setting, no assumptions are made on the relation between B, $c(e)$, and the number of packets input locally to a node. The network operates in a synchronous fashion with a delay of one time step for communication. This means that a packet sent in time step t arrives to its destination in time step $t + 1$.

Each packet is specified by a triple $r_i = (a_i, b_i, t_i)$, where $a_i \in V$ is the source node of the packet, $b_i \in V$ is the destination node, and $t_i \in \mathbb{N}$ is the time step in which the packet is input to a_i. Since we consider an online setting, no information is known about a packet r_i before time t_i. We consider packet routing without deadlines, namely, the algorithm is credited each time a packet arrives to its destination, regardless of the time it took it to travel.

In each time step, a node v considers the packets arriving via the local input, the packets arriving from incoming edges, and the packets stored in the buffer. Packets destined to node v are removed from the network (this is considered a success and no further routing of the packet is required). As for the other packets, the node determines which packets are sent along outgoing edges (i.e., forwarded), which packets are stored in the buffer, and which packets are dropped/rejected.

We use the following terminology. A packet is *injected* if it is locally input to a node and the nodes decides to store it or to forward it. A packet is *rejected* if it is locally input to a node and the node decides not to inject it. A packet is *dropped* if it was injected and a node decides not to store it or to forward it.

The task of *admission control* is to determine which packets are injected and which are rejected. An algorithm that drops packets is a *preemptive algorithm*; if an algorithm does not drop packets, then it is a *non-preemptive algorithm*.

2.2 Line Networks

A line network with n nodes is a directed path $G = (V, E)$. The vertices are denoted by $V = \{v_0, v_1, \ldots, v_{n-1}\}$. The edges are denoted by $E = \{(v_i, v_{i+1}) : 0 \le i \le n-2\}$. In a line network, the source a_i and the destination b_i of each packet satisfy $a_i < b_i$.

We assume that (i) all edges have identical capacities, denoted by c, and (ii) all nodes have the same buffer size, denoted by B.

2.3 Online Maximum Throughput in Line Networks

The *throughput* of a routing algorithm is the number of packets that are delivered to their destination. We consider the problem of maximizing the throughput of an online centralized randomized packet-routing algorithm.

Let Alg be a randomized online algorithm. Algorithm *Alg* is *ρ-competitive* with respect to an oblivious adversary if for every input sequence σ, $E(Alg) \ge \rho \cdot OPT(\sigma)$, where the expected value is over the random choices made by *Alg* [7].

3 Preliminaries

3.1 Space-Time Transformation

A *space-time transformation* is a method to map traffic in a directed graph over time into a directed acyclic graph. Consider a directed $G = (V, E)$ with edge capacities $c(e)$

and buffer size B. The space-time transformation of G is the acyclic directed graph $G^{st} = (V^{st}, E^{st})$ with edge capacities $c^{st}(e)$, where: (i) $V^{st} \triangleq V \times \mathbb{N}$. (ii) $E^{st} \triangleq E_0 \cup E_1$ where $E_0 \triangleq \{(u,t) \to (v,t+1) : (u,v) \in E, t \in \mathbb{N}\}$ and $E_1 \triangleq \{(u,t) \to (u,t+1) : u \in V, t \in \mathbb{N}\}$. (iii) If $(u,v) \in E$ then $c^{st}((u,t) \to (v,t+1)) \triangleq c(u,v)$. All edges in E_1 have capacity B.

For example, a packet that is stored in node i's buffer at time slot j for ℓ time slots is translated to a horizontal path that starts in the jth column, has length ℓ and is in the ith row of G^{st}. A packet that is delivered from node i to node $i+1$ at time j is translated to the diagonal edge $(i,j) \to (i+1, j+1)$ in G^{st}.

Space-time graphs have been used previously to model packet routing [5,1,6,11]. The idea is to map a route to a path in G^{st}. The space-time graph G^{st} of a line network $G = (V, E)$ is depicted in Fig. 1a. The rows correspond to vertices in V, and the columns correspond to time steps. Note that G^{st} has n rows and an infinite number of columns. The additional nodes per row are called sink-nodes, and are described below.

Adding sink nodes. Since we consider requests without deadlines, a request $r_i = (a_i, b_i, t_i)$ is routed along a path in G^{st} from (a_i, t_i) to a node in row b_i. Azar and Zachut [6] model the delivery of r_i to its destination by adding sink nodes as follows. For each node $v \in V$, add a sink node $\hat{v}$. Connect each vertex $(v,t) \in V^{st}$ to $\hat{v}$ by an edge of unbounded capacity. Thus, the path for r_i must end in $\hat{b}_i$.

3.2 Tiling

The term *tiling* refers to a partitioning of the nodes V^{st} of the space-time graph G^{st} into finite sets. The tilings we consider are obtained by an infinite packing of integral grid points by parallelograms (see Fig. 1b). Each parallelogram has horizontal length x and height y, and is referred to as a *tile*. We consider only nodes in G^{st}, namely points in the *positive stripe* defined by $\{(j,i) : 0 \leq j \leq n-1, i \geq 0\}$. In the vicinity of the boundaries of the stripe, the parallelograms are clipped. The tiling is specified by two additional parameters $\phi_x \in [0..(x-1)]$ and $\phi_y \in [0..(y-1)]$, called the *phase shifts*. The phase shifts determine the position of the "first" parallelogram; namely, the node (ϕ_y, ϕ_x) is the top left corner of the first parallelogram.

The clipped tiles are removed according to the following rule. Consider the top left quadrant (NW-quadrant, for north-west) of a tile. If the NW-quadrant does not intersect the positive stripe, then the tile is removed. Otherwise, it is clipped, as depicted in Fig. 1b.

3.3 The Sketch Graph

Consider a tiling $\mathcal{T}$ with a set T of tiles. A tiling defines a mapping $\tau : V^{st} \to T$ where $\tau(v)$ is the tile in T that contains the point v. The *sketch graph* is the graph $S = (T, E_S)$ induced by G^{st} and τ as follows (see Fig. 1c). A pair of tiles $(\hat{u}, \hat{v})$ is an edge in E_S if $\tau^{-1}(\hat{u}) \times \tau^{-1}(\hat{v})$ contains an edge in E^{st}. The capacity $\hat{c}(\hat{u}, \hat{v})$ is defined by $\sum\{c(e) : e \in E^{st} \cap (\tau^{-1}(\hat{u}) \times \tau^{-1}(\hat{v}))\}$, except for the horizontal edges in the bottom row that are assigned a capacity of $By/2$.

Proposition 1. *The capacities of the sketch edges satisfy the following property: (i) the capacity of each horizontal edge is in the range $(yB/2, yB]$, and (ii) the capacity of each diagonal edge is in the range $(xc/2, xc]$.*

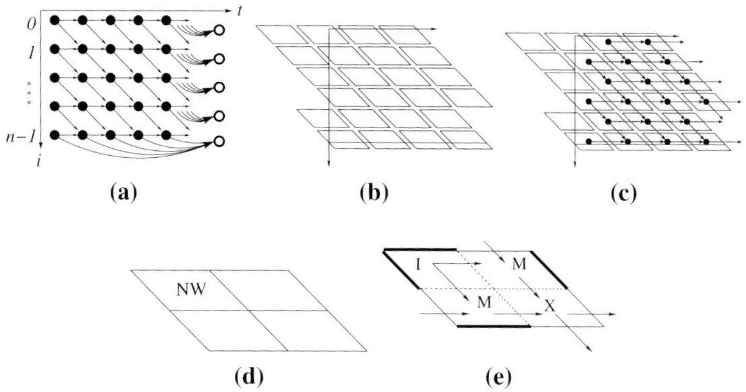

Fig. 1. (a) The space-time graph G^{st}. The x-axis is the (infinite) time axis and the y-axis is the (finite) node axis. Note the sink-nodes on the right, each of which is connected to every node in its row. (b) Tiling of the plane by parallelograms. Only the shaded tiles are nodes of the sketch graph. The parallelograms along the borders of the positive stripe are either removed or clipped. (c) The sketch graph over the tiles. (d) Partitioning of a tile into quadrants. (e) Allowed routes in parallelogram quadrants. Paths may not cross the thick lines.

3.4 Online Integral Packing of Paths

We consider the problem of integrally packing paths by a centralized online algorithm. The setting is taken from [8,9] who described a version of the setting in [4] in which demands are at most a logarithmic fraction of the edge capacities. Consider a graph $G = (V, E)$ with edge capacities $c(e)$. The adversary introduces a sequence of connection requests $\{r_i\}_i$, where each request is a source-destination pair (a_i, b_i). The online packing algorithm must either return a path p_i from a_i to b_i or reject the request. Since we are interested in maximizing throughput, the goal is to route as many requests as possible while respecting capacity constraints.

Consider a sequence $R = \{r_i\}_{i\in I}$ of requests. A sequence $P = \{p_i\}_{i\in J}$ is a (partial) *routing* with respect to R if $J \subseteq I$ and each path p_i (for $i \in J$) connects the source-destination pair r_i. The *load* of an edge e induced by a routing P is the ratio $|\{p_j : j \in J, e \in p_j\}|/c(e)$. A routing P with respect to R is called a *packing* if the load of each edge is at most 1. The *throughput* of a packing $P = \{p_i\}_{i\in J}$ is simply $|J|$.

A packing algorithm is said to be (α, β)-*competitive* if it computes a routing P with respect to the set of requests that satisfies: (i) the throughput of P is at least α times the maximum throughput over all packings, and (ii) the load of each edge is at most β.

A *fractional* packing is a multi-commodity flow. Namely, a request is a demand of a unit flow from the source to the destination. Each demand can be served by a combination of fractions of flows along paths. An optimal offline fractional packing can be computed by solving a linear program. Obviously, the throughput of an optimal fractional packing is an upper bound on the throughput of an optimal integral packing.

A reduction of (fractional) packet routing to (fractional) packing of paths was presented in [6]. In this reduction, a packet request $r_i{=}(a_i, b_i, t_i)$ is reduced to a connection request $r_i^{st} \triangleq ((a_i, t_i), \hat{b}_i)$ in the space-time graph G^{st}. This reduction preserves the (fractional) throughput.

It is important to observe that if multiple requests arrive simultaneously to the same node, then the optimal routing could inject at most $c + B$ packets among these packets. Since this limitation is imposed on the optimal solution, the path packing algorithm can abide this limitation as well without decreasing its competitiveness, i.e., by choosing the closest $c + B$ packets to the source node, as formalized in the following proposition.

Proposition 2. *W.l.o.g. each node accepts at most the closest $c + B$ requests at each time step.*

The proof of the following theorem is based on techniques from [4,8]. We refer to the online algorithm for online integral path packing by IPP.

Let $c_{\max} \triangleq \max_{e:c(e)<\infty} c(e)$ and let $c_{\min} \triangleq \min_{e:c(e)>0} c(e)$.

Theorem 1. *Consider an infinite graph with edge capacities such that $\frac{c_{\max}}{c_{\min}} \leq 4$. Consider an online path packing problem in which path lengths are bounded by $p_{\max}$. Assume that there is an oracle, that given edge weights and a connection request, finds a lightest path from the source to the destination among the paths of length at most $p_{\max}$. Then, there exists an $(O(1), O(\log p_{\max}))$-competitive online integral path packing algorithm. Moreover, the throughput is at least a constant fraction of the the maximum throughput over all fractional packings.*

Notation. Given a set R of packet requests, let $\text{OPT}(R)$ denote the maximum (offline) throughput. Let $\text{OPT}_f(R)$ denote the maximum fractional throughput.

4 Algorithm: Preprocessing

Tiling parameters. The parameters of the line network are: n nodes, buffer size B in each node, and link capacity c. We assume that $B, c \in [1, \log n]$. The parameters x, y of the tiling are defined as follows.

Definition 1. *(i) If $B \cdot c < \log n$, then $x = 2\lceil(\log n)/c\rceil$ and $y = 2 \cdot \lceil(\log n)/B\rceil$.*
(ii) If $B \cdot c \geq \log n$, then $x = 2B$ and $y = 2c$.

Proposition 3. *The choice of the tiling parameters implies the following:*

1. *$x + y = O(\log n)$.*
2. *The capacity of each sketch edge is at least $\log n$.*
3. *Sketch edges whose capacity is bounded have capacities in the interval $(\min\{xc/2, yB/2\}, \max\{xc, yB\})$. Thus the ratio between the maximum and the minimum capacity is bounded by 4.*

To simplify the presentation, we assume that $xc = yB$ and that the capacity of all sketch edges of bounded capacity equals xc (this is true up to a constant factor, as stated in Proposition 3).

Classification of requests. We partition each parallelogram into four "quadrants" as depicted Fig. 1d.

Note that side lengths x and y are even, so the North-West quadrant (NW-quadrant) of a tile is well defined.

The tiling defines the following classification of the requests. Let $Q_{x,y,\phi_x,\phi_y} \triangleq \{(a_i, t_i) \in \mathbb{N}^2 : (a_i, t_i) \text{ is in the NW-quadrant of the tile } \tau(a_i, t_i)\}$.

Definition 2. *Let $R^+ \subseteq R$ denote subset of requests such that $R^+ \triangleq \{r_i \in R : (a_i, t_i) \in Q_{x,y,\phi_x,\phi_y}\}$.*

The subset R^+ is further partitioned into two subsets *Far* and *Near*, defined by: *Near* $\triangleq \{r_i \in R^+ : \tau(a_i, t_i) = \tau(b_i, t_i)\}$ and *Far* $\triangleq R^+ \setminus$ *Near*.

A request $r_i \in$ *Far* must be routed along a path that crosses tiles. On the other hand, a request $r_i \in$ *Near* may be routed within a tile, although an optimal routing might route r_i along a path that crosses tiles.

Proposition 4. *If the phase shifts ϕ_x and ϕ_y are chosen independently and uniformly at random, then $E(\text{OPT}(R^+)) \geq \frac{1}{4} \cdot \text{OPT}(R)$. By a reverse Markov inequality, $\Pr\left[\text{OPT}(R^+) \geq \frac{1}{8} \cdot \text{OPT}(R)\right] \geq \frac{1}{7}$.*

5 Algorithm for Requests in *Far*

In this section we present an online algorithm for the requests in the subset *Far*.

5.1 Description of the *Far*-Algorithm

Let S denote the sketch graph induced by G^{st} and the tiling. Define $p_{\max}(\text{IPP})$ as follows:

$$p_{\max}(\text{IPP}) \triangleq \begin{cases} 7n & \text{if } B \cdot c > \log n, \\ 2 \cdot (n-1) \cdot (1 + B/c) & \text{otherwise.} \end{cases}$$

The input to the algorithm is a sequence of requests in *Far*. For simplicity we assume that at most one request arrives simultaneously at every node. The case of multiple simultaneous requests from the same node is discussed later.

Upon arrival of a request $r_i = (a_i, b_i, t_i)$, the algorithm proceeds as follows:

1. Call the online integral path packing algorithm IPP with the request $r_i^S \triangleq (\tau(a_i, t_i), \hat{b}_i)$ over the sketch graph S with path lengths at most $p_{\max}(\text{IPP})$. If r_i^S is rejected, then **reject** r_i. Otherwise, let $\hat{p}_i$ denote the the path computed by IPP.
2. Toss a biased 0-1 coin X_i such that $\Pr(X_i = 1) = p$. If $X_i = 0$, then **reject** r_i.
3. If the addition of $\hat{p}_i$ causes the load of any sketch edge to be at least $1/4$, then **reject** r_i.
4. Apply I-routing for r_i. If I-routing fails, then **reject** r_i. Otherwise, **inject** r_i with the sketch path $\hat{p}_i$.

We now elaborate on the steps of the algorithm. (1) The IPP algorithm computes an integral packing of paths under the constraint that the length of a path is at most $p_{\max}(\text{IPP})$. In Proposition 1, we show that this constraint reduces the optimal fractional throughput by a factor of at most two. Algorithm IPP remembers all accepted requests, even those that are rejected in subsequent steps. By Theorem 1, the computed paths constitute an $(O(1), k)$-competitive packing, for $k = O(\log n)$. The path oracle for the IPP algorithm finds a lightest path among the paths that contain at most $p_{\max}(\text{IPP})$ edges. (2) The probability p is set to $\frac{1}{\Theta(k)}$. (3) We maintain the invariant that after line 3, the load of every sketch edge is at most $1/4$. (4) I-routing deals with routing the request out of the initial NW-quadrant and is described in Sect. 5.2. We point out that the path p_i in G^{st} for the injected packet r_i can be computed before injection. To simplify the presentation, only its prefix is computed by I-routing. The rest of the path is computed based on the sketch path $\hat{p}_i$. This computation is performed locally on-the-fly by M- and X-routing (described in Sect. 5.2).

The Case of Multiple Simultaneous Requests From the Same Node. Upon arrival of requests $\{r_i\}_i = \{(a, b_i, t_i)\}_i$ to node $a \in E^{st}$, the algorithm first chooses the closest $c + B$ requests, rejects the rest, and then calls the online integral packing algorithm IPP on each of these chosen requests. Proposition 2 implies that limitation does not decrease the competitiveness of IPP.

Notation. We define a chain subsets of requests $R_{\text{inj}+} \subseteq R_{\text{inj}} \subseteq R_{\text{IPP}+} \subseteq R_{\text{IPP}}$, as follows. R_{IPP} is the subset of requests accepted by the IPP algorithm in line 1. $R_{\text{IPP}+} \subseteq R_{\text{IPP}}$ is the subset of requests for which $X_i = 1$. $R_{\text{inj}} \subseteq R_{\text{IPP}+}$ is the subset of requests whose addition did not cause a sketch edge to be at least $1/4$ loaded. $R_{\text{inj}+} \subseteq R_{\text{inj}}$ is the subset of requests that were successfully routed by I-routing.

5.2 Detailed Routing

The IPP Algorithm computes a sketch path $\hat{p}_i$. If we wish to route the packet, we need to compute a path p in G^{st}. We refer to this path as the *detailed path.* Let p_i denote the detailed path of a request $r_i \in R_{\text{inj}+}$. The packing $\{p_j\}_{\{j: r_j \in R_{\text{inj}+}\}}$ satisfies the following invariants (see Fig. 1e).

1. The source of p_j is in the NW-quadrant of a parallelogram.
2. The prefix of p_j till it exits the NW-quadrant of its first tile is without bends.
3. For every tile, p_j enters the tile only through the right half of the north side of the tile or the bottom half of the west side.
4. For every tile, p_j exits the tile only through the right half of the south side of the tile or the bottom half of the east side.
5. The load of every edge in G^{st} is at most one.

We decompose each tile into four quadrants and apply one of three detailed algorithms $(I, M$ or $X)$ to each quadrant as depicted in Fig. 1e.

I-Routing. I-routing deals with routing paths that start in the NW-quadrant of a tile. The goal is simply to exit the NW-quadrant either from its east side or its south side. I-routing considers only straight paths without bends.

By Proposition 2, at most $B + c$ requests are accepted at each node of G^{st} by Algorithm IPP. The set of simultaneous requests that arrive to the same node is ordered arbitrarily.

We consider each NW-quadrant as a three dimensional cube of dimensions $\frac{y}{2} \times \frac{x}{2} \times (B + c)$. The ith request that arrives to node (v, t) is represented by node (v, t, i) in the cube. We refer to each copy of the quadrant in the cube as a *plane*. The ith plane is the set of nodes (v, t, i) in the cube. I-routing deals with each $\frac{y}{2} \times \frac{x}{2}$ plane separately,

Let r denote the ith request to node (v, t). I-routing routes r either horizontally or diagonally according to the following cases:

1. If $1 \leq i \leq B$, then I-routing checks whether the horizontal path to the east side of the NW-quadrant is free in the ith plane. If it is free, then I-routing routes r and marks this horizontal path as occupied. If it is not free, then r is rejected.
2. If $B < i \leq B + c$, then I-routing checks whether the diagonal straight path to the south side of the NW-quadrant is free in the ith plane. If it is free, then I-routing routes r and marks this diagonal path as occupied. If it is not free, then r is rejected.

Finally, we need to limit the number of paths that emanate from each side of the NW-quadrant by $c^S/4$, where c^S denotes the capacity of the sketch edges to the neighboring parallelograms (i.e., not sink-nodes). Thus after $c^S/4$ requests have been successfully I-routed out of the NW-quadrant, all subsequent requests from this NW-quadrants fail.

Note that I-routing is computed before the packet is injected and does not preempt packets since precedence is given to existing paths.

M-routing. M-routing deals with routing paths that enter through two adjacent sides of a tile quadrant and exit through a third side. We show that M-routing is always successful.

Suppose that paths enter through the north and west sides of the quadrant, and should be routed to the south side of the quadrant. The detailed paths of north-to-south paths are simply diagonal without bends. The detailed paths of west-to-south paths are obtained by traveling eastward until a bend can be made, namely, the diagonal path to the south side is not saturated. Since both path types contain at most $c^S/4$ paths, and since $c^S/2$ paths can cross the south side of the quadrant, M-routing never fails.

X-routing. X-routing deals with routing paths that enter through two adjacent sides of a tile quadrant and exit through a the opposite sides. X-routing is implemented by super-positioning two instances of M-routing.

In X-routing, paths enter through the north and west sides, and should be routed either to the east or south sides. We apply M-routing for east-bound paths and M-routing for south-bound paths. Obviously, north-south paths and west-east paths are successful. On the other hand, if a north-east path intersects a west-south path, then they both "bend" and gain precedence over their route. Since there are at most $c^S/4$ east-bound paths, each north-east path is successfully routed. The same holds for west-south paths. Thus, X-routing is always successful.

Routing in The Bottom Row. First, note that no requests in *Far* start in the bottom row. Second, since the destination row in G^{st} is included in the last row of tiles, there are no east-west routes. Therefore, in the bottom row we only have incoming paths from the north side whose destination is within the tile. Thus, incoming paths from the north simply continue diagonally until they reach their destination.

5.3 Analysis

Consider a sequence R of requests for delivering packets in the line network G. We regard this sequence also as a sequence of requests for paths in the space-time graph G^{st}. The maximum throughput for the delivery of packets is upper bounded by the throughput of an optimal fractional path packing with respect to R. We now prove that the throughput of an optimal fractional path packing does not decrease by much if path lengths are bounded.

Formally, let $\text{OPT}_f(R|p_{\max})$ denote the throughput of an optimal fractional path packing with respect to R under the constraint that path lengths are at most $p_{\max}$. The following lemma shows that bounding path lengths to be at most $O(nB)$ decreases the fractional throughput by a factor of at most 2. The lemma extends the lemma from [6] to the case $c > 1$.

Lemma 1 ([6, Claim 4.5]). *Let* $p_{\max} \triangleq 2 \cdot (n-1) \cdot (1 + B/c)$*. Then,* $\text{OPT}_f(R|p_{\max}) \geq \frac{1}{2} \cdot \text{OPT}_f(R)$.

The following proposition justifies the limit of $7n$ on path lengths when the *Far*-Algorithm invokes IPP.

Proposition 5. *If the tile width x is not less than B, then every path p in G^{st} of length at most $2 \cdot (n-1) \cdot (1 + B/c)$ is mapped by τ to a path $\hat{p}$ in the sketch graph S of length at most $7n$.*

The following proposition shows that, in expectation over the biased coin tosses in Line 2, not too many additional paths are rejected due to line 3 in the *Far*-Algorithm.

Lemma 2. $E(|R_{\text{IPP}^+} \setminus R_{inj}|) \leq \frac{1}{4} \cdot |R_{\text{IPP}^+}|$.

The following lemma states that, in expectation, a constant fraction of the requests succeed in the I-routing and are injected.

Theorem 2. $E(|R_{inj^+}|) \geq \frac{p}{4} \cdot |R_{\text{IPP}}|$.

Let Alg_{far} denote the set of packet requests routed by the *Far*-Algorithm with respect to the requests in *Far*.

Theorem 3. $E(|Alg_{far}|) \geq \Omega(\frac{1}{\log n}) \cdot \text{OPT}(\text{Far})$.

6 Algorithm for Requests in *Near*

In this section we present an online algorithm for the requests in the subset *Near*. The algorithm is a straightforward greedy one-bend routing algorithm. Given a request $r_i \in$ *Near*, the algorithm searches for a path in G^{st} starting from (a_i, t_i) and ending in a node (b_i, t) such that (b_i, t) is in the same tile as (a_i, t_i). Thus, the goal is to reach any node in row b_i within the tile.

Upon arrival of a request $r_i \in$ *Near*, the computation of the path for r_i proceeds as follows:

1. Let $t = t_i$.
2. While the diagonal path from (a_i, t) to (b_i, t) is saturated:
   (a) If the horizontal edge is not saturated move to the right (i.e, $t \leftarrow t + 1$).
   (b) Else, if the horizontal edge saturated then **reject**.
   (c) If (a_i, t) is outside the tile, then **reject** r_i.
3. If a nonsaturated diagonal path is found, then the path consists of the concatenation of the horizontal path from (a_i, t_i) to (a_i, t) and the diagonal path from (a_i, t) to (b_i, t).

We emphasize that an optimal routing is not restricted to routing a request $r_i \in \mathit{Near}$ within the tile. Let $\mathit{Alg}_{\mathit{near}}$ denote the set of requests successfully routed by the *Near*-Algorithm with respect to the requests in *Near*. Let $\mathit{Alg}_{\mathit{near}}(s)$ denote the set of requests routed by the *Near*-Algorithm within the tile s. Let Near_s denote the set of requests in *Near* whose starting node is in the tile s.

Theorem 4. *For every tile* s, $|\mathit{Alg}_{\mathit{near}}(s)| \geq \Omega(\frac{1}{\log n}) \cdot \text{OPT}(\text{Near}_s)$.

Corollary 1. $|\mathit{Alg}_{\mathit{near}}| \geq \Omega(\frac{1}{\log n}) \cdot \text{OPT}(\text{Near})$.

7 Putting Things Together

The online randomized algorithm *Alg* for packet routing on a directed line proceeds as follows.

1. Choose the tiling parameters x, y according to Sect. 4.
2. Choose the phase shifts $\phi_x \in [0..x-1], \phi_y \in [0..y-1]$ of tiling independently and uniformly at random.
3. Flip a random fair coin $Z \in \{0, 1\}$.
4. If $Z = 1$, then consider only requests in *Far*, and apply the *Far*-algorithm to these requests.
5. If $Z = 0$, then consider only requests in *Near*, and apply the *Near*-algorithm to these requests.

Theorem 5. *If* $B, c \in [1, \log n]$, *then the competitive ratio of Alg is* $O(\log n)$.

8 Other Cases

The following cases are dealt with by simplifying the algorithm. The required modifications are mentioned in the full version.

Theorem 6. *If* $B > \log$ *and* $c \in \mathbb{N}$, *then the competitive ratio of the modified algorithm is* $O(\log n)$.

Theorem 7. *If* $B \in [\log n, n^{O(1)})$ *and* $c \in [\log n, \infty)$, *then the competitive ratio of the modified* deterministic *algorithm is* $O(\log n)$.

Theorem 8. *If* $B \in [1, \log n]$ *and* $c \in [\log n, \infty)$, *then the competitive ratio of the modified algorithm is* $O(\log n)$.

Acknowledgements

We thank Boaz Patt-Shamir, Adi Rosén and Niv Buchbinder for useful discussions.

References

1. Adler, M., Rosenberg, A.L., Sitaraman, R.K., Unger, W.: Scheduling time-constrained communication in linear networks. Theory Comput. Syst. 35(6), 599–623 (2002)
2. Aiello, W., Kushilevitz, E., Ostrovsky, R., Rosén, A.: Dynamic routing on networks with fixed-size buffers. In: SODA, pp. 771–780 (2003)
3. Angelov, S., Khanna, S., Kunal, K.: The network as a storage device: Dynamic routing with bounded buffers. Algorithmica 55(1), 71–94 (2009) (Appeared in APPROX-05)
4. Awerbuch, B., Azar, Y., Plotkin, S.: Throughput-competitive on-line routing. In: FOCS 1993: Proceedings of the 1993 IEEE 34th Annual Foundations of Computer Science, pp. 32–40. IEEE Computer Society, Washington (1993)
5. Awerbuch, B., Azar, Y., Fiat, A.: Packet routing via min-cost circuit routing. In: ISTCS, pp. 37–42 (1996)
6. Azar, Y., Zachut, R.: Packet routing and information gathering in lines, rings and trees. In: ESA, pp. 484–495 (2005), see also manuscript in `http://www.cs.tau.ac.il/~azar/`
7. Borodin, A., El-Yaniv, R.: Online computation and competitive analysis. Cambridge University Press, New York (1998)
8. Buchbinder, N., Naor, J.S.: Improved bounds for online routing and packing via a primal-dual approach. In: Annual IEEE Symposium on Foundations of Computer Science, pp. 293–304 (2006)
9. Buchbinder, N., Naor, J.S.: The design of competitive online algorithms via a primal-dual approach. Foundations and Trends in Theoretical Computer Science 3(2-3), 99–263 (2009)
10. Even, G., Medina, M.: Online Centralized Deterministic Packet-Routing with Preemptions: A Polylogarithmic Competitive Ratio for Grids (2010) (submitted)
11. Räcke, H., Rosén, A.: Approximation algorithms for time-constrained scheduling on line networks. In: SPAA, pp. 337–346 (2009)

A Topological Approach to Recognition

Mai Gehrke[1], Serge Grigorieff[2], and Jean-Éric Pin[2,⋆]

[1] Radboud University Nijmegen, The Netherlands
[2] LIAFA, University Paris-Diderot and CNRS, France

Abstract. We propose a new approach to the notion of recognition, which departs from the classical definitions by three specific features. First, it does not rely on automata. Secondly, it applies to any Boolean algebra (BA) of subsets rather than to individual subsets. Thirdly, topology is the key ingredient. We prove the existence of a *minimum recognizer* in a very general setting which applies in particular to any BA of subsets of a discrete space. Our main results show that this minimum recognizer is a uniform space whose completion is the dual of the original BA in Stone-Priestley duality; in the case of a BA of languages closed under quotients, this completion, called the *syntactic space* of the BA, is a compact monoid if and only if all the languages of the BA are regular. For regular languages, one recovers the notions of a syntactic monoid and of a free profinite monoid. For nonregular languages, the syntactic space is no longer a monoid but is still a compact space. Further, we give an equational characterization of BA of languages closed under quotients, which extends the known results on regular languages to nonregular languages. Finally, we generalize all these results from BAs to lattices, in which case the appropriate structures are partially ordered.

Recognizability is one of the most fruitful concepts in computer science [16,3]. Originally introduced for finite words, it has been successfully extended to infinite words, general algebras, finite and infinite trees and to many other structures. Roughly speaking, a set is recognizable if it is saturated by a congruence of finite index. A desirable property for any notion of recognition is the existence of a minimum recognizer. Here, the word "minimum" does not refer to algorithmic properties, like the minimal number of states of an automaton, but rather to a final object in a suitable category. For instance, there is a well defined notion of morphism of deterministic automata. Final objects exist in this category and are just the usual minimal automata. But no such notion is known for automata on infinite words, even for ω-regular languages. This problem has been overcome by using another type of recognizer. For languages of finite words, automata can be replaced by monoids, for which there is a minimal recognizer, the syntactic monoid. For ω-regular languages, ω-semigroups are a category in which minimal recognizers do exist again [9,17].

⋆ The authors acknowledge support from the AutoMathA programme of the European Science Foundation and from the programme *Research in Paris*.

S. Abramsky et al. (Eds.): ICALP 2010, Part II, LNCS 6199, pp. 151–162, 2010.

The aim of this paper is to propose a general definition of recognition for which each object has a *unique minimum recognizer*. Our approach departs from the classical definitions of recognition by three specific features:

(1) it does not rely at all on automata;
(2) it applies to Boolean algebras or more generally to lattices of subsets rather than to individual subsets;
(3) topology, and in particular Stone-Priestley duality, is the key ingredient.

Our most general definition is given in the category of uniform spaces, an abstraction of the notion of metric spaces well-known to topologists. We predominantly consider discrete spaces where the topology itself carries no valuable information. However, an appropriate uniformity gives rise by completion to a compact space, a common practice in mathematics, where it is often said that "compactness is the next best thing to finiteness".

We develop a notion of recognition in this general setting and prove that any Boolean algebra of subsets of a uniform space admits a *minimum recognizer*, which is again a uniform space, whose completion is the dual space of the original Boolean algebra in the sense of Stone-Priestley duality.

When the uniform space carries an algebraic structure for which the operations are at least separately uniformly continuous, it is natural to require that the recognizing maps be morphisms for the algebraic structure as well. In the case of a monoid, this amounts to working in the category of semiuniform monoids and imposes closure under quotients of the Boolean algebra. The minimum recognizer is then a semiuniform monoid whose completion is called the *syntactic space* of the Boolean algebra with quotients. We prove that this syntactic space is a compact monoid if and only if all the subsets of the Boolean algebra are recognizable. For a regular language, one recovers the classical notion of a syntactic monoid. For a variety of regular languages, one obtains the free profinite monoid of the corresponding variety of monoids. For nonregular languages, the syntactic space is no longer a monoid but is still a compact space. We also prove that any Boolean algebra of languages closed under quotient has an equational description. Finally, we generalize all these results from Boolean algebras to lattices and recover in this way the notion of a syntactic ordered monoid.

1 The Topological Setting

In this section, we recall the notions of topology needed to read this paper. We invite the reader to look at Wikipedia for an introduction and suitable references (notably the entries *uniform spaces* and *Stone-Čech compactification*).

Let X be a set. We denote by L^c the complement of a subset L of X. The subsets of $X \times X$ can be viewed as relations on X. Given a relation U, the *transposed relation* of U is the relation ${}^tU = \{(x,y) \in X \times X \mid (y,x) \in U\}$. We denote by UV the composition of two relations U and V on X. Thus

$$UV = \{(x,y) \in X \times X \mid \text{there exists } z \in X,\ (x,z) \in U \text{ and } (z,y) \in V\}.$$

Finally, if $x \in X$ and $U \subseteq X \times X$, we write $U(x)$ for the set $\{y \in X \mid (x,y) \in U\}$.

1.1 Uniform Spaces

Uniform spaces generalize metric spaces and enable the formalization of the notion of relative closeness. See [4] for a thorough discussion of these notions and [12] for a connection with Eilenberg's variety theory.

A *uniformity* on a set X is a nonempty set $\mathcal{U}$ of subsets of $X \times X$ satisfying the following properties:

(1) if a subset U of $X \times X$ contains an element of $\mathcal{U}$, then $U \in \mathcal{U}$,
(2) the intersection of any two elements of $\mathcal{U}$ is an element of $\mathcal{U}$,
(3) each element of $\mathcal{U}$ contains the diagonal of $X \times X$,
(4) for each $U \in \mathcal{U}$, there exists $V \in \mathcal{U}$ such that $VV \subseteq U$.
(5) for each $U \in \mathcal{U}$, ${}^tU \in \mathcal{U}$.

The elements of a uniformity are called *entourages*. The pair $(X,\mathcal{U})$ (or the set X if $\mathcal{U}$ is understood) is called a *uniform space*. The *discrete uniformity* on X is the unique uniformity which contains the diagonal of $X \times X$.

A *basis* of a uniformity $\mathcal{U}$ is a subset $\mathcal{B}$ of $\mathcal{U}$ such that each element of $\mathcal{U}$ contains an element of $\mathcal{B}$. In particular, $\mathcal{U}$ consists of all the relations on X containing an element of $\mathcal{B}$. We say that $\mathcal{U}$ is *generated* by $\mathcal{B}$.

A *subbasis* of a uniformity $\mathcal{U}$ is a subset $\mathcal{B}$ of $\mathcal{U}$ such that the finite intersections of members of $\mathcal{B}$ form a basis of $\mathcal{U}$.

If X and Y are uniform spaces, a function $\varphi\colon X \to Y$ is said to be *uniformly continuous* if, for each entourage V of Y, $(\varphi \times \varphi)^{-1}(V)$ is an entourage of X, or, equivalently, if for each entourage V of Y, there exists an entourage U of X such that $(\varphi \times \varphi)(U) \subseteq V$.

1.2 Pervin Uniformities

Pervin uniformities were first introduced in [10]. They play a key role in our definition of recognition given in Section 2.

For each subset L of a set X, consider the equivalence relation U_L on X:

$$U_L = (L \times L) \cup (L^c \times L^c) = \{(x, y) \in X \times X \mid x \in L \iff y \in L\}$$

Let $\mathcal{S}$ be a collection of subsets of X. The sets of the form U_L, for $L \in \mathcal{S}$, form the subbasis of a uniformity of X, called the *Pervin uniformity defined by* $\mathcal{S}$ and denoted by $\mathcal{U}_\mathcal{S}$. The space $(X,\mathcal{U}_\mathcal{S})$ is called a *Pervin space*.

1.3 Induced Topology

Let $\mathcal{U}$ be a uniformity on X. For each $x \in X$, let $\mathcal{U}(x) = \{\, U(x) \mid U \in \mathcal{U}\,\}$. There exists a unique topology on X, called the *topology induced* by $\mathcal{U}$, for which $\mathcal{U}(x)$ is the set of neighborhoods of x for each $x \in X$.

If $\mathcal{U}$ is a uniformity on X, the intersection of all its entourages is an equivalence relation $\sim$ on X, which is equal to the diagonal if and only if the topology induced by $\mathcal{U}$ is Hausdorff. Further, if $\pi : X \to X/{\sim}$ denotes the quotient map, then the sets of the form $(\pi \times \pi)(U)$, where U is an entourage of X, form a subbasis of a uniformity on $X/\sim$. This map is uniformly continuous and the Hausdorff uniform space $X/\sim$ is called the *Hausdorff quotient* of X.

Let $\mathcal{L}$ be a Boolean algebra of subsets of X. In the topology induced by the Pervin uniformity $\mathcal{U}_{\mathcal{L}}$, the neighborhoods of x are the supersets of the sets of $\mathcal{L}$ containing x.

1.4 Filters, Ultrafilters and Stone Duality

Let $\mathcal{L}$ be a Boolean algebra of subsets of X. A *filter* of $\mathcal{L}$ is a nonempty subset $\mathcal{F}$ of $\mathcal{L}$ such that:

(1) the empty set does not belong to $\mathcal{F}$,

(2) if $K \in \mathcal{F}$ and $K \subseteq L$, then $L \in \mathcal{F}$ (closure under extension),

(3) if $K, L \in \mathcal{F}$, then $K \cap L \in \mathcal{F}$ (closure under intersection).

An *ultrafilter* is a filter which is maximal for the inclusion. Recall that a filter is an ultrafilter if and only if, for every $L \in \mathcal{L}$, either $L \in \mathcal{F}$ or $L^c \in \mathcal{F}$. Let $S(\mathcal{L})$ be the set of ultrafilters of $\mathcal{L}$. For each $L \in \mathcal{L}$, let ω_L be the set of ultrafilters containing L. The set $\Omega = \{\omega_L \mid L \in \mathcal{L}\}$ is a Boolean algebra of subsets of $S(\mathcal{L})$, which defines a Pervin uniformity $\mathcal{U}_\Omega$. The uniform space $(S(\mathcal{L}), \mathcal{U}_\Omega)$ is called the *Stone dual space* of $\mathcal{L}$ and $S(\mathcal{L})$ with the induced topology is the Stone dual space of $\mathcal{L}$ in the topological sense. Note that Ω is a basis of clopen sets for the topology of $S(\mathcal{L})$ (recall that a set is *clopen* if it is both open and closed).

If X is a space, a filter of $\mathcal{P}(X)$ is simply called *a filter on* X. A filter $\mathcal{F}$ *converges* to a point x of X if, for each neighborhood U of x, there is a set B of $\mathcal{F}$ such that $B \subseteq U$. In this case, x is called a *limit* of $\mathcal{F}$.

1.5 Blocks

A subset L of a uniform space X is a *block* if U_L is an entourage. Intuitively, blocks are to uniformities what clopen sets are to topologies. Recall that the *characteristic function* of a subset L of X is the function χ_L from X to $\{0,1\}$ defined by $\chi_L(x) = 1$ if $x \in L$ and $\chi_L(x) = 0$ if $x \in L^c$.

Proposition 1.1. *Let X be a topological [uniform] space. A subset of X is clopen [a block] if and only if its characteristic function is a [uniformly] continuous function from X to the discrete [uniform] space $\{0,1\}$.*

In the same way, Pervin uniformities are the uniform analogs of zero-dimensional topologies: a topology is zero-dimensional [a uniformity is Pervin] if and only if it has a basis of clopen sets [blocks].

Proposition 1.2. *The blocks of a uniform space form a Boolean subalgebra of the Boolean algebra formed by the clopen sets. These two Boolean algebras coincide if the space is compact.*

The next result gives a simple description of the blocks of a Pervin uniformity.

Proposition 1.3. *Let $\mathcal{S}$ be a collection of subsets of X. The blocks of the Pervin uniformity defined by $\mathcal{S}$ form a Boolean algebra, equal to the Boolean algebra $\mathcal{L}$ generated by $\mathcal{S}$. Further, $\mathcal{S}$ and $\mathcal{L}$ define the same Pervin uniformity.*

1.6 Hausdorff Completion of a Uniform Space

Let X be a uniform space. A filter $\mathcal{F}$ on X is a *Cauchy filter* if, for every entourage U, there exists $B \in \mathcal{F}$ with $B \times B \subseteq U$. In Pervin spaces, Cauchy filters have a simple description.

Proposition 1.4. *Let $\mathcal{L}$ be a Boolean algebra of subsets of X. A filter $\mathcal{F}$ is Cauchy for the Pervin uniformity defined by $\mathcal{L}$ if and only if, for every $L \in \mathcal{L}$, either $L \in \mathcal{F}$ or $L^c \in \mathcal{F}$.*

A uniform space X is *complete* if every Cauchy filter converges. Every uniform space admits a unique *Hausdorff completion* [4]. More precisely, let X be a uniform space. Then there exist a complete Hausdorff uniform space $\widehat{X}$ and a uniformly continuous mapping $\imath\colon X \to \widehat{X}$ such that $\imath(X)$ is dense in $\widehat{X}$ and the following universal property holds: for each uniformly continuous mapping φ from X into a complete Hausdorff uniform space Y, there exists a unique uniformly continuous mapping $\hat{\varphi} : \widehat{X} \to Y$ such that $\hat{\varphi} \circ \imath = \varphi$. The image of X under $\imath$ is the Hausdorff quotient of X and $\imath$ is thus injective if and only if X is Hausdorff.

A uniform space is said to be *totally bounded* if, for each entourage U, there exists a finite cover $(B_i)_{i \in F}$ of X such that, for all $i \in F$, $B_i \times B_i$ is a subset of U. The interest of totally bounded uniformities lies in the following result [4, TG.II.29, Thm. 3]: a uniform space is totally bounded if and only if its completion is compact. This result applies in particular to Pervin spaces. Indeed, the subbasic entourages of the form U_L contain the sets $L \times L$ and $L^c \times L^c$ and $\{L, L^c\}$ is a finite cover of X. Thus we obtain

Proposition 1.5. *Any Pervin space is totally bounded.*

1.7 Pervin Completions

We now show that complete Pervin spaces are the uniform analogs of topological Stone spaces. Let $\mathcal{L}$ be a Boolean algebra of subsets of X and let $\mathcal{U}_{\mathcal{L}}$ be the Pervin uniformity defined by $\mathcal{L}$. By Proposition 1.5, the completion $\widehat{X}$ of X for this uniformity is compact. It consists of all *Cauchy filters* on X that are *minimal* for the inclusion order on filters. For each $x \in X$, $\imath(x)$ is the filter of neighborhoods of x in X and $\widehat{X}$ is equipped with the Pervin uniformity defined by the sets $\{\mathcal{F} \in \widehat{X} \mid L \in \mathcal{F}\}$, for each $L \in \mathcal{L}$. For this reason, we call $\widehat{X}$ the *Pervin completion of X with respect to $\mathcal{L}$*.

We now give an alternative description of $\widehat{X}$. If $\mathcal{G}$ is a filter on the Boolean algebra $\mathcal{L}$, we denote by $\uparrow\mathcal{G}$ the filter on X generated by $\mathcal{G}$.

Theorem 1.6. *The space $\widehat{X}$ is the dual space of $\mathcal{L}$ as defined in Section 1.4. Further, the maps $\mathcal{F} \mapsto \mathcal{F} \cap \mathcal{L}$ and $\mathcal{G} \mapsto \uparrow\mathcal{G}$ define mutually inverse uniformly continuous bijections between the set of minimal Cauchy filters on X and the set of ultrafilters of $\mathcal{L}$.*

The next series of results gives another natural correspondence between the blocks of X and the clopen sets of $\widehat{X}$. We shall use freely the following notation. Let χ_L be the characteristic function of some block L. By Proposition 1.1, χ_L is uniformly continuous. The universal property of the completion ensures that there is a unique uniformly continuous map $\widehat{\chi}_L : \widehat{X} \to \{0,1\}$ such that $\widehat{\chi}_L \circ \imath = \chi_L$. If L is a subset of X, we set $\tilde{L} = \imath^{-1}(\imath(L))$.

Theorem 1.7. *One has $\tilde{L} \in \mathcal{L}$ if and only if $\overline{\imath(L)}$ is clopen and $\overline{\imath(L)} \cap \imath(X) = \imath(L)$. If these conditions are satisfied, then $\overline{\imath(L)} = \widehat{\chi}_{\tilde{L}}^{-1}(1)$.*

If the space $(X,\mathcal{U}_{\mathcal{L}})$ is Hausdorff, then $\imath$ is the identity map and Theorem 1.7 can be simplified as follows:

Corollary 1.8. *Suppose that $(X,\mathcal{U}_{\mathcal{L}})$ is Hausdorff. Then $L \in \mathcal{L}$ if and only if $\overline{L}$ is clopen and $\overline{L} \cap X = L$. If these conditions are satisfied, then $\overline{L} = \widehat{\chi}_L^{-1}(1)$.*

Let us denote by $\mathrm{Clopen}(\widehat{X})$ the Boolean algebra of all clopen sets of $\widehat{X}$.

Theorem 1.9. *The maps $L \mapsto \overline{\imath(L)}$ and $K \mapsto \imath^{-1}(K \cap \imath(X))$ define mutually inverse isomorphisms between the Boolean algebras $\mathcal{L}$ and* $\mathrm{Clopen}(\widehat{X})$. *In particular, the following formulas hold, for all $L, L_1, L_2 \in \mathcal{L}$:*

(1) $\overline{\imath(L^c)} = \overline{\imath(L)}^c$,
(2) $\overline{\imath(L_1 \cup L_2)} = \overline{\imath(L_1)} \cup \overline{\imath(L_2)}$,
(3) $\overline{\imath(L_1 \cap L_2)} = \overline{\imath(L_1)} \cap \overline{\imath(L_2)}$,

2 Recognition in a Uniform Space

In this section, we define a notion of recognition for Boolean algebras of blocks of a uniform space. In spite of the analogy between clopen sets and blocks illustrated by Proposition 1.1, our definition can only be reformulated in terms of clopen sets and continuous maps if one moves to the Hausdorff completions. Indeed, there are nontrivial Pervin uniformities inducing the discrete topology.

2.1 Recognition of a Boolean Algebra

Let $(X,\mathcal{U})$ be a uniform space and let $\mathcal{L}$ be a Boolean algebra of blocks of X.

Definition 1. A [surjective] uniformly continuous map φ from X into a uniform space Y [*fully*] *recognizes* $\mathcal{L}$ if, for each $L \in \mathcal{L}$, $\varphi(L)$ is a block of Y and $\varphi^{-1}(\varphi(L)) = L$.

Let us state two important consequences of this definition. The first one shows that recognition preserves the Boolean structure and the second one is a transitivity property.

Proposition 2.1. *If φ recognizes $\mathcal{L}$, then φ induces an isomorphism of Boolean algebras between $\mathcal{L}$ and $\varphi(\mathcal{L})$.*

Proposition 2.2. *Let X, Y and Z be three uniform spaces and let $\mathcal{L}$ be a Boolean algebra of blocks of X. If $\mathcal{L}$ is [fully] recognized by $\varphi : X \to Y$ and $\varphi(\mathcal{L})$ is [fully] recognized by $\gamma : Y \to Z$, then $\mathcal{L}$ is [fully] recognized by $\gamma \circ \varphi$.*

2.2 Minimum Recognizer of a Boolean Algebra

If $\mathcal{L}$ is a Boolean algebra of blocks of X, the Pervin uniformity $\mathcal{U}_{\mathcal{L}}$ is contained in $\mathcal{U}$ and therefore, the identity on X is a uniformly continuous map from $(X,\mathcal{U})$ onto $(X,\mathcal{U}_{\mathcal{L}})$. The canonical map from $(X,\mathcal{U}_{\mathcal{L}})$ onto its Hausdorff quotient $X_{\mathcal{L}}$ is surjective and uniformly continuous. The composition of these two maps yields a surjective and uniformly continuous $\eta_{\mathcal{L}}$ from X onto $X_{\mathcal{L}}$, called the *minimum recognizing map* of $\mathcal{L}$. The space $X_{\mathcal{L}}$ is called the *minimum recognizer* of $\mathcal{L}$. This terminology is justified by the following universal property:

Proposition 2.3. *The map $\eta_{\mathcal{L}} : X \to X_{\mathcal{L}}$ fully recognizes $\mathcal{L}$. Further, if $\varphi : X \to Y$ fully recognizes $\mathcal{L}$, there exists a unique surjective uniformly continuous map $\pi : Y \to X_{\mathcal{L}}$ fully recognizing the Boolean algebra $\varphi(\mathcal{L})$ and such that $\pi \circ \varphi = \eta_{\mathcal{L}}$. Further, $\eta(\mathcal{L})$ is the set of blocks of $X_{\mathcal{L}}$.*

If X is a discrete space, then every subset is a block. It means that every Boolean algebra $\mathcal{L}$ of subsets of X admits a minimum recognizer. In this case, the space $X_{\mathcal{L}}$ is simply the quotient of X under the equivalence relation $\sim_{\mathcal{L}}$ defined by $u \sim_{\mathcal{L}} v$ if and only if, for each $L \in \mathcal{L}$, the conditions $u \in \mathcal{L}$ and $v \in \mathcal{L}$ are equivalent. But of course, the interesting part is the uniform structure of $X_{\mathcal{L}}$, inherited from the Pervin uniformity $\mathcal{U}_{\mathcal{L}}$ on X, which is in general nontrivial.

2.3 Recognition with Additional Algebraic Structure

The notion of recognition originates in the setting of monoids and automata. Recall that a subset of a monoid is *recognizable* if its syntactic monoid is finite. Equivalently, a subset is recognizable if and only if it has only finitely many distinct quotients. We now consider additional algebraic structure on uniform spaces. For this purpose, we require the operations to be separately uniformly continuous for each variable and the recognizing maps be morphisms for the algebraic structure. Theorem 2.4 below shows that this condition forces some structural conditions upon the Boolean algebra being recognized. Due to the lack of space, we only treat the case of monoids, which is sufficient to illustrate our ideas.

Let us define a *semiuniform monoid* as a monoid M equipped with a uniform structure for which the translations $x \mapsto xs$ and $x \mapsto sx$ are uniformly continuous for each $s \in M$. If the multiplication is jointly uniformly continuous, that is, if the map $(x, y) \mapsto xy$ is uniformly continuous, M is a *uniform monoid.*

Let L be a subset of M and let s and t be elements of M. The *quotient* $s^{-1}Lt^{-1}$ of L by s and t is defined by the formula $s^{-1}Lt^{-1} = \{x \in M \mid sxt \in L\}$. We can now state:

Theorem 2.4. *Let $\mathcal{L}$ be a Boolean algebra of blocks of M. Then $\mathcal{L}$ is closed under quotients if and only if $(M,\mathcal{U}_{\mathcal{L}})$ is a semiuniform monoid. If these conditions are satisfied, then the relation $\sim_{\mathcal{L}}$ is a congruence of monoids.*

Under the conditions of Theorem 2.4, the minimum recognizer $M_{\mathcal{L}}$ of $\mathcal{L}$ is a semiuniform monoid. This allows us to link our definition with the standard definition of a syntactic monoid. Suppose that M is a discrete monoid and let L be a subset of M. Consider the smallest Boolean algebra $\mathcal{L}$ containing L and closed under quotients. Since quotients commute with Boolean operations, this is also the Boolean algebra generated by the quotients of L. Now, the equivalence $\sim_{\mathcal{L}}$ defined at the end of Section 2.2 is the *syntactic congruence* of L, defined by $u \sim_L v$ if and only if, for all $x, y \in M$, the conditions $xuy \in L$ and $xvy \in L$ are equivalent. In summary, we obtain:

Proposition 2.5. *The minimum recognizer of the Boolean algebra generated by a set L and its quotients is the usual syntactic monoid of L enriched with a uniform structure which makes the translations uniformly continuous.*

3 Syntactic Monoid and Syntactic Space

We are now ready to introduce our second main definition.

Definition 2. Let $\mathcal{L}$ be a Boolean algebra of blocks of X. The completion of its minimum recognizer is called the *minimum space* of $\mathcal{L}$. If $\mathcal{L}$ is closed under quotients the minimum recognizer will be called the *syntactic monoid*, the minimum space the *syntactic space*, and the minimal recognizing map the *syntatic morphism*.

Since $X_{\mathcal{L}}$ is Hausdorff, it can be identified with a subset of $\widehat{X}_{\mathcal{L}}$. The minimum space has a universal property similar to that of the minimum recognizer. Let us say that a map $\varphi : X \to Y$ is *dense* if $\varphi(X)$ is dense in Y. A map *densely recognizes* $\mathcal{L}$ if it recognizes $\mathcal{L}$ and is dense. Then $\eta_{\mathcal{L}} : X \to \widehat{X}_{\mathcal{L}}$ is minimum among Hausdorff complete recognizers, in the following sense:

(1) $\eta_{\mathcal{L}} : X \to \widehat{X}_{\mathcal{L}}$ densely recognizes $\mathcal{L}$;

(2) if Y is an Hausdorff complete space and if $\varphi : X \to Y$ densely recognizes $\mathcal{L}$, there is a unique surjective uniformly continuous map $\pi : Y \to \widehat{X}_{\mathcal{L}}$ such that $\pi \circ \varphi = \eta_{\mathcal{L}}$.

The results of Section 1.7 show that the syntactic space is precisely the dual space of $\mathcal{L}$. Although the minimum recognizer $M_{\mathcal{L}}$ is a monoid, the product on $M_{\mathcal{L}}$ is not in general uniformly continuous and the completion of $M_{\mathcal{L}}$ is not in general a monoid. More precisely, the closure of the product is in general a ternary relation, as shown in Example 3.2.

Let us give a few examples of syntactic spaces.

Example 3.1. Let $\mathcal{P}(M)$ be the Boolean algebra of all subsets of a monoid M. Its minimum recognizer is M and its syntactic space is the Stone-Čech compactification of M, traditionally denoted by βM, and studied in detail in [7]. As foretold by Theorem 4.1 below, the closure in βM of the product on M is not a binary operation any longer. As a function from $\beta M \times \beta M$ into $\mathcal{P}(\beta M)$ it maps a pair of ultrafilters (p, q) to the family of ultrafilters extending the filter of supersets of $\{XY \mid X \in p, Y \in q\}$.

Example 3.2. The minimal recognizer of the language $\{u \in \{a,b\}^* \mid |u|_a = |u|_b\}$ is $(\mathbb{Z}, +)$. Its syntactic image is $\{0\}$ and its quotients are the sets $\{n\}$, where $n \in \mathbb{Z}$. The Boolean algebra generated by these quotients is the set of finite or cofinite subsets of $\mathbb{Z}$. The associated Pervin completion of $\mathbb{Z}$ is $\mathbb{Z} \cup \{\infty\}$: $\mathbb{Z}$ corresponds to the principal ultrafilters on $\mathcal{L}$ and ∞ is the ultrafilter of cofinite subsets of $\mathbb{Z}$.

The minimal recognizer of the language MAJORITY $= \{u \in \{a,b\}^* \mid |u|_a \geqslant |u|_b\}$ is also $(\mathbb{Z}, +)$ and its syntactic image is $[0, +\infty[$. Its quotients are $[n, +\infty[$, with $n \in \mathbb{Z}$, and they generate the Boolean algebra of all subsets of $\mathbb{Z}$ having a finite symmetric difference with one of the sets $\emptyset$, $\mathbb{Z}$, $-\mathbb{N}$ or $\mathbb{N}$. The associated Pervin completion of $\mathbb{Z}$ is $\mathbb{Z} \cup \{-\infty, +\infty\}$: again $\mathbb{Z}$ corresponds to the principal ultrafilters, and $+\infty$ $[-\infty]$ is the ultrafilter containing the cofinite subsets of $\mathbb{N}$ $[-\mathbb{N}]$.

Let us denote by $\widehat{\mathbb{Z}}$ the completion of $\mathbb{Z}$. Thus $\widehat{\mathbb{Z}} = \mathbb{Z} \cup \{\infty\}$ in the first case, and $\widehat{\mathbb{Z}} = \mathbb{Z} \cup \{-\infty, +\infty\}$ in the second case. The tables below describe the closure $\widehat{+}$ of the addition on $\mathbb{Z}$ for these two completions. These are not binary operations any longer. We give them as functions from $\widehat{\mathbb{Z}} \times \widehat{\mathbb{Z}}$ into $\mathcal{P}(\widehat{\mathbb{Z}})$.

$\widehat{+}$	i	∞
j	$\{i+j\}$	$\{\infty\}$
∞	$\{\infty\}$	$\widehat{\mathbb{Z}}$

$\widehat{+}$	i	$-\infty$	$+\infty$
j	$\{i+j\}$	$\{-\infty\}$	$\{+\infty\}$
$-\infty$	$\{-\infty\}$	$\{-\infty\}$	$\widehat{\mathbb{Z}}$
$+\infty$	$\{+\infty\}$	$\widehat{\mathbb{Z}}$	$\{+\infty\}$

4 Recognizable Boolean Algebras

When $\mathcal{L}$ is a Boolean algebra of regular languages of A^* its syntactic space is the *profinite monoid* attached to $\mathcal{L}$, in the sense of [1,6]. In particular, this syntactic space is a *compact monoid*, that is, a compact space equipped with a monoid operation which is jointly continuous. This is in fact characteristic, as we show in the following theorem. Let us say that a Boolean algebra of blocks of M is *recognizable* if all its members are recognizable.

Theorem 4.1. *Let $\mathcal{L}$ be a Boolean algebra of blocks of M closed under quotients. The following conditions are equivalent:*
1. *the syntactic monoid of $\mathcal{L}$ is a uniform monoid,*
2. *the syntactic space of $\mathcal{L}$ is a compact monoid,*
3. *the closure of the operation on the syntactic monoid of $\mathcal{L}$ is functional,*
4. *all the languages of $\mathcal{L}$ are recognizable.*

Example 4.1. In this example, we consider three Boolean algebras on $\mathbb{Z}$.

Let $\mathrm{Rec}(\mathbb{Z})$ be the Boolean algebra of all recognizable subsets of $\mathbb{Z}$, that is, the family of finite unions of congruence classes $\{a + n\mathbb{Z} \mid n \geqslant 1, 0 \leqslant a < n\}$. Its minimal recognizer is $\mathbb{Z}$ and its syntactic space $\widehat{\mathbb{Z}}$ is the free profinite group on one generator. Note that in this case, the closure of the addition is the usual addition on $\widehat{\mathbb{Z}}$. In the sequel, we denote by $i \mapsto \underline{i}$ the natural embedding from $\mathbb{Z}$ into $\widehat{\mathbb{Z}}$ and by $+$ the addition on $\widehat{\mathbb{Z}}$.

Consider now the Boolean algebra $\mathcal{L}$ generated by $\mathrm{Rec}(\mathbb{Z})$ and by the finite subsets of $\mathbb{Z}$. Its minimal recognizer is $\mathbb{Z}$ and its syntactic space is the disjoint union $\mathbb{Z} \cup \widehat{\mathbb{Z}}$: $\mathbb{Z}$ consists of the principal ultrafilters of $\mathcal{L}$ and the profinite group $\widehat{\mathbb{Z}}$ corresponds to the nonprincipal ones. The closure $\widehat{+}$ of the addition on $\mathbb{Z}$ is commutative but nonfunctional. It extends $+$ on $\mathbb{Z}$ and is such that, for $i \in \mathbb{Z}$ and $u, v \in \widehat{\mathbb{Z}}$, $i \mathbin{\widehat{+}} u = \underline{i} + u$ and $u \mathbin{\widehat{+}} v$ is $\{k, \underline{k}\}$ if $u + v = \underline{k}$ for some $k \in \mathbb{Z}$ and is $\{u + v\}$ otherwise.

Finally, let $\mathrm{Rat}(\mathbb{Z})$ be the Boolean algebra of rational subsets of $\mathbb{Z}$. Its minimal recognizer is again $\mathbb{Z}$ and its syntactic space is the disjoint union $(\widehat{\mathbb{Z}} \times \{-\}) \cup \mathbb{Z} \cup (\widehat{\mathbb{Z}} \times \{+\})$: as before $\mathbb{Z}$ stands for the principal ultrafilters and, for $\varepsilon \in \{+, -\}$, $\widehat{\mathbb{Z}} \times \{\varepsilon\}$ consists of the nonprincipal ones which contain $\varepsilon\mathbb{N}$. The closure $\widehat{+}$ of the addition on $\mathbb{Z}$ is commutative but nonfunctional. It extends the addition on $\mathbb{Z}$ and on each copy of $\widehat{\mathbb{Z}}$. Further, for $i \in \mathbb{Z}$ and $u, v \in \widehat{\mathbb{Z}}$, one has $i \mathbin{\widehat{+}} (u, \varepsilon) = (\underline{i} + u, \varepsilon)$ and

$$(u, +) \mathbin{\widehat{+}} (v, -) = \begin{cases} \{(\underline{k}, -), k, (\underline{k}, +)\} & \text{if } u + v = \underline{k} \text{ for some } k \in \mathbb{Z} \\ \{(u + v, -), (u + v, +)\} & \text{otherwise} \end{cases}$$

5 Equational Theory

Let A^* be a free monoid. We consider A^* as a uniform space, endowed with the Pervin uniformity defined by $\mathcal{P}(A^*)$. As we have seen, its completion is βA^*, the Stone-Čech compactification of A^*. Let $\mathcal{L}$ be a Boolean algebra of languages of A^* closed under quotients and let $\eta : A^* \to M_{\mathcal{L}}$ be its syntactic morphism. Then η extends uniquely to a uniformly continuous map $\widehat{\eta} : \beta A^* \to \widehat{M_{\mathcal{L}}}$. We denote by $\overline{L}$ the closure in βA^* of a language L of A^*.

Formally, an *equation* is a pair (u, v) of elements of βA^*. We say that $\mathcal{L}$ *satisfies the equation* $u = v$ if, for all $L \in \mathcal{L}$, and for all $x, y \in A^*$, the conditions $xuy \in \overline{L}$ and $xvy \in \overline{L}$ are equivalent. This is equivalent to stating that $\widehat{\eta}(u) = \widehat{\eta}(v)$. Given a set E of equations, the set of languages *defined by* E is the set of all languages of A^* satisfying all the equations of E. We are now ready to state our equational characterization of Boolean algebras closed under quotients, which extends the results of [6] to nonregular languages.

Theorem 5.1. *A set of languages of A^* is a Boolean algebra of languages closed under quotients if and only if it can be defined by a set of equations of the form $u = v$, where $u, v \in \beta A^*$.*

6 Lattices and Ordered Structures

Let us briefly indicate how to generalize these definitions and results to lattices. It consists mainly in extending the ideas developed in [11,12]. We treat directly the case of a monoid M.

Let $\mathcal{L}$ be a lattice of subsets of M. Define the *specialization preorder* on M given by $\mathcal{L}$ as the relation $\preccurlyeq$ defined by $x \preccurlyeq y$ if and only if for all $L \in \mathcal{L}$,

$$y \in L \implies x \in L$$

We define the preordered Pervin uniformity given by $\mathcal{L}$ to be $(M, \preccurlyeq, \mathcal{U}_{\mathcal{L}})$. The minimum recognizer of $\mathcal{L}$ is the Hausdorff quotient $(M_{\mathcal{L}}, \leqslant)$ with $\leqslant \, = \, \preccurlyeq / \sim$, where $\sim$ is the Hausdorff equivalence defined in Section 1.3 and the minimum space of $\mathcal{L}$ is the ordered completion $(\widehat{M_{\mathcal{L}}}, \leqslant)$ of $(M_{\mathcal{L}}, \leqslant)$. The latter is the uniform space version of the Priestley space of $\mathcal{L}$ [13]. If the syntactic space is a monoid, we obtain an ordered monoid. For instance, if L is a regular language, one gets the syntactic ordered monoid of L as defined in [11]. The order of the syntactic monoid of the language Majority considered in Example 3.2 is the usual order on $\mathbb{Z}$.

7 Conclusion and Perspectives

We have developed a topological approach to the notion of recognition which seems general enough to be applied not only to monoids but to more general algebras, notably those having finitely determined syntactic congruences in the sense of [5], including vector spaces, Boolean algebras, groups and rings.

Let us come back to finite words. The notion of a syntactic monoid has been extremely successful for regular languages and has developed into a rich theory. However, besides the noticeable exception of the theory of context-free groups [8], this notion is not doing so well beyond regular languages. The reason is that the syntactic monoid does not capture enough information. To work around this difficulty, Sakarovitch [14] proposed to use pointed monoids, a category which also admits minimal recognizers. The *pointed syntactic monoid* of a language is the pair formed by its syntactic monoid and by the image of the language in its syntactic monoid. Our new definition is an extension of this idea. However, instead of adding a "point" to the syntactic monoid, we attach to it a uniform structure (which also depends on the original language) and we consider its completion as a uniform space.

The power of topological methods opens new perspectives for the solution of problems beyond regular languages. Let us give a concrete example. Let AC^0 be the class of languages accepted by unbounded fan-in, polynomial size, constant-depth Boolean circuits. A famous result [2] states that a regular language belongs to AC^0 if and only if its syntactic monoid is quasi-aperiodic. It would be nice to prove this result (and the more general conjectures of this nature proposed by Straubing in his book [15]) by finding some suitable property of the syntactic space of AC^0.

Acknowledgments

The authors would like to thank the referees for many useful suggestions.

References

1. Almeida, J.: Profinite semigroups and applications, in Structural theory of automata, semigroups, and universal algebra. The Analysis of Concurrent Systems 207, 1–45 (2005)
2. Barrington, D.A.M., Compton, K., Straubing, H., Thérien, D.: Regular languages in NC^1. J. Comput. System Sci. 44(3), 478–499 (1992)
3. Bloom, S.L., Ésik, Z.: A Mezei-Wright theorem for categorical algebras. Theoret. Comput. Sci. 411(2), 341–359 (2010)
4. Bourbaki, N.: General topology. Elements of Mathematics (Berlin), ch. 1-4. Springer, Berlin (1998)
5. Clark, D.M., Davey, B.A., Freese, R.S., Jackson, M.: Standard topological algebras: syntactic and principal congruences and profiniteness. Algebra Universalis 52(2-3), 343–376 (2004)
6. Gehrke, M., Grigorieff, S., Pin, J.-E.: Duality and equational theory of regular languages. In: Aceto, L., Damgård, I., Goldberg, L.A., Halldórsson, M.M., Ingólfsdóttir, A., Walukiewicz, I. (eds.) ICALP 2008, Part II. LNCS, vol. 5126, pp. 246–257. Springer, Heidelberg (2008)
7. Hindman, N., Strauss, D.: Algebra in the Stone-Čech compactification, de Gruyter Expositions in Mathematics, vol. 27. Walter De Gruyter & Co., Berlin (1998) Theory and applications
8. Muller, D.E., Schupp, P.E.: Groups, the theory of ends, and context-free languages. J. Comput. System Sci. 26(3), 295–310 (1983)
9. Perrin, D., Pin, J.-E.: Infinite Words, Pure and Applied Mathematics, vol. 141. Elsevier, Amsterdam (2004)
10. Pervin, W.J.: Quasi-uniformization of topological spaces. Math. Ann. 147, 316–317 (1962)
11. Pin, J.-E.: A variety theorem without complementation. Russian Mathematics (Iz. VUZ) 39, 80–90 (1995)
12. Pin, J.-E., Weil, P.: Uniformities on free semigroups. International Journal of Algebra and Computation 9, 431–453 (1999)
13. Priestley, H.A.: Representation of distributive lattices by means of ordered Stone spaces. Bull London Math. Soc. 2, 186–190 (1970)
14. Sakarovitch, J.: An Algebraic Framework for the Study of the Syntactic Monoids Application to the Group Languages. In: Mazurkiewicz, A.W. (ed.) MFCS 1976. LNCS, vol. 45, pp. 510–516. Springer, Heidelberg (1976)
15. Straubing, H.: Finite automata, formal logic, and circuit complexity, Progress in Theoretical Computer Science. Birkhäuser Boston Inc, Boston (1994)
16. Thomas, W.: Uniform and nonuniform recognizability. Theoret. Comput. Sci. 292(1), 299–316 (2003); Selected papers in honor of Jean Berstel
17. Wilke, T.: An algebraic theory for regular languages of finite and infinite words. Int. J. Alg. Comput. 3, 447–489 (1993)

On $LR(k)$-Parsers of Polynomial Size
(Extended Abstract)

Norbert Blum

Informatik V, Universität Bonn
Römerstr. 164, D-53117 Bonn, Germany
blum@cs.uni-bonn.de

Abstract. Usually, a parser for an $LR(k)$-grammar G is a deterministic pushdown transducer which produces backwards the unique rightmost derivation for a given input string $x \in L(G)$. The best known upper bound for the size of such a parser is $O(2^{|G||\Sigma|^{k+1}})$ where $|G|$ and $|\Sigma|$ are the sizes of the grammar G and the terminal alphabet Σ, respectively. If we add to a parser the possibility to manipulate a directed graph of size $O(|G|n)$ where n is the length of the input then we obtain an extended parser. The graph is used for an efficient parallel simulation of all potential leftmost derivations of the current right sentential form such that the unique rightmost derivation of the input can be computed. Given an arbitrary $LR(k)$-grammar G, we show how to construct an extended parser of $O(|G| + \#LA|N|2^k k \log k)$ size where $|N|$ is the number of nonterminal symbols and $\#LA$ is the number of possible lookaheads with respect to the grammar G. As the usual parser, this extended parser uses only tables as data structure. Using some ingenious data structures and increasing the parsing time by a small constant factor, the size of the extended parser can be reduced to $O(|G|+\#LA|N|k^2)$. The parsing time is $O(ld(input) + k|G|n)$ where $ld(input)$ is the length of the derivation of the input. Moreover, we have constructed a one pass parser.

1 Introduction

Efficient implementations of parsers for context-free grammars play an important role with respect to the construction of compilers. Since practical algorithms for general context-free analysis need cubic time, during the sixties subclasses of the context-free grammars having linear time parsers were defined. The most important such subclasses are the $LR(k)$- and the $LL(k)$-grammars. But the size of linear $LR(k)$- and $LL(k)$-parsers might be exponential in the size of the underlying grammar. Indeed, Ukkonen [12] has constructed families of $LR(k)$- and $LL(k)$-grammars having only parsers of exponential size. The reason is that parsers read the input from left to right in one pass without backtrack and treat always the only possible derivation which can depend on the prefix of the input derived so far. Hence, the state of the parser has to include all necessary information about the prefix of the input read so far. Instead of the treatment of the only possible derivation one can consider a set of potential derivations which

S. Abramsky et al. (Eds.): ICALP 2010, Part II, LNCS 6199, pp. 163–174, 2010.

always contains the correct derivation in parallel. Hence, the following question arises: Is it possible to simulate an accurate set of derivations in parallel such that the correct derivation will be computed, the needed time remains linear and the modified parser uses on the input one pass without backtrack and has only polynomial size?

In [3] for $LL(k)$-grammars a positive answer to this question is given. In the case of $LR(k)$-grammers the situation is a little bit more complicated. The parser has to take into account all possible derivations of the current right sentential form. Hence, the state of the parser has to include all necessary information with respect to all possible derivations of the current rightmost sentential form from the start symbol. Instead of storing the whole needed information into the state the parser can treat simultaneously all potential leftmost derivations and also backwards the rightmost derivation which has to be computed. We will consider arbitrary $LR(k)$-grammars. The usual parser for an $LR(k)$-grammar $G = (V, \Sigma, P, S)$ is the so-called *canonical* $LR(k)$*-parser*. The best known upper bound for its size is $O(2^{|G||\Sigma|^{k+1}})$ [10]. Hence, DeRemer [6] has defined two subclasses of the class of $LR(k)$-grammars, the $SLR(k)$-grammars and the $LALR(k)$-grammars. Both classes allow smaller canonical LR-parsers. But the size of these parsers can still be $O(2^{|G|})$ [10]. Hence, the question posed above remains interesting for $SLR(k)$- and $LALR(k)$-grammers, too. We will give a positive answer to this question for arbitrary $LR(k)$-grammars. We assume that the reader is familiar with the elementary theory of $LR(k)$-parsing as written in standard text books (see e.g. [1,2,5,8,9,13]). The notations used in the subsequence are the same as in [1] and are reviewed in the full paper [4] . In Sections 2 and 3, the necessary background is given. Section 2 describes the canonical $LR(k)$-parser. Section 3 describes an efficient simulation of the pushdown automaton M_G designed for an arbitrary context-free grammar G. Section 4 combines the canonical $LR(k)$-parser and the efficient simulation of M_G for an arbitrary $LR(k)$-grammar G obtaining the extended $LR(k)$-parser for G.

2 The Canonical $LR(k)$-Parser

For a context-free grammar $G = (V, \Sigma, P, S)$, an integer k, and $\alpha \in V^*$ the set $FIRST_k(\alpha)$ contains all terminal strings of length $\leq k$ and all prefixes of length k of terminal strings which can be derived from α in G. A context-free grammar G is reduced if $P = \emptyset$ or, for each $A \in V$, $S \stackrel{*}{\Rightarrow} \alpha A \beta \stackrel{*}{\Rightarrow} w$ for some $\alpha, \beta \in V^*$, $w \in \Sigma^*$. Let $G = (V, \Sigma, P, S)$ be a reduced, context-free grammar and $k \geq 0$ be an integer. We say that G is $LR(k)$ if

1. $S \stackrel{*}{\Rightarrow} \alpha A w \Rightarrow \alpha \beta w$,
2. $S \stackrel{*}{\Rightarrow} \gamma B x \Rightarrow \alpha \beta y$, and
3. $FIRST_k(w) = FIRST_k(y)$

imply $\alpha = \gamma$, $A = B$, and $x = y$.

For the construction of a parser for an $LR(k)$-grammar G the following notations are useful: Let $S \stackrel{*}{\Rightarrow} \alpha A w \Rightarrow \alpha \beta w$ be a rightmost derivation in G. A prefix γ of $\alpha\beta$ is called *viable prefix* of G. A production in P with a dot on its right side is an *item*. More exactly, let $p = X \rightarrow X_1X_2\ldots X_{n_p} \in P$. Then $[p, i]$, $0 \leq i \leq n_p$ is an *item* which is represented by $[X \rightarrow X_1X_2\ldots X_i{\cdot}X_{i+1}\ldots X_{n_p}]$. If $p = X \rightarrow \varepsilon$ then we simpy write $[X \rightarrow \cdot]$. If we add to an item a terminal string of length $\leq k$ then we obtain an $LR(k)$-item. More formally, $[A \rightarrow \beta_1 \cdot \beta_2, u]$ where $A \rightarrow \beta_1\beta_2 \in P$ and $u \in \Sigma^{\leq k}$ is an $LR(k)$-*item*. An $LR(k)$-item $[A \rightarrow \beta_1 \cdot \beta_2, u]$ is *valid* for $\alpha\beta_1 \in V^*$ if there is a derivation $S \stackrel{*}{\Rightarrow} \alpha Aw \Rightarrow \alpha\beta_1\beta_2w$ with $u \in FIRST_k(\beta_2w)$. Note that by definition, an $LR(k)$-item can only be valid for a viable prefix of G.

The canonical LR-parser is a *shift-reduce parser*. A shift-reduce parser is a pushdown automaton which constructs a rightmost derivation backwards. We will give an informal description of such a pushdown automaton. Let $S \Rightarrow \alpha_0 \Rightarrow \alpha_1 \Rightarrow \ldots \Rightarrow \alpha_{m-1} \Rightarrow \alpha_m = x$ be a rightmost derivation of x from S. The shift-reduce parser starts with the right sentential form $\alpha_m := x$ as input and constructs successively the right sentential forms $\alpha_{m-1}, \alpha_{m-2}, \ldots, \alpha_1, \alpha_0, S$. The current right sentential form will always be the concatenation of the content of the pushdown store from the bottom to the top and the unread suffix of the input. At the beginning, the pushdown store is empty. Let y be the unexpended input and $\alpha_i = \gamma y$ be the current right sentential form. Then γ is the current content of the pushdown store where the last symbol of γ is the uppermost symbol of the pushdown store. Our goal is to construct the right sentential form α_{i-1} from α_i.

If $\alpha_i = \gamma_1\gamma_2y$ and $\alpha_{i-1} = \gamma_1Ay$ then the alternative γ_2 of the variable A expanded in the current step is on the top of the stack. If $\alpha_i = \gamma_1\gamma_2y_1y_2$ and $\alpha_{i-1} = \gamma_1Ay_2$ then a portion of the alternative of A is prefix of the unexpended input y. The goal of the shift-reduce parser is to take care that the alternative of the variable A expanded in α_{i-1} is on the top of the stack. If the alternative of A is on the top of the stack then the shift-reduce parser replaces this alternative by A. For doing this, the shift-reduce parser uses the following operations:

1. The next input symbol is read and shifted on the top of the pushdown store.
2. The shift-reduce parser identifies that the alternative of A is on the top of the stack and replaces this alternative by A. Therefore, a reduction is performed.

In each step, the shift-reduce parser can perform any of the two operations. In general, the shift-reduce parser is nondeterministic. $LR(k)$-grammars allow to make the shift-reduce parser deterministically. Moreover, the set of the $LR(k)$-items valid for the current content of the stack contains always the information which is sufficient to decide uniquely the next step of the shift-reduce parser.

Let γy be the current right sentential form; i.e., γ is the current content of the stack and y is the unread suffix of the input. Let $u := FIRST_k(y)$ be the current *lookahead*. Let $[A \rightarrow \beta_1 \cdot \beta_2, v]$ be an $LR(k)$-item which is valid for γ. Then β_1 is a suffix of γ. If $\beta_2 = \varepsilon$ then we have $v = u$ and the $LR(k)$-item $[A \rightarrow \beta_1\cdot, u]$ corresponds to a reduction which can be performed by the shift-reduce parser. If $\beta_2 \in \Sigma V^*$ and $u \in FIRST_k(\beta_2v)$ then the $LR(k)$-item $[A \rightarrow \beta_1 \cdot \beta_2, v]$ corresponds to a reading which can be performed by the shift-reduce parser. The following theorem tells us that the set of all $LR(k)$-items valid for γ corresponds to at most one step which can be performed by the shift-reduce parser.

Theorem 1. *Let $k \geq 0$ be an integer and $G = (V, \Sigma, P, S)$ be a context-free grammar. G is $LR(k)$ if and only if for all $u \in \Sigma^{\leq k}$ and all $\alpha\beta \in V^*$ the following property is fulfilled: If an $LR(k)$-item $[A \to \beta\cdot, u]$ is valid for $\alpha\beta$ then there exists no other $LR(k)$-item $[C \to \beta_1 \cdot \beta_2, v]$ valid for $\alpha\beta$ with $\beta_2 \in \Sigma V^* \cup \{\varepsilon\}$ and $u \in FIRST_k(\beta_2 v)$.*

The proof can be found in the full paper [4]. With respect to the shift-reduce parser, the theorem has the following implication: If during the construction of the rightmost derivation an $LR(k)$-item $[A \to \beta\cdot, u]$ is valid for the current content γ of the stack and u is the current lookahead then β is on the top of the pushdown store and the reduction corresponding to the production $A \to \beta$ is the only applicable step of the shift-reduce parser. If an $LR(k)$-item $[C \to \beta_1 \cdot \beta_2, v]$ with $\beta_2 \in \Sigma V^*$ is valid for the current content of the stack and the current lookahead u is in $FIRST_k(\beta_2 v)$ then the reading which corresponds to the first symbol of u is the only applicable step of the shift-reduce parser.

3 The Pushdown Automaton M_G

For the parallel simulation of all potential leftmost derivations we need the following pushdown automaton: Given any context-free grammar $G = (V, \Sigma, P, S)$, we will construct a pushdown automaton M_G with $L(M_G) = L(G)$ which produces a leftmost derivation. For a production $p \in P$, n_p denotes the length of the right side of p. Let $H_G = \{[p, i] \mid p \in P, 0 \leq i \leq n_p\}$ be the set of all items of G. Then $M_G = (Q, \Sigma, \Gamma, \delta, q_0, Z_0, F)$ is defined by

$$\begin{aligned}
&Q = H_G \cup \{[S' \to \cdot S], [S' \to S\cdot]\},\\
&q_0 = [S' \to \cdot S],\ F = \{[S' \to S\cdot]\},\\
&\Gamma = Q \cup \{\bot\},\ Z_0 = \bot, \text{ and}\\
&\delta : Q \times (\Sigma \cup \{\varepsilon\}) \times \Gamma \mapsto 2^{Q \times \Gamma^*}.
\end{aligned}$$

δ will be defined such that M_G simulates a leftmost derivation. With respect to δ, we distinguish three types of steps.

(E) *expansion*
$\delta([X \to \beta \cdot A\gamma], \varepsilon, Z) = \{([A \to \cdot\alpha], [X \to \beta \cdot A\gamma]Z) \mid A \to \alpha \in P\}$.
The leftmost variable in the left sentential form is replaced by one of its alternatives. The pushdown store is expanded.

(C) *reading*
$\delta([X \to \varphi \cdot a\psi], a, Z) = \{([X \to \varphi a \cdot \psi], Z)\}$.
The next input symbol is read.

(R) *reduction*
$\delta([X \to \alpha\cdot], \varepsilon, [W \to \mu \cdot X\nu]) = \{([W \to \mu X \cdot \nu], \varepsilon)\}$.
The whole alternative α is derived from X. Hence, the dot can be moved beyond X and the corresponding item can be removed from the pushdown store getting the new state. Therefore, the pushdown store is reduced.

The basis for the construction of a polynomial size extended $LR(k)$-parser is an efficient deterministic simulation of M_G.

Let $G = (V, \Sigma, P, S)$ be a reduced context-free grammar. $N := V \setminus \Sigma$ is the set of nonterminal symbols. Our goal is to develop a deterministic simulation of the pushdown automaton M_G. The algorithm which we will develop looks much like Earley's algorithm [7]. But in contrast to Earley's algorithm, the algorithm maintains the structure of the computation of the underlying pushdown automaton M_G. For the construction of the extended $LR(k)$-parser, this structure of the computation of M_G is needed. Tomita [11] has develloped a similiar approach the "graph-structured stack" which is restricted to non-cyclic grammars such that the graphs remain acyclic. Next we will describe the simulation of M_G.

If we write the current state of M_G always on the top of the stack then we have only to solve the problem of the deterministic simulation of the stack. The idea is to simulate all possible contents of the stack in parallel. Since an exponential number of different stacks are possible at the same time, the direct simulation of all stacks in parallel cannot be efficient. Observe that the grammar G and therefore the pushdown automaton M_G have a fixed size. Hence, at any time, at most a constant number of distinct items can be on the top of all stacks. Hence, there are only a constant number of possibilities to modify eventually an exponential number of different stacks. This observation suggests the following method:

We realize all stacks simultaneously by a directed graph $\mathcal{G} = (\mathcal{V}, \mathcal{E})$. Each node of the graph is marked by an item. We identify each node with its item. The graph contains exactly one node with indegree zero. This node is marked by the item $[S' \to \cdot S]$. We call this node the *start node* and nodes with outdegree zero *end nodes*. Everytime, we have a bijection of the paths from the start node to an end node and the possible contents of the stack. The algorithm separates into *phases*. During each phase, we treat all end nodes simultaneously. For doing this, we have the difficulty that with respect to different end nodes the kind of steps which have to be performed might be different; i.e., some end nodes have to be expanded, other end nodes have to be reduced, and some end nodes need a reading. Hence, it can be the case that with respect to different end nodes the unexpended input might be different. For the solution of this difficulty, we synchronize the computation using the following rules:

1. As long as there is an end node of the form $[A \to \alpha_1 \cdot B\alpha_2]$, $B \in N$ perform an expansion with respect to this end node.
2. If all end nodes are of the form $[A \to \alpha_1 \cdot \alpha_2]$, $\alpha_2 \in \Sigma V^* \cup \{\varepsilon\}$ then perform a reduction with respect to all end nodes with $\alpha_2 = \varepsilon$.
3. If all end nodes are of the form $[A \to \alpha_1 \cdot a\alpha_2]$, $a \in \Sigma$ then perform a reading with respect to all end nodes.

At the end of each phase exactly one input symbol has been read. Hence, we have n phases where n is the length of the input. We number these phases from 1 to n. Each phase separates into two subphases. During the first subphase, we perform all possible expansions and reductions. An end node of the form $[A \to \alpha_1 \cdot \alpha_2]$ with $\alpha_2 \in NV^*$ is called *expansible*, with $\alpha_2 \in \Sigma V^*$ is called *readable*, and with $\alpha_2 = \varepsilon$ is called *reducible*.

The first subphase is separated into rounds. In the first round, we perform as long as possible expansions. We call such a round *expansion step*. The same node is inserted only once. Instead of inserting the same node again, an edge pointing to the node inserted before is created. Since the alternative of an expanded nonterminal can be in NV^*, possibly we have to expand the new node again. Maybe, some cycles are constructed; e.g., the following chain of expansions would produce a cycle:

$$[A \to \alpha_1 \cdot B\alpha_2], [B \to \cdot C\beta_1], [C \to \cdot B\beta_2], [B \to \cdot C\beta_1].$$

In the second round, we perform all possible reductions. Such a round is called *reduction step*. According to the reductions, maybe some further expansions are possible. These are performed during a third round. If the alternative of the expanded variable is ε then this new end node is reducible and causes a reduction. All these reductions are performed in the next round a.s.o. New nodes are indexed by the number of the current phase. A reduction step is performed as follows: We remove all reducible nodes from the graph. Two cases with respect to a direct predecessor u of a removed node can arise:

1. All its successors are reducible and will be removed. Then u is of Type 1.
2. u has successors which will be not removed. Then u is of Type 2.

If u is of Type 1 then the dot of the item u will be moved by one position to the right. The index of u is changed to the number of the current phase. If u is of Type 2 then we copy the node u and all ingoing edges of u and move the dot of the copy u' of u by one position to the right. We index u' by the number of the current phase. Possibly, after moving the dot in u or in u', the node u or u' becomes reducible, expansible, or readable.

After the first subphase, all end nodes have a terminal symbol behind its dot. During the second subphase, we perform the reading step. Assume that the $(i+1)$th input symbol a_{i+1} is the first unread input symbol. End nodes where the terminal symbol behind the dot is unequal a_{i+1} cannot lead to an accepting computation of the pushdown automaton M_G. Hence, they can be removed from the graph. Nodes where all successors are removed can also be deleted. In end nodes with the first symbol behind the dot is a_{i+1}, we move the dot one position to the right and change the index of the current item to $i+1$.

Note that the graph $\mathcal{G} = (\mathcal{V}, \mathcal{E})$ can contain some cycles. The index of an item is equal to the length of the already read input. This index will be helpful for understanding the simulation algorithm and can be omited in any implementation of the algorithm. The correctness of the algorithm follows from the fact that after each performance of a phase there is a bijection between the paths from the start node to the end nodes and the possible contents of the stack. This can easily be proved by induction. It is also easy to prove that the algorithm uses $O(n^3)$ time and $O(n^2)$ space where n is the length of the input. If the context-free grammar G is unambiguous, the needed time reduces to $O(n^2)$.

4 The Construction of the Extended $LR(k)$-Parser

Let $k \geq 0$ be an integer and let $G = (V, \Sigma, P, S)$ be an arbitrary $LR(k)$-grammar. The idea is to combine the concept of the shift-reduce parser and the deterministic simulation of the pushdown automaton M_G. This means that for the construction of the extended parser P_G we use M_G under regard of properties of $LR(k)$-grammars. Just as for the construction of the canonical $LR(k)$-parser, Theorem 1 is the key for the construction of the extended $LR(k)$-parser. Note that Theorem 1 is a statement about valid $LR(k)$-items for a viable prefix of G. Hence, we are interested in all maximal viable prefixes represented by the current graph $\mathcal{G} = (\mathcal{V}, \mathcal{E})$ of the simulation algorithm of M_G. In the subsequence, we omit the indices of the items if they are not needed. Let $[A \rightarrow \alpha_1 \cdot \alpha_2]$ be an item. Then we call the portion α_1 left from the dot the *left side* of the item $[A \rightarrow \alpha_1 \cdot \alpha_2]$. Let P be any path from the start node to an end node in $\mathcal{G}$. Then the concatenation of the left sides of the items from the start node to the end node of P results in the maximal viable prefix $pref(P)$ with respect to P; i.e., if

$$P = [S' \rightarrow \cdot S], [S \rightarrow \alpha_1 \cdot A_2\beta_1], [A_2 \rightarrow \alpha_2 \cdot A_3\beta_2], \ldots, [A_t \rightarrow \alpha_t \cdot \beta_t]$$

then

$$pref(P) = \alpha_1\alpha_2 \ldots \alpha_t.$$

Next we will characterize valid $LR(k)$-items with respect to such a path P where the end node of P is reducible or readable; i.e., $\beta_t = \varepsilon$ or $\beta_t = a\beta'_t$ where $a \in \Sigma$ and $\beta'_t \in V^*$. Let $[B \rightarrow \alpha \cdot C\beta]$, $C \in N$, $\beta \in V^*$ be an item. Then we call β the *right side* of the item $[B \rightarrow \alpha \cdot C\beta]$. The *right side* of an item $[B \rightarrow \alpha \cdot a\beta]$, $a \in \Sigma$, $\beta \in V^*$ is $a\beta$. We obtain the *relevant suffix* $suf(P)$ with respect to P by concatenating the right sides from the end node to the start node of P; i.e.,

$$suf(P) = \begin{cases} \beta_{t-1}\beta_{t-2}\ldots\beta_1 & \text{if } \beta_t = \varepsilon \\ a\beta'_t\beta_{t-1}\beta_{t-2}\ldots\beta_1 & \text{if } \beta_t = a\beta'_t. \end{cases}$$

Let u be the current lookahead. The $LR(k)$-item $[A_t \rightarrow \alpha_t \cdot \beta_t, u]$ is *valid for the path P* iff $u \in FIRST_k(suf(P))$.

For an application of Theorem 1 to M_G it would be useful if all maximal viable prefixes of a path corresponding to any current stack would be the same. This shows the following Lemma:

Lemma 1. *Let $G = (V, \Sigma, P, S)$ be an $LR(k)$-grammar and let $\mathcal{G} = (\mathcal{V}, \mathcal{E})$ be the graph constructed by the deterministic simulation of $LR(k)$-M_G. Then at any time for any two paths P and Q from the start node $[S' \rightarrow \cdot S]$ to any end node it holds $pref(P) = pref(Q)$.*

The proof can be found in the full paper [4]. According to Lemma 1, we can incorporate Theorem 1 into the pushdown automaton M_G. We call the resulting pushdown automaton $LR(k)$-M_G. During the deterministic simulation of $LR(k)$-M_G the following invariant will be fulfilled:

1. Immediately before an expansion step, all end nodes of the graph $\mathcal{G}$ are of the form $[A \to \alpha \cdot B\beta]$ or $[A \to \alpha \cdot a\beta]$ where $\alpha, \beta \in V^*$, $B \in N$ and $a \in \Sigma$ is the next unread symbol of the input.
2. Immediately before a reduction/reading step, all end nodes of $\mathcal{G}$ are of the form $[A \to \cdot]$ or $[A \to \alpha \cdot a\beta]$ where $\alpha, \beta \in V^*$ and $a \in \Sigma$ is the next unread symbol of the input.

If the grammar G has no ε-production then every reduction/reading step starts with a reading. But after reading the next input symbol, some reductions are possible.

Before the first expansion step, the only node of $\mathcal{G}$ is the start node $[S' \to \cdot S]$. Hence, the invariant is fulfilled before the first expansion step. Assume that the invariant is fulfilled before the current expansion step. Let a be the next unread symbol of the input. Since an alternative $\alpha \in (\Sigma \setminus \{a\})V^*$ cannot lead to an accepting computation, all possible expansions are performed under the restriction that only alternatives in $NV^* \cup \{a\}V^* \cup \{\varepsilon\}$ are used. If a variable C of an end node $[B \to \alpha \cdot C\beta]$ has only alternatives in $(\Sigma \setminus \{a\})V^*$ then this end node cannot lead to an accepting computation. Hence, such an end node is deleted. Then, a *graph adjustment* is performed; i.e., as long as there is a node where all its successors are removed from the graph $\mathcal{G}$ this node is deleted, too. Obviously, the invariant is fulfilled after the expansion step and hence, before the next reduction/reading step.

Assume that the invariant is fulfilled before the current reduction/reading step. Let u be the current lookahead. Three cases can arise:

Case 1: There is a path P from the start node to an end node $[A \to \cdot]$ such that the $LR(k)$-item $[A \to \cdot, u]$ is valid for P.

Then according to Theorem 1, the corresponding reduction is the unique step performed by the parser. Hence, all other end nodes of the graph $\mathcal{G}$ are deleted. Then, a graph adjustment and the reduction with respect to the end node $[A \to \cdot]$ are performed. For each direct predecessor v of the node $[A \to \cdot]$ which has Type 1, we move the dot of the item v one position to the right. If v is of Type 2 then we copy v and all ingoing edges and move the dot of the copy v' one position to the right. The resulting items are the new end nodes of the graph and are of the form $[B \to \alpha A \cdot \beta]$ where $\beta \in V^*$. If $\beta \in NV^*$ then the item $[B \to \alpha A \cdot \beta]$ is expansible. If $\beta = \varepsilon$ then the resulting item $[B \to \alpha A \cdot]$ is reducible. If the $LR(k)$-item $[B \to \alpha A \cdot, u]$ is valid then the reduction with respect to the end node $[B \to \alpha A \cdot]$ is performed. Since after the expansion of any expansible end node each constructed reducible end node would be of the form $[C \to \cdot]$, by Theorem 1, all constructed end nodes cannot lead to a valid $LR(k)$-item. Hence, we need not perform the expansion of any expansible end node if the reduction of the end node $[B \to \alpha A \cdot]$ is performed such that all other end nodes are deleted from the graph. If the $LR(k)$-item $[B \to \alpha A \cdot, u]$ is not valid then the end node $[B \to \alpha A \cdot]$ is deleted. If $\beta \in (\Sigma \setminus \{a\})V^*$ then this end node cannot lead to an accepting computation and can be deleted from the graph. Then, a graph adjustment is performed. Hence, after the reduction step, all end nodes are of the form $[B \to \alpha A \cdot \beta]$ with $\beta \in NV^* \cup \{a\}V^*$. Therefore, the invariant is fulfilled before the next step.

Case 2: There is no such a path P but there is at least one end node with the terminal symbol a behind the dot.

Then, the corresponding reading step is the only possible step performed by the parser. All end nodes which do not correspond to this reading step are removed from the graph followed by a graph adjustment. Then we perform the reading step with respect to all remaining end nodes. This means that the next input symbol a is read and the dot is moved one position to the right with respect to all end nodes. The resulting items are of the form $[B \to \alpha a \cdot \beta]$ where $\beta \in V^*$. Let a' be the next unread input symbol and u' be the current lookahead. The same discussion as above shows that after the termination of the current reduction/reading step all end nodes are of the form $[B \to \alpha a \cdot \beta]$ with $\beta \in NV^* \cup \{a'\}V^*$. Hence, the invariant is fulfilled before the next step.

Case 3: None of the two cases described above is fulfilled.

Then, the $LR(k)$-grammar G does not generate the input.

5 The Implementation of the Simulation of $LR(k)$-M_G

How to realize the implementation of the simulation of $LR(k)$-M_G described above? Mainly, the following questions arise:

1. How to perform the expansions efficiently?
2. How to perform a reduction/reading step efficiently?

Let i be the index of the current phase and a be the next unread input symbol. Assume that $\gamma_1, \gamma_2, \ldots, \gamma_q$ are those alternatives of the variable A which are in $NV^* \cup \{a\}V^* \cup \{\varepsilon\}$. The expansion of an end node $[C \to \alpha \cdot A\beta]_i$ of the current graph $\mathcal{G}$ is performed in the following way:

(1) If the variable A is expanded during the current phase for the first time then add the nodes $[A \to \gamma_j]_i$, $1 \le j \le q$ to the current graph $\mathcal{G}$.
(2) Add the edges $([C \to \alpha \cdot A\beta]_i, [A \to \cdot\gamma_j]_i)$, $1 \le j \le q$ to the current graph $\mathcal{G}$.

If the variable A is expanded for the first time then q nodes and q edges are added to the graph. If after this expansion another end node $[C' \to \alpha' \cdot A\beta']_i$ has to be expanded we would add the q edges $([C' \to \alpha' \cdot A\beta']_i, [A \to \cdot\gamma_j]_i)$ to the graph. Therefore, the number of nodes of the graph $\mathcal{G}$ is bounded by $O(|G|n)$ but the number of edges can increase to $O(|G|^2 n)$. Hence, our goal is to reduce the number of edges in $\mathcal{G}$. The idea is to create an additional node A and the edges $(A, [A \to \cdot\gamma_j]_i)$, $1 \le j \le q$. Then, the expansion of an end node $[C \to \alpha \cdot A\beta]_i$ of the current graph $\mathcal{G}$ can be performed in the following way:

(1) If the variable A is expanded during the current phase for the first time then add the nodes A and $[A \to \gamma_j]_i$, $1 \leq j \leq q$ and the edges $(A, [A \to \cdot\gamma_j]_i)$, $1 \leq j \leq q$ to the current graph $\mathcal{G}$.
(2) Add the edge $([C \to \alpha \cdot A\beta]_i, A)$ to the current graph $\mathcal{G}$.

Then $q+1$ edges are inserted for the first expansion of the variable A. For each further expansion of A during the current phase only one edge is inserted. This will lead to an $O(|G|n)$ upper bound for the number of edges in $\mathcal{G}$. The expansion step transforms the graph $\mathcal{G}$ to a graph $\mathcal{G}'$.

After the expansion step, a reduction/reading step has to be performed. Let u be the current lookahead. First, we check if there is a path P from the start node to an end node $[A \to \cdot]$ or $[A \to \alpha \cdot a\beta]$ such that the $LR(k)$-item $[A \to \cdot, u]$ and $[A \to \alpha \cdot a\beta, u]$, respectively is valid for P. We call such a path P *suitable* for the end node $[A \to \cdot]$ and $[A \to \alpha \cdot a\beta]$, respectively. For doing this, we need an answer to the following question:

– Given such an end node $[A \to \cdot]$ or $[A \to \alpha \cdot a\beta]$ and a path P from the start node to this end node, how to decide efficiently if $u \in FIRST_k(suf(P))$?

The complexity of the reduction/reading step mainly depends on the length k of the lookahead u. Here, we only sketch the solution of the most simple case $k = 1$. This solution is extended to larger k in the full paper [4]. We distinguish two cases:

Case 1: There is an end node of the form $[A \to \alpha \cdot a\beta]$ where $\alpha, \beta \in V^*$ and $a \in \Sigma$.

According to the invariant which is fulfilled during the simulation of $LR(k)$-M_G, the terminal symbol a is the next unread symbol of the input. Obviously, $a \in FIRST_1(suf(P))$ for all paths P from the start node to the end node $[A \to \alpha \cdot a\beta]$. Hence, the $LR(k)$-item $[A \to \alpha \cdot a\beta, a]$ is valid for all such paths. Theorem 1 implies that no $LR(k)$-item which does not correspond to reading the next input symbol can be valid for a path from the start node to an end node.

Case 2: All end nodes of $\mathcal{G}'$ are of the form $[A \to \cdot]$.

Let P be a path from the start node to the end node $[A \to \cdot]$ and let $suf(P) = A_1A_2 \ldots A_r$. Then $A_i \in V$, $1 \leq i \leq r$. The $LR(k)$-item $[A \to \cdot, a]$ is valid for P iff $a \in FIRST_1(A_1A_2 \ldots A_r)$. Note that $a \in FIRST_1(A_1A_2 \ldots A_r)$ iff $a \in FIRST_1(A_1)$ or $\varepsilon \in FIRST_1(A_1)$ and $a \in FIRST_1(A_2A_3 \ldots A_r)$. Hence, $a \in FIRST_1(suf(P))$ iff there is $1 \leq i \leq r$ such that $\varepsilon \in FIRST_1(A_1A_2 \ldots A_{i-1})$ and $a \in FIRST_1(A_i)$. For the decision if $a \in FIRST_1(suf(P))$, we consider $A_1A_2 \ldots A_r$ from left to right. Assume that A_j is the current considered symbol. If $a \in FIRST_1(A_j)$ then $a \in FIRST_1(suf(P))$. Otherwise, if $\varepsilon \notin FIRST_1(A_j)$ or $j = r$ then $a \notin FIRST_1(suf(P))$. If $\varepsilon \in FIRST_1(A_j)$ and $j < r$ then the next symbol A_{j+1} of $suf(P)$ is considered.

Now we know how to decide if the current lookahead a is contained in $FIRST_1(suf(P))$ for a given path P from the start node to a readable or reducible end node. But we have to solve the following more general problem:

– Given an end node $[A \to \alpha \cdot a\beta]$ or $[A \to \cdot]$, how to decide if there is a path P from the start node to this end node with $a \in FIRST_1(suf(P))$?

The first case is trivial since for all paths P from the start node to the end node $[A \to \alpha \cdot a\beta]$ there holds $a \in FIRST_1(suf(P))$. In the second case, there can be a large number of paths from the start node to the end node $[A \to \cdot]$ such that we cannot answer this question by checking each such a path separately. Hence, we check all such paths simultaneously. The idea is to apply an appropriate graph search method to $\mathcal{G}'$.

A *topological search* on a directed graph is a search which visits only nodes with the property that all its predecessors are already visited. A *reversed search* on a directed graph is a search on the graph where the edges are traversed against their direction. A *reversed topolgical search* on a directed graph is a reversed search which visits only nodes where all its successors are already visited. Note that topological search and reversed topological search can only be applied to acyclic graphs.

It is useful to analyze the structure of the graph $\mathcal{G}(A)$ which is constructed according the expansion of the variable A. The graph $\mathcal{G}(A)$ depends only on the grammar and not on the current input of the parser. Note that $\mathcal{G}(A)$ has the unique start node A. The nodes without successors are the end nodes of $\mathcal{G}(A)$. An expansion step only inserts nodes where the left side of the corresponding item is ε. A successor $[C \to \cdot A\beta]$ of the start node A in $\mathcal{G}(A)$ is called *final node* of $\mathcal{G}(A)$. Observe that $([C \to \cdot A\beta], A)$ is an edge which closes a cycle in $\mathcal{G}(A)$. We call such an edge *closing edge*. Such cycles formed by closing edges are the only cycles in $\mathcal{G}'$.

The idea is to perform a reversed topological search on $\mathcal{G}'$ although $\mathcal{G}'$ is not acyclic. The following questions have to be answered:

1. What is the information which has to be transported through the graph during the search?
2. How to treat the cycles in $\mathcal{G}'$ during the reversed topological search?

The unambiguity of $LR(k)$-grammars is the key for the treatment of the cycles in $\mathcal{G}'$. An elaborated description of the reversed topological search is given in the full paper [4]. The parser only uses a table of size $O(|N||\Sigma|)$. This approach can be extended to larger k using a table of size $O(\#LA|N|2^k k \log k)$ where $\#LA$ denotes the number of possible lookaheads of length k. Obviously, $\#LA \leq |\Sigma|^k$.

If the size k of the lookahead is large then the size $\#LA|N|2^k k \log k$ of the table can be too large. Hence in [4], an implementation of $LR(k)$-M_G without the precomputation of these tables is described. We use tries instead of these tables. For an implementation of these tries, we need $O(\min\{\#LA|N|k^2, |\Sigma|^k|N|k\})$ space. Altogether, we have proved the following theorem:

Theorem 2. *Let $G = (V, \Sigma, P, S)$ be an $LR(k)$-grammar. Let $\#LA$ denote the number of possible lookaheads of length k with respect to G and let $ld(input)$ denote the length of the derivation of the input. Then there is an extended $LR(k)$-parser P_G for G which has the following properties:*

i) *The size of the parser is* $O(|G| + \#LA|N|2^k k \log k)$ *using only tables and* $O(|G| + \min\{\#LA|N|k^2, |\Sigma|^k|N|k)$ *if we use tries.*
ii) P_G *needs only the additional space for the manipulation of a directed graph of size* $O(|G|n)$ *where* n *is the length of the input.*
iii) *The parsing time ist bounded by* $O(ld(input) + k|G|n)$.

Since the unique derivation of the input is the output of the parser, the length of the derivation is a lower bound for the parsing time. In [1] it is shown that the length of the derivation is $O(n)$ where the constant depends on the size of the grammar. Hence, if the size of the grammar is considered as being constant then the parsing time is linear in the length of the input.

Altogether, we have constructed for $LR(k)$-grammars extended $LR(k)$-parsers of polynomial size. Hence, for small sizes of the lookahead (e.g. $k < 10$), $LR(k)$-grammars can be used instead of $LALR(1)$-grammars which are mostly used in practice. Moreover, if the number of lookaheads is not too large, $LR(k)$-grammars can also be used for large sizes of the lookahead. These possibilities open some new research directions.

Acknowledgements. The author thanks the referee of Review 1 for its exhaustive review which was helpful to improve the presentation.

References

1. Aho, A.V., Ullman, J.D.: The Theory of Parsing, Translation, and Compiling. Parsing, vol. I. Prentice-Hall, Englewood Cliffs (1972)
2. Blum, N.: Theoretische Informatik: Eine anwendungsorientierte Einführung. Oldenbourg Verlag (1998)
3. Blum, N.: On parsing LL-languages. TCS 267, 49–59 (2001)
4. Blum, N.: On LR(k)-parsers of polynomial size, Research report No. 85308, Dept. of Computer Science, University of Bonn (2010), `http://theory.cs.uni-bonn.de/blum/papers/lr4.pdf`
5. Chapman, N.P.: LR Parsing: Theory and Practice. Cambridge University Press, Cambridge (1987)
6. DeRemer, F.L.: Practical Translators for LR(k) Languages. Ph.D. Thesis, MIT, Harvard, Mass (1969)
7. Earley, J.: An efficient context-free parsing algorithm. CACM 13, 94–102 (1970)
8. Grune, D., Jacobs, C.J.H.: Parsing Techniques: A Practical Guide, 2nd edn. Monographs in Computer Science. Springer, Heidelberg (2008)
9. Sippu, S., Soisalon-Soininen, E.: Parsing Theory, vol. I: Languages and Parsing. EATCS Monographs on Theoretical Computer Science, vol. 15. Springer, Heidelberg (1988)
10. Sippu, S., Soisalon-Soininen, E.: Parsing Theory, vol. II: LR(k) and LL(k) Parsing. EATCS Monographs on Theoretical Computer Science, vol. 20. Springer, Heidelberg (1990)
11. Tomita, M.: An efficient context-free parsing algorithm for natural languages. In: IJCAI, pp. 756–764 (1985)
12. Ukkonen, E.: Lower bounds on the size of deterministic parsers. JCSS 26, 153–170 (1983)
13. Wilhelm, R., Maurer, D.: Compiler Design. Addison-Wesley, Reading (1995)

On Erasing Productions in Random Context Grammars

Georg Zetzsche

Universität Hamburg, Department Informatik
Vogt-Kölln-Straße 30, 22527 Hamburg
georg.zetzsche@informatik.uni-hamburg.de

Abstract. Three open questions in the theory of regulated rewriting are addressed. The first is whether every permitting random context grammar has a non-erasing equivalent. The second asks whether the same is true for matrix grammars without appearance checking. The third concerns whether permitting random context grammars have the same generative capacity as matrix grammars without appearance checking.

The main result is a positive answer to the first question. For the other two, conjectures are presented. It is then deduced from the main result that at least one of the two holds.

1 Introduction

Random context grammars (RCGs) were introduced by van der Walt in [8]. They extend context-free grammars by allowing every production to specify two sets of nonterminals, the *permitting* and the *forbidding* context. A production can then only be applied at a position if the rest of the sentential form contains none of the symbols in the forbidding context and contains every symbol from the permitting context. Such a grammar is called *permitting random context grammar* (PRCG) if every forbidding context is empty. Matrix grammars[1] extend context-free grammars by incorporating a finite set of finite sequences of context-free productions. Then, a word is part of the generated language if and only if it can be derived by a concatenation of some of these sequences.

For many grammar models, it is an important question whether erasing productions are necessary to generate all languages. This is due to the fact that non-erasing grammars can often easily be shown to generate only context-sensitive languages and thus have a linear bound on the space complexity of the membership problem.

The main result of this paper is that for every PRCG, there is an equivalent one that does not utilize erasing productions (aside from one that generates the empty word). Whether this is true was an open question until now (see Open Problems 1.3.1 in [3]). The result has a few interesting consequences. First, it follows that all properties of the languages of non-erasing PRCGs are shared by all languages generated by PRCGs. For example, it follows that the

[1] By matrix grammars, we always mean those without appearance checking.

S. Abramsky et al. (Eds.): ICALP 2010, Part II, LNCS 6199, pp. 175–186, 2010.

class of languages generated by arbitrary PRCGs is strictly contained in the class generated by non-erasing RCGs. Moreover, the pumping lemma from [5] is implied for arbitrary PRCGs. Second, all closure properties of the PRCGs can be carried over to the non-erasing PRCGs. Third, other grammar models can now be shown to be equivalent (for example, certain kinds of cooperating distributed grammar systems [1]). Fourth, we gain new insight into two other problems, which are still open. On the one hand, it is unknown whether non-erasing PRCGs have equal generative capacity as non-erasing matrix grammars. On the other hand, it is not known whether erasing productions can be eliminated in matrix grammars[2]. In section 4, we present two conjectures concerning these problems such that the main result of this paper implies that at least one of the two conjectures holds.

2 Random Context Grammars

In this section, we present some notation and the definition of RCGs.

A *monoid* is a set M together with an associative operation $\odot : M \times M \to M$ and a neutral element $e \in M$. For a monoid M with the operation $\odot$ and $m, m' \in M$, we write $m \sqsubseteq m'$ iff there is an $m'' \in M$ such that $m' = m \odot m''$. In this case, m is called a *prefix* of m'.

For a set Σ, we will write Σ^* for the set of words over Σ. The empty word is denoted by $\lambda \in \Sigma^*$. In particular, $\emptyset^* = \{\lambda\}$. Together with the concatenation as its operation, Σ^* is a monoid. We will regard every $x \in \Sigma$ as an element of Σ^*, namely the word consisting only of one occurence of x. For a symbol $x \in \Sigma$ and a word $w \in \Sigma^*$, let $|w|_x$ be the number of occurrences of x in w. For a subset $\Gamma \subseteq \Sigma$, let $|w|_\Gamma := \sum_{x \in \Gamma} |w|_x$. By $|w|$, we will refer to the length of w.

Furthermore, we write $\Sigma^\oplus$ for the set of *multisets* over the set Σ, that is, $\Sigma^\oplus$ is the set of mappings $\alpha : \Sigma \to \mathbb{N}$. The operation $+$ on $\Sigma^\oplus$ is defined by $(\alpha + \beta)(x) := \alpha(x) + \beta(x)$ for all $x \in \Sigma$. Together with the neutral element $\mathbf{0}$, defined by $\mathbf{0}(x) := 0$ for every $x \in \Sigma$, $\Sigma^\oplus$ is a (commutative) monoid. As in the case of words, we will regard Σ as a subset of $\Sigma^\oplus$ by identifying each $x \in \Sigma$ with $\mu_x \in \Sigma^\oplus$, which is defined by $\mu_x(x) = 1$ and $\mu_x(y) = 0$ for $y \in \Sigma$, $y \neq x$. For a multiset $\mu \in \Sigma^\oplus$, let $|\mu| := \sum_{x \in \Sigma} \mu(x)$. Here, $|\mu|$ is called the *size* of μ. For $\alpha \sqsubseteq \beta$, let $(\beta - \alpha)(x) := \beta(x) - \alpha(x)$. The *Parikh mapping* is the mapping $\Psi : \Sigma^* \to \Sigma^\oplus$ defined by $\Psi(w)(x) := |w|_x$ for all $w \in \Sigma^*$ and $x \in \Sigma$. For a set A, let $\mathcal{P}(A)$ denote the power set of A.

A *random context grammar* (RCG) is a tuple $G = (N, T, P, S)$, where N is an alphabet called the set of *nonterminals* (or *variables*), T is an alphabet called the set of *terminals*, P is a finite subset of $N \times (T \cup N)^* \times \mathcal{P}(N) \times \mathcal{P}(N)$, and $S \in N$ is the *start symbol*. The elements of P are its *productions*. An element $(A, w, U, W) \in P$ is also written as $(A \to w; U; W)$. In the case $W = \emptyset$, we also write $(A \to w; U)$. Furthermore, for $U = \{A_1, \ldots, A_n\}$, $(A \to w; A_1, \ldots, A_n)$

[2] In [4], p. 106, Theorem 2.1, it is claimed that erasing productions cannot be avoided. However, none of the given references contains a proof for this claim and in [2], the problem is again denoted as open.

will be used synonymously to $(A \to w; U; \emptyset)$. A is called the *left side*, w the *right side*, U the *permitting context*, and W the *forbidding context* of the production $(A \to w; U; W)$. Such a production is called *erasing* if w is the empty word. It is called *permitting* if $W = \emptyset$.

An RCG is a *permitting random context grammar* (PRCG) if it has only permitting rules. Furthermore, an RCG G is said to be *non-erasing* if it has no erasing rules or if $(S \to \lambda; \emptyset; \emptyset)$ is its only erasing rule and S does not appear on any right side.

The derivation relation $\Rightarrow_G$ for G is defined as follows. For words $u, v \in (T \cup N)^*$, it is $u \Rightarrow_G v$ iff there is a production $(A, w, U, W) \in P$ and words $r, s \in (T \cup N)^*$ such that $u = rAs$, $v = rws$, all the symbols from U occur in rs and no symbol from W occurs in rs. Then, the language generated by G is defined as

$$L(G) = \{w \in T^* \mid S \Rightarrow_G^* w\},$$

where $\Rightarrow_G^*$ denotes the reflexive transitive closure of $\Rightarrow_G$. The class of languages generated by RCGs, PRCGs, non-erasing RCGs, and non-erasing PRCGs is denoted by $\mathbf{RC}^\lambda$, $\mathbf{pRC}^\lambda$, $\mathbf{RC}$, $\mathbf{pRC}$, respectively.

A *derivation* for a grammar $G = (N, T, P, S)$ is a sequence $w_1, \ldots, w_n$ of words in $(T \cup N)^*$ such that $w_i \Rightarrow_G w_{i+1}$ for each i, $1 \leq i \leq n-1$. For such a derivation, the *derivation forest* is defined inductively, together with a correspondence between the the positions in w_n and the non-λ-labeled leaves. For $n = 1$, it consists of $|w_1|$ nodes, one for each position in w_1 and each labeled by the corresponding symbol in w_1. For $n > 1$, the derivation forest for $w_1, \ldots, w_n$ is extended in the following way. Let $(A \to v; U)$, $v = v_1 \cdots v_m$, $v_1, \ldots, v_m \in T \cup N$, be the production used in $w_n \Rightarrow_G w_{n+1}$ and let $w_n = rAs$, $w_{n+1} = rvs$. Futhermore, let x be the node corresponding to the position in w_n that was replaced to produce w_{n+1}. If $|v| \geq 1$, add a v_i-labeled node for each $1 \leq i \leq m$ and make these nodes children of x. Moreover, let the positions of the subword v of w_{n+1} correspond to these new nodes. If $v = \lambda$, then add one λ-labeled node and make it a child of x. Finally, let the positions in the subwords r, s in w_{n+1} correspond to the same nodes as the positions in the subwords r, s of w_n.

In the case $|w_1| = 1$, the derivation forest is a tree and thus called *derivation tree*. In every derivation tree $\mathcal{T}$, we have a partial order $\leq_\mathcal{T}$ on the nodes of $\mathcal{T}$, where $n_1 \leq_\mathcal{T} n_2$ for nodes n_1, n_2 iff n_1 lies on the (unique) path from the root of the tree to n_2. In a set M of nodes of $\mathcal{T}$, we call an element *maximal* if it is maximal among the elements of M with respect to $\leq_\mathcal{T}$.

Let $D : w_1 \Rightarrow_G \cdots \Rightarrow_G w_n$ be a derivation and $\mathcal{F}$ its derivation forest. Then the N-labeled nodes of $\mathcal{F}$ are also ordered by $\prec_D$, which is defined as follows. For each N-labeled node x, let $s(x)$ be the index i, $1 \leq i < n$, such that the position replaced in $w_i \Rightarrow_G w_{i+1}$ corresponds to x. Then, for nodes x_1, x_2, it is $x_1 \prec_D x_2$ iff $s(x_1) < s(x_2)$. As usual, let $x_1 \preceq_D x_2$ iff $x_1 = x_2$ or $x_1 \prec_D x_2$. Clearly, on the N-labeled nodes, $\preceq_D$ is a linear extension of $\leq_\mathcal{F}$. Note that a derivation tree $\mathcal{F}$ together with the order $\prec_D$ on its N-nodes contains enough information to reconstruct the derivation.

3 Erasing Productions

It is a well-known fact (see, for example, [7]) that in context-free grammars, erasing productions can be eliminated in the following way. Instead of producing symbols that will later be deleted, one avoids their production in the first place. This technique does not suffice for PRCGs, since here, in contrast to context-free grammars, the symbols that are not yet deleted may impact the rest of the derivation.

On the one hand, letting a symbol disappear too early can render the rest of the derivation impossible, in case its productions require this symbol to be present. On the other hand, a non-generated symbol could enable otherwise invalid derivations. This is the case when, in the original grammar, the symbol is only deletable when certain other symbols are present. (The presence of this symbol would thus demand that the other symbols have to appear once in order to obtain a terminal word).

Therefore, in order to preserve the generated language when avoiding the production of later-deleted symbols, we will need some mechanism to retain the influence of the these symbols on the derivation. This will be achieved by endowing the grammar with capabilities to avoid the generation of later-deleted symbols to a certain extent. The remaining occurrences of such symbols are then shown to be so rare that their influence can be accounted for by a mechanism that does not ultilize erasing.

In the construction for context-free grammars, one uses the set Λ of nonterminals that can be rewritten to the empty word. One then proceeds to allow the grammar to nondeterministically choose occurrences of such symbols and prevent them from being produced. Here, the role of Λ will be played by a set enjoying a similar property, which leads us to the first definition.

Definition 1. *A PRCG* $G = (N, T, P, S)$ *is in* erasing normal form *if there is a subset* $\Lambda \subseteq N$ *such that for every production* $(A \to w; U)$, *it is* $A \in \Lambda$ *if and only if* $w \in \Lambda^*$. *For a PRCG G in erasing normal form with subset* $\Lambda \subseteq N$, *we also write* $G = (N, \Lambda, T, P, S)$.

In a grammar that exhibits this form, the symbols in Λ can only be directly rewritten to words in Λ^*. Thus, the only terminal word derivable from a word in Λ^* is the empty word. The symbols in $N \setminus \Lambda$ on the other hand are rewritten to a word containing at least one symbol outside of Λ. Therefore, every terminal word derivable from symbols in $N \setminus \Lambda$ is non-empty.

The set Λ consists of all symbols that can *only* be rewritten to the empty word. In addition, we require that all symbols outside of Λ cannot be rewritten to λ. This means that, as opposed to the construction in the context-free case, the nondeterministic choice about which occurrence will indeed be rewritten to λ has already been made in a grammar in erasing normal form. That is, a symbol will be rewritten to the empty word if and only if it is in Λ. Furthermore, observe that a grammar that is in erasing normal form with $\Lambda = \emptyset$ is already non-erasing, since $\emptyset^* = \{\lambda\}$.

Lemma 1. *For every PRCG G with $\lambda \notin L(G)$, there is an equivalent PRCG G' in erasing normal form.*

Proof. Let $G' = (N', T, P', S)$, $\Lambda := \{\bar{A} \mid A \in N\}$, and $N' = N \cup \Lambda$, where $\bar{A}$ is a new symbol for each $A \in N$. We will need the mapping $\varphi : (T \cup N') \to (T \cup N)$, which is defined by $\varphi(\bar{A}) = A$, $\varphi(A) = A$, $\varphi(a) = a$ for $A \in N$ and $a \in T$. We will also need $\psi : N \to N'$, where $\psi(A) = \bar{A}$, $\psi(a) = a$ for each $A \in N$. The set of productions is $P' = P'_1 \cup P'_2$, where

$$P'_1 = \{(A \to w; U) \mid A \in N,\ w \in (N' \cup T)^* \setminus \Lambda^*,\ U \subseteq N',\ (A \to \varphi(w); \varphi(U)) \in P\},$$

$$P'_2 = \{(\psi(A) \to \psi(w); U) \mid A \in N,\ w \in N^*,\ U \subseteq N',\ (A \to w; \varphi(U)) \in P\}.$$

Clearly, with this set of productions, the grammar is in erasing normal form. In P'_1, the left side is always in $N' \setminus \Lambda$ and the right side is in $(N' \cup T)^* \setminus \Lambda^*$. In P'_2, the left side is always in Λ and the right side is in Λ^*.

It remains to be shown that $L(G') = L(G)$. Let $w_1 \Rightarrow_G w_2 \Rightarrow_G \cdots \Rightarrow_G w_n$, $w_1, \ldots, w_{n-1} \in (T \cup N)^*$, $w_n \in T^*$, be a derivation in G. We claim that there is a derivation $w'_1 \Rightarrow_{G'} w'_2 \Rightarrow_{G'} \cdots \Rightarrow_{G'} w'_n$, $w'_1, \ldots, w'_{n-1} \in (N' \cup T)^*$, $w_n \in T^*$, such that $\varphi(w'_i) = w_i$ for $i = 1, \ldots, n$.

For $n = 1$, this is trivial. For $n > 1$ assume that $w'_2 \Rightarrow_{G'} \cdots \Rightarrow_{G'} w'_n$ is such that $\varphi(w'_i) = w_i$, $i = 2, \ldots, n$. Now, w'_1 is obtained from w_1 in two steps. First, for every $A \in N$, replace every occurrence of A by $\bar{A}$ that is not rewritten in the derivation step $w_1 \Rightarrow_G w_2$ and that occurs as $\bar{A}$ in w'_2. Second, if the word in w'_2 corresponding to the right side of the applied production in $w_1 \Rightarrow_G w_2$ is contained in Λ^*, replace the left side A of this production in w_1 by $\bar{A}$. Then we have $w'_1 \Rightarrow_{G'} w'_2$ and the claim holds.

It follows that $L(G) \subseteq L(G')$. Indeed, let $w \in L(G)$ with $S = w_1 \Rightarrow_G \cdots \Rightarrow_G w_n = w$. Then, the derivation $w'_1 \Rightarrow_{G'} \cdots \Rightarrow_{G'} w'_n$ obtained by our claim satisfies $\varphi(w'_n) = w$ and thus $w'_n = w$, since $w \in T^*$. It is also $\varphi(w'_1) = S$, hence $w'_1 = \bar{S}$ or $w'_1 = S$. Since from sentential forms in Λ^*, the only derivable word in T^* is the empty word, $w'_1 = \bar{S}$ would imply $w = \lambda$, a contradiction. Therefore, $w'_1 = S$ and $w \in L(G')$.

Let $w \in L(G')$ with $S = w_1 \Rightarrow_{G'} \cdots \Rightarrow_{G'} w_n = w$. For every production $(A \to w; U) \in P'$, one clearly has $(\varphi(A) \to \varphi(w); \varphi(U)) \in P$ and thus $w_i \Rightarrow_{G'} w_{i+1}$ implies $\varphi(w_i) \Rightarrow_G \varphi(w_{i+1})$. Hence, $S = \varphi(w_1) \Rightarrow_G \cdots \Rightarrow_G \varphi(w_n) = w$, meaning $w \in L(G)$. □

As explained above, we cannot introduce productions that allow for the arbitrary prevention of the production of Λ-symbols without altering the generated language. Thus, in order to obtain an analogon for the productions that prevent Λ-symbols, we will have to use a somewhat restricted means. Therefore, we introduce the notion of a pruning grammar. In such a grammar, we are able to prevent an occurence of a Λ-symbol from being generated, and thus *prune* the derivation tree, provided that this symbol already appears in the sentential form at another position.

Definition 2. *A PRCG $G = (N, \Lambda, T, P, S)$ in erasing normal form is* pruning *if for every $(A \to w; U) \in P$ and every decomposition $w = rBs$, $r, s \in (T \cup N)^*$, $B \in \Lambda$, it is either*

1. *$|rs|_B \geq 1$ and $(A \to rs; U) \in P$ or*
2. *$|rs|_B = 0$ and $(A \to rs; U \cup \{B\}) \in P$.*

It is easy to see that for every PRCG $G = (N, \Lambda, T, P, S)$ in erasing normal form, there is a smallest set $\bar{P}$ of productions such that $P \subseteq \bar{P}$ and $\bar{G} := (N, \Lambda, T, \bar{P}, S)$ is pruning. With this, $\bar{G}$ is called the *closure* of G. For a production $(A \to rBs; U)$, if the productions $(A \to rs; U)$ and $(A \to rs; U \cup \{B\})$ exist, they are also called *variants* of $(A \to rBs; U)$.

Lemma 2. *For every PRCG G in erasing normal form, $L(\bar{G}) = L(G)$.*

Proof. It is clear that $L(G) \subseteq L(\bar{G})$. In order to prove the opposite inclusion, we use the *augmented grammar* $\hat{G}$. For a PRCG $G = (N, \Lambda, T, P, S)$, $\hat{G} := (N, \Lambda, T, \hat{P}, S)$ is obtained from G by adding the production $(A \to \lambda; A)$ for each $A \in \Lambda$. That is, if a symbol $A \in \Lambda$ appears at least twice in a given sentential form, one of the occurrences can be deleted in $\hat{G}$.

Every production added to G to make $\bar{G}$ can be simulated by a production from G and a sequence of productions of the form $(A \to \lambda; A)$, $A \in \Lambda$. Thus, $L(\bar{G}) \subseteq L(\hat{G})$. Therefore, proving $L(\hat{G}) \subseteq L(G)$ will be sufficient, since then $L(G) \subseteq L(\bar{G}) \subseteq L(\hat{G}) \subseteq L(G)$ and the lemma follows.

Let $w_1 \Rightarrow_{\hat{G}} \cdots \Rightarrow_{\hat{G}} w_n$ be a derivation in $\hat{G}$ such that $w_n \in T^*$. We will show by induction on n that $w_1 \Rightarrow_G^* w_n$, meaning $L(\hat{G}) \subseteq L(G)$.

In the case $n = 1$, there is nothing to do, so assume that $n > 1$ and that the rule applied in $w_1 \Rightarrow_{\hat{G}} w_2$ is $(A \to \lambda; A)$ for some $A \in \Lambda$. (This does not mean a restriction, since for rules not of this type, the induction step is trivial.) Let $\mathcal{F}$ be the derivation forest corresponding to the derivation $D : w_2 \Rightarrow_G^* w_n$, which exists by induction. Without loss of generality, we can write $w_1 = rAsAt$ and $w_2 = rsAt$, $r, s, t \in (T \cup N)^*$. The derivation $w_1 \Rightarrow_G^* w_n$ is obtained as follows. Let $\mathcal{T}$ be the tree in $\mathcal{F}$ whose root is the occurrence of A at position $|rs| + 1$ in w_2 (that is, the second occurrence of A that allowed us to apply the rule $(A \to \lambda; A)$). The new forest $\mathcal{F}'$ for the derivation $w_1 \Rightarrow_G^* w_n$ is obtained by inserting a copy of $\mathcal{T}$ into $\mathcal{F}$ at the position of the A deleted in $w_1 \Rightarrow_{\hat{G}} w_2$.

On the one hand, $\mathcal{F}'$ can be realized by using the derivation D, and, every time a production p is applied in D to a node in $\mathcal{T}$, by applying p again directly afterwards to its corresponding node in the copy of $\mathcal{T}$. This leads to a valid derivation, because the context condition of p can be satisfied out of occurrences that were already present in D, which means that they can be used by p again when applied to a node in the copy of $\mathcal{T}$.

On the other hand, the word derived by $\mathcal{F}'$ is obtained by inserting in w_n the word derived by $\mathcal{T}$. However, $\mathcal{T}$ derives the empty word, since its root is $A \in \Lambda$. Therefore, $\mathcal{F}'$ derives w_n and we have $w_1 \Rightarrow_G^* w_n$. □

Lemma 2 provides a grammar in which we can prevent the introduction of such symbols under certain circumstances. However, we might still need some of those symbols to fulfill context conditions. Thus, we will study means to rearrange derivations such that it becomes possible to prevent some Λ-symbols from being produced while still having enough to satisfy all context conditions. The notion of a context sufficient set of nodes will be used to fulfill the latter requirement. That is, a set of Λ-labeled nodes in a derivation tree is context sufficient if every context condition concerning Λ-symbols can be satisfied out of M.

Definition 3. *Let $S = w_1 \Rightarrow_G \cdots \Rightarrow w_n$ be a derivation in a PRCG $G = (N, \Lambda, T, P, S)$ in erasing normal form. A set M of Λ-labeled nodes in the derivation tree is called* context sufficient *if for every production $(A \to w; U)$ applied in the derivation to a sentential form w_i, every symbol in $U \cap \Lambda$ has an occurrence in w_i that corresponds to a node in M.*

Lemma 3. *Let $G = (N, \Lambda, T, P, S)$ be a pruning PRCG. For every $w \in L(G)$, there is a derivation with a context sufficient set M such that the maximal nodes of M have distinct labels.*

Proof. Let $w \in L(G)$ and $S = w_1 \Rightarrow_G \cdots \Rightarrow_G w_n = w$ be a derivation with derivation tree D_0. We construct a context sufficient set M_0 as follows. For each production $(A \to v; U)$ applied in w_i, $1 \leq i \leq n$, and each $B \in U \cap \Lambda$, choose an occurrence of B in w_i and include its node in M_0. The set M_0 is clearly context sufficient. We will construct a descending sequence $M_0 \supseteq M_1 \supseteq \cdots$ of sets and a sequence of derivations $D_0, D_1, \ldots$ such that each M_i is a context-sufficient set of nodes of D_i.

If the maximal nodes in M_i already have distinct labels, let $M_{i+1} = M_i$ and $D_{i+1} = D_i$. Otherwise, the set M_{i+1} is obtained from M_i as follows. First, include all non-maximal elements of M_i in M_{i+1}. Choose a $B \in \Lambda$ such that $|M_{i,B}| \geq 2$, where for each $A \in \Lambda$, $M_{i,A}$ is the set of maximal elements of M_i that are labeled with A. Now let $m_{i,B}$ be the $\preceq_{D_i}$-minimal element of $M_{i,B}$ and include it in M_{i+1}. Thus, $M_{i+1} = (M_i \setminus M_{i,B}) \cup \{m_{i,B}\}$.

D_{i+1} is obtained from D_i as follows. Let $\mathcal{F}$ be the derivation tree corresponding to D_i and let $\tilde{m}_{i,B}$ be the $\preceq_{D_i}$-maximal element of $M_{i,B}$. Moreover, let $\mathcal{T}$ be the subtree under $m_{i,B}$ and let $\tilde{\mathcal{T}}$ be the subtree under $\tilde{m}_{i,B}$. A new tree $\mathcal{F}'$ is constructed by replacing $\mathcal{T}$ with a copy $\tilde{\mathcal{T}}'$ of $\tilde{\mathcal{T}}$. That is, $\tilde{\mathcal{T}}'$ is isomorphic to $\tilde{\mathcal{T}}$ but has a new set of nodes such that the root of $\tilde{\mathcal{T}}'$ is identified with $m_{i,B}$. We will design D_{i+1} so as to make $\mathcal{F}'$ its derivation tree. In order to describe D_{i+1}, we shall present a word over the N-labeled nodes in $\mathcal{F}'$ and thus define a linear order on these nodes, which in turn defines D_{i+1}. Let X be the set of nodes of $\mathcal{F}$ such that the word $d \in X^*$ corresponds to the derivation D_i. Furthermore, let $Y, \tilde{Y}, \tilde{Y}' \subseteq X$, be the set of N-nodes in $\mathcal{T}$, $\tilde{\mathcal{T}}$, $\tilde{\mathcal{T}}'$, respectively. The isomorphism between $\tilde{\mathcal{T}}$ and $\tilde{\mathcal{T}}'$ induces a bijection $\alpha : \tilde{Y} \to \tilde{Y}'$. The homomorphism $h : X^* \to (\tilde{Y}' \cup X \setminus Y)^*$ is defined by $h(x) = \lambda$ for $x \in Y$, $h(x) = x\alpha(x)$ for $x \in \tilde{Y}$, and $h(x) = x$ otherwise. Then the word that defines the derivation D_{i+1} is $h(d)$. Thus in short, the occurrences corresponding to nodes in $\tilde{\mathcal{T}}'$ are rewritten directly after their counterparts in $\tilde{\mathcal{T}}$.

It remains to be shown that M_{i+1} is context sufficient. First, observe that M_i is still context sufficient in D_{i+1}. This is due to the fact that all the productions outside of $\tilde{\mathcal{T}}'$ can use the contexts they used in D_i. Furthermore, the productions in $\tilde{\mathcal{T}}$ did not need to use nodes in $\mathcal{T}$ as contexts, since $m_{i,B}$ was not present in D_i during the generation of $\tilde{\mathcal{T}}$. Therefore, these contexts can be reused by the productions in $\tilde{\mathcal{T}}'$ when applied directly after their counterparts in $\tilde{\mathcal{T}}$. Thus, M_i is context sufficient in D_{i+1}. In D_{i+1}, whenever there is a node from $M_{i,B}$ in a sentential form, the node $m_{i,B}$ is also present. This is due to the fact that $m_{i,B}$ is removed after the $\preceq_{D_i}$-maximal node of $M_{i,B}$. Therefore, in D_{i+1}, even $M_{i+1} = (M_i \setminus M_{i,B}) \cup \{m_{i,B}\}$ is context sufficient.

Since $M_0 \supseteq M_1 \supseteq \cdots$ is a descending sequence of finite sets, there is an index k such that $M_k = M_{k+1}$. In particular, all maximal nodes in M_k have distinct labels. Thus, $D := D_k$ and $M := M_k$ can serve as the claimed derivation and set of nodes. □

We are now able to construct derivations in which the number of Λ-symbols in the sentential forms is bounded by a constant that only depends on the grammar. This means in particular that a finite amount of space is sufficient to account for all the Λ-symbols.

Lemma 4. *Let $G = (N, \Lambda, T, P, S)$ be a pruning PRCG. Then there is a constant $k \in \mathbb{N}$ with the following property. Every $w \in L(G)$ has a derivation $S = w_1 \Rightarrow \cdots \Rightarrow w_n = w$ such that $|w_i|_\Lambda \leq k$, $i = 1, \ldots, n$.*

Proof. Let $w \in L(G)$. Lemma 3 provides a derivation D and a context sufficient set M of nodes such that the maximal nodes have distinct labels.

We construct a new derivation from D as follows. Since M is context sufficient, in order to fulfill all context conditions, we do not need subtrees in the derivation tree that contain no element of M. Let x be a Λ-labeled node in the derivation tree and v be the first sentential form that contains an occurrence corresponding to x. Then, we call x *prunable* if v contains more than one occurrence of the label of x and the subtree of x does not contain an M-node. If x is a prunable node produced by the production p, we say that we *prune* x if we replace p by a variant that does not create x (and thus remove x and its subtree from the derivation tree). That is, pruning is an operation that creates a new derivation. By definition, pruning a prunable node yields a valid derivation. Note that, since x is Λ-labeled, pruning does not change the derived word. The new derivation D' is obtained from D by pruning prunable nodes until there is no prunable node left.

Let $S = w_1 \Rightarrow_G \cdots \Rightarrow_G w_n = w$ be the derivation D'. Furthermore, let $J_i \subseteq \{1, \ldots, |w_i|\}$ be the set of positions in w_i that contain Λ-symbols. Each element of J_i corresponds to a Λ-labeled node in the derivation forest of D'. Let $K_i \subseteq J_i$ be the subset of elements that correspond to nodes whose subtree contains M-nodes. For each $j \in K_i$, let $\eta(j) \subseteq \Lambda$ be the set of labels of maximal M-nodes in the subtree of the node correspondig to j. Note that by the choice of K_i, the set $\eta(j)$ is non-empty for each $j \in K_i$. Since the maximal M-nodes have distinct labels, it is $\eta(j_1) \cap \eta(j_2) = \emptyset$ for every $j_1, j_2 \in K_i$ and thus $|K_i| \leq |\Lambda|$.

Each $j \in J_i \setminus K_i$ is the only occurrence in $J_i \setminus K_i$ of its symbol, since otherwise, one of these occurrences would have been prunable. Hence, $|J_i \setminus K_i| \leq |\Lambda|$. Therefore,

$$|w_i|_\Lambda = |J_i| = |J_i \setminus K_i| + |K_i| \leq 2|\Lambda|$$

and setting $k := 2|\Lambda|$ meets our requirements. □

Now, the main result of this paper can be proven. For every PRCG G, we will construct a non-erasing PRCG that simulates G in the following way. We assume G to be pruning. The constructed grammar will avoid the generation of symbols in Λ and instead store them in multisets 'attached' to the nonterminal symbols. Here, attached means that the new set of nonterminal symbols consists of pairs (A, μ), where A is a nonterminal symbol in G and μ is a multiset.

Theorem 1. $\mathbf{pRC} = \mathbf{pRC}^\lambda$.

Proof. In order to show $\mathbf{pRC}^\lambda \subseteq \mathbf{pRC}$, we can restrict ourselves to PRCGs G with $\lambda \notin L(G)$. Indeed, if $\lambda \in L(G)$, we can find a non-erasing grammar for $L(G) \cap T^+$ and then modify it so as to add the empty word to the generated language.

Thus, without loss of generality, let $G = (N, \Lambda, T, P, S)$ be a pruning PRCG and let k be the constant provided by Lemma 4. The homomorphisms $\delta : (T \cup N)^* \to (T \cup N \setminus \Lambda)^*$, $\rho : (T \cup N)^* \to \Lambda^*$ are those satisfying $\delta(x) = \lambda$ and $\rho(x) = x$ for $x \in \Lambda$ and $\delta(y) = y$ and $\rho(y) = \lambda$ for $y \in T \cup N \setminus \Lambda$. Let

$$N' := \{(A, \mu) \mid A \in T \cup N \setminus \Lambda,\ \mu \in \Lambda^\oplus,\ |\mu| \leq k\},$$

where (A, μ) is a new symbol for each A and μ. In order to describe how the simulation works, we need the homomorphisms α and β:

$$(T \cup N)^* \xrightarrow{\alpha} (T \cup N \setminus \Lambda)^* \times \Lambda^\oplus \xleftarrow{\beta} (T \cup N')^*.$$

Here, $(T \cup N \setminus \Lambda)^* \times \Lambda^\oplus$ is regarded as a monoid with the operation $(x_1, y_1)(x_2, y_2) = (x_1 x_2, y_1 + y_2)$ for $x_1, x_2 \in (T \cup N \setminus \Lambda)^*$ and $y_1, y_2 \in \Lambda^\oplus$. The homomorphisms are defined by $\alpha(v) = (\delta(v), \Psi(\rho(v)))$ for $v \in (T \cup N)^*$ and $\beta(a) = (a, \mathbf{0})$, $\beta((A, \mu)) = (A, \mu)$ for $a \in T$ and $(A, \mu) \in N'$. We say that $u \in (T \cup N')^*$ *represents* $v \in (T \cup N)^*$ if $\alpha(v) = \beta(u)$.

A symbol (A, μ) in the constructed grammar represents a word with one occurrence of A and $\mu(B)$ occurrences of B for every $B \in \Lambda$. Therefore, we say that A and the symbols $B \in \Lambda$ with $\mu(B) \geq 1$ *occur* in (A, μ). For a subset $W \subseteq N'$, let $\gamma(W) \subseteq N$ be the set of symbols occurring in some element of W. Note that, in a word $v \in (T \cup N)^*$, the permitting context $U \subseteq N$ is present if and only if, in a word $u \in (T \cup N')^*$ representing v, a permitting context $W \subseteq N'$ with $U \subseteq \gamma(W)$ can be found.

We will now describe the new set P' of productions. The homomorphism $\iota : (T \cup N)^* \to (T \cup N')^*$ is defined by $\iota(y) = (y, \mathbf{0})$ for $y \in T \cup N$. For a production $(A \to w; U) \in P$, we distinguish two cases.

– Suppose $A \in N \setminus \Lambda$. Then, $\delta(w) \neq \lambda$. Hence, write $\delta(w) = w_1 w'$, where $w_1 \in T \cup N \setminus \Lambda$ and $w' \in (T \cup N \setminus \Lambda)^*$. For the production $(A \to w; U)$, we include the production

$$((A, \mu) \to (w_1, \mu + \Psi(\rho(w)))\iota(w'); W) \tag{1}$$

for every $\mu \in \Lambda^{\oplus}$ such that $|\mu + \Psi(\rho(w))| \leq k$, and every $W \subseteq N'$ such that $U \subseteq \gamma(W)$.
– In the case $A \in \Lambda$, we have $\delta(w) = \lambda$ and the production

$$((B, \mu) \to (B, \mu - A + \Psi(w)); W) \tag{2}$$

is introduced for each $B \in T \cup N \setminus \Lambda$, each $\mu \in \Lambda^{\oplus}$ such that $\mu(A) \geq 1$ and $|\mu - A + \Psi(w)| \leq k$ and each $W \subseteq N'$ such that $U \subseteq \gamma(W)$. These productions achieve the replacement of an occurrence of A that is attached to another symbol.

Finally, we add productions $((a, \mathbf{0}) \to a; \emptyset)$ for each $a \in T$ in order to allow the grammar to produce terminal symbols. The new grammar is then $G' = (N', T, P', S')$, where $S' = (S, \mathbf{0})$.

Suppose $u_1 \in (T \cup N')^*$ represents $v_1 \in (T \cup N)^*$ and $u_1 \Rightarrow_{G'} u_2$ by applying a rule of the form (1) or (2). Observe that there is a $v_2 \in (T \cup N)^*$ such that $v_1 \Rightarrow_G v_2$ and u_2 represents v_2. For every $w \in L(G')$, there is a derivation $(S, \mathbf{0}) = u_1 \Rightarrow_{G'} \cdots \Rightarrow_{G'} u_n$ such that $u_n = \iota(w)$ and all the applied rules are of the form (1) or (2). By the aforementioned observation, there is a derivation $S = v_1 \Rightarrow_G \cdots \Rightarrow_G v_n$ such that u_i represents v_i for each $i = 1, \ldots, n$. In particular, $w = v_n \in L(G)$. This shows $L(G') \subseteq L(G)$.

Let $v_1 \Rightarrow_G v_2$ using the rule $(A \to w; U)$, where $v_1, v_2 \in (T \cup N)^*$ and $|v_1|_\Lambda, |v_2|_\Lambda \leq k$. Furthermore, assume that $u_1 \in (T \cup N')^*$ represents v_1. Using the fact that $|v_2|_\Lambda \leq k$ and depending on whether $A \in N \setminus \Lambda$ or $A \in \Lambda$, one can find a rule of form (1) or (2) that can be applied to u_1 to obtain a $u_2 \in (T \cup N')$ such that u_2 represents v_2. Assume $w \in L(G)$ and use Lemma 4 to find a derivation $S = v_1 \Rightarrow_G \cdots \Rightarrow_G v_n = w$ with $|v_i|_\Lambda \leq k$ for $i = 1, \ldots, n$. Then, we have a derivation $(S, \mathbf{0}) = u_1 \Rightarrow_{G'} \cdots \Rightarrow_{G'} u_n$ such that u_i represents v_i for $i = 1, \ldots, n$. In particular, $u_n = \iota(w)$ and thus the rules $((a, \mathbf{0}) \to a; \emptyset)$ can be used to derive $u_n \Rightarrow_{G'}^* w$. Therefore, $w \in L(G')$. This proves $L(G') = L(G)$. □

4 Consequences

Obviously, every closure property of $\mathbf{pRC}^\lambda$ also holds for **pRC**. A language class is a *semi-AFL* if it is closed under non-erasing homomorphisms, inverse homomorphisms, intersection with regular sets and union. A semi-AFL is said to be *full* if it is also closed under arbitrary homomorphisms. Since **pRC** is a semi-AFL (see Theorem 1.3.1 in [3]) and Theorem 1 implies its closure under arbitrary homomorphisms, we have the following result.

Corollary 1. *The semi-AFL* **pRC** *is full.*

In the following, the class of languages generated by (non-erasing) matrix grammars without appearance checking will be denoted by $\mathbf{MAT}^\lambda$ ($\mathbf{MAT}$). For a detailed definition of matrix grammars [3], we refer the reader to [9]. Our next corollary to Theorem 1 is not a new result.

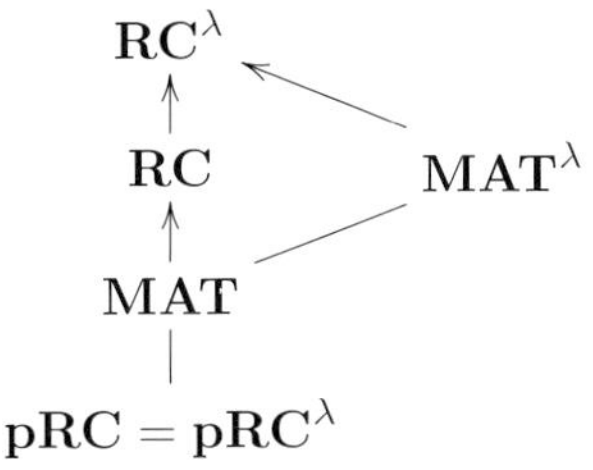

Fig. 1. Relations among language classes

Corollary 2. $\mathbf{pRC} \neq \mathbf{RC}$.

On the one hand, this can easily be deduced from the results in [6]. Since it is clear that $\mathbf{pRC} \subseteq \mathbf{MAT}$ and it is shown in [6] that all one-letter languages in $\mathbf{MAT}$ are regular, this also holds for $\mathbf{pRC}$. Furthermore, one can construct a non-erasing RCG generating a non-regular one-letter language (see Example 1.1.7 in [3]). Thus, the two classes differ. On the other hand, Ewert and van der Walt use their pumping lemma [5] to prove this inequality.

In the current paper, Corollary 2 can be obtained from Theorem 1 by observing that $\mathbf{pRC}$ is closed under erasing homomorphisms, while $\mathbf{RC}$ is not. The latter follows from the fact that $\mathbf{RC}$ only contains context-sensitive languages and $\mathbf{RC}^\lambda$ is the whole class of recursively enumerable languages (see, for example, Theorem 1.2.5 in [3]). Thus, the classes $\mathbf{pRC}$ and $\mathbf{RC}$ are not equal.

Corollary 3. $\mathbf{pRC}^\lambda$ *is contained in* $\mathbf{RC}$.

Theorem 1 can also be used to generalize the pumping lemma by Ewert and van der Walt [5] for non-erasing PRCGs. Since every PRCG has an equivalent non-erasing PRCG, we have the following corollary.

Corollary 4. *The pumping lemma from [5] holds for all languages generated by PRCGs.*

We will now present two conjectures regarding open problems in regulated rewriting. The first problem concerns the strictness of the inclusion $\mathbf{pRC} \subseteq \mathbf{MAT}$ (see Open Problems 1.2.2 in [3]). The language $L_1 = \{w \in \{a,b,c\}^* \mid |w|_a = |w|_b = |w|_c\}$ is contained in $\mathbf{MAT}$ (see Example 1.1.7 in [3] and use the fact that $\mathbf{MAT}$ is closed under permutation). However, L_1 does not seem to be contained in $\mathbf{pRC}$. This leads to the following conjecture.

Conjecture 1. $\mathbf{pRC} \neq \mathbf{MAT}$.

The second problem is whether there is a non-erasing matrix grammar for every language generated by a matrix grammar (see Open Problems 1.2.2 in [3]). The question is, in other words: is the inclusion $\mathbf{MAT} \subseteq \mathbf{MAT}^\lambda$ in fact an identity?

Conjecture 2. $\mathbf{MAT} = \mathbf{MAT}^\lambda$.

For more information on this problem, see [9].

Theorem 2. *Of the conjectures 1 and 2, at least one holds.*

[3] It should be noted here that in [9], non-erasing matrix grammars are allowed to generate the empty word. This difference aside, the definition in [3] is the same.

Proof. If **pRC** = **MAT**, then **MAT** is closed under arbitrary homomorphisms and thus equals $\mathbf{MAT}^\lambda$. □

A summary of the relations among the language classes is given in Figure 1. The lines (arrows) denote (proper) inclusions of the lower language classes into the upper language classes. Those that are not directly connected are not necessarily incomparable.

Acknowledgments. I would like to thank Matthias Jantzen, Manfred Kudlek, and Patrick Totzke for discussions and helpful comments.

References

1. Bordihn, H., Holzer, M.: Random context in regulated rewriting versus cooperating distributed grammar systems. In: Martín-Vide, C., Otto, F., Fernau, H. (eds.) LATA 2008. LNCS, vol. 5196, pp. 125–136. Springer, Heidelberg (2008)
2. Dassow, J.: Grammars with regulated rewriting. In: Martín-Vide, C., Mitrana, V., Păun, G. (eds.) Formal Languages and Applications, pp. 249–273. Springer, Berlin (2004)
3. Dassow, J., Păun, G.: Regulated rewriting in formal language theory. Springer, Berlin (1989)
4. Dassow, J., Păun, G., Salomaa, A.: Grammars with controlled derivations. In: Rozenberg, G., Salomaa, A. (eds.) Handbook of Formal Languages, vol. 2, pp. 101–154. Springer, Berlin (1997)
5. Ewert, S., van der Walt, A.: A pumping lemma for random permitting context languages. Theoretical Computer Science 270, 959–967 (2002)
6. Hauschildt, D., Jantzen, M.: Petri net algorithms in the theory of matrix grammars. Acta Informatica 31(8), 719–728 (1994)
7. Salomaa, A.: Formal Languages. Academic Press, New York (1973)
8. van der Walt, A.: Random context languages. In: Information Processing 71, Proceedings of the IFIP Congress 71, Foundations and Systems, vol. 1, pp. 66–68. North-Holland, Amsterdam (1972)
9. Zetzsche, G.: Erasing in Petri Net Languages and Matrix Grammars. In: Diekert, V., Nowotka, D. (eds.) DLT 2009, Stuttgart, Germany, June 30–July 3. LNCS, vol. 5583, pp. 490–501. Springer, Heidelberg (2009)

Game Semantics for Call-by-Value Polymorphism

James Laird

Department of Computer Science, University of Bath, UK
jiml@cs.bath.ac.uk

Abstract. A game semantic approach to interpreting call-by-value polymorphism is described, based on extending Hyland-Ong games (which have already proved a rich source of models for higher-order programming languages with computational effects) with explicit "copycat links". This captures universal quantification in a simple and concrete way; it is effectively presentable, and opens the possibility of extending existing model checking techniques to polymorphic types. In particular, we present a fully abstract semantics for a call-by-value language with general references and full higher-rank polymorphism, within which polymorphic objects, for example, may be represented. We prove full abstraction by showing that every universally quantified type is a *definable retract* of its instantiation with the type of natural numbers.

1 Introduction

This paper describes a denotational (games) semantics of higher-rank parametric polymorphism. Although semantic studies have successfully captured several aspects of this important paradigm, they have typically focused on a purely functional, call-by-name setting (in particular, the pure calculus System F [5,17]). However, polymorphism is also a key feature of languages with computational effects such as local state which are more naturally expressed in a call-by-value setting in which polymorphism is rather different to the phenomenon captured by System F. The aim of this paper is to explore a fully abstract model of a call-by-value polymorphic programming language with local state (general references) constructed using game semantics (itself a flexible way of describing many computational effects and features). The model is also quite concrete, notwithstanding the impredicative nature of second-order quantification.

Specifically, we shall study polymorphism in the context of a second-order extension of the language $\mathcal{L}$ introduced in [2]. This combines general references with a call-by-value functional language, and may be considered a core of ML. Although ML does not itself have full higher-rank polymorphism, such extension is possible [4] (the main issues, concerning type inference, are rather orthogonal to the semantic focus here). $\mathcal{L}$ was also proposed in [2] as a basis for describing *objects* with local state, making the extension with polymorphism a natural step towards describing object and subtype polymorphism. The same basic model

S. Abramsky et al. (Eds.): ICALP 2010, Part II, LNCS 6199, pp. 187–198, 2010.

has also been used to interpret *aspect-oriented* programs [18], with an associated (fully abstract) translation into $\mathcal{L}$.

Our model is (essentially[1]) a conservative extension of the semantics of $\mathcal{L}$ in [2], in which general references are interpreted by lifting the conditions of *innocence* and *visibility* applied in the original model of PCF [8]. The extension to polymorphic types is based on the observation, evident in earlier games models of e.g. propositional variables in proofs [3], that polymorphic proofs or programs correspond to *copycat strategies*: since such programs must behave uniformly over all instantiating types, all they can do is copy information between positive and negative occurrences. In our model, these "copycat links" are represented explicitly as pointers on sequences of moves, rather than by directly specifying behaviour at every possible type instantiation. Thus, determining equivalence of finitary program denotations is straightforward, and raises the possibility of using the semantics as the basis for more systematic model checking.

Related Work. Games models of (System F) polymorphism have been described by Hughes [7] and Abramsky and Jagadeesan [1]. The former captures full completeness for System F using a notion of *hypergame* allowing participants to import arenas instantiating variables. This closely reflects the syntax of System F; our semantics is more concrete and programming language oriented. The focus of the model in [1] is on *genericity* in the sense described in [13] — specifically it contains a rich collection of generic types (i.e. types such that instantiation into universally quantified types reflects denotational equivalence). The model described here also contains generic types: indeed every universal type is a retract of its instantiation with the type `nat`, a fact used to establish definability and full abstraction. A more direct comparison may be made with recent work by the author describing a fully abstract programming language based on extending System F with general references [10]— i.e. a call-by-name version of $\mathcal{L}^2$, although the more accurate distinction is between polymorphism of *value types* and *computation types* in the sense of [11]. A significant difference between the the two models is that copycat behaviour in the call-by-name case can be inferred from question/answer labelling via an extended bracketing condition, and so explicit pointers are not required. The work described here is also closely related to labelled transition systems for concurrent and sequential polymorphic languages, such as [12].

2 $\mathcal{L}^2$ — A Polymorphic Language with General References

We study polymorphism in the setting of $\mathcal{L}^2$, the second-order extension of the functional language with general references $\mathcal{L}$, modelled in [2]. Its types are given by the grammar:

[1] Its presentation is closer to Honda and Yoshida's model of the call-by-value λ-calculus [6], and also requires a further decomposition of moves as tuples of *atomic moves*, which are connected by copycat links.

Table 1. Evaluation Rules for $\mathcal{L}^2$

$$\frac{}{V,\mathcal{E}\Downarrow V,\mathcal{E}} \qquad \frac{M,\mathcal{E}\Downarrow\lambda x.M',\mathcal{E}' \quad N,\mathcal{E}'\Downarrow V,\mathcal{E}'' \quad M'[V/x],\mathcal{E}''\Downarrow U,\mathcal{E}'''}{M\,N,\mathcal{E}\Downarrow U,\mathcal{E}'''}$$

$$\frac{}{\mathtt{new}_T,\mathcal{E}\Downarrow a,(\mathsf{loc}\cup\{a\}),\mathcal{S}}\,a\notin\mathsf{loc} \qquad \frac{M,\mathcal{E}\Downarrow\Lambda(X).M',\mathcal{E}' \quad M'[T/X],\mathcal{E}'\Downarrow V,\mathcal{E}''}{M\{T\},\mathcal{E}\Downarrow M'[T/X],\mathcal{E}''}$$

$$\frac{M,\mathcal{E}\Downarrow a,\mathcal{E}' \quad N,\mathcal{E}'\Downarrow V,(\mathsf{loc},\mathcal{S})}{M{:=}N,\mathcal{E}\Downarrow(),(\mathsf{loc},\mathcal{S}[a\mapsto V])} \qquad \frac{M,\mathcal{E}\Downarrow a,(\mathsf{loc},\mathcal{S})}{!M,\mathcal{E}\Downarrow V,(\mathsf{loc},\mathcal{S})}\,\mathcal{S}(a)=V$$

$$X \mid \mathtt{unit} \mid \mathtt{nat} \mid \mathtt{bool} \mid S\times T \mid S\to T \mid \forall X.T$$

where X ranges over a set of type variables. The set of well-formed types over a given context of free type variables may be defined formally as for System F [5].

For any type T, we write $\mathtt{var}[T]$ for the type $(\mathtt{unit}\to T)\times(T\to\mathtt{unit})$ — the type of references to values of type T, corresponding to the product of the types of the two "methods" (*read* and *write*) for a reference object.

Terms are formed according to the rules of System F [5] (with products), extended with a collection of constants, including data values (numerals, truth values and a single value $()$: $\mathtt{unit}$), arithmetic operations including equality testing on $\mathtt{nat}$ — $\mathtt{eq}:\mathtt{nat}\times\mathtt{nat}\to\mathtt{bool}$ — a conditional $\mathtt{If}:\mathtt{bool}\to(T\times T)\to T$ — and constants $\mathtt{new}_T:\mathtt{var}[T]$ for declaring fresh references of type T. Given $M:\mathtt{var}[T]$, we write $!M$ for $\mathtt{fst}(M)$, and $M:=N$ for $\mathtt{snd}(M)\,N$. We omit typing annotations on variables and constants where they are arbitrary or may be inferred. Following [2], explicit recursion is omitted, since fixed points may be defined using self-referencing variables. The sublanguage $\mathcal{L}$ consists of all types constructed without using variables or quantification, and all terms in which each subterm is of such a type.

In [2], it was proposed that objects with local state could be represented as $\mathcal{L}$-terms: "The general scheme is that an object is represented by a term of the form $\mathsf{new}\,l_1 := v_1\ldots l_k := v_k\,\mathsf{in}\,\langle m_1,\ldots,m_p\rangle$ where $l_1,\ldots,l_k$ are the local variables of the object, and $m_1,\ldots,m_n$ are functions representing its methods." The example given in [2] is of a stack object, which has local variables representing a stack pointer and array storing the values on the stack, and functions *push* and *pop* representing its methods. This naturally extends to polymorphism — a polymorphic object may be represented as the *value* $\Lambda(X).\mathsf{new}\,l_1 := v_1\ldots l_k := v_k\,\mathsf{in}\,\langle m_1,\ldots,m_p\rangle$ — instantiating with a type creates a new object at that type — in the case of the stack example, this is the archetypal instance of a polymorphic object.

Operational Semantics. A *program* is a closed term of closed type of $\mathcal{L}^2$ extended with a set of location names (constants of closed type). *Values* are programs given by the grammar:

$$U,V ::= c \mid \lambda x.M \mid \Lambda x.M \mid (U,V)$$

where c is any constant except `new`. An environment is a pair $\mathcal{E} = (\mathsf{loc}, \mathcal{S})$ where loc is a set of location names and $\mathcal{S}$ is a partial function from loc to values. Key "big step" evaluation rules for evaluating a program and an environment to a value are given in Table 1. We write $M \Downarrow$ if $M, (\varnothing, \varnothing) \Downarrow V, \mathcal{E}$ for some $V, \mathcal{E}$ (this is conservative over the operational semantics of $\mathcal{L}$) and adopt standard definitions of contextual approximation and equivalence: given terms $M, N : T$, $M \lesssim N$ if for all closing contexts $C[\_]$, $C[M] \Downarrow$ implies $C[N] \Downarrow$. $M \approx N$ if $M \lesssim N$ and $N \lesssim M$. (This is also conservative over contextual equivalence for $\mathcal{L}$, which will be evident from the denotational semantics.)

3 Game Semantics of $\mathcal{L}$

We first recast the game semantics of $\mathcal{L}$ from [2] in a somewhat different presentation, required to enable the extension with polymorphism. As in [2], it is based on the dialogue games of Hyland and Ong [8]. However, we interpret the call-by-value λ-calculus in a *closed Freyd category* [16] using essentially the constructions of Honda and Yoshida [6] rather than the approach of [2] based on coproduct completion of a Cartesian closed category. The principal novelty here is a *decomposition* of the moves of call-by-value arenas as tuples of "atomic moves". Plays of the game will consist of sequences of these tuples or "compound moves", joined by justification pointers, with the "copycat links" introduced to interpret polymorphism connecting the atomic moves inside them.

Fix a "universal set of atomic moves $\mathcal{U}$ — this may be any set which contains a distinguished "context move" $\bullet$, a unit $*$, and the natural numbers, and such that $\mathcal{U} \oplus \mathcal{U} \subseteq \mathcal{U}$. A *decomposed arena* A over $\mathcal{U}$ is a tuple $(\mathsf{At}_A, M_A, \lambda_A, \mathsf{At}^I_A, \vdash_A)$, where $(\mathsf{At}_A, \lambda_A, \mathsf{At}^I_A, \vdash_A)$ is a labelled, bipartite, directed acyclic graph[2] presented as a set of nodes or *atomic moves* $\mathsf{At}_A \subseteq \mathcal{U}$, a question/answer labelling on At_A ($\lambda_A : M_A \to \{Q, A\}$), an explicit set of root nodes (initial moves), and an edge-relation ("enabling") $\vdash_A$, such that no two adjacent nodes are labelled as answers. Finally, $M_A \subseteq \bigcup\{\mathsf{At}^n_A \mid n \in \omega\}$ is a set of tuples of atomic moves (or "compound moves"), containing each atomic move at most once — i.e. $\pi_i(m) = \pi_j(n)$ implies $i = j$ and $m = n$, and such that any two atoms in the same compound move have the same labelling and polarity, and either both or neither are initial, so we may extend the question/answer, initial/non-initial and Player/Opponent designations to compound moves. We extend the enabling relation to M_A by stipulating that $\langle a_1, \ldots, a_m\rangle \vdash_A \langle b_1, \ldots, b_n\rangle$ if there exists a_i such that $a_i \vdash b_j$ for $j \leq n$. An A-rooted arena is one which every initial move is labelled as an answer, a Q-rooted arena is one in which every initial move is a question.

A justified sequence over a given set of (compound) moves is a sequence of such moves, together with at most one "justification pointer" from each move to a previously occurring move. A legal sequence over a Q-rooted arena A is a justified sequence over M_A such that each non-initial move has a pointer to an

[2] In which any two points with edges into a common node have edges coming from a common node.

occurrence of an enabling move, and which is *alternating* — Opponent moves are followed by Player moves and vice-versa —*well-opened* — there is at most one initial move — and *well-bracketed* — each answer move is justified by the most recent unanswered question.

Given decomposed A-rooted arenas A_1, A_2, we define a Q-rooted arena $A_1 \rightarrow A_2$ in which initial moves are the initial moves from A_1 relabelled as questions (to which the initial moves from A_2 are the answers).

- $\mathsf{At}_{A_1 \rightarrow A_2} = \mathsf{At}_{A_1} + \mathsf{At}_{A_2}$
- $M_{A_1 \rightarrow A_2} = \{\mathsf{in}_{\boldsymbol{i}}(\boldsymbol{a}) \mid \boldsymbol{a} \in M_{A_i} \wedge i \in \{1,2\}\}$
- $\lambda_{A_1 \rightarrow A_2}(a) = Q$, if $a \in \mathsf{At}^I_{A_1}$, $\lambda_{A_1 \rightarrow A_2}(\mathsf{in}_i(a)) = \lambda_{A_i}(a)$, otherwise,
- $\mathsf{At}^I_{A_1 \rightarrow A_2} = \{\mathsf{in}_1(a) \mid a \in \mathsf{At}^I_{A_1}\}$,
- $\vdash_{A_1 \rightarrow A_2} = \{\langle \mathsf{in}_i(a), \mathsf{in}_i(b)\rangle \mid i \in \{1,2\} \wedge a \vdash_{A_i} b\} \cup \{\langle \mathsf{in}_1(a), \mathsf{in}_2(b)\rangle \mid \langle a, b\rangle \in \mathsf{At}^I_{A_1} \times \mathsf{At}^I_{A_2}\}$.

Thus we may define a category $\mathcal{G}$ (relative to $\mathcal{U}$) in which objects are decomposed arenas over $\mathcal{U}$ and morphisms from A to B are (deterministic) *strategies* on $A \rightarrow B$ — non-empty, even-prefix-closed, even-branching sets of even-length legal sequences of $A \rightarrow B$. Strategies are composed as in [8,6]: given $\sigma : A \rightarrow B$, and $\tau : B \rightarrow C$, let $\sigma|\tau$ be the set of justified sequences s over $M_A + M_B + M_C$ such that $s\restriction A, B \in \sigma$ and $s \restriction B, C \in \tau$, then $\sigma;\tau : A \rightarrow C = \{s \in L_{A \rightarrow C} \mid \exists t \in \sigma|\tau . s = t\restriction A, C\}$. We may define *premonoidal* structure on $\mathcal{G}$, as in [6]:

- $\mathsf{At}_{A_1 \odot A_2} = \mathsf{At}_{A_1} + \mathsf{At}_{A_2}$
- $M_{A_1 \odot A_2} = \{\langle \mathsf{in}_{\mathbf{1}}(\boldsymbol{a}), \mathsf{in}_{\mathbf{2}}(\boldsymbol{b})\rangle \mid (\boldsymbol{a}, \boldsymbol{b}) \in M^I_{A_1} \times M^I_{A_2}\} \cup \{\mathsf{in}_{\boldsymbol{i}}(\boldsymbol{a}) \mid \boldsymbol{a} \in M_{A_i} \backslash M^I_{A_i}\}$
- $\lambda_{A_1 \odot A_2} = [\lambda_{A_1}, \lambda_{A_2}]$
- $\mathsf{At}^I_{A_1 \odot A_2} = \{\langle \mathsf{in}_1(a), \mathsf{in}_2(b)\rangle \mid a \in M_{A_1} \wedge b \in M_{A_2}\}$
- $\vdash_{A_1 \odot A_2} = \{\langle \mathsf{in}_i(a), \mathsf{in}_i(b)\rangle \mid a \vdash_{A_i} b\}$

The arena I, with a single (atomic and compound) move is the unit for $\odot$. For each arena A, an endofunctor $A \odot \_ : \mathcal{G} \rightarrow \mathcal{G}$ may be defined, along with symmetry and unit isomorphisms making $(\mathcal{G}, I, \odot)$ a symmetric premonoidal category (for further details see [6]).

We define a subcategory in which $\odot$ is a cartesian product by combining the notion of *totality* [6], with a form of *thread-independence* [2]: $\sigma : A \rightarrow B$ is total if $\tau;\sigma = \bot$ implies $\tau = \bot$ (where $\bot$ is the empty strategy) (i.e. σ responds to any initial question in A with an answer in B. A sequence in which this occurs is said to be total).

Given a total sequence $qas \in L_{A \rightarrow B}$, let $\sim$ be the reflexive, symmetric, transitive closure of the justification relation on s (not including qa). The *thread* of such a sequence is defined as follows:

$\mathsf{thread}(t) = t$ for $t \sqsubseteq qa$
$\mathsf{thread}(qasb) = \mathsf{thread}(qas)b$ if b is a Player move.
$\mathsf{thread}(qasbtc) = \mathsf{thread}(qasb)c$ if c is an Opponent move and b is the most recent move in $qasbt$ such that $b \sim c$.

A total strategy is *thread-independent* if for every sequence $s \in \sigma$, $\mathsf{thread}(s)$ is a legal sequence, and if $t \in \sigma$, with $\mathsf{thread}(tab) = \mathsf{thread}(s)$, then $tab \in \sigma$.

The composition of thread-independent total strategies is total and thread-independent (see [2]). So let $\mathcal{G}_t$ be the lluf subcategory of $\mathcal{G}$ consisting of such strategies. The premonoid $\odot$ restricts to $\mathcal{G}_t$, where it is a Cartesian product. Thus we have a Freyd category [16]; a Cartesian category $\mathcal{G}_t$ with an identity-on-objects strict symmetric premonoidal functor $J\_$ (in this case, inclusion) into a symmetric premonoidal category $\mathcal{G}$. Moreover, it is a *closed* Freyd category: for each A-rooted arena A, the functor $J(\_) \odot A : \mathcal{G}_t :\rightarrow \mathcal{G}$ has a right adjoint $A \rightharpoonup \_ : \mathcal{G} \rightarrow \mathcal{G}_t$. (Define $A \rightharpoonup B = \uparrow(A \rightarrow B)$, where $\uparrow\_$ adds a single initial answer move, enabling all of the initial moves of $A \rightarrow B$. Then there is an evident bijection from legal sequences on $A \odot B \rightarrow C$ to threads of total legal sequences on $A \rightarrow (B \rightharpoonup C)$ (sending $\langle \boldsymbol{a}, \boldsymbol{b}\rangle s$ to $\boldsymbol{a}\langle * \rangle \boldsymbol{b}s$) yielding the required adjunction.)

This yields a semantics of the call-by-value λ-calculus with products [15]. Concretely, this is equivalent to the semantics given in [2], based on a lifting monad $\mathbf{T}$ on a category of indexed families of Q-rooted arenas (equivalent to the action of $\mathbf{1} \rightharpoonup \_$ on $\mathcal{G}_t$). Constant types are interpreted as coproducts of the terminal object — e.g. $[\![\mathtt{nat}]\!] = \coprod_{i \in \mathtt{nat}} \mathbf{1}$. To complete the semantics of $\mathcal{L}$, the interpretation of the `new` declaration is given as the family of strategies $\mathsf{cell}_A : I \rightarrow (A \rightharpoonup I) \times (I \rightharpoonup A)$ defined in [2].

4 Polymorphic Arenas

We now describe the main contribution of this paper: further structure on decomposed arenas allowing the interpretation of type polymorphism, and in particular, the extension of the semantics of $\mathcal{L}$ to $\mathcal{L}^2$. We capture the fact that any strategy representing a generic program over a variable type can only play copycat between positive and negative occurrences of instantiating games in a uniform way by introducing a new kind of pointer, between *atomic* moves: a *copycat link*. A *copycat enabling* structure for the arena A is given by the following:

- A set of *contingent* atomic moves $\mathsf{Ct}_A \subseteq \mathsf{At}_A$ which can only be played with a copycat link to a previous move.
- A copycat enabling relation $\rhd \subseteq M_A \times \mathsf{At}_A \times \mathsf{Ct}_A$, such that if $(l, m) \rhd n$, then $\lambda^{OP}(l) = \lambda(m) = \overline{\lambda(n)}$, $l \vdash^* m$ and $l \vdash^* n$. (As well as the possible source (m) and target (n) of copycat links, this ternary relation also specified a "scoping move" (l).

A legal sequence on such an arena is a legal sequence on A together with a copycat link from each contingent atomic move c to a preceding atomic move b such that there exists a move a hereditarily justifying b and c with $(a, b) \lhd c$.

Context Arenas. Types with free variables will be interpreted as *context-arenas*. These are, in essence, arenas with sets of explicit "holes", into which any other game can be plugged (similar to the polymorphic arenas of [7]).

A notion of context *address* is a set of injections from $\mathcal{U}$ to $\mathcal{U}$, closed under composition with left and right tagging, and containing the identity. We assume such a notion (e.g. the set of finite sequences of right and left taggings).

Definition 1. *A n-context arena is given by an arena with copycat enabling $(\mathsf{At}_A, M_A, \lambda_A, \mathsf{At}^I_A, \vdash_A, \mathsf{Ct}_A, \rhd_A)$, and disjoint sets $C_A(1), \ldots, C_A(n)$ of addresses satisfying (for all $\phi, \psi \in \bigcup_{i \leq n} C_A(i)$):*

- $At_A \cap \phi(\mathcal{U}) \subseteq \{\phi(\bullet)\}$
- *If* $\phi \neq \psi$ *then* $\phi(\mathcal{U}) \cap \psi(\mathcal{U}) = \varnothing$.
- $\phi(\bullet) \notin \mathsf{Ct}_A$ *and* $(a, \phi(\bullet), b), (a, b, \phi(\bullet)) \notin \lhd_A$ *for all* $a, b \in \mathsf{At}_A$.

We write $H_A(i)$ for the set of atoms $\{\phi(\bullet) \mid \phi \in C_A(i)\}$, which are called *holes*: $H_A(i)$ is partitioned according to Player/Opponent labelling of A into sets $H^-_A(i)$ and $H^+_A(i)$ of Player and Opponent holes respectively.

The basic example of n-context arena is the arena X_i for $i \leq n$, containing a single atom, $\bullet$, a single (initial) compound move, $\langle\bullet\rangle$, with $C_{X_i}(i) = \{\mathsf{id}\}$ and $C_{X_i}(j) = \varnothing$ for $i \neq j$. The constructions $\rightarrow$, $\odot$ and $\rightharpoonup$ extend straightforwardly to n-context arenas by composing the address functions with left and right tagging: e.g. $C_{A \odot B}(i) = C_{A \rightarrow B}(i) = \{\phi_i; \mathsf{in}_1 \mid \phi \in C_A(i)\} \cup \{\phi; \mathsf{in}_2 \mid \phi \in C_B(i)\}$.

Given a Q-rooted n-context arena $(A, C_1, \ldots, C_n)$, (with $n > 0$) we define the *universal quantification* $\forall_n A$ to be the $n-1$-context arena obtained by adding the Player holes $H^-_A(n)$ as contingent moves with copycat enablings from the Opponent holes $H^+_A(n)$, with the scoping moves being any enabling initial moves:

- $\mathsf{At}_{\forall_n A} = \mathsf{At}_A$, $M_{\forall_n A} = M_A$, $\mathsf{At}^I_{\forall_n A} = \mathsf{At}^I_A$, $\vdash_{\forall_n A} = \vdash_A$,
- $\mathsf{Ct}_{\forall_n A} = \mathsf{Ct}_A \cup H^-_A(n)$
- $\rhd_{\forall_n A} = \rhd_A \cup (\mathsf{At}^I_A \times H^+_A(n) \times H^-_A(n))$.
- $C_{\forall_n} A(i) = C_A(i)$ for $i < n$.

We shall write $\forall A$ for the arena $\forall_1 \ldots \forall_n A$. For each k, we define a category $\mathcal{G}(k)$ in which objects are k-context arenas and morphisms from B to C are strategies on $\forall(A \rightarrow B)$. To extend the definition of composition to these morphisms, we stipulate that the restriction operation operates on sequences with copycat links by replacing the copycat link relation with its transitive closure over erased moves. Composition of $\sigma : A \rightarrow B$ and $\tau : B \rightarrow C$ is then just the same as for the underlying strategies. The *identity* $\mathsf{id}_A : A \rightarrow A$ is given by the set of copycat sequences on $\forall(A \rightarrow A)$ such that Player hole moves of $A \rightarrow A$ point to the corresponding preceding move. Similarly, the premonoidal structure on $\mathcal{G}$ may be extended to $\mathcal{G}(k)$, establishing:

Proposition 1. *For each $k \in \mathbb{N}$, $(\mathcal{G}(k), \mathcal{G}_t(k), I, \odot)$ is a closed Freyd category.*

For example, Figure 1 shows the sequences distinguishing the generic projection morphisms from $X_1 \times X_1$ to X_1 — in which only the copycat links differ. Figure 2 shows a typical sequence of a generic cell strategy cell_{X_1}. There are evident "identity on morphisms" functors:

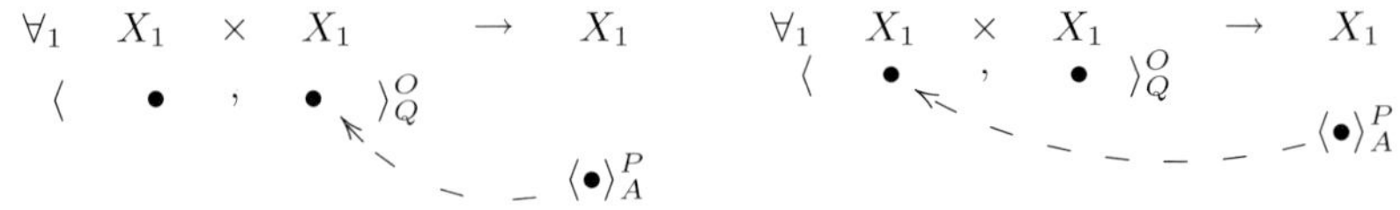

Fig. 1. Alternative Plays on $X \times X \to X$ with copycat links

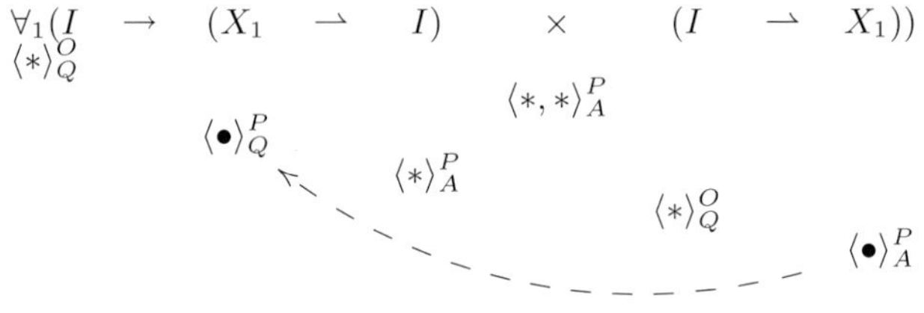

Fig. 2. Play of cell_X

- Contraction: $\delta_n : \mathcal{G}(n+1) \to \mathcal{G}(n)$ (sends $(A, C_A(1), \ldots, C_A(n+1))$ to $(A, C_A(1), \ldots, C_A(n) \cup C_A(n+1)))$.
- Permutation: $\theta_n^i : \mathcal{G}(n) \to \mathcal{G}(n)$ (sends $(A, C_A(1), \ldots, C_A(i), \ldots, C_A(n))$ to $(A, C_A(1), \ldots, C_A(n), \ldots, C_A(i)))$.
- Weakening: $K_n : \mathcal{G}(n) \to \mathcal{G}(n+1)$ (which sends $(A, C_A(1), \ldots, C_A(n))$ to $(A, C_A(1), \ldots, C_A(n), \varnothing))$.

The left adjoint to K_n (precomposed with the inclusion of $\mathcal{G}(k)_t$ into $\mathcal{G}(k)$) will be used to interpret type-variable abstraction.

Proposition 2. *The functor $K_n \cdot J : \mathcal{G}_t(n) \to \mathcal{G}(n+1)$ has a right adjoint Π_n.*

Proof. For any $n+1$-context arena B, let $\Pi_n B = \uparrow \forall_{n+1}(I \to B)$. For any n-context arena A, there is a (natural) correspondence between total, thread-independent strategies on $\forall(A \to \Pi_n B)$, and strategies on $\forall(K_n(A) \to B)$.

4.1 Composing Context Arenas

Instantiation of type variables with types is interpreted by replacing hole-moves with the corresponding context-arenas. Given an $n+1$-context arena A, and an m-context arena B, we define instantiation of B into the $n+1$th hole of A — the $n+m$-context arena $A[B]$ — by replacing the atomic move $\phi(\bullet)$ with the atomic moves $\phi(\mathsf{At}_B)$ for each $n+1$ hole address ϕ.

First, given a move $\boldsymbol{a} \in M_A$, we define the set of moves $\boldsymbol{a}[B]$ to be the set of tuples obtained by replacing occurrences of $\phi(\bullet)$ in $\boldsymbol{a}$ such that $\phi \in C_A(n+1)$ with $\boldsymbol{\phi(b)}$ for some $\boldsymbol{b} \in M_B^I$. Then:

- $\mathsf{At}_{A[B]} = (\mathsf{At}_A - H_A(n+1)) \cup \bigcup_{\phi \in C_A(n+1)} \phi(\mathsf{At}_B)$.
- $M_{A[B]} = \bigcup\{m[B] \mid m \in M_A\} \cup \{\boldsymbol{\phi(b)} \mid \boldsymbol{b} \in M_B - M_B^I \wedge \phi \in C_A(n+1)\}$
- $\lambda_{A[B]}(a) = \lambda_A(a)$ if $a \in \mathsf{At}_A - H_A(n+1)$,
  $\lambda_{A[B]}(\phi(b)) = \lambda_A(\phi(b))$, if $b \in \mathsf{At}_B - \mathsf{At}_B^I$
  $\lambda_{A[B]}(\phi(b)) = \lambda_B(\phi(\bullet))$, if $b \in \mathsf{At}_B^I$

- $\vdash_{A[B]} = \vdash_A \upharpoonright (M_A - H_A(n+1)) \cup \bigcup_{\phi \in C_A(n+1)} (\{(a, \phi(b) \mid a \vdash_A \phi(\bullet) \wedge b \in \mathsf{At}^I_B\} \cup \{(\phi(b), a \mid \phi(\bullet) \vdash_A a \wedge b \in \mathsf{At}^I_B\} \cup \{(\phi(b), \phi(b')) \mid b \vdash_B b'\}$.
- $\mathsf{Ct}_{A[B]} = \mathsf{Ct}_A \cup \bigcup_{\phi \in C_A(n+1)} \phi(\mathsf{Ct}_B)$
- $\rhd_{A[B]} = \rhd_A \cup \bigcup_{\phi \in C_n} \{(\phi(b), \phi(b'), \phi(b'')) \mid (b, b') \rhd_B b''\}$.
- $C_{A[B]}(i) = C_A(i)$ for $i \leq n$ and $C_{A[B]}(n+j) = \{\psi \cdot \phi \mid (\phi, \psi) \in C_A(n) \times C_B(j)\}$

We may observe that instantiation is associative — i.e. $A[B[C]] = (A[B])[C]$.

The corresponding instantiation of types for type variables in *terms* is interpreted by extending strategies to the expanded arenas by playing *copycat* between the copy of B substituted for a contingent Player hole move, and the copy of B substituted for the hole move to which it points. We define (by induction on sequence length) for each sequence $s \in L_{\forall(A[B] \rightarrow B[D])}$, a set of justified sequences $\widehat{s}$ on $L_{\forall(A \rightarrow D)}$ such that $s' \in \widehat{s}$ if it can be obtained from s by:

- Erasing non-initial B-moves in s.
- For each move $m \in M_{A \rightarrow D}$, replacing any move $\boldsymbol{a} \in m[B]$ with m.
- Adding copycat links between hole moves $\phi(\bullet) \in H^+_{A \rightarrow B}(n+1)$ and $\psi(\bullet) \in H^-_{A \rightarrow B}(n+1)$, if $\phi(\bullet)$ replaces $\boldsymbol{\phi(b)}$ and $\psi(\bullet)$ replaces $\boldsymbol{\psi(b)}$, where for all even prefixes $t \sqsubseteq^E s$ containing $\boldsymbol{\phi(b)}$, $\boldsymbol{\psi(b)}$, the subsequences of t consisting of compound moves of the form $\boldsymbol{\phi(b')}$ hereditarily justified by $\boldsymbol{\phi(b)}$ and of moves of the form $\boldsymbol{\psi(b')}$ hereditarily justified by $\boldsymbol{\psi(b)}$ are equal (up to the action of ϕ, ψ).

Given a strategy $\sigma : A \rightarrow D$ in $\mathcal{G}(n+1)$ we define $\sigma[B] : A[B] \rightarrow D[B]$ in $\mathcal{G}(n+m)$ to be the set of sequences s on $\forall(A[B] \rightarrow D[B])$ such that there exists $s' \in \widehat{s}$ with $s' \in \sigma$. We verify that this yields a deterministic strategy, and the action of instantiation into strategies is compositional.

Proposition 3. *For any m-context arena B, there is a functor (of closed Freyd categories) from $\mathcal{G}(n+1)$ to $\mathcal{G}(n+m)$ sending A to $A[B]$ and $\sigma : A \rightarrow D$ to $\sigma[B] : A[B] \rightarrow D[B]$.*

Using the permutation functor, we may define instantiation into any hole — i.e. $A[B]_i = \theta^i_n(\theta^i_{n+1}(A)[B])$ — and thus multiple instantiations: given a n-context arena A, and m-context arenas $B_1, \ldots, B_n$, we write $A[B_1, \ldots, B_n]$ for the m-context arena obtained by instantiation of B_i into hole i for each i, followed by contraction of each set of holes $\{i + j.m \mid j \leq m\}$ for each i.

5 Semantics of $\mathcal{L}^2$

We now have the constructions in place to define a *hyperdoctrine* model of $\mathcal{L}^2$, in the style of the Seely-Pitts formulation of $2\lambda\times$ hyperdoctrine model for System F [19,14]. We define an indexing category $\mathbf{B}$ in which objects are natural numbers and morphisms from m to n are n-tuples of m-context arenas. Composition of $\langle A_1, \ldots, A_m \rangle : l \rightarrow m$ with $\langle B_1, \ldots, B_n \rangle : m \rightarrow n$ is by instantiation to $\langle B_1[A_1, \ldots A_m], \ldots, B_n[A_1, \ldots A_m] \rangle$ (associativity follows from the unary case, with naturality of the functors for contraction and permutation). The identity on n is the tuple $\langle X_1, \ldots, X_n \rangle$. $\mathbf{B}$ has finite products, given by arithmetic sums, and is finitely generated from the object 1 by this product.

Let cFcat be the category of closed Freyd categories and structure-preserving functors (i.e. pairs of premonoidal structure preserving functors agreeing on objects and commuting with the specified identity-on-objects functor). We define a functor $\_^*$ from $\mathbf{B}^{\mathbf{OP}}$ into cFcat, sending n to $\mathcal{G}(n)$, and the tuple of context-arenas $\langle A_1, \ldots, A_n \rangle$ to the functor $\_[A_1, \ldots, A_n]$. The adjunctions between $\Pi_n\_ : \mathcal{G}(n+1) \to \mathcal{G}_t(n)$ and the reindexing $K_n \cdot J : \mathcal{G}(n+1) \to \mathcal{G}$ defined in Proposition 2 for each n form a fibred adjunction: i.e. for each reindexing $\alpha : m \to n$, $\Pi_n; J_n; \alpha^* = (\alpha \times \mathsf{id}_1)^*; \Pi_m; J_m$ (the *Beck-Chevalley* condition). Concretely, this is the requirement that $I \rightharpoonup \forall_{m+1} A[B_1, \ldots, B_n, X_{m+1}] = (I \rightharpoonup \forall_{n+1} A)[B_1, \ldots, B_n]$.

Thus we have an interpretation of term formation for $\mathcal{L}^2$, with terms over the free variables $X_1, \ldots, X_n$ interpreted in the fibre $\mathcal{G}(n)$. Constants of $\mathcal{L}$ are interpreted as in [2]. In particular, $\mathtt{new}_T$ is interpreted as the strategy $\mathsf{cell}_{[\![S]\!]}$ obtained by instantiating $[\![S]\!]$ into the generic strategy cell_{X_1} (Fig. 2). For constant S, this is the strategy defined in [2] and thus satisfies the key equational rules established there defining its behaviour under assignment and dereferencing. These are used, with the soundness of the hyperdoctrine semantics, to prove soundness of the model with respect to the operational semantics. *Computational Adequacy* is proved for an approximating semantics in which each cell can be dereferenced a bounded number of times (see [9]) using a reducibility predicate argument, which extends to the unbounded system by continuity.

Proposition 4. *$M \Downarrow$ if and only if $[\![M]\!] \neq \bot$.*

6 Full Abstraction

We prove that our semantics of $\mathcal{L}^2$ has the "finite definability property" — i.e. every finite strategy on a closed type is the denotation of a term (a. k. a. "intensional full abstraction") — by reduction to definability in $\mathcal{L}$, which was proved in [2]. The reduction to $\mathcal{L}$ is based on a strong form of the genericity property, described in [13] for models of System F: a type T is generic if instantiation of all universal types with T preserves denotational *inequivalence*. All types containing more than one distinguishable value, such as $\mathtt{bool}$, are generic with respect to our model of $\mathcal{L}^2$, although the unit type, for example, is not (instantiating $\forall X.X \times X \to X$ with $\mathtt{unit}$ equates left and right projection). Moreover, the type $\mathtt{nat}$ has a stronger "internal genericity" property — for any type $T(X)$, the instantiation $\lambda x^{\forall X.T}.\lambda y^{\mathtt{unit}}.x\{\mathtt{nat}\} : \forall X.T \to (\mathtt{unit} \to T[\mathtt{nat}])$ denotes a morphism with a definable retraction — i.e. a left-inverse which is the denotation of a term $\mathsf{inst}_T^{-1} : (\mathtt{unit} \to T[\mathtt{nat}]) \to \forall X.T$.

Informally, inst_T^{-1} denotes a strategy which plays copycat between $[\![\forall X.T[X]]\!]$ and $[\![\mathbf{1} \rightharpoonup T[\mathtt{nat}]]\!]$, except that each Opponent hole move a in $[\![T[X]]\!]$ is replaced with an atomic move representing a fresh natural number in $[\![\mathtt{unit} \to T[\mathtt{nat}]]\!]$. If Opponent subsequently plays a copy of this move in $[\![\mathtt{unit} \to T[\mathtt{nat}]]\!]$, then inst_T^{-1} plays a move with a copycat link to a. To define inst_T^{-1}, a counter is set up to supply fresh values of type nat, and an array for storing values of type X (a reference of type $\mathtt{nat} \to X$) is declared. Whenever a value of type X is encountered in $T[X]$, it is stored in the array at an index freshly generated by the counter, which is returned at the corresponding point in $T[\mathtt{nat}]$. Whenever a value of type nat is encountered in in $T[\mathtt{nat}]$, the value of type X stored at the corresponding index is returned.

Proposition 5. *For any type T, the morphism denoted by* $\mathsf{inst}_{\mathtt{nat}} : \forall X.T \to \mathbf{1} \to T[\mathtt{nat}]$ *has a definable retraction.*

Proof. Given $f : \mathtt{var}[\mathtt{nat} \to T]$, and $V : T$, define $f[n \to V] : \mathtt{unit} =_{df} f := \lambda y.\mathtt{If}\, y = n\, \mathtt{then}\, V\, \mathtt{else}\, (!f\ y)$. Given $c : \mathtt{var}[\mathtt{nat}]$, define $\mathtt{get}(c) = (a := \mathtt{succ}\ !a); !a$.

We define terms $f : \mathtt{var}[\mathtt{nat} \to X], c : \mathtt{var}[\mathtt{nat}] \vdash \mathsf{in}_T : T[X] \to A[\mathtt{nat}]$ and $f : \mathtt{var}[\mathtt{nat} \to X], c : \mathtt{var}[\mathtt{nat}] \vdash \mathsf{out}_A : A[\mathtt{nat}] \to T[X]$ by induction on T:

- $\mathsf{in}_X = \lambda x^{\mathtt{nat}}.(!f)\ x$, $\mathsf{out}_X = \lambda x^X.\mathtt{let}\, y^{\mathtt{nat}} = \mathtt{get}(c)\, \mathtt{in}\, f[y \mapsto x]; y$
- If $T = Y$ $(Y \neq X)$ or $T \in \{\mathtt{nat}, \mathtt{bool}, \mathtt{unit}\}$, then $\mathsf{in}_T = \mathsf{out}_T = \lambda x^T.x$.
- $\mathsf{in}_{S \times T} = \lambda x.\langle \mathsf{in}_S\ (\mathtt{fst} x), \mathsf{in}_T(\mathtt{snd} x)\rangle$, $\mathsf{out}_{S \times T} = \lambda x.\langle \mathsf{out}_S\ (\mathtt{fst} x), \mathsf{out}_T(\mathtt{snd} x)\rangle$
- $\mathsf{in}_{S \to T} = \lambda g.\lambda x.\mathsf{in}_T\ (g(\mathsf{out}_S\ x))$, $\mathsf{out}_{S \to T} = \lambda g.\lambda x.\mathsf{out}_T\ (g(\mathsf{in}_S\ x))$.

We may now define $\mathsf{inst}_T^{-1} = \lambda z^{\mathtt{unit} \to T[\mathtt{nat}]}.\Lambda(X).\mathtt{new}_{\mathtt{nat} \to X}\ f.\mathtt{new}_{\mathtt{nat}}\ c := 0.\mathsf{in}_T\ (z\ ())$.

Since the relation $\trianglelefteq$ is a precongruence on $\mathcal{L}^2$ types, every type of $\mathcal{L}^2$ is a definable retract of a type of $\mathcal{L}$ obtained by instantiating all universal types to nat. In combination with finite definability for $\mathcal{L}$ [2], this yields:

Theorem 1. *For any $\mathcal{L}^2$-type S, every finite strategy σ on $I \to [\![S]\!]$ is the denotation of a term $M_\sigma : S$*

This implies full abstraction for the collapse of the model under its *intrinsic preorder*. As in [2], it is straightforward to characterise the intrinsic preorder directly, by restricting strategies to their sets of *complete* sequences — i.e. those which contain equal numbers of questions and answers. Let $\mathsf{comp}(\sigma)$ be the set of complete sequences of the strategy σ. Then the following result is a corollary of finite definability (or equivalently, reduction to $\mathcal{L}$ via definable retraction).

Theorem 2. *For any terms M, N, $M \lesssim N \iff \mathsf{comp}([\![M]\!]) \subseteq \mathsf{comp}([\![N]\!])$.*

7 Conclusions and Further Directions

In recent work [10], we have shown how call-by-name polymorphism can be interpreted in a similar setting, but without explicit copycat links, using instead questions/answer labelling and the bracketing condition to infer them. This raises the problem of finding a semantics for a polymorphic version of a general typing system such as *call-by-push-value* [11]. Explicit copycat links do appear to make it simpler to describe strategies which are definable without general references — i.e. in polymorphic versions of call-by-value PCF or reduced ML, but this has yet to be worked out in detail. We have shown that the problem of determining observational equivalence in $\mathcal{L}^2$ is reducible to the same problem in $\mathcal{L}$ (which is, itself, a very expressive language). This leaves open the problem of finding fragments of $\mathcal{L}^2$ in which this problem is decidable. Finally, a more distant goal is an illuminating game semantics of subtype polymorphism.

References

1. Abramsky, S., Jagadeesan, R.: A game semantics for generic polymorphism. In: Gordon, A.D. (ed.) FOSSACS 2003. LNCS, vol. 2620, pp. 1–22. Springer, Heidelberg (2003)
2. Abramsky, S., Honda, K., McCusker, G.: A fully abstract games semantics for general references. In: Proceedings of the 13th Annual Symposium on Logic in Computer Science, LICS 1998 (1998)
3. Abramsky, S., Jagadeesan, R.: Games and full completeness for multiplicative linear logic. Journal of Symbolic Logic 59, 543–574 (1994)
4. Le Botlan, D., Rémy, D.: MLF: Raising ML to the power of System F. In: Proceedings of eighth ACM SIGPLAN conference of functional programming, pp. 27–38 (2003)
5. Girard, J.-Y.: Interprétation functionelle et elimination des coupures de l'arithmètique d'ordre supérieur. PhD thesis, Université Paris VII (1972)
6. Honda, K., Yoshida, N.: Game theoretic analysis of call-by-value computation. In: Degano, P., Gorrieri, R., Marchetti-Spaccamela, A. (eds.) ICALP 1997. LNCS, vol. 1256. Springer, Heidelberg (1997)
7. Hughes, D.J.D.: Hypergame Semantics: Full Completeness for System F. PhD thesis, University of Oxford (1999)
8. Hyland, J.M.E., Ong, C.-H.L.: On full abstraction for PCF: I, II and III. Information and Computation 163, 285–408 (2000)
9. Laird, J.: A categorical semantics of higher-order store. In: Proceedings of CTCS 2002. ENTCS, vol. 69. Elsevier, Amsterdam (2002)
10. Laird, J.: Game semantics for a polymorphic programming language. In: Proc. LICS 2010 (2010) (to appear)
11. Levy, P.B.: Call-By-Push-Value. In: Semantic Structures in Computation. Kluwer, Dordrecht (2004)
12. Levy, P.B., Lassen, S.: Typed normal form bisimulation for parametric polymorphism. In: Proceedings of LICS 2008, pp. 341–552. IEEE press, Los Alamitos (2008)
13. Longo, G., Milsted, K., Soloviev, S.: The genericity theorem and parametricity in the polymorphic λ-calculus. Theoretical Computer Science 121(1&2), 323–349 (1993)
14. Pitts, A.: Polymorphism is set-theoretic constructively. In: Pitt, D. (ed.) CTCS 1988. LNCS, vol. 283, Springer, Heidelberg (1988)
15. Power, J., Thielecke, H.: Environments in Freyd categories and κ-categories. In: Wiedermann, J., Van Emde Boas, P., Nielsen, M. (eds.) ICALP 1999. LNCS, vol. 1644. Springer, Heidelberg (1999)
16. Power, J., Robinson, E.: Premonoidal categories and notions of computation. Mathematical Structures in Computer Science (1997)
17. Reynolds, J.C.: Towards a theory of type structure. In: Robinet, B. (ed.) Programming Symposium. LNCS, vol. 19, Springer, Heidelberg (1974)
18. Sanjabi, S., Ong, C.-H.L.: Fully abstract semantics of additive aspects by translation. In: Proceedings of Sixth International ACM Conference on Aspect-Oriented Software Development, pp. 135–148 (2007)
19. Seely, R.A.G.: Categorical semantics for higher-order polymorphic lambda-calculus. Journal of Symbolic Logic 52(4), 969–989 (1987)

What Is a Pure Functional?

Martin Hofmann[1], Aleksandr Karbyshev[2], and Helmut Seidl[2]

[1] Institut für Informatik, Universität München, Oettingenstrasse 67, 80538 München, Germany
hofmann@ifi.lmu.de
[2] Fakultät für Informatik, Technische Universität München

Abstract. Given an ML function `f : (int->int)->int` how can we rigorously specify that `f` is pure, i.e., produces no side-effects other than those arising from calling its functional argument? We show that existing methods based on preservation of invariants and relational parametricity are insufficient for this purpose and thus define a new notion that captures purity in the sense that for any functional F that is pure in this sense there exists a corresponding question-answer strategy. This research is motivated by an attempt to prove algorithms correct that take such supposedly pure functionals as input and apply them to stateful arguments in order to inspect intensional aspects of their behaviour.

1 Introduction

Suppose we are given an unknown SML-function `f : (int->int)->int` as *input*. How can we rigorously specify that `f` does not cause side-effects other than those that might arise by applying `f` to a side-effecting argument? Our motivation for studying this question stems from an attempt to rigorously verify fixpoint solvers that take such a supposedly pure functional as input. Let us explain this application in some more detail.

Generic fixpoint solvers have successfully been used as the core algorithmic engine for program analyser frameworks both for logic programming languages [5, 7] and C [16], see also [11]. Such solvers take as input an arbitrary equation system over a set Var of variables and some complete lattice Dom. Each such system is specified as a function from the set Var of unknowns to their respective right-hand sides where each right-hand side is considered as a *function* of type $(\mathsf{Var} \to \mathsf{Dom}) \to \mathsf{Dom}$ which typically is implemented in some specification language. The generic local solver then starts from a set of interesting variables and explores the variable space Var only in so far as their values *contribute* to the values of the interesting variables. In order to evaluate as few right-hand sides as possible, any efficient fixpoint algorithm takes dependencies among variables into account. If right-hand sides, however, are just semantically given as functions, no static preprocessing is possible to identify (a superset of) such dependencies. Therefore, generic solvers such as [3, 9, 6] rely on *self-observation* to identify the variable dependencies when they are encountered during fixpoint iteration. Due to this reflective behaviour, these algorithms are quite involved and thus difficult to be proven correct. While they are formulated as being applicable to systems of equations using *arbitrary* functions as right-hand sides, they clearly can only work properly for right-hand sides which are sufficiently well-behaved.

S. Abramsky et al. (Eds.): ICALP 2010, Part II, LNCS 6199, pp. 199–210, 2010.

Other situations where supposedly pure functionals arise as input include Simpson's algorithm for exact integration [17] and the program transformations described in [10]. More distantly, we hope that our results might also contribute to the issue of purity in object-oriented specification [15] and be of interest to the Haskell community.

In this paper, we give an extensional semantic criterion for purity and show that it entails the existence of a strategy tree for the given functional. Thus, when trying to verify one of the aforementioned algorithms one can assume without loss of generality that the functional input is presented in the form of such a strategy tree which allows for a convenient proof by induction. Alternatively, one can use our extensional criterion directly for the verification and indeed we do so when verifying a recursive program that extracts a strategy tree from a given semantically pure functional.

Section 3 and 4 review classical parametricity and explain its weakness in the given context. Section 5 defines a new, stronger, notion of parametricity which by way of universal quantification yields our concept of semantic purity. Section 6 applies our notion to identify snapback (memorising and restoring the initial state) as impure, something that was hitherto impossible in a setting of total functions. Section 7 defines an inductive set of strategy trees which are shown in Sections 8 and 9 to represent pure functionals. Section 10 explains relations to Algol theory and game semantics.

The proofs except the one of Theorem 6 have been formalised in Coq. Moreover, one of us has just completed the formal verification (also in Coq) of a generic fixpoint algorithm using the results reported here. This will be published in a companion paper.

2 Preliminaries

For sets X and Y we denote by $X \times Y$ the Cartesian product and by $X \to Y$ the function space. We denote pairs by (x, y) and projections by $\mathit{fst}(x)$ and $\mathit{snd}(x)$. We use λ and juxtaposition for function abstraction and applications. We use the notations $f : X \to Y$ and $f \in X \to Y$ interchangeably. If $(X_i)_{i \in I}$ is a family of sets then we denote $\prod_{i \in I} X_i$ or simply $\prod_i X_i$ its Cartesian product. If $f \in \prod_i X_i$ then $f_i \in X_i$. We write $\mathbb{B}$ for the set $\{\mathsf{tt}, \mathsf{ff}\}$ of truth values. We use $\Rightarrow$ for logical implication; it binds weaker than the other logical connectives like $\wedge, \vee$. For sets X and S we define the *state monad* by

$$\mathsf{T}_S(X) := S \to S \times X \,.$$

We have the associated operations $\mathsf{val}_S : X \to \mathsf{T}_S(X)$ and $\mathsf{bind}_S : \mathsf{T}_S(X) \times (X \to \mathsf{T}_S(Y)) \to \mathsf{T}_S(Y)$ given by $\mathsf{val}_S(x)(s) = (s, x)$ and $\mathsf{bind}_S(f, g)(s) = g(x)(s_1)$ where $f(s) = (s_1, x)$. We tend to omit the index S whenever sensible.

If S is some set modelling global states, e.g., $S = \mathbb{Z} \times \mathbb{Z}$ in the case of two global variables of integer type, then an element f of $\mathsf{T}_S(X)$ may be viewed as a state-dependent and state-modifying expression of type X.

We let Var and Dom be two fixed sets, for example, $\mathsf{Var} = \mathsf{Dom} = \mathbb{Z}$. We fix elements $x_0 \in \mathsf{Var}$, $d_0 \in \mathsf{Dom}$. We define

$$\mathsf{Func} = \Pi_S.(\mathsf{Var} \to \mathsf{T}_S(\mathsf{Dom})) \to \mathsf{T}_S(\mathsf{Dom})$$

where the product Π_S ranges over a suitably large universe of sets. We do not intend to have the domain of the product to include Func itself so that we do not need to delve into the somewhat delicate issue of modelling impredicative polymorphism.

We view an element f of the function space $\mathsf{Var} \to \mathsf{T}_S(\mathsf{Dom})$ as a stateful function from Var to Dom: given $x \in \mathsf{Var}$ and a state $s \in S$ then $f(x)(s)$ yields a pair (s_1, d) thought of as final state (s_1) and result (d). The bind-construct models the application of such a function to a stateful expression of type Var, i.e., an element of $\mathsf{T}_S(\mathsf{Var})$.

3 Purity at First Order

A stateful function $f : \mathsf{Var} \to \mathsf{T}_S(\mathsf{Dom})$ may be considered "pure" (side-effect-free) if there exists a function $g : \mathsf{Var} \to \mathsf{Dom}$ such that $f(x)(s) = (s, g(x))$, i.e., f may be factored through $\mathsf{val}_S : \mathsf{Dom} \to \mathsf{T}_S(\mathsf{Dom})$. This intensional viewpoint can in this case be underpinned by a more extensional yet equivalent definition as follows:

Theorem 1. *Let $f : \mathsf{Var} \to \mathsf{T}_S(\mathsf{Dom})$ be given. The following are equivalent:*

1. *f factors through $\mathsf{val}_S : \mathsf{Dom} \to \mathsf{T}_S(\mathsf{Dom})$.*
2. *For all relations $R \subseteq S \times S$ and $x \in \mathsf{Var}$ and sRs' one has $v = v'$ and $s_1 R s_1$ where $(s_1, v) = f(x)(s)$ and $(s_1', v') = f(x)(s')$.*

Proof. The direction 1⇒ 2 is obvious. For the converse, pick $s_0 \in S$ (the boundary case $S = \emptyset$ is obvious) and define $g : \mathsf{Var} \to \mathsf{Dom}$ by $g(x) = \mathit{snd}(f(x)(s_0))$. We claim that $f = \mathsf{val} \circ g$. To see this, fix $x \in \mathsf{Var}$ and $s \in S$ and define $R = \{(s_0, s)\}$. If $(s_1, v) = f(x)(s_0)$ and $(s_1', v') = f(x)(s)$ then, since $s_0 R s$ we get $v = v'$ and $s_1' = s$. □

A functional $F : (\mathsf{Var} \to \mathsf{T}_S(\mathsf{Dom})) \to \mathsf{T}_S(\mathsf{Dom})$ can be applied to stateful functions. Intuitively, it should be called pure if when applied to a stateful function f then the only side-effects that $F(f) \in \mathsf{T}_S(\mathsf{Dom})$ will have are those caused by calls to f within F. In particular, if f is pure as described above, then $F(f)$ should be pure, too, i.e., of the form $\mathsf{val}_S(d)$ for some $d \in \mathsf{Dom}$.

It is tempting to conjecture that such "pure" F would stem from a functional $G : (\mathsf{Var} \to \mathsf{Dom}) \to \mathsf{Dom}$. However, there is no way of applying such a G to a stateful $f : \mathsf{Var} \to \mathsf{T}_S(\mathsf{Dom})$ and, indeed, such a G does not contain enough information to tell how to transport the state changes and dependencies caused by calls to the argument f.

4 Relational Parametricity

Let us therefore try to make progress with the relational approach. The following result may be encouraging.

Theorem 2. *Suppose that $F : (\{\star\} \to \mathsf{T}_S(\{\star\})) \to \mathsf{T}_S(\{\star\})$ is such that for all relations $R \subseteq S \times S$ the following is true: For all $k, k' : \{\star\} \to \mathsf{T}_S(\{\star\})$ such that for all $s, s' \in S$ sRs' implies $\mathit{fst}(k(\star)(s))\, R\, \mathit{fst}(k'(\star)(s'))$, one has that sRs' implies $\mathit{fst}(F(k)(s))\, R\, \mathit{fst}(F(k')(s'))$, for every $s, s' \in S$.*

Then there exists a natural number n such that $F = \mathit{it}_n$ where $\mathit{it}_0(k)(s) = (s, \star)$ and $\mathit{it}_{n+1}(k)(s) = k(\star)(\mathit{fst}(\mathit{it}_n(k)(s)))$.

Proof. We only show the case where $S = \mathbb{N}$, the general case is similar. We define $k_0(\star)(s) = (s+1,\star)$ and $n_0 = \mathit{fst}(F(k_0)(0))$. Intuitively, we assume that the state contains an integer variable which is incremented upon each call to k_0.

Now pick any k and s_0 and define $R = \{(n,\mathit{fst}(it_n(k)(s_0))) \mid n \in \mathbb{N}\}$. We have $(0, s_0)$ and whenever sRs' then $\mathit{fst}(k_0(\star)(s))\, R\, \mathit{fst}(k(\star)(s'))$. Therefore, by assumption $n_0 = \mathit{fst}(F(k_0))\, R\, \mathit{fst}(F(k))$. The claim follows from the definition of R. □

We remark that this result can also be obtained as a consequence of a Theorem in [18].

It is therefore tempting to generalise this approach to the type of our functionals (and sneaking in polymorphic quantification over state types) as follows:

Definition 1. *A functional* $F : \prod_S(\mathsf{Var} \to \mathsf{T}_S(\mathsf{Dom})) \to \mathsf{T}_S(\mathsf{Dom})$ *is* relationally parametric *if the following is true for all* S, S' *and relations* $R \subseteq S \times S'$.

For all $k : \mathsf{Var} \to \mathsf{T}_S(\mathsf{Dom})$ *and* $k' : \mathsf{Var} \to \mathsf{T}_{S'}(\mathsf{Dom})$ *such that for all* s, s'

$$sRs' \Rightarrow \mathit{fst}(k(x)(s))\, R\, \mathit{fst}(k'(x)(s')) \wedge \mathit{snd}(k(x)(s)) = \mathit{snd}(k'(x)(s'))$$

holds, one has that the following holds for all s, s'*:*

$$sRs' \Rightarrow \mathit{fst}(F_S(k)(s))\, R\, \mathit{fst}(F_{S'}(k')(s')) \wedge \mathit{snd}(F_S(k)(s)) = \mathit{snd}(F_{S'}(k')(s'))\,.$$

Definition 2 (Snapback). *Define* $F_{snap} : \prod_S(\mathsf{Var} \to \mathsf{T}_S(\mathsf{Dom})) \to \mathsf{T}_S(\mathsf{Dom})$ *by* $(F_{snap})_S(k)(s) = (s,d)$ *where* $(s_1,d) = k(x_0)(s)$*. Thus,* F_{snap} *invokes* k *but discards the resulting state and only keeps the resulting value in* d*. Instead, the initial state is restored.*

The following is direct.

Proposition 1. F_{snap} *is relationally parametric.* □

Therefore, relational parametricity is not strong enough to ensure purity in the intuitive sense because snapback cannot be considered pure. Let us introduce the following abbreviations:

Definition 3.
- *If* X, X' *are sets then* $\mathsf{Rel}(X,X')$ *denotes the set of binary relations between* X *and* X'*, i.e.,* $\mathcal{P}(X \times X')$*;*
- *if* X *is a set then* $\Delta_X \in \mathsf{Rel}(X,X)$ *is the equality on set* X*;*
- *if* $R \in \mathsf{Rel}(X,X')$ *and* $S \in \mathsf{Rel}(Y,Y')$ *then* $R{\to}S \in \mathsf{Rel}(X{\to}Y, X'{\to}Y')$ *is given by* $f\, R{\to}S\, f' \iff \forall x\, x'.\, xRx' \Rightarrow f(x) S f'(x')$*;*
- *if* $R \in \mathsf{Rel}(X,X')$ *and* $S \in \mathsf{Rel}(Y,Y')$ *then* $R{\times}S \in \mathsf{Rel}(X{\times}Y, X'{\times}Y')$ *is given by* $f\, R{\times}S\, f' \iff \mathit{fst}(f)\, R\, \mathit{fst}(f') \wedge \mathit{snd}(f)\, S\, \mathit{snd}(f')$*;*
- *if* $R \in \mathsf{Rel}(S,S')$ *and* $Q \in \mathsf{Rel}(X,X')$ *then* $\mathsf{T}_R^{\mathsf{param}}(Q) \in \mathsf{Rel}(\mathsf{T}_S(X), \mathsf{T}_{S'}(X'))$ *is given by* $\mathsf{T}_R^{\mathsf{param}}(Q) := R{\to}R{\times}Q$.

Now, $F \in \mathsf{Func}$ is relationally parametric if for all S, S' and $R \in \mathsf{Rel}(S,S')$ one has

$$(F_S, F_{S'}) \in (\Delta_{\mathsf{Var}} \to \mathsf{T}_R^{\mathsf{param}}(\Delta_{\mathsf{Dom}})) \to \mathsf{T}_R^{\mathsf{param}}(\Delta_{\mathsf{Dom}})\,.$$

5 A New Notion of Parametricity

We view the problem with snapback as a deficiency of the definition $\mathsf{T}_R^{\mathsf{param}}(Q)$. A stronger way of lifting a relation $Q \in \mathsf{Rel}(X, X')$ to $\mathsf{Rel}(\mathsf{T}_S(X), \mathsf{T}_{S'}(X'))$ is needed. Rather than tinkering with specific formats (of which we see examples later on), we jump to the most permissive notion of relation on sets of the form $\mathsf{T}_S(X)$.

Definition 4. *Fix sets S, S'. For each X, X' and $Q \in \mathsf{Rel}(X, X')$ fix a relation $\mathsf{T}^{\mathsf{rel}}(Q) \in \mathsf{Rel}(\mathsf{T}_S(X), \mathsf{T}_{S'}(X'))$. The family $(X, X', Q) \mapsto \mathsf{T}^{\mathsf{rel}}(Q)$ is an* acceptable monadic relation *if*

- *for all $X, X', Q \in \mathsf{Rel}(X, X'), x \in X, x' \in X'$:*

$$xQx' \Rightarrow \mathit{val}_S(x)\, \mathsf{T}^{\mathsf{rel}}(Q)\, \mathit{val}_{S'}(x')\,;$$

- *for all $X, X', Q \in \mathsf{Rel}(X, X')$, $Y, Y', P \in \mathsf{Rel}(Y, Y')$, $x \in \mathsf{T}_S(X)$, $x' \in \mathsf{T}_{S'}(X')$, $f : X \to \mathsf{T}_S(Y)$, $f' : X' \to \mathsf{T}_{S'}(Y')$:*

$$x\mathsf{T}^{\mathsf{rel}}(Q)x' \wedge f(Q{\to}\mathsf{T}^{\mathsf{rel}}(P))f' \Rightarrow \mathsf{bind}_S(x, f)\; \mathsf{T}^{\mathsf{rel}}(P)\; \mathsf{bind}_{S'}(x', f')\,.$$

The lifting of state relations known from relational parametricity forms an example of an acceptable monadic relation as stated in the next proposition. We will later see examples of acceptable monadic relations that are not of this form.

Proposition 2. *If $R \in \mathsf{Rel}(S, S')$ then $Q \mapsto \mathsf{T}_R^{\mathsf{param}}(Q)$ is an acceptable monadic relation.* □

It is now possible to state and prove a parametricity theorem to the effect that all functions definable from lambda calculus, bind, and val respect any acceptable monadic relation. The precise formulation and proof sketch is elided here for lack of space and may be found in the full paper.

Let us return to the specific example set Func. We can use the new parametricity notion to single out the pure elements of Func as follows.

Definition 5. *A functional $F \in$ Func is* pure *if*

$$(F_S, F_{S'}) \in (\Delta_{\mathsf{Var}} \to \mathsf{T}^{\mathsf{rel}}(\Delta_{\mathsf{Dom}})) \to \mathsf{T}^{\mathsf{rel}}(\Delta_{\mathsf{Dom}})$$

holds for all S, S' and for all acceptable monadic relations $\mathsf{T}^{\mathsf{rel}}$ for S, S'.

Notice that functionals arising as denotations of lambda terms involving "parametric" constants (i.e., those for which the parametricity theorem holds) are pure in this sense.

6 Ruling Out Snapback

Our aim in this section is to prove that the snapback functional from Def. 2 cannot be pure in the following positive sense:

Theorem 3. *Let $F \in$ Func be pure. Put Test$:=\mathbb{B}$ and define $k_{\mathsf{test}} : \mathsf{Var} \to \mathsf{T}_{\mathsf{Test}}(\mathsf{Dom})$ by $k_{\mathsf{test}}(x)(s) = (\mathsf{tt}, d_0)$. If $F_{\mathsf{Test}}(k_{\mathsf{test}})(\mathsf{ff}) = (\mathsf{ff}, d)$ then $F_S(k)(s) = (s, d)$, for all S, $s \in S$ and $k : \mathsf{Var} \to \mathsf{T}_S(\mathsf{Dom})$.*

We apply F to a stateful argument k_{test} which — when called — sets a global boolean variable. If this variable remains unset after the evaluation of $F_{\mathsf{Test}}(k_{\mathsf{test}})$ then F did not call its argument and must therefore be constant.

In order to prove the theorem we construct a specific monadic relation.

Definition 6. *Let S be a set and* $\mathsf{Test} = \mathbb{B}$. *For each X, X' and $Q \in \mathsf{Rel}(X, X')$ define* $\mathsf{T}_1^{\mathsf{rel}}(Q) \in \mathsf{Rel}(\mathsf{T}_{\mathsf{Test}}(X), \mathsf{T}_S(X'))$ *by*

$$\mathsf{T}_1^{\mathsf{rel}}(Q) = \{(f, f') \mid \forall s\ s'\ s_1\ s_1'\ x\ x'.f(s) = (s_1, x) \wedge f'(s') = (s_1', x') \Rightarrow \\ (\exists x_0'.\, xQx_0') \wedge (\exists x_0.\, x_0Qx') \wedge (s_1 = \mathsf{ff} \Rightarrow xQx' \wedge s' = s_1' \wedge s = \mathsf{ff})\,.$$

Note that the relations $\mathsf{T}_1^{\mathsf{rel}}(Q)$ are not of the usual form "related pre-states yield related post-states and related results". Rather, relatedness of results (x and x') is conditional on the final state having a specific property (here "being equal to ff").

Lemma 1. *The relations $\mathsf{T}_1^{\mathsf{rel}}(Q)$ form an acceptable monadic relation.*

Proof (Sketch). Let us abbreviate

$$Z(Q, s, s_1, s', s_1', x, x') \equiv \\ (\exists x_0'.\, xQx_0') \wedge (\exists x_0.\, x_0Qx') \wedge (s_1 = \mathsf{ff} \Rightarrow xQx' \wedge s' = s_1' \wedge s = \mathsf{ff})\,.$$

In the val-case we have $s = s_1$ and $s' = s_1'$ and xQx' by assumption. The claim $Z(Q, s, s_1, s', s_1', x, x')$ is then trivial.

For the bind-case assume $Z(\check{Q}, s, \check{s}, s', \check{s}', \check{x}, \check{x}')$ and $g\,(\check{Q} \to \mathsf{T}_1^{\mathsf{rel}}(Q))\,g'$. We put $(s_1, x) = g(\check{x})(\check{s})$ and $(s_1', x') = g'(\check{x}')(\check{s}')$. We should prove $Z(Q, s, s_1, s', s_1', x, x')$. Choose $\check{x}_0'$ such that $\check{x}\check{Q}\check{x}_0'$. The assumption on g yields $Z(Q, \check{s}, s_1, \check{s}', ?, x, ?)$ thus in particular the existence of x_0' such that xQx_0'. Similarly, we show $\exists x_0.\, x_0Qx'$.

Now assume $s_1 = \mathsf{ff}$. Applying $g\,(\check{Q} \to \mathsf{T}_1^{\mathsf{rel}}(Q))\,g'$ to $\check{x}\check{Q}x_0'$ yields $\check{s} = \mathsf{ff}$ (this step is the reason why we carry these $\exists$-clauses around). From $Z(\check{Q}, s, \check{s}, s', \check{s}', \check{x}, \check{x}')$ and $\check{s} = \mathsf{ff}$ we then conclude $\check{x}\check{Q}\check{x}'$ and also $s = \mathsf{ff}$. Using the assumption on g, g' *again* we then obtain the remaining bit x_1Qx_1'. □

Lemma 2. *Let S be a set and* $k : \mathsf{Var} \to \mathsf{T}_S(\mathsf{Dom})$. *We have* $(k_{\mathsf{test}}, k) \in \Delta_{\mathsf{Var}} \to \mathsf{T}_1^{\mathsf{rel}}(\Delta_{\mathsf{Dom}})$.

Proof. Suppose that $(s_1, d) = k_{\mathsf{test}}(x)(s)$ and $(s_1', d') = k(x)(s')$. Since $s_1 = \mathsf{tt}$ all we have to prove is $\exists x_0'.\, d = x_0'$ and $\exists x_0.\, x_0 = d'$ which is obvious. □

Note that the only relation R such that $k_{\mathsf{test}}\,(\Delta_{\mathsf{Var}} \to R {\to} R {\times} \Delta_{\mathsf{Dom}})\,k$ holds for all k is the empty relation but that is useless since it does not relate initial states to each other.

Proof (of Theorem 3). We prove $F_{\mathsf{Test}}(k_{\mathsf{test}})\ \mathsf{T}_1^{\mathsf{rel}}(\Delta_{\mathsf{Dom}})\ F_S(k)$ using purity of F together with Lemmas 1 and 2. This directly gives the desired result. □

7 Strategy Trees

In this section we show that pure elements of Func are in fact first-order objects, i.e., define a question-answer dialogue. We first define those dialogues that can be seen as strategies in a game leading to the computation of $F(k)$ for any given k. We associate with each such strategy t a pure functional *tree2fun*(t) in the obvious way. We then define a functional program *fun2tree* (see Appendix for ML code) that can extract a strategy from *any* functional whether pure or not.

However, the program might in general fail to terminate and produce "strategies" whose continuation functions do not terminate. We will first prove that *if* the program returns a proper strategy and the input functional is pure then the computed strategy corresponds to the input functional. To do this, we axiomatise the graph *Fun2tree* of the functional program restricted to proper strategies as a well-founded relation. Later in Section 9 we show that for pure input functional the program does indeed return a proper strategy, i.e., the well-founded relation defines a total function on pure functionals.

We focus on the set Func here since it comes from the intended applications to fixpoint solvers.

Definition 7 (Strategies). *The set* Tree *is inductively defined by the following clauses.*

- *If* $d \in \mathsf{Dom}$ *then* $\mathsf{answ}(d) \in \mathsf{Tree}$.
- *If* $x \in \mathsf{Var}$ *and* $f : \mathsf{Dom} \longrightarrow \mathsf{Tree}$ *then* $\mathsf{que}(x, f) \in \mathsf{Tree}$.

The function tree2fun : $\mathsf{Tree} \longrightarrow \mathsf{Func}$ *is (well-founded) recursively defined by:*

- $\mathit{tree2fun}(\mathsf{answ}(d))(k)(s) = (s, d)$;
- $\mathit{tree2fun}(\mathsf{que}(x, f))(k)(s) = \mathit{tree2fun}(f(d))(k)(\check{s})$ *where* $(\check{s}, d) = k(x)(s)$.

In order to extract an element of Tree from a given functional we define the state set

$$\mathsf{Test} = \mathsf{Dom}^* \times \mathsf{Var}^* \times \mathsf{Var} \times \mathbb{B}\,.$$

As usual, $(-)^*$ is Kleene star. We refer to the components of $s = (\vec{d}, \vec{x}, x, b)$ by $\vec{d} = s.\mathsf{ans}$, $\vec{x} = s.\mathsf{qns}$, $x = s.\mathsf{arg}$, $b = s.\mathsf{cal}$.

We write $s[\mathsf{qns} := \vec{x}']$ for $(\vec{d}, \vec{x}', a, b)$ and use similar notation for the other components. For $\vec{d} \in \mathsf{Dom}^*$ the initial state $r_{\vec{d}}$ is given by $(\vec{d}, \varepsilon, x_0, \mathsf{ff})$ (recall that x_0 and d_0 are the default elements of Var, Dom).

Definition 8. *The function* $k_{\mathsf{test}} : \mathsf{Var} \longrightarrow \mathsf{T}_{\mathsf{Test}}(\mathsf{Dom})$ *is given by:*

- $k_{\mathsf{test}}(x)(s) = (s, d_0)$, *if* $s.\mathsf{cal} = \mathsf{tt}$;
- $k_{\mathsf{test}}(x)(s) = (s[\mathsf{arg}{:=}x, \mathsf{cal}{:=}\mathsf{tt}], d_0)$, *if* $s.\mathsf{cal} = \mathsf{ff}$ *and* $s.\mathsf{ans} = \varepsilon$;
- $k_{\mathsf{test}}(x)(s) = (s[\mathsf{ans}{:=}\vec{d}, \mathsf{qns}{:=}\vec{x}x], d)$, *if* $s.\mathsf{cal} = \mathsf{ff}$, $s.\mathsf{ans} = d\vec{d}$ *and* $s.\mathsf{qns} = \vec{x}$;

where $d_0 \in \mathsf{Dom}$ *is the default element.*

Intuitively, so long as cal is not set, k_{test} reproduces the prerecorded answers from ans and stores the questions asked in qns. Once ans is empty the next question is stored in arg and cal is set preventing any further state modifications.

Definition 9. *The relation*

$$\mathit{Fun2treeAux} \subseteq ((\mathsf{Var}{\longrightarrow}\mathsf{T}_{\mathsf{Test}}(\mathsf{Dom})){\longrightarrow}\mathsf{T}_{\mathsf{Test}}(\mathsf{Dom})) \times \mathsf{Dom}^* \times \mathsf{Tree}$$

is inductively defined by the following clauses.

- *If* $F(k_{\mathsf{test}})(r_{\vec{d}}) = (r_1, d)$ *and* $r_1.\mathsf{cal} = \mathsf{ff}$ *then* $\mathit{Fun2treeAux}(F, \vec{d}, \mathsf{answ}(d))$.
- *If* $F(k_{\mathsf{test}})(r_{\vec{d}}) = (r_1, d)$ *and* $r_1.\mathsf{cal} = \mathsf{tt}$ *and* $r_1.\mathsf{arg} = x$ *and* $f : \mathsf{Dom} \to \mathsf{Tree}$ *is such that* $\mathit{Fun2treeAux}(F, \vec{db}, f(b))$, $b \in \mathsf{Dom}$, *holds then* $\mathit{Fun2treeAux}(F, \vec{d}, \mathsf{que}(x, f))$.

We also define

$$\mathit{Fun2tree}(F, t) \iff \mathit{Fun2treeAux}(F, \varepsilon, t)\,.$$

8 Strategy Trees for Pure Functionals

We will argue later in section 9 that for any pure F there always exists t such that $\mathit{Fun2tree}(F, t)$. Here, we merely show that *if* $\mathit{Fun2tree}(F, t)$ then $F = \mathit{tree2fun}(t)$, thus F is induced by a strategy tree.

Theorem 4. *Suppose that* $F \in \mathsf{Func}$ *is pure and that* $\mathit{Fun2tree}(F_{\mathsf{Test}}, t)$ *holds. Then* $F = \mathit{tree2fun}(t)$.

We prove a more general statement involving the auxiliary relation *Fun2treeAux*. For that, we relate sequences of questions to sequences of answers w.r.t. a given $k : \mathsf{Var} \to \mathsf{T}_S(\mathsf{Dom})$.

Definition 10. *Suppose* S *is a set and* $k : \mathsf{Var} \to \mathsf{T}_S(\mathsf{Dom})$. *We define* $\mathsf{Mat}_S(k) \subseteq \mathsf{Var}^* \times \mathsf{Dom}^* \times S \times S$ *inductively by:*

- $\mathsf{Mat}_S(k)(\varepsilon, \varepsilon, s, s)$ *for all* $s \in S$.
- *If* $\mathsf{Mat}_S(k)(\vec{x}, \vec{d}, s, \check{s})$ *and* $(s_1, d) = k(x)(\check{s})$ *then* $\mathsf{Mat}_S(k)(\vec{x}\,x, \vec{d}\,d, s, s_1)$.

Basically, $\mathsf{Mat}_S(k)(\vec{x}, \vec{d}, s, s_1)$ asserts that if we apply k successively to the arguments in $\vec{x}$ beginning in state s then (threading intermediate states through) we end up in state s_1 and the results we obtain along the way are recorded in $\vec{d}$.

Theorem 4 is a direct consequence of the following characterisation of *Fun2treeAux*.

Theorem 5. *Suppose that* $F \in \mathsf{Func}$ *is pure and that* $\mathit{Fun2treeAux}(F_{\mathsf{Test}}, \vec{d}, t)$ *holds. Suppose furthermore that* $F_{\mathsf{Test}}(k_{\mathsf{test}})(r_{\vec{d}}) = (r, \_)$ *and* $\mathsf{Mat}_S(k)(r.\mathsf{qns}, \vec{d}, s, \check{s})$ *holds. If* $F_S(k)(s) = (s_1, d_1)$ *and* $\mathit{tree2fun}(t, k, \check{s}) = (s_2, d_2)$ *then* $s_1 = s_2$ *and* $d_1 = d_2$.

The proof of Theorem 4 is by induction on *Fun2treeAux* and breaks down into the following two lemmas covering base case and inductive case.

Lemma 3 (Base case). *Let* F *be a pure functional. If* $F_{\mathsf{Test}}(k_{\mathsf{test}})(r_{\vec{d}}) = (r, v)$ *and* $\mathsf{Mat}_S(k)(r.\mathsf{qns}, \vec{d}, s, s_1)$ *and* $r.\mathsf{cal} = \mathsf{ff}$ *then* $F_S(k)(s) = (s_1, v)$.

This lemma is similar to Theorem 3 but is complicated by the fact that k_{test} only sets cal to tt after having worked off the pre-recorded answers $\vec{d}$. Accordingly, the Lemma requires that k match these prerecorded answers w.r.t. the questions asked on the way ($r.\mathsf{qns}$). The proof uses an acceptable monadic relation in the following general format.

Definition 11. *Let S, S' be sets. Let $Tr \in \mathsf{Rel}(S,S)$ and $Re, Gu \in \mathsf{Rel}(S \times S', S \times S')$ and $Q \in \mathsf{Rel}(X,X')$. The relation $\mathsf{T}^{\mathsf{rel}}_{Tr,Re,Gu}(Q) \in \mathsf{Rel}(\mathsf{T}_S(X), \mathsf{T}_{S'}(X'))$ is defined by*

$$\begin{array}{l} f\,\mathsf{T}^{\mathsf{rel}}_{Tr,Re,Gu}(Q)\,f' \iff \forall s\ s'\ s_1\ s_1'\ x\ x'. \\ \quad f(s) = (s_1, x) \wedge f'(s') = (s_1', x') \Rightarrow (\exists x_0'.\, xQx_0') \wedge (\exists x_0.\, x_0Qx') \wedge \\ \quad\quad Tr(s, s_1) \wedge (Re((s,s'),(s_1,s_1')) \Rightarrow xQx' \wedge Gu((s,s'),(s_1,s_1')))\,. \end{array}$$

Lemma 4. *If Tr, Gu are reflexive and transitive and furthermore*

$$\begin{array}{l} Re((s,s'),(s_1,s_1')) \wedge Tr(s,\check{s}) \wedge Tr(\check{s},s_1) \Rightarrow \\ \quad Re((s,s'),(\check{s},\check{s}')) \wedge (Gu((s,s'),(\check{s},\check{s}')) \Rightarrow Re((\check{s},\check{s}'),(s_1,s_1'))) \end{array}$$

holds then $Q \mapsto \mathsf{T}^{\mathsf{rel}}_{Tr,Re,Gu}(Q)$ is an acceptable monadic relation. □

We could have a more general format that also maintains a transition relation corresponding to Tr on the S'-component, but this is not needed for our present purpose.

Proof (of Lemma 3, Sketch). We instantiate Lemma 4 w.r.t. the state sets Test and S:

$$\begin{array}{ll} Tr(r, r_1) & \equiv \exists \vec{x}\ \vec{d}.\, TrP(r, r_1, \vec{x}, \vec{d})\,, \\ Re((r,s),(r_1,s_1)) & \equiv r_1.\mathsf{cal} = \mathsf{ff} \wedge \forall \vec{x}\ \vec{d}.\, TrP(r, r_1, \vec{x}, \vec{d}) \Rightarrow \exists \check{s}.\, \mathsf{Mat}_S(k)(\vec{x}, \vec{d}, s, \check{s})\,, \\ Gu((r,s),(r_1,s_1)) & \equiv \exists \vec{x}\ \vec{d}.\, TrP(r, r_1, \vec{x}, \vec{d}) \wedge \mathsf{Mat}_S(k)(\vec{x}, \vec{d}, s, s_1)\,, \\ TrP(r, r_1, \vec{x}, \vec{d}) & \equiv r_1.\mathsf{cal} = \mathsf{ff} \Rightarrow r.\mathsf{cal} = \mathsf{ff} \wedge r_1.\mathsf{arg} = r.\mathsf{arg} \wedge |\vec{x}| = |\vec{d}| \wedge \\ & \qquad r_1.\mathsf{qns} = r.\mathsf{qns}\,\vec{x} \wedge r.\mathsf{ans} = \vec{d}\,r_1.\mathsf{ans}\,. \end{array}$$

One must now show that these definitions meet the conditions of Lemma 4 and that the resulting monadic relation relates $k_{\mathsf{test}}(x)$ to $k(x)$ for all x. Note that via $\mathsf{Mat}_S(k)$ the definition of the monadic relation is dependent on the k in question. This was not the case in the proof of Theorem 3. The result then follows. □

Lemma 5 (Inductive Case). *Let F be a pure functional. If $F_{\mathsf{Test}}(k_{\mathsf{test}})(r_{\vec{d}}) = (r, v)$ and $F_{\mathsf{Test}}(k_{\mathsf{test}})(r_{\vec{d}\,d}) = (t', v')$ and $r.\mathsf{cal} = \mathsf{tt}$ then $r'.\mathsf{qns} = r.\mathsf{qns}\ r.\mathsf{arg}$.*

Notice that the inductive case no longer involves the state set S and k but operates entirely on the specific state set Test.

We use an acceptable monadic relation obeying the following generic format that does not seem to be an instance of the previous one used for the base case.

Definition 12. *Let S, S' be sets. Let $Tr \in \mathsf{Rel}(S,S)$, $Tr' \in \mathsf{Rel}(S',S')$ and $St1, St2 \in \mathsf{Rel}(S,S')$. The relation $\mathsf{T}^{\mathsf{rel}}_{Tr,Tr',St1,St2}(Q) \in \mathsf{Rel}(\mathsf{T}_S(X), \mathsf{T}_{S'}(X'))$ is defined by*

$$\begin{array}{l} f\,\mathsf{T}^{\mathsf{rel}}_{Tr,Tr',St1,St2}(Q)\,f' \iff \forall s\ s'\ s_1\ s_1'\ x\ x'. \\ \quad f(s) = (s_1, x) \wedge f'(s') = (s_1', x') \Rightarrow (\exists x_0'.\, xQx_0') \wedge (\exists x_0.\, x_0Qx') \wedge \\ \quad\quad Tr(s, s_1) \wedge Tr'(s', s_1') \wedge (St1(s,s') \Rightarrow St1(s_1,s_1') \wedge xQx' \vee St2(s_1,s_1'))\,. \end{array}$$

Lemma 6. *If Tr, Tr' are reflexive and transitive and furthermore*

$$St2(s,s') \wedge Tr(s,s_1) \wedge Tr'(s',s_1') \Rightarrow St2(s_1,s_1')$$

then $Q \mapsto \mathsf{T}^{\mathsf{rel}}_{Tr,Tr',St1,St2}(Q)$ is an acceptable monadic relation. □

Proof (of Lemma 5 (Sketch)). We instantiate the framework with state sets $S :=$ Test and $S' :=$ Test and

$$\begin{aligned}
Tr(r, r_1) &\equiv Tr'(r, r_1) \equiv \\
&\quad (r_1.\mathsf{cal} = \mathsf{ff} \Rightarrow r.\mathsf{cal} = \mathsf{ff}) \wedge (r.\mathsf{cal} = \mathsf{tt} \Rightarrow r = r_1) \wedge \\
&\quad (r.\mathsf{ans} = \varepsilon \Rightarrow r = r_1 \vee r_1.\mathsf{ans} = \varepsilon \wedge r_1.\mathsf{cal} = \mathsf{tt} \wedge r_1.\mathsf{qns} = r.\mathsf{qns}), \\
St1(t, t') &\equiv r.\mathsf{cal} = \mathsf{ff} \wedge r'.\mathsf{cal} = \mathsf{ff} \wedge r'.\mathsf{ans} = r.\mathsf{ans}\, d \wedge r'.\mathsf{qns} = r.\mathsf{qns}, \\
St2(r, r') &\equiv r.\mathsf{cal} = \mathsf{tt} \wedge r.\mathsf{ans} = \varepsilon \wedge r'.\mathsf{ans} = \varepsilon \wedge r'.\mathsf{qns} = r.\mathsf{qns}\, r.\mathsf{arg}\,.
\end{aligned}$$

The main result is then a fairly direct consequence. □

Theorem 4 is proved by induction on *Fun2treeAux* employing Lemmas 3 and 5. □

9 Existence of Strategy Trees

We will now show that for any pure functional one can indeed find a corresponding strategy tree in the sense of *Fun2tree*. By the results of the previous section this then implies that any pure functional can be represented by or seen as a strategy tree.

Admittedly, this result came as a certain surprise to us: we believed for a long time that existence of strategy trees could only be guaranteed under some additional continuity assumptions. For example, the minimum functional $Min : (\mathbb{N} \to \mathbb{N}) \to \mathbb{N}$ given by $Min(f) = \min\{f(n) \mid n\}$ is not continuous and cannot be represented by a strategy tree. However, there is no pure functional (with $\mathsf{Var} = \mathsf{Dom} = \mathbb{N}$) because it would have to make infinitely many calls to its argument which could be tracked by a suitable set S: consider, for instance, the application of such putative pure functional F to a $k : \mathbb{N} \to \mathsf{T}_{\mathbb{N}}(\mathbb{N})$ that increments a global variable upon each call.

Theorem 6. *Let $F \in$ Func be pure. There exists t such that $Fun2tree(F_{\mathsf{Test}}, t)$.*

Proof (Sketch). Assume for a contradiction that no such t exists. By studying an unsuccessful attempt at constructing such a t (formally this involves the use of the axiom of choice) we can construct an infinite sequence $d_1, d_2, d_3, \ldots$ of elements of Dom such that $(fst(F_{\mathsf{Test}}(k_{\mathsf{test}})(s_{\vec{d}_n})).\mathsf{cal} = \mathsf{tt}$ for all n where $\vec{d}_n = d_1 d_2 d_3 \ldots d_{n-1}$.

Now let Test^∞ be defined like Test except that the ans-component may contain finite as well as infinite lists over Dom. Let k^∞_{test} be the extension of k_{test} to Test^∞. By a simulation argument using Proposition 2 one finds $F_{\mathsf{Test}^\infty}(k^\infty_{\mathsf{test}})(s) = F_{\mathsf{Test}}(k_{\mathsf{test}})$ whenever $s \in \mathsf{Test} \subseteq \mathsf{Test}^\infty$. The following facts are proved using a mild generalisation of the acceptable monadic relation used in the proof of Lemma 3:

- $F_{\mathsf{Test}^\infty}(k_{\mathsf{test}})(r_{\vec{d}}) = (r_1, d) \wedge r_1.\mathsf{cal} = \mathsf{tt} \Rightarrow r_1.\mathsf{ans} = \varepsilon$;
- $F_{\mathsf{Test}^\infty}(k_{\mathsf{test}})(r_{\vec{d}}) = (r_1, d) \Rightarrow \exists ans \in Dom^*.\vec{d} = ans\; r_1.\mathsf{ans}$;
- $F_{\mathsf{Test}^\infty}(k_{\mathsf{test}})(r_{\vec{d}}) = (r_1, d) \wedge r_1.\mathsf{cal} = \mathsf{ff} \Rightarrow (F_{\mathsf{Test}^\infty}(k_{\mathsf{test}})(r_{\vec{d}\upharpoonright})).\mathsf{cal} = \mathsf{ff}$ where $\vec{d}\upharpoonright$ comprises the first $|r_1.\mathsf{qns}|$ elements of $\vec{d}$.

Let $\vec{d}$ be the infinite list of the d_i and write $(r_1, d) = F_{\mathsf{Test}^\infty}(k_{\mathsf{test}})(r_{\vec{d}})$. By the first and second fact we must have $r_1.\mathsf{cal} = \mathsf{ff}$. Thus, by the third fact, there exists n (namely $|r_1.\mathsf{qns}|$) with $(fst(F_{\mathsf{Test}}(k_{\mathsf{test}})(s_{\vec{d}_n})).\mathsf{cal} = \mathsf{tt}$, a contradiction. □

10 Related Work

Relational parametricity has been introduced by Reynolds [13, 14] as a means for restricting the range of polymorphic type quantification. Wadler then popularised Reynolds' results in his famous [18].

Relational parametricity has also been used in order to justify program equivalences in *Idealized Algol* a higher-order call-by-name language with local variables and stateful integer expressions. The equivalences of interest rely on the fact that a procedure cannot modify or read a local variable declared in a disjoint scope. In this context, an alternative extension of relational parametricity has been developed which can also rule out snapback functionals: *strict logical relations* [12]. It works in the setting of monotone continuous functions on Scott domains and relies crucially on the following "built-in" parametricity property of such functions: if $F(\lambda x.\bot) = x \neq \bot$ then $F(k) = x$ for all k. Loc. cit. also relates certain functionals to strategy trees (there called resumptions).

The differences to our work are twofold: (1) we address all types of computational lambda calculus in particular allow to return functions as results; (2) we work in a total, set-theoretic framework whereas strict logical relations can only operate in the presence of $\bot$ and monotonicity.

The strategy trees are reminiscent of game semantics [1, 2, 8] and can be traced back even further to Berry-Curiens sequential algorithms [4] and even to Kleene's. The new aspect here is the construction of a strategy tree for any set-theoretic functional that is pure in an extensional sense defined by preservation of structure rather than by existence of intensional representations. It would be very interesting to investigate to what extent our notion of purity which makes sense at all types of the computational lambda calculus entails existence of strategies in the sense of game semantics or sequential algorithms also at those higher types.

References

1. Abramsky, S., Jagadeesan, R., Malacaria, P.: Full abstraction for PCF (extended abstract). In: Hagiya, M., Mitchell, J.C. (eds.) TACS 1994. LNCS, vol. 789, pp. 1–15. Springer, Heidelberg (1994)
2. Abramsky, S., McCusker, G.: Linearity, sharing and state: a fully abstract game semantics for idealized algol with active expressions. Electr. Notes Theor. Comput. Sci. 3 (1996)
3. Le Charlier, B., Van Hentenryck, P.: A Universal Top-Down Fixpoint Algorithm. Technical Report CS-92-25, Brown University, Providence, RI 02912 (1992)
4. Berry, G., Curien, P.-L.: Sequential algorithms on concrete data structures. Theor. Comput. Sci. 20, 265–321 (1982)
5. Fecht, C.: GENA - A Tool for Generating Prolog Analyzers from Specifications. In: Mycroft, A. (ed.) SAS 1995. LNCS, vol. 983, pp. 418–419. Springer, Heidelberg (1995)
6. Fecht, C., Seidl, H.: A faster solver for general systems of equations. Sci. Comput. Program. 35(2), 137–161 (1999)
7. Hermenegildo, M.V., Puebla, G., Marriott, K., Stuckey, P.J.: Incremental analysis of constraint logic programs. ACM Trans. Program. Lang. Syst. 22(2), 187–223 (2000)

8. Hyland, J.M.E., Luke Ong, C.-H.: On full abstraction for pcf: I, ii, and iii. Inf. Comput. 163(2), 285–408 (2000)
9. Jorgensen, N.: Finding Fixpoints in Finite Function Spaces Using Neededness Analysis and Chaotic Iteration. In: LeCharlier, B. (ed.) SAS 1994. LNCS, vol. 864, pp. 329–345. Springer, Heidelberg (1994)
10. Longley, J.: When is a functional program not a functional program? In: ICFP, pp. 1–7 (1999)
11. Nielson, H.R., Nielson, F.: Flow logics for constraint based analysis. In: Koskimies, K. (ed.) CC 1998. LNCS, vol. 1383, pp. 109–127. Springer, Heidelberg (1998)
12. O'Hearn, P.W., Reynolds, J.C.: From algol to polymorphic linear lambda-calculus. J. ACM 47(1), 167–223 (2000)
13. Reynolds, J.: Types, abstraction and parametric polymorphism. In: Information Processing, IFIP. North-Holland, Amsterdam (1983)
14. Reynolds, J.C., Plotkin, G.D.: On functors expressible in the polymorphic typed lambda calculus. Technical Report ECS-LFCS-88-53, University of Edinburgh (May 1988)
15. Rudich, A., Darvas, Á., Müller, P.: Checking well-formedness of pure-method specifications. In: Cuellar, J., Maibaum, T., Sere, K. (eds.) FM 2008. LNCS, vol. 5014, pp. 68–83. Springer, Heidelberg (2008)
16. Seidl, H., Vojdani, V.: Region analysis for race detection. In: Palsberg, J., Su, Z. (eds.) Static Analysis. LNCS, vol. 5673, pp. 171–187. Springer, Heidelberg (2009)
17. Simpson, A.K.: Lazy functional algorithms for exact real functionals. In: Brim, L., Gruska, J., Zlatuška, J. (eds.) MFCS 1998. LNCS, vol. 1450, pp. 456–464. Springer, Heidelberg (1998)
18. Wadler, P.: Theorems for free! In: FPCA, pp. 347–359 (1989)

Example-Guided Abstraction Simplification

Roberto Giacobazzi[1] and Francesco Ranzato[2]

[1] University of Verona, Italy
[2] University of Padova, Italy

Abstract. In static analysis, approximation is typically encoded by abstract domains, providing systematic guidelines for specifying approximate semantic functions and precision assessments. However, it may well happen that an abstract domain contains redundant information for the specific purpose of approximating a given semantic function modeling some behavior of a system. This paper introduces Example-Guided Abstraction Simplification (EGAS), a methodology for simplifying abstract domains, i.e. removing abstract values from them, in a maximal way while retaining exactly the same approximate behavior of the system under analysis. We show that, in abstract model checking and predicate abstraction, EGAS provides a simplification paradigm of the abstract state space that is guided by examples, meaning that it preserves spuriousness of examples (i.e., abstract paths). In particular, we show how EGAS can be integrated with the well-known CEGAR (CounterExample-Guided Abstraction Refinement) methodology.

1 Introduction

In static analysis and verification, model-driven *abstraction refinement* has emerged in the last decade as a fundamental method for improving abstractions towards more precise yet efficient analyses. The basic idea is simple: given an abstraction modeling some observational behavior of the system to analyze, refine the abstraction in order to remove the artificial computations that may appear in the approximate analysis by considering how the concrete system behaves when false alarms or spurious traces are encountered. The general concept of using spurious counterexamples for refining an abstraction stems from CounterExample-Guided Abstraction Refinement (CEGAR) [4,5]. The model here drives the automatic identification of prefixes of the counterexample path that do not correspond to an actual trace in the concrete model, by isolating abstract (failure) states that need to be refined in order to eliminate that spurious counterexample. Model-driven refinements, such as CEGAR, provide algorithmic methods for achieving abstractions that are complete (i.e., precise [17,14]) with respect to some given property of the concrete model.

We investigate here the dual problem of *abstraction simplification*. Instead of refining abstractions in order to eliminate spurious traces, our goal is to simplify an abstraction A towards a simpler (ideally, the simplest) model A_s that maintains the same approximate behavior as A does. In abstract model checking, this abstraction simplification has *to keep the same examples* of the concrete system in the following sense. Recall that an abstract path π in an abstract transition system is *spurious* when no real concrete path is

S. Abramsky et al. (Eds.): ICALP 2010, Part II, LNCS 6199, pp. 211–222, 2010.

abstracted to π. Assume that a given abstract state space A of a system $\mathcal{A}$ gets simplified to A_s and thus gives rise to a more abstract system $\mathcal{A}_s$. Then, we say that $\mathcal{A}_s$ keeps the same examples of $\mathcal{A}$ when the following condition is satisfied: if π_{A_s} is a spurious path in the simplified abstract system $\mathcal{A}_s$ then there exists a spurious path π_A in the original system $\mathcal{A}$ that is abstracted to π_{A_s}. Such a methodology is called EGAS, Example-Guided Abstraction Simplification, since this abstraction simplification does not add spurious paths, namely, does keep examples, since each spurious path in $\mathcal{A}_s$ comes as an abstraction of a spurious path in $\mathcal{A}$. Let us illustrate how EGAS works through a simple example.

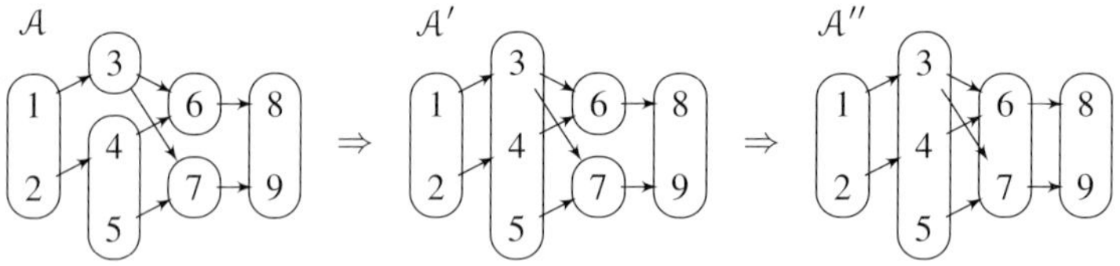

Let us consider the above abstract transition system $\mathcal{A}$, where concrete states are numbers which are abstracted by blocks of a state partition. The abstract state space of $\mathcal{A}$ is simplified by merging the abstract states $[3]$ and $[4,5]$: EGAS ensures that this can be safely done because $\mathrm{pre}^\sharp([3]) = \mathrm{pre}^\sharp([4,5])$ and $\mathrm{post}^\sharp([3]) = \mathrm{post}^\sharp([4,5])$, where $\mathrm{pre}^\sharp$ and $\mathrm{post}^\sharp$ denote, resp., the abstract predecessor and successor functions. This abstraction simplification leads to the above abstract system $\mathcal{A}'$. Let us observe that the abstract path $\langle [1,2],[3,4,5],[7],[8,9]\rangle$ in $\mathcal{A}'$ is spurious and it is the abstraction of the spurious path $\langle [1,2],[4,5],[7],[8,9]\rangle$ in $\mathcal{A}$. On the other hand, consider the path $\pi' = \langle [1,2],[3,4,5],[6],[8,9]\rangle$ in $\mathcal{A}'$ and observe that all the paths in $\mathcal{A}$ that are abstracted to π', i.e. $\langle [1,2],[3],[6],[8,9]\rangle$ and $\langle [1,2],[4,5],[6],[8,9]\rangle$, are not spurious. This is consistent with the fact that π' actually is not spurious. Likewise, $\mathcal{A}'$ can be further simplified to the abstract system $\mathcal{A}''$ where $[6]$ and $[7]$ are merged into a new abstract state $[6,7]$ and this transformation also keeps examples because now there is no spurious path in $\mathcal{A}''$. Let us also notice that if $\mathcal{A}$ would get simplified to $\mathcal{A}'''$ by merging $[1,2]$ and $[3]$ into a new abstract state $[1,2,3]$ then this transform would not keep examples because we would obtain the spurious loop path $\langle [1,2,3],[1,2,3],[1,2,3],...\rangle$ in $\mathcal{A}'''$ while no corresponding spurious abstract path would exist in $\mathcal{A}$.

EGAS is formalized within the standard abstract interpretation framework [8,9]. This ensures that EGAS can be applied both in abstract model checking and in abstract interpretation. Consider for instance the abstract domains $A_1 \triangleq \{\mathbb{Z},\mathbb{Z}_{\leq 0},\mathbb{Z}_{\geq 0},0\}$ and $A_2 \triangleq \{\mathbb{Z},\mathbb{Z}_{\geq 0}\}$ for sign analysis of an integer variable. Recall that in abstract interpretation the best correct approximation of a semantic function f on an abstract domain A that is specified through abstraction/concretization maps α/γ is given by $f^A \triangleq \alpha \circ f \circ \gamma$. Consider a simple operation of increment x++ on an integer variable x. In this case, the best correct approximations on A_1 and A_2 are as follows:

$$\text{++}^{A_1} = \{0 \mapsto \mathbb{Z}_{\geq 0},\ \mathbb{Z}_{\leq 0} \mapsto \mathbb{Z},\ \mathbb{Z}_{\geq 0} \mapsto \mathbb{Z}_{\geq 0},\ \mathbb{Z} \mapsto \mathbb{Z}\},$$
$$\text{++}^{A_2} = \{\mathbb{Z}_{\geq 0} \mapsto \mathbb{Z}_{\geq 0},\ \mathbb{Z} \mapsto \mathbb{Z}\}.$$

We observe that the best correct approximations of ++ in A_1 and A_2 encode the same function, meaning that the approximations of ++ in A_1 and A_2 are equivalent, the latter being clearly simpler. In other terms, the abstract domain A_1 contains some "irrelevant" elements for approximating the increment operation, that is, 0 and $\mathbb{Z}_{\leq 0}$. We formalize this simplification of an abstract domain relatively to a semantic function in the most general abstract interpretation setting. This allows us to provide, for generic continuous semantic functions, a systematic and constructive method, that we call *correctness kernel*, for simplifying a given abstraction A relatively to a given semantic function f towards the unique minimal abstract domain that induces an equivalent approximate behavior of f as in A. EGAS is then designed by iteratively applying the correctness kernel to abstractions. We show how EGAS can be embedded within the CEGAR methodology by providing a novel refinement heuristics in a CEGAR iteration step which turns out to be more accurate than the basic refinement heuristics [5]. We also describe how EGAS may be applied in predicate abstraction-based model checking [11,18] for reducing the search space without applying Ball et al.'s [2] Cartesian abstractions, which typically yield additional loss of precision.

2 Correctness Kernels

As usual in standard abstract interpretation [8,9], abstract domains (or abstractions) are specified by Galois connections/insertions (GCs/GIs for short). A GC/GI of the abstract domain A into the concrete domain C through abstraction and concretization maps $\alpha : C \to A$ and $\gamma : A \to C$ is denoted by (α, C, A, γ). It is known that $\mu_A \triangleq \gamma \circ \alpha : C \to C$ is an upper closure operator (uco) on C and that abstract domains can be equivalently defined as uco's. GIs of a common concrete domain C are preordered w.r.t. precision as usual: $\mathcal{G}_1 = (\alpha_1, C, A_1, \gamma_1) \sqsubseteq \mathcal{G}_2 = (\alpha_2, C, A_2, \gamma_2)$ — i.e. A_1/A_2 is a refinement/simplification of A_2/A_1 — iff $\gamma_1 \circ \alpha_1 \sqsubseteq \gamma_2 \circ \alpha_2$. Moreover, $\mathcal{G}_1$ and $\mathcal{G}_2$ are equivalent when $\mathcal{G}_1 \sqsubseteq \mathcal{G}_2$ and $\mathcal{G}_2 \sqsubseteq \mathcal{G}_1$. We denote by $\mathrm{Abs}(C)$ the family of abstract domains of C up to the above equivalence. It is well known that $\langle \mathrm{Abs}(C), \sqsubseteq \rangle$ is a complete lattice, so that one can consider the most concrete simplification (i.e., lub $\sqcup$) and the most abstract refinement (i.e., glb $\sqcap$) of any family of abstract domains. Let us also recall that the lattice of abstract domains $\langle \mathrm{Abs}(C), \sqsubseteq \rangle$ is isomorphic to the lattice of uco's on C $\langle \mathrm{uco}(C), \sqsubseteq \rangle$.

Let $A \in \mathrm{Abs}(C)$, $f : C \to C$ be some concrete semantic function — for simplicity, we consider 1-ary functions — and $f^\sharp : A \to A$ be a corresponding abstract function. $\langle A, f^\sharp \rangle$ is a sound abstract interpretation when $\alpha \circ f \sqsubseteq f^\sharp \circ \alpha$. The abstract function $f^A \triangleq \alpha \circ f \circ \gamma : A \to A$ is called the best correct approximation (b.c.a.) of f on A because $\langle A, f^\sharp \rangle$ is sound iff $f^A \sqsubseteq f^\sharp$.

2.1 The Problem

Given a semantic function $f : C \to C$ and an abstract domain $A \in \mathrm{Abs}(C)$, does there exist the *most abstract domain* that induces the same best correct approximation of f as A does?

Let us formalize the above question. Consider two abstractions $A, B \in \mathrm{Abs}(C)$. We say that A and B induce the same best correct approximation of f when f^A and f^B are the same function up to isomorphic representations of abstract values, i.e., if μ_A and

μ_B are the corresponding uco's then $\mu_A \circ f \circ \mu_A = \mu_B \circ f \circ \mu_B$. In order to keep the notation easy, this is denoted simply by $f^A = f^B$. Also, if $F \subseteq C \longrightarrow C$ is a set of concrete functions then $F^A = F^B$ means that for any $f \in F$, $f^A = f^B$. Hence, given $A \in \text{Abs}(C)$ and by defining

$$A_s \triangleq \sqcup\{B \in \text{Abs}(C) \mid F^B = F^A\}$$

the question is whether $F^{A_s} = F^A$ holds or not.

It is worth remarking that the dual question on the existence of the *most concrete domain* that induces the same best correct approximation of f as A has a negative answer, as shown by the following simple example.

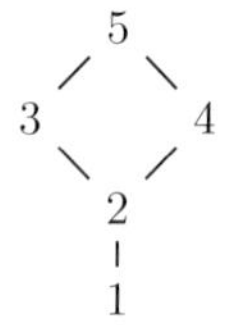

Example 2.1. Consider the lattice C depicted on the right, the monotonic function $f : C \to C$ defined as $f \triangleq \{1 \mapsto 1, 2 \mapsto 1, 3 \mapsto 5, 4 \mapsto 5, 5 \mapsto 5\}$ and the domain $\mu \in \text{uco}(C)$ defined as $\mu \triangleq \{1, 5\}$. We have that $\mu \circ f \circ \mu = \{1 \mapsto 1, 2 \mapsto 5, 3 \mapsto 5, 4 \mapsto 5, 5 \mapsto 5\}$. Consider the domains $\rho_1 \triangleq \{1, 3, 5\}$ and $\rho_2 \triangleq \{1, 4, 5\}$ and observe that $\rho_i \circ f \circ \rho_i = \mu \circ f \circ \mu$. However, $\rho_1 \sqcap \rho_2 = \lambda x.x$, so that $(\rho_1 \sqcap \rho_2) \circ f \circ (\rho_1 \sqcap \rho_2) = f \neq \mu \circ f \circ \mu$. Thus, we have that the most concrete domain that induces the same best correct approximation of f as μ does not exist. □

2.2 The Solution

Our key technical result is the following *constructive* characterization of the property of "having the same b.c.a." for two comparable abstract domains. In the following, given a poset A and $S \subseteq A$, $\max(S) \triangleq \{x \in S \mid \forall y \in S.\ x \leq_A y \Rightarrow x = y\}$ denotes the set of maximal elements of S in A.

Lemma 2.2. *Let $f : C \to C$, $A, B \in \text{Abs}(C)$ such that $B \subseteq A$ and $f \circ \mu_A$ is continuous (i.e., preserves lub's of chains). Then,*

$$f^B = f^A \;\Leftrightarrow\; \text{img}(f^A) \cup \textstyle\bigcup_{y \in A} \max(\{x \in A \mid f^A(x) \leq_A y\}) \subseteq B.$$

It is important to remark that the proof of the above result basically consists in reducing the equality $f^A = f^B$ between b.c.a.'s to a standard property of completeness of the abstract domains A and B for the function f and then in exploiting the constructive characterization of completeness of abstract domains by Giacobazzi et al. [17, Section 4]. In this sense, the proof itself is particularly interesting because it provides an unexpected reduction of best correct approximations as a completeness problem.

Definition 2.3. Given $F \subseteq C \longrightarrow C$ define: $\mathcal{K}_F : \text{Abs}(C) \to \text{Abs}(C)$ as

$$\mathcal{K}_F(A) \triangleq \sqcup\{B \in \text{Abs}(C) \mid F^B = F^A\}.$$

If $F^{\mathcal{K}_F(A)} = F^A$ then $\mathcal{K}_F(A)$ is called the *correctness kernel* of A for F. □

As a consequence of Lemma 2.2 we obtain the following constructive result of existence for correctness kernels. If $X \subseteq A$ then $\mathrm{Cl}_\wedge(X) \triangleq \{\wedge S \in A \mid S \subseteq X\}$ denotes the glb-closure of X in A (note that $\wedge\varnothing = \top_A \in \mathrm{Cl}_\wedge(X)$), while $\mathrm{Cl}_\vee(X)$ denotes the dual lub-closure.

Theorem 2.4. *Let $A \in \mathrm{Abs}(C)$ and $F \subseteq C \to C$ such that, for any $f \in F$, $f \circ \mu_A$ is continuous. Then, the correctness kernel of A for F exists and it is*

$$\mathcal{K}_F(A) = \mathrm{Cl}_\wedge\Big(\bigcup_{f\in F} \mathrm{img}(f^A) \cup \textstyle\bigcup_{y\in \mathrm{img}(f^A)} \max(\{x \in A \mid f^A(x) = y\})\Big).$$

Example 2.5. Consider sets of integers $\wp(\mathbb{Z})_\subseteq$ as concrete domain and the square operation $sq : \wp(\mathbb{Z}) \to \wp(\mathbb{Z})$ as concrete function, i.e., $sq(X) \triangleq \{x^2 \mid x \in X\}$, which is obviously additive and therefore continuous. Consider the abstract domain $\mathrm{Sign} \in \mathrm{Abs}(\wp(\mathbb{Z})_\subseteq)$, depicted in the figure, that represents the sign of an integer variable. Sign induces the following best correct approximation of sq:

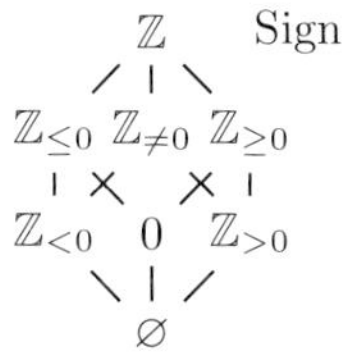

$$\begin{aligned} sq^{\mathrm{Sign}} = \{&\varnothing \mapsto \varnothing, \mathbb{Z}_{<0} \mapsto \mathbb{Z}_{>0}, 0 \mapsto 0, \mathbb{Z}_{>0} \mapsto \mathbb{Z}_{>0}, \mathbb{Z}_{\leq 0} \mapsto \mathbb{Z}_{\geq 0},\\ &\mathbb{Z}_{\neq 0} \mapsto \mathbb{Z}_{>0}, \mathbb{Z}_{\geq 0} \mapsto \mathbb{Z}_{\geq 0}, \mathbb{Z} \mapsto \mathbb{Z}_{\geq 0}\}.\end{aligned}$$

Let us characterize the correctness kernel $\mathcal{K}_{sq}(\mathrm{Sign})$ by Theorem 2.4. We have that $\mathrm{img}(sq^{\mathrm{Sign}}) = \{\varnothing, \mathbb{Z}_{>0}, 0, \mathbb{Z}_{\geq 0}\}$. Moreover,

$$\begin{aligned} \max(\{x \in \mathrm{Sign} \mid sq^{\mathrm{Sign}}(x) = \varnothing\}) &= \{\varnothing\}\\ \max(\{x \in \mathrm{Sign} \mid sq^{\mathrm{Sign}}(x) = \mathbb{Z}_{>0}\}) &= \{\mathbb{Z}_{\neq 0}\}\\ \max(\{x \in \mathrm{Sign} \mid sq^{\mathrm{Sign}}(x) = 0\}) &= \{0\}\\ \max(\{x \in \mathrm{Sign} \mid sq^{\mathrm{Sign}}(x) = \mathbb{Z}_{\geq 0}\}) &= \{\mathbb{Z}\}\end{aligned}$$

Hence, $\cup_{y\in \mathrm{img}(sq^{\mathrm{Sign}})} \max(\{x \in \mathrm{Sign} \mid sq^{\mathrm{Sign}}(x) = y\}) = \{\varnothing, \mathbb{Z}_{\neq 0}, 0, \mathbb{Z}\}$ so that, by Theorem 2.4:

$$\mathcal{K}_{sq}(\mathrm{Sign}) = \mathrm{Cl}_\cap(\{\varnothing, \mathbb{Z}_{>0}, 0, \mathbb{Z}_{\geq 0}, \mathbb{Z}_{\neq 0}, \mathbb{Z}\}) = \mathrm{Sign} \smallsetminus \{\mathbb{Z}_{<0}, \mathbb{Z}_{\leq 0}\}.$$

Thus, it turns out that we can safely remove the abstract values $\mathbb{Z}_{<0}$ and $\mathbb{Z}_{\leq 0}$ from Sign and still preserve the same b.c.a. as Sign does. Besides, we cannot remove further abstract elements otherwise we do not retain the same b.c.a. as Sign. For example, this means that Sign-based analyses of programs like

$x := k$; **while** condition **do** $x := x * x$;

can be carried out by using the simpler domain $\mathrm{Sign} \smallsetminus \{\mathbb{Z}_{<0}, \mathbb{Z}_{\leq 0}\}$, providing the same input/output abstract behavior. □

It is also worth remarking that in Theorem 2.4 the hypothesis of continuity is crucial for the existence of correctness kernels as shown by the following example.

Example 2.6. Let us consider as concrete domain C the $\omega + 2$ ordinal, i.e., $C \triangleq \{x \in Ord \mid x < \omega\} \cup \{\omega, \omega+1\}$, and let $f : C \longrightarrow C$ be defined as follows: for any $x < \omega$, $f(x) \triangleq \omega$, and $f(\omega) = f(\omega+1) \triangleq \omega + 1$. Let $\mu \in \mathrm{uco}(C)$ be the identity $\lambda x.x$, so that $\mu \circ f \circ \mu = f$. For any $k \geq 0$, consider $\rho_k \in \mathrm{uco}(C)$ defined as $\rho_k \triangleq C \smallsetminus [0, k[$ and observe that for any k, we have that $\rho_k \circ f \circ \rho_k = f = \mu \circ f \circ \mu$. However, it turns out that $\sqcup_{k \geq 0} \rho_k = \{\omega, \omega + 1\}$ and $(\sqcup_{k\geq 0}\rho_k) \circ f \circ (\sqcup_{k \geq 0} \rho_k) = \lambda x.\omega + 1 \neq \mu \circ f \circ \mu$. Hence, the correctness kernel of μ for f does not exist. Observe that $\mu \circ f = f$ is not continuous and therefore this example is consistent with Theorem 2.4. □

3 Correctness Kernels in Abstract Model Checking

Following [19], partitions can be viewed as particular abstract domains of the concrete domain $\wp(\Sigma)$. Let $\mathrm{Part}(\Sigma)$ denote the set of partitions of Σ. A partition $P \in \mathrm{Part}(\Sigma)$ can be considered an abstract domain by means of the following Galois insertion $(\alpha_P, \wp(\Sigma)_\subseteq, \wp(P)_\subseteq, \gamma_P)$: $\alpha_P(S) \triangleq \{B \in P \mid B \cap S \neq \varnothing\}$ and $\gamma_P(\mathcal{B}) \triangleq \cup_{B \in \mathcal{B}} B$. Hence, $\alpha_P(S)$ encodes the minimal over-approximation of a set S of states through blocks of P.

Consider a Kripke structure $\mathcal{K} = \langle \Sigma, \rightarrow, \ell \rangle$ and a corresponding abstract Kripke structure $\mathcal{A} = \langle P, \rightarrow^\sharp, \ell^\sharp \rangle$ defined over a state partition $P \in \mathrm{Part}(\Sigma)$.[1] Fixpoint-based verification of a temporal specification on the abstract model $\mathcal{A}$ involves the computation of least/greatest fixpoints of operators defined using Boolean connectives (union, intersection, complementation) on abstract states and abstract successor/predecessor functions $\mathrm{post}^\sharp$/$\mathrm{pre}^\sharp$ on the abstract transition system $\langle P, \rightarrow^\sharp \rangle$. The key point here is that sucessor/predecessor functions are defined as best correct approximations on the abstract domain P of the corresponding concrete successor/predecessor functions. In standard abstract model checking [1,6,7], the abstract transition relation is defined as the existential/existential relation $\rightarrow^{\exists\exists}$ between blocks of P:

$$B \rightarrow^{\exists\exists} C \text{ iff } \exists x \in B. \exists y \in C.\, x \rightarrow y$$
$$\mathrm{post}^{\exists\exists}(B) \triangleq \{C \in P \mid B \rightarrow^{\exists\exists} C\};\ \mathrm{pre}^{\exists\exists}(C) \triangleq \{B \in P \mid B \rightarrow^{\exists\exists} C\}.$$

It turns out [19] that $\mathrm{pre}^{\exists\exists}$ and $\mathrm{post}^{\exists\exists}$ are the best correct approximations of, resp., pre and post on the abstract domain $(\alpha_P, \wp(\Sigma)_\subseteq, \wp(P)_\subseteq, \gamma_P)$. In fact, for a block $C \in P$,

$$\alpha_P(\mathrm{pre}(\gamma_P(C))) = \{B \in P \mid B \cap \mathrm{pre}(C) \neq \varnothing\} = \mathrm{pre}^{\exists\exists}(C)$$

and an analogous equation holds for post. We thus have that $\mathrm{pre}^{\exists\exists} = \alpha_P \circ \mathrm{pre} \circ \gamma_P$ and $\mathrm{post}^{\exists\exists} = \alpha_P \circ \mathrm{post} \circ \gamma_P$.

This abstract interpretation-based framework allows us to apply correctness kernels in the context of abstract model checking. The abstract transition system $\mathcal{A} = \langle P, \rightarrow^{\exists\exists} \rangle$ is viewed as the abstract interpretation defined by the abstract domain $(\alpha_P, \wp(\Sigma)_\subseteq, \wp(P)_\subseteq, \gamma_P)$ and the corresponding abstract functions $\mathrm{pre}^{\exists\exists} = \alpha_P \circ \mathrm{pre} \circ \gamma_P$ and $\mathrm{post}^{\exists\exists} = \alpha_P \circ \mathrm{post} \circ \gamma_P$. Then, the correctness kernel of $\wp(P)$ for the concrete predecessor/successor $\{\mathrm{pre}, \mathrm{post}\}$, that we denote simply by $\mathcal{K}_\rightarrow(P)$ (this clearly exists

[1] Equivalently, the abstract Kripke structure $\mathcal{A}$ can be defined over an abstract state space A determined by a surjective abstraction function $h : \Sigma \longrightarrow A$.

by Theorem 2.4 since pre and post are additive), provides a simplification of the abstract domain $\wp(P)$ that preserves the best correct approximations of predecessor and successor. This simplification of the abstract state space works as follows:

Corollary 3.1. *$\mathcal{K}_{\rightarrow}(P)$ merges two blocks $B_1, B_2 \in P$ if and only if for any $A \in P$, $A \rightarrow^{\exists\exists} B_1 \Leftrightarrow A \rightarrow^{\exists\exists} B_2$ and $B_1 \rightarrow^{\exists\exists} A \Leftrightarrow B_2 \rightarrow^{\exists\exists} A$.*

4 EGAS and CEGAR

Let us discuss how correctness kernels give rise to an Example-Guided Abstraction Simplification (EGAS) paradigm in abstract transition systems.

Let us first recall some basic notions of CEGAR [4,5]. Consider an abstract transition system $\mathcal{A} = \langle P, \rightarrow^{\exists\exists} \rangle$ defined over a state partition $P \in \mathrm{Part}(\Sigma)$ and a finite abstract path $\pi = \langle B_1, ..., B_n \rangle$ in $\mathcal{A}$. Typically, this is a path counterexample to the validity of a temporal formula that has been given as output by a model checker (for simplicity we do not consider here loop path counterexamples). The set of concrete paths that are abstracted to π are defined as follows: $\mathrm{paths}(\pi) \triangleq \{\langle s_1, ..., s_n \rangle \in \Sigma^n \mid \forall i \in [1, n].s_i \in B_i \;\&\; \forall i \in [1, n).s_i \rightarrow s_{i+1}\}$. The abstract path π is *spurious* when $\mathrm{paths}(\pi) = \varnothing$. The sequence of sets of states $\mathrm{sp}(\pi) = \langle S_1, ..., S_n \rangle$ is inductively defined as follows: $S_1 \triangleq B_1$; $S_{i+1} \triangleq \mathrm{post}(S_i) \cap B_{i+1}$. As shown in [5], it turns out that π is spurious iff there exists a least $k \in [1, n-1]$ such that $S_{k+1} = \varnothing$. In such a case, the partition P is refined by splitting the block B_k. The three following sets partition the block B_k:

dead-end states: $B_k^{\mathrm{dead}} \triangleq S_k \neq \varnothing$
bad states: $B_k^{\mathrm{bad}} \triangleq B_k \cap \mathrm{pre}(B_{k+1}) \neq \varnothing$
irrelevant states: $B_k^{\mathrm{irr}} \triangleq B_k \smallsetminus (B_k^{\mathrm{dead}} \cup B_k^{\mathrm{bad}})$

The split of the block B_k must separate dead-end states from bad states, while irrelevant states may be joined indifferently with dead-end or bad states. However, the problem of finding the coarsest refinement of P that separates dead-end and bad states is NP-hard [5] and thus some refinement heuristics are used. According to the basic heuristics in [5, Section 4], B_k is simply split into B_k^{dead} and $B_k^{\mathrm{bad}} \cup B_k^{\mathrm{irr}}$. Let us see a simple example.

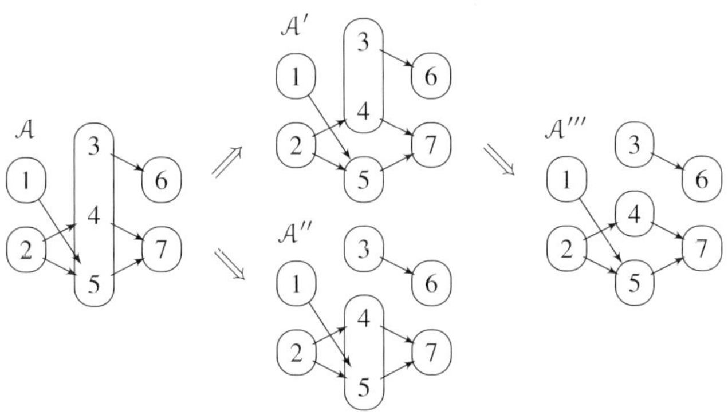

Consider the abstract path $\pi = \langle [1], [345], [6] \rangle$ in $\mathcal{A}$. This is a spurious path and the block $[345]$ is therefore partitioned as follows: $[5]$ dead-end states, $[3]$ bad states and $[4]$ irrelevant states. The refinement heuristics of CEGAR tells us that irrelevant states are joined with bad states so that $\mathcal{A}$ is refined to $\mathcal{A}'$. In turn, consider the spurious path $\pi' = \langle [2], [34], [6] \rangle$ in $\mathcal{A}'$, so that CEGAR refines $\mathcal{A}'$ to $\mathcal{A}'''$ by splitting the block $[34]$. In the first abstraction refinement, let us observe that if irrelevant states would have been joined together with dead-end states rather than with bad states we would have obtained the abstract system $\mathcal{A}''$, and $\mathcal{A}''$ does not contain spurious paths so that it surely does not need to be further refined.

EGAS can be integrated within the CEGAR loop thanks to the following remark. If π_1 and π_2 are paths, resp., in $\langle P_1, \rightarrow^{\exists\exists} \rangle$ and $\langle P_2, \rightarrow^{\exists\exists} \rangle$, where $P_1, P_2 \in \mathrm{Part}(\Sigma)$ and $P_1 \preceq P_2$, then π_1 is abstracted to π_2, denoted by $\pi_1 \sqsubseteq \pi_2$, when $\mathrm{length}(\pi_1) = \mathrm{length}(\pi_2)$ and for any $j \in [1, \mathrm{length}(\pi_1)]$, $\pi_1(j) \subseteq \pi_2(j)$.

Corollary 4.1. *Consider an abstract transition system $\mathcal{A} = \langle P, \rightarrow^{\exists\exists} \rangle$ over a partition $P \in \mathrm{Part}(\Sigma)$ and its simplification $\mathcal{A}_s = \langle \mathcal{K}_{\rightarrow}(P), \rightarrow^{\exists\exists} \rangle$ induced by the correctness kernel $\mathcal{K}_{\rightarrow}(P)$. If π is an abstract path in $\mathcal{A}_s$ such that $\mathrm{paths}(\pi) = \varnothing$ then there exists an abstract path π' in $\mathcal{A}$ such that $\pi' \sqsubseteq \pi$ and $\mathrm{paths}(\pi') = \varnothing$.*

Thus, the abstraction simplification induced by the correctness kernel does not add spurious paths.

The above observations suggest us a new refinement strategy within the CEGAR loop. Let $\pi = \langle B_1, ..., B_n \rangle$ be a spurious path in $\mathcal{A}$ and $\mathrm{sp}(\pi) = \langle S_1, ..., S_n \rangle$ such that $S_{k+1} = \varnothing$ for some minimum $k \in [1, n-1]$, so that the block B_k needs to be split. The set of irrelevant states B_k^{irr} is partitioned as follows. We first define the subset of *bad-irrelevant* states $B_k^{\text{bad-irr}}$. Let $\mathrm{pre}^{\exists\exists}(B_k^{\mathrm{bad}}) = \{A_1, ..., A_j\}$ and $\mathrm{post}^{\exists\exists}(B_k^{\mathrm{bad}}) = \{C_1, ..., C_l\}$. Then,

$$B_k^{\text{bad-irr}} \triangleq \big(\mathrm{post}(A_1 \cup ... \cup A_j) \cap \mathrm{pre}(C_1 \cup ... \cup C_l)\big) \cap B_k^{\mathrm{irr}}.$$

The underlying idea is simple: $B_k^{\text{bad-irr}}$ contains the irrelevant states that: (1) can be reached from a block that reaches some bad state and (2) reach a block that is also reached by some bad state. By Corollary 4.1, it is therefore clear that by merging $B_k^{\text{bad-irr}}$ and B_k^{bad} no spurious path is added w.r.t. the abstract system where they are kept separate. The subset of *dead-irrelevant* states $B_k^{\text{dead-irr}}$ is analogosly defined: If $\mathrm{pre}^{\exists\exists}(B_k^{\mathrm{dead}}) = \{A_1, ..., A_j\}$ and $\mathrm{post}^{\exists\exists}(B_k^{\mathrm{dead}}) = \{C_1, ..., C_l\}$ then

$$B_k^{\text{dead-irr}} \triangleq \big(\mathrm{post}(A_1 \cup ... \cup A_j) \cap \mathrm{pre}(C_1 \cup ... \cup C_l)\big) \cap B_k^{\mathrm{irr}}.$$

It may happen that: (A) an irrelevant state is both bad- and dead-irrelevant; (B) an irrelevant state is neither bad- nor dead-irrelevant. From the viewpoint of EGAS, the states of case (A) can be equivalently merged with bad or dead states since in both cases no spurious path is added. On the other hand, the states of case (B) are called *fully-irrelevant* because EGAS does not provide a merging strategy with bad or dead states. For these states, one could use, for example, the basic refinement heuristics of CEGAR that merge them with bad states.

In the above example, for the spurious path $\langle [1], [345], [6] \rangle$ in $\mathcal{A}$, the block $B = [345]$ needs to be refined: $B^{\mathrm{bad}} = [3]$, $B^{\mathrm{dead}} = [5]$ and $B^{\mathrm{irr}} = [4]$. Here, 4 is a dead-irrelevant state and so it is merged in $\mathcal{A}''$ with the dead-end state 5.

5 Correctness Kernels in Predicate Abstraction

Let us show how correctness kernels can be also used in the context of predicate abstraction-based model checking [11,18]. Following Ball et al. [2], predicate abstraction can be formalized by abstract interpretation as follows. Let us consider a program P with k integer variables $x_1,...,x_k$. The concrete domain of computation of P is $\langle\wp(\mathrm{States}), \subseteq\rangle$ where $\mathrm{States} \triangleq \{x_1, ..., x_k\} \to \mathbb{Z}$. Values in States are denoted by tuples $\langle z_1, ..., z_k\rangle \in \mathbb{Z}^k$. The program P generates a transition system $\langle\mathrm{States}, \to\rangle$ so that the concrete semantics of P is defined by the corresponding successor function $\mathrm{post} : \wp(\mathrm{States}) \to \wp(\mathrm{States})$.

A finite set $\mathcal{P} = \{p_1, ..., p_n\}$ of state predicates is considered, where each predicate p_i denotes the subset of states that satisfy p_i, i.e. $\{s \in \mathrm{States} \mid s \models p_i\}$. These predicates give rise to the so-called Boolean abstraction $B \triangleq \langle\wp(\{0,1\}^n), \subseteq\rangle$ which is related to $\wp(\mathrm{States})$ through the following abstraction/concretization maps (here, $s \models p_i$ is understood in $\{0, 1\}$) that give rise to a disjunctive (i.e., γ preserves lub's) Galois connection:

$$\alpha_B(S) \triangleq \{\langle s \models p_1, ..., s \models p_n\rangle \in \{0,1\}^n \mid s \in S\},$$
$$\gamma_B(V) \triangleq \{s \in \mathrm{States} \mid \langle s \models p_1, ..., s \models p_n\rangle \in V\}.$$

Verification of reachability properties based on predicate abstraction consists in computing the least fixpoint of the best correct approximation of post on the Boolean abstraction B, namely, $\mathrm{post}^B \triangleq \alpha_B \circ \mathrm{post} \circ \gamma_B$. As argued in [2], the Boolean abstraction B may be too costly for the purpose of reachability verification, so that one usually abstracts B through the so-called Cartesian abstraction. This latter abstraction formalizes precisely the abstract post operator computed by the verification algorithm of the c2bp tool in SLAM [3]. However, the Cartesian abstraction of B may cause a loss of precision, so that this abstraction is successively refined by reduced disjunctive completion and the so-called focus operation, and this formalizes the bebop tool in SLAM [2].

Let us consider the example program in Figure 1, taken from [2], where the goal is that of verifying that the assert at line $(*)$ is never reached, regardless of the context in which *foo*() is called. Ball et al. [2] consider the following set of predicates

```
int x, y, z, w;

void foo() {
  do {
    z := 0; x := y;
    if (w) { x++; z := 1; }
  } while (!(x = y))
  if (z)
    assert(0); // (*)
}
```

Fig. 1. An example program

$\mathcal{P} \triangleq \{p_1 \equiv (z = 0), p_2 \equiv (x = y)\}$ so that the Boolean abstraction is $B = \wp(\{\langle 0,0\rangle, \langle 0,1\rangle, \langle 1,0\rangle, \langle 1,1\rangle\})_{\subseteq}$. Clearly, the analysis based on B allows to conclude that line $(*)$ is not reachable. This comes as a consequence of the fact that the least fixpoint of the best correct approximation post^B for the do-while-loop provides as result $\{\langle 0,0\rangle, \langle 1,1\rangle\} \in B$ because:

$$\varnothing \xrightarrow{z:=0;\ x:=y} \{\langle 1,1\rangle\} \xrightarrow{\mathbf{if}(w)\{x\text{++};\ z:=1;\}} \{\langle 1,1\rangle, \langle 0,0\rangle\}$$

so that at the exit of the do-while-loop one can conclude that

$$\{\langle 1,1\rangle, \langle 0,0\rangle\} \cap p_2 = \{\langle 1,1\rangle, \langle 0,0\rangle\} \cap \{\langle 0,1\rangle, \langle 1,1\rangle\} = \{\langle 1,1\rangle\}$$

holds, hence p_1 is satisfied, so that $z = 0$ and therefore line $(*)$ cannot be reached.

Let us characterize the correctness kernel of the Boolean abstraction B. Let $S_1 \triangleq z := 0;\ x := y$ and $S_2 \triangleq x\text{++};\ z := 1$. The best correct approximations of post_{S_1} and post_{S_2} on the abstract domain B turn out to be as follows:

$$\begin{aligned}\alpha_B \circ \mathrm{post}_{S_1} \circ \gamma_B = \Big\{&\langle 0,0\rangle \mapsto \{\langle 1,1\rangle\}, \langle 0,1\rangle \mapsto \{\langle 1,1\rangle\}, \langle 1,0\rangle \mapsto \{\langle 1,1\rangle\},\\ &\langle 1,1\rangle \mapsto \{\langle 1,1\rangle\}\Big\}\\ \alpha_B \circ \mathrm{post}_{S_2} \circ \gamma_B = \Big\{&\langle 0,0\rangle \mapsto \{\langle 0,0\rangle, \langle 0,1\rangle\}, \langle 0,1\rangle \mapsto \{\langle 0,0\rangle\},\\ &\langle 1,0\rangle \mapsto \{\langle 0,0\rangle, \langle 0,1\rangle\}, \langle 1,1\rangle \mapsto \{\langle 0,0\rangle\}\Big\}\end{aligned}$$

Thus, we have that $\mathrm{img}(\alpha_B \circ \mathrm{post}_{S_1} \circ \gamma_B) = \{\{\langle 1,1\rangle\}\}$ and $\mathrm{img}(\alpha_B \circ \mathrm{post}_{S_2} \circ \gamma_B) = \{\{\langle 0,0\rangle, \langle 0,1\rangle\}, \{\langle 0,0\rangle\}\}$ so that

$$\begin{aligned}\max\left(\{V \in B \mid \alpha_B(\mathrm{post}_{S_1}(\gamma_B(V))) = \{\langle 1,1\rangle\}\}\right) &= \{\{\langle 0,0\rangle, \langle 0,1\rangle, \langle 1,0\rangle, \langle 1,1\rangle\}\}\\ \max\left(\{V \in B \mid \alpha_B(\mathrm{post}_{S_2}(\gamma_B(V))) = \{\langle 0,0\rangle, \langle 0,1\rangle\}\}\right) &= \{\{\langle 0,0\rangle, \langle 0,1\rangle, \langle 1,0\rangle, \langle 1,1\rangle\}\}\\ \max\left(\{V \in B \mid \alpha_B(\mathrm{post}_{S_2}(\gamma_B(V))) = \{\langle 0,0\rangle\}\}\right) &= \{\{\langle 0,1\rangle, \langle 1,1\rangle\}\}\end{aligned}$$

Hence, by Theorem 2.4, the kernel $\mathcal{K}_F(B)$ of B for $F \triangleq \{\mathrm{post}_{S_1}, \mathrm{post}_{S_2}\}$ is:

$$\begin{aligned}\mathrm{Cl}_\cap\Big(\mathrm{Cl}_\cup\big(\{\{\langle 0,0\rangle\}, \{\langle 1,1\rangle\}, \{\langle 0,0\rangle, \langle 0,1\rangle\}, \{\langle 0,1\rangle, \langle 1,1\rangle\},\\ \{\langle 0,0\rangle, \langle 0,1\rangle, \langle 1,0\rangle, \langle 1,1\rangle\}\}\big)\Big) = \mathrm{Cl}_\cup\Big(\{\{\langle 0,0\rangle\}, \{\langle 0,1\rangle\}, \{\langle 1,1\rangle\}\}\Big)\end{aligned}$$

This means that $\mathcal{K}_F(B)$ can be represented as

$$\langle \wp(\{\langle 0,0\rangle, \langle 0,1\rangle, \langle 1,1\rangle\}) \cup \{\langle 0,0\rangle, \langle 0,1\rangle, \langle 1,0\rangle, \langle 1,1\rangle\}, \subseteq\rangle$$

and therefore $\mathcal{K}_F(B)$ is a proper abstraction of B that, for example, is not able to express the property $p_1 \wedge \neg p_2 \equiv (z = 0) \wedge (x \neq y)$.

It is interesting to compare this correctness kernel $\mathcal{K}_F(B)$ with Ball et al.'s [2] Cartesian abstraction of B. The Cartesian abstraction is defined as $C \triangleq \langle \{0,1,*\}^n \cup \{\bot_C\}, \leq\rangle$, where $\leq$ is pointwise ordering between tuples of values in $\{0,1,*\}$ ordered by $0 < *$ and $1 < *$ ($\bot$ is the bottom element that represents the empty set of states). The concretization function $\gamma_C : C \to \wp(\mathrm{States})$ is as follows:

$$\gamma_C(\langle v_1, ..., v_n \rangle) \triangleq \{s \in \text{States} \mid \langle s \models p_1, ..., s \models p_n \rangle \leq \langle v_1, ..., v_n \rangle\}.$$

These two abstractions are not comparable: for instance, $\langle 1, 0 \rangle \in C$ represents $p_1 \wedge \neg p_2$ which is instead not represented by $\mathcal{K}_F(B)$, while $\{\langle 0, 0 \rangle, \langle 1, 1 \rangle\} \in \mathcal{K}_F(B)$ represents $(\neg p_1 \wedge \neg p_2) \vee (p_1 \wedge p_2)$ which is not represented in C. However, while the correctness kernel guarantees no loss of information in analyzing the program P, the analysis of P with the Cartesian abstraction C is inconclusive because:

$$\bot_C \xrightarrow{z:=0;\ x:=y} \langle 1, 1 \rangle \xrightarrow{\textbf{if}(w)\{x\text{++};\ z:=1;\}} \langle 0, 0 \rangle \vee_C \langle 1, 1 \rangle = \langle *, * \rangle$$

where $\gamma_C(\langle *, * \rangle) = \text{States}$, so that at the exit of the do-while-loop one cannot infer that line $(*)$ cannot be reached.

6 Related and Future Work

Few examples of abstraction simplifications are known. A general notion of domain simplification and compression in abstract interpretation has been introduced in [12,15] as a dual of abstraction refinement. This duality has been further exploited in [13] to include semantics transformations in a general theory for transforming abstractions and semantics based on abstract interpretation. Our domain transformation does not fit directly in this framework. Following [15], given a property $\mathcal{P}$ of abstract domains, the core of an abstract domain A, when it exists, provides the most concrete simplification of A that satisfies the property $\mathcal{P}$, while the compressor of A, when it exists, provides the most abstract simplification of A that induces the same refined abstraction in $\mathcal{P}$ as A does. Examples of compressors include the least disjuctive basis [16], where $\mathcal{P}$ is the abstract domain property of being disjunctive, and examples of cores include the completeness core [17], where $\mathcal{P}$ is the domain property of being complete for some semantic function. The correctness kernel defined in this paper is neither an instance of a domain core nor an instance of domain compression. The first because, given an abstraction A, the correctness kernel of A characterizes the most abstract domain that induces the same best correct approximation of a function f on A, whilst the notion of domain core for the domain property $\mathcal{P}_A$ of inducing the same b.c.a. as A would not be meaningful, as this would trivially yield A itself. The second because there is no (unique) maximal domain refinement of an abstract domain which induces the same property $\mathcal{P}_A$.

The EGAS methodology opens some stimulating directions for future work, such as (1) the formalization of a precise relationship between EGAS and CEGAR and (2) an experimental evaluation of the integration in the CEGAR loop of the EGAS-based refinement strategy of Section 4. It is here useful to recall that some work formalizing CEGAR in abstract interpretation has already been done [10,14]. On the one hand, [14] shows that CEGAR corresponds to iteratively compute a so-called complete shell [17] of the underlying abstract model A with respect to the concrete successor transformer, while [10] formally compares CEGAR with an abstraction refinement strategy based on the computations of abstract fixpoints in an abstract domain. These works can therefore provide a starting point for studying the relationship between EGAS and CEGAR in a common abstract interpretation setting.

Acknowledgements. This work was carried out during a visit of the authors to the Equipe "Abstraction" lead by P. and R. Cousot, at École Normale Supérieure, Paris. This work was partially supported by the PRIN 2007 Project "*AIDA2007: Abstract Interpretation Design and Applications*" and by the University of Padova under the Project "*Analysis, verification and abstract interpretation of models for concurrency*".

References

1. Baier, C., Katoen, J.-P.: Principles of Model Checking. The MIT Press, Cambridge (2008)
2. Ball, T., Podelski, A., Rajamani, S.K.: Boolean and Cartesian abstraction for model checking C programs. Int. J. Softw. Tools Technol. Transfer 5, 49–58 (2003)
3. Ball, T., Rajamani, S.K.: The SLAM Project: Debugging system software via static analysis. In: Proc. 29th ACM POPL, pp. 1–3 (2002)
4. Clarke, E.M., Grumberg, O., Jha, S., Lu, Y., Veith, H.: Counterexample-guided abstraction refinement. In: Emerson, E.A., Sistla, A.P. (eds.) CAV 2000. LNCS, vol. 1855, pp. 154–169. Springer, Heidelberg (2000)
5. Clarke, E.M., Grumberg, O., Jha, S., Lu, Y., Veith, H.: Counterexample-guided abstraction refinement for symbolic model checking. J. ACM 50(5), 752–794 (2003)
6. Clarke, E.M., Grumberg, O., Long, D.: Model checking and abstraction. ACM Trans. Program. Lang. Syst. 16(5), 1512–1542 (1994)
7. Clarke, E.M., Grumberg, O., Peled, D.A.: Model checking. The MIT Press, Cambridge (1999)
8. Cousot, P., Cousot, R.: Abstract interpretation: a unified lattice model for static analysis of programs by construction or approximation of fixpoints. In: Proc. 4th ACM POPL, pp. 238–252 (1977)
9. Cousot, P., Cousot, R.: Systematic design of program analysis frameworks. In: Proc. 6th ACM POPL, pp. 269–282 (1979)
10. Cousot, P., Ganty, P., Raskin, J.-F.: Fixpoint-guided abstraction refinements. In: Riis Nielson, H., Filé, G. (eds.) SAS 2007. LNCS, vol. 4634, pp. 333–348. Springer, Heidelberg (2007)
11. Das, S., Dill, D.L., Park, S.: Experience with predicate abstraction. In: Halbwachs, N., Peled, D.A. (eds.) CAV 1999. LNCS, vol. 1633, pp. 160–171. Springer, Heidelberg (1999)
12. Filé, G., Giacobazzi, R., Ranzato, F.: A unifying view of abstract domain design. ACM Comp. Surveys 28(2), 333–336 (1996)
13. Giacobazzi, R., Mastroeni, I.: Transforming abstract interpretations by abstract interpretation (Invited Lecture). In: Alpuente, M., Vidal, G. (eds.) SAS 2008. LNCS, vol. 5079, pp. 1–17. Springer, Heidelberg (2008)
14. Giacobazzi, R., Quintarelli, E.: Incompleteness, counterexamples, and refinements in abstract model checking. In: Cousot, P. (ed.) SAS 2001. LNCS, vol. 2126, pp. 356–373. Springer, Heidelberg (2001)
15. Giacobazzi, R., Ranzato, F.: Refining and compressing abstract domains. In: Degano, P., Gorrieri, R., Marchetti-Spaccamela, A. (eds.) ICALP 1997. LNCS, vol. 1256, pp. 771–781. Springer, Heidelberg (1997)
16. Giacobazzi, R., Ranzato, F.: Optimal domains for disjunctive abstract interpretation. Sci. Comp. Program. 32, 177–210 (1998)
17. Giacobazzi, R., Ranzato, F., Scozzari, F.: Making abstract interpretations complete. J. ACM 47(2), 361–416 (2000)
18. Graf, S., Saïdi, H.: Construction of abstract state graphs with PVS. In: Grumberg, O. (ed.) CAV 1997. LNCS, vol. 1254, pp. 72–83. Springer, Heidelberg (1997)
19. Ranzato, F., Tapparo, F.: Generalized strong preservation by abstract interpretation. J. Logic and Computation 17(1), 157–197 (2007)

Compositional Closure for Bayes Risk in Probabilistic Noninterference

Annabelle McIver[1], Larissa Meinicke[1], and Carroll Morgan[2,⋆]

[1] Dept. Computer Science, Macquarie University, NSW 2109 Australia
[2] School of Comp. Sci. and Eng., Univ. New South Wales, NSW 2052 Australia

Abstract. We give a quantitative sequential model for noninterference security with probability (but not demonic choice), and a novel *refinement* order that we prove to be the *greatest* compositional relation consistent with an "elementary" order based on Bayes Risk. This *compositional closure* complements our earlier work defining refinement similarly for qualitative noninterference with demonic choice (but not probability).

The *Three-Judges Protocol* illustrates our model's utility: with compositionality, the embedded sub-protocols can be treated in isolation.

1 Introduction

Noninterference analysis splits a state space into high- and low-security portions and determines whether high-security values can be inferred from observation of low-security values and behaviours [5]. If **probability** is present, however, the question becomes "how much" rather than "whether" — and thus in that case we address the *likelihood* with which high-security values can be inferred from low-security observations. Here, we *compare* programs for that likelihood.

For programs S, I we say that $S \preceq I$ if S and I are functionally equivalent and the **Bayes Risk** (defined below) associated with implementation I is no worse than the Risk associated with specification S. If for all $S \preceq I$ and context $\mathcal{C}$ we had $\mathcal{C}(S) \preceq \mathcal{C}(I)$, then we would say that $(\preceq)$ is compositional.

Our TECHNICAL CONTRIBUTION is that we (i) give a sequential semantics for probabilistic noninterference, (ii) define the above "less likely to leak" order $(\preceq)$ based on Bayes Risk, (iii) show it is *not* compositional, (iv) identify a **compositional** subset of it, a *refinement* order $(\sqsubseteq)$ such that $S \sqsubseteq I$ implies $\mathcal{C}(S) \preceq \mathcal{C}(I)$ for all contexts $\mathcal{C}$ and (v) show that $(\sqsubseteq)$ is in fact the compositional **closure** of $(\preceq)$, so that we have $S \not\sqsubseteq I$ *only* when $\mathcal{C}(S) \not\preceq \mathcal{C}(I)$ for some $\mathcal{C}$.

Our GENERAL CONTRIBUTION is to further the goal of structuring secure protocols hierarchically and then designing/verifying them in separate pieces.

⋆ We acknowledge the support of the Australian Research Council Grant DP0879529.

S. Abramsky et al. (Eds.): ICALP 2010, Part II, LNCS 6199, pp. 223–235, 2010.

2 A Probabilistic, Noninterference Sequential Semantics

We distinguish *visible* variables (low-security), typically v in some finite type $\mathcal{V}$, and *hidden* variables (high-security), typically h in finite $\mathcal{H}$. Variables are in sans serif to avoid confusion with (decorated) values $v{:}\,\mathcal{V}, h{:}\,\mathcal{H}$ they might contain.

For example, let $\mathsf{h}{:}\,\{0,1,2\}$ represent one of three boxes: Box 0 has no white balls and two black; Box 1 has one of each; and Box 2 has two white. Let $\mathsf{v}{:}\,\{w,b,\bot\}$ represent a ball colour: *white*, *black*, *unknown*. Program S, informally written $\mathsf{h}{:=}\,0{\oplus}1{\oplus}2; \mathsf{v}{:\in}\, \{\!\{w^{@\frac{\mathsf{h}}{2}}, b^{@1-\frac{\mathsf{h}}{2}}\}\!\}; \mathsf{v}{:=}\,\bot$ chooses box h uniformly, then draws a ball v from that box: it has probability $\mathsf{h}/2$ of being white, and $1{-}\mathsf{h}/2$ of being black. Finally it replaces the ball. A typical security concern is then "How much information about h was revealed by the assignments to v?"

Below we give syntax and semantics to make the above program precise, providing the framework for asking –and answering– such security questions.

First however we introduce *distribution* notation, generalising set notations.

2.1 Distributions: Explicit, Implicit and Expected Values over Them

We write function application as $f.x$, with "." associating to the left. Operators without their operands are written between parentheses, as $(\preceq)$ for example.

By $\mathbb{D}X$ we mean the set of *discrete sub-distributions* on set X that sum to no more than one, and by $\mathsf{D}X$ we mean the *full* distributions that sum to one exactly. The *support* $\lceil\delta\rceil$ of (sub-)distribution $\delta{:}\,\mathbb{D}X$ is those elements x in X with $\delta.x{\neq}0$. Distributions can be scaled and summed according to the usual pointwise extension of multiplication and addition to real-valued functions.

Here are our notations for *explicit* distributions (cf. set enumerations):

multiple. We write $\{\!\{x^{@p}, y^{@q}, \cdots, z^{@r}\}\!\}$ for the distribution assigning probabilities $p, q, \cdots, r$ to elements $x, y, \cdots, z$ respectively, with $p{+}q{+}\cdots{+}r \leq 1$.

uniform. When explicit probabilities are omitted they are uniform: thus $\{\!\{x\}\!\}$ is the point distribution $\{\!\{x^{@1}\}\!\}$, and $\{\!\{x,y,z\}\!\}$ is $\{\!\{x^{@\frac{1}{3}}, y^{@\frac{1}{3}}, z^{@\frac{1}{3}}\}\!\}$.

We write $(\odot\, d{:}\,\delta \bullet E)$ for the *expected value* $\sum_{d:\,\lceil\delta\rceil}(\delta.d {*} E)$ of expression E interpreted as a random variable in d over distribution δ.[1] If however E is Boolean, then it is taken to be 1 if E holds and 0 otherwise, so that the expected value is then just the combined probability in δ of all elements d satisfying E.

We write *implicit* distributions (cf. set comprehensions) as $\{\!\{d{:}\,\delta \mid R \bullet E\}\!\}$, for distribution δ, real expression R and expression E, meaning

$$(\odot\, d{:}\,\delta \bullet R * \{\!\{E\}\!\}) \;/\; (\odot\, d{:}\,\delta \bullet R) \tag{1}$$

where, first, an expected value is formed in the numerator by scaling and adding point-distribution $\{\!\{E\}\!\}$ as a real-valued function: this gives another distribution.

[1] It is a dot-product between the distribution and the random variable as vectors.

The scalar denominator then normalises to give a distribution yet again. A missing E is implicitly d itself; and missing R is implicitly 1, effectively removing the denominator if δ is full (i.e. sums to one).

For example $\{\!\{d\colon \delta \bullet E\}\!\}$ *maps* expression E in d over distribution δ to make a new distribution on E's type. And a Boolean R is converted to 0,1; in that case $\{\!\{d\colon \delta \mid R\}\!\}$ is δ's *conditioning* over formula R as predicate on d, if δ is full.

Finally, for *Bayesian belief revision* let δ be an a-priori distribution over some D and let expression R for each d in D be the probability of a certain subsequent result if that d is chosen. Then $\{\!\{d\colon \delta \mid R\}\!\}$ is the a-posteriori distribution over D when that result actually occurs. Thus in the three-box program S let the value first assigned to v be $\hat{v}$. The a-priori distribution δ over h is uniform, and the probability of $\hat{v}{=}w$ is therefore $1/3*(0/2+1/2+2/2) = 1/2$. But the a-posteriori distribution of h *given that* $\hat{v}{=}w$ is $\{\!\{h\colon \delta \mid h/2\}\!\}$, which from (1) we calculate

$$= \quad (\odot\, h\colon \{\!\{0,1,2\}\!\} \bullet \frac{h}{2} * \{\!\{h\}\!\}) \;/\; (\odot\, h\colon \{\!\{0,1,2\}\!\} \bullet \frac{h}{2}) \quad = \quad \{\!\{1^{@\frac{1}{6}}, 2^{@\frac{1}{3}}\}\!\} \;/\; \frac{1}{2}\,,$$

that is $\{\!\{1^{@\frac{1}{3}}, 2^{@\frac{2}{3}}\}\!\}$. Thus if a white ball is drawn ($\hat{v}{=}w$) then the chance it came from Box 2 is 2/3, the probability of $\mathsf{h}{=}2$ in the a-posteriori distribution.

2.2 Program Denotations over a Visible/Hidden "Split" State-Space

With *visible* and *hidden* partitioning of the finite state space $\mathcal{V}{\times}\mathcal{H}$, probabilistic states in our new model are *split-states* of type $\mathcal{V}{\times}\mathsf{D}\mathcal{H}$, whose typical element (v,δ) indicates that we know $\mathsf{v}{=}v$ exactly, but all we know about h –which is not directly observable– is that it takes value h with probability $\delta.h$.

Programs are functions $(\mathcal{V}{\times}\mathsf{D}\mathcal{H}) \rightarrow \mathsf{D}(\mathcal{V}{\times}\mathsf{D}\mathcal{H})$ from split-states to distributions over them, called *hyper-distributions* since they are distributions with other distributions inside them: the outer distribution is directly visible but the inner distribution(s) over $\mathcal{H}$ are not. Thus for a program P, the application $[\![P]\!].(v,\delta)$ is the distribution of final split-states produced from initial (v,δ). Each (v',δ') in that outcome, with probability p say in the outer- (left-hand) D in $\mathsf{D}(\mathcal{V}{\times}\mathsf{D}\mathcal{H})$, means that with probability p an attacker will observe that v is v' and simultaneously be able to deduce that h has distribution δ'.

2.3 Program Syntax and Semantics

The programming language syntax and semantics is given in Fig. 1. Assignments to v or h can use an expression $E.\mathsf{v}.\mathsf{h}$ or a distribution $D.\mathsf{v}.\mathsf{h}$; and assignments to v might reveal information about h. For example, we have that

(i) A direct assignment of h to v reveals everything about h:
$$[\![\mathsf{v}{:=}\,\mathsf{h}]\!].(v,\delta) = \{\!\{h\colon \delta \bullet (h, \{\!\{h\}\!\})\}\!\}$$

(ii) Choosing v from a distribution independent of h reveals nothing about h:
$$[\![\mathsf{v}{:=}\,0\;{}_{1/3}{\oplus}\;1]\!].(v,\delta) = \{\!\{(0,\delta)^{@\frac{1}{3}}, (1,\delta)^{@\frac{2}{3}}\}\!\}$$

(iii) Partially h-dependent assignments to v might reveal something about h:
$$[\![\mathsf{v}{:=}\,\mathsf{h}\;\mathbf{mod}\;2]\!].(v,\{\!\{0,1,2\}\!\}) = \{\!\{(0,\{\!\{0,2\}\!\})^{@\frac{2}{3}}, (1,\{\!\{1\}\!\})^{@\frac{1}{3}}\}\!\}$$

Program type	Program text P	Semantics $[\![P]\!].(v,\delta)$
Identity	**skip**	$\{\!\{\ (v,\delta)\ \}\!\}$
Assign to visible	v:= E.v.h	$\{\!\{\ h{:}\,\delta \bullet (E.v.h, \{\!\{h'{:}\,\delta \mid E.v.h'{=}E.v.h\}\!\})\ \}\!\}$
Assign to hidden	h:= E.v.h	$\{\!\{\ (v, \{\!\{h{:}\,\delta \bullet E.v.h\}\!\})\ \}\!\}$
Choose prob. visible	v:∈ D.v.h	$\{\!\{\ v'{:}\,(\odot\, h{:}\,\delta \bullet D.v.h) \bullet (v', \{\!\{h'{:}\,\delta \mid D.v.h'.v'\}\!\})\}\!\}$
Choose prob. hidden	h:∈ D.v.h	$\{\!\{\ (v, (\odot\, h{:}\,\delta \bullet D.v.h))\ \}\!\}$
Composition	$P_1; P_2$	$(\odot\,(v',\delta'){:}\,[\![P_1]\!].(v,\delta) \bullet\ [\![P_2]\!].(v',\delta'))$
Probabilistic choice	$P_1\ {}_p\!\oplus P_2$	$p * [\![P_1]\!].(v,\delta) + (1{-}p) * [\![P_2]\!].(v,\delta)$ p is constant
Conditional choice p is $(\odot\, h{:}\,\delta \bullet G.v.h)$	**if** G.v.h **then** P_t **else** P_f **fi**	$p * [\![P_t]\!].(v, \{\!\{h{:}\,\delta \mid G.v.h\}\!\})$ $+\ (1{-}p) * [\![P_f]\!].(v, \{\!\{h{:}\,\delta \mid \neg G.v.h\}\!\})$

For simplicity let $\mathcal{V}$ and $\mathcal{H}$ have the same type $\mathcal{X}$. Expression E.v.h is then of type $\mathcal{X}$, distribution D.v.h is of type $\mathsf{D}\mathcal{X}$ and expression G.v.h is Boolean. Also we assume here that the p in ${}_p\!\oplus$ is constant — but it can in general depend on v and h.

For distributions in *program texts* we allow the more familiar infix notation ${}_p\!\oplus$, so that we can write h:= $0\,{}_{\frac{1}{3}}\!\oplus 1$ for h:∈ $\{\!\{0^{@\frac{1}{3}}, 1^{@\frac{2}{3}}\}\!\}$ and h:= $0\oplus 1$ for the uniform h:∈ $\{\!\{0,1\}\!\}$. The degenerate cases h:= 0 and h:∈ $\{\!\{0\}\!\}$ are then equivalent, as they should be.

Fig. 1. Split-state semantics of commands

On the other hand, assignments to h affect δ directly. Thus choosing h might

(i) increase our uncertainty of h: $[\![\text{h:= }0\oplus 1\oplus 2]\!].(v, \{\!\{0,1\}\!\}) = \{\!\{(v, \{\!\{0,1,2\}\!\})\}\!\}$
(ii) or reduce it: $[\![\text{h:= }0\oplus 1]\!].(v, \{\!\{0,1,2\}\!\}) = \{\!\{(v, \{\!\{0,1\}\!\})\}\!\}$
(iii) or leave it unchanged: $[\![\text{h:= }2{-}\text{h}]\!].(v, \{\!\{0,1,2\}\!\}) = \{\!\{(v, \{\!\{2,1,0\}\!\})\}\!\}$

Assignment statements are "atomic" — an attacker may not directly witness the evaluation of the right-hand side. For instance, the atomic probabilistic choice v:= h⊕¬h does *not* reveal which of the equally likely operands of (⊕) was used. We show elsewhere [11] how atomicity can be controlled more generally.

2.4 A Strong Attacker: Perfect Recall, and Implicit Flow

Our definition $[\![P_1; P_2]\!]$ of *sequential composition*[2] gives an attacker **perfect recall** after P_2 of the visible variable v as it was after P_1. Compare Program S (above) with Program I_1 defined h:= $0\oplus 1\oplus 2$; v:= $\perp$ in which no ball is drawn: the final hyper-distributions are

$$\{\!\{\ (\perp, \{\!\{1^{@\frac{1}{3}}, 2^{@\frac{2}{3}}\}\!\}),\ (\perp, \{\!\{0^{@\frac{2}{3}}, 1^{@\frac{1}{3}}\}\!\})\ \}\!\} \qquad (\Delta'_S)$$

and

$$\{\!\{\ (\perp, \{\!\{0,1,2\}\!\})\}\!\}\ . \qquad (\Delta'_{I_1})$$

In neither case does the final value $\perp$ of v reveal anything about h. But Δ'_S, unlike Δ'_{I_1}, has separated pairs which recall implicitly the intermediate value $\hat{v}$ of v. Generally, if two final pairs (v', δ'_1) and (v', δ'_2) occur with $\delta'_1 \neq \delta'_2$ then it

[2] It is effectively the Kleisli composition over the outer distribution.

means an attacker can deduce whether h's distribution is δ'_1 or δ'_2 even though v has the same final value v' in both cases. Although the direct evidence $\hat{v}$ has been overwritten, the separated pairs preserve the attacker's deductions from it.

The meaning of *probabilistic choice* $P_1 \,{}_p\!\oplus P_2$ makes it behave like $[\![P_1]\!]$ with probability p and $[\![P_2]\!]$ with the remaining probability. (In Fig. 1 we gave the definition only for constant p; but in general p can be an expression over v, h.) The definition allows an attacker to observe which branch was taken: thus unlike (ii) above we have $[\![h{:=}\,0 \oplus h{:=}\,1]\!].(v,\delta) = \{\!\{(v, \{\!\{0\}\!\}), (v, \{\!\{1\}\!\})\}\!\}$, which is an example of **implicit flow**. *Conditional choice* has the same effect, revealing G.v.h.

Both perfect recall and implicit flow are built-in because, in our earlier "Shadow" semantics of noninterference and demonic- rather than probabilistic choice [13, 14], we found via program-algebraic *gedanken* experiments that compositionality (equivalently, monotonicity of refinement) required the adversary to be treated as if it had those two abilities.

3 The Bayes-Risk Based Elementary Testing Order

The elementary testing order has both traditional, functional characteristics and specialised, information-based security characteristics.

Say that two programs are *functionally equivalent* iff from the same input they produce the same *overall* output distribution [8, 12], defined for hyper-distribution Δ' to be $\mathsf{ft}.\Delta' {:=} \{\!\{(v',\delta')\colon \Delta'; h'\colon \delta' \;\bullet\; (v',h')\}\!\}$. We consider state-space $\mathcal{V}{\times}\mathcal{H}$ jointly, i.e. not only $\mathcal{V}$, because differing distributions over h alone can be revealed by the context $(-\,;\ \mathsf{v}{:=}\,\mathsf{h})$ that appends an assignment v:= h.

We measure the *security* of a program with "Bayes Risk" [1–3, 18], an attacker's chance of guessing the final value of h in one try. The most effective such attack is to determine which split-state (v',δ') in a final hyper-distribution actually occurred, and then to guess that h has some value h' that maximises δ', i.e. so that $\delta'.h' = \sqcup\delta'$. For a whole hyper-distribution we average the attacks over its elements, weighted by the probability it gives to each, and so we we define the **Bayes Risk** of Δ' to be $\mathsf{br}.\Delta' {:=} (\odot\, (v',\delta')\colon \Delta' \bullet \sqcup\delta')$.[3]

For Program S the Risk is the chance of guessing h by remembering v's intermediate value, say $\hat{v}$, and then guessing that h at that point had the value most likely to have produced that $\hat{v}$: when $\hat{v}{=}w$ (probability 1/2), guess h=2; when $\hat{v}{=}b$, guess h=0. Via $\mathsf{br}.\Delta'_S$ that Risk is $1/2{*}2/3 + 1/2{*}2/3 = 2/3$. For I_1 however, where there is no "leaking" $\hat{v}$, the Risk is the lower $\mathsf{br}.\Delta'_{I_1} = 1/3$.

The elementary testing order on (final) hyper-distributions is then defined so that $\Delta'_S {\preceq} \Delta'_I$ just when $\mathsf{ft}.\Delta'_S{=}\mathsf{ft}.\Delta'_I$ and $\mathsf{br}.\Delta'_S{\geq}\mathsf{br}.\Delta'_I$, and it extends pointwise to the **elementary testing order** on whole programs. That is, we say that $S{\preceq}I$ just when for corresponding inputs (i) S, I are functionally equivalent and (ii) the Risk for I is no more than the Risk for S. Thus $S{\preceq}I_1$ because they are functionally equivalent and the Risks of S, I_1 are $2/3, 1/3$ resp.

---

[3] "Greatest chance of leak" is more convenient than the dual (and more usual) "least chance of no leak." Our definition corresponds to *vulnerability* [18, for example].

4 Non-compositionality of the Elementary Testing Order

For stepwise development we require more than just $S \preceq I$: we must ensure that $\mathcal{C}(S) \preceq \mathcal{C}(I)$ holds for all contexts $\mathcal{C}(\cdot)$ in which S, I might be placed — and we do not know in advance what those contexts might be.

Consider Program I_2 in which also Box 1 has two black balls, defined by the code $\mathsf{h}{:=}\, 0 \oplus 1 \oplus 2; \mathsf{v}{:\in} \{\!\{ w^{@(\mathsf{h} \div 2)}, b^{@1-(\mathsf{h} \div 2)} \}\!\}; \mathsf{v}{:=}\, \bot$ with final hyper-distribution

$$\{\!\{\ (\bot, \{\!\{2\}\!\})^{@\frac{1}{3}}\ ,\ (\bot, \{\!\{0,1\}\!\})^{@\frac{2}{3}}\ \}\!\}\ . \qquad (\Delta'_{I_2})$$

The Risk for I_2 is $1/3{*}1 + 2/3{*}1/2$, again $2/3$ so that $S \preceq I_2$. Now if context $\mathcal{C}$ is defined $(-\,;\ \mathsf{h}{:=}\,\mathsf{h} \div 2)$, the Risk for $\mathcal{C}(S)$ is $1/2{*}2/3 + 1/2{*}1 = 5/6$: it is more than for S alone because there are fewer final h-values to choose from. But for $\mathcal{C}(I_2)$ it is greater still, at $1/3{*}1 + 2/3{*}1 = 1$.

Since $S \preceq I_2$ but $\mathcal{C}(S) \not\preceq \mathcal{C}(I_2)$, the order $(\preceq)$ is not compositional (monotonic).

5 The Refinement Order, and Compositional Closure

To address the non-compositionality exposed just above, we seek the *compositional closure* of $(\preceq)$, the unique *refinement* relation $(\sqsubseteq)$ such that (*soundness*) if $S \sqsubseteq I$ then for all $\mathcal{C}$ we have $\mathcal{C}(S) \preceq \mathcal{C}(I)$; and (*completeness*) if $S \not\sqsubseteq I$ then for some $\mathcal{C}$ we have $\mathcal{C}(S) \not\preceq \mathcal{C}(I)$. Soundness gives refinement the property (refer §4) we need for stepwise development; and completeness makes refinement as liberal as possible consistent with that.

We found above that $S \not\sqsubseteq I_2$; we show later (§6.1) that we do have $S \sqsubseteq I_1$.

6 Constructive Definition of the Refinement Order $(\sqsubseteq)$

We give a detailed example to help introduce our definition. Let $x\ \mathbf{rnd}\ n$ be a distribution over the multiple(s) of n closest to x, weighted inversely by their distance: thus $1\mathbf{rnd}4$ is $(0_{3/4}\oplus 4)$ and $3\mathbf{rnd}4$ is $(0_{1/4}\oplus 4)$; but $2\mathbf{rnd}4$ is $(0_{1/2}\oplus 4)$. When x divides n exactly, the outcome is definite: thus $2\ \mathbf{rnd}\ 2 = \{\!\{2\}\!\}$. Now consider the two programs

$$\begin{array}{rll} & P_2{:=} & \mathsf{h}{:=}\,1 \oplus 2 \oplus 3;\ \mathsf{v}{:\in}\,\mathsf{h}\ \mathbf{rnd}\ 2;\ \mathsf{v}{:=}\,\mathsf{h}\ \mathbf{mod}\ 2 \\ \text{and} & P_4{:=} & \mathsf{h}{:=}\,1 \oplus 2 \oplus 3;\ \mathsf{v}{:\in}\,\mathsf{h}\ \mathbf{rnd}\ 4;\ \mathsf{v}{:=}\,\mathsf{h}\ \mathbf{mod}\ 2\ . \end{array} \qquad (2)$$

Both reveal $\mathsf{h}\,\mathbf{mod}2$ in v's final value v', but each P_n also reveals in the overwritten visible $\hat{v}$, say, something about $\mathsf{h}\ \mathbf{rnd}\ n$; and intuition suggests that $P_n \sqsubseteq P_m$ for $n \leq m$ only. Yet the Risk is $5/6$ for both $P_{2,4}$, which we can see from the final hyper-distributions; they are

$$\{\!\{\ (0,\{\!\{2\}\!\})^{@\frac{1}{3}},\ (1,\{\!\{1\}\!\})^{@\frac{1}{6}}, (1,\{\!\{1,3\}\!\})^{@\frac{1}{3}}, (1,\{\!\{3\}\!\})^{@\frac{1}{6}}\ \}\!\} \qquad (\Delta'_{P_2})$$

$$\{\!\{\ (0,\{\!\{2\}\!\})^{@\frac{1}{3}}, \underbrace{(1,\{\!\{1^{@\frac{3}{4}},3^{@\frac{1}{4}}\}\!\})^{@\frac{1}{3}}}, (1,\{\!\{1^{@\frac{1}{4}},3^{@\frac{3}{4}}\}\!\})^{@\frac{1}{3}}\ \}\!\} \qquad (\Delta'_{P_4})$$

With overall probability $1/3{*}3/4 + 1/3{*}1/4 = 1/3$ the final v' will be 1 and $\hat{v}$ will be 0; since v' is 1 then h must be 1 or 3; but if $\hat{v}$ was 0 that h is three times as likely to have been 1.

so that e.g. indeed $1/3{*}1+1/3{*}3/4+1/3{*}3/4=5/6$ for P_4. The overall distribution of (v',h') is $\{\!\{(0,2),(1,1),(1,3)\}\!\}$ in both cases, so that $P_{2,4}$ are functionally equivalent; but they have different residual uncertainties of h.

Now we consider just the h-distributions associated with $v'{=}1$ and, by multiplying through their associated probabilities from the hyper-distributions, present them as a collection of *fractions*, sub-distributions over $\mathcal{H}$. We call such collections *partitions* and here they are given for P_2 and P_4 respectively by

$$\text{when } v'{=}1 \quad \left\{ \begin{array}{ll} \Pi'_{P_2}: & \langle \{\!\{1^{@\frac{1}{6}}\}\!\}, \{\!\{1^{@\frac{1}{6}}, 3^{@\frac{1}{6}}\}\!\}, \{\!\{3^{@\frac{1}{6}}\}\!\} \rangle \\ \Pi'_{P_4}: & \langle \{\!\{1^{@\frac{1}{4}}, 3^{@\frac{1}{12}}\}\!\}, \{\!\{1^{@\frac{1}{12}}, 3^{@\frac{1}{4}}\}\!\} \rangle\,. \end{array} \right. \tag{3}$$

Fractions can be summed, so that e.g. $\{\!\{1^{@\frac{1}{6}}\}\!\} + \{\!\{1^{@\frac{1}{6}}, 3^{@\frac{1}{6}}\}\!\}$ gives $\{\!\{1^{@\frac{1}{3}}, 3^{@\frac{1}{6}}\}\!\}$.

6.1 Constructive Definition of Refinement

Let the function $\mathsf{fracs}.\Delta.v$ for hyper-distribution Δ and value v give the partition of fractions extracted from Δ for $\mathsf{v}{=}v$. Say that one partition is *finer* than another if its fractions can be summed in groups to realise the *coarser* one. It is *sim-finer* if only fractions that are multiples of each other are summed.

Definition 1. *Secure refinement* We say that hyper-distribution Δ_S is secure-refined by Δ_I, written $\Delta_S \sqsubseteq \Delta_I$, just when for every v there is some intermediate partition Π of fractions so that both (i) Π is sim-finer than $\mathsf{fracs}.\Delta_S.v$ and (ii) Π is finer than $\mathsf{fracs}.\Delta_I.v$.[4] Refinement of hyper-distributions extends pointwise to the programs that produce them. □

Note that the (sim-)finer relation preserves the sum of *all* a partition's fractions, so that ($\sqsubseteq$) from Def. 1 implies functional equality.

Referring to Δ'_S, we get $\mathsf{fracs}.\Delta'_S.\bot = \langle \{\!\{1^{@\frac{1}{6}}, 2^{@\frac{1}{3}}\}\!\}, \{\!\{0^{@\frac{1}{3}}, 1^{@\frac{1}{6}}\}\!\} \rangle$ by multiplying through, and $\mathsf{fracs}.\Delta'_{I_1}.\bot = \langle \{\!\{0^{@\frac{1}{3}}, 1^{@\frac{1}{3}}, 2^{@\frac{1}{3}}\}\!\} \rangle$. The two fractions of the former sum to the single fraction of the latter, and so $S{\sqsubseteq}I_1$ according to our definition Def. 1 of secure refinement.

For the more detailed $\Delta'_{P_2}{\sqsubseteq}\Delta'_{P_4}$ and $v'{=}1$, we need the intermediate partition $\Pi{:=}\ \langle \{\!\{1^{@\frac{1}{6}}\}\!\}, \{\!\{1^{@\frac{1}{12}}, 3^{@\frac{1}{12}}\}\!\}, \{\!\{1^{@\frac{1}{12}}, 3^{@\frac{1}{12}}\}\!\}, \{\!\{3^{@\frac{1}{6}}\}\!\} \rangle$, whose middle two fractions turn out to be equal: summing them gives the middle $\{\!\{1^{@\frac{1}{6}}, 3^{@\frac{1}{6}}\}\!\}$ of Π'_{P_2}. Summing the first two gives $\{\!\{1^{@\frac{1}{4}}, 3^{@\frac{1}{12}}\}\!\}$, the first fraction of Π'_{P_4}; and the last two give the second fraction of Π'_{P_4}. Partition $\langle \{\!\{2^{@\frac{1}{3}}\}\!\} \rangle$ deals trivially with $v'{=}0$, and so indeed $P_2{\sqsubseteq}P_4$. In §7.2 and in §B we show however that $P_4{\not\sqsubseteq}P_2$.

Refinement ($\sqsubseteq$) is a partial order, and our programs preserve it [11]:

Lemma 1. *Monotonicity of refinement.* If $S{\sqsubseteq}I$ then $\mathcal{C}(S){\sqsubseteq}\mathcal{C}(I)$ for all contexts $\mathcal{C}$ built from programs as defined in Fig. 1. □

---

[4] In our earlier *qualitative* work [14] refinement reduces to taking unions of equivalence classes of hidden values, so-called "Shadows." Köpf et al. observe similar effects [7].

7 Refinement ($\sqsubseteq$) Is the Compositional Closure of ($\preceq$)

7.1 Soundness (Sketch)

Our approach shows first that $\Delta_S \sqsubseteq \Delta_I$ implies $\Delta_S \preceq \Delta_I$, using arithmetic properties of maximum, and the addition and multiplication by non-negative scalars that occur in the operations (i,ii) of Def. 1. Since $S \sqsubseteq I$ implies $\mathcal{C}(S) \sqsubseteq \mathcal{C}(I)$ from Lem. 1, the above gives $\mathcal{C}(S) \preceq \mathcal{C}(I)$ as required. The full proof is in §A.1.

7.2 Completeness (Sketch)

Here from $S \not\sqsubseteq I$ we must discover a context $\mathcal{C}$ such that $\mathcal{C}(S) \not\preceq \mathcal{C}(I)$. This is done by reformulating the set of *all* refinements of specification S as a convex subset X_S of (higher-dimensional) Euclidean space, and the implementation I as a single point x_I in that space: the refinement-failure then becomes $x_I \notin X_S$.

The *Separating Hyperplane Lemma* [19] then gives us a hyperplane having all of X_S on one side and x_I on the other, and the coefficients of its normal M determine the parameters of a context $(- ; C)$ that assigns conditionally to h and distinguishes x_I from all x_S's in X_S. For example, if we take C to be

$$\begin{array}{l}\textbf{if } \mathsf{v}{=}1 \textbf{ then } \mathsf{h}{:}{\in} \ (\{\!\{1^{@\frac{1}{2}}, 2^{@\frac{1}{4}}, 3^{@\frac{1}{4}}\}\!\} \textbf{ if } \mathsf{h}{=}1 \textbf{ else } \{\!\{2^{@\frac{1}{2}}, 3^{@\frac{1}{2}}\}\!\}) \\ \qquad\quad \textbf{else } \ \mathsf{h}{:=}1 \textbf{ fi} \ , \end{array} \tag{4}$$

whose probabilities $\frac{1}{2}, \frac{1}{4}, \frac{1}{4}$ and $0, \frac{1}{2}, \frac{1}{2}$ come from just such an M (Fig. 4 in §B), then we can concentrate on $v'{=}1$ and use (3,4) to give the partitions

$$v'{=}1 \left\{ \begin{array}{ll} \Pi'_{P_2;C}: & \langle \{\!\{1^{@\frac{1}{12}}, 2^{@\frac{1}{24}}, 3^{@\frac{1}{24}}\}\!\}, \{\!\{1^{@\frac{1}{12}}, 2^{@\frac{1}{8}}, 3^{@\frac{1}{8}}\}\!\}, \{\!\{2^{@\frac{1}{12}}, 3^{@\frac{1}{12}}\}\!\} \rangle \\ \Pi'_{P_4;C}: & \langle \{\!\{1^{@\frac{1}{8}}, 2^{@\frac{5}{48}}, 3^{@\frac{5}{48}}\}\!\}, \{\!\{1^{@\frac{1}{24}}, 2^{@\frac{7}{48}}, 1^{@\frac{7}{48}}\}\!\} \rangle \ . \end{array} \right.$$

Now the Risk of a partition on its own is obtained by simple summing of maxima, since its constituent fractions have been scaled already: thus at (3) above for Π'_{P_2} we get $1/6{+}1/6{+}1/6 = 1/2$, and for Π'_{P_4} we get $1/4{+}1/4 = 1/2$, the same. But for partition $\Pi'_{P_2;C}$ we get $1/12{+}1/8{+}1/12 = 7/24$; and for $\Pi'_{P_4;C}$ we get $1/8{+}7/48 = 13/48$, just smaller. Since the other partition (for $v'{=}0$) is $\langle \{\!\{1^{@\frac{1}{3}}\}\!\} \rangle$ in both cases, we establish $(P_4; C) \not\preceq (P_2; C)$. The full proof is in §A.2.

8 Case Study: The *Three Judges* Protocol

The **motivation** for our case study is to suggest and illustrate techniques for reasoning compositionally from specification to implementation of noninterference [6]. Our previous examples include (unboundedly many) Dining Cryptographers [4, 6, `Morgan:06`], Oblivious Transfer [16, 14] and Multi-Party Shared Computation [20, 13]. All of them however used our *qualitative* model for compositional noninterference [14, 13, 6, `Morgan:06`]; here we have instead a *quantitative* model.

To demonstrate the utility of our approach, we invented the following example. Three judges A, B, C are to give a majority decision, innocent or guilty, by exchanging messages but concealing their individual votes.[5] We describe this protocol with a program fragment, a **specification** which captures exactly the functional and security properties we want. Its variables are Boolean, equivalently $\{0,1\}$ and, including some notational conventions explained below, it evaluates $(\mathsf{a}+\mathsf{b}+\mathsf{c} \geq 2)$ atomically, and assigns it to visible j:

$$\begin{array}{ll} \textbf{vis}\ \mathsf{j};\ \textbf{vis}_A\ \mathsf{a};\ \textbf{vis}_B\ \mathsf{b};\ \textbf{vis}_C\ \mathsf{c}; & \leftarrow \text{These are global variables.} \\ \quad \mathsf{j}{:=}\,(\mathsf{a}+\mathsf{b}+\mathsf{c} \geq 2)\ . & \leftarrow \text{Atomic assignment.} \end{array} \tag{5}$$

We borrow features introduced in our earlier case studies to extend the reach of our technique without essentially changing its character, a sort of "syntactic sugaring." They include a convention –used in (5) above– that allows us to treat multiple-observer systems: annotation **vis** declares a variable visible to all observers, whereas e.g. $\textbf{vis}_A$ declares visiblity to the observer "Judge A" only. Furthermore, we allow multiple variables so that, in terms of Fig. 1, for A's view we would have (j,a) as v jointly and (b,c) as h; similarly for Judge B we treat (j,b) as v and (a,c) as h.

Although the **vis**-convention suggests that protocol development, e.g. as in §8.2 to come, requires proofs for each observer (since the patterns of variables' visibility might differ), in fact we can usually follow a single chain of reasoning whose steps are shown to be valid for two or even all three observers at once.

We also allow *local* variables, with which (as usual) implementations introduce extra structure that does not appear in the specification and so escapes any requirements of *functional* correctness. But local variables are still *security* risks as much as global variables, especially when they are used to describe message passing: with perfect recall, their visibility is not affected by their being local.

8.1 The Encryption Lemma: Qualitative vs. Quantitative Reasoning

Rather than appeal constantly to the basic semantics (Fig. 1) instead we have accumulated, with experience, a repertoire of identities –a program algebra– which we use to reason at the source level. Those identities themselves are proved directly in the semantics but, after that, they become permanent members of the designer's toolkit. One of the most common is the *Encryption Lemma.*

Let statement $(\mathsf{v}\nabla\mathsf{h}){:=}\,E$ set Booleans v,h so that their exclusive-or $\mathsf{v}\nabla\mathsf{h}$ equals Boolean E: there are exactly two possible ways of doing so. In our earlier work [14], we proved that when the choice is made demonically, on a single run nothing is revealed about E; in our refinement style we express that as

$$\textbf{skip} \quad = \quad |[\ \textbf{vis}\ \mathsf{v};\textbf{hid}\ \mathsf{h};\ (\mathsf{v}\nabla\mathsf{h}){:=}\,E\ ]|\ , \tag{6}$$

where equality is "refinement both ways," and the "begin-end" brackets $|[\cdots]|$ enclose local declarations. In our current model we can prove that *exactly the same identity holds* if the choice is made uniformly [11]. That means that extant

[5] The generalised dining cryptographers would instead reveal the *actual number* of guilty votes. Here we reveal only the majority, a more difficult job [6, `Morgan:09a`].

qualitative source-level proofs that rely only on "upgradeable identities" like (6) can be used *as is* for quantitative results provided the demonic choices involved are converted to uniform choice. And that is the case with our current example.

Beyond the *Encryption Lemma*, we use *Two-party Conjunction* [20, 13] and *Oblivious Transfer* [16, 14] in our implementation, but in our development we refer *only to their specifications*. Just as for the Encryption Lemma, the algebraic proofs of their implementations [14, 13] apply quantitatively provided we interpret the (formerly) demonic choice as uniform.

8.2 The Three-Judges *Development* (Sketch)

Here we present only a sketch of the steps used to take specification (5) to an implementation (Fig. 2); details are given elsewhere [11].

We begin with a two-party conjunction [20, 13] which sets variables $\mathsf{b}_0, \mathsf{c}_0$ so that their exclusive-or equals the conjunction of two other variables b, c. We show how to implement this elsewhere [13]; but here we need only refer to its specification to check –via (6)– that the introduction of the two-party conjunction into (5) preserves both its functional and secure correctness. We have

$$\mathsf{j}{:=}\,(\mathsf{a}{+}\mathsf{b}{+}\mathsf{c} \geq 2) \quad = \quad \mathbf{skip};\ \mathsf{j}{:=}\,(\mathsf{a}{+}\mathsf{b}{+}\mathsf{c} \geq 2) \qquad \text{"}\mathbf{skip}\text{ is identity"}$$

$$= \quad |[\![\ \mathbf{vis}_B\ \mathsf{b}_0; \mathbf{vis}_C\ \mathsf{c}_0;\ (\mathsf{b}_0 \nabla \mathsf{c}_0){:=}\,\mathsf{b} \wedge \mathsf{c};\ ]\!]|;\ \ \mathsf{j}{:=}\ (\mathsf{a}{+}\mathsf{b}{+}\mathsf{c} \geq 2)\ \ldots \qquad \text{"Introduce two-party conjunction: correctness trivial for } A\text{; use (6) for } B, C.\text{"}$$

We must justify this step for all three observers: for A the introduced block equals **skip** since all assignments are to local variables hidden from A; for B the block is equivalent to **skip** because it is an instance of the Encryption Lemma with v as b_0 and h as c_0; for C it is as for B, but reversed. With similar reasoning we introduce a two-party disjunction and reorganise:

$$\begin{aligned} \ldots = \quad & |[\![\ \mathbf{vis}_B\ \mathsf{b}_0; \mathbf{vis}_C\ \mathsf{c}_0;\ (\mathsf{b}_0 \nabla \mathsf{c}_0){:=}\,\mathsf{b} \wedge \mathsf{c};\ ]\!]|; \\ & |[\![\ \mathbf{vis}_B\ \mathsf{b}_1; \mathbf{vis}_C\ \mathsf{c}_1;\ (\mathsf{b}_1 \nabla \mathsf{c}_1){:=}\,\mathsf{b} \vee \mathsf{c};\ ]\!]|; \\ & \mathsf{j}{:=}\,(\mathsf{a}{+}\mathsf{b}{+}\mathsf{c} \geq 2) \end{aligned} \qquad \text{"Introduce two-party disjunction with same justification as above."}$$

$$\begin{aligned} = \quad & |[\![\ \mathbf{vis}_B\ \mathsf{b}_0, \mathsf{b}_1; \mathbf{vis}_C\ \mathsf{c}_0, \mathsf{c}_1; \\ & \quad (\mathsf{b}_0 \nabla \mathsf{c}_0){:=}\,\mathsf{b} \wedge \mathsf{c};\ (\mathsf{b}_1 \nabla \mathsf{c}_1){:=}\,\mathsf{b} \vee \mathsf{c}; \\ & \quad \mathsf{j}{:=}\,(\mathsf{a}{+}\mathsf{b}{+}\mathsf{c} \geq 2)\ ]\!]| \end{aligned} \qquad \text{"Reorganise declarations and scoping"}$$

$$\begin{aligned} = \quad & |[\![\ \mathbf{vis}_B\ \mathsf{b}_0, \mathsf{b}_1; \mathbf{vis}_C\ \mathsf{c}_0, \mathsf{c}_1; \\ & \quad (\mathsf{b}_0 \nabla \mathsf{c}_0){:=}\,\mathsf{b} \wedge \mathsf{c};\ (\mathsf{b}_1 \nabla \mathsf{c}_1){:=}\,\mathsf{b} \vee \mathsf{c}; \\ & \quad \mathsf{j}{:=}\,\mathsf{b}_\mathsf{a} \nabla \mathsf{c}_\mathsf{a}\ ]\!]|\ \ldots \end{aligned} \qquad \text{"Boolean algebra; expression } \mathsf{b}_\mathsf{a} \nabla \mathsf{c}_\mathsf{a} \text{ abbreviates } \mathsf{b}_1 \nabla \mathsf{c}_1\ \mathbf{if}\ \mathsf{a}\ \mathbf{else}\ \mathsf{b}_0 \nabla \mathsf{c}_0.\text{"}$$

Now since its being assigned to j will reveal $\mathsf{b}_a \nabla \mathsf{c}_a$ to everyone, and thus to A in particular, it does no harm first to capture that value in variables visible to A alone and then to have Agent A reveal those to everyone else:

$$
\begin{array}{lll}
& |||[\ \mathbf{vis}_A\ \mathsf{a}_0,\mathsf{a}_1;\ \mathbf{vis}_B\ \mathsf{b}_0,\mathsf{b}_1;\ \mathbf{vis}_C\ \mathsf{c}_0,\mathsf{c}_1; & \\
\text{two party conjunction} \left\{ \begin{array}{l} \rightarrow \\ \\ \\ \rightarrow \end{array} \right. &
\begin{array}{l}
\mathsf{b}_0{:=}\,\mathsf{true} \oplus \mathsf{false}; \\
\mathsf{b}_1{:=}\,\mathsf{true} \oplus \mathsf{false}; \\
\\
\mathsf{c}_0{:=}\ (\mathsf{b}\nabla\mathsf{b}_0\ \mathbf{if}\ \mathsf{c}\ \mathbf{else}\ \mathsf{b}_0); \\
\mathsf{c}_1{:=}\ (\neg\mathsf{b}_1\ \mathbf{if}\ \mathsf{c}\ \mathbf{else}\ \mathsf{b}\nabla\mathsf{b}_1); \\
\mathsf{a}_0{:=}\ (\mathsf{b}_1\ \mathbf{if}\ \mathsf{a}\ \mathbf{else}\ \mathsf{b}_0); \\
\mathsf{a}_1{:=}\ (\mathsf{c}_1\ \mathbf{if}\ \mathsf{a}\ \mathbf{else}\ \mathsf{c}_0);
\end{array}
&
\begin{array}{l}
\leftarrow \text{These are } \textit{uniform} \text{ choices.} \\
\leftarrow \\
\\
\left.\begin{array}{l}\\ \\ \\ \\ \end{array}\right\} \begin{array}{l} \textit{Four oblivious transfers:} \\ \text{each one's implementation} \\ \text{contains further uniform choices.}\end{array}
\end{array} \\
& \mathsf{j}{:=}\,\mathsf{a}_0\nabla\mathsf{a}_1\ ]]|| &
\end{array}
$$

We replace the two Two-Party 'junctions by their implementations as oblivious transfers [13]: each becomes two statements instead of one. The uniformly random flipping of bits $\mathsf{b}_{\{0,1\}}$ is then collected at the start. Correctness is preserved by compositionality.

Fig. 2. Three-Judges Protocol assuming Oblivious Transfers as primitives

$$
\begin{array}{lll}
\ldots = & |||[\ \mathbf{vis}_A\ \mathsf{a}_0,\mathsf{a}_1;\ \mathbf{vis}_B\ \mathsf{b}_0,\mathsf{b}_1;\ \mathbf{vis}_C\ \mathsf{c}_0,\mathsf{c}_1; & \text{“Introduce private variables of } A\text{”} \\
& \quad (\mathsf{b}_0\nabla\mathsf{c}_0){:=}\,\mathsf{b}\wedge\mathsf{c};\ (\mathsf{b}_1\nabla\mathsf{c}_1){:=}\,\mathsf{b}\vee\mathsf{c}; & \\
& \quad (\mathsf{a}_0\nabla\mathsf{a}_1){:=}\,\mathsf{b_a}\nabla\mathsf{c_a};\quad (\dagger) & \\
& \quad \mathsf{j}{:=}\ \mathsf{a}_0\nabla\mathsf{a}_1\ ]]||\ . &
\end{array}
$$

The point of using two variables $\mathsf{a}_{\{0,1\}}$ rather than one is to separate the communication $(B,C){\rightarrow}A$ at (†) into two oblivious transfers $B{\rightarrow}A$ and $C{\rightarrow}A$ [16]. Our last step does that [11], giving finally the code of Fig. 2.

A full implementation at the level of assignments is indicated in Fig. 5 of §C.

9 Conclusions — And an Open Question

There are many alternatives for a definition of "elementary testing." Bayes Risk measures how difficult it is to determine h using only one query $\mathsf{h}{=}h$, while *Marginal Guesswork* [15, 7] allows multiple queries of that form. And *Shannon Entropy* [17] can be related to multiple queries of the form $\mathsf{h}{\in}H$. Other measures, such as *Guessing Entropy* [9, 7], are further variations.

No single one of these elementary testing orderings is objectively the best. Although Shannon Entropy is a well-accepted measure of uncertainty, Pliam observes [15] that e.g. Marginal Guesswork might be better for measuring vulnerability to brute-force attacks; he also shows that there can be no general ordering between these two measures. Smith compares Bayes Risk and Shannon Entropy, speculating that also those measures are mutually incomparable [18].

Whichever definition of elementary testing is chosen, a crucial *practical* concern is to determine whether compositional reasoning can be based on it. Smith suggested that Bayes Risk might not be compositional [18]; we *prove* it isn't compositional — and then we identify a subset ($\sqsubseteq$) of it that is. Further, we have given a practical –and non-trivial– example of how useful that can be (§8).

Our refinement ensures that uncertainty cannot decrease for Marginal Guesswork, Shannon- or Guessing Entropy [11]: it is sound for those three as well as for Bayes Risk (§7). This means that –in spite of the speculations above– in fact the orders *are* comparable: *with contexts*, Bayes Risk is at least as discriminating as any of the others. **Still open is whether ($\sqsubseteq$) is complete for those others.** If it were, then –again, with contexts– *they would all be equally discriminating.*

With concurrency over visible- and hidden actions giving attackers strong capabilities as we do (§2.4), Braun et al. [1] identify *safe* contexts $\mathcal{C}_{\text{safe}}$ such that I "$\preceq$" $\mathcal{C}_{\text{safe}}(I)$; with our emphasis on implementations I *and* their specifications S, by analogy we would be looking for $S{\preceq}I$ implies $\mathcal{C}_{\text{safe}}(S){\preceq}\mathcal{C}_{\text{safe}}(I)$. But rather than restrict *contexts* $\mathcal{C}$ to $\mathcal{C}_{\text{safe}}$'s, instead we restrict the *testing-relation* ($\preceq$) to a subset ($\sqsubseteq$), keeping contexts as they are — a complementary approach.

We are not aware of others' having identified a refinement relation that is either sound or complete with respect to all contexts in their language.

The semantics presented here is similar to a Hidden Markov Model (HMM) augmented with an ordering which determines when a program yields more or less information about the hidden state than another. Whether the established techniques of HMM's apply here (and *vice versa*) has not yet been explored.

Finally the merits of compositional refinement and its relationship to other treatments of noninterference are discussed in detail elsewhere [14, 11, 6].

The Appendices §A,§B,§C to this paper may be found online [10, 11].

References

1. Braun, C., Chatzikokolakis, K., Palamidessi, C.: Compositional methods for information-hiding. In: Amadio, R.M. (ed.) FOSSACS 2008. LNCS, vol. 4962, pp. 443–457. Springer, Heidelberg (2008)
2. Braun, C., Chatzikokolakis, K., Palamidessi, C.: Quantitative notions of leakage for one-try attacks. In: Proc. MFPS. ENTCS, vol. 249, Elsevier, Amsterdam (2009)
3. Chatzikokolakis, K., Palamidessi, C., Panangaden, P.: Probability of error in information-hiding protocols. In: Proc. CSF, pp. 341–354. IEEE, Los Alamitos (2007)
4. Chaum, D.: The Dining Cryptographers problem: Unconditional sender and recipient untraceability. Jnl. Cryptol. 1(1), 65–75 (1988)
5. Goguen, J.A., Meseguer, J.: Unwinding and inference control. In: Proc. IEEE Symp on Security and Privacy, pp. 75–86. IEEE, Los Alamitos (1984)
6. Probabilistic Systems Group, `http://www.cse.unsw.edu.au/~carrollm/probs`
7. Köpf, B., Basin, D.: An information-theoretic model for adaptive side-channel attacks. In: Proc. 14th ACM Conf. Comp. Comm. Security (2007)
8. Kozen, D.: A probabilistic PDL. Jnl. Comp. Sys. Sci. 30(2), 162–178 (1985)
9. Massey, J.L.: Guessing and entropy. In: Proc. IEEE International Symposium on Information Theory, p. 204 (1994)
10. McIver, A.K., Meinicke, L.A., Morgan, C.C.: Draft of this paper including its appendices [6, McIver:10]
11. McIver, A.K., Meinicke, L.A., Morgan, C.C.: Draft full version of this paper, `http://www.comp.mq.edu.au/~lmeinick/icalp.pdf`
12. McIver, A.K., Morgan, C.C.: Abstraction, Refinement and Proof for Probabilistic Systems. Tech. Mono. Computer Science. Springer, Heidelberg (2005)

13. McIver, A.K., Morgan, C.C.: Sums and lovers: Case studies in security, compositionality and refinement. In: Cavalcanti, A., Dams, D. (eds.) Proc. FM 2009. LNCS, vol. 5850, Springer, Heidelberg (2009), Treats Two-Party Secure Computation
14. Morgan, C.C.: The Shadow Knows: Refinement of ignorance in sequential programs. Science of Computer Programming 74(8) (2009), Treats Oblivious Transfer
15. Pliam, J.O.: On the incomparability of entropy and marginal guesswork in brute-force attacks. In: Roy, B., Okamoto, E. (eds.) INDOCRYPT 2000. LNCS, vol. 1977, pp. 67–79. Springer, Heidelberg (2000)
16. Rivest, R.: Unconditionally secure commitment and oblivious transfer schemes using private channels and a trusted initialiser. Technical report, M.I.T. (1999), `http://theory.lcs.mit.edu/~rivest/Rivest-commitment.pdf`
17. Shannon, C.E.: A mathematical theory of communication. Bell System Technical Journal 27, 379–423, 623–656 (1948)
18. Smith, G.: Adversaries and information leaks. In: Barthe, G., Fournet, C. (eds.) TGC 2007 and FODO 2008. LNCS, vol. 4912, pp. 383–400. Springer, Heidelberg (2008)
19. Trustrum, K.: Linear Programming. Library of Mathematics. Routledge and Kegan Paul, London (1971)
20. Yao, A.C.: Protocols for secure computations (extended abstract). In: Proc. FOCS 1982, pp. 160–164. IEEE, Los Alamitos (1982)

Asynchronous Throughput-Optimal Routing in Malicious Networks*

Paul Bunn[1,**] and Rafail Ostrovsky[1,2,***]

[1] UCLA Department of Mathematics
paulbunn@math.ucla.edu
[2] UCLA Department of Computer Science
rafail@cs.ucla.edu

Abstract. We demonstrate the feasibility of throughput-efficient routing in a highly unreliable network. Modeling a network as a graph with vertices representing nodes and edges representing the links between them, we consider two forms of unreliability: unpredictable edge-failures, and deliberate deviation from protocol specifications by corrupt nodes. The first form of unpredictability represents networks with dynamic topology, whose links may be constantly going up and down; while the second form represents malicious insiders attempting to disrupt communication by deliberately disobeying routing rules in an arbitrary manner, for example by introducing junk messages or deleting or altering messages. We present a robust routing protocol for end-to-end communication that is simultaneously resilient to both forms of unreliability, achieving provably optimal throughput performance.

Keywords: Network Routing, Fault Localization, Multi-Party Computation in Presence of Dishonest Majority, Communication Complexity, End-to-End Communication, Competitive Analysis, Asynchronous Protocols.

1 Introduction

With the immense range of applications and the multitude of networks encountered in practice, there has been an enormous effort to study routing in various settings. For the purpose of developing network models in which routing protocols can be developed and formally analyzed, networks are typically modeled as a graph with vertices representing nodes (processors, routers, etc.) and edges representing the connections between them. Beyond this basic structure, additional assumptions and restrictions are then made in attempt to capture various

* Full version of the paper is available on-line [18].

** Supported in part by Lockheed Martin Corporation and NSF grants 0716835, 0716389, 0830803, 0916574.

*** Supported in part by Lockheed Martin Corporation, IBM Faculty Award, Xerox Innovation Group Award, the Okawa Foundation Award, Intel, Teradata, NSF grants 0716835, 0716389, 0830803, 0916574 and U.C. MICRO grant.

S. Abramsky et al. (Eds.): ICALP 2010, Part II, LNCS 6199, pp. 236–248, 2010.

features that real-world networks may display. In deciding which network model is best-suited to a particular application, developers must make a choice with respect to each of the following considerations: 1) Synchronous or Asynchronous; 2) Static or Dynamic Topology; 3) Global Control or Distributed/Local Control; 4) Connectivity/Liveness Assumptions; 5) Existence of Faulty/Malicious Nodes.

Notice that in each option above there is an inherent trade-off between generality/applicability of the model verses optimal performance within the model. For instance, a protocol that assumes a fixed network topology will likely outperform a protocol designed for a dynamic topology setting, but the former protocol may not work in networks subject to edge-failures. Similarly, a protocol that protects against the existence of faulty or deliberately malicious nodes will likely be out-performed in networks with no faulty behavior by a protocol that assumes all nodes act honestly.

From both a theoretical and a practical standpoint, it is important to understand how each (combination) of the above listed factors affects routing performance. In this paper, we explore the feasibility of end-to-end routing in highly unreliable networks, i.e. networks that simultaneously consider *all* of the more general features: Asynchronous, Dynamic Topology, Local Control, no Connectivity Assumptions, and the presence of Malicious Nodes. In this "worst-case" model it is unlikely that any protocol will perform well, and stronger assumption(s) must be made to achieve a reasonable level of performance. However, understanding behavior in the worst case, even with respect to the most basic task of end-to-end communication, is important to determine how much (if any) the addition of each assumption improves optimal protocol performance.

1.1 Previous Work

As mentioned above, development and analysis of routing protocols relies heavily on the choices made for the network model. To date, all network models have guaranteed at least one (and more commonly multiple) "reliability" assumption(s) with respect to the above list of five network characteristics. In this section, we explore various combinations of assumptions that have been made in recent work, highlighting positive and negative results with respect to each network model, and emphasizing clearly which assumptions are employed in each case. Since our work focuses on theoretical results, for space considerations we do not discuss below the vast amount of research and analysis of routing issues for specific network systems encountered in practice, e.g. the Internet. Still, the amount of research regarding network routing and analysis of routing protocols is extensive, and as such we include only a sketch of the most related work, indicating how their models differ from ours and providing references that offer more detailed descriptions.

End-to-End Communication: One of the most relevant research directions to our paper is the notion of End-to-End communication in distributed networks, where two nodes (sender and receiver) wish to communicate through a network. While there is a multitude of problems that involve end-to-end communication (e.g. End-to-End Congestion Control, Path-Measurement, and Admission Control), we discuss here work that consider networks whose only task is to facilitate communication between sender and receiver. Some of these include a line of work developing the *Slide* protocol (the starting point of our protocol) of Afek, Gafni and Rosén [3] (see also Afek et al. [1].) The Slide protocol (and its variants) have been studied in a variety of network settings, including multi-commodity flow (Awerbuch and Leighton [11]), networks controlled by an online bursty adversary (Aiello et al. [4]), and networks that allow corruption of nodes (Amir et al. [7]). However, prior to our work there was no version of Slide that considered routing in the "worst case" network setting: only [7] considers networks with corruptible nodes, but their network model assumes synchronous communication and demands minimal connectivity guarantees.

FAULT DETECTION AND LOCALIZATION PROTOCOLS: There have been a number of papers that explore the possibility of corrupt nodes that deliberately disobey protocol specifications in order to disrupt communication. In particular, there is a recent line of work that considers a network consisting of a *single path* from the sender to the receiver, culminating in the recent work of Barak et al. [13] (for further background on fault localization see references therein). In this model, the adversary can corrupt any node (except the sender and receiver) in a dynamic and malicious manner. Since corrupting any node on the path will sever the honest connection between sender and receiver, the goal of a protocol in this model is *not* to guarantee that all messages sent are received. Instead, the goal is to *detect* faults when they occur and *localize* the fault to a single edge.

Goldberg et al. [19] show that a protocol's ability to detect faults relies on the assumption that One-Way Functions (OWF) exist, and Barak et al. [13] show that the (constant factor) overhead (in terms of communication cost) incurred for utilizing cryptographic tools (such as MACs or Signature Schemes) is mandatory for any fault-localization protocol. Awerbuch et al. [10] also explore routing in the Byzantine setting, although they do not present a formal treatment of security, and indeed a counter-example that challenges their protocol's security is discussed in the appendix of [13].

Fault Detection and Localization protocols focus on very restrictive network models (typically synchronous networks with fixed topology and some connectivity assumptions), and throughput-performance is usually not considered when analyzing fault detection/localization protocols.

COMPETITIVE ANALYSIS: Competitive Analysis was introduced by Sleator and Tarjan [22] as a mechanism for measuring the *worst-case* performance of a protocol, in terms of how badly the given protocol may be out-performed by an *off-line* protocol that has access to perfect information. Recall that a given protocol has *competitive ratio* $1/\lambda$ (or is λ-*competitive*) if an ideal off-line protocol has advantage over the given protocol by at most a factor of λ. One place competitive analysis has been used to evaluate performance is the setting of distributed algorithms in asynchronous shared memory computation, including the work of Ajtai et al. [6]. This line of work has a different flavor than the problem considered in the present paper due to the nature of the algorithm being analyzed (computation algorithm verses network routing protocol). In particular, network topology is not a consideration in this line of work (and malicious deviation of processors is not considered). Competitive Analysis also plays a role in Adversarial Queuing Theory, see, for example [15]. (We discuss this aspect in greater detail below.)

Competitive analysis is a useful tool for evaluating protocols in unreliable networks (e.g. asynchronous networks and/or networks with no connectivity guarantees), as it provides best-possible standards (since absolute performance guarantees may be impossible due to the lack of network assumptions). For a thorough description of competitive analysis, see [14].

MAX-FLOW AND MULTI-COMMODITY FLOW: The Max-flow and multi-commodity flow models assume synchronous networks with connectivity/liveness guarantees and have incorruptible nodes (max-flow networks also typically have fixed topology and are global-control). There has been a tremendous amount of work in these areas, see e.g. Leighton et al. [21] for a discussion of the two models and a list of results, as well as Awerbuch and Leighton [11] who show optimal throughput-competitive ratio for the network model in question.

ADMISSION CONTROL AND ROUTE SELECTION: The admission control/route selection model differs from the multi-commodity flow model in that the goal of a protocol is not to meet the demand of all ordered pairs of nodes (s, t), but rather the protocol must decide which requests it can/should honor, and then designate a path for honored requests. There are numerous models that are concerned with questions of admission control and route selection: The Asynchronous Transfer Model (see e.g. Awerbuch et al. [9]), Queuing Theory (see e.g. Borodin and Kleinberg [15] and Andrews et al. [8]), Adversarial Queuing Theory (see e.g. Broder et al. [16] and Aiello et al. [5]).

The admission control/route selection model assumes synchronous communication and incorruptible nodes and makes connectivity/liveness guarantees. Among the other options (fixed or dynamic topology, global or local control), each combination has been considered by various authors, see the above references for further details and results within each specific model.

1.2 Our Results

In this paper, we consider the feasibility of end-to-end routing in unreliable networks controlled by a malicious adversary with polynomial computing power. In particular, we present a local-control protocol that achieves optimal throughput in asynchronous networks with untrustworthy nodes and dynamic topology with no connectivity guarantees.

The first step in obtaining our result is to first consider networks where nodes are guaranteed to behave honestly, but otherwise the network demonstrates all of the unreliability features. In these networks, we have the following matching upper and lower bounds on throughput performance:

Theorem 1 (Informal). *The best competitive-ratio that any protocol can achieve in a distributed asynchronous network with dynamic topology (and no connectivity assumptions) is $1/n$ (where n is the number of nodes). In particular, given any protocol $\mathcal{P}$, there exists an alternative protocol $\mathcal{P}'$, such that $\mathcal{P}'$ will out-perform $\mathcal{P}$ by a factor of at least n.*

Theorem 2 (Informal). *There exists a protocol that achieves a competitive ratio of $1/n$ in a distributed asynchronous network with dynamic topology (and no connectivity assumptions).*

Due to space constraints, we do not prove Theorems 1 and 2 here, but refer the reader to [17] for full details of the proofs of each of these. In this paper, we focus on the following result, which extends Theorem 2 to networks in which nodes are no longer assumed to behave honestly; i.e. they may deviate from the specified protocol in any desired manner to disrupt communication as much as possible. Somewhat surprisingly, we show that this increased level of unreliability does not affect optimal throughput performance; indeed, we demonstrate a protocol that achieves $1/n$ competitive ratio, matching the lower-bound of Theorem 1.

Theorem 3 (MAIN THEOREM, Informal). *Assuming Public-Key Infrastructure, there exists a protocol with competitive ratio $1/n$ in a distributed asynchronous network with dynamic topology (and no connectivity assumptions), even if a polynomially bounded adversary can dynamically corrupt an arbitrary set of nodes.*

2 The Model

In this section, we describe formally the model in which we will be analyzing routing protocols. We begin by modeling the network as a graph G with n vertices (or *nodes*). Two of these nodes are designated as the *sender* and *receiver*, and the sender has a stream of messages $\{m_1, m_2, \dots\}$ that it wishes to transmit through the network to the receiver.

Asynchronous communication networks vary from synchronous networks in that the transmission time across an edge in the network is not fixed (even along the same edge, from one message transmission to the next). Since there is no common global clock or mechanism to synchronize events, an asynchronous network is often said to be "message driven," in that the actions of the nodes occur exactly (and only) when they have just sent/received a message.

Asynchronous networks are commonly modeled by introducing a scheduling adversary that controls the edges of the network as follows. Informally, we focus on a single edge $E(u, v)$, and then a "round" consists of allowing the edge to deliver a message in both directions.[1] To model unpredictable delivery times across each edge, we have each node u decide on the next message to send to v

[1] An adversary that is allowed to deliver messages in only *one* direction can be modelled by defining a round to consist of (at least) one communication in each direction. Since competitive analysis can be used to show that acknowledgements of some kind are requisite for a finite competitive-ratio, it is natural to define a round as above.

immediately after receiving a message from v, and this message is then sent to the adversary who stores it until the next time he activates edge $E(u,v)$.

Formally, we define a round to consist of a single edge $E(u,v)$ in the network chosen by the adversary in which two sequential events occur: 1a) Among the packets from u to v that the adversary is storing, it will choose one (in any manner it likes) and deliver it to v; 1b) Similarly, the adversary chooses one of the packets it is storing from v to u and delivers it to u; 2a) After seeing the delivered packet, u sends requests of the form $(u,v,m) =$ (sending node, target node, message) to the adversary, which will be stored by the adversary and may be delivered the *next* time $E(u,v)$ is made a round; 2b) Similarly for v.

Modeling asynchronicity in this manner captures the intuition that a node has no idea how long a message "sent" to an adjacent node will take to arrive, and this definition also captures the "worst-case" asynchronicity, in that a (potentially deliberately malicious) adversary controls the scheduling of rounds/edges.

Aside from obeying the above specified rules, we place no restriction on the scheduling adversary. In other words, it may activate whatever edges it likes (this models the fact our network makes no connectivity assumptions), wait indefinitely long between activating the same edge twice (modeling both the dynamic and asynchronous features of our network), and do anything else it likes (so long as it respects steps (1) and (2) above each time it activates an edge) in attempt to hinder the performance of a routing protocol.

Our model also allows a polynomially bounded node-controlling adversary to corrupt the *nodes* in the network. The node-controlling adversary is malicious, meaning that takes complete control over the nodes he corrupts, and can therefore force them to deviate from any protocol in whatever manner he likes. We also allow for a dynamic adversary, which means that he can corrupt nodes at any stage of the protocol, deciding which nodes to corrupt based on what he has observed thus far. We do not impose any "access-structure" limitations on the adversary. That is, the adversary may corrupt any nodes it likes (although if the sender and/or receiver is corrupt, secure routing between them is impossible). Because integrity of the messages received by the receiver is now a concern (as corrupt nodes can delete and/or modify messages), we will say a routing protocol is secure if the receiver eventually gets all of the messages sent by the sender, in order and without duplication or modification.

The separation of the adversaries into two distinct entities is solely for conceptual reasons. Note that the scheduling adversary cannot be controlled or eliminated: edges themselves are not inherently "good" or "bad," so identifying an unresponsive edge does not allow us to forever refuse the protocol to utilize this edge. By contrast, our protocol will limit the amount of influence the node-controlling adversary has in the network. Specifically, we will show that if a node deviates from the protocol in a sufficiently destructive manner (in a well-defined sense), then our protocol will be able to identify it as corrupted in a timely fashion. Once a corrupt node has been identified, it will be eliminated from the network by excluding it from all future communication.

Note that our network model is on-line and distributed, in that we do not assume that the nodes have access to any information (including future knowledge of the adversary's schedule) aside from the packets they receive. Also, we insist that nodes have bounded memory which is at least $\Omega(n^2)$.[2]

Our mechanism for evaluating protocols will be to measure their throughput, a notion we can now define formally in the context of rounds and the scheduling adversary. In particular, let $f_{\mathcal{P}}^{\mathcal{A}} : \mathbb{N} \to \mathbb{N}$ be a function that measures, for a given protocol $\mathcal{P}$ and adversary $\mathcal{A}$, the number of packets that the receiver has received as a function of the number of rounds that have passed. Note that in this paper, we will consider only deterministic protocols, so $f_{\mathcal{P}}^{\mathcal{A}}$ is well-defined. The function $f_{\mathcal{P}}^{\mathcal{A}}$ formalizes our notion of throughput.

As mentioned in the Introduction, we utilize competitive analysis to gauge the performance (with respect to throughput) of a given protocol against all possible competing protocols. In particular, for any fixed adversary $\mathcal{A}$, we may consider the ideal "off-line" protocol $\mathcal{P}'$ which has perfect information: knowledge of all future decisions of the scheduling adversary, as well as knowledge of which nodes are/will become corrupt. That is, for any fixed round x, there exists an ideal off-line protocol $\mathcal{P}'(\mathcal{A}, x)$ such that $f_{\mathcal{P}'}^{\mathcal{A}}(x)$ is maximal. We demand that the ideal protocol $\mathcal{P}'$ never utilizes corrupt nodes once they have been corrupted (this restriction is not only reasonable, it is necessary, as it can easily be shown that allowing $\mathcal{P}'$ to utilize corrupt nodes will result in *every* on-line protocol having competitive ratio $1/\infty$).

Definition 1. *We say that a protocol $\mathcal{P}$ has competitive ratio $1/\lambda$ (respectively is λ-competitive) if there exists a constant k and function $g(n, C)$ (C is the memory bound per node) such that for all adversaries $\mathcal{A}$ and for all $x \in \mathbb{N}$:*[3]

$$f_{\mathcal{P}'}^{\mathcal{A}}(x) \leq (k \cdot \lambda) \cdot f_{\mathcal{P}}^{\mathcal{A}}(x) + g(n, C) \tag{1}$$

We assume a Public-Key Infrastructure (PKI) that allows digital signatures. In particular, this allows the sender and receiver to sign messages to each other that cannot be forged (except with negligible probability in the security parameter) by any other node in the system. It also allows nodes to verify/sign communications with their neighbors (see Section 3.2).

3 Description of Protocol

In this section we present an on-line protocol that enjoys competitive ratio $1/n$ in the network model of Section 2. Our protocol uses as its starting point the "Slide" protocol (or *gravitational-flow*), which was first introduced by Afek, Gafni, and Rosén [3], and further developed in a series of work [1], [20], and [17]. As is shown in [17], Slide+ enjoys competitive ratio $1/n$ in networks in which all nodes behave

---

[2] For simplicity, we assume that all nodes have the same memory bound, although our argument can be readily extended to handle the more general case.

[3] Typically, λ is a function of the number of nodes in the network n, and Definition 1 implicitly assumes the minimal value of λ for which (1) holds.

honestly (but otherwise the network is as modelled here). We first describe this protocol in Section 3.1, and then in Section 3.2 describe how we modify this protocol to address networks allowing misbehaving nodes.

3.1 Description of the Slide+ Protocol

Recall that we model an asynchronous network via a scheduling adversary that maintains a buffer of requests of the form (u, v, p), which is a request from node u to send packet p to node v. The scheduling adversary proceeds in a sequence of activated edges (called rounds), and a protocol can be completely described by the actions of node u (and symmetrically v) during a round $E(u, v)$. Let C denote the size of each node's memory, then Slide+ requires that $C \geq 8n^2$, and for simplicity we will assume that $C/n \in \mathbb{N}$.

During activated edge $E(u, v)$, let $(v, u, (p', h'))$ denote the message that u receives from v in Step 1 of the round (via the scheduling adversary). Also, u has recorded the request $(u, v, (p, h))$ that it made during Step 2 of the previous round in which $E(u, v)$ was activated; note that v will be receiving this message during Step 1 of the current round. Then during round $E(u, v)$, u does:

1. If u is the Sender, then:
   (a) If $h < C$: u deletes packet p from his input stream $\{p_1, p_2, \dots\}$, ignores the received p', and proceeds to Step (1c)
   (b) If $h' \geq C$: u keeps p, ignores the received p', and proceeds to Step (1c)
   (c) The Sender finds the next packet $p_i \in \{p_1, p_2, \dots\}$ that has not been deleted and is not currently an outstanding request already sent to the adversary, and sends the request $(u, v, (p_i, C + \frac{C}{n} - n))$ to the adversary.
2. If u is the Receiver, then u sends the request $(u, v, (\perp, \frac{-C}{n} - 2n + 1))$ to the adversary. Meanwhile, if $p' \neq \perp$, then u stores/outputs p' as a packet successfully received.
3. If u is any internal node, then:
   (a) If $h \geq h' + (C/n + 2n)$: u ignores p', deletes p, updates height $h = h - 1$, and proceeds to Step (3d)
   (b) If $h \leq h' - (C/n + 2n)$: u keeps both p and p', updates height $h = h + 1$, and proceeds to Step (3d)
   (c) If $|h - h'| < C/n + 2n$: u ignores packet p', keeps p, and proceeds to Step (3d)
   (d) Node u finds a packet p'' that it has not already committed in an outstanding request to the adversary, and sends the request $(u, v, (p'', h))$ to the adversary

3.2 Our Protocol

Our protocol extends the Slide+ protocol described above to provide security against the node-controlling adversary by using digital signatures in the following two ways:

1. The sender signs every packet, so that honest nodes do not waste resources on modified or junk packets, and so that packets the receiver gets are unmolested
2. Communication between nodes will be signed by each node. This information will be used later by the sender (if there has been malicious activity) to hold nodes accountable for their actions, and ultimately eliminate corrupt nodes

The routing rules for each internal node are the same as in the Slide+ protocol, except that whenever a node u sends a packet to a neighbor v, there will be four parts to this communication:

(a) The packet itself, i.e. a packet from the sender intended for the receiver
(b) The current height of u, i.e. how many packets u is currently storing
(c) A signature on the communication that u has had with v, as described below
(d) Signatures from other nodes that the sender requested, as described below

The first two parts of each communication are identical to the Slide+ protocol, so it remains to discuss the second two items, which are used for the identification of corrupt nodes. Note that the second two items each consist of a signature on some quantity; for this reason we will require that the bandwidth of each edge is large enough to allow for simultaneous transmission of two signatures (plus the packet itself). The signature that u includes on his communications with v for Item (c) above pertains to the following four items:

Sig1 The total number of packets u has sent to v so far
Sig2 The total number of times the previous packet p that was exchanged between them has crossed the edge $E(u, v)$ (can be more than once)
Sig3 The cumulative difference in u and v's heights, measured from each time u and v exchanged a packet
Sig4 An index representing how many times $E(u, v)$ has been activated, to serve as a time-stamp on the above three items

It remains to explain Item (d) from above, for which it will be useful to first describe from a high-level how our protocol handles malicious activity by corrupt nodes. Since secure routing is impossible if either the sender or receiver is corrupted, we will assume that they remain uncorrupted through the protocol, and they will be responsible for regulation of the network (e.g. identifying and eliminating corrupt nodes). Also, because our definition of security (see Section 2) requires that the receiver gets all of the packets sent by the sender, we will use error-correction and first expand the messages into codewords so that the receiver can reconstruct each message if he has a constant fraction of the codeword packets. See e.g. [7] for a specific description of how this can be done. We note that because the definition of throughput only cares about asymptotic performance (i.e. constants are absorbed in the k that appears in Definition 1), the use of error-correction will not affect the throughput of our protocol.

From a high-level, the protocol attempts to transfer one message (codeword), consisting of $\Theta(nC)$ bits, at a time (this is called a message/codeword transmission). The sender will continue inserting packets corresponding to the same codeword until one of the following occurs:

S1 Sender gets a message indicating the receiver decoded the current codeword
F2 Sender gets a message alerting him of inconsistencies in height differences
F3 Sender has inserted all packets corresponding to the current codeword
F4 Sender gets a message indicating the receiver got the same packet twice
F5 Sender is able to identify a corrupt node

Cases S1, F2, and F4 come from messages sent by the receiver, a process we do not explicitly describe due to space constraints. In the case of S1 (successful codeword transmission), the sender will begin inserting packets corresponding to the next codeword. In the case of F5, the sender will eliminate the identified node (i.e. alert all nodes in the network to forever ignore the corrupt node), and begin anew transmitting packets corresponding to the current codeword. The other three cases correspond to failed attempts to transfer the current codeword due to corrupt nodes disobeying protocol rules, and in each case the sender will use the signed information from Item (c) above to identify a corrupt node.

In cases F2-F4, the sender will begin anew transmitting packets corresponding to the current codeword. Before nodes are allowed to participate in transferring the codeword packets, they must first learn that the last transmission failed, the reason for failure (F2-F4), and the sender must receive all of *the signatures the node was storing from its neighbors*, called the node's status report (i.e. all signed information from Item (c) above). Note that the network itself is the only medium of communication available for relaying the signatures a node is storing to the sender, and hence part of the bandwidth of each edge (and part of the storage capacity of each node) is devoted to returning these pieces of signed information to the sender (this is Item (d) from the above list).

Until the sender has received a node's status report for a failed transmission, the node will remain on the **blacklist**. That is, no honest node u will transfer any codeword packets to another node v until u obtains verification from the sender that the sender has received v's status report.

4 Analysis of Our Protocol

We use competitive analysis to evaluate the throughput performance of the above protocol. To this end, let $(\mathcal{A}, \mathcal{P}')$ denote an adversary/off-line protocol pair for which we compare our routing protocol $\mathcal{P}$. Due to space constraints, we provide only a proof sketch of Theorem 3 (see [18] for details):

Theorem 3. *If at any time $\mathcal{P}'$ has received $\Theta(xn)$ messages, then $\mathcal{P}$ has received $\Omega((x - n^2))$ messages. Thus, if the number of messages $x \in \Omega(n^2)$, then our protocol has competitive ratio $1/n$.*

Theorem 3 will follow immediately from the following three Lemmas:

Lemma 1. *Suppose transmission* T *failed and at some later time (after* T *but before any nodes are eliminated) the sender has the status report from all nodes not on the blacklist during* T*. Then the sender can eliminate a corrupt node.*

Proof. (Sketch) We split the proof into the three cases of transmission failure:

Handling Case F2. If a misbehaving node u tries to jam the network by duplicating packets, then there will be a discrepancy between the recorded values of cumulative height differences from packets transferred from u's neighbors *to* u and packets transferred *from* u to its neighbors. Therefore, if the sender has Sig3 from all of u's neighbors, the he can identify u as corrupt.

Handling Case F3. The number of packets per codeword ($\Theta(nC)$) is chosen so that even if nC packets are missing, the receiver can still decode. Therefore, since the capacity of the network is bounded by nC, if the sender has inserted all of the codeword packets and the receiver cannot decode, then necessarily a corrupt node is deleting packets. The information from the status reports (in particular information from Sig1) can be used to identify such a node.

Handling Case F4. A corrupt node is duplicating packets, and the status reports (in particular information from Sig2) can be used to identify such a node.

Lemma 2. *There can be at most $n-1$ (not necessarily consecutive) failed codeword transmissions $\{\mathtt{T}_i\}_{i=1}^{n-1}$ (i.e. cases F2-F4) before there is necessarily some $\mathtt{T}_i$ such that the sender has gathered the complete* ***status report*** *from every node that was not on the blacklist during $\mathtt{T}_i$.*

Proof. (Sketch) A node is not allowed to participate in a transmission (it is placed on the blacklist) until the sender has received the node's status report(s) for all previous failed transmissions. Thus, for each failed transmission $\mathtt{T}_i$ for which the sender has not collected all status reports, there is (at least) one *distinct* node whose status report is missing, and hence this node will be on the blacklist for all later transmissions until the sender gets this report. Since there are $n-1$ nodes (excluding the sender), this can happen at most $n-1$ times.

The final lemma guarantees that one of the cases S1-F5 necessarily happens by the time the off-line protocol $\mathcal{P}'$ has delivered $O(n^2C)$ packets. For any transmission $\mathtt{T}$, let $Y_{\mathtt{T}}^{\mathcal{P}}$ and $Z_{\mathtt{T}}^{\mathcal{P}}$ (respectively $Y_{\mathtt{T}}^{\mathcal{P}'}$ and $Z_{\mathtt{T}}^{\mathcal{P}'}$) denote the set of packets sent and received during $\mathtt{T}$ by protocol $\mathcal{P}$ (respectively by $\mathcal{P}'$).

Lemma 3. *In any transmission $\mathtt{T}$, $|Z_{\mathtt{T}}^{\mathcal{P}'}| = O(n^2C)$. If the transmission was successful (as in case S1), then $|Z_{\mathtt{T}}^{\mathcal{P}}| = \Theta(nC)$.*

Proof. (Sketch) The second statement of the theorem is immediate, since the receiver requires $\Theta(nC)$ packets to decode a codeword. For the first statement, we first fix a transmission $\mathtt{T}$, and split the packets of $Z^{\mathcal{P}'}$ (we will suppress subscripts $\mathtt{T}$) into subsets as follows. We can view the scheduling adversary $\mathcal{A}$ as simply a schedule (order) of edges that the adversary will honor. We will imagine a *virtual* world, in which $\mathcal{P}$ and $\mathcal{P}'$ are run simultaneously. Let $Z_3^{\mathcal{P}'}$ denote the set of packets in $Z^{\mathcal{P}'}$ that traveled between two ***honest*** nodes in some round of $\mathtt{T}$, and $\mathcal{P}$ did not transfer a packet in this round because (at least) one of these nodes was on the blacklist. Define $Z_1^{\mathcal{P}'}$ to be the subset of $Z^{\mathcal{P}'} \setminus Z_3^{\mathcal{P}'}$ consisting of packets p' for which there exists at least one round $E(u, v)$ such that both p' *and* some packet $p \in Y^{\mathcal{P}}$ were both transferred this round.[4] Set $Z_2^{\mathcal{P}'} = Z^{\mathcal{P}'} \setminus (Z_1^{\mathcal{P}'} \cup Z_3^{\mathcal{P}'})$. Also, let $T^{\mathcal{P}}$ denote the number of packet transfers in $\mathcal{P}$ between two ***honest*** nodes during T. Then Lemma 3 follows from:

Claim. (1) $T^{\mathcal{P}}{=}O(n^2C)$, (2) $|Z_1^{\mathcal{P}'}| \le T^{\mathcal{P}}_,$ (3) $|Z_2^{\mathcal{P}'}| \le T^{\mathcal{P}}_,$ (4) $|Z_3^{\mathcal{P}'}|{=}O(n^2C)$

Proof. (Sketch) (1) follows from transfer rules: a packet transfer corresponds to a packet dropping in height by C/n, so this can happen n times per inserted packet, and there are $\Theta(nC)$ packets per codeword. (2) is immediate, and (4) comes from the fact that by the time $O(nC)$ packets have reached any honest node u, the sender will necessarily have received any outstanding status report of u. (3) is the most difficult to obtain, and is done using potential function arguments together with the following observations: 1) when any packet $p' \in Z_2^{\mathcal{P}'}$ is first inserted, it was necessarily inserted into some node u such that *with respect to* $\mathcal{P}$, u had height $\approx C$ (otherwise $\mathcal{P}$ would have also inserted a packet this round, and then $p' \in Z_1^{\mathcal{P}'}$). Similarly, when $p' \in Z_2^{\mathcal{P}'}$ is received by the Receiver from some node v, then *with respect to* $\mathcal{P}$, v had height zero. The idea will then be to assign a potential function $\varphi_{p'}$ to every packet $p' \in Z_2^{\mathcal{P}'}$ that represents the current height *with respect to* $\mathcal{P}$ of the node in which p' is currently stored. Thus, when a packet $p' \in Z_2^{\mathcal{P}'}$ is first inserted, $\varphi_{p'} = C$, and when $p' \in Z_2^{\mathcal{P}'}$ is received, $\varphi_{p'} = 0$. Then roughly speaking, we show that for each $p' \in Z_2^{\mathcal{P}'}$, decreases in $\varphi_{p'}$ can be linked to decreases in height of packets transferred by $\mathcal{P}$.

References

1. Afek, Y., Awerbuch, B., Gafni, E., Mansour, Y., Rosen, A., Shavit, N.: Slide– The Key to Poly. End-to-End Communication. J. of Algo's 22, 158–186 (1997)
2. Afek, Y., Gafni, E.: End-to-End Communication in Unreliable Networks. In: PODC (1988)
3. Afek, Y., Gafni, E., Rosén, A.: The Slide Mechanism with Applications in Dynamic Networks. In: Proc. 11th ACM SODA, pp. 35–46 (1992)
4. Aiello, W., Kushilevitz, E., Ostrovsky, R., Rosén, A.: Adaptive Packet Routing For Bursty Adversarial Traffic. J. Comput. Syst. Sci. 60(3), 482–509 (2000)
5. Aiello, W., Ostrovsky, R., Kushilevitz, E., Rosén, A.: Dynamic Routing on Networks with Fixed-Size Buffers. In: Proc. 14th ACM SODA, pp. 771–780 (2003)
6. Ajtai, M., Aspnes, J., Dwork, C., Waarts, O.: A Theory of Competitive Analysis for Distributed Algorithms. In: Proc. 35th IEEE FOCS, pp. 32–40 (1994)
7. Amir, Y., Bunn, P., Ostrovsky, R.: Authenticated Adversarial Routing. In: 6th Theory of Crypt. Conf., pp. 163–182 (2009)
8. Andrews, M., Awerbuch, B., Fernández, A., Kleinberg, J., Leighton, T., Liu, Z.: Universal Stability Results for Greedy Contention-Resolution Protocols. In: Proc. 37th IEEE FOCS, pp. 380–389 (1996)
9. Awerbuch, B., Azar, Y., Plotkin, S.: Throughput-Competitive On-Line Routing. In: Proc. 34th IEEE FOCS, pp. 401–411 (1993)
10. Awerbuch, B., Holmer, D., Nina-Rotaru, C., Rubens, H.: An On-Demand Secure Routing Protocol Resilient to Byzantine Failures. In: Proc. of 2002 Workshop on Wireless Security, pp. 21–30 (2002)

[4] Note that we make no condition that the two packets traveled in the same direction.

11. Awerbuch, B., Leighton, T.: Improved Approximation Algorithms for the Multi-Commodity Flow Problem and Local Competitive Routing in Dynamic Networks. In: Proc. 26th ACM STOC, pp. 487–496 (1994)
12. Awerbuch, B., Mansour, Y., Shavit, N.: End-to-End Communication With Polynomial Overhead. In: Proc. of the 30th IEEE FOCS, pp. 358-363 (1989)
13. Barak, B., Goldberg, S., Xiao, D.: Protocols and Lower Bounds for Failure Localization in the Internet. In: Smart, N.P. (ed.) EUROCRYPT 2008. LNCS, vol. 4965, pp. 341–360. Springer, Heidelberg (2008)
14. Borodin, A., El-Yaniv, R.: Online Computation and Competitive Analysis. Camb. Univ Press, Cambridge (1998)
15. Borodin, A., Kleinberg, J., Raghavan, P., Sudan, M., Williamson, D.: Adversarial Queuing Theory. In: Proc. 28th ACM STOC, pp. 376–385 (1996)
16. Broder, A., Frieze, A., Upfal, E.: A General Approach to Dynamic Packet Routing with Bounded Buffers. In: Proc. 37th IEEE FOCS, pp. 390–399 (1996)
17. Bunn, P., Ostrovsky, R.: Throughput in Asynchronous Networks. arXiv Technical Report, arXiv:0910.4572 (2009)
18. Bunn, P., Ostrovsky, R.: Asynchronous Throughput Optimal Routing in Malicious Networks. IACR Eprint Archive, Report 2010/231. April 2010 (2010)
19. Goldberg, S., Xiao, D., Tromer, E., Barak, B., Rexford, J.: Path-Quality Monitoring in the Presence of Adversaries. SIGMETRICS 36, 193–204 (2008)
20. Kushilevitz, E., Ostrovsky, R., Rosén, A.: Log-Space Polynomial End-to-End Communication. SIAM Journal of Computing 27(6), 1531–1549 (1998)
21. Leighton, T., Makedon, F., Plotkin, S., Stein, C., Tardos, É., Tragoudas, S.: Fast Approximation Algorithms for Multicommodity Flow Problem. In: Proc. 23rd ACM STOC, pp. 101–111 (1991)
22. Sleator, D., Tarjan, R.: Amortized Efficiency of List Update and Paging Rules. Commun. ACM 28(2), 202–208 (1985)

Improved Fault Tolerance and Secure Computation on Sparse Networks

Nishanth Chandran[1,⋆], Juan Garay[2], and Rafail Ostrovsky[3,⋆⋆]

[1] Department of Computer Science, UCLA
nishanth@cs.ucla.edu
[2] AT&T Labs – Research, Florham Park, NJ
garay@research.att.com
[3] Departments of Computer Science & Mathematics, UCLA
rafail@cs.ucla.edu

Abstract. In the problem of *almost-everywhere agreement* (denoted a.e. agreement), introduced by Dwork, Peleg, Pippenger, and Upfal [STOC '86], n parties want to reach agreement on an initially held value, despite the possible disruptive and malicious behavior of up to t of them. So far this is reminiscent of the classical *Byzantine agreement* problem, except that in the alternative formulation the underlying connectivity graph is *sparse*—i.e., not all parties share point-to-point reliable channels—thus modeling the actual connectivity of real communication networks. In this setting, one may not be able to guarantee agreement amongst all honest parties, and some of them, say x, must be given up. Thus, in this line of work the goal is to be able to tolerate a high value for t (a constant fraction of n is the best possible) while minimizing x. As shown in the original paper, the dependency on d, the degree of the network, to achieve this goal is paramount.

Indeed, the best polynomial-time a.e. agreement protocol tolerating a constant fraction of corruptions $t = \alpha n$, for some constant $\alpha > 0$ (presented in the original paper, over two decades ago) has parameters, $d = n^{\epsilon}$ for constant $\epsilon > 0$ and $x = \mu t$ for some constant $\mu > 1$. In this work, we significantly improve on the above parameters obtaining a protocol with $t = \alpha n$, $d = \mathcal{O}(\log^q n)$, for constant $q > 0$ and $x = \mathcal{O}(\frac{t}{\log n})$. Our approach follows that of Dwork *et al.* of reducing the a.e. agreement problem to constructing a reliable transmission scheme between pairs of nodes for a large fraction of them; however, given our setting's more stringent conditions—poly-logarithmic degree and a linear number of corruptions, such a task is significantly harder.

We also consider the problem of *secure computation* on partially connected networks, as formulated by Garay and Ostrovsky [Eurocrypt '08], and as a corollary to our main result obtain an almost-everywhere secure multi-party computation protocol with the same parameters as above, again significantly improving on the bound on the number of left-out

⋆ Work partly done while visiting AT&T Labs – Research. Supported in part by NSF grants 0716835, 0716389, 0830803, 0916574.

⋆⋆ Supported in part by IBM Faculty Award, Xerox Innovation Group Award, the Okawa Foundation Award, Intel, Teradata, NSF grants 0716835, 0716389, 0830803, 0916574 and U.C. MICRO grant.

S. Abramsky et al. (Eds.): ICALP 2010, Part II, LNCS 6199, pp. 249–260, 2010.

parties—$x = \mathcal{O}(\frac{t}{\log n})$ for $t \leq \alpha n$ corruptions, as opposed to $x = \mathcal{O}(t)$ in the original work.

1 Introduction

Clearly, partially connected networks are far more realistic than fully connected networks, especially as the number of nodes grows. Indeed, essentially all deployed practical networks do not have dedicated links between each pair of nodes, and instead rely on routing and multi-hop message transmission protocols. In a seminal paper, Dwork, Peleg, Pippenger and Upfal [10] introduced the notion of *almost-everywhere agreement* (a.e. agreement for short) in an effort to model the reality of communication networks, as well as to capture the impact of limited connectivity on the properties of fundamental fault-tolerant distributed tasks, such as *Byzantine agreement* [21,18], which requires that parties agree on a value based on initial inputs held by each of them, despite the disruptive behavior of some of the nodes, and which so far had only been studied assuming full connectivity amongst the parties.

Instead, in the Dwork *et al.* formulation, the n parties, or nodes, are connected by a graph G. Nodes that are connected by an edge in G share a point-to-point reliable channel with each other; other nodes have to communicate by transmitting messages over the paths that might be available to them, through other nodes in the network. Clearly, in such a setting, one may not be able to guarantee agreement for all nodes in the network, even if they are honest. For example, if an honest node is connected only to misbehaving (or "corrupt") nodes, then guaranteeing that this node reaches agreement with other honest nodes is impossible. In other words, these honest nodes have to be "given up" (hence the term "almost-everywhere" agreement) and its number becomes a new relevant parameter to the problem. Thus, the added goal of fault-tolerant protocols for partially connected settings, besides tolerating the maximal number of faults or corruptions, is to minimize the number of such excluded parties—a task which, as shown in [10], heavily depends on the degree of the graph.

Indeed, Dwork *et al.* constructed a.e. agreement protocols for several classes of partially connected networks, which make the interplay between the various parameters apparent. For example, they presented a protocol for a.e. agreement on a constant-degree graph tolerating up to $t = \mathcal{O}(\frac{n}{\log n})$ corrupt nodes, while guaranteeing that no more than $x = \mathcal{O}(t)$ are left out. They also constructed a protocol on a graph of degree n^ϵ for constant ϵ tolerating up to $t = \mathcal{O}(n)$ corrupt nodes, with $x = \mathcal{O}(t)$. The main problem left open in [10] was to construct graphs of low degree tolerating $t = \mathcal{O}(n)$ corrupt nodes with $x = \mathcal{O}(t)$ (or even lower) excluded nodes. In a remarkable result, Upfal [22] showed the existence of an a.e. agreement protocol on constant-degree graphs tolerating a constant fraction of corrupt nodes, while giving up a linear (in t) number of honest nodes. Unfortunately, the protocol of [22] runs in exponential time (in n).

In this work, we construct graphs of poly-logarithmic degree ($\mathcal{O}(\log^q n)$, for constant $q > 0$), on which we show an efficient (i.e., polynomial-time) a.e.

agreement protocol tolerating up to a constant fraction of corrupt nodes; further, and in contrast to previous results, we only give up $\mathcal{O}(\frac{t}{\log n})$ nodes, as opposed to linear (in t). Thus, our protocol is the first significant (in fact, *exponential*) improvement on the degree of graphs, as well as on the number of given-up nodes from a constant fraction to a sub-constant, admitting deterministic polynomial-time protocols since the work of [10] more than 20 years ago. We remark that, similarly to [22], we construct a specific graph of poly-logarithmic degree along with an a.e. agreement protocol on this graph network.

We also consider the problem of (unconditional, or information-theoretic) *secure multi-party computation* (MPC) [2,8] in the context of partially connected networks, as formulated by Garay and Ostrovsky [13]. By applying our new a.e. agreement protocol to the construction of [13], we immediately obtain an a.e. MPC protocol for graphs of poly-logarithmic degree, tolerating a linear number of corruptions, while giving up only $\mathcal{O}(\frac{t}{\log n})$ parties from the secure computation.

Related work. We already mentioned above the formulation of the a.e. agreement problem by Dwork *et al.* [10], and the result, albeit inefficient, by Upfal [22] for constant-degree graphs tolerating a constant fraction of corruptions and yet guaranteeing agreement also for a constant fraction of the nodes. Berman and Garay [4,5], improved the efficiency of the protocols from [10], while Ben-Or and Ron [3] considered the problem in which faults are random and not adversarially chosen. Bagchi *et al.* [1] considered a related problem of obtaining a large connected component of a graph (that avoids all adversarial nodes), such that this connected component has high expansion given that the original graph had high expansion. This result can be applied to improve the bounds obtained by Upfal [22]. However, the algorithm for obtaining this large connected component also does not run in polynomial time (in addition to the exponential-time protocol from [22] that one would have to run on this connected component).

An alternative view to limited network connectivity is to try to minimize the communication costs of fault-tolerant distributed tasks ($\Omega(n^2)$ in the case of Byzantine agreement [9]) for scalability purposes. In that vein, King *et al.* [17] constructed a *randomized* a.e. agreement protocol with low communication and parameters similar to ours, i.e., their protocol tolerates linear number of corruptions and gives up $\mathcal{O}(\frac{t}{\log n})$ honest nodes. However, besides being non-error-free and requiring parties to have access to private random bits (something unavoidable if the communication complexity lower bound is to be overcome), the protocol is only able to tolerate *static* corruptions (meaning which parties are corrupted must be specified before the protocol execution starts); in contrast, our protocol enjoys *adaptive* security, allowing an adversary to use information obtained from a set of corrupted parties at one round to determine which node(s) to corrupt next. In the fully connected network model, further work by King and Saia [16] builds on [17] in the sense of avoiding all-to-all communication, and yet achieve full agreement at a lower communication cost. The work of [16] also differs from our setting in the following ways – it considers a fully connected network, utilizes private random bits, and considers only static corruptions.

Overview of our techniques. We will call the honest nodes for which we guarantee agreement the *privileged* nodes, and the honest nodes for which we do not the *doomed* nodes. Effectively, we follow the general approach of [10] and [22] for a.e. agreement by constructing a reliable remote message transmission scheme between any two nodes in a large set of privileged nodes. However, given only poly-logarithmic degree and a linear number of corruptions, this is significantly harder than in [10]. On the other hand, the technique used by Upfal [22] is to simply "flood" all the paths with the message, and showing that at least one uncorrupted path exists; one can then exhaustively search for the set of corrupted nodes and obtain the message m, which leads to an exponential-time algorithm. In contrast, we will need to obtain polynomially many good paths between two privileged nodes using just poly-logarithmic degree, even though a linear number of nodes may be corrupted.

Further, unlike the transmission schemes of [10] and [22], nodes along the path in our scheme will be more "proactive" and will not just simply forward the message being sent. This is necessary in order to ensure that the correct message keeps being transmitted along majority of the paths at the different stages. This will then enable us to get a polynomial-time reliable message transmission scheme, which in turn will be sufficient both for our result on a.e. agreement as well as for a.e. MPC.

Our starting point is the reliable remote message transmission scheme $\mathrm{TS}_{\mathrm{dppu}}$ from [10] mentioned above for constant degree networks, which tolerates $t = \mathcal{O}(\frac{n}{\log n})$ number of corruptions and gives reliable communication between any two nodes from a set of privileged nodes of size $n - \mathcal{O}(t)$. At a high level, the scheme associates with every node u in the graph a *fan-in* set and a *fan-out* set of a fixed (but not necessarily constant) size. In addition, (not necessarily vertex-disjoint) paths from a node to its sets are specified, as well as (vertex-disjoint) paths for all ordered pairs of one node's fan-out set to any other node' fan-in set. When node u wants to send a message to node v, $\mathrm{TS}_{\mathrm{dppu}}$ consists of three phases: first u sends the message to all members of its fan-out set; each member then sends the message to its connected (via a path) pair in v's fan-in set; and finally each member in v's set forwards the message to v, who accepts the value resulting from the majority of received values.

Given such a scheme, our construction proceeds as follows. We start with the technique of forming partially overlapping "committees," introduced by Bracha [6] and used in several other contexts (e.g., [20,23,15,11]). However, while this is a somewhat standard first step, we need to make use of several additional tools in order for the technique to be successful in our a.e. agreement context. Our construction works through the following steps:

1. We create $N = n \log^{k'} n$ committees (for some constant k') such that at most $\mathcal{O}(\frac{N}{\log N})$ of these committees are "bad" (by "bad" here we mean that some threshold fraction of the nodes in the committee are corrupted).

2. For every node in the graph, we assign a poly-logarithmic number of these committees as the *helper committees* for this node. We view these committees as "super-nodes" that can be connected by "super-edges"; when two committees are connected by a super-edge, we have to connect node i in the first committee with node i in the second, ordering nodes in each committee lexicographically.

3. Now, if we assume that these N committees are nodes connected by edges as per the graph G_{dppu} from [10], then using the transmission scheme TS_{dppu}, one can obtain a large set of committees (call them the "privileged" committees) such that any two committees can reliably communicate between themselves. This is because only $\mathcal{O}(\frac{N}{\log N})$ of the committees are corrupt. But, for this to work, committees need to be able to communicate across super-edges in exactly the same way as nodes communicate across edges. In order to achieve this task, we will make use of a suitable *differential agreement* protocol, specified in Section 2.3. The validity condition of this agreement protocol has the property that if many honest nodes begin the protocol with some value v then at the end of the protocol all honest nodes will output v. In this way, reliable message transmission across a super-edge can be obtained by having nodes in one committee send the message to nodes in the other committee and running the above differential agreement protocol amongst the nodes of the second committee.

4. We next show that for $n-t-\mathcal{O}(\frac{t}{\log n})$ nodes (those are the "privileged" nodes), most helper committees assigned to these nodes are also privileged committees.

5. The idea now is to first make a privileged sender node u_s send the message m to all its helper committees (most of which are privileged). Second, these helper committees can communicate with the privileged committees in the helper-committee set of the receiver node u_r using the protocol TS_{dppu}. Finally, u_r can obtain the value m from its set of helper committees.

Organization of the paper. We begin in Section 2 with the description of our model, as well as the definitions and building blocks needed for our protocol. Section 3 is dedicated to our main result: the construction of our poly-logarithmic degree graph, and presentation of our protocol for reliable remote message transmission. Due to space limitations, some of the background material, the "reduction" of a.e. agreement and secure computation on sparse networks to our reliable remote message transmission protocol, as well as proofs, are given in the full version [7] of this paper.

2 Model, Definitions and Building Blocks

Let $G = (V, E)$ denote a graph with n nodes (i.e., $|V| = n$). We also refer to the nodes of the network as parties. The edges of the graph model communication links or channels. We assume a synchronous network and assume that the communication is divided into rounds. In every round, a player can send (possibly different) messages on its incident edges; these messages are delivered before the next round. An adversary $\mathcal{A}$ can corrupt a set of nodes $\mathcal{T}$ in the network such that $\mathcal{T} \subset V, |\mathcal{T}| \leq t$. $\mathcal{A}$ has unlimited computational power, can corrupt nodes adaptively (i.e., can use information obtained from a set of corrupted parties at one round to determine which node(s) to corrupt next) and is *rushing* (i.e., $\mathcal{A}$ can learn messages sent by honest parties before deciding the messages to be sent by corrupted parties in a particular round).

2.1 Expander Graphs

Expander graphs are graphs with the property that for any (not too large) subset of nodes S, the number of outgoing edges from this set is proportional to its size. Expander graphs can also be viewed as bipartite graphs. When we wish to consider this representation, we will use the following definition.

Definition 1. *A* bipartite multi-graph *with n left vertices and m right vertices, where every left vertex has degree d, can be specified by a function $\Gamma : [n] \times [d] \rightarrow [m]$, where $\Gamma(u, r)$ denotes the rth neighbor of vertex $u \in [n]$. For a set $S \subseteq [n]$, we write $\Gamma(S)$ to denote the set of neighbors of S. That is, $\Gamma(S) = \{\Gamma(x, y) : x \in S, y \in [d]\}$.*

Definition 2. *A bipartite graph $\Gamma : [n] \times [d] \rightarrow [m]$ is an (n, m, d, l, A)*-expander, *if for every set $S \subseteq [n]$, with $|S| = l$, we have $|\Gamma(S)| \geq A \cdot l$. Γ is an $(n, m, d, \leq l_{max}, A)$ expander if it is an (n, m, d, l, A) expander for every $l \leq l_{max}$.*

A bipartite expander is *balanced* if $m = n$. It is *right-regular* if all nodes on the right also have the same degree D (nodes on the left all have degree d). We will make use of constant-degree balanced expander graphs[1] that are right D-regular, where $A = \epsilon' d$ for some constant ϵ', $l_{\max} \leq \theta n$ for constant θ and $D = \mathcal{O}(d)$. Such graphs can be constructed using any constant-degree unbalanced ($m < n$) expander following the work of Guruswami *et al.* [14].

2.2 Almost-Everywhere Agreement

The problem of *almost-everywhere agreement* (a.e. agreement for short) was introduced by Dwork *et al.* [10]. A.e. agreement "gives up" certain honest nodes in the network, which is unavoidable due to their poor connectivity with other honest nodes. We refer to the given-up nodes as *doomed* nodes; the honest nodes for which we guarantee agreement are referred to as *privileged* nodes. Let the set of doomed nodes be denoted by $\mathcal{X}$ and the set of privileged nodes by $\mathcal{P}$. Note that the sets $\mathcal{P}$ and $\mathcal{X}$ are a function of the set of corrupted nodes ($\mathcal{T}$) and the underlying graph. Let $|\mathcal{X}| = x$ and $|\mathcal{P}| = p$. Clearly, we have $p + x + t = n$. We begin with the formal definition of a.e. agreement.

Definition 3. *A protocol for parties $\{P_1, P_2, \cdots, P_n\}$, each holding initial value v_i, is an* almost-everywhere agreement *protocol if the following conditions hold for any adversary $\mathcal{A}$ that corrupts a set of nodes $\mathcal{T}$ with $|\mathcal{T}| \leq t$:*

AGREEMENT: *All nodes in $\mathcal{P}$ output the same value.*
VALIDITY: *If for all nodes in $\mathcal{P}$, $v_i = v$, then all nodes in $\mathcal{P}$ output v.*

The difference with respect to standard Byzantine agreement is that in the latter the two conditions above are enforced on *all* honest nodes, as opposed to only the nodes in $\mathcal{P}$. For brevity, we keep the same names.

[1] Strictly speaking, we do not require the expander to be balanced, only that $n = m \log^s m$, for some constant $s \geq 0$.

In the context of a.e. agreement, one would like the graph G to have as small a degree as possible (i.e., in relation to the size of the graph and to the number of corrupted parties). We would like the protocol to guarantee agreement amongst $n - \mathcal{O}(t)$ parties, while allowing $t = \alpha n$ for some constant $0 < \alpha < 1$.

Dwork *et al.* constructed graphs with *constant degree* tolerating at most $t = \mathcal{O}(\frac{n}{\log n})$ corruptions and at the same time guaranteeing agreement amongst $n - \mathcal{O}(t)$ nodes in the network. That is, the graph $G_{\text{dppu}} = (V_{\text{dppu}}, E_{\text{dppu}})$ on n nodes has constant degree. The number of corrupted parties t, tolerated by the protocol can be at most $\mathcal{O}(\frac{n}{\log n})$, while the number of doomed nodes is a constant times t. The idea behind the protocol is to simulate a complete graph on the set of privileged nodes. The theorem from [10] is as follows:

Theorem 1. *There exist constants μ and d independent of n and t, an n-vertex d-regular graph G_{dppu} that can be explicitly constructed, and a communication protocol* TS_{dppu} *such that for any set of adversarial nodes $\mathcal{T}$ in G_{dppu} such that $|\mathcal{T}| = t = \mathcal{O}(\frac{n}{\log n})$, the communication protocol guarantees reliable communication between all pairs of nodes in a set of honest nodes $\mathcal{P}$ of size $\geq n - \mu t$, for constant $\mu > 1$. The protocol generates polynomial (in n) number of messages and has polynomial (in n) running time.*

Given the above theorem, Dwork *et al.* observe that one can run any Byzantine agreement protocol designed for a fully connected graph on G_{dppu} by simulating all communication between nodes in the network with the communication protocol TS_{dppu}. We remark that this results in a slow down of the agreement protocol by a factor proportional to the diameter of the graph. (A high-level idea of how TS_{dppu} works was given in the overview of our techniques in Section 1; we refer the reader to [10] for further details.)

As a result, let μ, d, and t be as defined above and let $\text{BA}(n, t')$ be an agreement protocol for a complete network with up to $t' = \mu t$ faulty processors. Then, simulating the protocol $\text{BA}(n, t')$ on the network G_{dppu} using the communication protocol TS_{dppu}, guarantees agreement among at least $n - \mu t$ honest nodes in the presence of up to $t = \mathcal{O}(\frac{n}{\log n})$ faulty nodes.

2.3 Differential Agreement

Fitzi and Garay [12] introduced the problem of δ-*differential agreement* (also, "consensus") developing on the so-called "strong consensus" problem [19], in which every party begins with an input v from a larger (than binary) domain $\mathcal{D}$.[2] We describe the problem below and state the results from [12].

In the standard Byzantine agreement problem, n parties attempt to reach agreement on some value v (either 0 or 1). Let c_v denote the number of honest parties whose initial value is v, and δ be a non-negative integer. δ-differential agreement is defined as follows:

[2] In contrast to standard Byzantine agreement, the validity condition in the strong consensus problem states that the output value v must have been the input of some honest party P_i (which is implicit in the case of binary Byzantine agreement).

Definition 4. *A protocol for parties $\{P_1, P_2, \cdots, P_n\}$, each holding initial value v_i, is a δ-*differential agreement *protocol if the following conditions hold for any adversary $\mathcal{A}$ that corrupts a set $\mathcal{T}$ of parties with $|\mathcal{T}| \leq t$:*

AGREEMENT: *All honest parties output the same value.*
δ-DIFFERENTIAL VALIDITY: *If the honest parties output v, then $c_v + \delta \geq c_{\bar{v}}$.*

Theorem 2. *[12] In a synchronous, fully connected network, δ-differential agreement is impossible if $n \leq 3t$ or $\delta < t$. On the other hand, there exists an efficient (i.e., polynomial-time) protocol that achieves t-differential agreement for $n > 3t$ in $t + 1$ rounds.*

Let $\text{DA}(n, t, \delta)$ denote a δ-differential agreement protocol for a fully connected network tolerating up to t faulty processors.

3 Reliable Remote Communication on Sparse Networks

In this section we show how to build a reliable message transmission scheme, TS_{low}, between any two nodes u_i and u_j that are in a large set of privileged nodes $\mathcal{P}$, on a low-degree (i.e., poly-logarithmic) graph. We begin with the construction of the graph, followed by the description of the transmission scheme, followed by its proof of correctness.

Given only poly-logarithmic degree and a linear number of corruptions, constructing a reliable remote message transmission scheme is significantly harder than in the case of [10]. As mentioned before, the technique used by Upfal [22] of simply "flooding" all the paths with the message, and showing that at least one corrupted path exists, leads to an exponential-time algorithm. To avoid that, we will need to obtain multiple good paths between two privileged nodes using just poly-logarithmic degree, even though a linear number of nodes may be corrupted. A salient feature of our transmission scheme compared to those of [10] and [22] will be that nodes along the path in our scheme play and active role and do not just simply forward the message being sent. This is done in order to ensure that the correct message is transmitted along a majority of the paths.

3.1 The Low-Degree Graph Construction

The graph $G = (V, E)$ that we construct is as follows. Let the nodes in V be denoted by $u_1, u_2, \cdots, u_n$. Let $G_{\text{exp}} = (V, E_{\text{exp}})$ be an (n, d, ϵ)-expander graph for constants $d, \epsilon > 0$ on the nodes $u_1, u_2, \cdots, u_n$. We begin, by first forming partial overlapping "virtual committees." The notion of such committees was introduced by Bracha [6] in the context of Byzantine agreement and has since been used in the construction of several protocols for other problems, including leader election, secure message transmission and secure multi-party computation [20,23,15,11].

We form committees in the following manner. Start at any node $u_i \in V$, and consider all possible walks of length $\gamma = k \log \log n$ starting at this node. Group nodes in each walk to form a committee C_j. We repeat this procedure beginning at every node in V. Let $k' = k \log d$. Note that, by the above procedure, we create $N = n\log^{k'} n$ committees $C = \{C_1, \cdots, C_N\}$, each of size $\gamma = k \log\log n$. We construct the set of edges E in graph G in the following three ways:

1. First, If $u_i, u_j \in C_l$ for some C_l, then we connect u_i and u_j by an edge. In other words, we connect all nodes within a committee by a clique.
2. Next, let $G_{\text{dppu}} = (V_{\text{dppu}}, E_{\text{dppu}})$ be a constant-degree r-regular graph on the "nodes" $C = \{C_1, C_2, \cdots, C_N\}$ as constructed in the work of [10]. Now, if $(C_i, C_j) \in E_{\text{dppu}}$, then for all $1 \leq l \leq \gamma$, we connect the lth node in C_i with the lth node in C_j, ordering nodes in C_i and C_j lexicographically; we say "C_i and C_j are connected by a super-edge" to express this.
3. Finally, let G_{biexp} be a $(N, N, d', \leq \theta N, \epsilon' d')$ bipartite expander graph that is right D-regular for constants $d', \epsilon', \theta, D > 0$. Let the nodes on the left of this graph (call it V_l) represent the nodes of G (i.e., V) where each node $u_i \in V$ appears in V_l a $(\log^{k'} n)$ number of times; we use $u_{i,1}, \cdots, u_{i,\log^{k'} n}$ to denote these $\log^{k'} n$ nodes. Let the nodes on the right of this graph (call it V_r) represent the N committees formed by the above outlined method. Now, if $(u_{i,m}, C_j)$, $1 \leq m \leq \log^{k'} n$, is an edge in G_{biexp}, we connect u_i and all nodes in C_j by an edge.

This completes the construction of graph $G = (V, E)$. In the full version [7], we show that the degree of every node in G is poly-logarithmic in n.

3.2 The Reliable Remote Message Transmission Scheme

We begin with a high-level description of our reliable remote message transmission scheme, TS_{low}.

High-level intuition. Let the number of nodes in the network be n and let the number of corrupt nodes be $t = \alpha n$. Using the n nodes of G, following our graph construction above we formed $N = n\log^{k'} n$ committees each of size $k \log\log n$. We call a committee *bad* if the number of corrupted nodes in it is $\geq \frac{k \log\log n}{4}$; otherwise, we call a committee *good*. Now, again according to our graph construction, nodes within each committee are connected by a clique and hence can run any standard Byzantine agreement protocol successfully within themselves if the number of corrupted nodes in them is less than $\frac{1}{4}^{\text{th}}$ fraction. In other words, any honest node in a good committee can agree upon a value with other honest nodes in the committee.

We begin by showing that the number of bad committees (or super-nodes) is at most $T = \frac{N}{c\mu \log N}$, for constants $\mu, c > 1$. Recall that the N committees are connected by the graph G_{dppu}. Therefore, out of these N committees, at least $N - \mu T$ of them are "privileged" and hence any two privileged committees can execute reliable remote message transmission between themselves.

In order to do this, we will describe a protocol for simulating the transmission of message m across a super-edge that connects two good committees. In particular, we need to make sure that while transmitting a message across a path consisting of committees, the number of honest players holding the message m in every committee along the path, remains the same. For this, we make use of a differential agreement protocol (Section 2.3).

Now that we have the guarantee that any two privileged committees can reliably communicate, we can outline our transmission scheme. Recall that every node u_i is connected to $\beta = d' \log^{k'} n$ committees according to the bipartite expander graph G_{biexp}. Let these β committees be called *helpers* (or *helper committees*) of node u_i. We will show that for at least $n - \frac{\mu' t}{\log n}$ (for some constant μ') of the nodes in V (this will be the set of privileged nodes $\mathcal{P}$), more than $\frac{5\beta}{6}$ of the nodes' helpers are privileged committees. This means that for every privileged node u_i, more than a $\frac{5}{6}^{\text{th}}$ fraction of u_i's helper committees are privileged according to the [10] graph connecting the committees.

Suppose now that $u_i \in \mathcal{P}$ wishes to send message m reliably to $u_j \in \mathcal{P}$. u_i first sends m to all its helper committees; call these helper committees $C_1^{u_i}, \cdots, C_\beta^{u_i}$. Let u_j's helper committees be denoted by $C_1^{u_j}, \cdots, C_\beta^{u_j}$. Next, for all $1 \le l \le \beta$, $C_l^{u_i}$ sends message m to $C_l^{u_j}$ using the transmission scheme TS_{dppu} simulating the communication across super-edges with the (differential agreement-based) protocol mentioned before. Since we have the guarantee that more than a $\frac{5}{6}^{\text{th}}$ fraction of u_i and u_j's helper committees are privileged and any two privileged committees can reliably send messages to each other (according to [10]), we have that a $\frac{2}{3}^{\text{rds}}$ majority ($> \frac{1}{2}$) of the helper committees of u_j receive the message m. Since in a privileged committee, greater than a $\frac{3}{4}^{\text{ths}}$ fraction of the nodes are honest, a simple majority ($> \frac{2}{3} \times \frac{3}{4}$) of the nodes (these nodes are honest) in the helper committees of u_j receive message m. Finally, u_i simply receives a value from all its helper committees and takes a majority of the values received. We now describe the transmission scheme in detail.

Message transmission between committees. We begin by describing the protocol for reliable remote message transmission executed by committees. We have a set of N committees, $\mathcal{C} = \{C_1, \cdots, C_N\}$, each of size $\gamma = k \log \log n$. Nodes within a committee are connected by a clique. The N committees are connected through super-edges according to a constant degree graph G_{dppu} from [10]. A super-edge between two committees C_i and C_j is obtained by connecting the lth node in C_i to the lth node in C_j (for all $1 \le l \le \gamma$), ordering the nodes in C_i and C_j lexicographically. A committee is *bad* if at least $\frac{k \log \log n}{4}$ of the nodes in it are corrupt. Let the number of bad committees be denoted by $\mathcal{T}_C$, with $|\mathcal{T}_C| = T$. We have a sender committee C_s and a receiver committee C_r. Both these committees are good and furthermore are "privileged" according to the graph G_{dppu}. All honest nodes in C_s begin the protocol with a message m. We require that at the end of the protocol all honest nodes in C_r output the same message m. Furthermore, we require that the set of privileged committees $\mathcal{P}_C$ be large; i.e., at least $N - \mu T$ for some constant $\mu > 0$. We outline such a protocol below, which essentially consists of running the TS_{dppu} transmission scheme, but at a committee level:

$\text{TS}_{\text{dppu}}^{\mathcal{C}}(\mathbf{C_s}, \mathbf{C_r}, \mathbf{T}, \mu, \mathbf{m})$:

1. Committees $\{C_1, \cdots, C_N\}$ view themselves as nodes in the graph G_{dppu}. C_s uses the reliable remote message transmission scheme TS_{dppu} to send message

m to C_r. However, whenever committee C_i is supposed to send message m to committee C_j, such that C_i and C_j are connected by a super-edge, the committees execute the protocol $\text{Send}^{\mathcal{C}}(C_i, C_j, m)$ described below.

2. Let the output of committee C_r be m_r from the above protocol. Every node $u \in C_r$ outputs m_r as the output of the protocol.

$\text{Send}^{\mathcal{C}}(\mathbf{C_i}, \mathbf{C_j}, \mathbf{m})$:

1. Let the nodes in C_i be denoted by $u_1^i, \cdots, u_\gamma^i$ and the nodes in C_j be denoted by $u_1^j, \cdots, u_\gamma^j$. u_l^i sends message m to u_l^j across the edge connecting the two nodes, for all $1 \le l \le \gamma$. Let the value received by u_l^j be denoted by m_l^j.
2. The nodes $u_1^j, \cdots, u_\gamma^j$ execute a differential agreement protocol $\text{DA}(\gamma, \lceil \frac{\gamma}{4} \rceil - 1, \lceil \frac{\gamma}{4} \rceil - 1)$ with inputs $m_1^j, \cdots, m_\gamma^j$. Let the value agreed by honest nodes in C_j be denoted by m'. The output of the committee C_j in the protocol is m'.

The main protocol. Let $u_i, u_j \in V$ be two privileged nodes. u_i is connected to $\beta = d' \log^{k'} n$ helper committees $C_1^{u_i}, \cdots, C_\beta^{u_i}$. In turn, let the nodes in $C_l^{u_i}$ be denoted by $C_l^{u_i}[1], \cdots, C_l^{u_i}[\gamma]$, where $\gamma = k \log \log n$ (likewise for u_j). The protocol for reliable remote message transmission between two privileged nodes u_i and u_j is given below.

$\text{TS}_{\text{low}}(\mathbf{u_i}, \mathbf{u_j}, \mathbf{m})$:

1. For all $1 \le l \le \beta, 1 \le w \le \gamma$, u_i sends $C_l^{u_i}[w]$ the value m using the edge connecting u_i and $C_l^{u_i}[w]$.
2. For all $1 \le l \le \beta$, $C_l^{u_i}$ sends $C_l^{u_j}$ message m using protocol $\text{TS}^{\mathcal{C}}_{\text{dppu}}(C_l^{u_i}, C_l^{u_j}, T, \mu, m)$.
3. For all $1 \le l \le \beta, 1 \le w \le \gamma$, let $m_l^{u_j}[w]$ denote the output of node $C_l^{u_j}[w]$ after execution of protocol $\text{TS}^{\mathcal{C}}_{\text{dppu}}(C_l^{u_i}, C_l^{u_j}, T, \mu, m)$. For all $1 \le l \le \beta, 1 \le w \le \gamma$, $C_l^{u_j}[w]$ sends node u_j the value $m_l^{u_j}[w]$ using the edge connecting $C_l^{u_j}[w]$ and u_j.
4. u_j takes the majority of all $m_l^{u_j}[w]$ values received and outputs this majority (call it m') as the output of the protocol.

3.3 Proof of Correctness

We prove the correctness of our transmission scheme (theorem below) through a series of lemmas that can be found in the full version [7] of this paper.

Theorem 3. *Let u_i and u_j be two privileged nodes in graph G. Then $\text{TS}_{\text{low}}(u_i, u_j, m)$ is a reliable remote message transmission protocol between u_i and u_j.*

To conclude, following the approaches of [10,13], we show in the full version [7] how to use our transmission scheme to achieve a.e. agreement on graph G, and a.e. secure computation on a graph with degree a constant times G's.

References

1. Bagchi, A., Bhargava, A., Chaudhary, A., Eppstein, D., Scheideler, C.: The effect of faults on network expansion. Theory Comput. Syst. 39(6), 903–928 (2006)
2. Ben-Or, M., Goldwasser, S., Wigderson, A.: Completeness theorems for non-cryptographic fault-tolerant distributed computation (extended abstract). In: STOC 1988, pp. 1–10 (1988)
3. Ben-Or, M., Ron, D.: Agreement in the presence of faults, on networks of bounded degree. Information Processing Letters 57, 329–334 (1996)
4. Berman, P., Garay, J.: Asymptotically optimal distributed consensus (extended abstract). In: Ronchi Della Rocca, S., Ausiello, G., Dezani-Ciancaglini, M. (eds.) ICALP 1989. LNCS, vol. 372, pp. 80–94. Springer, Heidelberg (1989)
5. Berman, P., Garay, J.: Fast consensus in networks of bounded degree (extended abstract). In: van Leeuwen, J., Santoro, N. (eds.) WDAG 1990. LNCS, vol. 486, pp. 321–333. Springer, Heidelberg (1991)
6. Bracha, G.: An $O(\log n)$ expected rounds randomized Byzantine generals protocol. In: STOC 1985, pp. 316–326 (1985)
7. Chandran, N., Garay, J., Ostrovsky, R.: Improved fault tolerance and secure computation on sparse networks. CoRR (2010), `http://arxiv.org/`
8. Chaum, D., Crépeau, C., Damgård, I.: Multiparty unconditionally secure protocols (abstract). In: STOC 1988, pp. 11–19 (1988)
9. Dolev, D., Reischuk, R.: Bounds on information exchange for byzantine agreement. In: PODC 1982, pp. 132–140 (1982)
10. Dwork, C., Peleg, D., Pippenger, N., Upfal, E.: Fault tolerance in networks of bounded degree (preliminary version). In: STOC 1986, pp. 370–379 (1986)
11. Fitzi, M., Franklin, M., Garay, J., Vardhan, S.: Towards optimal and efficient perfectly secure message transmission. In: Vadhan, S.P. (ed.) TCC 2007. LNCS, vol. 4392, pp. 311–322. Springer, Heidelberg (2007)
12. Fitzi, M., Garay, J.: Efficient player-optimal protocols for strong and differential consensus. In: PODC 2003, pp. 211–220 (2003)
13. Garay, J., Ostrovsky, R.: Almost-everywhere secure computation. In: Smart, N.P. (ed.) EUROCRYPT 2008. LNCS, vol. 4965, pp. 307–323. Springer, Heidelberg (2008)
14. Guruswami, V., Lee, J., Razborov, A.: Almost euclidean subspaces of ℓ_1^N via expander codes. In: SODA 2008, pp. 353–362 (2008)
15. Hirt, M., Maurer, U.: Player simulation and general adversary structures in perfect multiparty computation. Journal of Cryptology 13(1), 31–60 (2000)
16. King, V., Saia, J.: From almost everywhere to everywhere: Byzantine agreement with $\tilde{O}(n^{3/2})$ bits. In: Keidar, I. (ed.) DISC 2009. LNCS, vol. 5805, pp. 464–478. Springer, Heidelberg (2009)
17. King, V., Saia, J., Sanwalani, V., Vee, E.: Towards secure and scalable computation in peer-to-peer networks. In: FOCS 2006, pp. 87–98 (2006)
18. Lamport, L., Shostak, R., Pease, M.: The Byzantine generals problem. ACM Transactions on Programming Languages and Systems 4(3), 382–401 (1982)
19. Neiger, G.: Distributed consensus revisited. Information Processing Letters 49(4), 195–201 (1994)
20. Ostrovsky, R., Rajagopalan, S., Vazirani, U.: Simple and efficient leader election in the full information model. In: STOC 1994, pp. 234–242 (1994)
21. Pease, M., Shostak, R., Lamport, L.: Reaching agreement in the presence of faults. Journal of the ACM 27, 228–234 (1980)
22. Upfal, E.: Tolerating linear number of faults in networks of bounded degree. In: PODC 1992, pp. 83–89 (1992)
23. Zuckerman, D.: Randomness-optimal sampling, extractors, and constructive leader election. In: STOC 1996, pp. 286–295 (1996)

Sparse Reliable Graph Backbones

Shiri Chechik[1,⋆], Yuval Emek[2,3], Boaz Patt-Shamir[3,⋆⋆], and David Peleg[1,⋆]

[1] Department of Computer Science and Applied Mathematics,
Weizmann Institute of Science, Rehovot, Israel
[2] Microsoft Israel R&D Center, Herzelia, Israel
[3] School of Electrical Engineering, Tel Aviv University, Tel Aviv, Israel

Abstract. Given a connected graph G and a failure probability $p(e)$ for each edge e in G, the *reliability* of G is the probability that G remains connected when each edge e is removed independently with probability $p(e)$. In this paper it is shown that every n-vertex graph contains a sparse *backbone*, i.e., a spanning subgraph with $O(n \log n)$ edges whose reliability is at least $(1 - n^{-\Omega(1)})$ times that of G. Moreover, for any pair of vertices s, t in G, the (s,t)*-reliability* of the backbone, namely, the probability that s and t remain connected, is also at least $(1 - n^{-\Omega(1)})$ times that of G. Our proof is based on a polynomial time randomized algorithm for constructing the backbone. In addition, it is shown that the constructed backbone has nearly the same *Tutte polynomial* as the original graph (in the quarter-plane $x \geq 1$, $y > 1$), and hence the graph and its backbone share many additional features encoded by the Tutte polynomial.

Keywords: network reliability, sparse subgraphs, Tutte polynomial.

1 Introduction

Finding a sparse subgraph that approximately preserves some key attribute of the original graph is fundamental to network algorithms: any lazy network manager would find the capability to maintain fewer links in a large network a precious gift. This can also be considered from the perspective of identifying a set of redundant edges in a graph. Whether an edge is redundant or not depends of course on the attributes that should be preserved. Spanners [14,15] for example, approximately preserve pairwise distances in graphs, with a trade-off spectrum between the quality of approximation and the number of edges in the spanner. The general graph attribute we focus on in the current paper is connectivity under random edge failures.

Specifically, we consider the classical setting of *network reliability*, defined over a graph G whose edges e are associated with *failure* probabilities $p(e)$. The *reliability* of G is the probability that G remains connected when each edge e of G is removed independently with probability $p(e)$. Clearly, the reliability of

⋆ Supported in part by a France-Israel cooperation grant ("Mutli-Computing" project) and by the Israel Science Foundation (grant 894/09).

⋆⋆ Supported in part by the Israel Science Foundation (grant 1372/09) and by the Israel Ministry of Science and Technology.

S. Abramsky et al. (Eds.): ICALP 2010, Part II, LNCS 6199, pp. 261–272, 2010.

a graph is monotone non-increasing with respect to edge removal. We seek a sparse spanning subgraph (containing all vertices and only a small subset of the edges) of G, referred to henceforth as a *backbone*, whose reliability is almost as good as that of G.

Our main result is a randomized algorithm for constructing a backbone with $O(n \log n)$ edges that approximates the reliability of G to within a (multiplicative) factor of $1 - n^{-\Omega(1)}$, where n denotes the number of vertices. The randomized algorithm allows edge multiplicities, so G may have significantly more than $\binom{n}{2}$ edges. This construction is tight: we show that there are graphs whose reliability cannot be approximated to within any positive factor by any subgraph with significantly less than $n \log n$ edges. Moreover, the backbone graph approximates not only the *all-terminal* variant of the reliability (the probability that the whole graph remains connected), but also the *(s, t)-reliability* of G for any two vertices s and t, defined as the probability that s and t remain in the same connected component. Our construction is presented first for the *homogeneous* case, where the failure probability of every edge is some constant $0 < p < 1$, and then extended to the general *heterogeneous* case, assuming that there aren't "too many" edges whose failure probabilities are very close to 1 (see Sect. 3.1 for a precise statement).

It turns out that our backbone also provides a good approximation for the *Tutte polynomial*[1]. Specifically, in the quarter-plane $x \geq 1$, $y > 1$ the Tutte polynomial of the backbone approximates the Tutte polynomial of the original graph to within a factor of $1 \pm n^{-\Omega(1)}$ after multiplying by a (trivially calculated) normalizing factor that accounts for the different number of edges. Since the Tutte polynomial encodes many interesting features of the graph (including its reliability), this result seems to indicate that our backbone construction provides a good representation of the graph in some deeper sense.

Related Work. Network reliability is a fundamental problem in operations research since the early days of that discipline [13]; see the survey [2] for a comprehensive account. It is also well-known in the area of computational complexity; various versions of the network reliability problem are listed among the 14 basic #P-complete problems[2] presented in [18]. In particular, both the all-terminal reliability problem and the (s, t)-reliability problem are known to be #P-hard even when the failure probabilities $p(e)$ are homogeneous. [10] establishes a fully polynomial time randomized approximation scheme (FPRAS) for the problem of evaluating the probability that the graph disconnects under random edge failures. Although this disconnection probability is simply one minus the reliability of the graph, the algorithm of [10] does not translate to a (multiplicative) approximation for the problem of evaluating the reliability. In fact, the approximability of the all-terminal reliability and the (s, t)-reliability problems is still an open question.

[1] The Tutte polynomial $T_G(x, y)$ is a bivariate polynomial whose coefficients are determined by the graph G. See Sect. 5 for details.

[2] The complexity class #P consists of the counting problems whose decision versions are in NP.

A notion somewhat related to ours is that of graph *sparsifiers* [16,17]: An n vertex weighted graph H is said to be a *κ-sparsifier* of an n vertex weighted graph G if $x^T L_G x \leq x^T L_H x \leq \kappa \cdot x^T L_G x$ for every vector $x \in \mathbb{R}^n$, where L_H and L_G are the Laplacian matrices of H and G, respectively. Sparsifiers are a generalization of the *cut-preservers* of [3], that approximately preserve the total weight of edges crossing any cut in the graph. Indeed, the cut-preserving condition corresponds to the sparsifier condition restricted to vectors $x \in \{0,1\}^n$.

One is interested in constructing sparse sparsifiers (hence the name) and the state of the art in that context is the recent construction of $(1+\epsilon)$-sparsifiers with $O(n)$ edges presented in [6]. Note that unlike the backbone constructed in the current paper, sparsifiers are not required to be subgraphs of the original graph. Furthermore, even if a sparsifier edge is present in the original graph, its weight may be different. In fact, there exist unweighted graphs for which every good sparsifier must introduce edges of widely varying weights [17].

A brief overview of the Tutte polynomial is given in Sect. 5. Here we comment that the computational complexity of evaluating the Tutte polynomial on various points $(x, y) \in \mathbb{R}^2$ is almost completely understood. The problem admits an efficient algorithm if $(x, y) \in \{(1,1), (-1,-1), (0,1), (-1,0)\}$ or if $(x-1)(y-1) = 1$; otherwise it is #P-hard [8]. An FPRAS exists for the $y > 0$ portion of the "Ising" hyperbola $(x-1)(y-1) = 2$ [9]; and unless RP = NP, an FPRAS does not exist if $x < -1$ or if $y < -1$ except for the aforementioned easy-to-compute points, the ray $x < -1$, $y = 1$, and the $y < -1$ portion of the hyperbola $(x-1)(y-1) = 2$ [7]. An FPRAS also exists for the quarter-plane $x \geq 1$, $y \geq 1$ if the minimum degree in G is $\Omega(n)$ [1] and for the half-plane $y > 1$ if the size of a minimum cut in G is $\Omega(\log n)$ [10].

Technique. Our backbone construction samples each edge with probability inverse proportional to its *strength*, a parameter closely related to edge connectivity. This technique was introduced in [3] for the construction of sparse cut-preservers. In [3], the weights of the selected edges are then modified to meet the cut-preserving condition. This cannot be done when constructing a backbone: we can only remove edges, and we cannot change intrinsic attributes (namely failure probabilities) of the remaining edges. Nevertheless, we show that with high probability, the resulting backbone approximately preserves the reliability of the original graph. The main ingredient in our analysis is the fact that graphs with logarithmic edge connectivity are highly reliable [12,10]. (Note that we do not make any assumptions on the connectivity of the original graph.) The Tutte polynomial analysis is slightly more involved and it essentially relies on an observation of [1] combined with a theorem of [10].

Paper Organization. The remainder of this paper is organized as follows. Section 2 includes the preliminaries used throughout the paper. The backbone construction is presented in Sect. 3 and the matching lower bound is established in Sect. 4. In Sect. 5 we prove that our backbone also provides a good approximation for the Tutte polynomial.

2 Preliminaries

Unless stated otherwise, all graphs mentioned in this paper are undirected and not necessarily simple (i.e., they may contain parallel edges and self loops). We denote the vertex set and edge set of a graph G by $V(G)$ and $E(G)$, respectively. The graph *induced* on G by a vertex subset $U \subseteq V(G)$ is $G(U) = (U, E(G) \cap (U \times U))$. The graph *induced* on G by an edge subset $F \subseteq E(G)$ is simply $G(F) = (V(G), F)$. Consider some partition of $V(G)$ into $V(G) = U_1 \cup \cdots \cup U_r$ and let $\mathcal{U} = \{U_1, \ldots, U_r\}$. We refer to the edges in $E(G) \cap \bigcup_{i=1}^{r} U_i \times U_i$ as the *internal* edges of $\mathcal{U}$ and to the edges in $E(G) \cap \bigcup_{i \neq j} U_i \times U_j$ as the *external* edges of $\mathcal{U}$.

A *cut* C of a graph G is a partition of $V(G)$ into two non-empty subsets, that is, $C = \{U_1, U_2\}$, where $U_1 \cap U_2 = \emptyset$ and $U_1 \cup U_2 = V(G)$. We say that an edge $e \in E(G)$ *crosses* C if $e \in U_1 \times U_2$. The set of edges crossing C is denoted by $E(C)$. The cardinality $|E(C)|$ is referred to as the *size* of C; if the edges of G are associated with weights, then the total weight of all edges in $E(C)$ is referred to as the *weight* of C. A *min cut* (respectively, *min weight cut*) is a cut of minimum size (resp., weight).

3 Backbone Construction and Reliability Analysis

A *network reliability* instance consists of a connected graph G and a *failure* probability $0 < p(e) < 1$ associated with each edge $e \in E(G)$. The network is assumed to occasionally undergo an *edge failure event* $\mathcal{F}$. Upon such an event, each edge $e \in E(G)$ *fails*, i.e., is removed from the graph, with probability $p(e)$ independently of all other edges. In the *all terminal network reliability* problem, one is interested in the probability that G remains connected following the failure event $\mathcal{F}$, whereas in the *two terminal network reliability* problem one is interested in the probability that two designated vertices s and t remain in the same connected component of G following the event $\mathcal{F}$. The former probability, denoted $\mathrm{REL}(G, p)$, is referred to as the *reliability* of G and the latter, denoted $\mathrm{REL}(G, s, t, p)$, is referred to as the *reliability* of s and t in G.

Our goal in this section is to establish the existence of a backbone with $O(n \log n)$ edges that approximates the reliability of the original graph. We first focus on homogeneous failure probabilities, proving Theorem 1. The extension to heterogeneous failure probabilities is discussed in Sect. 3.1.

Theorem 1. *There exists an efficient randomized algorithm that given a connected graph G, failure probability $0 < p < 1$, and performance parameters $\delta_1, \delta_2 \geq 1$, outputs a backbone G' of G that satisfies the following three requirements with probability $1 - O(n^{-\delta_1})$:*

(1) $|E(G')| = O\left(n \log n \cdot \left(\delta_1 + \frac{\delta_2}{1-p}\right)\right)$*;*
(2) $\mathrm{REL}(G', p) \geq \mathrm{REL}(G, p) \cdot \left(1 - O\left(n^{-\delta_2}\right)\right)$*; and*
(3) $\mathrm{REL}(G', s, t, p) \geq \mathrm{REL}(G, s, t, p) \cdot \left(1 - O\left(n^{-\delta_2}\right)\right)$ *for every* $s, t \in V(G)$*.*

Our technique derives from that presented in [3]; for completeness, we describe some ingredients in detail.

Strong Components. A graph G is said to be *k-connected* if the size of every cut in G is at least k. Fix some vertex subset $U \subseteq V(G)$. The vertex induced subgraph $G(U)$ is called a *k-strong component* of G if it is k-connected and $G(U')$ is not k-connected for any vertex subset $U' \subseteq V(G)$ such that $U' \supsetneq U$. If $G(U_1)$ and $G(U_2)$ are k-strong components of G, then U_1 and U_2 must be disjoint, as otherwise $G(U_1 \cup U_2)$ is k-connected. Therefore if the size of a minimum cut in G is c, then the k-strong components of G for $k = c, c+1, \ldots$ define a laminar family over $V(G)$, that is, G itself is the sole c-strong component, and for every $k \geq c$, the collection $\mathcal{U}_k$ of vertex sets of the k-strong components forms a partition of $V(G)$, refined by the partition $\mathcal{U}_{k+1}$.

The *strength* of an edge $e = (u, v) \in E(G)$, denoted k_e, is defined to be the maximum k such that u and v belong to the same k-strong component of G. Note that $k_e \geq k$ for every internal edge of $\mathcal{U}_k$ and $k_e < k$ for every external edge of $\mathcal{U}_k$. Moreover, if $G(U)$ is a k-strong component, then the strength in $G(U)$ of every edge $e \in E(G) \cap (U \times U)$ is equal to its original strength k_e in G.

Edge Sampling. Consider some n-vertex graph G and let $q : E(G) \to [0, 1]$ be a mapping that assigns some *sampling probability* $q(e)$ to each edge $e \in E(G)$. Given some edge subset $F \subseteq E(G)$, let F^q be a random subset of F that contains each edge $e \in F$ with probability $q(e)$ independently of all other edges and let $G^q = (V(G), E(G)^q)$ be the random graph obtained from G by selecting each edge $e \in E(G)$ in that manner. The *expected graph* $\bar{G}^q$ of G^q is the weighted graph obtained from G by associating a weight $q(e)$ with each edge $e \in E(G)$. As the name implies, for each cut C in G, the weight of C in $\bar{G}^q$ reflects the expected size of C in G^q. The following theorem, established in [11], guarantees that if every cut in the expected graph is sufficiently heavy, then the sizes of cuts in G^q can be "predicted" with high probability.

Theorem 2 ([11]). *Let $\bar{c}$ be the weight of a min weight cut in $\bar{G}^q$ and fix some $0 < \epsilon < 1$ and $d > 0$. If $\bar{c} \geq 3(d + 2)\ln(n)/\epsilon^2$, then with probability $1 - O(n^{-d})$, every cut in G^q has size between $1 - \epsilon$ and $1 + \epsilon$ times its expected size (i.e., its weight in $\bar{G}^q$).*

Consider some r disjoint graphs $G_1, \ldots, G_r$. Let $n_i = |V(G_i)|$ for every $1 \leq i \leq r$ and let $n = \sum_{i=1}^{r} n_i$. For $i = 1, \ldots, r$, let $q_i : E(G_i) \to [0, 1]$ be a mapping that assigns some probability $q_i(e)$ to each edge $e \in E(G_i)$. The statement of Theorem 2 can be extended to hold for all graphs G_i simultaneously:

Corollary 1. *Let $\bar{c}_i$ be the weight of a min weight cut in $\bar{G}_i^{q_i}$ for $i = 1, \ldots, r$ and fix some $0 < \epsilon < 1$ and $d > 0$. If $\min_{1 \leq i \leq r} \bar{c}_i \geq 3(d + 2)\ln(n)/\epsilon^2$, then with probability $1 - O(n^{-d})$, every cut in $G_i^{q_i}$ has size between $1 - \epsilon$ and $1 + \epsilon$ times its expected size (i.e., its weight in $\bar{G}_i^{q_i}$) for all $1 \leq i \leq r$.*

Sampling Edges by their Strength. We now turn to describe Algorithm **SRGB**, performing the actual construction of the sparse reliable backbone.

The algorithm is given an n-vertex graph G with edge failure probability p and two performance parameters $\delta_1, \delta_2 \geq 1$. Let

$$\rho = \left\lceil 12 \ln n \cdot \max\left\{\delta_1 + 2,\, 2\,\frac{\delta_2 + 2}{1 - p}\right\}\right\rceil \tag{1}$$

and define $q(e) = \min\{1, \rho/k_e\}$ for all $e \in E(G)$, where k_e is the strength of e in G. The algorithm constructs the backbone G' of G by selecting each edge $e \in E(G)$ independently with probability $q(e)$, namely, $G' \leftarrow G^q$.

We need to show that Algorithm **SRGB** guarantees the requirements of Theorem 1. The authors of [3] analyze a very similar construction[3] and show, among other things, that $\mathbb{E}[|E(G')|] = \rho(n-1)$. By Chernoff's inequality, the probability that $|E(G')|$ is greater than, say, twice its expected value is exponentially small. Part (1) of Theorem 1 follows. Our goal in the remainder of this section is to prove that with probability $1 - O(n^{-\delta_1})$, the random graph G' satisfies $\mathrm{REL}(G', p) \geq \mathrm{REL}(G, p) \cdot (1 - O(n^{-\delta_2}))$. Proving Part (3) of the theorem, namely, showing that with probability $1 - O(n^{-\delta_1})$ the random graph G' satisfies $\mathrm{REL}(G', s, t, p) \geq \mathrm{REL}(G, s, t, p) \cdot (1 - O(n^{-\delta_2}))$ for every $s, t \in V(G)$, is analogous.

Let $G(U_1), \ldots, G(U_r)$ be the ρ-strong components of G and consider some $G(U_i)$, $1 \leq i \leq r$. Let C be a cut in $G(U_i)$ and let e be some edge in $E(C)$. Recall that the strength of e in $G(U_i)$ is equal to its strength in G, denoted k_e. Since e crosses a cut of size $|C|$ in $G(U_i)$, it follows that $k_e \leq |C|$, thus $\sum_{e \in E(C)} 1/k_e \geq 1$. On the other hand, $G(U_i)$ is ρ-connected, hence $k_e \geq \rho$ and $q(e) = \rho/k_e$. Therefore the weight of C in the expected graph $\bar{G}^q$ is

$$\sum_{e \in E(C)} q(e) = \rho \sum_{e \in E(C)} 1/k_e \geq \rho\,.$$

By Eq. (1), $\rho \geq 12(\delta_1 + 2) \ln n$, so Corollary 1 can be applied to $G(U_1), \ldots, G(U_r)$ to conclude that with probability $1 - O(n^{-\delta_1})$, every cut in $G'(U_i)$, $1 \leq i \leq r$, has size at least $\rho/2$ (probability is w.r.t. the random choices of Algorithm **SRGB**). Since Eq. (1) also implies that $(1-p)\rho/2 \geq 12(\delta_2 + 2) \ln n$, an application of Corollary 1 to $G'(U_1), \ldots, G'(U_r)$ derives[4] that with probability $1 - O(n^{-\delta_2})$, all of these components remain connected following an edge failure event $\mathcal{F}$ (in fact, the size of all cuts decreases by at most half).

Let A (respectively, A') denote the event that G (resp., G') remains connected after an edge failure event $\mathcal{F}$ and let B (resp., B') denote the event that all the components $G(U_1), \ldots, G(U_r)$ (resp., $G'(U_1), \ldots, G'(U_r)$) remain connected after an edge failure event $\mathcal{F}$. We argue that $\mathbb{P}(A') \geq \mathbb{P}(A) \cdot (1 - O(n^{-\delta_2}))$. We know that $\mathbb{P}(B') \geq 1 - O(n^{-\delta_2})$ and by definition, $\mathbb{P}(B') \leq \mathbb{P}(B) \leq 1$. Let $\mathcal{E}_X \subseteq E(G)$ be the set of all edges external to $\{U_1, \ldots, U_r\}$. Note that every

[3] The construction in [3] assigns (new) weights to the edges of the random graph, and hence its analysis requires some additional complications.

[4] The fact that components of large edge connectivity admit high reliability was originally discovered by [12] and later on restated in [10]. Using their frameworks instead of Corollary 1 would have resulted in slightly better constants.

edge $e \in \mathcal{E}_X$ has strength $k_e < \rho$ in G, and therefore was selected by Algorithm **SRGB** with probability 1. It follows that all those edges are included in G', i.e., $\mathcal{E}_X \subseteq E(G')$, and thus $\mathbb{P}(A' \mid B') = \mathbb{P}(A \mid B) \geq \mathbb{P}(A \mid \neg B)$. The argument follows by rewriting

$$\mathbb{P}(A') \geq \mathbb{P}(A' \mid B') \cdot \mathbb{P}(B') \geq \mathbb{P}(A \mid B) \cdot (1 - O(n^{-\delta_2}))$$

and

$$\mathbb{P}(A) \leq \mathbb{P}(A \mid B) + \mathbb{P}(A \mid \neg B) \cdot \mathbb{P}(\neg B) \leq \mathbb{P}(A \mid B) \cdot (1 + O(n^{-\delta_2})) .$$

This completes the proof of part (2) of Theorem 1 as $\mathrm{REL}(G, p) = \mathbb{P}(A)$ and $\mathrm{REL}(G', p) = \mathbb{P}(A')$.

Las-Vegas Implementation. As discussed above, our algorithm satisfies all three requirements with very high probability. However, once invoking the algorithm on some instance graph G, one may wish to *ensure* that indeed all three requirements are satisfied. As stated above, the approximability of the all-terminal reliability and (s, t)-reliability problems is still an open question. So, it may seem hopeless to be able to check if requirements (2) and (3) indeed hold for a specific invocation of our algorithm. However, following our line of arguments, one can see that to guarantee that requirements (2) and (3) hold, it suffices to check that the minimal cut in all ρ-strong components $G(U_1), \ldots, G(U_r)$ is at least $\rho/2$. This, of course, can be done in polynomial time.

Running Time. The running time of our algorithm is dominated by finding the strength of the edges. It is not hard to see that this can be done in polynomial time (by hierarchically decomposing the graph via n minimum cut computations). However, this could be too slow for certain applications. Luckily, our algorithm does not require the exact values k_e; rather, one can settle for approximate values $\tilde{k}_e$ satisfying some properties. This can be done, using some ideas presented in [3], so as to improve the overall running time to $O(m \log^2 n)$.

3.1 Heterogeneous Failure Probabilities

We now turn to discuss the heterogeneous case, where each edge e has a different failure probability $p(e)$. It's not hard to verify that setting $\rho = \left\lceil 12 \ln n \cdot \max\left\{\delta_1 + 2,\, 2\, \frac{\delta_2 + 2}{1 - \hat{p}}\right\}\right\rceil$, where $\hat{p}$ is the highest failure probability in G, yields the same analysis and results as for the homogeneous case. However, if $\hat{p}$ is close to 1, then this would result in a backbone G' with too many edges. Consider, for example, an arbitrary graph G^- where all edges have the same (constant) failure probability $0 < p < 1$, and augment it into a graph G by adding a single new edge with very high failure probability, say, $\hat{p} = 1 - 1/n^2$. Clearly, applying Algorithm **SRGB** to G^- will generate, with probability at least $1 - O(n^{-\delta_1})$, a backbone G'^- with $O(n \log n)$ edges such that $\mathrm{REL}(G'-, p) \geq \mathrm{REL}(G, p) \cdot (1 - O(n^{-\delta_2}))$. Using the algorithm with $\hat{p}$, however, will yield a very high value for ρ, and the resulting backbone G' is likely to contain $\Omega(n^2)$ edges.

Hence we are interested in constructing a backbone G' with $O(n \log n)$ edges that approximates the reliability of G even when some of the failure probabilities are close to 1. We show that if the average failure probability of every cut in G is at most $\bar{p}$, then it is possible to construct a backbone G' such that with probability at least $1 - O(n^{-\delta_1})$, G' has $O\left(\frac{n \log n}{1-\bar{p}}\left(\delta_1 + \frac{\delta_2}{1-\bar{p}}\right)\right)$ edges and $\mathrm{REL}(G', p) \geq \mathrm{REL}(G, p) \cdot (1 - O(n^{-\delta_2}))$. This is depicted by the following theorem whose proof is deferred to the full version of this paper.

Theorem 3. *There exists an efficient randomized algorithm that given a connected graph G, failure probability $p(e)$ for each $e \in E(G)$, where the average failure probability of every cut in G is at most $\bar{p}$, and performance parameters $\delta_1, \delta_2 \geq 1$, outputs a backbone G' of G that satisfies the following three requirements with probability $1 - O(n^{-\delta_1})$:*

(1) $|E(G')| = O\left(\frac{n \log(n)}{1-\bar{p}}\left(\delta_1 + \frac{\delta_2}{1-\bar{p}}\right)\right)$*;*
(2) $\mathrm{REL}(G', p) \geq \mathrm{REL}(G, p) \cdot \left(1 - O\left(n^{-\delta_2}\right)\right)$*; and*
(3) $\mathrm{REL}(G', s, t, p) \geq \mathrm{REL}(G, s, t, p) \cdot \left(1 - O\left(n^{-\delta_2}\right)\right)$ *for every choice of* $s, t \in V(G)$*.*

4 A Tight Lower Bound

We now turn to show that the $O(n \log n)$ upper bound on the number of edges is indeed tight. Consider some graph G and let $\mathcal{S}_G$ be the collection of all spanning subgraphs of G. Given some failure probability $0 < p < 1$ and some real $\epsilon > 0$, let

$$\psi_{p,\epsilon}(G) = \max\left\{\mathrm{REL}(H, p) \mid H \in \mathcal{S}_G, |E(H)| \leq (1-\epsilon) n \log_{1/p} n\right\} .$$

We establish the following theorem.

Theorem 4. *For every failure probability $0 < p < 1$, the family $\{K_{n,n}\}_{n=1}^{\infty}$ of complete bipartite graphs with n vertices on each side satisfies*

(1) $\lim_{n\to\infty} \mathrm{REL}(K_{n,n}, p) = 1$*; and*
(2) for every constant $\epsilon > 0$, $\lim_{n\to\infty} \psi_{p,\epsilon}(K_{n,n}) = 0$.

Proof. Requirement (1) is immediately satisfied by Theorem 2, so it remains to establish requirement (2). To that end, fix some n and consider some constant $\epsilon > 0$ and some spanning subgraph H of $K_{n,n}$ such that $|E(H)| \leq (1-\epsilon) n \log_{1/p} n$. The subgraph H is bipartite as well; let $Z = \{v_1, \ldots, v_k\}$ be the set of vertices of degree at most $(1 - \epsilon/2) \log_{1/p} n$ on its left side. By a straightforward counting argument, $k \geq n\left(1 - \frac{1-\epsilon}{1-\epsilon/2}\right) > \epsilon n/2$.

Let A_i be the event that v_i becomes an isolated vertex under an edge failure event $\mathcal{F}$. By definition, $\mathbb{P}(A_i) \geq p^{(1-\epsilon/2)\log_{1/p} n} = n^{-(1-\epsilon/2)}$. Since H is bipartite, the events $A_1, \ldots, A_k$ are independent (each determined by a disjoint set of edges), hence the probability that none of them occurs is at most

$$\left(1 - n^{-(1-\epsilon/2)}\right)^k \leq \left(1 - n^{-(1-\epsilon/2)}\right)^{\epsilon n/2} \leq e^{-\epsilon n^{\epsilon/2}/2} ,$$

which tends to 0 as $n \to \infty$. The assertion follows as $\mathrm{REL}(H, p) \leq \mathbb{P}(\neg A_1 \wedge \cdots \wedge \neg A_k)$. □

5 The Tutte Polynomial of the Backbone

The Tutte polynomial, introduced by W.T. Tutte, is a bivariate polynomial whose coefficients are determined by a given graph. The Tutte polynomial is a central concept in algebraic graph theory, as it captures many interesting properties of the graph from which it is derived. [4] gives a relatively updated treatment of the concept. Below, we only review the basic definitions and some key results.

Let G be a graph. The Tutte polynomial of G at point $(x, y) \in \mathbb{R}^2$, denoted $T_G(x, y)$, is defined by

$$T_G(x, y) = \sum_{F \subseteq E(G)} (x-1)^{K(F)-K(G)} (y-1)^{K(F)+|F|-n} ,$$

where $n = |V(G)|$, and for $F \subseteq E(G)$, $K(F)$ denotes the number of connected components in the graph $(V(G), F)$, and $K(G) = K(E(G))$. The Tutte polynomial contains many interesting points and lines that capture combinatorial features of the graph G, including:

- $T_G(1, 1)$ counts the number of spanning trees of G.
- $T_G(2, 1)$ counts the number of spanning forests of G.
- $T_G(1, 2)$ counts the number of connected spanning subgraphs of G.
- At $y = 0$ and $x = 1-\lambda$ for positive integer λ, the Tutte polynomial specializes to yield the *chromatic polynomial* $\chi_G(\lambda) = (-1)^{n-K(G)} \lambda^{K(G)} T_G(1-\lambda, 0)$ that counts the number of legal vertex colorings of G using λ colors.
- At $x = 1$ and $y = 1/(1-p)$ for $0 < p < 1$, the Tutte polynomial specializes to yield the reliability of G, $\mathrm{REL}(G, p) = (1-p)^{|E(G)|-n+1} p^{n-1} T_G(1, 1/(1-p))$.
- Along the hyperbolas $(x-1)(y-1) = s$ for any positive integer s, the Tutte polynomial specializes to the partition function of the s-state *Potts model* of statistical mechanics.

The reader is referred to the survey [5] for more interpretations.

Our goal in this section is to prove the following theorem.

Theorem 5. *For every point (x, y) in the quarter-plane $x \geq 1$, $y > 1$, there exists an efficient randomized algorithm that given a connected graph G and performance parameters $\delta_1, \delta_2 \geq 1$, outputs a backbone G' of G that satisfies the following two requirements with probability $1 - O(n^{-\delta_1})$:*

(1) $|E(G')| = O\left(n\log(n)\left(\delta_1 + \frac{\delta_2}{1-1/y}\right)\right)$; *and*
(2) $T_G(x,y) \cdot \left(1 - O\left(n^{-\delta_2}\right)\right) \le y^{|E(G)|-|E(H)|} \cdot T_{G'}(x,y) \le T_G(x,y) \cdot \left(1 + O\left(n^{-\delta_2}\right)\right)$.

Note first that along the ray $x = 1$, $y > 1$, the Tutte polynomial of G specializes to the reliability of G following the identity

$$\mathrm{REL}(G,p) = (1-p)^{|E(G)|-n+1}p^{n-1}T_G(1, 1/(1-p)) .$$

Therefore when $x = 1$, Theorem 5 follows directly from Theorem 1. Assume hereafter that $x > 1$.

Fix $q = 1-1/y$. The construction of G' is identical to that described in Sect. 3 when setting $p = 1 - q$. In Sect. 3 we argued that with very high probability, $|E(G')| = O(n\rho)$, which implies requirement (1) of Theorem 5 by the choice of ρ. Our goal in the remainder of this section is to prove that requirement (2) holds with probability $1 - O(n^{-\delta_1})$.

The authors of [1] observe that in the quarter-plane $x > 1$, $y > 1$, the Tutte polynomial of a connected graph G with n vertices and m edges can be expressed as

$$T_G(x,y) = \frac{y^m}{(x-1)(y-1)^n}\mathbb{E}\left[z^{K(G^q)}\right] ,$$

where $z = (x-1)(y-1)$. Theorem 5 will be established by showing that $\mathbb{E}[z^{K(G^q)}] \approx \mathbb{E}[z^{K(G'^q)}]$.

Let $G(U_1), \ldots, G(U_r)$ be the ρ-strong components of G and Let $\mathcal{E}_X \subseteq E(G)$ be the set of all edges external to $\{U_1, \ldots, U_r\}$. Consider the collection $\mathcal{H}$ of all spanning subgraphs H of G such that

(1) $\mathcal{E}_X \subseteq E(H)$; and
(2) $H(U_i)$ is $(\rho/2)$-connected for every $1 \le i \le r$.

By definition, G itself is in $\mathcal{H}$. Recall that G' contains all edges whose strength in G is smaller than ρ. Eq. (1) implies that $\rho \ge 12(\delta_1+2)\ln n$, thus we can follow the line of arguments used in Sect. 3 and apply Corollary 1 to $G(U_1), \ldots, G(U_r)$ to conclude that with probability $1-O(n^{-\delta_1})$, G' is also in $\mathcal{H}$, where the probability is taken with respect to the random choices of Algorithm **SRGB**. Our analysis relies on showing that $\mathbb{E}[z^{K(H^q)}]$ is approximately the same for all graphs $H \in \mathcal{H}$.

Consider an arbitrary graph $H \in \mathcal{H}$. Partition the edges of H into $E(H) = \mathcal{E}_I \cup \mathcal{E}_X$, where $\mathcal{E}_I = \bigcup_{i=1}^{r} E(H) \cap (U_i \times U_i)$ and $\mathcal{E}_X = E(H) - \mathcal{E}_I$. We express $\mathbb{E}[z^{K(H^q)}]$ as

$$\mathbb{E}\left[z^{K(H^q)}\right] = \sum_{F \subseteq \mathcal{E}_X} \mathbb{E}\left[z^{K(H^q)} \mid \mathcal{E}_X^q = F\right] \cdot \mathbb{P}\left(\mathcal{E}_X^q = F\right)$$

and establish Theorem 5 by proving that

$$\mathbb{E}\left[z^{K(H^q)} \mid \mathcal{E}_X^q = F\right] = z^{K_F}\left(1 \pm O\left(n^{-\delta_2}\right)\right)$$

for every $F \subseteq \mathcal{E}_X$, where $K_F = K(V(H), \mathcal{E}_I \cup F)$ denotes the number of connected components in the graph induced on H by the edges in $\mathcal{E}_I \cup F$.

Assume first that $0 < z \leq 1$. By Eq. (1), $q\rho/2 \geq 12(\delta_2+2)\ln n$, thus an application of Corollary 1 to $H(U_1),\ldots,H(U_r)$ implies that with probability $1-O(n^{-\delta_2})$, all these components remain connected, where the probability is taken with respect to the experiment H^q. Therefore

$$z^{K_F}\left(1-O\left(n^{-\delta_2}\right)\right) \leq \mathbb{E}\left[z^{K(H^q)} \mid \mathcal{E}_X^q = F\right] \leq z^{K_F}$$

which establishes the assertion.

Now, assume that $z > 1$ and fix some edge subset $F \subseteq \mathcal{E}_X$. Let $\Gamma = (V(H), \mathcal{E}_I^q \cap F)$ be the random graph obtained from H by taking the edges in F and selecting each edge $e \in \mathcal{E}_I$ independently with probability q. Let $H_I = (V(H), \mathcal{E}_I)$ be the graph induced on H by the edges in $\mathcal{E}_I$ and let $\kappa = K(H_I^q) - K(H_I)$ be a random variable that takes on the number of connected components "added" to H_I due to the experiment H_I^q. We have

$$\begin{aligned}
z^{K_F} \leq \mathbb{E}\left[z^{K(H^q)} \mid \mathcal{E}_X^q = F\right] &= \sum_{j\geq 0} \mathbb{P}\left(K(\Gamma) = K_F + j\right) \cdot z^{K_F+j} \\
= z^{K_F} \cdot \sum_{j\geq 0} \mathbb{P}\left(K(\Gamma) = K_F + j\right) \cdot z^j &\leq z^{K_F} \cdot \sum_{j\geq 0} \mathbb{P}\left(K(\Gamma) \geq K_F + j\right) \cdot z^j \\
\leq z^{K_F} \cdot \sum_{j\geq 0} \mathbb{P}\left(\kappa \geq j\right) \cdot z^j &= z^{K_F}\left(1 + \sum_{j\geq 1} \mathbb{P}\left(\kappa \geq j\right) \cdot z^j\right),
\end{aligned}$$

where the last inequality follows from the definition of κ as the event $K(\Gamma) \geq K_F + j$ cannot occur unless $\kappa \geq j$. It remains to show that $\sum_{j\geq 1} \mathbb{P}(\kappa \geq j) \cdot z^j = O(n^{-\delta_2})$. The following theorem is established in [10].

Theorem 6 ([10]). *Let G be a connected n-vertex graph and let c be the size of a minimum cut in G. Fix some reals $d > 1$ and $q \in [0,1]$ and integer $t \geq 2$. If $c \geq (d+2)\log_{1/(1-q)} n$, then $\mathbb{P}(K(G^q) \geq t) < n^{-dt/2}$.*

Theorem 6 can be extended to yield the following corollary by following the same "black-box" type of argument employed in the proof of Corollary 1.

Corollary 2. *Consider some r disjoint graphs $G_1,\ldots,G_r$. Let $n_i = |V(G_i)|$ for every $1 \leq i \leq r$ and let $n = \sum_{i=1}^r n_i$. Let c_i be the size of a minimum cut in G_i for $i = 1,\ldots,r$. Set $\tilde{G} = (\bigcup_{i=1}^r V(G_i), \bigcup_{i=1}^r E(G_i))$. Fix some reals $d > 1$ and $q \in [0,1]$ and integer $t \geq 2$. If $\min_{1\leq i\leq r} c_i \geq (d+2)\log_{1/(1-q)} n$, then $\mathbb{P}(K(\tilde{G}^q) \geq r+t-1) < n^{-dt/2}$.*

Recall that we wish to show that $\sum_{j\geq 1} \mathbb{P}(\kappa \geq j) \cdot z^j = O(n^{-\delta_2})$. Eq. (1) yields $\rho/2 \geq 12(\delta_2+2)\ln(n)/q > (\delta_2+2)\log_{1/(1-q)} n$, so we can use Corollary 2 to deduce that $\mathbb{P}(\kappa \geq j) < n^{-\delta_2(j+1)/2}$. Therefore

$$\begin{aligned}
\sum_{j\geq 1} \mathbb{P}(\kappa \geq j) \cdot z^j < \sum_{j\geq 1} n^{-\delta_2(j+1/2)} \cdot z^j &= z^{-1} \cdot \sum_{j\geq 2}\left(zn^{-\delta_2/2}\right)^j \\
&= z^{-1} \cdot \frac{\left(zn^{-\delta_2/2}\right)^2}{1-zn^{-\delta_2/2}} \leq 2zn^{-\delta_2},
\end{aligned}$$

where the last inequality follows by assuming that n is sufficiently large so that $zn^{-\delta_2/2} \leq 1/2$. This completes the proof of Theorem 5.

References

1. Alon, N., Frieze, A., Welsh, D.: Polynomial time randomized approximation schemes for Tutte-Gröthendieck invariants: the dense case. Random Struct. Algorithms 6(4), 459–478 (1995)
2. Ball, M.O., Colbourn, C.J., Provan, J.S.: Network reliability. In: Handbook of Operations Research: Network Models, pp. 673–762. Elsevier North-Holland (1995)
3. Benczúr, A., Karger, D.R.: Approximating $s-t$ minimum cuts in $\tilde{O}(n^2)$ time. In: Proc. 28th ACM Symp. on the Theory of Computing (STOC), pp. 47–55 (1996)
4. Bollobás, B.: Modern Graph Theory. Graduate texts in mathematics. Springer, Berlin (1998)
5. Brylawski, T.H., Oxley, J.G.: The Tutte polynomial and its applications. In: White, N. (ed.) Matroid Applications, pp. 123–225. Cambridge Univ. Press, Cambridge (1992)
6. Batson, J.D., Spielman, D.A., Srivastava, N.: Twice-ramanujan sparsifiers. In: Proc. of the 41st ACM Symp. on Theory of Computing (STOC), pp. 255–262 (2009)
7. Goldberg, L.A., Jerrum, M.: Inapproximability of the Tutte polynomial. Inf. Comput. 206(7), 908–929 (2008)
8. Jaeger, F., Vertigan, D.L., Welsh, D.J.A.: On the computational complexity of the Jones and Tutte polynomials. Math. Proc. Camb. Phil. SOC. 108, 35–53 (1990)
9. Jerrum, M., Sinclair, A.: Polynomial-time approximation algorithms for the Ising model. SIAM J. Comput. (SICOMP) 22(5), 1087–1116 (1993)
10. Karger, D.R.: A randomized fully polynomial time approximation scheme for the all-terminal network reliability problem. SIAM J. Comput. (SICOMP) 29(2), 492–514 (1999)
11. Karger, D.R.: Random sampling in cut, flow, and network design problems. Mathematics of Operations Research (MOR) 24(2), 383–413 (1999)
12. Lomonosov, M.V., Polesskii, V.P.: Lower bound of network reliability. Probl. Peredachi Inf. 8(2), 47–53 (1972)
13. Moore, E.F., Shannon, C.E.: Reliable circuits using less reliable relays. J. Franklin Inst. 262, 191–208, 263, 281–297 (1956)
14. Peleg, D., Schäffer, A.A.: Graph spanners. J. of Graph Theory 13, 99–116 (1989)
15. Peleg, D., Ullman, J.D.: An optimal synchronizer for the hypercube. SIAM J. on Computing 18, 740–747 (1989)
16. Spielman, D.A., Teng, S.-H.: Nearly-linear time algorithms for graph partitioning, graph sparsification, and solving linear systems. In: Proc. of the 36th ACM Symp. on Theory of Computing (STOC), pp. 81–90 (2004)
17. Spielman, D.A., Teng, S.-H.: Spectral sparsification of graphs (2008), `http://arxiv.org/abs/0808.4134`
18. Valiant, L.G.: The complexity of enumeration and reliability problems. SIAM J. Comput. (SICOMP) 8(3), 410–421 (1979)

Approximation Algorithms for Diversified Search Ranking

Nikhil Bansal[1], Kamal Jain[2], Anna Kazeykina[3], and Joseph (Seffi) Naor[4,⋆]

[1] IBM Research, Yorktown Heights, NY 10598
nikhil@us.ibm.com
[2] Microsoft Research, Redmond, WA 98052
kamalj@microsoft.com
[3] Moscow State University, Moscow, Russian Federation
filledesoleil@gmail.com
[4] Computer Science Dept., Technion, Haifa, Israel
naor@cs.technion.ac.il

Abstract. A fundamental issue in Web search is ranking search results based on user logs, since different users may have different preferences and intents with regards to a search query. Also, in many search query applications, users tend to look at only the top part of the ranked result list in order to find relevant documents. The setting we consider contains various types of users, each of which is interested in a subset of the search results. The goal is to rank the search results of a query providing highly ranked relevant results. Our performance measure is the *discounted cumulative gain* which offers a graded relevance scale of documents in a search engine result set, and measures the usefulness (gain) of a document based on its position in the result list. Based on this measure, we suggest a general approach to developing approximation algorithms for ranking search results that captures different aspects of users' intents. We also take into account that the relevance of one document cannot be treated independently of the relevance of other documents in a collection returned by a search engine. We first consider the scenario where users are interested in only a single search result (e.g., navigational queries). We then develop a polynomial time approximation scheme for this case. We further consider the general case where users have different requirements on the number of search results, and develop efficient approximation algorithms. Finally, we consider the problem of choosing the top k out of n search results and show that for this problem $(1-1/e)$ is indeed the best approximation factor achievable, thus separating the approximability of the two versions of the problem.

1 Introduction

Satisfying users querying a search engine has become immensely complex given the rapid growth of the Internet, its content diversity, and its usage as a primary

⋆ Most of this work was done while visiting Microsoft Research, Redmond, WA. This work was partly supported by ISF grant 1366/07.

S. Abramsky et al. (Eds.): ICALP 2010, Part II, LNCS 6199, pp. 273–284, 2010.

source of information. The satisfaction of users with search results has traditionally been characterized by the notion of *relevance* of a document. Since users tend to look only at the top part of a ranked result list in order to find relevant documents, ranking search results is a fundamental problem in Web search. The goal is to rank the search results of a query providing highly ranked relevant results. A common performance metric for relevance is the *discounted cumulative gain* [8,10] which offers a graded relevance scale of documents in a search engine result set, and measures the usefulness (gain) of a document based on its position in the result list. The gain is accumulated cumulatively, starting from the top of the result list, with the gain of each result discounted at lower ranks.

Recent approaches to ranking search results have placed more emphasis on inferring relevance and intents of queries from user logs and understanding the distribution of users running a query. One major issue that arises here is that most queries have multiple intents[1], since different users may have different preferences, and therefore a ranking system should provide diverse results that cover a wide spectrum of intents.

It is common practice to partition search queries into three broad categories [10]. The first one is an *informational query*, in which users typically try to assimilate information from multiple web pages. The second one is a *navigational query* where a user looks for a particular (single) website among the search results. The third one is a *transactional query* which is typically a prelude to a transaction on the web. Note that the categories differ (among other things) in the number of search results needed to satisfy a user.

We suggest the following approach for quantifying aggregate user satisfaction. Assume that for a particular search query a set of search results is obtained. There are several user types, corresponding to the multiple intents associated with the query, each of which is a-priori known to be interested in a (known) subset of the results. For each user type we assume that we know the number of relevant search results needed to satisfy it. This number depends, among other things, on the category to which the query belongs. The question is which order should the search results be ranked in, so that all user types are satisfied, and the discounted cumulative gain is maximized. As explained later, this problem turns out to be computationally intractable, and thus we develop approximation algorithms for it.

So far we have made the common assumption that the relevance of one document can be treated independently of the relevance of other documents in the collection returned by a search engine. Carbonell and Goldstein [4] were among the first to note that documents retrieved by a search engine are not necessarily informationally independent and are frequently characterized by a high level of redundancy. Thus, the relevance of a document should be replaced by its

[1] For example, users searching for "cricket" could be interested in different things: the insect, the sport, the wireless company, ..., etc. Similarly, even for unambiguous queries such as for some researcher's name, say "John Smith", different users might have different intents. Some might be interested in his list of publications, some in his Facebook account, some in his personal web page and so on.

marginal relevance with respect to other documents in a collection [4,11,14]. In [4] it is suggested to maximize marginal relevance (MMR), which is a ranking method that maximizes a linear combination of the relevance of a document and its novelty (a measure of diversity) with respect to already retrieved documents. User studies have shown that MMR is generally preferred to a standard ranking algorithm.

Chen and Karger [6] introduced a probabilistic approach to the relevance problem in which, given a probabilistic metric, the expected value of the metric is optimized. For a variety of metrics used in information retrieval (search length, reciprocal rank, %no, and instance recall), they showed that the optimization problem is computationally intractable. They empirically studied the performance of greedy algorithms and suggested the study of more sophisticated approximation techniques as future work on the topic.

The work of Agrawal et al. [1] is the closest to ours. The authors define their objective function as maximizing the probability of satisfying an average user. They observed that the optimized function is submodular and proposed to use a greedy algorithm to obtain a $(1 - 1/e)$-approximate solution. However, [1] implicitly assumed that users study all the documents returned by a search engine with equal attention, while (as we argued) it is more reasonable to assume the attention decreases while going through the list of results from top to bottom.

1.1 The Model

We assume that there exists a taxonomy of information, and that user intents are modeled at the topical level of this taxonomy. Let us focus on a single search query. Denote the search results by $e_1, \ldots, e_n$ and suppose that there are m user types, or intents. For each user type there is a subset of the search results which are relevant to this type. We model our setting as a hypergraph or an instance of the hitting set problem. The search results correspond to elements $e_1, \ldots, e_n$ in a universe U and each user type corresponds to a set, or a hyperedge, containing the elements in which the user type is interested. The collection of sets is denoted by $\mathcal{S} = \{S_1, \ldots, S_m\}$. For each set S there is a coverage requirement, denoted by $k(S)$, corresponding to the number of relevant search results needed to satisfy user type S. Recall that $k(S) = 1$ corresponds to a navigational query, and $k(S)$ corresponds to an informational query. Given an ordering ϕ of the elements $e_1, \ldots, e_n$, set S is covered at the earliest time (position) $t(S)$ in which $k(S)$ elements from S have already appeared. The goal is to find an ordering maximizing the discounted cumulative gain (DCG):

$$\mathrm{DCG} = \sum_{S} \frac{1}{\log(t(S) + 1)}.$$

The logarithmic factor in the denominator is to the base e and it is the *discount factor* of the gain of each search result. Intuitively, elements that can provide coverage to many sets should be placed in the beginning of the ordering ϕ so as to maximize the objective function. One can consider more general discounting functions but the logarithmic discounting seems to be most commonly considered in practice [8, Chapter 8.4.3]. We consider this problem in two settings. First, when there is an bound on the number of elements k that must be chosen. This is motivated by the problem of choosing which query results to display on the first page. Second, when there is no bound on the number of pages to display.

In the case of $k(S) = 1$, we can further consider a more general model when one can model correlations between different search results using information theoretical tools. Given a query q and the set of search results $e_1, e_2, \ldots, e_n$, we define the information function $H_q(e_1, e_2, \ldots, e_n)$ that captures the overall knowledge about q that can be obtained from observing all the search results in the set. For any subset S of search results define $H_q(S)$ to be the function capturing the information about query q contained in S. We assume that $H_q(S)$ has the following entropy properties:

1. $H_q(\emptyset) = 0$;
2. $H_q(S) \leq H_q(T), \quad \forall S \subseteq T$ (*monotonicity*);
3. $H_q(S \cup e) - H_q(S) \geq H_q(T \cup e) - H_q(T), \quad \forall S \subseteq T,\ e \notin T$ (*submodularity*).

For a ranked list of search results, the *marginal relevance* (MR) of result e_i is:

$$\mathrm{MR}(e_i) = H_q(\{e_1, \ldots, e_i\}) - H_q(\{e_1, \ldots, e_{i-1}\}).$$

Since most currently used evaluation metrics in information retrieval make use of relevance labels assigned to search results, we get a natural generalization of these metrics by substituting the relevance of e_i by its marginal relevance $\mathrm{MR}(e_i)$. Then, the generalization of DCG is:

$$\mathrm{GDCG} = \sum_{i=1}^{n} \frac{H_q(\{e_1, \ldots, e_i\}) - H_q(\{e_1, \ldots, e_{i-1}\})}{\log(i+1)}. \tag{1}$$

Note that GDCG captures the model of Agrawal et al. [1], as well as probabilistic ranking models.

1.2 Our Results

We first consider the problem of *choosing* and *ordering* the top k out of n search results so as to maximize the DCG, where k is an input to the problem. We show that for the case in which users are only interested in a single search result, a natural greedy algorithm achieves an approximation factor of $(1 - 1/e) \approx 0.632$. Moreover, we show that this is the best approximation factor achievable, assuming P $\neq$ NP. Our $(1 - 1/e)$ approximation also holds for the more general GDCG measure where each user type can have a monotone submodular utility function (satisfying the properties stated in Section 1.1) over the set of search results. Finally, for the case where the users can be interested in an arbitrary number of search results, i.e. $k(S)$ is arbitrary, we show that the problem is hard in the following sense. It is at least as hard as the notorious Densest-k-Subgraph problem for which the best known approximation is only $O(n^{1/3})$ [9].

Next, we consider the above models in the setting where there is no restriction on the number of search results that we wish to display. Most of our paper is devoted to this setting. In particular, the goal is to simply to find an ordering of all n results maximizing GDCG.

For the case of $k(S) = 1$ (i.e., navigational queries), we develop an approximation algorithm that yields a polynomial-time approximation scheme (ptas). That is, the algorithm achieves a $(1 + \varepsilon)$ approximation given any arbitrarily small constant $\epsilon > 0$, and has running time polynomial in n. This approximation scheme also generalizes to the more general GDCG setting. (I.e., with the Informational function $H_q(S)$.)

For the case of arbitrary values of $k(S)$, we give a linear programming based $O(\log \log n)$-approximation. We also show how to adapt these ideas to obtain a quasi-polynomial time approximation scheme[2]. The natural linear programming relaxations for this problem have a large integrality gap. We go around this by strengthening the relaxation by adding exponentially many so-called *knapsack cover inequalities* [5]. Even though the number of constraints is exponential, it can be solved optimally in polynomial time. Our approximation algorithm is based on rounding these fractional solutions and exploits various properties of the problem structure. While our approach is related to recent work of [3], there are major differences. In particular, while [3] considers a minimization problem, ours is a maximization problem, which does not seem amenable to a local term-by-term analysis as in [3], and we need a much more complex and global analysis.

Our results can be viewed as showing a strong separation between the two versions of the problem, depending on whether the number of search results to be displayed is fixed or not.

1.3 Related Work

Our modeling of user types as hyperedges with a covering demand follows the work of Azar et al. [2]. They defined a model for re-ranking search results where the goal is to minimize the average time (in a certain sense) of satisfying user types. Their model generalizes classic problems like minimum sum set cover and minimum latency. They developed logarithmic approximation factors for their problem using a linear programming formulation. The approximation factor was improved to a constant by Bansal et al. [3] who strengthened the linear program by adding knapsack cover constraints.

Generating a diverse set of search result is a well studied topic and we mention a few relevant papers. Accounting for different meanings of ambiguous queries and document redundancy was considered by Zhai et al. [14], who proposed a generalization of the classic precision and recall metrics. Ziegler et al. [15] considered the diversification of personalized recommendation lists by reducing the intralist similarity (the sum of pairwise similarities between items in the list). Their user study showed that increased diversity of the recommendation list improved user satisfaction, but also revealed that human perception can capture the level of diversification inherent to a list only to some extent. Beyond that point, increasing diversity remains unnoticed.

[2] A $(1 + \epsilon)$-approximation for any constant $\epsilon > 0$ with a running time of $n^{\mathrm{polylog}(n)}$.

Radlinski and Dumais [11] studied the problem in the context of query reformulations. They proposed to build a diversified set of related queries and then provide the top N results retrieved for each query as an input to a standard ranking algorithm. Relevant studies were also carried out in the domain of online shopping, relational databases [13], and online learning algorithms [12].

In the field of question answering, Clarke et al. [7] developed a probabilistic ranking principle by viewing documents as sets of "information nuggets". They measured the relevance of a document as the probability that it contains at least one relevant and new information nugget. Then, they presented a generalization of the DCG metric and proved that the computation of the ideal gain is NP-hard.

2 Unit Covering Requirements

In this section we consider the case when all the covering requirements $k(S)$ are equal to 1. We will give an approximation scheme for maximizing GDCG. However, it will be easier to describe the scheme in the simpler setting of independent search results where we maximize DCG. The generalization to GDCG is quite straightforward.

2.1 Top k Out of n Documents

We first describe a simple and efficient greedy algorithm for maximizing the gain (GDCG) by choosing and ordering k out of n documents. The greedy algorithm simply chooses at each step the element that maximizes the incremental profit. The proof of the next statement is left out due to lack of space.

Statement 1. *The greedy algorithm for GDCG is a* $(1 - 1/e)$*-approximation.*

Perhaps not too surprisingly, our analysis is similar to that of the classical max k-coverage problem defined as follows: We are given a set of elements $U = \{e_1, \ldots, e_n\}$ and a collection of sets $\mathcal{S} = \{S_1, \ldots, S_m\}$ defined over U. The goal is to choose k elements that cover the maximum number of sets. A set S is said to be covered if some element from S is chosen. This problem is NP-hard and it is well known that the greedy algorithm, that at any point of time chooses the element that covers the maximum number of uncovered sets thus far, gives a $(1 - 1/e)$-approximation.

It is somewhat surprising that the greedy algorithm still achieves a $(1 - 1/e)$ approximation even in the more general setting of using a submodular information function (e.g. $H_q(S)$) together with a logarithmic discount function, instead of maximizing cardinality. This generalization allows for generalizing the approximation to GDCG. We note that we can also show that this result is best possible unless P=NP.

2.2 No Restriction on the Number of Documents

We do not have here a restriction on the number of documents we can display and the goal is simply to order the pages so as to maximize DCG. A $(1 - 1/e)$-approximation follows by setting $k = n$ in Statement 1. We now describe how to adapt it to obtain a polynomial time approximation scheme (ptas).

The Approximation Scheme. Consider the following algorithm.

- Given the parameter $\epsilon > 0$, we consider all possible candidate choices for the ordering of the first $g(\epsilon) = (2/\epsilon^2)^{(1/\epsilon)}$ elements. There are at most $\binom{n}{g(\epsilon)} g(\epsilon)! \leq n^{g(\epsilon)}$ such choices. Such a choice is determined by the set of elements G and permutation π.
- For each choice G of elements above, let $\mathcal{S}_G$ denote the collection of sets covered by G. Apply the following algorithm to the system $U \setminus G, \mathcal{S} \setminus \mathcal{S}_G$ to obtain the sets $A_0, A_1, \ldots$.
  - Initialize: Let $T_0 = \emptyset$. In general, T_i denotes the sets covered before phase i begins.
  - Phase: For $i = 0, 1, \ldots, \lceil \log n \rceil$, apply the following steps.
    1. Consider the max k-coverage instance defined on the universe $U \setminus G$ and the set collection $(\mathcal{S} \setminus \mathcal{S}_G) \setminus T_i$. Let $k = 2^i$.
    2. Apply the greedy algorithm to the instance above and let A_i denote the $k = 2^i$ elements chosen.
    3. Let $\mathcal{S}_i$ denote the sets in $\mathcal{S} \setminus T_i$ that are covered by elements in A_i. Set $T_{i+1} = T_i \cup \mathcal{S}_i$.
  - Output: Concatenate the lists $\pi(G)$, A_0,A_1,... in that order. Within each set A_i the elements can be ordered arbitrarily.
- Over all choices of G and π, output the ordering with the maximum gain.

Analysis. Consider the case when G consists of the first $g(\epsilon)$ elements in the optimum ordering Π_{opt}, and the elements in G are also ordered as in Π_{opt}. Let alg_1 and opt_1 denote the gain obtained by the first $g(\epsilon)$ elements in the respective orderings and let $\mathsf{alg}_2 = \mathsf{alg} - \mathsf{alg}_1$ and $\mathsf{opt}_2 = \mathsf{opt} - \mathsf{opt}_1$ denote the respective gain from the remaining elements (that lie after the first $g(\epsilon)$ elements).

Theorem 1. *The above scheme is a polynomial-time approximation scheme.*

Proof. Clearly $\mathsf{alg}_1 = \mathsf{opt}_1$. We will show that $\mathsf{alg}_2 \geq (1-\epsilon)\mathsf{opt}_2$. Let O_i denote the sets covered by elements that appear in Π_{opt} in positions $[2^i, 2^{i+1}-1]$ after the first $g(\epsilon)$ elements (i.e. in absolute positions $[g(\epsilon)+2^i, g(\epsilon)+2^{i+1}-1]$). Similarly, let T_{i+1} denote the sets covered by elements $A_0 \cup \ldots, A_i$. We claim the following without proof (due to lack of space).

Claim. For any $0 \leq i \leq n$, after phase i, the number of sets covered by the algorithm, i.e. $|T_{i+1}|$, satisfies

$$|T_{i+1}| \geq \sum_{j=0}^{i} (1 - e^{j-i})|O_j|. \tag{2}$$

$$\mathsf{alg}_2 \geq \sum_{i=0}^{\infty} \frac{(|T_{i+1}| - |T_i|)}{\log(g(\epsilon) + 2^{i+1})}$$

$$= \sum_{i=0}^{\infty} \left(\frac{1}{\log(g(\epsilon) + 2^{i+1})} - \frac{1}{\log(g(\epsilon) + 2^{i+2})} \right) |T_{i+1}|$$

$$\geq \sum_{i=0}^{\infty} \left(\frac{1}{\log(g(\epsilon) + 2^{i+1})} - \frac{1}{\log(g(\epsilon) + 2^{i+2})} \right) \cdot \sum_{j=0}^{i} (1 - e^{j-i}) |O_j|$$

$$= \sum_{j=0}^{\infty} \sum_{i=j}^{\infty} (1 - e^{j-i}) \cdot \left(\frac{1}{\log(g(\epsilon) + 2^{i+1})} - \frac{1}{\log(g(\epsilon) + 2^{i+2})} \right) |O_j|$$

$$\geq \sum_{j=0}^{\infty} \sum_{i=j+2\ln(1/\epsilon)}^{\infty} (1 - \epsilon^2) \cdot \left(\frac{1}{\log(g(\epsilon) + 2^{i+1})} - \frac{1}{\log(g(\epsilon) + 2^{i+2})} \right) |O_j|$$

$$= \sum_{j=0}^{\infty} (1 - \epsilon^2) \frac{1}{\log(g(\epsilon) + (2^{j+1}/\epsilon^2))} |O_j|. \tag{3}$$

The last step follows since the terms are telescoping.

To complete the proof, we note that the contribution of O_j to the optimum ordering is at most $|O_j|/(\log(g(\epsilon) + 2^i + 1))$. On the other hand, by (3) the contribution of O_j to alg_2 is at least:

$$(1 - \epsilon^2)(1/\log(g(\epsilon) + 2^{j+1}/\epsilon^2))|O_j| \geq (1 - \epsilon^2)(1/\log((g(\epsilon) + 2^j)(2/\epsilon^2))|O_j|$$

$$= (1 - \epsilon^2) \frac{1}{\log(g(\epsilon) + 2^j) + \log(2/\epsilon^2)} |O_j| \geq (1 - \epsilon) \frac{1}{\log(g(\epsilon) + 2^j)} |O_j|.$$

The last step follows as $\log(2/\epsilon^2) \leq \epsilon \log(g(\epsilon)) \leq \epsilon \log(g(\epsilon) + 2^j)$ by our choice of $g(\epsilon)$. ■

The algorithm has a huge running time of $n^{2^{O(1/\epsilon)}}$, but this is still a polynomial-time approximation scheme. It would be an interesting open problem to see if the dependence of the running time on ϵ can be made to be singly exponential.

3 General Requirements

In this section we consider the scenario when $k(S)$ can be arbitrary. We first consider the setting where only k documents can be displayed, and show that the problem is extremely hard even for very special cases of the problem. We then consider the case when there is no bound on the number of documents that can be displayed. We describe an $O(\log \log n)$-approximation for maximizing DCG in this setting. Our algorithm is based on an LP formulation using knapsack cover inequalities. Finally, we will show how to adapt the algorithm to obtain a quasi-polynomial time approximation scheme.

3.1 Top k Out of n Documents

We show that in this setting, the DCG problem already captures the notoriously hard densest k-subgraph problem. In the densest k-subgraph problem, we are given an undirected graph $G = (V, E)$ and the goal is to find a subset of k vertices V' that maximizes the number of induced edges (i.e. edges that have both end points in V'). The best known algorithm for the densest k-subgraph problem essentially achieves a guarantee of only $n^{1/3}$ [9]. It is an outstanding open question whether this bound can be improved. To see the connection to Densest-k-Subgraph, consider the following for a given graph $G = (V, E)$. Define the elements as the vertices V and sets S as the edges E, where each S has a covering requirement of $k(S) = 2$. Clearly, finding k elements that cover the maximum number of sets for this instance is equivalent to solving the densest k-subgraph problem. Since the $1/\log(t+1)$ term in the objective function of the DCG is bounded between 1 and $\log(k+1)$ this implies that the problem is as hard to approximate as the Densest-k-Subgraph problem within an $O(\log(k))$ factor. Moreover, note that this is a very special case of our problem, since $k(S) = 2$ for all sets, and each set has size 2.

3.2 No Restriction on the Number of Documents

Given the discussion above, we note that the approach taken in the previous section of solving the max k-coverage problem for geometrically increasing values of k, and then concatenating the resulting sets, will yield a very poor approximation. Given this limitation, our approximation algorithm will use quite different ideas which are based on a linear programming (LP) formulation of the problem. In particular, we will strongly use the fact that we do not have a bound on the number of elements we need to choose (i.e., we can avoid the max k-coverage approach), and also exploit the specific nature of our objective function.

Our approach is based on the recent work of [3], however, there are crucial differences. Most notably, [3] considers a minimization problem, while here we are interested in a maximization problem. Our LP formulation, described below, is based on *knapsack cover inequalities* first introduced by [5]. It is known that a naive LP relaxation for our problem that does not use these inequalities can have a very large integrality gap (we defer this discussion here, and refer the interested reader to [3]).

An LP Relaxation. Let $[n] = \{1, 2, \ldots, n\}$, where $n = |U|$, the number of elements in the universe. In the following, x_{et} is the indicator variable for whether element $e \in U$ is selected at time $t \in [n]$, and y_{St} is the indicator variable for whether set S has been covered by time $t \in [n]$.

$$\text{Maximize} \quad \sum_{1 \le t \le |U|} \sum_{S \in \mathcal{S}} (y_{S,t} - y_{S,t-1}) / \log(t+1)$$

$$\text{subject to} \quad \sum_{e \in U} x_{et} = 1 \qquad \forall t \in [n] \tag{4}$$

$$\sum_{t \in [n]} x_{et} = 1 \qquad \forall e \in U \tag{5}$$

$$\sum_{e \in S \setminus A} \sum_{t' < t} x_{et'} \ge (k(S) - |A|) \cdot y_{St} \tag{6}$$

$$\forall S \in \mathcal{S}, \forall A \subseteq S, \forall t \in [n]$$
$$x_{et}, y_{St} \in [0,1] \qquad \forall e \in U,\ S \in \mathcal{S},\ t \in [n]$$

If x_{et} and y_{St} are restricted to take $\{0,1\}$ values, then this is easily seen to be a valid formulation for the problem. Constraints (4) require that only one element can be assigned to a time slot and constraints (5) require that each element must be assigned to some time slot. Constraints (6) correspond to the knapsack cover inequalities and require that if $y_{St} = 1$, then for every subset of elements A, at least $k(S) - |A|$ elements must be chosen from $S \setminus A$ before time t.

The Algorithm. Let (x^*, y^*) denote an optimal (fractional) solution to the above linear programming formulation and let opt denote its value. Clearly, opt is an upper bound on an integral optimal solution. Our rounding algorithm proceeds in $O(\log n)$ stages, with the ith stage operating in the time interval $[1, 2^{i+1} - 1]$. In stage i, for $i = 0, 1, \ldots$, we perform one round of randomized rounding (as described below) on the fractional solution restricted to the interval $[1, 2^{i+1} - 1]$ and obtain a set A_i of elements. At the conclusion of these stages, we output the elements of A_0, followed by the elements of A_1, and then $A_2, \ldots,$, with the elements of any set A_j being output in an arbitrary order.

The rounding process for stage i that generates set A_i is the following:

- Let $t_i = 2^i$.
- Define the fractional extent to which e is selected before time t_i, for each $e \in U$, to be: $z_{e,i} \leftarrow \sum_{t' \leq t_i} x^*_{et'}$.
- Define for all $e \in U$, $p_{e,i} \leftarrow \min(1, 8\log^2(n+1) z_{e,i})$.
- Pick each element $e \in U$ independently with probability $p_{e,i}$. Let A_i be the set of these elements. If $A_i > 16\log^2(n+1) \cdot 2^i$, then set $A_i = \emptyset$.

Analysis. In the solution (x^*, y^*), for each set S, let $t^*(S)$ denote the earliest time that S has been allocated to an extent of $1/\log(n+1)$, i.e., $y_{t^*(S),S} \geq 1/\log(n+1)$. The next lemma shows that $t^*(S)$ is a good estimate for the time when a set is covered.

Lemma 1. $\mathsf{opt} \leq \sum_S 2/\log(t^*(S)+1)$.

Proof. Since any set S is covered to an extent of at most $1/\log(n+1)$ by time $t^*(S)$, this fraction can yield a gain of at most $(1/\log(n+1)) \cdot (1/\log 2) \leq 1/\log(n+1)$. This is at most $(1/\log(t^*(S)+1))$, since $t^*(S) \leq n$ (as each set is covered by time n). The remaining $1 - 1/\log(n+1)$ portion can yield a total gain of at most $(1 - 1/\log(n+1)) \cdot (1/\log(t^*(S)+1)) \leq (1/\log(t^*(S)+1))$. Thus, the total gain is at most $2/\log(t^*(S)+1)$. ■

Due to space constraints we state the next lemma without proof.

Lemma 2. *For any set S and any stage i such that $t^i \geq t^*_S$, the probability that $k(S)$ elements from S are not picked in stage i is at most $1 - 2/n^2$.*

Theorem 2. *The algorithm above is an $O(\log\log n)$-approximation.*

Proof. Since $|A_i| \leq 16\log^2(n+1)2^i$, each element in A_i appears no later than time $16\log^2(n+1)(2^{i+1}-1)$ in the ordering produced by the algorithm. By Lemma 2, with probability at least $1-2/n^2$, each set S appears in a set A_i where $i \in [t^*(S), 2t^*(S)-1]$. Thus, with probability $1-2/n^2$, set S appears in the ordering of the algorithm by time $64\log^2(n+1)t^*(S)-1$.

Thus, the expected contribution of set S to the algorithm is at least

$$\left(1-\frac{1}{n^2}\right)\cdot\left(\frac{t^*(S)}{\log 64\log^2(n+1)}\right) = \Omega\left(\frac{1}{\log\log n}\cdot\log(t^*+1)\right).$$

By Lemma 1, opt can obtain a gain of at most $2/(\log(t^*+1))$, and hence we get an $O(\log\log n)$-approximation. ■

Next, we show that the algorithm can be modified to obtain a quasi-polynomial time approximation scheme. That is, a $(1+\epsilon)$-approximation for any $\epsilon > 0$, but with running time $O(n^{\mathrm{polylog}(n)})$.

A Quasi-Polynomial Time Approximation Scheme. We modify the algorithm above to first guess (by trying out all possibilities) the first $f(\epsilon) = (\log n)^{4/\epsilon}$ elements in the ordering of opt. Let us assume that $n \geq 1/\epsilon \geq 8$ (otherwise the problem can be solved trivially in $O(1)$ time).

Given the optimum LP solution, let us define $t^*(S)$ to be the earliest time when set S is covered to extent $\epsilon/\log n$. A slight modification of Lemma 1 implies that opt $\leq (1+\epsilon)/\log(t^*+1)$.

The analysis of our rounding algorithm guarantees that the expected contribution of set S to the algorithm is at least

$$\left(1-\frac{1}{n^2}\right)\cdot\left(\frac{t^*(S)}{\log 64\log^2(n+1)}\right) \geq \frac{1-\epsilon^2}{\log t^*(S)+4(\log\log(n+1)},$$

since $n \geq 1/\epsilon \geq 8$. If $\log t^*(S) \leq (4/\epsilon)\log\log n)$, or equivalently $t^*(S) \leq \log n^{4/\epsilon}$, the contribution of S to the algorithm is at least $(1-\epsilon)$ times its contribution to opt. Thus, we can apply the same idea as the one used for obtaining a ptas for the case of $k(S) = 1$, and guess the first $f(\epsilon) = (\log n)^{4/\epsilon}$ positions in the ordering of opt.

4 Conclusions

A natural question is to consider more general forms of discounting in the definition of DCG, beyond just $\gamma(t) = 1/\log(t+1)$. In [8, Chapter 8.4.3] it is mentioned that the choice of the logarithmic discount function is somewhat arbitrary and has no theoretical justification, although it does provide a relatively smooth (gradual) reduction. It is easily seen that our $(1-1/e)$-approximation for unit covering requirements works for any monotonically decreasing $\gamma(t)$. In the case when there is no limit on the number of documents returned, our ptas can also be extended to the case where $\gamma(t)$ satisfies the following property. For any ϵ, the inequality $\gamma(2t) \geq \gamma(t)/(1+\epsilon)$ holds for all but $\ell = O_\epsilon(1)$ integers t.

In this case our algorithm has running time $n^{O(\ell)}$. Note that for the logarithmic function, $\ell = 2^{O(1/\epsilon)}$. The above condition is satisfied for any $\gamma(t)$ of the type $1/\text{polylog}(t)$, but it is not satisfied for a polynomial such as $f(t) = 1/t^{\delta}$.

References

1. Agrawal, R., Gollapudi, S., Halverson, A., Ieong, S.: Diversifying search results. In: WSDM 2009, pp. 5–14 (2009)
2. Azar, Y., Gamzu, I., Yin, X.: Multiple intents re-ranking. In: STOC 2009: Proceedings of the 41st Annual ACM Symposium on Theory of Computing, pp. 669–678. ACM, New York (2009)
3. Bansal, N., Gupta, A., Krishnaswamy, R.: A constant factor approximation algorithm for generalized min-sum set cover. In: Symposium on Discrete Algorithms, SODA (2010)
4. Carbonell, J., Goldstein, J.: The use of MMR, diversity-based reranking for reordering documents and producing summaries. In: SIGIR 1998, pp. 335–336 (1998)
5. Carr, R., Fleischer, L., Leung, V., Phillips, C.: Strengthening integrality gaps for capacitated network design and covering problems. In: Symposium on Discrete Algorithms (SODA), pp. 106–115 (2000)
6. Chen, H., Karger, D.R.: Less is more: probabilistic models for retrieving fewer relevant documents. In: SIGIR 2006, pp. 429–436 (2006)
7. Clarke, C.L.A., Kolla, M., Cormack, G.V., Vechtomova, O., Ashkan, A., Bttcher, S., MacKinnon, I.: Novelty and diversity in information retrieval evaluation. In: SIGIR '08, pp. 659–666 (2008)
8. Croft, B., Metzler, D., Strohman, T.: Search Engines: Information Retrieval in Practice. Addison-Wesley, Reading (2009)
9. Feige, U., Peleg, D., Kortsarz, G.: The dense k-subgraph problem. Algorithmica 29(3), 410–421 (2001)
10. Manning, C.D., Raghavan, P., Schuetze, H.: Introduction to Information Retrieval. Cambridge University Press, New York (2008)
11. Radlinski, F., Dumais, S.T.: Improving personalized web search using result diversification. In: SIGIR 2006, pp. 691–692 (2006)
12. Radlinski, F., Kleinberg, R., Joachims, T.: Learning diverse rankings with multi-armed bandits. In: ICML 2008, pp. 784–791 (2008)
13. Vee, E., Srivastava, U., Shanmugasundaram, J., Bhat, P., Yahia, S.A.: Efficient computation of diverse query results. In: ICDE 2008, pp. 228–236 (2008)
14. Zhai, C., Cohen, W.W., Lafferty, J.D.: Beyond independent relevance: methods and evaluation metrics for subtopic retrieval. In: SIGIR 2003, pp. 10–17 (2003)
15. Ziegler, C.-N., McNee, S.M., Konstan, J.A., Lausen, G.: Improving recommendation lists through topic diversification. In: WWW 2005, pp. 22–32 (2005)

Rewriting Measurement-Based Quantum Computations with Generalised Flow

Ross Duncan[1,⋆] and Simon Perdrix[2]

[1] Oxford University Computing Laboratory
ross.duncan@comlab.ox.ac.uk
[2] CNRS, LIG, Université de Grenoble
Simon.Perdrix@imag.fr

Abstract. We present a method for verifying measurement-based quantum computations, by producing a quantum circuit equivalent to a given deterministic measurement pattern. We define a diagrammatic presentation of the pattern, and produce a circuit via a rewriting strategy based on the generalised flow of the pattern. Unlike other methods for translating measurement patterns with generalised flow to circuits, this method uses neither ancilla qubits nor acausal loops.

1 Introduction

The one-way quantum computer (1WQC) [1] is model of quantum computation which is a very promising candidate for physical implementation, and also has many interesting theoretical properties (in complexity theory, for instance [2,3]). The basis of the 1WQC is an entangled resource state, which is gradually consumed by performing local measurements upon it. By careful choice of measurements, any quantum computation can be performed. In this paper we address the task of verifying properties of one-way computations by using rewriting strategies in a graphical framework, which originates in categorical analyses of quantum mechanics [4].

The main task is to verify the correctness of a given one-way computation—presented in the pattern syntax of the *measurement calculus* [5]—by producing an equivalent quantum circuit. We will also verify that the pattern can be carried out deterministically: that is, we check that the non-deterministic effects of quantum measurement are properly corrected by the pattern.

The question of determinism in the one-way model has been previously addressed by *flow techniques*; see [6,7]. These techniques examine the resource state: if it has the correct geometry then any errors introduced by the non-deterministic nature of quantum measurements can be corrected, and the resulting computation will be deterministic. Both causal flow [6] and generalised flow [7] do not address any concrete pattern, rather they simply assert the existence of a deterministic computation using the given resource state. In fact, generalised flow (gflow) characterises the notion of *uniform determinism*, where the actual

⋆ Supported by EPSRC postdoctoral fellowship EP/E045006/1.

S. Abramsky et al. (Eds.): ICALP 2010, Part II, LNCS 6199, pp. 285–296, 2010.

choice of the measurements is irrelevant. (Causal flow provides a sufficient condition.) Our work relaxes the uniformity restriction and derive correctness proofs in cases where the choice of measurement is significant.

The problem of producing a circuit equivalent to a given measurement-based quantum computation is of great importance. In [8], an automated translation has been proposed for measurement-based computations which have a causal flow. In [9], the author presents a similar technique based on causal flow and notes that her method produces circuits with "time-like loops" if applied on measurement-based computations which do not have a causal flow. In this work we rely on the bialgebraic structure induced by quantum complementarity to produce equivalent circuits from measurement-based quantum computations which do not have causal flow. Unlike other translations from 1WQC, the circuits we generate do not make use of any ancilla qubits.

The diagrammatic calculus we employ draws from the long tradition of graphical representations of monoidal categories. Aside from providing a very intuitive notation for reasoning about information flow, the categorical approach to quantum computation (see for example [10,11,12]), provides a clearer view of the structure of quantum informatic phenomena than conventional approaches. The particular system of this paper is essentially that of [4], and the bialgebraic relations between complementary quantum observables exposed there form the core of the main lemma of this paper[1].

The structure of this paper is as follows: in Section 2, we introduce the diagrammatic syntax and its semantics; in Section 3 we introduce the rewrite system used to derive our results. This rewrite system has no particularly nice properties—it is neither confluent nor terminating—but in the rest of the paper we will define strategies to achieve our results. Section 4 introduces the measurement calculus and its translation into diagrams, and Section 5 how to derive the circuit-like form Due to space restrictions, the proofs have been omitted.

Notational conventions. When u, v are vertices in some graph G, we write $u \sim v$ to indicate that they are adjacent. The *neighbourhood* of u, denoted $N_G(u)$, is defined $N_G(u) = \{v \in V \ : \ u \sim v\}$. Given some $K \subseteq V$, the *odd neighbourhood of* K is defined by $\mathrm{Odd}_G(K) = \{v \in V \ : \ |N_G(v) \cap K| = 1 \mod 2\}$, i.e. $\mathrm{Odd}_G(K)$ is the set of vertices which have an odd number of neighbours in K. We use Dirac notation to denote vectors, e.g. $|\psi\rangle$. The standard basis for $\mathbb{C}^2$ is denoted $|0\rangle = \begin{pmatrix}1\\0\end{pmatrix}$, $|1\rangle = \begin{pmatrix}0\\1\end{pmatrix}$; we will also use the complementary basis $|+\rangle = \frac{1}{\sqrt{2}}\begin{pmatrix}1\\1\end{pmatrix}$, $|-\rangle = \frac{1}{\sqrt{2}}\begin{pmatrix}1\\-1\end{pmatrix}$.

2 Diagrams

Definition 1. *An* open graph *is a triple* (G, I, O) *consisting of an undirected graph* $G = (V, E)$ *and distinguished subsets* $I, O \subseteq V$ *of* input *and* output

[1] The calculus has been implemented in a mechanised rewriting tool: see [13].

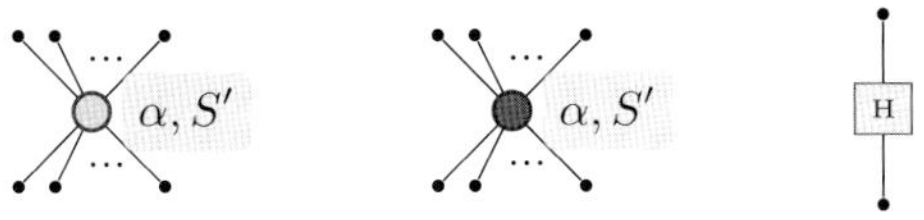

Fig. 1. Permitted interior vertices

vertices I and O. The set of vertices $I \cup O$ is called the boundary *of G, and $V \setminus (I \cup O)$ is the* interior *of G.*

Definition 2. *Let S be some set of variables. A* formal diagram over *S is an open graph whose boundary vertices are always of degree 1, and whose interior vertices are restricted to the following types:*

- *Z vertices, labelled by an angle $\alpha \in [0, 2\pi)$ and some collection of variables $S' \subseteq S$; these are shown as (light) green circles,*
- *X vertices, labelled by an angle $\alpha \in [0, 2\pi)$ and some collection of variables $S' \subseteq S$; these are shown as (dark) red circles,*
- *H (or Hadamard) vertices, restricted to degree 2; shown as squares.*

The allowed vertices are shown in Figure 1.

Diagrams are oriented such that the inputs are at the top and the outputs are at the bottom, and hence the implied temporal (partial) order of the components is from top to bottom.

If an X or Z vertex is labelled by $\alpha = 0$ then the label is omitted. In the case where S' is not empty then the corresponding vertex is called *conditional*; if no conditional vertices occur in a diagram it is *unconditional*. For each S the formal diagrams over S form a symmetric monoidal category (in fact compact closed) in the evident way: the objects of the category are sets and an arrow $g : A \to B$ is a diagram whose underlying open graph is (G, A, B). The tensor product is disjoint union, and composition $g \circ f$ is defined by identifying the output vertices of f with the input vertices of g. For more details see [14,15]. Denote this category $\mathbb{D}(S)$; we denote the category $\mathbb{D}(\emptyset)$ of unconditional diagrams by $\mathbb{D}$. Note that the components shown in Figure 1 are the generators of $\mathbb{D}(S)$.

Informally, the edges of a diagram are interpreted as qubits, though some caution is required. Different edges can represent the same physical qubit at different stages of the computation, and certain edges do not represent qubits at all: they encode correlations between different parts of the system. Example 7 shows how 2-qubit gates are encoded using such correlations. The vertices of the diagram are interpreted as local operations, possibly conditioned on the variables, so that the entire diagram yields a superoperator from its inputs to its outputs. We define an interpretation functor to make this intuition precise.

Definition 3. *Call $v : S \to \{0, 1\}$ a* valuation *of S; for each valuation v, we define a functor $\hat{v} : \mathbb{D}(S) \to \mathbb{D}$ which simply instantiates the labels of Z and X vertices occurring in each diagram. If a vertex z is labelled by α and S', then $\hat{v}(z)$ is labelled by 0 if $\prod_{s \in S'} v(s) = 0$ and α otherwise.*

Definition 4. *Let* $[\![\cdot]\!] : \mathbb{D} \to$ ***FDHilb*** *be a traced monoidal functor; define its action on objects by* $[\![A]\!] = \mathbb{C}^{2^n}$ *whenever* $n = |A|$*; define its action on the generators as:*

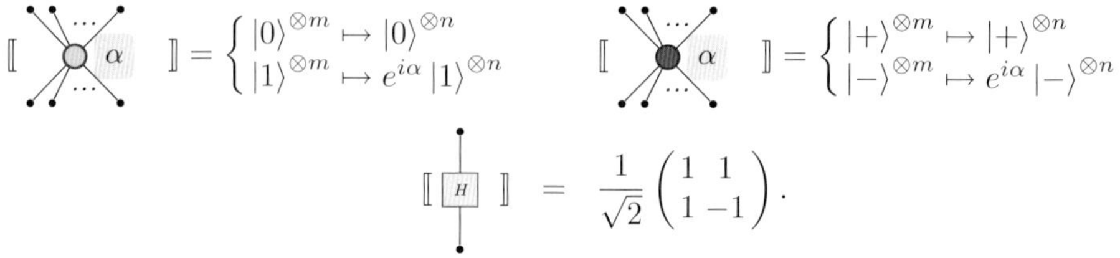

$$[\![\cdot]\!] = \begin{cases} |0\rangle^{\otimes m} \mapsto |0\rangle^{\otimes n} \\ |1\rangle^{\otimes m} \mapsto e^{i\alpha} |1\rangle^{\otimes n} \end{cases} \qquad [\![\cdot]\!] = \begin{cases} |+\rangle^{\otimes m} \mapsto |+\rangle^{\otimes n} \\ |-\rangle^{\otimes m} \mapsto e^{i\alpha} |-\rangle^{\otimes n} \end{cases}$$

$$[\![\cdot]\!] = \frac{1}{\sqrt{2}} \begin{pmatrix} 1 & 1 \\ 1 & -1 \end{pmatrix}.$$

The value of $[\![\cdot]\!]$ *on all other arrows is then fixed by the requirement that it be a traced monoidal functor*[2].

Definition 5. *The denotation of a diagram D over variables S is a superoperator constructed by summing over all the valuations of S:*

$$\rho \mapsto \sum_{v \in 2^S} [\![\hat{v}(D)]\!] \rho [\![\hat{v}(D)]\!]^\dagger .$$

Example 6 (Pauli Matrices). The Pauli X and Z matrices can be defined by degree 2 vertices:

$$[\![\cdot]\!] = \begin{pmatrix} 0 & 1 \\ 1 & 0 \end{pmatrix} \qquad [\![\cdot]\!] = \begin{pmatrix} 1 & 0 \\ 0 & -1 \end{pmatrix}$$

Example 7 (2-qubit gates). Composing an X with a Z vertex yields the 2-qubit $\wedge X$ (controlled-NOT) gate where the Z vertex is the control qubit. The $\wedge Z$ gate is defined similarly.

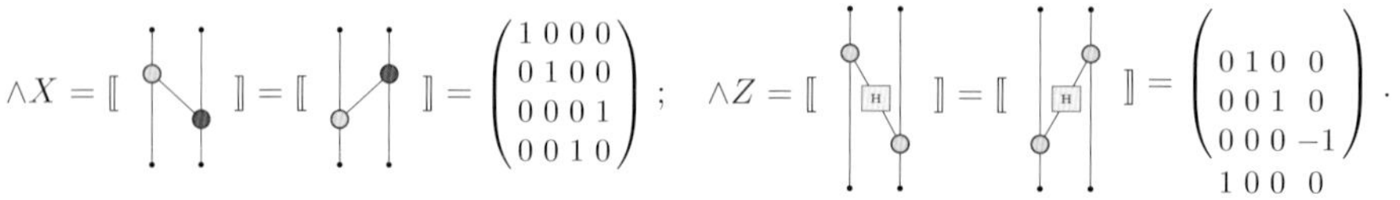

$$\wedge X = [\![\cdot]\!] = [\![\cdot]\!] = \begin{pmatrix} 1&0&0&0 \\ 0&1&0&0 \\ 0&0&0&1 \\ 0&0&1&0 \end{pmatrix}; \quad \wedge Z = [\![\cdot]\!] = [\![\cdot]\!] = \begin{pmatrix} 0&1&0&0 \\ 0&0&1&0 \\ 0&0&0&-1 \end{pmatrix} \\ 1\ 0\ 0\ 0 .$$

In both cases, the diagonal edge connecting the two sides of the diagram produces the correlation of the two physical qubits represented by the vertical edges.

Example 8 (Preparing and measuring qubits). The preparation of a fresh qubit is represented by a single vertex with no input edges and one output edge:

$$[\![\cdot]\!] = \begin{pmatrix} 1 \\ 0 \end{pmatrix} = |0\rangle ; \qquad [\![\cdot]\!] = \frac{1}{\sqrt{2}} \begin{pmatrix} 1 \\ 1 \end{pmatrix} = |+\rangle .$$

To encode a projection we use a dual diagram to preparation; the non-determinism of measurement is represented using a conditional operation whose two possible valuations correspond to the two possible outcomes:

[2] Again, the full details of this construction regarding cyclic graphs and traces can be found in [14].

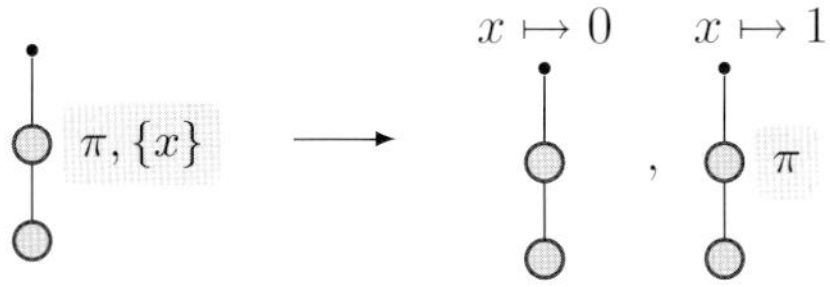

$$\rho \mapsto \langle +|\,\rho\,|+\rangle + \langle +|\,Z\rho Z\,|+\rangle \\ = \langle +|\,\rho\,|+\rangle + \langle -|\,\rho\,|-\rangle$$

From the preceding examples, it will be obvious that our diagrammatic language can represent a universal set of quantum gates, and hence can represent all quantum circuits. However, not every diagram corresponds to a quantum circuit.

Definition 9. *A diagram is called* circuit-like *if (1) all of its boundary, X, and Z vertices can be covered by a set $\mathcal{P}$ of disjoint paths, each of which ends in an output; (2) every cycle in the diagram traverses at least one edge covered by $\mathcal{P}$ in the direction opposite to that induced by the path; and, (3) it is weakly 3-coloured in the following sense: in every connected subgraph whose vertices are all the same type, no two (non-boundary) vertices are labelled by the same set S of variables.*

The paths mentioned in the condition (1) represent the physical qubits of a quantum circuit, and condition (2) prevents information being fed from a later part of the circuit to an earlier part. Notice that condition (1) allows, but does not require, H vertices to be covered by the path; hence the $\wedge Z$ example above is circuit-like. Condition (3) is a requirement that circuit-like diagrams are normal with respect to certain rewrite rules introduced in Section 3.

The path-cover $\mathcal{P}$ of a circuit-like diagram gives a factorisation of the diagram into unitary gates, thus defining a quantum circuit, possibly with some part of its input fixed. More precisely, every such diagram can be obtained from a circuit by the rewrite rules of the following section. The following is an immediate consequence.

Proposition 10. *If D is unconditional and circuit-like then $[\![D]\!]$ is a unitary embedding.*

3 Rewrites

The map $[\![\cdot]\!]$ gives an interpretation of diagrams as linear maps. This interpretation, however, is not injective: there are numerous diagrams which denote the same linear map. To address this difficulty, an equational theory on $\mathbb{D}$ is required. We will now introduce such a theory via a set of rewriting rules.

Definition 11. *Let R be least transitive and reflexive relation on $\mathbb{D}$ generated by the local rewrite rules shown in Figure 2. Let $\leftrightarrow^*$ denote the symmetric closure of R.*

The diagrammatic syntax, and the equations of the rewrite rules are derived from those introduced in [4]. The Z family of vertices correspond to operations

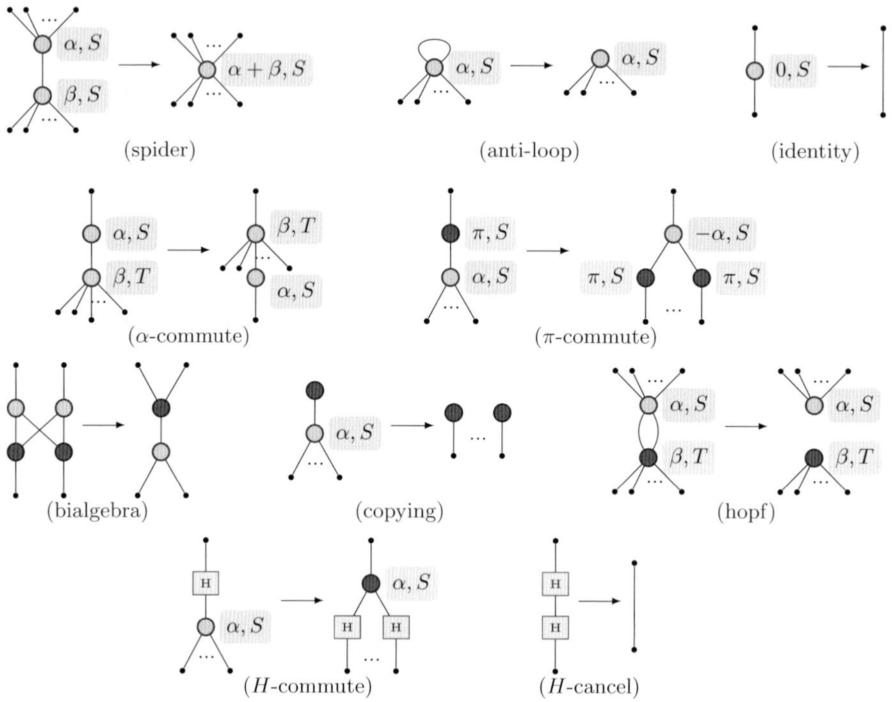

Fig. 2. Rewrite rules for system R. We present the rules for the Z subsystem; to obtain the complete set of rules exchange the colours in the rules shown above.

defined with respect to the eigenbasis of the Pauli Z operator; a copying operation for this basis and phase rotations which leave it fixed. Similarly the X family are defined with respect to the Pauli X. The H vertices represent the familiar 1-qubit Hadamard, which maps sends each family onto the other. Each family individually forms a special Frobenius algebra, and together they form a Hopf algebra with trivial antipode. Space does not permit a more thorough justification of these particular operations and rules, beyond the following:

Proposition 12. *The rewrite system R is sound with respect to the interpretation map $[\![\cdot]\!]$.*

Despite its soundness, this rewrite system does not have many good properties. It is not complete with respect to the interpretation in Hilbert space; an example of an unprovable true equation is discussed in [16]. It is manifestly not terminating since several of the rules are reversible, for example the α-commutation rule; other rules can generate an infinite sequence of rewrites, for example the π-commutation rule. The subsystem without H is known to be neither confluent nor terminating [17]. Rather than attempt to remedy these defects by tinkering with the system, in this paper we will use particular rewrite strategies to produce circuit-like diagrams.

Proposition 10 implies that any unconditional circuit-like diagram has a natural interpretation as a quantum circuit, hence the existence of such a reduct for a given diagram shows that the diagram is equivalent to the derived circuit. In the following sections we will see how to apply this idea to the verification of one-way quantum computations.

Lemma 13 (Main Lemma). *Given a diagram D, let $\mathcal{X} = \{x_0, \ldots x_k\}$ and $\mathcal{Z} = \{z_0, \ldots, z_\ell\}$ be sets of its X and Z vertices respectively, such that the subdiagram G, induced by $\mathcal{Z} \cup \mathcal{X}$, is bipartite—that is, for all i, j, we have $x_i \not\sim x_j$ and $z_i \not\sim z_j$ in G.*

Define a new graph G' with vertices $V_{G'} = V_G \cup \{u_1, \ldots u_\ell\} \cup \{v_1, \ldots, v_\ell\}$, and such that for any $0 \leq i \leq k$ and $1 \leq j \leq \ell$,

- *there are edges (u_j, v_j), (u_j, x_{j-1}) and $(u_j, x_j) \in G'$;*
- *there is an edge $(x_i, z_0) \in G'$ iff $x_i \in \mathrm{Odd}_G(\mathcal{Z})$*
- *there is an edge $(x_i, v_j) \in G'$ iff $x_i \in \mathrm{Odd}_G(\{z_j, \ldots z_\ell\})$.*

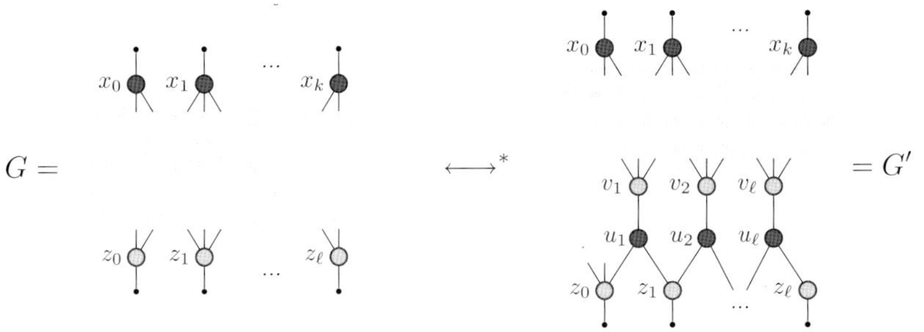

Then $G \leftrightarrow^* G'$.

Note that there is an edge between an X vertex x and a Z vertex z in G if and only if there is an odd number of paths between x and z in G'.

A direct proof of the lemma can be given using rewrites or R, although we note that is a special case of the well known normal form theorem for Hopf algebras (see [18] for a nice version).

Each instance of the Main Lemma provides a new admissible rule $G \longrightarrow G'$; since $\leftrightarrow^*$ is just the equivalence relation generated by R, these new rules are sound with respect to the interpretation map $[\![\cdot]\!]$. One way to view the lemma is as a new set of rewrite rules S compatible with R.

Example 14. An admissible rule from the schema S. :

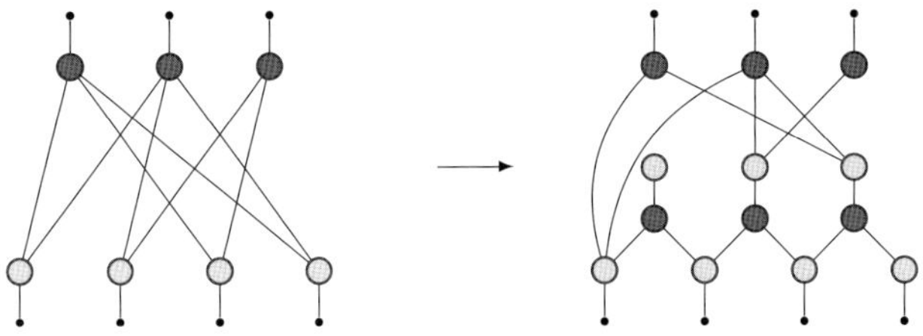

4 The Measurement Calculus

The *measurement calculus*, introduced by Danos, Kashefi and Panangaden [5], is a formal calculus for one-way quantum computations [1]. We review here the basic features of the calculus; for a complete exposition see [5].

Definition 15. *A* measurement pattern *consists of a set V of qubits, with distinguished subsets I and O of inputs and outputs respectively, and, in addition, a sequence of* commands *chosen from the following operations.*

- *1-qubit preparations, N_i, which prepare the qubit $i \notin I$ to the state $|+\rangle$.*
- *2-qubit entangling operations, E_{ij}, which applies a $\wedge Z$ to qubits i and j.*
- *1-qubit measurements, ${}^s[M_i^\alpha]^t$, which act as destructive measurements on the qubit $i \notin O$, in the basis $|0\rangle \pm e^{(-1)^s i\alpha + t\pi} |1\rangle$, where $s, t \in \{0, 1\}$ are boolean values called* signals.
- *1-qubit corrections X_i^s and Z_j^t, which act as the Pauli X and Z operators on qubits i and j, if the signals s and t, respectively, are equal to 1; otherwise the corrections have no effect.*

A qubit is measured if and only if it is not an output. The set of signals is in bijection with the set $V \setminus O$ of measured qubits: signal s is set to 0 if the corresponding measurement yields the +1 eigenstate, and 1 otherwise.

Each pattern can be interpreted as a superoperator $\mathbb{C}^{2^{|I|}} \to \mathbb{C}^{2^{|O|}}$ via a linear map, called the *branch map*, for each possible vector of measurement outcomes, much as in Def. 5. Indeed each pattern can be translated into diagram with the same semantics.

Remark 16. The measurement operation ${}^s[M_i^\alpha]^t$ is equivalent to the sequence $M_i^\alpha X_i^s Z_i^t$. The following assumes that all measurements have been so decomposed.

Definition 17. *Let $\mathfrak{P}$ be a pattern. Define a diagram $D_{\mathfrak{P}}$ over $V \setminus O$ by translating the command sequence according to table 1, and composing in these elements in the the evident way.*

Example 18. The ubiquitous CNOT operation can be computed by the pattern $\mathfrak{P} = X_4^3 Z_4^2 Z_1^2 M_3^0 M_2^0 E_{13} E_{23} E_{34} N_3 N_4$ [5]. This yields the diagram,

Table 1. Translation from pattern to diagram

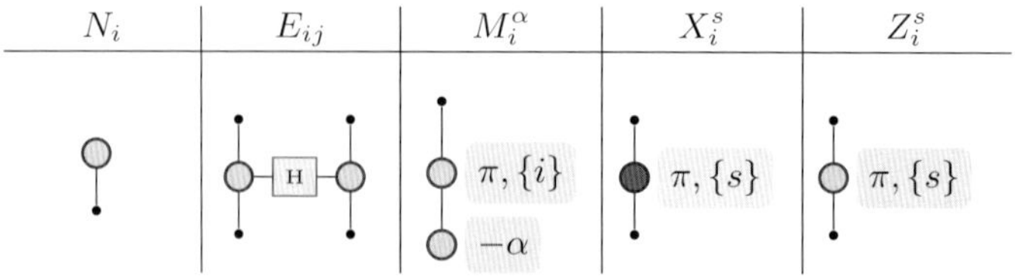

$D_{\mathfrak{P}} =$ 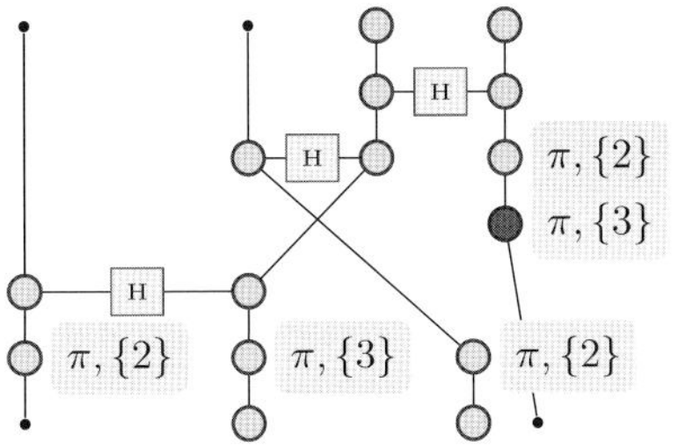

,

where each qubit is represented by a vertical "path" from top to bottom, with qubit 1 the leftmost, and qubit 4 is the rightmost.

By virtue of the soundness of R and Proposition 10, if $D_{\mathfrak{P}}$ can be rewritten to a circuit-like diagram without any conditional operations, then the rewrite sequence constitutes a proof that the pattern computes the same operation as the derived circuit.

Example 19. Returning to the CNOT pattern of Example 18, there is a rewrite sequence, the key steps of which are shown below, which reduces the $D_{\mathfrak{P}}$ to the unconditional circuit-like pattern for CNOT introduced in Example 7. This proves two things: firstly that $\mathfrak{P}$ indeed computes the CNOT unitary, and that the pattern $\mathfrak{P}$ is *deterministic.*

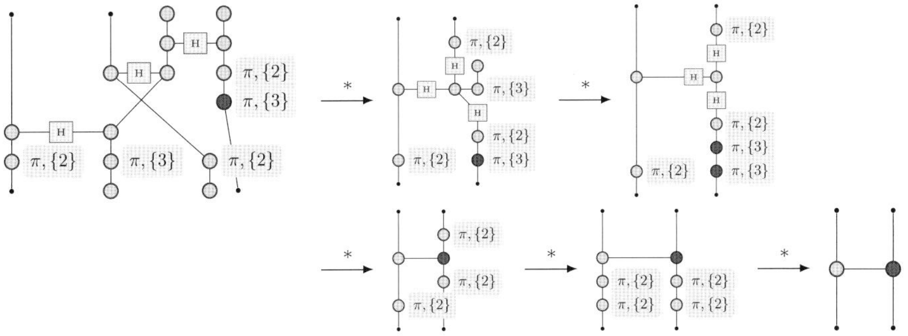

One can clearly see in this example how the non-determinism introduced by measurements is corrected by conditional operations later in the pattern. The possibility of performing such corrections depends on the *geometry* of the pattern, the entanglement graph implicitly defined by the pattern.

Definition 20. *Let $\mathfrak{P}$ be a pattern; the* geometry *of $\mathfrak{P}$ is an open graph $\gamma(\mathfrak{P}) = (G, I, O)$ whose vertices are the qubits of $\mathfrak{P}$ and where $i \sim j$ iff E_{ij} occurs in the command sequence of $\mathfrak{P}$.*

Definition 21. *Given a geometry $\Gamma = ((V, E), I, O)$ we can define a diagram $D_\Gamma = ((V_D, E_D), I_D, O_D)$ as follows:*

- $V_D = V + E + I + O$*, coloured such that:*
  - $v \in V$ *is an unconditional Z vertex in D_Γ, labelled by $\alpha = 0$;*

- *$e \in E$ is an H vertex;*
- *$b \in I + O$ is a boundary vertex.*

– *The edge relation is as follows:*
- *if $v \in I$, or $v \in O$, in Γ then $v_I \sim v_V$, respectively $v_O \sim v_V$, in D_Γ;*
- *if $e = (v, v')$ in Γ, then $e_E \sim v_V$ and $e_E \sim v'_V$ in D_Γ;*

– *$v_I \in I_D$ and $v_O \in O_D$.*

The Z vertices of $D_{\gamma(\mathfrak{P})}$ are in bijective correspondence with the qubits of $\mathfrak{P}$.

Example 22. Let $\mathfrak{P} = E_{12}E_{13}E_{23}N_1N_2N_3$. This pattern has no inputs or measurements: it simply prepares a triangular graph state. Notice that $D_{\gamma(\mathfrak{P})}$ is a reduct of $D_{\mathfrak{P}}$.

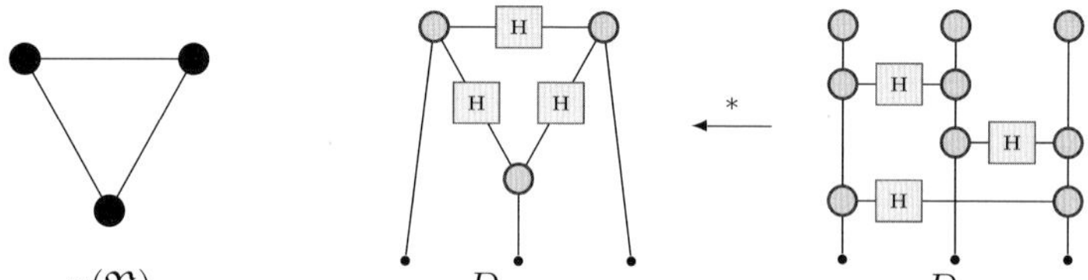

$\gamma(\mathfrak{P})$ $D_{\gamma(\mathfrak{P})}$ $D_{\mathfrak{P}}$

Given $D_{\gamma(\mathfrak{P})}$, we can adjoin measurements to construct a diagram $D^*_{\mathfrak{P}}$, such that $D_{\mathfrak{P}} \xrightarrow{*} D^*_{\mathfrak{P}}$. Justified by this, we shall use $D_{\gamma(\mathfrak{P})}$ in place of $D_{\mathfrak{P}}$, to allow properties based on the geometry to be imported directly. The most important such property is the generalised flow, or gflow.

Definition 23. *Let (G, I, O) be an open graph; a* generalised flow *(or* gflow*) is a pair $(g, \prec)$, with $\prec$ a partial order and g a function $g : O^c \to \mathcal{P}(I^c)$ which associates with every non output vertex a set of non input vertices such that:*

(G1). if $j \in g(i)$ then $i \prec j$;
(G2). if $j \in \mathrm{Odd}_G(g(i))$ then $j = i$ or $i \prec j$;
(G3). $i \in \mathrm{Odd}_G(g(i))$.

In the special case that $|g(v)| = 1$ for all vertices v, the gflow is called a causal flow*, or simply a* flow*.*

Theorem 24 ([7]). *If (G, I, O) has a gflow, then there exists a pattern $\mathfrak{P}_0$ such that $\gamma(\mathfrak{P}_0) = (G, I, O)$ and $\mathfrak{P}_0$ is deterministic, in the sense that all of its branch maps are equal. Further, this property does not depend on the angle of any measurement in $\mathfrak{P}_0$.*

Since different patterns may have the same geometry, it may be that $\gamma(\mathfrak{P}) = \gamma(\mathfrak{P}')$ but one is deterministic and the other is not. In the next section we describe how to produce a circuit-like diagram from $D_{\gamma(\mathfrak{P})}$ using a rewrite strategy based on the existence of a gflow.

5 Rewriting to Circuits

Now we relate the various flow structures on a geometry, to the possibility that the corresponding pattern is deterministic.

Notice that Def. 23 can be readily adapted to define a gflow over an unconditional diagram: simply replace the vertices of the geometry with the non-H vertices of the diagram, and replace "adjacent" with "reachable via a path of zero or more H vertices". It is easy to see that the original definition on $\gamma(\mathfrak{P})$ and the modified version on $D_{\gamma(\mathfrak{P})}$ exactly coincide.

Now we demonstrate a rewriting strategy that will perform two tasks at once. If the open graph has a gflow, we will discover it. And, we will, in the process, transform the graph into a new graph which has a casual flow.

Lemma 25. *There is a convergent rewriting strategy such that if* $\mathfrak{P}$ *has a gflow then* $D_{\gamma(\mathfrak{P})}\downarrow$ *is circuit like.*

Proof (Sketch). Suppose we know the gflow on $D_{\gamma(\mathfrak{P})}$. For every non-output qubit i, the sets $g(i)$ and $\{i\} \cup \{j \in V : j \prec i\}$ provide the situation of the main lemma, hence we can rewrite the diagram according the induced rules. The new graph has again a gflow, and further, the overall size of the sets $g(i)$ has been reduced. It just remains to find the gflow if it exists; for this we can essentially simulate the method of [7] by the choice of admissible rules S.

Lemma 26. $\mathfrak{P}$ *has a causal flow if and only if* $D_{\gamma(\mathfrak{P})}$ *is circuit like.*

Theorem 27. *If a geometry* Γ *has a gflow then* D_Γ *can be rewritten to a circuit like diagram.*

Example 28. The existence of a gflow is a sufficient condition for a pattern $\mathfrak{P}$ to be circuit-like, but not necessary. For instance, although the pattern $\mathfrak{P} = M_3^0 M_2^\alpha E_{23} E_{12} N_2 N_3$ has no gflow, it can be rewritten to a circuit-like diagram:

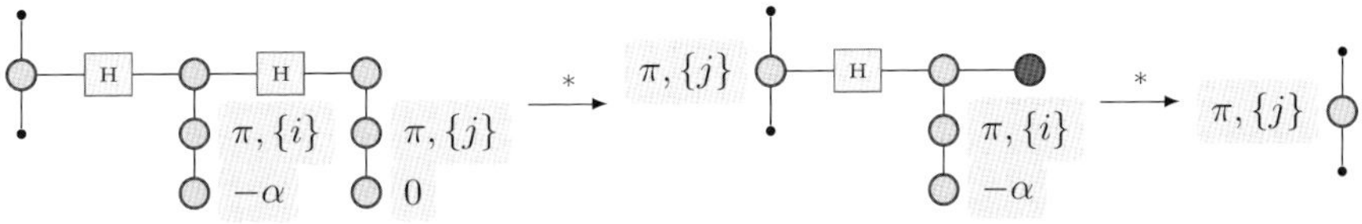

This example shows that the verification using our rewriting technique is more powerful than the static gflow condition: the rewriting techniques can verify non-uniform properties, i.e. properties which depend on the actual measurement angles.

6 Conclusions, Extensions, and Future Work

We have shown how to represent the measurement calculus in a diagrammatic form, and demonstrated how rewriting of these diagrams can prove the equivalence of computations. Our main result describes a rewriting strategy for transforming a measurement pattern it into a circuit-like diagram, which furthermore uses no ancilla qubits. Although space limitations prevent its description here, this result can be extended. We can rewrite the resulting diagram to an unconditional diagram if and only if the given *pattern* is in fact deterministic—that is, free of programming errors. Indeed by suitable annotations of the diagram this strategy can discover where additional corrections should be added to the pattern to make it deterministic, effectively debugging the pattern. These techniques extend outside the realm of gflow since we can also show non-uniform determinism, as discussed in at the end of Section 5. One important area which we have not treated here is the depth complexity of the circuits constructed by our strategy. This will be examined in future work.

References

1. Raussendorf, R., Briegel, H.J.: A one-way quantum computer. Phys. Rev. Lett. 86, 5188–5191 (2001)
2. Anne Broadbent, J.F., Kashefi, E.: Universal blind quantum computation. In: Proc. FoCS 2009 (2009)
3. Browne, D.E., Kashefi, E., Perdrix, S.: Computational depth complexity of measurement-based quantum computation (2009) preprint: arXiv:0909.4673
4. Coecke, B., Duncan, R.: Interacting quantum observables. In: Aceto, L., Damgård, I., Goldberg, L.A., Halldórsson, M.M., Ingólfsdóttir, A., Walukiewicz, I. (eds.) ICALP 2008, Part II. LNCS, vol. 5126, pp. 298–310. Springer, Heidelberg (2008)
5. Danos, V., Kashefi, E., Panangaden, P.: The measurement calculus. J. ACM 54(2) (2007)
6. Danos, V., Kashefi, E.: Determinism in the one-way model. Phys. Rev. A 74(052310) (2006)
7. Browne, D., Kashefi, E., Mhalla, M., Perdrix, S.: Generalized flow and determinism in measurement-based quantum computation. New J. Phys. 9 (2007)
8. Duncan, R.: Verifying the measurement calculus by rewriting. In: DCM 2007 (2007) (Oral presentation)
9. Kashefi, E.: Lost in translation. In: Proc. DCM 2007 (2007)
10. Abramsky, S., Coecke, B.: A categorical semantics of quantum protocols. In: Proc. LiCS 2004, pp. 415–425. IEEE Computer Society Press, Los Alamitos (2004)
11. Coecke, B., Pavlovic, D.: Quantum measurements without sums. In: Chen, G., Kauffman, L.H., Lomonaco Jr., S.J. (eds.) The Mathematics of Quantum Computation and Technology. Taylor and Francis, Abington (2007)
12. Coecke, B., Paquette, E.O.: POVMs and Naimark's theorem without sums. In: Proceedings of QPL 2006 (2006)
13. Dixon, L., Duncan, R., Kissinger, A.: Quantomatic. Project home page, `http://dream.inf.ed.ac.uk/projects/quantomatic/`
14. Duncan, R.: Types for Quantum Computing. PhD thesis, Oxford University (2006)
15. Dixon, L., Duncan, R.: Graphical reasoning in compact closed categories for quantum computation. Ann. Math. Artif. Intel. 56(1), 23–42 (2009)
16. Duncan, R., Perdrix, S.: Graph states and the necessity of Euler decomposition. In: Ambos-Spies, K., Löwe, B., Merkle, W. (eds.) CiE 2009. LNCS, vol. 5635, pp. 167–177. Springer, Heidelberg (2009)
17. Kissinger, A.: Graph rewrite systems for complementary classical structures in †-symmetric monoidal categories. Master's thesis, Oxford University (2008)
18. Lack, S.: Composing PROPs. Theor. Appl. Categ. 13(9), 147–163 (2004)

The Compositional Structure of Multipartite Quantum Entanglement

Bob Coecke and Aleks Kissinger*

Oxford University Computing Laboratory

Abstract. Multipartite quantum states constitute a (if not the) key resource for quantum computations and protocols. However obtaining a generic, structural understanding of entanglement in N-qubit systems is a long-standing open problem in quantum computer science. Here we show that multipartite quantum entanglement admits a compositional structure, and hence is subject to modern computer science methods.

Recall that two N-qubit states are SLOCC-equivalent if they can be inter-converted by stochastic local (quantum) operations and classical communication. There are only two SLOCC-equivalence classes of genuinely entangled 3-qubit states, the GHZ-class and the W-class, and we show that these exactly correspond with two kinds of internal commutative Frobenius algebras on $\mathbb{C}^2$ in the symmetric monoidal category of Hilbert spaces and linear maps, namely 'special' ones and 'anti-special' ones. Within the graphical language of symmetric monoidal categories, the distinction between 'special' and 'anti-special' is purely topological, in terms of 'connected' vs. 'disconnected'.

These GHZ and W Frobenius algebras form the primitives of a graphical calculus which is expressive enough to generate and reason about representatives of arbitrary N-qubit states. This calculus refines the graphical calculus of complementary observables in [5, ICALP'08], which has already shown itself to have many applications and admit automation. Our result also induces a generalised graph state paradigm for measurement-based quantum computing.

1 Introduction

Spatially separated compound quantum systems exhibit correlations under measurement which cannot be explained by classical physics. Bipartite states are used in protocols such as quantum teleportation, quantum key distribution, superdense coding, entanglement swapping, and many other typically quantum phenomena. The tripartite *GHZ-state* allows for a purely qualitative Bell-type argument demonstrating the non-locality of quantum mechanics [17], a phenomenon which has recently been exploited to boost computational power [2]. In one-way quantum computing, multipartite *graph states* which generalise GHZ-states constitute a resource for universal quantum computing [19]. There are

* This work is supported by EPSRC Advanced Research Fellowship EP/D072786/1, by a Clarendon Studentship, by US Office of Naval Research Grant N00014-09-1-0248 and by EU FP6 STREP QICS. We thank Jamie Vicary for useful feedback.

S. Abramsky et al. (Eds.): ICALP 2010, Part II, LNCS 6199, pp. 297–308, 2010.

also many other applications of GHZ-states and graph states in the areas of fault-tolerance and communication protocols [24]. The tripartite *W-state*, which is qualitatively very different from the GHZ-state, supports distributed leader-election [12]. However, very little is known about the structure and behaviours of general multipartite quantum states.

What is known is that the variety of different possible behaviours is huge. For example, there is an infinite number of 4-qubit states which are not inter-convertible by *stochastic local* (quantum) *operations* and *classical communication* (SLOCC) [28]. States that are not SLOCC-equivalent correspond to incomparable forms of 'distributed quantum-ness,' so each will have distinct behaviours and applications.

For three qubits there are only two non-degenerate SLOCC-classes [16], one that contains the GHZ-state and another one that contains the W-state:

$$|GHZ\rangle = |000\rangle + |111\rangle \qquad |W\rangle = |100\rangle + |010\rangle + |001\rangle\,.$$

We will now argue that *tripartite qubit states can be seen as algebraic operations on* $\mathbb{C}^2$. The most fundamental operations in nearly all branches of algebra have two inputs and one output. Quantum protocols like gate teleportation have taught us not to care much about distinguishing inputs and outputs, as there is little distinction between information flowing forward through an operation and flowing 'horizontally' across an entangled state. Hence the 'total arity' (inputs + outputs) becomes a cogent feature. In this sense, tripartite states, regarded as operations with zero inputs and three outputs, are analogous to binary algebraic operations.

In this paper, we show that GHZ-states and W-states play a foundational role in the composition of multipartite entangled states. Just as $+$ and $*$ can be used to generate arbitrary polynomials, W and GHZ can be used to generate arbitrary N-partite qubit states.

These results are presented in the context of *categorical quantum mechanics*, initiated by Abramsky and one of the authors in [1, LiCS'04]. An appealing feature of this framework is its formulation in symmetric monoidal categories, which admit a rich graphical calculus [25,18,27]. Frobenius algebras, specifically in their categorical formulation due to Carboni and Walters [4], have become a key focus of categorical quantum mechanics by accounting for observables and corresponding classical data flows [8,9,7,10]. This picture of complementarity observables was axiomatised by Coecke and Duncan in [5, ICALP'08], resulting in a powerful graphical calculus, which we shall refer to here as the *Z/X-calculus*. It has since had applications in quantum foundations [6], in measurement-based quantum computation [5, ICALP'08], [14] and [15, ICALP'10], and for the analysis of quantum cryptographic protocols [11,10]. There is also a software tool called `quantomatic` [13], developed by Dixon, Duncan and Kissinger, which performs semi-automated reasoning within the Z/X-calculus.

Section 2 reviews commutative Frobenius algebras in a categorical context. In section 3 we introduce a calculus which is similar to Z/X-calculus, in that it also has two commutative Frobenius algebras (CFAs) as its main ingredients. However, while in Z/X-calculus the CFAs are both special [21], here we introduce 'anti-special' CFAs which will account for the W-state behaviour. We then show in section 4 that this calculus is a powerful tool for generating and reasoning about multipartite states. In section 5 we show how the W/GHZ-calculus actually *refines* Z/X-calculus, by reconstructing the latter's generators and relations. Since Z/X-calculus subsumes reasoning with graph states [14], GHZ/W-calculus provides a generalised graph state paradigm, and could also lead to a generalised measurement-based quantum computational model, among many other potential applications. We conclude by noting how the `quantomatic` software can easily be adjusted to semi-automate reasoning within the more powerful GHZ/W-calculus, giving a computational handle on this much richer language.

We formally don't distinguish 'states' from 'vectors'; it should be clear to the reader that by 'state $|\psi\rangle$' we mean the ray spanned by the vector $|\psi\rangle$. By $|i\rangle$ we refer to a vector of a chosen orthonormal basis, also referred to as the *computational basis.* It is in this basis that our GHZ- and W-states are expressed.

An extended version of this paper, `arXiv:1002.2540`*, contains all proofs.*

2 Background: Commutative Frobenius Algebras

Let $\mathbf{C}$ be a symmetric monoidal category. We work within the induced graphical calculus and take associativity and unit laws to be strict. A *commutative Frobenius algebra* (CFA) in $\mathbf{C}$ is an object A and morphisms $\mu, \eta, \delta, \epsilon$ such that:

- $(A, \mu : A \otimes A \to A, \eta : I \to A)$ is an internal commutative monoid,
- $(A, \delta : A \to A \otimes A, \epsilon : A \to I)$ is an internal cocommutative comonoid, and
- $(1 \otimes \mu) \circ (\delta \otimes 1) = \delta \circ \mu$.

Depicting μ, δ, η, ϵ respectively as , ,  and  the *Frobenius identity* becomes:

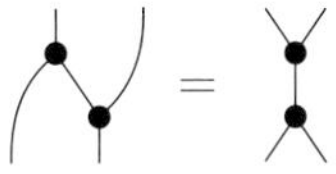

Definition 1. For a CFA $A = (A, \mu, \eta, \delta, \epsilon)$, an A-*graph* is a morphism obtained from the following maps: 1_A, $\sigma_{A,A}$ (the swap map), μ, η, δ, and ϵ, combined with composition and the tensor product. An A-graph is said to be *connected* precisely when its graphical representation is connected.

The following is a well-known result about Frobenius algebras, for a proof, see e.g. [21].

Proposition 1. *The Frobenius identity guarantees that any connected A-graph is uniquely determined by its number of inputs, outputs, and its number of loops.*[1]

[1] Here, the *number of loops* is the maximum number of edges one can remove without disconnecting the graph. Equivalently, it is the number of holes in the corresponding cobordism [21].

This makes CFA's highly topological, in that A-graphs are invariant under deformations that respect the number of loops. In the special case where there are 0 loops, we make the following notational simplification, called *spider*-notation.

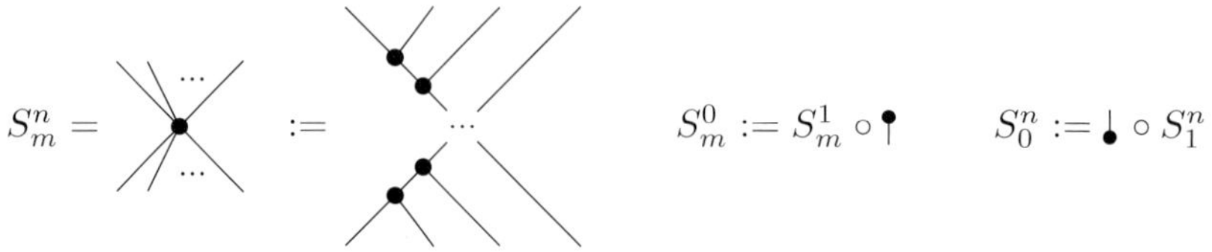

For example, we can use this notation to construct the following maps:

$S_2^0 =$ '*cap*' $=$  $S_0^2 =$ '*cup*' $=$ 

We usually omit the dots from caps and cups when there is no ambiguity, e.g.

Definition 2. A CFA is *special* (a *SCFA*), resp. *anti-special* (an *ACFA*) iff:

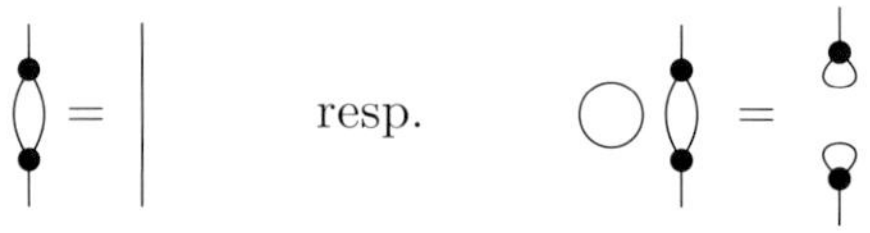

While the notion of special Frobenius algebras is standard, that of anti-special ones seems new. For CFAs we assume that circles admit an inverse [2] i.e. ◯∘⊖ = ⊖∘◯ $= 1_I$. Interpreting maps $I \to I$ as scalars, this just means ◯ is non-zero.

3 GHZ- and W-States as Commutative Frobenius Algebras

Let Σ be a distributed N-qubit system. A *local operation* on Σ is an operation on a single subsystem of Σ.[3] Two states of Σ are *SLOCC-equivalent* if with some non-zero probability they can be inter-converted with only local physical operations and classical communication. We shall use the following important theorem to characterise such states.

Theorem 1 ([16]). *Two states $|\Psi\rangle, |\Phi\rangle$ of Σ are SLOCC-equivalent iff there exist invertible linear maps $L_i : \mathcal{H}_i \to \mathcal{H}_i$ such that $|\Psi\rangle = (L_1 \otimes \ldots \otimes L_N)|\Phi\rangle$.*

By the *induced tripartite state* of a CFA we mean $S_3^0 =$ . We denote the symmetric monoidal category of finite-dimensional Hilbert spaces, linear maps, the tensor product and with $\mathbb{C}$ as the tensor unit by **FHilb**. In **FHilb**, any morphism $\psi : \mathbb{C} \to \mathcal{H}$ uniquely defines a vector $|\psi\rangle := \psi(1) \in \mathcal{H}$ and vice versa.

[2] In **FHilb**, ◯ $= D$, the dimension of the underlying space. Therefore ⊖ $= 1/D$.

[3] These may also be generalised measurements, i.e. those arising when measuring the system together with an ancillary system by means of a projective measurement, as well unitary operations applied to extended systems.

Theorem 2. *For each SCFA (resp. ACFA) on* $\mathbb{C}^2$ *in* **FHilb** *its induced tripartite state is SLOCC-equivalent to* $|GHZ\rangle$ *(resp.* $|W\rangle$*). Conversely, any symmetric state in* $\mathbb{C}^2 \otimes \mathbb{C}^2 \otimes \mathbb{C}^2$ *that is SLOCC-equivalent to* $|GHZ\rangle$ *(resp.* $|W\rangle$*) is the induced tripartite state for some SCFA (resp. ACFA) on* $\mathbb{C}^2$ *in* **FHilb**.

Each SCFA on $\mathcal{H}$ in **FHilb** induces a state that is SLOCC-equivalent to $|GHZ\rangle$ because the *copied states* $|\psi_i\rangle \in \mathcal{H}$, that is, those satisfying $\delta(|\psi_i\rangle) = |\psi_i\rangle \otimes |\psi_i\rangle$, form a basis of $\mathcal{H}$ (see [9]§6). The induced tripartite state is then $\sum_i |\psi_i\psi_i\psi_i\rangle$ which is evidently SLOCC-equivalent to $\sum_i |iii\rangle$.

For the GHZ-state the induced SCFA is:

 $= |0\rangle\langle 00| + |1\rangle\langle 11|$  $= |+\rangle := |0\rangle + |1\rangle$

 $= |00\rangle\langle 0| + |11\rangle\langle 1|$  $= \langle +| := \langle 0| + \langle 1|$ (1)

and for the W-state the induced ACFA is:

 $= |1\rangle\langle 11| + |0\rangle\langle 01| + |0\rangle\langle 10|$  $= |1\rangle$

 $= |00\rangle\langle 0| + |01\rangle\langle 1| + |10\rangle\langle 1|$  $= \langle 0|$ (2)

We know from [16] that W and GHZ are the *only* genuine tripartite qubit states, up to SLOCC-equivalence. Thus, the result above offers an exhaustive classification of CFA's on $\mathbb{C}^2$, up to local operations.

Corollary 1. *Any CFA on* $\mathbb{C}^2$ *in* **FHilb** *is 'locally equivalent' to a SCFA or an ACFA. Concretely, there exists an invertible linear map* $L : \mathbb{C}^2 \to \mathbb{C}^2$ *such that the induced maps*

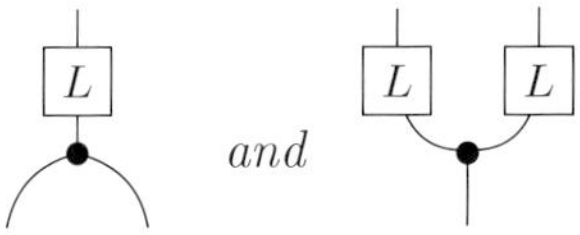

define a CFA that is either special or anti-special.

Corollary 2. *Every (commutative) monoid on* $\mathbb{C}^2$ *in* **FHilb** *extends to a CFA.*

We now show that an SCFA and an ACFA each admit a normal form. By the previous theorem these govern the graphical calculi associated to GHZ and W SLOCC-class states.

Theorem 3. *Let* **C** *be any symmetric monoidal category. For an SCFA on* **C**, *any connected CFA-morphism is equal to a spider, for an ACFA, any connected CFA-morphism is either equal to a spider or is of the following form:*

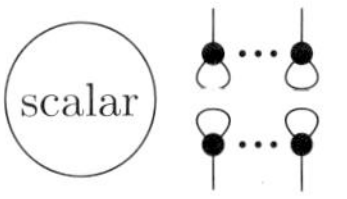

where the scalar is some tensor product of , , *and* . *The total number of loops minus the number of*  *is moreover preserved.*

A key ingredient in the proof is that δ (resp. μ) 'copies'  (resp. ).

Proposition 2. *For any ACFA we have:* 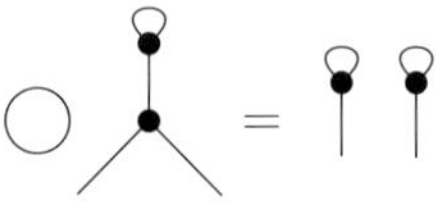

Thm 2 shows that the structure of either an SCFA or an ACFA alone generates relatively few morphisms, and the only non-degenerate multipartite states which arise are the canonical n-qubit analogous to the GHZ- and W-state. However, when combining these two a wealth of states emerges, as we show now.

4 Generating General Multipartite States

For the specific cases of the GHZ-SCFA and the W-ACFA as in Eqs (1) and (2) there are many equations which connect (, , ,) and (, , ,). A small subset of these provide us with a calculus that helps us to realise the main goal of this section, to show that representatives of all known multipartite SLOCC-classes arise from the interaction of a SCFA with an ACFA.

The cups and caps induced by each CFA in general do not coincide, e.g.

$|10\rangle + |01\rangle =$ 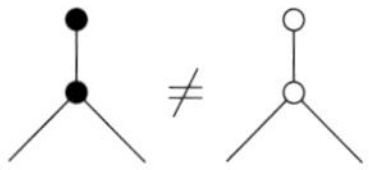 $= |00\rangle + |11\rangle$

Therefore we always place dots on caps and cups in order to distinguish them, except in the case of and , which are always assumed to consist of a (co) multiplication and a cap or cup of the same colour.

Definition 3. A *GHZ/W-pair* consists of a SCFA (, , ,) and an ACFA (, , ,) which satisfy the following four equations.

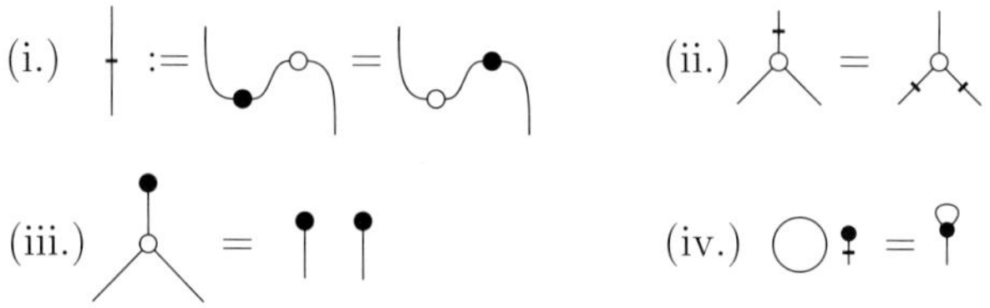

In **FHilb** these conditions have a clear interpretation. By compactness of cups and caps, the first condition implies that a 'tick' on a wire is self-inverse which together with the second condition implies that it is a permutation of the copied states of the SCFA (see [7]§3.4). The third condition asserts that is a copiable point. The fourth condition implies that is also a (scaled) copiable point since it is the result of applying a permutation to a scalar multiple of .

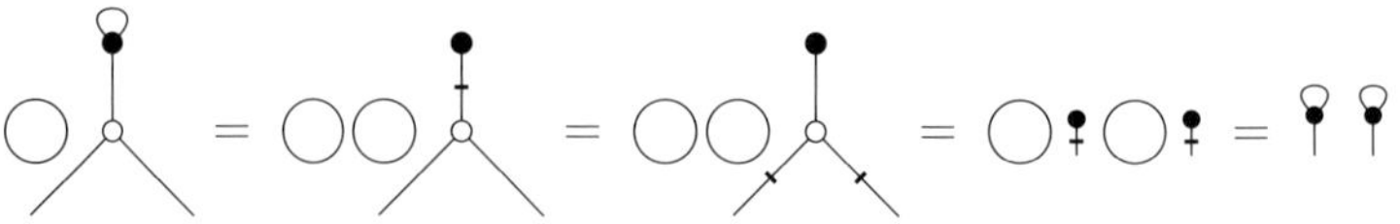

We have shown abstractly that the ACFA structure defines the copiable points of the SCFA structure, which uniquely determines the structure itself.

Theorem 4. *For any SCFA $\mathcal{G}$ on $\mathbb{C}^2$, there is a unique ACFA $\mathcal{W}$ such that $(\mathcal{G}, \mathcal{W})$ forms a GHZ/W-pair. Furthermore, for any ACFA $\mathcal{W}'$ on $\mathbb{C}^2$, there is a unique SCFA $\mathcal{G}'$ such that $(\mathcal{G}', \mathcal{W}')$ forms a GHZ/W-pair.*

There is necessarily an infinite number of SLOCC classes when $N \geq 4$ [16]. To obtain finite classification results many authors have expanded to talk about SLOCC *super-classes*, or families of SLOCC classes parameterised by one or more continuous variables. An example of this approach is [22], where the authors introduce a classification scheme based upon the right singular subspace of a pure state. They begin with the observation that a column vector with 2^N entries has the same data as a $2^{(N-1)} \times 2$ matrix. Therefore, they treat a pure state on N qubits as a map from $\bigotimes^{(N-1)} \mathbb{C}^2$ to $\mathbb{C}^2$. Performing a singular value decomposition on such a matrix yields a 1- or 2-dimensional right singular subspace, spanned by vectors in $\bigotimes^{N-1} \mathbb{C}^2$. The SLOCC super-class of this state is then labeled by the SLOCC super-classes of these spanning vectors, thus performing the inductive step. The base case is $\mathbb{C}^2 \otimes \mathbb{C}^2$, where the only two SLOCC classes are represented by the product state and the Bell state.

An alternative way of looking at this scheme is to consider N-partite states as "controlled" $(N-1)$-partite states. That is to say, the right singular space of a state is spanned by $\{|\Psi\rangle, |\Phi\rangle\}$ iff there exists a SLOCC-equivalent state of the form $|0\Psi\rangle + |1\Phi\rangle$. This provides an operational description of a SLOCC super-class. Namely, a state $|\Theta\rangle$ is in the SLOCC superclass $\{|\Psi\rangle, |\Phi\rangle\}$ if there exists *some* (two-dimensional, possibly non-orthogonal) basis B such that projecting the first qubit on to an element of B yields a state that is SLOCC-equivalent to $|\Psi\rangle$ for outcome 1 and $|\Phi\rangle$ for outcome 2. From this point of view, we can show that the language of GHZ/W-pairs realises the inductive step.

Theorem 5. *In* **FHilb**, *when considering the GHZ/W-pair on $\mathbb{C}^2$ as in Eqs (1) and (2), the linear map*

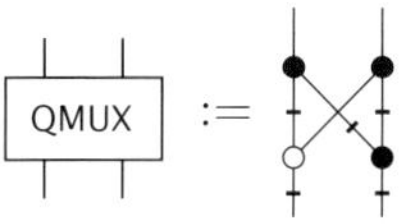

(3)

takes states $|\psi\rangle \otimes |\phi\rangle$ to a state that is SLOCC-equivalent to $\langle 1|\phi\rangle|0\psi\rangle + \langle 1|\psi\rangle|1\phi\rangle$. From this it follows that more generally,

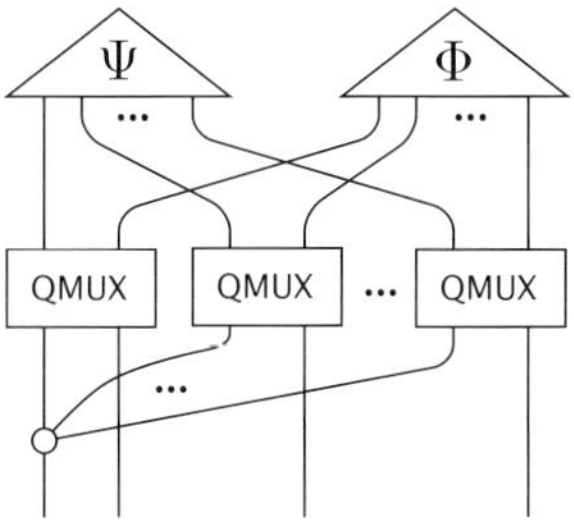

takes the states $|\Psi\rangle \otimes |\Phi\rangle \in \left(\bigotimes^{N-1} \mathbb{C}^2\right) \otimes \left(\bigotimes^{N-1} \mathbb{C}^2\right)$ to

$$\langle \underbrace{1 \ldots 1}_{N-1} |\Phi\rangle|0\Psi\rangle + \langle \underbrace{1 \ldots 1}_{N-1} |\Psi\rangle|1\Phi\rangle \, .$$

Proof. We show this by using axioms (i.)-(iv.). We only require the result to hold up to SLOCC-equivalence, so we shall disregard the scalars and . Note that $\langle 0| =$ and $\langle 1| =$:

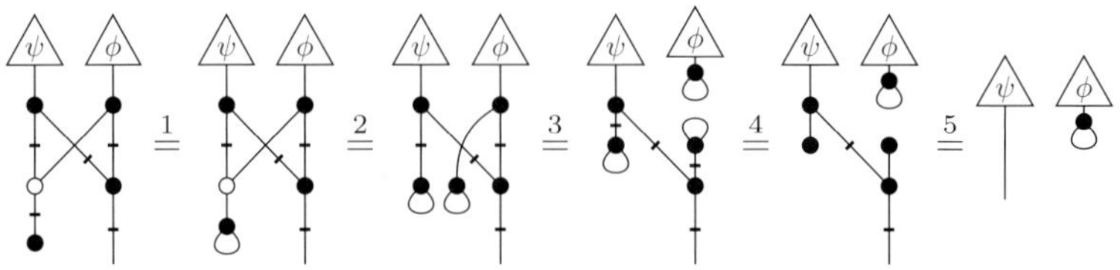

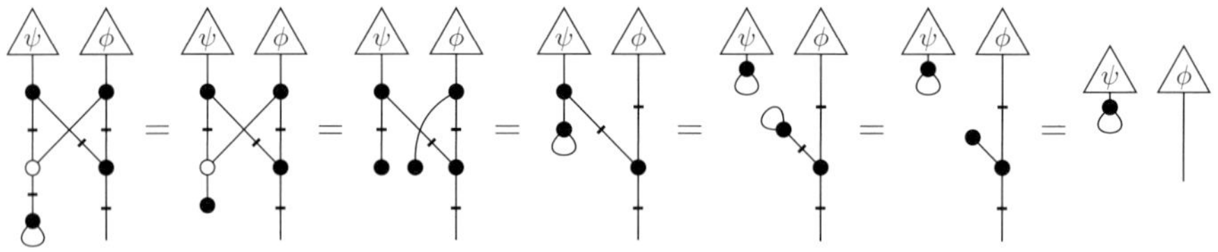

We shall explain the first sequence of equalities. The second proceeds similarly. Step 1 is due to axiom (iv.). For step 2, we can show that is a copiable point of (c.f. the remark following Def 3). Step 3 is due to anti-specialness and step 4 to axiom (iv.). Step 5 is two applications of the unit and axiom (i.), which implies that is involutive. □

Scalars $\langle 1 \ldots 1|\Psi\rangle$ and $\langle 1 \ldots 1|\Phi\rangle$ are be assumed to be non-zero. If this is not the case we vary the representatives of SLOCC-classes. It is an easy exercise to show that any state is SLOCC-equivalent to a state that is not orthogonal to $|1 \ldots 1\rangle$.

Theorem 6. *In* **FHilb***, when considering the GHZ/W-pair on* $\mathbb{C}^2$ *as in Eqs (1) and (2), a linear map* $L : \mathbb{C}^2 \to \mathbb{C}^2$ *can always be realised either as:*

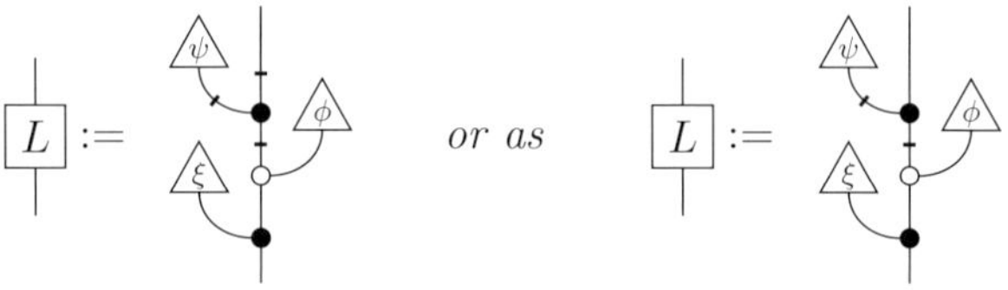

for some single-qubit states ψ*,* ϕ *and* ξ*. Consequently, given a representative of a SLOCC-class we can reproduce the whole SLOCC-class when we augment the GHZ/W-calculus with 'variables', i.e. single-qubit states.*

Since we can produce a witness for any SLOCC-class, as well as any other multipartite state that is SLOCC-equivalent to it, we can produce any multipartite state. Via map-state duality, from arbitrary $N + M$-qubit states we obtain arbitrary linear maps $L : \bigotimes^N \mathbb{C}^2 \to \bigotimes^M \mathbb{C}^2$.

Corollary 3. *If we adjoin variables to the graphical language of GHZ/W-pairs then any* N*-qubit entangled state and consequently also any linear map* $L : \bigotimes^N \mathbb{C}^2 \to \bigotimes^M \mathbb{C}^2$ *can be written in graphical language.*

What is important here, since all variables are local, is that all genuine new kinds of entanglement arise from the GHZ/W-calculus only.

Of course, the graphs that we obtain in the above prescribed manner are not at all the simplest representatives of a SLOCC-superclass. With 4 qubits, for example, it is easy to construct much simpler representatives of distinct SLOCC-superclasses. Here are representatives of five distinct superclasses:

where:

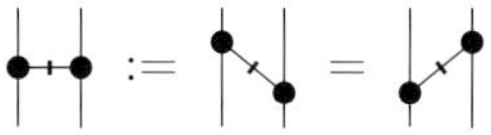

The first two are the 4 qubit GHZ- and W-state respectively for which we have:

- $|GHZ_4\rangle = |0\rangle|000\rangle + |1\rangle|111\rangle$
- $|W_4\rangle = |0\rangle|W\rangle + |1\rangle|000\rangle$

and one easily verifies that the other three are:

- $|0\rangle \underbrace{(|000\rangle + |101\rangle + |010\rangle)}_{\overset{\text{SLOCC}}{\simeq}|W\rangle} + |1\rangle(|0\rangle \underbrace{(|01\rangle + |10\rangle)}_{\overset{\text{SLOCC}}{\simeq}|Bell\rangle})$
- $|0\rangle|000\rangle + |1\rangle(|1\rangle \underbrace{(|01\rangle + |10\rangle)}_{\overset{\text{SLOCC}}{\simeq}|Bell\rangle})$
- $|0\rangle \underbrace{(|000\rangle + |111\rangle)}_{\overset{\text{SLOCC}}{\simeq}|GHZ\rangle} + |1\rangle|010\rangle$

respectively, from which we can read off the corresponding right singular vectors.

We can also obtain examples of fully parametrized SLOCC-superclasses. That is, the values of the variables yield all SLOCC-classes that the superclass contains. For example, the following figure corresponds with the given SLOCC superclass.

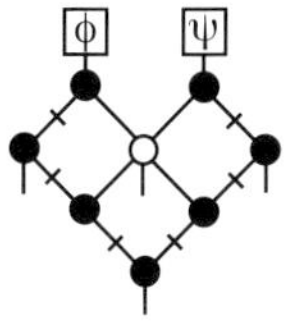

$$= |0\rangle(\underbrace{(|00\rangle + |1\psi\rangle)}_{\overset{\text{SLOCC}}{\simeq}|Bell\rangle}|\phi\rangle) + |1\rangle|0\rangle|Bell\rangle$$

So in addition to providing an inductive method to generate arbitrary multipartite states, the graphical calculus provides an intuitive tool to produce and reason about multipartite states. Since individual components exhibit well-defined primitive behaviours via the graph rewriting, one could imagine constructing composite states to meet specific, complex behavioural specifications in a quantum algorithm or protocol.

5 Induced Z/X-Calculus

Z/X-pairs (also called complementary classical structures) provide a graphical means to reason about the behaviour of interacting, maximally non-commuting observables in a quantum system. Here, we show how (in two dimensions) the theory of GHZ/W-pairs *subsumes* the theory of Z/X-pairs.

Definition 4. A *Z/X-pair* consists of two SCFAs (, , ,) and (, , ,) which satisfy the following equations:

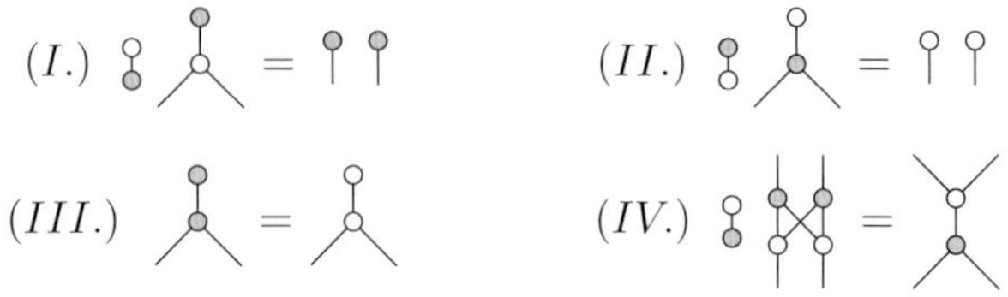

as well as the horizontal mirror image of these equations.

The key example of a Z/X-pair on $\mathbb{C}^2$ in **FHilb** are the SCFAs corresponding to the Z- and the X-eigenstates, i.e. a pair of *complementary observables*. By composition one for example obtains:

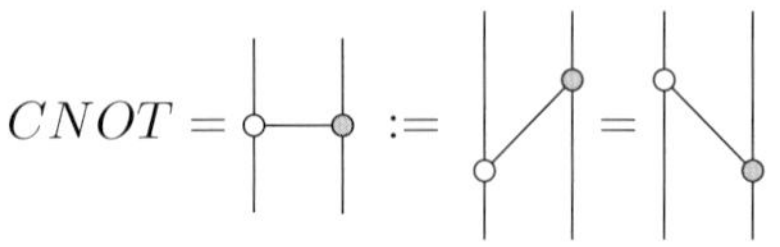

and the calculus then enables to reason about circuits, measurement-based quantum computing, QKD and many other things [5,14,6,15,11]. Meanwhile there is the `quantomatic` software which semi-automates reasoning within Z/X-calculus.

Theorem 7. *Under the assumption of the 'plugging rule':*[4]

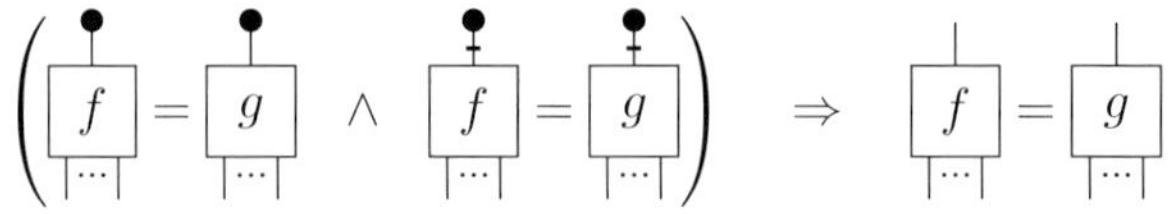

(4)

and for $\sqrt{\bigcirc} : I \to I$ *an isomorphism such that* $\sqrt{\bigcirc}\sqrt{\bigcirc} = \bigcirc$, *and with inverse* $\sqrt{\ominus} : I \to I$, *each GHZ/W-pair induces a Z/X-pair, in particular:*

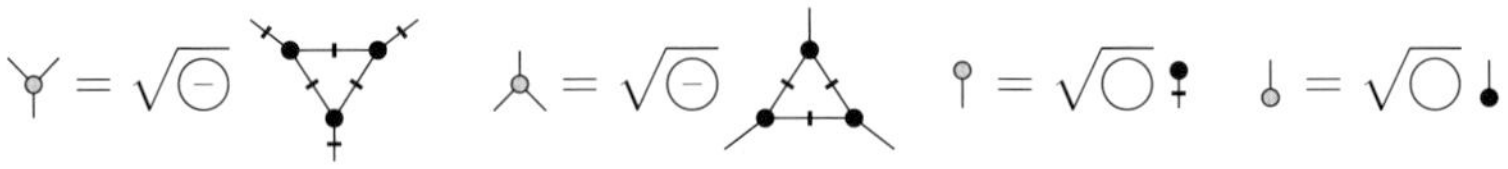
(5)

One particular application of Z/X-calculus is that it enables to write down graph states and reason about them. Graph states constitute the main resource in measurement-based quantum computing. What is particular appealing about them is that they relate physical properties to combinatorial properties of graphs.

Z/X-graph	graph state
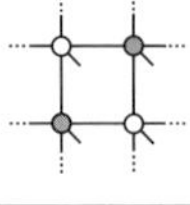	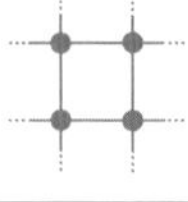

[4] In **FHilb**, this condition can be read as "the vectors { , } span $\mathbb{C}^2$."

The results in this section tell us that the GHZ/W-calculus gives rise to a more powerful generalised notion of graph state.

6 Conclusion and Outlook

In the light of the results in Sec 5, and given the power of the graphical calculus of complementary observables, we expect even more to come from our GHZ/W-calculus. As the W-state and the GHZ-state have very different kinds of applications [17,12] we expect their blend to give rise to a wide range of new possibilities. The graphical paradigm has been very successful in measurement-based quantum computing [19,3,15] and other areas [24], and our generalised graphical paradigm would substantially expand the scope of this practice, which with support of a forthcoming `quantomatic mark II` can be semi-automated.

We can now ask which fragment of equations that hold for Hilbert space quantum mechanics can be reproduced with GHZ/W-calculus, augmented with the plugging rule Eq (4). Does there exist an extension which provides a completeness result? This question is less ambitious than it may sound at first, given Selinger's theorem that dagger compact closed categories are complete with respect to finite-dimensional Hilbert spaces [26]. The obvious next step is to explore the states representable in this theory, and the types of (provably correct) protocols they can implement.

References

1. Abramsky, S., Coecke, B.: A categorical semantics of quantum protocols. In: LiCS (2004), Revision: arXiv:quant-ph/0808.1023
2. Anders, J., Browne, D.E.: Computational power of correlations. Physical Review Letters 102 (2009), 050502. arXiv:0805.1002
3. Browne, D.E., Kashefi, E., Mhalla, M., Perdrix, S.: Generalized flow and determinism in measurement-based quantum computation. New Journal Physics 9, 250 (2007), arXiv:quant-ph/0702212
4. Carboni, A., Walters, R.F.C.: Cartesian bicategories I. Journal of Pure and Applied Algebra 49, 11–32 (1987)
5. Coecke, B., Duncan, R.W.: Interacting quantum observables. In: Aceto, L., Damgård, I., Goldberg, L.A., Halldórsson, M.M., Ingólfsdóttir, A., Walukiewicz, I. (eds.) ICALP 2008, Part II. LNCS, vol. 5126, pp. 298–310. Springer, Heidelberg (2008); Extended version: arXiv:0906.4725
6. Coecke, B., Edwards, B., Spekkens, R.W.: Phase groups and the origin of non-locality for qubits. In: QPL 2009. ENTCS (to appear, 2010), arXiv:1003.5005
7. Coecke, B., Paquette, E.O., Pavlovic, D.: Classical and quantum structuralism. In: Mackie, I., Gay, S. (eds.) Semantic Techniques for Quantum Computation, pp. 29–69. Cambridge University Press, Cambridge (2009), arXiv:0904.1997
8. Coecke, B., Pavlovic, D.: Quantum measurements without sums. In: Chen, G., Kauffman, L., Lamonaco, S. (eds.) Mathematics of Quantum Computing and Technology, pp. 567–604. Taylor and Francis, Abington (2007), arXiv:quant-ph/0608035
9. Coecke, B., Pavlovic, D., Vicary, J.: A new description of orthogonal bases (2008), arXiv:0810.0812

10. Coecke, B., Perdrix, S.: Environment and classical channels in categorical quantum mechanics (2010) arXiv:1004.1598
11. Coecke, B., Wang, B.-S., Wang, Q.-L., Wang, Y.-J., Zhang, Q.-Y.: Graphical calculus for quantum key distribution. In: QPL 2009. ENTCS (to appear, 2010)
12. D'Hondt, E., Panangaden, P.: The computational power of the W and GHZ states. Quantum Information and Computation 6, 173–183 (2006)
13. Dixon, L., Duncan, R., Kissinger, A.: quantomatic, `http://dream.inf.ed.ac.uk/projects/quantomatic/`
14. Duncan, R., Perdrix, S.: Graph states and the necessity of Euler decomposition. In: CiE 2009. LNCS, vol. 5635. Springer, Heidelberg (2009) arXiv:0902.0500
15. Duncan, R., Perdrix, S.: Rewriting measurement-based quantum computations with generalised flow. Accepted for ICALP 2010 (2010)
16. Dür, W., Vidal, G., Cirac, J.I.: Three qubits can be entangled in two inequivalent ways. Phys. Rev. A 62 (2000), 62314.arXiv:quant-ph/0005115
17. Greenberger, D.M., Horne, M.A., Shimony, A., Zeilinger, A.: Bell's theorem without inequalities. American Journal of Physics 58, 1131–1143 (1990)
18. Joyal, A., Street, R.: The Geometry of tensor calculus I. Advances in Mathematics 88, 55–112 (1991)
19. Hein, M., Dür, W., Eisert, J., Raussendorf, R., Van den Nest, M., Briegel, H.-J.: Entanglement in graph states and its applications (2006) arXiv:quant-ph/0602096v1
20. Kelly, G.M., Laplaza, M.L.: Coherence for compact closed categories. Journal of Pure and Applied Algebra 19, 193–213 (1980)
21. Kock, J.: Frobenius Algebras and 2D Topological Quantum Field Theories. Cambridge University Press, Cambridge (2003)
22. Lamata, L., Leon, J., Salgado, D., Solano, E.: Inductive entanglement classification of four qubits under SLOCC. Physical Review A 75, 22318 (2007) arXiv:quant-ph/0610233
23. Lamata, L., Leon, J., Salgado, D., Solano, E.: Inductive classification of multipartite entanglement under SLOCC. Physical Review A 74, (2006), 52336.arXiv:quant-ph/0603243
24. Markham, D., Sanders, B.C.: Graph states for quantum secret sharing. Physical Review A 78 (2008), 42309.arXiv:0808.1532
25. Penrose, R.: Applications of negative dimensional tensors. In: Welsh, D. (ed.) Combinatorial Mathematics and its Applications, pp. 221–244. Academic Press, London (1971)
26. Selinger, P.: Finite dimensional Hilbert spaces are complete for dagger compact closed categories. In: QPL 2008. ENTCS (to appear, 2010)
27. Selinger, P.: A survey of graphical languages for monoidal categories. In: Coecke, B. (ed.) New Structures for Physics, pp. 275–337. Springer, Heidelberg (2009), arXiv:0908.3347
28. Verstraete, F., Dehaene, J., De Moor, B., Verschelde, H.: Four qubits can be entangled in nine different ways. Physical Review A 65 (2002) 52112.arXiv:quant-ph/0109033

Compositionality in Graph Transformation

Arend Rensink

Department of Computer Science, Universiteit Twente
rensink@cs.utwente.nl

Abstract. Graph transformation works under a whole-world assumption. In modelling realistic systems, this typically makes for large graphs and sometimes also large, hard to understand rules. From process algebra, on the other hand, we know the principle of reactivity, meaning that the system being modelled is embedded in an environment with which it continually interacts. This has the advantage of allowing modular system specifications and correspondingly smaller descriptions of individual components. Reactivity can alternatively be understood as enabling *compositionality*: the specification of components and subsystems are composed to obtain the complete model.

In this work we show a way to ingest graph transformation with compositionality, reaping the same benefits from modularity as enjoyed by process algebra. In particular, using the existing concept of graph interface, we show under what circumstances rules can be decomposed into smaller subrules, each working on a subgraph of the complete, whole-world graph, in such a way that the effect of the original rule is precisely captured by the synchronisation of subrules.

1 Introduction

Graph transformation has shown to be a very useful specification formalism, enabling the rapid modelling of systems of all kinds, ranging from physical systems to protocols and concrete software. However, one drawback of graph transformation systems is that they require a "whole-world" view of the system to be modelled: the model at hand always describes the entire system, and thus can grow very large. There is no support for component submodels which can be analysed individually and composed later.

This is a consequence of the fact that graph transformation, like all rewriting techniques, has a *reductive* semantics: applying a graph transformation rule involves finding a match in the current model (the host graph) and making local changes in the model without any reference to an external environment (a step which in some contexts is called a reduction). This is in contrast to the *reactive* semantics enjoyed by, for instance, process algebra: there the application of a rule typically involves communication with an environment that is unknown at the moment (often called a reaction); the overall system behaviour results from synchronisation of different models, in which one plays the role of environment for the other.

In this paper we study a notion of reactivity for graph transformation. We compose individual models by "gluing them together" along a predefined interface; the result is like union, where the interface identifies the parts that are are merged. (Technically, this comes down to constructing pushouts in an appropriate category.) Transformation rules

S. Abramsky et al. (Eds.): ICALP 2010, Part II, LNCS 6199, pp. 309–320, 2010.

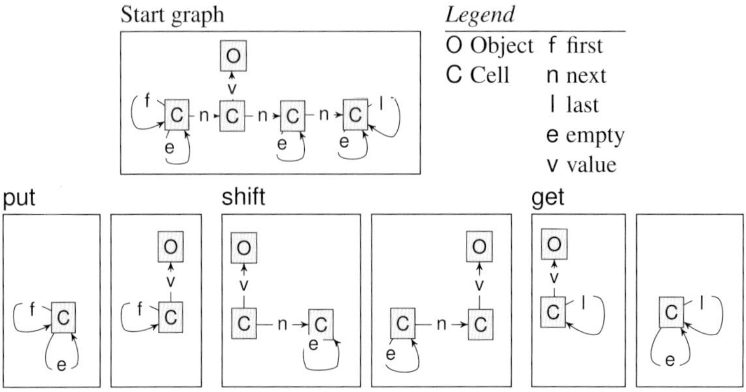

Fig. 1. Start graph and transformation rules for a simple, 4-cell buffer

are glued together in a similar fashion. Let us use the symbol '+' to represent composition (which is partial since only objects with compatible interfaces can be composed). We then compare transitions of individual components, $G_i \xrightarrow{p_i} H_i$ for $i = 1, 2$, where the G_i and H_i are graphs and the p_i transformation rules, to transitions $G_1 + G_2 \xrightarrow{p} H$ of the composed system. We then investigate the following crucial properties (or actually a slightly more involved version that also takes matches into account):

Soundness. Compatible local transitions always give rise to global transitions: when the G_i and p_i are compatible, then $G_i \xrightarrow{p_i} H_i$ for $i = 1, 2$ implies that the H_i are compatible and that $G_1 + G_2 \xrightarrow{p_1+p_2} H_1 + H_2$.

Completeness. All global transitions can be obtained by composing compatible local transitions: $G_1 + G_2 \xrightarrow{p} H$ implies that there are compatible p_i for $i = 1, 2$ such that $G_i \xrightarrow{p_i} H_i$, $p = p_1 + p_2$ and $H = H_1 + H_2$.

We illustrate the results on a simple example of a buffer. The whole-world model with corresponding rules (consisting of a left hand side and a right hand side graph) is given in Fig. 1. The intuitive meaning of the rules is that a match is found for the left hand side, which is then replaced by the right hand side. A modular specification will allow us to specify the behaviour per cell (with sufficient context information to glue the cells together). For instance, Fig. 2 shows how the original graph can be decomposed into four individual cells, and also shows the decomposition of the rules.

The structure of the paper is as follows: Sect. 2 defines concrete graphs and their composition; subsequently, Sect. 3 generalises this to the more abstract setting of adhesive categories. We prove soundness and state sufficient conditions for completeness. Sect. 4 concludes the paper with an overview of related work and open questions.

A somewhat extended version of the paper, including all the proofs, can be found in the report [15].

2 Graph Composition

In this section we introduce a concrete definition of graphs with interfaces, called *marked graphs*, as well as the rules to transform them.

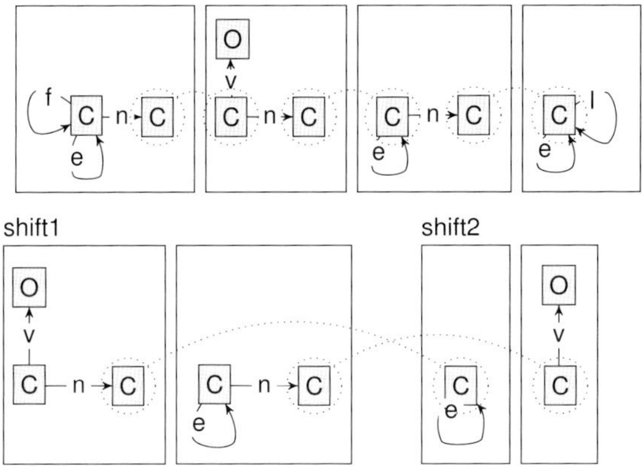

Fig. 2. Decomposed start graph and shift-rule. Dotted lines indicate sharing

2.1 Graphs and Their Transformation

Throughout this paper we assume global (countable) disjoint universes N of nodes, E of edges, and L of labels, with (also globally defined) functions $src, tgt\colon \mathsf{E} \to \mathsf{N}$ and $lab\colon \mathsf{E} \to \mathsf{L}$. In particular, for every combination of $v, w \in \mathsf{N}$ and $a \in \mathsf{L}$, there are assumed to be countably many $e \in \mathsf{E}$ such that $src(e) = v$, $tgt(e) = w$ and $lab(e) = a$.

Furthermore, we will use *structure-preserving functions* over $\mathsf{N} \cup \mathsf{E}$, which are functions $f = f_V \cup f_E$ with $f_V\colon V \to \mathsf{N}$ for some $V \subseteq \mathsf{N}$ and $f_E\colon E \to \mathsf{E}$ for some $E \subseteq \mathsf{E}$ such that $src \circ f_E = f_V \circ src \upharpoonright E$, $tgt \circ f_E = f_V \circ tgt \upharpoonright E$ and $lab \circ f_E = lab \upharpoonright E$. Note that this implies $src(E) \cup tgt(E) \subseteq V$.

Definition 1 (graph)

- *A graph is a finite set* $G \subseteq \mathsf{N} \cup \mathsf{E}$, *such that* $src(G \cap \mathsf{E}) \cup tgt(G \cap \mathsf{E}) \subseteq G$. *We often write* V_G *for* $G \cap \mathsf{N}$ *and* E_G *for* $G \cap \mathsf{E}$, *or just* V *and* E *if the index* G *is clear from the context.*
- *Given graphs* G, H, *a* graph morphism $f\colon G \to H$ *is a structure-preserving function. If* f *is bijective we also call it an* isomorphism *and* G *and* H isomorphic.

We often use the pointwise extension of morphisms to sets of elements. Due to the use of globally defined sets of nodes and edges, graphs are closed under union and intersection, but not under set difference: $G \setminus H$ may contain "dangling edges". Moreover, for a morphism $f\colon G \to H$ and a subgraph $H' \subseteq H$, $f^{-1}(H')$ is also a graph.

Definition 2 (rule). *A graph transformation rule is a tuple* $p = \langle L, R \rangle$, *consisting of a left hand side (LHS) graph* L *and a right hand side (RHS) graph* R. *The intersection* $I = L \cap R$ *is often called the* interface *of* p.

Let $p = \langle L, R \rangle$ be a transformation rule. p is *applicable* to a graph G (often called the *host graph*) if there exists a *match* $m\colon L \to G$, which is a graph morphism satisfying

No dangling edges: For all $e \in E_G$, $src(e) \in m(L \setminus R)$ or $tgt(e) \in m(L \setminus R)$ implies $e \in m(L \setminus R)$;

No delete conflicts: $m(L \setminus I) \cap m(I) = \emptyset$.

The intuition is that the elements of G that are in $m(L)$ but not in $m(I)$ are scheduled to be deleted by the production. If a node is deleted, then so must its incident edges, or the result would not be a graph. Note that, due to the absence of delete conflicts, $m(L \setminus R) = m(L \setminus I) = m(L) \setminus m(I)$. Given such a match m, the *application* of p to G is defined by extending m to a morphism $m' \colon L \cup R \to H'$, where $H' \supseteq G$ and all elements of $R \setminus L$ have distinct, fresh images under m', and defining

$$H = (G \setminus m(L)) \cup m'(R) \ .$$

H is called the *target* of the production; we write $G \xrightarrow{p,m} H$ to denote that m is a valid match on host graph G, giving rise to target graph H, and $G \xrightarrow{p} H$ to denote that there is a match m such that $G \xrightarrow{p,m} H$. Note that H is not uniquely defined for a given p and m, due to the freedom in choosing the fresh images for $R \setminus L$; however, it is well-defined modulo isomorphism. From now on we assume that the fresh images are chosen in some deterministic fashion, depending on the element of $R \setminus L$ that triggers their introduction as well as the elements that have been generated "so far". (This is a kind of requirement that is quite hard to formalise but easy to realise in any implementation.)

2.2 Marked Graphs and Their Composition

We now define the notion of graphs and rules with interfaces, discussed above.

Definition 3 (marked graphs and rules)

- *A* marked graph G *is a pair of graphs* $(\underline{G}, \overline{G})$ *with* $\underline{G} \subseteq \overline{G}$. $\underline{G}$ *is called the* inner graph *or* subgraph, *and* $\overline{G}$ *the* outer graph. *Two marked graphs* G, H *are called* compatible *if* $\underline{G} = \underline{H} = \overline{G} \cap \overline{H}$; *in that case, we use* $G + H$ *to denote the graph* $\overline{G} \cup \overline{H}$.
- *A* marked morphism *between two marked graphs* G, H *is a pair of morphisms* $m = (\underline{m} \colon \underline{G} \to \underline{H}, \overline{m} \colon \overline{G} \to \overline{H})$ *such that* $\underline{m} = \overline{m} \upharpoonright \underline{G}$. *We write* $m \colon G \to H$.
- *A* marked rule p *is a pair of marked graphs* (L, R), *such that* $\underline{L} \cap \overline{R} = \overline{L} \cap \underline{R}$. *This can alternatively be interpreted as a pair of rules* $(\underline{p}, \overline{p})$ *with* $\underline{p} = (\underline{L}, \underline{R})$ *and* $\overline{p} = (\overline{L}, \overline{R})$. *As before,* $\underline{p}$ *is called the* inner rule *or* subrule *and* $\overline{p}$ *the* outer rule. *Two marked rules* p, q *are compatible if* L_p *and* L_q *as well as* R_p *and* R_q *are compatible; the composition is denoted* $p + q$ $(= (L_p + L_q, R_p + R_q))$.

Obviously, the intention is that a marked rule should act upon a marked graph by applying the outer rule to the outer graph and the inner rule to the inner graph. The outcome should be a new marked graph. For this purpose, we define a (marked) match of a marked rule p into a marked graph G as a marked morphism $m \colon L \to G$ such that $\overline{m}$ is a match of $\overline{p}$ into $\overline{G}$ (meaning that there are no dangling edges or delete conflicts) and in addition the following condition is satisfied:

Delete consistency: $\overline{m}(\overline{L}) \cap \underline{G} \subseteq \overline{m}(\underline{L} \cup \overline{I})$

Delete consistency essentially states that elements deleted from the outer graph (by the outer rule) should either not occur in the inner graph in the first place, or be explicitly deleted from the inner graph (by the inner rule). The following states that delete consistency is a necessary and sufficient conditions for marked rule application to yield a new marked graph.

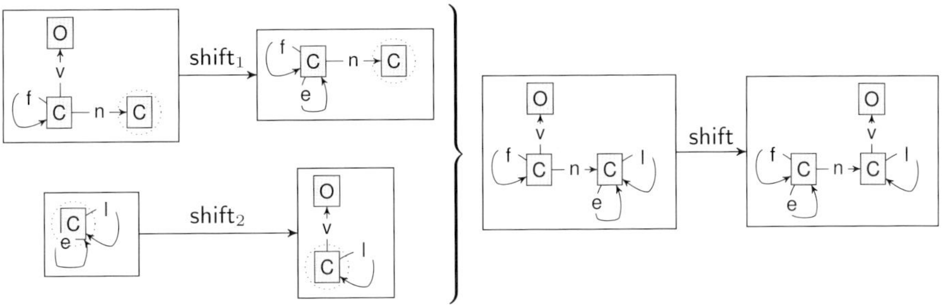

Fig. 3. Composition of two transformations

Proposition 4. *Let p be a marked rule, G a marked graph, and $m\colon L \to G$ a marked morphism. m is a marked match if and only if the pair $H = (\underline{H}, \overline{H})$ defined by $\underline{G} \xrightarrow{p,m} \underline{H}$ and $\overline{G} \xrightarrow{p,m} \overline{H}$ is a marked graph. We write $G \xrightarrow{p,m} H$.*

2.3 Soundness and Completeness

We can now formulate the notion of composition of graph transformations that is central to this paper. Composition is defined only for compatible marked transformations, where two marked transformations $G_i \xrightarrow{p_i,m_i} H_i$ for $i = 1, 2$ are called compatible if (G_1, G_2), (p_1, p_2) and (m_1, m_2) are compatible pairs. The assumption of determinism then implies that H_1 and H_2 are also compatible.

As discussed in the introduction, the crucial properties that we are after are soundness and completeness of subgraph transformations with respect to transformation of the complete graph. Soundness holds for all marked matches: the following theorem is a consequence of the more general Th. 14 proved in the next section.

Theorem 5 (soundness for graphs). *Any compatible pair of marked transformations is composable; i.e., if $G_i \xrightarrow{p_i,m_i} H_i$ for $1 = 1, 2$ are compatible marked transformations, then $G_1 + G_2 \xrightarrow{p_1+p_2,m_1+m_2} H_1 + H_2$.*

For instance, Fig. 3 shows how transformations on two marked fragments of a buffer, using the shift$_i$-rules of Fig. 2, give rise to a global transformation using the composed rule shift of Fig. 1. As before, the common subgraphs are indicated by dotted lines.

Completeness, on the other hand, only holds under an additional constraint. This is due to the fact that rules cannot be decomposed arbitrarily. We give a sufficient condition for decomposability, based on the concept of *accommodation*.

Definition 6 (accommodation of graphs). *Let p be a rule, and $m\colon L \to G$ a match of p in G. A subgraph $G' \subseteq G$* accommodates *a subgraph $R' \subseteq R$ under m if $L \cap R' = R \cap m^{-1}(G')$.*

Intuitively, G' accommodates R' if for all edges created according to R' (with respect to L), the end nodes are either themselves created by p or matched in G'. This ensures that a subrule p' of p exists with RHS R' and LHS $m^{-1}(G')$ (being the largest subgraph of L

that matches into G'). For instance, in a match of the rule shift of Fig. 1 in a graph G, the subgraph $G' \subseteq G$ consisting only of the image of the right hand C-node accommodates the subgraph of R_{shift} consisting of the v-edge and its end nodes, since the other end node (the O-node) is itself created. On the other hand, consider the following variation:

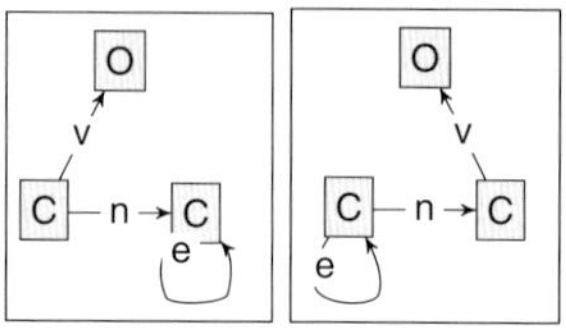

(1)

Here the O-node is not created by the rule: hence, in order to accommodate the RHS' v-edge, a subgraph must include an image of the O-node.

The completeness result for the concrete graphs studied in this section is given by the following theorem, the proof of which follows from the more general Th. 17 below.

Theorem 7 (completeness for graphs). *Let G_i be compatible marked graphs for $i = 1, 2$. A transformation $G_1 + G_2 \xrightarrow{p,m} H$ can be decomposed into marked transformations $G_i \xrightarrow{p_i,m_i} H_i$ if there exist graphs $\overline{R}_i$ for $i = 1, 2$ such that (i) $R = \overline{R}_1 \cup \overline{R}_2$ and (ii) $\overline{G}_i$ accommodates $\overline{R}_i$ under m.*

For our running example, the rules in Fig. 1 are such that all created edges have precisely one pre-existing end node; for that reason, the conditions for decomposability are always satisfied, meaning that we can soundly and completely decompose all transformations under arbitrary decompositions of the graphs. Indeed, the following (fixed) rule decomposition turns out to be sufficient:

- put is decomposed into put_1, which is identical to put, and an empty rule put_2;
- shift is decomposed into shift_1 and shift_2;
- get is decomposed into get_1, which is empty, and get_2, which is identical to get.

An example is shown in Fig. 4. To the left is the transition system T resulting from the repeated application of the composed rules to an initial graph consisting of two empty cells. To the right are the transition systems T_1 and T_2 generated from subgraphs consisting of one cell each, and the subrules discussed above. The matches are not included. The correctness of the (de)composition can be seen from the fact that T is the product of T_1 and T_2 in the automata sense, where x_i-transitions ($x = \mathsf{put}, \mathsf{shift}, \mathsf{get}$ and $i = 1, 2$) are synchronised and relabelled to x.

3 Composition for Marked Objects

We now lift the framework for concrete graphs presented above to a more abstract, categorical level, and we prove the soundness and completeness results on this level.

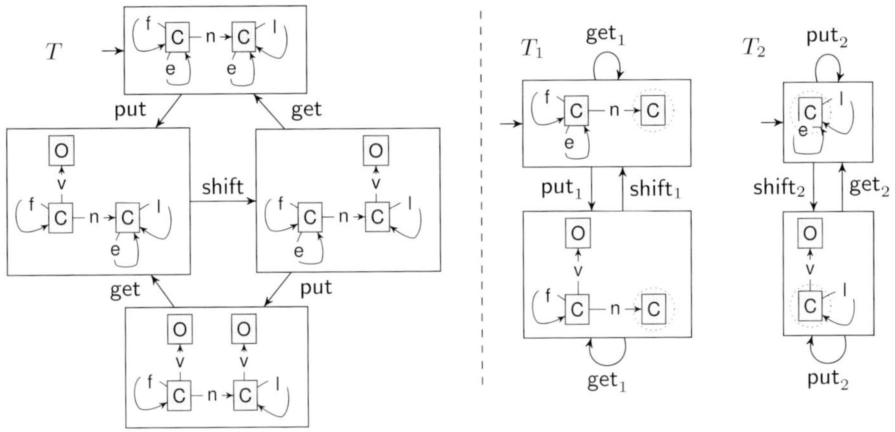

Fig. 4. Transformations of a complete and decomposed 2-cell buffer

3.1 Transformation in Adhesive Categories

Unfortunately, there is no space to recall the concepts from category theory used in this section (but see the report version [15]). We now recall the definitions of adhesive and quasiadhesive categories from [11,10]:

Definition 8 ((quasi-)adhesive category). *A category C is* quasiadhesive *if it satisfies the following properties:*

1. *C has pushouts along regular monomorphisms;*
2. *C has pullbacks;*
3. *Pushouts along regular monomorphisms are Van Kampen squares.*

A quasiadhesive category is called adhesive *if all monos are regular.*

For those that are not familiar with this theory, the following intuitions may be helpful:

- A regular mono $f\colon A \to B$ identifies a subobject of B that is isomorphic to A;
- The pushout of $B \xleftarrow{f} A \xrightarrow{g} C$ may be thought of as the union of B and C, where the shared subset is given by A and its "embedding" in B and C;
- The pullback of $B \xrightarrow{h} D \xleftarrow{k} C$ may be thought of as the intersection of B and C, where their "embedding" in D determines which elements they have in common.

It has been shown in [11,10] that (quasi-)adhesive categories form a nice, general framework in which properties of graph transformation systems can be proved abstractly; they generalise in some part the High-Level Replacement systems studied in, e.g., [4]. The graphs used in the previous section fall into this framework.

Proposition 9. *Graphs with graph morphisms form an adhesive category* Graph.

The notion of transformation rule used in the previous section generalises to categories in the standard way: the pair (L, R) turns into a span $L \hookleftarrow I \hookrightarrow R$, where I acts as the interface between L and R — which in the setting of the previous section corresponds to the intersection $L \cap R$. We also introduce morphisms over rules.

Definition 10 (rule). *Let C be a quasiadhesive category.*

- *A rule p is a span of regular monos $L \xleftarrow{l} I \xrightarrow{r} R$.*
- *A rule p is applicable to a given graph G if there exists a morphism $m\colon L \to G$ such that $I \hookrightarrow L \xrightarrow{m} G$ has a pushout complement. In that case, the application of p to G is defined by the diagram*

$$\begin{array}{ccccc} L & \xleftarrow{\;l\;} & I & \xrightarrow{\;r\;} & R \\ {\scriptstyle m}\downarrow & \mathsf{PO} & \downarrow{\scriptstyle k} & \mathsf{PO} & \downarrow{\scriptstyle m'} \\ G & \xleftarrow[\;g\;]{} & K & \xrightarrow[\;h\;]{} & H \end{array}$$

- *A rule morphism $f\colon p \to q$ is a triple of regular monomorphisms $\langle f_L, f_I, f_R\rangle$ such that the following diagram commutes and both squares are pullbacks:*

$$\begin{array}{ccccc} L_p & \xleftarrow{\;l_p\;} & I_p & \xrightarrow{\;r_p\;} & R_p \\ {\scriptstyle f_L}\downarrow & \mathsf{PB} & \downarrow{\scriptstyle f_I} & \mathsf{PB} & \downarrow{\scriptstyle f_R} \\ L_q & \xleftarrow[\;l_q\;]{} & I_q & \xrightarrow[\;r_q\;]{} & R_q \end{array}$$

The purpose of insisting that the squares of a rule morphism are pullbacks is to ensure that I_p is essentially the intersection of L_p and I_q, or alternatively, of R_p and I_q. This implies that elements preserved by the target rule (q) will also be preserved by the source rule (p). For an arbitrary (quasiadhesive) category C, the rules with rule morphisms form a category $\mathsf{Rule}(C)$.

3.2 Marked Objects

We now define the general notion of a marked object. As in the concrete case of graphs, a marked object is a monomorphism from an inner object to an outer object. The inner object is an interface used to glue marked objects together: gluing two marked objects with the same interface comes down to taking the pushout of the corresponding span.

Definition 11 (marked object). *Let C be an arbitrary category.*

- *A* marked object *X is a monomorphism $e_X : \underline{X} \hookrightarrow \overline{X}$. $\underline{X}$ is called the inner object and $\overline{X}$ the outer object.*
- *Given two marked objects X, Y, a marked morphism $f\colon X \to Y$ is a pair of morphisms $\underline{f}\colon \underline{X} \to \underline{Y}$ and $\overline{f}\colon \overline{X} \to \overline{Y}$ such that the resulting square commutes:*

$$\begin{array}{ccc} \underline{X} & \xrightarrow{\;\underline{f}\;} & \underline{Y} \\ {\scriptstyle e_X}\downarrow & & \downarrow{\scriptstyle e_Y} \\ \overline{X} & \xrightarrow{\;\overline{f}\;} & \overline{Y} \end{array}$$

- *Two marked objects X, Y are* compatible *if $\underline{X} = \underline{Y}$. If this is the case, we will use $X + Y$ to refer to the pushout object in the diagram*

$$\begin{array}{ccc} \underline{Y} = \underline{X} & \xrightarrow{\;e_X\;} & \overline{X} \\ {\scriptstyle e_Y}\downarrow & \mathsf{PO} & \downarrow \\ \overline{Y} & \hookrightarrow & X + Y \end{array}$$

For a category C, we use C^{M} to denote the category consisting of marked C-objects and marked C-morphisms. This construction is a special case of the *Artin gluing* studied in [10]. From that paper we may infer

Corollary 12 ([10, Th. 24]). *If C is an adhesive category, then C^{M} is a quasiadhesive category in which the regular monos are pullbacks of monos in C.*

This means that transformation of marked objects is well-defined, and that rules in C^{M} correspond to arrows in $\mathsf{Rule}(C)$ (cf. Def. 11). In the remainder of this section, unless stated otherwise we implicitly restrict ourselves to adhesive categories C. The following proposition states how the transformation of marked objects works: it essentially consists of the individual transformation of the inner and outer objects.

Proposition 13. *For any marked rule p, marked object G and marking consistent morphism $m\colon L \to G$, $G \xrightarrow{p,m} H$ if and only if $\underline{G} \xrightarrow{\underline{p},m} \underline{H}$ and $\overline{G} \xrightarrow{\overline{p},\overline{m}} \overline{H}$.*

In the full paper [15], we also take a look at the existence of pushout complements for marked objects. We give a sufficient criterion for their existence, which in the case of Graph is implied by the delete consistency defined in Sect. 2.2.

3.3 Soundness and Completeness

We now arrive at the main results of this paper, which establish the relation between marked transformations of marked subgraphs and global transformations of the composed graph. The first main result of this paper states that we can compose arbitrary (compatible) marked transformations.

Theorem 14 (soundness). *For $i = 1,2$, let G_i be compatible marked objects and p_i compatible marked rules. If $G_i \xrightarrow{p_i,m_i} H_i$ for $i = 1,2$ such that $\underline{m_1} = \underline{m_2}$, then $G_1 + G_2 \xrightarrow{p_1+p_2,m_1+m_2} H_1 + H_2$.*

The second main result states that, under some circumstances, we can also decompose global transformations into transformations of subgraphs. The circumstances involve that the decomposition into subgraphs allows an analogous decomposition of the rule's RHS. To formulate this precisely, we lift the notion of accommodation, defined in Def. 6, to the categorical level.

Definition 15 (accommodation). *Let p be a rule, G an object and $m\colon L \to G$ a morphism. A subobject $G' \hookrightarrow G$* accommodates *a subobject $R' \hookrightarrow R$ if they give rise to the following diagram:*

$$
\begin{array}{ccccccc}
G & \xleftarrow{m} & L & \hookleftarrow & I & \hookrightarrow & R \\
\uparrow & & PB & & \uparrow & PB & \uparrow \\
G' & \longleftarrow & & & I' & \hookrightarrow & R'
\end{array}
$$

This notion of accommodation generalises the one of Def. 6. The intuition is the same: the intersection of R' and I (given by the right hand pullback), which determines where to connect the elements to be created according to R', should coincide with the part of I that matches into G'.

Proposition 16. *Accommodation in* Graph *coincides with the property in Def. 6.*

We can now formulate the generalised completeness theorem:

Theorem 17 (completeness). *Let p be a rule and for $i = 1, 2$ let G_i be compatible marked objects. If $G_1 + G_2 \xrightarrow{p,m} H$, and $R = R_1 + R_2$ for marked graphs R_i ($i = 1, 2$) such that $\overline{G}_i$ accommodates $\overline{R}_i$ under m, then there are marked transformations $G_i \xrightarrow{p_i,m_i} H_i$ for $i = 1, 2$ such that $p = p_1 + p_2$, $m = m_1 + m_2$ and $H = H_1 + H_2$.*

The accommodation criterion in Def. 15 is sufficient but not necessary for a transformation to be decomposable. This can be seen by observing that the construction in the proof of Th. 17 always gives rise to marked matches m_i that are actually pullback squares in C; but composition also works for "ordinary" matches. In particular, it is quite possible to have component rules p_i of which the outer LHS $\overline{L}_i$ is not the pullback of $\overline{G}_i$ and L, but some subgraph of this pullback. The search for a more precise criterion is future work (see below).

4 Conclusion

We have defined a notion of composition for graph transformations that acts on graphs as well as rules. We have proved that composition is sound, and have given sufficient conditions under which it is complete. This is a first, and essential, ingredient for enabling graph transformation to move from a purely reductive, whole-world specification formalism to a reactive, compositional formalism.

4.1 Related Work

Though we believe our aims and approach to be completely original, there is a number of loosely related topics, which we review here.

Synchronised Hyperedge Replacement. This is a paradigm in which graph transformation rules (more specifically, hyperedge replacement rules) can be synchronised based one the adjacency of their occurrences within a graph; see [9,7]. The synchronised rules are not themselves understood as graph transformation rules, an consequently the work does not address the type of compositionality issues that we have studied here. Still, it is interesting to see whether SHR synchronisation can be understood as a special type of composition in our sense.

History-Dependent Automata. This is a behavioural model in which states are enriched with a set of *names* (see [13] for an overview). Transitions expose names to the environment, and can also record the deletion, creation and permutation of names. HD-automata can be composed while synchronising their transitions: this provides a model for name passing. Transition systems induced by graph transformation rules (such as the ones depicted in Fig. 4) can be understood as a variant of HD-automata where the states are enriched with graphs rather than just sets, and the information on the transitions is extended accordingly. We intend to investigate this connection in the future.

Rule amalgamation. Studied first in [3] and later, much more extensively, in [16], the principle of rule amalgamation provides a general mechanism for rule (de)composition.

This is a sub-problem of the one we have addressed here (we study composition of the graphs as well as the rules), and indeed for that sub-problem our approach is entirely based on amalgamation.

Borrowed contexts. Like our paper, the work on borrowed contexts [5,1] uses a setting where only part of a graph is available, and studies the application of rules to such subgraphs in a way that is compatible with the original, reductive semantics. In contrast to our approach, however, they do not decompose rules: instead, when a rule is applied to a graph in which some of the required structure ("context") for the match is missing, this is imported ("borrowed") as part of the transformation. As a result, in this paradigm the subgraphs grow while being transformed, incorporating ever more context information. This is quite different from the basic intuitions behind our approach.

Summarising, where only rules are (de)composed in rule amalgamation, and only graphs in borrowed contexts, in our approach both rules and graphs are subject to (de)composition.

Compositional model transformation. The recent [2] studies a notion of compositionality in model transformation. Though on the face of it this sounds similar, in fact they study a different question altogether, namely whether a transformation affects the *semantics* of a model (given as a separate mapping to a semantic domain) in a predictable (compositional) manner. This is in sharp contrast with our work, which rather addresses the compositionality of the graph transformation framework itself.

4.2 Open Issues

Adhesive HLR categories. Adhesive categories as a foundation for graph transformation have been generalised to classes of categories with weaker assumptions; for instance, adhesive HLR categories in [6] and weak adhesive HLR categories in [14]. A natural question is whether our results also carry over to this generalisation.

Negative application conditions. For the use of graph transformation in practice, negative application conditions (NACs) as introduced in [8] have shown to be extremely useful. We plan to investigate the extension of our results to a setting with NACs.

Improved criteria for completeness. Th. 17 only gives a sufficient criterion for decomposing a transformation. It is not clear if this is weak enough to be usable in practice. From a theoretical point of view, in any case it would be interesting to have a more precise, necessary and sufficient criterion.

More general types of synchronisation. Our notion of composition requires marked rules to be compatible, meaning that they have a common subrule. This implies that joint nodes can only be created and deleted from subgraphs simultaneously. In other words, it is not possible to *hand over* a node from one subgraph to another. This is illustrated by the non-decomposable rule in (1) (page 314). Since such hand-over is definitely a desirable feature (used, e.g., in mobile calculi [12] to communicate channel names), we intend to study a generalisation of our framework that does not synchronise on subrules.

The larger picture. We have studied decomposition for individual rules. We want to extend this to rule systems; ideally, it should be possible to give a fixed decomposition of a rule system which is guaranteed to remain correct for arbitrary sequences of transitions. At that point, also the connection with SOS semantics for process algebra (which was our starting point, see Sect. 1) should be strengthened.

References

1. Baldan, P., Ehrig, H., König, B.: Composition and decomposition of DPO transformations with borrowed context. In: Corradini, A., Ehrig, H., Montanari, U., Ribeiro, L., Rozenberg, G. (eds.) ICGT 2006. LNCS, vol. 4178, pp. 153–167. Springer, Heidelberg (2006)
2. Bisztray, D., Heckel, R., Ehrig, H.: Compositionality of model transformations. In: Aldini, A., ter Beek, M., Gadducci, F. (eds.) 3rd International Workshop on Views On Designing Complex Architectures (VODCA). ENTCS, vol. 236, pp. 5–19 (2009)
3. Boehm, P., Fonio, H.R., Habel, A.: Amalgamation of graph transformations: A synchronization mechanism. J. Comput. Syst. Sci. 34(2/3), 377–408 (1987)
4. Ehrig, H., Habel, A., Kreowski, H.J., Parisi-Presicce, F.: From graph grammars to high level replacement systems. In: Ehrig, H., Kreowski, H.-J., Rozenberg, G. (eds.) Graph Grammars 1990. LNCS, vol. 532, pp. 269–291. Springer, Heidelberg (1991)
5. Ehrig, H., König, B.: Deriving bisimulation congruences in the DPO approach to graph rewriting with borrowed contexts. Mathematical Structures in Computer Science 16(6), 1133–1163 (2006)
6. Ehrig, H., Padberg, J., Prange, U., Habel, A.: Adhesive high-level replacement systems: A new categorical framework for graph transformation. Fundam. Inform. 74(1), 1–29 (2006)
7. Ferrari, G.L., Hirsch, D., Lanese, I., Montanari, U., Tuosto, E.: Synchronised hyperedge replacement as a model for service oriented computing. In: de Boer, F.S., Bonsangue, M.M., Graf, S., de Roever, W.-P. (eds.) FMCO 2005. LNCS, vol. 4111, pp. 22–43. Springer, Heidelberg (2006)
8. Habel, A., Heckel, R., Taentzer, G.: Graph grammars with negative application conditions. Fundam. Inform. 26(3/4), 287–313 (1996)
9. Hirsch, D., Montanari, U.: Synchronized hyperedge replacement with name mobility. In: Larsen, K.G., Nielsen, M. (eds.) CONCUR 2001. LNCS, vol. 2154, pp. 121–136. Springer, Heidelberg (2001)
10. Johnstone, P.T., Lack, S., Sobocinski, P.: Quasitoposes, quasiadhesive categories and Artin glueing. In: Mossakowski, T., Montanari, U., Haveraaen, M. (eds.) CALCO 2007. LNCS, vol. 4624, pp. 312–326. Springer, Heidelberg (2007)
11. Lack, S., Sobocinski, P.: Adhesive categories. In: Walukiewicz, I. (ed.) FOSSACS 2004. LNCS, vol. 2987, pp. 273–288. Springer, Heidelberg (2004)
12. Milner, R., Parrow, J., Walker, D.: A calculus of mobile processes, I. Inf. Comput. 100(1), 1–40 (1992)
13. Montanari, U., Pistore, M.: History-dependent automata: An introduction. In: Bernardo, M., Bogliolo, A. (eds.) SFM-Moby 2005. LNCS, vol. 3465, pp. 1–28. Springer, Heidelberg (2005)
14. Prange, U., Ehrig, H.: From algebraic graph transformation to adhesive HLR categories and systems. In: Bozapalidis, S., Rahonis, G. (eds.) CAI 2007. LNCS, vol. 4728, pp. 122–146. Springer, Heidelberg (2007)
15. Rensink, A.: A first study of compositionality in graph transformation. Technical Report TR-CTIT-10-08, Centre for Telematics and Information Technology, University of Twente (2010)
16. Taentzer, G.: Parallel high-level replacement systems. TCS 186(1-2), 43–81 (1997)

On p-Optimal Proof Systems and Logics for PTIME

Yijia Chen[1] and Jörg Flum[2]

[1] Shanghai Jiaotong University, China
yijia.chen@cs.sjtu.edu.cn
[2] Albert-Ludwigs-Universität Freiburg, Germany
joerg.flum@math.uni-freiburg.de

Abstract. We prove that TAUT has a p-optimal proof system if and only if a logic related to least fixed-point logic captures polynomial time on all finite structures. Furthermore, we show that TAUT has no *effective* p-optimal proof system if $\mathrm{NTIME}(h^{O(1)}) \not\subseteq \mathrm{DTIME}(h^{O(\log h)})$ for every time constructible and increasing function h.

1 Introduction

As the title already indicates, this paper relates two topics which at first glance seem to be unrelated. On the one hand we consider optimal proof systems. A *proof system* in the sense of Cook and Reckhow [6], say for the class TAUT of tautologies of propositional logic, is a polynomial time computable function defined on $\{0,1\}^*$ and with TAUT as range. A proof system is *p-optimal* if it simulates any other proof system in polynomial time.[1] In their fundamental paper [13] Krajíček and Pudlák derive a series of statements equivalent to the existence of a p-optimal proof system for TAUT and state the conjecture:

Conjecture 1. There is no p-optimal proof system for TAUT.

On the other hand, the question of whether there is a logic capturing polynomial time remains the central open problem in descriptive complexity. There are artificial logics capturing polynomial time, but they do not fulfill a natural requirement to logics in this context:

> There is an algorithm that decides whether $\mathcal{A}$ is a model of φ for all structures $\mathcal{A}$ and sentences φ of the logic and that does this for fixed φ in time polynomial in the size $\|\mathcal{A}\|$ of $\mathcal{A}$. (1)

If this condition is fulfilled for a logic capturing polynomial time, we speak of a P-bounded logic for P. In [10] Gurevich states the conjecture:

Conjecture 2. There is no P-bounded logic for P.

The conjecture is false if one waives the effectivity condition (1). This is shown in [10, Section 7, CLAIM 2]) by considering a logic introduced by Blass and Gurevich and which we denote by $L_{\leq}$. For any vocabulary the sentences of $L_{\leq}$ are the sentences

[1] All notions will be defined in a precise manner in Section 2.

S. Abramsky et al. (Eds.): ICALP 2010, Part II, LNCS 6199, pp. 321–332, 2010.

of least fixed-point logic in a vocabulary with an additional binary relation symbol for orderings. In $L_{\leq}$ for a structure $\mathcal{A}$ to be a model of φ it is required that in all structures of cardinality less than or equal to that of $\mathcal{A}$, the validity of φ (as a sentence of least fixed-point logic) does not depend on the chosen ordering, and $\mathcal{A}$ with some ordering satisfies φ.

As $L_{\leq}$ satisfies all requirements of a P-bounded logic for P except (1), Gurevich implicitly states the conjecture:

Conjecture 2a. $L_{\leq}$ is not a P-bounded logic for P.

The main result of this paper (cf. Theorem 6) tells us that

$$\text{Conjecture 1 is true} \iff \text{Conjecture 2a is true.} \tag{2}$$

We mentioned that at first glance "p-optimal proof systems for TAUT" and "logics for P" seem to be unrelated topics. However, there are reformulations of Conjecture 1 and Conjecture 2 that are alike. In fact, it is known [15] that TAUT has a p-optimal proof system if and only if there is a (computable) enumeration of all subsets of TAUT that are in P by means of Turing machines that decide them. And it is not hard to see that there is a P-bounded logic for P if and only if there is an enumeration of all polynomial time decidable classes of graphs closed under isomorphisms, again an enumeration in terms of Turing machines that decide these classes. In fact the question for a logic for P was stated in this way by Chandra and Harel [2] in the context of an analysis of the complexity and expressiveness of query languages.

Hence one consequence of (2) (which we only mention in this Introduction) is:

Theorem 1. *If there is an enumeration of all polynomial time decidable subsets of* TAUT, *then there is an enumeration of all polynomial time decidable classes of graphs closed under isomorphisms.*

Using a special feature of the semantics of the logic $L_{\leq}$, one can construct (cf. Proposition 11) a logic that is an *effectively* P-bounded logic for P, if $L_{\leq}$ is a P-bounded logic for P. Here this "effectively" means that in (1) we can *compute* from φ a polynomial bounding the time to decide whether $\mathcal{A}$ is a model of φ. In this way we can strengthen the conclusion of Theorem 1 by requiring that every Turing machine in the enumeration comes with a polynomial time clock. Apparently this is a strengthening, while from any enumeration of the polynomial time decidable subsets of TAUT we obtain one with polynomial time clocks in a trivial manner, namely by systematically adding such clocks.

In general, the experts tend to believe Conjecture 1, as the existence of a p-optimal proof system for TAUT would have various consequences which seem to be unlikely (see [12,13]). It is worthwhile to emphasize that we show that Conjecture 1 is equivalent to Conjecture 2a and do not claim its equivalence to Conjecture 2. The situation with Conjecture 2 is quite different; no known consequences of the existence of a P-bounded logic for P seem to be implausible. Moreover, due to results showing that there are logics capturing polynomial time on always larger classes of structures, Grohe [9] "mildly leans towards believing" that there is a P-bounded logic for P.

In [3] we have shown that $L_{\leq}$ is not an effectively P-bounded logic for P under the assumption NP[TC] $\not\subseteq$ P[TC$^{\log \text{TC}}$], which means that NTIME($h^{O(1)}$) $\not\subseteq$ DTIME($h^{O(\log h)}$) for every time constructible and increasing function h. Under this assumption, we get (see Theorem 15) that TAUT has no effectively p-optimal proof system. Here a proof system P for TAUT is *effectively* p-optimal if from every other proof system for TAUT we can *compute* a polynomial time simulation by P.

On the other hand, Krajíček and Pudlák [13] showed, assuming E = NE, that TAUT has a p-optimal proof system. Using our result [3] that under the assumption E = NE the logic $\big(L_{=}$ and hence$\big)$ $L_{\leq}$ is an effectively P-bounded logic for P, we can derive (see Corollary 17) that TAUT has an *effectively* p-optimal proof system if E = NE.

In [5] we extract the main idea underlying the proof of (2), apply it to other problems, and generalize it to the "nondeterministic case," thus obtaining statements equivalent to the existence of an optimal (not necessarily p-optimal) proof system for TAUT.

2 Preliminaries

In this section we recall concepts and results from complexity theory and logic that we will use later and fix some notation.

2.1 Complexity

We denote the alphabet $\{0, 1\}$ by Σ. The length of a string $x \in \Sigma^*$ is denoted by $|x|$. We identify problems with subsets Q of Σ^*. Clearly, as done mostly, we present concrete problems in a verbal, hence uncodified form. We denote by P the class of problems Q such that $x \in Q$ is solvable in polynomial time.

All Turing machines have Σ as their alphabet and are deterministic ones if not stated otherwise explicitly. If necessary we will not distinguish between a Turing machine and its code, a string in Σ^*. If $\mathbb{M}$ is a Turing machine we denote by $\|\mathbb{M}\|$ the length of its code.

By $m^{O(1)}$ we denote the class of polynomially bounded functions from $\mathbb{N}$ to $\mathbb{N}$. Sometimes statements containing a formulation like "there is $d \in \mathbb{N}$ such that for all $x \in \Sigma^*$: $\ldots \leq |x|^d$" can be wrong for $x \in \Sigma^*$ with $|x| \leq 1$. We trust the reader's common sense to interpret such statements reasonably.

Optimal proof systems, almost optimal algorithms and enumerations of P-easy subsets. A *proof system* for a problem $Q \subseteq \Sigma^*$ is a surjective function $P : \Sigma^* \to Q$ computable in polynomial time. The proof system P for Q is *polynomially optimal* or *p-optimal* if for every proof system P' for Q there is a polynomial time computable $T : \Sigma^* \to \Sigma^*$ such that for all $w \in \Sigma^*$

$$P(T(w)) = P'(w).$$

If $\mathbb{A}$ is any algorithm we denote by $t_{\mathbb{A}}(x)$ the number of steps of the run of $\mathbb{A}$ on input x; if $\mathbb{A}$ on x does not stop, then $t_{\mathbb{A}}(x)$ is not defined.

An algorithm $\mathbb{A}$ deciding Q is *almost optimal* or *optimal on positive instances of Q* if for every algorithm $\mathbb{B}$ deciding Q there is a polynomial $p \in \mathbb{N}[X]$ such that for all $x \in Q$

$$t_{\mathbb{A}}(x) \leq p(t_{\mathbb{B}}(x) + |x|)$$

(note that nothing is required of the relationship between $t_{\mathbb{A}}(x)$ and $t_{\mathbb{B}}(x)$ for $x \notin Q$).

By definition a subset Q' of Q is P-*easy* if $Q' \in$ P. An *enumeration of* P-*easy subsets of* Q is a computable function $M : \mathbb{N} \to \Sigma^*$ such that

- for every $i \in \mathbb{N}$ the string $M(i)$ is a polynomial time Turing machine deciding a P-easy subset of Q;
- for every P-easy subset Q' of Q there is $i \in \mathbb{N}$ such that $M(i)$ decides Q'.

We denote by TAUT the class of tautologies of propositional logic. The following theorem is well-known (cf. [13] for the equivalence of the first two statements and [15] for the equivalence to the third one):

Theorem 2. *The following are equivalent:*
(1) TAUT *has a p-optimal proof system.*
(2) TAUT *has an almost optimal algorithm.*
(3) TAUT *has an enumeration of the* P-*easy subsets.*

2.2 Logic

A *vocabulary* τ is a finite set of relation symbols. Each relation symbol has an *arity*. A *structure* $\mathcal{A}$ of vocabulary τ, or τ-*structure* (or, simply structure), consists of a nonempty set A called the *universe*, and an interpretation $R^{\mathcal{A}} \subseteq A^r$ of each r-ary relation symbol $R \in \tau$. *All structures in this paper are assumed to have finite universe.*

For a structure $\mathcal{A}$ we denote by $\|\mathcal{A}\|$ the size of $\mathcal{A}$, that is, the length of a reasonable encoding of $\mathcal{A}$ as a string in Σ^* (e.g., cf. [8] for details). We only consider properties of structures that are invariant under isomorphisms, so it suffices that from the encoding of $\mathcal{A}$ we can recover $\mathcal{A}$ up to isomorphism. We can assume that there is a computable function lgth such that for every vocabulary τ and $m \geq 1$:

- $\|\mathcal{A}\| = \text{lgth}(\tau, m)$ for every τ-structure $\mathcal{A}$ with universe of cardinality m;
- for fixed τ, the function $m \mapsto \text{lgth}(\tau, m)$ is computable in time $m^{O(1)}$;
- $\text{lgth}(\tau \cup \{R\}, m) = O(\text{lgth}(\tau, m) + m^r)$ for every r-ary relation symbol R not in τ.

We assume familiarity with first-order logic and its extension *least fixed-point logic* LFP (e.g. see [7]). We denote by LFP[τ] the set of sentences of vocabulary τ of LFP. As we will introduce further semantics for the formulas of least fixed-point logic, we write $\mathcal{A} \models_{\text{LFP}} \varphi$ if the structure $\mathcal{A}$ is a model of the LFP-sentence φ. An algorithm based on the inductive definition of the satisfaction relation for LFP shows (see [17]):

Proposition 3. *The model-checking problem* $\mathcal{A} \models_{\text{LFP}} \varphi$ *for structures* $\mathcal{A}$ *and* LFP-*sentences* φ *can be solved in time*

$$\|\mathcal{A}\|^{O(|\varphi|)}.$$

Logics capturing polynomial time. For our purposes a *logic* L consists

- of an algorithm that for every vocabulary τ and every string ξ decides whether ξ is in the set $L[\tau]$, the set of *L-sentences of vocabulary* τ;
- of a *satisfaction relation* $\models_L$; if $(\mathcal{A}, \varphi) \in \models_L$, then $\mathcal{A}$ is a τ-structure and $\varphi \in L[\tau]$ for some vocabulary τ; furthermore for each τ and $\varphi \in L[\tau]$ the class of structures $\mathcal{A}$ with $\mathcal{A} \models_L \varphi$ is closed under isomorphisms.

We say that $\mathcal{A}$ is a *model* of φ if $\mathcal{A} \models_L \varphi$ (that is, if $(\mathcal{A}, \varphi) \in \models_L$). We set $\text{Mod}_L(\varphi) := \{\mathcal{A} \mid \mathcal{A} \models_L \varphi\}$ and say that φ *axiomatizes* the class $\text{Mod}_L(\varphi)$.

Definition 4. Let L be a logic.

(a) *L is a logic for* P if for all vocabularies τ and all classes C (of encodings) of τ-structures closed under isomorphisms we have

$$C \in \text{P} \iff C = \text{Mod}_L(\varphi) \text{ for some } \varphi \in L[\tau].$$

(b) *L is a* P*-bounded logic for* P if (a) holds and if there is an algorithm $\mathbb{A}$ deciding $\models_L$ (that is, for every structure $\mathcal{A}$ and L-sentence φ the algorithm $\mathbb{A}$ decides whether $\mathcal{A} \models_L \varphi$) and if moreover $\mathbb{A}$, for every fixed φ, polynomial in $\|\mathcal{A}\|$.

Hence, if L is a P-bounded logic for P, then for every L-sentence φ the algorithm $\mathbb{A}$ witnesses that $\text{Mod}_L(\varphi) \in$ P. However, we do not necessarily know ahead of time a bounding polynomial.

(c) *L is an effectively* P*-bounded logic for* P if L is a P-bounded logic for P and if in addition to the algorithm $\mathbb{A}$ as in (b) there is a computable function that assigns to every L-sentence φ a polynomial $q \in \mathbb{N}[X]$ such that $\mathbb{A}$ decides whether $\mathcal{A} \models_L \varphi$ in $\leq q(\|\mathcal{A}\|)$ steps.

The logic $L_\leq$ and invariant sentences. In this section we introduce the logic $L_\leq$, a variant of least fixed-point logic.

For every vocabulary τ we let $\tau_< := \tau \cup \{<\}$, where $<$ is a binary relation symbol not in τ chosen in some canonical way. We set

$$L_\leq[\tau] = \text{LFP}[\tau_<]$$

for every vocabulary τ. Before we define the satisfaction relation for $L_\leq$ we introduce the notion of $\leq m$-invariant sentence.

Definition 5. Let φ be an $L_\leq[\tau]$-sentence.

– For $m \geq 1$ we say that φ is *$\leq m$-invariant* if for all structures $\mathcal{A}$ with $|A| \leq m$ and all orderings $<_1$ and $<_2$ on A we have

$$(\mathcal{A}, <_1) \models_{\text{LFP}} \varphi \iff (\mathcal{A}, <_2) \models_{\text{LFP}} \varphi.$$

– φ is *invariant* if it is $\leq m$-invariant for all $m \geq 1$.

Finally we introduce the semantics for the logic $L_\leq$ by

$$\mathcal{A} \models_{L_\leq} \varphi \iff \Big(\varphi \text{ is } \leq |A|\text{-invariant and } (\mathcal{A}, <) \models_{\text{LFP}} \varphi \text{ for some ordering } < \text{ on } A\Big).$$

Immerman [11] and Vardi [16] have shown that LFP is an effectively P-bounded logic for P *on the class of ordered structures*, a result we will not need in the proof of our main theorem. However, using it one can easily show that $L_\leq$ is a logic for P.

For later purposes we remark that for every $L_{\leq}[\tau]$-sentence φ and $m \geq 1$ we have

$$\varphi \text{ is } \leq m\text{-invariant} \iff \neg\varphi \text{ is } \leq m\text{-invariant},$$

and thus for every τ-structure $\mathcal{A}$

$$\varphi \text{ is } \leq |A|\text{-invariant} \iff \big(\mathcal{A} \models_{L_{\leq}} \varphi \text{ or } \mathcal{A} \models_{L_{\leq}} \neg\varphi\big).$$

In particular,

$$\varphi \text{ is } \leq m\text{-invariant} \iff \big(\mathcal{A}(\tau, m) \models_{L_{\leq}} \varphi \text{ or } \mathcal{A}(\tau, m) \models_{L_{\leq}} \neg\varphi\big),$$

where $\mathcal{A}(\tau, m)$ is the τ-structure with universe $\{1, \ldots, m\}$, where every relation symbol in τ is interpreted by the empty relation of the corresponding arity.

Finally we remark that it can happen for $L_{\leq}$-sentences φ and ψ and a structure $\mathcal{A}$ that $\mathcal{A} \models_{L_{\leq}} (\varphi \wedge \psi)$ but neither $\mathcal{A} \models_{L_{\leq}} \varphi$ nor $\mathcal{A} \models_{L_{\leq}} \psi$.

3 The Main Theorem

In this section we want to show:

Theorem 6. TAUT *has a p-optimal proof system iff* $L_{\leq}$ *is a* P*-bounded logic for* P.

In view of Theorem 2 we get one direction of Theorem 6 with the following lemma.

Lemma 7. *If* $L_{\leq}$ *is a* P*-bounded logic for* P*, then there is an enumeration of the* P*-easy subsets of* TAUT.

Proof. It is easy to introduce a vocabulary τ such that in polynomial time we can associate with every propositional formula α a τ-structure $\mathcal{A}(\alpha)$ such that

- every propositional variable X of α corresponds to two distinct elements a_X, b_X of $\mathcal{A}(\alpha)$ and there is a unary relation symbol $P \in \tau$ such that $P^{\mathcal{A}(\alpha)} = \{a_X \mid X \text{ variable of } \alpha\}$;
- there is an LFP-sentence $\varphi(\text{PROP})$ of vocabulary τ axiomatizing the class

$$\{\mathcal{B} \mid \mathcal{B} \cong \mathcal{A}(\alpha) \text{ for some } \alpha \in \text{PROP}\}$$

  (by PROP we denote the class of formulas of propositional logic);
- if $\mathcal{B} \models \varphi(\text{PROP})$, then one can determine the unique $\alpha \in \text{PROP}$ with $\mathcal{B} \cong \mathcal{A}(\alpha)$ in polynomial time.

Again let $\tau_< := \tau \cup \{<\}$ with a new binary $<$. Note that a $\tau_<$-structure of the form $(\mathcal{A}(\alpha), <)$ yields an assignment of the variables of α, namely the assignment sending a variable X to TRUE if and only if $a_X < b_X$. There is an LFP[$\tau_<$]-formula $\varphi(\text{sat})$ that for every $\alpha \in \text{PROP}$ expresses in $(\mathcal{A}(\alpha), <)$ that the assignment given by $<$ satisfies α.

We introduce the $L_{\leq}[\tau]$-sentence

$$\varphi_0 := \big(\varphi(\text{PROP}) \rightarrow \varphi(\text{sat})\big).$$

By the definition of $\models_{L_\leq}$ we see that for every $\alpha \in$ PROP and every $L_\leq[\tau]$-sentence φ

$$\text{if } \mathcal{A}(\alpha) \models_{L_\leq} (\varphi_0 \wedge \varphi), \text{ then } \alpha \in \text{TAUT}. \tag{3}$$

We claim that the class of models of $(\varphi_0 \wedge \varphi)$, more precisely,

$$Q(\varphi) := \{\alpha \in \text{PROP} \mid \mathcal{A}(\alpha) \models_{L_\leq} (\varphi_0 \wedge \varphi)\},$$

where φ ranges over all $L_\leq[\tau]$-sentences, yields the desired enumeration of P-easy subsets of TAUT. By (3), we have $Q(\varphi) \subseteq$ TAUT.

For $\varphi \in L_\leq[\tau]$ let the Turing machine $\mathbb{M}_\varphi$, given an input $\alpha \in$ PROP, first construct $\mathcal{A}(\alpha)$ and then check whether $\mathcal{A}(\alpha) \models_{L_\leq} (\varphi_0 \wedge \varphi)$. Clearly, $\mathbb{M}_\varphi$ decides $Q(\varphi)$ and does this in polynomial time, as $L_\leq$ is a P-bounded logic for P.

Conversely, let Q be a P-easy subset of TAUT. If Q is finite, it is easy to see that $Q = Q(\varphi)$ for some $\varphi \in L_\leq[\tau]$. Now let Q be infinite. The class

$$\{\mathcal{B} \mid \mathcal{B} \cong \mathcal{A}(\alpha) \text{ for some } \alpha \in Q\}$$

is in P, and therefore it is axiomatizable by an $L_\leq[\tau]$-sentence φ. As the class contains arbitrarily large structures, the formula φ is invariant. We show that $Q = Q(\varphi)$.

Assume first that $\alpha \in Q(\varphi)$, i.e., $\mathcal{A}(\alpha) \models_{L_\leq} (\varphi_0 \wedge \varphi)$. Then, by invariance of φ, we have $\mathcal{A}(\alpha) \models_{L_\leq} \varphi$ and thus $\alpha \in Q$. Conversely, assume that $\alpha \in Q$. Then $\mathcal{A}(\alpha) \models_{L_\leq} \varphi$. As $\alpha \in$ TAUT, in order to get $\mathcal{A}(\alpha) \models_{L_\leq} (\varphi_0 \wedge \varphi)$ $\big($and hence, $\alpha \in Q(\varphi)\big)$ it suffices to show that $(\varphi_0 \wedge \varphi)$ is $\leq |A(\alpha)|$-invariant. So let $\mathcal{B}$ be a τ-structure with $|B| \leq |A(\alpha)|$. If $\mathcal{B} \not\models_{L_\leq} \varphi$, then, by invariance of φ, we have $(\mathcal{B}, <^B) \not\models_{\text{LFP}} (\varphi_0 \wedge \varphi)$ for all orderings $<^B$ on B; if $\mathcal{B} \models_{L_\leq} \varphi$, then $\mathcal{B} \cong \mathcal{A}(\beta)$ for some $\beta \in Q \subseteq$ TAUT. Hence, $(\mathcal{B}, <^B) \models_{\text{LFP}}$ $(\varphi_0 \wedge \varphi)$ for all orderings $<^B$ on B. □

Remark 8. In the previous proof we have used the definition of the satisfaction relation $\models_{L_\leq}$ in order to express the universal second-order quantifier in the statement "all assignments satisfy α." Similarly, we can do with every Π^1_1-sentence $\forall R\varphi$, where φ is a first-order formula or (equivalently) LFP-formula and show in this way that there is an enumeration of the P-easy subsets closed under isomorphisms of the class of models of $\forall R\varphi$, if $L_\leq$ is a P-bounded logic for P. In fact, let k be the arity of R. If a structure $\mathcal{A}$ has n elements, we consider a structure $\mathcal{B}$ with additional disjoint unary relations $U^{\mathcal{B}}, P_0^{\mathcal{B}}, P_1^{\mathcal{B}}$ such that

$$B = U^{\mathcal{B}} \cup P_0^{\mathcal{B}} \cup P_1^{\mathcal{B}}, \quad U^{\mathcal{B}} = A, \quad |P_0^{\mathcal{B}}| = n^k \quad |P_1^{\mathcal{B}}| = n^k$$

and with an ordering $<^{\mathcal{B}}$.

With the elements in $P_0^{\mathcal{B}}$ interpreted as 0s and the elements in $P_1^{\mathcal{B}}$ interpreted as 1s, the first n^k-elements of the ordering in $P_0^{\mathcal{B}} \cup P_1^{\mathcal{B}}$ represent a natural number $< 2^{n^k}$ and thus a k-ary relation R on A, which we can compute in polynomial time (polynomial in n); hence we can define R by an LFP-formula. As in this way, by changing the ordering, we have access to all such k-ary relations R on A, we can express the quantifier $\forall R$ using the invariance requirement of $\models_{L_\leq}$.

For example, let C be the class of all pairs $(\mathcal{G},\mathcal{H})$ of graphs such that $\mathcal{H}$ is *not* a homomorphic image of $\mathcal{G}$. By the previous observation, we see that there is an enumeration of the P-easy subclasses of C closed under isomorphisms if $L_{\leq}$ is a P-bounded logic for P. Of course, a subclass D of C is closed under isomorphisms if

$$\mathcal{G} \cong \mathcal{G}', \ \mathcal{H} \cong \mathcal{H}' \text{ and } (\mathcal{G},\mathcal{H}) \in D \text{ imply } (\mathcal{G}',\mathcal{H}') \in D.$$

As the models of such a Π^1_1-sentence corresponds to a problem Q in co-NP, a simple complexity-theoretic argument shows that there is an enumeration of the P-easy subsets of Q provided there is one for the P-easy subsets of TAUT (see also [1]). However, in this way, in the previous example we would not get an enumeration of those P-easy subclasses that are *closed under isomorphisms*.

In view of Theorem 2 the remaining direction in Theorem 6 is provided by the following result.

Lemma 9. *If* TAUT *has an almost optimal algorithm, then* $L_{\leq}$ *is a* P*-bounded logic for* P.

Proof. We assume that TAUT has an almost optimal algorithm $\mathbb{O}$ and have to show that there is an algorithm that decides $\mathcal{B} \models_{L_{\leq}} \varphi$ and does this for fixed φ in time $\|\mathcal{B}\|^{O(1)}$.

By the definition of $\mathcal{B} \models_{L_{\leq}} \varphi$ and Proposition 3 it suffices to show the existence of an algorithm $\mathbb{A}$ that for every $L_{\leq}$-sentence φ and every $m \in \mathbb{N}$ decides whether φ is $\leq m$-invariant and does this for fixed φ in time $m^{O(1)}$.

We set

$$Q := \Big\{ \big(\chi, \ell, \text{lgth}(\tau,\ell)^{|\chi|}\big) \ \Big|\ \tau \text{ a vocabulary, } \chi \in \text{LFP}[\tau],\ \ell \geq 1,\ \text{lgth}(\tau,\ell)^{|\chi|} \text{ in unary, there is a } \tau\text{-structure } \mathcal{B} \text{ with } \big(|B| \leq \ell \text{ and } \mathcal{B} \models_{\text{LFP}} \chi\big) \Big\}$$

(compare Section 2.2 for the definition of the function lgth). By Proposition 3, $Q \in$ NP. Thus there is a polynomial time reduction $R : Q \leq^p$ SAT. We can assume that from $R(x)$ we can recover x in polynomial time.

Let φ be an $L_{\leq}[\tau]$-sentence. Then

$$\begin{aligned} \varphi \text{ is not} \leq m\text{-invariant} &\iff \text{there is a } \tau\text{-structure } \mathcal{B} \text{ and orderings } <_1, <_2 \text{ with} \\ &\qquad \big(|B| \leq m \text{ and } (\mathcal{B}, <_1, <_2) \models_{\text{LFP}} \underbrace{(\varphi(<_1) \wedge \neg\varphi(<_2))}_{\varphi^*}\big) \\ &\iff \left(\varphi^*, m, \text{lgth}(\tau \cup \{<_1, <_2\}, m)^{|\varphi^*|}\right) \in Q \\ &\iff R\left(\varphi^*, m, \text{lgth}(\tau \cup \{<_1, <_2\}, m)^{|\varphi^*|}\right) \in \text{SAT}. \end{aligned}$$

We set $\alpha(\varphi, m) := R\left(\varphi^*, m, \text{lgth}(\tau \cup \{<_1, <_2\}, m)^{|\varphi^*|}\right)$. Hence

$$\varphi \text{ is} \leq m\text{-invariant} \iff \neg\alpha(\varphi, m) \in \text{TAUT}. \tag{4}$$

It is clear that there is an algorithm that on input (φ, m) computes $\alpha(\varphi, m)$ and for fixed φ

$$\text{it computes } \alpha(\varphi, m) \text{ in time } m^{O(1)}, \text{ in particular, } |\alpha(\varphi, m)| \leq m^{O(1)}, \tag{5}$$

as for fixed τ, the function $m \mapsto \text{lgth}(\tau, m)$ is polynomial in m.

Let $\mathbb{S}$ be the algorithm that on input φ by systematically going through all τ-structures with universe $\{1\}$, all with universe $\{1, 2\}$,... and all orderings of these universes computes $m(\varphi)$:= the least m such that φ is not $\leq m$-invariant. If φ is invariant, then $m(\varphi)$ is not defined and $\mathbb{S}$ does not stop.

We show that the following algorithm $\mathbb{A}$ has the desired properties.

$\mathbb{A}(\varphi, m)$
// φ an $L_{\leq}$-sentence, $m \in \mathbb{N}$

1. Compute $\alpha(\varphi, m)$.
2. In parallel simulate $\mathbb{S}$ on input φ and $\mathbb{O}$ on input $\neg\alpha(\varphi, m)$.
3. **if** $\mathbb{O}$ stops first, **then** output its answer.
4. **if** $\mathbb{S}$ stops first, **then**
5. **if** $m < m(\varphi)$ **then** accept **else** reject.

By our assumptions on $\mathbb{O}$ and $\mathbb{S}$ and by (4), it should be clear that $\mathbb{A}$ on input (φ, m) decides whether φ is $\leq m$-invariant. We have to show that for fixed φ it does it in time $m^{O(1)}$.

Case "φ is invariant": Then for all m we have $\neg\alpha(\varphi, m) \in$ TAUT. Thus the following algorithm $\mathbb{O}_\varphi$ decides TAUT: on input $\beta \in$ PROP the algorithm $\mathbb{O}_\varphi$ checks whether $\beta = \neg\alpha(\varphi, m)$ for some $m \geq 1$. If so, it accepts and otherwise it runs $\mathbb{O}$ on input β and answers accordingly. By (5), we have

$$t_{\mathbb{O}_\varphi}(\neg\alpha(\varphi, m)) \leq m^{O(1)}. \tag{6}$$

As $\mathbb{O}$ is optimal, we know that there is a constant d such that for all $\beta \in$ TAUT

$$t_{\mathbb{O}}(\beta) \leq \left(|\beta| + t_{\mathbb{O}_\varphi}(\beta)\right)^d. \tag{7}$$

In particular, we have

$$t_{\mathbb{O}}(\neg\alpha(\varphi, m)) \leq \left(|\neg\alpha(\varphi, m)| + t_{\mathbb{O}_\varphi}(\neg\alpha(\varphi, m))\right)^d \leq m^{O(1)}.$$

By this inequality, (5) and (6), we see that for invariant φ we have $t_{\mathbb{A}}(\varphi, m) \leq m^{O(1)}$.

Case "φ is not invariant": Then $\mathbb{S}$ will stop on input φ. Thus, in the worst case, $\mathbb{A}$ on input (φ, m) has to wait till the simulation of $\mathbb{S}$ on φ stops and then must check whether the result $m(\varphi)$ of the computation of $\mathbb{S}$ is bigger than m or not and answer accordingly. So the algorithm $\mathbb{A}$ at most takes time $m^{O(1)} + O(t_{\mathbb{S}}(\varphi) + m) \leq m^{O(1)}$ (note that we fix φ, so that $t_{\mathbb{S}}(\varphi)$ is a constant). □

Corollary 10. *If* TAUT *has a p-optimal proof system, then there is an effectively* P-*bounded logic for* P.

This result follows from Theorem 6 using the following proposition:

Proposition 11. *If* $L_\leq$ *is a* P*-bounded logic for* P*, then there is an effectively* P*-bounded logic for* P.

Proof. In Section 2.2 we have seen that for every $L_\leq$-sentence φ and $m \geq 1$ it holds that

$$\varphi \text{ is } \leq m\text{-invariant} \iff \big(\mathcal{A}(\tau, m) \models_{L_\leq} \varphi \text{ or } \mathcal{A}(\tau, m) \models_{L_\leq} \neg\varphi\big), \tag{8}$$

where $\mathcal{A}(\tau, m)$ denotes the "empty structure" of vocabulary τ with universe $\{1, \ldots, m\}$.

Now assume that $L_\leq$ is a P-bounded logic for P and let $\mathbb{A}$ be an algorithm witnessing that $L_\leq$ is a P-bounded logic for P. By (8), there is a function h assigning to every $L_\leq$-sentence φ a polynomial $h(\varphi) \in \mathbb{N}[X]$ such that $\mathbb{A}$ decides whether φ is $\leq m$-invariant in time $h(\varphi)(m)$.

We consider the logic $T(L_\leq)$, *time-clocked* $L_\leq$, defined as follows:

– for every vocabulary τ

$$T(L_\leq)[\tau] := \{(\varphi, p) \mid \varphi \in L_\leq[\tau] \text{ and } p \in \mathbb{N}[X]\};$$

– $\mathcal{A} \models_{T(L_\leq)} (\varphi, p)$ iff (a) and (b) are fulfilled, where
  (a) $\mathbb{A}$ shows via (8) in $\leq p(|A|)$ steps that φ is $\leq |A|$-invariant;
  (b) $(\mathcal{A}, <) \models_{\mathrm{LFP}} \varphi$ for some ordering $<$, say with the ordering of A given by the encoding of $\mathcal{A}$.

It is not hard to verify that $T(L_\leq)$ is an effectively P-bounded logic for P. □

Remark 12. In a slightly different way but using the same idea one can define the time-clocked version $T(L)$ for any P-bounded logic L for P. However, in general, $T(L)$ is not even a logic, as it can happen that the class of models of a $T(L)$-sentence is not closed under isomorphisms. In the case of $T(L_\leq)$ this is guaranteed by the fact that condition (a) in the definition of $\mathcal{A} \models_{T(L_\leq)} (\varphi, p)$ only refers to the cardinality of the universe of $\mathcal{A}$.

There is a further consequence of Theorem 6. By a reformulation of the statement "$L_\leq$ is a P-bounded logic for P" due to Nash et al. [14] (see [3] for a proof), we get:

Theorem 13. *The following are equivalent:*

(a) TAUT *has a p-optimal proof system.*
(b) There is an algorithm deciding for every nondeterministic Turing machine $\mathbb{M}$ *and every natural number* m *whether* $\mathbb{M}$ *accepts the empty input tape in* $\leq m$ *steps and the algorithm does this for every fixed* $\mathbb{M}$ *in time* $m^{O(1)}$.

4 Effective Versions

Let NP[TC] $\not\subseteq$ P[TC$^{\log \text{TC}}$] mean that NTIME($h^{O(1)}$) $\not\subseteq$ DTIME($h^{O(\log h)}$) for every time constructible and increasing function h. In [3] we have shown:

Proposition 14. *Assume that* $\mathrm{NP}[\mathrm{TC}] \not\subseteq \mathrm{P}[\mathrm{TC}^{\log \mathrm{TC}}]$. *Then* $L_{\leq}$ *is not an effectively* P-*bounded logic for* P.

Are there *natural* effective versions of the properties of TAUT listed in Theorem 2 equivalent to the statement "$L_{\leq}$ is not an effectively P-bounded logic for P" and which therefore, by Proposition 14, could not hold under the assumption $\mathrm{NP}[\mathrm{TC}] \not\subseteq \mathrm{P}[\mathrm{TC}^{\log \mathrm{TC}}]$? We did not find them. However, by analyzing the proof of Proposition 14, we isolate a property of an effective P-bounded logic for P that cannot be fulfilled if $\mathrm{NP}[\mathrm{TC}] \not\subseteq \mathrm{P}[\mathrm{TC}^{\log \mathrm{TC}}]$. It turns out that this is equivalent to natural effective versions of the properties on TAUT under consideration. We already state the result we aim at and then define the concepts appearing in it and present the generalization of Theorem 2 on which its proof is based. Due to space limitations all proofs of results in this section will be given in the full version of the paper.

Theorem 15. *If* $\mathrm{NP}[\mathrm{TC}] \not\subseteq \mathrm{P}[\mathrm{TC}^{\log \mathrm{TC}}]$, *then* TAUT *has no effectively p-optimal proof system.*

Let $Q \subseteq \Sigma^*$. A proof system P for Q is *effectively p-optimal* if there are two computable functions $S : \Sigma^* \times \mathbb{N}[X] \to \Sigma^*$ and $b : \Sigma^* \times \mathbb{N}[X] \to \mathbb{N}[X]$ such that for every proof system P' for Q with time bound $p \in \mathbb{N}[X]$ and every $w' \in \Sigma^*$, we have

$$P'(w') = P\big(S(P', p)(w')\big),$$

where $S(P', p)$ is (the code of) a Turing machine with time bound $b(P', p)$ and $S(P', p)(w')$ denotes the output of $S(P', p)$ on input w'.

An algorithm $\mathbb{A}$ deciding Q is *effectively almost optimal* if there is a computable function $b : \Sigma^* \to \mathbb{N}[X]$ such that for every algorithm $\mathbb{B}$ deciding Q we have for every $x \in Q$ we have

$$t_{\mathbb{A}}(x) \leq b(\mathbb{B})\big(t_{\mathbb{B}}(x) + |x|\big).$$

We say that Q has an *effective enumeration of* P-*easy subsets*, if it has an enumeration $M : \mathbb{N} \to \Sigma^*$ of P-easy subsets of Q such that there are functions $I : \Sigma^* \times \mathbb{N}[X] \to \mathbb{N}$ and $b : \Sigma^* \times \mathbb{N}[X] \to \mathbb{N}[X]$ such that for every Turing machine $\mathbb{M}$ and polynomial $p \in \mathbb{N}[X]$,

> if the Turing machine $\mathbb{M}$ recognizes a subset $Q' \subseteq Q$ with time bound p, then the machine $M(I(\mathbb{M}, p))$ recognizes Q' with time bound $b(\mathbb{M}, p)$.

We can prove the effective analogue of Theorem 2:

Theorem 16. *The following are equivalent:*

(1) TAUT *has an effectively p-optimal proof system.*
(2) TAUT *has an effectively almost optimal algorithm.*
(3) TAUT *has an effective enumeration of the P-easy subsets.*

In [3] we have shown that if E = NE, then (the logic $L_{=}$ and hence) $L_{\leq}$ are effectively P-bounded logics for P. The proof of the previous result shows that TAUT has an effectively p-optimal proof system if $L_{\leq}$ is an effectively P-bounded logic for P. Therefore we obtain the following "effective version" of a result due to Krajíček and Pudlák.

Corollary 17. *If* E = NE, *then* TAUT *has an effectively p-optimal proof system.*

Acknowledgement. This research has been partially supported by the National Nature Science Foundation of China (60970011) and the Sino-German Center for Research Promotion (GZ400).

References

1. Beyersdorff, O., Sadowski, Z.: Characterizing the existence of optimal proof systems and complete sets for promise classes. In: Frid, A., Morozov, A., Rybalchenko, A., Wagner, K.W. (eds.) CSR 2009. LNCS, vol. 5675, pp. 47–58. Springer, Heidelberg (2009)
2. Chandra, A.K., Harel, D.: Structure and complexity of relational queries. Journal of Computer and System Sciences 25, 99–128 (1982)
3. Chen, Y., Flum, J.: A logic for PTIME and a parameterized halting problem. In: Proceedings of the 24th IEEE Symposium on Logic in Computer Science (LICS 2009), pp. 397–406 (2009)
4. Chen, Y., Flum, J.: On the complexity of Gödel's proof predicate. The Journal of Symbolic Logic 75(1), 239–254 (2010)
5. Chen, Y., Flum, J.: On slicewise monotone parameterized problems and optimal proof systems for TAUT (2010), `http://basics.sjtu.edu.cn/~chen/papers`
6. Cook, S., Reckhow, R.: The relative efficiency of propositional proof systems. The Journal of Symbolic Logic 44, 36–50 (1979)
7. Ebbinghaus, H.-D., Flum, J.: Finite Model Theory, 2nd edn. Springer, Heidelberg (1999)
8. Flum, J., Grohe, M.: Parameterized Complexity Theory. Springer, Heidelberg (2006)
9. Grohe, M.: Fixed-point definability and polynomial time. In: Grädel, E., Kahle, R. (eds.) CSL 2009. LNCS, vol. 5771, pp. 20–23. Springer, Heidelberg (2009)
10. Gurevich, Y.: Logic and the challenge of computer science. In: Current Trends in Theoretical Computer Science, pp. 1–57. Computer Science Press, Rockville (1988)
11. Immerman, N.: Relational queries computable in polynomial time. Information and Control 68, 86–104 (1986)
12. Köbler, J., Messner, J., Torán, J.: Optimal proof systems imply complete sets for promise classes. Information and Computation 184, 71–92 (2003)
13. Krajíček, J., Pudlák, P.: Propositional proof systems, the consistency of first order theories and the complexity of computations. The Journal of Symbolic Logic 54, 1063–1088 (1989)
14. Nash, A., Remmel, J., Vianu, V.: PTIME queries revisited. In: Eiter, T., Libkin, L. (eds.) ICDT 2005. LNCS, vol. 3363, pp. 274–288. Springer, Heidelberg (2005)
15. Sadowski, Z.: On an optimal propositionl proof system and the structure of easy subsets. Theoretical Computer Science 288(1), 181–193 (2002)
16. Vardi, M.Y.: The complexity of relational query languages. In: Proceedings of the 14th ACM Symposium on Theory of Computing (STOC 1982), pp. 137–146 (1982)
17. Vardi, M.Y.: On the complexity of bounded-variable queries. In: Proceedings of the 14th ACM Symposium on Principles of Database Systems (PODS 1995), pp. 266–276 (1995)

Placing Regenerators in Optical Networks to Satisfy Multiple Sets of Requests*

George B. Mertzios[1], Ignasi Sau[2], Mordechai Shalom[3], and Shmuel Zaks[2]

[1] Department of Computer Science, RWTH Aachen University, Aachen, Germany
mertzios@cs.rwth-aachen.de
[2] Department of Computer Science, Technion, Haifa, Israel
{ignasi,zaks}@cs.technion.ac.il
[3] TelHai Academic College, Upper Galilee, 12210, Israel
cmshalom@telhai.ac.il

Abstract. The placement of regenerators in optical networks has become an active area of research during the last years. Given a set of lightpaths in a network G and a positive integer d, regenerators must be placed in such a way that in any lightpath there are no more than d hops without meeting a regenerator. While most of the research has focused on heuristics and simulations, the first theoretical study of the problem has been recently provided in [10], where the considered cost function is the number of *locations* in the network hosting regenerators. Nevertheless, in many situations a more accurate estimation of the real cost of the network is given by the *total* number of regenerators placed at the nodes, and this is the cost function we consider. Furthermore, in our model we assume that we are given a finite set of p possible traffic patterns (each given by a set of lightpaths), and our objective is to place the minimum number of regenerators at the nodes so that each of the traffic patterns is satisfied. While this problem can be easily solved when $d = 1$ or $p = 1$, we prove that for any fixed $d, p \geq 2$ it does not admit a PTAS, even if G has maximum degree at most 3 and the lightpaths have length $\mathcal{O}(d)$. We complement this hardness result with a constant-factor approximation algorithm with ratio $\ln(d \cdot p)$. We then study the case where G is a path, proving that the problem is NP-hard for any $d, p \geq 2$, even if there are two edges of the path such that any lightpath uses at least one of them. Interestingly, we show that the problem is polynomial-time solvable in paths when all the lightpaths share the first edge of the path, as well as when the number of lightpaths sharing an edge is bounded. Finally, we generalize our model in two natural directions, which allows us to capture the model of [10] as a particular case, and we settle some questions that were left open in [10].

Keywords: optical networks, regenerators, overprovisioning, approximation algorithms, hardness of approximation.

* This research was supported by the Israel Science Foundation (grant No. 1249/08) and by the British Council (grant No. UKTELHAI09).

S. Abramsky et al. (Eds.): ICALP 2010, Part II, LNCS 6199, pp. 333–344, 2010.

1 Introduction

1.1 Background

In modern optical networks, high-speed signals are sent through optical fibers using WDM (Wavelength Division Multiplexing) technology. Networks with each fiber typically carrying around 80 wavelengths are operational, whereas networks with a few hundreds wavelengths per fiber are already experimental. As the energy of the signal decreases with the traveled distance, optical amplifiers are required every some fixed distance (a typical value being around 100 km). However, optical amplifiers introduce noise into the signal, so after a certain number of amplifications, the optical signal needs to be regenerated in order to keep the SNR (Signal-to-Noise Ratio) above a specified threshold. In current technology, the signal is regenerated as follows. An ROADM (Reconfigurable Optical Add-Drop Multiplexer) has the capability of inserting/extracting a given number of wavelengths (typically, around 4) to/from the optical fiber. Then, for each extracted wavelength, an optical regenerator is needed to regenerate the signal carried by that wavelength. That is, at a given optical node, one needs as many regenerators as wavelengths one wants to regenerate. See Fig. 1 for a simplified illustration of the aforementioned devices in the case when the network is a path and the fiber carries 3 wavelengths.

The problem of placing regenerators in optical networks has attracted the attention of several recent research works [5,8,9,13,18,19,22,23]. Mostly, these articles propose heuristics and run simulations in order to reduce the number of regenerators, but no theoretical analysis is presented. Recently, the first theoretical study of the problem has been done by Flammini *et al.* in [10]. In the next paragraph we discuss how our model differs from the one studied in [10].

Nowadays the cost of a regenerator is considerably higher than the cost of an ROADM (as an example, \$160K vs \$50K). Moreover, the regenerator cost is per wavelength, as opposed to ROADM cost that is payed once per several wavelengths. Therefore the *total* number of regenerators seems to be the right cost to minimize. Another possible criterion is to minimize the number of *locations* (that is, the number of nodes) in which optical regenerators are placed. This measure is the one assumed in [10], which makes sense when the dominant

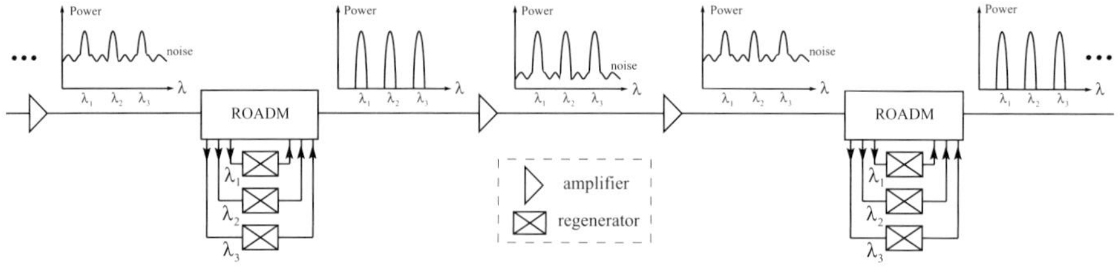

Fig. 1. A simplified optical network: amplifiers introduce noise into the signal, which needs to be regenerated after at most $d = 3$ hops. When the signal is regenerated through an ROADM, a different regenerator is needed for each wavelength.

cost is given by the set-up of new optical nodes, or when the equipment to be placed at each node is the same for all nodes. Nevertheless, the total number of regenerators seem to be a better estimate of the real cost of the network, and therefore we consider this cost in this article.

It is worth mentioning here that when all the connection requests are known a priori, minimizing the number of regenerators is an easy task. Indeed, suppose that the maximum number of hops a lightpath can make without meeting a regenerator is an integer d (in the example of Fig. 1, we have $d = 3$). Then, for each lightpath ℓ, we need to place one regenerator every d consecutive vertices in ℓ, to get an optimal solution.

Unfortunately, when designing a network, it is usually the case that the traffic requests are not known in advance. For instance, the traffic in a given network may change dramatically depending on whether in the foreseeable future an Internet supplier or an email storage server opens or closes a site within the area of the network. In such a situation of uncertain traffic forecast, a common approach in order to minimize capital expenses is to predeploy (or overprovision) resources [12,14,15,17]. That is, the network is designed to satisfy several possible traffic patterns. A similar setting arises in networks in which there are several possible traffic configurations that alternate according to some phenomena, like the weather, the season, an overflow of the capacity of another network, or a breakdown. In that case, the network must be designed so that it can satisfy each of the traffic configurations independently.

In our model, we assume that we are given a finite set of p possible traffic patterns (each given by a set of lightpaths), and our objective is to place the minimum total number of regenerators at the nodes so that each of the traffic patterns is satisfied. That is, the number of regenerators that must be placed at a node of the network is the maximum of the number of regenerators needed by any of the traffic patterns at that node. We aim at minimizing the total number of regenerators placed at the network. We formally define the problem in Section 1.2.

1.2 Definitions

Given an undirected underlying graph $G = (V, E)$ that corresponds to the network topology, a *lightpath* is a simple path in G. That is, we assume that the routing of the requests is given (see [10] for complexity results when the routing of the requests is not given). We also assume that lightpaths sharing an edge use different wavelengths. That is, we deal with optical networks without traffic grooming [2]. The *length* of a lightpath is the number of edges it contains. We consider *symmetric* lightpaths, that is, a lightpath with endpoints u and v consists of a request from u to v and a request from v to u. The *internal vertices* (resp. *edges*) of a lightpath or a path ℓ are the vertices (resp. edges) in ℓ different from the first and the last one. Given an integer d, a lightpath ℓ is *d-satisfied* if there are no d consecutive internal vertices in ℓ without a regenerator. A set of lightpaths is *d-satisfied* if each of its lightpaths is d-satisfied. Given p sets of lightpaths $L_1, \ldots, L_p$, with $L_i = \{\ell_{i,j} \mid 1 \leq j \leq x_i\}$, we consider the union of all lightpaths in the p sets $\cup L_i = \{\ell_{i,j} \mid 1 \leq i \leq p, 1 \leq j \leq x_i\}$. An *assignment* of regenerators is a function $\text{reg} : V \times \cup L_i \to \{0,1\}$, where $\text{reg}(v,\ell) = 1$ if and only if a regenerator is used at vertex v by lightpath ℓ.

We study the following problem: given $p \geq 1$ sets of lightpaths, and a distance $d \geq 1$, determine the smallest number of regenerators that d-satisfy each of the p sets. Formally, for two fixed integers $d, p \geq 1$, the optimization problem we study is defined as follows.

(d,p)-TOTAL REGENERATORS ((d,p)-TR)

Input: A graph $G = (V, E)$ and p sets of lightpaths $\mathcal{L} = \{L_1, \ldots, L_p\}$.

Output: A function $\text{reg} : V \times \cup L_i \to \{0,1\}$ such that each lightpath in $\cup L_i$ is d-satisfied.

Objective: Minimize $\sum_{v \in V} \text{reg}(v)$, where $\text{reg}(v) = \max_{1 \leq i \leq p} \sum_{\ell \in L_i} \text{reg}(v,\ell)$.

Note that, as mentioned in Section 1.1, in the case $p = 1$ (that is, when there is a single set of requests) the problem is trivially solvable in polynomial time, as the regenerators can be placed for each lightpath independently. The case $d = 1$ is not interesting either, as for each internal vertex $v \in V$ and each $\ell \in \cup L_i$, $\text{reg}(v,\ell) = 1$, so there is only one feasible solution, which is optimal.

1.3 Our Contribution

In this article we provide hardness results and approximation algorithms for the (d,p)-TOTAL REGENERATORS problem ((d,p)-TR for short). We first prove in Section 3 that for any two fixed integers $d, p \geq 2$, (d,p)-TR does not admit a PTAS unless P = NP, even if the underlying graph G has maximum degree at most 3, and the lightpaths have length at most $\lceil \frac{7d}{2} \rceil$. In Section 4 we complement this hardness result with a constant-factor approximation algorithm with ratio $\min\{p, H_{d \cdot p} - 1/2\}$, where $H_n = \sum_{i=1}^{n} \frac{1}{i}$ is the n-th harmonic number. Section 5 is devoted to the case where the underlying graph is a path. In Section 5.1 we prove that (d,p)-TR is NP-hard in paths for any fixed $d, p \geq 2$, even if there are two edges of the path such that any lightpath uses at least one of them. Interestingly, we show in Section 5.2 that the problem is polynomial-time solvable in paths when all the lightpaths share the first (or the last) edge, as well as when the maximum number of lightpaths sharing an edge is bounded. In Section 6 we generalize the model presented in Section 1.2 in two natural directions. This generalization allows us to capture the model of [10] as a particular case, and to settle some complexity issues that were left open in [10]. (Since we need some further definitions, we defer the precise statement of these results to Section 6.) Finally, in Section 7 we conclude the article and present a number of interesting avenues for further research. We first provide in Section 2 some standard preliminaries. Due to space limitations, almost all proofs are omitted in this extended abstract (except that of Proposition 1); they can be found in [16].

2 Preliminaries

We use standard terminology concerning graphs, complexity, and algorithms; see for instance [7,11,21], respectively.

Graphs. All the graphs considered in this article are simple and undirected. Given a graph G we denote by $V(G)$ and $E(G)$ the sets of vertices and edges of G, respectively. If H is a subgraph of G, we denote it by $H \subseteq G$. Given a graph G and $F \subseteq E(G)$, we denote by $G[F]$ the subgraph of G induced by the edges in F together with their endpoints. Given a a subset $S \subseteq V(G)$, we define $N_G[S]$ to be the set of vertices of $V(G)$ at distance at most 1 from at least one vertex of S. If $S = \{v\}$, we simply use the notation $N_G[v]$. We also define $N_G(v) = N_G[v] \setminus \{v\}$. The *degree* of a vertex $v \in V(G)$ is defined as $\deg_G(v) = |N_G(v)|$. A graph is *cubic* if all its vertices have degree 3. The *maximum degree* of G is defined as $\Delta(G) = \max_{v \in V(G)} \deg_G(v)$. A *matching* in a graph is a set of disjoint edges, and a *vertex cover* is a set of vertices that contains at least one endpoint of every edge. The *girth* of a graph is the length of a shortest cycle. Given an edge $e = \{u, v\}$, by *subdividing* e we denote the operation of deleting the edge $e = \{u, v\}$, adding a new vertex w, and making it adjacent to both u and v.

Complexity and approximation algorithms. Given an NP-hard minimization problem Π, we say that a polynomial-time algorithm $\mathcal{A}$ is an α-approximation algorithm for Π, with $\alpha \geq 1$, if for any instance of Π, algorithm $\mathcal{A}$ finds a feasible solution with cost at most α times the cost of an optimal solution. For instance, a maximal matching constitutes a 2-approximation algorithm for the Minimum Vertex Cover problem. In complexity theory, the class APX (Approximable) contains all NP-hard optimization problems that can be approximated within a constant factor. The subclass PTAS (Polynomial Time Approximation Scheme) contains the problems that can be approximated in polynomial time within a ratio $1 + \varepsilon$ for *any* fixed $\varepsilon > 0$. In some sense, these problems can be considered to be *easy* NP-hard problems. Since, assuming P $\neq$ NP, there is a strict inclusion of PTAS in APX (for instance, Minimum Vertex Cover $\in$ APX $\setminus$ PTAS), an APX-hardness result for a problem implies the non-existence of a PTAS unless P = NP.

3 Hardness Results for General Graphs

In this section we prove that, unless P = NP, (d, p)-TR does not admit a PTAS for any $d, p \geq 2$, even if the underlying graph G has maximum degree at most 3 and the lightpaths have length $\mathcal{O}(d)$. Before this, we need two technical results to be used in the reductions.

Minimum Vertex Cover is known to be APX-hard in cubic graphs [1]. By a simple reduction, we prove in the following lemma that Minimum Vertex Cover is also APX-hard in a class of graphs with degree at most 3 and high girth, which will be used in the sequel.

Lemma 1. Minimum Vertex Cover *is* APX*-hard in the class of graphs* $\mathcal{H}$ *obtained from cubic graphs by subdividing each edge twice.*

Thomassen proved [20] that the edges of any cubic graph can be two-colored such that each monochromatic connected component is a path of length at most 5. In addition, the aforementioned coloring can be found in polynomial time [20]. Note that in such a coloring of a cubic graph, each vertex appears exactly once as an endpoint of a path, and exactly once as an internal vertex of another path. We next show that this result can be easily extended to graphs with maximum degree at most 3.

Lemma 2. *The edges of any graph with maximum degree at most 3 can be two-colored such that each monochromatic connected component is a path of length at most 5.*

We are now ready to announce the main results of this section. For the sake of presentation, we first present in Proposition 1 the result for $d = p = 2$, and then we show in Theorem 1 how to extend the reduction to any fixed $d, p \geq 2$.

Proposition 1. $(2,2)$-TR *does not admit a* PTAS *unless* P = NP, *even if* G *has maximum degree at most 3 and the lightpaths have length at most 7.*

Proof. The reduction is from Minimum Vertex Cover (VC for short) in the class of graphs $\mathcal{H}$ obtained from cubic graphs by subdividing each edge twice, which does not admit a PTAS by Lemma 1 unless P = NP. Note that by construction any graph in $\mathcal{H}$ has girth at least 9. Given a graph $H \in \mathcal{H}$ as instance of Vertex Cover, we proceed to build an instance of $(2,2)$-TR. We set $G = H$, so G has maximum degree at most 3.

To define the two sets of lightpaths L_1 and L_2, let $\{E_1, E_2\}$ be the partition of $E(H)$ given by the two-coloring of Lemma 2. Therefore, each connected component of $H[E_1]$ and $H[E_2]$ is a path of length at most 5. Each such path in $H[E_1]$ (resp. $H[E_2]$) will correspond to a lightpath in L_1 (resp. L_2), which we proceed to define. A key observation is that, as the paths of the two-coloring have length at most 5, if any endpoint v of a such path P had one neighbor in $V(P)$, it would create a cycle of length at most 6, a contradiction to the fact that the girth of H is at least 9. Therefore, as the vertices of H have degree 2 or 3, any endpoint v of a path P has at least one neighbor in $V(H) \setminus V(P)$.

We are now ready to define the lightpaths. Let P be a path with endpoints u, v, and let u' (resp. v') be a neighbor of u (resp. v) in $V(H) \setminus V(P)$, such that $u' \neq v'$ (such distinct vertices u', v' exist by the above observation and by the fact that H has girth at least 9). The lightpath associated with P consists of the concatenation of $\{u', u\}$, P, and $\{v, v'\}$. Therefore, the length of each lightpath is at most 7. This completes the construction of the instance of $(2,2)$-TR. Observe that since we assume that $d = 2$, regenerators must be placed in such a way that all the internal edges of a lightpath (that is, all the edges except the first and the last one) have a regenerator in at least one of their endpoints. We can assume without loss of generality that no regenerator serves at the endpoints of a lightpath, as the removal of such regenerators does not alter the feasibility of a solution. Note that in our construction, each vertex of G appears as an internal vertex in at most two lightpaths, one (possibly) in L_1 and the other one (possibly) in L_2, so we can assume that $\text{reg}(v) \leq 1$ for any $v \in V(G)$.

We now claim that $\text{OPT}_{\text{VC}}(H) = \text{OPT}_{(2,2)-\text{TR}}(G, \{L_1, L_2\})$.

Indeed, let first $S \subseteq V(H)$ be a vertex cover of H. Placing one regenerator at each vertex belonging to S defines a feasible solution to $(2,2)$-TR in G with cost $|S|$, as at least one endpoint of each internal edge of each lightpath contains a regenerator. Therefore, $\text{OPT}_{\text{VC}}(H) \geq \text{OPT}_{(2,2)-\text{TR}}(G, \{L_1, L_2\})$.

Conversely, suppose we are given a solution to (2,2)-TR in G using r regenerators. Since E_1 and E_2 are a partition of $E(G) = E(H)$ and the set of internal edges of the lightpaths in L_1 (resp. L_2) is equal to E_1 (resp. E_2), the regenerators placed at the endpoints of the internal edges of the lightpaths constitute a vertex cover of H of size at most r. Therefore, $\text{OPT}_{\text{VC}}(H) \leq \text{OPT}_{(2,2)-\text{TR}}(G, \{L_1, L_2\})$.

Summarizing, since $\text{OPT}_{\text{VC}}(H) = \text{OPT}_{(2,2)-\text{TR}}(G, \{L_1, L_2\})$ and any feasible solution to $\text{OPT}_{(2,2)-\text{TR}}(G, \{L_1, L_2\})$ using r regenerators defines a vertex cover of H of size at most r, the existence of a PTAS for $(2,2)$-TR would imply the existence of a PTAS for Vertex Cover in the class of graphs $\mathcal{H}$, which is a contradiction by Lemma 1, unless P = NP. □

Theorem 1. (d,p)-TR *does not admit a* PTAS *for any* $d \geq 2$ *and any* $p \geq 2$ *unless* P = NP, *even if the underlying graph* G *satisfies* $\Delta(G) \leq 3$ *and the lightpaths have length at most* $\lceil \frac{7d}{2} \rceil$.

4 Approximation Algorithms for General Graphs

We have seen in Section 3 that (d,p)-TR does not admit a PTAS for $d, p \geq 2$ unless P = NP. In this section we complement this result with a constant-factor approximation algorithm for (d,p)-TR in general graphs.

Theorem 2. *For any fixed* $d, p \geq 2$, *there is a polynomial-time approximation algorithm for the* (d,p)-TR *problem with ratio* $\min\{p, H_{d \cdot p} - 1/2\}$, *where* $H_{d \cdot p} = \sum_{i=1}^{d \cdot p} \frac{1}{i}$.

Note that for big d, p, $H_{d \cdot p} \approx \ln d + \ln p + 1/2$, so comparing both approximation ratios, we have that $p < \ln d + \ln p$ when $d = \Omega(2^p)$.

5 The Case of the Path

In this section we focus on the case where the network topology is a path, which is one of the most important topologies in real networks, as well as one of the most natural and apparently simplest underlying graphs to study. Clearly, hardness results obtained for this topology will carry over all topologies. We first present in Section 5.1 an NP-hardness result, and then we present in Section 5.2 polynomial-time optimal algorithms for two families of instances.

5.1 Hardness Result

The model of [10] turns out to be polynomial-time solvable when the underlying topology is a tree. Surprisingly enough, in this section we show that our model remains NP-hard even if the network is a path, for any $d \geq 2$ and any $p \geq 2$.

Theorem 3. *(d, p)-TR is NP-hard in paths for any $d, p \geq 2$, even if each vertex is the endpoint of at most 10 lightpaths and there are two edges of the path such that any lightpath uses at least one of them.*

5.2 Polynomial-Time Solvable Cases

In this section we present polynomial-time optimal algorithms in path networks for two restricted sets of instances, namely when all the lightpaths go through a common edge, and when the *load* of the path (that is, the maximum number of lightpaths in any set L_i crossing an edge of the path) is bounded by a logarithmic function of the input size.

Edge instances. In an *edge instance* there is an edge $e \in E(G)$ that is used by all the lightpaths. Note that the instance built in the reduction used in the proof of Theorem 3 contains two edges intersecting all the lightpaths.

Proposition 2. *For any fixed $d, p \geq 2$, there is a polynomial-time algorithm solving the (d, p)-TR problem for edge instances in a path where all the lightpaths share the first edge.*

Bounded load. From Theorem 3 it follows that (d, p)-TR remains hard in paths even if each vertex is the endpoint of at most 10 lightpaths. It turns out that if we further impose that not only the number of lightpaths per vertex is bounded, but also the load of the path is bounded by an appropriate function of the size of the instance, then the problem is solvable in polynomial time. Intuitively, this special case of instances is in the opposite extreme of the edge instances, where there is an edge with unbounded load.

Proposition 3. *For any fixed $d, p \geq 2$, (d, p)-TR is polynomial-time solvable in paths if the load is $\mathcal{O}\left(\frac{\log |I| - \log p}{2p \cdot \log d}\right) = \mathcal{O}(\log |I|)$, where $|I|$ is the size of the instance.*

6 More General Settings

In this section we generalize the (d, p)-TR problem in two natural directions. Namely, in Section 6.1 we allow the number p of traffic patterns to be unbounded, and in Section 6.2 we introduce a parameter k that bounds the number of regenerators that can be placed at a vertex. Technologically, the latter constraint captures the fact of having a bounded number of ROADMs per vertex, as the number of wavelengths (and therefore, the number of regenerators) an ROADM can handle is usually not too big (see Section 1.1).

6.1 Unbounded Number of Sets of Lightpaths

If p is part of the input, then (d,p)-TR contains as a particular case the model studied in [10] (the so-called *location* problem, denoted RPP/∞/+ in [10]). Indeed, if each set of lightpaths consists of a single lightpath (that is, when p is the number of lightpaths), then the objective is to place the minimum number of regenerators such that each lightpath is satisfied. Therefore, the hardness results stated in [10] also apply to this more general setting, in particular an approximation lower bound of $\Omega(\log(d \cdot p))$ unless NP can be simulated in subexponential time. Note that this hardness bound matches the approximation ratio given by Theorem 2. Nevertheless, note also that the approximation algorithm presented in Theorem 2 runs in polynomial time only for bounded p.

We now reformulate the problem studied in [10] using our terminology. Let $d \geq 1$ be a fixed integer.

d-Regenerators Location (d-RL)

Input: An undirected graph $G = (V, E)$ and a set of lightpaths L.

Output: A function $\text{reg} : V \times L \to \{0,1\}$ such that each lightpath $\ell \in L$ is d-satisfied.

Objective: Minimize $\sum_{v \in V} \text{reg}(v)$, where $\text{reg}(v) = \max_{\ell \in L} \text{reg}(v, \ell)$.

Note that in the above problem, $\text{reg}(v) \in \{0,1\}$. We now focus on the case $d = 2$ of d-RL.

Remark 1. *Given an instance of* 2-RL *in a graph G, the problem can be reduced to a* Minimum Vertex Cover *problem in a subgraph of G. Indeed, given a set of lightpaths L, remove the first and the last edge of each lightpath, and let H be the subgraph of G defined by the union of the edges in the modified lightpaths. It is then clear that the minimum number of regenerators to 2-satisfy all the lightpaths in L equals the size of a minimum vertex cover of H.*

By Remark 1 and König's theorem [7], it follows that 2-RL can be solved in polynomial time in bipartite graphs. This result extends the results of [10] for $d = 2$, where it is proved that for any $d \geq 2$, d-RL is polynomial-time solvable in trees and rings. Finally, it also follows from Remark 1 that 2-RL admits a PTAS in planar graphs [4] and, more generally, in any family of minor-free graphs [6].

6.2 Bounded Number of Regenerators per Vertex

From a technological point of view, it makes sense to introduce a parameter k that limits the number of regenerators that can be used at a single vertex. Adding this restriction to the d-RL problem, we get the following problem, which is actually the so-called *k-location* problem and denoted RPP/k/+ in [10].

Again, we restate the problem using our terminology. Let $d, k \geq 1$ be two fixed integers.

(d,k)-REGENERATORS LOCATION ((d,k)-RL)
Input: An undirected graph $G = (V, E)$ and a set of lightpaths L.
Output: A function $\text{reg} : V \times L \rightarrow \{0, 1\}$ such that each lightpath $\ell \in L$ is d-satisfied and $\text{reg}(v) \leq k$, where $\text{reg}(v) = \sum_{\ell \in L} \text{reg}(v, \ell)$.
Objective: Minimize $|\{v \in V \mid \text{reg}(v) > 0\}|$.

We now resolve two questions that were left open in [10]. Namely, it is proved in [10] that given an instance of $(3,1)$-RL, it is NP-complete to decide whether there exists a feasible solution for it, which in particular implies that the $(3,1)$-RL problem itself is NP-hard to approximate within any ratio. In the following we prove that, surprisingly, the situation changes for $d = 2$ and $k = 1$. More precisely, it is in P to decide whether there exists a feasible solution for an instance of $(2,1)$-RL, while finding an optimal one is NP-hard.

Proposition 4. *Given an instance of* $(2,1)$-RL, *it can be decided in polynomial time whether there exists a feasible solution for it, while the* $(2,1)$-RL *problem itself (that is, finding an optimal solution) is* NP*-hard.*

7 Conclusions and Further Research

In this article we presented a theoretical study of the problem of placing regenerators in optical networks, so that on each lightpath we must put a regenerator every at most d hops. The cost is the total number of regenerators. We considered the case when p possible traffic patters are given (each by a set of lightpaths), and the objective is to place the minimum number of regenerators satisfying each of these patterns. This setting arises naturally when designing real networks under uncertain traffic forecast. The problem is called (d,p)-TOTAL REGENERATORS problem, or (d,p)-TR for short. We now summarize our results and propose a number of lines for further research.

We proved that for any fixed $d, p \geq 2$, (d,p)-TR does not admit a PTAS unless P = NP, even if the network topology has maximum degree at most 3, by reduction from MINIMUM VERTEX COVER in cubic graphs. It would be interesting to determine which is the explicit approximation lower bound given by Theorem 1. The recent results of Austrin *et al.* [3] about the hardness of MINIMUM VERTEX COVER in graphs of bounded degree may shed some light on this question. We provided an approximation algorithm for (d,p)-TR with constant ratio $\ln(d \cdot p)$, by reducing it to MINIMUM SET COVER. Finding a polynomial-time approximation algorithm matching the hardness lower bound given by Theorem 1 seems to be a challenging task.

We proved that (d,p)-TR is NP-hard in paths for any $d, p \geq 2$, by reduction from the problem of whether the edges of a tripartite graph can be partitioned into triangles. It is easy to see that the proof of Theorem 3 can be adapted to the case when the network is a ring. In fact, the optimization version where the objective is to find the maximum number of edge-disjoint triangles is APX-hard in tripartite graphs [2]. Nevertheless, the proof of Theorem 3 does not allow – at least, without major modifications – to prove that (d,p)-TR does not admit a PTAS in paths, although we believe that this is indeed the case. Therefore, the existence of a PTAS for (d,p)-TR in paths, trees, rings, or even planar graphs, remains open.

The NP-hardness result for paths holds even if there are two edges of the path such that each lightpath uses at least one of them. In order to better understand what makes the problem hard, we proved that when all lightpaths use the first (or the last) edge of the path, then (d,p)-TR becomes polynomial-time solvable for any $d, p \geq 2$. Between these two cases, it only remains to settle the complexity of the case when the edge shared by all lightpaths is an internal edge of the path, which could be polynomial or NP-hard.

Still in the path, but in the opposite extreme of the type of instances, we also proved that (d,p)-TR can be solved in polynomial time when the maximum number of lightpaths using an edge is logarithmically bounded by the size of the instance. It may be possible to extend our dynamic programming approach to trees with instances having this property, and even to graphs with bounded treewidth.

We generalized our model by allowing the number of sets of lightpaths to be unbounded, and by introducing a parameter k that bounds the number of regenerators that can be placed at a node. This way, the model studied in [10] becomes a particular case. We settled several complexity questions that were left open in [10] concerning the case $k = 1$ and $d = 2$. As future work, it seems to be of high importance to consider the parameter k in the original statement of our (d,p)-TR problem.

Acknowledgement. We would like to express our gratitude to Ori (Ornan) Gerstel from CISCO, Israel, for sharing with us the new trends concerning the placement of regenerators in optical networks, and especially for suggesting this research direction concerning multiple sets of requests.

References

1. Alimonti, P., Kann, V.: Some APX-completeness results for cubic graphs. Theoretical Computer Science 237(1-2), 123–134 (2000)
2. Amini, O., Pérennes, S., Sau, I.: Hardness and Approximation of Traffic Grooming. Theoretical Computer Science 410(38-40), 3751–3760 (2009)
3. Austrin, P., Khot, S., Safra, M.: Inapproximability of Vertex Cover and Independent Set in Bounded Degree Graphs. In: Proc. of the 24th IEEE Computational Complexity Conference (CCC), pp. 74–80 (2009)
4. Baker, B.S.: Approximation algorithms for NP-complete problems on planar graphs. Journal of the ACM 41(1), 153–180 (1994)
5. Chen, S., Raghavan, S.: The regenerator location problem. In: Proc. of the International Network Optimization Conference, INOC (2007); Full version to appear in Networks
6. Demaine, E., Hajiaghayi, M., Kawarabayashi, K.-I.: Algorithmic Graph Minor Theory: Decomposition, Approximation and Coloring. In: Proc. of the 46th Annual IEEE Symposium on Foundations of Computer Science (FOCS), pp. 637–646 (2005)

7. Diestel, R.: Graph Theory. Springer, Heidelberg (2005)
8. Fedrizzi, R., Galimberti, G.M., Gerstel, O., Martinelli, G., Salvadori, E., Saradhi, C.V., Tanzi, A., Zanardi, A.: A Framework for Regenerator Site Selection Based on Multiple Paths. In: Prooceedings of IEEE/OSA Conference on Optical Fiber Communications, OFC (to appear, 2010)
9. Fedrizzi, R., Galimberti, G.M., Gerstel, O., Martinelli, G., Salvadori, E., Saradhi, C.V., Tanzi, A., Zanardi, A.: Traffic Independent Heuristics for Regenerator Site Selection for Providing Any-to-Any Optical Connectivity. In: Proc. of IEEE/OSA Conference on Optical Fiber Communications, OFC (to appear, 2010)
10. Flammini, M., Marchetti-Spaccamela, A., Monaco, G., Moscardelli, L., Zaks, S.: On the complexity of the regenerator placement problem in optical networks. In: Proc. of the 21st Annual ACM Symposium on Parallel Algorithms and Architectures (SPAA), pp. 154–162 (2009)
11. Garey, M., Johnson, D.: Computers and Intractability: A Guide to the Theory of NP-Completeness. W. H. Freeman, New York (1979)
12. Gerstel, O., Raza, H.: Predeployment of Resources in Agile Photonic Networks. IEEE/OSA Journal of Lightwave Technology 22(10), 2236–2244 (2004)
13. Kim, S.W., Seo, S.W.: Regenerator placement algorithms for connection establishment in all-optical networks. IEE Proceedings Communications 148(1), 25–30 (2001)
14. Korotki, S.K.: An Overview of the Global Network Expectation Model. In: Prooceedings of IEEE/OSA Conference on Optical Fiber Communications, OFC (2004)
15. Korotki, S.K., Oikonomou, K.N.: Scaling of Most-Likely Traffic Patterns of Hose- and Cost-Constrained Ring and Mesh Networks. In: Prooceedings of IEEE/OSA Conference on Optical Fiber Communications, OFC (2006)
16. Mertzios, G.B., Sau, I., Shalom, M., Zaks, S.: Placing Regenerators in Optical Networks to Satisfy Multiple Sets of Requests. Technical Report CS-2010-07, Technion, Israel Institute of Technology (2010), `www.cs.technion.ac.il/users/wwwb/cgi-bin/tr-info.cgi?2010/CS/CS-2010-07`
17. Murthy, C.S.R., Sinha, S.: Information Theoretic Approach to Traffic Adaptive WDM Networks. IEEE/ACM Transactions on Networking 13(4), 881–894 (2005)
18. Pachnicke, S., Paschenda, T., Krummrich, P.M.: Physical Impairment Based Regenerator Placement and Routing in Translucent Optical Networks. In: Optical Fiber Communication Conference and Exposition and The National Fiber Optic Engineers Conference (Optical Society of America, paper OWA2) (2008)
19. Sriram, K., Griffith, D., Su, R., Golmie, N.: Static vs. dynamic regenerator assignment in optical switches: models and cost trade-offs. In: Workshop on High Performance Switching and Routing (HPSR), pp. 151–155 (2004)
20. Thomassen, C.: Two-Coloring the Edges of a Cubic Graph Such That Each Monochromatic Component Is a Path of Length at Most 5. J. Comb. Theory, Ser. B 75(1), 100–109 (1999)
21. Vazirani, V.V.: Approximation algorithms. Springer, Heidelberg (2001)
22. Yang, X., Ramamurthy, B.: Dynamic routing in translucent WDM optical networks. In: Proc. of the IEEE International Conference on Communications (ICC), pp. 955–971 (2002)
23. Yang, X., Ramamurthy, B.: Sparse Regeneration in Translucent Wavelength-Routed Optical Networks: Architecture, Network Design and Wavelength Routing. Photonic Network Communications 10(1), 39–53 (2005)

Maximal Decidable Fragments of Halpern and Shoham's Modal Logic of Intervals

Angelo Montanari[1], Gabriele Puppis[2], and Pietro Sala[1]

[1] Department of Mathematics and Computer Science, Udine University, Italy
{angelo.montanari,pietro.sala}@dimi.uniud.it
[2] Computing Laboratory, Oxford University, England
gabriele.puppis@comlab.ox.ac.uk

Abstract. In this paper, we focus our attention on the fragment of Halpern and Shoham's modal logic of intervals (HS) that features four modal operators corresponding to the relations "meets", "met by", "begun by", and "begins" of Allen's interval algebra ($\mathsf{A\bar{A}B\bar{B}}$ logic). $\mathsf{A\bar{A}B\bar{B}}$ properly extends interesting interval temporal logics recently investigated in the literature, such as the logic $\mathsf{B\bar{B}}$ of Allen's "begun by/begins" relations and propositional neighborhood logic $\mathsf{A\bar{A}}$, in its many variants (including metric ones). We prove that the satisfiability problem for $\mathsf{A\bar{A}B\bar{B}}$, interpreted over finite linear orders, is decidable, but not primitive recursive (as a matter of fact, $\mathsf{A\bar{A}B\bar{B}}$ turns out to be maximal with respect to decidability). Then, we show that it becomes undecidable when $\mathsf{A\bar{A}B\bar{B}}$ is interpreted over classes of linear orders that contains at least one linear order with an infinitely ascending sequence, thus including the natural time flows $\mathbb{N}$, $\mathbb{Z}$, $\mathbb{Q}$, and $\mathbb{R}$.

1 Introduction

For a long time, the role of interval temporal logics in computer science has been controversial. On the one hand, it is commonly recognized that they provide a natural framework for representing and reasoning about temporal properties in many computer science areas (quoting Kamp and Reyle [11], "truth, as it pertains to language in the way we use it, relates sentences not to instants but to temporal intervals"), including specification and design of hardware components, concurrent real-time processes, event modeling, temporal aggregation in databases, temporal knowledge representation, systems for temporal planning and maintenance, qualitative reasoning, and natural language semantics [9]. On the other hand, the computational complexity of most interval temporal logics proposed in the literature has been a barrier to their systematic investigation and their extensive use in practical applications. This is the case with the modal logic of time intervals HS introduced by Halpern and Shoham in [10]. HS makes it possible to express all basic binary relations that may hold between any pair of intervals (the so-called Allen's relations [1]) by means of four unary modalities, namely, $\langle \mathsf{B} \rangle$, $\langle \mathsf{E} \rangle$ and their transposes $\langle \bar{\mathsf{B}} \rangle$, $\langle \bar{\mathsf{E}} \rangle$, corresponding to Allen's relations "begun by", "ended by" and their inverses "begins", "ends", provided

S. Abramsky et al. (Eds.): ICALP 2010, Part II, LNCS 6199, pp. 345–356, 2010.

that singleton intervals are included in the temporal structure [21]. HS turns out to be highly undecidable under very weak assumptions on the class of linear orders over which its formulas are interpreted [10]. In particular, undecidability holds for any class of linear orders that contains at least one linear order with an infinitely ascending or descending sequence, thus including the natural time flows $\mathbb{N}$, $\mathbb{Z}$, $\mathbb{Q}$, and $\mathbb{R}$. In fact, undecidability occurs even without infinitely ascending/descending sequences: undecidability also holds for any class of linear orders with unboundedly ascending sequences, that is, for any class such that for every n, there is a structure in the class with an ascending sequence of length at least n, e.g., for the class of all finite linear orders. In [12], Lodaya sharpens the undecidability of HS showing that the two modalities $\langle B \rangle, \langle E \rangle$ suffice for undecidability over dense linear orders (in fact, the result applies to the class of all linear orders [9]).

The recent identification of expressive decidable fragments of HS, whose decidability does not depend on simplifying semantic assumptions such as locality and homogeneity [9], shows that such a trade-off between expressiveness and decidability of interval temporal logics can actually be overcome. The most significant ones are the logic $B\bar{B}$ (resp., $E\bar{E}$) of Allen's "begun by/begins" (resp., "ended by/ends") relations [9], the logic $A\bar{A}$ of temporal neighborhood, whose modalities correspond to Allen's "meets/met by" relations (it can be easily shown that Allen's "before/after" relations can be expressed in $A\bar{A}$) [8], and the logic $D\bar{D}$ of the subinterval/superinterval relations, whose modalities correspond to Allen's "contains/during" relations [14]. In this paper, we focus our attention on the logic $A\bar{A}B\bar{B}$ that joins $B\bar{B}$ and $A\bar{A}$ (the case of $A\bar{A}E\bar{E}$ is fully symmetric). The decidability of $B\bar{B}$ (resp., $E\bar{E}$) can be proved by translating it into the point-based propositional temporal logic of linear time with temporal modalities F (sometime in the future) and P (sometime in the past), which has the finite (pseudo-)model property and is decidable [9]. Unfortunately, such a reduction to point-based temporal logics does not work for most interval temporal logics as their propositional variables are evaluated over pairs of points and translate into binary relations. This is the case with $A\bar{A}$. Unlike the case of $B\bar{B}$ (resp., $E\bar{E}$), when dealing with $A\bar{A}$ one cannot abstract away from the left (resp., right) endpoint of intervals, as contradictory formulas may hold over intervals with the same right (resp., left) endpoint and a different left (resp., right) one. The decidability of $A\bar{A}$, over various classes of linear orders, has been proved by Bresolin et al. [3] by reducing its satisfiability problem to that of the two-variable fragment of first-order logic over the same classes of linear orders [17]. An optimal (NEXPTIME) tableau-based decision procedure for $A\bar{A}$ over the integers has been given in [5] and later extended to the classes of all (resp., dense, discrete) linear orders [6], while a decidable metric extension of the future fragment of $A\bar{A}$ over the natural numbers has been proposed in [7] and later extended to the full logic [4]. Finally, a number of undecidable extensions of $A\bar{A}$ have been given in [2, 3].

In [16], Montanari et al. consider the effects of adding the modality $\langle A \rangle$ to $B\bar{B}$, interpreted over the natural numbers. They show that $AB\bar{B}$ retains the simplicity of its constituents, but it improves a lot on their expressive power. In particular, besides making it possible to easily encode the until operator of point-based temporal logic (this is possible neither with $\mathsf{B\bar{B}}$ nor with A), $\mathsf{AB\bar{B}}$ allows one to express accomplishment conditions as well as metric constraints. Such an increase in expressiveness is achieved at the cost of an increase in complexity: the satisfiability problem for $\mathsf{AB\bar{B}}$ is EXPSPACE-complete (that for A is NEXPTIME-complete). In this paper, we show that the addition of the modality $\langle \bar{\mathsf{A}} \rangle$ to $\mathsf{AB\bar{B}}$ drastically changes the characteristics of the logic. First, decidability is preserved (only) if $\mathsf{A\bar{A}B\bar{B}}$ is interpreted over finite linear orders, but the satisfiability problem is not primitive recursive anymore. Moreover, we show that the addition of any modality in the set $\{\langle \mathsf{D} \rangle, \langle \bar{\mathsf{D}} \rangle, \langle \mathsf{E} \rangle, \langle \bar{\mathsf{E}} \rangle, \langle \mathsf{O} \rangle, \langle \bar{\mathsf{O}} \rangle\}$ (modalities $\langle \mathsf{O} \rangle, \langle \bar{\mathsf{O}} \rangle$ correspond to Allen's "overlaps/overlapped by" relations) to $\mathsf{A\bar{A}B\bar{B}}$ leads to undecidability. This allows us to conclude that $\mathsf{A\bar{A}B\bar{B}}$, interpreted over finite linear orders, is maximal with respect to decidability. Next, we prove that the satisfiability problem for $\mathsf{A\bar{A}B\bar{B}}$ becomes undecidable when it is interpreted over any class of linear orders that contains at least one linear order with an infinitely ascending sequence, thus including the natural time flows $\mathbb{N}$, $\mathbb{Z}$, $\mathbb{Q}$, and $\mathbb{R}$. As matter of fact, we prove that the addition of B to $\mathsf{A\bar{A}}$ suffices to yield undecidability (the proof can be easily adapted to the case of $\bar{\mathsf{B}}$). Paired with undecidability results in [2, 3], this shows the maximality of $\mathsf{A\bar{A}}$ with respect to decidability when interpreted over these classes of linear orders.

2 The Interval Temporal Logic $\mathsf{A\bar{A}B\bar{B}}$

In this section, we first give syntax and semantics of the logic $\mathsf{A\bar{A}B\bar{B}}$. Then, we introduce the basic notions of atom, type, and dependency. We conclude the section by providing an alternative interpretation of $\mathsf{A\bar{A}B\bar{B}}$ over labeled grid-like structures (such an interpretation is quite common in the interval temporal logic setting).

2.1 Syntax and Semantics

Given a set $\mathcal{P}rop$ of propositional variables, formulas of $\mathsf{A\bar{A}B\bar{B}}$ are built up from $\mathcal{P}rop$ using the boolean connectives $\neg$ and $\vee$ and the unary modal operators $\langle \mathsf{A} \rangle$, $\langle \bar{\mathsf{A}} \rangle$, $\langle \mathsf{B} \rangle$, $\langle \bar{\mathsf{B}} \rangle$. As usual, we shall take advantage of shorthands like $\varphi_1 \wedge \varphi_2 = \neg(\neg\varphi_1 \vee \neg\varphi_2)$, $[\mathsf{A}]\varphi = \neg\langle \mathsf{A} \rangle\neg\varphi$, $[\mathsf{B}]\varphi = \neg\langle \mathsf{B} \rangle\neg\varphi$, $\top = p \vee \neg p$, and $\bot = p \wedge \neg p$, with $p \in \mathcal{P}rop$. Hereafter, we denote by $|\varphi|$ the size of φ.

We interpret formulas of $\mathsf{A\bar{A}B\bar{B}}$ in interval temporal structures over finite linear orders with the relations "meets", "met by", "begins", and "begun by". Precisely, given $N \in \mathbb{N}$, we define $\mathbb{I}_N$ as the set of all (non-singleton) closed intervals $[x, y]$, with $0 \leq x < y \leq N$. For any pair of intervals $[x, y], [x', y'] \in \mathbb{I}_N$, Allen's relations "meets" A, "met by" $\bar{\mathsf{A}}$, "begun by" B, and "begins" $\bar{\mathsf{B}}$ are defined as follows:

- **"meets":** $[x, y] \; \mathsf{A} \; [x', y']$ iff $y = x'$;
- **"met by":** $[x, y] \; \bar{\mathsf{A}} \; [x', y']$ iff $x = y'$;

- **"begun by":** $[x, y] \, B \, [x', y']$ iff $x = x'$ and $y' < y$;
- **"begins":** $[x, y] \, \bar{B} \, [x', y']$ iff $x = x'$ and $y < y'$.

Given an *interval structure* $\mathcal{S} = (\mathbb{I}_N, A, \bar{A}, B, \bar{B}, \sigma)$, where $\sigma : \mathbb{I}_N \to \mathscr{P}(\mathcal{P}rop)$ is a labeling function that maps intervals in $\mathbb{I}_N$ to sets of propositional variables, and an initial interval I, we define the semantics of an $A\bar{A}B\bar{B}$ formula as follows:

- $\mathcal{S}, I \models a$ iff $a \in \sigma(I)$, for any $a \in \mathcal{P}rop$;
- $\mathcal{S}, I \models \neg\varphi$ iff $\mathcal{S}, I \not\models \varphi$;
- $\mathcal{S}, I \models \varphi_1 \vee \varphi_2$ iff $\mathcal{S}, I \models \varphi_1$ or $\mathcal{S}, I \models \varphi_2$;
- for every relation $R \in \{A, \bar{A}, B, \bar{B}\}$, $\mathcal{S}, I \models \langle R \rangle \varphi$ iff there is an interval $J \in \mathbb{I}_N$ such that $I \, R \, J$ and $\mathcal{S}, J \models \varphi$.

Given an interval structure $\mathcal{S}$ and a formula φ, we say that $\mathcal{S}$ *satisfies* φ if there is an interval I in $\mathcal{S}$ such that $\mathcal{S}, I \models \varphi$. We say that φ is *satisfiable* if there exists an interval structure that satisfies it. We define the *satisfiability problem* for $A\bar{A}B\bar{B}$ as the problem of establishing whether a given $A\bar{A}B\bar{B}$-formula φ is satisfiable.

2.2 Atoms, Types, and Dependencies

Let $\mathcal{S} = (\mathbb{I}_N, A, \bar{A}, B, \bar{B}, \sigma)$ be an interval structure and φ be a formula of $A\bar{A}B\bar{B}$. In the sequel, we shall compare intervals in $\mathcal{S}$ with respect to the set of subformulas of φ they satisfy. To do that, we introduce the key notions of φ-atom and φ-type.

First of all, we define the *closure* $\mathcal{C}l(\varphi)$ of φ as the set of all subformulas of φ and of their negations (we identify $\neg\neg\alpha$ with α, $\neg\langle A \rangle \alpha$ with $[A]\neg\alpha$, etc.). For technical reasons, we also introduce the *extended closure* $\mathcal{C}l^+(\varphi)$, which is defined as the set of all formulas in $\mathcal{C}l(\varphi)$ plus all formulas of the forms $\langle R \rangle \alpha$ and $\neg\langle R \rangle \alpha$, with $R \in \{A, \bar{A}, B, \bar{B}\}$ and $\alpha \in \mathcal{C}l(\varphi)$.

A φ-*atom* is any non-empty set $F \subseteq \mathcal{C}l^+(\varphi)$ such that (i) for every $\alpha \in \mathcal{C}l^+(\varphi)$, we have $\alpha \in F$ iff $\neg\alpha \notin F$ and (ii) for every $\gamma = \alpha \vee \beta \in \mathcal{C}l^+(\varphi)$, we have $\gamma \in F$ iff $\alpha \in F$ or $\beta \in F$ (intuitively, a φ-*atom* is a maximal *locally consistent* set of formulas chosen from $\mathcal{C}l^+(\varphi)$). Note that the cardinalities of both sets $\mathcal{C}l(\varphi)$ and $\mathcal{C}l^+(\varphi)$ are *linear* in the number $|\varphi|$ of subformulas of φ, while the number of φ-atoms is *at most exponential* in $|\varphi|$ (precisely, we have $|\mathcal{C}l(\varphi)| = 2|\varphi|$, $|\mathcal{C}l^+(\varphi)| = 18|\varphi|$, and there are at most $2^{9|\varphi|}$ distinct atoms).

We also associate with each interval $I \in \mathcal{S}$ the set of all formulas $\alpha \in \mathcal{C}l^+(\varphi)$ such that $\mathcal{S}, I \models \alpha$. Such a set is called φ-*type* of I and it is denoted by $\mathcal{T}ype_{\mathcal{S}}(I)$. We have that every φ-type is a φ-atom, but not vice versa. Hereafter, we shall omit the argument φ, thus calling a φ-atom (resp., a φ-type) simply an atom (resp., a type).

Given an atom F, we denote by $\mathcal{O}bs(F)$ the set of all *observables* of F, namely, the formulas $\alpha \in \mathcal{C}l(\varphi)$ such that $\alpha \in F$. Similarly, given an atom F and a relation $R \in \{A, \bar{A}, B, \bar{B}\}$, we denote by $\mathcal{R}eq_R(F)$ the set of all R-*requests* of F, namely, the formulas $\alpha \in \mathcal{C}l(\varphi)$ such that $\langle R \rangle \alpha \in F$. Note that, for every pair of intervals $I = (x, y)$ and $J = (x', y')$ in $\mathcal{S}$, if $y = y'$ (resp., $x = x'$) holds, then $\mathcal{R}eq_A(\mathcal{T}ype_{\mathcal{S}}(I)) = \mathcal{R}eq_A(\mathcal{T}ype_{\mathcal{S}}(J))$ (resp., $\mathcal{R}eq_{\bar{A}}(\mathcal{T}ype_{\mathcal{S}}(I)) = \mathcal{R}eq_{\bar{A}}(\mathcal{T}ype_{\mathcal{S}}(J))$)

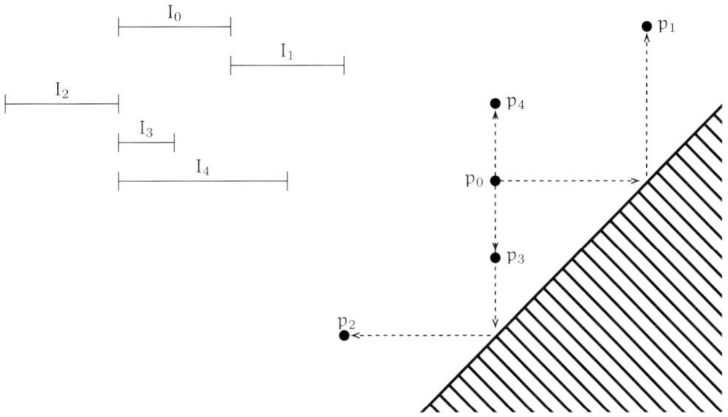

Fig. 1. A compass structure

follows. Taking advantage of the above sets, we can define the following relations between atoms F and G:

$$F \xmapsto{A} G \quad \text{iff} \quad \begin{cases} \mathcal{R}eq_A(F) = \mathcal{O}bs(G) \cup \mathcal{R}eq_{\bar{B}}(G) \\ \mathcal{R}eq_B(G) = \varnothing \\ \mathcal{O}bs(F) \subseteq \mathcal{R}eq_{\bar{A}}(G) \end{cases}$$

$$F \xmapsto{B} G \quad \text{iff} \quad \begin{cases} \mathcal{R}eq_B(F) = \mathcal{O}bs(G) \cup \mathcal{R}eq_B(G) \\ \mathcal{R}eq_{\bar{B}}(G) = \mathcal{O}bs(F) \cup \mathcal{R}eq_{\bar{B}}(F). \end{cases}$$

Note that the above relations satisfy a *view-to-type dependency*, namely, for every pair of intervals $I = [x, y]$ and $I' = [x', y']$, we have

$$\begin{array}{lll} x' = y \ \wedge y' = y + 1 & \text{implies} & \mathcal{T}ype_{\mathcal{S}}(I) \xmapsto{A} \mathcal{T}ype_{\mathcal{S}}(I') \\ x' = x \ \wedge y' = y - 1 & \text{implies} & \mathcal{T}ype_{\mathcal{S}}(I) \xmapsto{B} \mathcal{T}ype_{\mathcal{S}}(I'). \end{array}$$

2.3 Compass Structures

The logic $A\bar{A}B\bar{B}$ can be equivalently interpreted over the so-called compass structures [20], namely, over grid-like structures. Such an alternative interpretation exploits the existence of a natural bijection between the intervals $I = [x, y]$ and the points $p = (x, y)$ of an $N \times N$ grid such that $x < y$. As an example, Figure 1 depicts five intervals $I_0, ..., I_4$ such that I_0 A I_1, I_0 $\bar{A}$ I_2, I_0 B I_3, and I_0 $\bar{B}$ I_4, together with the corresponding points $p_0, ..., p_4$ of a discrete grid (note that the four Allen's relations $A, \bar{A}, B, \bar{B}$ between intervals are mapped to corresponding spatial relations between points; for the sake of readability, we name the latter ones as the former ones).

Definition 1. *Given an* $A\bar{A}B\bar{B}$ *formula* φ, *a (finite, consistent, and fulfilling)* compass *(φ-)*structure *of length* $N \in \mathbb{N}$ *is a pair* $\mathcal{G} = (\mathbb{P}_N, \mathcal{L})$, *where* $\mathbb{P}_N$ *is the set of points* $p = (x, y)$, *with* $0 \le x < y \le N$, *and* $\mathcal{L}$ *is function that maps any point* $p \in \mathbb{P}_N$ *to a (φ-)atom* $\mathcal{L}(p)$ *in such a way that*

- *for every relation* $R \in \{A, \bar{A}, B, \bar{B}\}$ *and every pair of points* $p, q \in \mathbb{P}_N$ *such that* $p \; R \; q$*, we have* $\mathcal{O}bs(\mathcal{L}(q)) \subseteq \mathcal{R}eq_R(\mathcal{L}(p))$ *(***consistency***);*
- *for every relation* $R \in \{A, \bar{A}, B, \bar{B}\}$*, every point* $p \in \mathbb{P}_N$*, and every formula* $\alpha \in \mathcal{R}eq_R(\mathcal{L}(p))$*, there is a point* $q \in \mathbb{P}_N$ *such that* $p \; R \; q$ *and* $\alpha \in \mathcal{O}bs(\mathcal{L}(q))$ *(***fulfillment***).*

It is easy to see that the (finite, consistent, and fulfilling) compass structures are exactly those structures $\mathcal{G} = (\mathbb{P}_N, \mathcal{L})$, with $N \in \mathbb{N}$, that satisfy the following conditions for all pair of points p, q in $\mathcal{G}$:

i) if $p = (x, y)$ and $q = (y, y+1)$, then $\mathcal{L}(p) \xmapsto{A} \mathcal{L}(q)$;
ii) if $p = (x, y)$ and $q = (x, y+1)$, then $\mathcal{L}(q) \xmapsto{B} \mathcal{L}(p)$;
iii) if $p = (y-1, y)$, then $\mathcal{R}eq_{\bar{A}}(\mathcal{L}(p)) = \bigcup_{0 \le x < y-1} \mathcal{O}bs(\mathcal{L}(x, y-1))$;
iv) if $p = (x, N)$, then $\mathcal{R}eq_A(\mathcal{L}(p)) = \varnothing$ and $\mathcal{R}eq_{\bar{B}}(\mathcal{L}(p)) = \varnothing$.

We say that a compass structure $\mathcal{G} = (\mathbb{P}_N, \mathcal{L})$ *features* a formula α if there is a point $p \in \mathbb{P}_N$ such that $\alpha \in \mathcal{L}(p)$. We conclude the section with the following basic result (the proof is straightforward and thus omitted).

Proposition 1. *An* $A\bar{A}B\bar{B}$*-formula* φ *is satisfied by some finite interval structure iff it is featured by some finite* φ*-compass structure.*

3 Decidability and Complexity of the Satisfiability Problem for $A\bar{A}B\bar{B}$ over Finite Linear Orders

In this section, we prove that the satisfiability problem for $A\bar{A}B\bar{B}$ interpreted over *finite* linear orders is decidable, but not primitive recursive. In order to do that, we use a technique similar to [16], namely, we fix a formula φ and a finite compass structure $\mathcal{G} = (\mathbb{P}_N, \mathcal{L})$ satisfying φ and we show that, under suitable conditions, $\mathcal{G}$ can be reduced in length while preserving the existence of atoms featuring φ. For the sake of brevity, we call *contraction* the operation that reduces the length of a given compass structure $\mathcal{G}$ while preserving the existence of atoms featuring φ. Such an operation has been introduced in its simple variant in [16] and it precisely consists of removing the portion of the compass structure $\mathcal{G}$ included between two distinguished rows y_0 and y_1 and selecting a subset of atoms from the upper row y_1 that match with the atoms of the lower row y_0. Hereafter, we refer the reader to Figure 2 for an intuitive account of the contraction operation (the colored nodes represent the atoms associated with the points of $\mathcal{G}$). According to the definition given in [16], the contraction operation is applicable whenever the set of atoms of the lower row y_0 is included in the set of atoms of the upper row y_1 (the arrows in Figure 2 represent a matching function f between the atoms of the lower row y_0 and the atoms of the upper row y_1). Such a condition on the set of atoms associated with the rows y_0 and y_1 guarantees the correctness of the contraction operation with respect to the definition of consistent and fulfilling compass structure, provided that the use of the modal operator $\langle \bar{A} \rangle$ is avoided. However, in the presence of the

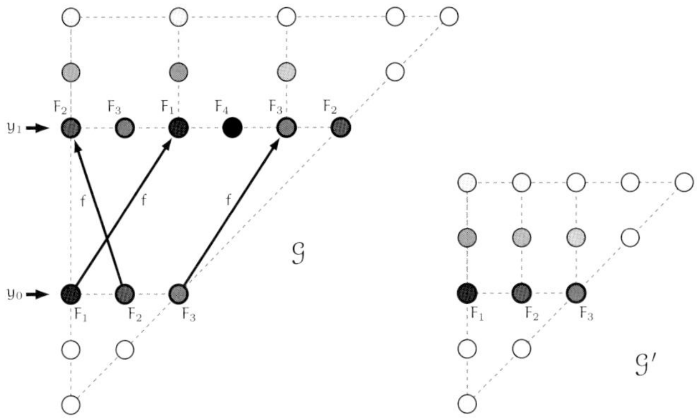

Fig. 2. Contraction of a compass structure

modal operator $\langle \bar{A} \rangle$, things get more involved, since some points $p = (x, y_1)$ from the upper row y_1 (e.g., the one labeled by F_4 in Figure 2) might be necessary in order to fulfill the $\bar{A}$-requests enforced by other points $p' = (x', y')$, with $x' = y_1$ and $y' > y_1$. In the following, we describe a suitable variant of the contraction operation which is applicable to models of $A\bar{A}B\bar{B}$ formulas.

Let us fix an $A\bar{A}B\bar{B}$ formula φ that is featured by a finite compass structure $\mathcal{G} = (\mathbb{P}_N, \mathcal{L})$. Without loss of generality, we can assume that φ is of the form $(\phi \wedge [B]\bot) \vee (\langle \bar{B} \rangle \phi) \vee (\langle \bar{B} \rangle \langle A \rangle \phi)$ and, furthermore, it belongs to the atom associated with the point $p = (0, 1)$ at the bottom of the structure $\mathcal{G}$. Before turning to our main result, we need to introduce some preliminary notation and terminology. For every $1 \leq y \leq N$, we denote by $\mathcal{R}ow_{\mathcal{G}}(y)$ the row y of $\mathcal{G}$, namely, the set of all points $p = (x, y)$ of $\mathcal{G}$. We associate with each row y the set $\mathcal{S}hading_{\mathcal{G}}(y) = \mathcal{L}(\mathcal{R}ow_{\mathcal{G}}(y))$, which consists of the atoms associated with the points in $\mathcal{R}ow_{\mathcal{G}}(y)$. Clearly, for every pair of atoms F, G in $\mathcal{S}hading_{\mathcal{G}}(y)$, we have $\mathcal{R}eq_A(F) = \mathcal{R}eq_A(G)$. We also associate with the row y the function $\mathcal{C}ount_{\mathcal{G}}(y)$, which maps an atom F to the number $\mathcal{C}ount_{\mathcal{G}}(y)(F)$ of F-labeled points in $\mathcal{R}ow_{\mathcal{G}}(y)$.

In order to deal with $\bar{A}$-requests, we need to introduce the notion of cover of a compass structure. Intuitively, this is a selection of points that fulfills all $\bar{A}$-requests coming from other points (hence the points in a cover should not disappear during the operation of contraction). Formally, a *cover* of a compass structure $\mathcal{G} = (\mathbb{P}_N, \mathcal{L})$ is a subset C of $\mathbb{P}_N$ that satisfies the following two conditions:

- if $(x, y) \in C$ and $x < y - 1$, then $(x, y - 1) \in C$ as well;
- for every point $q = (y - 1, y) \in \mathbb{P}_N$, the set $\mathcal{R}eq_{\bar{A}}(\mathcal{L}(q))$ coincides with the union of the sets $\mathcal{O}bs(\mathcal{L}(p))$ for all $p = (x, y - 1) \in C$.

Given a cover C of $\mathcal{G}$, we extend the notations $\mathcal{R}ow_{\mathcal{G}}(y)$, $\mathcal{S}hading_{\mathcal{G}}(y)$, and $\mathcal{C}ount_{\mathcal{G}}(y)$ respectively to $\mathcal{R}ow_{\mathcal{G}|C}(y)$, $\mathcal{S}hading_{\mathcal{G}|C}(y)$, and $\mathcal{C}ount_{\mathcal{G}|C}(y)$, having the obvious meaning (e.g., $\mathcal{R}ow_{\mathcal{G}|C}(y)$ is the set of all points of $\mathcal{G}$ along the row y that also belong to C). Moreover, we say that a cover is *minimal* if it does not

```
let ϕ be an input formula
let φ be (ϕ ∧ [B]⊥) ∨ (⟨B̄⟩ϕ) ∨ (⟨B̄⟩⟨A⟩ϕ)

proc CheckRows(F_Δ, S_Δ, C_Δ, F_{Δ+1}, S_{Δ+1}, C_{Δ+1})
  S⁺_{Δ+1} ← S_{Δ+1} ∪ {F_{Δ+1}}
  if there is F ∈ S⁺_{Δ+1} such that F ↦A/ F_Δ
    then return false
  S^cov_{Δ+1} ← {F : C_{Δ+1}(F) > 0}
  if Req_Ā(F_Δ) ≠ ⋃Obs(S^cov_{Δ+1})
    then return false
  f ← any function from S⁺_{Δ+1} to S_Δ
  if there is F ∈ S⁺_{Δ+1} such that f(F) ↦B/ F
    then return false
  M_Δ ← {(F,i) : F ∈ S_Δ, 1 ≤ i ≤ C_Δ(F)}
  M⁺_{Δ+1} ← {(F,i) : F ∈ S⁺_{Δ+1}, 1 ≤ i ≤ C_{Δ+1}(F)}
  g ← any injective function
        from M_Δ to M⁺_{Δ+1}
  if there is (F,i) ∈ M_Δ and (F′,i′) = g(F,i)
     such that F ↦B/ F′
    then return false
  return true

proc CheckContraction(F_1, S_1, C_1, ..., F_Δ, S_Δ, C_Δ)
  if S_Δ ≠ ∅ and there is 1 ≤ Δ′ < Δ such that
     S_Δ ∪ {F_Δ} ⊆ S_Δ′ ∪ {F_Δ′} and C_Δ ≥ C_Δ′
    then return true
  return false

main
  Δ ← 1
  F_1 ← any φ-atom F such that
        Req_A(F) = Req_B̄(F) = Req_B(F) = ∅
  S_1 ← any set of φ-atoms F such that
        Req_A(F) = Req_B̄(F) = ∅, Req_B(F) ≠ ∅
  C_1 ← the function C : S_1 ∪ {F_1} → ℕ such
        that C(F) = 0 for all F ∈ S_1 ∪ {F_1}

  while S_Δ ≠ ∅ or φ ∉ F_Δ
  do
    F_{Δ+1} ← any φ-atom F
              such that Req_B(F) = ∅
    S_{Δ+1} ← any set of φ-atoms F
              such that Req_B(F) ≠ ∅
    C_{Δ+1} ← any C : S_{Δ+1} ∪ {F_{Δ+1}} → ℕ such
              that  { 0 ≤ C(F_{Δ+1}) ≤ 1
                    { Σ_F C(F) ≥ Σ_{F≠F_Δ} C_Δ(F)
                    { Σ_F C(F) ≤ Σ_F C_Δ(F) + |φ|
    if not CheckRows(F_Δ, S_Δ, C_Δ, F_{Δ+1}, S_{Δ+1}, C_{Δ+1})
      then return false
    if CheckContraction(F_1, S_1, C_1, ..., F_{Δ+1}, S_{Δ+1}, C_{Δ+1})
      then return false
    Δ ← Δ + 1
  return true
```

Fig. 3. Decision algorithm for the satisfiability problem over finite linear orders

include properly any other cover. We can easily verify that every *minimal* cover C of $\mathcal{G} = (\mathbb{P}_N, \mathcal{L})$ satisfies

$$\begin{aligned} &\mathcal{R}ow_{\mathcal{G}|C}(N) = \varnothing \\ &\left|\mathcal{R}ow_{\mathcal{G}|C}(y)\right| - 1 \leq \left|\mathcal{R}ow_{\mathcal{G}|C}(y-1)\right| \leq \left|\mathcal{R}ow_{\mathcal{G}|C}(y)\right| + |\varphi|. \end{aligned} \tag{1}$$

The following proposition shows that, under suitable conditions, a given compass structure $\mathcal{G}$ can be reduced in length while preserving the existence of atoms featuring φ. Note that such a result can be thought of as a strenghtening of the original "contraction lemma" for structures over the signature $A, B, \bar{B}$ (indeed, if the logic does not allow the modal operator $\langle \bar{A} \rangle$, then the empty set is the unique minimal cover of any compass structure $\mathcal{G}$ and hence the proposition below becomes equivalent to Lemma 3.2 in [16]). For the sake of brevity, hereafter we use $\leq$ to denote the componentwise partial order between functions that map atoms to natural numbers, i.e., $f \leq g$ iff $f(F) \leq g(F)$ holds for all atoms F.

Proposition 2. *Let $\mathcal{G} = (\mathbb{P}_N, \mathcal{L})$ be a compass structure that features a formula φ in its bottom row. If there exist a cover C of $\mathcal{G}$ and two rows y_0 and y_1 in $\mathcal{G}$, with $1 < y_0 < y_1 \leq N$, such that*
i) $\mathcal{S}hading_{\mathcal{G}}(y_0) \subseteq \mathcal{S}hading_{\mathcal{G}}(y_1)$,
ii) $\mathcal{C}ount_{\mathcal{G}}(y_0) \geq \mathcal{C}ount_{\mathcal{G}|C}(y_1)$,
then there exists a compass structure $\mathcal{G}'$ of length $N' < N$ that features φ.

On the grounds of Proposition 2, it makes sense to restrict ourselves to the *minimal* models of φ and, in particular, to those compass structures $\mathcal{G} = (\mathbb{P}_N, \mathcal{L})$

that feature φ $(= (\phi \wedge [B]\bot) \vee (\langle\bar{B}\rangle\phi) \vee (\langle\bar{B}\rangle\langle A\rangle\phi))$ in the bottom row and that cannot be contracted. The above argument leads to a non-deterministic procedure that decides whether a given formula ϕ is satisfied by a (contraction-free) interval structure $\mathcal{S}$. The pseudo-code of such an algorithm is given in Figure 3: the variable Δ represents the value $N - y + 1$, where N is the length of the model $\mathcal{G}$ to be guessed and y is the current row (note that we cannot use y in place of Δ since there is no a priori bound on the length N of the model), the variable F_Δ represents the atom associated with the rightmost point $p = (y-1, y)$ along the current row y, the variable S_Δ represents an *over-approximation* of the set $\mathit{Shading}_{\mathcal{G}}(y)$, and the variable C_Δ represents the function $\mathit{Count}_{\mathcal{G}|C}(y)$ for a suitable cover C of $\mathcal{G}$ (note that the content of such a variable can be guessed because the sum of its values is bounded in virtue of Equation 1).

The decidability of the satisfiability problem for $A\bar{A}B\bar{B}$ interpreted over finite linear orders is thus reduced to a proof of termination, soundness, and completeness for the algorithm given in Figure 3 as formally stated by Theorem 1 (its proof is reported in [15]). As a matter of fact, termination relies on the following crucial lemma, which is often attributed to Dickson.

Lemma 1 (Dickson's Lemma). *Let* $(\mathbb{N}^k, \leq)$ *be the* k*-dimensional vector space over* $\mathbb{N}$ *equipped with the componentwise partial order* $\leq$*. Then,* $(\mathbb{N}^k, \leq)$ *admits no infinite anti-chains, namely, every subset of* $\mathbb{N}^d$ *that consists of pairwise* $\leq$*-incomparable vectors must be finite.*

Theorem 1. *The satisfiability problem for* $A\bar{A}B\bar{B}$*, interpreted over finite linear orders, is decidable.*

We conclude the section by analyzing the complexity of the satisfiability problem for $A\bar{A}B\bar{B}$. In [16], Montanari et al. show that the satisfiability problem for $AB\bar{B}$ is EXPSPACE-complete. Here we prove that, quite surprisingly, the satisfiability problem for $A\bar{A}B\bar{B}$ (in fact, also that for the fragment $A\bar{A}B$) has much higher complexity, precisely, it is not primitive recursive.

Theorem 2. *The satisfiability problem for* $A\bar{A}B$*, and hence that for* $A\bar{A}B\bar{B}$*, interpreted over finite linear orders, is not primitive recursive.*

The proof of Theorem 2 is given in the Appendix and it is based on a reduction from the reachability problem for lossy counter machines, which is known to have strictly non-primitive recursive complexity [19], to the satisfiability problem for $A\bar{A}B$. In particular, it shows that there is an $A\bar{A}B$ formula that defines a set of encodings of all possible computations of a given lossy counter machine. The key ingredients of the proof are as follows. First, we represent the value $c(t)$ of each counter c, at each instant t of a computation, by means of a sequence consisting of exactly $c(t)$ unit-length intervals labeled by c. Then, we guarantee that suitable disequalities of the form $c(t+1) \leq c(t) + h$, with $h \in \{-1, 0, 1\}$, hold between the values of the counter c at consecutive time instants. This can be done by enforcing the existence of a surjective partial function g from the set of c-labeled unit-length intervals corresponding to the time instant t to the set of c-labeled unit-length intervals corresponding to the next time instant $t+1$. Finally, we exploit the fact that surjective partial functions between sets of unit-length intervals can be specified in the logic $\mathsf{A\bar{A}B}$.

4 Undecidabiliy Is the Rule, Decidability the Exception

We conclude the paper by proving that $\mathsf{A\bar{A}B\bar{B}}$, interpreted over finite linear orders, is maximal with respect to decidability. The addition of a modality for any one of the remaining Allen's relations, that is, of any modality in the set $\{\langle \mathsf{D}\rangle, \langle \bar{\mathsf{D}}\rangle, \langle \mathsf{E}\rangle, \langle \bar{\mathsf{E}}\rangle, \langle \mathsf{O}\rangle, \langle \bar{\mathsf{O}}\rangle\}$, indeed leads to undecidability. The proof of the following theorem can be found in [15].

Theorem 3. *The satisfiability problem for the logic* $\mathsf{A\bar{A}B\bar{B}D}$ *(resp.,* $\mathsf{A\bar{A}B\bar{B}\bar{D}}$, $\mathsf{A\bar{A}B\bar{B}E}$, $\mathsf{A\bar{A}B\bar{B}\bar{E}}$, $\mathsf{A\bar{A}B\bar{B}O}$, $\mathsf{A\bar{A}B\bar{B}\bar{O}}$*), interpreted over finite linear orders, is undecidable.*

It is possible to show that the satisfiability problem for $\mathsf{A\bar{A}B\bar{B}}$ (in fact, this holds for its proper fragment $\mathsf{A\bar{A}B}$) becomes undecidable if we interpret it over any class of linear orders that contains at least one linear order with an infinitely ascending sequence. It follows that, in particular, it is undecidable when $\mathsf{A\bar{A}B\bar{B}}$ is interpreted over natural time flows like $\mathbb{N}$, $\mathbb{Z}$, $\mathbb{Q}$, and $\mathbb{R}$. We first consider the satisfiability problem for $\mathsf{A\bar{A}B}$ interpreted over $\mathbb{N}$. By definition, φ is satisfiable over $\mathbb{N}$ if there exists an interval structure of the form $\mathcal{S} = (\mathbb{I}_\omega, A, \bar{A}, B, \sigma)$, with $\mathbb{I}_\omega = \{[x, y] : 0 \leq x < y < \omega\}$ and $\sigma : \mathbb{I}_\omega \rightarrow \mathscr{P}(\mathcal{P}rop)$, that satisfies it. A straightforward adaptation of the proof of Theorem 2 (see the proof of Theorem 4 in [15]) shows that an undecidable variant of the universal reachability problem for lossy counter machines, called "structural termination" [13], is reducible to the satisfiability problem for $\mathsf{A\bar{A}B}$ interpreted over interval structures of the form $\mathcal{S} = (\mathbb{I}_\omega, A, \bar{A}, B, \sigma)$. It immediately follows that the latter problem is undecidable as well. Such a negative result can be easily transferred to any class of linear orders that contains at least one linear order with an infinitely ascending sequence.

Theorem 4. *The satisfiability problem for the logic* $\mathsf{A\bar{A}B}$*, and hence that for the logic* $\mathsf{A\bar{A}B\bar{B}}$*, interpreted over over any class of linear orders that contains at least one linear order with an infinitely ascending sequence is undecidable.*

5 Conclusions

In this paper, we proved that the satisfiability problem for $\mathsf{A\bar{A}B\bar{B}}$, interpreted over finite linear orders, is decidable, but not primitive recursive. We also showed that all proper extensions of $\mathsf{A\bar{A}B\bar{B}}$ with a modality corresponding to one of the remaining Allen's relations yields undecidability, thus proving maximality of $\mathsf{A\bar{A}B\bar{B}}$ with respect to finite linear orders. Moreover, we proved that the satisfiability problem for $\mathsf{A\bar{A}B}$ (in fact, the proof for $\mathsf{A\bar{A}B}$ can be adapted to $\mathsf{A\bar{A}\bar{B}}$), interpreted over any class of linear orders that contains at least one linear order with an infinitely ascending sequence, is undecidable. The same results hold for

$\mathsf{A\bar{A}E}$ and $\mathsf{A\bar{A}\bar{E}}$, provided that we replace the infinitely ascending sequence by an infinitely descending one. As Bresolin et al. already proved that the extension of $\mathsf{A\bar{A}}$ with the operator $\langle \mathsf{D} \rangle$ (resp., $\langle \bar{\mathsf{D}} \rangle$, $\langle \mathsf{O} \rangle$, $\langle \bar{\mathsf{O}} \rangle$) is undecidable [2, 3], maximality of $\mathsf{A\bar{A}}$, interpreted over any class of linear orders that contains at least one linear order with an infinitely ascending/descending sequence, immediately follows. As a matter of fact, this is the first case in the interval temporal logic setting where the decidability/undecidability of a logic depends on the class of linear orders in which it is interpreted (a similar result has been proved by Ouaknine and Worrell for point-based metric temporal logics [18]).

Acknowledgments

We would like to acknowledge the financial support from the PRIN project *Innovative and multi-disciplinary approaches for constraint and preference reasoning* and the GNCS project *Logics, automata, and games for the formal verification of complex systems*.

References

[1] Allen, J.F.: Maintaining knowledge about temporal intervals. Communications of the Association for Computing Machinery 26(11), 832–843 (1983)

[2] Bresolin, D., Della Monica, D., Goranko, V., Montanari, A., Sciavicco, G.: Decidable and undecidable fragments of Halpern and Shoham's interval temporal logic: towards a complete classification. In: Cervesato, I., Veith, H., Voronkov, A. (eds.) LPAR 2008. LNCS (LNAI), vol. 5330, pp. 590–604. Springer, Heidelberg (2008)

[3] Bresolin, D., Goranko, V., Montanari, A., Sciavicco, G.: Propositional interval neighborhood logics: expressiveness, decidability, and undecidable extensions. Annals of Pure and Applied Logic 161(3), 289–304 (2009)

[4] Bresolin, D., Della Monica, D., Goranko, V., Montanari, A., Robinson, C., Sciavicco, G.: Metric Propositional Neighborhood Logics. Research Report UDMI/2010/02, Dept. of Mathematics and Computer Science, University of Udine (2010), `http://users.dimi.uniud.it/~angelo.montanari/rr201002.pdf`

[5] Bresolin, D., Montanari, A., Sala, P.: An optimal tableau-based decision algorithm for Propositional Neighborhood Logic. In: Thomas, W., Weil, P. (eds.) STACS 2007. LNCS, vol. 4393, pp. 549–560. Springer, Heidelberg (2007)

[6] Bresolin, D., Montanari, A., Sala, P., Sciavicco, G.: Tableau-based decision procedures for Propositional Neighborhood Logic. Research Report UDMI/2010/01, Dept. of Mathematics and Computer Science, University of Udine (2010), `http://users.dimi.uniud.it/~angelo.montanari/rr201001.pdf`

[7] Bresolin, D., Goranko, V., Montanari, A., Sciavicco, G.: Right propositional neighborhood logic over natural numbers with integer constraints for interval lengths. In: Proc. of the 7th IEEE Int. Conference on Software Engineering and Formal Methods (SEFM), pp. 240–249. IEEE Comp. Society Press, Los Alamitos (2009)

[8] Goranko, V., Montanari, A., Sciavicco, G.: Propositional interval neighborhood temporal logics. Journal of Universal Computer Science 9(9), 1137–1167 (2003)

[9] Goranko, V., Montanari, A., Sciavicco, G.: A road map of interval temporal logics and duration calculi. Applied Non-classical Logics 14(1-2), 9–54 (2004)

[10] Halpern, J.Y., Shoham, Y.: A propositional modal logic of time intervals. Journal of the ACM 38, 279–292 (1991)

[11] Kamp, H., Reyle, U.: From Discourse to Logic: Introduction to Model-theoretic Semantics of Natural Language, Formal Logic and Discourse Representation Theory. Studies in Linguistics and Philosophy, vol. 42. Springer, Heidelberg (1993)

[12] Lodaya, K.: Sharpening the undecidability of interval temporal logic. In: He, J., Sato, M. (eds.) ASIAN 2000. LNCS, vol. 1961, pp. 290–298. Springer, Heidelberg (2000)

[13] Mayr, R.: Undecidable problems in unreliable computations. Theoretical Computer Science 297(1-3), 337–354 (2003)

[14] Montanari, A., Puppis, G., Sala, P.: A decidable spatial logic with cone-shaped cardinal directions. In: Grädel, E., Kahle, R. (eds.) CSL 2009. LNCS, vol. 5771, pp. 394–408. Springer, Heidelberg (2009)

[15] Montanari, A., Puppis, G., Sala, P.: Maximal decidable fragments of Halpern and Shoham's modal logic of intervals. Research Report UDMI/2010/04, Dept. of Mathematics and Computer Science, University of Udine (2010), `http://users.dimi.uniud.it/~angelo.montanari/rr201004.pdf`

[16] Montanari, A., Puppis, G., Sala, P., Sciavicco, G.: Decidability of the interval temporal logic $AB\bar{B}$ over the natural numbers. In: Proc. of the 27th Int. Symposium on Theoretical Aspects of Computer Science (STACS), pp. 597–608 (to appear, 2010)

[17] Otto, M.: Two variable first-order logic over ordered domains. Journal of Symbolic Logic 66(2), 685–702 (2001)

[18] Ouaknine, J., Worrell, J.: On the decidability and complexity of metric temporal logic over finite words. Logical Methods in Computer Science 3(1), 1–27 (2007)

[19] Schnoebelen, P.: Verifying lossy channel systems has nonprimitive recursive complexity. Information Processing Letters 83(5), 251–261 (2002)

[20] Venema, Y.: Two-dimensional modal logics for relation algebras and temporal logic of intervals. ITLI prepublication series LP-89-03, University of Amsterdam (1989)

[21] Venema, Y.: A modal logic for chopping intervals. Journal of Logic and Computation 1(4), 453–476 (1991)

B and D Are Enough to Make the Halpern–Shoham Logic Undecidable

Jerzy Marcinkowski, Jakub Michaliszyn, and Emanuel Kieroński

Institute of Computer Science,
University Of Wroclaw,
ul. Joliot-Curie 15, 50-383 Wroclaw, Poland
{jma,jmi,kiero}@cs.uni.wroc.pl

Abstract. The Halpern–Shoham logic is a modal logic of time intervals. Some effort has been put in last ten years to classify fragments of this beautiful logic with respect to decidability of its satisfiability problem. We contribute to this effort by showing (among other results), that the *BD* fragment (where only the operators "begins" and "during" are allowed) is undecidable over discrete structures.

1 Introduction

In classical temporal logic structures are defined by assigning properties (propositional variables) to points of time (which is an ordering, discrete or dense). However, not all phenomena can be well described by such logics. Sometimes we need to talk about actions (processes) that take some time and we would like to be able to say that one such action takes place, for example, during or after another.

The Halpern–Shoham logic [11], which is the subject of this paper, is one of the modal logics of time intervals. Judging by the number of papers published, and by the amount of work devoted to the research on it, this logic is probably the most influential of time interval logics. But historically it was not the first one. Actually, the earliest papers about intervals in context of modal logic were written by philosophers, e.g., [10]. In computer science, the earliest attempts to formalize time intervals were process logic [15,17] and interval temporal logic [13]. Relations between intervals in linear orders from an algebraic point of view were first studied systematically by Allen [1].

The Halpern–Shoham logic is a modal temporal logic, where the elements of a model are no longer — like in classical temporal logics — points in time, but rather pairs of points in time. Any such pair — call it $[p, q]$, where q is not earlier than p — can be viewed as a (closed) time interval, that is, the set of all time points between p and q. HS logic does not assume anything about order — it can be discrete or continuous, linear or branching, complete or not.

Halpern and Shoham introduce six modal operators, acting on intervals. Their operators are "begins" B, "during" D, "ends" E, "meets" A, "later" L, "overlaps"

S. Abramsky et al. (Eds.): ICALP 2010, Part II, LNCS 6199, pp. 357–368, 2010.

O and the six inverses of those operators: $\bar{B}$, $\bar{D}$, $\bar{E}$, $\bar{A}$, $\bar{L}$, $\bar{O}$. It is easy to see that the set of operators is redundant: D can be expressed using B and E (a prefix of my suffix is my infix), L can be expressed by A ("later" means "meets an interval that meets") and O can be expressed using E and $\bar{B}$.

In their paper, Halpern and Shoham show that (satisfiability of formulae of) their logic is undecidable. Their proof requires logic with five operators (B, E and A are explicitly used in the formulae and, as we mentioned above, once B, E and A are allowed, D and L come for free) so they state a question about decidable fragments of their logic.

Some effort has been put since this time to settle this question. First, it was shown [12] that the BE fragment is undecidable. Recently, negative results were also given for the classes $B\bar{E}$, $\bar{B}\bar{E}$, $\bar{B}E$, $A\bar{A}D$, $\bar{A}D^*\bar{B}$, $\bar{A}D^*B$ [3,7]. Another surprising negative result was that $O\bar{O}$ is undecidable over discrete orders [4,5].

On the positive side, it was shown that some small fragments, like $B\bar{B}$ or $E\bar{E}$, are decidable and easy to translate into standard, point-based modal logic [9]. The fragment using only A and $\bar{A}$ is a bit harder and its decidability was only recently shown [7,8]. Obviously, this last result implies decidability of $L\bar{L}$ as L is expressible by A. The last remaining fragment with just one operator is D — in this case, it was only shown that satisfiability is decidable over dense structures ([2,6]). Another interesting decidable fragment is $AB\bar{B}$ [14].

In this paper we show that the BD fragment (and so DE) is undecidable. To make the presentation simpler, instead of D we consider the operator $D_{\subset}$ (see Section 2.1), which is more convenient for our purposes. As explained later, our technique can be easily modified to handle the case of D.

In Sections 2.2 – 2.4 we present the proof of the following result:

Theorem 1. *Satisfiability of the $BD_{\subset}$ fragment of the HS logic is undecidable over the class of all finite orders.*

In Section 2.5 we show how to modify the proof of Theorem 1 to get:

Theorem 2. *Satisfiability of the $BD_{\subset}$ fragment of the HS logic is undecidable over the class of all discrete orderings.*

Finally, in Section 2.6 we formulate, as exercises for the reader, more results that can be proved by slight modifications of our technique. They concern some logics similar to $BD_{\subset}$, most importantly BD, but also $\bar{B}D$, DE and others, and different classes of orderings. In Exercise 5 we show that Theorem 2 remains true even if the class of all discrete orderings is replaced by any nontrivial class of discrete orderings.

What remains open is the status of the D fragment over discrete orders — a slightly more expressible fragment BD is shown undecidable in this paper, but on the other hand the $D\bar{D}$ fragment over dense orderings is known to be decidable ([2,6]).

2 Technical Part

2.1 Preliminaries

Orderings. As in [11], we say that a total[1] order $\langle \mathbb{D}, \leq \rangle$ is *discrete* if each element is either minimal (maximal) or has a unique predecessor (successor); in other words for all $a, b \in \mathbb{D}$, if $a < b$, then there exist points a', b' such that $a < a'$, $b' < b$ and there exists no c with $a < c < a'$ or $b' < c < b$.

Semantics of the logic HS. Let $\langle \mathbb{D}, \leq \rangle$ be a discrete ordered set[2].

An *interval* over $\mathbb{D}$ is a pair $[a, b]$ with $a, b \in \mathbb{D}$ and $a \leq b$. A *labeling* is a function $\gamma : \mathrm{I}(\mathbb{D}) \to \mathcal{P}(\mathcal{V}ar)$, where $\mathrm{I}(\mathbb{D})$ is a set of all intervals over $\mathbb{D}$ and $\mathcal{V}ar$ is a finite set of variables. A structure of the form $\mathrm{M} = \langle \mathrm{I}(\mathbb{D}), \gamma \rangle$ is called a *model.*

The truth values of formulae are determined by the following (natural) semantic rules:

1. For all $v \in \mathcal{V}ar$ we have $\mathrm{M}, [a, b] \models v$ iff $v \in \gamma([a, b])$.
2. $\mathrm{M}, [a, b] \models \neg\varphi$ iff $\mathrm{M}, [a, b] \not\models \varphi$.
3. $\mathrm{M}, [a, b] \models \varphi_1 \wedge \varphi_2$ iff $\mathrm{M}, [a, b] \models \varphi_1$ and $\mathrm{M}, [a, b] \models \varphi_2$.
4. $\mathrm{M}, [a, b] \models \langle B \rangle \varphi$ iff there exists an interval $[a, b']$ such that $b' < b$ and $\mathrm{M}, [a, b'] \models \varphi$.
5. $\mathrm{M}, [a, b] \models \langle E \rangle \varphi$ iff there exists an interval $[a', b]$ such that $a < a'$ and $\mathrm{M}, [a', b] \models \varphi$.

Boolean connectives $\vee, \Rightarrow, \Leftrightarrow$ are introduced in the standard way. We also use the operators $\langle D \rangle \varphi \equiv \langle B \rangle \langle E \rangle \varphi$ and $\langle D_{\subset} \rangle \varphi \equiv \langle D \rangle \varphi \vee \langle E \rangle \varphi$. For $X \in \{B, E, D, D_{\subset}\}$ we abbreviate $\neg \langle X \rangle \neg \varphi$ by $[X]\varphi$. By $\bar{B}, \bar{D}, \bar{D}_{\subset}$, and $\bar{E}$ we denote inversed operators.

A formula φ is said to be *satisfiable* with respect to a class of orderings $\mathcal{D}$ if there exist a structure $\mathbb{D} \in \mathcal{D}$, a labeling γ, and an interval $[a, b]$ such that $\langle \mathrm{I}(\mathbb{D}), \gamma \rangle, [a, b] \models \varphi$. A formula is satisfiable in a given ordering $\mathbb{D}$ if it is satisfiable with respect to $\{\mathbb{D}\}$.

2.2 Convenient Automata

As for the tool in our undecidability proofs, we are going to use undecidability of the problem of establishing whether a given two-counter automaton with a finite set Q of states, starting from a given initial state q_0 and two empty counters, will ever halt. An instruction of such an automaton has the format:

if the current state is q, 1st counter is/isn't 0, 2nd counter is/isn't 0, then change state to q' and increase/decrease 1st/2nd counter

Notice that we assume, for simplicity, that exactly one counter is changed in a single step.

---

[1] Halpern and Shoham consider also partial orders. Our techniques can be easily modified to handle them. See Exercise 7 in Section 2.6.

[2] To keep the notation light, we will identify the order $\langle \mathbb{D}, \leq \rangle$ with the set $\mathbb{D}$

There is, however, from the point of view of our encoding, a slight inconvenience in this format: being in the configuration after step $k+1$ of the computation, we will not be able to easily check if the counters after step k were empty or not. For this reason we introduce the following notion of a *convenient two-counter finite automaton* (or just a *convenient automaton*):

A convenient automaton is given by four **disjoint** sets of states Q_{00}, Q_{01}, Q_{10}, and Q_{11}, and by a set of instructions of the form:

if the current state is q, then increase/decrease 1st/2nd counter and change the state to one of $\{q^{00}, q^{01}, q^{10}, q^{11}\}$, where $q^{ij} \in Q_{ij}$ for $i, j \in \{0, 1\}$

We assume here that there is exactly one instruction of this form for each non-final state q. For each *final state* there is exactly one instruction of the form "remain in the current state and do not change the counters".

Formally, the state-transition relation is given by a set $\mathcal{C} \subseteq Q^2$, where $Q = Q_{00} \cup Q_{01} \cup Q_{10} \cup Q_{11}$, and a function $\nu : Q \to \{d_f, d_s, i_f, i_s, \bot\}$, where $d/i_{f/s}$ means "decrease/increase first/second counter", respectively, and $\bot$ means "do nothing". We assume that there is no $q \in Q_{00} \cup Q_{01}$ with $\nu(q) = d_f$ and there is no $q \in Q_{00} \cup Q_{10}$ with $\nu(q) = d_s$.

Definition 1. *A configuration $\langle q, x, y \rangle$ of a convenient automaton is* admissible, *with $q \in Q_{ij}$ being a state and x, y being the numbers on the counters, if $i = 0 \Leftrightarrow x = 0$ and $j = 0 \Leftrightarrow y = 0$. We assume that $q_0 \in Q_{00}$, where q_0 is the initial state of the automaton.*

The halting problem is the problem of establishing whether, for a given convenient automaton with a single final state q_F, there exists a computation starting from $\langle q_0, 0, 0 \rangle$, consisting only of admissible configurations, and ending in a configuration with the final state. By an obvious simulation of a standard two-counter automaton we get:

Lemma 1. *The halting problem for convenient automata is undecidable.*

In Section 2.4 we are going to write, for a given convenient automaton with a single final state, a formula of logic $BD_{\subset}$ which will be satisfiable if and only if the automaton halts.

In Section 2.5 we will consider automata with two final states q_F and q_G. We say that q_F accepts and q_G rejects. The formula we are going to write for such an automaton will be satisfiable if and only if the automaton does not reject. Clearly, checking if an automaton does not reject is also an undecidable problem.

2.3 Finite Orders: Intervals, Slices, and Configurations

In this and the next section, we will prove Theorem 1. Suppose a convenient automaton $\mathcal{A}$, with the set of states $Q = Q_{00} \cup Q_{01} \cup Q_{10} \cup Q_{11}$, is given. We consider any finite total order consisting of $N+1$ elements $0, \ldots N$, in this order. Let $\mathrm{I}(\mathbb{D})$ be the set of all the intervals with endpoints in the set $\mathbb{D} = \{0, \ldots N\}$. The intervals will be labeled with a set $\mathcal{V}ar$ of propositional variables consisting of the following elements

- A variable q for every $q \in Q$. Variables of this kind will be called, not surprisingly, *states*.
- A variable $c_{q,q'}$ for each pair q, q' such that there is an instruction in $\mathcal{A}$, allowing changing a state from q to q'. Variables of this sort will be called *step controllers*. The set of all step controllers will be denoted as $\mathcal{C}$.
- Variables $f_0, f_1, f_0^l, f_1^l, f_0^u, f_1^u$, called *$f$-marks*. Variables f_1, f_1^l, f_1^u will be also called *f-ones* and f_0, f_0^l, f_0^u will be also called *f-nulls*. Variables f_1^u, f_0^u will be called *f-upper critical* and variables f_1^l, f_0^l will be called *f-lower critical.*
- Variables $s_0, s_1, s_0^l, s_1^l, s_0^u, s_1^u$ called *s-marks*. Variables s_1, s_1^l, s_1^u will be also called *s-ones* and s_0, s_0^l, s_0^u will be also called *s-nulls*.

The letter f above stands for "the first counter" and the letter s stands for "the second counter". From now on, we will usually only bother with first counter — the way one deals with second one is completely analogous.

For any i, with $0 \leq i \leq N$, the set of intervals $v_i = \{[i,i], [i,i+1], \dots [i,N]\}$ will be called a *slice*. Slices are going to serve us as devices to store the configurations of $\mathcal{A}$. Slices v_i and v_{i-1} will be called *consecutive*. We will force consecutive slices to store consecutive configurations of $\mathcal{A}$. Notice that if slices w and w' are consecutive, then w' is longer by one element than w — this is as it should be, since to store future configurations of $\mathcal{A}$ we may possibly need more and more room for counters (notice that the direction of time is slightly counterintuitive here).

Definition 2. *Let $\gamma : \mathrm{I}(\mathbb{D}) \to \mathcal{P}(\mathcal{V}ar)$ be a labeling of intervals with propositional variables. We will say that γ is slicewise correct if for each slice v_i there exist $q, q' \in Q$, with $c_{q',q} \in \mathcal{C}$, such that the following conditions hold:*

(i) *$q \in \gamma([i,i])$ and for all other pairs q'', j, where $q'' \in Q$ and $i \leq j \leq N$, we have $q'' \notin \gamma([i,j])$.*

(ii) *$c_{q',q} \in \gamma([i,i+1])$ and for all other tuples q_1, q_2, j, where $q_1, q_2 \in Q$ and $i \leq j \leq N$, we have $c_{q_1,q_2} \notin \gamma([i,j])$.*

(iii) *For each j, where $i \leq j \leq N$, there is exactly one f-mark y such that $y \in \gamma([i,j])$.*

(iv) *If $y \in \gamma([i,j])$ for some $j > i$ and $y \in \{f_1, f_0^l, f_1^l\}$, then $f_1 \in \gamma([i,k])$ for each $i \leq k < j$. If $y \in \gamma([i,j])$ for some $j > i$ and $y \in \{f_0^u, f_1^u\}$, then for all $i \leq k < j$ if $z \in \gamma([i,k])$ then $z \in \{f_1, f_0^l, f_1^l\}$.*

(v) *If $f_0 \in \gamma([i,j])$ for some $j > i$, then $y \in \gamma([i,k])$ for some $i \leq k < j$ and upper-critical y. If $y \in \gamma([i,j])$ for some $j > i$ and upper-critical y, then $z \in \gamma([i,k])$ for some $i \leq k < j$ and lower-critical z.*

(vi) *Let $y \in \gamma([i,i])$ be an f-mark. Then y is an f-null if and only if $q \in Q_{00} \cup Q_{01}$.*

(vii) *Let $y \in \gamma([i,j])$ for some f-upper critical y. Then $y = f_1^u$ if and only if the instruction of $\mathcal{A}$ concerning the action from the state q' tells that the first counter must be increased (i.e. $\nu(q') = i_f$).*

(viii) Let $y \in \gamma([i,j])$ *for some* f*-lower critical* y*. Then* $y = f_0^l$ *if and only if the instruction of* $\mathcal{A}$ *concerning the action from the state* q' *tells that the first counter must be decreased (i.e.* $\nu(q') = d_f$*).*

(ix) Conditions (iii)-(viii) hold analogously for s*-marks and the second counter.*

The way the conditions are written is not the simplest possible one. Actually, they are not meant to be simple. They are meant to be expressible in the logic $BD_{\subset}$ (we will make use of it in Section 2.4). So we feel we owe the reader some explanation.

A labeled slice which satisfies the conditions from the above definition can naturally be understood as an admissible configuration of the convenient automaton $\mathcal{A}$. We imagine v_i as a tape of $N - i + 1$ cells, where the interval $[i, i]$ represents the first cell, $[i, i+1]$ represents the second, and so on. If the labeling is slicewise correct, then in each of those cells we keep one f-mark (and one s-mark). The number of f-ones on the tape is understood to be the value of the first counter. Conditions (iii)-(v) imply that the marks occur in some fixed order: first there are f-ones in the cells $[i, i]$ to $[i, j]$, for some j, and then f-nulls in the cells $[i, j+1]$ to $[j+1, N]$. Most of those f-marks are either equal f_1 or f_0 — only near the border between ones and nulls typically there are two f-critical marks: one lower, and one upper (this follows from the conditions (iv) and (v)). Those critical marks can be both ones, both nulls or the lower can be a one and the upper a null — depending on the action of $\mathcal{A}$ in the state q' which is assumed to be the previous state of $\mathcal{A}$. This is a crucial part of a mechanism that will be used in Lemma 2. In fact, for technical reasons, in some borderline cases (namely, in slices representing initial configurations, and successor configurations of configurations with empty counter) one of critical marks will not appear.

Notice that the condition (vi) together with its counterpart concerning the second counter, imply that the configuration described by the labeling is admissible (in the sense of Definition 1).

In the figure below we present a slicewise correct labeling of $\mathrm{I}(\mathbb{D})$ for $\mathbb{D} = \{0, 1, \ldots, 8\}$. The intervals are arranged in the triangular table, such that interval $[i, j]$, is located in the i-th row and j-th column. Notice that each row corresponds to a slice. For transparency we do not present the values of s-marks.

0	1	2	3	4	5	6	7	8	
f_0^l, q_8	f_0^u, c_{q_7,q_8}	f_0	f_0	f_0	f_0	f_0	f_0	f_0	0
	f_1, q_7	f_0^l, c_{q_6,q_7}	f_0^u	f_0	f_0	f_0	f_0	f_0	1
		f_1, q_6	f_1, c_{q_5,q_6}	f_0^l	f_0^u	f_0	f_0	f_0	2
			f_1, q_5	f_1, c_{q_4,q_5}	f_1^l	f_0^u	f_0	f_0	3
				f_1, q_4	f_1^l, c_{q_3,q_4}	f_1^u	f_0	f_0	4
					f_1, q_3	f_1^l, c_{q_2,q_3}	f_0^u	f_0	5
						f_1^l, q_2	f_1^u, c_{q_1,q_2}	f_0	6
							f_1^u, q_1	f_0, c_{q_0,q_1}	7
								f_0^u, q_0	8

In fact, this model represents the following computation of an automaton (again, we consider only one counter): $q_0 \xrightarrow{+1} q_1 \xrightarrow{+1} q_2 \xrightarrow{=} q_3 \xrightarrow{+1} q_4 \xrightarrow{=} q_5 \xrightarrow{-1} q_6 \xrightarrow{-1} q_7 \xrightarrow{-1} q_8$. It appears that the labeling is also *stepwise correct* in the following sense.

Definition 3. *Let $\gamma : \mathrm{I}(\mathbb{D}) \to \mathcal{P}(\mathcal{V}ar)$ be a labeling of intervals with propositional variables. We will say that γ is stepwise correct if it is slicewise correct and for each two consecutive slices v_{i+1}, v_i the following conditions hold:*

(i) If q, q' are states, such that $q \in \gamma([i+1, i+1])$ and $q' \in \gamma([i,i])$, then $c_{q,q'} \in \gamma([i, i+1])$.
(ii) For each j, where $i < j \leq N$, the two conditions are equivalent:
  - *$y \in \gamma([i+1, j])$ for some y being an f-null;*
  - *$f_0 \in \gamma([i, j])$.*

(iii) Same as (ii) but for the second counter.

The following crucial lemma establishes the correspondence between stepwise correct labelings and computations of the automaton $\mathcal{A}$.

Lemma 2. *Let γ be a slicewise correct labeling. The following two conditions are equivalent:*

(1) γ is stepwise correct.
(2) Any pair of consecutive slices v_{i+1}, v_i represents two consecutive (in the sense of the transitions of the convenient automaton $\mathcal{A}$) admissible configurations of $\mathcal{A}$.

Due to the space limit we are not able to present all details of the formal proof. Instead, using our example, we only illustrate the mechanism required for the $\Rightarrow$ direction.

Consider for example the transition from slice v_5, which represents the automaton in the configuration in state q_3 and the counter equal to 2. At this point our automaton should increase the value of its counter. Let us see that v_4 needs to look exactly as in our figure. Conditions (i) and (ii) of Definition 2 and condition (i) of Definition 3 say that the state variable and the step controller of v_4 agree with the transition function, so in our case they have to be q_4 and c_{q_3,q_4}, respectively. By condition (ii) of Definition 3, the two rightmost positions in v_4 must be f_0-s. The same condition forbids f_0-s at earlier positions in v_4. By condition (v) of Definition 2, f_0-s have to be preceded by a lower-critical and by an upper-critical marks. Since we impose a specific order on marks, they have to be located exactly at intervals $[4, 5]$ and $[4, 6]$. By (vii) and (viii) those critical marks have to be f_1^l and f_1^u, respectively. Finally, by (iv) the critical positions may be proceeded by f_1-s only.

Once we know how to simulate the steps of the automaton, it is time for:

Definition 4. *Let $\gamma : \mathrm{I}(\mathbb{D}) \to \mathcal{P}(\mathcal{V}ar)$ be a labeling of intervals with propositional variables. We will say that γ is globally correct if it is stepwise correct and there exist $0 \leq i < j \leq N$ such that $q_0 \in \gamma([j, j])$ and $q_F \in \gamma([i, i])$.*

By Lemma 2, a globally correct labeling γ of $\mathbb{D}$ exists for some N if and only if the convenient automaton $\mathcal{A}$ halts after at most N computation steps.

What remains to be done, in order to end the proof of Theorem 1, is writing down a formula of logic $BD_{\subset}$ which is satisfiable if and only if a globally correct labeling γ exists for some N.

2.4 Finite Orders: The formula

The formula ϕ we are going to write will be of the form $\phi^1 \wedge \phi^2 \wedge \phi^3$, where ϕ^1 will be satisfied in models whose labeling is slicewise correct, ϕ^2 will be satisfied in models whose labeling is stepwise correct, provided it is slicewise correct, and ϕ^3 will be satisfied in models whose labeling is globally correct, provided it is stepwise correct. Formulae ϕ^1 and ϕ^3 are straightforward to write. To be able to write ϕ^2 we need one more easy lemma:

Lemma 3. *Let γ be a stepwise correct labeling, and let $0 \leq i < j \leq N$. Then the following two conditions are equivalent:*

(1) $y \in \gamma([i+1, j])$, for some f-null y.
(2) There exists $i < k \leq j$ and an f-null variable x such that $x \in \gamma([k, j])$

Proof. Obviously (1) implies (2). Implication in the opposite direction follows from condition (ii) of Definition 3. But one can also think, that it reflects the fact, that if the first counter (in v_k) stored a number smaller than $j - k + 1$ $k - i - 1$ moves ago, then now (in v_{i+1}) it stores a number smaller than $j - i$. □

First notice that we can define, as $\langle B_G \rangle \psi = \psi \vee \langle B \rangle \psi$, an operator saying that ψ holds true in some (interval which is) prefix of the current interval. Let also $atMostOne(X) = \bigwedge_{x \in X}(x \Rightarrow \bigwedge_{x' \in X \setminus \{x\}} \neg x')$ be an operator saying that at most one variable from the set X is true in the current interval. Another useful abbreviation is the operator "globally" $[G]\varphi = \varphi \wedge [D_{\subset}]\varphi \wedge [B]\varphi$ - it says that φ is satisfied in every (reachable) interval.

Now we are able to write ϕ. Define $\phi^1 = \phi^1_{(i)} \wedge \phi^1_{(ii)} \wedge \ldots \wedge \phi^1_{(viii)} \wedge \phi^1_{(ix)}$, where the subformulae mimic the conditions from Definition 2:

$$\phi^1_{\text{(i)}} = [G](([B]\bot \Leftrightarrow \bigvee_{q \in Q} q) \wedge atMostOne(Q))$$

$$\phi^1_{\text{(ii)}} = [G](\bigvee_{c \in \mathcal{C}} c \Leftrightarrow \langle B \rangle \top \wedge [B] \bigvee_{q \in Q} q) \wedge [G]atMostOne(\mathcal{C})$$

$$\phi^1_{\text{(iii)}} = [G](atMostOne(\{f_1, f_0, f^l_1, f^u_1, f^l_0, f^u_0\}) \wedge (f_1 \vee f_0 \vee f^l_1 \vee f^u_1 \vee f^l_0 \vee f^u_0))$$

$$\phi^1_{\text{(iv)}} = [G]((f_1 \vee f^l_1 \vee f^l_0) \Rightarrow [B]f_1) \wedge [G]((f^u_0 \vee f^u_1) \Rightarrow [B](f_1 \vee f^l_1 \vee f^l_0))$$

$$\phi^1_{\text{(v)}} = [G](\langle B \rangle \top \Rightarrow (f_0 \Rightarrow \langle B \rangle (f^u_1 \vee f^u_0)) \wedge ((f^u_0 \vee f^u_1) \Rightarrow \langle B \rangle (f^l_1 \vee f^l_0)))$$

$$\phi^1_{\text{(vi)}} = [G]([B]\bot \wedge (f_0 \vee f^l_0 \vee f^u_0) \Leftrightarrow \bigvee_{q \in Q_{00} \cup Q_{01}} q)$$

Let us split $\mathcal{C}$ into $\mathcal{C}_{if}, \mathcal{C}_{is}, \mathcal{C}_{df}, \mathcal{C}_{ds}, \mathcal{C}_{\perp}$ where $\mathcal{C}_{if}$ contains variables related to instructions that increase the first counter, $\mathcal{C}_{df}$ contains variables related to instructions that decrease the first counter, $\mathcal{C}_{is}$ and $\mathcal{C}_{ds}$ contain variables related to instructions increasing and decreasing second counter, respectively, and $\mathcal{C}_{\perp}$ contains variables related to the remaining instructions.

$$\phi^1_{(\mathrm{vii})} = [G]\left((\bigwedge_{c \in \mathcal{C}_{if}} \langle B_G \rangle c \Rightarrow \neg \langle B_G \rangle f^u_0) \wedge (\bigwedge_{c \in \mathcal{C} \setminus \mathcal{C}_{if}} \langle B_G \rangle c \Rightarrow \neg \langle B_G \rangle f^u_1) \right)$$

$$\phi^1_{(\mathrm{viii})} = [G]\left((\bigwedge_{c \in \mathcal{C}_{df}} \langle B_G \rangle c \Rightarrow \neg \langle B_G \rangle f^l_1) \wedge (\bigwedge_{c \in \mathcal{C} \setminus \mathcal{C}_{df}} \langle B_G \rangle c \Rightarrow \neg \langle B_G \rangle f^l_0) \right)$$

And $\phi^1_{(\mathrm{ix})}$ is analogous to the conjunction of $\phi^1_{(iii)}$ to $\phi^1_{(viii)}$, but concerns the second counter.

Define $\phi^2 = \phi^2_{(i)} \wedge \phi^2_{(ii)}$ where $\phi^2_{(i)}$ reflects condition (i) from Definition 3 and $\phi^2_{(ii)}$ reflects conditions (ii) and (iii):

$\phi^2_{(i)} = [G] \left(\bigwedge_{c_{q_1,q_2} \in \mathcal{C}} c_{q_1,q_2} \Rightarrow \langle B \rangle q_2 \wedge \langle D_{\subset} \rangle q_1 \right)$

$\phi^2_{(ii)} = [G] \left(f_0 \Leftrightarrow \langle D_{\subset} \rangle (f^l_0 \vee f^u_0 \vee f_0) \right) \wedge [G] \left(s_0 \Leftrightarrow \langle D_{\subset} \rangle (s^l_0 \vee s^u_0 \vee s_0) \right)$

Finally, let $\phi^3 = \langle B \rangle q_F \wedge \langle D_{\subset} \rangle q_0$.

Now, it follows from the construction, that the formula ϕ is satisfiable *over some finite ordering* if and only if the convenient automaton $\mathcal{A}$ halts. This ends the proof of Theorem 1.

2.5 Infinite Discrete Orders

The formula ϕ we wrote in Section 2.4 works fine for orders in which each interval (with endpoints among the elements of the ordered set) contains only finitely many points — for example for finite sets. But if arbitrary discrete orders are allowed, then it may very well happen that ϕ will be satisfiable even if $\mathcal{A}$ does not halt. Actually, as the following example shows, it will be satisfiable if there exists a configuration c of $\mathcal{A}$, which is final, in the sense that the state is q_F, and such that there exists an "infinite computation" which ends in c but never begins (we mean here an infinite sequence $c = c_0, c_1, c_2 \dots$ of configurations, such that for each i the configuration c_i is the result of one computation step performed in c_{i+1}).

Example. Fix an "infinite computation" as above and imagine the order $\langle V, \leq \rangle$ consisting of elements $a_0, a_1, a_2, \dots$ and $b_0, b_1, b_2, \dots$ with $a_i < a_j$ and $b_j < b_i$ for $i < j$ and with $a_i < b_j$ for any i, j. Let $d \in V$. Like in Section 2.3, we can view the set of sequences $\{[d, x] : x \leq b_0\}$ as a slice, and encode any configuration of A as a labeling of this slice. Let us label the slice $\{[a_i, x] : x \leq b_0\}$ as the configuration c_i of the above infinite sequence, and the slice $\{[b_i, x] : x \leq b_0\}$ as the configuration which is reached by $\mathcal{A}$ after i computation steps, if started in the beginning configuration. The described labeling turns out to satisfy ϕ.

Obviously, some details are left here for the reader to fill — for example how to label the intervals of the form $[a_j, b_j]$. □

Still, the proof of Theorem 1 from Sections 2.2 - 2.4 can be easily modified so that it proves Theorem 2.

It is enough to consider convenient automaton with two final states: q_F (the accepting state) and q_G (the rejecting state). Let us remind that we assume that there is one instruction of automaton for each state — also for the two final states — but in the final states the instruction tells the automaton to freeze, that is to leave the counters unchanged and remain in the same state.

The undecidable problem we will use now, is the problem if this new convenient automaton $\mathcal{A}$ ever rejects. More precisely, we write a formula ϕ' such that ϕ' is satisfiable in some discrete order if and only if $\mathcal{A}$ (started from the beginning configuration and visiting only admissible configurations) does not reject (i.e. it accepts or runs forever). As it turns out, the only change we need to make in ϕ concerns the subformula ϕ^3: let $\phi' = \phi^1 \wedge \phi^2 \wedge \psi^3$, where $\psi^3 = \langle B \rangle q_F \wedge \langle D_{\subset} \rangle q_0 \wedge \neg \langle D_{\subset} \rangle q_G$.

Now, suppose $\mathcal{A}$ does not reject. There are two possible cases: either it accepts (after some finite number of steps reaches a configuration with q_F) or it does not halt. In the former case we can build a finite model, like in Section 2.3. In the latter, we proceed like in the example above — notice that, since the automaton can freeze in the state q_F, we can be sure that an "infinite computation" $\mathbf{c}$ exists.

What remains to be proved is that if $\mathcal{A}$ rejects then ϕ' does not have a model. Suppose it rejects after N steps, and that there is a model $\langle \mathrm{I}(\mathbb{D}), \gamma \rangle$ of ϕ' where $a < b$ are such elements of $\mathbb{D}$ that $q_F \in \gamma([a,a])$ and $q_0 \in \gamma([b,b])$. Let q^i be the state of $\mathcal{A}$ after i steps of the rejecting computation (so that $q^0 = q_0$ and $q^N = q_G$.)

Let $b_0 = b$ and let b_{i+1}, for $0 \leq i < N$, be the predecessor of b_i in the order, if such a predecessor exists. Actually, this is exactly what we need q_F for — to make sure that there are many enough elements of $\mathbb{D}$ (smaller than b), to accommodate the rejecting computation:

Lemma 4. *Let* $0 \leq i \leq N$

(1) If b_i *exists then* $q^i \in \gamma([b_i, b_i])$.
(2) If b_i *exists and* $0 \leq j \leq i$ *then* $q_F \notin \gamma([b_j, b_j])$.
(3) If b_i *exists then* $a < b_i$.
(4) If b_i *exists then* b_{i+1} *exists.*
(5) b_N *exists, and* $q_G \in \gamma([b_N, b_N])$.

The proof of the lemma is by easy induction. Claim (1) of the induction step follows from the construction of ϕ' — remember that the interval $[b_i, b]$ is finite and all the arguments from Section 2 apply. Claim (2) follows from (1), and from the fact that a rejecting computation of $\mathcal{A}$ never enters the state q_F. Claim (3) follows from (2) and from the inequality $a < b$. Claim (4) follows from (3) and from the assumption that each element of $\mathbb{D}$ is either the smallest or has a predecessor. Finally, since $q^N = q_G$ claim (5) follows from (4).

But it follows from the lemma, that there exists $d \in \mathbb{D}$ such that $q_G \in \gamma([d,d])$, which is not allowed by ϕ'. This contradiction ends the proof of Theorem 2.

2.6 More Results (in Exercises)

Exercise 1. Show that the satisfiability problem for the logic $BD_{\subseteq}$ over discrete orderings is undecidable, where $D_{\subseteq}$ is the *reflexive* variant of D, i.e., $\mathrm{M}, [a,b] \models \langle D_{\subseteq}\rangle\varphi$ iff there exist a', b' such that $a \leq a' \leq b' \leq b''$, and $\mathrm{M}, [a',b'] \models \varphi$. Similarly for the logic $BD_{\sqsubset}$, where $D_{\sqsubset}$ is the *proper* variant of D, i.e., $\mathrm{M}, [a,b] \models \langle D_{\subseteq}\rangle\varphi$ iff there exist a', b' such that $a \leq a' \leq b' \leq b''$, $[a,b] \neq [a',b']$ and $\mathrm{M}, [a',b'] \models \varphi$. *Hint*: In our proof we use the convenient property that intervals visible by B are not visible by $D_{\subset}$. The analogous fact does not hold for $BD_{\subseteq}$ and $BD_{\sqsubset}$. Use an additional variable p and formulae $[G]((\langle B\rangle p \to p) \wedge [G]((\langle B\rangle\neg p \to \neg p)$ and $[G]((\bigvee_{c\in C} C) \Rightarrow \langle D\rangle p \wedge \langle D\rangle\neg p)$. This will allow to distinguish between the current slice and the previous one.

Exercise 2. Show that the satisfiability problem for the logic BD over discrete orderings is undecidable. Recall that $\langle D\rangle\varphi \equiv \langle B\rangle\langle E\rangle\varphi$. Such variant of D is called *strict*. *Hint*: The idea is to use three "critical levels" instead of two.

Exercise 3. Show that the satisfiability problem for the logic $\bar{B}D$ over discrete orderings is undecidable. *Hint*: Modify the formula for BD. The formula ϕ^1, can be easily expressed — use $\bar{B}$ to define the order on the marks and D to label intervals with the states and the step controllers (note that the property $\phi^1_{(\mathrm{V})}$ needs to be slightly modified). Finally, formula ϕ^3 can be replaced by $\langle D\rangle(q_F \wedge \langle \bar{B}\rangle\langle D\rangle q_0)$, and $\phi^2_{(i)}$ can be adjusted in the same way.

Exercise 4. Show that the satisfiability problem for logic DE and $D\bar{E}$ over discrete orderings is undecidable. *Hint*: Actually, no hint is needed here. Just replace every occurrence of B by E in the formula.

Exercise 5. Show that for any class of discrete orderings $\mathcal{D}$, BD is undecidable over $\mathcal{D}$ iff $\mathcal{D}$ contains orderings with arbitrarily large chains. *Hint*: For undecidability result, consider two cases: if there exist $\mathbb{D} \in \mathcal{D}$ and $a, b \in \mathbb{D}$ such that $\{c | a \leq c \leq b\}$ if infinite, then you can use the proof of Theorem 2, otherwise you can use the proof of Theorem 1. For decidability result observe that the number of non-isomorphic chains with bounded size is bounded.

Exercise 6. Show that $BD\bar{D}$ logic is undecidable over the class of all orderings. *Hint*: Consider the formula $[G](length_0 \Rightarrow \langle\bar{D}\rangle(p \wedge length_1) \wedge \langle\bar{D}\rangle(\neg p \wedge length_1))$, where $length_i$ is true in intervals with the length i.

Exercise 7. In this paper we focused on total orderings. Originally, HS logic was defined for any order that satisfy the following condition. For each a_1, a_2, a_3, a_4 if $a_1 \leq a_2$, $a_1 \leq a_3$, $a_2 \leq a_4$, and $a_3 \leq a_4$, then $a_2 \leq a_3$ or $a_3 \leq a_2$. Show that our theorems still hold in this case. *Hint*: Again, no hint is needed here — just read carefully the definition above.

References

1. Allen, J.F.: Maintaining knowledge about temporal intervals. Communications of the ACM 26(11), 832–843 (1983)
2. Montanari, A., Puppis, G., Sala, P.: A decidable spatial logic with cone-shaped cardinal directions. In: Grädel, E., Kahle, R. (eds.) CSL 2009. LNCS, vol. 5771, pp. 394–408. Springer, Heidelberg (2009)
3. Bresolin, D., Della Monica, D., Goranko, V., Montanari, A., Sciavicco, G.: Decidable and Undecidable Fragments of Halpern and Shoham's Interval Temporal Logic: Towards a Complete Classification. In: Cervesato, I., Veith, H., Voronkov, A. (eds.) LPAR 2008. LNCS (LNAI), vol. 5330, pp. 590–604. Springer, Heidelberg (2008)
4. Bresolin, D., DellaMonica, D., Goranko, V., Montanari, A., Sciavicco, G.: Undecidability of Interval Temporal Logics with the Overlap Modality. In: Proc. of 16th International Symposium on Temporal Representation and Reasoning - TIME 2009, pp. 88–95. IEEE Computer Society Press, Los Alamitos (2009)
5. Bresolin, D., DellaMonica, D., Goranko, V., Montanari, A., Sciavicco, G.: Undecidability of the Logic of Overlap Relation over Discrete Linear Orderings. In: Proceedings of M4M 6: 6th Workshop on Methods for Modalities (November 2009)
6. Bresolin, D., Goranko, V., Montanari, A., Sala, P.: Tableau-based decision procedures for the logics of subinterval structures over dense orderings. Journal of Logic and Computation 20(1), 133–166 (2010)
7. Bresolin, D., Goranko, V., Montanari, A., Sciavicco, G.: Propositional Interval Neighborhood Logics: Expressiveness, Decidability, and Undecidable Extensions. Annals of Pure and Applied Logic 161(3), 289–304 (2009)
8. Bresolin, D., Montanari, A., Sala, P., Sciavicco, G.: Optimal Tableaux for Right Propositional Neighborhood Logic over Linear Orders. In: Hölldobler, S., Lutz, C., Wansing, H. (eds.) JELIA 2008. LNCS (LNAI), vol. 5293, pp. 62–75. Springer, Heidelberg (2008)
9. Goranko, V., Montanari, A., Sciavicco, G.: A road map of interval temporal logics and duration calculi. Journal of Applied Non-Classical Logics 14(1-2), 9–54 (2004)
10. Hamblin, C.L.: Instants and intervals. Studium Generale 27, 127–134 (1971)
11. Halpern, J., Shoham, Y.: A propositional modal logic of time intervals. Journal of the ACM 38(4), 935–962 (1991)
12. Lodaya, K.: Sharpening the undecidability of interval temporal logic. In: He, J., Sato, M. (eds.) ASIAN 2000. LNCS, vol. 1961, pp. 290–298. Springer, Heidelberg (2000)
13. Moszkowski, B.C.: Reasoning about Digital Circuits. PhD thesis, Stanford University, Computer Science Department (July 1983)
14. Montanari, A., Puppis, G., Sala, P., Sciavicco, G.: Decidability of the Interval Temporal Logic $AB\bar{B}$ on Natural Numbers. In: Proc. of the 27th Symposium on Theoretical Aspects of Computer Science (STACS 2010), pp. 597–608 (2010)
15. Parikh, R.: A decidability result for second order process logic. In: Proc. 19th FOCS, pp. 177–183. IEEE, Los Alamitos (October 1978)
16. Pnueli, A.: A temporal logic of programs. In: Proc. 18th FOCS, pp. 46–57. IEEE, Los Alamitos (1977)
17. Pratt, V.R.: Process logic. In: Proc. 6th POPL, pp. 93–100. ACM, New York (1979)
18. Prior, A.N.: Past, Present and Future. Clarendon Press, Oxford (1967)

Parameterized Modal Satisfiability

Antonis Achilleos, Michael Lampis, and Valia Mitsou

Computer Science Department,
Graduate Center, City University of New York,
365 5th Ave New York, NY 10016 USA
antach@corelab.ntua.gr, mlampis@gc.cuny.edu, vmitsou@cs.gc.cuny.edu

Abstract. We investigate the parameterized computational complexity of the satisfiability problem for modal logic and attempt to pinpoint relevant structural parameters which cause the problem's combinatorial explosion, beyond the number of propositional variables v. To this end we study the modality depth, a natural measure which has appeared in the literature, and show that, even though modal satisfiability parameterized by v and the modality depth is FPT, the running time's dependence on the parameters is a tower of exponentials (unless P=NP). To overcome this limitation we propose possible alternative parameters, namely diamond dimension and modal width. We show fixed-parameter tractability results using these measures where the exponential dependence on the parameters is much milder (doubly and singly exponential respectively) than in the case of modality depth thus leading to FPT algorithms for modal satisfiability with much more reasonable running times. We also give lower bound arguments which prove that our algorithms cannot be improved significantly unless the Exponential Time Hypothesis fails.

1 Introduction

In this paper we consider the computational complexity of deciding formula satisfiability, for modal logics, focusing on the standard modal logic K. We attempt to present a new point of view on this important topic by making use of the parameterized complexity framework, which was pioneered by Downey and Fellows. Although the complexity of satisfiability for modal logic has been studied extensively in the past, to the best of our knowledge this is the first time this has been done from an explicitly parameterized perspective. Moreover, the parameterized complexity of logic problems has been a fruitful field of research and we hope to extend this success to modal logic (some examples are the celebrated theorem of Courcelle [3] or the results of [7]; for an excellent survey on the interplay between logic, graph problems and parameterized complexity see [8]).

Modal logic is a family of systems of formal logic where the truth value of a sentence ϕ can be qualified by modality operators, usually denoted by $\Box$ and $\Diamond$. Depending on the specific modal logic and the application one considers, $\Box\phi$ and $\Diamond\phi$ can be informally read to mean, for example, "it is necessary that ϕ", or "it is known that ϕ" for $\Box$ and "it is possible that ϕ" for $\Diamond$. The fundamental

S. Abramsky et al. (Eds.): ICALP 2010, Part II, LNCS 6199, pp. 369–380, 2010.

normal modal logic system is known as K, while other common variations of this logic system include T, D, S4, S5. Modal logic systems provide a diverse universe of logics able to fit many modern applications in computer science (for example in AI or in game theory), making modal logic a widespread topic of research. The interested reader in the recent state of modal logic and its applications is directed to [1].

As in propositional logic, the satisfiability problem for modal logic is one of the most important and fundamental problems considered and many results are known about its (traditional) computational complexity. Ladner in [11] showed that satisfiability for K, T and S4 is PSPACE-complete, while for S5 the problem is NP-complete. Furthermore, in [2] it is shown that satisfiability for K and K4 is PSPACE-complete even for formulae without any variables. It should be noted that the satisfiability of propositional logic is a subcase of satisfiability for any normal modal logic, thus for any normal modal logic the problem is NP-hard. In this paper we will focus on the standard modal logic K. For an introduction to modal logic and its complexity see [10,5].

Traditional computational complexity theory attempts to characterize the complexity of a problem as a function of the input size n. The notion of parameterized complexity introduces to every hard problem a structural parameter k, which attempts to capture the aspect of the problem which causes its intractability. The central notion of tractability in this theory is called fixed-parameter tractability (FPT): an algorithm is called FPT if it runs in time $O(f(k) \cdot n^c)$, where f is any recursive function and c a constant. For an introduction to the vast area of parameterized complexity see [4,6].

Because the definition of FPT allows for any recursive function $f(k)$, fixed-parameter tractable problems can have complexities which depend on k in very different ways, ranging from sub-exponential to non-elementary. Thus, it is one of the main goals of parameterized complexity research to find the best possible $f(k)$ for every problem and this will be one of the main concerns of our work.

Our Contribution. In this paper we study the complexity of modal satisfiability from a parameterized, or multi-variate, point of view. Just as parameterized complexity attempts to refine traditional complexity theory by more specifically identifying the aspects of an intractable problem which cause the problem's unavoidable combinatorial explosion, we attempt to identify some structural aspects of modal formulae which can have an impact on the solvability of satisfiability.

One natural parameter for the satisfiability problem (in any logic) is the number of propositional letters in the formula, which we denote by v. In propositional logic, when v is taken as a parameter, the propositional satisfiability problem trivially becomes fixed-parameter tractable. As was already mentioned, this does not generally hold in the case of satisfiability for modal logics where the problem is hard even for constant number of variables.

On the other hand since the satisfiability problem for modal logics is a generalization of the same problem for propositional logics, considering the modal satisfiability problem without bounding the number of variables or imposing some other propositional restriction on the formulae will result in an intractable problem. Although it would be interesting to investigate modal satisfiability when certain structural propositional restrictions are placed (for example, we could say we are interested in formulae such that removing all modality symbols leaves a 2-CNF or a Horn formula, which are tractable cases of propositional satisfiability) this goes beyond the scope of this work[1]. In this paper we will focus on strictly modal structural formula restrictions and therefore we will assume that the best way to make propositional satisfiability tractable is to restrict the number of variables. For our purposes the conclusion is that for modal satisfiability to become tractable, bounding v is necessary but not sufficient.

Motivated by the above we take the approach of a double parameterization: we investigate the complexity of satisfiability when v is considered a parameter and at the same time some other aspect contributing to the problem's complexity is identified and bounded.

We first study a natural notion of formula complexity called modality depth or modal depth. This complexity measure was already known in [9] where in fact a fixed-parameter tractability result was shown when the problem is parameterized by the sum of v and the modality depth of the formula. However, since parameterized complexity was not well-known at the time, in [9] it is only pointed out that the problem is solvable in linear time for fixed values of the parameters, without mentioning how different values of v and the depth affect the running time. We address this by upper bounding the running time by an exponential tower of height equal to the modality depth of the formula. More importantly, we show a lower bound argument which proves that even though the problem is FPT, this exponential tower in the running time cannot be avoided unless P=NP (Theorem 2). Our hardness proof follows an approach of encoding a propositional formula into a modal formula with very small modality depth. This draws a nice connection with previously known lower bound results of this form which also use a similar idea to prove the hardness of some (non-modal) model checking problems for first and second-order logic ([7] and the relevant chapter in [6]).

This result indicates that modal depth is unlikely to be a very useful parameter because even for formulae where the depth is very moderate the satisfiability problem is still very hard. This begs the natural question of whether there is a way to work around the lower bound of Theorem 2 by using another formula complexity measure in the place of modal depth. We show that this is indeed possible by introducing two alternative formula complexity notions.

Specifically, we define the notion of diamond dimension and show that satisfiability is FPT when parameterized by v and the diamond dimension and the dependence on the parameters is (only) doubly exponential. We then demonstrate a lower bound argument which proves that this dependence cannot be significantly improved unless the Exponential Time Hypothesis fails, that is, unless there exists an algorithm for n-variable 3-CNF-SAT running in time $2^{o(n)}$.

---

[1] However, see [12] for related (non-parameterized) complexity results.

Then we define a measure called modal width and show that satisfiability is FPT when parameterized by v and the modal width and the dependence on the parameters is now just singly exponential.

Thus, our work shows that there exist many natural formula complexity parameters worth examining in the context of modal satisfiability and what's more that their complexity behavior can be vastly different and this could be an interesting field of study. Let us also note in passing that our results for modal width and depth directly apply also to satisfiability's dual problem, formula validity, since the validity of a formula can be solved by checking the satisfiability of its negation and every formula has the same width and depth as its negation. Our results for diamond dimension can also be extended for this problem by defining a dual "box dimension" measure, suitable for the validity problem.

Due to space constraints, several proofs have been omitted. Results with omitted proofs are denoted with a *.

Notation. The modal language of logic K contains exactly the formulae that can be constructed using propositional variables, the standard propositional operators $\wedge, \vee, \neg$ (and the operators which can be defined using these, such as $\rightarrow, \leftrightarrow$) and the unary modality operators ($\Box, \Diamond$). Standard Kripke semantics are considered here: a Kripke frame is a set of states W and an accessibility relation R between states. A Kripke frame together with a valuation of propositional letters in each state is called a Kripke model or a Kripke structure. A modal formula's truth value in a state is defined in the usual way, as in propositional logic, with the addition of $\Box\phi$ being true in s iff ϕ is true in every accessible state. $\Diamond\phi$ is true in s iff ϕ is true in some accessible state. We implicitly assume that our language includes the constants $\bot$ and $\top$, for false and true, but these too can also be considered shorthand for $x \wedge \neg x$ and $x \vee \neg x$ respectively. When a formula ϕ is true (satisfied) in a state s of a Kripke structure $\mathcal{M}$ we write $(\mathcal{M}, s) \models \phi$. A formula ϕ is said to be satisfiable if there exists a Kripke structure $\mathcal{M}$ and a state s of that structure that satisfy the formula. A formula ϕ is said to be valid if any Kripke structure $\mathcal{M}$ and state s of that structure satisfy the formula.

2 Modal Depth

In this section we give the definition of modality depth. As we will see, a fixed-parameter tractability result can be obtained when satisfiability is parameterized by v and the modality depth of the input formula. This was first observed in [9], but in this section we more precisely bound the running time (in [9] it was simply noted that the running time is linear for constant depth and constant v with a hidden constant which "may be huge"). More importantly we show that the "huge constant" cannot be significantly improved by giving a hardness proof which shows that, if the running time of an algorithm for modal satisfiability is significantly less than an exponential tower of height equal to the modality depth, then P=NP.

Definition 1. *The modality depth of a modal formula ϕ is defined inductively as follows:*

- $md(p) = 0$, *if p is a propositional letter,*
- $md(\Diamond\phi) = md(\Box\phi) = 1 + md(\phi)$,
- $md(\phi_1 \vee \phi_2) = md(\phi_1 \wedge \phi_2) = \max\{md(\phi_1), md(\phi_2)\}$,
- $md(\neg\phi) = md(\phi)$

Theorem 1. *[*]([9]) Modal satisfiability for the logic K is FPT when parameterized by v and $md(\phi)$.*

The running time of the algorithm of [9] is $O(f_v(\text{md}(\phi))|\phi|)$ where $f_v(d)$ is the function recursively defined as $f_v(0) = 2^v$ and $f_v(d+1) = 2^{f_v(d)+v}$.

Lower Bound. Let us now proceed to the main result of this section, which is that even though modal satisfiability is fixed-parameter tractable, the exponential tower in the running time cannot be avoided. Specifically, we will show that solving modal satisfiability parameterized by modality depth, even for constant v, requires a running time which is a tower of exponentials with height linear in the modality depth. We will prove this under the assumption that P≠NP, by reducing the problem of propositional satisfiability to our problem. Our proof follows ideas similar to those found in [7].

Suppose that we are given a propositional CNF formula ϕ_p with variables $x_1, \ldots, x_n$ and we need to check whether there exists a satisfying assignment for it. We will encode ϕ_p into a modal formula with small depth and a constant number of variables. In order to do so we inductively define a sequence of modal formulae.

- In order to encode the variables of ϕ_p we need some formulae to encode numbers (the indices of the variables). The modal formula v_i is defined inductively as follows: $v_0 \equiv \Box\bot$ and $v_n \equiv \bigwedge_{i:n_i=1} \Diamond v_i$ where by n_i we denote the i-th bit of n when n is written in binary and the least significant bit is numbered 0. So, for example $v_1 = \Diamond v_0$, $v_2 = \Diamond v_1$, $v_5 = \Diamond v_2 \wedge \Diamond v_0 = (\Diamond\Diamond v_1) \wedge \Diamond v_0$ and so on. Observe that v_0 can only be true in a state with no successor states. Also, what is important is that these formulae allow us to encode very large numbers using only a very small modality depth and no variables (or just one variable if $\bot$ is considered short for $x \wedge \neg x$).
- Next, we need to encode the literals of ϕ_p. The modal formula $\mathcal{L}(x_i)$ is defined as $\mathcal{L}(x_i) \equiv \Diamond v_i \wedge \Box v_i$. The formula $\mathcal{L}(\neg x_i)$ is defined as $\mathcal{L}(\neg x_i) \equiv \Diamond v_i \wedge \Diamond v_0 \wedge \Box (v_i \vee v_0)$.
- Now, to encode clauses we set $\mathcal{C}(l_1 \vee l_2 \vee \ldots \vee l_k) \equiv \left(\bigwedge_{i=1}^{k} \Diamond\mathcal{L}(l_i)\right) \wedge \Box\left(\bigvee_{i=1}^{k} \mathcal{L}(l_i)\right)$.
- Finally, to encode the whole formula we use $\mathcal{F}(c_1 \wedge c_2 \wedge \ldots \wedge c_m) \equiv \bigwedge_{i=1}^{m} \Diamond\mathcal{C}(c_i)$

So far we have described how to construct a modal formula $\mathcal{F}(\phi_p)$ from ϕ_p. $\mathcal{F}(\phi_p)$ encodes the structure of ϕ_p. Now we need to add two more ingredients: we must describe with a modal formula that ϕ_p is satisfied by an assignment and that the assignment is consistent among clauses. We give two more formulae, $\mathcal{S}$ and $\mathcal{CA}(n)$, which play the previously described roles respectively:

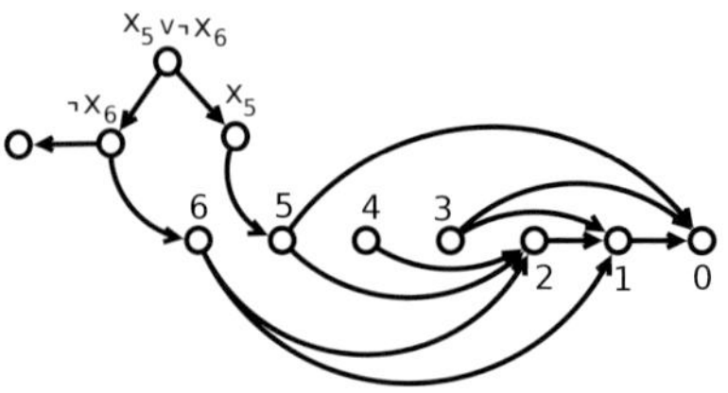

Fig. 1. A partial example, illustrating our construction for a specific clause. For the encoding of the clause $(x_5 \vee \neg x_6)$ we build the formula $\mathcal{C}(x_5 \vee \neg x_6)$ which holds in the state at the top of the depicted model.

- $\mathcal{S} \equiv \Box\Diamond\left[((\Diamond v_0) \rightarrow (\Box\neg y)) \wedge ((\neg\Diamond v_0) \rightarrow (\Box y))\right]$, where we have introduced a single variable y.
- $\mathcal{CA}(n) \equiv \bigwedge_{i=1}^{n} (\Diamond\Diamond\Diamond(y \wedge v_i) \leftrightarrow \neg\Diamond\Diamond\Diamond(\neg y \wedge v_i))$

Our full construction is, given a propositional CNF formula ϕ_p with n variables named $x_1, \dots, x_n$, we create the modal formula $\phi_m \equiv \mathcal{F}(\phi_p) \wedge \mathcal{S} \wedge \mathcal{CA}(n)$.

Lemma 1. *ϕ_p is satisfiable if and only if ϕ_m is satisfiable in K.*

Proof. Suppose that ϕ_m is true in a state s of some Kripke structure. Then $\mathcal{CA}(n)$ is true in s therefore for each i we have either $\Diamond\Diamond\Diamond(y \wedge v_i)$ is true in s or $\Diamond\Diamond\Diamond(\neg y \wedge v_i)$ is true in s. From this we create a satisfying assignment: for those i for which the first holds we set $x_i = \top$ and for the rest $x_i = \bot$. We will show that this assignment satisfies ϕ_p.

Suppose that it does not, therefore there is some clause c_i which is not satisfied. However, since $\mathcal{F}(\phi_p)$ is true in s there exists a state p with sRp such that $\mathcal{C}(c_i)$ is true in p. In every successor state of p we have that $\mathcal{L}(l_j)$ is true for some literal l_j of c_i and there exists such a state for every literal of c_i. Also, in s we have that $\mathcal{S}$ is true, therefore in p we have $\Diamond\left[((\Diamond v_0) \rightarrow (\Box\neg y)) \wedge ((\neg\Diamond v_0) \rightarrow (\Box y))\right]$. Therefore, in some q such that pRq we have $((\Diamond v_0) \rightarrow (\Box\neg y)) \wedge ((\neg\Diamond v_0) \rightarrow (\Box y))$ and we also have that $\mathcal{L}(l_j)$ is true for some literal l_j of c_i. Suppose that l_j is a negated literal, that is $l_j \equiv \neg x_k$. Then $\mathcal{L}(l_j) \equiv \Diamond v_k \wedge \Diamond v_0 \wedge \Box(v_k \vee v_0)$. Therefore, since $\Diamond v_0$ is true in q this means that $\Box\neg y$ is true. Because $\Diamond v_k$ and $\Box\neg y$ are both true in q there exists an r such that qRr and $v_k \wedge \neg y$ is true in r. But then $\Diamond\Diamond\Diamond(v_k \wedge \neg y)$ is true in s which implies that our assignment gives the value false to x_k. Since c_i contains $\neg x_k$ it must be satisfied by our assignment, a contradiction. Similarly, if $l_j \equiv x_k$ then $\mathcal{L}(l_j) \equiv \Diamond v_k \wedge \Box v_k$. Clearly, v_0 and v_k cannot be true in the same state for $k > 0$ therefore in q we have $\neg\Diamond v_0$ which implies $\Box y$. Therefore in some r with qRr we have $y \wedge v_k$ which implies that our assignment sets x_k to true and since c_i has the literal x_k it must be satisfied.

The other direction is easier. We build a Kripke structure where for each v_i there exists a state such that v_i holds in that state. We start by introducing a state without successors, in which v_0 holds. Then, for each $i \in \{1, \dots, n\}$ we add a state with appropriate transitions to states previously introduced so that v_i holds in that state (see Figure 1 for an example).

Now the completion of the Kripke structure so that ϕ_m is satisfied is straightforward. For every i with $1 \leq i \leq n$ we create two more states: the first has as its only successor the state where v_i is true. The other has two successors: the state where v_i is true and a state without successors (where v_0 holds). Thus, for each i we have a state where $\mathcal{L}(x_i)$ is true and a state where $\mathcal{L}(\neg x_i)$ is true. For every clause we create a state and for each literal l_j in the clause we add a transition to the state where $\mathcal{L}(l_j)$ is true. Therefore, for each clause c_i we have a state where $\mathcal{C}(c_i)$ is true. Finally, we add a state and transitions to all the states where some $\mathcal{C}(c_i)$ is true. Clearly, $\mathcal{F}(\phi_p)$ is true in that state, which we call the root state. It is not hard to see that $\mathcal{CA}(n)$ will also be satisfied independent of where y is true, because for every $i \in \{1, \ldots, n\}$ we have made a unique state p_i where v_i is true and p_i is at distance exactly 3 from the root.

Take a satisfying assignment; for every x_i which is true set the variable y to true in the states of the Kripke structure where v_i is true. Set y to false in every other state. Now, we must show that $\mathcal{S}$ is true in the root state. This is not hard to verify because for every clause in the original formula there is a true literal, call it l. If that literal is not negated then in the state where $\mathcal{L}(l)$ is true we have $\neg\Diamond v_0$ (because the literal is not negated) and $\Box y$ (because the literal is true, so its variable is true thus we must have set y to true in the variable's corresponding state). Therefore $(\neg\Diamond v_0 \rightarrow \Box y) \wedge (\Diamond v_0 \rightarrow \Box\neg y)$ is true in the literal's corresponding state and $\Diamond\,[(\neg\Diamond v_0 \rightarrow \Box y) \wedge (\Diamond v_0 \rightarrow \Box\neg y)]$ is true in the clause's corresponding state. Similar arguments can be made for a negated literal. Since we start with a satisfying assignment the same can be said for every clause, thus $\mathcal{S}$ is also true in the root state. $\Box$

Now, we need to show that the produced modal formula has very small depth and the hardness result will follow in a way very similar to the results of [7].

Lemma 2. *[*] Suppose that ϕ_p is a propositional CNF formula with n variables. Then, if $tow(h) \geq n$ the formula $\phi_m \equiv \mathcal{F}(\phi_p) \wedge \mathcal{S} \wedge \mathcal{CA}(n)$ has modality depth at most $4 + h$, where $tow(h)$ is the inductively defined function $tow(0) = 0$ and $tow(h+1) = 2^{tow(h)}$.*

Theorem 2. *[*] There is no algorithm which can solve modal satisfiability in K for formulae with a single variable and modality depth d in time $f(d) \cdot poly(|\phi|)$ with $f(d) = O(tow(d-5))$, unless P=NP.*

3 Diamond Dimension

In this Section we propose a structural characteristic of modal formulae called diamond dimension. This is an alternative natural formula complexity measure which intuitively bounds the size of a model required to satisfy a formula. As we will see the parameter dependence of a satisfiability algorithm for formulae of small diamond dimension is doubly exponential, immensely lower than the dependence for modal depth. However, we will also show a lower bound indicating that it is unlikely that an algorithm with singly exponential parameter dependence could exist for this measure.

Definition 2. *Let ϕ be a modal formula in negation normal form, that is, with the $\neg$ symbol appearing only directly before propositional variables. Then its diamond dimension, denoted by $\mathrm{d}_\Diamond(\phi)$ is defined inductively as follows:*

- $\mathrm{d}_\Diamond(p) = \mathrm{d}_\Diamond(\neg p) = 0$, *if p is a propositional letter*
- $\mathrm{d}_\Diamond(\phi_1 \wedge \phi_2) = \mathrm{d}_\Diamond(\phi_1) + \mathrm{d}_\Diamond(\phi_2)$
- $\mathrm{d}_\Diamond(\phi_1 \vee \phi_2) = \max\{\mathrm{d}_\Diamond(\phi_1), \mathrm{d}_\Diamond(\phi_2)\}$
- $\mathrm{d}_\Diamond(\Box\phi) = \mathrm{d}_\Diamond(\phi)$
- $\mathrm{d}_\Diamond(\Diamond\phi) = 1 + \mathrm{d}_\Diamond(\phi)$

Our goal with this measure is to prove that if $\mathrm{d}_\Diamond(\phi)$ is small then ϕ's satisfiability can be checked in models with few states. This is why the two properties of ϕ which can increase $\mathrm{d}_\Diamond(\phi)$ are $\Diamond$ (which requires the creation of a new state) and $\wedge$ (which requires the creation of states for both parts of the conjunction).

Lemma 3. *[*] If a modal formula ϕ is satisfiable and $\mathrm{d}_\Diamond(\phi) \leq k$ then there exists a Kripke structure with $O(2^{k/2})$ states which satisfies ϕ.*

Theorem 3. *Given a modal formula ϕ with v variables and diamond dimension $\mathrm{d}_\Diamond(\phi) = k$ we can solve the satisfiability problem for ϕ in time $2^{O(2^k \cdot v)} \cdot |\phi|$.*

Proof. From Lemma 3 it follows that if ϕ is satisfiable, this can be verified in a model of $O(2^{k/2})$ states. There are at most $2^{O(2^k)}$ Kripke frames from which we can get such models. For each we just enumerate through all possible assignments to the v variables in the $O(2^{k/2})$ states, a total of $2^{O(2^{k/2} \cdot v)}$ different assignments. Once we have fixed a model deciding if ϕ holds can be done in bilinear time. $\Box$

Lower Bound. We will now present a lower bound argument showing that, under reasonable complexity assumptions, the results we have shown for diamond dimension cannot be improved significantly. We will once again encode a propositional 3-CNF formula into a modal formula, this time with a goal of achieving small diamond dimension. We will also use a small number of propositional variables. We assume without loss of generality that we are given a 3-CNF formula ϕ_p with n variables, where n is a power of 2.

Let $\Box^j$ be short-hand for j consecutive repetitions of $\Box$, with $\Box^0\phi$ being equivalent to ϕ. We recursively define the formulae $F(i)$ as $F(0) = \Box\bot$ and $F(i) = \left(\Diamond(\bigwedge_{j=0}^{i-1} \Box^j b_i)\right) \wedge \left(\Diamond(\bigwedge_{j=0}^{i-1} \Box^j \neg b_i)\right) \wedge \Box F(i-1)$, where b_i are propositional variables. It is not hard to see that $\mathrm{d}_\Diamond(F(i)) = 2i$ and also that $F(i)$ can only be satisfied in a model with at least 2^i states. The model to keep in mind here is a complete binary tree of height i.

We will use the formula $F(\log n)$ to encode a 3-CNF formula with n variables and each leaf of the tree that must be constructed to satisfy it will correspond to a variable. It is now natural to encode the variables of the original formula using their binary representation. We define $B(x_m) = \bigwedge_{m_i=1} b_i \wedge \bigwedge_{m_i=0} \neg b_i$, where once again m_i denotes the i-th bit in the binary representation of m, now with the least significant bit numbered 1.

Our modal formula will also have a propositional variable y which will be true in leaves that correspond to variables of the 3-CNF formula that must be set to true. We encode a literal consisting of the variable x_m as $L_1(x_m) \equiv \Box^{\log n}(B(m) \rightarrow y)$. The corresponding negated literal is $L_2(\neg x_m) \equiv \Box^{\log n}(B(m) \rightarrow \neg y)$. A clause is encoded as the disjunction of the encodings of its three literals. Our final modal formula ϕ_m is a conjunction of $F(\log n)$ with the encodings of all the clauses of the propositional formula ϕ_p.

Lemma 4. *Given a propositional 3-CNF formula ϕ_p the modal formula ϕ_m is satisfiable in K iff ϕ_p is satisfiable.*

Proof. Suppose that ϕ_p is satisfiable. We construct a binary tree of height $\log n$ as our model and ϕ_m will be made true at the root. It is not hard to satisfy $F(\log n)$ at the root: simply set $b_{\log n}$ to be true on all states on one of the subtrees of height $\log n - 1$ and false in all states of the other, then proceed to satisfy $F(\log n - 1)$ at the subtrees recursively in the same manner. Every leaf of the model corresponds to a variable of ϕ if we read the variables b_i as encoding the binary representation of the index of the variable. We set y to be true in the leaves that correspond to variables which are true in a satisfying assignment. It is not hard to see that this satisfies the encoding of all the clauses on the assumption that we started with an assignment satisfying ϕ_p.

Now for the other direction, suppose that ϕ_m is satisfied in a state of some model. A first observation is that for all $i \in \{1, \ldots, n\}$ there must exist a state in which $B(i)$ holds and is at distance $\log n$ from the state where ϕ_m holds, as this is required for $F(\log n)$ to hold. From this we can infer that $\Box^{\log n}(B(i) \rightarrow y)$ and $\Box^{\log n}(B(i) \rightarrow \neg y)$ cannot both hold in the state where ϕ_m holds. Therefore, we can extract a consistent assignment for the variables of ϕ from the model, by setting to true the x_i for which $\Box^{\log n}(B(i) \rightarrow y)$ holds. It is not hard to see that this assignment must satisfy ϕ_p because its clauses are encoded in ϕ_m. □

Now that we have described how to embed a 3-CNF formula into a modal formula with only logarithmically many variables and logarithmic diamond dimension we can use this fact to prove a lower bound. This time we rely on the stronger, but widely believed, assumption that 3-CNF SAT with n variables cannot be solved in time $2^{o(n)}$, also known as the Exponential Time Hypothesis. This allows us to obtain a much sharper bound than simply assuming that P≠NP.

Theorem 4. *There is no algorithm which can decide the satisfiability in K of a modal formula ϕ with v variables and $\mathrm{d}_{\Diamond}(\phi) = k$ in time $2^{2^{o(v+k)}}$ poly($|\phi|$) unless the Exponential Time Hypothesis (ETH) fails (this is a standard assumption, see for example [13]).*

Proof. Suppose that an algorithm running in time $2^{2^{o(v+k)}}$*poly*($|\phi|$) did exist. Then we could use the described construction to decide 3-CNF satisfiability for any formula with n variables. It is not hard to see that $v + k = O(\log n)$ and that the size of the produced modal formula is polynomial in the size of the 3-CNF formula, thus this would give an algorithm running in time $2^{o(n)}$, contradicting the ETH. □

4 Modal Width

In this section we give another structural parameter for modal formulae called modal width in an attempt to solve modal satisfiability more efficiently. We will show that satisfiability can be solved in time only singly exponential in the modal width and v.

First we define inductively the function $s(\phi)$ which given a modal formula returns a set of modal formulae. Intuitively, whether ϕ holds in a given state s of a Kripke structure depends on two things: the values of the propositional variables in s and the truth values of some formulae ψ_i in the successor states of s. These formulae are informally the subformulae of ϕ which appear at modal depth 1. $s(\phi)$ gives us exactly this set of formulae.

- $s(p) = \emptyset$ if p is a propositional letter
- $s(\neg\phi) = s(\phi)$, $s(\phi_1 \vee \phi_2) = s(\phi_1 \wedge \phi_2) = s(\phi_1) \cup s(\phi_2)$
- $s(\Box\psi) = s(\Diamond\psi) = \{\psi\}$

Now we inductively define the set $S_i(\phi)$, which intuitively corresponds to the set of subformulae of ϕ at depth i.

- $S_1(\phi) = s(\phi)$
- $S_{i+1}(\phi) = \bigcup_{\psi\in S_i(\phi)} s(\psi)$

Finally, we can now define the modal width of a formula ϕ at depth i as $\mathrm{mw}_i(\phi) = |S_i(\phi)|$ and the modal width of a formula as $\mathrm{mw}(\phi) = \max_i \mathrm{mw}_i(\phi)$.

Theorem 5. *[*] There exists an algorithm which decides the satisfiability of a modal formula ϕ with v variables, $md(\phi) = d$ and $mw(\phi) = w$ in time $O(2^{2^{v+3w}} \cdot d \cdot w \cdot |\phi|)$.*

To give some intuition, the modal width measures how many different modal subformulae our formula contains at depth i. The idea is that the truth value of the subformulae of depth i at some state s depends only on the truth value of the subformulae of depth $i+1$ at the successors of s. If the maximum width of the formula is bounded we can exhaustively check all possible truth values for subformulae at the next level of depth and decide if some particular truth assignment to the subformulae of depth i is possible. Using this idea it is possible to obtain an algorithm with the promised running time if we use a dynamic programming technique.

Lower Bound. Intuitively, one would probably not expect that a significantly better algorithm is possible in this case, since the algorithm we have described is singly exponential in the parameter $v + w$. Indeed, it follows if one accepts the ETH that for formulae of width 0 (that is, propositional formulae) it is not possible to achieve time $2^{o(v+w)}$. Nevertheless, this kind of lower bound argument is not entirely satisfactory for our purposes, since it completely neglects the contribution of the modal width to the problem's hardness. For all we know, the best algorithm's dependence on w alone may be sub-exponential, though this would be surprising.

However, a more careful examination of the lower bound arguments we have presented for diamond dimension is useful here. The formulae constructed there have a logarithmic number of variables and linear modal width. Therefore, an algorithm which in general runs in $2^{O(v)+o(w)}$ would in this case give an algorithm running in time $2^{o(n)}$ for propositional SAT, contradicting the ETH. In addition, even if one assumes a constant v, things cannot improve much. A second reading of the lower bound argument for modal depth shows that our construction has modal width $O(n \cdot polylog(n))$. This implies that any algorithm which runs in $2^{O(w^c)}$ for any $c < 1$ in the case of constant v would imply a $2^{o(n)}$ algorithm for SAT, again contradicting the ETH. Thus, the existence of an algorithm with significantly better dependence on w than the one presented here is unlikely.

5 Conclusions and Open Problems

In this paper we defined and studied several modal formula complexity measures and investigated how each can be used to attack cases of modal satisfiability. Our results show that proving fixed-parameter tractability is only a first step in such problems, because the dependence on the parameters can vary significantly and some parameters offer much better algorithmic footholds than others.

It is worthy of remark that the measures of formula complexity we have discussed are not directly comparable; for example it is possible to construct a formula with small modality depth and very high modal width, or vice-versa. In this sense it is not possible to infer solely from our results which formula complexity measure is the "best", since each corresponds to a different family of modal formulae. However, our results can be seen as a first attempt at drawing a complexity "map" for different modal formula parameters, looking for areas where satisfiability becomes more or less tractable. This perspective creates a nice connection between this work and for example the research area of graph widths, where the complexity of model checking problems on graphs is explored in different graph families depending on a graph complexity measure. This is a well-developed area whose insights may be applicable and helpful in the study of the problems of this paper. (For a summary of the current complexity "map" for graph width parameters see Figure 8.1 in [8])

A possible future direction is the investigation of yet more natural formula complexity measures. Additionally, extending our results to other modal logics, such as modal logics where Kripke structures are required to be reflexive or transitive (e.g. S4) would also be an interesting next step.

References

1. Blackburn, P., van Benthem, J.F.A.K., Wolter, F.: Handbook of Modal Logic. Studies in Logic and Practical Reasoning, vol. 3. Elsevier Science Inc., New York (2006)
2. Chagrov, A.V., Rybakov, M.N.: How Many Variables Does One Need to Prove PSPACE-hardness of Modal Logics. In: Balbiani, P., Suzuki, N.-Y., Wolter, F., Zakharyaschev, M. (eds.) Advances in Modal Logic, pp. 71–82. King's College Publications (2002)

3. Courcelle, B.: The Monadic Second-Order Logic of Graphs. I. Recognizable Sets of Finite Graphs. Inf. Comput. 85(1), 12–75 (1990)
4. Downey, R.G., Fellows, M.R.: Parameterized complexity. Springer, Heidelberg (1999)
5. Fagin, R., Halpern, J.Y., Moses, Y., Vardi, M.Y.: Reasoning About Knowledge. The MIT Press, Cambridge (1995)
6. Flum, J., Grohe, M.: Parameterized complexity theory. Springer, New York (2006)
7. Frick, M., Grohe, M.: The complexity of first-order and monadic second-order logic revisited. Ann. Pure Appl. Logic 130(1-3), 3–31 (2004)
8. Grohe, M.: Logic, graphs, and algorithms. In: Electronic Colloquium on Computational Complexity (ECCC), vol. 14(091) (2007)
9. Halpern, J.Y.: The effect of bounding the number of primitive propositions and the depth of nesting on the complexity of modal logic. Artif. Intell. 75(2), 361–372 (1995)
10. Halpern, J.Y., Moses, Y.: A guide to completeness and complexity for modal logics of knowledge and belief. Artif. Intell. 54(3), 319–379 (1992)
11. Ladner, R.E.: The computational complexity of provability in systems of modal propositional logic. SIAM J. Comput. 6(3), 467–480 (1977)
12. Nguyen, L.A.: On the complexity of fragments of modal logics. Advances in Modal Logic 5, 249–268 (2005)
13. Woeginger, G.: Exact algorithms for NP-hard problems: A survey. Combinatorial OptimizationEureka, You Shrink!, 185–207

Automata for Coalgebras: An Approach Using Predicate Liftings*

Gaëlle Fontaine, Raul Leal, and Yde Venema

Institute for Logic, Language and Computation, Universiteit van Amsterdam, Science Park 904, 1098XH Amsterdam, The Netherlands

Abstract. Universal Coalgebra provides the notion of a *coalgebra* as the natural mathematical generalization of state-based evolving systems such as (infinite) words, trees, and transition systems. We lift the theory of parity automata to this level of abstraction by introducing, for a set Λ of predicate liftings associated with a set functor $\mathcal{T}$, the notion of a Λ-automata operating on coalgebras of type $\mathcal{T}$. In a familiar way these automata correspond to extensions of coalgebraic modal logics with least and greatest fixpoint operators.

Our main technical contribution is a general bounded model property result: We provide a construction that transforms an arbitrary Λ-automaton $\mathbb{A}$ with nonempty language into a small pointed coalgebra $(\mathbb{S}, s)$ of type $\mathcal{T}$ that is recognized by $\mathbb{A}$, and of size exponential in that of $\mathbb{A}$. $\mathbb{S}$ is obtained in a uniform manner, on the basis of the winning strategy in our satisfiability game associated with $\mathbb{A}$. On the basis of our proof we obtain a general upper bound for the complexity of the non-emptiness problem, under some mild conditions on Λ and $\mathcal{T}$. Finally, relating our automata-theoretic approach to the tableaux-based one of Cîrstea et alii, we indicate how to obtain their results, based on the existence of a complete tableau calculus, in our framework.

Keywords: coalgebra, modal logic, parity automata, predicate lifitings, fixpoint logic.

1 Introduction

The theory of finite automata, seen as devices for classifying (possibly) infinite structures [6], combines a rich mathematical theory, dating back to the seminal work of Büchi and Rabin, with an wide range of applications, particularly in areas related to program verification and synthesis. The main purpose of our paper is to contribute to this theory by showing that some of its fundamental ideas can be lifted to a coalgebraic level of generality.

Universal Coalgebra [14] provides the notion of a *coalgebra* as the natural mathematical generalization of state-based evolving systems such as streams,

* The research of the authors has been made possible by VICI grant 639.073.501 of the Netherlands Organization for Scientific Research (NWO).

S. Abramsky et al. (Eds.): ICALP 2010, Part II, LNCS 6199, pp. 381–392, 2010.

(infinite) trees, Kripke models, (probabilistic) transition systems, and many others. Formally, a coalgebra is a pair $\mathbb{S} = (S, \sigma)$, where S is the carrier or state space of the coalgebra, and $\sigma : S \longrightarrow \mathcal{T}S$ is its unfolding or transition map. This approach combines simplicity with generality and wide applicability: many features, including input, output, nondeterminism, probability, and interaction, can easily be encoded in the coalgebra type $\mathcal{T}$ (formally an endofunctor on the category Set of sets as objects with functions as arrows).

Logic enters the picture if one wants to specify and reason about *behavior*, one of the most fundamental notions admitting a coalgebraic formalization. With Kripke structures constituting key examples of coalgebras, it should come as no surprise that most coalgebraic logics are some kind of modification or generalization of *modal logic*.

Moss [11] introduced a modality $\nabla_{\mathcal{T}}$ generalizing the so-called 'cover modality' from Kripke structures to coalgebras of arbitrary type. This approach is uniform in the functor $\mathcal{T}$, but as a drawback only works properly if $\mathcal{T}$ satisfies a certain category-theoretic property (viz., it should preserve weak pullbacks); also the nabla modality is syntactically rather nonstandard. As an alternative, Pattinson [12] and others developed coalgebraic modal formalisms, based on a completely standard syntax, that work for coalgebras of arbitrary type. In this approach, the semantics of each modality is determined by a so-called *predicate lifting* (see Definition 3 below). Many well-known variations of modal logic in fact arise as the coalgebraic logic ML_Λ associated with a set Λ of such predicate liftings; examples include both standard and (monotone) neighborhood modal logic, graded and probabilistic modal logic, coalition logic, and conditional logic. The theory of coalgebraic modal logic has developed rather rapidly; to mention just one example, it presently includes generic PSPACE upper bounds for the satisfiability problem [15].

The fact that ordinary modal formulas have a finite *depth* severely restricts the expressive power of plain coalgebraic modal logic, and thus limits its usefulness as a language for specifying *ongoing* behavior. For the latter purpose one needs to extend the language with *fixpoint operators*, generalizing the modal μ-calculus [9]. A coalgebraic fixpoint language on the basis of Moss' modality was introduced by Venema [16]. Recently, Cîrstea, Kupke and Pattinson [5] introduced the *coalgebraic μ-calculus* $\mu\mathrm{ML}_\Lambda$ parametrized by a set Λ of predicate liftings for a functor $\mathcal{T}$.

Given the success of automata-theoretic approaches towards fixpoint logics, one may expect a rich and elegant *universal automata theory* that generalizes the theory of specific devices for streams, trees or graphs, by dealing with automata that operate on coalgebras. A first step in this direction was the introduction of so-called *coalgebra automata* by Venema [16]. Kupke & Venema [10] generalized many results in automata theory, such as closure properties of recognizable languages, to this class of automata. However, coalgebra automata are related to fixpoint languages based on Moss' modality ∇, and do not correspond directly to coalgebraic modal languages associated with predicate liftings (such as the graded modal μ-calculus). In addition, the theory of coalgebra automata needs the *type* of the coalgebras to be a functor that preserves weak pullbacks, and hence cannot be applied as generally as possible.

This paper introduces automata for coalgebras of *arbitrary* type (Definition 4). More precisely, given a set Λ of monotone predicate liftings, we introduce Λ-automata as devices that accept or reject pointed $\mathcal{T}$-coalgebras (that is, coalgebras with an explicitly specified starting point) on the basis of so-called *acceptance games*. Λ-automata provide the counterpart to the coalgebraic μ-calculus for Λ. In particular, there is a construction transforming a μML_Λ-formula into an equivalent Λ-automaton (of size quadratic in the length of the formula). Hence we may use the theory of Λ-automata in order to obtain results about coalgebraic modal fixpoint logic.

The main technical contribution of this paper concerns a *small model property* for Λ-automata (Theorem 3). We show that any Λ-automaton $\mathbb{A}$ with a non-empty language recognizes a pointed coalgebra $(\mathbb{S}, s)$ that can be obtained from $\mathbb{A}$ via some uniform construction involving a satisfiability game (Definition 7) that we associate with $\mathbb{A}$. The size of $\mathbb{S}$ is exponential in the size of $\mathbb{A}$. On the basis of our proof, in Theorem 4 we give a doubly exponential bound on the complexity of the satisfiability problem of μML_Λ-formulas in $\mathcal{T}$-coalgebras (provided that the one-step satisfiability problem of Λ over $\mathcal{T}$ has a reasonable complexity).

Compared to the work of Cîrstea, Kupke and Pattinson [5], our results are more general in the sense that they do not depend on the existence of a complete tableau calculus. On the other hand, the cited authors obtain a much better complexity result: Under some mild conditions on the efficiency of their complete tableau calculus (conditions that are met by e.g. the modal μ-calculus and the graded μ-calculus), they establish an EXPTIME upper bound for the satisfiability problem of the μ-calculus for Λ. However, in Section 5 below we shall make a connection between our satisfiability game and their tableau game, and on the basis of this connection one may obtain the same complexity bound as in [5] (if one assumes the same conditions on the existence and nature of the tableau system).

2 Preliminaries

We assume familiarity with basic notions from category theory such as categories, functors, natural transformations. We let Set denote the category with sets as objects and functions as arrows. For convenience, and without loss of generality [2], we assume our functors to be standard i.e to preserve set inclusions.

Definition 1. *Let* $\mathcal{T} : \mathsf{Set} \longrightarrow \mathsf{Set}$ *be a functor. A* $\mathcal{T}$-coalgebra *is a pair* (S, σ) *where* S *is a set and* σ *is a function* $\sigma : S \longrightarrow \mathcal{T}S$*. A* morphism of $\mathcal{T}$-coalgebras *from* $\mathbb{S}$ *to* $\mathbb{S}'$*, written* $f : \mathbb{S} \longrightarrow \mathbb{S}'$*, is a function* $f : S \longrightarrow S'$ *such that* $T(f)\sigma = \sigma' f$*. The* size of a coalgebra $\mathbb{S}$ *is the cardinality of the set* S*.*

1. We write $\mathcal{Q} : \mathsf{Set}^{op} \longrightarrow \mathsf{Set}$ for the contravariant power set functor, and $\mathcal{P}$ for the covariant power set functor. Coalgebras for $\mathcal{P}$ are Kripke frames [1].

2. The monotone neighborhood functor $\mathcal{M}$ maps a set X to $\mathcal{M}(X) = \{U \in \mathcal{QQ}(X) \mid U \text{ is upwards closed}\}$, and a function f to $\mathcal{M}(f) = \mathcal{QQ}(f) = (f^{-1})^{-1}$. Coalgebras for this functor are monotone neighborhood frames [7].
3. We write $\mathcal{D}$ for the distribution functor which maps a set X to $\mathcal{D}(X) = \{\mu : X \longrightarrow [0,1] \mid \sum_{x \in X} \mu(x) = 1\}$ and a function f to the function $\mathcal{D}(f) : \mathcal{D}(X) \longrightarrow \mathcal{D}(Y)$ which maps a probability distribution μ to $\mathcal{D}(f)(\mu)(y) = \sum_{f(x)=y} \mu(x)$. In this case coalgebras correspond to Markov chains [3].
4. We write $\mathcal{B}$ for the bags, or multiset, functor which maps a set X to $\overline{\mathbb{N}}^X$, where $\overline{\mathbb{N}} = \mathbb{N} + \{\infty\}$, the action on arrows is similar to that of $\mathcal{D}$. Coalgebras for $\mathcal{B}$ are often referred to as multigraphs [17].

We assume familiarity with the basic notions of the theory of automata and infinite games [6]. Here we fix some notation and terminology.

Definition 2. *(1) Given a set A, we let A^* and A^ω denote, respectively, the set of* words *(finite sequences) and* streams *(infinite sequences) over A. Automata operating on streams will be called* stream automata *(rather than ω-automata). Given $\pi \in A^* + A^\omega$ we write $Inf(\pi)$ for the set of elements in A that appear infinitely often in π.*

(2) A graph game *is a tuple $\mathbb{G} = (G_\exists, G_\forall, E, Win)$ where $G_\exists$ and $G_\forall$ are disjoint sets, and (with $G := G_\exists + G_\forall$) we have $E \subseteq G^2$, and $Win \subseteq G^\omega$. In case $\mathbb{G}$ is a parity game, that is, Win is given by a parity function $\Omega : G \longrightarrow \mathbb{N}$, we write $\mathbb{G} = (G_\exists, G_\forall, E, \Omega)$.*

(3) A strategy *for a player P in a game $\mathbb{G} = (G_\exists, G_\forall, E, Win)$ is a map $\alpha : G^* \longrightarrow G$. A $\mathbb{G}$-match $\pi = v_0 v_1 \dots$ is α-*conform *if $v_{i+1} = \alpha(v_0 \dots v_i)$ for all $i \geq 0$ such that $v_i \in G_\exists$. A strategy α is* winning *for a player P if all α-conform matches are winning for P.*

(4) A strategy α is a finite memory strategy *if there is a finite* memory set *M, an element $m_I \in M$ and a map $(\alpha_1, \alpha_2) : G \times M \longrightarrow G \times M$ such that for all pairs of sequences $v_0 \dots v_k \in V^*$ and $m_0 \dots m_k \in M^*$ if $m_0 = m_I$, $v_k \in G_\exists$ and $m_{i+1} = \alpha_2(v_i, m_i)$ (for all $i < k$), then $\alpha(v_0 \dots v_k) = \alpha_1(v_k, m_k)$.*

(5) A game $\mathbb{G} = (G_\exists, G_\forall, E, Win)$ is called regular *if there exists an ω-regular language L over a finite alphabet C, and a map $col : G \longrightarrow C$, such that $Win = \{v_0 v_1 \dots \in G^\omega : col(v_0) col(v_1) \dots \in L\}$.*

The following fact on regular games can be proved by putting together various known results from [4] and [8].

Fact 1. *Let $\mathbb{G} = (G_\exists, G_\forall, E, Win)$ be a regular game, let $col : G \longrightarrow C$ be a coloring of G, and let $\mathbb{B}$ be a deterministic parity stream automaton such that $Win = \{v_0 v_1 \dots \in G^\omega \mid col(v_0) col(v_1) \dots \in L(\mathbb{B})\}$. Let n, m, and b be the size of G, E, and $\mathbb{B}$, respectively, and let d be the index of $\mathbb{B}$. Then for each player P we may assume winning strategies for P to be finite memory ones, with memory of size b. In addition, the problem, whether a given position $v \in G$ is winning for P, is decidable in time $\mathcal{O}\left(d \cdot m \cdot b \cdot \left(\frac{n \cdot b}{\lfloor d/2 \rfloor}\right)^{\lfloor d/2 \rfloor}\right)$.*

3 Automata for the Coalgebraic μ-Calculus

As mentioned in the introduction, the following notion is fundamental in the development of coalgebraic modal logic.

Definition 3. *An n-ary* predicate lifting *for $\mathcal{T}$ is a natural transformation*

$$\lambda : \mathcal{Q}^n \longrightarrow \mathcal{Q}\mathcal{T}.$$

Such a predicate lifting is monotone *if for each set S, the operation $\lambda_S : (\mathcal{Q}(S))^n \longrightarrow \mathcal{Q}(S)$ preserves the (subset) order in each coordinate. The (Boolean)* dual *of a predicate lifting $\lambda : \mathcal{Q}^n \longrightarrow \mathcal{Q}\mathcal{T}$ is the lifting $\overline{\lambda} : \mathcal{Q}^n \longrightarrow \mathcal{Q}\mathcal{T}$ given by $\overline{\lambda}_S(A_1, \ldots, A_n) = S \setminus \lambda_S(S \setminus A_1, \ldots, S \setminus A_n)$.*

Predicate liftings allow one to see coalgebras as (polyadic) neighborhood frames. Accordingly, with each n-ary predicate lifting we will associate an n-ary *modality* $\heartsuit_\lambda$. Its semantics in a coalgebra $\mathbb{S}$ is given by the following:

$$[\![\heartsuit_\lambda(\phi_1, \ldots, \phi_n)]\!]_{\mathbb{S}} = \sigma^{-1}\lambda_S([\![\phi_1]\!]_{\mathbb{S}}, \ldots, [\![\phi_n]\!]_{\mathbb{S}}) \tag{1}$$

where we inductively assume that $[\![\phi_i]\!]_{\mathbb{S}} \subseteq S$ is the meaning of the formula ϕ_i in $\mathbb{S}$. In words, $\heartsuit_\lambda(\phi_1, \ldots, \phi_n)$ is true at a state s iff the unfolding $\sigma(s)$ belongs to the set $\lambda_S([\![\phi_1]\!]_{\mathbb{S}}, \ldots, [\![\phi_n]\!]_{\mathbb{S}})$.

Example 1. (1) In case of the covariant power set functor the predicate lifting given by $\lambda_S(U) = \{V \in \mathcal{P}S \mid V \subseteq U\}$ induces the usual universal modality $\Box$, i.e. $[\![\heartsuit_\lambda \phi]\!]^\sigma_V = [\![\Box\phi]\!]^\sigma_V$, on Kripke Frames.

(2) Consider the monotone neighborhood functor. We can obtain the standard modalities as predicate liftings. The universal modality is given by $\lambda_S(U) = \{N \in \mathcal{M}(S) \mid U \in N\}$.

(3) Let k be a natural number. A graded modality can be seen as a predicate lifting for the multiset functor; $\lambda^k_S(U) = \{B : S \longrightarrow \mathbb{N} \mid \sum_{x \in U} B(x) \geq k\}$. In this case $\mathbb{S}, V, s \Vdash \heartsuit^k_\lambda \phi$ holds iff s has at least k many successors satisfying ϕ.

(4) Let p be an element in the closed interval $[0,1]$. The following defines a predicate lifting for the distribution functor $\lambda^p_S(U) = \{\mu : S \longrightarrow [0,1] \mid \sum_{x \in U} \mu(x) \geq p\}$. In this case $\mathbb{S}, V, s \Vdash \heartsuit^p_\lambda \phi$ holds if the probability that s has a successor satisfying ϕ is at least p.

(5) Propositional information can be provided by predicate liftings for the functor $\mathcal{P}(\mathsf{P}) \times \mathcal{T}$, where P is a fixed set of proposition letters. The semantics of the proposition letter $p \in \mathsf{P}$ is given by the predicate liftings $\lambda^p_S(U) = \{(X,t) \in \mathcal{P}(\mathsf{P}) \times \mathcal{T}(S) \mid p \in X\}$, and $\lambda^{\neg p}_S(U) = \{(X,t) \in \mathcal{P}(\mathsf{P}) \times \mathcal{T}(S) \mid p \notin X\}$.

Convention 2 *In the remainder of this paper we fix a functor $\mathcal{T}$ on* Set, *and a set Λ of monotone predicate liftings that we assume to be closed under taking Boolean duals. In case we are dealing with a language containing proposition letters, these are supposed to be encoded in appropriate liftings, as in Example 1(5).*

We can now introduce coalgebraic modal fixpoint logic, or the coalgebraic μ-calculus. We fix a set X of variables, and define the set $\mu\mathrm{ML}_\Lambda$ of fixpoint formulas ϕ, ϕ_i as follows:

$$\phi ::= x \in X \mid \bot \mid \top \mid \phi_0 \wedge \phi_1 \mid \phi_0 \vee \phi_1 \mid \heartsuit_\lambda(\phi_0, \ldots, \phi_n) \mid \mu x.\phi \mid \nu x.\phi$$

where $\lambda \in \Lambda$. Syntactic notions pertaining to formulas, such as alternation depth, are defined as usual. The size of a formula is defined as its length (with the proviso that if Λ is infinite, to each occurrence of a modality we add a weight associated with its index, as in [15]).

The semantics of this language is completely standard. Let $\mathbb{S} = (S, \sigma)$ be a $\mathcal{T}$-coalgebra. Given a valuation $V : X \longrightarrow \mathcal{P}(S)$, we define the *meaning* $[\![\phi]\!]_{\mathbb{S},V}$ of a formula ϕ by a standard induction which includes the following clauses:

$$[\![x]\!]_{\mathbb{S},V} := V(x), \qquad [\![\mu x.\phi]\!]_{\mathbb{S},V} := \mathsf{LFP}.\phi_x^{\mathbb{S},V}, \qquad [\![\nu x.\phi]\!]_{\mathbb{S},V} := \mathsf{GFP}.\phi_x^{\mathbb{S},V}.$$

Here $\mathsf{LFP}.\phi_x^{\mathbb{S},V}$ and $\mathsf{GFP}.\phi_x^{\mathbb{S},V}$ are the least and greatest fixpoint, respectively, of the monotone map $\phi_x^{\mathbb{S},V} : \mathcal{P}(S) \longrightarrow \mathcal{P}(S)$ given by $\phi_x^{\mathbb{S},V}(A) := [\![\phi]\!]_{\mathbb{S},V[x\mapsto A]}$ (with $V[x \mapsto A](x) = A$ and $V[x \mapsto A](y) = V(y)$ for $y \neq x$). For *sentences*, that is, formulas without free variables, the valuation does not matter; we write $\mathbb{S}, s \Vdash \phi$ iff $s \in [\![\phi]\!]_{\mathbb{S},V}$ for some/any valuation V.

By Convention 2, we may assume that the language $\mu\mathrm{ML}_\Lambda$ contains proposition letters and their negations, and we may see negation itself as a definable connective.

Before we can turn to the definition of our automata we need some preliminary notions. Given a set X, we denote the set of positive propositional formulas, or lattice terms, over X, by $\mathcal{L}_0(X)$:

$$\phi ::= x \in X \mid \bot \mid \top \mid \phi_0 \wedge \phi_1 \mid \phi_0 \vee \phi_1,$$

and we let $\Lambda(X)$ denote the set $\{\heartsuit_\lambda(x_1, \cdots, x_n) \mid \lambda \in \Lambda, x_i \in X\}$. Elements of the set $\mathcal{L}_0\Lambda\mathcal{L}_0(X)$ will be called *depth-one* formulas over X.

Any valuation $V : X \longrightarrow \mathcal{P}(S)$ can be extended to a meaning function $[\![-]\!]_V : \mathcal{L}_0X \longrightarrow \mathcal{P}(S)$ in the usual manner. We write $S, V, s \Vdash \phi$ to indicate $s \in [\![\phi]\!]_V$. The meaning function $[\![-]\!]_V$ naturally induces a map $[\![-]\!]_V^1 : \mathcal{L}_0\Lambda\mathcal{L}_0(X) \longrightarrow \mathcal{P}(\mathcal{T}S)$ interpreting depth-one formulas as subsets of $\mathcal{T}S$. This map is defined inductively, with

$$[\![\heartsuit_\lambda(\phi_1, \ldots, \phi_n)]\!]_V^1 = \lambda_S([\![\phi_1]\!]_V, \ldots, [\![\phi_n]\!]_V) \tag{2}$$

being the clause for the modalities, and with the standard clauses for the boolean connectives. We write $\mathcal{T}S, V, \tau \Vdash^1 \phi$ to indicate $\tau \in [\![\phi]\!]_V^1$, and refer to this relation as the *one-step semantics*.

We are now ready for the definition of the key structures of this paper, viz., Λ-automata, and their semantics.

Definition 4 (Λ-automata). *A Λ-automaton $\mathbb{A}$ is a quadruple $\mathbb{A}=(A, a_I, \delta, \Omega)$, where A is a finite set of states, $a_I \in A$ is the initial state, $\delta : A \longrightarrow \mathcal{L}_0\Lambda(A)$ is the transition map, and $\Omega : A \longrightarrow \mathbb{N}$ is a parity map. The size of $\mathbb{A}$ is defined as its number of states, and its index as the size of the range of Ω.*

The acceptance game of Λ-automata proceeds in *rounds* moving from one basic position in $A \times S$ to another. In each round, at position (a, s) first $\exists$ picks a valuation V that makes the depth-one formula $\delta(a)$ true at $\sigma(s)$. Looking at this $V : A \longrightarrow \mathcal{P}S$ as a binary relation $\{(a', s') \mid s' \in V(a')\}$ between A and S, $\forall$ closes the round by picking an element of this relation.

Definition 5 (Acceptance game). *Let $\mathbb{S} = (S, \sigma)$ be a $\mathcal{T}$-coalgebra and let $\mathbb{A} = (A, a_I, \delta, \Omega)$ be a Λ-automaton. The associated acceptance game $Acc(\mathbb{A}, \mathbb{S})$ is the parity game given by the table below.*

Position	*Player*	*Admissible moves*	*Priority*
$(a, s) \in A \times S$	$\exists$	$\{V : A \longrightarrow \mathcal{P}(S) \mid \mathbb{S}, V, \sigma(s) \Vdash^1 \delta(a)\}$	$\Omega(a)$
$V \in \mathcal{P}(S)^A$	$\forall$	$\{(a', s') \mid s' \in V(a')\}$	*0*

A pointed coalgebra $(\mathbb{S}, s_0)$ is accepted *by the automaton $\mathbb{A}$ if the pair (a_I, s_0) is a winning position for player $\exists$ in $Acc(\mathbb{A}, \mathbb{S})$.*

As expected, and generalizing the automata-theoretic perspective on the modal μ-calculus as in [6], Λ-automata are the counterpart of the coalgebraic μ-calculus associated with Λ. As a formalization of this we need the following Proposition, the proof of which is routine, and deferred to the Appendix. Here we say that a Λ-automaton $\mathbb{A}$ is *equivalent* to a sentence $\phi \in \mu\mathrm{ML}_\Lambda$ if any pointed $\mathcal{T}$-coalgebra $(\mathbb{S}, s)$ is accepted by $\mathbb{A}$ iff $\mathbb{S}, s \Vdash \phi$.

Proposition 1. *There is an effective procedure transforming a sentence ϕ in $\mu\mathrm{ML}_\Lambda$ into an equivalent Λ-automaton $\mathbb{A}_\phi$ of size dn and index d, where n is the size and d is the alternation depth of ϕ.*

4 Finite Model Property

In this section we show that $\mu\mathrm{ML}_\Lambda$ has the small model property. The key tool in our proof is a satisfiability game that characterizes whether the class of pointed coalgebras accepted by a given Λ-automaton, is empty or not.

Definition 6. *Let A be a finite set and Ω a map from A to $\mathbb{N}$. Given a sequence $R_0 \ldots R_k$ in $(\mathcal{P}(A \times A))^*$ the set of* traces through *$R_0 \ldots R_k$ is defined as $Tr(R_0 \ldots R_k) := \{a_0 \ldots a_{k+1} \in A^* \mid (a_i, a_{i+1}) \in R_i$ for all $i \leq k.\}$. Similarly $Tr(R_0 R_1 \ldots) \subseteq A^\omega$ denotes the set of (infinite) traces through $R_0 R_1 \ldots$. With $NBT(A, \Omega)$ we denote the set of $R_0 R_1 \cdots \in (\mathcal{P}(A \times A))^\omega$ that contain no* bad trace, *that is, no trace $a_0 a_1 \ldots$ such that* $\max\{\Omega(a) \mid a \in Inf(a_0 a_1 \ldots)\}$ *is odd.*

Definition 7 (Satisfiability game). *The satisfiability game $Sat(\mathbb{A})$ associated with an automaton $\mathbb{A} = (A, a_I, \delta, \Omega)$ is the graph game given by the rules of the tableau below. Here for an element $a \in A$ and for a collection $\mathcal{R} \subseteq \mathcal{P}(A \times A)$, $\varsigma^a : A \longrightarrow A \times A$ maps b to (a, b) and $U_\mathcal{R} : A \times A \longrightarrow \mathcal{P}(\mathcal{R})$ denotes the valuation given by such that $U_\mathcal{R}(a, b) = \{R \in \mathcal{R} \mid (a, b) \in R\}$. The range of a relation R is denoted by $Ran(R)$.*

Position	*Player*	*Admissible moves*
$R \subseteq A \times A$	$\exists$	$\{\mathcal{R} \in \mathcal{PP}(A \times A) \mid [\![\bigwedge\{\varsigma^a \delta(a) \mid a \in Ran(R)\}]\!]^1_{U_\mathcal{R}} \neq \emptyset\}$
$\mathcal{R} \in \mathcal{PP}(A \times A)$	$\forall$	$\{R \mid R \in \mathcal{R}\}$

Unless specified otherwise, we assume $\{(a_I, a_I)\}$ *to be the starting position of* $Sat(\mathbb{A})$. *An infinite match* $R_0\mathcal{R}_0R_1\ldots$ *is winning for* $\exists$ *if* $R_0R_1\ldots \in NBT(A, \Omega)$.

We leave it for the reader to verify that $Sat(\mathbb{A})$ is a regular game, and that its winning condition is an ω-regular language L of which the complement is recognized by a nondeterministic parity stream automaton of size $|A|$ and index $|Ran(\Omega)|$. So by [13], L is recognized by a deterministic parity stream automaton of size exponential in $|A|$ and index polynomial in $|A|$.

We are now ready to state and prove our main result.

Theorem 3. *Given a* Λ*-automaton* $\mathbb{A}$*, the following are equivalent.*
(1) $L(\mathbb{A})$ *is not empty.*
(2) $\exists$ *has a winning strategy in the game* $Sat(\mathbb{A})$.
(3) $L(\mathbb{A})$ *contains a finite pointed coalgebra of size exponential in the size of* $\mathbb{A}$.

Proof. Details for the implication $(1 \Rightarrow 2)$ are in the appendix, and $(3 \Rightarrow 1)$ is immediate. We focus on the hardest implication $(2 \Rightarrow 3)$. Suppose that $\exists$ has a winning strategy in the game $Sat(\mathbb{A}) = (G_\exists, G_\forall, E, Win)$. By the remark following Definition 7 and by Fact 1, we may assume this strategy to use finite memory only: there is a finite set M, $m_I \in M$ and maps $\alpha_1 : G_\exists \times M \longrightarrow G$ and $\alpha_2 : G_\exists \times M \longrightarrow M$ which satisfy the conditions of Definition 2(3). Moreover, the size of M is at most exponential in the size of $\mathbb{A}$. Without loss of generality, we may assume that for all $(R, m) \in G_\exists \times M$, $\alpha_2(R, m) = m$.

We denote by $W_\exists$ the set of pairs $(R, m) \in G_\exists \times M$ satisfying the following: For all $Sat(\mathbb{A})$-matches $R_0\mathcal{R}_0R_1\mathcal{R}_1\ldots$ for which there exists a sequence $m_0m_1\ldots$ with $R_0 = R, m_0 = m$ and for all $i \in \mathbb{N}$, $\mathcal{R}_i = \alpha_1(R_i, m_i)$, $m_{i+1} = \alpha_2(R_i, m_i)$, we have that $R_0\mathcal{R}_0R_1\mathcal{R}_1\ldots$ is won by $\exists$.

The finite coalgebra in $L(\mathbb{A})$ that we are looking for will have the set $G_\exists \times M$ as its carrier. Therefore we first define a coalgebra map $\xi : G_\exists \times M \longrightarrow \mathcal{T}(G_\exists \times M)$. We base this construction on two observations.

First, let (R, m) be an element of $W_\exists$, and write $\mathcal{R} := \alpha_1(R, m)$; then by the rules of the satisfiability game, there is an object $g(R, m) \in \mathcal{T}\mathcal{R}$ such that for every $a \in Ran(R)$, the formula $\varsigma^a\delta(a)$ is true at $g(R, m)$ under the valuation $U_\mathcal{R}$. Note that $\mathcal{R} \subseteq G_\exists$, and thus we may think of the above as defining a function $g : W_\exists \longrightarrow \mathcal{T}G_\exists$. Choosing some dummy values for elements $(R, m) \in (G_\exists \times M)\backslash W_\exists$, the domain of this function can be extended to the full set $G_\exists \times M$. To simplify our notation we will also let g denote the resulting map, with domain $G_\exists \times M$ and codomain $\mathcal{T}G_\exists$. Second, consider the map $add_m : G_\exists \longrightarrow G_\exists \times M$, given by $add_m(R) = (R, m)$. Based on this map we define the function $h : \mathcal{T}(G_\exists) \times M \longrightarrow \mathcal{T}(G_\exists \times M)$ such that $h(\tau, m) = \mathcal{T}(add_m)(\tau)$.

We let $\mathbb{S}$ be the coalgebra $(G_\exists \times M, \xi)$, where $\xi : G_\exists \times M \longrightarrow \mathcal{T}(G_\exists \times M)$ is the map $\xi := h \circ (g, \alpha_2)$. Observe that the size of $\mathbb{S}$ is at most exponential in the size of $\mathbb{A}$, since $G_\exists$ is the set $\mathcal{P}(A \times A)$ and M is at most exponential in the size of A. As the designated point of $\mathbb{S}$ we take the pair (R_I, m_I), where $R_I := \{(a_I, a_I)\}$.

It is left to prove that the pointed coalgebra $(\mathbb{S}, (R_I, m_I))$ is accepted by $\mathbb{A}$. That is, using $\exists$'s winning strategy α in the satisfiability game we need to find a winning strategy for $\exists$ in the acceptance game for the automaton $\mathbb{A}$ with starting position $(a_I, (R_I, m_I))$. We will define this strategy by induction on the length of a partial match, simultaneously setting up a shadow match of the satisfiability game. Inductively we maintain the following relation between the two matches: (*) If $(a_0, (R_0, m_0)), \ldots, (a_k, (R_k, m_k))$ is a partial match of the acceptance game (during which $\exists$ plays the inductively defined strategy), then $a_I a_0 \ldots a_k$ is a trace through $R_0 \ldots R_k$ (and so in particular, a_k belongs to $Ran(R_k)$), and for all $i \in \{0, \ldots, k-1\}$, $R_{i+1} \in \alpha_1(R_i, m_i)$ and $m_{i+1} = \alpha_2(R_i, m_i)$.

Setting up the induction, it is easy to see that the above condition is met at the start $(a_0, (R_0, m_0)) = (a_I, (R_I, m_I))$ of the acceptance match: $a_I a_I$ is the (unique) trace through the one element sequence R_I.

Inductively assume that, with $\exists$ playing as prescribed, the play of the acceptance game has reached position $(a_k, (R_k, m_k))$. By the induction hypothesis, we have $a_k \in Ran(R_k)$ and the position (R_k, m_k) is a winning position for $\exists$ in the acceptance game. Abbreviate $\mathcal{R} := \alpha_1(R_k, m_k)$ and $n := \alpha_2(R_k, m_k)$. As the next move for $\exists$ we propose the valuation $V : A \longrightarrow \mathcal{P}(G_\exists \times M)$ such that $V(a) := \{(R, n) \mid (a_k, a) \in R \text{ and } R \in \mathcal{R}\}$.

Claim. V is a legitimate move at position $(a_k, (R_k, m_k))$.

Proof of Claim. We need to show that $\mathbb{S}, V, (R_k, m_k) \Vdash^1 \delta(a_k)$. First, recall that (R_k, m_k) belongs to $W_\exists$. Hence, the element $\gamma := g(R_k, m_k)$ of $\mathcal{T}\mathcal{R}$ satisfies the formula $\varsigma^{a_k}\delta(a_k)$ under the valuation $U := U_\mathcal{R}$ (where $U_\mathcal{R}$ is defined as in Definition 7). That is $\mathcal{T}\mathcal{R}, U_\mathcal{R}, \gamma \Vdash^1 \varsigma^{a_k}\delta(a_k)$. Thus in order to prove the claim it clearly suffices to show that

$$\mathbb{S}, V, (R_k, m_k) \Vdash^1 \phi \text{ iff } \mathcal{T}\mathcal{R}, U, \gamma \Vdash^1 \varsigma^{a_k}\phi \tag{3}$$

for all formulas ϕ in $\mathcal{L}_0(\Lambda(A))$. The proof of (3) proceeds by induction on the complexity of ϕ. We only consider a simplified version of the base step, where ϕ is of the form $\heartsuit_\lambda a$. We can prove (3) as follows (recall that $n = \alpha_2(R_k, m_k)$):

$$\begin{aligned}
\mathbb{S}, V, (R_k, m_k) \Vdash^1 \heartsuit_\lambda b &\iff \xi(R_k, m_k) \in \lambda_{G_\exists \times M}([\![b]\!]_V). && \text{(definition of } \Vdash^1\text{)}\\
&\iff (\mathcal{T}\, add_n)(\gamma) \in \lambda_{G_\exists \times M}([\![b]\!]_V). && \text{(definition of } \xi\text{)}\\
&\iff \gamma \in (\mathcal{T}\, add_n)^{-1}(\lambda_{G_\exists \times M}[\![b]\!]_V) && \text{(definition of } (\cdot)^{-1}\text{)}\\
&\iff \gamma \in \lambda_{G_\exists}(add_n^{-1}([\![b]\!]_V)) && \text{(naturality of } \lambda\text{)}\\
&\iff \gamma \in \lambda_\mathcal{R}([\![(a_k, b)]\!]_U) && (\ddagger)\\
&\iff \mathcal{T}\mathcal{R}, U, \gamma \Vdash^1 \heartsuit_\lambda(a_k, b) && \text{(definition of } \Vdash^1\text{)}\\
&\iff \mathcal{T}\mathcal{R}, U, \gamma \Vdash^1 \varsigma^{a_k}\heartsuit_\lambda b && \text{(definition of } \varsigma^{a_k}\text{)}
\end{aligned}$$

For (‡), consider the following valuation $U' : A \times A \longrightarrow \mathcal{P}(G_\exists)$ such that $U'(a', b') := U(a', b') \cap \mathcal{R}$. It follows from $\mathcal{R} \subseteq G_\exists$ and standardness that $\lambda_\mathcal{R}[\![a]\!]_U = \lambda_{G_\exists}[\![a]\!]_{U'}$. But then (‡) follows because $add_n^{-1}([\![b]\!]_V) = [\![(a, b)]\!]_{U'}$, which holds by a relatively routine proof. *This finishes the proof of the Claim.*

We leave it for the reader to verify that with this definition of a strategy for $\exists$, the inductive hypothesis (including the relation (*) between the two matches) remains true. In particular this shows that $\exists$ will never get stuck. Hence in order to verify that the strategy is winning for $\exists$, we may confine our attention to infinite matches of $Acc(\mathbb{A}, \mathbb{S})$. Let $\pi = (a_0, (R_0, m_0))(a_1, (R_1, m_1))\dots$ be such a match, then it follows from (*) that $a_I a_0 a_1 \dots$ is a trace through $R_0 R_1 \dots$, and so we may infer from the assumption that (α_1, α_2) is a winning strategy for $\exists$ in $Sat(\mathbb{A})$, that $a_I a_0 a_1 \dots$ is not bad. This means that the match π is won by $\exists$.

Putting this theorem together with Proposition 1, we obtain a small model property for the coalgebraic μ-calculus, for *every* set of predicate liftings.

Corollary 1. *If $\phi \in \mu\mathrm{ML}_\Lambda$ is satisfiable in a $\mathcal{T}$-coalgebra, it is satisfiable in a $\mathcal{T}$-coalgebra of size exponential in the size of ϕ.*

Moreover, given some mild condition on Λ and $\mathcal{T}$, we obtain the following complexity result.

Definition 8. *Given sets A and $\mathcal{X} \subseteq \mathcal{P}A$, let $U_\mathcal{X} : A \longrightarrow \mathcal{P}\mathcal{X}$ be the valuation given by $U_\mathcal{X} : a \mapsto \{B \in \mathcal{X} \mid a \in B\}$. The* one-step satisfiability problem for Λ over $\mathcal{T}$ *is the problem whether, for fixed A and $\mathcal{X}$, a given formula ϕ is satisfiable in $\mathcal{T}\mathcal{X}$ under $U_\mathcal{X}$.*

Theorem 4. *If Λ has an EXPTIME one-step satisfiability problem over $\mathcal{T}$, then the satisfiability problem of $\mu\mathrm{ML}_\Lambda$ over $\mathcal{T}$-coalgebras is decidable in 2EXPTIME.*

Proof. Let ϕ be a given sentence in $\mu\mathrm{ML}_\Lambda$ of size n, and let $\mathbb{A}_\phi$ be the Λ-automaton associated with ϕ, as in Proposition 1. On the basis of the remark following Definition 7, the reader may easily check that $Sat(\mathbb{A}_\phi)$ is a regular game of size doubly exponential in n, and with a winning condition that is recognizable by a deterministic parity stream automaton of size exponential in n and index polynomial in n. Hence by Fact 1 the problem of determining the winner of this game can be solved in doubly exponential time.

However, the game $Sat(\mathbb{A}_\phi)$ has to be *constructed* in doubly exponential time as well. The problem here concerns the complexity of the problem whether a given pair $(R, \mathcal{R})$ is an edge of the game graph. Under the assumption of the Theorem, this can be done in time doubly exponential in n — note that the *length* of the one-step formulas in the range of the transition function of $\mathbb{A}_\phi$ may be exponential in n.

5 One-Step Tableau Completeness

In this section we show how our satisfiability game relates to the work of Cîrstea, Kupke and Pattinson [5]. We need some definitions — for reasons of space limitations we omit proofs and refer to *opus cit.* for motivation and examples.

Definition 9. *A one-step rule* d *for* Λ *is of the form*

$$\frac{\Gamma_0}{\gamma_1 \quad \cdots \quad \gamma_n}$$

where $\Gamma_0 \subseteq_\omega \Lambda(X)$ *and* $\gamma_1, \ldots, \gamma_n \subseteq_\omega X$, *every propositional variable occurs at most once in* Γ_0 *and all variables occurring in each of the* γ_i*'s* $(i > 0)$ *also occur in* Γ_0. *We write* $Conc(\mathsf{d})$ *for the set* Γ_0 *and* $Prem(\mathsf{d})$ *for the set* $\{\gamma_i \mid 1 \leq i \leq n\}$.

Given $\Gamma, \{\phi\} \subseteq_\omega \mathcal{L}_0\Lambda(X)$, *we say that* Γ propositionally entails ϕ, *notation:* $\Gamma \vdash_{PL} \phi$, *if there are* $\Gamma', \{\phi'\} \subseteq_\omega \mathcal{L}_0(Y)$ *and a substitution* $\tau : Y \longrightarrow \Lambda(X)$ *such that* $\tau[\Gamma'] = \Gamma$, $\tau(\phi') = \phi$ *and* $\Gamma' \vdash \phi'$ *in propositional logic,.*

For a set of such rules, with an automaton $\mathbb{A}$ we associate a so-called *tableau game*, in which the rules themselves are part of the game board.

Definition 10. *Let* $\mathbb{A} = (A, a_I, \delta, \Omega)$ *be a* Λ*-automaton and let* D *be a set of one-step rules for* Λ. *The game* $Tab(\mathbb{A}, \mathsf{D})$ *is the two-player graph game given by the table below.*

Position	*Player*	*Admissible moves*
$R \in \mathcal{P}(A \times A)$	$\exists$	$\{\Gamma \subseteq_\omega \Lambda(A \times A) \mid (\forall a \in ran(R))(\Gamma \vdash_{PL} \varsigma^a\delta(a)\}$
$\Gamma \subseteq_\omega \Lambda(A \times A)$	$\forall$	$\left\{(\mathsf{d}, \tau) \in \mathsf{D} \times (A \times A)^X \mid \tau[Conc(\mathsf{d})] \subseteq \Gamma)\right\}$
$(\mathsf{d}, \tau) \in \mathsf{D} \times (A \times A)^X$	$\exists$	$\{\tau[\gamma] \mid \tau : X \longrightarrow A \times A, \gamma \in Prem(\mathsf{d})\}$

Unless specified differently, the starting position is $\{(a_I, a_I)\}$. *An infinite match* $R_0\Gamma_0(\mathsf{d}_0, \tau_0)R_1\Gamma_1(\mathsf{d}_1, \tau_1)\ldots$ *is won by* $\exists$ *if* $R_0R_1\ldots$ *belongs to* $NBT(A, \Omega)$.

Given the connection of Proposition 1 between formulas and automata, one may show that our tableau games are virtually the same as the ones in [5]. Our tableau game $Tab(\mathbb{A}, \mathsf{D})$ is (in some natural sense) *equivalent* to the satisfiability game for $\mathbb{A}$ if we assume the set D to be *one-step complete* with respect to $\mathcal{T}$.

Definition 11. *A set* D *of one-step rules is* one-step complete *for* $\mathcal{T}$ *if for any set* Y *of variables, any set* S, $\Gamma \subseteq_\omega \Lambda(Y)$ *and valuation* $V : Y \longrightarrow \mathcal{P}(S)$ *the following are equivalent:*
(a) $[\![\bigwedge \Gamma]\!]^1_V \neq \emptyset$
(b) for all rules $\mathsf{d} \in \mathsf{D}$ *and all substitutions* $\tau : X \longrightarrow Y$ *with* $\tau[Conc(d)] \subseteq_\omega \Gamma$, *there exists* $\gamma_i \in Prem(\mathsf{d})$ *such that* $[\![\bigwedge \tau[\gamma_i]]\!]^1_V \neq \emptyset$.

The proof of the following equivalence is deferred to the appendix.

Theorem 5. *Let* $\mathbb{A}$ *be a* Λ*-automaton and let* D *be a set of one-step rules for* Λ. *If* D *is one-step complete with respect to* $\mathcal{T}$, *then* $\exists$ *has a winning strategy in* $Sat(\mathbb{A})$ *iff* $\exists$ *has a winning strategy in* $Tab(\mathbb{A}, \mathsf{D})$.

For the purpose of obtaining good complexity results for the coalgebraic μ-calculus, in case we have a nice set D of derivation rules at our disposal, then the tableau game has considerable advantages over the satisfiability game. The point is that starting from a sentence $\phi \in \mu\mathrm{ML}_\Lambda$, the *size* of the game board of $Tab(\mathbb{A}, \mathsf{D})$ is not necessarily *doubly* exponential in the size of ϕ. If we follow exactly the ideas of [5], with a suitable restriction of D, some further manipulations may in fact yield a *single exponential* size game board, which may also be constructed in single exponential time (in the size of the original sentence). More specifically, in our framework of Λ-automata we may prove the main result of [5] stating that if Λ admits a so-called *exponentially tractable*, *contraction closed* one-step complete set D of rules, then the satisfiability problem for $\mu\mathrm{ML}_\Lambda$-sentences over $\mathcal{T}$-coalgebras may be solved in exponential time.

References

1. Aczel, P.: Non-Well-Founded Sets. CSLI Publications, Stanford (1988)
2. Adámek, J., Trnková, V.: Automata and Algebras in Categories. Kluwer Academic Publishers, Dordrecht (1990)
3. Bartels, F., Sokolova, A., de Vink, E.: A hierarchy of probabilistic system types. Theoretical Computer Science 327, 3–22 (2004)
4. Büchi, J.R., Landweber, L.H.: Solving sequential conditions by finite state strategies. Transactions of the American Mathematical Society 138, 295–311 (1969)
5. Cîrstea, C., Kupke, C., Pattinson, D.: EXPTIME tableaux for the coalgebraic μ-calculus. In: Grädel, E., Kahle, R. (eds.) CSL 2009. LNCS, vol. 5771, pp. 179–193. Springer, Heidelberg (2009)
6. Grädel, E., Thomas, W., Wilke, T. (eds.): Automata, Logics, and Infinite Games. LNCS, vol. 2500. Springer, Heidelberg (2002)
7. Hansen, H., Kupke, C.: A coalgebraic perspective on monotone modal logic. Electronic Notes in Theoretical Computer Science 106, 121–143 (2004); Proceedings of the Workshop on Coalgebraic Methods in Computer Science (CMCS)
8. Jurdziński, M.: Small progress measures for solving parity games. In: Reichel, H., Tison, S. (eds.) STACS 2000. LNCS, vol. 1770, pp. 290–301. Springer, Heidelberg (2000)
9. Kozen, D.: Results on the propositional μ-calculus. Theoretical Computer Science 27(3), 333–354 (1983)
10. Kupke, C., Venema, Y.: Coalgebraic automata theory: basic results. Logical Methods in Computer Science 4, 1–43 (2008)
11. Moss, L.: Coalgebraic logic. Annals of Pure and Applied Logic 96, 277–317 (1999); Erratum published APAL 99, 241–259, 1999
12. Pattinson, D.: Coalgebraic modal logic: Soundness, completeness and decidability of local consequence. Theoretical Computer Science 309, 177–193 (2003)
13. Piterman, N.: From nondeterministic Büchi and Streett automata to deterministic parity automata. In: Proceedings of the Twentyfirst Annual IEEE Symposium on Logic in Computer Science (LICS 2006), pp. 255–264. IEEE Computer Society, Los Alamitos (2006)
14. Rutten, J.: Universal coalgebra: A theory of systems. Theoretical Computer Science 249, 3–80 (2000)
15. Schröder, L., Pattinson, D.: PSPACE bounds for rank–1 modal logics. ACM Transactions on Computational Logic 10, 1–32 (2009)
16. Venema, Y.: Automata and fixed point logic: a coalgebraic perspective. Information and Computation 204, 637–678 (2006)
17. Visser, A., D'Agostino, G.: Finality regained: A coalgebraic study of Scott-sets and multisets. Archive for Mathematical Logic 41, 267–298 (2002)

Resolving the Complexity of Some Data Privacy Problems

Jeremiah Blocki[1,⋆] and Ryan Williams[2,⋆⋆]

[1] Carnegie Mellon University
jblocki@cs.cmu.edu
[2] IBM Almaden Research Center
ryanwill@us.ibm.com

Abstract. We formally study two methods for data sanitation that have been used extensively in the database community: k-anonymity and ℓ-diversity. We settle several open problems concerning the difficulty of applying these methods optimally, proving both positive and negative results:

- 2-anonymity is in P.
- The problem of partitioning the edges of a triangle-free graph into 4-stars (degree-three vertices) is NP-hard. This yields an alternative proof that 3-anonymity is NP-hard even when the database attributes are all *binary*.
- 3-anonymity with only 27 attributes per record is MAX SNP-hard.
- For databases with n rows, k-anonymity is in $O(4^n \cdot \text{poly}(n)))$ time for all $k > 1$.
- For databases with ℓ attributes, alphabet size c, and n rows, k-Anonymity can be solved in $2^{O(k^2(2c)^\ell)} + O(n\ell)$ time.
- 3-diversity with binary attributes is NP-hard, with one sensitive attribute.
- 2-diversity with binary attributes is NP-hard, with three sensitive attributes.

1 Introduction

The topic of *data sanitization* has received enormous attention in recent years. The high-level idea is to release a database to the public in such a manner that two conflicting goals are achieved: (1) the data is useful to benign researchers who want to study trends and identify patterns in the data, and (2) the data is not useful to malicious parties who wish to compromise the privacy of individuals. Many different models for data sanitization have been proposed in the literature, and they can be roughly divided into two kinds: *output perturbative* models (e.g., [2,8]) and *output abstraction* models (e.g., [16,17,12]). In perturbative models, some or all of the output data is perturbed in a way that no longer

⋆ Supported by an NSF Graduate Research Fellowship.
⋆⋆ Supported by the Josef Raviv Memorial Postdoctoral Fellowship.

S. Abramsky et al. (Eds.): ICALP 2010, Part II, LNCS 6199, pp. 393–404, 2010.

corresponds precisely to the input data (the perturbation is typically taken to be a random variable with nice properties). This include work which assumes *interaction* between the prospective data collector and the database, such as differential privacy. In abstraction models, some of the original data is suppressed or generalized (*e.g.* an age becomes an age range) in a way that preserves data integrity. The latter models are preferred in cases where data integrity is the highest priority, or when the data is simply non-numerical.

In this work, we formally study two data abstraction models from the literature, and determine which cases of the problems are efficiently solvable. We study k-anonymity and ℓ-diversity.

1.1 K-Anonymity

The method of k-anonymization, introduced in [16,17], is a popular method in the database community for publicly releasing part of a database while protecting individual identities in that database. Formally speaking, an instance of the k-anonymity problem is a matrix (a.k.a. database) with n rows and m columns with entries drawn from an underlying alphabet. Intuitively, the rows correspond to individuals and the columns correspond to various attributes of them. For hardness results, we study a special case called the *suppression model*, where the goal is to replace entries in the matrix with a special symbol $\star$ (called a 'star'), until each row is identical to at least $k-1$ other rows. The intuition is that the information released does not explicitly identify any individual in the database, but rather identifies at worst a group of size k.[1]

A trivial way to k-anonymize a database is to suppress every entry (replacing all entries with $\star$), but this renders the database useless. In order to maximize the utility of the database, one would like to suppress the fewest entries—this is the k-ANONYMITY problem with suppression. Meyerson and Williams [13] proved that in the most general case, this is a difficult task: k-ANONYMITY is NP-hard for $k \geq 3$, provided that the size of the alphabet is $\Omega(n)$. Aggarwal *et al.* [1] improved this, showing that 3-ANONYMITY remains NP-hard even when the alphabet size is 3. Bonizzoni *et al.* [5] further improved the result to show that 3-ANONYMITY is APX-hard, even with a binary alphabet. They also showed that 4-ANONYMITY with a constant number of attributes per record is NP-hard. In a related, but independent work, Chakaravarthy *et al.* showed that 7-ANONYMITY is MAX SNP-hard with just 3 attributes [6]. Two basic questions remain:

1. How difficult is 3-anonymity with a small number of attributes per record?
2. How difficult is the 2-anonymity problem?

Addressing the two questions above, we discover both a positive and negative result. On the positive side, in Section 3 we present a polynomial time algorithm for 2-ANONYMITY, applying a result of Anshelevich and Karagiozova [3]:

[1] This intuition can break down when combined with background knowledge [12]. However, our intent in this paper is not to critique the security/insecurity of these methods, but rather to understand their feasibility.

Theorem 1. 2-ANONYMITY *is in* P.

The polynomial time algorithm works not only for the simple suppression model, but also for the most general version of k-anonymity, where for each attribute we are given a *generalization hierarchy* of ways to withhold data.

In Section 4, we consider k-anonymity in databases where the number of attributes per record is constant. This setting seems to be the most relevant for practice: in a database of users, the number of attributes per user is often dwarfed by the number of users in the database. We find a surprisingly strong negative result.

Theorem 2. 3-ANONYMITY *with just 27 attributes per record is* MAX SNP-*hard. Therefore,* 3-ANONYMITY *does not have a polynomial time approximation scheme in this case, unless* P = NP.

Our proof uses an alphabet with $\Omega(n)$ cardinality. This motivates the question: how efficiently can we solve k-anonymity with a small alphabet and constant number of attributes per record? Here we can prove a positive result, showing that when the number of attributes is small and the alphabet is constant, there are subexponential algorithms for optimal k-anonymity for every $k > 1$.

Theorem 3. *For every* $k > 2$, k-ANONYMITY *can be solved in* $O(4^n poly(n))$ *time, where* n *is the total number of rows in the database.*

Theorem 4. *Let* ℓ *be the number of attributes in a database, let* c *be the size of its alphabet, and let* n *be the number of rows. Then* k-ANONYMITY *can be solved in* $2^{O(k^2(2c)^{\ell})} + O(n\ell)$ *time.*

This improves on results in [9]. Theorem 4 implies that k-ANONYMITY is solvable in polynomial time when $\ell \leq (\log\log n)/\log c$ and $c \leq \log n$. Theorem 4 also implies that for $c = n^{o(1)}$ and $\ell = O(1)$, optimal k-anonymity is in *subexponential time*. Therefore it is unlikely that we can tighten the unbounded alphabet constraint of Theorem 2, for otherwise all of NP has $2^{n^{o(1)}}$ time algorithms.

In the full version of the paper, we provide an alternative proof that BINARY 3-ANONYMITY, the special case of the problem where all of the attributes are binary-valued, is NP-hard. This result is weaker than [5] who recently showed that BINARY 3-ANONYMITY is APX-hard. However, our proof also shows that a certain edge partitioning problem is NP-complete, which to the best of our knowledge is new.[2] Let EDGE PARTITION INTO TRIANGLES AND 4-STARS be the problem of partitioning the edges of a given graph into 3-cliques (triangles) and 4-stars (graphs with three degree-1 nodes and one degree-3 node).

Theorem 5. EDGE PARTITION INTO TRIANGLES & 4-STARS *is* NP-*complete.*

Theorem 5 implies that the TERNARY 3-ANONYMITY hardness reduction given in [1] is sufficient to conclude that BINARY 3-ANONYMITY is NP-hard.

[2] EDGE PARTITION INTO TRIANGLES is NP-Complete as is EDGE PARTITION INTO 4-STARS [7], but this does not imply that EDGE PARTITION INTO TRIANGLES AND 4-STARS is NP-Complete.

1.2 L-Diversity

In the full version of the paper, we also consider the method of ℓ-diversity introduced in [12], which has also been well-studied. This method refines the notion of k-anonymity to protect against knowledge attacks on particular sensitive attributes.

We will work with a simplified definition of ℓ-diversity that captures the essentials. Similar to k-anonymity, we think of an ℓ-diversity instance as a table (database) with m rows (records) and n columns (attributes). However, each attribute is also given a label q or s, inducing a partition of the attributes into two sets Q and S. Q is called the set of quasi-identifier attributes and S called the set of sensitive attributes.

Definition 1. *A database D is said to be* ℓ-diverse *if for every row u_0 of D there are (at least) $\ell - 1$ distinct rows $u_1, ..., u_{\ell-1}$ of D such that:*

1. $\forall q \in Q, 0 \leq i < j < \ell$ *we have* $u_i[s] = u_j[s]$
2. $\forall s \in S, 0 \leq i < j < \ell$ *we have* $u_i[s] \neq u_j[s]$

Constraint 1 is essentially the same as k-anonymity. Any row must have at least $k - 1$ other rows whose (non sensitive) attributes are identical. Intuitively, Constraint 2 prevents anyone from definitively learning any row's sensitive attribute; in the worst case, an individual's attribute can be narrowed down to a set of at least ℓ choices. Similar to k-anonymity with suppression, we allow stars to be introduced to achieve the two constraints.

We can show rather strong hardness results for ℓ-diversity.

Theorem 6. *Optimal* 2*-diversity with binary attributes and three sensitive attributes is* NP*-hard.*

Theorem 7. *Optimal* 3*-diversity with binary attributes and one sensitive attribute is* NP*-hard.*

Independent of their applications in databases, k-anonymity and ℓ-diversity are also interesting from a theoretical viewpoint. They are natural combinatorial problems with a somewhat different character from other standard NP-hard problems. They are a kind of discrete partition task that has not been studied much: *find a partition where each part is intended to "blend in the crowd."* Such problems will only become more relevant in the future, and we believe the generic techniques developed in this paper should be useful in further analyzing these new partition problems.

2 Preliminaries

We use poly(n) to denote a quantity that is polynomial in n.

Definition 2. *Let n and m be positive integers. Let Σ be a finite set. A* database *with n* rows *(records) and m* columns *(attributes) is a matrix from $\Sigma^{n \times m}$. The* alphabet *of the database is Σ.*

Definition 3. *Let k be a positive integer. A database is said to be* k-anonymous *or* k-anonymized *if for every row r_i there exist at least $k-1$ identical rows.*

As mentioned earlier, there are two methods of achieving k-anonymity: suppression and generalization. In the suppression model, cells from the table are replaced with stars until the database is k-anonymous. Informally, the generalization model allows the entry of an individual cell to be replaced by a broader category. For example, one may change a numerical entry to a range, *e.g.* (Age: 26 → Age: [20-30]). A formal definition is given in Section 8.

In our hardness results, we consider k-anonymity with suppression. Since suppression is a special case of generalization, the hardness results also apply to k-anonymity with generalization. Interestingly, our polynomial time 2-anonymity algorithm works under both models.

Definition 4. *Under the suppression model, the* cost *of a k-anonymous solution to a database is the number of stars introduced.*

We let $Cost_k^\star(D)$ denote the minimum cost of k-anonymizing database D.

For our inapproximability results, we need the notion of an L-reduction [14].

Definition 5. *Let A and B be two optimization problems and let $f : A \to B$ be a polynomial time computable transformation. f is an* L-reduction *if there are positive constants α and β such that*

1. $OPT(f(I)) \leq \alpha \cdot OPT(I)$
2. *For every solution of $f(I)$ of cost c_2 we can in polynomial time find a solution of I with cost c_1 such that*

$$|OPT(I) - c_1| \leq \beta \cdot |OPT(f(I)) - c_2|$$

3 Polynomial Time Algorithm for 2-Anonymity

Because 3-anonymity is hard even for binary attributes, it is natural to wonder if 2-anonymity is also difficult. However it turns out that achieving optimal 2-anonymity is polynomial time solvable. The resulting algorithm is nontrivial and would require heavy machinery to implement. We rely on a special case of hypergraph matching called Simplex Matching, introduced in [3].

Definition 6. Simplex Matching*: Given a hypergraph $H = (V, E)$ with hyperedges of size 2 and 3 and a cost function $c : E \to \mathbb{N}$ such that*

1. $(u, v, w) \in E(H) \Longrightarrow (u, v), (v, w), (u, w) \in E(H)$ *and*
2. $c(u, v) + c(v, w) + c(u, w) \leq 2 \cdot c(u, v, w)$

find $M \subseteq E$ such that for all $v \in V$ there is a unique $e \in M$ containing v, and $\sum_{e \in M} c(e)$ is minimized.

Anshelevich and Karagiozova gave a polynomial time algorithm to solve SIMPLEX MATCHING. We show that 2-ANONYMITY can be efficiently reduced to a simplex matching.

Reminder of Theorem 1. 2-ANONYMITY *is in* P.

Proof. Given a database D with rows $r_1, \ldots, r_n$, let $C_{i,j}$ denote the number of stars needed to make rows r_i and r_j. Similarly define $C_{i,j,k}$ to be the number of stars needed to make r_i, r_j, r_k all identical. Observe that in a 2-anonymization, any group with more than three identical rows could simply be split into subgroups of size two or three without increasing the anonymization cost. Therefore we may assume (without loss of generality) that the optimal 2-anonymity solution partitions the rows into groups of size two or three.

Construct a hypergraph H as follows:

1. For every row r_i of D, add a vertex v_i.
2. For every pair r_i, r_j, add the 2-edge $\{v_i, v_j\}$ with cost $c(v_i, v_j) = C_{i,j}$.
3. For every triple r_i, r_j, r_k, add the 3-edge $\{v_i, v_j, v_k\}$ with cost $c(v_i, v_j, v_k) = C_{i,j,k}$.

Thus H is a hypergraph with n vertices and $O(n^3)$ edges. We claim that H meets the conditions of the simplex matching problem. The first condition is trivially met. Suppose we anonymize the pair of rows r_i, r_j with cost $C_{i,j}$, so both rows have $\frac{1}{2}C_{i,j}$ stars when anonymized. Observe that if we decided to anonymize the group r_i, r_j, r_k, the number of stars introduced per row would not decrease. That is, for all i, j, k we have

$$\frac{1}{3} \cdot C_{i,j,k} \geq \frac{1}{2} \cdot C_{i,j}.$$

By symmetry, we also have

$$\frac{1}{3} \cdot C_{i,j,k} \geq \frac{1}{2} \cdot C_{j,k}, \ \frac{1}{3} \cdot C_{i,j,k} \geq \frac{1}{2} \cdot C_{i,k}.$$

Adding the three inequalities together,

$$C_{i,j,k} \geq \frac{1}{2}(C_{i,j} + C_{j,k} + C_{i,k}).$$

Therefore H is an instance of the simplex matching problem.

Finally, observe that any simplex matching of H directly corresponds to a 2-anonymization of D with the same cost, and vice-versa. □

In the full version of this paper [4], we show that the proof of Theorem 1 also carries over to the most general case of 2-ANONYMITY, where instead of only suppressing entries with stars, we have a *generalization hierarchy* of possible values to write to an entry.

Theorem 8. *For every generalization hierarchy T, k-*ANONYMITY-*T is in* P.

4 k-Anonymity with Few Attributes

We now turn to studying the complexity of k-Anonymity with a constant number of attributes. First we show that for an unbounded alphabet, the 3-anonymity problem is still hard even with only 27 attributes. We use the following MAX SNP-hard problem in our proof.

Definition 7. MAX 3DM-3 (Maximum 3-Dimensional Matching With 3 Occurrences)
INSTANCE: *A set $M \subseteq W \times X \times Y$ of ordered triples where W, X and Y are disjoint sets. The number of occurrences in M of any element in W, X or Y is bounded by 3. Let*

$$C_{3DM}(M') = \frac{3|M'|}{|W| + |X| + |Y|}.$$

GOAL: *Maximize $C_{3DM}(M')$ over all $M' \subseteq M$ such that no two elements of M' agree in any coordinate.*

Reminder of Theorem 2. 3-ANONYMITY *with just 27 attributes per record is* MAX SNP*-hard. Therefore,* 3-ANONYMITY *does not have a polynomial time approximation scheme in this case, unless* P = NP*.*

Proof. To show 3-anonymity is MAX SNP-hard, we show that there is an L-reduction from MAX 3DM-3 to 3-ANONYMITY WITH 27 ATTRIBUTES [14], since it is known that MAX 3DM-3 is MAX SNP-complete [11].

Given a MAX 3DM-3 instance $I = (M, W, X, Y)$, construct a 3-ANONYMITY instance D as follows:

1. Define $\Sigma = M \bigcup W \bigcup X \bigcup Y$, so that it contains a special symbol for each triple in $t \in M$ and each element $r \in W \bigcup X \bigcup Y$.
2. Add a row to D corresponding to each element $r_i \in W \bigcup X \bigcup Y$, as follows. For $r \in W \bigcup X \bigcup Y$, let $t_{r,1}, t_{r,2}, t_{r,3} \in M$ be the three triples of M which contain r (if there are less than three triples then simply introduce new symbols).
   - If $r \in W$ then add the following row to D:

$t_{r,1}$	$t_{r,1}$	$t_{r,1}$	$t_{r,1}$	$t_{r,1}$	$t_{r,1}$	$t_{r,1}$	$t_{r,1}$	$t_{r,1}$	$t_{r,2}$	$t_{r,2}$	$\ldots$	$t_{r,3}$

   That is, the row contains nine copies of $t_{r,1}$, nine copies of $t_{r,2}$, then nine copies of $t_{r,3}$.
   - If $r \in X$, then add the row:

$t_{r,1}$	$t_{r,1}$	$t_{r,1}$	$t_{r,2}$	$t_{r,2}$	$t_{r,2}$	$t_{r,3}$	$t_{r,3}$	$t_{r,3}$	$t_{r,1}$	$t_{r,1}$	$\ldots$	$t_{r,3}$

   - If $r \in Y$, then add the row:

$t_{r,1}$	$t_{r,2}$	$t_{r,3}$	$t_{r,1}$	$t_{r,2}$	$t_{r,3}$	$t_{r,1}$	$t_{r,2}$	$t_{r,3}$	$t_{r,1}$	$t_{r,2}$	$\ldots$	$t_{r,3}$

Suppose $w_i \in W, x_j \in X, y_k \in Y$ are arbitrary. Then the corresponding three rows in the database have the form:

w_i	$t_{w_i,1}$	$t_{w_i,1}$	$t_{w_i,1}$	$t_{w_i,1}$	$t_{w_i,1}$	$t_{w_i,1}$	$t_{w_i,1}$	$t_{w_i,1}$	$t_{w_i,1}$	$\ldots$	$t_{w_i,3}$
x_j	$t_{x_j,1}$	$t_{x_j,1}$	$t_{x_j,1}$	$t_{x_j,2}$	$t_{x_j,2}$	$t_{x_j,2}$	$t_{x_j,3}$	$t_{x_j,3}$	$t_{x_j,3}$	$\ldots$	$t_{x_j,3}$
y_k	$t_{y_k,1}$	$t_{y_k,2}$	$t_{y_k,3}$	$t_{y_k,1}$	$t_{y_k,2}$	$t_{y_k,3}$	$t_{y_k,1}$	$t_{y_k,2}$	$t_{y_k,3}$	$\ldots$	$t_{y_k,3}$

Observe that D has a total of $27n$ entries, where $n = |X| + |W| + |Y|$. Recall $Cost_3^\star(D)$ is the optimal number of stars needed to 3-anonymize D. It is useful to redefine 3-Anonymity as a maximization problem (where one maximizes the information released). Let P be a 3-anonymous solution to D, and define

$$C_{3ANON}(P) = 1 - \frac{Cost_3^\star(P)}{27n},$$

so that $OPT(D) = \max_P\{C_{3ANON}(P)\}$.

Suppose $D = \{r_1, \ldots, r_n\}$ is an instance of 3-Anonymity obtained from the above reduction. Three properties are immediate from the construction of D:

1. For any x rows r_i, r_j, r_k, r_l, where $x \geq 4$, the cost of anonymizing these rows is
$$C_{i,j,k,l} = 27x$$
because there is no alphabet symbol that is used in all 4 rows.
2. If $\{r_i, r_j, r_k\} \notin M$ then the cost of anonymizing the three corresponding rows is
$$C_{i,j,k} = 27 \cdot 3 = 81$$
because there is no alphabet symbol that is used in all 3 rows.
3. If $\{r_i, r_j, r_k\} \in M$ then the cost of anonymizing the three corresponding rows is
$$C_{i,j,k} = 26 \cdot 3 = 78$$
because the three rows match in exactly one of the 27 columns.

These properties lead directly to the lemma:

Lemma 1. *There is a polynomial time mapping g from 3DM-3 feasible solutions to 3-anonymity feasible solutions, such that if $M' \subseteq M$ is a 3DM-3 feasible solution then $C_{3DM}(M') = 27 \cdot C_{3ANON}(g(M'))$.*

The proof of Lemma 1 can be found in the full version of the paper [4].

It remains for us to show that the above reduction is in fact an L-reduction. Let I be a Max 3DM-3 instance, with corresponding 3-Anonymity instance $f(I)$, and set $\alpha = \frac{1}{27}, \beta = 27$. Now by Lemma 1

$$OPT(f(I)) = \frac{1}{27} OPT(I) \leq \alpha OPT(I)$$

so that condition (1) of an L-reduction holds. Similarly, if we have a solution of $f(I)$ of cost c_2, then again by Lemma 1 we can quickly compute a solution to I of cost $c_1 = 27c_2$. Therefore,

$$|OPT(I) - c_1| = |27OPT(f(I)) - 27c_2| = \beta|OPT(f(I)) - c_2|$$

so that condition (2) also holds. □

To complement the above bad news, we now give an efficient algorithm for optimal k-anonymity when the number of attributes and the size of the alphabet are both small. Along the way, we also give an algorithm for the general k-anonymity problem that runs in about 4^n time.

A naive algorithm for k-anonymity would take an exorbitant amount of time, trying all possible partitions of n rows into groups with cardinality between k and $2k-1$. We can reduce this greatly using a divide-and-conquer recursion.

Reminder of Theorem 3. *For every $k > 2$, k-ANONYMITY can be solved in $O(4^n poly(n))$ time, where n is the total number of rows in the database.*

Proof. Interpret our k-anonymity instance S as a multiset of n vectors drawn from $|\Sigma|^\ell$. Define $S_k = \{T : T \subseteq S, |T| \in [\frac{n}{2}, \frac{n}{2} + 2k]\}$. That is, S_k contains all multisubsets which have approximately $n/2$ elements. Then

$$Cost_k(S) = argmin_{T \in S_k} \left[Cost_k(S - T) + Cost_k(T)\right], \qquad (1)$$

where $Cost_k(S)$ is the cost of the optimal k-anonymous solution for S. Equation (1) holds because (without loss of generality) any k-anonymized group of rows in a database is at most $2k-1$, so we can always partition the k-anonymized groups of a database into two multisets where their cardinalities are in the interval $[n/2 - 2k, n/2 + 2k]$.

Suppose we compute the optimal k-anonymity solution by evaluating equation (1) recursively, for all eligible multisubsets T. In the base case when $|S| \in [k, 2k-1]$, we add a minimum number of stars that make all rows in S identical, and return that solution.

We can simply enumerate all 2^n possible subcollections of rows in S to produce all possible T in equation (1). The time recurrence of the resulting algorithm is

$$T(n) \leq 2^{n+1} \cdot T(n/2 + 2k) + 2^n.$$

This recurrence solves to $T(n) \leq O(4^n \cdot \text{poly}(n))$ for constant k. □

Reminder of Theorem 4. *Let ℓ be the number of attributes in a database, let c be the size of its alphabet, and let n be the number of rows. Then k-ANONYMITY can be solved in $2^{O(k^2(2c)^\ell)} + O(n\ell)$ time.*

If ℓ and c are constants then there are at most c^ℓ possible rows. To specify a group G of k-anonymized rows we write $G = \langle r', t\rangle$ where t is the number of times the anonymized row r' occurs in the group. We can think of a k-anonymous solution as a partition of the rows into such anonymized groups. The following lemma will be useful for our algorithm.

Lemma 2. *Suppose that our database D contained at least $k(2k-1)2^\ell$ copies of a row r. Then the optimal k-anonymity solution must contain a group containing only row r, i.e. $G = \langle r, t\rangle$ where $t \geq k$.*

Proof. Suppose for contradiction that D contains at least $k(2k-1)2^\ell$ copies of row r, but that the optimal solution did not contain a group $G = \langle r, t\rangle$. Without loss of generality we can assume $k \le t \le 2k-1$ for each group, since larger groups could be divided into two groups without increasing the cost. Therefore, we must have at least $k2^\ell$ groups of the form $\langle r', t\rangle$ which contain the row r. Notice that each attribute of r' either matches r or is a $\star$. Hence there are at most 2^ℓ possible values of r'. By the pigeonhole principle there must be at least k groups $G_i = \langle r', t_i\rangle$ containing r where the anonymized rows r' are all identical. Note r' must contain at least one star, since we assumed there was no group of the form $\langle r, t\rangle$. Merge the groups G_i into one big group $G = \langle r', \Sigma_{i=1}^k t_i\rangle$ at no extra cost. Each of the original k groups contained at least one copy of the row r, so we can split G into two groups $\langle r, k\rangle$ and $\langle r', \left(\Sigma_{i=1}^k t_i\right) - k\rangle$ while saving at least k stars. Hence, our original solution was not optimal, a contradiction. □

For each row r, define $Index(r)$ to be a unique index between 0 and $c^l - 1$, by interpreting r as an ℓ-digit number in base c. Using Lemma 2, the following algorithm can be used to obtain a *kernelization* of k-Anonymity, in the sense of parameterized complexity [10].

Algorithm 1. k-anonymize a database D with small alphabet and attributes

Require: $rowCount[i] = |\{r \in D \mid Index(r) = i\}|$
Require: c, ℓ small
  $T \leftarrow k(2k-1)2^\ell$
  for Row $r \in D$ **do**
    $i \leftarrow Index(r)$
    if $rowCount[i] \ge T$ **then**
      print "$\langle r, k\rangle$" {By Lemma 2}
      $rowCount[i] \leftarrow rowCount[i] - k$
    end if
  end for
  {Now $\forall i$, $rowCount[i] < T$, so there are at most $k(2k)2^\ell(c^\ell) = k(2k)(2c)^\ell$ rows remaining}

Lemma 3. *Algorithm 1 runs in $O(n\ell)$ time on a database D and outputs a database D' with at most $O(k^2(2c)^\ell)$ rows, with the property that an optimal k-anonymization for D' can be extended to an optimal k-anonymization for D in $O(n\ell)$ time.*

That is, for the parameter $k+c+\ell$, the k-anonymity problem is not only fixed parameter tractable, but can also be kernelized in linear time.

Proof. (Sketch) By implementing rowCount as a hash table, each $Index(r)$ and lookup operation takes $O(\ell)$ time. Hence, the initialization takes $O(n\ell)$ time as does the loop. By Lemma 2 there must be an optimal k-anonymity solution containing $\langle r, t\rangle$ with $t \ge k$, when r occurs at least $k(2k-1)2^\ell$ times in D'. Therefore, if r occurs at least $k(2k)2^\ell > k + k(2k-1)2^\ell$ times in D then there is an optimal k-anonymity solution which contains the groups $\langle r, k\rangle$ and $\langle r, t\rangle$, so adding back k copies of row r to D' does not change the optimal k-anonymization, except for the extra $\langle r, k\rangle$ group. □

Proof of Theorem 4. By Lemma 3, Algorithm 1 takes an arbitrary k-anonymity instance D and reduces it to a new instance D' with $m \leq k(2k)(2c)^{\ell}$ rows in time $O(n\ell)$. We can then apply Theorem 3 to k-anonymize the instance D' in time $O(4^m \cdot \text{poly}(m))$. The total running time is $2^{O(k^2(2c)^{\ell})} + O(n\ell)$. □

5 Conclusion

We have demonstrated the hardness and feasibility of several methods used in database privacy, settling several open problems on the topic. The upshot is that most of these problems are difficult to solve optimally, even in very special cases; however in some interesting cases these problems can be solved faster. Several interesting open questions address possible ways around this intractability:

- To what degree can the hard problems be approximately solved? For example, the best known approximation algorithm for k-anonymity, given by Park and Shim [15], suppresses no more than $O(\log k)$ times the optimal number of entries. Could better approximation ratios be achieved when the number of attributes is small?
- The best known running time for Simplex Matching is $O(n^3 + n^2m^2)$ steps [3]. Here, n is the number of nodes and m is the number of hyperedges in the hypergraph. In our algorithm for 2-anonymity, n is also the number of rows in the database while $m = \binom{n}{3} = O(n^3)$ because we add a hyperedge for every triples. Hence our algorithm for 2-Anonymity has running time $O(n^8)$. Can this exponent be reduced to a more practical running time?

Acknowledgements. We thank Manuel Blum, Lenore Blum and Anupam Gupta for their help and guidance during this work.

References

1. Aggarwal, G., Feder, T., Kenthapadi, K., Motwani, R., Panigrahy, R., Thomas, D., Zhu, A.: Anonymizing tables. In: Eiter, T., Libkin, L. (eds.) ICDT 2005. LNCS, vol. 3363, pp. 246–258. Springer, Heidelberg (2004)
2. Agrawal, R., Srikant, R.: Privacy-preserving data mining. ACM SIGMOD Rec. 29(2), 439–450 (2000)
3. Anshelevich, E., Karagiozova, A.: Terminal backup, 3D matching, and covering cubic graphs. In: Proceedings of the 39th ACM Symposium on Theory of Computing, pp. 391–400 (2007)
4. Blocki, J., Williams, R.: Resolving the Complexity of Some Data Privacy Problems. arXiv:1004.3811 (2010)
5. Bonizzoni, P., Della Vedova, G., Dondi, R.: The k-anonymity problem is hard. In: Gębala, M. (ed.) FCT 2009. LNCS, vol. 5699, pp. 26–37. Springer, Heidelberg (2009)
6. Chakaravarthy, V., Pandit, V., Sabharwal, Y.: On the Complexity of the k-Anonymization Problem. arXiv:1004.4729 (2010)

7. Dor, D., Tarsi, M.: Graph decomposition is NPC - A complete proof of Holyer's conjecture. In: Proceedings of the 24th ACM Symposium on Theory of Computing, pp. 252–263 (1992)
8. Dwork, C.: Differential privacy. In: Bugliesi, M., Preneel, B., Sassone, V., Wegener, I. (eds.) ICALP 2006. LNCS, vol. 4052, pp. 1–12. Springer, Heidelberg (2006)
9. Evans, P., Chaytor, R., Wareham, T.: Fixed-parameter tractability of anonymizing data by suppressing entries. Journal of Combinatorial Optimization 18(4), 362–375 (2009)
10. Flum, J., Grohe, M.: Parameterized complexity theory. Springer, New York (2006)
11. Kann, V.: Maximum bounded 3-dimensional matching is MAX SNP-complete. Information Processing Letters 37(1), 27–35 (1991)
12. Machanavajjhala, A., Kifer, D., Gehrke, J., Venkitasubramaniam, M.: L-diversity: Privacy beyond k-anonymity. ACM Transactions on Knowledge Discovery from Data 1(1) (2007)
13. Meyerson, A., Williams, R.: On the complexity of optimal K-anonymity. In: Proceedings of the 23rd ACM SIGMOD-SIGACT-SIGART Symposium on Principles of Database Systems, pp. 223–228 (2004)
14. Papadimitriou, C., Yannakakis, M.: Optimization, approximation, and complexity classes. In: Proceedings of the 20th ACM Symposium on Theory of Computing, pp. 229–234 (1988)
15. Park, H., Shim, K.: Approximate algorithms for K-anonymity. In: Proceedings of the ACM SIGMOD International Conference on Management of Data, pp. 67–78 (2007)
16. Samarati, P.: Protecting respondents' identities in microdata release. IEEE Transactions on Knowledge and Data Engineering, 1010–1027 (2001)
17. Sweeney, L.: k-anonymity: a model for protecting privacy. International Journal on Uncertainty, Fuzziness and Knowledge-based Systems 10(5), 557–570 (2002)

Private and Continual Release of Statistics

T.-H. Hubert Chan[1], Elaine Shi[2], and Dawn Song[3]

[1] The University of Hong Kong
[2] PARC
[3] UC Berkeley

Abstract. We ask the question – *how can websites and data aggregators continually release updated statistics, and meanwhile preserve each individual user's privacy?* Given a stream of 0's and 1's, we propose a differentially private continual counter that outputs at every time step the approximate number of 1's seen thus far. Our counter construction has error that is only poly-log in the number of time steps. We can extend the basic counter construction to allow websites to continually give top-k and hot items suggestions while preserving users' privacy.

1 Introduction

Websites such as online retailers, search engines and social networks commonly publish aggregate statistics about their users to realize valuable social and economic utilities. Moreover, the published statistics are continually updated over time as new data arrive. Such practices are ubiquitous and we name a few examples below. Sites such as Amazon, IMDB, Delicious and Flickr recommend popular items to users to enhance their browsing experience and engage their interests. Search engines such as Google and Yahoo help a user to auto-complete her search query by suggesting the most frequent search terms matching the prefix specified by the user. During political campaigns, websites survey the population and continually update the support rates for candidates.

Releasing aggregate information about users may seem harmless at first glance. However, previous work has shown that such statistical disclosures can expose sensitive information about an individual user [3, 11]. In particular, sites that continually update the published statistics over time can give even more leverage to the adversary and result in more severe privacy leakage [1].

In this paper, we ask the question – *how can we guarantee the users' privacy when a website must continually publish new statistics as new data arrive?* Independent from our work, Dwork *et.al.* also consider essentially the same problem, and they phrase the problem as *"differential privacy under continual observation"* [6, 9, 10].

The setting we consider is different from the traditional setting in which differential privacy was studied. The traditional setting assumes a static database, and a curator who must answer k interactive queries or publish some sanitized statistics of the database non-interactively. In our setting, the database is dynamic and evolves over time, and a mechanism must update the published statistics as new data items arrive. Therefore, traditional differentially private mechanisms either fail to apply directly to our setting, or result in an unsatisfactory loss in terms of utility or privacy if applied naively.

S. Abramsky et al. (Eds.): ICALP 2010, Part II, LNCS 6199, pp. 405–417, 2010.

1.1 Contributions

Differentially private continual counter with poly-log error. We consider the *continual counting problem*. Assume that the input stream $\sigma \in \{0,1\}^{\mathbb{N}}$ is a sequence of bits. The bit $\sigma(t)$ at time $t \in \mathbb{N}$ may denote whether an event of interest occurred at time t, e.g., whether a user purchased an item at time t. At every time step $t \in \mathbb{N}$, the mechanism must output an approximate count of the number of 1's seen thus far.

We design an ϵ-differentially private continual counter with small error. Specifically, for each $t \in \mathbb{N}$, with probability at least $1 - \delta$, we guarantee $O(\frac{1}{\epsilon} \cdot (\log t)^{1.5} \cdot \log \frac{1}{\delta})$ error[1]. In an independent work by Dwork *et.al.* [9], they also show a similar upper bound of $O(\frac{1}{\epsilon} \cdot (\log t)^{1.5})$ (omitting the δ term). The above upper bound is almost tight, since Dwork *et.al.* [9] show that any ϵ-differentially private mechanism will for some stream, with probability at least δ, make an error of at least $\Omega(\frac{1}{\epsilon}(\log T + \log \frac{1}{\delta}))$ at some time before T.

Our mechanism achieves *time unboundedness*, i.e., the mechanism does not require a priori knowledge of an upper bound on the time for which it will run, and provides guarantees even when it is run indefinitely. This represents an improvement over the work by Dwork *et.al.* [6] – their mechanism requires a priori knowledge of an upper bound on the number of time steps.

Pan privacy. Dwork *et.al.* first introduced the notion of pan privacy [6, 10]. A mechanism is pan privacy if it can preserve differential privacy even when an adversary can observe snapshots of the mechanism's internal states, e.g., in subpoenas. We show how to modify our mechanism to achieve pan privacy, without incurring any loss in the asymptotic guarantees (Section 5).

Applications. Our continual counter construction has immediate practical applications. As mentioned earlier, it is a common practice for websites to suggest to users the most popular movies, news items or photos. We show how websites can continually make such top-k or hot items suggestions in a differentially private manner. Due to limited space, we describe applications in the full version of the paper [18].

The counter is also an important primitive in numerous data streaming algorithms [2, 14, 16]. Our differentially private continual counter is an initial step towards designing a broad class of streaming algorithms that continually report outputs over time.

1.2 Related Work

Most closely related work. Independent from our work, Dwork *et.al.* show a similar result in a recent paper [9]. They also construct a differentially private continual counter with error $O(\frac{1}{\epsilon} \cdot (\log t)^{1.5})$ where t is the number of timesteps. Moreover, they show a lower bound of $\Omega(O(\frac{1}{\epsilon} \cdot (\log t))$, indicating that the upper bound is almost tight. A preliminary version of the result was revealed at the SODA'10 conference [6] in an

[1] For large values of t, we can actually get a better bound $O(\frac{1}{\epsilon} \cdot (\log t)^{1.5} \cdot \sqrt{\log \frac{1}{\delta}})$. To get a high probability statement, we can set $\delta := \frac{1}{\mathrm{poly}(t)}$ and the corresponding error becomes $O((\log t)^2/\epsilon)$.

invited talk by Dwork. The preliminary result contains a slightly looser upper bound – a differentially private continual counter with error square root in the number of 1's seen thus far.

Dwork, Naor, Pitassi and Rothblum [10] recently propose the notion of pan privacy, i.e., how to achieve differential privacy even in the presence of intrusions, in which the adversary is allowed access to the mechanism's internal states. Dwork *et.al.* used the notion of pan privacy in the continual counter mechanism [6, 9], and showed how to make their counter mechanism resilient against a single unannounced intrusion. Inspired by their techniques, we also convert our mechanism to a pan private version that is immune to a single unannounced intrusion or multiple afterwards announced intrusions.

Differential privacy in the traditional setting. In the traditional setting, a trusted curator who holds a large data set must respond to queries *interactively* or publish sanitized statistics about the data *non-interactively*. The notion of differential privacy was first proposed and studied by Dwork *et.al.* [4, 8]. An extensive literature has since emerged, studying the different tradeoffs between utility and privacy. To better understand the motivation and state-of-the-art of this line of research, we recommend the readers to these excellent survey papers by Dwork [5, 7].

Researchers have also applied theoretical results in differential privacy to real-world applications. For example, McSherry and Mironov show how to build privacy into the Netflix database published for the Netflix contest [15]. Korolova *et.al.* show how to release search logs and click logs privately [13].

Attacks against privacy. A complementary line of research is attacks against privacy. Narayanan *et.al.* show how to de-anonymize the Netflix data set [17]. Jones *et.al.* show how to break the privacy of query log bundles [12]. More relevant to this work, Calandrino *et.al.* [1] recently demonstrate that by observing continual updates from websites such as Amazon over a period of time, an adversary can learn individual user behavior at a fine level of granularity. Our work is partly inspired by the problem they expose.

2 Preliminaries

2.1 Definitions

We consider streams of 0's and 1's. Formally, a stream $\sigma \in \{0,1\}^{\mathbb{N}}$ is a bit-string of countable length, where $\mathbb{N} := \{1, 2, 3, \ldots\}$ is the set of positive integers. Specifically, $\sigma(t) \in \{0,1\}$ denotes the bit at time $t \in \mathbb{N}$. We write $[T] := \{1, 2, 3, \ldots, T\}$ and $\sigma_T \in \{0,1\}^T$ is the length T prefix of the stream σ. We will use the term *item* to refer to a bit in the stream.

At every time t, we wish to output the number of 1's that have arrived up to time t.

Definition 1 (Continual Counting Query). *Given a stream* $\sigma \in \{0,1\}^{\mathbb{N}}$, *the count for the stream is a mapping* $c_\sigma : \mathbb{N} \to \mathbb{Z}$ *such that for each* $t \in \mathbb{N}$, $c_\sigma(t) := \sum_{i=1}^{t} \sigma(i)$. *We write* c *instead of* c_σ *when there is no risk of ambiguity on the stream* σ *in question.*

We now formally define the notion of a continual counting mechanism which continually outputs the number of 1's seen thus far.

Definition 2 (Counting Mechanism). *A counting mechanism $\mathcal{M}$ takes a stream $\sigma \in \{0,1\}^{\mathbb{N}}$ and produces a (possibly randomized) mapping $\mathcal{M}(\sigma) : \mathbb{N} \to \mathbb{R}$. Moreover, for all $t \in \mathbb{N}$, $\mathcal{M}(\sigma)(t)$ is independent of all $\sigma(i)$'s for $i > t$. We can also view $\mathcal{M}(\sigma)$ as a point in $\mathbb{R}^{\mathbb{N}}$. When there is no risk of ambiguity on the stream σ in question, we drop the dependence on σ and use $\mathcal{M}(t)$ to mean $\mathcal{M}(\sigma)(t)$.*

Definition 3 (Time-bounded Mechanism). *A counting mechanism $\mathcal{M}$ is unbounded, if it accepts streams of indefinite lengths, i.e., given any stream σ, $\mathcal{M}(\sigma) \in \mathbb{R}^{\mathbb{N}}$. Given $T \in \mathbb{N}$, a mechanism $\mathcal{M}$ is T-bounded if it only accepts streams of lengths at most T and returns $\mathcal{M}(\sigma) \in \mathbb{R}^T$. In other words, the mechanism needs to know the value T in advance and only looks at the length T prefix of any given stream.*

We would like the mechanism to be useful, that is, its output should well approximate the true count at any point of time. We formally define the notion of utility below.

Definition 4 (Utility). *A counting mechanism $\mathcal{M}$ is (λ, δ)-useful at time t, if for any stream σ, with probability at least $1-\delta$, we have $|c_\sigma(t) - \mathcal{M}(\sigma)(t)| \leq \lambda$. Note that λ may be a function of δ and t.*

Intuitively, a mechanism is differentially private if it cannot be used to distinguish two streams that are almost the same. In other words, an adversary is unable to determine whether an event of interest took place or not by observing the output of the mechanism over time. For example, the adversary is unable to determine whether a user purchased an item at some time t.

Definition 5 (Differential Privacy). *Two streams σ and σ' are adjacent if they differ at exactly one time t. A counting mechanism $\mathcal{M}$ is ϵ-differentially private (or preserves ϵ-differential privacy) if for any adjacent streams σ and σ', and any measurable subset $S \subseteq \mathbb{R}^{\mathbb{N}}$ (or $S \subseteq \mathbb{R}^T$ for T-bounded mechanisms), $\Pr[\mathcal{M}(\sigma) \in S] \leq \exp(\epsilon) \cdot \Pr[\mathcal{M}(\sigma') \in S]$.*

2.2 Tools

In the design of differentially private mechanisms, the Laplace distribution is often used to introduce random noise [4, 8]. We use $\mathsf{Lap}(b)$ to denote the Laplace distribution with mean 0 and variance $2b^2$. Its probability density function is $x \mapsto \frac{1}{2b}\exp(-\frac{|x|}{b})$.

Dwork *et.al.* showed that if we mask the true answer of a query with Laplacian noise proportional to the sensitivity of the query function, such a mechanism preserves differential privacy for static databases [4, 8]. This is stated formally in the Fact 1.

Fact 1 (Laplace Distribution Maintains Differential Privacy). *Let $a, b \in \mathbb{R}$ and $|a - b| \leq \Delta$. Let $\gamma \sim \mathsf{Lap}(\frac{\Delta}{\epsilon})$ be a random variable having Laplace distribution. Then, for any measurable subset $S \subseteq \mathbb{R}$, $\Pr[a + \gamma \in S] \leq \exp(\epsilon) \cdot \Pr[b + \gamma \in S]$.*

In the constructions that we propose, the noise may not come from a single Laplace distribution, but rather is the sum of multiple independent Laplace distributions. We now derive a property of the sum of independent Laplace distributions.

Lemma 1 (Sum of Independent Laplace Distributions). *Suppose γ_i's are independent random variables, where each γ_i has Laplace distribution* $\mathsf{Lap}(b_i)$. *Suppose* $Y := \sum_i \gamma_i$, *and* $b_M := \max_i b_i$. *Let* $\nu \geq \sqrt{\sum_i b_i^2}$ *and* $0 < \lambda < \frac{2\nu^2}{b_M}$. *Then,* $\Pr[Y > \lambda] \leq \exp(-\frac{\lambda^2}{8\nu^2})$.

The proof to Lemma 1 is a Chernoff-like argument using moment generating functions. We provide the detailed proof in the full version [18].

Corollary 1 (Measure Concentration). *Let* Y, ν, $\{b_i\}_i$ *and* b_M *be defined as in Lemma 1. Suppose* $0 < \delta < 1$ *and* $\nu > \max\{\sqrt{\sum_i b_i^2}, b_M\sqrt{2\ln\frac{2}{\delta}}\}$. *Then,* $\Pr[|Y| > \nu\sqrt{8\ln\frac{2}{\delta}}] \leq \delta$.

To simplify our presentation and improve readability, we choose $\nu := \sqrt{\sum_i b_i^2} \cdot \sqrt{2\ln\frac{2}{\delta}}$ *and use the following slightly weaker result: with probability at least* $1-\delta$, *the quantity* $|Y|$ *is at most* $O(\sqrt{\sum_i b_i^2}\log\frac{1}{\delta})$.

3 Time-Bounded Counting Mechanisms

In this section, we describe mechanisms that require a priori knowledge of an upper bound on time. In Section 4, we show how to remove this requirement, and achieve unbounded counting mechanisms.

3.1 Simple Counting Mechanisms

To aid the understanding of our contributions and techniques, we first explain two simple constructions.

Simple Counting Mechanism I. The mechanism is given a stream $\sigma \in \{0,1\}^{\mathbb{N}}$, a differential privacy parameter $\epsilon > 0$, and an upper bound T on time. At each time step t, the mechanism samples a fresh independent random variable $\gamma_t \sim \mathsf{Lap}(\frac{1}{\epsilon})$, and releases $\alpha_t = c(t) + \gamma_t$, where $c(t)$ is the true count at time step t. It is not hard to see that the above mechanism is $O(T\epsilon)$-differentially private, and at each time step, the error is $O(\frac{1}{\epsilon})$ with high probability. Alternatively, one can substitute $\epsilon' = \epsilon/T$, and add much bigger noise $\sim \mathsf{Lap}(\frac{1}{\epsilon'})$ at every time step. In this way, we get ϵ differential privacy; however, now the error at each time step is $O(\frac{T}{\epsilon})$.

Simple mechanism I is a straightforward extension of the Laplace mechanism proposed by Dwork *et.al.* [4, 8]. Basically, at every time step, the mechanism answers a new query, and randomizes the answer with fresh independent noise. The down side of this approach is that the privacy loss grows linearly with respect to the number of queries, which is t in our setting.

Simple Counting Mechanism II. In essence, Simple Counting Mechanism II produces a "sanitized" stream by adding independent Laplacian noise to each item in the stream. Suppose the mechanism is given a stream $\sigma \in \{0,1\}^{\mathbb{N}}$ and a differential privacy parameter $\epsilon > 0$. For each time step $t \in \mathbb{N}$, the mechanism samples an independent random variable γ_t with Laplace distribution $\mathsf{Lap}(\frac{1}{\epsilon})$. Define $\alpha_t := \sigma(t) + \gamma_t$. Then, the mechanism $\mathcal{M}$ gives the output $\mathcal{M}(\sigma)(t) := \sum_{i \leq t} \alpha_i$ at time t. A similar idea has been proposed as a survey technique by Warner [19].

It is not hard to see that Simple Mechanism II can be implemented with $O(1)$ words of memory and is unbounded and ϵ-differentially private. We use Corollary 1 to analyze the utility of the mechanism. Fix some time T. Observe that $\mathcal{M}(\sigma)(T) - c_\sigma(T) = \sum_{t \leq T} \gamma_t =: Y$. In this case, all $\gamma_t \sim \mathsf{Lap}(\frac{1}{\epsilon})$. Hence, all $b_t := \frac{1}{\epsilon}$.

Theorem 1. *Let* $0 < \delta < 1$, $\epsilon > 0$. *the Simple Counting Mechanism II is* ϵ*-differentially private, and is* $(O(\frac{\sqrt{t}}{\epsilon} \cdot \log \frac{1}{\delta}), \delta)$*-useful at any time* $t \in \mathbb{N}$.

3.2 Intuition

We will describe the Two-Level Counting Mechanism and the Binary Counting Mechanism. Informally, the Two-Level Mechanism achieves ϵ-differential privacy and $O(t^{\frac{1}{4}})$ error. The Binary Mechanism is a further improvement, and achieves $O((\log t)^{1.5})$ error while maintaining ϵ-differential privacy. We now explain the intuitions for the Two-Level Mechanism and the Binary Mechanism.

A framework for describing mechanisms. We will describe our counting mechanisms using a common framework. Recall that the job of the mechanism is to output an approximate count at every time. However, from now on, we will think of our mechanisms as releasing noisy "p-sums" instead of counts. One can think of p-sums as intermediate results from which an observer can estimate the count at every time step herself.

Definition 6 (p-sum). *A* p-sum *is a partial sum of consecutive items. Let* $1 \leq i \leq j$. *We use the notation* $\Sigma[i,j] := \sum_{k=i}^{j} \sigma(k)$ *to denote a partial sum involving items* i *through* j.

Furthermore, once we add noise to a p-sum, we obtain a noisy p-sum denoted as $\widehat{\Sigma}$.

The mechanisms we consider will release noisy versions of these p-sums as new items arrive. When an observer sees the sequence of p-sums, she can compute an estimate for the count at each time step, in particular, by summing up an appropriate selection of p-sums. For example, if an observer sees a noisy p-sum $\widehat{\Sigma}[1,k] = \Sigma[1,k] + \textit{noise}$ released at time step k, and another noisy p-sum $\widehat{\Sigma}[k+1,t] = \Sigma[k+1,t] + \textit{noise}$ released at time step t, then she can estimate the count at time t by summing up these two noisy p-sums, i.e., $\widehat{\Sigma}[1,k] + \widehat{\Sigma}[k+1,t]$. Notice that the observer needs to be able to do this not only for a specific time t, but also for every time step in $\mathbb{N}$.

Now we rethink Simple Mechanism I using this framework. The noisy p-sums released are noisy versions of the true count for each time step, that is, $\{\widehat{\Sigma}[1,t] = \Sigma[1,t] + \textit{noise}\}_{1 \leq t \leq T}$, where $\Sigma[1,t] = c(t)$ is the true count at time t. In this case, the $\widehat{\Sigma}[1,t]$ itself is the estimated count at time t; and therefore can be regarded as a sum of noisy p-sums (with only one summand). Notice that each item $\sigma(t)$ appears in $O(T)$ of these p-sums. This means that when you flip an item in the incoming stream, $O(T)$ of these p-sums will be affected – this is the reason why the privacy loss is linear in T.

Now consider Simple Mechanism II. The noisy p-sums released are noisy versions of each item $\widehat{\Sigma}_t = \Sigma[t,t] + \textit{noise}$, where $\Sigma[t,t] = \sigma(t)$ is the t-th item itself. In this

Table 1. Informal intuition for the Two-Level Mechanism and the Binary Mechanism. For simplicity, we omit the parameters ϵ and δ from the bounds.

Mechanism	**Each item appears in ? p-sums**	**Each count is the sum of ? p-sums**	**Asymptotic error** (while maintaining ϵ diff. priv.)
Simple I	$O(T)$	$O(1)$	$O(T)$
Simple II	$O(1)$	$O(T)$	$O(\sqrt{T})$
Two-Level	$O(1)$	$O(\sqrt{T})$	$O(T^{\frac{1}{4}})$
Binary	$O(\log T)$	$O(\log T)$	$O((\log T)^{1.5})$

case, each item appears in only one p-sum, however, each count is the sum of $O(T)$ p-sums. More specifically, to estimate the count at time t, the observer sums up t noisy p-sums $\widehat{\Sigma}_1, \ldots \widehat{\Sigma}_t$. As each noisy p-sum contains some fresh independent noise, the noises add up. In fact, over t time steps, the error would be $O(\sqrt{t})$ with high probability.

Observation 1. *(Informal.) Suppose a mechanism $\mathcal{M}$ adds $\mathsf{Lap}(\frac{1}{\epsilon})$ noise to every p-sum before releasing it. In $\mathcal{M}$, each item in the stream appears in at most x p-sums, and each estimated count is the sum of at most y p-sums. Then, the mechanism $\mathcal{M}$ achieves $x \cdot \epsilon$ differential privacy. Moreover, from Corollary 1, the error is $O(\frac{\sqrt{y}}{\epsilon})$ with high probability. Alternatively, to achieve ϵ-differential privacy, one can scale appropriately by having $\epsilon' = \frac{\epsilon}{x}$. Now if the mechanism instead adds $\mathsf{Lap}(\frac{1}{\epsilon'})$ noise to each p-sum, we achieve ϵ-differential privacy, and $O(\frac{x\sqrt{y}}{\epsilon})$ error with high probability.*

Goal. From the above analysis, it appears that an inherent tension exists between utility (i.e., small error) and privacy, and our challenge is how to strike a balance between the two conflicting goals. We would like to achieve the following goals.

- *Each item appears in a small number of* p-sums . Intuitively, this limits the influence of any item and guarantees small privacy loss. More specifically, when one flips an item in the incoming stream, not too many p-sums will be affected.
- *Each count is a sum of a small number of* p-sums . Each noisy p-sum contains some noise, and the noises add up as one sums up several noisy p-sums. If each output count is the sum of a small number of noisy p-sums, the accumulation of noises is bounded. In this way, we can achieve small error.

3.3 Two-Level Counting Mechanism

We can use the p-sum idea to construct a Two-level Mechanism. As this is not our main construction, we give an overview of the Two-level mechanism below and leave details of the construction to the full version [18]. The basic idea is to release two types of noisy p-sums: 1) a noisy p-sum for every item, that is, $\widehat{\Sigma}[1,1]$, $\widehat{\Sigma}[2,2]$, ..., $\widehat{\Sigma}[T,T]$ where T is an upper bound on the number of time steps; and 2) a noisy p-sum for each contiguous block of $B = \Theta(\sqrt{T})$ items, namely, $\widehat{\Sigma}[kB+1,(k+1)B]$ for $k \geq 0$. It is not hard to see that each item appears in only 2 p-sums, and each count can be expressed as the sum of $O(\sqrt{T})$ p-sums. According to Observation 1, such a mechanism is 2ϵ-differentially private, and achieves $O(T^{\frac{1}{4}}/\epsilon)$ error with high probability.

3.4 Binary Counting Mechanism

We could extend the idea of the Two-Level Counting Mechanism to a Multi-level Counting Mechanism, and compute the optimal number of levels given an upper bound on time. However, we take a better approach called the Binary Mechanism. The idea is that at any time t, the counting mechanism internally groups the items that have arrived to form p-sums of different sizes. The precise grouping of the items depends on the binary representation of the number t – hence the name Binary Mechanism.

Given any number $t \in N$, let $\mathsf{Bin}_i(t) \in \{0,1\}$ be the ith digit in the binary representation of t, where $\mathsf{Bin}_0(t)$ is the least significant digit. Hence, $t = \sum_i \mathsf{Bin}_i(t) \cdot 2^i$. Informally, if $\mathsf{Bin}_i(t) = 1$, then there is a p-sum involving 2^i items. We formally describe the Binary Mechanism in Figure 1.

Input: A time upper bound T, a privacy parameter ϵ, and a stream $\sigma \in \{0,1\}^T$.
Output: At each time step t, output estimate $\mathcal{B}(t)$.
Initialization: Each α_i and $\widehat{\alpha_i}$ are (implicitly) initialized to 0.
$\epsilon' \leftarrow \epsilon / \log T$
for $t \leftarrow 1$ **to** T **do**

Express t in binary form: $t = \sum_j \mathsf{Bin}_j(t) \cdot 2^j$.
Let $i := \min\{j : \mathsf{Bin}_j(t) \neq 0\}$.

$$\alpha_i \leftarrow \sum_{j<i} \alpha_j + \sigma(t) \quad (1)$$

// previous value (if any) of α_i is overwritten
// $\alpha_i = \Sigma[t-2^i+1, t]$ is a p-sum of involving 2^i items
for $j \leftarrow 0$ **to** $i-1$ **do**

$$\alpha_j \leftarrow 0, \quad \widehat{\alpha_j} \leftarrow 0$$

end

$$\widehat{\alpha_i} \leftarrow \alpha_i + \mathsf{Lap}(\frac{1}{\epsilon'}) \quad (2)$$

// $\widehat{\alpha_i}$ is the noisy p-sum $\widehat{\Sigma}[t-2^i+1, t]$
Output the estimate at time t**:**

$$\mathcal{B}(t) \leftarrow \sum_{j:\mathsf{Bin}_j(t)=1} \widehat{\alpha_j} \quad (3)$$

end

Fig. 1. Binary Mechanism $\mathcal{B}$

Binary mechanism: the p-sum *view.* The best way to understand the Binary Mechanism is to think in terms of the p-sum framework described earlier. Basically, instead of outputting the estimated counts, the mechanism could equivalently release a sequence of noisy p-sums which provide sufficient information for an observer to estimate the count at each time step t. In particular, at any time t, the Binary Mechanism "releases" a new noisy p-sum $\widehat{\Sigma}[t - 2^i + 1, t]$ of length 2^i and ending at position t, where i denotes the position of the least significant non-zero bit in the binary representation of t. This p-sum and its noisy version are (temporarily) saved in the variables α_i and $\widehat{\alpha}_i$.

It remains to specify how to estimate the count at each time step from previously "released" noisy p-sums. Let $i_1 < i_2 < \ldots < i_m$ denote the positions of non-zero bits in the binary representation of t. It is not hard to see that the count at time t is the sum of m p-sums of size $2^{i_1}, 2^{i_2}, \ldots, 2^{i_m}$ respectively. They correspond to the values of variables $\alpha_{i_1}, \ldots, \alpha_{i_m}$ maintained by the mechanism at time t. Specifically, the p-sums are 1) α_{i_1}, of the most recent 2^{i_1} items; 2) α_{i_2}, of the preceding 2^{i_2} items; 3) α_{i_3}, of the further preceding 2^{i_3} items and so on.

In the full version [18], we show that the Binary Mechanism can be implemented with small memory, as the mechanism can reuse the variables α's and $\widehat{\alpha}$'s.

Differential Privacy. Consider an item arriving at $t \in [T]$. We analyze which of the p-sums would be affected if $\sigma(t)$ is flipped. It is not hard to see that the item $\sigma(t)$ can be in at most $\log T$ p-sums. In particular, it can be in at most 1 p-sum of size 2^j, where $j \leq \log T$. Observe that each noisy p-sum maintains $\frac{\epsilon}{\log T}$-differential privacy by Fact 1. Hence, we can conclude the ϵ-differential privacy of the Binary Mechanism.

Theorem 2 (Differential Privacy). *For $T \in \mathbb{N}$, the Binary Mechanism preserves T-bounded ϵ-differential privacy.*

Utility. We next consider the usefulness of the Binary Mechanism. Each estimated count $\mathcal{B}(t)$ is the sum of at most $\log T$ noisy p-sums, and each noisy p-sum contains fresh, independent Laplace noise $\mathsf{Lap}(\frac{\log T}{\epsilon})$. Therefore, the error at time t is the summation of at most $O(\log t)$ i.i.d. Laplace distributions $\mathsf{Lap}(\frac{\log T}{\epsilon})$. We use the Corollary 1 to conclude the mechanism's usefulness.

Theorem 3 (Utility). *For each $t \in [T]$, the T-bounded Binary Mechanism is $(O(\frac{1}{\epsilon}) \cdot (\log T) \cdot \sqrt{\log t} \cdot \log \frac{1}{\delta}, \delta)$-useful at time $t \in [T]$.*

4 Unbounded Counting Mechanisms

Previously, we mainly considered time-bounded mechanisms, i.e., the mechanism requires a priori knowledge of an upper bound on the time. We now describe how to remove this assumption and derive unbounded counting mechanisms.

We describe the Hybrid Mechanism which gives a generic way to convert any time-bounded mechanism $\mathcal{M}$ into an unbounded one by running two mechanisms in parallel: (1) an unbounded mechanism that only outputs counts at time steps t being powers of 2; (2) a time-bounded mechanism $\mathcal{M}$ to take care of items arriving at time steps between successive powers of 2.

Logarithmic Counting Mechanism. First, consider an unbounded mechanism which only reports the estimated counts at sparse intervals, in particular, when t is a power of 2. We would expect such a mechanism to have better guarantees than one that has to report at every time step.

So what do we do when t is not a power of 2? We know the approximate count $\widehat{c}_1$ for the time period $[1, T]$ where $T = 2^k$ for some non-negative integer k. Suppose we also know the approximate count $\widehat{c}_2$ for the time period $[T+1, t]$ where $T + 1 \leq t \leq 2T$. Then we can estimate the count at time t as $\widehat{c}_1 + \widehat{c}_2$. Therefore, it remains for us to count the 1's between $[T, t]$ for any $t \in [T + 1, 2T]$, We can simply apply a T-bounded mechanism (e.g., the Binary Mechanism) for this task.

We now design an unbounded mechanism called the *Logarithmic Mechanism* which reports the count only when the time t is a power of 2.

```
Input: Differential privacy parameter ε, and a stream σ ∈ {0,1}^ℕ.
Output: ∀k ∈ ℤ, at time t = 2^k, output estimate ℒ(t).
Initialization: β ← 0.
foreach t ∈ ℕ do
    β ← β + σ(t)
    if t = 2^k for some k ∈ ℤ then
        β ← β + Lap(1/ε)
        Output ℒ(t) ← β
    end
end
```

Fig. 2. Logarithmic Mechanism $\mathcal{L}$

The idea for the Logarithmic Mechanism is quite simple. The mechanism internally keeps a value β which is initialized to 0. β is used to keep track of the approximate count at any point of time. As an item comes in, its value is added to β. At t equal to a power of 2, the mechanism adds fresh randomness to the value β (on top of randomness previously added), and outputs β.

If t is a power of 2, it is clear that the accumulated error at time t is a sum of $O(\log t)$ independent Laplace distributions $\mathsf{Lap}(\frac{1}{\epsilon})$. Hence, we have the following guarantee from Corollary 1.

Theorem 4. *The Logarithmic Counting Mechanism is unbounded, preserves ϵ-differential privacy and is $(O(\frac{1}{\epsilon}) \cdot \sqrt{\log t} \cdot \log \frac{1}{\delta}, \delta)$-useful at time $t = 2^k$ for some $k \geq 0$.*

Logarithmic Mechanism: the p-sum *view.* The Logarithmic Mechanism also has a p-sum interpretation. Equivalently, one can think of it as releasing the noisy p-sums $\widehat{\alpha}_0 = \widehat{\Sigma}[1, 1]$, as well as $\widehat{\alpha}_k = \widehat{\Sigma}[2^{k-1} + 1, 2^k]$ for every $k \geq 1$, Now an observer can estimate the count at time $t = 2^k$ as $\sum_{i=0}^{k} \widehat{\alpha}_i$.

Hybrid Mechanism. We combine the Logarithmic Mechanism and a time-bounded counting mechanism to process a given stream σ. We run one copy of $\frac{\epsilon}{2}$-differentially private Logarithmic Mechanism, which reports an approximate count when t is a power of 2. Suppose the Logarithmic Mechanism has reported count $\mathcal{L}(T)$ at $T = 2^k$ for some non-negative integer k. For time t in the range $T + 1 \leq t \leq 2T$, we run an

$\frac{\epsilon}{2}$-differentially private T-bounded counting mechanism denoted as $\mathcal{M}$ to count the number of 1's in the range $[T+1, t]$. We write $\tau = t - T$. At time t, let $\mathcal{M}(\tau)$ be the number of 1's in $[T+1, T+\tau]$ reported by the T-bounded counting mechanism $\mathcal{M}$. Then, the hybrid mechanism reports $\mathcal{L}(T) + \mathcal{M}(\tau)$ at time t.

Input: Differential privacy parameter ϵ, a stream $\sigma \in \{0,1\}^{\mathbb{N}}$, Logarithmic Mechanism $\mathcal{L}$, and a time-bounded mechanism $\mathcal{M}$.
Output: For each $t \in \mathbb{N}$, output estimate $\mathcal{H}(t)$.
Initialization: $T \leftarrow 1$.
Initiate the mechanism $\mathcal{L}$ with privacy parameter $\frac{\epsilon}{2}$ on stream σ.
foreach $t \in \mathbb{N}$ **do**
  Feed $\sigma(t)$ to mechanism $\mathcal{L}$.
  if $t = 2^k$ *for some* $k \in \mathbb{Z}$ **then**
    Output $\mathcal{H}(t) \leftarrow \mathcal{L}(t)$
    $T \leftarrow t$
    Initiate an instance of the T-bounded mechanism $\mathcal{M}_T$ with time upper bound T, privacy parameter $\frac{\epsilon}{2}$ and stream $\sigma^{(T)} \in \{0,1\}^T$, where $\sigma^{(T)}(\tau) := \sigma(\tau + T)$ for $\tau \in [1, T]$.
  else
    $\tau \leftarrow t - T$
    Feed $\sigma^{(T)}(\tau) := \sigma(t)$ to mechanism $\mathcal{M}_T$.
    Output $\mathcal{H}(t) \leftarrow \mathcal{L}(T) + \mathcal{M}_T(\tau)$
  end
end
// At time t, T is the largest power of 2 no bigger than t.
// $\sigma^{(T)}$ is the sub-stream of σ for the duration $[T+1, 2T]$.
// $\mathcal{M}_T$ is a time-bounded mechanism that runs for $[T+1, 2T]$.

Fig. 3. Hybrid Mechanism $\mathcal{H}$ (with Mechanism $\mathcal{M}$)

Theorem 5. *Assume that given any $\epsilon > 0$ and $0 < \delta < 1$, Logarithmic Mechanism $\mathcal{L}$ is ϵ-differentially private and is $(f(\epsilon, t, \delta), \delta)$-useful at time t. Similarly, assume that given any $\epsilon > 0$, the T-bounded mechanism $\mathcal{M}$ is ϵ-differentially private and is $(g(\epsilon, T, \tau, \delta), \frac{\delta}{2})$-useful at time $\tau \in [T]$, where g is monotonically increasing with T and τ. Then, the Hybrid Mechanism described above is unbounded, preserves ϵ-differential privacy, and is $(f(\frac{\epsilon}{2}, t, \frac{\delta}{2}) + g(\frac{\epsilon}{2}, t, t, \frac{\delta}{2}), \delta)$-useful at time t.*

The proof of Theorem 5 can be found in the full version [18].

Corollary 2. *If we instantiate the Hybrid Mechanism using the Binary Mechanism as the T-bounded mechanism, the resulting Hybrid Mechanism is unbounded, preserves ϵ-differential privacy, and is $(O(\frac{1}{\epsilon}) \cdot (\log t)^{1.5} \cdot \log \frac{1}{\delta}, \delta)$-useful at time t.*

For simplicity, in the remainder of the paper, when we refer to the Hybrid Mechanism, we mean the Hybrid Mechanism instantiated with the Binary Mechanism.

Hybrid Mechanism: the p-sum *view.* One can also interpret the Hybrid Mechanism naturally using the p-sum framework. Basically, one can equivalently think of the Hybrid Mechanism as releasing the union of the noisy p-sums of the Logarithmic Mechanism and the Binary Mechanism. From this set of noisy p-sums, an observer can compute the approximate count at every time step $t \in \mathbb{N}$.

5 Pan Privacy

Dwork *et.al.* formalized the notion of pan privacy [6, 10] to deal with intruders who can observe snapshots of the mechanism's internal states, e.g., in a subpoena. For mechanisms in the p-sum framework, we can apply techniques similar to those proposed in the work [6] to make them pan private against a single unannounced intrusion, with only a constant-factor loss in the error term. Furthermore, we extend the idea to construct pan private counting mechanisms resilient against multiple announced (afterwards) intrusions. The error scales with a square root factor on the number of intrusions made. We provide detailed definitions of pan privacy and constructions in the full version [18].

References

[1] Calandrino, J.A., Narayanan, A., Felten, E.W., Shmatikov, V.: Don't review that book: Privacy risks of collaborative filtering. Manuscript (2009)

[2] Demaine, E.D., López-Ortiz, A., Munro, J.I.: Frequency estimation of internet packet streams with limited space. In: Möhring, R.H., Raman, R. (eds.) ESA 2002. LNCS, vol. 2461, p. 348. Springer, Heidelberg (2002)

[3] Dinur, I., Nissim, K.: Revealing information while preserving privacy. In: PODS (2003)

[4] Dwork, C.: Differential privacy. In: Bugliesi, M., Preneel, B., Sassone, V., Wegener, I. (eds.) ICALP 2006. LNCS, vol. 4052, pp. 1–12. Springer, Heidelberg (2006)

[5] Dwork, C.: The differential privacy frontier. In: Reingold, O. (ed.) TCC 2009. LNCS, vol. 5444, pp. 496–502. Springer, Heidelberg (2009)

[6] Dwork, C.: Differential privacy in new settings. In: Invited presentation at ACM-SIAM Symposium on Discrete Algorithms, SODA (2010)

[7] Dwork, C.: A firm foundation for private data analysis. Communications of the ACM (2010)

[8] Dwork, C., McSherry, F., Nissim, K., Smith, A.: Calibrating noise to sensitivity in private data analysis. In: Halevi, S., Rabin, T. (eds.) TCC 2006. LNCS, vol. 3876, pp. 265–284. Springer, Heidelberg (2006)

[9] Dwork, C., Naor, M., Pitassi, T., Rothblum, G.N.: Differential privacy under continual observation. In: STOC (2010)

[10] Dwork, C., Naor, M., Pitassi, T., Rothblum, G.N., Yekhanin, S.: Pan-private streaming algorithms. In: Innovations in Computer Science, ISC (2010)

[11] Dwork, C., Yekhanin, S.: New efficient attacks on statistical disclosure control mechanisms. In: Wagner, D. (ed.) CRYPTO 2008. LNCS, vol. 5157, pp. 469–480. Springer, Heidelberg (2008)

[12] Jones, R., Kumar, R., Pang, B., Tomkins, A.: Vanity fair: privacy in querylog bundles. In: CIKM (2008)

[13] Korolova, A., Kenthapadi, K., Mishra, N., Ntoulas, A.: Releasing search queries and clicks privately. In: WWW (2009)

[14] Manku, G.S., Motwani, R.: Approximate frequency counts over data streams. In: VLDB (2002)
[15] McSherry, F., Mironov, I.: Differentially private recommender systems: building privacy into the netflix prize contenders. In: KDD (2009)
[16] Metwally, A., Agrawal, D., Abbadi, A.E.: Efficient computation of frequent and top-k elements in data streams. In: Eiter, T., Libkin, L. (eds.) ICDT 2005. LNCS, vol. 3363, pp. 398–412. Springer, Heidelberg (2004)
[17] Narayanan, A., Shmatikov, V.: Robust de-anonymization of large sparse datasets. In: IEEE Symposium on Security and Privacy (2008)
[18] Song, D., Hubert Chan, T.-H., Shi, E. Private and continual release of statistics (2010), http://eprint.iacr.org/2010/076.pdf
[19] Warner, S.L.: Randomized response: A survey technique for eliminating evasive answer bias. Journal of the American Statistical Association (1965)

Envy-Free Pricing in Multi-item Markets

Ning Chen[1] and Xiaotie Deng[2]

[1] Division of Mathematical Sciences, School of Physical and Mathematical Sciences, Nanyang Technological University, Singapore
ningc@ntu.edu.sg

[2] Department of Computer Science, City University of Hong Kong, Hong Kong
csdeng@cityu.edu.hk

Abstract. In this paper, we study the revenue maximization envy-free pricing in multi-item markets: there are m items and n potential buyers where each buyer is interested in acquiring one item. The goal is to determine allocations (a matching between buyers and items) and prices of all items to maximize the total revenue given that all buyers are envy-free.

We give a polynomial time algorithm to compute a revenue maximization envy-free pricing when every buyer evaluates at most two items a positive valuation, by reducing it to an instance of weighted independent set in a perfect graph and applying the Strong Perfect Graph Theorem. We complement our result by showing that the problem becomes NP-hard if some buyers are interested in at least three items.

Next we extend the model to allow buyers to demand a subset of consecutive items, motivated from TV advertising where advertisers are interested in different consecutive slots with different valuations and lengths. We show that the revenue maximization envy-free pricing in this setting can be computed in polynomial time.

1 Introduction

In a multi-item market [20,10], there are m homogeneous items and n potential buyers where each buyer i is interested in acquiring one item at different valuations $v_i(\cdot)$. As an output of the market, an allocation (i.e., a matching between buyers and items) and a price vector are specified; the goal of the market designer is to find allocation and price vectors to satisfy certain fairness conditions. *Walrasian market equilibrium* [21], one of the most classical economic goals, says that all buyers are envy-free for the given price vector and the market clears (i.e., all unallocated items are priced at zero). Walrasian equilibrium captures both the fairness condition for buyers and market clearing condition for the market from a global point of view. It is observed by Shapley and Shubik [20] that in multi-item settings, a Walrasian equilibrium always exists; later Demange, Gale and Sotomayor [10] propose a dynamic auction process that converges to an equilibrium. Multi-item markets are of particular importance nowadays due to huge applications in advertising markets.

While Walrasian equilibrium has long been recognized as an elegant tool and benchmark for the analysis of competitive markets in economics, it may not

S. Abramsky et al. (Eds.): ICALP 2010, Part II, LNCS 6199, pp. 418–429, 2010.

exist in general and even when one exists, the revenue it generates (i.e., the total price paid by buyers) can be rather low. The latter is a critical business concern for market designers, e.g., search engines like Google and Yahoo!. As a relaxation to Walrasian equilibrium, envy-free pricing [17] was proposed to focus on the revenue aspect of the market. *Envy-free pricing* does not require the market clearing condition and only insists on the fairness condition in Walrasian equilibrium. As a result, an envy-free pricing always exists (for example all prices are infinite); our goal is to find an envy-free pricing with maximum revenue.

In this paper, we study revenue maximization envy-free pricing in multi-item matching markets. In terms of the terminologies of envy-free pricing, our problem falls into the setting of unit-demand and unit-supply[1]. Despite of the recent surge in studies of envy-free pricing [17,18,5,9,14,1,12,2,4,6,7,13], surprisingly, it has not been received much attention in multi-item matching markets.

1.1 Our Results

Our main result relies on a polynomial time algorithm to compute revenue maximization envy-free pricing when every buyer evaluates at most two items a positive valuation, i.e., $|\{j \mid v_i(j) > 0\}| \leq 2$ (such number is called the *degree* of a buyer). Note that such implication of small degrees does happen in applications like housing market and keywords advertising. We complement our result by showing an NP-hardness result of computing revenue maximization envy-free pricing when the maximum degree of buyers is at least three. Our results imply the limits of tractability of envy-free pricing in multi-item matching markets. Note that by adding identical copies for items with multiple supplies, the hardness proof of unit-demand setting given by Guruswami et al. [17] implies that the problem is NP-hard when the maximum degree of buyers is eight.

At a high level view of the algorithm, we reduce the envy-free pricing problem to an instance of weighted independent set on a Berge graph and apply the Strong Perfect Graph Theorem [8], which says that a graph is perfect if and only if it is a Berge graph. While the weighted independent set problem is NP-hard in general, it can be solved in polynomial time in perfect graphs by the seminal result of Grötschel, Lovász and Schrijver [15]. Such reduction to independent set on perfect graphs turns out to be a powerful approach in solving revenue maximization envy-free pricing problems and has been used in [6,13]. The reduction in our setting, however, is more complicated and very different from that of [6]. In the setting of [6], there is a metric space among items behind all valuations, which implies a transitivity property: if buyer i prefers (to buy the item at) location j and buyer j prefers location k, then i prefers k as well. Such transitivity property is crucial to derive a directed acyclic graph, and based on which it is shown that the constructed graph is perfect. In our setting, however, we do not have such transitivity condition as the valuations can be arbitrary. Therefore,

[1] If items have multiple supplies, we can make the same number of identical copies for each item so that buyers demand all these copies at the same value. In this way, the envy-free pricing of the two instances are equivalent.

we need to explore the structure of the problem in more depth to obtained the desired result.

In general, envy-free pricing is easy if we simply look for a feasible solution. The complication arises when the envy-free condition is imposed on the top of revenue maximization — it has the tradeoff between whether it is more profitable to charge a higher price from a buyer for an item or charge a lower price and make up the difference in volume (since more buyers would be able to afford the item, which forces them to win other items). A fundamental observation in our setting is that in any revenue maximization solution, if buyer i wins item j with a price equal to its full value $v_i(j)$, due to the fact that the degree of buyers is at most 2, it effectively uniquely determines the allocations and prices of some other items through a *chain structure* (i.e., if i' demands j and j' and $v_{i'}(j) > v_i(j)$, then i' has to win j'). The chain structure allows us to translate envy-free pricing to the problem of finding buyer-item pairs where the buyer is fully charged at price $v_i(j)$ (such a pair is called a *price-setter*). The chain structure and price-setters play a critical role in constructing the perfect graph and inspire the connection between revenue maximization and independent set. Although the chain structure does not have transitivity, it has other nice properties like semi-Euclidean (Lemma 3) and transitivity or symmetry (Lemma 4). These properties are the keys for our reduction and proving the constructed graph is perfect.

Finally, we extend the unit-demand setting to allow buyers to demand a subset of consecutive items, motivated from TV advertising [19] where advertisers are interested in different consecutive slots with different values and lengths. Note that when there are unlimited supplies for each item, this is precisely the "highway" problem introduced in [17] and shown to be strongly NP-hard [11]. For our setting, we show that the revenue maximization envy-free solution can be computed in polynomial time. Instead of describing the algorithm explicitly, we show a stronger result — a Walrasian equilibrium always exists and can be computed in polynomial time — by proving that the demand matrix is totally unimodular, from which we know that a Walrasian equilibrium always exists [3]. Further, by the seminal result of Gul and Stacchetti [16], a Walrasian equilibrium always maximizes social welfare (and therefore revenue in our setting).

1.2 Related Work

The problem of revenue maximization envy-free pricing was initiated by Guruswami et al. [17]; it was shown that computing an optimal envy-free pricing is APX-hard, even items have unlimited supply and buyers are unit-demand or single-minded (i.e., demand a fixed subset of items). Briest [4] showed that given appropriate complexity assumptions (the hardness of the balanced bipartite independent set problem in constant degree graphs or refuting random 3CNF formulas), the envy-free pricing problem in general can not be approximated within $O(\log^{\epsilon} n)$ for some $\epsilon > 0$.

For the unit-demand setting, Guruswami et al. [17] gave an $O(\log n)$ approximation algorithm. Chen et al. [6] provided a polynomial time algorithm to compute a revenue maximization envy-free pricing when there is a metric space behind all items. For the multi-unit demand setting, [6] gave an $O(\log D)$ approximation algorithm under the same metric space assumption, where D is the maximum demand, and Briest [4] showed that the problem is hard to approximate within a ratio of $O(n^\epsilon)$ for some ϵ, unless $NP \subseteq \bigcap_{\epsilon>0} BPTIME(2^{n^\epsilon})$.

When buyers are single-minded, Guruswami et al. [17] and Balcan et al. [2] gave an $O(\log m + \log n)$-approximation algorithm for unlimited supplies. An almost tight lower bound was derived by Demaine et al. [9]. A number of special cases has been studied, such as the highway problem [17,1,5,11], the tollbooth problem [17,14,5] where buyers desire paths in a graph, and the graph vertex pricing problem [1] where each buyer requests the two endpoints of an edge in a given graph. When items have limited supply, Cheung and Swamy [7] showed an $O(\sqrt{m}\log u_{\max})$-approximation algorithm, where $u_{\max}$ is the maximum supply of items, and an $O(\log u_{\max})$-approximation algorithm for the highway problem.

2 Model and Main Results

There are a set A of m homogeneous items with unit supply each and n potential buyers where each buyer i is interested in acquiring one item. For each buyer i and item j, there is a value $v_{i,j}$ denoting the maximum amount that i is willing to pay for j. Let $A_i = \{j \in A \mid v_{i,j} > 0\}$ be the set of items that buyer i is interested in. We denote by $|A_i|$ the *degree* of buyer i.

An output of the market is composed of an allocation vector $\mathbf{x} = (x_1, \ldots, x_n)$, where x_i is the item that i wins, and a price vector $\mathbf{p} = (p_1, \ldots, p_m)$ for all items. If i does not win any item, denote $x_i = 0$. Note that $x_i \neq x_{i'}$ for any $i \neq i'$ unless $x_i = x_{i'} = 0$. Given an output $(\mathbf{x}, \mathbf{p})$, if buyer i wins item j, i.e., $x_i = j$, we say i is a *winner* and his *utility* is defined to be $v_{i,j} - p_j$; otherwise, his utility is defined to be 0. An output $(\mathbf{x}, \mathbf{p})$ is *envy-free* if the utility of everyone is maximized for the given prices $\mathbf{p}$, i.e., $v_{i,x_i} - p_{x_i} \geq v_{i,j} - p_j$ for any item j (denote $v_{i,0} = p_0 = 0$).

Our main focus is to consider the complexity of computing an *optimal* envy-free pricing that maximizes the total *revenue*, i.e., $\sum_{i=1}^{n} p_{x_i}$. Note that in our model, for any given price vector, due to envy-freeness, we can find a corresponding allocation that maximizes the total revenue by a matching technique or conclude that there is no feasible solution. Hence, for simplicity we will ignore allocations in the output and only focus on pricing. We have the following hardness result.

Theorem 1. *The optimal envy-free pricing is NP-hard when the maximum degree of buyers is at least 3, even when each buyer has the same valuation towards all his desired items.*

On a positive side, if the degree of all buyers is at most 2, i.e., $|A_i| \leq 2$, an optimal envy-free pricing can be solved in polynomial time, as the following claim states. (Details of the algorithm are given in the following section.)

Theorem 2. *There is a polynomial time algorithm to compute an optimal envy-free pricing when the degree of all buyers is at most 2.*

3 Main Algorithm

In this section, we will describe our polynomial time algorithm to compute an optimal envy-free pricing when $|A_i| \leq 2$. The main idea of the algorithm is as follows: We define the notion of a "price-setter" as a pair of a buyer i and an item j such that i wins j at a price equal to his full valuation $p_j = v_{i,j}$. By envy-freeness, such assignment determines the allocations and prices for several other buyers and items. Then, we can consider the total revenue collected from all these items together, and assign them to the price-setter pairs. By considering a graph of all pairs that can be simultaneously price setters, we reduce the revenue maximization problem to weighted independent set. Our main insight is that the graph is perfect, and the independent set can thus be found in polynomial time.

We will first introduce the notion of chain structure in Section 3.1 and analyze its properties in Section 3.2. We will reduce an optimal envy-free pricing to a weighted independent set problem in Section 3.3 and show that the constructed graph is perfect in Section 3.4.

3.1 Price-Setter and Chain Structure

We first establish the following observation for an optimal envy-free pricing.

Lemma 1. *Let* $\mathbf{p}$ *be an optimal envy-free pricing. If buyer* i *wins item* j *and* $v_{i,j} > p_j$*, then there is a buyer* $i' \neq i$ *and an item* $j' \neq j$ *such that* i' *wins* j' *and* $v_{i,j} - p_j = v_{i,j'} - p_{j'}$.

Proof. By the given condition, buyer i wins item j and $v_{i,j} > p_j$. As we cannot increase p_j to obtain more revenue, there must be another item, say $j' \neq j$, such that i desires j' as well (i.e., $A_i = \{j, j'\}$) and $v_{i,j'} - p_{j'} = v_{i,j} - p_j$. In this case, there must be another buyer, say $i' \neq i$, who wins j'. Otherwise, we can increase the price of p_j and $p_{j'}$ by a sufficiently small amount $\epsilon > 0$ such that i still prefers to buy j. In the new pricing solution, the allocation and envy-freeness of all other buyers will not change, and it generates a larger revenue, which contradicts the optimality of $\mathbf{p}$. □

The above lemma implies a chain structure, illustrated by Figure 1:

- If i_1 wins j_1 and $v_{i_1,j_1} > p_{j_1}$, there is j_2 such that $v_{i_1,j_1} - p_{j_1} = v_{i_1,j_2} - p_{j_2}$.
- If i_2 wins j_2 and $v_{i_2,j_2} > p_{j_2}$, there is j_3 such that $v_{i_2,j_2} - p_{j_2} = v_{i_2,j_3} - p_{j_3}$.
- If i_3 wins j_3 and $v_{i_3,j_3} > p_{j_3}$, there is j_4 such that $v_{i_3,j_3} - p_{j_3} = v_{i_3,j_4} - p_{j_4}$.
- ...
- There is i_ℓ such that i_ℓ wins j_ℓ and $v_{i_\ell,j_\ell} = p_{j_\ell}$.

We claim that items $j_1, \ldots, j_\ell$ are all different and there is no loop in the above structure. This is because, if $j_\alpha = j_\beta$, where $1 \leq \alpha < \beta \leq \ell$, then $S \triangleq \{i_\alpha, \ldots, i_{\beta-1}\}$ and $A' \triangleq \{j_\alpha, \ldots, j_{\beta-1}, j_\beta\}$ form a self-contained system: As the degree of all buyers in S is 2, their desired items are in A' and all items in A' are allocated to buyers in S. By the construction of the chain structure, $v_{i,j}$

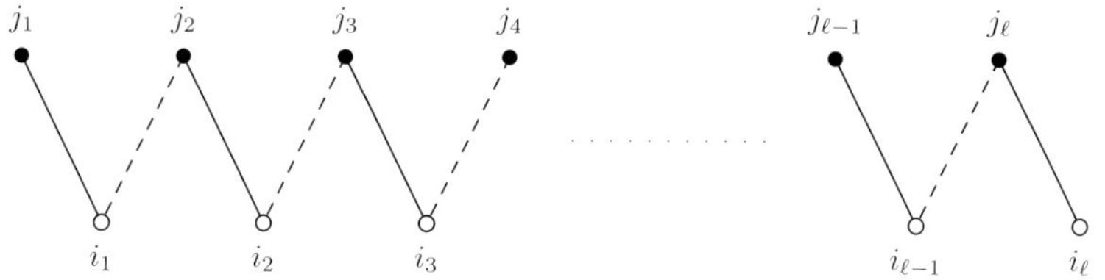

Fig. 1. The chain structure

is strictly larger than p_j for any $i \in S$ and $j \in A_i$. Hence, we can increase each price p_j, for $j \in A'$, by $\epsilon > 0$ such that all buyers in S are still satisfied with their allocations, from which we get a higher revenue, a contradiction.

Note that at the end of the chain, i_ℓ wins j_ℓ at a price equal to his value for j_ℓ. In other words, the price and allocation of j_ℓ effectively determine the entire structure of the chain. In particular, the prices of $j_1, \ldots, j_{\ell-1}$ cannot be increased due to envy-freeness. All items and buyers in Figure 1 form a chain structure when $[i_\ell, j_\ell]$ is a price-setter, as defined below.

Definition 1 (PRICE-SETTER AND CHAIN STRUCTURE). *We say a tuple $[i,j]$ a* price-setter *if buyer i wins item j at price $p_j = v_{i,j}$. We say $[j_1, i_1, j_2, i_2, \ldots, j_\ell, i_\ell]$ forms a* chain structure *if $[i_\ell, j_\ell]$ is a price-setter and for $k = 1, \ldots, \ell - 1$, i_k wins j_k and $v_{i_k,j_k} - p_{j_k} = v_{i_k,j_{k+1}} - p_{j_{k+1}} > 0$.*

By the above definition, if $[j_1, i_1, j_2, i_2, \ldots, j_\ell, i_\ell]$ forms a chain structure, then for any $1 \le r \le \ell$, $[j_r, i_r, \ldots, j_\ell, i_\ell]$ forms a chain structure as well. Intuitively, $[i,j]$ being a price-setter illustrates the fact that the seller charges a full value from buyer i for the given allocation towards the goal of revenue maximization. The effect of setting a price-setter is captured by a collection of chain structures where the prices and allocations of those items are effectively uniquely determined.

For each buyer i and item $j \in A_i$, given the condition that i wins j at price $v_{i,j}$ (i.e., $[i,j]$ is a price-setter), we define $H[i,j] \subseteq A$ and $w[i,j] \in \mathbb{R}$ as follows:

- If making $[i,j]$ as a price setter leads to a contradiction[2], let $H[i,j] = \emptyset$ and $w[i,j] = -\infty$.
- Otherwise, define $H[i,j] \subseteq A$ to be the subset of items where $j' \in H[i,j]$ if there are items $j' = j_1, j_2, \ldots, j_\ell = j$ and buyers $i_1, i_2, \ldots, i_\ell = i$ such that $[j_1, i_1, j_2, i_2, \ldots, j_\ell, i_\ell]$ forms a chain structure. (Note that in such a case, $\{j_1, \ldots, j_\ell\} \subseteq H[i,j]$.) Let $w[i,j]$ denote the total revenue obtained from items in $H[i,j]$, given that $[i,j]$ is a price-setter.

Figure 2 shows an example of the definitions. For instance, when $[i_1, j_2]$ is a price-setter, i_3 has to win j_3 at a price no more than 0.5. Due to envy-freeness,

[2] That is, given that $[i,j]$ is a price-setter, it will lead to a situation where a buyer cannot be satisfied. In other words, through the effect of the chain structure starting from $[i,j]$, eventually either at least two buyers request the same item or i desires the other item rather than j.

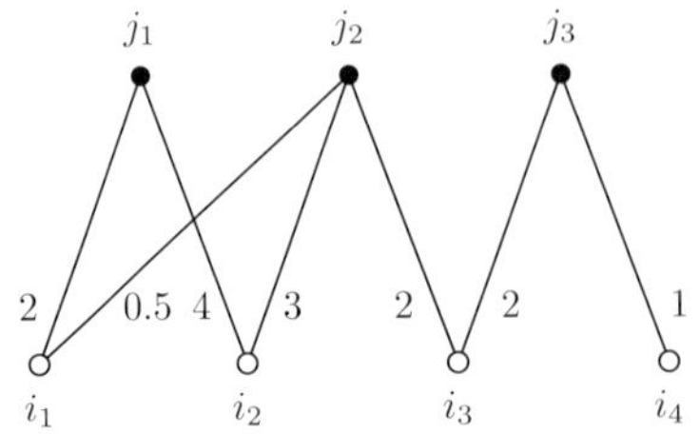

$H[i_1, j_1] = \{j_1, j_2, j_3\}$ $w[i_1, j_1] = 4$
$H[i_2, j_1] = \{j_1\}$ $w[i_2, j_1] = 4$
$H[i_1, j_2] = \emptyset$ $w[i_1, j_2] = -\infty$
$H[i_2, j_2] = \{j_2\}$ $w[i_2, j_2] = 3$
$H[i_3, j_2] = \{j_1, j_2\}$ $w[i_3, j_2] = 5$
$H[i_3, j_3] = \{j_3\}$ $w[i_3, j_3] = 2$
$H[i_4, j_3] = \{j_1, j_2, j_3\}$ $w[i_4, j_3] = 4$

Fig. 2. Definition of $H[\cdot, \cdot]$ and $w[\cdot, \cdot]$

i_4 has to win j_3 as well, which is impossible. Hence, $H[i_1, j_2] = \emptyset$. As another example, when $[i_1, j_1]$ is a price-setter, $p_{j_1} = v_{i_1, j_1} = 2$ and we obtain a revenue of 2 from i_1, which implies that i_2 must win j_2 at price 1 and i_3 must win j_3 at price 1. Hence, $H[i_1, j_1] = \{j_1, j_2, j_3\}$ and $w[i_1, j_1] = 4$.

Note that $H[i, j]$ and $w[i, j]$ can be computed in polynomial time. This is because for each new item (with its price and allocation determined) added into $H[i, j]$, we can check in polynomial time if it leads any buyer unsatisfied, from which we either can conclude that there is no feasible solution or need to add more items. Further, the definition of $H[i, j]$ and $w[i, j]$ is independent of any specific optimal envy-free pricing — it says that for *any* optimal solution where $[i, j]$ is a price-setter, due to envy-freeness, the price and allocation of all items in $H[i, j]$ are effectively uniquely determined, so as the total revenue obtained from these items.

The following result implies that to find an optimal envy-free pricing, it suffices to find the collection of price-setters of that pricing solution.

Lemma 2. *Let S be the collection of price-setters of an optimal envy-free pricing* $\mathbf{p}$. *Let A' be the set of items not allocated to any buyer. Then (i) $A' \cap H[i, j] = \emptyset$ for any $[i, j] \in S$, (ii) $H[i, j] \cap H[i', j'] = \emptyset$ for any $[i, j], [i', j'] \in S$, $[i, j] \neq [i', j']$, and (iii) $\bigcup_{[i,j] \in S} H[i, j] = A \setminus A'$. That is, the collection of $H[i, j]$ of all price-setters plus A' defines a partition of all items.*

Proof. Consider any item $k \in H[i, j]$ for any $[i, j] \in S$; there are items $k = j_1, j_2, \ldots, j_\ell = j$ and buyers $i_1, i_2, \ldots, i_\ell = i$ such that $[j_1, i_1, j_2, i_2, \ldots, j_\ell, i_\ell]$ forms a chain structure. Thus, k is allocated to buyer i_1 in the chain, which implies that $A' \cap H[i, j] = \emptyset$. By the following semi-Euclidean property of Lemma 3, k cannot be in another chain with a different price-setter, which implies that $H[i, j] \cap H[i', j'] = \emptyset$ for any $[i', j'] \in S$.

It remains to show that the collection of $H[i, j]$ of all price-setters plus A' covers all items. Consider any item j'. Assume that buyer i' wins j' (if there is no such a buyer, then $j' \in A'$). If $p_{j'} = v_{i', j'}$, then $[i', j']$ itself is a price-setter, which implies that $[i', j'] \in S$ and $j' \in H[i', j']$. If $p_{j'} < v_{i', j'}$, by the argument of Figure 1 above, there must be a chain structure connecting i' and j' to some price-setter $[i, j]$, which implies that $j' \in H[i, j]$. □

3.2 Properties of $H[\cdot,\cdot]$

For each item $j \in A$, let $T(j) = \{i \mid v_{i,j} > 0\}$ be the set of buyers that are interested in j. We have the following properties of $H[\cdot,\cdot]$, which will be used crucially in the following discussions.

Lemma 3. (Semi-Euclidean) *If there is an item $k \in H[i,j] \cap H[i',j']$, where $i \neq i'$ and $j \neq j'$, then either $j' \in H[i,j]$ or $j \in H[i',j']$.*

Lemma 4. *Assume that $j' \in H[i,j]$, $j' \neq j$, where the corresponding chain is $C = [j' = j_1, i_1, \ldots, j_{\ell-1}, i_{\ell-1}, j_\ell = j, i_\ell = i]$. Let the price of each item j_r defined by C be p_r, $r = 1, \ldots, \ell$. For any $i' \in T(j')$,*

- (Transitivity) *if $k \in H[i',j']$ and $v_{i',j'} > p_{j'}$, then $k \in H[i,j]$. Further, if $A_{i'} = \{j', j''\}$, then $j'' \in H[i,j]$ when $v_{i',j'} > p_{j'}$.*
- (Symmetry) *if $H[i',j'] \neq \emptyset$ and $v_{i',j'} \leq p_{j'}$, then $j \in H[i',j']$.*

3.3 Construction of Graph G

We define a node-weighted graph $G = (V,E)$ as follows: For each buyer $i \in T(j)$, we include a vertex, denoted by $i(j)$, with weight $w(i(j)) = w[i,j]$. Let $V = \{i(j) \mid i \in T(j), j \in A\}$. The set of edges E is defined by the following three categories Γ_1, Γ_2 and Γ_3:

- Γ_1: For each $i, i' \in T(j)$, there is an edge between $i(j)$ and $i'(j)$. That is, all vertices in $T(j)$ form a complete subgraph.
- Γ_2: For each buyer i, if $A_i = \{j, j'\}$ (i.e., $i \in T(j) \cap T(j')$), connect $i(j)$ and $i(j')$.
- Γ_3: For each pair $i(j), i'(j') \in V$, $j \neq j'$, there is an edge between $i(j)$ and $i'(j')$ if $j' \in H[i,j]$. For the simplicity of the analysis below, we define the direction of this type of edges to be $i(j) \to i'(j')$.

Figure 3 gives an example of the construction of G of the instance given by Figure 2. In the definition above, $\Gamma_1 \cap (\Gamma_2 \cup \Gamma_3) = \emptyset$. Further, it is possible that there are edges in both Γ_2 and Γ_3 (e.g., $(i_1(j_1), i_1(j_2))$ in Figure 3). In this case, we will refer the edges to be in Γ_3. A straightforward implication of the definition of Γ_3 is that if $j' \in H[i,j]$, there is an edge $i(j) \to i'(j')$ for any $i' \in T(j')$.

Roughly speaking, edges in G capture the price-setter relation of the two endpoints. That is, if there is an edge between $i(j)$ and $i'(j')$, then at most one of $[i,j]$ and $[i',j']$ can be a price-setter. This idea is illustrated by the following key connection between envy-free pricing and graph G.

Theorem 3. *Computing the optimal envy-free pricing is equivalent to finding the maximum weighted independent set of $G = (V,E)$.*

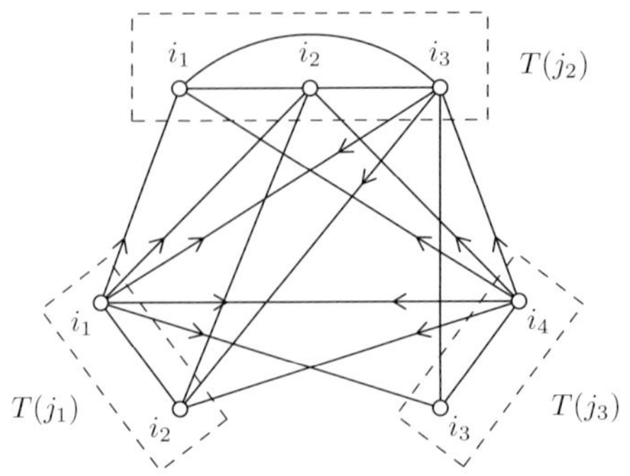

Fig. 3. Construction of graph G

3.4 G Is a Perfect Graph

Let C_n denote a cycle composed of n nodes, and co-C_n be the complement of C_n (with respect to the complete graph with n nodes). A subgraph G' of a graph G is said to be *induced* if, for any pair of vertices i and j of G', (i, j) is an edge of G' if and only if (i, j) is an edge of G. A graph is called a *Berge* graph if it does not contain C_n and co-C_n as an induced subgraph, for odd numbers $n = 5, 7, 9, \ldots$.

Lemma 5. *G does not have C_n and co-C_n as an induced subgraph, for odd numbers $n = 5, 7, 9, \ldots$.*

From the above lemma, we know that G is a Berge graph. A graph is said to be *perfect* if the chromatic number (i.e., the least number of colors needed to color the graph) of every induced subgraph equals the clique number of that subgraph. By the seminal Strong Perfect Graph Theorem [8], which states that a graph is a perfect graph if and only if it is a Berge graph, we have the following corollary:

Corollary 1. *G is a perfect graph.*

We know that the maximum weighted independent set problem can be solved in polynomial time on perfect graphs by the seminal result of Grötschel et al. [15]. Combining all of these, we know the optimal envy-free pricing can be computed in polynomial time, which completes the proof of Theorem 2.

4 The TV Advertising Problem

In this section, we extend the unit-demand setting to a special single-minded setting motivated from TV advertising [19]: items $j = 1, \ldots, m$ are consecutive for a given order and each buyer i desires a subset of consecutive items. That is, for each buyer i, there are α_i and β_i, where $1 \leq \alpha_i \leq \beta_i \leq m$, such that i demands the whole subset $S_i = \{\alpha_i, \alpha_i + 1, \ldots, \beta_i\}$ at value v_i. (For instance, different advertisers are interested in different consecutive slots with different values and lengths.)

Similar to the multi-item matching markets, the output here is composed of an allocation vector $\mathbf{x} = (x_1, \ldots, x_n)$ and a price vector $\mathbf{p} = (p_1, \ldots, p_m)$, where $x_i = 1$ if buyer i wins all items in S_i at price $p(S_i) = \sum_{j \in S_i} p_j$ and $x_i = 0$ if i does not win anything. We require that $x_i = x_j = 1$ implies $S_i \cap S_j = \emptyset$ for any $i \neq j$. An allocation $\mathbf{x} = (x_1, \ldots, x_n)$ is called *efficient* if it maximizes *social welfare*, i.e., $\sum_i v_i x_i$. The output $(\mathbf{x}, \mathbf{p})$ is *envy-free* if $v_i \geq p(S_i)$ when $x_i = 1$ and $v_i \leq p(S_i)$ when $x_i = 0$.

To study the revenue maximization envy-free solution, we consider a stronger notion — Walrasian equilibrium: a tuple $(\mathbf{x}, \mathbf{p})$ is called a *Walrasian equilibrium* if every buyer is envy-free and all unallocated items are priced at 0. In general, Walrasian equilibrium may not exist; however, once it exists, it is well-known that the allocation $\mathbf{x}$ is efficient [16].

The efficient allocation can be written by the following integer program (IP):

$$\begin{aligned} \max \quad & \sum_{i=1}^{n} v_i x_i \\ s.t. \quad & \sum_{i=1}^{n} a_{i,j} x_i \leq 1, \quad \forall\, 1 \leq j \leq m \\ & x_i \in \{0, 1\}, \quad \forall\, 1 \leq i \leq n \end{aligned}$$

where $a_{i,j} = 1$ if item $j \in S_i$ and $a_{i,j} = 0$ otherwise. Let $M = (a_{i,j})_{n \times m}$ be the coefficient matrix. Note that matrix M has the property that all 1's are consecutive in each row. We have the following observation.

Lemma 6. *Any* 0-1 *matrix* $M = (a_{i,j})_{n \times m}$ *where all 1's are consecutive in each row is totally unimodular, where a matrix is called* totally unimodular *if each square sub-matrix has determinant equal to* $0, +1,$ *or* -1.

Therefore, the linear program relaxation (LPR) of the above IP has an optimal integral solution and thus the IP can be solved in polynomial time. Further, the optimal solution of LPR being equal to IP gives an sufficient and necessary condition for the existence of Walrasian equilibrium [3]. Hence, a Walrasian equilibrium always exists in our setting. Further, for any given efficient allocation $\mathbf{x}$, an equilibrium pricing can be computed by the following linear inequalities system (plus the condition where $p_j = 0$ if j is unallocated), which always has a feasible solution [16]:

$$\begin{aligned} & \sum_{j \in S_i} p_j \leq v_i, \ \forall\, i: \ x_i = 1 \\ & \sum_{j \in S_i} p_j \geq v_i, \ \forall\, i: \ x_i = 0 \end{aligned}$$

Now return back to envy-freeness: for any optimal envy-free solution $(\mathbf{x}, \mathbf{p})$, it can be seen that the revenue obtained from each winner i is exactly v_i (otherwise, we can always increase p_j for some $j \in S_i$ to obtain more revenue). Thus, the total revenue obtained is $\sum_i v_i x_i$, which is equal to social welfare. Therefore, a Walrasian equilibrium also gives an optimal envy-free solution. In summary, we have the following result:

Theorem 4. *The optimal envy-free solution can be computed in polynomial time for the TV advertising problem.*

Finally, we remark that for the general single-minded buyers with unit-supply setting, it is tempting to think that in any optimal envy-free solution $(\mathbf{x}, \mathbf{p})$, the allocation $\mathbf{x}$ is efficient. However, as the following example shows, this is not true: There are three items j_1, j_2, j_3 and four buyers with $S_1 = \{j_1, j_2, j_3\}$, $v_1 = 4$; $S_2 = \{j_1, j_2\}$, $v_2 = 3$; $S_3 = \{j_2, j_3\}$, $v_3 = 3$; and $S_4 = \{j_1, j_3\}$, $v_4 = 3$. In the efficient allocation, the first buyer wins S_1. To guarantee envy-freeness, there must be $p_1 + p_2 + p_3 \leq 4$, $p_1 + p_2 \geq 3$, $p_2 + p_3 \geq 3$ and $p_1 + p_3 \geq 3$, which has no feasible solution. Indeed, a Walrasian equilibrium does not exist in this example and the optimal envy-free solution will allocate, e.g., j_1 and j_2 to the second buyer and charge $p_1 = p_2 = 1.5$ and $p_3 = \infty$, which gives a total revenue of 3.

5 Conclusions and Future Research

We study the revenue maximization envy-free pricing in a multi-item matching setting, showing that the problem is in polynomial time solvable if the degree of very buyer is at most 2 (i.e., evaluates at most two items a positive valuation) and becomes NP-hard if some buyers have degree of at least 3. Our results imply the limits of tractability for envy-free pricing in multi-item markets. The reduction from revenue maximization envy-free pricing to independent set in perfect graphs turns out to be a powerful approach in solving algorithmic pricing problems [6,13]. It is interesting to explore other applications of this approach in either envy-free pricing or other equilibrium pricing concepts. Further, from a practical point of view (e.g., towards applications in keywords advertising), it would be interesting to develop better approximation results when the degrees of buyers are small constants.

Acknowledgements

This work is supported by a DON project supported by Comet Electronics (HK) Ltd and Hong Kong UGC (Project No DON9220046), an REF Grant (CityU 112909) of Research Grants Council of Hong Kong SAR, as well as Future Networking Centre (FNC) [Project 9681001].

References

1. Balcan, M., Blum, A.: Approximation Algorithms and Online Mechanisms for Item Pricing. In: EC 2006, pp. 29–35 (2006)
2. Balcan, M., Blum, A., Mansour, Y.: Item Pricing for Revenue Maximization. In: EC 2008, pp. 50–59 (2008)

3. Bikhchandani, S., Mamer, J.W.: Competitive Equilibrium in An Economy with Indivisibilities. Journal of Economic Theory 74, 385–413 (1997)
4. Briest, P.: Uniform Budgets and the Envy-Free Pricing Problem. In: Aceto, L., Damgård, I., Goldberg, L.A., Halldórsson, M.M., Ingólfsdóttir, A., Walukiewicz, I. (eds.) ICALP 2008, Part I. LNCS, vol. 5125, pp. 808–819. Springer, Heidelberg (2008)
5. Briest, P., Krysta, P.: Single-Minded Unlimited Supply Pricing on Sparse Instances. In: SODA 2006, pp. 1093–1102 (2006)
6. Chen, N., Ghosh, A., Vassilvitskii, S.: Optimal Envy-Free Pricing with Metric Substitutability. In: EC 2008, pp. 60–69 (2008)
7. Cheung, M., Swamy, C.: Approximation Algorithms for Single-Minded Envy-Free Profit-Maximization Problems with Limited Supply. In: FOCS 2008, pp. 35–44 (2008)
8. Chudnovsky, M., Robertson, N., Seymour, P., Thomas, R.: The Strong Perfect Graph Theorem. Annals of Mathematics 164(1), 51–229 (2006)
9. Demaine, E., Hajiaghayi, M., Feige, U., Salavatipour, M.: Combination Can be Hard: Approximability of the Unique Coverage Problem. In: SODA 2006, pp. 162–171 (2006)
10. Demange, G., Gale, D., Sotomayor, M.: Multi-Item Auctions. Journal of Political Economy 94(4), 863–872 (1986)
11. Elbassioni, K., Raman, R., Ray, S.: On Profit-Maximizing Pricing for the Highway and Tollbooth Problems, arXiv:0901.1140 (2009)
12. Elbassioni, K., Sitters, R., Zhang, Y.: A Quasi-PTAS for Profit-Maximizing Pricing on Line Graphs. In: Arge, L., Hoffmann, M., Welzl, E. (eds.) ESA 2007. LNCS, vol. 4698, pp. 451–462. Springer, Heidelberg (2007)
13. Fiat, A., Wingarten, A.: Envy, Multi Envy, and Revenue Maximization. In: Leonardi, S. (ed.) WINE 2009. LNCS, vol. 5929, pp. 498–504. Springer, Heidelberg (2009)
14. Grigoriev, A., van Loon, J., Sitters, R., Uetz, M.: How to Sell a Graph: Guidelines for Graph Retailers. In: Fomin, F.V. (ed.) WG 2006. LNCS, vol. 4271, pp. 125–136. Springer, Heidelberg (2006)
15. Grötschel, M., Lovász, L., Schrijver, A.: The Ellipsoid Method and its Consequences in Combinatorial Optimization. Combinatorica 1(2), 169–197 (1981)
16. Gul, F., Stacchetti, E.: Walrasian Equilibrium with Gross Substitutes. Journal of Economic Theory 87, 95–124 (1999)
17. Guruswami, V., Hartline, J., Karlin, A., Kempe, D., Kenyon, C., McSherry, F.: On Profit-Maximizing Envy-Free Pricing. In: SODA 2005, pp. 1164–1173 (2005)
18. Hartline, J., Koltun, V.: Near-Optimal Pricing in Near-Linear Time. In: Dehne, F., López-Ortiz, A., Sack, J.-R. (eds.) WADS 2005. LNCS, vol. 3608, pp. 422–431. Springer, Heidelberg (2005)
19. Nisan, N., Bayer, J., Chandra, D., Franji, T., Gardner, R., Matias, Y., Rhodes, N., Seltzer, M., Tom, D., Varian, H., Zigmond, D.: Google"s auction for TV ads. In: Albers, S., Marchetti-Spaccamela, A., Matias, Y., Nikoletseas, S., Thomas, W. (eds.) ICALP 2009. LNCS, vol. 5556, pp. 309–327. Springer, Heidelberg (2009)
20. Shapley, L.S., Shubik, M.: The Assignment Game I: The Core. International Journal of Game Theory 1(1), 111–130 (1971)
21. Walras, L.: Elements of Pure Economics. Harvard University Press, 1954 (1877)

Contention Resolution under Selfishness

George Christodoulou[1,⋆], Katrina Ligett[2], and Evangelia Pyrga[3,⋆⋆]

[1] University of Liverpool, Liverpool, UK
[2] Cornell University, Ithaca, NY
[3] Ludwig-Maximilians-Universität München, Germany
gchristo@liv.ac.uk, katrina@cs.cornell.edu, pyrga@tcs.ifi.lmu.de

Abstract. In many communications settings, such as wired and wireless local-area networks, when multiple users attempt to access a communication channel at the same time, a conflict results and none of the communications are successful. Contention resolution is the study of distributed transmission and retransmission protocols designed to maximize notions of utility such as channel utilization in the face of blocking communications.

An additional issue to be considered in the design of such protocols is that selfish users may have incentive to deviate from the prescribed behavior, if another transmission strategy increases their utility. The work of Fiat et al. [8] addresses this issue by constructing an asymptotically optimal incentive-compatible protocol. However, their protocol assumes the cost of any single transmission is zero, and the protocol completely collapses under non-zero transmission costs.

In this paper, we treat the case of non-zero transmission cost c. We present asymptotically optimal contention resolution protocols that are robust to selfish users, in two different channel feedback models. Our main result is in the Collision Multiplicity Feedback model, where after each time slot, the number of attempted transmissions is returned as feedback to the users. In this setting, we give a protocol that has expected cost $2n + c\log n$ and is in $o(1)$-equilibrium, where n is the number of users.

1 Introduction

Consider a set of sources, each with a data packet to be transmitted on a shared channel. The channel is time-slotted; that is, the transmissions are synchronized and can only take place at discrete steps. The packets are of fixed length and each fits within one time slot. If only one user transmits in a given slot, the transmission is successful. If more than one user attempts to transmit messages in the same slot, a collision occurs, and all transmissions for that time step fail; the failed packets will need to be retransmitted later. Typically, the goal of the system designer is to optimize global notions of performance such as channel utilization or average throughput. If all of the sources were under centralized control, avoiding collisions would be simple: Simply allow one source to transmit at each time step, alternating in a round-robin or other "fair" fashion.

⋆ Partially supported by DFG grant Kr 2332/1-3 within Emmy Noether Program and by EPSRC grant EP/F069502/1.

⋆⋆ This research has been conducted while this author was at the Max-Planck-Institut für Informatik, Saarbrücken, Germany.

S. Abramsky et al. (Eds.): ICALP 2010, Part II, LNCS 6199, pp. 430–441, 2010.

What happens, though, if the transmission protocol must be executed in a distributed fashion, with minimal additional communication? Further, what happens if each source selfishly wishes to minimize the expected time before she transmits successfully, and will only obey a protocol if it is in her best interest? Can we still design good protocols in this distributed, adversarial setting? What information does each user need to receive on each time step in order for such protocols to function efficiently?

In this game theoretic contention resolution framework, Fiat et al. [8] design an incentive-compatible transmission protocol which guarantees that (w.h.p.) all players will transmit successfully in time linear in the total number of users. One of the nice features of their protocol is that it only needs a very simple feedback structure to work: They assume only that each player receives feedback of the form $0/1/2^+$ after each time step (*ternary* feedback), indicating whether zero, one, or more than one transmission was attempted. This positive result is actually based on a very negative observation, that the price of anarchy [15] in this model is unbounded: If transmission costs are assumed to be zero, it is an equilibrium strategy for all users to transmit on all time steps! Clearly, this is an undesirable equilibrium. Fiat et al. [8] construct their efficient equilibrium using this bad equilibrium quite cleverly as a "threat"— the players agree that if not all players have exited the game by a certain time, they will default to the always-transmit threat strategy for a very large time interval. This harsh penalty then incentivizes good pre-deadline behavior.

It is natural, however, to assume that players incur some transmission cost $c > 0$ (attributable to energy consumption; see, for example, [17,24]) every time they attempt a transmission, in addition to the costs they incur due to the total length of the protocol. If the cost of transmitting is even infinitesimally non-zero, though, the threat strategy used in [8] is no longer at equilibrium, and the protocol breaks down. We address this here, by developing efficient contention resolution protocols that are ε-incentive-compatible even under *strictly positive transmission costs*.

In this work, we consider the model of Collision Multiplicity Feedback (CMF). After each collision, while the identity of the collided packets is lost, the *number* of the packets that participated in the collision is broadcast to all users. This information can be estimated (with small error) by a number of energy detectors. The CMF model has gained substantial attention in the literature because it admits significantly better throughput results than can be achieved with ternary feedback. In this setting, we present an efficient contention resolution protocol that is robust to selfish players. We also propose a contention resolution protocol for a *perfect information* feedback model, where all players can identify *which* players transmitted.

1.1 Our Results

There are three main technical challenges we address:

1. Separating players by developing unique ids. Our protocols differ from previous incentive-compatible contention resolution protocols in that they are *history dependent*; that is, the protocol uses the transmission history in order to construct a random ordering of the users. We will use algorithmic techniques similar to those for "tree"-style protocols, originally developed by Capetanakis [7,6] and later further developed in the information theory and networks literatures.

2. Developing a "threat". Like Fiat et al. [8], we use a threat strategy to incentivize good behavior. However, the threat they use collapses under nonzero transmission costs[1]. On the other hand, we use a weaker threat strategy and need to develop efficient protocols that are incentive compatible despite our weaker punishment.
3. Detecting deviations. In order for a threat to be effective, the players need to be able to detect and punish when one of them cheats. Our protocol employs a system of checksums and transmissions whose purpose is to communicate information on cheating—despite the fact that a "transmission" gives no other information to the players than its presence or absence.

We address these challenges in two different feedback models, described below. In each feedback model we consider, we present asymptotically optimal protocols that guarantee to each user expected average cost that is linear in the total number of users. Our protocols are in ε-equilibrium, where ε goes to 0 as the number of players grows. This form of approximate equilibrium is a very reasonable equilibrium notion in our setting, as games with a large number of players are technically the only interesting case—if there were only a constant number of players, one could simply play the exact time-independent equilibrium that appears in [8], although this has exponential cost.

Perfect Information. First, in Section 3, we consider the feedback model of *perfect information*, where each user finds out after each time step what subset of sources attempted a transmission. Perfect information is a very common assumption in non-cooperative game theory. Making this strong assumption allows us to highlight the game theoretic aspects of the problem, and the insight we develop in the context of this strong feedback model is useful in developing algorithms under more restrictive feedback.

Unlike the trivial protocol under global ids, the randomized protocol that we present is *fair* in the sense that all users have the same expected cost, regardless of how each individual chooses to label them with local ids. Protocol PERFECT has expected cost $n/2 + \log n$ and is a $o(1)$-equilibrium w.r.t. the number of players n.

Collision Multiplicity. Next, in Section 4, we present the main result of this work. Here, we study a model with Collision Multiplicity Feedback (CMF), (otherwise known as M-ary feedback; see e.g. [25,20,23]), in which after each time slot, users find out the exact number of packets which were transmitted during the slot, but not the identities of the transmitting players. In some practical situations, this feedback can be measured as the total energy on the channel during one slot, by means of a number of energy detectors. Our protocol MULTIPLICITY has expected cost $2n + c\log n$, where c is the transmission cost, and is a $o(1)$-equilibrium.

1.2 Related Work

Contention resolution for communication networks is a well-studied problem. The ALOHA protocol [1], given by Abramson in 1970 (and modified by Roberts [22] to its slotted version), is one of the most famous multiaccess communication protocols.

[1] Remember from the earlier description that the threat of Fiat et al. requires that all remaining players will be transmitting in every step with probability 1 for a large number of steps. This is an equilibrium only when the cost of a transmission is zero.

However, Aloha leads to poor channel utilization due to an unnecessarily large number of collisions. Many subsequent papers study the efficiency of multiaccess protocols when packets are generated by some stochastic process (see for example [12,11,21]). Such statistical arrival models are very useful, but cannot capture worst-case scenarios of bursty inputs, as in [5], where batched arrivals are modeled by all n packets arriving at the same time. To model this worst-case scenario, one needs n nodes, each of which must simultaneously transmit a packet; this is also the model we use in this work.

One class of contention resolution protocols explicitly deals with conflict resolution; that is, if $k \geq 2$ users collide (out of a total of n users), then a resolution algorithm is called on to resolve this conflict (it makes sure that all the packets that collided are successfully transmitted), before any other source is allowed to use the channel. For example, [7,6,14,26] describe *tree algorithms* whose main idea is to iteratively give priority to smaller groups, until all conflicts are resolved, with $\Theta(k + k\log(n/k))$ makespan. We use a similar splitting technique in the algorithms we present here.

A variety of upper and lower bounds for the efficiency of various protocols have been shown. For the binary model (transmitting players learn whether they succeed or fail; non-transmitting players receive no feedback) when k is known, [10] provides an $O(k + \log k \log n)$ algorithm, while [18] provides a matching lower bound. For the ternary model, [13] provides a bound of $\Omega(k(\log n/\log k))$ for all deterministic algorithms. In all of the results mentioned so far in this subsection, it is assumed that players will always follow the protocol given to them, even if it is not in their own best interest.

The CMF model we consider in this paper was first considered by Tsybakov [25], where he proposed a protocol with throughput 0.533. Later Pippenger [20] showed, using a random-coding existential argument, that the capacity of the channel is 1. Ruszinkó and Vanroose later in [23] gave a constructive proof of the same result, by designing a particular protocol reaching the throughput 1. Georgiadis and Papantoni-Kazakos [9] considered the case when the collision multiplicity can be estimated by energy detectors, up to an upper bound.

More recently, a variety of *game theoretic* models of slotted Aloha have also been proposed and studied in an attempt to understand selfish users; see for example [2,16,3]; also [17,2] for models that include non-zero transmission costs. Much of the prior game theoretic work only considers transmission protocols that always transmit with the same fixed probability (a function of the number of players in the game). By contrast, we consider more complex protocols, where a player's transmission probability is allowed to be an arbitrary function of her play history and the sequence of feedback she has received. Other game theoretic approaches have considered pricing schemes [27] and cases in which the channel quality changes with time and players must choose their transmission levels accordingly [19,28], and [4] for a related model.

As discussed above, Fiat et al. [8] study a model very similar to the one we present here; while the feedback mechanism they assume is not as rich as ours, crucially, their model does not incorporate transmission costs. The idea of a threat is used both in [8] and in our work, as a way to incentivize the players to be obedient. However, the technical issues involved are completely different in the two papers. [8] uses a threat in a form of a *deadline*, while ours use a *cheat detection* mechanism to identify the fact that someone deviated from the protocol. The protocol in Fiat et al. [8] relies for its threat on the existence of an extremely inefficient equilibrium, where all players constantly transmit their packets for an exponentially long period. This equilibrium is used as an artificial deadline, that is, the protocol switches to that inefficient equilibrium after linear time. This threat is history independent, in the sense that it will take place after a linear number of time steps, regardless of any transmission history of the players. This history-independent threat relies critically on the absence of transmission costs. On the other hand, our threat is history dependent and makes use of a cheat-detection mechanism: any deviation from the protocol is identified with at least constant probability, and the existence of a deviation is communicated to all players. In response, all players switch their transmission strategy according to the exponential time-independent equilibrium (all players transmit at every slot with probability $\Theta(1/\sqrt{n})$).

The communication allowed by the feedback models we employ is critical in allowing us to perform cheat detection and in allowing us to communicate the presence of a cheater, so that she can be punished. Although we are not aware of lower bound results that explicitly rule this out, we suspect that the ternary feedback mechanism used by Fiat et al. [8] is not rich enough to allow such communication.

2 Definitions

Game structure. Let $N = \{1,2,\ldots,n\}$ be the set of players in the game. Every player carries a single packet of information that she wants to send through a common channel, and all players (and all packets) are present at the start of the protocol. We assume that time t is discretized, divided into slots $t = 1,2,\ldots$. At any given slot t, a pending player i has two available pure strategies: She can either try to transmit her packet in that slot or stay quiet. We represent the action of a player i by an indicator variable X_{it} that takes the value 1 if player i transmitted at time t, and 0 otherwise. The transmission vector X_t at time t is represented by $X_t = (X_{1t}, X_{2t}, \ldots, X_{nt})$, while the number of attempted transmissions at time t is denoted by $Y_t = \sum_{i=1}^{n} X_{it}$. The transmission sequence X^t is the sequence of transmission vectors of time up to t: $X^t = (X_1, X_2, \ldots, X_t)$. In a (mixed) strategy p_i, a player transmits at time t with probability $p_{it} = Pr[X_{it} = 1]$. If exactly one player transmits in a given slot, we say that the transmission is *successful*, and the player who transmitted leaves the game;[2] the game then continues with the rest of the players. If two or more players attempt to transmit at the same slot, then they all fail and remain in the game. The game ends when all players have successfully transmitted.

Feedback. At every time step t, the actual transmission vector is X_t. However, individual players do not have access to this complete information. Instead, after playing at step t, each player i receives some feedback I_{it} that is a function of X_t. The feedback is symmetric, i.e., every player who receives feedback gets the same information, i.e., $I_{jt} = I_{kt} = I_t$. At any time step t, a player's selected action is a (randomized) function of the entire sequence of actions she has taken so far and the *history* $H_{it} = (I_{i1}, \ldots, I_{i(t-1)})$ of the feedback that she has received from the channel. For convenience, we define a player i's *personal history* $h_{it} = (X_{i1}, X_{i2}, \ldots, X_{it})$ as the sequence of actions she took.

We distinguish between two different feedback structures: (1) *Perfect information:* After each time step t, all players receive as feedback the identities of the players who

[2] Alternatively, we can assume the player transmits with $p_{it} = 0$ on all subsequent rounds.

attempted a transmission, i.e., $I_{it} = X_t, \forall i \in N$. However, there are not shared global ids for the players; each player potentially has a different local ordering on the player set, so, for example, the concept of the "lexicographically first player" has no common meaning. (2) *Collision Multiplicity Feedback (CMF):* After each time step t, all players receive as feedback the cardinality of the set of players who attempted a transmission, but do not find out their identities. Here, $I_{it} = Y_t = \sum_{j=1}^{n} X_{jt}, \forall i \in N$.

Transmission protocols. We define f_{it}, a *decision rule* for player i at time t, as a function that maps a pair $(h_{i(t-1)}, H_{i(t-1)})$ to a probability p_{it}. A *protocol* f_i for player i is simply a sequence of decision rules $f_i = f_{i1}, f_{i2}, \cdots$. A protocol is *symmetric* or *anonymous* and is denoted by $f = f_1 = \ldots = f_n$ iff the decision rule assigns the same probabilities to all players with the same personal history. In other words, if $h_{it} = h_{jt}$ for two players $i \neq j$, it holds that $f_{i,t+1}(h_{it}, H_{it}) = p_{i(t+1)} = p_{j(t+1)} = f_{j,t+1}(h_{jt}, H_{jt})$.[3]

Individual utility. Given a transmission sequence X^T wherein all players eventually transmit successfully, define the *latency* or *success time* S_i of agent i as $\arg\min_t (X_{it} = 1, X_{jt} = 0, \ \forall j \neq i)$. The cost to player i is made up of costs for the time-to-success and transmission costs: $C_i(X^T) = S_i + c\sum_{t \leq S_i} X_{it}$. Given a transmission sequence X^T of actions so far, a decision rule f induces a probability distribution over sequences of further transmissions. In that case, we write $E_i^f(X^T)$ for the expected total cost incurred by a sequence of transmissions that starts with X^T and then continues based on f. In particular, for $X^0 := \emptyset$, $E_i^f(X^0)$ is the expected cost of the sequence induced by f.

Equilibria. The objective of every player is to minimize her expected cost. We say that a protocol f is in *equilibrium* if for any transmission sequence X^t the players cannot decrease their cost by unilaterally deviating; that is, for all players i, $E_i^f(X^t) \leq E_i^{(f_i', f_{-i})}(X^t)$, for all f_i', t. Similarly, we say that a protocol f is in an ε*-equilibrium* if for any transmission history X^t $E_i^f(X^t) \leq (1+\varepsilon)E_i^{(f_i', f_{-i})}(X^t)$, for all f_i', t.

Social utility. We are interested in providing the players with a symmetric protocol that is in equilibrium (or ε-equilibrium, for some small $\varepsilon > 0$) such that the average expected cost[4] $E_i^f(X^0)$ of any player i is low.

3 Perfect Information

In this section we consider the perfect information setting, where in every time slot t, every user i receives feedback $I_{it} = X_t$, the exact vector of transmissions in t. It is important to note that although in this setting each player can distinguish between her opponents, we do not assume that the players have globally visible id numbers.[5] Instead, we assume that each player has a set of local id numbers to distinguish among her opponents, but one player's local labeling of all other players may be independent of another's. Unlike global ids, local ids do not pose very hard implementation constraints;

[3] Notice that since the feedback is symmetric, $h_{it} = h_{jt}$ implies $H_{it} = H_{jt}$.

[4] Since we are interested in symmetric protocols, then the average expected cost is equal to the expected cost of any player, and hence the social utility coincides with the individual utility.

[5] In fact, if the identities of the players were common knowledge, then simply transmitting in lexicographic order would be incentive-compatible and achievable.

for instance, in sensor networks or ad-hoc mobile wireless networks, users may be able to derive local ids for the other players based on relative topological position.

The main idea of the protocol we present here is to generate unique, random ids for each player based on her transmission history. Next, with the use of those random ids, the players are synchronized in a fair manner, and can exit the game within short time.

As mentioned earlier, this section is presented with transmission costs c as some negligible, nonzero ε, rather than treating general nonzero costs. This greatly simplifies the presentation of this section and allows us to focus on the main ideas that the more complicated protocol of Section 4 is based on. No such assumption on c will be made when describing the protocol for the more restricted (and thus more challenging) feedback model. Further, non negligible transmission costs can be incorporated into this protocol as well. Due to lack of space, however, the details are omitted.

3.1 Protocol PERFECT

Protocol PERFECTworks in rounds. In each round k there is exactly one *split* slot and some $\ell_k \geq 0$ *leave* slots. In a split slot, all pending players (i.e., the players that are still in the game) transmit with probability $1/2$, independently of each other and their personal history. We define the id $id_i(k)$ of player i, after the kth split slot has taken place, as a binary string of length k that represents the transmission history of player i only on the split slots. When, after some round k, a player i manages to obtain a unique id, i.e., $id_i(k) \neq id_j(k)$, for all $i \neq j$, she will be assigned a leave slot. During a leave slot a single prescribed player transmits with probability 1, while all other players stay quiet. Such a player has a successful transmission and exits the game.

We will now describe what happens in a round in more detail. Consider the beginning of round $k+1$, for $k \geq 0$. The first slot s is a split slot. Let n_T be the total number of players that transmitted in s. Every player observes the actions of all other players in slot s, and updates their ids: The id of player j is updated by appending "1" or "0" at the end of $id_j(k)$, depending on whether j transmitted in s or not. If there are players that obtained unique ids within slot s then they must be assigned leave slots. Let U_{k+1} be the set containing those players. The order in which those players will be assigned leave slots depends on the number n_T of players that transmitted in s: The players in U_{k+1} are assigned leave slots in order of increasing id if n_T is even, and in order of decreasing id otherwise. All players in U_{k+1} will transmit successfully and exit the game.[6]

The order in which the players in U_{k+1} are assigned leave slots is not fixed, so as to avoid giving incentive to a player to strategically create an id, instead of obtaining a random one. If the players in U_{k+1} were always assigned leave slots in order of increasing id, then players would have incentive to remain quiet in split slots, as this would result in an id of smaller value (they append a "0" to their id) than if they transmitted (they would append a "1" to their id). To avoid this, the protocol prescribes the order to be increasing or decreasing with equal probability (since n_T is equally likely to be even or odd); this way the players have nothing to gain by choosing any specific id.

[6] A player i who is currently assigned a leave slot, keeps transmitting until she succeeds. This technical detail ensures that the protocol will not collapse if some other player j tries to transmit at that slot. This might happen only in the case that j deviates from the protocol and transmits in the leave slot assigned to i.

Fixing a player i, any player j (including i) is equally likely to obtain a unique id in any round k, regardless of whether i transmits or stays quiet during the split slot of round k. Therefore, i cannot reduce the expected number of rounds she needs until she obtains a unique id, nor the expected number of players that will be assigned leave slots before she does. Also, due to the assumption of arbitrarily small transmission cost c, player i has no incentive to deterministically stay quiet during a split so as to save on the transmission costs she incurs. Therefore, if no player could succeed during a split slot (i.e, have a successful transmission due to being the single player transmitting in a split), then the expected cost of i would have been exactly the same, whether i transmits or stays quiet in a split. (Player i has no reason to deviate from the protocol in a leave round, as this can only increase her total cost.) The possibility of players succeeding during a split, creates an imbalance between the expected costs a player has per step when she transmits and when she stays quiet during the split. However, the following Theorem suggests that the maximum gain over all possible deviations is very small.

Theorem 1. *Protocol* PERFECT *is a $o(1)$-equilibrium. Moreover, the expected total cost of a player i is $E_i(X^0) = n/2 + \log n$.*

Regarding the expected cost, note that player i is expected to obtain a unique id in $\log n$ rounds and the players are equally likely to be assigned the k-th leave slot, for all $1 \leq k \leq n$. Due to space limitations the proof of Theorem 1 is omitted.

4 Collision Multiplicity Feedback

In this section, we present the main result of the paper, Protocol MULTIPLICITY. This protocol works under the CMF channel model, in which, after each slot t, all players are informed about the number of attempted transmissions, i.e., $Y_t = \sum_{i \in N} X_{it}$. This information can be provided by a number of energy detectors, and it is broadcast to all users. CMF is a well-studied and important feedback model in information theory, with many nice theoretical results (see e.g. [25,20,9,23]).

Here we give an overview of the main ideas of Protocol MULTIPLICITY and we will describe it in detail in Section 4.1. Protocol PERFECT presented in Section 3.1 crucially relies on users knowing how each player acts at every time step, and thus does not work under this feedback model. Instead, we design a different $o(1)$-equilibrium protocol that overcomes this difficulty and has expected average cost $2n + c\log n$. Recall that in Protocol PERFECT the *id* of a player is a string denoting all the random choices the player had to make during split slots. For every time t, the players are partitioned into groups according to their ids, i.e., all the players in the same group share the same id. Moreover, all players perform a split at the same time, regardless of the group they belong to. The protocol MULTIPLICITY that we present here, again uses the idea of randomly generated ids, but here, each group splits separately, in a sequential manner. Each split is followed by a *validation* slot, whose aim is to verify that the split has been performed "correctly".

In the CMF model, the players have an incomplete view of history. This might give incentive to some players to "cheat" and pretend to belong to a different group (of smaller size), in order to exit the game sooner. We discourage such a behavior using a "threat": if any deviation from the protocol is observed, then all players switch their transmission strategy according to a costly equilibrium strategy. Finally, a *cheat-detecting* mechanism is needed. The validation slots accomplish exactly this task; the cheating is noted *by all players* if some validation step fails. In that case, all the players get punished by switching to an exponential-cost time-independent equilibrium protocol (punishment protocol):

The punishment protocol. Fiat, Mansour and Nadav [8] show that, for transmission cost $c = 0$ and k pending players, the time-independent symmetric protocol where every player transmits with probability $p = \Theta(1/\sqrt{k})$ is in equilibrium. It gives average packet latency $e^{\Theta(\sqrt{k})}$, and thus switching to this protocol can be used as a high-cost punishment for detected defections. For our punishment protocol, we adapt this protocol to the general case of transmission cost $c \geq 0$: the transmission probability becomes $p_c = \Theta(1/\sqrt{k(1+c)})$ and the expected cost is $(1+c)e^{\Theta(\sqrt{k/(1+c)})}$.

4.1 Protocol MULTIPLICITY

The protocol works in rounds. Every round consists of a sequence of *split* and *validation* slots such that each player *participates* in exactly one split slot in each round. We say that a player participates in a split slot s, if the protocol requires the player to decide randomly whether she will transmit in s or not.[7]

Assume that at the end of round $k \geq 0$, there are M_k different groups (each group consists of players that have the same transmission history with respect to the split slots they have participated in).[8] Let $G_{j,k}$ be the jth group. The players do not know which players belong to group $G_{j,k}$, but they will be aware of the size $|G_{j,k}|$ of the group.

Consider round $k+1$. At the beginning of the round, the players decide, using (as in the perfect information setting) the parity of the total number x_k of players that transmitted during all the split slots of round k, whether groups will split in increasing or decreasing order of ids. According to this order, every group will perform a split, followed by a validation. Let $G_{j,k}$ be the current group performing a split and validation.

Split slot. When it is group $G_{j,k}$'s turn, all players that belong to this group (and only these players) will transmit with probability $1/2$. All players (regardless of whether they belong in $G_{j,k}$ or not) note the number $n_{T,j}$ of the members of $G_{j,k}$ that transmitted in this slot. These $n_{T,j}$ players will form one of the new subgroups of $G_{j,k}$.

Validation slot. The immediately next slot is a *validation* slot. All players of $G_{j,k}$ that transmitted in the previous split slot must now stay quiet, while those that did *not*, must now transmit. This second set of players will form the other subgroup of $G_{j,k}$. Again all players can see their number $n_{Q,j}$.

Right after the validation step has happened (and before the next group's turn comes), all players check if the members of $G_{j,k}$ were properly split into the two new subgroups, by checking that the sum of the sizes of the two subgroups equals $|G_{j,k}|$. If that is true, this group is properly divided, and the next group will split.

If the check failed, then there is some player that deviated from the protocol: Either one of the members of $G_{j,k}$ did not transmit in any of the split or validation slots of

[7] As opposed to a player that the protocol instructs to stay quiet during s with probability 1.

[8] At round 0 all players belong to the same group, i.e., $M_0 = 1$.

group $G_{j,k}$ (or even transmitted in both slots); or, some player that did not belong in $G_{j,k}$ transmitted in either of these two slots. All players note therefore the fact that someone has deviated, and they all switch to the punishment protocol.

We note that since now each group splits separately, there is no longer the need for explicit leave-slots. A user that obtains a unique id in round k will transmit successfully when her group $G_{j,k}$ performs a split if she is the only one to transmit (i.e., if she was the only member of $G_{j,k}$ to append a '1' to her id); or she will transmit successfully when her group performs the validation step if she was the only from $G_{j,k}$ that stayed quiet in the split (i.e., she was the only member of $G_{j,k}$ to append a '0' to her id).

If all players of a group $G_{j,k}$ transmitted during their corresponding split, the validation that normally follows will be skipped. The reason is that if all players of $G_{j,k}$ transmitted in the split, no one would transmit in the validation slot. All players would know that this slot should be empty, which would provide an incentive to "attack", i.e., transmit during that slot, disobeying the protocol.

4.2 Analysis

Theorem 2. *The expected cost of Protocol* MULTIPLICITY *for any player is* $2n + c\log n$.

Proof. The expected number of split-slots required for a player to obtain a unique id, is $\log n$. Consider a round k. Every player will transmit exactly once during this round (either in the split slot corresponding to her group, or in the validation slot immediately following that split). If M_{k-1} is the number of groups that have formed by the end of round $k-1$, then the duration of round k is at most $2M_{k-1}$ slots, where $M_{k-1} \leq 2^{k-1}$. Therefore the total expected cost for i is bounded by $2n + c\log n$.

Theorem 3. *Protocol* MULTIPLICITY *is a* $o(1)$*-equilibrium.*

Proof. First, we will show that no player has an incentive to cheat. We say that a player "cheats" if she transmits during a slot she was not supposed to or did not transmit when she was expected to do so. If a player belonging to group $G_{j,k}$, for some j,k, did not transmit at the split slot of $G_{j,k}$, nor at the corresponding validation slot, then the sum $n_{T,j} + n_{Q,j}$ will be found less than $|G_{j,k}|$. This will make all players switch to the (high cost) punishment protocol. Similarly, if a player transmits to the validation slot of group $G_{j,k}$ when she was not supposed to, then $n_{T,j} + n_{Q,j} > |G_{j,k}|$.

The remaining case is when a player $i \notin G_{j,k}$ cheats by transmitting during the split slot[9] of group $G_{j,k}$. Assume that i cheats when there are $n' \leq n$ pending players in total. She will get caught with probability at least $1/4$ (if $G_{j,k}$ is of minimum size, i.e. 2).[10] In that case she will have expected future cost $(1+c)e^{\Theta(\sqrt{n'/(1+c)})}$, worse than the corresponding cost of following the protocol, i.e., $O(n')$. Therefore, the expected cost of i becomes larger if she deviates instead of following the protocol.

9 Validation slots only happen if there is at least one player from $G_{j,k}$ that is supposed to transmit in them. Thus, a player cannot have a successful transmission by attacking a validation slot.

10 If none of the members of $G_{j,k}$ transmitted during the split slot, then i has a successful transmission. If all members but one transmitted, then the cheating does not get caught (and i only had a failed transmission). In this case, it looks as if all members of $G_{j,k}$ transmitted, and the validation slot is skipped. In all other cases, i gets caught.

We note that a player cannot gain by deterministically choosing to stay quiet during a split she participates in. She cannot save on the transmission cost c, as she would have to transmit during the validation slot anyway. Moreover, staying quiet or transmitting in the split does not affect the number of rounds a player must wait until she obtains a unique id: Consider a player i belonging to some group $G_{j,k}$. All other players from $G_{j,k}$ transmit during the corresponding split slot with probability $1/2$; the expected sizes of the two new groups to be formed are the same and i has exactly the same probability of obtaining a unique id, whether she transmits in the split, or stays quiet.

On the other hand, splits always happen before the corresponding validations. If i obtains a unique id during round k, then she exits the game earlier if she was the only player of her group transmitting at the split, than if she were the only quiet player. This implies that "always transmit" gives a smaller expected (future) cost. It is therefore the optimal strategy. Nevertheless, if p_τ is the probability for a player that transmits during split slots to succeed at the time step τ, then p_τ is also the probability for a player that stays quiet during split slots to succeed at the time step $\tau+1$ (since validation slots occur immediately after split slots). Let X^t be any transmission history, and suppose that $t+1$ is a split slot that i participates in (otherwise i's optimal strategy is to behave according to the protocol). Let $A(X^t) = t + \sum_{\tau \le t} X_{i\tau}$ be the actual cost incurred by i until time t, and let $T(X^t), Q(X^t)$ be the total expected cost of player i if she always transmits, stays quiet, respectively, in all future split slots she participates in. Then,

$$T(X^t) - A(X^t) = \textstyle\sum_{\tau=t+1}^{\infty} \tau p_\tau$$
$$Q(X^t) - A(X^t) = \textstyle\sum_{\tau=t+1}^{\infty} (\tau+1) p_\tau = \sum_{\tau=t+1}^{\infty} (\tau p_\tau + p_\tau) = T(X^t) - A(X^t) + 1,$$

and therefore, $\frac{Q(X^t)}{T(X^t)} = \frac{T(X^t)+1}{T(X^t)} = 1 + o(1)$.

$Q(X^t)$ is an upper bound on the total expected cost of the protocol: Staying quiet in split slots is always worse than transmitting; according to the protocol a player stays quiet only in half (in expectation) of the future split slots she participates in. Thus, Protocol MULTIPLICITY is a $o(1)$-equilibrium.

References

1. Abramson, N.: The ALOHA system: Another alternative for computer communications. In: Proceedings of the Fall Joint Computer Conference, November 17-19, pp. 281–285. ACM, New York (1970)
2. Altman, E., El Azouzi, R., Jiménez, T.: Slotted aloha as a game with partial information. Comput. Netw. 45(6), 701–713 (2004)
3. Altman, E., Barman, D., Benslimane, A., El Azouzi, R.: Slotted aloha with priorities and random power. In: Proc. IEEE Infocom (2005)
4. Auletta, V., Moscardelli, L., Penna, P., Persiano, G.: Interference games in wireless networks. In: Papadimitriou, C., Zhang, S. (eds.) WINE 2008. LNCS, vol. 5385, pp. 278–285. Springer, Heidelberg (2008)
5. Bender, M., Farach-Colton, M., He, S., Kuszmaul, B., Leiserson, C.: Adversarial contention resolution for simple channels. In: SPAA 2005, pp. 325–332. ACM, New York (2005)
6. Capetanakis, J.: Generalized tdma: The multi-accessing tree protocol. IEEE Transactions on Communications 27(10), 1476–1484 (1979)

7. Capetanakis, J.: Tree algorithms for packet broadcast channels. IEEE Transactions on Information Theory 25(5), 505–515 (1979)
8. Fiat, A., Mansour, Y., Nadav, U.: Efficient contention resolution protocols for selfish agents. In: SODA 2007, pp. 179–188. SIAM, Philadelphia (2007)
9. Georgiadis, L., Papantoni-Kazakos, P.: A collision resolution protocol for random access channels with energy detectors. IEEE Transactions on Communications COM-30, 2413–2420 (1982)
10. Geréb-Graus, M., Tsantilas, T.: Efficient optical communication in parallel computers. In: SPAA 1992, pp. 41–48. ACM, New York (1992)
11. Goldberg, L.A., MacKenzie, P.D.: Analysis of practical backoff protocols for contention resolution with multiple servers. J. Comput. Syst. Sci. 58(1), 232–258 (1999)
12. Goldberg, L.A., Mackenzie, P.D., Paterson, M., Srinivasan, A.: Contention resolution with constant expected delay. J. ACM 47(6), 1048–1096 (2000)
13. Greenberg, A., Winograd, S.: A lower bound on the time needed in the worst case to resolve conflicts deterministically in multiple access channels. J. ACM 32(3), 589–596 (1985)
14. Hayes, J.: An adaptive technique for local distribution. IEEE Transactions on Communications 26(8), 1178–1186 (1978)
15. Koutsoupias, E., Papadimitriou, C.H.: Worst-case equilibria. In: Meinel, C., Tison, S. (eds.) STACS 1999. LNCS, vol. 1563, pp. 404–413. Springer, Heidelberg (1999)
16. Ma, R.T., Misra, V., Rubenstein, D.: Modeling and analysis of generalized slotted-aloha mac protocols in cooperative, competitive and adversarial environments. In: ICDCS 2006, Washington, DC, USA, p. 62. IEEE, Los Alamitos (2006)
17. MacKenzie, A., Wicker, S.: Stability of multipacket slotted aloha with selfish users and perfect information (2003)
18. MacKenzie, P.D., Plaxton, C.G., Rajaraman, R.: On contention resolution protocols and associated probabilistic phenomena. J. ACM 45(2), 324–378 (1998)
19. Menache, I., Shimkin, N.: Efficient rate-constrained nash equilibrium in collision channels with state information. In: INFOCOM 2008, pp. 403–411 (2008)
20. Pippenger, N.: Bounds on the performance of protocols for a multiple-access broadcast channel. IEEE Transactions on Information Theory 27(2), 145–151 (1981)
21. Raghavan, P., Upfal, E.: Stochastic contention resolution with short delays. Technical report, Weizmann Science Press of Israel, Jerusalem, Israel, Israel (1995)
22. Roberts, L.: Aloha packet system with and without slots and capture. SIGCOMM Comput. Commun. Rev. 5(2), 28–42 (1975)
23. Ruszinko, M., Vanroose, P.: How an erdöos-rényi-type search approach gives an explicit code construction of rate 1 for random access with multiplicity feedback. IEEE Transactions on Information Theory 43(1), 368–372 (1997)
24. Srivastava, V., Neel, J.A., MacKenzie, A.B., Hicks, J.E., DaSilva, L.A., Reed, J.H., Gilles, R.P.: Using game theory to analyze wireless ad hoc networks. IEEE Communications Surveys and Tutorials 7(5), 46–56 (2005)
25. Tsybakov, B.: Resolution of a conflict of known multiplicity. Problemy Peredachi Informatsii (1980)
26. Tsybakov, B.S., Mikhailov, V.A.: Free synchronous packet access in a broadcast channel with feedback. Problems of Information Transmission 14(4), 259–280 (1978)
27. Wang, D., Comaniciu, C., Tureli, U.: Cooperation and fairness for slotted aloha. Wirel. Pers. Commun. 43(1), 13–27 (2007)
28. Zheng, D., Ge, W., Zhang, J.: Distributed opportunistic scheduling for ad-hoc communications: an optimal stopping approach. In: MobiHoc 2007, pp. 1–10. ACM, New York (2007)

On the Expressiveness of Polyadic and Synchronous Communication in Higher-Order Process Calculi

Ivan Lanese[1], Jorge A. Pérez[2], Davide Sangiorgi[1], and Alan Schmitt[3]

[1] Laboratory FOCUS (University of Bologna/INRIA)
[2] CITI - Department of Computer Science, FCT New University of Lisbon
[3] INRIA

Abstract. *Higher-order process calculi* are calculi in which processes can be communicated. We study the expressiveness of *strictly* higher-order process calculi, and focus on two issues well-understood for first-order calculi but not in the higher-order setting: *synchronous* vs. *asynchronous* communication and *polyadic* vs. *monadic* communication. First, and similarly to the first-order setting, synchronous process-passing is shown to be encodable into asynchronous process-passing. Then, the absence of name-passing is shown to induce a hierarchy of higher-order process calculi based on the arity of polyadic communication, thus revealing a striking point of contrast with respect to first-order calculi. Finally, the passing of *abstractions* (i.e., functions from processes to processes) is shown to be more expressive than process-passing alone.

1 Introduction

Higher-order process calculi are calculi in which processes can be communicated. In this paper, we study the expressive power of *strictly* higher-order process calculi, and concentrate on fundamental questions of expressiveness in process calculi at large: *asynchronous* vs. *synchronous* communication and *polyadic* vs. *monadic* communication. These are well-understood issues for first-order process calculi: several works (see, e.g., [1,2,3]) have studied the *asynchronous π-calculus* [4,5] and its relationship with the (synchronous) π-calculus. Also, the encoding of polyadic communication into monadic communication in the π-calculus [6] is simple and very robust [7,8]. However, analogous studies are lacking for calculi in the higher-order setting.

We approach these questions in the context of HOπ, a *strictly* higher-order process calculus (i.e., it has no name-passing features) [9]. HOπ is very expressive: it is Turing complete and several modelling idioms are expressible in it as derived constructs. Hence, answers to the questions we are interested in are far from obvious. We shall consider SHO and AHO, the synchronous and asynchronous variants of HOπ with polyadic communication (Section 2). SHO and AHO represent two *families* of higher-order process calculi: given $n \geq 0$, SHO^n (resp. AHO^n) denotes the synchronous (resp. asynchronous) higher-order process calculus with n-adic communication.

A fundamental consideration in strictly higher-order process calculi is that scope extrusions have a limited effect. In a process-passing setting, received processes can only be executed, forwarded, or discarded. Hence, an input context cannot gain access to the (private) names of the processes it receives; to the context, received processes are

S. Abramsky et al. (Eds.): ICALP 2010, Part II, LNCS 6199, pp. 442–453, 2010.

much like a "black box". Although higher-order communications might lead to scope extrusion of the private names *contained* in the transmitted processes, such extrusions are of little significance: without name-passing, a receiving context can only use the names contained in a process in a restricted way, namely the way decreed by the sender process.[1] In a process-passing setting, sharing of (private) names is thus rather limited.

We begin by investigating the relationship between synchrony and asynchrony. Our first contribution is an *encodability* result: an encoding of SHO^n into AHO^n (Section 4). This reveals a similarity between first- and higher-order process calculi. Intuitively, a synchronous output is encoded by an asynchronous output that communicates both the communication object and its continuation. In Section 5 we move to examine the situation for polyadic communication. We consider variants of SHO with different arity in communications, and study their relative expressive power. Interestingly, in the case of polyadic communication, the absence of name-passing causes a loss in expressive power. Our second contribution is a *non-encodability* result: for every $n > 1$, SHO^n cannot be encoded into SHO^{n-1}. We thus obtain a *hierarchy* of higher-order process calculi of strictly increasing expressiveness. Hence, polyadic communication is a striking point of contrast between first- and higher-order process calculi. Finally, in Section 6 we consider the extension of SHO with *abstraction-passing*. An abstraction is an expression parametric on processes; the expressiveness of abstraction-passing is thus specific to the higher-order setting. We consider SHO^n_a, the extension of SHO^n with abstractions of order one (i.e., functions from processes to processes). We show that SHO^n can be encoded into SHO^1_a. Our final contribution uses this result to show that there is no encoding of SHO^n_a into SHO^m for $n, m > 0$.

Our notion of encoding exploits a refined account of internal actions: in SHO, the internal actions that result from synchronizations on restricted names are distinguished from those resulting from synchronizations on public names. Only the former are considered as internal actions; the latter are regarded as visible actions. While this distinction might appear as demanding in the light of recent proposals for "good encodings" (e.g., [10]), we find it useful to focus on *compositional* encodings that are *robust with respect to interferences*, that is, encodings that work in an arbitrary context of the target language (i.e., not necessarily a context in the image of the encoding). Further, the distinction is crucial in certain technical details of our proofs.

Extended discussions and full technical details can be found in [11, Chapter 6].

2 The Calculi

We define SHO^n and AHO^n, the two families of higher-order process calculi we shall be working with.

Definition 1. *Let x, y range over process variables, and $a, b, \ldots r, s, \ldots$ denote names. The language of* SHO *processes is given by the following syntax:*

$$P, Q, \ldots ::= a(\widetilde{x}).\, P \;\big|\; \bar{a}\langle \widetilde{Q} \rangle.\, P \;\big|\; P_1 \parallel P_2 \;\big|\; \nu r\, P \;\big|\; x \;\big|\; \mathbf{0}$$

[1] Here we refer to process-passing *without* passing of abstractions, i.e. functions from processes to processes. As we shall see, the situation is rather different with abstraction-passing.

$$\textsc{Inp}\ \frac{}{a(\widetilde{x}).\,P \xrightarrow{a(\widetilde{x})} P} \qquad \textsc{Out}\ \frac{}{\overline{a}\langle\widetilde{Q}\rangle.\,P \xrightarrow{\overline{a}\langle\widetilde{Q}\rangle} P} \qquad \textsc{Act1}\ \frac{P_1 \xrightarrow{\alpha} P_1' \quad \mathsf{cond}(\alpha, P_2)}{P_1 \parallel P_2 \xrightarrow{\alpha} P_1' \parallel P_2}$$

$$\textsc{Res}\ \frac{P \xrightarrow{\alpha} P' \quad r \notin \mathsf{n}(\alpha)}{\nu r\, P \xrightarrow{\alpha} \nu r\, P'} \qquad \textsc{Open}\ \frac{P \xrightarrow{(\nu\widetilde{s})\overline{a}\langle\widetilde{P''}\rangle} P' \quad r \neq a,\ r \in \mathsf{fn}(\widetilde{P''}) - \widetilde{s}}{\nu r\, P \xrightarrow{(\nu r\widetilde{s})\overline{a}\langle\widetilde{P''}\rangle} P'}$$

$$\textsc{Tau1}\ \frac{P_1 \xrightarrow{(\nu\widetilde{s})\overline{a}\langle\widetilde{P}\rangle} P_1' \quad P_2 \xrightarrow{a(\widetilde{x})} P_2' \quad \widetilde{s} \cap \mathsf{fn}(P_2) = \emptyset}{P_1 \parallel P_2 \xrightarrow{a\tau} \nu\widetilde{s}\,(P_1' \parallel P_2'\{\widetilde{P}/\widetilde{x}\})} \qquad \textsc{IntRes}\ \frac{P \xrightarrow{a\tau} P'}{\nu a\, P \xrightarrow{\tau} \nu a\, P}$$

Fig. 1. The LTS of SHO. Symmetric rules ACT2 and TAU2 are omitted.

Using standard notations and properties for tuples of syntactic elements, polyadicity in process-passing is interpreted as expected: an output prefixed process $\overline{a}\langle\widetilde{Q}\rangle.\,P$ sends the tuple of processes $\widetilde{Q}$ on name (or channel) a and then continues as P; an input prefixed process $a(\widetilde{x}).\,P$ can receive a tuple $\widetilde{Q}$ on name a and continue as $P\{\widetilde{Q}/\widetilde{x}\}$. In both cases, a is said to be the *subject* of the action. We write $|\,\widetilde{x}\,|$ for the length of tuple $\widetilde{x}$; the length of the tuples that are passed around determines the actual *arity* in polyadic communication. In interactions, we assume inputs and outputs have the same arity; we shall rely on notions of *types* and *well-typed processes* as in [9]. Parallel composition allows processes to interact, and $\nu r\, P$ makes r private (or restricted) to the process P. Notions of bound and free names and variables ($\mathsf{bn}(\cdot)$, $\mathsf{fn}(\cdot)$, $\mathsf{bv}(\cdot)$, and $\mathsf{fv}(\cdot)$, resp.) are defined in the usual way: an input $a(\widetilde{x}).\,P$ binds the free occurrences of variables in $\widetilde{x}$ in P; similarly, $\nu r\, P$ binds the free occurrences of name r in P. We abbreviate $a(\widetilde{x}).\,P$ as $a.\,P$ when none of the variables in $\widetilde{x}$ is in $\mathsf{fv}(P)$; $\overline{a}\langle\widetilde{\mathbf{0}}\rangle.\,P$ as $\overline{a}.\,P$; $\overline{a}\langle Q\rangle.\,\mathbf{0}$ as $\overline{a}\langle Q\rangle$; and $\nu a\, \nu b\, P$ as $\nu a\, b\, P$. Notation $\prod^k P$ stands for k copies of process P in parallel.

The semantics for SHO is given by the Labelled Transition System (LTS) in Figure 1; we use $\mathsf{cond}(\alpha, P)$ to abbreviate $\mathsf{bv}(\alpha) \cap \mathsf{fv}(P) = \emptyset \wedge \mathsf{bn}(\alpha) \cap \mathsf{fn}(P) = \emptyset$. As anticipated, we distinguish between *internal* and *public* synchronizations. The former are given by synchronizations on *restricted* names, are the only source of internal behavior, and are denoted as $\xrightarrow{\tau}$. The latter are given by synchronization on *public* names: a synchronization on the public name a leads to the visible action $\xrightarrow{a\tau}$. We thus have four kinds of transitions: in addition to internal and public synchronizations, there are input transitions $P \xrightarrow{a(\widetilde{x})} P'$, and output transitions $P \xrightarrow{(\nu\widetilde{s})\overline{a}\langle\widetilde{Q}\rangle} P'$ (with extrusion of the tuple of names $\widetilde{s}$), which have the expected meaning. We use α to range over actions. The *signature* of α, $\mathsf{sig}(\alpha)$, is defined as $\mathsf{sig}(a(\widetilde{x})) = a\,\mathsf{in}$, $\mathsf{sig}((\nu\widetilde{s})\overline{a}\langle\widetilde{Q}\rangle) = a\,\mathsf{out}$, $\mathsf{sig}(a\tau) = a\tau$, $\mathsf{sig}(\tau) = \tau$, and is undefined otherwise. Notions of bound/free names and variables extend to actions as expected. We use $\vec{\alpha}$ to denote a sequence of actions $\alpha_1, \ldots, \alpha_n$. Weak transitions are defined in the usual way. We write $\Rightarrow$ for the reflexive, transitive closure of $\xrightarrow{\tau}$. Given an action $\alpha \neq \tau$, notation $\xRightarrow{\alpha}$ stands for $\Rightarrow\xrightarrow{\alpha}\Rightarrow$ and $\xRightarrow{\tau}$ stands for $\Rightarrow$. Given a sequence $\vec{\alpha} = \alpha_1, \ldots, \alpha_n$, we define $\xRightarrow{\vec{\alpha}}$ as $\xRightarrow{\alpha_1} \cdots \xRightarrow{\alpha_n}$.

By varying the arity in polyadic communication, Definition 1 actually gives a *family* of higher-order process calculi. We have the following notational convention:

Convention 1. *For each $n > 0$,* SHO^n *corresponds to the calculus obtained from the syntax given in Definition 1 in which polyadic communication has arity at most n.*

Definition 2. AHO *corresponds to the fragment of* SHO *where output actions have no continuations. All the definitions extend to* AHO *processes as expected;* AHO^n *is thus the asynchronous calculus with n-adic communication.*

The following definition is standard.

Definition 3 (Barbs). *Given a process P and a name a, we write (i) $P \downarrow_a$ —a* strong input barb— *if P can perform an input action with subject a; and (ii) $P \downarrow_{\overline{a}}$ —a* strong output barb— *if P can perform an output action with subject a. Given $\mu \in \{a, \overline{a}\}$, we define a* weak *barb $P \Downarrow_\mu$ if, for some P', $P \Rightarrow P' \downarrow_\mu$.*

3 The Notion of Encoding

Our definition of encoding is inspired by the notion of "good encoding" in [10]. We say that a *language* $\mathcal{L}$ is given by: (i) an algebra of *processes* $\mathcal{P}$, with an associated function $\mathsf{fn}(\cdot)$; (ii) a labeled transition relation $\longrightarrow$ on $\mathcal{P}$, i.e., a structure $(\mathcal{P}, \mathcal{A}, \longrightarrow)$ for some set $\mathcal{A}$ of *actions* (or *labels*) with an associated function $\mathsf{sig}(\cdot)$; and (iii) a weak behavioral equivalence $\approx$ such that: if $P \approx Q$ and $P \stackrel{\alpha}{\Longrightarrow} P'$ then $Q \stackrel{\alpha'}{\Longrightarrow} Q'$, $P' \approx Q'$, and $\mathsf{sig}(\alpha) = \mathsf{sig}(\alpha')$. Given languages $\mathcal{L}_\mathsf{s} = (\mathcal{P}_\mathsf{s}, \longrightarrow_\mathsf{s}, \approx_\mathsf{s})$ and $\mathcal{L}_\mathsf{t} = (\mathcal{P}_\mathsf{t}, \longrightarrow_\mathsf{t}, \approx_\mathsf{t})$, a *translation* of $\mathcal{L}_\mathsf{s}$ into $\mathcal{L}_\mathsf{t}$ is a function $[\![\cdot]\!] : \mathcal{P}_\mathsf{s} \to \mathcal{P}_\mathsf{t}$. We shall call *encoding* any translation that satisfies the following syntactic and semantic conditions.

Definition 4 (Syntactic Conditions). *Let $[\![\cdot]\!] : \mathcal{P}_\mathsf{s} \to \mathcal{P}_\mathsf{t}$ be a translation of $\mathcal{L}_\mathsf{s}$ into $\mathcal{L}_\mathsf{t}$. We say that $[\![\cdot]\!]$ is:*

1. compositional *if for every k-ary operator* op *of $\mathcal{L}_\mathsf{s}$ and for all $S_1, \ldots, S_k$ with* $\mathsf{fn}(S_1, \ldots, S_k) = N$*, there exists a k-ary context $C^N_{\mathsf{op}} \in \mathcal{P}_\mathsf{t}$ that depends on N and* op *such that* $[\![\mathsf{op}(S_1, \ldots, S_k)]\!] = C^N_{\mathsf{op}}[[\![S_1]\!], \ldots, [\![S_k]\!]]$;
2. name invariant *if $[\![\sigma(P)]\!] = \sigma([\![P]\!])$, for any injective renaming of names σ.*

Definition 5 (Semantic Conditions). *Let $[\![\cdot]\!] : \mathcal{P}_\mathsf{s} \to \mathcal{P}_\mathsf{t}$ be a translation of $\mathcal{L}_\mathsf{s}$ into $\mathcal{L}_\mathsf{t}$. We say that $[\![\cdot]\!]$ is:*

1. complete *if for every $S, S' \in \mathcal{P}_\mathsf{s}$ and $\alpha \in \mathcal{A}_\mathsf{s}$ such that $S \stackrel{\alpha}{\Longrightarrow}_\mathsf{s} S'$, it holds that $[\![S]\!] \stackrel{\beta}{\Longrightarrow}_\mathsf{t} \approx_\mathsf{t} [\![S']\!]$, where $\beta \in \mathcal{A}_\mathsf{t}$ and $\mathsf{sig}(\alpha) = \mathsf{sig}(\beta)$;*
2. sound *if for every $S \in \mathcal{P}_\mathsf{s}$, $T \in \mathcal{P}_\mathsf{t}$, $\beta \in \mathcal{A}_\mathsf{t}$ such that $[\![S]\!] \stackrel{\beta}{\Longrightarrow}_\mathsf{t} T$ there exists an $S' \in \mathcal{P}_\mathsf{s}$ and an $\alpha \in \mathcal{A}_\mathsf{s}$ such that $S \stackrel{\alpha}{\Longrightarrow}_\mathsf{s} S'$, $T \Rightarrow \approx_\mathsf{t} [\![S']\!]$, and $\mathsf{sig}(\alpha) = \mathsf{sig}(\beta)$;*
3. adequate *if for every $S, S' \in \mathcal{P}_\mathsf{s}$, if $S \approx_\mathsf{s} S'$ then $[\![S]\!] \approx_\mathsf{t} [\![S']\!]$;*
4. diverge-reflecting *if for every $S \in \mathcal{P}_\mathsf{s}$, $[\![S]\!]$ diverges only if S diverges.*

Adequacy is crucial to obtain *composability* of encodings (see Prop. 1 below). We stress that we always use *weak* behavioral equivalences. Some properties of our notion of encoding are given in the following proposition, whose proof we omit for space reasons.

Proposition 1. *Let* $[\![\cdot]\!]$ *be an encoding of* $\mathcal{L}_s$ *into* $\mathcal{L}_t$. *Then* $[\![\cdot]\!]$ *satisfies:*

Barb preservation. *For every* $S \in \mathcal{P}_s$ *it holds that* $S \Downarrow_{\overline{a}}$ *(resp.* $S \Downarrow_a$*) if and only if* $[\![S]\!] \Downarrow_{\overline{a}}$ *(resp.* $[\![S]\!] \Downarrow_a$*).*

Preservation of free names. *Let* a *be a name. If* $a \in \mathsf{fn}(P)$ *then* $a \in \mathsf{fn}([\![P]\!])$.

Composability. *If* $\mathcal{C}[\![\cdot]\!]$ *is an encoding of* $\mathcal{L}_1$ *into* $\mathcal{L}_2$, *and* $\mathcal{D}[\![\cdot]\!]$ *is an encoding of* $\mathcal{L}_2$ *into* $\mathcal{L}_3$ *then their composition* $(\mathcal{D} \cdot \mathcal{C})[\![\cdot]\!]$ *is an encoding of* $\mathcal{L}_1$ *into* $\mathcal{L}_3$.

4 An Encodability Result for Synchronous Communication

Here we study the relationship between synchronous and asynchronous communication. While it is easy to define an encoding of SHO^n into AHO^{n+1} (i.e., by sending the communication object and the continuation of the output action in a single synchronization, the continuation being an additional parameter), an encoding of asynchronous process-passing into synchronous communication of the *same arity* is much more challenging. We now describe such an encoding. Intuitively, the idea is to send a *single process* consisting of a guarded choice between a communication object and the continuation of the synchronous output. For the monadic case the encoding is as follows:

$$[\![\overline{a}\langle P\rangle.\, S]\!] = \nu k\, l\, (\overline{a}\langle k.\, ([\![P]\!] \parallel \overline{k}) + l.\, ([\![S]\!] \parallel \overline{k})\rangle \parallel \overline{l}) \quad [\![a(x).\, R]\!] = a(x).\, (x \parallel [\![R]\!])$$

where "+" stands for the encoding of disjoint choice proposed for HOCORE [12]; k, l are names not in $\mathsf{fn}(P, S)$; and $[\![\cdot]\!]$ is an homomorphism for the other operators in SHO^1. The encoding exploits the fact that the continuation should be executed exactly once, while the communication object can be executed zero or more times. In fact, there is only one copy of $\overline{l}$, the trigger that executes the encoding of the continuation. Notice that $\overline{l}$ releases both the encoding of the continuation and a trigger for executing the encoding of the communication object (denoted $\overline{k}$); such an execution will only occur when the choice sent by the encoding of output appears at the top level. This way, it is easy to see that a trigger $\overline{k}$ is always available. This idea can be generalized as follows:

Definition 6 (Synchronous to Asynchronous). *For each* $n > 0$, *the encoding of* SHO^n *into* AHO^n *is defined as follows:*

$$[\![\overline{a}\langle P_1, \ldots, P_n\rangle.\, S]\!] = \nu k\, l\, (\overline{a}\langle [\![P_1]\!], \ldots, [\![P_{n-1}]\!], T_{k,l}[\, [\![P_n]\!], [\![S]\!]\,]\rangle \parallel \overline{l})$$
$$[\![a(x_1, \ldots, x_n).\, R]\!] = a(x_1, \ldots, x_n).\, (x_n \parallel [\![R]\!])$$

with $T_{k,l}[M_1, M_2] \stackrel{def}{=} k.\, (M_1 \parallel \overline{k}) + l.\, (M_2 \parallel \overline{k})$, $\{k, l\} \cap \mathsf{fn}(P_1, \ldots, P_n, S) = \emptyset$, *and where* $[\![\cdot]\!]$ *is an homomorphism for the other operators in* SHO^n.

Correctness of the encoding (i.e. proofs that the encoding satisfies the conditions in Section 3) is presented in [11]. The encoding provides compelling evidence on the expressive power of (asynchronous) process-passing. The observation that the encoding of synchronous into asynchronous communication is a particular case of that of polyadic into monadic communication leaves open the possibility that an encoding as in the π-calculus might exist in a process-passing setting. In the next section we prove that this is *not* the case.

5 Separation Results for Polyadic Communication

Here we present the separation results for SHO. Section 5.1 introduces the notion of *disjoint forms*, which are useful to capture a number of *stability conditions*, i.e., invariant properties of higher-order processes with respect to their sets of private names. Stability conditions are essential in defining the hierarchy of SHO calculi based on polyadic communication, which is reported in Section 5.2.

5.1 Disjoint Forms

The *disjoint forms* for SHO processes are intended to capture the invariant structure of processes along communications, focusing on the private names shared among the participants. Their definition exploits *contexts*, that is, processes with a hole. We shall consider *multi-hole contexts*, that is, contexts with more than one hole. More precisely, a multi-hole context is n-ary if at most n different holes $[\cdot]_1, \ldots, [\cdot]_n$, occur in it. (A process is a 0-ary multi-hole context.) We will assume that any hole $[\cdot]_i$ can occur more than once in the context expression. Notions of free and bound names for contexts are as expected and denoted $\mathsf{bn}(\cdot)$ and $\mathsf{fn}(\cdot)$, respectively.

Definition 7. *The syntax of (guarded, multihole) contexts is defined as:*

$$C, C', \ldots ::= a(x).\, D \;\big|\; \bar{a}\langle D\rangle.\, D \;\big|\; C \parallel C \;\big|\; \nu r\, C \;\big|\; P$$
$$D, D', \ldots ::= [\cdot]_i \;\big|\; C \;\big|\; D \parallel D \;\big|\; \nu r\, D$$

Definition 8 (Disjoint Form). *Let $T \equiv \nu\widetilde{n}(P \parallel C[\widetilde{R}])$ be a* SHO^m *process where*

1. *$\widetilde{n}$ is a set of names such that $\widetilde{n} \subseteq \mathsf{fn}(P, \widetilde{R})$ and $\widetilde{n} \cap \mathsf{fn}(C) = \emptyset$;*
2. *C is a k-ary (guarded, multihole) context;*
3. *$\widetilde{R}$ contains k closed processes.*

*We then say that T is in k-*adic disjoint form with respect to $\widetilde{n}$, $\widetilde{R}$, and P.

A disjoint form captures the fact that processes $\widetilde{R}$ and context C do not share private names, i.e., that their sets of names are *disjoint*. A disjoint form can arise as the result of the communication between two processes that do not share private names; processes $\widetilde{R}$ would be then components of some process P_0 that evolved into P by communicating $\widetilde{R}$ to C. The above definition decrees an arbitrary (but fixed) arity for the context. We shall say that processes in such a form are in *n-adic disjoint form*, or NDF. By restricting the arity of the context, this general definition can be instantiated:

Definition 9 (Monadic and Zero-adic Disjoint Forms). *Let T be a process in disjoint form with respect to some $\widetilde{n}$, $\widetilde{R}$, and P. If $\mid \widetilde{R} \mid = 1$ then T is said to be in* monadic disjoint form *(or* MDF*) with respect to $\widetilde{n}$, R, and P. If $\mid \widetilde{R} \mid = 0$ then T is said to be in* zero-adic disjoint form *(or* ZDF*) with respect to $\widetilde{n}$ and P.*

Proposition 2 (Encodings preserve ZDFs). *Let $[\![\cdot]\!]$ be an encoding. If T is in ZDF with respect to some $\widetilde{n}$ and P then $[\![T]\!]$ is in ZDF with respect to $\widetilde{n}$ and $[\![P]\!]$.*

Properties of Disjoint Forms I: Stability Conditions. Stability conditions are central to capture the following insight: without name-passing, the set of names private to a process remains invariant along computations. Hence, two processes that interact respecting the stability conditions and do not share any private name will never be able to establish a private link. The distinction on internal actions is essential to define stability conditions for internal synchronizations (Lemma 1) and output actions (Lemma 2).

Lemma 1. *Let* $T \equiv \nu\widetilde{n}\,(P \parallel C[\widetilde{R}])$ *be a process in NDF with respect to* $\widetilde{n}$, $\widetilde{R}$, *and* P. *If* $T \xrightarrow{\tau} T'$ *then:* $T' \equiv \nu\widetilde{n}\,(P' \parallel C'[\widetilde{R}])$; $\mathsf{fn}(P', \widetilde{R}) \subseteq \mathsf{fn}(P, \widetilde{R})$ *and* $\mathsf{fn}(C') \subseteq \mathsf{fn}(C)$; T' *is in NDF with respect to* $\widetilde{n}$, $\widetilde{R}$, *and* P'.

The following results state that there is a stability condition for output actions, and the way in which a ZDF evolves after a *public* synchronization.

Lemma 2. *Let* $T \equiv \nu\widetilde{n}\,(P \parallel C[\widetilde{R}])$ *be a process in NDF with respect to* $\widetilde{n}$, $\widetilde{R}$, *and* P. *If* $T \xrightarrow{(\nu\widetilde{s})\overline{a}\langle Q\rangle} T'$ *then: there exist* P', C', $\widetilde{n}'$ *such that* $T' \equiv \nu\widetilde{n}'\,(P' \parallel C'[\widetilde{R}])$; $\mathsf{fn}(P', \widetilde{R}) \subseteq \mathsf{fn}(P, \widetilde{R})$, $\mathsf{fn}(C') \subseteq \mathsf{fn}(C)$ *and* $\widetilde{n}' \subseteq \widetilde{n}$ *hold;* T' *is in NDF with respect to* $\widetilde{n}'$, $\widetilde{R}$, *and* P'.

Lemma 3. *Let* T *be a* SHO^n *process in ZDF with respect to* $\widetilde{n}$ *and* P. *Suppose* $T \xrightarrow{a\tau} T'$ *where* $\xrightarrow{a\tau}$ *is a public* n*-adic synchronization with* $P \xrightarrow{(\nu\widetilde{n})\overline{a}\langle\widetilde{R}\rangle} P'$ *as a premise. Then* T' *is in* n*-adic disjoint form with respect to* $\widetilde{n}$, $\widetilde{R}$, *and* P'.

Properties of Disjoint Forms II: Origin of Actions. We now give some properties regarding the order and origin of internal and output actions of processes in DFs.

Definition 10. *Let* $T = \nu\widetilde{n}\,(A \parallel C[\widetilde{R}])$ *be a process in NDF with respect to* $\widetilde{n}$, $\widetilde{R}$, *and* A. *Suppose* $T \xrightarrow{\alpha} T'$ *for some action* α.

- *Let* α *be an output action. We say that* α originates in A *if* $A \xrightarrow{\alpha'} A'$ *occurs as a premise in the derivation of* $T \xrightarrow{\alpha} T'$, *and that* α originates in C *if* $C[\widetilde{R}] \xrightarrow{\alpha'} C'[\widetilde{R}]$ *occurs as a premise in the derivation of* $T \xrightarrow{\alpha} T'$. *In both cases,* $\alpha = (\nu\widetilde{s})\alpha'$ *for some* $\widetilde{s}$.
- *Let* $\alpha = \tau$. *We say that* α originates in A *if, for some* $a \in \widetilde{n}$, $A \xrightarrow{a\tau} A'$ *occurs as a premise in the derivation of* $T \xrightarrow{\alpha} T'$, *or if* $A \xrightarrow{\tau} A'$ *occurs as a premise in the derivation of* $T \xrightarrow{\alpha} T'$. *We say that* α originates in C *if* $C[\widetilde{R}] \xrightarrow{\tau} C'[\widetilde{R}]$ *occurs as a premise in the derivation of* $T \xrightarrow{\alpha} T'$.

The lemma below formalizes when two actions of a disjoint form can be *swapped*.

Lemma 4 (Swapping Lemma). *Let* $T = \nu\widetilde{n}\,(A \parallel C[\widetilde{R}])$ *be a process in NDF with respect to* $\widetilde{n}$, $\widetilde{R}$, *and* A. *Consider two actions* α *and* β *that can be either output actions or internal synchronizations. Suppose that* α *originates in* A, β *originates in* C, *and that there exists a* T' *such that* $T \xrightarrow{\alpha}\xrightarrow{\beta} T'$. *Then* $T \xrightarrow{\beta}\xrightarrow{\alpha} T'$ *also holds, i.e., action* β *can be performed before* α *without affecting the final behavior.*

The converse of the Swapping Lemma does not hold: since an action β originated in C can enable an action α originated in A, these cannot be swapped. We now generalize the Swapping Lemma to a sequence of internal synchronizations and output actions.

Lemma 5 (Commuting Lemma). *Let $T = \nu\widetilde{n}\,(A \parallel C[\widetilde{R}])$ be a NDF with respect to $\widetilde{n}$, $\widetilde{R}$, and A. Suppose $T \stackrel{\vec{\alpha}}{\Longrightarrow} T'$, where $\vec{\alpha}$ is a sequence of output actions and internal synchronizations. Let $\vec{\alpha}_C$ (resp. $\vec{\alpha}_A$) be its subsequence without actions originated in A (resp. C) or in its derivatives. Then, there exists a process T_1 such that*

1. $T \stackrel{\vec{\alpha}_C}{\Longrightarrow} T_1 \stackrel{\vec{\alpha}_A}{\Longrightarrow} T'$.
2. $T_1 \equiv \nu\widetilde{n}'\,(A \parallel \prod^{m_1} R_1 \parallel \cdots \parallel \prod^{m_k} R_k \parallel C'[\widetilde{R}])$, *for some* $m_1, \ldots, m_k \geq 0$.

5.2 A Hierarchy of Synchronous Higher-Order Process Calculi

We introduce a hierarchy of synchronous higher-order process calculi. The hierarchy is defined in terms of the impossibility of encoding SHO^n into SHO^{n-1}. We first present the result that sets the basic case of the hierarchy, namely that biadic process-passing cannot be encoded into monadic process-passing (Theorem 1). The proof exploits the notion of MDF and its associated stability conditions. We then state the general result, i.e., the impossibility of encoding SHO^{n+1} into SHO^n (Theorem 2).

Theorem 1. *There is no encoding of* SHO^2 *into* SHO^1.

Proof (Sketch). Assume, towards a contradiction, that an encoding $[\![\cdot]\!] : \mathrm{SHO}^2 \to \mathrm{SHO}^1$ does indeed exist. In what follows, we use i, j to range over $\{1, 2\}$, assuming that $i \neq j$. Assume processes $S_1 = \overline{s_1}$ and $S_2 = \overline{s_2}$. Consider the SHO^2 process $P = E^{(2)} \parallel F^{(2)}$, where $E^{(2)}$ and $F^{(2)}$ are defined as follows:

$$E^{(2)} = \overline{a}\langle S_1,\, S_2\rangle.\,\mathbf{0}$$
$$F^{(2)} = \nu b\,(a(x_1, x_2).\,(\overline{b}\langle \overline{b_1}.\,x_1\rangle.\,\mathbf{0} \parallel \overline{b}\langle \overline{b_2}.\,x_2\rangle.\,\mathbf{0} \parallel b(y_1).\,b(y_2).\,y_1))$$

where both $b_1, b_2 \notin \mathsf{fn}(E^{(2)})$ (with $b_1 \neq b_2$) and $s_1, s_2 \notin \mathsf{fn}(F^{(2)})$ (with $s_1 \neq s_2$) hold. P can perform only the following computations:

$$P \xrightarrow{a\tau} P_0 \xrightarrow{\tau}\xrightarrow{\tau} P_1 \xrightarrow{\overline{b_1}} P_2 \xrightarrow{\overline{s_1}} \mathbf{0} \qquad (1)$$
$$P \xrightarrow{a\tau} P_0 \xrightarrow{\tau}\xrightarrow{\tau} P_1' \xrightarrow{\overline{b_2}} P_2' \xrightarrow{\overline{s_2}} \mathbf{0}\,. \qquad (2)$$

In P_0 there is an internal choice on b, which has direct influence on: (i) the output action on b_i and (ii) the output action on s_i. Notice that each of these actions enables the following one, and that an output on b_i precludes the possibility of actions on b_j and s_j. The behavior of $[\![P]\!]$ —the encoding of P— can thus be described as follows:

$$[\![P]\!] \stackrel{a\tau}{\Longrightarrow}\approx [\![P_0]\!] \Rightarrow\approx [\![P_1]\!] \stackrel{\overline{b_1}}{\Longrightarrow}\approx [\![P_2]\!] \stackrel{\overline{s_1}}{\Longrightarrow}\approx \mathbf{0} \quad \text{and} \qquad (3)$$
$$[\![P]\!] \stackrel{a\tau}{\Longrightarrow}\approx [\![P_0]\!] \Rightarrow\approx [\![P_1']\!] \stackrel{\overline{b_2}}{\Longrightarrow}\approx [\![P_2']\!] \stackrel{\overline{s_2}}{\Longrightarrow}\approx \mathbf{0}\,. \qquad (4)$$

Actually, outputs may have parameters, but this does not change our results. The first (weak) transition, namely $[\![P]\!] \stackrel{a\tau}{\Longrightarrow}\approx [\![P_0]\!]$, is the same in both possibilities. For SHO[1] processes T, T', and T_0, it holds

$$[\![P]\!] \Rightarrow T \xrightarrow{a\tau} T' \Rightarrow T_0 \approx [\![P_0]\!]\,. \tag{5}$$

By examining the disjoint forms in the processes in (5) and using the stability conditions (Prop. 2, Lemma 3, Lemma 1) one can show that T_0 is in MDF with respect to a set of names $\widetilde{l}$, and some processes R and A_0. Indeed, for some context C_0 (with private name b), we have that $T_0 = \nu\widetilde{l}\,(A_0 \parallel C_0[R])$. Notice that (5) ensures that $T_0 \approx [\![P_0]\!]$. Hence, by definition of $\approx$, T_0 should be able to match each action from $[\![P_0]\!]$ by performing either the sequence of actions given in (3) or the one in (4). Crucially, both (3) and (4) involve only internal synchronizations and output actions. Therefore, by Lemmas 1 and 2, every derivative of T_0 intended to mimic the behavior of $[\![P_0]\!]$ (and its derivatives) is in MDF with respect to R, some l_i and some A_i.

By analyzing the bisimilarity game between T_0 and $[\![P_0]\!]$, it is possible to infer the following behavior starting in T_0:

$$T_0 \Rightarrow T_1 \stackrel{\overline{b_1}}{\Longrightarrow} T_2 \stackrel{\overline{s_1}}{\Longrightarrow}\approx \mathbf{0} \quad \text{and} \tag{6}$$

$$T_0 \Rightarrow T_1' \stackrel{\overline{b_2}}{\Longrightarrow} T_2' \stackrel{\overline{s_2}}{\Longrightarrow}\approx \mathbf{0}. \tag{7}$$

where, by definition of $\approx$, $[\![P_i]\!] \approx T_i$ for $i \in \{0,1,2\}$ and $[\![P_j']\!] \approx T_j'$ for $j \in \{1,2\}$. Call C_2 and C_2' the derivatives of C_0 in T_2 and T_2', respectively. It is worth noticing that by conditions on names, output actions on s_1 and s_2 cannot originate in C_2 and C_2'.

The behavior of T_0 described in (6) and (7) can be equivalently described as $T_0 \stackrel{\alpha_1}{\Longrightarrow} \mathbf{0}$ and $T_0 \stackrel{\alpha_2}{\Longrightarrow} \mathbf{0}$, where α_1 contains outputs on b_1 and s_1, and α_2 contains outputs on b_2 and s_2, respectively. Using the Commuting Lemma (Lemma 5) on T_0, we know there exist processes T_1^*, and T_2^* such that

1. $T_1^* \equiv \nu\widetilde{n}_1\,(A_0 \parallel \prod^m R \parallel C_1^*[R])$ and $T_2^* \equiv \nu\widetilde{n}_2\,(A_0 \parallel \prod^{m'} R \parallel C_2^*[R])$, for some $m, m' \geq 0$. Recall that T_1^* and T_2^* are the results of performing every output action and internal synchronization originated in C_0. Since the encoding does not introduce divergence, we have that $C_1^*[R] \not\rightarrow$ and $C_2^*[R] \not\rightarrow$.
2. T_1^* (resp. T_2^*) can only perform an output action on s_1 (resp. s_2) and internal actions. Hence, we have that $T_1^* \Downarrow_{\overline{s_1}}$, $T_1^* \not\Downarrow_{\overline{s_2}}$ and $T_2^* \Downarrow_{\overline{s_2}}$, $T_2^* \not\Downarrow_{\overline{s_1}}$ should hold.

Item (1) allows to observe that the only difference between T_1^* and T_2^* is in the number of copies of R (the sets of restricted names are also different, but these do not involve the names we are interested in). This number has direct influence on performing an output action on s_1 or on s_2; as such, it has influence on the bisimulation game between $[\![P_2]\!]$ and T_2, and that between $[\![P_2']\!]$ and T_2'. More precisely, we have both $T_0 \stackrel{\overline{b_1}}{\Longrightarrow} T_1^*$ (with $T_1^* \Downarrow_{\overline{s_1}}$) and $T_0 \stackrel{\overline{b_2}}{\Longrightarrow} T_2^*$ (with $T_2^* \Downarrow_{\overline{s_2}}$). By assuming $m > m'$, we obtain that T_1^* corresponds to the composition of T_2^* and a number of copies of R. Hence, $T_1^* \Downarrow_{\overline{s_2}}$ and $T_0 \stackrel{\overline{b_1}}{\Longrightarrow} T^*$ with $T^* \downarrow_{\overline{s_2}}$. By operational correspondence, we have $P_0 \stackrel{\overline{b_1}}{\Longrightarrow} P'$ such that $T^* \Rightarrow T'$ with $T' \approx [\![P']\!]$. Notice that since the strong barb on s_2 in T^* cannot disappear (there is no reception on s_2), it is still in T'. Thus P' has a weak barb on s_2, which is impossible. □

The scheme used in the proof of Theorem 1 can be generalized for calculi with arbitrary polyadicity. Therefore we have the following.

Theorem 2. *For every $n > 1$, there is no encoding of* SHO^n *into* SHO^{n-1}.

Remark 1 (A hierarchy for *asynchronous* calculi). *Theorem 2 holds for calculi in* AHO *as well. The main structure of the proof is the same, but one needs to adapt the different pieces.*

6 The Expressive Power of Abstraction-Passing

In this section we show that abstraction-passing, i.e., the communication of parameterizable processes, is strictly more expressive than process-passing. We consider SHO^n_a, the extension of SHO^n with the communication of abstractions of order one, i.e., functions from processes to processes. The language of SHO^n_a processes is obtained by extending the syntax of SHO^n processes (Definition 1) in the following way:

$$P, Q, \ldots ::= \cdots \;\big|\; (x)P \;\big|\; P_1\lfloor P_2 \rfloor$$

That is, we consider *abstractions* $(x)P$ and *applications* $P_1\lfloor P_2\rfloor$, that allow to apply an abstraction P_1 to an argument P_2. As usual, $(x_1)\ldots(x_n)P$ is abbreviated as $(x_1, \ldots, x_n)P$. The LTS of SHO^n_a extends that of SHO^n with the rule:

$$\text{App}\ \frac{}{(x)P\lfloor Q\rfloor \xrightarrow{\tau} P\{Q/x\}}\,.$$

Moreover, for SHO^n_a we rely on types and well-typed processes as in [9]; roughly speaking, the type system ensures consistent uses of application w.r.t. abstractions.

We now show that abstraction-passing increases the expressive power of pure process-passing in SHO. The result is based on the encoding below.

Definition 11 (Monadic abstraction-passing can encode polyadic communication). *The encoding* $[\![\cdot]\!] : \mathrm{SHO}^2 \to \mathrm{SHO}^1_a$ *is defined as:*

$$\begin{aligned}
[\![\overline{a}\langle P_1, P_2\rangle.\, R]\!] &= a(z).\, ([\![R]\!] \parallel \nu m\, n\, c\, (\overline{n} \parallel z\lfloor n.\, (\overline{c} \parallel \overline{m}) + m.\, ([\![P_1]\!] \parallel \overline{m})\rfloor \\
&\qquad\qquad \parallel c.\, z\lfloor [\![P_2]\!]\rfloor))\\
[\![a(x_1, x_2).\, Q]\!] &= \nu b\, (\overline{a}\langle (y)\overline{b}\langle y\rangle\rangle \parallel b(x_1).\, (x_1 \parallel b(x_2).\, [\![Q]\!]))
\end{aligned}$$

where $[\![\cdot]\!]$ is an homomorphism for the other operators in SHO^2.

The encoding is correct, except that it does not preserve signatures (as inputs are translated into outputs and viceversa); a correct encoding can be written by resorting to abstractions with abstractions as parameters. This encoding leads also to the separation result below. The result is remarkable since it formalizes the fact that the expressive power of abstraction-passing is beyond any arity of polyadic communication.

Theorem 3. *For every $n, m > 1$, there is no encoding of* SHO_a^n *into* SHO^m.

Proof. Suppose, for the sake of contradiction, there is an encoding $\mathcal{A}[\![\cdot]\!] : \mathrm{SHO}_a^n \rightarrow \mathrm{SHO}^m$. Thanks to Def. 11, we have an encoding $\mathcal{B}[\![\cdot]\!] : \mathrm{SHO}^{m+1} \rightarrow \mathrm{SHO}_a^n$.[2] Now, the composition of two encodings is an encoding (Prop. 1), and so $(\mathcal{A} \cdot \mathcal{B})[\![\cdot]\!]$ is an encoding of SHO^{m+1} into SHO^m. However, by Theorem 2 such an encoding does not exist, and we reach a contradiction. □

7 Concluding Remarks

Summary. In first-order process calculi (a)synchronous and polyadic communication are well-understood mechanisms. In this paper, we have studied the expressiveness of these mechanisms in the context of *strictly higher-order* process calculi. Our results strengthen and complement expressiveness studies for higher-order process calculi in [12,13,11,9,14]. We have studied two families of higher-order process calculi: the first one, called AHO^n, is the asynchronous higher-order process calculus with n-adic communication; the second, called SHO^n, is the synchronous variant of AHO^n. Our first contribution was an *encodability* result of SHO^n into AHO^n. We then moved to analyze polyadic communication, and showed that in this case the absence of name-passing does entail a loss in expressiveness; this is represented by the impossibility of encoding SHO^n into SHO^{n-1}. This *non-encodability* result induces a *hierarchy* of higher-order process calculi based on the arity allowed in process-passing communications. This hierarchy holds for AHO as well. Finally, we showed an encoding of SHO^n into SHO^1 extended with abstraction-passing, and used it in our final contribution: the non-existence of an encoding of abstraction-passing into process-passing of any arity.

Related Work. Sangiorgi [9] proposed a hierarchy of HOπ fragments, based on the degree of the abstractions allowed (the level of arrow nesting in the type of the abstraction). This hierarchy is shown to match the expressiveness of a hierarchy of first-order calculi with only internal mobility. The argument that the hierarchy is strict is however intensional, counting the causal dependencies among names. In contrast, the hierarchy we consider here is given by the size of the tuples that can be passed around in polyadic communications. Also related are [12,13,11], in which expressiveness/decidability issues of HOCORE—roughly, the fragment of HOπ without restriction— are addressed.

Other works have used the distinction between internal and public synchronizations that we have used in the LTS for SHO. In [15], labels of internal actions are annotated with the name on which the synchronization occurs so as to define *located* semantics for the π-calculus; such semantics are then used to study concurrent semantics using a standard LTS. In the higher-order setting, [16] defines a variant of CHOCS in which synchronizations on so-called *activation channels* (i.e., the fresh channels used in the encoding of CHOCS into the π-calculus to trigger a copy of a process) are distinguished from other synchronizations. An LTS based on such a distinction is shown to be finitely branching; its induced bisimilarity is shown to coincide with bisimulation in CHOCS.

[2] The fact that the encoding does not preserve signatures can be overcome with a direct proof.

Future Work. It would be interesting to explore whether the hierarchy in Section 5 can be presented without resorting to the distinction on internal actions. This would require to formalize the concept of encoding robust with respect to interferences. Also, the result in Section 6 gives the base case of a hierarchy based on abstraction-passing. Here we have considered abstractions of order one; we plan to generalize such a result to abstractions of arbitrary order so as to define a hierarchy based on abstraction-passing.

Acknowledgments. We are grateful to J. Aranda and F. Valencia for discussions on the topics of this paper, and to the anonymous reviewers for their suggestions. This research was carried out while the second author was a PhD student at University of Bologna. This research has been partially supported by INRIA Equipe Associée BACON, by Project FP7- 231620 HATS, and by FCT / MCTES (CMU-PT/NGN44-2009-12).

References

1. Palamidessi, C.: Comparing the expressive power of the synchronous and asynchronous pi-calculi. Mathematical Structures in Computer Science 13(5), 685–719 (2003)
2. Nestmann, U.: What is a good encoding of guarded choice? Inf. Comput. 156(1-2), 287–319 (2000); A preliminary version appeared in EXPRESS (1997)
3. Cacciagrano, D., Corradini, F., Palamidessi, C.: Separation of synchronous and asynchronous communication via testing. Theor. Comput. Sci. 386(3), 218–235 (2007)
4. Boudol, G.: Asynchrony and the π-calculus (note). Technical report, Rapport de Recherche 1702, INRIA, Sophia-Antipolis (1992)
5. Honda, K., Tokoro, M.: An object calculus for asynchronous communication. In: America, P. (ed.) ECOOP 1991. LNCS, vol. 512, pp. 133–147. Springer, Heidelberg (1991)
6. Milner, R.: The Polyadic pi-Calculus: A Tutorial. Technical Report ECS-LFCS-91-180, University of Edinburgh (1991)
7. Quaglia, P., Walker, D.: Types and full abstraction for polyadic pi-calculus. Inf. Comput. 200(2), 215–246 (2005)
8. Yoshida, N.: Graph types for monadic mobile processes. In: Chandru, V., Vinay, V. (eds.) FSTTCS 1996. LNCS, vol. 1180, pp. 371–386. Springer, Heidelberg (1996)
9. Sangiorgi, D.: π-calculus, internal mobility and agent-passing calculi. Theor. Comput. Sci. 167(2), 235–274 (1996)
10. Gorla, D.: Towards a unified approach to encodability and separation results for process calculi. In: van Breugel, F., Chechik, M. (eds.) CONCUR 2008. LNCS, vol. 5201, pp. 492–507. Springer, Heidelberg (2008)
11. Pérez, J.A.: Higher-Order Concurrency: Expressiveness and Decidability Results. PhD thesis, University of Bologna (2010) Draft in `http://www.japerez.phipages.com/`
12. Lanese, I., Pérez, J.A., Sangiorgi, D., Schmitt, A.: On the expressiveness and decidability of higher-order process calculi. In: Proc. of LICS 2008, pp. 145–155. IEEE Computer Society, Los Alamitos (2008)
13. Di Giusto, C., Pérez, J.A., Zavattaro, G.: On the expressiveness of forwarding in higher-order communication. In: Leucker, M., Morgan, C. (eds.) ICTAC 2009. LNCS, vol. 5684, pp. 155–169. Springer, Heidelberg (2009)
14. Sangiorgi, D.: Expressing Mobility in Process Algebras: First-Order and Higher-Order Paradigms. PhD thesis CST–99–93, University of Edinburgh, Dept. of Comp. Sci. (1992)
15. Lanese, I.: Concurrent and located synchronizations in *pi*-calculus. In: van Leeuwen, J., Italiano, G.F., van der Hoek, W., Meinel, C., Sack, H., Plášil, F. (eds.) SOFSEM 2007. LNCS, vol. 4362, pp. 388–399. Springer, Heidelberg (2007)
16. Amadio, R.M.: On the reduction of Chocs bisimulation to π-calculus bisimulation. In: Best, E. (ed.) CONCUR 1993. LNCS, vol. 715, pp. 112–126. Springer, Heidelberg (1993)

On Bisimilarity and Substitution in Presence of Replication*

Daniel Hirschkoff[1] and Damien Pous[2]

[1] ENS Lyon, Université de Lyon, CNRS, INRIA
[2] CNRS, Laboratoire d'Informatique de Grenoble

Abstract. We prove a new congruence result for the π-calculus: bisimilarity is a congruence in the sub-calculus that does not include restriction nor sum, and features top-level replications. Our proof relies on algebraic properties of replication, and on a new syntactic characterisation of bisimilarity. We obtain this characterisation using a rewriting system rather than a purely equational axiomatisation. We then deduce substitution closure, and hence, congruence. Whether bisimilarity is a congruence when replications are unrestricted remains open.

1 Introduction

We study algebraic properties of behavioural equivalences, and more precisely, of strong bisimilarity ($\sim$). This has long been an important question in concurrency theory, with a particular focus on the search for axiomatisations of bisimilarity (see [1] for a survey). Our primary goal is to establish congruence results for the π-calculus [14]. At the heart of the π-calculus is the mechanism of *name-passing*, which is the source of considerable expressive power. Name-passing however introduces substitutions in the formalism, and these in turn lead to irregularities in the behavioural theory of processes: due to the input prefix, we need bisimilarity to be closed under substitutions for it to be a congruence.

To establish substitution closure, we exploit a new axiomatisation of bisimilarity. Several axiomatisation results for process calculi that feature an operator of parallel composition ($|$) have been derived by decomposing this operator using sum, and possibly left merge [4,3,1]. We, on the contrary, are interested in treating parallel composition as a primitive operator. One reason for this is that the sum operator is often absent from the π-calculus since it can be encoded [10], under certain conditions. More importantly, this operator makes substitution closure fail [14,2], so that existing axiomatisations of bisimilarity in calculi featuring sum do not help when it comes to reason about congruence in the π-calculus.

In the present paper, we focus on properties of the replication operator [9], denoted by '!'. As [14,2] shows, bisimilarity is not substitution closed when both replication and name restriction are present in the calculus, and we have established in [6] that it is when we renounce to replication. To our knowledge,

* Work partially funded by the French ANR projects "Curry-Howard pour la Concurrence" CHOCO ANR-07-BLAN-0324 and COMPLICE ANR-08-BLANC-0211-01.

S. Abramsky et al. (Eds.): ICALP 2010, Part II, LNCS 6199, pp. 454–465, 2010.

congruence of bisimilarity in the restriction-free π-calculus with replication is an open problem [14]; we provide here a partial answer.

Behavioural properties of replication. Replication is an "infinitary version" of parallel composition. Structural congruence traditionally contains the following *structural laws*: $!a.P \mid a.P \equiv !a.P$ and $!a.P \mid !a.P \equiv !a.P$ (given here for CCS), so that a replicated process acts as an unbounded number of parallel copies of that process. A contribution of this work is an analysis of *behavioural laws* capturing other properties of replication. For example, for any context C, we have

$$!a.P \mid C[a.P] \sim !a.P \mid C[\mathbf{0}] \qquad \text{and} \qquad !a.C[a.C[\mathbf{0}]] \sim !a.C[\mathbf{0}] \ .$$

The left-hand side law is a generalisation the first structural congruence law: a replicated process can erase one of its copies arbitrarily deep in a term. The right-hand side law is more involved: read from right to left, it shows that a replicated process is able to replicate itself. Its most trivial instance is $!a.a \sim !a$.

Although the above laws are the basic ingredients we need in order to characterise bisimilarity in our setting, they do not form a complete axiomatisation of bisimilarity, as the following example shows:

$$P_1 = !a.(b|a.c) \mid !a.(c|a.b) \ \sim \ !a.b \mid !a.c = P_2 \ .$$

P_1 can be obtained from P_2 by inserting a copy of $a.b$ inside $!a.c$, and, symmetrically, a copy of $a.c$ inside $!a.b$. It seems reasonable to consider P_2 as a kind of normal form of P_1; however, P_1 and P_2 cannot be related using the above laws. Describing this phenomenon of "mutual replication" in all its generality leads to complicated equational schemata, so that we take another approach.

Overview. Our first contribution is a syntactic characterisation of bisimilarity on a fragment of CCS with top-level replications. This characterisation relies on a rewriting system for processes (such that P_1 above rewrites into P_2). An important technical notion we need to introduce is that of *seed*: a seed of P is a process bisimilar to P of minimal size; for example, P_2 is a seed of P_1. Our proof goes by characterising bisimilarity on seeds, and establishing that any process P can be rewritten into a seed of P.

Our second contribution is congruence of bisimilarity in the corresponding fragment of the π-calculus. Concretely, we prove that bisimilarity is substitution closed by considering *visible* bisimilarity (sometimes called *io*-bisimilarity [8]), the equivalence obtained by disallowing challenges along internal communications. Visible bisimilarity is inherently substitution closed, and our characterisation allows us to show that it coincides with bisimilarity.

We provide detailed proofs and present most intermediate steps for CCS. We indeed view the reasonings we use in our proofs as an important contribution of this work. In particular, we make use of both algebraic and coinductive reasoning, notably using "up-to techniques" for bisimulation [13,11,12]. On the contrary, we omit most of the technical developments that lead to congruence in the π-calculus: they follow to a large extent the path of our proofs for CCS. We collect these proofs in an extended version of this abstract [5].

Outline. We describe the subset of CCS we work with and we prove general properties of replication in Sect. 2. In Sect. 3, we introduce the notion of seed, and give a characterisation of bisimilarity on seeds. The rewriting system is defined in Sect. 4, where we show that any process can be rewritten into a seed, and where we characterise strong bisimilarity. We present our new congruence result for the π-calculus in Sect. 5. Section 6 suggests directions for future work.

2 General Setting, and Properties of Replication

We let a, b range over a countable set of *names*; we work in a fragment of CCS which we call mCCS (pronounced 'miniCCS'), defined by the following grammar:

$$\begin{array}{rlrl} \alpha, \beta ::= a \mid \overline{a} & \mu ::= \alpha \mid \tau & & \text{(actions and labels)} \\ E, F ::= \mathbf{0} \mid \alpha.F \mid F|F & P, Q ::= F \mid !\alpha.F \mid P|P & & \text{(processes)} \\ D ::= [] \mid \alpha.D \mid D|F & C ::= D \mid !\alpha.D \mid C|P & & \text{(contexts)} \end{array}$$

This calculus features no restriction, no sum, and allows only top-level replicated prefixes. Note that the τ prefix is not included in the syntax, and only appears in *labels* (μ); we return to this point in Rmk. 19. We use P, Q to range over processes; according to the syntax, a *finite* process (F) is a process which does not contain an occurrence of the replication operator ($!\alpha.$). We omit trailing occurrences of $\mathbf{0}$, and write, e.g., $\alpha.\beta$ for $\alpha.\beta.\mathbf{0}$. We shall sometimes write $\prod_{i \in [1..k]} \alpha_i.F_i$ for $\alpha_1.F_1 \mid \ldots \mid \alpha_k.F_k$. We extend the syntactic operator of replication to a function defined over processes by letting

$$!\mathbf{0} \triangleq \mathbf{0} \qquad\qquad !(P|Q) \triangleq !P|!Q \qquad\qquad !!\alpha.F \triangleq !\alpha.F \ .$$

In particular, $!F$ will always denote a process having only replicated (parallel) components. We let C range over single-hole *contexts*, mapping finite processes to processes, and similarly for *finite contexts*, ranged over using D. Note that the hole cannot occur immediately under a replication in C.

The following labelled transition system (LTS) for mCCS is standard (we omit symmetric rules for parallel composition).

$$\frac{}{\alpha.F \xrightarrow{\alpha} F} \qquad \frac{}{!\alpha.F \xrightarrow{\alpha} !\alpha.F \mid F} \qquad \frac{P \xrightarrow{\mu} P'}{P|Q \xrightarrow{\mu} P'|Q} \qquad \frac{P \xrightarrow{\overline{a}} P' \qquad Q \xrightarrow{a} Q'}{P|Q \xrightarrow{\tau} P'|Q'}$$

This LTS yields the following standard notion of *bisimilarity*, ($\sim$). We also define *visible bisimilarity* ($\dot{\sim}$), where silent transitions are not taken into account.

Definition 1. Strong bisimilarity ($\sim$) *is the largest symmetric binary relation over processes such that whenever $P \sim Q$ and $P \xrightarrow{\mu} P'$, there exists Q' such that $P' \sim Q'$ and $Q \xrightarrow{\mu} Q'$.* Visible bisimilarity ($\dot{\sim}$) *is defined similarly, by restricting challenges to the cases where $\mu \neq \tau$.*

Both bisimilarities are congruences. They are moreover preserved by the extended replication function, and we have $\sim \subseteq \dot{\sim}$. On finite processes, bisimilarity and visible bisimilarity coincide and can be characterised using the following *distribution law*, where there are as many occurrences of F on both sides [6]:

$$\alpha.(F|\alpha.F|\dots|\alpha.F) \sim \alpha.F|\alpha.F|\dots|\alpha.F \;. \tag{D}$$

We now present some important properties of replicated processes w.r.t. bisimilarity. The following proposition allows us to obtain the two laws from the introduction, that involve copying replicated sub-terms.

Proposition 2. *If* $C[\mathbf{0}] \sim !\alpha.F|P$*, then* $C[\mathbf{0}] \sim C[\alpha.F]$.

Proof. We show that $\mathcal{R}= \{(C[\mathbf{0}], C[\alpha.F]) \;/\; \forall C \text{ s.t. } C[\mathbf{0}] \sim !\alpha.F|P \text{ for some } P\}$ is a bisimulation up to transitivity [11,12]. There are several cases to consider:

- the hole occurs at top-level in the context ($C = [\,]|Q$) and the right-hand side process does the following transition: $C[\alpha.F] \xrightarrow{\alpha} F|Q$. By hypothesis, $Q \sim !\alpha.F|P$ so that we find Q' such that $Q \xrightarrow{\alpha} Q'$ and $Q' \sim !\alpha.F|F|P$. Injecting the latter equality gives $Q' \sim Q|F$, so that Q' closes the diagram.
- the hole occurs under a replicated prefix of the context ($C = !\beta.D|Q$) that is fired: we have $C[\mathbf{0}] \xrightarrow{\beta} P_l = C[\mathbf{0}]|D[\mathbf{0}]$ and $C[\alpha.F] \xrightarrow{\beta} P_r = C[\alpha.F]|D[\alpha.F]$. This is where we reason up to transitivity: these processes are not related by $\mathcal{R}$ (we work with single-hole contexts), but we have $P_l \;\mathcal{R}\; P_c \;\mathcal{R}\; P_r$, for $P_c = C[\mathbf{0}]|D[\alpha.F]$, using contexts $C_{lc} = C[\mathbf{0}]|D$ and $C_{cr} = C|D[\alpha.F]$.
- the hole occurs under a non-replicated prefix in the context ($C = \beta.D|Q$), or the context triggers a transition that does not involve or duplicate the hole; it suffices to play the bisimulation game.
- we are left with the cases where a synchronisation is played; they can be handled similarly (in particular because contexts have a single hole). □

As a consequence, we obtain the validity of the following laws. We shall see in the sequel that together with the distribution law (D), they capture the essence of bisimilarity in our calculus.

$$!\alpha.F \mid C[\alpha.F] \sim !\alpha.F \mid C[\mathbf{0}] \tag{A}$$

$$!\alpha.D[\alpha.D[\mathbf{0}]] \sim !\alpha.D[\mathbf{0}] \tag{A'}$$

(Note that Prop. 2 and the above laws hold for full CCS and for the π-calculus, as long as the hole does not occur as argument of a sum in C and D, and C and D do not bind names occurring in $\alpha.F$.) We now give two useful cancellation properties of visible bisimilarity; they are actually also valid for bisimilarity ($\sim$).

Lemma 3. *If* $!F \dot{\sim} P|Q$*, then* $!F \dot{\sim} !F|P$.

Proof. We reason purely algebraically: we replicate both sides of $!F \dot{\sim} P|Q$, and add P in parallel (since $!P \dot{\sim} !P|P$): this gives $!F \dot{\sim} !P|!Q \dot{\sim} !P|!Q|P$. We deduce $!F \dot{\sim} !F|P$ by injecting the first equivalence into the second one. □

Proposition 4. *If* $!F|F_0 \dot{\sim} !E|E_0$ *with* F_0, E_0 *finite, then* $!F \dot{\sim} !E$.

Proof. By emptying F_0 on the left-hand side[1], we find a finite process E_1 such that $!F \dot{\sim} !E|E_1$ $(*)$. Similarly, by emptying E_0 on the right-hand side we find F_1 such that $!F|F_1 \dot{\sim} !E$ $(**)$. By injecting the former equivalence in the latter, we have $!E|E_1|F_1 \dot{\sim} !E$ $(\dagger)$. By Lemma 3, $(**)$ gives $!E \dot{\sim} !E|F_1$, that we can inject into $(*)$ to obtain $!E|E_1|F_1 \dot{\sim} !F$. We finally deduce $!E \dot{\sim} !F$ from $(\dagger)$. □

Again, these properties are not specific to the subset of CCS we focus on: Prop. 4 holds provided that both F_0 and E_0 can be reduced to the empty process using transitions (this is the case, e.g., for the *normed* processes of [7]). The counterpart of this cancellation property does not hold; the replicated parts of bisimilar processes cannot always be cancelled: we cannot deduce $a \dot{\sim} \mathbf{0}$ from $!a|a \dot{\sim} !a|\mathbf{0}$.

3 Seeds

Definition 5 (Size, seed). *The* size of P, *noted* $\sharp P$, *is the number of prefixes in* P. *A* seed of P *is a process* Q *of least size such that* $P \dot{\sim} Q$, *whose number of replicated components is largest among the processes of least size. When* P *is a seed of* P, *we simply say that* P *is a seed.*

We show how to rewrite an arbitrary process into a seed in Sect. 4; in this section, we give a characterisation of bisimilarity on seeds (Prop. 11).

Definition 6 (Distribution congruence). *We call* distribution congruence *the smallest congruence relation* $\equiv$ *that satisfies the laws of an abelian monoid for* $(|, \mathbf{0})$ *and the distribution law* (D).

Fact 7. *We have* $\equiv \subseteq \sim \subseteq \dot{\sim}$*; the latter equivalence is substitution closed; on finite processes, the three relations coincide.*

Proof. See [5], where we exploit some results about finite processes from [6]. □

It is easy to show that distribution congruence is decidable, and only relates processes having the same size. In the sequel, we always work modulo distribution congruence. We shall prove that on seeds, bisimilarity actually coincides with distribution congruence. Thanks to Prop. 4, the replicated parts of bisimilar seeds are necessarily bisimilar. As a consequence, in the remainder of this section, we fix a seed S having only replicated components: $S = \prod_i !\alpha_i.S_i$, and we study processes obtained by composing S with finite processes.

Definition 8 (Clean process, residual). *A finite process* F *is* clean w.r.t. S, *written* $S\#F$, *if* F *does not contain a sub-term of the form* $\alpha_i.S_i$*: for all* i *and finite context* D, $F \not\equiv D[\alpha_i.S_i]$. *A finite process* R *is a* residual of S, *written* $S \rightsquigarrow R$, *when there exist* $k > 0$, $\alpha_1, .., \alpha_k$, *and* $P_1, .., P_k$ *such that* $S \xrightarrow{\alpha_1} P_1 \dots \xrightarrow{\alpha_k} P_k \equiv S|R$. *We shall use* R *to range over such residual processes.*

[1] In the present case, "emptying F_0" means playing all prefixes of F_0 in the bisimulation game between $!F|F_0$ and $!E|E_0$. We shall reuse this terminology in some proofs below; note that this is possible only with finite processes.

Note that if $S \rightsquigarrow R$, then R is a parallel composition of sub-terms of the S_is. We can also remark that residuals and clean processes are stable under transitions: if $S\#F$ (resp. $S \rightsquigarrow F$) and $F \xrightarrow{\alpha} F'$, then $S\#F'$ (resp. $S \rightsquigarrow F'$). As shown by the following lemma, a seed cannot absorb its non-trivial residuals (ii), and sub-terms of seeds are clean (i,iii):

Lemma 9. *(i) If $S|F$ is a seed, then $S\#F$.*
(ii) If $S \rightsquigarrow R$ and $S \dot{\sim} S|R$, then $R \equiv \mathbf{0}$.
(iii) If $S \rightsquigarrow R$, then $S\#R$.

Proof. (i) By contradiction: if $F \equiv D[\alpha_i.S_i]$, then $S|F \sim S|D[\mathbf{0}]$ by law (A), which contradicts the minimality hypothesis about $S|F$.

(ii) Suppose by contradiction $R \equiv \alpha.R_0|R_1$. Lemma 3 gives $S \dot{\sim} S|\alpha.R_0$, hence $S \dot{\sim} S|!\alpha.R_0$ $(*)$ by replicating all processes. Moreover, $S \rightsquigarrow \alpha.R_0$, so that we have i, D such that $S_i \equiv D[\alpha.R_0]$. Therefore, by $(*)$ and law (A), we obtain $S \dot{\sim} \prod_{j \neq i} !\alpha_j.S_j|!\alpha_i.D[\mathbf{0}]|!\alpha.R_0$. The latter process has the same size as S, but it has strictly more replicated components, which contradicts the fact that S is a seed (Def. 5).

(iii) By contradiction, suppose that $R \equiv D[\alpha_i.S_i]$. By emptying the prefixes of D, we have $S \rightsquigarrow \alpha_i.S_i$. Since $S \dot{\sim} S|\alpha_i.S_i$, this contradicts (ii). □

The third point above leads to the following cancellation result:

Lemma 10. *If $S|F \dot{\sim} S|E$, $S\#F$, and $S\#E$, then $F \equiv E$.*

Proof. We prove the following stronger property, by induction on n: for all n, F, E such that $\sharp F, \sharp E \leq n$, $S\#F$, and $S\#E$, we have:

$$\begin{cases} (i) & \forall P, S|F \dot{\sim} P|E \text{ entails } \sharp E \leq \sharp F\,; \\ (ii) & S|F \dot{\sim} S|E \text{ entails } F \equiv E\,. \end{cases}$$

The case $n = 0$ is trivial; assume $n > 0$.

(i) Suppose $\sharp F < \sharp E$ by contradiction. By emptying F, we get P', E' such that $S \dot{\sim} P'|E'$, with $0 < \sharp E' \leq \sharp E$. Write $E' = \alpha.E_0|E_1$, then $S \dot{\sim} S|\alpha.E_0$ by Lemma 3, and $S|S_i \dot{\sim} S|E_0$ for some i with $\alpha_i = \alpha$. Necessarily, $\sharp S_i \leq \sharp E_0$: otherwise, by emptying E_0, we would obtain a non empty residual R such $S|R \dot{\sim} S$, which would contradict Lemma 9(ii). Since $\sharp E_0 < \sharp E' \leq \sharp E \leq n$, we can use the induction hypothesis, so that $S_i \equiv E_0$, and hence $\alpha_i.S_i \equiv \alpha.E_0$, which contradicts $S\#E$.

(ii) By the above point, $\sharp F = \sharp E$. We show that $\mathcal{R} \triangleq \{(F, E)\} \cup \equiv$ is a visible bisimulation. If $F \xrightarrow{\alpha} F'$, then $S|F \xrightarrow{\alpha} S|F'$, and $S|E$ can answer this challenge: $S|E \xrightarrow{\alpha} S|E'$ with $S|F' \dot{\sim} S|E'$. If the answer comes from E, we are done by induction: $\sharp E' = \sharp F' = \sharp F - 1 \leq n - 1$. Otherwise, i.e., if $S|F' \dot{\sim} S|S_i|E$ for some i, we get a contradiction with (i): we would have $\sharp E \leq \sharp F' = \sharp E - 1$. Challenges of E are handled symmetrically. □

We can now characterise bisimilarity on seeds:

Proposition 11. *For all seeds P, P', $P \dot{\sim} P'$ iff $P \sim P'$ iff $P \equiv P'$.*

Proof. By Fact 7, it suffices to show that $P \dot{\sim} P'$ entails $P \equiv P'$. Write P and P' as $S|F$ and $S'|F'$, where S, S' are replicated processes. By Prop. 4, $S \dot{\sim} S'$. Moreover, S and S' are necessarily seeds because P and P' are (hence the notation). Write $S \equiv \prod_{i \leq m} !\alpha_i.S_i$ and $S' \equiv \prod_{j \leq n} !\alpha'_j.S'_j$, play each prefix on the left-hand side and apply Lemma 10 to show that there exists a map $\sigma : [1..m] \to [1..n]$, such that $\alpha_i.S_i \equiv \alpha'_{\sigma i}.S'_{\sigma i}$ (recall that $S\#S_j$ by Lemma 9(iii)). This map is bijective: we could otherwise construct a smaller seed. Therefore, $S \equiv S'$. By Lemma 9(i), $S\#F$ and $S'\#F'$, which allows us to deduce $F \equiv F'$, using Lemma 10. Finally, $P \equiv P'$. □

We conclude this section by the following remark: seeds are stable under transitions, so that they actually form a proper sub-calculus of mCCS.

Proposition 12. *If P is a seed and $P \xrightarrow{\mu} P'$, then P' is a seed.*

4 Rewriting Processes to Normal Forms

By Prop. 11, the seed of a process P is unique up to distribution congruence ($\equiv$); in the sequel, we denote it by $\mathsf{s}(P)$. In this section, we show that the seed of a process can be obtained using a rewriting system. This entails two important properties of mCCS: visible and strong bisimilarity coincide and bisimilarity is closed under substitutions (i.e., bisimilar processes remain bisimilar when applying an arbitrary name substitution).

Definition 13 (Rewriting). *Any process T induces a relation between processes, written $\xrightarrow{T}$, defined by the following rules, modulo $\equiv$:*

$$\frac{T \equiv\, !\alpha.F \mid Q}{C[\alpha.F] \xrightarrow{T} C[\mathbf{0}]}\ (\text{R1}) \qquad\qquad \frac{}{!\alpha.F \mid !\alpha.F \mid P \xrightarrow{T}\, !\alpha.F \mid P}\ (\text{R2})$$

The reflexive transitive closure of $\xrightarrow{T}$ is written $\xrightarrow{T}{}^{*}$.

We give some intuitions about how the rewriting rules work. First, only the replicated part of T matters when rewriting with $\xrightarrow{T}$. Relation $\xrightarrow{T}$ is nevertheless defined for an arbitrary process T in order to facilitate the presentation of some results below. Then, we observe that it is only sensible to rewrite P using $\xrightarrow{T}$ when T is a seed of P. This means in particular that the rewriting system does not provide a direct way to compute the seed of a process (since the seed has to be guessed). It is rather a procedure to check that some process T is a "simplification" of P—Lemma 14 below validates this intuition. Rule (R2) is rather self-explanatory. The rewriting rule (R1) is related to laws (A) and (A′); we illustrate its use by considering the following examples:

$$!a.b \mid !b \mid b.a \xrightarrow{!a|!b} !a.b \mid !b \mid b \xrightarrow{!a|!b} !a.b \mid !b \xrightarrow{!a|!b} !a \mid !b \qquad (1)$$

$$!a.(b \mid a.b) \xrightarrow{!a.b} !a.b \qquad (2)$$

$$!a.b \mid !b.a \xrightarrow{!a|!b} !a.b \mid !b \xrightarrow{!a|!b} !a \mid !b \qquad (3)$$

$$!a|!a.b \xrightarrow{!a|!b} !a|!a \xrightarrow{!a|!b} !a \qquad (4)$$

(1) The first example shows how (R1) can be used to "implement" law (A) and erase redundant sub-terms. At each rewrite step, a copy of a component of the seed (here, $!a|!b$) is erased. In the third rewriting step, simplification occurs in a replicated component.
(2) Law (A′) is applied: a replicated component can be "simplified with itself".
(3) This example illustrates how the rewriting system solves the problem we exposed in the introduction (processes P_1 and P_2), where two replicated components have to simplify each other: by guessing the seed ($!a|!b$), we are able to apply the two simplifications in sequence.
(4) Here, we make a wrong guess about the seed: when assuming that $!b$ is part of the seed, we can erase the prefix b in $!a.b$. However, at the end, we are not able to validate this assumption: $!b$ does not appear in the normal form.

Accordingly, we introduce the following correctness criterion:

Lemma 14 (Soundness). *If $P \xrightarrow{T}{}^{*} T$, then $P \sim T$.*

Definition 15 (Joinability). *We say that processes P and Q are* joinable, *written $P \curlyvee Q$, if there exists a process T such that $P \xrightarrow{T}{}^{*} T$ and $Q \xrightarrow{T}{}^{*} T$.*

By Lemma 14, $\curlyvee \subseteq \sim$; the other property which is required in order to characterise bisimilarity is *completeness* of the rewriting system, i.e., that all bisimilar processes can be joined. For this, we show that any process can be rewritten into a seed. The proof necessitates the following technical lemma (recall that $\mathsf{s}(P)$ denotes the seed of P):

Lemma 16. *For all P, either P is a seed, or $P \xrightarrow{\mathsf{s}(P)} P'$ for some P' s.t. $P \sim P'$.*

Proof. Write $P \equiv !F|F^P$ and $\mathsf{s}(P) \equiv S|F^S$, with $F \equiv \prod_i \beta_i.F_i$ and $S \equiv \prod_j !\alpha_j.S_j$. By Prop. 4, and since $P \dot{\sim} \mathsf{s}(P)$, $!F \dot{\sim} S$ (∗).

Any transition at β_i by $!F$ is answered by S at some $\alpha_{\sigma i}$, yielding equivalence $!F|F_i \;\dot{\sim}\; S|S_{\sigma i}$, which in turn gives $S|F_i \;\dot{\sim}\; S|S_{\sigma i}$, by injecting (∗). By Lemma 10, either (a) $F_i \equiv S_{\sigma i}$, or (b) $\neg(S \# F_i)$. In the latter case, (b), this means that P admits some $\alpha_j.S_j$ as a sub-term, and can be rewritten using rule (R1), the resulting process being bisimilar to P, by Prop. 2.

Suppose now that we are in case (a) for all transitions from $!F$, that is, for all i, there exists σi such that $\beta_i.F_i \equiv \alpha_{\sigma i}.S_{\sigma i}$. We observe that the converse (associating a ηj to all js) also holds, and that the number of parallel components in $!F$ is necessarily greater than the number of components in S (otherwise, we would obtain a smaller seed). In the case where this number is strictly greater, this means a replicated component appears twice in $!F$, so that P can be rewritten using rule (R2). We are left with the case where the two processes have the same number of components, which entails that they are equated by $\equiv$.

To sum up, either P can be rewritten, or $!F \equiv S$. In the latter case, we deduce $S \mid F^P \dot{\sim} S \mid F^S$ from (∗), and since $S \# F^S$ by Lemma 9(i), there are two cases according to Lemma 10: either $F^P \equiv F^S$, in which case $P \equiv \mathsf{s}(P)$: P is a seed; or $\neg(S \# F^P)$, i.e., F^P admits some $\alpha_j.S_j$ as a sub-term, and we can rewrite P using (R1), getting a process bisimilar to P by Prop. 2. □

Proposition 17 (Completeness). *For all P, $P \xrightarrow{\mathsf{s}(P)}{}^{*} \mathsf{s}(P)$.*

Thanks to our characterisation of bisimilarity on seeds (Prop. 11), we obtain:

Theorem 18 (Characterisation). *In mCCS, visible and strong bisimilarity coincide with joinability: $P \dot{\sim} Q$ iff $P \sim Q$ iff $P \curlyvee Q$.*

Proof. We have $\curlyvee \subseteq \sim \subseteq \dot{\sim}$ by Lemma 14. Then, $P \dot{\sim} Q$ entails $\mathsf{s}(P) \equiv \mathsf{s}(Q)$ by Prop. 11. Since $P \xrightarrow{\mathsf{s}(P)}{}^{*} \mathsf{s}(P)$ and $Q \xrightarrow{\mathsf{s}(Q)}{}^{*} \mathsf{s}(Q)$ by Prop. 17, we get $P \curlyvee Q$. □

This result has several consequences. First, we do not need to play silent transitions in bisimulation games (recall the absence of τ prefix). Second, bisimilarity is substitution closed in mCCS. Third, bisimilarity is decidable in mCCS: the definition of joinability is a priori not effective (we are not told how to find T); however, according to the proof of Thm. 18, it suffices to search for T among the processes whose size is smaller than both P and Q to test whether $P \curlyvee Q$.

It should be noted that Christensen et al. already proved decidability of bisimilarity in a larger subset of CCS [3], so that the latter consequence is not surprising. However, their axiomatisation exploits the expansion law, so that it cannot be used to establish substitution closure in our setting.

Remark 19. *The τ prefix is not included in our presentation of mCCS. We extend our results in [5] to handle this prefix. The overall strategy is the same, but the proof involves some non-trivial additional technicalities. Basically, difficulties arise when a process answers to a transition emanating from a τ-prefix using a synchronisation (consider, e.g., $!a|!\overline{a}|\tau \sim !a|!\overline{a}$). From the point of view of the axiomatisation, it suffices to extend the rewriting system using the following law:*

$$!a.E \mid !\overline{a}.F \mid !\tau.(E \mid F) \sim !a.E \mid !\overline{a}.F$$

5 Congruence of Strong Bisimilarity in the π-Calculus

In this section, we adapt the previous results from CCS to the π-calculus in order to obtain closure of bisimilarity under substitutions, and deduce congruence in the restriction-free π-calculus with only top-level replications.

In moving from CCS to π, some care has to be taken. The first reason for that is that "being a sub-term of" is more subtle in π than in CCS, because of issues related to binding and α-conversion. The second reason is that the LTS for the π-calculus involves substitutions, and we must choose how to handle these in the definition of behavioural equivalence. Among the various notions of bisimilarity that exist for π, we shall actually adopt the simplest and coarsest one, namely ground bisimilarity: when ground bisimilarity is closed under substitutions, the ground, early and late versions of the equivalence coincide [14].

We let x, y, a, b range over a countable set of *names*. We work in the subset of the π-calculus, called $m\pi$, defined by replacing actions from the syntax of mCCS (Sect. 2) with the following productions: $\alpha, \beta ::= a(x) \mid \overline{a}\langle b\rangle$. As usual,

$$\frac{}{\overline{a}\langle b\rangle.F \xrightarrow{\overline{a}\langle b\rangle} F} \qquad \frac{}{!\overline{a}\langle b\rangle.F \xrightarrow{\overline{a}\langle b\rangle} !\overline{a}\langle b\rangle.F \mid F} \qquad \frac{P \xrightarrow{\mu} P' \qquad \mathrm{bn}(\mu) \cap \mathrm{fn}(Q) = \emptyset}{P|Q \xrightarrow{\mu} P'|Q}$$

$$\frac{y \notin \mathrm{fn}(a(x).F)}{a(x).F \xrightarrow{a(y)} F\{y/x\}} \qquad \frac{y \notin \mathrm{fn}(a(x).F)}{!a(x).F \xrightarrow{a(y)} !a(x).F \mid F\{y/x\}} \qquad \frac{P \xrightarrow{\overline{a}\langle b\rangle} P' \qquad Q \xrightarrow{a(x)} Q'}{P|Q \xrightarrow{\tau} P'|Q'\{b/x\}}$$

Fig. 1. Labelled Transition System for $m\pi$

the operator of input prefix is binding, we write $\mathrm{fn}(P)$ for the set of free names of P, $\mathrm{bn}(\alpha)$ for the set of names bound by α, and we let $P\{y/x\}$ stand for the capture-avoiding substitution of x with y in P. Note that contexts (C) can bind names (e.g., $a(x).[]$). The LTS for $m\pi$ is presented on Fig. 1, where symmetric rules for parallel composition are omitted. The conditions involving freshness of names ensure that $P \xrightarrow{a(x)} P'$ entails $x \notin \mathrm{fn}(P)$; this allows us to give a simple definition of ground bisimilarity:

Definition 20. Ground bisimilarity, *denoted by* $\sim$, *is the largest symmetric binary relation such that* $P \sim Q$ *entails that* $\mathrm{fn}(P) = \mathrm{fn}(Q)$, *and that whenever* $P \xrightarrow{\mu} P'$, *there exists* Q' *s.t.* $Q \xrightarrow{\mu} Q'$ *and* $P' \sim Q'$. Visible ground bisimilarity ($\dot{\sim}$) *is defined similarly, by restricting challenges to the cases where* $\mu \neq \tau$.

Since we lack the restriction operator, the condition on free names is actually enforced by standard notions of bisimilarity. In particular, this definition coincides with the standard definition of ground bisimilarity on $m\pi$ [14]: input prefixes are tested with fresh names. On finite $m\pi$-processes, ground bisimilarity is a substitution closed congruence [6], so that it coincides with early and late bisimilarities. We need to show that it also coincides with visible bisimilarity (the proof, given in [5], exploits some technical results from [6]):

Theorem 21. *On finite* $m\pi$ *processes,* $\dot{\sim}$ *and* $\sim$ *coincide.*

As for CCS, we then establish that visible and ground bisimilarities coincide on all $m\pi$ processes. Since visible bisimilarity is easily shown to be substitution closed (Prop. 22 below), this allows us to deduce congruence and coincidence with the other notions of bisimilarity (Thm. 23).

Proposition 22. *Visible bisimilarity is a substitution closed congruence.*

The reasoning goes along the same lines as for CCS, so that we only review the main differences, referring to [5] for detailed proofs. We need to adapt the definition of distribution congruence, and we rely on Thm. 21 to prove that distribution congruence is contained in ground bisimilarity. As expected, we need to impose conditions on names when stating results involving contexts; for example, in Prop. 2, C should not bind free names of $\alpha.F$. Note moreover that we need to go against a Barendregt convention to perform some rewriting steps. For example, we want to allow $!a(x).a(x) \xrightarrow{!a(x)} !a(x)$. We finally obtain coincidence of visible and ground bisimilarities, which yields congruence:

Theorem 23 (Characterisation and congruence). *In $m\pi$, early, late, visible and ground bisimilarity coincide and define a substitution closed congruence.*

6 Conclusions and Future Work

We have presented a characterisation of strong bisimilarity in the restriction- and sum-free fragment of CCS, where replications are only allowed at top-level (Thm. 18). This has allowed us to put forward important algebraic properties of replication w.r.t. bisimilarity. By extending this result to the π-calculus, we have established congruence of bisimilarity in the corresponding fragment (Thm. 23).

We would like to generalise our results further, by finding extensions of the calculi we have studied for which bisimilarity is substitution closed. A counterexample involving the operators of restriction and replication is presented in [2] to establish non-congruence of bisimilarity. Therefore, in light of [6, Corollary 5.9] and Thm. 23, we can think of two paths to explore: either add a limited usage of restriction to the language, or study the full replication operator.

Adding the restriction operator. The counterexample of [2] suggests that restrictions occurring immediately under replications are problematic. A natural extension of mCCS would therefore consist in adding restriction only to the grammar for finite processes—we indeed know from [6] that restriction does not break substitution closure on finite processes. Adding the τ prefix is a first step (cf. [5] and Rmk. 19) in this direction: this prefix can be encoded as $(\nu c)\,(\overline{c}|c.P)$, for a fresh c. However, an important difficulty in adapting our proofs is the definition and analysis of a counterpart of visible bisimilarity in presence of restriction.

Beyond top-level replications. Handling arbitrary replications seems really challenging. We have started investigating the case where replication is not at top-level, but where nested replications (i.e., replications that occur under replications) are forbidden. The law

$$\alpha.C[!\alpha.C[\mathbf{0}]] \ \sim\ !\alpha.C[\mathbf{0}]$$

seems important to capture bisimilarity in this setting: it somehow generalises the distribution law (D) to replicated processes, and it allows one to equate processes like $!a$ and $a.!a$. We do not know at the moment whether this law, together with the laws presented above, is sufficient to characterise bisimilarity. One of the difficulties in studying this richer language is that seeds are no longer stable under reduction (Prop. 12): for example, $!a.b|c.!b$ is a seed while its reduct along c, $!a.b|!b$, is not, being bisimilar to $!a|!b$.

Related to this question is the work on HOcore [8], a restriction-free higher-order π-calculus where strong bisimilarity is characterised by the distribution law. In this calculus, replication can be encoded using the higher-order features. The encoding is not fully abstract, however, so that it does not entail substitution closure in presence of "standard" replication.

Weak bisimilarity. Rather complex laws appear when moving from the strong to the weak case. For example, the following laws are valid for weak bisimilarity:

$$!\overline{a}.a \mid a.b \approx\ !\overline{a}.a \mid a \mid b\ , \qquad\qquad !\overline{a} \mid !a.b \approx\ !\overline{a} \mid !a \mid !b\ .$$

In both cases, although the related processes have the same size, the right-hand side process could be considered as a seed. We do not know how to generalise the first equivalence. For the second one, the following law, where $\langle P \rangle_a$ is defined homomorphically, except for $\langle a.P \rangle_a = \langle \overline{a}.P \rangle_a = \langle P \rangle_a$, is an interesting candidate:

$$!\overline{a}.P \mid !a.Q \approx\ !\overline{a} \mid !a \mid !\langle P \rangle_a \mid !\langle Q \rangle_a\ .$$

Acknowledgements. We are grateful to the anonymous referees for their numerous and valuable comments.

References

1. Aceto, L., Fokkink, W.J., Ingolfsdottir, A., Luttik, B.: Finite equational bases in process algebra: Results and open questions. In: Middeldorp, A., van Oostrom, V., van Raamsdonk, F., de Vrijer, R. (eds.) Processes, Terms and Cycles: Steps on the Road to Infinity. LNCS, vol. 3838, pp. 338–367. Springer, Heidelberg (2005)
2. Boreale, M., Sangiorgi, D.: Some congruence properties for π-calculus bisimilarities. Theoretical Computer Science 198, 159–176 (1998)
3. Christensen, S., Hirshfeld, Y., Moller, F.: Decidable subsets of CCS. Computer Journal 37(4), 233–242 (1994)
4. Hennessy, M., Milner, R.: Algebraic laws for nondeterminism and concurrency. Journal of ACM 32(1), 137–161 (1985)
5. Hirschkoff, D., Pous, D.: Extended version of this abstract, `http://hal.archives-ouvertes.fr/hal-00375604/`
6. Hirschkoff, D., Pous, D.: A distribution law for CCS and a new congruence result for the pi-calculus. Logial Methods in Computer Science 4(2) (2008)
7. Hirshfeld, Y., Jerrum, M.: Bisimulation equivalence is decidable for normed process algebra. In: Wiedermann, J., Van Emde Boas, P., Nielsen, M. (eds.) ICALP 1999. LNCS, vol. 1644, pp. 412–421. Springer, Heidelberg (1999)
8. Lanese, I., Pérez, J.A., Sangiorgi, D., Schmitt, A.: On the expressiveness and decidability of higher-order process calculi. In: LICS, pp. 145–155. IEEE, Los Alamitos (2008)
9. Milner, R.: Functions as Processes. J. of Mathematical Structures in Computer Science 2(2), 119–141 (1992)
10. Nestmann, U., Pierce, B.C.: Decoding choice encodings. Information and Computation 163, 1–59 (2000)
11. Pous, D.: Complete lattices and up-to techniques. In: Shao, Z. (ed.) APLAS 2007. LNCS, vol. 4807, pp. 351–366. Springer, Heidelberg (2007)
12. Pous, D.: Techniques modulo pour les bisimulations. PhD thesis, ENS Lyon (2008)
13. Sangiorgi, D.: On the bisimulation proof method. J. of Mathematical Structures in Computer Science 8, 447–479 (1998)
14. Sangiorgi, D., Walker, D.: The π-calculus: a Theory of Mobile Processes. Cambridge University Press, Cambridge (2001)

The Downward-Closure of Petri Net Languages*

Peter Habermehl[1], Roland Meyer[1], and Harro Wimmel[2]

[1] LIAFA, Paris Diderot University & CNRS
{peter.habermehl,roland.meyer}@liafa.jussieu.fr
[2] Department of Computing Science, University of Rostock
harro.wimmel@uni-rostock.de

Abstract. We show that the downward-closure of a Petri net language is effectively computable. This is mainly done by using the notions defined for showing decidability of the reachability problem of Petri nets. In particular, we rely on Lambert's construction of marked graph transition sequences — special instances of coverability graphs that allow us to extract constructively the simple regular expression corresponding to the downward-closure. We also consider the remaining language types for Petri nets common in the literature. For all of them, we provide algorithms that compute the simple regular expressions of their downward-closure. As application, we outline an algorithm to automatically analyse the stability of a system against attacks from a malicious environment.

1 Introduction

Petri nets or the very similar vector addition systems are a popular fundamental model for concurrent systems. Deep results have been obtained in Petri net theory, among them and perhaps most important decidability of the reachability problem [6,10,8], whose precise complexity is still open.

Petri nets have also been studied in formal language theory, and several notions of Petri net languages have been introduced. The standard notion to which we simply refer as *Petri net language* accepts sequences of transition labels in a run from an initial to a final marking. Other notions are the *prefix language* considering all markings to be final, the *covering language* where sequences leading to markings that dominate a given final marking are accepted, and *terminal languages* where all sequences leading to a deadlock are computed.

We study the *downward-closure* of all these languages wrt. the subword ordering [4]. It is well known that given a language L over some finite alphabet its downward-closure is regular; it can always be written as the complement of an upward-closed set, which in turn is characterised by a finite set of minimal elements. Even more, downward-closed languages correspond to *simple regular expressions* [1]. However, such an expression is not always effectively computable. This depends on L. For example, the reachability set of lossy channel systems is downward-closed but not effectively computable [11], even though membership

* The first authors were supported by the French ANR projects Averiss and Veridyc.

S. Abramsky et al. (Eds.): ICALP 2010, Part II, LNCS 6199, pp. 466–477, 2010.

in the set is decidable. On the contrary, for pushdown-automata the problem has been solved positively by Courcelle [2].

We show as our main result that the downward-closure of Petri net languages is *effectively computable*. This is done by a careful inspection of the *proof of decidability of the reachability problem* due to Lambert [8]. From his so-called perfect marked graph transition sequences (MGTS) we directly extract the simple regular expression corresponding to the downward-closure of the language. Key to this is an iteration argument that employs Lambert's pumping lemma for Petri nets and the particular structure of MGTS in a non-trivial way.

We also establish computability of the downward-closure for the remaining language types. For terminal languages we rely on the previous result, whereas for covering and prefix languages we directly construct the expressions from the coverability tree of the Petri net.

To be able to compute the downward-closure of a language is important for several reasons. For example, it is precisely what an environment observes from a language in an asynchronous interaction. A component which periodically observes the actions (or alternatively states) of another process will see exactly the downward-closure of the language of actions the partner issues. Another application of the downward-closure of a language is the use as a regular overapproximation of the system behaviour, allowing for safe inclusion checks between a Petri net language and all types of languages for which inclusion of a regular language (or even only simple regular expressions) is decidable.

We apply our results to automatically analyse the stability of a system against attacks. Consider a malicious environment that tries to force the system into an undesirable state. Then the downward-closure of the environment's language provides information about the intrusions the system can tolerate.

The paper is organised as follows. In Section 2, we provide preliminary definitions concerning Petri nets, languages, and downward-closed sets. In Section 3, we state our main result. The downward-closure of Petri net languages is effectively computable. In Section 4, we investigate the other language types. In Section 5 we illustrate an application of our result before concluding in Section 6.

2 Petri Nets and Their Languages

Petri nets generalise finite automata by distributed states and explicite synchronisation of transitions. A *Petri net* is a triple (P, T, F) with finite and disjoint sets of *places* P and *transitions* T. The *flow function* $F : (P \times T) \cup (T \times P) \to \mathbb{N}$ determines the mutual influence of places and transitions.

States of Petri nets, typically called *markings*, are functions $M \in \mathbb{N}^P$ that assign a natural number to each place. We say that a place p *has* k *tokens under* M if $M(p) = k$. A marking M *enables* a transition t, denoted by $M[t\rangle$, if the places carry at least the number of tokens required by F, i.e., $M(p) \geq F(p,t)$ for all $p \in P$. A transition t that is enabled in M may be *fired* and yields marking M' with $M'(p) = M(p) - F(p,t) + F(t,p)$ for all $p \in P$. The firing relation is extended inductively to transition sequences $\sigma \in T^*$.

Let symbol ω represent an unbounded number and abbreviate $\mathbb{N} \cup \{\omega\}$ by $\mathbb{N}_\omega$. The usual order $\leq$ on natural numbers extends to $\mathbb{N}_\omega$ by defining $n \leq \omega$ for all $n \in \mathbb{N}$. Similar to markings, ω-markings are functions in $\mathbb{N}_\omega^P$. The ordering $\preceq_\omega \subseteq \mathbb{N}_\omega^P \times \mathbb{N}_\omega^P$ defines the precision of ω-markings. We have $M \preceq_\omega M'$ if $M(p) = M'(p)$ or $M'(p) = \omega$.

To adapt the firing rule to ω-markings, we define $\omega - n := \omega =: \omega + n$ for any $n \in \mathbb{N}$. The relation defined above can now be applied to ω-markings, and firing a transition will never increase or decrease the number of tokens for a place p with $M(p) = \omega$. An ω-marking M' is *reachable* from an ω-marking M in a net N if there is a firing sequence leading from M to M'. We denote the set of ω-markings reachable from M by $\mathcal{R}(M)$.

Definition 1. *The* reachability problem **RP** *is the set*

$$\mathbf{RP} := \{(N, M, M') \mid N = (P, T, F), M, M' \in \mathbb{N}_\omega^P, \text{ and } M' \in \mathcal{R}(M)\}.$$

The reachability problem **RP** is known to be decidable. This was first proved by Mayr [9,10] with an alternative proof by Kosaraju [6]. In the '90s, Lambert [8] presented another proof, which can also be found in [13].

To deal with reachability, reachability graphs and coverability graphs were introduced in [5]. Consider $N = (P, T, F)$ with an ω-marking $M_0 \in \mathbb{N}_\omega^P$. The *reachability graph* R of (N, M_0) is the edge-labelled graph $R = (\mathcal{R}(M_0), E, T)$, where a t-labelled edge $e = (M_1, t, M_2)$ is in E whenever $M_1[t\rangle M_2$.

A *coverability graph* $C = (V, E, T)$ of (N, M_0) is defined inductively. First, M_0 is in V. Then, if $M_1 \in V$ and $M_1[t\rangle M_2$, check for every M on a path from M_0 to M_1 if $M \leq M_2$. If the latter holds, change $M_2(s)$ to ω whenever $M_2(s) > M(s)$. Add, if not yet contained, the modified M_2 to V and (M_1, t, M_2) to E. The procedure is repeated, until no more nodes and edges can be added.

Reachability graphs are usually infinite, whereas coverability graphs are always finite. But due to the inexact ω-markings, coverability graphs do not allow for deciding reachability. However, the concept is still valuable in dealing with reachability, as it allows for a partial solution to the problem. A marking M is not reachable if there is no M' with $M' \geq M$ in the coverability graph. For a complete solution of the reachability problem, coverability graphs need to be extended as discussed in Section 3.

Our main contributions are procedures to compute representations of Petri net languages. Different language types have been proposed in the literature that we shall briefly recall in the following definition [12].

Definition 2. *Consider a Petri net $N = (P, T, F)$ with initial and final markings $M_0, M_f \in \mathbb{N}^P$, Σ a finite alphabet, and $h \in (\Sigma \cup \{\epsilon\})^T$ a labelling that is extended homomorphically to T^*. The* language *of N accepts firing sequences to the final marking:*

$$\mathcal{L}_h(N, M_0, M_f) := \{h(\sigma) \mid M_0[\sigma\rangle M_f \text{ for some } \sigma \in T^*\}.$$

We write $\mathcal{L}(N, M_0, M_f)$ if h is the identity. The prefix language *of the net accepts all transition sequences:*

$$\mathcal{P}_h(N, M_0) := \{h(\sigma) \mid M_0[\sigma\rangle M \text{ for some } \sigma \in T^* \text{ and } M \in \mathbb{N}^P\}.$$

The terminal language *of the Petri net accepts runs to deadlock markings, i.e., markings where no transition is enabled:*

$$\mathcal{T}_h(N, M_0) := \{h(\sigma) \mid M_0[\sigma\rangle M \text{ with } \sigma \in T^*, M \in \mathbb{N}^P, \text{ and } M \text{ is a deadlock}\}.$$

The covering language *requires domination of the final marking:*

$$\mathcal{C}_h(N, M_0, M_f) := \{h(\sigma) \mid M_0[\sigma\rangle M \geq M_f \text{ for some } \sigma \in T^* \text{ and } M \in \mathbb{N}^P\}.$$

Note that the prefix language $\mathcal{P}_h(N, M_0)$ is the covering language of the marking that assigns zero to all places, $\mathcal{P}_h(N, M_0) = \mathcal{C}_h(N, M_0, \mathbf{0})$.

We are interested in the downward-closure of the above languages wrt. the subword ordering $\preceq \subseteq \Sigma^* \times \Sigma^*$. The relation $a_1 \dots a_m \preceq b_1 \dots b_n$ requires word $a_1 \dots a_m$ to be embedded in $b_1 \dots b_n$, i.e., there are indices $i_1, \dots, i_m \in \{1, \dots, n\}$ with $i_1 < \dots < i_m$ so that $a_j = b_{i_j}$ for all $j \in \{1, \dots, m\}$. Given a language L, its downward-closure is $L\!\downarrow := \{w \mid w \preceq v \text{ for some } v \in L\}$. A downward-closed language is a language L such that $L\!\downarrow = L$. Every downward-closed language is regular since it is the complement of an upward-closed set which can be represented by a finite number of minimal elements with respect to $\preceq$. This follows from the fact that the subword relation is a well-quasi-ordering on words [4]. More precisely, every downward-closed set can be written as a *simple regular expression* over Σ (see [1]): We call an atomic expression any regular expression e of the form $(a + \epsilon)$ where $a \in \Sigma$, or of the form $(a_1 + \dots + a_m)^*$ where $a_1, \dots, a_m \in \Sigma$. A product p is either the empty word ϵ or a finite sequence $e_1 e_2 \dots e_n$ of atomic expressions. A simple regular expression is then either $\emptyset$ or a finite union $p_1 + \dots + p_k$ of products.

3 Downward-Closure of Petri Net Languages

Fix a Petri net $N = (P, T, F)$ with initial and final markings $M_0, M_f \in \mathbb{N}^P$ and labelling $h \in (\Sigma \cup \{\epsilon\})^T$. We establish the following main result.

Theorem 1. *$\mathcal{L}_h(N, M_0, M_f)\!\downarrow$ is computable as (♣) below.*

Recall that any downward-closed language is representable by a simple regular expression [1]. We show that in case of Petri net languages these expressions can be computed effectively. In fact, they turn out to be rather natural; they correspond to the transition sets in the precovering graphs of the net. To see this, we shall need some insight into the decidability proof for reachability in Petri nets. We follow here essentially the presentation given in [14] for solving the infinity problem of intermediate states in Petri nets.

3.1 A Look at the Decidability of RP

We present here some main ideas behind the proof of decidability of **RP** according to Lambert [8,13]. The proof is based on marked graph transition sequences (MGTS), which are sequences of special instances of coverability graphs C_i alternating with transitions t_j of the form $G = C_1.t_1.C_2 \dots t_{n-1}.C_n$. These special instances of coverability graphs are called *precovering graphs* in [8] and have additional structure from which we shall only use strong connectedness. Each precovering graph C_i is augmented by two additional ω-markings, the *input* $m_{i,in}$ and the *output* $m_{i,out}$. The *initial marking* M_i of C_i is less concrete than input and output, $m_{i,in} \preceq_\omega M_i$ and $m_{i,out} \preceq_\omega M_i$. The transitions $t_1, \ldots, t_{n-1}$ in an MGTS connect the output $m_{i,out}$ of one precovering graph to the input $m_{i+1,in}$ of the next, see Figure 1.

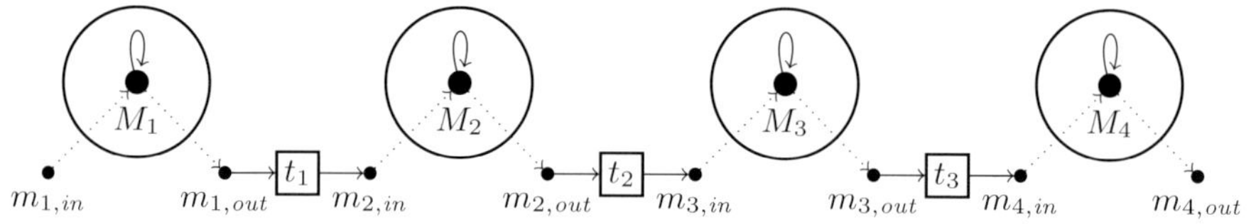

Fig. 1. A marked graph transition sequence $C_1.t_1.C_2 \ldots t_3.C_4$. Dots represent markings and circles represent strongly connected precovering graphs with in general more than one node. The initial marking is depicted in the center. Solid lines inside these circles are transition sequences that must be firable in the Petri net. Dotted lines show the entry to and exit from precovering graphs, which do not change the actual marking in the Petri net. Both $m_{i,in} \preceq_\omega M_i$ and $m_{i,out} \preceq_\omega M_i$ hold for every i.

A *solution* of an MGTS is by definition a transition sequence leading through the MGTS. In Figure 1 it begins with marking $m_{1,in}$, leads in cycles through the first precovering graph until marking $m_{1,out}$ is reached, then t_1 can fire to reach $m_{2,in}$, from which the second coverability graph is entered and so on, until the MGTS ends. Whenever the marking of some node has a finite value for some place, this value *must be reached exactly* by the transition sequence. If the value is ω, there are no such conditions. The *set of solutions* of an MGTS G is denoted by $\mathcal{L}(G)$ [8, page 90].

An instance $RP = (N, M_0, M_f)$ of the reachability problem can be formulated as the problem of finding a solution for the special MGTS G_{RP} depicted in Figure 2. The node $\boldsymbol{\omega}$ (with all entries ω) is the only node of the coverability graph, i.e., we allow for arbitrary ω-markings and firings of transitions between $m_{1,in} = M_0$ and $m_{1,out} = M_f$, but the sequence must begin exactly at the (concrete) initial

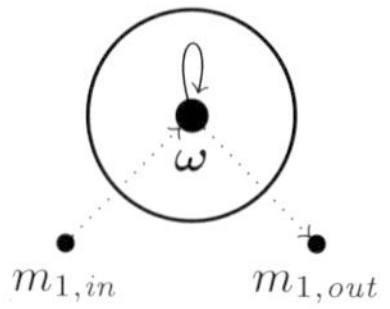

Fig. 2. MGTS representation of an instance $(N, m_{1,in}, m_{1,out})$ of the reachability problem. The MGTS consists of one precovering graph with a single node $\boldsymbol{\omega}$ which represents the ω-marking where all places have an unbounded number of tokens and from which every transition can fire. A solution for this MGTS is a transition sequence from $m_{1,in}$ to $m_{1,out}$.

marking of the net and end at its final marking. The solutions to this MGTS are precisely the runs in the net N leading from M_0 to M_f:

$$\mathcal{L}(N, M_0, M_f) = \mathcal{L}(G_{RP}).$$

Hence, to decide **RP** it is sufficient to solve arbitrary MGTS. Lambert defines for each MGTS a characteristic equation that is fulfilled by all its solutions. In other words, the equation is a necessary condition for solutions of the MGTS. More precisely, the author derives a system of linear equations $Ax = b$ where A and b range over integers. It encodes the firing behaviour of the precovering graphs and intermediary transitions and can become quite large. There is one variable for every marking entry $m_{i,in}$ and $m_{i,out}$ (including zero and ω entries) as well as one variable for each edge in every precovering graph. Since markings must not become negative, solutions sought must be semi-positive. This (possibly empty) set of semi-positive solutions can always be computed [7].

If the characteristic equation was sufficient for the existence of solutions of an MGTS, **RP** would have been solved immediately. While not valid in general, Lambert provides precise conditions for when this implication holds. Generally speaking, a solution to the characteristic equation yields a solution to the MGTS if the variables for the edges and the variables for all ω-entries of the markings are unbounded in the solution space. An MGTS with such a sufficient characteristic equation is called *perfect* and denoted by $\mathbb{G}$. Unboundedness of the variables can be checked effectively [7].

Since not all MGTS are perfect, Lambert presents a decomposition procedure [8]. It computes from one MGTS G a new set of MGTS that are to a greater degree perfect and have the same solutions as G. This means each transition sequence leading through the original MGTS and solving it will also lead through at least one of the derived MGTS and solve it, and vice versa. The degree of perfectness is discrete and cannot be increased indefinitely. Therefore the decomposition procedure terminates and returns a finite set Γ_G of perfect MGTS. With the assumption that $m_{1,in}$ and $m_{n,out}$ are ω-free, the corresponding decomposition theorem is simplified to the following form.

Theorem 2 (Decomposition [8,13]). *An MGTS G can be decomposed into a finite set Γ_G of perfect MGTS with the same solutions, $\mathcal{L}(G) = \bigcup_{\mathbb{G} \in \Gamma_G} \mathcal{L}(\mathbb{G})$.*

When we apply the decomposition procedure to the MGTS G_{RP} for the instance $RP = (N, m_{1,in}, m_{1,out})$ of the reachability problem (Figure 2), we obtain a set $\Gamma_{G_{RP}}$ of perfect MGTS. For each of these perfect MGTS $\mathbb{G}$ we can decide whether it has solutions, i.e., whether $\mathcal{L}(\mathbb{G}) \neq \emptyset$. If at least one has a solution, we obtain a positive answer to the reachability problem, otherwise a negative answer. This means, the following algorithm decides **RP**:

> **input** $RP = (N, m_{1,in}, m_{1,out})$
> `create` G_{RP} according to Figure 2
> `decompose` G_{RP} into $\Gamma_{G_{RP}}$ with $\mathbb{G}$ perfect for all $\mathbb{G} \in \Gamma_{G_{RP}}$
> **if** $\exists \mathbb{G} \in \Gamma_{G_{RP}}$ `with` $\mathcal{L}(\mathbb{G}) \neq \emptyset$ **answer** `yes` **else answer** `no`.

The reachability problem is not only decidable. If it has a solution, it is also possible to calculate a solving transition sequence. Consider a perfect MGTS $\mathbb{G} = C_1.t_1.C_2 \ldots t_{n-1}.C_n$ and let each precovering graph have the initial marking M_i (cf. Figure 1). We search for covering sequences u_i that indefinitely increase the token count on ω-places of M_i. More precisely, u_i is a transition sequence from M_i to M_i with the following properties.

- The sequence u_i is enabled under marking $m_{i,in}$.
- If $M_i(s) = \omega > m_{i,in}(s)$, then u_i will add tokens to place s.
- If $M_i(s) = m_{i,in}(s) \in \mathbb{N}$, then u_i will not change the token count on place s.

In case $M_i(s) = \omega = m_{i,in}(s)$, no requirements are imposed. Sequence u_i is accompanied by a second transition sequence v_i with similar properties, except that the reverse of v_i must be able to fire backwards from $m_{i,out}$. This decreases the token count on ω-places and lets v_i reach the output node $m_{i,out}$ from M_i. Having such pairs of covering sequences $((u_i, v_i))_{1\leq i\leq n}$ available for all precovering graphs, the following theorem yields a solution to the perfect MGTS.

Theorem 3 (Lambert's Iteration Lemma [8,13]). *Consider some perfect MGTS $\mathbb{G}$ with at least one solution and let $((u_i, v_i))_{1\leq i\leq n}$ be covering sequences satisfying the above requirements. We can compute $k_0 \in \mathbb{N}$ and transition sequences β_i, w_i from M_i to M_i such that* for every $k \geq k_0$ *the sequence*

$$(u_1)^k\beta_1(w_1)^k(v_1)^k t_1(u_2)^k\beta_2(w_2)^k(v_2)^k t_2 \ldots t_{n-1}(u_n)^k\beta_n(w_n)^k(v_n)^k$$

is a solution of $\mathbb{G}$.

Lambert proved that such covering sequences u_i, v_i always exist and that at least one can be computed [8]. Firing u_i repeatedly, at least k_0 times, pumps up the marking to the level necessary to execute $\beta_i(w_i)^k$. Afterwards v_i pumps it down to reach $m_{i,out}$. Transition t_i then proceeds to the next precovering graph.

3.2 Computing the Downward-Closure

According to the decomposition theorem, we can represent the Petri net language $\mathcal{L}(N, M_0, M_f)$ by the decomposition of the corresponding MGTS G_{RP}. We shall restrict our attention to perfect MGTS $\mathbb{G}$ that have a solution, i.e., $\mathcal{L}(\mathbb{G}) \neq \emptyset$. They form the subset $\Gamma^{\checkmark}_{G_{RP}}$ of $\Gamma_{G_{RP}}$. As the labelled language just applies a homomorphism, we derive

$$\mathcal{L}_h(N, M_0, M_f) = h(\mathcal{L}(N, M_0, M_f)) = h(\bigcup_{\mathbb{G}\in\Gamma^{\checkmark}_{G_{RP}}} \mathcal{L}(\mathbb{G})) = \bigcup_{\mathbb{G}\in\Gamma^{\checkmark}_{G_{RP}}} h(\mathcal{L}(\mathbb{G})).$$

Since downward-closure $-\downarrow$ and the application of h commute, and since downward-closure distributes over $\cup$, we obtain

$$\mathcal{L}_h(N, M_0, M_f)\downarrow = \bigcup_{\mathbb{G}\in\Gamma^{\checkmark}_{G_{RP}}} h(\mathcal{L}(\mathbb{G})\downarrow).$$

The main result in this section is a characterisation of $\mathcal{L}(\mathbb{G})\downarrow$ as a simple regular expression $\phi_{\mathbb{G}}$. By the previous argumentation this solves the representation problem of $\mathcal{L}_h(N, M_0, M_f)\downarrow$ and hence proves Theorem 1. We compute $\phi_{\mathbb{G}}$ for the language of every perfect MGTS $\mathbb{G} \in \Gamma^{\checkmark}_{G_{RP}}$. Then we apply the homomorphism to these expressions, $h(\phi_{\mathbb{G}})$, and end up in a finite disjunction

$$\mathcal{L}_h(N, M_0, M_f)\downarrow = \mathcal{L}(\sum_{\mathbb{G}\in\Gamma^{\checkmark}_{G_{RP}}} h(\phi_{\mathbb{G}})). \qquad (\clubsuit)$$

We spend the remainder of the section on the representation of $\mathcal{L}(\mathbb{G})\downarrow$. Surprisingly, the simple regular expression turns out to be just the sequence of transition sets in the precovering graph,

$$\phi_{\mathbb{G}} := T_1^*.(t_1 + \epsilon).T_2^* \ldots (t_{n-1} + \epsilon).T_n^*,$$

where $\mathbb{G} = C_1.t_1.C_2 \ldots t_{n-1}.C_n$ and C_i contains the transitions T_i.

Proposition 1. $\mathcal{L}(\mathbb{G})\downarrow = \mathcal{L}(\phi_{\mathbb{G}})$.

The inclusion from left to right is trivial. The proof of the reverse direction relies on the following key observation about Lambert's iteration lemma. The sequences u_i can always be chosen in such a way that they contain all transitions of the precovering graph C_i. By iteration we obtain all sequences u_i^k. Since u_i contains all transitions in T_i, we derive

$$T_i^* \subseteq (\bigcup_{k\in\mathbb{N}} u_i^k)\downarrow = \bigcup_{k\in\mathbb{N}} u_i^k\downarrow .$$

Hence, all that remains to be shown is that u_i can be constructed so as to contain all edges of C_i and consequently all transitions in T_i. Lets start with a covering sequence u_i' that satisfies the requirements stated above and that can be found with Lambert's procedure [8]. Since C_i is strongly connected, there is a finite path z_i from M_i to M_i that contains all edges of C_i. The corresponding transition sequence may have a negative effect on the ω-places, say at most $m \in \mathbb{N}$ tokens are removed. Concrete token counts are, by construction of precovering graphs, reproduced exactly. Since u_i' is a covering sequence, we can repeat it $m+1$ times. By the second requirement, this adds at least $m+1$ tokens to every ω-place. If we now append z_i, we may decrease the token count by m but still guarantee a positive effect of $m + 1 - m = 1$ on the ω-places. This means

$$u_i := {u_i'}^{m+1}.z_i$$

is a covering sequence that we may use instead of u_i' and that contains all transitions. This concludes the proof of Proposition 1.

4 Downward-Closure of Other Language Types

We consider the downward-closure of terminal and covering languages. For terminal languages that accept via deadlocks we provide a reduction to the previous computability result. For covering languages, we avoid solving reachability and give a direct construction of the downward-closure from the coverability tree.

4.1 Terminal Languages

Deadlocks in a Petri net $N = (P', T, F)$ are characterised by a finite set $\mathcal{P}$ of partially specified markings where the token count on some places is arbitrary, $M_P \in \mathbb{N}^P$ with $P \subseteq P'$. Each such partial marking corresponds to a case where no transition can fire. Hence, the terminal language is a finite union of partial languages that accept by a partial marking, $\mathcal{T}_h(N, M_0) = \bigcup_{M_P \in \mathcal{P}} \mathcal{L}_h(N, M_0, M_P)$. We now formalise the notion of a partial language and then prove computability of its downward-closure. With the previous argumentation, this yields a representation for the downward-closure of the terminal language.

A partial marking $M_P \in \mathbb{N}^P$ with $P \subseteq P'$ denotes a potentially infinite set of markings M that coincide with M_P in the places in P, $M|_P = M_P$. The *partial language* is therefore defined to be $\mathcal{L}_h(N, M_0, M_P) := \bigcup_{M|_P = M_P} \mathcal{L}_h(N, M_0, M)$. We apply a construction due to Hack [3] to compute this union.

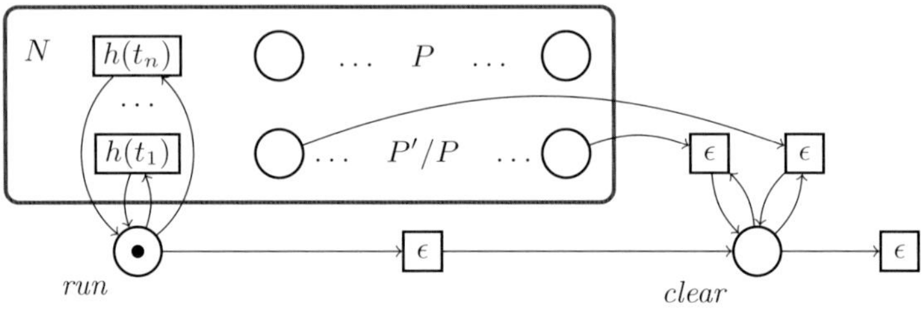

Fig. 3. Hack's construction to reduce partial Petri net languages to ordinary languages

We extend the given net $N = (P', T, F)$ to $N_e = (P' \cup P_e, T \cup T_e, F_e)$ as illustrated in Figure 3. The idea is to guess a final state by removing the *run* token and then empty the places outside $P \subseteq P'$. As a result, the runs in N from M_0 to a marking M with $M|_P = M_P$ are precisely the runs in N_e from M_0^r to the marking M_f, up to the token removal phase in the end. Marking M_0^r is M_0 with an additional token on the *run* place. Marking M_f coincides with M_P and has no tokens on the remaining places. Projecting away the new transitions t with $h_e(t) = \epsilon$ characterises the partial language by an ordinary language.

Lemma 1. $\mathcal{L}_h(N, M_0, M_P) = \mathcal{L}_{h \cup h_e}(N_e, M_0^r, M_f)$.

Combined with Theorem 1, a simple regular expression ϕ_{M_p} is computable that satisfies $\mathcal{L}_h(N, M_0, M_P)\downarrow = \mathcal{L}(\phi_{M_p})$. As a consequence, the downward-closure of the terminal language is the (finite) disjunction of these expressions.

Theorem 4. $\mathcal{T}_h(N, M_0)\downarrow = \mathcal{L}(\Sigma_{M_P \in \mathcal{P}}\, \phi_{M_p})$.

Note that the trick we employ for the partially specified final markings also works for partial input markings. Hence, we can compute the language and the terminal language also for nets with partially specified input markings.

4.2 Covering Languages

We extend the coverability tree to a finite automaton where the downward-closure coincides with the downward-closure of the covering-language. Hence, the desired regular expression is computable. The idea is to add edges to the coverability tree that represent the domination of markings by their successors and thus, by monotonicity of Petri nets, indicate cyclic behaviour. The final states reflect domination of the final marking. In the remainder, fix $N = (P, T, F)$ with initial and final markings M_0 and M_f and labelling $h \in (\Sigma \cup \{\epsilon\})^T$.

The coverability tree $CT = (V, E, \lambda)$ is similar to the coverability graph discussed in Section 2 but keeps the tree structure of the computation. Therefore, the vertices are labelled by extended markings, $\lambda(v) \in (\mathbb{N} \cup \{\omega\})^P$, and the edges $e \in E \subseteq V \times V$ by transitions, $\lambda(e) \in T$. A path is truncated as soon as it repeats an already visited marking.

We extend CT to a finite automaton $FA = (V, v_0, V_f, E \cup E', \lambda \cup \lambda')$ by adding backedges. The root of CT is the initial state v_0. States that cover M_f are final, $V_f := \{v \in V \mid \lambda(v) = M \geq M_f\}$. If the marking of v dominates the marking of an E-predecessor v', $\lambda(v) = M \geq M' = \lambda(v')$, we add a backedge $e' = (v, v')$ to E' and label it by $\lambda'(e') = \epsilon$. The downward-closed language of this automaton is the downward-closed covering language without labelling.

Lemma 2. $\mathcal{L}(FA)\downarrow = \mathcal{C}(N, M_0, M_f)\downarrow$.

To compute $\mathcal{L}(FA)\downarrow$ we represent the automaton as tree of its strongly connected components $SCC(FA)$. The root is the component C_0 that contains v_0. We need two additional functions to compute the regular expression. For two components $C, C' \in SCC(FA)$, let $\gamma_{C,C'} = (t + \varepsilon)$ if there is a t-labelled edge from C to C', and let $\gamma_{C,C'} = \emptyset$ otherwise. Let $\tau_C = \varepsilon$ if C contains a final state and $\tau_C = \emptyset$ otherwise. Concatenation with $\gamma_{C,C'} = \emptyset$ or $\tau_C = \emptyset$ suppresses further regular expressions if there is no edge or final state, respectively. Let T_C denote the transitions occurring in component C as edge labels. We recursively define regular expressions ϕ_C for the downward-closed languages of components:

$$\phi_C := T_C^*.\big(\tau_C + \sum_{C' \in SCC(FA)} \gamma_{C,C'}.\phi_{C'}\big).$$

Due to the tree structure, all regular expressions are well-defined. The following lemma is easy to prove.

Lemma 3. $\mathcal{L}(FA)\downarrow = \mathcal{L}(\phi_{C_0})$.

As the application of h commutes with the downward-closure, a combination of Lemma 2 and 3 yields the desired representation.

Theorem 5. $\mathcal{C}_h(N, M_0, M_f)\downarrow = \mathcal{L}(h(\phi_{C_0}))$.

Note that $h(\phi_{C_0})$ can be transformed into a simple regular expression by distributivity of concatenation over $+$ and removing possible occurrences of $\emptyset$.

5 Applications to Stability Analysis

Consider a system modelled as a Petri net N_s. It typically interacts with some potentially malicious environment. This means, $N_s = (P_s, T_s, F_s)$ is embedded[1] in a larger net $N = (P, T, F)$ where the environment changes the token count or restricts the firing behaviour in the subnet N_s. Figure 3 illustrates the situation. The environment is Hack's gadget that may stop the Petri net and empty some places. The results obtained in this paper allow us to approximate the attacks system N_s can tolerate without reaching undesirable states.

Consider an initial marking M_0^s of N_s and a bad marking M_b^s that should be avoided. For the full system N we either use $M_0^s, M_b^s \in \mathbb{N}^{P_s}$ as partially specified markings or assume full initial and final markings, $M_0, M_b \in \mathbb{N}^P$ with $M_0|_{P_s} = M_0^s$ and $M_b|_{P_s} = M_b^s$. The stability of N_s is estimated as follows.

Proposition 2. *An upward-closed language is computable that underapproximates the environmental behaviour N_s tolerates without reaching M_b^s from M_0^s.*

We consider the case of full markings M_0 and M_b of N. For partially specified markings, Hack's construction in Section 4.1 reduces the problem to this one. Let the full system N be labelled by h. Relabelling all transitions of N_s to ϵ yields a new homomorphism h' where only environmental transitions are visible. By definition, the downward-closure always contains the language itself, $\mathcal{L}_{h'}(N, M_0, M_b)\downarrow \supseteq \mathcal{L}_{h'}(N, M_0, M_b)$. This is, however, equivalent to

$$\overline{\mathcal{L}_{h'}(N, M_0, M_b)\downarrow} \subseteq \overline{\mathcal{L}_{h'}(N, M_0, M_b)}.$$

By Theorem 1, the simple regular expression for $\mathcal{L}_{h'}(N, M_0, M_b)\downarrow$ is computable. As regular languages are closed under complementation, the expression for $\overline{\mathcal{L}_{h'}(N, M_0, M_b)\downarrow}$ is computable as well. The language is upward-closed and underapproximates the attacks the system can tolerate.

Likewise, if we consider instead of M_b a desirable good marking M_g, then language $\mathcal{L}_{h'}(N, M_0, M_g)\downarrow$ overapproximates the environmental influences required to reach it. The complement of the language provides behaviour that definitely leads away from the good marking. Note that for covering instead of reachability similar arguments apply that rely on Theorem 5.

6 Conclusion

We have shown that the downward-closures of all types of Petri net languages are effectively computable. As an application of the results, we outlined an algorithm to estimate the stability of a system towards attacks from a malicious environment. In the future, we plan to study further applications. Especially in concurrent system analysis, our results should yield fully automated algorithms for the verification of asynchronous compositions of Petri nets with other models

[1] Formally, $N = (P, T, F)$ is *embedded* in $N' = (P', T', F')$ if $P \subseteq P'$, $T \subseteq T'$, and $F'|_{(S\times T)\cup(T\times S)} = F$. If homomorphism h labels N and h' labels N' then $h'|_T = h$.

like pushdown-automata. A different application domain is compositional verification of Petri nets. For an observer of a system, it is sufficient to check whether it reaches a critical state in the composition with the downward-closure of the system's language. However, cyclic proof rules are challenging.

References

1. Abdulla, P.A., Collomb-Annichini, A., Bouajjani, A., Jonsson, B.: Using forward reachability analysis for verification of lossy channel systems. Form. Methods Syst. Des. 25(1), 39–65 (2004)
2. Courcelle, B.: On constructing obstruction sets of words. Bulletin of the EATCS 44, 178–186 (1991)
3. Hack, M.: Decidability questions for Petri nets. Technical report, Cambridge, MA, USA (1976)
4. Higman, G.: Ordering by divisibility in abstract algebras. Proc. London Math. Soc. 2(3), 326–336 (1952)
5. Karp, R.M., Miller, R.E.: Parallel program schemata. J. Comput. Syst. Sci. 3(2), 147–195 (1969)
6. Kosaraju, S.R.: Decidability of reachability in vector addition systems (preliminary version). In: STOC, pp. 267–281. ACM, New York (1982)
7. Lambert, J.L.: Finding a partial solution to a linear system of equations in positive integers. Comput. Math. Applic. 15(3), 209–212 (1988)
8. Lambert, J.L.: A structure to decide reachability in Petri nets. Theor. Comp. Sci. 99(1), 79–104 (1992)
9. Mayr, E.W.: An algorithm for the general Petri net reachability problem. In: STOC, pp. 238–246. ACM, New York (1981)
10. Mayr, E.W.: An algorithm for the general Petri net reachability problem. SIAM J. Comp. 13(3), 441–460 (1984)
11. Mayr, R.: Undecidable problems in unreliable computations. Theor. Comp. Sci. 297(1-3), 337–354 (2003)
12. Peterson, J.L.: Petri nets. ACM Computing Surveys 9(3), 223–252 (1977)
13. Priese, L., Wimmel, H.: Petri-Netze. Springer, Heidelberg (2003)
14. Wimmel, H.: Infinity of intermediate states is decidable for Petri nets. In: Cortadella, J., Reisig, W. (eds.) ICATPN 2004. LNCS, vol. 3099, pp. 426–434. Springer, Heidelberg (2004)

Reachability Games on Extended Vector Addition Systems with States

Tomáš Brázdil[1,⋆], Petr Jančar[2,⋆⋆], and Antonín Kučera[1,⋆⋆⋆]

[1] Faculty of Informatics, Masaryk University, Botanická 68a,
60200 Brno, Czech Republic
{brazdil,kucera}@fi.muni.cz
[2] Center of Applied Cybernetics, Dept. of Computer Science, FEI,
Technical University of Ostrava, 17. listopadu 15, 70833 Ostrava, Czech Republic
Petr.Jancar@vsb.cz

Abstract. We consider two-player turn-based games with zero-reachability and zero-safety objectives generated by extended vector addition systems with states. Although the problem of deciding the winner in such games in undecidable in general, we identify several decidable and even tractable subcases of this problem obtained by restricting the number of counters and/or the sets of target configurations.

1 Introduction

Vector addition systems with states (VASS) are an abstract computational model equivalent to Petri nets (see, e.g., [27,29]) which is well suited for modelling and analysis of distributed concurrent systems. Roughly speaking, a *k-dimensional VASS*, where $k \geq 1$, is a finite-state automaton with k unbounded counters which can store non-negative integers. Depending on its current control state, a VASS can choose and perform one of the available transitions. A given transition changes the control state and updates the vector of current counter values by adding a fixed vector of integers which *labels* the transition. For simplicity, we assume that transition labels can increase/decrease each counter by at most one. Since the counters cannot become negative, transitions which attempt to decrease a zero counter are disabled. Configurations of a given VASS are written as pairs $p\boldsymbol{v}$, where p is a control state and $\boldsymbol{v} \in \mathbb{N}^k$ a vector of counter values. In this paper, we consider *extended VASS games* which enrich the modelling power of VASS in two orthogonal ways.

(1) Transition labels can contain *symbolic* components (denoted by ω) whose intuitive meaning is "add an arbitrarily large non-negative integer to a given counter". For example, a single transition $p \rightarrow q$ labeled by $(1, \omega)$ represents an infinite number of "ordinary" transitions labeled by $(1, 0)$, $(1, 1)$, $(1, 2)$, ... A natural source of motivation for introducing symbolic labels are systems with multiple resources that can be consumed and produced simultaneously by performing a transition. The ω components can then be conveniently used to model an unbounded "reloading" of resources.

⋆ Supported by the Institute for Theoretical Computer Science (ITI), project No. 1M0545.
⋆⋆ Supported by the Czech Ministry of Education, project No. 1M0567.
⋆⋆⋆ Supported by the Czech Science Foundation, grant No. P202/10/1469.

S. Abramsky et al. (Eds.): ICALP 2010, Part II, LNCS 6199, pp. 478–489, 2010.

(2) To model the interaction between a system and its environment, the set of control states is split into two disjoint subsets of *controllable* and *environmental* states, which induces the corresponding partition of configurations. Transitions from the controllable and environmental configurations then correspond to the events generated by the system and its environment, respectively.

Hence, the semantics of a given extended VASS game $\mathcal{M}$ is a possibly infinitely-branching turn-based game $G_{\mathcal{M}}$ with infinitely many vertices that correspond to the configurations of $\mathcal{M}$. The game $G_{\mathcal{M}}$ is initiated by putting a token on some configuration $p\boldsymbol{v}$. The token is then moved from vertex to vertex by two players, $\Box$ and $\Diamond$, who select transitions in the controllable and environmental configurations according to some strategies. Thus, they produce an infinite sequence of configurations called a *play*. Desired properties of $\mathcal{M}$ can be formalized as *objectives*, i.e., admissible plays. The central problem is the question whether player $\Box$ (the system) has a *winning* strategy which ensures that the objective is satisfied for every strategy of player $\Diamond$ (the environment). We refer to, e.g., [32,13,35] for more comprehensive expositions of results related to games in formal verification. In this paper, we are mainly interested in *zero-safety* objectives consisting of plays where no counter is decreased to zero, i.e., a given system never reaches a situation when some of its resources are insufficient. Player $\Box$ always aims at satisfying a given zero-safety objective, while player $\Diamond$ aims at satisfying the dual *zero-reachability* objective.

As a simple example, consider a workshop which "consumes" wooden sticks, screws, wires, etc., and produces puppets of various kinds which are then sold at the door. From time to time, the manager may decide to issue an order for screws or other supplies, and thus increase their number by a finite but essentially unbounded amount Controllable states can be used to model the actions taken by workshop employees, and environmental states model the behaviour of unpredictable customers. We wonder whether the workshop manager has a strategy which ensures that at least one puppet of each kind is always available for sell, regardless of what the unpredictable customers do. Note that a winning strategy for the manager must also resolve the symbolic ω value used to model the order of screws by specifying a *concrete number* of screws that should be ordered.

Technically, we consider extended VASS games with *non-selective* and *selective* zero-reachability objectives, where the set of target configurations that should be reached by player $\Diamond$ and avoided by player $\Box$ is either Z and Z_C, respectively. Here, the set Z consists of all $p\boldsymbol{v}$ such that $\boldsymbol{v}_\ell = 0$ for some ℓ (i.e., some counter is zero); and the set Z_C, where C is a subset of control states, consists of all $p\boldsymbol{v} \in Z$ such that $p \in C$.

Our main results can be summarized as follows:

(a) The problem of deciding the winner in k-dimensional extended VASS games (where $k \geq 2$) with Z-reachability objectives is in **(k-1)-EXPTIME**.
(b) A finite description of the winning region for each player (i.e., the set of all vertices where the player wins) is computable in $(k-1)$-exponential time.
(c) Winning strategies for both players are finitely and effectively representable.

We note that the classical result by Lipton [24] easily implies **EXPSPACE**-hardness (even in the case when player $\Diamond$ has no influence). These (decidability) results are complemented by noting the following straightforward undecidability:

(d) The problem of deciding the winner in 2-dimensional VASS games with "ordinary" (non-symbolic) transitions and Z_C-reachability objectives is undecidable. The same problem for 3-dimensional *extended* VASS games is *highly* undecidable (beyond the arithmetical hierarchy).

Further, we consider the special case of one-dimensional extended VASS games, where we provide the following (tight) complexity results:

(e) The problem of deciding the winner in one-dimensional extended VASS games with Z-reachability objectives is in **P**. Both players have "counterless" winning strategies constructible in polynomial time.
(f) The problem of deciding the winner in one-dimensional extended VASS games with Z_C-reachability objectives is **PSPACE**-complete. A finite description of the winning regions is computable in exponential time.

To the best of our knowledge, these are the first positive decidability/tractability results about a natural class of *infinitely branching* turn-based games, and some of the underlying observations are perhaps of broader interest (in particular, we obtain slight generalizations of the "classical" results about self-covering paths achieved by Rackoff [28] and elaborated by Rosier&Yen [30]).

To build some intuition behind the technical proofs of (a)–(f), we give a brief outline of these proofs and sketch some of the crucial insights. The details are available in [4].

A proof outline for (a)–(c). Observe that if the set of environmental states that are controlled by player $\Diamond$ is empty, then the existence of a winning strategy for player $\Box$ in $p\boldsymbol{v}$ is equivalent to the existence of a *self-covering zero-avoiding path* of the form $p\boldsymbol{v} \rightarrow^* q\boldsymbol{u} \rightarrow^+ q\boldsymbol{u}'$, where $\boldsymbol{u} \leq \boldsymbol{u}'$ and the counters stay positive along the path. The existence and the size of such paths has been studied in [28,30] (actually, these works mainly consider the existence of an *increasing self-covering path* where $\boldsymbol{u}'$ is *strictly* larger than $\boldsymbol{u}$ in at least one component, and the counters *can* be decreased to zero in the intermediate configurations). One can easily generalize this observation to the case when the set of environmental states is non-empty and show that the existence of a winning strategy for player $\Box$ in $p\boldsymbol{v}$ is equivalent to the existence of a *self-covering zero-avoiding tree* initiated in $p\boldsymbol{v}$, which is a finite tree, rooted in $p\boldsymbol{v}$, describing a strategy for player $\Box$ where each maximal path is self-covering and zero-avoiding.

We show that the existence of a self-covering zero-avoiding tree initiated in a given configuration of a given extended VASS is decidable, and we give some complexity bounds. Let us note that this result is more subtle than it might seem; one can easily show that the existence of a self-covering (but not necessarily zero-avoiding) tree for a given configuration is already *undecidable*. Our algorithm constructs all *minimal* $p\boldsymbol{v}$ (w.r.t. component-wise ordering) where player $\Box$ has a winning strategy. Since this set is necessarily finite, and the winning region of player $\Box$ is obviously upwards-closed, we obtain a finite description of the winning region for player $\Box$. The algorithm can be viewed as a concrete (but not obvious) instance of a general approach, which is dealt with, e.g., in [33,10,11]. First, we compute all control states p such that player $\Box$ can win in *some* configuration $p\boldsymbol{v}$. Here, a crucial step is to observe that if this is *not* the case, i.e., player $\Diamond$ can win in every $p\boldsymbol{v}$, then player $\Diamond$ has a *counterless* winning strategy which depends only on the current control state (since there are only finitely many counterless strategies, they can be tried out one by one). This computation also gives an initial bound B such that for every control state p we have that if player □ wins in *some* $p\boldsymbol{v}$, then he wins in all $p\boldsymbol{v}'$ where $\boldsymbol{v}'_\ell \geq B$ for all indexes (counters) $\ell \in \{1, 2, \ldots, k\}$. Then the algorithm proceeds inductively, explores the situations where at least one counter is less than B, computes (bigger) general bounds for the other $k-1$ counters, etc.

A finite description of a strategy for player □ which is winning in every configuration of his winning region is obtained by specifying the moves in all minimal winning configurations (observe that in a non-minimal winning configuration $p(\boldsymbol{v}+\boldsymbol{u})$ such that $p\boldsymbol{v}$ is minimal, player □ can safely make a move $p(\boldsymbol{v}+\boldsymbol{u}) \rightarrow q(\boldsymbol{v}'+\boldsymbol{u})$ where $p\boldsymbol{v} \rightarrow q\boldsymbol{v}'$ is the move associated to $p\boldsymbol{v}$). Note that this also resolves the issue with ω components in transitions performed by player □. Since the number of minimal winning configurations is finite, there is a finite and effectively computable constant c such that player □ never needs to increase a counter by more than c when performing a transition whose label contains a symbolic component (and we can even give a simple "recipe" which gives an optimal choice for the ω values for every configuration separately).

The winning region of player ◇ is just the complement of the winning region of player □. Computing a finite description of a winning strategy for player ◇ is somewhat trickier and relies on some observations made in the "inductive step" discussed above (note that for player ◇ it is not sufficient to stay in his winning region; he also needs to make some progress in approaching zero in some counter).

A proof outline for (d). The undecidability result for 2-dimensional VASS games is obtained by a straightforward reduction from the halting problem for Minsky machines with two counters initialized to zero, which is undecidable [26] (let us note that this construction is essentially the same as the one for monotonic games presented in [1]). After some minor modifications, the same construction can be also used to establish the undecidability of other natural problems for VASS and extended VASS games, such as boundedness or coverability. The high undecidability result for 3-dimensional extended VASS games is proven by reducing the problem whether a given nondeterministic Minsky machine with two counters initialized to zero has an infinite computation such that the initial instruction is executed infinitely often (this problem is known to be Σ_1^1-complete [15]). This reduction is also straightforward, but at least it demonstrates that symbolic transitions do bring some extra power (note that for "ordinary" VASS games, a winning strategy for player ◇ in a given $p\boldsymbol{v}$ can be written as a finite tree, and hence the existence of such a strategy is semidecidable).

A proof outline for (e)–(f). The case of one-dimensional extended VASS games with zero-reachability objectives is, of course, simpler than the general case, but our results still require some effort. In the case of Z-reachability objectives, we show that the winning region of player ◇ can be computed as the least fixed point of a monotonic function over a finite lattice. Although the lattice has exponentially many elements, we show that the function reaches the least fixed point only after a quadratic number of iterations. The existence and efficient constructibility of counterless winning strategies is immediate for player □, and we show that the same is achievable for player ◇. The results about Z_C-reachability objectives are obtained by applying known results about the emptiness problem for alternating finite automata with one letter alphabet [16] (see also [21]) and the emptiness problem for alternating two-way parity word automata [31], together with some additional observations.

Related work. As already mentioned, some of our results and proof techniques use and generalize the ones from [28,30]. VASS games can be also seen as a special case of *monotonic* games considered in [1], where it is shown that the problem of deciding the winner in monotonic games with reachability objectives is undecidable (see the proof outline for (d) above). Let us note that the results presented in [1] mainly concern the so-called *downward-closed* games, which is a model different from ours. Let us also mention that (extended) VASS games are different from another recently studied model of *branching vector addition systems* [34,6] which has different semantics and different algorithmic properties (for example, the coverability and boundedness problems for branching vector addition systems are complete for **2-EXPTIME** [6]). Generic procedures applicable to upward-closed sets of states are studied in, e.g., [3,12,33,10,11].

Note that one-dimensional VASS games are essentially one-counter automata where the counter cannot be tested for zero explicitly (that is, there are no transitions enabled only when the counter reaches zero). Such one-counter automata are also called *one-counter nets* because they correspond to Petri nets with just one unbounded place. The models of one-counter automata and one-counter nets have been intensively studied [18,20,22,2,7,9,19,31,14]. Many problems about equivalence-checking and model-checking one-counter automata are known to be decidable, but only a few of them are solvable efficiently. From this point of view, we find the polynomial-time result about one-dimensional extended VASS games with Z-reachability objectives encouraging.

2 Definitions

In this paper, the sets of all integers, positive integers, and non-negative integers are denoted by $\mathbb{Z}$, $\mathbb{N}^{>0}$, and $\mathbb{N}$, respectively. For every finite or countably infinite set M, the symbol M^* denotes the set of all finite words (i.e., finite sequences) over M. The length of a given word w is denoted by $|w|$, and the individual letters in w are denoted by $w(0), w(1), \ldots$. The empty word is denoted by ε, where $|\varepsilon| = 0$. We also use M^+ to denote the set $M^* \setminus \{\varepsilon\}$. A *path* in $\mathcal{M} = (M, \rightarrow)$, for a binary relation $\rightarrow \subseteq M \times M$, is a finite or infinite sequence $w = w(0), w(1), \ldots$ such that $w(i) \rightarrow w(i{+}1)$ for every i. A given $n \in M$ is *reachable* from a given $m \in M$, written $m \rightarrow^* n$, if there is a finite path from m to n. A *run* is a maximal path (infinite, or finite which cannot be prolonged). The sets of all finite paths and all runs in $\mathcal{M}$ are denoted by $FPath(\mathcal{M})$ and $Run(\mathcal{M})$, respectively. Similarly, the sets of all finite paths and runs that start in a given $m \in M$ are denoted by $FPath(\mathcal{M}, m)$ and $Run(\mathcal{M}, m)$, respectively.

Definition 1. *A* game *is a tuple* $G = (V, \mapsto, (V_\Box, V_\Diamond))$ *where* V *is a finite or countably infinite set of* vertices, $\mapsto \subseteq V \times V$ *is an* edge relation, *and* $(V_\Box, V_\Diamond)$ *is a partition of* V.

A game is played by two players, $\Box$ and $\Diamond$, who select the moves in the vertices of $V_\Box$ and $V_\Diamond$, respectively. Let $\odot \in \{\Box, \Diamond\}$. A *strategy* for player $\odot$ is a (partial) function which to each $wv \in V^* V_\odot$, where v has at least one outgoing edge, assigns a vertex v' such that $v \mapsto v'$. The set of all strategies for player $\Box$ and player $\Diamond$ is denoted by Σ and Π, respectively. We say that a strategy τ is *memoryless* if $\tau(wv)$ depends just on the last vertex v. In the rest of this paper, we consider memoryless strategies as (partial) functions from $V_{\odot}$ to V.

A *winning objective* is a set of runs $\mathcal{W} \subseteq Run(G)$. Every pair of strategies $(\sigma, \pi) \in \Sigma \times \Pi$ and every initial vertex $v \in V$ determine a unique run $G^{(\sigma,\pi)}(v) \in Run(G, v)$ which is called a *play*. We say that a strategy $\sigma \in \Sigma$ is *$\mathcal{W}$-winning for player $\Box$* in a given $v \in V$ if for every $\pi \in \Pi$ we have that $G^{(\sigma,\pi)}(v) \in \mathcal{W}$. Similarly, a strategy $\pi \in \Pi$ is $\mathcal{W}$-winning for player $\Diamond$ if for every $\sigma \in \Sigma$ we have that $G^{(\sigma,\pi)}(v) \in \mathcal{W}$. The set of all vertices where player $\odot$ has a $\mathcal{W}$-winning strategy is called the *winning region* of player $\odot$ and denoted by $Win(\odot, \mathcal{W})$.

In this paper, we only consider *reachability* and *safety* objectives, which are specified by a subset of target vertices that should or should not be reached by a run, respectively. Formally, for a given $T \subseteq V$ we define the sets of runs $\mathcal{R}(T)$ and $\mathcal{S}(T)$, where $\mathcal{R}(T) = \{w \in Run(G) \mid w(i) \in T \text{ for some } i\}$, and $\mathcal{S}(T) = Run(G) \smallsetminus \mathcal{R}(T)$. We note that the games with reachability and safety objectives are *determined* [25], i.e., $Win(\Box, \mathcal{S}(T)) = V \smallsetminus Win(\Diamond, \mathcal{R}(T))$, and each player has a *memoryless* winning strategy in every vertex of his winning region.

Definition 2. *Let $k \in \mathbb{N}^{>0}$. A k-dimensional* vector addition system with states (VASS) *is a tuple $\mathcal{M} = (Q, T, \alpha, \beta, \delta)$ where $Q \neq \emptyset$ is a finite set of* control states, *$T \neq \emptyset$ is a finite set of* transitions, *$\alpha : T \to Q$ and $\beta : T \to Q$ are the* source *and* target *mappings, and $\delta : T \to \{-1, 0, 1\}^k$ is a* transition displacement *labeling. For technical convenience, we assume that for every $q \in Q$ there is some $t \in T$ such that $\alpha(t) = q$.*

An extended VASS (eVASS for short) *is a VASS where the transition displacement labeling is a function $\delta : T \to \{-1, 0, 1, \omega\}^k$.*

A VASS game *(or* eVASS game*) is a tuple $\mathcal{M} = (Q, (Q_{\Box}, Q_{\Diamond}), T, \alpha, \beta, \delta)$ where $(Q, T, \alpha, \beta, \delta)$ is a VASS (or eVASS) and $(Q_{\Box}, Q_{\Diamond})$ is a partition of Q.*

A *configuration* of $\mathcal{M}$ is an element of $Q \times \mathbb{N}^k$. We write $p\mathbf{v}$ instead of $(p, \mathbf{v})$, and the ℓ-th component of $\mathbf{v}$ is denoted by $\mathbf{v}_\ell$. For a given transition $t \in T$, we write $t : p \to q$ to indicate that $\alpha(t) = p$ and $\beta(t) = q$, and $p \xrightarrow{\mathbf{v}} q$ to indicate that $p \to q$ and $\delta(t) = \mathbf{v}$. A transition $t \in T$ is *enabled* in a configuration $p\mathbf{v}$ if $\alpha(t) = p$ and for every $1 \leq \ell \leq k$ such that $\delta(t)_\ell = -1$ we have $\mathbf{v}_\ell \geq 1$.

Every k-dimensional eVASS game $\mathcal{M} = (Q, (Q_{\Box}, Q_{\Diamond}), T, \alpha, \beta, \delta)$ induces a unique infinite-state game $G_{\mathcal{M}}$ where $Q \times \mathbb{N}^k$ is the set of vertices partitioned into $Q_{\Box} \times \mathbb{N}^k$ and $Q_{\Diamond} \times \mathbb{N}^k$, and $p\mathbf{v} \mapsto q\mathbf{u}$ iff the following condition holds: There is a transition $t \in T$ enabled in $p\mathbf{v}$ such that $\beta(t) = q$ and for every $1 \leq \ell \leq k$ we have that $\mathbf{u}_\ell - \mathbf{v}_\ell$ is either non-negative or equal to $\delta(t)_\ell$, depending on whether $\delta(t)_\ell = \omega$ or not, respectively. Note that any play can get stuck only when a counter is zero, because there is at least one enabled transition otherwise.

In this paper, we are interested in VASS and eVASS games with *non-selective* and *selective* zero-reachability objectives. Formally, for every $C \subseteq Q$ we define the set $Z_C = \{p\mathbf{v} \in Q \times \mathbb{N}^k \mid p \in C \text{ and } \mathbf{v}_i = 0 \text{ for some } 0 \leq i \leq k\}$ and we also put $Z = Z_Q$. Selective (or non-selective) zero-reachability objectives are reachability objectives where the set T of target configurations is equal to Z_C for some $C \subseteq Q$ (or to Z, respectively).

As we have already noted, our games with reachability objectives are memoryless determined and this result of course applies also to eVASS games with zero-reachability objectives. However, since eVASS games have infinitely many vertices, not all memoryless strategies are finitely representable. In this paper we will often deal with a simple form of memoryless strategies, where the decision is independent of the current counter values; such strategies are called *counterless strategies*.

Definition 3. *Given an eVASS* $\mathcal{M} = (Q, (Q_\Box, Q_\Diamond), T, \alpha, \beta, \delta)$*, a* strategy τ *of player* $\odot \in \{\Box, \Diamond\}$ *is* counterless *if it determines a (fixed) transition* t_p *for each* $p \in Q_\odot$*, together with (fixed) values* $c_{p,\ell} \in \mathbb{N}$ *for all those* ℓ *for which* $\delta(t_p)_\ell = \omega$*, so that* $\tau(p\boldsymbol{v})$ *is the configuration obtained by performing* t_p *in* $p\boldsymbol{v}$ *where* ω*'s are instantiated with* $c_{p,\ell}$*.*

3 VASS and eVASS Games with Zero-Reachability Objectives

In this section, we analyze VASS and eVASS games with zero-reachability objectives (full proofs can be found in [4]). We first note that the problems of our interest are undecidable for $\mathcal{R}(Z_C)$ objectives; this can be shown by standard techniques.

Proposition 4. *The problem of deciding the winner in 2-dimensional VASS games with* $\mathcal{R}(Z_C)$ *objectives is undecidable. For 3-dimensional eVASS games, the same problem is* highly *undecidable (i.e., beyond the arithmetical hierarchy).*

Let us note that Proposition 4 does not hold for one-dimensional eVASS games, which are analyzed later in this section. Further, by some trivial modifications of the proof of Proposition 4 we also get the undecidability of the boundedness/coverability problems for 2-dimensional VASS games.

Now we turn our attention to $\mathcal{R}(Z)$ objectives. For the rest of this section, we fix a k-dimensional eVASS game $\mathcal{M} = (Q, (Q_\Box, Q_\Diamond), T, \alpha, \beta, \delta)$. Since we are interested only in $\mathcal{R}(Z)$ objectives, we may safely assume that every transition $p \xrightarrow{\boldsymbol{v}} q$ of $\mathcal{M}$ where $p \in Q_\Diamond$ satisfies $\boldsymbol{v}_\ell \neq \omega$ for every $1 \leq \ell \leq k$ (if there are some ω-components in $\boldsymbol{v}$, they can be safely replaced with 0). We also use d to denote the *branching degree* of $\mathcal{M}$, i.e, the least number such that every $q \in Q$ has at most d outgoing transitions.

Let $\leq$ be the partial order on the set of configurations of $\mathcal{M}$ defined by $p\boldsymbol{u} \leq q\boldsymbol{v}$ iff $p = q$ and $\boldsymbol{u} \leq \boldsymbol{v}$ (componentwise). For short, we write $Win_\Diamond$ instead of $Win(\Diamond, \mathcal{R}(Z))$ and $Win_\Box$ instead of $Win(\Box, \mathcal{S}(Z))$. Obviously, if player $\Diamond$ has a winning strategy in $q\boldsymbol{v}$, then he can use "essentially the same" strategy in $q\boldsymbol{u}$ for every $\boldsymbol{u} \leq \boldsymbol{v}$ (behaving in $q'\boldsymbol{v}'$ as previously in $q'(\boldsymbol{v}' + \boldsymbol{v} - \boldsymbol{u})$, which results in reaching 0 in some counter possibly even earlier). Similarly, if $q\boldsymbol{v} \in Win_\Box$ then $q\boldsymbol{u} \in Win_\Box$ for every $\boldsymbol{u} \geq \boldsymbol{v}$. Hence, the sets $Win_\Diamond$ and $Win_\Box$ are downwards closed and upwards closed w.r.t. $\leq$, respectively. This means that the set $Win_\Box$ is finitely representable by its subset $Min_\Box$ of *minimal elements* (note that $Min_\Box$ is necessarily finite because there is no infinite subset of $\mathbb{N}^k$ with pairwise incomparable elements, as Dickson's Lemma shows). Technically, it is convenient to consider also *symbolic configurations* of $\mathcal{M}$ which are introduced in the next definition.

Definition 5. *A* symbolic configuration *is a pair* $q\boldsymbol{v}$ *where* $q \in Q$ *and* $\boldsymbol{v} \in (\mathbb{N} \cup \{\omega\})^k$*. We say that a given index* $\ell \in \{1, 2, \ldots, k\}$ *is* precise *in* $q\boldsymbol{v}$ *if* $\boldsymbol{v}_\ell \in \mathbb{N}$*, otherwise it is* symbolic *in* $q\boldsymbol{v}$*. The* precision *of* $q\boldsymbol{v}$*, denoted by* $P(q\boldsymbol{v})$*, is the number of indexes that are precise in* $q\boldsymbol{v}$*. We say that a configuration* $p\boldsymbol{u}$ matches *a symbolic configuration* $q\boldsymbol{v}$ *if* $p = q$ *and* $\boldsymbol{u}_\ell = \boldsymbol{v}_\ell$ *for every* ℓ *precise in* $q\boldsymbol{v}$*. Similarly, we say that* $p\boldsymbol{u}$ matches $q\boldsymbol{v}$ above *a given bound* $B \in \mathbb{N}$ *if* $p\boldsymbol{u}$ *matches* $q\boldsymbol{v}$ *and* $\boldsymbol{u}_\ell \geq B$ *for every* ℓ *symbolic in* $q\boldsymbol{v}$*.*

We extend the set $Win_\Box$ by all symbolic configurations $q\boldsymbol{v}$ such that some configuration matching $q\boldsymbol{v}$ belongs to $Win_\Box$. Similarly, the set $Win_\Diamond$ is extended by all symbolic configurations $q\boldsymbol{v}$ such that all configurations matching $q\boldsymbol{v}$ belong to $Win_\Diamond$ (note that every symbolic configuration belongs either to $Win_\Box$ or to $Win_\Diamond$). We also extend the previously fixed ordering on configurations to symbolic configurations by stipulating that $\omega \leq \omega$ and $n < \omega$ for all $n \in \mathbb{N}$. Obviously, this extension does not influence the set $Min_\Box$, and the winning region $Win_\Diamond$ can be now represented by its subset $Max_\Diamond$ of all maximal elements, which is necessarily finite.

Our ultimate goal is to compute the sets $Min_\Box$ and $Max_\Diamond$. Since our reachability games are determined, it actually suffices to compute just one of these sets. In the following we show how to compute $Min_\Box$.

We start with an important observation about winning strategies for player $\Box$, which in fact extends the "classical" observation about self-covering paths in vector addition systems presented in [28]. Let $q \in Q$ be such that $q\boldsymbol{v} \in Win_\Box$ for some $\boldsymbol{v}$, i.e., $q(\omega, \ldots, \omega) \in Win_\Box$. This means that there is a strategy of player $\Box$ that prevents unbounded decreasing of the counters; we find useful to represent the strategy by a finite *unrestricted self-covering tree for q*. The word "unrestricted" reflects the fact that we also consider configurations with negative and symbolic counter values. More precisely, an unrestricted self-covering tree for q is a finite tree $\mathcal{T}$ whose nodes are labeled by the elements of $Q \times (\mathbb{Z} \cup \{\omega\})^k$ satisfying the following (ω is treated in the standard way, i.e., $\omega + \omega = \omega + c = \omega$ for every $c \in \mathbb{Z}$):

- The root of $\mathcal{T}$ is labeled by $q(0, \ldots, 0)$.
- If n is a non-leaf node of $\mathcal{T}$ labeled by $p\boldsymbol{u}$, then
  - if $p \in Q_\Box$, then n has only one successor labeled by some $r\boldsymbol{t}$ such that $\mathcal{M}$ has a transition $p \xrightarrow{\boldsymbol{v}} r$ where $\boldsymbol{t} = \boldsymbol{u} + \boldsymbol{v}$;
  - if $p \in Q_\Diamond$, then there is a one-to-one correspondence between the successors of n and transitions of $\mathcal{M}$ of the form $p \xrightarrow{\boldsymbol{v}} r$. The node which corresponds to a transition $p \xrightarrow{\boldsymbol{v}} r$ is labeled by $r\boldsymbol{t}$ where $\boldsymbol{t} = \boldsymbol{u} + \boldsymbol{v}$.
- If n is a leaf of $\mathcal{T}$ labeled by $p\boldsymbol{u}$, then there is another node m (where $m \neq n$) on the path from the root of $\mathcal{T}$ to n which is labeled by $p\boldsymbol{t}$ for some $\boldsymbol{t} \leq \boldsymbol{u}$.

The next lemma bounds the depth of such a tree.

Lemma 6. *Let $q(\omega, \ldots, \omega) \in Win_\Box$ (i.e., $q\boldsymbol{v} \in Win_\Box$ for some $\boldsymbol{v}$). Then there is an unrestricted self-covering tree for q of depth at most $f(|Q|, d, k) = 2^{(d-1)\cdot|Q|} \cdot |Q|^{c\cdot k^2}$, where c is a fixed constant independent of $\mathcal{M}$, and d is the branching degree of $\mathcal{M}$.*

Lemma 6 thus implies that if $q(\omega, \ldots, \omega) \in Win_\Box$, then $q\boldsymbol{u} \in Win_\Box$ for all $\boldsymbol{u}$ with $\boldsymbol{u}_\ell \geq f(|Q|, d, k)$ for all $\ell \in \{1, 2, \ldots, k\}$ (recall that each counter can be decreased at most by one in a single transition). The next lemma shows that we can compute the set of all $q \in Q$ such that $q(\omega, \ldots, \omega) \in Win_\Box$ (the lemma is formulated "dually", i.e., for player $\Diamond$).

Lemma 7. *The set of all $q \in Q$ such that $q(\omega, \ldots, \omega) \in Win_\Diamond$ is computable in space bounded by $g(|Q|, d, k)$, where g is a polynomial in three variables.*

An important observation, which is crucial in our proof of Lemma 7 and perhaps interesting on its own, is that if $q(\omega, \ldots, \omega) \in Win_\Diamond$, then player $\Diamond$ has a *counterless* strategy which is winning in every configuration matching $q(\omega, \ldots, \omega)$.

To sum up, we can compute the set of all $q(\omega, \ldots, \omega) \in Win_\Box$ and a bound B which is "safe" for all $q(\omega, \ldots, \omega) \in Win_\Box$ in the sense that all configurations matching $q(\omega, \ldots, \omega)$ above B belong to $Win_\Box$. Intuitively, the next step is to find out what happens if one of the counters, say the first one, stays bounded by B. Obviously, there is the *least* $j \leq B$ such that $q(j, \omega, \ldots, \omega) \in Win_\Box$, and there is a bound $D > B$ such that all configurations matching $q(j, \omega, \ldots, \omega)$ above D belong to $Win_\Box$. If we manage to compute the minimal j (also for the other counters, not just for the first one) and the bound D, we can go on and try to bound *two* counters simultaneously by D, find the corresponding minima, and construct a new "safe" bound. In this way, we eventually bound all counters and compute the set $Min_\Box$. In our next definition, we introduce some notions that are needed to formulate the above intuition precisely. (Recall that $P(q\mathbf{v})$ gives the number of precise, i.e. non-ω, elements of $\mathbf{v}$.)

Definition 8. *For a given* $0 \leq j \leq k$, *let* $SymMin_\Box^j$ *be the set of all minimal* $q\mathbf{v} \in Win_\Box$ *such that* $P(q\mathbf{v}) = j$. *Further, let* $SymMin_\Box = \bigcup_{i=0}^{k} SymMin_\Box^i$. *We say that a given* $B \in \mathbb{N}$ *is* safe for precision j, *where* $0 \leq j \leq k$, *if for every* $q\mathbf{v} \in \bigcup_{i=0}^{j} SymMin_\Box^i$ *we have that* $\mathbf{v}_\ell \leq B$ *for every precise index* ℓ *in* $\mathbf{v}$, *and every configuration matching* $q\mathbf{v}$ *above* B *belongs to* $Win_\Box$.

Obviously, every $SymMin_\Box^j$ (and hence also $SymMin_\Box$) is finite, and $Min_\Box = SymMin_\Box^k$. Also observe that $SymMin_\Box^0$ is computable in time exponential in $|Q|$ and k by Lemma 7, and a bound which is safe for precision 0 is computable in polynomial time by Lemma 6. Now we design an algorithm which computes $SymMin_\Box^{j+1}$ and a bound safe for precision $j{+}1$, assuming that $SymMin_\Box^i$ for all $i \leq j$ and a bound safe for precision j have already been computed.

Lemma 9. *Let* $0 \leq j < k$, *and let us assume that* $\bigcup_{i=0}^{j} SymMin_\Box^i$ *has already been computed, together with some bound* $B \in \mathbb{N}$ *which is safe for precision* j. *Then* $SymMin_\Box^{j+1}$ *is computable in time exponential in* $|Q| \cdot B^{j+1}$, d, *and* $k{-}j{-}1$, *and the bound* $B + f(|Q| \cdot B^{j+1}, d, k{-}j{-}1)$ *is safe for precision* $j+1$ *(here* f *is the function of Lemma 6 and* d *is the branching degree of* $\mathcal{M}$*).*

Now we can easily evaluate the total complexity of computing $SymMin_\Box$ (and hence also $Min_\Box$). If we just examine the recurrence of Lemma 9, we obtain that the set $SymMin_\Box$ is computable in k-exponential time. However, we can actually decrease the height of the tower of exponentials by one when we incorporate the results presented later in this section, which imply that for one-dimensional eVASS games, the depth of an unrestricted self-covering tree can be bounded by a *polynomial* in $|Q|$ and d, and the set of all $q \in Q$ where $q(\omega) \in Win_\Diamond$ is computable in *polynomial time*. Hence, we actually need to "nest" Lemma 9 only $k{-}1$ times. Thus, we obtain the following (where 0-exponential time denotes polynomial time):

Theorem 10. *For a given k-dimensional eVASS, the set* $Min_\Box$ *is computable in* $(k{-}1)$*-exponential time.*

Let us note a substantial improvement in complexity would be achieved by improving the bound presented in Lemma 6. Actually, it is not so important what is the depth of an unrestricted self-covering tree, but what are the minimal numbers that allow for applying the strategy described by this tree without reaching zero (i.e., what is the maximal decrease of a counter in the tree). A more detailed complexity analysis based on the introduced parameters reveals that if the maximal counter decrease was just polynomial in the number of control states (which is our conjecture), the complexity bound of Theorem 10 would be *polynomial* for every fixed dimension k (see also Section 4).

Note that after computing the set $Min_\Box$, we can easily compute a finite description of a strategy σ for player $\Box$ which is winning in every configuration of $Win_\Box$. For every $p\boldsymbol{v} \in Min_\Box$ such that $p \in Q_\Box$, we put $\sigma(p\boldsymbol{v}) = q\boldsymbol{v}'$, where $q\boldsymbol{v}'$ is (some) configuration such that $q\boldsymbol{v}' \geq q\boldsymbol{t}$ for some $q\boldsymbol{t} \in Min_\Box$. Note that there must be at least one such $q\boldsymbol{v}'$ and it can be computed effectively. For every configuration $p\boldsymbol{u}$ such that $p\boldsymbol{u} \geq p\boldsymbol{v}$ for some $p\boldsymbol{v} \in Min_\Box$, we put $\sigma(p\boldsymbol{u}) = q(\boldsymbol{v}'+\boldsymbol{u}-\boldsymbol{v})$ where $\sigma(p\boldsymbol{v}) = q\boldsymbol{v}'$ (if there are more candidates for $p\boldsymbol{v}$, any of them can be chosen). It is easy to see that σ is winning in every configuration of $Win_\Box$. Also observe that if we aim at constructing a winning strategy for player $\Box$ which minimizes the concrete numbers used to substitute ω's, we can use $Min_\Box$ to construct an "optimal" choice of the values which are sufficient (and necessary) to stay in the winning region of player $\Box$.

Now we present the promised results about the special case of one-dimensional VASS and eVASS games with zero-reachability objectives. Let us fix a one-dimensional eVASS game $\mathcal{M} = (Q, (Q_\Box, Q_\Diamond), T, \alpha, \beta, \delta)$ and $C \subseteq Q$. For every $i \in \mathbb{N}$, let $Win_\Diamond(C, i) = \{p \in Q \mid p(i) \in Win(\Diamond, \mathcal{R}(Z_C))\}$. It is easy to see that if $Win_\Diamond(C, i) = Win_\Diamond(C, j)$ for some $i, j \in \mathbb{N}$, then also $Win_\Diamond(C, i{+}1) = Win_\Diamond(C, j{+}1)$. Let m_C be the least $i \in \mathbb{N}$ such that $Win_\Diamond(C, i) = Win_\Diamond(C, j)$ for some $j > i$, and let n_C be the least $i > 0$ such that $Win_\Diamond(C, m_C) = Win_\Diamond(C, m_C{+}i)$. Obviously, $m_c + n_c \leq 2^{|Q|}$ and for every $i \geq m_c$ we have that $Win_\Diamond(C, i) = Win_\Diamond(C, m_C + ((i - m_C) \mod n_C))$. Hence, the winning regions of both players are fully characterized by all $Win_\Diamond(C, i)$, where $0 \leq i < m_C + n_C$.

The selective subcase is analyzed in the next theorem. The **PSPACE** lower bound is obtained by reducing the emptiness problem for alternating finite automata with one letter alphabet, which is known to be **PSPACE** complete [16] (see also [21] for a simpler proof). The **PSPACE** upper bound follows by employing the result of [31] which says that the emptiness problem for alternating two-way parity word automata (2PWA) is in **PSPACE** (we would like to thank Olivier Serre for providing us with relevant references). The effective constructability of the winning strategies for player $\Box$ and player $\Diamond$ follows by applying the results on non-selective termination presented below.

Theorem 11. *The problem whether $p(i) \in Win(\Diamond, \mathcal{R}(Z_C))$ is **PSPACE**-complete. Further, there is a strategy σ winning for player $\Box$ in every configuration of $Win(\Box, \mathcal{S}(Z_C))$ such that for all $p \in Q_\Box$ and $i \geq m_C$ we have that $\sigma(p(i)) = \sigma(p(m_C + ((i - m_C) \mod n_C)))$. The numbers m_C, n_C and the tuple of all $Win_\Diamond(C, i)$ and $\sigma(p(i))$, where $0 \leq i < m_C{+}n_C$ and $p \in Q_\Box$, are constructible in time exponential in $|\mathcal{M}|$.*

In the non-selective subcase, the situation is even better. The winning regions for both players are monotone, which means that $m_Q \leq |Q|$ and $n_Q = 1$. Further, all of the considered problems are solvable in polynomial time.

Theorem 12. *The problem whether* $p(i) \in Win(\Diamond, \mathcal{R}(Z))$ *is in* **P**. *Further, there are counterless strategies* σ *and* π *such that* σ *is winning for player* $\Box$ *in every configuration of* $Win(\Box, \mathcal{S}(Z))$ *and* π *is winning for player* $\Diamond$ *in every configuration of* $Win(\Diamond, \mathcal{R}(Z))$. *The tuple of all* $Win_{\Diamond}(Q, i)$, $\sigma(p)$, *and* $\pi(q)$, *where* $0 \leq i \leq m_C$, $p \in Q_{\Box}$, *and* $q \in Q_{\Diamond}$, *is constructible in time polynomial in* $|\mathcal{M}|$.

4 Conclusions, Future Work

Technically, the most involved result presented in this paper is Theorem 10. This decidability result is not obvious, because most of the problems related to formal verification of Petri nets (equivalence-checking, model-checking, etc.) are undecidable [8,17,23,5]. Since the upper complexity bound given in Theorem 10 is complemented only by the **EXPSPACE** lower bound, which is easily derivable from [24], there is a complexity gap which constitutes an interesting challenge for future work.

References

1. Abdulla, P.A., Bouajjani, A., d'Orso, J.: Monotonic and downward closed games. Journal of Logic and Computation 18(1), 153–169 (2008)
2. Abdulla, P.A., Čerāns, K.: Simulation is decidable for one-counter nets. In: Sangiorgi, D., de Simone, R. (eds.) CONCUR 1998. LNCS, vol. 1466, pp. 253–268. Springer, Heidelberg (1998)
3. Abdulla, P.A., Čerāns, K., Jonsson, B., Tsay, Y.-K.: General decidability theorems for infinite-state systems. In: Proceedings of LICS 1996, pp. 160–170. IEEE Computer Society Press, Los Alamitos (1996)
4. Brázdil, T., Jančar, P., Kučera, A.: Reachability games on extended vector addition systems with states. CoRR abs/1002.2557 (2010)
5. Burkart, O., Caucal, D., Moller, F., Steffen, B.: Verification on infinite structures. Handbook of Process Algebra, 545–623 (2001)
6. Demri, S., Jurdziński, M., Lachish, O., Lazić, R.: The covering and boundedness problems for branching vector addition systems. In: Proceedings of FST&TCS 2009. Leibniz International Proceedings in Informatics, vol. 4, pp. 181–192. Schloss Dagstuhl–Leibniz-Zentrum für Informatik (2009)
7. Demri, S., Lazic, R., Sangnier, A.: Model checking freeze LTL over one-counter automata. In: Amadio, R.M. (ed.) FOSSACS 2008. LNCS, vol. 4962, pp. 490–504. Springer, Heidelberg (2008)
8. Esparza, J.: Decidability of model checking for infinite-state concurrent systems. Acta Informatica 34, 85–107 (1997)
9. Etessami, K., Wojtczak, D., Yannakakis, M.: Quasi-birth-death processes, tree-like QBDs, probabilistic 1-counter automata, and pushdown systems. In: Proceedings of 5th Int. Conf. on Quantitative Evaluation of Systems (QEST 2008). IEEE Computer Society Press, Los Alamitos (2008)
10. Finkel, A., Goubault-Larrecq, J.: Forward analysis for WSTS, Part I: Completions. In: Proceedings of STACS 2009. Leibniz International Proceedings in Informatics, vol. 3, pp. 433–444. Schloss Dagstuhl–Leibniz-Zentrum für Informatik (2009)
11. Finkel, A., Goubault-Larrecq, J.: Forward analysis for WSTS, Part II: Complete WSTS. In: Albers, S., Marchetti-Spaccamela, A., Matias, Y., Nikoletseas, S., Thomas, W. (eds.) ICALP 2009. LNCS, vol. 5556, pp. 188–199. Springer, Heidelberg (2009)

12. Finkel, A., Schnoebelen, P.: Well structured transition systems everywhere? Theoretical Computer Science 256(1-2), 63–92 (2001)
13. Grädel, E., Thomas, W., Wilke, T.: Automata, Logics, and Infinite Games. LNCS, vol. 2500. Springer, Heidelberg (2002)
14. Haase, C., Kreutzer, S., Ouaknine, J., Worrell, J.: Reachability in succinct and parametric one-counter automata. In: Bravetti, M., Zavattaro, G. (eds.) CONCUR 2009. LNCS, vol. 5710, pp. 369–383. Springer, Heidelberg (2009)
15. Harel, D.: Effective transformations on infinite trees with applications to high undecidability dominoes, and fairness. Journal of the Association for Computing Machinery 33(1) (1986)
16. Holzer, M.: On emptiness and counting for alternating finite automata. In: Developments in Language Theory II, pp. 88–97. World Scientific, Singapore (1995)
17. Jančar, P.: Undecidability of bisimilarity for Petri nets and some related problems. Theoretical Computer Science 148(2), 281–301 (1995)
18. Jančar, P.: Decidability of bisimilarity for one-counter processes. Information and Computation 158(1), 1–17 (2000)
19. Jančar, P., Kučera, A., Moller, F.: Simulation and bisimulation over one-counter processes. In: Reichel, H., Tison, S. (eds.) STACS 2000. LNCS, vol. 1770, pp. 334–345. Springer, Heidelberg (2000)
20. Jančar, P., Kučera, A., Moller, F., Sawa, Z.: DP lower bounds for equivalence-checking and model-checking of one-counter automata. Information and Computation 188(1), 1–19 (2004)
21. Jančar, P., Sawa, Z.: A note on emptiness for alternating finite automata with a one-letter alphabet. Information Processing Letters 104(5), 164–167 (2007)
22. Kučera, A.: The complexity of bisimilarity-checking for one-counter processes. Theoretical Computer Science 304(1-3), 157–183 (2003)
23. Kučera, A., Jančar, P.: Equivalence-checking on infinite-state systems: Techniques and results. Theory and Practice of Logic Programming 6(3), 226–264 (2006)
24. Lipton, R.: The reachability problem requires exponential space. Technical report 62, Yale University (1976)
25. Martin, D.A.: Borel determinacy. Annals of Mathematics, Second Series 102(2), 363–371 (1975)
26. Minsky, M.L.: Computation: Finite and Infinite Machines. Prentice-Hall, Englewood Cliffs (1967)
27. Peterson, J.L.: Petri Net Theory and the Modelling of Systems. Prentice-Hall, Englewood Cliffs (1981)
28. Rackoff, C.: The covering and boundedness problems for vector addition systems. Theoretical Computer Science 6, 223–231 (1978)
29. Reisig, W.: Petri Nets—An Introduction. Springer, Heidelberg (1985)
30. Rosier, L.E., Yen, H.-C.: A multiparameter analysis of the boundedness problem for vector addition systems. Journal of Computer and System Sciences 32, 105–135 (1986)
31. Serre, O.: Parity games played on transition graphs of one-counter processes. In: Aceto, L., Ingólfsdóttir, A. (eds.) FOSSACS 2006. LNCS, vol. 3921, pp. 337–351. Springer, Heidelberg (2006)
32. Thomas, W.: Infinite games and verification. In: Hunt Jr., W.A., Somenzi, F. (eds.) CAV 2003. LNCS, vol. 2725, pp. 58–64. Springer, Heidelberg (2003)
33. Valk, R., Jantzen, M.: The residue of vector sets with applications to decidability problems in Petri nets. Acta Informatica 21, 643–674 (1985)
34. Verma, K.N., Goubault-Larrecq, J.: Karp-Miller trees for a branching extension of VASS. Discrete Mathematics & Theoretical Computer Science 7(1), 217–230 (2005)
35. Walukiewicz, I.: A landscape with games in the background. In: Proceedings of LICS 2004, pp. 356–366. IEEE Computer Society Press, Los Alamitos (2004)

Modelling Mobility: A *Discrete* Revolution⋆
(Extended Abstract)

Andrea E.F. Clementi[1], Angelo Monti[2], and Riccardo Silvestri[2]

[1] Dipartimento di Matematica, Università di Roma "Tor Vergata"
{clementi,pasquale}@mat.uniroma2.it
[2] Dipartimento di Informatica, Università di Roma "La Sapienza"
silvestri@di.uniroma1.it

Abstract. We introduce a new approach to model and analyze *Mobility*. It is fully based on discrete mathematics and yields a class of mobility models, called the *Markov Trace* Model. This model can be seen as the discrete version of the *Random Trip* Model: including all variants of the *Random Way-Point* Model [14].

We derive fundamental properties and *explicit* analytical formulas for the *stationary distributions* yielded by the Markov Trace Model. Such results can be exploited to compute formulas and properties for concrete cases of the Markov Trace Model by just applying counting arguments.

We apply the above general results to the discrete version of the *Manhattan Random Way-Point* over a square of bounded size. We get formulas for the total stationary distribution and for two important *conditional* ones: the agent spatial and destination distributions.

Our method makes the analysis of complex mobile systems a feasible task. As a further evidence of this important fact, we first model a complex vehicular-mobile system over a set of crossing streets. Several concrete issues are implemented such as parking zones, traffic lights, and variable vehicle speeds. By using a *modular* version of the Markov Trace Model, we get explicit formulas for the stationary distributions yielded by this vehicular-mobile model as well.

1 Introduction

A crucial issue in modeling mobility is to find a good balance between the goal of implementing important features of concrete scenarios and the possibility to study the model from an analytical point of view. Several interesting approaches have been introduced and studied over the last years [3,12,16,14]. Among them, we focus on those models where *agents* move independently and according to some random process, i.e., random mobility models. Nice examples of such random models are the random-way point and the walker models [3,5,12,14,16] which are, in turn, special cases of a family of mobility models known as random trip model [14]. Mobile networks are complex dynamical systems whose analysis

⋆ Partially supported by the Italian MIUR *COGENT*.

S. Abramsky et al. (Eds.): ICALP 2010, Part II, LNCS 6199, pp. 490–501, 2010.

is far to be trivial. In particular, deriving explicit formulas of the relative stationary probabilistic distributions, such as the agent spatial one, requires very complex integral calculus [4,6,14,15].

We propose a new approach to model and analyse mobility. This approach is based on a simple observation over concrete network scenarios:

> It is not so important to record every position of the agents at every instant of time and it thus suffices to discretize the space into a set of cells and record the current agent cell at discrete time steps.

We exploit the above observation to get a class of fully-discrete mobility models based on *agent movement-traces* (in short, traces). A *trace* is the representation of an agent trajectory by means of the sequence of visited cells. Similarly to the Random Trip Model, our mobile model is defined by fixing the set of feasible traces and the criterium the agent adopts to select the next trace after arriving at the end of the current trace.

We define the *(Discrete) Markov Trace Model* (in short, MTM) where, at every time step, an agent either is (deterministically) following the selected trace or is choosing at random (according to a given probability distribution) the next trace over a set of feasible traces, all starting from the final cell of the previous trace. It is important to observe that the same trajectory run at different speeds yields different traces (cell-sequences are in general ordered multi-sets): so, it is possible to model variable agent speeds that may depend on the specific area traffic or on other concrete issues. A detailed description of the MTM is given in Section 2. We here discuss its major features and benefits. Any MTM $\mathcal{D}$ determines a discrete-time *Markov chain* $\mathcal{M}_{\mathcal{D}}$ whose generic state is a pair $\langle T, i \rangle$: an agent has chosen trace T and, at that time step, she is in position $T(i)$. We first study the stationary distribution(s) of the Markov chain $\mathcal{M}_{\mathcal{D}}$ (in what follows we will say shortly: "stationary distribution of $\mathcal{D}$"). We show evidence of the generality of our model, derive an explicit form of the stationary distribution(s), and establish *existence* and *uniqueness* conditions for the stationary distributions of an MTM. We then give a necessary and sufficient condition for *uniformness* of the stationary distribution of an MTM. The above results for the stationary phase can be applied to get explicit formulas for the stationary *(agent) spatial distribution* and the stationary *(agent) destination* one. The former gives the probability that an agent lies in a given cell, while the latter gives the probability that an agent, *conditioned* to stay in a cell v, has *destination* cell w, for any choice of v and w. The knowledge of such distributions is crucial to achieve *perfect simulation*, to derive connectivity properties of Mobile Ad-hoc NETworkS (MANETS) defined over the mobility model, and for the study of information spreading over such MANETS [7,8,11]. We emphasize that all the obtained explicit formulas can be computed by counting arguments (it mainly concerns calculating the number of feasible traces passing over or starting from a cell). If the agent's behaviour can be described by using a limited set of *typical* traces (this happens in most of MANETS applications), then such formulas can be computed by a computer in few minutes.

Our MTM model can thus serve as a general framework that allows an analytical study of concrete mobility scenarios. We provide two examples that show its power and applicability.

In the first one, we consider the *Manhattan Random Way-Point* (MRWP) model [11,5,14]. This version of the *Random Way-Point* model is motivated by scenarios where agents travel over an urban zone and try to minimize the number of *turns* while keeping the chosen route as short as possible. We then implement this model as a specific MTM and we derive explicit formulas for its stationary distributions. In particular, we provide the spatial and the destination distributions for any choice of the cell resolution parameter $\epsilon > 0$. We observe that, by taking the limit for $\epsilon \to 0$, our explicit formula of the spatial distribution coincides to that computed by using rather complex integral calculus in [11] for the continuous space-time MRWP model (in terms of *probability density functions*).

Finally, we give, for the first time, the destination distribution of the continuous space-time MRWP model as well. Both these formulas have been recently used to derive the first analytical bounds on flooding time for the MRWP model [10].

Our approach can make the analysis of complex scenarios much simpler: it is just a matter of modelling objects and events as ingredients of an MTM. After doing that, you do not need to prove new properties or new formulas, you can just apply ours.

As a second concrete example of this fact, we consider a more complex vehicular-mobility scenario: The *Down-Town* model where a set of horizontal and vertical streets cross each other and they alternate with building blocks (see Fig 1). Agents (i.e. vehicles) move over the streets according to *Manhattan-like* paths and park on the border of the streets (a detailed description of the model is given in Section 4.1). Different agent speeds and red and green events of traffic lights can be implemented by considering different traces over the same street path.

Thanks to a *modular* version of our MTM model, we are also able to analyze this more complex scenario. In fact, the main advantage of our approach is that a given scenario can be analyzed by simply modelling objects and events as "ingredient" of an MTM, thus obtaining the stationary probability distributions directly from our formulas.

2 The Markov Trace Model

The mobility model we are introducing is discrete with respect to time and space. The positions an agent can occupy during her movement belong to the set of *points* (also called *cells*) $\mathcal{R}$ and they are traced at discrete time steps. The set $\mathcal{R}$ might be a subset of $\mathbb{R}^d$, for some $d = 1, 2, \ldots$, or it might be some other set. It is only assumed that $\mathcal{R}$ is a metric space.

A *movement trace*, or simply a *trace*, is any (finite) sequence $T{=}(u_0, u_1, \ldots, u_k)$ of at least two points. When we mention points we tacitly assume that they belong to $\mathcal{R}$. The points of a trace are not necessarily distinct. The length of a trace T (i.e., the number of points of T) is denoted by $|T|$ and, for each $i = 0, 1, \ldots |T| - 1$, let $T(i)$ denote the i-th point of the trace T. A trace T can be interpreted as the recording of the movement of an agent starting from some initial time t_0: for every $i = 0, 1, \ldots, |T| - 1$, $T(i)$ is the traced position of the agent at time $t_0 + i \cdot \tau$, where $\tau > 0$ is the duration of a time step.

In our model, an agent can move along trajectories that are represented by traces. For any trace T, let T_{start} and T_{end} denote, respectively, the starting point and the ending point of the trace. Let $\mathcal{T}$ be any set (possibly infinite) of traces. We say that $\mathcal{T}$ is *endless* if for every trace $T \in \mathcal{T}$, there is a trace $T' \in \mathcal{T}$ such that $T'_{start} = T_{end}$.

For any point $u \in \mathcal{R}$, $\mathcal{T}^{\text{out}}(u)$ denotes the subset of traces of $\mathcal{T}$ whose starting point is u. Let

$$P(\mathcal{T}) = \{u \mid \mathcal{T}^{\text{out}}(u) \neq \emptyset\} \quad \text{and} \quad S(\mathcal{T}) = \{\langle T, i \rangle \mid T \in \mathcal{T} \wedge 1 \leqslant i \leqslant |T| - 1\}$$

A *Markov Trace Model* (*MTM*) is a pair $\mathcal{D} = (\mathcal{T}, \Psi)$ such that:

i) $\mathcal{T}$ is an endless trace set such that $|P(\mathcal{T})| < \infty$;
ii) Ψ is a *Trace Selecting Rule for* $\mathcal{T}$ (*TSR*), that is, Ψ is a family of probability distributions $\{\psi_u\}_{u \in P(\mathcal{T})}$ such that for each point $u \in P(\mathcal{T})$, ψ_u is a probability distribution over $\mathcal{T}^{\text{out}}(u)$.

Similarly to the random trip model [14], any MTM $\mathcal{D}$ determines a Markov chain $\mathcal{M}_{\mathcal{D}} = (S(\mathcal{T}), P[\mathcal{T}, \Psi])$ whose state space is $S(\mathcal{T})$ and the transition probabilities $P[\mathcal{T}, \Psi]$ are defined as follows: for every $T \in \mathcal{T}$,

- *Deterministic-move Rule.* For every i with $1 \leqslant i < |T| - 1$, $\mathbf{Pr}\left(\langle T, i \rangle \to \langle T, i+1 \rangle\right) = 1$;
- *Next-trace Rule.* For every T' in $\mathcal{T}^{\text{out}}(T_{end})$, $\mathbf{Pr}\left(\langle T, |T| - 1 \rangle \to \langle T', 1 \rangle\right) = \psi_{T_{end}}(T')$;

all the other transition probabilities are 0. It is immediate to verify that for any $s \in S(\mathcal{T})$ it holds that $\sum_{r \in S(\mathcal{T})} \mathbf{Pr}\left(s \to r\right) = 1$.

Stationary Properties. We first introduce some notions that are useful in studying the stationary distributions of a MTM. For any $u, v \in \mathcal{R}$, $\mathcal{T}(u, v)$ denotes the subset of traces of $\mathcal{T}$ whose starting point is u and whose ending point is v. Define also $\mathcal{T}^{\text{in}}(u) = \{T \in \mathcal{T} \mid T_{end} = u\}$.

Let $\mathcal{D} = (\mathcal{T}, \Psi)$ be a MTM. For any two distinct points $u, v \in P(\mathcal{T})$, we say that u is *connected to* v in $\mathcal{D}$ if there exists a sequence of points of $P(\mathcal{T})$ $(z_0, z_1, \ldots, z_k)$ such that $z_0 = u$, $z_k = v$, and, for every $i = 0, 1, \ldots, k - 1$, $\sum_{T \in \mathcal{T}(z_i, z_i+1)} \psi_{z_i}(T) > 0$ Informally, this can be interpreted as saying that if an agent is in u then, with positive probability, she will reach v. We say that $\mathcal{D}$ is *strongly connected* if, for every $u, v \in P(\mathcal{T})$, u is connected to v. Observe that if $\mathcal{D}$ is not strongly connected then at least a pair of points $u, v \in P(\mathcal{T})$ exists such that u is not connected to v. In the full version of this work [9], by applying standard results concenring Markov chains, we prove that: i) Any MTM $\mathcal{D}$ always admits a stationary probability distribution; If D is strongly connected then it has a unique stationary distribution. Let $\mathcal{D} = (\mathcal{T}, \Psi)$ be any MTM. We say that $\mathcal{D}$ is *uniformly selective* if $\forall u \in P(\mathcal{T})$, ψ_u is a uniform distribution. We say that $\mathcal{D}$ is *balanced* if $\forall u \in P(\mathcal{T})$, $|\mathcal{T}^{\text{in}}(u)| = |\mathcal{T}^{\text{out}}(u)|$ Observe that if a MTM $\mathcal{D} = (\mathcal{T}, \Psi)$ has a uniform stationary distribution then it must be the case that $|S(\mathcal{T})| < \infty$ or, equivalently, $|\mathcal{T}| < \infty$. We also prove that an MTM $\mathcal{D} = (\mathcal{T}, \Psi)$ has a uniform stationary distribution iff it is both uniformly selective and balanced.

Stationary Spatial and Destination Distributions. We use the following notations. For any trace $T \in \mathcal{T}$ and for any $u \in \mathcal{R}$, define

$$\#_{T,u} = |\{i \in \mathbb{N} \mid 1 \leqslant i < |T| - 1 \ \wedge \ T(i) = u\}| \ \text{ and } \ \mathcal{T}_u = \{T \in \mathcal{T} \mid \#_{T,u} \geqslant 1\}$$

- We now derive the function $\mathfrak{s}(u)$ representing the probability that an agent lies in point $u \in \mathcal{R}$ w.r.t. the stationary distribution π. This is called *Stationary (Agent) Spatial Distribution.* By definition, for any point $u \in \mathcal{R}$, it holds that

$$\mathfrak{s}(u) = \sum_{\langle T,i\rangle \in S(\mathcal{T}) \wedge T(i)=u} \pi(\langle T,i\rangle) = \sum_{T \in \mathcal{T}_u} \#_{T,u} \cdot \pi(\langle T,1\rangle)$$

If the stationary distribution π is uniform, then $\mathfrak{s}(u) = (1/|S(\mathcal{T})|) \cdot \sum_{T \in \mathcal{T}_u} \#_{T,u}$. We say that an MTM is *simple* if, for any trace $T \in \mathcal{T}$ and $u \in \mathcal{R}$, $\#_{T,u} \leqslant 1$. Then, if the MTM is simple *and* π is uniform, then it holds

$$\mathfrak{s}(u) = \frac{|\mathcal{T}_u|}{|S(\mathcal{T})|} \tag{1}$$

- Another important distribution is given by function $\mathfrak{d}_u(v)$ representing the probability that an agent has destination v under the condition she is in position u. This function will be called *Stationary (Agent) Destination Distribution.* By definition, it holds that

$$\mathfrak{d}_u(v) = \frac{\sum_{\langle T,i\rangle \in S(\mathcal{T}) \wedge T(i)=u \wedge T_{end}=v} \pi(\langle T,i\rangle)}{\mathfrak{s}(u)} = \frac{\sum_{T \in \mathcal{T}_u \wedge T_{end}=v} \#_{T,u} \cdot \pi(\langle T,1\rangle)}{\mathfrak{s}(u)}$$

We define $\Gamma_u(v) = |\mathcal{T}_u \cap \mathcal{T}^{\text{in}}(v)|$ and $\Gamma_u = |\mathcal{T}_u|$ and observe that, if the MTM is simple *and* π is uniform, then

$$\mathfrak{d}_u(v) = \frac{\Gamma_u(v)}{\Gamma_u} \tag{2}$$

3 The Manhattan Random-Way Point

In this section, we study a mobility model, called *Manhattan Random-Way Point,* an interesting variant of the Random-Way Point that has been recently studied in [11].

Consider a finite 2-dimensional square of edge length $L > 0$. In order to formally define the MTM, we introduce the following *support graph* $G_\epsilon(V_\epsilon, E_\epsilon)$ where $V_\epsilon = \{(i\epsilon, j\epsilon) \ : \ i,j \in \{0,1,\ldots,N-1\}\}$ and $E_\epsilon = \{(u,v) \ : \ u,v \in V_\epsilon \ \wedge \ d(u,v) = \epsilon\}$ where, here and in the sequel, $N = \lceil L/\epsilon \rceil$ and $d(\cdot,\cdot)$ is the Euclidean distance.

Now, given any point $v \in V_\epsilon$, we define a set $\mathcal{C}(v)$ of feasible paths from v as follows. For any point u, $\mathcal{C}(v)$ includes the (at most) two Manhattan paths having exactly one corner point. More precisely, let $v = (x, y)$ and $u = (x', y')$ we consider the path having first the horizontal segment from (x, y) to (x', y) and then the vertical segment to (x', y'). The second path is symmetrically formed by the vertical segment from (x, y) to (x, y') and the horizontal segment to (x', y'). Observe that if $x = x'$ or $y = y'$, then the two paths coincides. We are now able to define the *Manhattan Markov Trace Model* (in short MANHATTAN-MTM) $(\mathcal{T}_\epsilon, \Psi_\epsilon)$, where $\mathcal{T}_\epsilon = \{T \mid T$ is the point sequence of a path in $\mathcal{C}(v)$ for some $v \in V_\epsilon\}$, and Ψ_ϵ is the *uniform* TSR for $\mathcal{T}_\epsilon$. It is easy to verify the MANHATTAN-MTM enjoys the following properties. The MANHATTAN-MTM is balanced, uniformly-selective and strongly-connected. So, the MANHATTAN-MTM has a unique stationary distribution and it is the uniform one. Moreover, since the MANHATTAN-MTM is simple, the stationary spatial and the destination distributions are given by Eq.s 1 and 2, respectively.

So, we just have to count the size of some subsets of traces (i.e paths in $G_\epsilon(V_\epsilon, E_\epsilon)$). The point $(i\epsilon, j\epsilon)$ will be denoted by its grid coordinates (i, j). The stationary spatial distribution for $(\mathcal{T}_\epsilon, \Psi_\epsilon)$ is

$$\mathfrak{s}_\epsilon(i, j) = \frac{3((4N^2 - 6N + 2)(i + j) - (4N - 2)(i^2 + j^2) + 6N^2 - 8N + 3)}{(N^4 - N^2)(4N - 2)} \tag{3}$$

We now study the Manhattan Random-Way Point over grids of arbitrarily high *resolution*, i.e. for $\epsilon \to 0$ in order to derive the *probability densitiy* functions of the stationary distributions. We first compute the probability that an agent lies into a square of center (x, y) (where x and y are the Euclidean coordinates of a point in V_ϵ) and side length 2δ w.r.t. the spatial distribution; then, we take the limits as $\delta, \epsilon \to 0$. We thus get the *probability density function* of the spatial distribution

$$s(x, y) = \frac{3}{L^3}(x + y) - \frac{3}{L^4}(x^2 + y^2) \tag{4}$$

This is also the formula obtained in [11] for the classic (real time-space) MRWP model.

- The stationary destination density function can be computed very similarly by applying Eq. 2. The probability density $f_{(x_0,y_0)}(x, y)$ that an agent, conditioned to stay in position (x_0, y_0), has destination (x, y) is

$$f_{(x_0,y_0)}(x, y) = \begin{cases} \frac{2L - x_0 - y_0}{4L(L(x_0+y_0)-(x_0^2+y_0^2))} & \text{if } x < x_0 \text{ and } y < y_0 \\ \frac{x_0 + y_0}{4L(L(x_0+y_0)-(x_0^2+y_0^2))} & \text{if } x > x_0 \text{ and } y > y_0 \\ \frac{L - x_0 + y_0}{4L(L(x_0+y_0)-(x_0^2+y_0^2))} & \text{if } x < x_0 \text{ and } y > y_0 \\ \frac{L + x_0 - y_0}{4L(L(x_0+y_0)-(x_0^2+y_0^2))} & \text{if } x > x_0 \text{ and } y < y_0 \\ +\infty & \text{if } x = x_0 \text{ and } y = y_0 \\ +\infty & \text{if } x = x_0 \text{ and } y < y_0 \text{ (South Case)} \\ +\infty & \text{if } x < x_0 \text{ and } y = y_0 \text{ (West Case)} \\ +\infty & \text{if } x = x_0 \text{ and } y > y_0 \text{ (North Case)} \\ +\infty & \text{if } x > x_0 \text{ and } y = y_0 \text{ (East Case)} \end{cases} \tag{5}$$

It is also possible to derive the probability that an agent, visiting point (x_0, y_0), has destination in one of the last four cases (south, west, north, and east)

$$\phi^{\text{south}}_{(x_0,y_0)} = \phi^{\text{north}}_{(x_0,y_0)} = \frac{y_0(L-y_0)}{4L(x_0+y_0)-4(x_0^2+y_0^2)}, \quad \phi^{\text{west}}_{(x_0,y_0)} = \phi^{\text{east}}_{(x_0,y_0)} = \frac{x_0(L-x_0)}{4L(x_0+y_0)-4(x_0^2+y_0^2)}$$

We observe that the resulting *cross* probability, (i.e. the probability an agent has destination over the *cross* centered on its current position), is equal to 1/2 despite the fact that this region (i.e. the cross) has area 0. This is crucial for getting an upper bound on flooding time [10].

4 Modular Trace Models

Defining a MTM whose aim is the approximate representation of a concrete mobility scenario might be a very demanding task. We thus introduce a technique that makes the definition of MTMs easier when the mobility scenario is *modular*. For example, consider vehicular mobility in a city. Any mobility trace can be viewed as formed by the concatenation of *trace segments* each of which is the segment of the trace that lies on a suitable segment of a street (e.g., the segment of a street between two crossings). Moreover, given a street segment we can consider all the trace segments that lies on it. Then, it is reasonable to think that two alike street segments (e.g., two rectilinear segments approximately of the same length), have similar collections of trace segments. This leads us to the insight that all the traces can be defined by suitably combining the collection of trace segments relative to street segments. It works just like combining *Lego* blocks.

In the sequel, we use the term *trace segment* to mean a trace that is a part of longer traces. Given a trace (or a trace segment) T, the *shadow of* T, denoted by S_T, is the sequence of points obtained from T by replacing each maximal run of repetitions of a point u by a single occurrence of u. For example, the shadow of (u, u, v, w, w, w, u) is (u, v, w, u) (where u, v, w are distinct points). Given any two sequences of points T and T' (be them traces, trace segments, or shadows), the *combination* of T and T', in symbols $T \cdot T'$, is the concatenation of the two sequences of points. Moreover, we say that T and T' are *disjoint* if no point occurs in both T and T'. Given any multiset X we denote the cardinality of X by $|X|$, including repeated memberships.

A *bundle* B is any non-empty finite multiset of trace segments such that, for every $T, T' \in B$, $S_T = S_{T'}$. The common shadow of all the trace segments in B is called the *shadow of* B and it is denoted by S_B.

Two bundles B and B' are *non-overlapping* if S_B and $S_{B'}$ are disjoint. Given two non-overlapping bundles B and B' the *combination* of B and B', in symbols $B \cdot B'$, is the bundle consisting of all the trace segments $T \cdot T'$ for all the T, T' with $T \in B$ and $T' \in B'$. Notice that, since B and B' are non-overlapping, it holds that $S_{B \cdot B'} = S_B \cdot S_{B'}$. Moreover, it holds that $|B \cdot B'| = |B| \cdot |B'|$.

A *bundle-path* is a sequence of bundles $P = (B_1, B_2, \ldots, B_k)$ such that any two consecutive bundles of P are non-overlapping. A bundle-path P determines a bundle $\mathsf{Bundle}(P) = B_1 \cdot B_2 \cdots B_k$. Observe that $|\mathsf{Bundle}(P)| = \prod_{i=1}^{k} |B_i|$. Given a bundle-path P, let P_{start} and P_{end} denote, respectively, the starting point and the ending point of the traces belonging to $\mathsf{Bundle}(P)$.

A *route* R is a multiset of bundle-paths all having the same starting point R_{start} and the same ending point R_{end} (i.e. there exist points R_{start} and R_{end} such that for every bundle-path P in R it holds $P_{start} = R_{start}$ and $P_{end} = R_{end}$).

Informally speaking, a bundle-path is formed by traces having the same shadow; introducing such different traces allows to model agents travelling on the same path at different speeds (in this way, it is also possible to change speed around cross-ways and modeling other concrete events). Moreover, routes are introduced to allow different bundle-paths connecting two points. By introducing more copies of the same bundle-path into a route, it is possible to determine paths having more agent traffic. As described below, all such issues can be implemented without making the system analysis much harder: it still mainly concerns counting traces visiting a given bundle.

A *Route System* is a pair $\mathfrak{R} = (\mathcal{B}, \mathcal{R})$ where: (i) $\mathcal{B}$ is a set of bundles, and (ii) $\mathcal{R}$ is a multiset of routes over the bundles of $\mathcal{B}$ such that, for every $R \in \mathcal{R}$, there exists $R' \in \mathcal{R}$ with $R'_{start} = R_{end}$.

We need some further notations. Let $\mathcal{R}_u$ be the multiset $\{R \in \mathcal{R} | R_{start} = u\}$. $\#_{P,T}$ is the multiplicity of trace T in $\mathsf{Bundle}(P)$. $\#_{P,B}$ is the number of occurrences of bundle B in the bundle-path P. Moreover $\#_{R,B} = \sum_{p \in R} \#_{P,B}$ and $\#_{B,u} = \sum_{T \in B} \#_{T,u}$, where the sums vary over all the elements, including repeated memberships. Let $\#B$ denote the total number of occurrences of points in all the trace segments of B, including repeated memberships, that is,

$$\#B = \sum_{u \text{ in } S_B} \#_{B,u}$$

A Route System $\mathfrak{R} = (\mathcal{B}, \mathcal{R})$ defines a MTM $\mathcal{D}[\mathfrak{R}] = (\mathcal{T}[\mathfrak{R}], \Psi[\mathfrak{R}])$ where

(i) $\mathcal{T}[\mathfrak{R}] = \{T \mid \exists R \in \mathcal{R}\ \exists P \in R : \ T \in \mathsf{Bundle}(P)\}$ Notice that $\mathcal{T}[\mathfrak{R}]$ is a set not a multiset. (ii) for every $u \in P(\mathcal{T}[\mathfrak{R}])$ and for every $T \in \mathcal{T}[\mathfrak{R}]^{\text{out}}(u)$,

$$\psi[\mathfrak{R}]_u(T) = \frac{1}{|\mathcal{R}_u|} \sum_{R \in \mathcal{R}_u} \frac{1}{|R|} \sum_{P \in R} \frac{\#_{P,T}}{|\mathsf{Bundle}(P)|}$$

The above probability distribution assigns equal probability to routes starting from u, then it assigns equal probability to every bundle path of the same route and, finally, it assigns equal probability to every trace occurrence of the same bundle path.

The "stationary" formulas for general route systems are given in the full version of the paper [9]. We here give the simpler formulas for balanced route systems. A Route System $\mathfrak{R} = (\mathcal{B}, \mathcal{R})$ is *balanced* if, for every $u \in \mathcal{S}$, it holds that

$$|\{R \in \mathcal{R} | R_{start} = u\}| = |\{R \in \mathcal{R} | R_{end} = u\}|.$$

We are now able to derive the explicit formulas for the spatial and the destination distributions; observe that such formulas can be computed by counting arguments or by computer calculations.

Proposition 1 *Let $\mathfrak{R} = (\mathcal{B}, \mathcal{R})$ be a balanced Route System such that the associated MTM $\mathcal{D}[\mathfrak{R}] = (\mathcal{T}[\mathfrak{R}], \Psi[\mathfrak{R}])$ is strongly connected. Then, (i) The stationary spatial distribution $\mathfrak{s}$ of $\mathcal{D}[\mathfrak{R}]$ is, for every $u \in \mathcal{S}$,*

$$\mathfrak{s}(u) = \frac{1}{\Lambda_{\mathrm{b}}[\mathfrak{R}]} \sum_{B \in \mathcal{B}} \frac{\#_{B,u}}{|B|} \sum_{R \in \mathcal{R}} \frac{\#_{R,B}}{|R|} \quad \textit{with} \quad \Lambda_{\mathrm{b}}[\mathfrak{R}] = \sum_{B \in \mathcal{B}} \frac{\#B}{|B|} \sum_{R \in \mathcal{R}} \frac{\#_{R,B}}{|R|}$$

(ii) the stationary destination distributions $\mathfrak{d}$ *of* $\mathcal{D}[\mathfrak{R}]$ *are, for every* $u, v \in \mathcal{S}$,

$$\mathfrak{d}_u(v) = \frac{1}{\mathfrak{s}(u)\Lambda_{\mathrm{b}}[\mathfrak{R}]} \sum_{B \in \mathcal{B}} \frac{\#_{B,u}}{|B|} \sum_{R \in \mathcal{R} \wedge R_{end} = v} \frac{\#_{R,B}}{|R|}$$

4.1 Application: The DownTown Model

We now use the Modular Trace Model to describe vehicles that move over a squared *city-like* support. This support consists of a square of $(n+1) \times (n+1)$ crossing *streets* (horizontal and vertical) and *buildings* (where n is an even number). Buildings are interdicted zones, while veichles move and park on the streets. Streets are in turn formed by *parking* and *transit* cells and every transit cells of a given street has its own direction (see Fig.s 1 and 2). Moreover, a parking cell has its natural direction given by the direction of its closest transit cells.

A vehicle (agent) moves from one parking cell (the *start*) to another parking one (the *destination*) by choosing at random one of the feasible paths. To every feasible path, a set of traces is uniquely associated that models the different ways a vehicle may run over that path: this will also allow to simulate traffic lights on the cross-ways.

Every street is an alternating sequence of *cross-ways* and *blocks*. We enumerate horizontal streets by an increasing even index $\{0, 2, \ldots, n\}$, starting from the left-top corner. We do the same for vertical streets as well. In this way, every cross-way gets a pair of coordinates (i, j). We say that a direction is *positive* over a horizontal street if it goes from left to right and while the opposite direction is said to be *negative*. As for vertical streets, the positive direction is the one going from top to bottom and the opposite is said to be negative (see Fig.s 1 and 2).

Then, the blocks of a horizontal street i will be indexed from left to right with coordinates $(i, 1), (i, 3), (i, 5), \ldots$. Similarly, the block of a vertical street j will be indexed from top to bottom with coordinates $(1, j), (3, j), \ldots$.

We now formally introduce the *DownTown Route System* $\mathfrak{R}^D = \langle \mathcal{B}^D, \mathcal{R}^D \rangle$; let's start with the bundle set $\mathcal{B}^D$. We here only describe the bundle shadows; the complete description is given in the full version [9].

[Blocks.] Each (street) block is formed by 4 stripes of m cells each with indexing shown in Fig. 2. Two stripes are for transit while the two external ones are for parking use. The parking stripe adjacent to the transit stripe with positive direction is said *positive parking stripe* while the other one is said *negative parking stripe.*

For every $0 \leqslant i, j \leqslant n$ such that $(i$ odd $\wedge\, j$ even $) \vee (i$ even $\wedge\, j$ odd $)$, Block (i, j) has the following bundles. Bundle $B_T^+(i, j)$ whose shadow is the stripe having positive direction; Bundle $B_T^-(i, j)$ is symmetric to $B_T^+(i, j)$ for the negative direction; For each parking cell of index k, there are four start-Bundles $B_{S,k}^{++}(i, j)$, $B_{S,k}^{+-}(i, j)$, $B_{S,k}^{--}(i, j)$, and $B_{S,k}^{-+}(i, j)$; For each parking cell of index k,

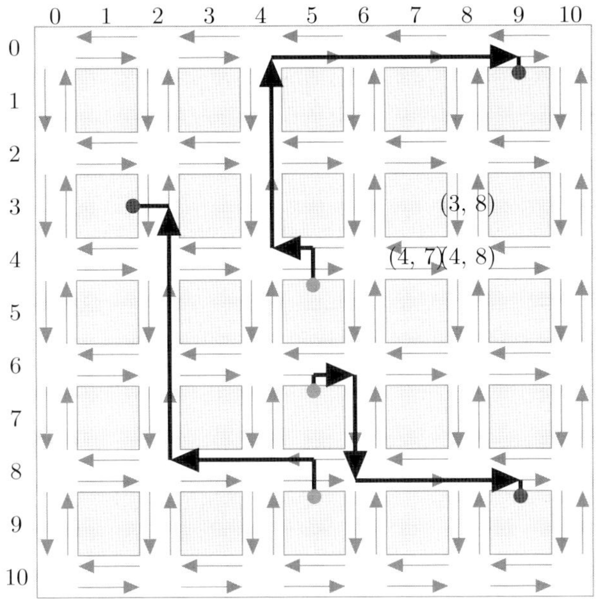

Fig. 1. The DownTown model with $n = 10$. Directions for each block are shown in gray. In blue are shown three possible routes. The starting cells are in green and the ending cells are in red.

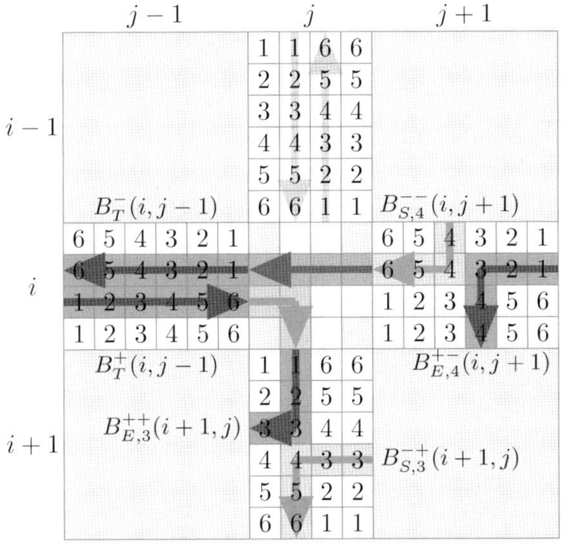

Fig. 2. The cross way at (i, j) and its four adjacent blocks are shown, with $m = 6$. The shadows of two transit bundles are shown blue. The shadows of start bundles, $--$ and $-+$, are shown in green, the other two cases (i.e., $++$, and $+-$) are symmetric. The shadows of end bundles, $++$ and $+-$, are shown in red, the other two cases are symmetric. The shadow of $B_C^{H,-}(i, j)$ is shown in violet, the other three straight cross bundles are symmetric. The shadow of $B_C^{H,++}(i, j)$ is shown in orange, the other seven turn cross bundles are symmetric.

there are four end-Bundles $B_{E,k}^{++}(i,j)$, $B_{E,k}^{+-}(i,j)$, $B_{E,k}^{--}(i,j)$, and $B_{E,k}^{-+}(i,j)$. The shadows of the above bundles are shown in Fig. 2.

[Cross-Ways.] A cross-way is formed by 12 cells as shown in Fig. 2. We have two types of associated bundles.

For every $0 \leqslant i,j \leqslant n$ such that (i even $\wedge\, j$ even), we have: The 4 straight bundles $B_C^{H,+}(i,j)$, $B_C^{H,-}(i,j)$, $B_C^{V,+}(i,j)$, and $B_C^{V,-}(i,j)$; The 8 turn bundles $B_C^{H,++}(i,j)$, $B_C^{H,+-}(i,j)$, $B_C^{H,--}(i,j)$ $B_C^{H,-+}(i,j)$; Moreover, $B_C^{V,++}(i,j)$, $B_C^{V,+-}(i,j)$, $B_C^{V,--}(i,j)$, and $B_C^{V,-+}(i,j)$. The relative shadows are shown in Fig. 2. Observe that the first sign indicates the sign of the in-direction and the other indicates the out-direction.

The set of DownTown routes $\mathcal{R}^D$ formed by combining the bundles described above are depicted in Fig. 1 (a formal description is given in the full version). Notice that some paths are not the shortest ones.

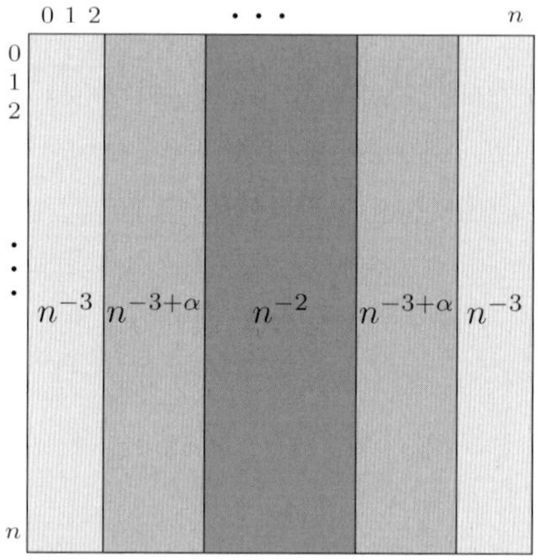

Fig. 3. Asymptotical behaviour of the spatial probability distribution of horizontal positive transit cells ($0 < \alpha < 1$). The role of vertical coordinate i is almost negligible since the only transit direction of such cells is the *positive horizontal* one. This representation takes no care about the slowness of the cells. Clearly, in vertical positive cells, the roles of i and j interchange.

Let $\Lambda = \Lambda_{\mathrm{b}}[\mathfrak{R}^{\mathfrak{D}}]/m^2$ be the normalization constant with $\Lambda_{\mathrm{b}}[\mathfrak{R}^{\mathfrak{D}}]$ defined in Prop 1. Let u be a transit cell of index k (with any $k \in \{1,\ldots,m\}$) in the *positive transit stripe* of the horizontal transit block (i,j) (i.e. i even and j odd). (with $i \notin \{0,n\}$). By calculations provided in the full version, we obtain the formula of the stationary spatial distribution

$$\mathfrak{s}(u) = \frac{\mathsf{slow}(k)}{\Lambda}\left(a(i,j) + \frac{k}{m}b(j) + \frac{1}{m}c(j)\right) \quad \text{where}$$

$$a(i,j) = (n-j)(2nj+j+n-i-1) + (n-2)j - \frac{n}{2} + i - 2,$$

$$b(j) = n(n+1) + \frac{n}{2} - 2(n+1)j, \quad \text{and} \quad c(j) = (n+1)(n+j) + n - 3$$

where $\mathsf{slow}(k)$ is the *slowness* parameter that summarizes the impact of trace segments on the transit bundles (see the full version). An informal representation of the asymptotical behaviour of the above function is given in Fig. 3.

Acknowledgements. We are very grateful to Paolo Penna for useful comments.

References

1. Koberstein, J., Peters, H., Luttenberger, N.: Graph-based mobility model for urban areas fueled with real world datasets. In: Proc. of the 1st SIMUTOOLS 2008, pp. 1–8 (2008)
2. Aldous, D., Fill, J.: Reversible Markov Chains and Random Walks on Graphs (2002), http://stat-www.berkeley.edu/users/aldous/RWG/book.html
3. Camp, T., Boleng, J., Davies, V.: A survey of mobility models for ad hoc network research. Wireless Communication and Mobile Computing 2(5), 483–502 (2002)
4. Baccelli, F., Brémaud, P.: Palm Probabilities and Stationary Queues. Springer, Heidelberg (1987)
5. Bettstetter, C., Resta, G., Santi, P.: The Node Distribution of the Random Waypoint Mobility Model for Wireless Ad Hoc Networks. IEEE Transactions on Mobile Computing 2, 257–269 (2003)
6. Camp, T., Navidi, W., Bauer, N.: Improving the accuracy of random waypoint simulations through steady-state initialization. In: Proc. of 15th Int. Conf. on Modelling and Simulation, pp. 319–326 (2004)
7. Clementi, A., Monti, A., Pasquale, F., Silvestri, R.: Information spreading in stationary markovian evolving graphs. In: Proc. of 23rd IEEE IPDPS, pp. 1–12 (2009)
8. Clementi, A., Pasquale, F., Silvestri, R.: MANETS: High mobility can make up for low transmission power. In: Albers, S., Marchetti-Spaccamela, A., Matias, Y., Nikoletseas, S., Thomas, W. (eds.) ICALP 2009. LNCS, vol. 5556, pp. 387–398. Springer, Heidelberg (2009)
9. Clementi, A., Monti, A., Silvestri, R.: Modelling Mobility: A Discrete Revolution. Techn. Rep. arXiv.org, Tech. Rep. arXiv:1002.1016v1 (2010)
10. Clementi, A., Monti, A., Silvestri, R.: Fast Flooding over Manhattan. In: Proc. of 29th ACM PODC (to appear, 2010)
11. Crescenzi, P., Di Ianni, M., Marino, A., Rossi, G., Vocca, P.: Spatial Node Distribution of Manhattan Path Based Random Waypoint Mobility Models with Applications. In: Kutten, S. (ed.) SIROCCO 2009. LNCS, vol. 5869, pp. 154–166. Springer, Heidelberg (2009)
12. Diaz, J., Perez, X., Serna, M.J., Wormald, N.C.: Walkers on the cycle and the grid. SIAM J. Discrete Math. 22(2), 747–775 (2008)
13. Diaz, J., Mitsche, D., Perez-Gimenez, X.: On the connectivity of dynamic random geometric graphs. In: Proc. of the 19th ACM-SIAM SODA 2008, pp. 601–610 (2008)
14. Le Boudec, J.-Y., Vojnovic, M.: The Random Trip Model: Stability, Stationary Regime, and Perfect Simulation. IEEE/ACM Transaction on Networking 16(6), 1153–1166 (2006)
15. Le Boudec, J.-Y.: Understanding the simulation of mobility models with Palm calculus. Performance Evaluation 64, 126–147 (2007)
16. Le Boudec, J.-Y., Vojnovic, M.: Perfect simulation and the stationarity of a class of mobility models. In: Proc. of the 24th IEEE INFOCOM, pp. 2743–2754 (2005)

Tell Me Where I Am So I Can Meet You Sooner
(Asynchronous Rendezvous with Location Information)

Andrew Collins[1], Jurek Czyzowicz[2], Leszek Gąsieniec[1], and Arnaud Labourel[3]

[1] University of Liverpool
[2] Université du Québec
[3] Université de Bordeaux

Abstract. In this paper we study efficient rendezvous of two mobile agents moving asynchronously in the Euclidean 2D-space. Each agent has limited visibility, permitting it to see its neighborhood at unit range from its current location. Moreover, it is assumed that each agent knows its own initial position in the plane given by its coordinates. The agents, however, are not aware of each others position. The agents possess coherent compasses and the same unit of length, which permit them to consider their current positions within the same system of coordinates. The cost of the rendezvous algorithm is the sum of lengths of the trajectories of both agents. This cost is taken as the maximum over all possible asynchronous movements of the agents, controlled by the adversary.

We propose an algorithm that allows the agents to meet in a local neighborhood of diameter $O(d)$, where d is the original distance between the agents. This seems rather surprising since each agent is unaware of the possible location of the other agent. In fact, the cost of our algorithm is $O(d^{2+\varepsilon})$, for any constant $\varepsilon > 0$. This is almost optimal, since a lower bound of $\Omega(d^2)$ is straightforward. The only up to date paper [12] on asynchronous rendezvous of bounded-visibility agents in the plane provides the feasibility proof for rendezvous, proposing a solution exponential in the distance d and in the labels of the agents. In contrast, we show here that, when the identity of the agent is based solely on its original location, an almost optimal solution is possible.

An integral component of our solution is the construction of a novel type of non-simple *space-filling curves* that preserve locality. An infinite curve of this type visits specific grid points in the plane and provides a route that can be adopted by the mobile agents in search for one another. This new concept may also appear counter-intuitive in view of the result from [22] stating that for any simple space-filling curve, there always exists a pair of close points in the plane, such that their distance along the space-filling curve is arbitrarily large.

1 Introduction

1.1 The Problem and the Model

A pair of identical mobile agents is located at two points in the plane. Each agent has limited visibility, permitting it to see its neighborhood at unit range from its current location. We assume that each agent knows its own *initial position* in the

S. Abramsky et al. (Eds.): ICALP 2010, Part II, LNCS 6199, pp. 502–514, 2010.

plane given by its coordinates, i.e., it is *location aware*. However, the agents do not know each others position. We also assume that the agents possess coherent compasses and the same unit of length, which permit them to consider their current positions within the same system of coordinates. Therefore each agent may consider its initial location as its unique ID.

The *route* of each agent is a sequence of segments which are subsequently traversed during its movement. The entire route of the agent depends uniquely on its initial position. The actual *walk* of each agent along every segment is *asynchronous*, i.e., it is controlled by an adversary. The agents meet if they eventually get within the visibility range of each other, i.e., at some point in time the distance between their current positions will not be greater than one.

We now define more precisely the power of the adversary. The adversary initially places both agents at any two points in the plane. Given its initial location a_0, the route chosen by the agent is a sequence of segments $(e_1, e_2, \ldots)$, such that in stage i the agent traverses segment $e_i = [a_{i-1}, a_i]$, starting at a_{i-1} and ending at a_i. Stages are repeated indefinitely (until rendezvous). We assume that each agent may start its walk at any time, but both agents are placed by the adversary at their respective initial positions at the same moment, and since that time any moving agent may find the other agent, even if the other agent didn't start its walk yet.

We describe the walk f of an agent on its route, similarly as in [12]: let $R = (e_1, e_2, \ldots)$ be the route of an agent. Let $(t_1, t_2, \ldots)$, where $t_1 = 0$, be an increasing sequence of reals, chosen by the adversary, that represent points in time. Let $f_i : [t_i, t_{i+1}] \rightarrow [a_i, a_{i+1}]$ be any continuous function, chosen by the adversary, such that $f_i(t_i) = a_i$ and $f_i(t_{i+1}) = a_{i+1}$. For any $t \in [t_i, t_{i+1}]$, we define $f(t) = f_i(t)$. The interpretation of the walk f is as follows: at time t the agent is at the point $f(t)$ of its route. The adversary may arbitrarily vary the speed of the agent, as long as the walk of the agent in each segment is continuous, eventually bringing the agent from the starting endpoint to the other endpoint of the corresponding segment of its route[1].

Agents with routes R_1 and R_2 and with walks $f^{(1)}$ and $f^{(2)}$ meet at time t, if points $f^{(1)}(t)$ and $f^{(2)}(t)$ are identical. A rendezvous is guaranteed for routes R_1 and R_2, if the agents using these routes meet at some time t, regardless of the walks chosen by the adversary. The cost of the rendezvous algorithm is measured by the sum of the lengths of the trajectories of both agents from their starting locations until the time t of the rendezvous. Since the actual portions of these trajectories may vary depending on the adversary, we consider the maximum of this sum, i.e., the worst-case over all possible walks chosen for both agents by the adversary. In this paper we are looking for the rendezvous algorithm of the smallest possible cost with respect to the original distance d between the agents.

[1] This defines a very powerful adversary. Notice that the presented algorithm is valid even with this powerful adversary, and the lower bound argument works also for a weaker adversary that can only speed up or slow down the robot, without moving it back (corresponding to a walk function f which must be additionally monotonous). Hence our results also hold in this (perhaps more realistic) model.

1.2 Related Work

The rendezvous problem is often presented as a search game involving two players (or agents) which cooperate in order to meet as quickly as possible. An extensive presentation of the large literature on rendezvous can be found in the excellent book [2]. The majority of research concern deterministic algorithms, which is also the model adopted in this paper. Most papers on rendezvous assume either the graph environment, e.g., [2,3] or the geometric environment. In the geometric scenario the agents move in some geometric terrain, e.g. line [6,7,20], plane [4,5,12], or unknown bounded environment [11,21].

One of the fundamental issues in the deterministic rendezvous algorithms is the problem of *symmetry breaking*, since identical agents starting at some symmetric positions may never meet, indefinitely performing symmetric moves. One possible way to break symmetry is to have agents identified with different *labels*. For the case of agents which are unlabeled, i.e., *anonymous*, [19] studied rendezvous in trees, assuming that agents have bounded memory. However, trees are a special case in which rendezvous is often feasible, supposing that neither nodes nor agents are labeled or marked. The rendezvous in a graph is feasible, see [13], if and only if the starting positions of the anonymous agents are asymmetric, i.e., the views of the graph from the initial positions of the agents are distinguishable, cf. [30]. In [31] the problem of gathering many agents with unique labels was studied. In [15,23] deterministic rendezvous in graphs with labeled agents was considered. One usual approach used for labeled agents consists in finding a (usually non simple) cycle in the graph, computable by an agent placed at any starting vertex, and an integer bijection f on the set of labels. The agent A goes $f(A)$ times around such cycle and different agents are forced to meet (see e.g. [11,13,14,23]). In [13] it was proved that the log-space memory is sufficient in order to decide whether a given instance of the rendezvous problem is feasible for any graph and any initial positions of the agents.

However, in most of the papers above, the *synchronous* setting was assumed. In the *asynchronous* setting it is assumed that the timing of each action may be arbitrarily slowed down by an adversary. The efficiency of the asynchronous algorithms is determined by the worst-case possible behavior of the adversary. Asynchronous gathering in geometric environments has been studied, e.g., in [10,18] in different models than ours: anonymous agents are oblivious (they can not remember past events), but they are assumed to have at least partial visibility of the scene. The first paper to consider deterministic asynchronous rendezvous in graphs was [14], where the complexity of rendezvous in simple classes of graphs, such as rings and infinite lines, was studied for labeled agents. In [12] the feasibility of asynchronous rendezvous for labeled agents was considered both for graphs and the 2D-space. It was proved that rendezvous is feasible in any connected (even countably infinite) graph. For this purpose, an enumeration of all quadruples containing possible pairs of agent labels and their starting positions is considered. According to this enumeration, the routes of the agents involved in each quadruple is extended in such a way that their meeting is always ensured. If the graph is unknown, the enumeration is constructed while the graph is explored. The cost of the rendezvous algorithm is exponential in the original distance between the agents. On the other hand, asynchronous rendezvous is unfeasible for agents starting at arbitrary positions in the plane, unless the agents have an $\epsilon > 0$ visibility range, see [12]. The assumption that the agents operating in the geometric environment has a bounded, non-zero visibility range is very natural (cf. [4,5,12,21]).

The assumption that the distributed mobile entities know their initial location in the geometric environment was considered in the past, e.g., in the context of geometric routing, see, e.g., [1,8,24,25], where it is typically assumed that the source node knows the position of the destination as well as its own position, or broadcasting [16,17], where the position awareness of only the broadcasting node is admitted. Such assumption, partly fueled by the expansion of the Global Positioning System (GPS), is sometimes called *location awareness* of agents or nodes of the network, and it often leads to better bounds of the proposed solutions. A technique consisting in the construction of the partition of the plane into bounded diameter cells is usually used here.

An interesting context of this work is its relationship to *space-filling curves* extensively studied at various contexts in the literature, see, e.g., [9,22,26,29]. One of the most important attributes of space-filling curves is sometimes called the *preservation of locality*, i.e., that if two points are close in the 2D-space they are also closely located on the space-filling curve. In this context, however, Gotsman and Lindenbaum pointed out in [22] that space-filling curves fail in preserving the locality in the worst case. They show that, for any space-filling curve, there always exist some close points in the 2D-space that are arbitrarily far apart on the space-filling curve. In this paper we show that such deficiency of space-filling curves comes from a very strong assumption that curves visit each point in a discrete 2D-space exactly once. We propose an alternative to space-filling curves that preserves locality also in the worst case. Namely, we introduce *space-covering sequences* that traverse points in a discrete 2D-space multiple times. We show that, for any $\varepsilon > 0$, there exists a space-covering sequence, s.t., for any two points located at distance d in the 2D-space there are well defined and efficiently computable instances of these two points in the sequence at distance $O(d^{2+\varepsilon})$ apart.

2 Efficient Construction of Space-Covering Sequences

The trajectories constructed in the paper follow grid lines except for their initial segments by which each agent, starting from its *arbitrary* initial position, reaches its closest grid point. It is possible that the first agent traverses an arbitrarily long portion of its route, while the adversary holds the other agent on its initial segment being not visible from any grid line. To prevent this we assume, w.l.o.g., that the 2D-space is rescaled so that the value of $\frac{\sqrt{2}}{2}$ corresponds to the unit length of the 2D-space. This way the considered grid is fine enough, and the agent visiting an integer grid point v will see another agent, situated in any interior point of a unit grid square with vertex v.

The fundamental concept used in the design of the rendezvous algorithm is the *space-covering sequence* on which both robots are walking until rendezvous. The space-covering sequence is infinite in both directions. It is formed of short segments with the endpoints located at the integer grid points. Every point of the integer grid is visited by the space-covering sequence infinitely many times. Each agent starting from its arbitrary initial position in the plane walks first to the closest grid point and then it starts making a special zigzag movement on the sequence, each time covering more and more distance. The actual points at which the agent changes the direction of its movement are determined by the coordinates of the initial position of the agent and the purpose of our algorithm is to determine them so that an efficient rendezvous will always be possible.

The construction of the space-covering sequence utilizes a hierarchy of infinite grids of squares of increasing sizes This hierarchy is an amalgamate $\mathcal{H}_{QC}$ of two complementary hierarchies of square partitions: the *quad-tree partition hierarchy* $\mathcal{H}_Q$ and the *central square partition hierarchy* $\mathcal{H}_C$. For the clarity of presentation we first demonstrate an argument leading to the rendezvous algorithm of cost $O(d^4)$ and later extend it to obtain a $O(d^{2+\varepsilon})$ cost solution.

Quad-tree hierarchy $\mathcal{H}_Q$: The first hierarchy of partitions $\mathcal{H}_Q$ has a form of an infinite *quad-tree* like structure, (for information on quad-trees see, e.g., [28]) in which the central point of the partition from each layer is aligned with the origin $(0,0)$ of the plane. The ith layer L_Q^i of the hierarchy, for $i = 0, 1, 2, ...$, is formed of an infinite grid of squares of size 2^i. Hence the lowest level of the hierarchy $\mathcal{H}_Q$ corresponds to the standard integer grid. In layer L_Q^i we denote by $S_Q^i(x,y)$ a square with the corners located at points (listed in the clockwise order counting from the top-left corner) $(x\cdot 2^i, y\cdot 2^i)$, $((x+1)\cdot 2^i, y\cdot 2^i)$, $((x+1)\cdot 2^i, (y-1)\cdot 2^i)$ and $(x\cdot 2^i, (y-1)\cdot 2^i)$. The overlapping squares at two neighboring layers L_Q^i and L_Q^{i+1} are engaged in a parent-child relationship. In particular, a square $S_Q^{i+1}(x,y)$ at layer L_Q^{i+1} has four children squares $S_Q^i(2x,2y)$, $S_Q^i(2x+1,2y)$, $S_Q^i(2x+1,2y-1)$ and $S_Q^i(2x,2y-1)$ at the layer L_Q^i, for $i = 0, 1, 2, \ldots$

Central-square hierarchy $\mathcal{H}_C$: The second hierarchical partition $\mathcal{H}_C$ is formed of (infinitely many) enumerated layers, where the ith layer L_C^i is an infinite grid with squares of size 2^i, for $i = 1, 2, \ldots$ Each layer in $\mathcal{H}_C$ is aligned, s.t., the origin $(0,0)$ of the plane is associated with the center of one of the squares in this layer. In particular, in layer L_C^i we denote by $S_C^i(x,y)$ a square with the corners located at points (listed in the clockwise order counting from the top-left corner) $((x\cdot 2^i) - 2^{i-1}, (y\cdot 2^i) + 2^{i-1})$, $((x\cdot 2^i) + 2^{i-1}, (y\cdot 2^i) + 2^{i-1})$, $((x\cdot 2^i) + 2^{i-1}, (y\cdot 2^i) - 2^{i-1})$, and $((x\cdot 2^i) - 2^{i-1}, (y\cdot 2^i) - 2^{i-1})$.

Hierarchy $\mathcal{H}_{QC}$: By $\mathcal{H}_{QC}$ we understand the infinite sequence of plane partitions

$$\pi_1 = L_Q^0, \pi_2 = L_C^1, \pi_3 = L_Q^1, \pi_4 = L_C^2, \pi_5 = L_Q^2, \ldots$$

Hence π_i is a grid partition of the 2D-space into squares of size $2^{\lfloor i/2 \rfloor}$, with grid point having each coordinate of the form $2^{\lfloor i-1/2 \rfloor} + k2^{\lfloor i/2 \rfloor}$, for any integer k. To assure that each layer of $\mathcal{H}_{QC}$ forms an exact partition, we assume that each square contains, besides its interior points, its right and top open sides as well as the top-right vertex.

Intuitively, the hierarchical partition $\mathcal{H}_{QC}$ provides a mechanism used to guarantee that any two points p_1 and p_2 located at distance d in the 2D-space are covered by some square of size $O(d)$ in either $\mathcal{H}_Q$ or in $\mathcal{H}_C$. The smallest square in the hierarchical structure with this property is referred to as the *rendezvous square* $R(p_1, p_2)$.

We state two lemmas directly following from the definitions of $\mathcal{H}_Q$ and $\mathcal{H}_C$.

Lemma 1. *Any square $S^i_C(x,y)$ located in layer L^i_C, for $i = 1, 2, \ldots$, encapsulates exactly four squares $S^{i-1}_Q(2x-1, 2y+1)$, $S^{i-1}_Q(2x, 2y+1)$, $S^{i-1}_Q(2x, 2y)$, and $S^{i-1}_Q(2x-1, 2y)$, in layer L^{i-1}_Q.*

Lemma 2. *Any square $S^i_Q(x,y)$ located in layer L^i_Q, for $i = 1, 2, \ldots$, overlaps with exactly four squares $S^i_C(x,y)$, $S^i_C(x+1,y)$, $S^i_C(x+1,y-1)$ and $S^i_C(x,y-1)$ in layer L^i_C.*

The following tree-like structure $\mathcal{T}_{QC}$ is useful to visualize the functioning of our approach: each square of every layer of $\mathcal{H}_{QC}$ is a node of $\mathcal{T}_{QC}$. For every such square S from layer $i > 1$ of $\mathcal{H}_{QC}$ the squares from layer $i-1$ intersecting S are children of S in $\mathcal{T}_{QC}$. By lemmas 1 and 2 $\mathcal{T}_{QC}$ is a quaternary tree. $\mathcal{T}_{QC}$ is infinite (does not a have a root) and its leaves are unit squares of the integer grid.

The observation stated in the following lemma is the basis of the complexity proof of our algorithm.

Lemma 3. *For any two points p_1 and p_2 located at distance d in the 2D-space there exists a square in $\mathcal{H}_{QC}$ of size $O(d)$ that contains p_1 and p_2.*

Proof. Assume that $2^{i-1} < d \le 2^i$. Consider five consecutive layers from $\mathcal{H}_{QC}$, L^i_Q, L^{i+1}_C, L^{i+1}_Q, L^{i+2}_C, and L^{i+2}_Q, where i meets the condition stated. Since any layer in $\mathcal{H}_{QC}$ forms a partition of the 2D-space into squares, within the layer L^{i+2}_Q there exists a unique square $S^{i+2}_Q(x,y)$ containing p_1. Since four quad-tree children of $S^{i+2}_Q(x,y)$ partition it, exactly one of them, a square belonging to L^{i+1}_Q also contains p_1. Similarly, there is exactly one square from L^i_Q, one of the sixteen grandchildren of $S^{i+2}_Q(x,y)$ in the quad-tree, which contains p_1, see Figure 1. Let $S^* \in L^i_Q$ denote the square containing p_1. Note that, since $d \le 2^i$, the d-neighborhood of S^* intersects nine squares of L^i_Q - the square S^* itself and eight squares surrounding S^*. Hence p_2 must belong to one of these nine squares.

We consider now the cases depending which of these sixteen squares is S^*. Due to the symmetry of the five layers in $\mathcal{H}_{QC}$, w.l.o.g., we can consider only one, e.g., the top-left quadrant of $S^{i+2}_C(x,y)$, which contains four squares at L^i_Q. One of the three possible cases can occur.

Case 1. If S^* containing p_1 corresponds to the square depicted by α_1, then p_2 must be located within $S^{i+2}_C(x,y)$, since $S^{i+2}_C(x,y)$ contains the entire d-neighborhood of α_1.

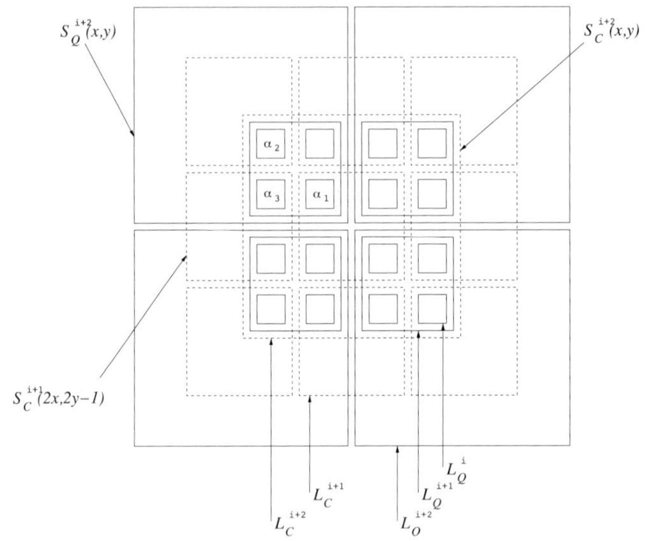

Fig. 1. The symmetric structure of layers $L_Q^i, L_C^{i+1}, L_Q^{i+1}, L_C^{i+2}$ and L_Q^{i+2}

Case 2. If S^* corresponds to the square depicted by α_2 then p_2 must be located within $S_Q^{i+2}(x, y)$.

Case 3. If S^* is one of the two remaining, symmetrically located squares within the selected quadrant depicted by α_3, then p_2 is located either in $S_Q^{i+2}(x, y)$, $S_C^{i+2}(x, y)$ or in $S_C^{i+1}(2x, 2y - 1)$.

Thus in all three cases there exists a square within layers L_Q^i, L_C^{i+1}, L_Q^{i+1}, L_C^{i+2}, and L_Q^{i+2}, that contains both p_1 and p_2. Moreover, since squares at those layers are of size $O(d)$, the thesis of the lemma follows. □

In fact a stronger result holds too.

Corollary 1. *Take any fragment of $\mathcal{H}_{QC}$ formed of three consecutive layers L_Q^i, L_Q^{i+1}, and L_Q^{i+2} in $\mathcal{H}_Q$ interleaved with two respective layers L_C^{i+1} and L_C^{i+2} in $\mathcal{H}_C$, s.t., $d \leq 2^i$. This fragment contains also a square that contains p_1 and p_2.*

Proof. The three cases from Lemma 3 also apply here. □

Space-covering sequences. Recall, that at the lowest layer of the structure $\mathcal{H}_{QC}$ there is partition π_1 containing *unit squares* of L_Q^0. On the basis of unit squares, we form *atomic* space-covering sequences, constituting basic components of length $O(1)$. The atomic sequence based on a point p belonging to a unit square in the 2D-space is referred to as the source $s(p)$ of p. We suppose that $s(p)$ is the sequence formed of a single point, being the top left corner of the unit square containing p. At any higher layer π_i we recursively form a longer sequence associated with each square S from this layer by concatenating the sequences from layer π_{i-1}, corresponding to the children of S in the tree $\mathcal{T}_{QC}$ (i.e., for even i - squares from π_{i-1} that are covered by S^*, see Lemma 1, and, for odd i - squares from π_{i-1} that overlap with S^*, see Lemma 2). To perform such construction we need to define *connectors* linking together the portions of the space-covering curve already created for the squares at the lower level. For the simplicity of presentation we suppose that the portion of the space-covering curve corresponding to any square S starts and ends at the top left corner of S. We assume that the children of the same parent of $\mathcal{T}_{QC}$ are arranged in the clockwise order starting from the top left child. The connectors are the line segments joining the top left corners of the siblings. The connectors are used twice, once in the increasing order of the siblings (which, by convention, corresponds to the left-to-right traversal of the space-covering sequence) and the other time in the decreasing order. For example connectors A, B, C link, respectively, squares $S_Q^i(2x-1, 2y+1)$, $S_Q^i(2x, 2y+1)$, $S_Q^i(2x, 2y)$ and $S_Q^i(2x-1, 2y)$ in Figure 2 (a) and squares $S_C^i(x, y)$, $S_C^i(x+1, y)$, $S_C^i(x+1, y-1)$ and $S_C^i(x, y-1)$ in Figure 2(b). Note that, in the former case, the obtained curve already starts and ends at the top left corner of the parent square $S_C^{i+1}(x, y)$. In the latter case, we also add connector D (cf. Fig. 2 (b)), taken twice, in order to make the constructed portion start and end at the top left corner of the parent square $S_Q^i(x, y)$. This process can be iterated for as long as it is required. The space-covering sequence associated with the *rendezvous square* $R(p_1, p_2)$ will be used to obtain rendezvous of two participating agents located initially at points p_1 and p_2. In what follows, we show how to explore the space-covering sequence efficiently during the rendezvous process.

Note that, since each layer in $\mathcal{H}_{QC}$ is a partition of the 2D-space into squares, every point p in the 2D-space can be associated with a unique infinite *list of squares* $S_1(p), S_2(p), \ldots$ from the consecutive layers $\pi_1(p), \pi_2(p), \ldots$ in $\mathcal{H}_{QC}$, respectively, s.t., each square contains p. Note also, that the space-covering sequence associated with $S_i(p)$, for each $i \geq 1$ forms a contiguous segment of positions in the space-covering sequence associated with $S_{i+1}(p)$. Let $left(S)$ and $right(S)$ denote, respectively, the leftmost and the rightmost position on the space-covering sequence corresponding to square S. Then we have $left(S_{i+1}(p)) \leq left(S_i(p)) \leq right(S_i(p)) \leq right(S_{i+1}(p))$.

Lemma 4. *For any two points p_1 and p_2 at distance d in the 2D-space, the space-covering sequence associated with the rendezvous square $R(p_1, p_2)$, is of length $O(d^4)$.*

Proof. Recall that the lengths of space-covering sequences associated with squares in $\pi_1 = L_Q^0$ are $O(1)$. Assume now that the sequences associated with squares of size 2^{k-1} at layer L_Q^{k-1} are of size $f(2^{k-1})$, for some positive integer function f. Note that the connectors from layer k, used for linking the endpoints of the space-covering sequences for the squares from layer $k-1$, are of length $O(2^k)$. Thus the space-covering sequences associated with squares in L_C^k have length $4 \cdot f(2^{k-1}) + O(2^k)$. Similarly, we

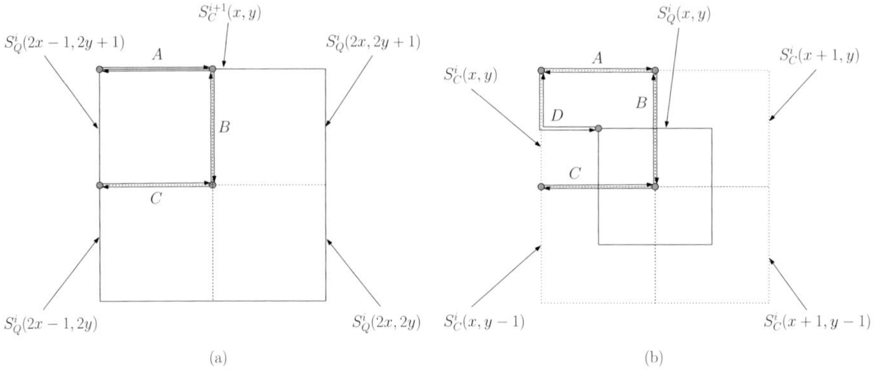

Fig. 2. Connectors between siblings (dotted line squares) and parent (solid lines). In case (a) parent comes from $\mathcal{H}_C$ family and in case (b) parent comes from $\mathcal{H}_Q$.

associate the squares in layer L_Q^k with space-covering sequences of length $4(4 \cdot f(2^{k-1}) + O(2^k)) + O(2^k) = 16 \cdot f(2^{k-1}) + O(2^k)$. Thus the length of the space-covering sequences associated with the squares in L_Q^k (also in L_C^k) can be described by the recurrence:

(1) $f(2^1) = O(1)$,
(2) $f(2^k) = 16 \cdot f(2^{k-1}) + O(2^k)$, for any integer $k > 1$.

Since, by Lemma 3, the rendezvous square $R(p_1, p_2)$ is of size $O(d)$, the recurrence will be applied at most $\log d + O(1)$ times. Thus the total length of the space-covering sequences for the squares from the layers L_Q^k and L_C^k is $O(d^4)$. □

We show now, that we can remove from $\mathcal{H}_{QC}$ certain layers coming from $\mathcal{H}_C$, obtaining a new hierarchy $\mathcal{H}_{QC}^*$, such that the distance separating p_1 and p_2 on the corresponding space-covering sequence can be reduced to $O(d^{2+\varepsilon})$, for any constant $\varepsilon > 0$.

Hierarchy $\mathcal{H}_{QC}^*$: Fix a natural number z. $\mathcal{H}_{QC}^*$ is formed of a sequence of blocks, each block containing $z+4$ layers. The i-th block, for $i = 0, 1, \ldots,$ contains z consecutive layers of $\mathcal{H}_Q$ - $L_Q^{i(z+2)}, L_Q^{i(z+2)+1}, \ldots, L_Q^{i(z+2)+z-1}$, followed by four layers $L_C^{i(z+2)+z}, L_Q^{i(z+2)+z}, L_C^{i(z+2)+z+1}, L_Q^{i(z+2)+z+1}$. E.g., the portion of $\mathcal{H}_{QC}^*$ corresponding to the first two blocks is

$$L_Q^0, L_Q^1, ..., L_Q^{z-1}, L_C^z, L_Q^z, L_C^{z+1}, L_Q^{z+1}, L_Q^{z+2}, ..., L_Q^{2z+1}, L_C^{2z+2}, L_Q^{2z+2}, L_C^{2z+3}, L_Q^{2z+3}$$

Note that, if some layer of $\mathcal{H}_{QC}^*$ comes from $\mathcal{H}_C$, i.e., it is L_C^k, for some value of k, its predecessor in $\mathcal{H}_{QC}^*$ is L_Q^{k-1}, hence Lemma 1 directly applies. On the other hand, for any layer of $\mathcal{H}_{QC}^*$ coming from $\mathcal{H}_Q$, say L_Q^k, its predecessor in $\mathcal{H}_{QC}^*$ is either L_C^k or L_Q^{k-1}. In the former case Lemma 2 directly applies. In the latter case each square from L_C^k partitions exactly into four squares of L_Q^{k-1}, hence the claim of Lemma 2 is true as well. Therefore the tree $\mathcal{T}^*_{QC}$ representing hierarchy $\mathcal{H}^*_{QC}$ may be obtained and the space-covering sequences are constructed similarly as in the case of $\mathcal{H}_{QC}$, where in case of missing layers from $\mathcal{H}_C$ the concatenation process is performed according to the structure of squares located in the hierarchical partition $\mathcal{H}_Q$. Similarly, in $\mathcal{H}^*_{QC}$ the rendezvous square $R(p_1, p_2)$ of two points p_1 and p_2 is the square on a lowest layer which contains the two points. The following lemma holds.

Lemma 5. *For any constant $\varepsilon > 0$, there exists $\mathcal{H}^*_{QC}$ in which the space-covering sequence associated with the rendezvous square $R(p_1, p_2)$ of two arbitrary points p_1 and p_2 located at distance d in the* 2D*-space is of length $O(d^{2+\varepsilon})$.*

Proof. According to Corollary 1, $R(p_1, p_2)$ - the rendezvous square for p_1 and p_2 is present in $\mathcal{H}^*_{QC}$. Moreover, $R(p_1, p_2)$ belongs to layer k, such that $k = \log d + z + O(1) = \log d + O(1)$, for some constant z, meaning that the size of the rendezvous square is still $O(d)$. The size of the space-covering sequence at layer k in $\mathcal{H}^*_{QC}$ is then bounded by $O(4^k \cdot 4^{2 \cdot \frac{k}{z+2}})$, where contribution $O(4^k)$ comes from the structure of $\mathcal{H}_Q$ and $O(4^{2 \cdot \frac{k}{z+2}})$ comes from $\mathcal{H}_C$. Note that we can choose the constant z, s.t., the exponent in the second term is the smallest constant that we require. Also since $k = \log d + z + O(1)$ the second term translates to

$$O(4^{2 \cdot \frac{\log d + z + O(1)}{z+2}}) \leq O(4^{2 \cdot \frac{\log d + z + O(1)}{z}}) = O(4^{\frac{2}{z} \cdot \log d}) = O(d^{\frac{4}{z}}).$$

Thus for any $\varepsilon > 0$, we can find an integer constant $z \geq \frac{4}{\varepsilon}$, s.t., the length of the space-covering sequence in $\mathcal{H}^*_{QC}$ for any two points at distance d in the 2D-space is $O(d^{2+\varepsilon})$. □

3 The Rendezvous Algorithm

Our rendezvous algorithm utilizes the nested structure of space-covering sequences associated with the list of squares defined for each point p in the 2D-space. The agent determines the list of squares in $\mathcal{H}^*_{QC}$ according to its initial location p. Then, for each square $S_i(p)$ from the list, the agent visits the leftmost and the rightmost point on the space-covering sequence, corresponding to the computed traversal of S_i, until it encounters the other agent.

Algorithm. `RV` (point $p \in$ 2D-space)

1. visit an integer grid point of the 2D-space which the closest to p;
2. $i \leftarrow 1$;
3. **repeat**
4.   Let $S_i(p)$ be the square from layer i of $\mathcal{H}^*_{QC}$ containing p;
5.   Go right on the space-covering curve until reaching $right(S_i(p))$;
6.   Go left on the space-covering curve until reaching $left(S_i(p))$;
7. $i \leftarrow i + 1$;
8. **until** rendezvous is reached ;

Theorem 1. *Two location aware agents located in points p_1 and p_2 at distance d in the 2D-space executing algorithm* RV *will meet after traversing asynchronously a trajectory of length $O(d^{2+\varepsilon})$, for any constant $\varepsilon > 0$.*

Proof. By Corollary 1, there exists the square $R(p_1, p_2)$ in $\mathcal{H}^*_{QC}$ containing p_1 and p_2. This square is on the list of squares considered in step 4 of the algorithm by each agent. Suppose, by symmetry, that agent $\mathcal{A}_1$ is the first one to terminate at time t step 6 of the algorithm for the iteration i during which $S_i(p_1) = R(p_1, p_2)$. If agent $\mathcal{A}_2$ has not yet completed its execution of step 1 of the algorithm, it must belong to $S_1(p_2)$ - a unit square included in $R(p_1, p_2)$ - and $\mathcal{A}_1$ completing step 6 must meet $\mathcal{A}_2$. Hence we may assume that, at time t agent $\mathcal{A}_2$ must be traversing a portion of the space-covering sequence, corresponding to some square included in $R(p_1, p_2)$. All intermediate space-covering sequences associated with the predecessors of $R(p_1, p_2)$ in the lists of squares for p_2 form the space-covering sequences included in the interval $[left(R(p_1, p_2)), right(R(p_1, p_2))]$. Hence, while agent $\mathcal{A}_1$ traverses this interval in step 6, it must meet agent $\mathcal{A}_2$, which, by our assumption, is within this segment at time t. The total length of the trajectory adopted by the agents is linear in the size of the space-covering sequence due to exponential growth of intermediate sequences associated with the consecutive squares in the list of squares. □

Remark. Note that there are $\Omega(d^2)$ integer grid points within distance d from any point in the 2D-space. Therefore, since the adversary can keep one of the agents immobile, the rendezvous implies that the other agent has to explore its d-environment, adopting a route of length $\Omega(d^2)$. Thus the cost of our algorithm is almost optimal.

4 Final Comments and Open Problems

Our algorithm may be extended in a standard way in order to solve *gathering* of a set of agents. However, instead of instantly stopping while a meeting occurs, a group of $n \geq 2$ agents involved in the meeting chooses a leader (e.g. the agent with the lexicographically smallest initial position) and all agents follow its route. If the total number of agents is known in advance they gather after traversing a route of length $O(d^{2+\varepsilon})$, provided they were initially within a d-neighborhood of some point in the 2D-space.

References

1. Abraham, I., Dolev, D., Malkhi, D.: LLS: a locality aware location service for mobile ad hoc networks. In: Proc. DIALM-POMC 2004, pp. 75–84 (2004)
2. Alpern, S.: The rendezvous search problem. SIAM J. Control and Optimization 33, 673–683 (1995)
3. Alpern, S., Baston, V., Essegaier, S.: Rendezvous search on a graph. J. App. Probability 36, 223–231 (1999)

4. Anderson, E., Lin, J., Morse, A.S.: The Multi-Agent Rendezvous Problem - The Asynchronous Case. In: 43rd IEEE Conf. on Decision and Control, pp. 1926–1931 (2004)
5. Anderson, E., Fekete, S.: Two-dimensional rendezvous search. Operations Research 49, 107–118 (2001)
6. Anderson, E., Essegaier, S.: Rendezvous search on the line with indistinguishable players. SIAM J. on Control and Optimization 33, 1637–1642 (1995)
7. Baston, V., Gal, S.: Rendezvous on the line when the players' initial distance is given by an unknown probability distribution. SIAM J. on Control and Optimization 36, 1880–1889 (1998)
8. Bose, P., Morin, P., Stojmenovic, I., Urrutia, J.: Routing with guaranteed delivery in ad hoc wireless networks. Wireless Networks 7(6), 609–616 (2001)
9. Buchin, K.: Constructing Delaunay Triangulations along Space-Filling Curves. In: Fiat, A., Sanders, P. (eds.) ESA 2009. LNCS, vol. 5757, pp. 119–130. Springer, Heidelberg (2009)
10. Cieliebak, M., Flocchini, P., Prencipe, G., Santoro, N.: Solving the Robots Gathering Problem. In: Baeten, J.C.M., Lenstra, J.K., Parrow, J., Woeginger, G.J. (eds.) ICALP 2003. LNCS, vol. 2719, pp. 1181–1196. Springer, Heidelberg (2003)
11. Czyzowicz, J., Ilcinkas, D., Labourel, A., Pelc, A.: Asynchronous deterministic rendezvous in bounded terrains. In: SIROCCO (2010)
12. Czyzowicz, J., Labourel, A., Pelc, A.: How to meet asynchronously (almost) everywhere. In: Proc. of SODA 2010, pp. 22–30 (2010)
13. Czyzowicz, J., Kosowski, A., Pelc, A.: How to Meet when you Forget: Log-space Rendezvous in Arbitrary Graphs. In: Proc. of 29th Ann. Symp. on Principles of Distributed Computing, PODC 2010 (to appear, 2010)
14. De Marco, G., Gargano, L., Kranakis, E., Krizanc, D., Pelc, A., Vaccaro, U.: Asynchronous deterministic rendezvous in graphs. Th. Comp. Sc. 355, 315–326 (2006)
15. Dessmark, A., Fraigniaud, P., Kowalski, D., Pelc, A.: Deterministic rendezvous in graphs. Algorithmica 46, 69–96 (2006)
16. Emek, Y., Gasieniec, L., Kantor, E., Pelc, A., Peleg, D., Su, C.: Broadcasting in UDG radio networks with unknown topology. Distributed Computing 21(5), 331–351 (2009)
17. Emek, Y., Kantor, E., Peleg, D.: On the effect of the deployment setting on broadcasting in Euclidean radio networks. In: Proc. PODC 2008, pp. 223–232 (2008)
18. Flocchini, P., Prencipe, G., Santoro, N., Widmayer, P.: Gathering of asynchronous oblivious robots with limited visibility. In: Ferreira, A., Reichel, H. (eds.) STACS 2001. LNCS, vol. 2010, pp. 247–258. Springer, Heidelberg (2001)
19. Fraigniaud, P., Pelc, A.: Deterministic rendezvous in trees with little memory. In: Taubenfeld, G. (ed.) DISC 2008. LNCS, vol. 5218, pp. 242–256. Springer, Heidelberg (2008)
20. Gal, S.: Rendezvous search on the line. Operations Research 47, 974–976 (1999)
21. Ganguli, A., Cortés, J., Bullo, F.: Multirobot rendezvous with visibility sensors in nonconvex environments. IEEE Transactions on Robotics 25(2), 340–352 (2009)
22. Gotsman, C., Lindenbaum, M.: On the metric properties of discrete space-filling curves. IEEE Transactions on Image Processing 5(5), 794–797 (1996)
23. Kowalski, D., Malinowski, A.: How to meet in anonymous network. Th. Comp. Science 399, 141–156 (2008)
24. Kozma, G., Lotker, Z., Sharir, M., Stupp, G.: Geometrically aware communication in random wireless networks. In: Proc. PODC 2004, pp. 310–319 (2004)
25. Kuhn, F., Wattenhofer, R., Zhang, Y., Zollinger, A.: Geometric ad-hoc routing: theory and practice. In: Proc. PODC 2003, pp. 63–72 (2003)

26. Moon, B., Jagadish, H.V., Faloutsos, C., Saltz, J.H.: Analysis of the Clustering Properties of the Hilbert Space-Filling Curve. IEEE Transactions on Knowledge Data Engineering 14(1), 124–141 (2001)
27. Paterson, M.S., Yao, F.F.: Efficient binary space partitions for hidden-surface removal and solid modeling. Discr. and Comp. Geom. 5(5), 485–503 (1990)
28. Samet, H.: The quadtree and related hierarchical data structures. Surveys 16(2), 187–260 (1984)
29. Xu, B., Chen, D.Z.: Density-Based Data Clustering Algorithms for Lower Dimensions Using Space-Filling Curves. In: Zhou, Z.-H., Li, H., Yang, Q. (eds.) PAKDD 2007. LNCS (LNAI), vol. 4426, pp. 997–1005. Springer, Heidelberg (2007)
30. Yamashita, M., Kameda, T.: Computing on Anonymous Networks: Part I-Characterizing the Solvable Cases. IEEE Trans. Parallel Dist. Syst. 7, 69–89 (1996)
31. Yu, X., Yung, M.: Agent rendezvous: a dynamic symmetry-breaking problem. In: Meyer auf der Heide, F., Monien, B. (eds.) ICALP 1996. LNCS, vol. 1099, pp. 610–621. Springer, Heidelberg (1996)

Rendezvous of Mobile Agents without Agreement on Local Orientation

Jérémie Chalopin and Shantanu Das

LIF, CNRS & Aix Marseille Université,
39 rue Joliot Curie, 13453 Marseille cedex 13, France
jeremie.chalopin@lif.univ-mrs.fr, shantanu.das@acm.org

Abstract. The exploration of a connected graph by multiple mobile agents has been previously studied under different conditions. A fundamental coordination problem in this context is the gathering of all agents at a single node, called the *Rendezvous* problem. To allow deterministic exploration, it is usually assumed that the edges incident to a node are locally ordered according to a fixed function called local orientation. We show that having a fixed local orientation is not necessary for solving rendezvous; Two or more agents having possibly distinct local orientation functions can rendezvous in all instances where rendezvous is solvable under a common local orientation function. This result is surprising and extends the known characterization of solvable instances for rendezvous and leader election in anonymous networks. On one hand, our model is more general than the anonymous port-to-port network model and on the other hand it is less powerful than qualitative model of Barrière et al. [4,9] where the agents have distinct labels. Our results hold even in the simplest model of communication using identical tokens and in fact, we show that using two tokens per agent is necessary and sufficient for solving the problem.

Keywords: Distributed Coordination, Mobile Agents, Rendezvous, Synchronization, Anonymous Networks, Incomparable Labels.

1 Introduction

Consider an undirected connected graph G that is explored by some mobile entities (called agents) that move along the edges of G. Such a setting occurs in many practical scenarios such as network monitoring, search and rescue operations, intruder detection and exploration of unknown territories by robots. The objective of the agents may be to gather information, search for some resource or make periodic visits to the vertices of G. When there are multiple autonomous agents operating in such an environment, it may be sometimes necessary to gather all the agents at a single location, for example to exchange information or for assignment of duties to the agents. This is a fundamental problem in distributed coordination, known as the *Rendezvous* problem and there is a long history of research on achieving rendezvous in graphs using either deterministic or probabilistic means (see [1] for a survey). This paper focusses on the deterministic

S. Abramsky et al. (Eds.): ICALP 2010, Part II, LNCS 6199, pp. 515–526, 2010.

setting. Notice that if the nodes of the graph G have distinct labels (and the agents can perceive these labels), then rendezvous can be achieved trivially by moving to a predetermined location. The more challenging problem is to rendezvous in a graph where the nodes do not have distinct identifiers. This problem relates to the more general question of what can be computed in a distributed network of anonymous processors [2,3,16].

As an example, consider the case of agents moving on an asynchronous ring, starting from distinct nodes. Clearly, rendezvous is not possible here if the agents keep following each other on the cycle forever. To facilitate rendezvous in such situations, each agent can be equipped with a marking device called the token (or pebble)[1] which can be used to mark the starting location of the agent [5]. Even with the capability of marking nodes, it is not always possible to deterministically solve rendezvous. We are interested in algorithms that achieve rendezvous whenever it is solvable, and otherwise detect and report the fact that is not solvable for the given instance. Such an algorithm is said to solve the *Rendezvous with Detect* problem.

Solving the rendezvous problem requires the agent to explore the graph G. In order to allow the agents to navigate through the graph G, it is usually assumed that the edges incident at any node v are locally ordered as $1, 2, \ldots d$ where d is the degree of v. While local orientation (or port numbering) is usually introduced to ensure navigability, it is inadvertently assumed that the agents agree on the local orientation, and a common order on the port numbers is then used to break symmetries. In this paper, we show that with or without agreement on the local orientation, rendezvous can be solved in the same distributed environments. In general, the edges of G may be assigned labels from some set Γ which is unknown to the algorithm designer and thus there may not be a predetermined order on the set of labels. Each agent, depending on its perceptions of the labels it encounters, may choose some arbitrary order on the set of labels. We define the rendezvous problem in this setting as "*Rendezvous without (agreement on) common port numbering*" or, **RVwA** to distinguish it from the usual setting where all agents agree on a common port numbering. The latter problem, which is a special case of the former, would be called "*Rendezvous with common port numbering*" or, **RVCP**.

Notice that the traversal path followed by the agent would vary depending on the port numbering used by that agent. Thus, it is no longer possible to determine the actions of an agent based only on the starting location of the agent in the graph. This is an important distinction between the two models (i.e. with or without common port numbering). In the former model, each agent can determine the so called *view* [16] of the other agents based on its traversal path and one common strategy for rendezvous is to compare the views of the agents and elect a leader. Such a strategy is no longer possible in our model and we require completely different techniques for solving the problem.

[1] The tokens can not be used for identifying an agent, since all agents carry identical tokens.

Our model is similar to the qualitative model of computation [4,9] where the incident edges at a node have distinct labels but the agents do not agree on a total order on these labels (i.e. the labels are said to *incomparable*). However, the model considered in the above papers also assume the agents to be distinct (i.e. distinguishable) and gives them the ability to write messages on public *white-boards* available at each node. We, on the other hand, consider the much weaker model where the agents are indistinguishable from each other and have to rendezvous in an anonymous network using only tokens to mark the nodes (and no explicit communication). In fact, we show that the problem of **RVwA** is solvable in exactly those instances where rendezvous with common port numbering is possible. In contrast, in the qualitative model of Barrière et al. [4,9] the class of solvable instances is much larger.

Our Results: We present an algorithm for solving rendezvous of mobile agents in arbitrary graphs when there is no agreement on a common port numbering. Our algorithm solves the problem whenever a deterministic solution is possible and otherwise detects the impossibility of rendezvous. This gives us a characterization of the solvable instances for the **RVwA** problem. Surprisingly, it turns out that this characterization coincides with that for the conventional version of the problem (**RVCP**) where a common port numbering is assumed. In other words, our result shows that for solving rendezvous, the assumption of a common port numbering is not necessary (it is sufficient that the incident edges are distinguishable).

The algorithm presented in this paper uses exactly two tokens per agent and we show that two tokens are necessary for solving the problem in the absence of other capabilities (e.g. whiteboards or distant communication). This contrasts nicely with the simpler problem of **RVCP**, where a single token per agent is known to be necessary and sufficient (e.g. see [12]). In fact, our algorithm uses two tokens because we need to synchronize between the actions of the agents[2]. We believe our synchronization technique, using tokens, will be useful for solving other problems in asynchronous settings.

Related Results: Our work is related to a long line of research on computability in anonymous environments starting from the work of Angluin [2]. Many researchers have focussed on characterizing the conditions under which distributed coordination problems (such as leader election) can be solved in the absence of unique identifiers for the participating entities. Characterizations of the solvable instances for leader election in *message passing systems* have been provided by Boldi *et al.* [3] and by Yamashita and Kameda [16] among others. In the message-passing model with port-to-port communication, each vertex of the graph is associated with a single agent; the agents are stationary and can send and receive messages over the incident edges to communicate with neighbors. The leader election problem in message-passing systems is equivalent to the rendezvous problem in the mobile agent model [7].

[2] Note that for synchronous environments, our algorithm can be adapted to use only one token.

In the deterministic setting, initial solutions for rendezvous were for synchronous environments with the prior knowledge of the topology [18]. An interesting line of research is determining what minimum capabilites allow the agents to solve rendezvous. For instance, Fraigniaud and Pelc [13] consider agents with small memory while Klasing et al. [14] consider robots with no memory of previous steps (though these robots can see at each step, the complete graph and the current location of the other robots). Recently, Czyzowicz et al. [10] considered a model where the agents have unique identifiers, but they have no way to communicate with each other (they cannot leave messages or tokens on the nodes).

2 Definitions and Notations

The Model: The environment is represented by a simple undirected connected graph $G = (V(G), E(G))$ and a set $\mathcal{E}$ of mobile agents that are located in the nodes of G. The initial placement of the agents is denoted by the function $p : \mathcal{E} \to V(G)$. We denote such a distributed mobile environment by $(G, \mathcal{E}, p)$ or by (G, χ_p) where χ_p is a vertex-labelling of G such that $\chi_p(v) = 1$ if there exists an agent a such that $p(a) = v$, and $\chi_p(v) = 0$ otherwise.

In order to enable navigation of the agents in the graph, at each node $v \in V(G)$, the edges incident to v are distinguishable to any agent arriving at v. For each agent $a \in \mathcal{E}$, there is a bijective function $\delta_{(a,v)} : \{(v, u) \in E(G) : u \in V(G)\} \to \{1, 2, \dots d(v)\}$ which assigns unique labels to the edges incident at node v (where $d(v)$ is the degree of v). In the literature, it is generally assumed that all agents have a common local orientation function: in that case, there exists a port numbering δ such that for each agent a, $\delta_a = \delta$. The nodes of G do not have visible identities by which the agents can identify them. Each agent carries some identical tokens. Each node v of G is equipped with a stack and any agent that is located at v can insert tokens or remove tokens from the stack. Access to the stack at each node, is in fair mutual exclusion Each time an agent gains access to the stack, the agent can see the number of tokens in the stack, and depending on this number, it may put a token, remove a token, or do nothing. Initially no node contains any token and each agent has exactly two tokens. The system is asynchronous; an agents may start at the any time and every action it performs may take an unpredictable (but finite) amount of time. The agents have no means of direct communication with each other. An agent can see another agent only when they are both located at the same node (and not when they are traversing the same edge). All agents start in *active* state, but during the algorithm an agent a may become *passive* and return to its homebase $p(a)$ to *sleep*. Any other agent located at the same node can see a *sleeping* agent and can initiate a process to wake-up such a *sleeping* agent. Note that the agents can distinguish a *sleeping* agent a from any other agent that may be waiting (actively) at the node v.

We also assume that initially each agent knows n, the size of G. We will explain in Section 5, how we can weaken this hypothesis. The agents have no other prior knowledge about the environment (e.g. the topology, the number of agents, are both unknown a priori).

Graph Coverings and Automorphisms: We now present some definitions and results related to coverings of directed graphs (or multigraphs, since we allow multiple arcs). A directed graph(digraph) $D = (V(D), A(D), s, t)$ possibly having parallel arcs and self-loops, is defined by a set $V(D)$ of vertices, a set $A(D)$ of arcs and by two maps s and t that assign to each arc two elements of $V(D)$: a source and a target. A *symmetric* digraph D is a digraph endowed with a symmetry, i.e. an involution $Sym : A(D) \to A(D)$ such that for every $a \in A(D), s(a) = t(Sym(a))$. We now define the notion of graph coverings, borrowing the terminology of Boldi and Vigna [6]. A *covering projection* is a homomorphism φ from a digraph D to a digraph D' satisfying the following: For each arc a' of $A(D')$ and for each vertex v of $V(D)$ such that $\varphi(v) = v' = t(a')$ (resp. $\varphi(v) = v' = s(a')$) there exists a unique arc a in $A(D)$ such that $t(a) = v$ (resp. $s(a) = v$) and $\varphi(a) = a'$. If a covering projection $\varphi : D \to D'$ exists, D is said to be a *covering* of D' via φ and D' is called the base of φ. For symmetric digraphs D, D', φ is a *symmetric covering* if $\forall a \in A(D), \varphi(Sym(a)) = Sym(\varphi(a))$. A digraph D is *symmetric-covering-minimal* if there does not exist any graph D' not isomorphic to D such that D is a symmetric covering of D'.

We consider labelled (di)graphs: a (di)graph G whose vertices are labelled over L will be denoted by (G, λ), where $\lambda\colon V(G) \to L$ is the labelling function[3]. We will consider homomorphisms which preserve the labelling on the vertices. Given a connected undirected graph $G = (V(G), E(G))$, we can associate it with a symmetric strongly connected digraph denoted by $Dir(G)$ and defined as follows: $V(Dir(G)) = V(G)$ and for each edge $\{u, v\} \in E(G)$, there exist two arcs $a_{(u,v)}, a_{(v,u)} \in A(Dir(G))$ such that $s(a_{(u,v)}) = t(a_{(v,u)}) = u$, $t(a_{(u,v)}) = s(a_{(v,u)}) = v$ and $Sym(a_{(u,v)}) = a_{(v,u)}$. A distributed mobile environment $(G, \mathcal{E}, p)$ can be represented by the symmetric labelled digraph $(Dir(G), \chi_p)$.

For simple connected undirected graph, Yamashita and Kameda [16] introduced the concept of views which we present below:

Definition 1. *Given a labelled graph (G, λ) with a port numbering δ, the* view *of a node v is the infinite rooted tree denoted by $T_G(v)$ defined as follows. The root of $T_G(v)$ represents the node v and for each neighbor u_i of v, there is a vertex x_i in $T_G(v)$ (labelled by $\lambda(u_i)$) and an edge from the root to x_i with the same labels as the edge from v to u_i in (G, δ). The subtree of $T_G(v)$ rooted at x_i is again the view $T_G(u_i)$ of node u_i.*

It is known that from the view of any vertex v truncated to depth $2n$, one can construct a labelled digraph (D, μ_D) such that $(Dir(G), \delta)$ is a symmetric covering of (D, μ_D) (See e.g. [3]). The digraph (D, μ_D) corresponds to the *quotient graph* in Yamashita and Kameda's work [16].

[3] Note that this labelling is not necessarily injective, i.e. two vertices may have the same label.

For any labelled undirected graph (G, λ), two vertices $v, v' \in V(G)$ are *similar* (we write $v \sim v'$) if there exists a label-preserving automorphism σ of $(Dir(G), \lambda)$ such that $v = \sigma(v')$. The relation $\sim$ is an equivalence relation over the vertices of G; the equivalence class of $v \in V(G)$ is denoted by $[v]$. For two disjoint subsets of vertices $V, V' \subseteq V(G)$, $G[V]$ denotes the subgraph of G induced by the vertices in V and $G[V, V']$ denotes the bipartite subgraph of G defined as follows. The vertices of $G[V, V']$ are $V \cup V'$ and there is an edge $\{v, v'\}$ in $G[V, V']$ if and only if $v \in V, v' \in V'$ and $\{v, v'\} \in E(G)$.

3 Characterization for Rendezvous

We present the following theorem that relates the various existing characterizations [6,16,17] of distributed mobile environments where the **RVCP** problem can be solved. Note that some of these characterizations were initially given for the problem of leader election in message passing systems.

Theorem 1 ([6,16,17]). *For any distributed mobile environment $(G, \mathcal{E}, p)$, the following statements are equivalent:*
1. *For any common port-numbering function δ, Rendezvous with common port-numbering can be solved in $(G, \mathcal{E}, p, \delta)$;*
2. *For any port-numbering function δ, all vertices of (G, χ_p, δ) have a different view;*
3. *There is no partition $V_1, V_2, \dots V_k$ of $V(G)$ with $k \in [1, |V(G)| - 1]$ such that for any distinct $i, j \in [1, k]$, the following conditions hold:*
   (i) $G[V_i]$ is d-regular for some d, and if d is odd, it contains a perfect matching,
   (ii) $G[V_i, V_j]$ is regular.
4. *$(Dir(G), \chi_p)$ is symmetric-covering-minimal.*

Since the **RVCP** problem is a special case of the **RVwA** problem, the conditions of Theorem 1 are also necessary for solving rendezvous when the agents do not agree on the local orientation. The following theorem is the main result of our paper; it shows that when each agent is supplied with a sufficient number of (identical) tokens, **RVwA** can be solved in $(G, \mathcal{E}, p)$ if and only if **RVCP** can be solved in $(G, \mathcal{E}, p)$. We prove the theorem by providing an algorithm that achieves this result.

Theorem 2. *There exists an algorithm for rendezvous without common port-numbering in a distributed mobile environment $(G, \mathcal{E}, p)$ if and only if $(Dir(G), \chi_p)$ is symmetric-covering-minimal.*

4 Our Rendezvous Algorithm

We present an algorithm for achieving rendezvous in the absence of a common port numbering (see Algorithm 1). The algorithm has an initialization round and multiple rounds of marking where the agents collectively try to break the symmetry among the vertices of the graph, until a single vertex can be chosen as the rendezvous location. Figure 1 illustrates the execution of the algorithm on a small toy-graph.

Initialization and Map Construction: At the beginning of the algorithm, each agent a puts a token on its homebase and constructs its view up to depth $2n$ (recall that the agent knows n, the number of vertices of G). Since the other agents may not have started at the same time, agent a may reach a homebase containing a *sleeping* agent. In that case agent a wakes-up the sleeping agent and waits until this agent puts a token on the node.

Algorithm 1. RDV (n)

```
Put a token on your own homebase ;
(D, μ) := ConstructMap(n) ;
/* Each agent computes (D, μ) such that (Dir(G), χ_p) covers (D, μ)   */
if (G, χ_p) is not symmetric-covering-minimal then
|   Terminate and report that rendezvous cannot be solved in (G, ℰ, p) ;
else
    /* Each agent knows a rooted map of (G, μ) = (G, χ_p)              */
    Synchronize ;
    Construct equivalence partition of (G, μ) ;
    repeat
        H := The minimal class that contains active homebases ;
        /* H defines the set of active agents for this round           */
        Active agents wait for passive agents to return to their homebases;
        if there exists a class C such that |H| > |C| then
            /* We split the class H into two                           */
            C := minimal class such that |H| > |C| ;
            Active agents (i.e. whose homebase ∈ H) try to mark vertices in C ;
            /* The ones that do not succeed become passive             */
            Synchronize ;
            Distinguish active homebases from passive homebases;
            Refine the labelling μ to give fresh labels to passive homebases;
        else if there exists C = [v] such that |H| < |C| then
            /* We split the class C in two.                            */
            C := minimal class such that |H| < |C| ;
            Each active agent mark a vertex in C ;
            Synchronize ;
            Refine the labelling μ to give fresh labels to marked vertices ;
        Re-construct equivalence partition of (G, μ);
    until There is only one vertex in each class ;
    h := The active homebase with minimum label ;
    The agent whose homebase is h, marks h and wakes up all the other agents;
    All other agents go to the only marked vertex, when woken up;
```

As mentioned before, the information contained in the view is sufficient to construct the quotient graph (D, μ) such that $(Dir(G), \chi_p)$ is a symmetric covering of (D, μ). Since each agent initially knows $n = |V(G)|$, it can determine whether (G, χ_p) is symmetric covering minimal or not. In the former case, the agent has obtained a map of (G, χ_p), while in the latter case, the agent reports that rendezvous is not solvable and terminates the algorithm.
Each agent r executes the following steps during the initialization procedure:

(Step A) Agent r puts a token on its homebase.
(Step B) Agent r constructs its view and builds the quotient graph. If $(Dir(G), \chi_p)$ is not minimal, agent r detects it and terminates the algorithm.
(Step C) Agent r puts a second token on its homebase
(Step D) Agent r checks that all agents have put zero or two tokens on their homebases.
(Step E) Agent r removes the two tokens from its homebase
(Step F) Agent r goes to each homebase h, and waits until either there is no token on h, or there is a sleeping agent on h.

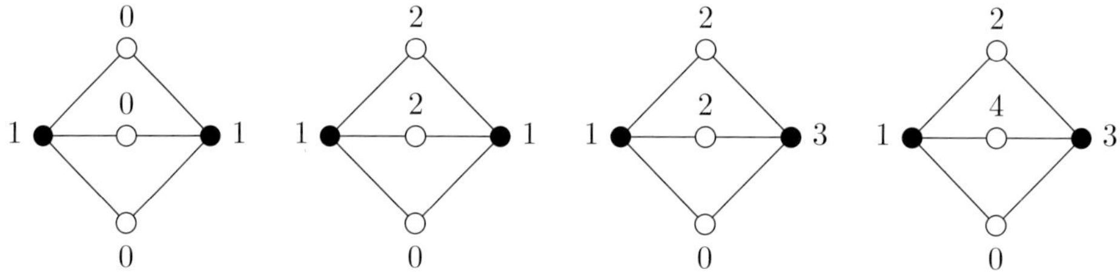

Fig. 1. The different labellings of a graph G computed by the agents during one particular execution of our algorithm on the distributed environment $(G, \mathcal{E}, p)$ represented on the left (black vertices represent homebases)

Constructing an order on equivalence classes: Given any vertex-labelled graph (G, μ), there exists standard procedures for partitioning the vertex set of G to obtain an ordered sequence of equivalence classes that respect the labelling. (See [4,9] for example.) Note that since the agents start with the same labelled graph (G, μ), they compute the same ordered sequence of equivalence classes.

Synchronization Procedure: We now describe the procedure for the marking round. At the beginning of each marking round, the agents choose two classes H and C, where H is the class of active homebases and C is the class of vertices to be marked by the agents during this round. Since the agents agree on the order of the equivalence classes, they also agree on the choice of H and C. (H is the first class in the sequence that contains active homebases and C is the first class whose size is either larger or smaller than that of H).

An agent whose homebase belongs to the class H is active during the current round. Each active agent r executes the following instructions. We suppose that at the beginning of the round, each agent carries its two tokens.

(Step 0) Agent r goes to the homebase of each passive agent (i.e. any homebase $\notin H$) and waits until there is a sleeping agent at that node.

(Step 1) Agent r traverses the graph G using its map, and if it arrives at a node $c \in C$ where there is no token, it puts a token at c and sets its state to SUCCESS. If agent r does not manage to mark any vertex of C (this can happen only when $|C| < |H|$), then it puts a token on any vertex c of C (that has already been marked by another agent). Such an agent sets its state to FAIL.

(Step 2) The agent r does a traversal of the graph and counts the total number of tokens on the vertices $\in C$. If there are strictly less tokens on vertices of C than the number of active agents (because some other agent has not finished the previous step), then agent goes back to its homebase and sleeps until it is woken up by another agent; On wake-up, agent r traverses the graph again to count the number of tokens on the vertices of C. When agent r completes this step, all other agents must have completed the previous step.

(Step 3) The agent r puts the second token on its homebase.

(Step 4) The agent r does a traversal of the graph and each time it arrives on the homebase h of another active agent r', it waits until there is a token or a sleeping agent at h. If there is a sleeping agent at h, agent r wakes it up and waits until there is a token on node h.

(Step 5) The agent goes back to the vertex $c \in C$ where it placed a token during Step 1 and removes a token from c.

(Step 6) The agent r does a traversal of the network. Each time it arrives on a vertex $c' \in C$, it waits until all tokens have been removed from c'.

(Step 7) The agent r removes the token from on its homebase. If the state of the agent is FAIL, then it becomes passive (goes to sleep). Otherwise the agent executes the next step.

(Step 8) The agent r does a traversal of the network. Each time it arrives on the homebase h of an active agent r', it waits until there is no token or there is a sleeping agent at h.

Let us consider two different scenarios.

If $|\mathbf{C}| > |\mathbf{H}|$, then the class C will be partitioned into marked and unmarked vertices. Moreover, each agent knows from the information it has stored on the map at Step 2 which vertices of C has been marked in this round. The agents would relabel the marked vertices to obtain the new labelling μ.

If $|\mathbf{C}| < |\mathbf{H}|$, then there would be two categories of agents: those whose state=SUCCESS and those whose state=FAIL. The former would remain active but the latter would become passive at the end of this procedure. In order to distinguish the active homebases in H from the passive homebases another procedure (explained below) is executed by the active agents.

Distinguishing Active from Passive Homebases: The following procedure is used for partitioning the class H in a round where the class C is smaller than the class of homebases H. The active agents (i.e. those who were successful in the marking process) can put tokens on their homebases to distinguish them. However, in order to avoid conflicts during consecutive rounds, the active agents must first mark vertices of C and not of H. Indeed, when an agent starts this procedure, there may be another agent that is still performing Step 8 of the synchronization procedure. The following steps are followed by an active agent r during this procedure (Note that exactly $|C|$ agents execute this procedure).

(Step 1') Agent r traverses the graph and puts a token on a vertex c of C that contains no token.
(Step 2') The agent r does a traversal of the graph and on each vertex c of C, the agent waits until there is a token on c.
(Step 3') The agent r puts a token on its homebase.
(Step 4') The agent r does a traversal of the graph and at each node $h \in H$, agent r waits until there is a token or there is a sleeping agent. Note that if node h is homebase of an active agent r', then agent r' will eventually complete Step 3' and thus there will be a token at h. Otherwise if h is the homebase of a passive agent r'' then agent r'' will eventually complete the previous procedure and return to its homebase to sleep.
(Step 5') The agent r goes to the node c that it marked in Step 1' and removes the token.
(Step 6') The agent r does a traversal of the network. Each time it arrives on a vertex c' of C, it waits until there is no token on c'.
(Step 7') The agent r removes the token from its homebase.
(Step 8') The agent r does a traversal of the graph and at each node $h \in H$, agent r waits until there is no token at h or there is a sleeping agent at h.

At the end of this procedure each active agent knows which homebases are still active. Hence the agent can relabel the passive homebases to obtain the new labelling μ (i.e. the class H is partitioned into two subclasses).

Refining the Vertex Labelling μ of (G, μ): During the algorithm, each agent keeps track of the labels assigned to the vertices of G by writing them in its local map. Since all active agents agree on the order of equivalence classes, they would agree on the label-assignment.

During each round, some class C_j is split into two sub-classes and vertices in the first subclass are assigned a new label (e.g. the smallest integer not yet used as a label). At the end of a round, the vertex set is repartitioned while respecting the labels assigned to the vertices and after the repartitioning the labelling is refined accordingly. If the new labelling is injective, the algorithm terminates; Otherwise the next round is started.

Correctness of the Algorithm: During our algorithm, the equivalence partitioning is refined in each round using two classes of distinct sizes. We consider now a configuration such that all equivalence classes have the same size. Let q be the maximum number appearing on a vertex of (G, μ); the vertices from G are labelled by numbers in $[0, q]$. Let $V_0, V_1, \ldots, V_q$ be the partition of $V(G)$ defined by μ, i.e., $v \in V_i$ if $\mu(v) = i$. For any distinct $i, j \in [0, q]$, since V_i and V_j are equivalence classes of (G, μ), all vertices in V_i (resp. V_j) have the same number $d_{(i,j)}$ (resp. $d_{(j,i)}$) of neighbors in V_j (resp. V_i). Since the number of edges in $G[V_i, V_j]$ is $|V_i|d_{(i,j)} = |V_j|d_{(j,i)}$ and since $|V_i| = |V_j|$, $d_{(i,j)} = d_{(j,i)}$ and thus $G[V_i, V_j]$ is regular. For any $i \in [0, q]$, since V_i is an equivalence class, $G[V_i]$ is vertex-transitive and thus d_i-regular for some d_i. From Gallai-Edmonds decomposition (see [15]), we know that any vertex-transitive graph of odd degree admits a perfect matching. Consequently, if d_i is odd, we know that $G[V_i]$ admits a perfect matching. Thus, from the characterization of Yamashita and Kameda [17] given in Theorem 1, and since we know that (G, χ_p) is symmetric-covering-minimal, we know that each V_i contains exactly one vertex. In other words, the labelling μ is injective. Thus, the algorithm succeeds in selecting a unique rendezvous location whenever (G, χ_p) is symmetric-covering-minimal.

5 Further Remarks

In this section we justify some of the assumption made in this paper. Based on Angluin's impossibility result [2] (see also [8]), we know that there does not exist any universal algorithm that solves rendezvous with detect. Thus, some prior knowledge about the environment is necessary. We assumed the knowledge of n, the size of the graph; However we can easily adapt our algorithm to use only a bound on the size of the graph instead.

Proposition 1. *If the agents initially know a tight bound $B \in [n, 2n-1]$ on the size of G, the agents can rendezvous in $(G, \mathcal{E}, p)$, or detect it is impossible. Further, if the agents initially know that $(Dir(G), \chi_p)$ is symmetric-covering-minimal then knowledge of an arbitrary bound $B \geq n$ on the size of G is sufficient to solve rendezvous in $(G, \mathcal{E}, p)$.*

Our algorithm presented in Section 4 requires two identical tokens per agent. Under the assumption that each agent knows only the size of G, but has no information on the number of agents, we show that two tokens (per agent) are necessary to solve **RVwA**. However, it remains open to determine if two tokens are still necessary when the agents know completely the environment $(G, \mathcal{E}, p)$.

Proposition 2. *There exists graphs G such that there is no algorithm using one token per agent such that for each distributed mobile environment $(G, \mathcal{E}, p)$, either the agents solve rendezvous in $(G, \mathcal{E}, p)$, or detect that it is impossible.*

Finally, we consider the cost of solving **RVwA** in terms of the number of moves made by the agents. Our algorithm requires an additional $O(n^2k)$ moves for solving rendezvous without common port numbering, compared to the solution for rendezvous with common port-numbering [12] using tokens.

References

1. Alpern, S., Gal, S.: The Theory of Search Games and Rendezvous. Kluwer, Dordrecht (2003)
2. Angluin, D.: Local and global properties in networks of processors. In: Proc. 12th Symposium on Theory of Computing (STOC 1980), pp. 82–93 (1980)
3. Boldi, P., Codenotti, B., Gemmell, P., Shammah, S., Simon, J., Vigna, S.: Symmetry breaking in anonymous networks: characterizations. In: Proc. 4th Israeli Symp. on Theory of Computing and Systems (ISTCS 1996), pp. 16–26 (1996)
4. Barrière, L., Flocchini, P., Fraigniaud, P., Santoro, N.: Can we elect if we cannot compare? In: Proc. 15th Symp. on Parallel Algorithms and Architectures (SPAA), pp. 324–332 (2003)
5. Baston, V., Gal, S.: Rendezvous search when marks are left at the starting points. Naval Research Logistics 48(8), 722–731 (2001)
6. Boldi, P., Vigna, S.: Fibrations of graphs. Discrete Mathematics 243(1-3), 21–66 (2002)
7. Chalopin, J., Godard, E., Métivier, Y., Ossamy, R.: Mobile agent algorithms versus message passing algorithms. In: Shvartsman, M.M.A.A. (ed.) OPODIS 2006. LNCS, vol. 4305, pp. 187–201. Springer, Heidelberg (2006)
8. Chalopin, J., Godard, E., Métivier, Y., Tel, G.: About the termination detection in the asynchronous message passing model. In: van Leeuwen, J., Italiano, G.F., van der Hoek, W., Meinel, C., Sack, H., Plášil, F. (eds.) SOFSEM 2007. LNCS, vol. 4362, pp. 200–211. Springer, Heidelberg (2007)
9. Chalopin, J.: Election and rendezvous with incomparable labels. Theoretical Computer Science 399(1-2), 54–70 (2008)
10. Czyzowicz, J., Labourel, A., Pelc, A.: How to meet asynchronously (almost) everywhere. In: Proc. ACM Symp. on Discrete Algorithms (SODA 2010), pp. 22–30 (2010)
11. Das, S., Flocchini, P., Nayak, A., Kutten, S., Santoro, N.: Map Construction of Unknown Graphs by Multiple Agents. Theoretical Computer Science 385(1-3), 34–48 (2007)
12. Das, S., Flocchini, P., Nayak, A., Santoro, N.: Effective elections for anonymous mobile agents. In: Asano, T. (ed.) ISAAC 2006. LNCS, vol. 4288, pp. 732–743. Springer, Heidelberg (2006)
13. Fraigniaud, P., Pelc, A.: Deterministic rendezvous in trees with little memory. In: Taubenfeld, G. (ed.) DISC 2008. LNCS, vol. 5218, pp. 242–256. Springer, Heidelberg (2008)
14. Klasing, R., Kosowski, A., Navarra, A.: Taking advantage of symmetries: Gathering of asynchronous oblivious robots on a ring. In: Baker, T.P., Bui, A., Tixeuil, S. (eds.) OPODIS 2008. LNCS, vol. 5401, pp. 446–462. Springer, Heidelberg (2008)
15. Lovász, L., Plummer, M.D.: Matching Theory. Annals of Discrete Mathematics, vol. 29. North-Holland, Amsterdam (1986)
16. Yamashita, M., Kameda, T.: Computing on anonymous networks: Part I - characterizing the solvable cases. IEEE Transactions on Parallel and Distributed Systems 7(1), 69–89 (1996)
17. Yamashita, M., Kameda, T.: Leader election problem on networks in which processor identity numbers are not distinct. IEEE Transactions on Parallel and Distributed Systems 10(9), 878–887 (1999)
18. Yu, X., Yung, M.: Agent rendezvous: A dynamic symmetry-breaking problem. In: Meyer auf der Heide, F., Monien, B. (eds.) ICALP 1996. LNCS, vol. 1099, pp. 610–621. Springer, Heidelberg (1996)

Probabilistic Automata on Finite Words: Decidable and Undecidable Problems

Hugo Gimbert[1] and Youssouf Oualhadj[2]

[1] LaBRI, CNRS, France
hugo.gimbert@labri.fr
[2] LaBRI, Université Bordeaux 1, France
youssouf.oualhadj@labri.fr

Abstract. This paper tackles three algorithmic problems for probabilistic automata on finite words: the Emptiness Problem, the Isolation Problem and the Value 1 Problem. The *Emptiness Problem* asks, given some probability $0 \leq \lambda \leq 1$, whether there exists a word accepted with probability greater than λ, and the *Isolation Problem* asks whether there exist words whose acceptance probability is arbitrarily close to λ. Both these problems are known to be undecidable [11,4,3]. About the Emptiness problem, we provide a new simple undecidability proof and prove that it is undecidable for automata with as few as two probabilistic transitions. The *Value* 1 *Problem* is the special case of the Isolation Problem when $\lambda = 1$ or $\lambda = 0$. The decidability of the Value 1 Problem was an open question. We show that the Value 1 Problem is undecidable. Moreover, we introduce a new class of probabilistic automata, $\sharp$-*acyclic automata*, for which the Value 1 Problem is decidable.

Introduction

Probabilistic automata on finite words are a computation model introduced by Rabin [12]. Like deterministic automata on finite words, a probabilistic automaton reads finite words from a finite alphabet A. Each time a new letter $a \in A$ is read, a transition from the current state $s \in Q$ to a new state $t \in Q$ occur. In a deterministic automaton, t is a function of s and a. In a probabilistic automaton, a lottery determines the new state, according to transition probabilities which depend on the current state s and letter a.

Since the seminal paper of Rabin, probabilistic automata on finite words have been extensively studied, see [6] for a survey of 416 papers and books about probabilistic automata published in the 60s and 70s.

Quite surprisingly, relatively few *algorithmic* results are known about probabilistic automata on finite words and almost all of them are undecidability results. There are two main algorithmic problems for probabilistic automata on finite words: the Emptiness Problem and the Isolation Problem. The *Emptiness Problem* asks, given some probability $0 \leq \lambda \leq 1$, whether there exists a word accepted with probability greater than λ, while the *Isolation Problem* asks whether there exist words whose acceptance probability is arbitrarily close

S. Abramsky et al. (Eds.): ICALP 2010, Part II, LNCS 6199, pp. 527–538, 2010.

to λ. Both these problems were shown undecidable, respectively by Paz [11] and Bertoni [4,3]. To our knowledge, most decidability results known for probabilistic automata on *finite* words are rather straightforward: they either apply to one-letter probabilistic automata, in other words Markov chains, or to problems where the probabilistic nature of the automaton is not taken into account. A notable exception is the decidability of language equality [13].

In contrast, several algorithmic results were proved for probabilistic automata on *infinite* words. The existence of an infinite word accepted with probability 1 is decidable [1]. For probabilistic Büchi automata [2], the emptiness problem may be decidable or not depending on the acceptance condition. A class of probabilistic Büchi automata which recognize exactly ω-regular languages was presented in [7]. In this paper, we only consider automata on finite words but several of our results seem to be extendable to probabilistic automata on infinite words.

Our contributions are the following.

First, we provide in Section 2.1 a new proof for the undecidability of the Emptiness Problem.

Second, we strengthen the result of Paz: the Emptiness Problem is undecidable even for automata with as few as two probabilistic transitions (Proposition 4).

Third, we solve an open problem: Bertoni's result shows that for any fixed cut-point $0 < \lambda < 1$, the Isolation Problem is undecidable. However, as stated by Bertoni himself, the proof seems hardly adaptable to the symmetric cases $\lambda = 0$ and $\lambda = 1$. We show that both these cases are undecidable as well, in other words the Value 1 Problem is undecidable (Theorem 4).

Fourth, we introduce a new class of probabilistic automata, *♯-acyclic automata*, for which the Value 1 Problem is decidable (Theorem 5 in Section 4). To our opinion, this is the main contribution of the paper. Moreover, this result is a first step towards the design of classes of stochastic games with partial observation for which the value 1 problem is decidable.

These undecidability results show once again that probabilistic automata are very different from deterministic and non-deterministic automata on finite or infinite words, for which many algorithmic problems are known to be decidable (e.g. emptiness, universality, equivalence). Surprisingly maybe, we remark that several natural decision problems about deterministic and non-deterministic automata are undecidable as well (Corollaries 1 and 2).

Due to space restrictions most proofs are omitted, a long version is available online.

1 Probabilistic Automata

A probability distribution on Q is a mapping $\delta \in [0,1]^Q$ such that $\sum_{s \in S} \delta(s) = 1$. The set $\{s \in Q \mid \delta(s) > 0\}$ is called the support of δ and denoted $\mathrm{Supp}(\delta)$. For every non-empty subset $S \subseteq Q$, we denote δ_S the uniform distribution on S defined by $\delta(q) = 0$ if $q \notin S$ and $\delta(q) = \frac{1}{|S|}$ if $q \in S$. We denote $\mathcal{D}(Q)$ the set of probability distributions on Q.

Formally, a probabilistic automaton is a tuple $\mathcal{A} = (Q, A, (M_a)_{a\in A}, q_0, F)$, where Q is a finite set of states, A is the finite input alphabet, $(M_a)_{a\in A}$ are the transition matrices, q_0 is the initial state and F is the set of accepting states. For each letter $a \in A$, $M_a \in [0,1]^{Q\times Q}$ defines transition probabilities: $0 \le M_a(s,t) \le 1$ is the probability to go from state s to state t when reading letter a. Of course, for every $s \in S$ and $a \in A$, $\sum_{t\in S} M_a(s,t) = 1$, in other word in the matrix M_a, the line with index s is a probability distribution on Q.

Transition matrices define a natural action of A^* on $\mathcal{D}(Q)$. For every word $a \in A$ and $\delta \in \mathcal{D}(S)$, we denote $\delta \cdot a$ the probability distribution in $\mathcal{D}(Q)$ defined by $(\delta \cdot a)(t) = \sum_{s\in Q} \delta(s) \cdot M_a(s,t)$. This action extends naturally to words of A^*: $\forall w \in A^*, \forall a \in A, \delta \cdot (wa) = (\delta \cdot w) \cdot a$.

The computation of $\mathcal{A}$ on an input word $w = a_0 \dots a_n \in A^*$ is the sequence $(\delta_0, \delta_1, \dots, \delta_n) \in \mathcal{D}(Q)^{n+1}$ of probability distributions over Q such that $\delta_0 = \delta_{\{q_0\}}$ and for $0 \le i < n, \delta_{i+1} = \delta_i \cdot a_i$.

For every state $q \in Q$ and for every set of states $R \subseteq Q$, we denote $\mathbb{P}_\mathcal{A}(q \xrightarrow{w} R) = \sum_{r\in R}(\delta_q \cdot w)(r)$ the probability to reach the set R from state q when reading the word w.

Definition 1 (Value and acceptance probability). *The* acceptance probability *of a word $w \in A^*$ by $\mathcal{A}$ is $\mathbb{P}_\mathcal{A}(w) = \mathbb{P}_\mathcal{A}(q_0 \xrightarrow{w} F)$. The* value *of $\mathcal{A}$, denoted $val(\mathcal{A})$, is the supremum acceptance probability: $val(\mathcal{A}) = \sup_{w\in A^*} \mathbb{P}_\mathcal{A}(w)$.*

2 The Emptiness Problem

Rabin defined the language recognized by a probabilistic automaton as $\mathcal{L}_\mathcal{A}(\lambda) = \{w \in A^* \mid \mathbb{P}_\mathcal{A}(w) \ge \lambda\}$, where $0 \le \lambda \le 1$ is called the cut-point. Hence, a canonical decision problem for probabilistic automata is:

Problem 1 (Emptiness Problem) *Given a probabilistic automaton $\mathcal{A}$ and $0 \le \lambda \le 1$, decide whether there exists a word w such that $\mathbb{P}_\mathcal{A}(w) \ge \lambda$.*

The *Strict Emptiness Problem* is defined the same way except the large inequality $\mathbb{P}_\mathcal{A}(w) \ge \lambda$ is replaced by a strict inequality $\mathbb{P}_\mathcal{A}(w) > \lambda$.

The special cases where $\lambda = 0$ and $\lambda = 1$ provide a link between probabilistic and non-deterministic automata on finite words. First, the Strict Emptiness Problem for $\lambda = 0$ reduces to the emptiness problem of non-deterministic automata, which is decidable in non-deterministic logarithmic space. Second, the Emptiness Problem for $\lambda = 1$ reduces to the universality problem for non-deterministic automata, which is PSPACE-complete [9]. The two other cases are trivial: the answer to the Emptiness Problem for $\lambda = 0$ is always yes and the answer to the Strict Emptiness Problem for $\lambda = 1$ is always no.

In the case where $0 < \lambda < 1$, both the Emptiness and the Strict Emptiness Problems are undecidable, which was proved by Paz [11]. The proof of Paz is a reduction from an undecidable problem about free context grammars. An alternative proof was given by Madani, Hanks and Condon [10], based on a reduction from the emptiness problem for two counter machines. Since Paz was focusing on expressiveness aspects of probabilistic automata rather than on algorithmic questions, his undecidability proof is spread on the whole book [11], which makes it arguably hard to read. The proof of Madani et al. is easier to read but quite long and technical.

In the next section, we present a new simple undecidability proof of the Emptiness Problem.

2.1 New Proof of Undecidability

In this section we show the undecidability of the (Strict) Emptiness Problem for the cut-point $\frac{1}{2}$ and for a restricted class of probabilistic automata called *simple* probabilistic automata:

Definition 2 (Simple automata). *A probabilistic automaton is called* simple *if every transition probability is in* $\{0, \frac{1}{2}, 1\}$.

The proof is based on a result of Bertoni [4]: the undecidability of the Equality Problem.

Problem 2 (Equality problem) *Given a simple probabilistic automaton* $\mathcal{A}$*, decide whether there exist a word* $w \in A^*$ *such that* $\mathbb{P}_{\mathcal{A}}(w) = \frac{1}{2}$.

Proposition 1 (Bertoni). *The equality problem is undecidable.*

The short and elegant proof of Bertoni is a reduction of the Post Correspondence Problem (PCP) to the Equality Problem.

Problem 3 (PCP) *Let* $\varphi_1 : A \to \{0,1\}^*$ *and* $\varphi_2 : A \to \{0,1\}^*$ *two functions, naturally extended to* A^*. *Is there a word* $w \in A^*$ *such that* $\varphi_1(w) = \varphi_2(w)$*?*

Roughly speaking, the proof of Proposition 1 consists in encoding the equality of two words in the decimals of transition probabilities of a well-chosen probabilistic automaton. While the reduction of PCP to the Equality problem is relatively well-known, it may be less known that there exists a simple reduction of the Equality problem to the Emptiness and Strict Emptiness problems:

Proposition 2. *Given a simple probabilistic automaton* $\mathcal{A}$*, one can compute probabilistic automata* $\mathcal{B}$ *and* $\mathcal{C}$ *whose transition probabilities are multiple of* $\frac{1}{4}$ *and such that:*

$$\left(\exists w \in A^+, \mathbb{P}_{\mathcal{A}}(w) = \frac{1}{2}\right) \iff \left(\exists w \in A^+, \mathbb{P}_{\mathcal{B}}(w) \geq \frac{1}{4}\right) \tag{1}$$

$$\iff \left(\exists w \in A^+, \mathbb{P}_{\mathcal{C}}(w) > \frac{1}{8}\right) . \tag{2}$$

Proof. The construction of $\mathcal{B}$ such that (1) holds is based on a very simple fact: a real number x is equal to $\frac{1}{2}$ if and only if $x(1-x) \geq \frac{1}{4}$. Consider the automaton $\mathcal{B}$ which is the cartesian product of $\mathcal{A}$ with a copy of $\mathcal{A}$ whose accepting states are the non accepting states of $\mathcal{A}$. Then for every word $w \in A^*$, $\mathbb{P}_{\mathcal{A}_1}(w) = \mathbb{P}_{\mathcal{A}}(w)(1 - \mathbb{P}_{\mathcal{A}}(w))$, thus (1) holds.

The construction of $\mathcal{C}$ such that (2) holds is based on the following idea. Since $\mathcal{A}$ is simple, transition probabilities of $\mathcal{B}$ are multiples of $\frac{1}{4}$, thus for every word w of length $|w|$, $\mathbb{P}_{\mathcal{B}}(w)$ is a multiple of $\frac{1}{4^{|w|}}$. As a consequence, $\mathbb{P}_{\mathcal{B}}(w) \geq \frac{1}{4}$ if and only if $\mathbb{P}_{\mathcal{B}}(w) > \frac{1}{4} - \frac{1}{4^{|w|}}$. Adding three states to $\mathcal{B}$, one obtains easily a probabilistic automaton $\mathcal{C}$ such that for every non-empty word $w \in A^*$ and letter $a \in A$, $\mathbb{P}_{\mathcal{C}}(aw) = \frac{1}{2} \cdot \mathbb{P}_{\mathcal{B}}(w) + \frac{1}{2} \cdot \frac{1}{4^{|w|}}$, thus (2) holds. To build $\mathcal{C}$, simply add a new initial state that goes with equal probability $\frac{1}{2}$ either to the initial state of $\mathcal{B}$ or to a new accepting state q_f. From q_f, whatever letter is read, next state is q_f with probability $\frac{1}{4}$ and with probability $\frac{3}{4}$ it is a new non-accepting absorbing sink state q_*. □

As a consequence:

Theorem 1 (Paz). *The emptiness and the strict emptiness problems are undecidable for probabilistic automata. These problems are undecidable even for simple probabilistic automata and cut-point* $\lambda = \frac{1}{2}$.

To conclude this section, we present another connection between probabilistic and non-probabilistic automata on finite words.

Corollary 1. *The following problem is undecidable. Given a* non-deterministic *automaton on finite words, does there exists a word such that at least half of the computations on this word are accepting?*

We do not know a simple undecidability proof for this problem which does not make of use of probabilistic automata.

2.2 Probabilistic Automata with Few Probabilistic Transitions

Hirvensalo [8] showed that the emptiness problem is undecidable for probabilistic automata which have as few as 2 input letters and 25 states, see also [5] for similar result about the isolation problem.

On the other hand, the emptiness problem is decidable for *deterministic* automata. This holds whatever the number of states, as long as there are no probabilistic transition in the automaton. Formally, a probabilistic transition is a couple (s, a) of a state $s \in S$ and a letter $a \in A$ such that for at least one state $t \in S$, $0 < M_a(s, t) < 1$.

This motivates the following question: *what is the minimal number of probabilistic transitions for which the emptiness problem is undecidable?*

The following undecidability result is a rather surprising answer:

Proposition 3. *The emptiness problem is undecidable for probabilistic automata with two probabilistic transitions.*

Moreover, a slight variant of the emptiness problem for probabilistic automata with *one* probabilistic transition is undecidable:

Proposition 4. *The following problem is undecidable: given a simple probabilistic automaton over an alphabet A with one probabilistic transition and given a rational language of finite words $L \subseteq A^*$, decide whether $\mathbb{P}_{\mathcal{A}}(w) \geq \frac{1}{2}$ for some word $w \in L$.*

For probabilistic automata with a unique probabilistic transition, we do not know whether the emptiness problem is decidable or not.

3 Undecidability of the Value 1 Problem

In his seminal paper about probabilistic automata [12], Rabin introduced the notion of *isolated cut-points.*

Definition 3. *A real number $0 \leq \lambda \leq 1$ is an isolated cut-point with respect to a probabilistic automaton $\mathcal{A}$ if:*

$$\exists \varepsilon > 0,\ \ \forall w \in A^*,\ \ |\mathbb{P}_{\mathcal{A}}(w) - \lambda| \geq \varepsilon\ .$$

Rabin motivates the introduction of this notion by the following theorem:

Theorem 2 (Rabin). *Let $\mathcal{A}$ a probabilistic automaton and $0 \leq \lambda \leq 1$ a cut-point. If λ is isolated then the language $\mathcal{L}_{\mathcal{A}}(\lambda) = \{u \in A^* \mid \mathbb{P}_{\mathcal{A}}(u) \geq \lambda\}$ is rational.*

This result suggests the following decision problem.

Problem 4 (Isolation Problem) *Given a probabilistic automaton $\mathcal{A}$ and a cut-point $0 \leq \lambda \leq 1$, decide whether λ is isolated with respect to $\mathcal{A}$.*

Bertoni [4] proved that the Isolation Problem is undecidable in general:

Theorem 3 (Bertoni). *The Isolation Problem is undecidable for probabilistic automata with five states.*

A closer look at the proof of Bertoni shows that the Isolation Problem is undecidable for a fixed λ, provided that $0 < \lambda < 1$.

However the same proof does not seem to be extendable to the cases $\lambda = 0$ and $\lambda = 1$. This was pointed out by Bertoni in the conclusion of [4]:

> "Is the following problem solvable: $\exists \delta > 0, \forall x, (p(x) > \delta)$? For automata with 1-symbol alphabet, there is a decision algorithm bound with the concept of transient state [11]. We believe it might be extended but have no proof for it".

The open question mentioned by Bertoni is the Isolation Problem for $\lambda = 0$. The case $\lambda = 1$ is essentially the same, since 0 is isolated in an automaton $\mathcal{A}$ if and only if 1 is isolated in the automaton obtained from $\mathcal{A}$ by turning final states into non-final states and vice-versa. When $\lambda = 1$, the Isolation Problem asks whether there exists some word accepted by the automaton with probability arbitrarily close to 1. We use the game-theoretic terminology and call this problem the Value 1 Problem.

The open question of Bertoni can be rephrased as the decidability of the following problem:

Problem 5 (Value 1 Problem) *Given a probabilistic automaton* $\mathcal{A}$*, decide whether* $\mathcal{A}$ *has value* 1.

Unfortunately,

Theorem 4. *The Value* 1 *Problem is undecidable.*

The proof of Theorem 4 is a reduction of the Strict Emptiness Problem to the Value 1 Problem. It is similar to the proof of undecidability of the Emptiness Problem for probabilistic Büchi automata of Baier et al. [2]. The core of the proof is the following proposition.

Proposition 5. *Let* $0 < x < 1$ *and* $\mathcal{A}_x$ *be the probabilistic automaton depicted on Fig. 1. Then* $\mathcal{A}_x$ *has value* 1 *if and only if* $x > \frac{1}{2}$.

The proof of Theorem 4 relies on the fact that there is a natural way to combine $\mathcal{A}_x$ with an arbitrary automaton $\mathcal{B}$ so that the resulting automaton has value 1 if and only if some word is accepted by $\mathcal{B}$ with probability strictly greater than $\frac{1}{2}$.

The value 1 problem for simple probabilistic automata can be straigntforwardly rephrased as a "quantitative" decision problem about non-deterministic automaton on finite words, which shows that:

Corollary 2. *This decision problem is undecidable: given a* non-deterministic *automaton on finite words, does there exists words such that the proportion of of non-accepting computation pathes among all computation pathes is arbitrarily small?*

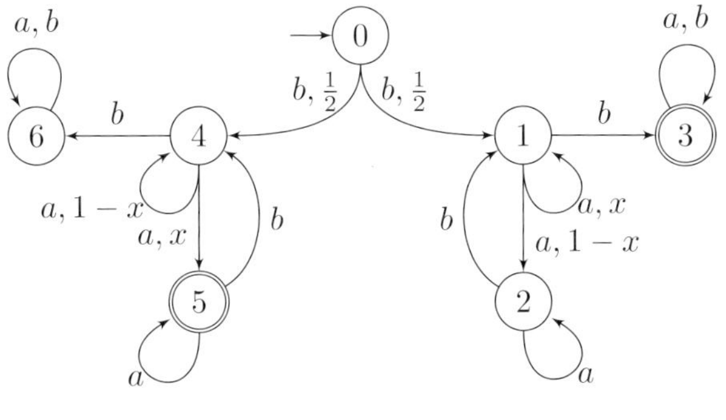

Fig. 1. This automaton has value 1 if and only if $x > \frac{1}{2}$

4 The Class of $\sharp$-acyclic Probabilistic Automata

In this section, we introduce a new class of probabilistic automata, $\sharp$-*acyclic probabilistic automata*, for which the value 1 problem is decidable.

To get a decision algorithm for the value 1 problem, our starting point is the usual subset construction for non-deterministic automata, defined by mean of the natural action of letters on subsets of Q. However the quantitative aspect of the Value 1 Problem stressed in Corollary 2 suggests that the subset construction needs to be customized. Precisely, we use not only the usual action $S \cdot a$ of a letter a on a subset $S \subseteq Q$ of states but consider also another action $a^\sharp$. Roughly speaking, $a^\sharp$ deletes states that are transient when reading letter a forever.

Definition 4 (Actions of letters and $\sharp$-reachability). *Let $\mathcal{A}$ a probabilistic automaton with alphabet A and set of states Q. Given $S \subseteq Q$ and $a \in A$, we denote:*

$$S \cdot a = \{t \in Q \mid \exists s \in S, M_a(s,t) > 0\} \ .$$

A state $t \in Q$ is a-reachable from $s \in Q$ if for some $n \in \mathbb{N}$, $\mathbb{P}_{\mathcal{A}}(s \xrightarrow{a^n} t) > 0$. A state $s \in Q$ is a-recurrent if for any state $t \in Q$,

$$(t \text{ is } a\text{-reachable from } s) \implies (s \text{ is } a\text{-reachable from } t) \ ,$$

in other words s is a-recurrent if it belongs to a bottom strongly connected component of the graph of states and a-transitions.

A set $S \subseteq Q$ is a-stable if $S = S \cdot a$. If S is a-stable, we denote:

$$S \cdot a^\sharp = \{s \in S \mid s \text{ is } a\text{-recurrent}\} \ .$$

The support graph *$\mathcal{G}_{\mathcal{A}}$ of a probabilistic automaton $\mathcal{A}$ with alphabet A and set of states Q is the directed graph whose vertices are the non-empty subsets of Q and whose edges are the pairs (S,T) such that for some letter $a \in A$, either $(S \cdot a = T)$ or $(S \cdot a = S$ and $S \cdot a^\sharp = T)$.*

Reachability in the support graph of $\mathcal{A}$ is called $\sharp$-reachability in $\mathcal{A}$.

The class of $\sharp$-acyclic probabilistic automata is defined as follows.

Definition 5 ($\sharp$-acyclic probabilistic automata). *A probabilistic automaton is* $\sharp$-acyclic *if the only cycles in its support graph are self-loops.*

Obviously, this acyclicity condition is quite strong. However, it does not forbid the existence of cycles in the transition table, see for example the automaton depicted on Fig. 2. Note also that the class of $\sharp$-acyclic automata enjoys good properties: it is closed under cartesian product and parallel composition.

4.1 The Value 1 Problem Is Decidable for $\sharp$-acyclic Automata

For $\sharp$-acyclic probabilistic automata, the value 1 problem is decidable:

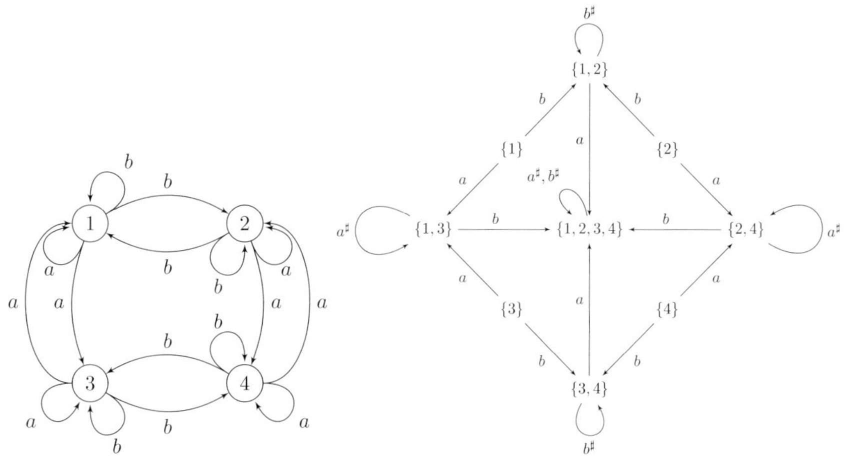

Fig. 2. A ♯-acyclic automaton (on the left) and its support graph (on the right). All transition probabilities are equal to $\frac{1}{2}$.

Theorem 5. *Let $\mathcal{A}$ be a probabilistic automaton with initial state q_0 and final states F. Suppose that $\mathcal{A}$ is ♯-acyclic . Then $\mathcal{A}$ has value 1 if and only if F is ♯-reachable from $\{q_0\}$ in $\mathcal{A}$.*

The support graph can be computed on-the-fly in polynomial space thus deciding whether a probabilistic automaton is ♯-acyclic and whether an ♯-acyclic automaton has value 1 are PSPACE decision problems.

The rest of this section is dedicated to the proof of Theorem 5. This proof relies on the notion of limit-paths.

Definition 6 (Limit paths and limit-reachability). *Let $\mathcal{A}$ be a probabilistic automaton with states Q and alphabet A. Given two subsets S, T of Q, we say that T is limit-reachable from S in $\mathcal{A}$ if there exists a sequence $w_0, w_1, w_2, \ldots \in A^*$ of finite words such that for every state $s \in S$:*

$$\mathbb{P}_{\mathcal{A}}(s \xrightarrow{w_n} T) \xrightarrow[n\to\infty]{} 1 \ .$$

The sequence $w_0, w_1, w_2, \ldots$ is called a limit path *from S to T, and T is said to be limit-reachable from S in $\mathcal{A}$.*

In particular, an automaton has value 1 is and only if F is limit-reachable from $\{q_0\}$.

To prove Theorem 5, we show that in ♯-acyclic automata, ♯-reachability and limit-reachability coincide. The following proposition shows that ♯-reachability always implies limit-reachability, may the automaton be ♯-acyclic or not.

Proposition 6. *Let $\mathcal{A}$ be a probabilistic automaton with states Q and $S, T \subseteq Q$. If T is ♯-reachable from S in $\mathcal{A}$ then T is limit-reachable from S in $\mathcal{A}$.*

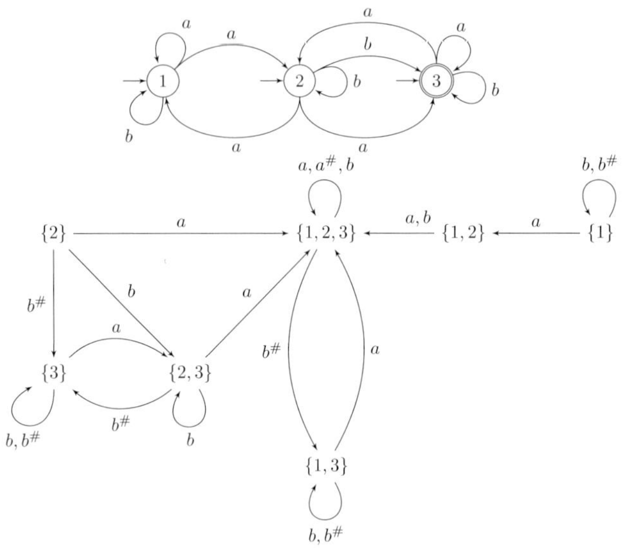

Fig. 3. This automaton has value 1 and is not ♯-acyclic

The converse implication is not true in general. For example, consider the automaton depicted on Fig. 3. There is only one final state, state 3. The initial state is not represented, it leads with equal probability to states 1, 2 and 3. The transitions from states 1, 2 and 3 are either deterministic or have probability $\frac{1}{2}$.

It turns out that the automaton on Fig. 3 has value 1, because $((b^n a)^n)_{n \in \mathbb{N}}$ is a limit-path from $\{1,2,3\}$ to $\{3\}$. However, $\{3\}$ is *not* reachable from $\{1,2,3\}$ in the support graph. Thus, limit-reachability does not imply ♯-reachability in general. This automaton is *not* ♯-acyclic , because his support graph contains a cycle of length 2 between $\{1,2,3\}$ and $\{1,3\}$. It is quite tempting to add an edge labelled $(ab^\sharp)^\sharp$ between $\{1,3\}$ and $\{3\}$.

Now we prove that for ♯-acyclic automata, limit-reachability implies ♯-reachability.

Definition 7 (Stability and ♯-stability). *Let $\mathcal{A}$ be a probabilistic automaton with states Q. The automaton $\mathcal{A}$ is* stable *if for every letter $a \in A$, Q is a-stable. A stable automaton $\mathcal{A}$ is* ♯-stable *if for every letter $a \in A$ $Q \cdot a^\sharp = Q$.*

The proof relies on the three following lemmata.

Lemma 1 (Blowing lemma). *Let $\mathcal{A}$ be a ♯-acyclic probabilistic automaton with states Q and $S \subseteq Q$. Suppose that $\mathcal{A}$ is ♯-acyclic and ♯-stable. If Q is limit-reachable from S in $\mathcal{A}$, then Q is ♯-reachable from S as well.*

Proof (of the blowing lemma). If $S = Q$ there is nothing to prove. If $S \neq Q$, we prove that there exists $S_1 \subseteq Q$ such that (i) S_1 is ♯-reachable from S, (ii) $S \subsetneq S_1$, and (iii) Q is limit-reachable from S_1. Since $S \subsetneq Q$ and since there exists a limit-path from S to Q there exists at least one letter a such that S is not a-stable, i.e. $S \cdot a \not\subseteq S$. Since $\mathcal{A}$ is $\sharp$-acyclic , there exists $n \in \mathbb{N}$ such that $S \cdot a^{n+1} = S \cdot a^n$ i.e. $S \cdot a^n$ is a-stable. We choose $S_1 = (S \cdot a^n) \cdot a^\sharp$ and prove (i),(ii) and (iii) First, (i) is obvious.

To prove (ii), we prove that S_1 contains both S and $S \cdot a$. Let $s \in S$. By definition, every state t of $S \cdot a^n$ is a-accessible from s. Since $\mathcal{A}$ is $\sharp$-stable, state s is a-recurrent and by definition of a-recurrence, s is a-accessible from t. Since $t \in S \cdot a^n$ and $S \cdot a^n$ is a-stable, $s \in S \cdot a^n$ and since s is a-recurrent $s \in (S \cdot a^n) \cdot a^\sharp = S_1$. The proof that $S \cdot a \subseteq S_1$ is similar.

If $S_1 = Q$ the proof is complete, because (i) holds. If $S_1 \subsetneq Q$, then (iii) holds because $S \subseteq S_1$ thus Q is limit-reachable not only from S but from S_1 as well, using the same limit-path. As long as $S_n \neq Q$, we use (iii) to build inductively an increasing sequence $S \subsetneq S_1 \subsetneq S_2 \subsetneq \ldots \subsetneq S_n = Q$ such that for every $1 \leq k < n$, S_{k+1} is $\sharp$-reachable from S_k. Since $\sharp$-reachability is transitive this completes the proof of the blowing lemma. □

Next lemma shows that in a $\sharp$-stable and $\sharp$-acyclic automata, once a computation has flooded the whole state space, it cannot shrink back.

Lemma 2 (Flooding lemma). *Let $\mathcal{A}$ be a probabilistic automaton with states Q. Suppose that $\mathcal{A}$ is $\sharp$-acyclic and $\sharp$-stable. Then Q is the only set of states limit-reachable from Q in $\mathcal{A}$.*

Now, we turn our attention to leaves of the acyclic support graph.

Definition 8. *Let $\mathcal{A}$ be a probabilistic automaton with states Q. A non-empty subset $R \subseteq Q$ is called a leaf if for every letter $a \in A$, $R \cdot a = R$ and $R \cdot a^\sharp = R$.*

In a stable $\sharp$-acyclic automaton, there is a unique leaf:

Lemma 3 (Leaf lemma). *Let $\mathcal{A}$ be a probabilistic automaton with states Q. Suppose that $\mathcal{A}$ is $\sharp$-acyclic .Then there exists a unique leaf $\sharp$-accessible from Q. Every set limit-reachable from Q contains this leaf.*

To prove that limit-reachability implies $\sharp$-reachability, we proceed by induction on the depth in the support graph. The inductive step is:

Lemma 4 (Inductive step). *Let $\mathcal{A}$ be a probabilistic automaton with states Q and $S_0, T \subseteq Q$. Suppose that $\mathcal{A}$ is $\sharp$-acyclic and T is limit-reachable from S_0. Then either $S_0 = T$ or there exists $S_1 \neq S_0$ such that S_1 is $\sharp$-reachable from S_0 in $\mathcal{A}$ and T is limit-reachable from S_1 in $\mathcal{A}$.*

Repeated use of Lemma 4 gives:

Proposition 7. *Let $\mathcal{A}$ be a probabilistic automaton with states Q and $S_0, T \subseteq Q$. Suppose that $\mathcal{A}$ is $\sharp$-acyclic. If T is limit-reachable from S_0 in $\mathcal{A}$, then T is $\sharp$-reachable from S_0 as well.*

Thus, limit-reachability and $\sharp$-reachability coincide in $\sharp$-acyclic automata and Theorem 5 holds.

Is the maximal distance between two $\sharp$-reachable sets in the support graph bounded by a polynomial function of $|A|$ and $|Q|$? The answer to this question could lead to a simpler proof and/or algorithm.

Conclusion. Whether the emptiness problem is decidable for probabilistic automata with a unique probabilistic transition is an open question.

The class of ♯-acyclic automata can be probably extended to a larger class of automata for which the value 1 problem is still decidable.

Acknowledgments. We thank the anonymous referees as well as A. Muscholl and I. Walukiewicz for finding a flaw in the previous version of this manuscript. We thank Benedikt Bollig for his valuable comments during the final preparation of this manuscript.

References

1. Alur, R., Courcoubetis, C., Yannakakis, M.: Distinguishing tests for nondeterministic and probabilistic machines. In: STOC, pp. 363–372. ACM, New York (1995)
2. Baier, C., Bertrand, N., Größer, M.: On decision problems for probabilistic büchi automata. In: Amadio, R.M. (ed.) FOSSACS 2008. LNCS, vol. 4962, pp. 287–301. Springer, Heidelberg (2008)
3. Bertoni, A., Mauri, G., Torelli, M.: Some recursive unsolvable problems relating to isolated cutpoints in probabilistic automata. In: Salomaa, A., Steinby, M. (eds.) ICALP 1977. LNCS, vol. 52, pp. 87–94. Springer, Heidelberg (1977)
4. Bertoni, A.: The solution of problems relative to probabilistic automata in the frame of the formal languages theory. In: Siefkes, D. (ed.) GI 1974. LNCS, vol. 26, pp. 107–112. Springer, Heidelberg (1975)
5. Blondel, V., Canterini, V.: Undecidable problems for probabilistic automata of fixed dimension. Theory of Computing Systems 36, 231–245 (2003)
6. Bukharaev, R.G.: Probabilistic automata. Journal of Mathematical Sciences 13(3), 359–386 (1980)
7. Chadha, R., Prasad Sistla, A., Viswanathan, M.: Power of randomization in automata on infinite strings. In: Bravetti, M., Zavattaro, G. (eds.) CONCUR 2009. LNCS, vol. 5710, pp. 229–243. Springer, Heidelberg (2009)
8. Hirvensalo, M.: Improved undecidability results on the emptiness problem of probabilistic and quantum cut-point languages. In: van Leeuwen, J., Italiano, G.F., van der Hoek, W., Meinel, C., Sack, H., Plášil, F. (eds.) SOFSEM 2007. LNCS, vol. 4362, pp. 309–319. Springer, Heidelberg (2007)
9. Kozen, D.: Lower bounds for natural proofs systems. In: Proc. of 18th Symp. Foundations of Comp. Sci., pp. 254–266 (1977)
10. Madani, O., Hanks, S., Condon, A.: On the undecidability of probabilistic planning and related stochastic optimization problems. Artificial Intelligence 147, 5–34 (2003)
11. Paz, A.: Introduction to probabilistic automata (Computer science and applied mathematics). Academic Press, Inc., Orlando (1971)
12. Rabin, M.O.: Probabilistic automata. Information and Control 6(3), 230–245 (1963)
13. Tzeng, W.-G.: A polynomial-time algorithm for the equivalence of probabilistic automata. SIAM J. Comput. 21(2), 216–227 (1992)

Space-Efficient Scheduling of Stochastically Generated Tasks

Tomáš Brázdil[1,⋆], Javier Esparza[2], Stefan Kiefer[3,⋆⋆], and Michael Luttenberger[2]

[1] Faculty of Informatics, Masaryk University, Brno, Czech Republic
[2] Institut für Informatik, Technische Universität München, Germany
[3] Oxford University Computing Laboratory, UK

Abstract. We study the problem of scheduling tasks for execution by a processor when the tasks can stochastically generate new tasks. Tasks can be of different types, and each type has a fixed, known probability of generating other tasks. We present results on the random variable S^σ modeling the maximal space needed by the processor to store the currently active tasks when acting under the scheduler σ. We obtain tail bounds for the distribution of S^σ for both offline and online schedulers, and investigate the expected value $\mathbb{E}[S^\sigma]$.

1 Introduction

We study the problem of scheduling tasks that can stochastically generate new tasks. We assume that the execution of a task τ can generate a set of subtasks. Tasks can be of different types, and each type has a fixed, known probability of generating new subtasks. Systems of tasks can be described using a notation similar to that of stochastic grammars. For instance

$$X \xhookrightarrow{0.2} \langle X, X\rangle \qquad X \xhookrightarrow{0.3} \langle X, Y\rangle \qquad X \xhookrightarrow{0.5} \emptyset \qquad Y \xhookrightarrow{0.7} \langle X\rangle \qquad Y \xhookrightarrow{0.3} \langle Y\rangle$$

describes a system with two types of tasks. Tasks of type X can generate 2 tasks of type X, one task of each type, or zero tasks with probabilities 0.2, 0.3, and 0.5, respectively (angular brackets denote multisets). Tasks of type Y can generate one task, of type X or Y, with probability 0.7 and 0.3. Tasks are executed by one processor. The processor repeatedly selects a task from a pool of unprocessed tasks, processes it, and puts the generated subtasks (if any) back into the pool. The pool initially contains one task of type X_0, and the next task to be processed is selected by a *scheduler*.

We study random variables modeling the time and space needed to *completely* execute a task τ, i.e., to empty the pool of unprocessed tasks assuming that initially the pool only contains task τ. We assume that processing a task takes one time unit, and storing it in the pool takes a unit of memory. So the *completion time* is given by the total number of tasks processed, and the *completion space* by the maximum size reached by the pool during the computation. The completion time has been studied in [13], and so the bulk of the paper is devoted to studying the distribution of the completion space for different classes of schedulers.

⋆ Supported by Czech Science Foundation, grant No. P202/10/1469.
⋆⋆ Supported by the EPSRC project *Automated Verification of Probabilistic Programs*.

S. Abramsky et al. (Eds.): ICALP 2010, Part II, LNCS 6199, pp. 539–550, 2010.

Our computational model is abstract, but relevant for different scenarios. In the context of search problems, a task is a problem instance, and the scheduler is part of a branch-and-bound algorithm (see e.g. [18]). In the more general context of multithreaded computations, a task models a thread, which may generate new threads. The problem of scheduling multithreaded computations space-efficiently on *multi*processor machines has been extensively studied (see e.g. [21,6,2,1]). These papers assume that schedulers know nothing about the program, while we consider the case in which stochastic information on the program behaviour is available (obtained from sampling).

We study the performance of *online* schedulers that know only the past of the computation, and compare them with the *optimal offline* scheduler, which has complete information about the future. Intuitively, this scheduler has access to an oracle that knows how the stochastic choices will be resolved. The oracle can be replaced by a machine that inspects the code of a task and determines which subtasks it will generate (if any).

We consider task systems with completion probability 1, which can be further divided into those with finite and infinite expected completion time, often called *subcritical* and *critical*. Many of our results are related to the probability generating functions (pgfs) associated to a task system. The functions for the example above are $f_X(x, y) = 0.2x^2 + 0.3xy + 0.5$ and $f_Y(x, y) = 0.7x + 0.3y$, and the reader can easily guess the formal definition. The completion probability is the least fixed point of the system of pgfs [17].

Our first results (Section 3) concern the distribution of the completion space S^{op} of the optimal offline scheduler op on a fixed but arbitrary task system with $\boldsymbol{f}(\boldsymbol{x})$ as pgfs (in vector form). We exhibit a very surprising connection between the probabilities $\Pr[S^{op} = k]$ and the *Newton approximants* to the least fixed point of $\boldsymbol{f}(\boldsymbol{x})$ (the approximations to the least fixed point obtained by applying Newton's method for approximating a zero of a differentiable function to $\boldsymbol{f}(\boldsymbol{x}) - \boldsymbol{x} = \mathbf{0}$ with seed $\mathbf{0}$). This connection allows us to apply recent results on the convergence speed of Newton's method [19,12], leading to tail bounds of S^{op}, i.e., bounds on $\Pr[S^{op} \geq k]$. We then study (Section 4) the distribution of S^{σ} for an online scheduler σ, and obtain upper and lower bounds for the performance of *any* online scheduler in subcritical systems. These bounds suggest a way of assigning weights to task types reflecting how likely they are to require large space. We study *light-first* schedulers, in which "light" tasks are chosen before "heavy" tasks with larger components, and obtain an improved tail bound.

So far we have assumed that there are no dependencies between tasks, requiring a task to be executed before another. We study in Section 4.3 the case in which a task can only terminate after all the tasks it has (recursively) spawned have terminated. These are the *strict* computations studied in [6]. The optimal scheduler in this case is the *depth-first* scheduler, i.e., the one that completely executes the child task before its parent, resulting in the familiar stack-based execution. Under this scheduler our tasks are equivalent to special classes of recursive state machines [15] and probabilistic pushdown automata [14]. We determine the exact asymptotic performance of depth-first schedulers, hereby making use of recent results [8].

We restrict ourselves to the case in which a task has at most two children, i.e., all rules $X \overset{p}{\hookrightarrow} \langle X_1, \ldots, X_n \rangle$ satisfy $n \leq 2$. This case already allows to model the forking-mechanism underlying many multithreaded operating systems, e.g. Unix-like systems.

Related work. Space-efficient scheduling for search problems or multithreaded computations has been studied in [18,21,6,2,1]. These papers assume that nothing is known about the program generating the computations. We study the case in which statistical information is available on the probability that computations split or die. The theory of *branching processes* studies stochastic processes modeling populations whose members can reproduce or die [17,4]. In computer science terminology, all existing work on branching processes assumes that the number of processors is *unbounded* [3,7,20,22,24,26]. To our knowledge, we are the first to study the 1-processor case.

Structure of the paper. The rest of the paper is structured as follows. The preliminaries in Section 2 formalize the notions from the introduction and summarize known results on which we build. In Section 3 we study optimal offline schedulers. Section 4 is dedicated to online schedulers. First we prove performance bounds that hold uniformly for all online schedulers, then we prove improved bounds for light-first schedulers, and finally we determine the exact asymptotic behaviour of depth-first schedulers. In Section 5 we obtain several results on the expected space consumption under different schedulers. Section 6 contains some conclusions. Full proofs can be found in [9].

2 Preliminaries

Let A be a finite set. We regard elements of $\mathbb{N}^A$ and $\mathbb{R}^A$ as *vectors* and use boldface (like $\boldsymbol{u}, \boldsymbol{v}$) to denote vectors. The vector whose components are all 0 (resp. 1) is denoted by $\mathbf{0}$ (resp. $\mathbf{1}$). We use angular brackets to denote multisets and often identify multisets over A and vectors indexed by A. For instance, if $A = \{X, Y\}$ and $\boldsymbol{v} \in \mathbb{N}^A$ with $\boldsymbol{v}_X = 1$ and $\boldsymbol{v}_Y = 2$, then $\boldsymbol{v} = \langle X, Y, Y\rangle$. We often shorten $\langle a\rangle$ to a. $M_A^{\leq 2}$ denotes the multisets over A containing at most 2 elements.

Definition 2.1. *A* task system *is a tuple* $\Delta = (\Gamma, \hookrightarrow, Prob, X_0)$ *where* Γ *is a finite set of* task types, $\hookrightarrow \subseteq \Gamma \times M_\Gamma^{\leq 2}$ *is a set of* transition rules, *Prob is a function assigning positive probabilities to transition rules so that for every* $X \in \Gamma$ *we have* $\sum_{X \hookrightarrow \alpha} Prob((X, \alpha)) = 1$, *and* $X_0 \in \Gamma$ *is the* initial type.

We write $X \overset{p}{\hookrightarrow} \alpha$ whenever $X \hookrightarrow \alpha$ and $Prob((X, \alpha)) = p$. Executions of a task system are modeled as family trees, defined as follows. Fix an arbitrary total order $\preceq$ on Γ. A *family tree* t is a pair (N, L) where $N \subseteq \{0,1\}^*$ is a finite binary tree (i.e. a prefix-closed finite set of words over $\{0,1\}$) and $L : N \hookrightarrow \Gamma$ is a labelling such that every node $w \in N$ satisfies one of the following conditions: w is a leaf and $L(w) \hookrightarrow \varepsilon$, or w has a unique child $w0$, and $L(w)$ satisfies $L(w) \hookrightarrow L(w0)$, or w has two children $w0$ and $w1$, and $L(w0), L(w1)$ satisfy $L(w) \hookrightarrow \langle L(w0), L(w1)\rangle$ and $L(w0) \preceq L(w1)$. Given a node $w \in N$, the subtree of t rooted at w, denoted by t_w, is the family tree (N', L') such that $w' \in N'$ iff $ww' \in N$ and $L'(w') = L(ww')$ for every $w' \in N'$. If a tree t has a subtree t_0 or t_1, we call this subtree a *child* of t. (So, the term *child* can refer to a node or a tree, but there will be no confusion.)

We define a function Pr which, loosely speaking, assigns to a family tree $t = (N, L)$ its probability (see the assumption below). Assume that the root of t is labeled by X. If t consists only of the root, and $X \overset{p}{\hookrightarrow} \varepsilon$, then $\Pr[t] = p$; if the root has only one child (the

$$X \xhookrightarrow{0.25} \langle Y, Z\rangle \qquad Y \xhookrightarrow{0.1} \langle X, Z\rangle \qquad Z \xhookrightarrow{0.4} \langle Y\rangle$$
$$X \xhookrightarrow{0.75} \emptyset \qquad Y \xhookrightarrow{0.9} \emptyset \qquad Z \xhookrightarrow{0.6} \emptyset$$

(a)

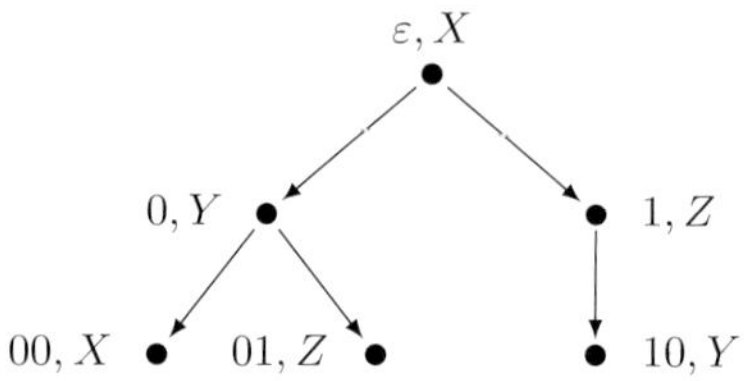

(b)

Fig. 1. (a) A task system. (b) A family tree.

node 0) labeled by Y, and $X \xhookrightarrow{p} Y$, then $\mathrm{Pr}[t] = p \cdot \mathrm{Pr}[t_0]$; if the root has two children (the nodes 0 and 1) labeled by Y and Z, and $X \xhookrightarrow{p} \langle Y, Z\rangle$, then $\mathrm{Pr}[t] = p \cdot \mathrm{Pr}[t_0] \cdot \mathrm{Pr}[t_1]$. We denote by $\mathcal{T}_X$ the set of all family trees whose root is labeled by X, and by Pr_X the restriction of Pr to $\mathcal{T}_X$. We drop the subscript of Pr_X if X is understood.

Example 2.2. Figure 1 shows (a) a task system with $\Gamma = \{X, Y, Z\}$; and (b) a family tree t of the system with probability $\mathrm{Pr}[t] = 0.25 \cdot 0.1 \cdot 0.75 \cdot 0.6 \cdot 0.4 \cdot 0.9$. The name and label of a node are written close to it.

Assumptions. Throughout the paper we assume that a task system $\Delta = (\Gamma, \hookrightarrow, \mathit{Prob}, X_0)$ satisfies the following two conditions for every type $X \in \Gamma$: (1) X is *reachable* from X_0, meaning that some tree in $\mathcal{T}_{X_0}$ contains a node labeled by X, and (2) $\mathrm{Pr}[\mathcal{T}_X] = \sum_{t \in \mathcal{T}_X} \mathrm{Pr}[t] = 1$. So we assume that $(\mathcal{T}_X, \mathrm{Pr}_X)$ is a discrete probability space with $\mathcal{T}_X$ as set of elementary events and Pr_X as probability function. This is the formal counterpart to assuming that every task is completed with probability 1.

Proposition 2.3. *It can be decided in polynomial time whether assumptions (1) and (2) are satisfied.*

Proof. (1) is trivial. For (2) let the *probability generating function* (pgf) of the task system be defined as the function $\boldsymbol{f} : \mathbb{R}^\Gamma \to \mathbb{R}^\Gamma$ of Δ where for every $X \in \Gamma$

$$\boldsymbol{f}_X(\boldsymbol{v}) = \sum_{X \xhookrightarrow{p} \langle Y, Z\rangle} p \cdot \boldsymbol{v}_Y \cdot \boldsymbol{v}_Z + \sum_{X \xhookrightarrow{p} \langle Y\rangle} p \cdot \boldsymbol{v}_Y + \sum_{X \xhookrightarrow{p} \emptyset} p \,.$$

It is well known (see e.g. [17]) that (2) holds iff the least nonnegative fixed point of $\boldsymbol{f}$ equals $\mathbf{1}$, which is decidable in polynomial time [15]. □

Derivations and schedulers. Let $t = (N, L)$ be a family tree. A *state* of t is a maximal subset of N in which no node is a proper prefix of another node (graphically, no node is a proper descendant of another node). The elements of a state are called *tasks*. If s is a state and $w \in s$, then the *w-successor of s* is the uniquely determined state s' defined as follows: if w is a leaf of N, then $s' = s \setminus \{w\}$; if w has one child $w0$, then $s' = (s \setminus \{w\}) \cup \{w0\}$; if w has two children $w0$ and $w1$, then $s' = (s \setminus \{w\}) \cup \{w0, w1\}$. We write $s \Rightarrow s'$ if s' is the w-successor of s for some w. A *derivation of t* is a sequence $s_1 \Rightarrow \ldots \Rightarrow s_k$ of states such that $s_1 = \{\epsilon\}$ and $s_k = \emptyset$. A *scheduler* is a mapping σ that assigns to a family tree t a derivation $\sigma(t)$ of t. If $\sigma(t) = (s_1 \Rightarrow \ldots \Rightarrow s_k)$, then for every $1 \leq i < k$ we denote by $\sigma(t)[i]$ a task of s_i such that s_{i+1} is the $\sigma(t)[i]$-successor of s_i. Intuitively, $\sigma(t)[i]$ is the task of s_i scheduled by σ. This definition allows for schedulers that know the tree, and so how future tasks will behave. In Section 4 we define and study online schedulers which only know the past of the computation. Notice that schedulers are deterministic (non-randomized).

Example 2.4. A scheduler σ_1 may schedule the tree t in Figure 1 as follows: $\{\varepsilon\} \Rightarrow \{0,1\} \Rightarrow \{0,10\} \Rightarrow \{0\} \Rightarrow \{00,01\} \Rightarrow \{01\} \Rightarrow \{\}$. Let σ_2 be the scheduler which always picks the least unprocessed task w.r.t. the lexicographical order on $\{0,1\}^*$. (This is an example of an online scheduler.) It schedules t as follows: $\{\varepsilon\} \Rightarrow \{0,1\} \Rightarrow \{00,01,1\} \Rightarrow \{01,1\} \Rightarrow \{1\} \Rightarrow \{10\} \Rightarrow \{\}$.

Time and space. Given $X \in \Gamma$, we define a random variable T_X, the *completion time of* X, that assigns to a tree $t \in \mathcal{T}_X$ its number of nodes. Assuming that tasks are executed for one time unit before its generated subtasks are returned to the pool, T_X corresponds to the time required to completely execute X. Our assumption (2) guarantees that T_X is finite with probability 1, but its expectation $\mathbb{E}[T_X]$ may or may not be finite. A task system Δ is called *subcritical* if $\mathbb{E}[T_X]$ is finite for every $X \in \Gamma$. Otherwise it is called *critical*. If Δ is subcritical, then $\mathbb{E}[T_X]$ can be easily computed by solving a system of linear equations [13]. The notion of criticality comes from the theory of branching processes, see e.g. [17,4]. Here we only recall the following results:

Proposition 2.5 ([17,15]). *Let Δ be a task system with pgf $\boldsymbol{f}$. Denote by $\boldsymbol{f}'(\mathbf{1})$ the Jacobian matrix of partial derivatives of $\boldsymbol{f}$ evaluated at* $\mathbf{1}$. *If Δ is critical, then the spectral radius of $\boldsymbol{f}'(\mathbf{1})$ is equal to* 1; *otherwise it is strictly less than* 1. *It can be decided in polynomial time whether Δ is critical.*

A state models a pool of tasks awaiting to be scheduled. We are interested in the maximal size of the pool during the execution of a derivation. So we define the random *completion space* S_X^σ as follows. If $\sigma(t) = (s_1 \Rightarrow \ldots \Rightarrow s_k)$, then $S_X^\sigma(t) := \max\{|s_1|, \ldots, |s_k|\}$, where $|s_i|$ is the cardinality of s_i. Sometimes we write $S^\sigma(t)$, meaning $S_X^\sigma(t)$ for the type X labelling the root of t. If we write S^σ without specifying the application to any tree, then we mean $S_{X_0}^\sigma$.

Example 2.6. For the schedulers of Example 2.4 we have $S^{\sigma_1}(t) = 2$ and $S^{\sigma_2}(t) = 3$.

3 Optimal (Offline) Schedulers

Let S^{op} be the random variable that assigns to a family tree the minimal completion space of its derivations. We call $S^{op}(t)$ the *optimal completion space* of t. The optimal scheduler assigns to each tree a derivation with optimal completion space. In the multithreading scenario, it corresponds to a scheduler that can inspect the code of a thread and decide whether it will spawn a new thread or not. Note that, although the optimal scheduler "knows" how the stochastic choices are resolved, the optimal completion space $S^{op}(t)$ is still a random variable, because it depends on a random tree. The following proposition characterizes the optimal completion space of a tree in terms of the optimal completion space of its children.

Proposition 3.1. *Let t be a family tree. Then*

$$S^{op}(t) = \begin{cases} \min \left\{ \begin{array}{l} \max\{S^{op}(t_0)+1, S^{op}(t_1)\}, \\ \max\{S^{op}(t_0), S^{op}(t_1)+1\} \end{array} \right\} & \text{if } t \text{ has two children } t_0,\, t_1 \\ S^{op}(t_0) & \text{if } t \text{ has exactly one child } t_0 \\ 1 & \text{if } t \text{ has no children.} \end{cases}$$

Proof sketch. The only nontrivial case is when t has two children t_0 and t_1. Consider the following schedulings for t, where $i \in \{0,1\}$: Execute first all tasks of t_i and then all tasks of t_{1-i}; within both t_i and t_{1-i}, execute tasks in optimal order. While executing t_i, the root task of t_{1-i} remains in the pool, and so the completion space is $s(i) = \max\{S^{op}(t_i)+1, S^{op}(t_{1-i})\}$. The optimal scheduler chooses the value of i that minimizes $s(i)$. □

Given a type X, we are interested in the probabilities $\Pr[S_X^{op} \le k]$ for $k \ge 1$. Proposition 3.1 yields a recurrence relation which at first sight seems difficult to handle. However, using results of [11,10] we can exhibit a surprising connection between these probabilities and the pgf $\boldsymbol{f}$.

Let $\boldsymbol{\mu}$ denote the least fixed point of $\boldsymbol{f}$ and recall from the proof of Proposition 2.3 that $\boldsymbol{\mu} = \mathbf{1}$. Clearly, $\mathbf{1}$ is a zero of $\boldsymbol{f}(\boldsymbol{x}) - \boldsymbol{x}$. It has recently been shown that $\boldsymbol{\mu}$ can be computed by applying to $\boldsymbol{f}(\boldsymbol{x}) - \boldsymbol{x}$ Newton's method for approximating a zero of a differentiable function [15,19]. More precisely, $\boldsymbol{\mu} = \lim_{k\to\infty} \boldsymbol{\nu}^{(k)}$ where

$$\boldsymbol{\nu}^{(0)} = \mathbf{0} \quad \text{and} \quad \boldsymbol{\nu}^{(k+1)} = \boldsymbol{\nu}^{(k)} + (I - \boldsymbol{f}'(\boldsymbol{\nu}^{(k)}))^{-1} \left(\boldsymbol{f}(\boldsymbol{\nu}^{(k)}) - \boldsymbol{\nu}^{(k)} \right)$$

and $\boldsymbol{f}'(\boldsymbol{\nu}^{(k)})$ denotes the Jacobian matrix of partial derivatives of $\boldsymbol{f}$ evaluated at $\boldsymbol{\nu}^{(k)}$ and I the identity matrix. Computing $\boldsymbol{\mu}$, however, is in our case uninteresting, because we already know that $\boldsymbol{\mu} = \mathbf{1}$. So, why do we need Newton's method? Because the sequence of Newton approximants provides exactly the information we are looking for:

Theorem 3.2. $\Pr[S_X^{op} \le k] = \boldsymbol{\nu}_X^{(k)}$ *for every type X and every $k \ge 0$.*

Proof sketch. We illustrate the proof idea on the one-type task system with pgf $f(x) = px^2 + q$, where $q = 1 - p$. Let $\mathcal{T}_{\le k}$ and $\mathcal{T}_{=k}$ denote the sets of trees t with $S^{op}(t) \le k$ and $S^{op}(t) = k$, respectively. We show $\Pr[\mathcal{T}_{\le k}] = \nu^{(k)}$ for all k by induction on k. The case $k = 0$ is trivial. Assume that $\nu^{(k)} = \Pr[\mathcal{T}_{\le k}]$ holds for some $k \ge 0$. We prove $\Pr[\mathcal{T}_{\le k+1}] = \nu^{(k+1)}$. Notice that

$$\nu^{(k+1)} := \nu^{(k)} + \frac{f(\nu^{(k)}) - \nu^{(k)}}{1 - f'(\nu^{(k)})} = \nu^{(k)} + (f(\nu^{(k)}) - \nu^{(k)}) \cdot \textstyle\sum_{i=0}^{\infty} f'(\nu^{(k)})^i .$$

Let $\mathcal{B}_{k+1}^{(0)}$ be the set of trees that have two children both of which belong to $\mathcal{T}_{=k}$, and, for every $i \ge 0$, let $\mathcal{B}_{k+1}^{(i+1)}$ be the set of trees with two children, one belonging to $\mathcal{T}_{\le k}$, the other one to $\mathcal{B}_{k+1}^{(i)}$. By Proposition 3.1 we have $\mathcal{T}_{\le k+1} = \bigcup_{i\ge 0} \mathcal{B}_{k+1}^{(i)}$. We prove $\Pr\left[\mathcal{B}_{k+1}^{(i)}\right] = f'(\nu^{(k)})^i \, (f(\nu^{(k)} - \nu^{(k)})$ by an (inner) induction on i, which completes the proof. For the base $i = 0$, let $\mathcal{A}_{\le k}$ be the set of trees with two children in $\mathcal{T}_{\le k}$; by induction hypothesis we have $\Pr[\mathcal{A}_{\le k}] = p\nu^{(k)}\nu^{(k)}$. In a tree of $\mathcal{A}_{\le k}$ either (a) both children belong to $\mathcal{T}_{=k}$, and so $t \in \mathcal{B}^{(0)}_{k+1}$, or (b) at most one child belongs to $\mathcal{T}_{=k}$. By Proposition 3.1, the trees satisfying (b) belong to $\mathcal{T}_{\leq k}$. In fact, a stronger property holds: a tree of $\mathcal{T}_{\leq k}$ either satisfies (b) or it has one single node. Since the probability of the tree with one node is q, we get $\Pr[\mathcal{A}_{\leq k}] = \Pr\left[\mathcal{B}^{(0)}_{k+1}\right] + \Pr[\mathcal{T}_{\leq k}] - q$. Applying the induction hypothesis again we obtain $\Pr\left[\mathcal{B}^{(0)}_{k+1}\right] = p\nu^{(k)}\nu^{(k)} + q - \nu^{(k)} = f(\nu^{(k)}) - \nu^{(k)}$. For the induction step, let $i > 0$. Divide $\mathcal{B}^{(i)}_{k+1}$ into two sets, one containing the trees whose left (right) child belongs to $\mathcal{B}^{(i)}_{k+1}$ (to $\mathcal{T}_{\leq k}$), and the other the trees whose left (right) child belongs to $\mathcal{T}_{\leq k}$ (to $\mathcal{B}^{(i)}_{k+1}$). Using both induction hypotheses, we get that the probability of each set is $p\nu^{(k)} f'(\nu^{(k)})^i (f(\nu^{(k)}) - \nu^{(k)})$. So $\Pr\left[\mathcal{B}^{(i+1)}_{k+1}\right] = (2p\nu^{(k)}) \cdot f'(\nu^{(k)})^i (f(\nu^{(k)}) - \nu^{(k)})$. Since $f(x) = px^2 + q$ we have $f'(\nu^{(k)}) = 2p\nu^{(k)}$, and so $\Pr\left[\mathcal{B}^{(i+1)}_{k+1}\right] = f'(\nu^{(k)})^{i+1} (f(\nu^{(k)} - \nu^{(k)})$ as desired. □

Example 3.3. Consider the task system $X \overset{p}{\hookrightarrow} \langle X, X \rangle$, $X \overset{q}{\hookrightarrow} \emptyset$ with pgf $f(x) = px^2 + q$, where p is a parameter and $q = 1 - p$. The least fixed point of f is 1 if $p \leq 1/2$ and q/p otherwise. So we consider only the case $p \leq 1/2$. The system is critical for $p = 1/2$ and subcritical for $p < 1/2$. Using Newton approximants we obtain the following recurrence relation for the distribution of the optimal scheduler, where $p_k := \Pr[S^{op} \geq k] = 1 - \nu^{(k-1)}$: $p_{k+1} = (pp_k^2)/(1 - 2p + 2pp_k)$. In particular, for the critical value $p = 1/2$ we get $p_k = 2^{1-k}$ and $\mathbb{E}[S^{op}] = \sum_{k \geq 1} \Pr[S^{op} \geq k] = 2$.

Theorem 3.2 allows to compute the probability mass function of S^{op}. As a Newton iteration requires $\mathcal{O}(|\Gamma|^3)$ arithmetical operations, we obtain the following corollary, where by the unit cost model we refer to the cost in the Blum-Shub-Smale model, in which arithmetic operations have cost 1 independently of the size of the operands [5].

Corollary 3.4. $\Pr[S^{op}_X = k]$ *can be computed in time* $\mathcal{O}(k \cdot |\Gamma|^3)$ *in the unit cost model.*

It is easy to see that Newton's method converges quadratically for subcritical systems (see e.g. [23]). For critical systems, it has recently been proved that Newton's method still converges linearly [19,12]. These results lead to tail bounds for S^{op}_X:

Corollary 3.5. *For any task system* Δ *there are real numbers* $c > 0$ *and* $0 < d < 1$ *such that* $\Pr[S^{op}_X \geq k] \leq c \cdot d^k$ *for all* $k \in \mathbb{N}$. *If* Δ *is subcritical, then there are real numbers* $c > 0$ *and* $0 < d < 1$ *such that* $\Pr[S^{op}_X \geq k] \leq c \cdot d^{2^k}$ *for all* $k \in \mathbb{N}$.

4 Online Schedulers

From this section on we concentrate on online schedulers that only know the past of the computation. Formally, a scheduler σ is *online* if for every tree t with $\sigma(t) = (s_1 \Rightarrow \ldots \Rightarrow s_k)$ and for every $1 \leq i < k$, the task $\sigma(t)[i]$ depends only on $s_1 \Rightarrow \ldots \Rightarrow s_i$ and on the restriction of the labelling function L to $\bigcup_{j=1}^{i} s_j$.

Compact Task Systems. Any task system can be transformed into a so-called *compact* task system such that for every scheduler of the compact task system we can construct a scheduler of the original system with nearly the same properties. A type W is *compact* if there is a rule $X \hookrightarrow \langle Y, Z \rangle$ such that X is reachable from W. A task system is *compact* if all its types are compact. *From now on we assume that task systems are compact.* This assumption is essentially without loss of generality, as we argue in [9].

4.1 Tail Bounds for Online Schedulers

The following main theorem gives computable lower and upper bounds which hold uniformly for all online schedulers σ.

Theorem 4.1. *Let Δ be subcritical.*

- *Let $\boldsymbol{v}, \boldsymbol{w} \in (1, \infty)^\Gamma$ be vectors with $\boldsymbol{f}(\boldsymbol{v}) \leq \boldsymbol{v}$ and $\boldsymbol{f}(\boldsymbol{w}) \geq \boldsymbol{w}$. Denote by $\boldsymbol{v}_{min}$ and $\boldsymbol{w}_{max}$ the least component of $\boldsymbol{v}$ and the greatest component of $\boldsymbol{w}$, respectively. Then*
$$\frac{\boldsymbol{w}_{X_0} - 1}{\boldsymbol{w}_{max}^{k+2} - 1} \leq \Pr[S^\sigma \geq k] \leq \frac{\boldsymbol{v}_{X_0} - 1}{\boldsymbol{v}_{min}^{k} - 1} \text{ for all online schedulers } \sigma.$$
- *Vectors $\boldsymbol{v}, \boldsymbol{w} \in (1, \infty)^\Gamma$ with $\boldsymbol{f}(\boldsymbol{v}) \leq \boldsymbol{v}$ and $\boldsymbol{f}(\boldsymbol{w}) \geq \boldsymbol{w}$ exist and can be computed in polynomial time.*

Proof sketch. Choose $h > 1$ and $\boldsymbol{u} \in (0, \infty)^\Gamma$ such that $h^{\boldsymbol{u}_X} = \boldsymbol{v}_X$ for all $X \in \Gamma$. Define for all $i \geq 1$ the variable $m^{(i)} = \boldsymbol{z}^{(i)} \bullet \boldsymbol{u}$ where "$\bullet$" denotes the scalar product, i.e., $m^{(i)}$ measures the number of tasks at time i weighted by types according to $\boldsymbol{u}$. One can show that $h^{m^{(1)}}, h^{m^{(2)}}, \ldots$ is a supermartingale for any online scheduler σ, and, using the Optional Stopping Theorem [27], that $\Pr\left[\sup_i m^{(i)} \geq x\right] \leq (\boldsymbol{v}_{X_0} - 1)/(h^x - 1)$ for all x (see [9] for the details and [16,25] for a similar argument on random walks). As each type has at least weight $\boldsymbol{u}_{min}$, we have that $S^\sigma \geq k$ implies $\sup_i m^{(i)} \geq k\boldsymbol{u}_{min}$. Hence $\Pr[S^\sigma \geq k] \leq \Pr\left[\sup_i m^{(i)} \geq k\boldsymbol{u}_{min}\right] \leq (\boldsymbol{v}_{X_0} - 1)/(\boldsymbol{v}_{min}^k - 1)$. The lower bound is shown similarly. □

All online schedulers perform within the bounds of Theorem 4.1. For an application of the upper bound, assume one wants to provide as much space as is necessary to guarantee that, say, 99.9% of the executions of a task system can run without needing additional memory. This can be accomplished, regardless of the scheduler, by providing k space units, where k is chosen such that the upper bound of Theorem 4.1 is at most 0.001.

A comparison of the lower bound with Corollary 3.5 proves for subcritical task systems that the asymptotic performance of any online scheduler σ is far away from that of the optimal offline scheduler: the ratio $\Pr[S^\sigma \geq k] / \Pr[S^{op} \geq k]$ is unbounded.

Example 4.2. Consider again the task system with pgf $f(x) = px^2 + q$. For $p < 1/2$ the pgf has two fixed points, 1 and q/p. In particular, $q/p > 1$, so q/p can be used to obtain both an upper and a lower bound for online schedulers. Since there is only one type of tasks, vectors have only one component, and the maximal and minimal components coincide; moreover, in this case the exponent $k+2$ of the lower bound can be improved to k. So the upper and lower bounds coincide, and we get $\Pr[S^\sigma \geq k] = \frac{q/p - 1}{(q/p)^k - 1}$ for every online scheduler σ. In particular, as one intuitively expects, all online schedulers are equivalent.[1]

[1] For this example $\Pr[S^\sigma \geq k]$ can also be computed by elementary means.

4.2 Tail Bounds for Light-First Schedulers

We present a class of online schedulers for which a sharper upper bound than the one given by Theorem 4.1 can be proved. It may be intuitive that a good heuristic is to pick the task with the smallest expected completion time. If we compute a vector $\boldsymbol{v}$ with $\boldsymbol{f}(\boldsymbol{v}) \leq \boldsymbol{v}$ in polynomial time according to the proof of Theorem 4.1, then the type X_{min} for which $\boldsymbol{v}_{X_{min}} = \boldsymbol{v}_{min}$ holds turns out to be the type with smallest expected completion time. This suggests choosing the active type X with smallest component in $\boldsymbol{v}$. So we look at $\boldsymbol{v}$ as a vector of weights, and always choose the lightest active type. In fact, for this (intuitively good) scheduler we obtain two different upper bounds.

Given a vector $\boldsymbol{v}$ with $\boldsymbol{f}(\boldsymbol{v}) \leq \boldsymbol{v}$ we denote by $\sqsubseteq$ a total order on Γ such that whenever $X \sqsubseteq Y$ then $\boldsymbol{v}_X \leq \boldsymbol{v}_Y$. If $X \sqsubseteq Y$, then we say that X is lighter than Y. The *$\boldsymbol{v}$-light-first scheduler* is an online scheduler that, in each step, picks a task of the lightest type available in the pool according to $\boldsymbol{v}$. Theorem 4.3 below strengthens the upper bound of Theorem 4.1 for light-first schedulers. For the second part of Theorem 4.3 we use the notion of *$\boldsymbol{v}$-accumulating types*. A type $X \in \Gamma$ is $\boldsymbol{v}$-accumulating if for every $k \geq 0$ the $\boldsymbol{v}$-light-first scheduler has a nonzero probability of reaching a state with at least k tasks of type X in the pool.

Theorem 4.3. *Let Δ be subcritical and $\boldsymbol{v} \in (1,\infty)^\Gamma$ with $\boldsymbol{f}(\boldsymbol{v}) \leq \boldsymbol{v}$. Let σ be a $\boldsymbol{v}$-light-first scheduler. Let $\boldsymbol{v}_{minmax} := \min_{X \hookrightarrow \langle Y,Z \rangle} \max\{\boldsymbol{v}_Y, \boldsymbol{v}_Z\}$ (here the minimum is taken over all transition rules with two types on the right hand side). Then $\boldsymbol{v}_{minmax} \geq \boldsymbol{v}_{min}$ and for all $k \geq 1$*

$$\Pr[S^\sigma \geq k] \leq \frac{\boldsymbol{v}_{X_0} - 1}{\boldsymbol{v}_{min}\boldsymbol{v}_{minmax}^{k-1} - 1}.$$

Moreover, let $\boldsymbol{v}_{minacc} := \min\{\boldsymbol{v}_X \mid X \in \Gamma,\ X \text{is } \boldsymbol{v}\text{-accumulating}\}$. Then $\boldsymbol{v}_{minacc} \geq \boldsymbol{v}_{minmax}$, $\boldsymbol{v}_{minacc}$ can be computed in polynomial time, and there is an integer ℓ such that for all $k \geq \ell$

$$\Pr[S^\sigma \geq k] \leq \frac{\boldsymbol{v}_{X_0} - 1}{\boldsymbol{v}_{min}^{\ell}\boldsymbol{v}_{minacc}^{k-\ell} - 1}.$$

Proof sketch. Recall the proof sketch of Theorem 4.1 where we used that $S^\sigma \geq k$ implies $\sup_i m^{(i)} \geq k\boldsymbol{u}_{min}$, as each type has at least weight $\boldsymbol{u}_{min}$. Let ℓ be such that no more than ℓ tasks of non-accumulating type can be in the pool at the same time. Then $S^\sigma \geq k$ implies $\sup_i m^{(i)} \geq \ell\boldsymbol{u}_{min} + (k-\ell)\boldsymbol{u}_{minacc}$ which leads to the final inequality of Theorem 4.3 in a way analogous to the proof sketch of Theorem 4.1. □

Intuitively, a light-first scheduler "works against" light tasks by picking them as soon as possible. In this way it may be able to avoid the accumulation of some light types, so it may achieve $\boldsymbol{v}_{minacc} > \boldsymbol{v}_{min}$. This is illustrated in the following example.

Example 4.4. Consider the task system with 2 task types and pgfs $x = a_2xy + a_1y + a_0$ and $y = b_2xy + b_1y + b_0$, where $a_2 + a_1 + a_0 = 1 = b_2 + b_1 + b_0 = 1$. The system is subcritical if $a_1b_2 < a_2b_1 - a_2 + b_0$. The pgfs have a greatest fixed point $\boldsymbol{v}$ with $\boldsymbol{v}_X = (1-a_2-b_1-a_1b_2+a_2b_1)/b_2$ and $\boldsymbol{v}_Y = (1-b_1-b_2)/(a_2+a_1b_2-a_2b_1)$. We have $\boldsymbol{v}_X \leq \boldsymbol{v}_Y$ iff $a_2-b_2 \leq a_2b_1-a_1b_2$, and so the light-first scheduler chooses X before Y if this condition holds, and Y before X otherwise. We show that the light-first scheduler is asymptotically optimal. Assume w.l.o.g. $\boldsymbol{v}_X \leq \boldsymbol{v}_Y$. Then X is not accumulating (because X-tasks are picked as soon as they are created), and so $\boldsymbol{v}_{minacc} = \boldsymbol{v}_Y$. So the upper bound for the light-weight scheduler yields a constant c_2 such that $\Pr[S^\sigma \geq k] \leq c_2/\boldsymbol{v}_Y^k$. But the general lower bound for arbitrary online schedulers states that there is a constant c_1 such that $\Pr[S^\sigma \geq k] \geq c_1/\boldsymbol{v}_Y^k$, so we are done.

4.3 Tail Bounds for Depth-First Schedulers

Space-efficient scheduling of multithreaded computations has received considerable attention [21,6,2,1]. The setting of these papers is slightly different from ours, because they assume data dependencies among the threads, which may cause a thread to wait for a result from another thread. In this sense our setting is similar to that of [18], where, in thread terminology, the threads can execute independently.

These papers focus on *depth-first* computations, in which if thread A has to wait for thread B, then B was spawned by A or by a descendant of A. The optimal scheduler is the one that, when A spawns B, interrupts the execution of A and continues with B; this online scheduler produces the familiar stack-based execution [6,21].

We study the performance of this *depth-first* scheduler. Formally, a depth-first scheduler σ_λ is determined by a function λ that assigns to each rule $r = X \hookrightarrow \langle Y, Z\rangle$ either YZ or ZY. If $\lambda(r) = YZ$, then Z models the continuation of the thread X, while Y models a new thread for whose termination Z waits. The depth-first scheduler σ_λ keeps as an internal data structure a word $w \in \Gamma^*$, a "stack", such that the Parikh image of w is the multiset of the task types in the pool. If $w = Xw'$ for some $w' \in \Gamma^*$, then σ picks X. If a transition rule $X \hookrightarrow \alpha$ "fires", then σ_λ replaces Xw' by $\beta w'$ where $\beta = \lambda(X \hookrightarrow \alpha)$.

Using techniques of [8] for *probabilistic pushdown systems*, we obtain the following:

Theorem 4.5. *Let Δ be subcritical and σ be any depth-first scheduler. Then $\Pr[S^\sigma = k]$ can be computed in time $\mathcal{O}(k \cdot |\Gamma|^3)$ in the unit-cost model. Moreover, there is $0 < \rho < 1$ such that $\Pr[S^\sigma \geq k] \in \Theta(\rho^k)$, i.e, there are $c, C > 0$ such that $c\rho^k \leq \Pr[S^\sigma \geq k] \leq C\rho^k$ for all k. Furthermore, ρ is the spectral radius of a nonnegative matrix $B \in \mathbb{R}^{\Gamma\times\Gamma}$, where B can be computed in polynomial time.*

While the proof of Theorem 4.5 does not conceptually require much more than the results of [8], the technical details are delicate. The proof can be found in [9].

5 Expectations

In this section we study the expected completion space, i.e., the expectation $\mathbb{E}[S^\sigma]$ for both offline and online schedulers. Fix a task system $\Delta = (\Gamma, \hookrightarrow, Prob, X_0)$.

Optimal (Offline) Schedulers. The results of Section 3 allow to efficiently approximate the expectation $\mathbb{E}[S^{op}]$. Recall that for any random variable R with values in the natural numbers we have $\mathbb{E}[R] = \sum_{i=1}^{\infty} \Pr[R \geq i]$. So we can (under-) approximate $\mathbb{E}[R]$ by $\sum_{i=1}^{k} \Pr[R \geq i]$ for finite k. We say that *k terms compute b bits of* $\mathbb{E}[S^{op}]$ if $\mathbb{E}[S^{op}] - \sum_{i=0}^{k-1}(1 - \boldsymbol{\nu}_{X_0}^{(i)}) \leq 2^{-b}$.

Theorem 5.1. *The expectation* $\mathbb{E}[S^{op}]$ *is finite (no matter whether* Δ *is critical or subcritical). Moreover,* $\mathcal{O}(b)$ *terms compute* b *bits of* $\mathbb{E}[S^{op}]$*. If the task system* Δ *is subcritical, then* $\log_2 b + \mathcal{O}(1)$ *terms compute* b *bits of* $\mathbb{E}[S^{op}]$*. Finally, computing* k *terms takes time* $\mathcal{O}(k \cdot |\Gamma|^3)$ *in the unit cost model.*

Online Schedulers. The main result for online schedulers states that the finiteness of $\mathbb{E}[S^\sigma]$ does not depend on the choice of the online scheduler σ.

Theorem 5.2. *If* Δ *is subcritical, then* $\mathbb{E}[S^\sigma]$ *is finite for every online scheduler* σ*. If* Δ *is critical, then* $\mathbb{E}[S^\sigma]$ *is infinite for every online scheduler* σ*.*

Proof sketch. The first assertion follows from Theorem 4.1. Let Δ be critical. For this sketch we focus on the case where X_0 is reachable from every type. By Proposition 2.5 the spectral radius of $\boldsymbol{f}'(\mathbf{1})$ equals 1. Then Perron-Frobenius theory guarantees the existence of a vector $\boldsymbol{u}$ with $\boldsymbol{f}'(\mathbf{1})\boldsymbol{u} = \boldsymbol{u}$ and $\boldsymbol{u}_X > 0$ for all X. Using a martingale argument, similar to the one of Theorem 4.1, one can show that the sequence $m^{(1)}, m^{(2)}, \ldots$ with $m^{(i)} := \boldsymbol{z}^{(i)} \bullet \boldsymbol{u}$ is a martingale for every scheduler σ, and, using the Optional-Stopping Theorem, that $\Pr[S^\sigma \geq k] \geq \boldsymbol{u}_{X_0}/(k+2)$. So we have $\mathbb{E}[S^\sigma] = \sum_{k=1}^{\infty} \Pr[S^\sigma \geq k] \geq \sum_{k=1}^{\infty} \boldsymbol{u}_{X_0}/(k+2) = \infty$. □

Since we can decide in polynomial time whether a system is subcritical or critical, we can do the same to decide on the finiteness of the expected completion time.

Depth-first Schedulers. To approximate $\mathbb{E}[S^\sigma]$ for a given depth-first scheduler σ, we can employ the same technique as for optimal offline schedulers, i.e., we approximate $\mathbb{E}[S^\sigma]$ by $\sum_{i=1}^{k} \Pr[S^\sigma \geq i]$ for finite k. We say that *k terms compute b bits of* $\mathbb{E}[S^\sigma]$ if $\mathbb{E}[S^\sigma] - \sum_{i=1}^{k} \Pr[S^\sigma \geq i] \leq 2^{-b}$.

Theorem 5.3 (see Theorem 19 of [8]). *Let* Δ *be subcritical, and let* σ *be a depth-first scheduler. Then* $\mathcal{O}(b)$ *terms compute* b *bits of* $\mathbb{E}[S^\sigma]$*, and computing* k *terms takes time* $\mathcal{O}(k \cdot |\Gamma|^3)$ *in the unit cost model.*

6 Conclusions

We have initiated the study of scheduling tasks that can stochastically generate other tasks. We have provided strong results on the performance of both online and offline schedulers for the case of one processor and task systems with completion probability 1. It is an open problem how to compute and analyze online schedulers which are optimal in a sense. While we profited from the theory of branching processes, the theory considers (in computer science terms) systems with an unbounded number of processors, and therefore many questions had not been addressed before or even posed.

Acknowledgement. We thank the referees for their helpful comments.

References

1. Agrawal, K., Leiserson, C.E., He, Y., Hsu, W.J.: Adaptive work-stealing with parallelism feedback. ACM TOCS 26(3) (2008)
2. Arora, N.S., Blumofe, R.D., Plaxton, C.G.: Thread scheduling for multiprogrammed microprocessors. Theory of Computing Systems 34, 115–144 (2001)

3. Athreya, K.B.: On the maximum sequence of a critical branching process. Annals of Probability 16, 502–507 (1988)
4. Athreya, K.B., Ney, P.E.: Branching Processes. Springer, Heidelberg (1972)
5. Blum, L., Cucker, F., Shub, M., Smale, S.: Complexity and Real Computation. Springer, Heidelberg (1998)
6. Blumofe, R.D., Leiserson, C.E.: Scheduling multithreaded computations by work stealing. Journal of the ACM 46(5), 720–748 (1999)
7. Borovkov, K.A., Vatutin, V.A.: On distribution tails and expectations of maxima in critical branching processes. Journal of Applied Probability 33(3), 614–622 (1996)
8. Brázdil, T., Esparza, J., Kiefer, S.: On the memory consumption of probabilistic pushdown automata. In: Proceedings of FSTTCS, pp. 49–60 (2009)
9. Brázdil, T., Esparza, J., Kiefer, S., Luttenberger, M.: Space-efficient scheduling of stochastically generated tasks. Technical report (2010), `http://arxiv.org/abs/1004.4286`
10. Esparza, J., Kiefer, S., Luttenberger, M.: An extension of Newton's method to ω-continuous semirings. In: Harju, T., Karhumäki, J., Lepistö, A. (eds.) DLT 2007. LNCS, vol. 4588, pp. 157–168. Springer, Heidelberg (2007)
11. Esparza, J., Kiefer, S., Luttenberger, M.: On fixed point equations over commutative semirings. In: Thomas, W., Weil, P. (eds.) STACS 2007. LNCS, vol. 4393, pp. 296–307. Springer, Heidelberg (2007)
12. Esparza, J., Kiefer, S., Luttenberger, M.: Convergence thresholds of Newton's method for monotone polynomial equations. In: STACS 2008, pp. 289–300 (2008)
13. Esparza, J., Kučera, A., Mayr, R.: Quantitative analysis of probabilistic pushdown automata: Expectations and variances. In: LICS 2005, pp. 117–126. IEEE, Los Alamitos (2005)
14. Esparza, J., Kučera, A., Mayr, R.: Model checking probabilistic pushdown automata. In: LICS 2004, pp. 12–21. IEEE Computer Society Press, Los Alamitos (2004)
15. Etessami, K., Yannakakis, M.: Recursive markov chains, stochastic grammars, and monotone systems of nonlinear equations. Journal of the ACM 56(1), 1–66 (2009)
16. Feller, W.: An introduction to probability theory and its applications, vol. I. John Wiley & Sons, Chichester (1968)
17. Harris, T.E.: The Theory of Branching Processes. Springer, Heidelberg (1963)
18. Karp, R.M., Zhang, Y.: Randomized parallel algorithms for backtrack search and branch-and-bound computation. Journal of the ACM 40(3), 765–789 (1993)
19. Kiefer, S., Luttenberger, M., Esparza, J.: On the convergence of Newton's method for monotone systems of polynomial equations. In: STOC 2007, pp. 217–226. ACM, New York (2007)
20. Lindvall, T.: On the maximum of a branching process. Scandinavian Journal of Statistics 3, 209–214 (1976)
21. Narlikar, G.J., Belloch, G.E.: Space-efficient scheduling of nested parallelism. ACM TOPLAS 21(1), 138–173 (1999)
22. Nerman, O.: On the maximal generation size of a non-critical galton-watson process. Scandinavian Journal of Statistics 4(3), 131–135 (1977)
23. Ortega, J.M., Rheinboldt, W.C.: Iterative solution of nonlinear equations in several variables. Academic Press, London (1970)
24. Pakes, A.G.: A limit theorem for the maxima of the para-critical simple branching process. Advances in Applied Probability 30, 740–756 (1998)
25. Spitzer, F.: Principles of Random Walk. Springer, Heidelberg (1976)
26. Spătaru, A.: A maximum sequence in a critical multitype branching process. Journal of Applied Probability 28(4), 893–897 (1991)
27. Williams, D.: Probability with Martingales. Cambridge University Press, Cambridge (1995)

Exponential Lower Bounds for Policy Iteration

John Fearnley

Department of Computer Science, University of Warwick, UK
john@dcs.warwick.ac.uk

Abstract. We study policy iteration for infinite-horizon Markov decision processes. It has recently been shown policy iteration style algorithms have exponential lower bounds in a two player game setting. We extend these lower bounds to Markov decision processes with the total reward and average-reward optimality criteria.

1 Introduction

The problem of finding an optimal policy for infinite-horizon Markov decision process has been widely studied [8]. Policy iteration is one method that has been developed for this task [5]. This algorithm begins by choosing an arbitrary policy, and then iteratively improves that policy by modifying the policy so that it uses different actions. For each policy, the algorithm computes a set of actions that are switchable, and it then chooses some subset of these actions to be switched. The resulting policy is guaranteed to be an improvement.

The choice of which subset of switchable actions to switch in each iteration is left up to the user: different variants of policy iteration can be created by giving different rules that pick the subset. Traditionally, policy iteration algorithms use a greedy rule that switches every state with a switchable action. Greedy policy iteration will be the focus of this paper.

Policy iteration has been found to work well in practice, where it is used as an alternative to linear programming. Linear programming is known to solve the problem in polynomial time. However, relatively little is known about the complexity of policy iteration. Since each iteration yields a strictly improved policy, the algorithm can never consider the same policy twice. This leads to a natural exponential bound on the number of iterations before the algorithm arrives at the optimal policy. The best upper bounds have been provided by Mansour and Singh [6], who showed that greedy policy iteration will terminate in $O(k^n/n)$ iterations, where k is the maximum number of outgoing actions from a state.

Melekopoglou and Condon have shown exponential lower bounds for some simple variants of policy iteration [7]. The policy iteration algorithms that they consider switch only a single action in each iteration. They give a family of examples upon which these policy iteration algorithms take $2^n - 1$ steps. It has been a long standing open problem as to whether exponential lower bounds could be shown for greedy policy iteration. The best lower bound that has been shown so far is $n + 6$ iterations [2].

S. Abramsky et al. (Eds.): ICALP 2010, Part II, LNCS 6199, pp. 551–562, 2010.

Policy iteration is closely related to the technique of strategy improvement for two player games. Friedmann [4] has recently found a family of parity games upon which the strategy improvement algorithm of Vöge and Jurdziński [9] takes an exponential number of steps. It has been shown that these examples can be generalized to obtain exponential lower bounds for strategy improvement algorithms on other prominent types of two player game [1].

Our contribution. Friedmann's example relies on the fact that there are two players in a parity game. We show how Friedmann's example can be adapted to provide exponential lower bounds for policy iteration on Markov decision processes. We present an example that provides an exponential lower bound for the total reward criterion, and we also argue that the same example provides an exponential lower bound for the average-reward criterion.

2 Preliminaries

A Markov decision process consists of a set of states S, where each state $s \in S$ has an associated set of actions A_s. For a given state $s \in S$ and action $a \in A_s$ the function $\mathrm{r}(s, a)$ gives an integer reward for when the action a in chosen at the state s. Given two states s and s', and an action $a \in A_s$, the function $\mathrm{p}(s'|s, a)$ gives the probability of moving to state s' when the action a is chosen in state s. This is a probability distribution, so $\sum_{s' \in S} \mathrm{p}(s'|s, a) = 1$ for all s and $a \in A_s$.

A deterministic memoryless policy $\pi : S \to A_s$ is a function that selects one action at each state. It has been shown that there is always a policy with this form that maximizes the optimality criteria that we are interested in. Therefore, we restrict ourselves to policies of this form for the rest of the paper. For a given starting state s_0, a run that is consistent with a policy π is an infinite sequence of states $\langle s_0, s_1, \ldots \rangle$ such that $p(s_{i+1}|s_i, \pi(s_i)) > 0$ for all i. The set $\Omega^{\pi}_{s_0}$ contains every consistent run from s_0 when π is used. A probability space can be defined over these runs using the σ-algebra that is generated by the cylinder sets of finite paths starting at s_0. The cylinder set of a finite path contains every infinite path that has the finite path as a prefix. If we fix the probability of the cylinder set of a finite path $\langle s_0, s_1, s_2, \ldots s_k \rangle$ to be $\prod_{i=0}^{k-1}(s_{i+1}|s_i, \pi(s_i))$, then standard techniques from probability theory imply that there is a unique extension to a probability measure $\mathbb{P}^{\pi}_{s_0}(\cdot)$ on the σ-algebra [3]. Given a function that assigns a value to each consistent run $f : \Omega \to \mathbb{R}$, we define $\mathbb{E}^{\pi}_{s_0}\{f\}$ to be the expectation of this function in the probability space.

The value of a state s when a policy π is used varies according to the choice of optimality criterion. In the total reward criterion the value is $\mathrm{Val}^{\pi}(s) = \mathbb{E}^{\pi}_{s}\{\sum_{i=0}^{\infty} \mathrm{r}(s_i, s_{i+1})\}$, and for the average-reward criterion the value is $\mathrm{Val}^{\pi}_{\mathcal{A}}(s) = \mathbb{E}^{\pi}_{s}\{\liminf_{N \to \infty} \frac{1}{N} \sum_{i=0}^{N} \mathrm{r}(s_i, s_{i+1})\}$. It should be noted that the value of some policies may not exist under the total reward criterion. Our examples will be carefully constructed to ensure that the value does exist. The computational objective is to find the optimal policy π^*, which is the policy that maximizes the value function for every starting state. We define the value of a state to be the value of that state when an optimal policy is being used. That is, we define $\text{Val}(s) = \text{Val}^{\pi*}(s)$ and $\text{Val}_{\mathcal{A}}(s) = \text{Val}_{\mathcal{A}}^{\pi*}(s)$ for every state s.

For each optimality criterion, it has been shown that the value of each state can be characterised by the solution of a system of optimality equations [8]. For the total reward criterion these optimality equations are, for every state s:

$$V(s) = \max_{a \in A_s} \left(\mathrm{r}(s, a) + \sum_{s' \in S} p(s'|s, a) \cdot V(s') \right) \tag{1}$$

For the average-reward criterion we have two types of optimality equation, which must be solved simultaneously. The first of these are called the gain equations:

$$G(s) = \max_{a \in A_s} \left(\sum_{s' \in S} p(s'|s, a) \cdot G(s') \right) \tag{2}$$

Secondly we have the bias equations. If $M_s = \{a \in A_s \ : \ G(s) = \sum_{s' \in S} p(s'|s, a) \cdot G(s')\}$ is the set of actions that satisfy the gain equation at the state s, then the bias equations are defined as:

$$B(s) = \max_{a \in M_s} \left(\mathrm{r}(s, a) - G(s) + \sum_{s' \in S} p(s'|s, a) \cdot B(s') \right) \tag{3}$$

It has been shown that the solution to these optimality equations is unique, and that this solution characterises the value of each state. That is, we have $\text{Val}(s) = V(s)$ and $\text{Val}_{\mathcal{A}}(s) = G(s)$, for every state s. We can also obtain an optimal policy by setting $\pi^*(s) = a$, where a is an action that achieves the maximum in the optimality equation.

3 Policy Iteration

Policy iteration is a method for solving the optimality equations presented in Section 2. We begin by describing policy iteration for the total reward criterion. For every policy π that the algorithm considers, it computes the value $\text{Val}^{\pi}(s)$ of the policy at every state s, and checks whether this is a solution of the optimality equation (1). The value of the policy can be obtained by solving:

$$\text{Val}^{\pi}(s) = \mathrm{r}(s, \pi(s)) + \sum_{s' \in S} p(s'|s, \pi(s)) \cdot \text{Val}^{\pi}(s') \tag{4}$$

If the value of π satisfies the optimality equation (1) at every state, then a solution has been found and the algorithm terminates. Otherwise, we define the appeal for each action $a \in A_s$ in the policy π to be: $\text{Appeal}^{\pi}(s, a) = \mathrm{r}(s, a) + \sum_{s' \in S} p(s'|s, a) \cdot \text{Val}^{\pi}(s')$. If the policy π does not satisfy the optimality equation there must be at least one action a at a state s such that $\text{Appeal}^{\pi}(s, a) > \text{Val}^{\pi}(s)$. We say that an action with this property is switchable in π. Switching an action $a \in A_t$ in a policy π creates a new policy π' where $\pi'(s) = a$ if $s = t$, and $\pi'(s) = \pi(s)$ for all other states s. It can be shown that switching any subset of switchable actions will create an improved policy.

Theorem 1 ([8]). *If π is a policy and π' is a policy that is obtain by switching some subset of switchable actions in π then* $\text{Val}^{\pi'}(s) \geq \text{Val}^{\pi}(s)$ *for every state s, and there is some state in which the inequality is strict.*

Policy iteration begins at an arbitrary policy. In each iteration it computes the set of switchable actions, and picks some subset of these actions to switch. This creates a new policy to be considered in the next iteration. Since policy iteration only switches switchable actions, Theorem 1 implies that it cannot visit the same policy twice. This is because repeating a policy would require the value of some state to decrease. Since there are a finite number of policies, the algorithm must eventually arrive at a policy with no switchable actions. This policy satisfies the optimality equation (1), and policy iteration terminates.

Note that any subset of switchable actions can be chosen in each iteration of the algorithm, and the choice of subset affects the behaviour of the algorithm. In this paper we study the greedy policy iteration algorithm, which selects the most appealing switchable action at every state. For every state s where equation (1) is not satisfied, the algorithm will switch the action: $\text{argmax}_{a \in A_s}(\text{Appeal}^{\pi}(s, a))$.

Policy iteration for the average-reward criterion follows the same pattern, but it uses optimality equations (2) and (3) to decide which actions are switchable in a given policy. For each policy it computes a solution to:

$$G^{\pi}(s) = \sum_{s' \in S} p(s'|s, \pi(s)) \cdot G^{\pi}(s)$$

$$B^{\pi}(s) = \text{r}(s, \pi(s)) - G^{\pi}(s) + \sum_{s' \in S} p(s'|s, \pi(s)) \cdot B^{\pi}(s')$$

An action $a \in A_s$ is switchable if either $\sum_{s' \in S} p(s'|s, a) \cdot G^{\pi}(s') > G^{\pi}(s)$ or if $\sum_{s' \in S} p(s'|s, a) \cdot G^{\pi}(s') = G^{\pi}(s)$ and: $\text{r}(s, a) - G^{\pi}(s) + \sum_{s' \in S} p(s'|s, a) > B^{\pi}(s)$.

4 Exponential Lower Bounds for the Total Reward Criterion

In this section we will describe a family of examples that force greedy policy iteration for the total reward criterion to take an exponential number of steps. Due to the size and complexity of our examples, we will break them down into several component parts, which will be presented separately.

Our examples will actually contain very few actions that are probabilistic. An action $a \in A_s$ is deterministic if there is some state s' such that $\text{p}(s'|s, a) = 1$. For the sake of convenience, we will denote actions of this form as (s, s'). We also overload our previous notations: the notation $\pi(s) = s'$ indicates that π chooses the deterministic action from s to s', the function $\text{r}(s, s')$ gives the reward of this action, and $\text{Appeal}^{\pi}(s, s')$ gives the appeal of this action under the policy π.

Since we are working with the total reward criterion, care must be taken to ensure that the value of a policy remains well defined. For this purpose, our examples will contain a sink state c_{n+1} that has a single action (c_{n+1}, c_{n+1}) with reward 0. This will be an absorbing state, in the sense that every run of the

MDP from every starting state will eventually arrive at the state c_{n+1}, for every policy that is considered by policy iteration. This will ensure that the value of each state remains finite throughout the execution of the algorithm.

We will give diagrams for parts our examples, such as the one given in Figure 1. States are drawn as boxes, and the name of a state is printed on the box. Actions are drawn as arrows: deterministic actions are drawn as an arrow between states, and probabilistic actions are drawn as arrows that split, and end at multiple states. The probability distribution is marked after the arrow has split, and the reward of the action is marked before the arrow has split.

Our goal is to construct a set of examples that force policy iteration to mimic the behaviour of a binary counter. Each policy will be associated with some configuration of this counter, and the exponential lower bound will be established by forcing policy iteration to consider one policy for every configuration of the counter. In the rest of this section, we construct an example that forces policy iteration to mimic the behaviour of a binary counter with n bits.

If the bits of our counter are indexed 1 through n, then there are two conditions that are sufficient enforce this behaviour. Firstly, a bit with index i should become 1 only after all bits with index $j < i$ are 1. Secondly, when the bit with index i becomes 1, every bit with index $j < i$ must be set to 0. Our exposition will follow this structure: in section 4.1 we describe how each policy corresponds to a configuration of a binary counter, in section 4.2 we show how the first condition is enforced, and in section 4.3 we show how the second condition is enforced.

4.1 A Bit

The example will contain n instances of structure shown in Figure 1, which will represent the bits. We will represent the configuration of a binary counter as a set $B \subseteq \{1, 2, \ldots n\}$ that contains the indices of the bits that are 1. A policy π represents a configuration B if $\pi(b_i) = a_i$ for every index $i \in B$, and $\pi(b_i) \neq a_i$ for every every index $i \notin B$. For a set of natural numbers B we define $B^{>i}$ to be the set $B \setminus \{k \in \mathbb{N} : k \leq i\}$. We define analogous notations for $<$, $\geq$, and $\leq$.

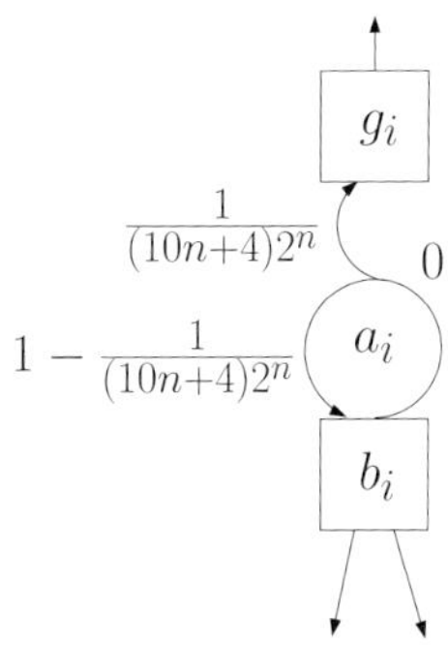

Fig. 1. The structure for the bit with index i

The actions a_i are the only probabilistic actions in the example. When the action a_i is chosen at b_i the effect, under the total reward criterion, is identical to a deterministic action (b_i, g_i) with reward 0. The fact that it takes an expected $(10n + 4)2^n$ steps to move from b_i to the g_i using the action a_i is irrelevant because the reward of a_i is 0, and these steps have no effect on the total reward.

Proposition 2. *For every policy π, if $\pi(b_i) = a_i$ then* $\text{Val}^\pi(b_i) = \text{Val}^\pi(g_i)$.

The reason why the given probabilities have been chosen for the action a_i is that the value of the state g_i will never exceed $(10n + 4)2^n$. Therefore, we make the following assumption, which we will later show to be true.

Assumption 3. *For every policy π we have* $\text{Val}^\pi(b_i) > 0$ *and* $\text{Val}^\pi(g_i) \leq (10n+4)2^n$.

Although the action a_i behaves like a deterministic action when it is chosen at b_i, it behaves differently when it is not chosen. A deterministic action (b_i, g_i) would have $\text{Appeal}^\pi(b_i, g_i) = \text{Val}^\pi(g_i)$ in every policy. By contrast, when a_i is not chosen by a policy π, we can show that the appeal of a_i is at most $\text{Val}^\pi(b_i) + 1$.

Proposition 4. *Suppose that Assumption 3 holds. If π is a policy such that $\pi(b_i) \neq a_i$ then* $\text{Appeal}^\pi(b_i, a_i) < \text{Val}^\pi(b_i) + 1$.

This is the key property that will allow us to implement a binary counter. The value of the state g_i could be much larger than the value of b_i. However, we are able to prevent policy iteration from switching the action a_i by ensuring that there is always some other action x such that $\text{Appeal}(b_i, x) \geq \text{Val}^\pi(b_i) + 1$.

4.2 Switching the Smallest Bit

In this section we fully describe the example, and we show how policy iteration can only switch a_i at b_i after it has switched a_j at every state b_j with $j < i$.

Figure 2 shows a key structure, which is called a deceleration lane. Previously we argued that an action (b_i, x) with $\text{Appeal}^\pi(b_i, x) \geq \text{Val}^\pi(b_i) + 1$ is required in every policy π with $\pi(b_i) \neq a_i$ to prevent policy iteration from switching the action a_i. The deceleration is the structure that ensures these actions will exist.

The states x and y both have outgoing actions that will be specified later. For now, we can reason about the behaviour of the deceleration lane by assuming that the value of y is larger than the value of x.

Assumption 5. *For every policy π we have* $\text{Val}^\pi(y) > \text{Val}^\pi(x)$.

The initial policy for the deceleration lane is the one in which every state d_k chooses (d_k, y). It is not difficult to see that the only switchable action in this policy is (d_1, d_0). This is a general trend: the action (d_j, d_{j-1}) can only be switched after every action (d_k, d_{k-1}) with $1 \leq k < j$ has been switched. Therefore, policy

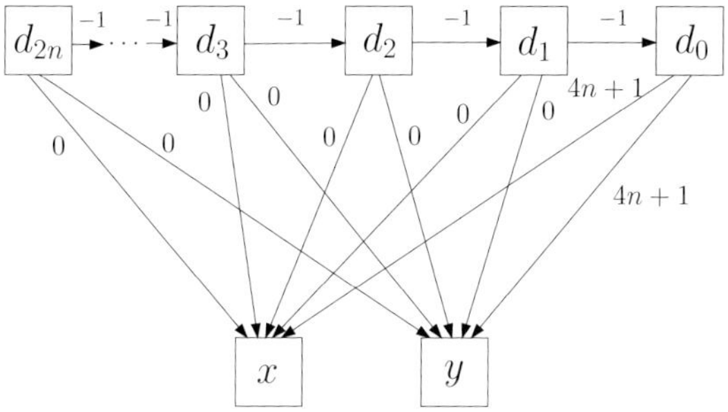

Fig. 2. The deceleration lane

iteration will take $2n$ steps to arrive at the optimal policy for the deceleration lane. Formally, for every j in the range $0 \leq j \leq 2n$ we define a partial policy:

$$\pi_j(s) = \begin{cases} d_{k-1} & \text{if } s = d_k \text{ and } 1 \leq k \leq j, \\ y & \text{otherwise.} \end{cases} \tag{5}$$

Proposition 6. *Suppose that Assumption 5 holds. Applying policy iteration to* π_0 *produces the sequence of policies* $\langle \pi_0, \pi_1, \ldots, \pi_{2n} \rangle$.

Figure 3 shows how each state b_i is connected to the deceleration lane. Of course, since we have not yet specified the outgoing actions from the states f_i, we cannot reason about their appeal. These actions will be used later to force the state b_i to switch away from the action a_i as the binary counter moves between configurations. For now, we can assume that these actions are not switchable.

Assumption 7. *We have* $\text{Appeal}^{\pi}(b_i, f_j) < \text{Val}^{\pi}(b_i)$ *for every policy* π *and every action* (b_i, f_j).

We now describe the behaviour of policy iteration for every index $i \notin B$. The initial policy for the state b_i will choose the action (b_i, y). In the first iteration the action (b_i, d_{2i}) will be switched, but after this the action chosen at b_i follows the

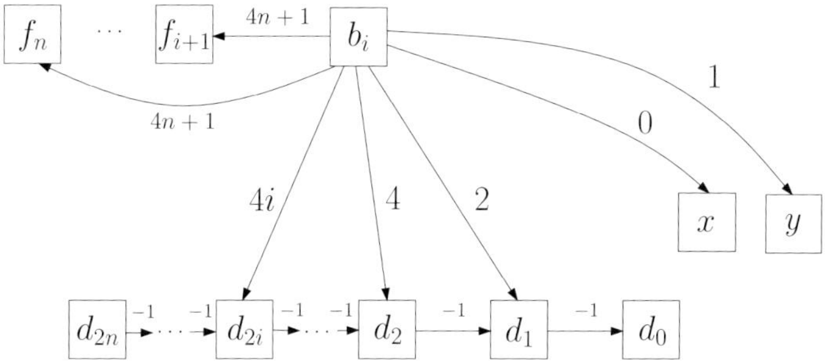

Fig. 3. The outgoing actions from the state b_i

deceleration lane: policy iteration will switch the action (b_i, d_k) in the iteration immediately after it switches the action (d_k, d_{k-1}). Since $\mathrm{r}(b_i, d_k) + \mathrm{r}(d_k, d_{k-1}) = \mathrm{r}(b_i, d_{k-1}) + 1$, this satisfies the condition that prevents the action a_i being switched at b_i. Formally, for every j in the range $0 \leq j \leq 2i + 1$ we define a partial policy:

$$\pi_j^o(s) = \begin{cases} \pi_j(s) & \text{if } s = d_k \text{ for some } k, \\ y & \text{if } j = 0 \text{ and } s = b_i \\ d_{2i} & \text{if } j = 1 \text{ and } s = b_i \\ d_{j-1} & \text{if } 2 \leq j \leq 2i + 1 \text{ and } s = b_i. \end{cases}$$

Proposition 8. *Suppose that Assumptions 3, 5, and 7 hold. When policy iteration is applied to* π_0^o *it will produce* $\langle \pi_0^o, \pi_1^o, \dots \pi_{2i+1}^o \rangle$.

We can now see why a bit with index i can only be set to 1 after all bits with index j such that $j < i$ have been set to 1. Since each state b_i has $2i$ outgoing actions to the deceleration lane, policy iteration is prevented from switching the action a_i for $2i + 2$ iterations. Therefore, policy iteration can switch a_i at the state b_i at least two iterations before it can switch a_j at a state b_j with $j > i$.

The second important property of the deceleration lane is that it can be reset. If at any point policy iteration arrives at a policy π_j^o in which $\mathrm{Val}^{\pi_j^o}(x) > \mathrm{Val}^{\pi_j^o}(y) + 6n + 1$ then policy iteration will switch the actions (d_k, x) for all k and the action (b_i, x) for every $i \in B$, to create a policy π'. The reason why these actions must be switched is that the largest value that a state d_k or b_i can obtain in a policy π_j^o is $\mathrm{Val}^{\pi_j^o}(y) + 6n + 1$. Now suppose that $\mathrm{Val}^{\pi'}(y) > \mathrm{Val}^{\pi'}(x) + 4n$. If this is true, then policy iteration will switch the actions (d_k, y) and the action (b_i, y), and it therefore arrives at the policy π_0^o. The ability to force the deceleration lane to reset by manipulating the difference between the values of y and x will be used in the next section.

We now turn our attention to the states b_i where $i \in B$. Policy iteration should never switch away from the action a_i at these states irrespective of the state of the deceleration lane. Since we have not yet specified the outgoing actions of g_i, we need to assume that the value of b_i is large enough to prevent the actions (b_i, d_k) being switchable.

Assumption 9. *For every policy* π, *if* $i \in B$ *then* $\mathrm{Val}^{\pi}(b_i) > \mathrm{Val}^{\pi}(y) + 6n + 1$.

When this assumption holds, the state b_i will not be switched away from the action a_i. Formally, for j in the range $2 \leq j \leq 2i$ we define a partial policy:

$$\pi_j^c(s) = \begin{cases} \pi_j(s) & \text{if } s = d_k \text{ for some } k, \\ a_i & \text{if } s = b_i. \end{cases}$$

Proposition 10. *Suppose that Assumptions 5, 7, and 9 hold. When policy iteration is applied to* π_0^c *it will produce the sequence* $\langle \pi_0^c, \pi_1^c, \dots \pi_{2i}^c \rangle$.

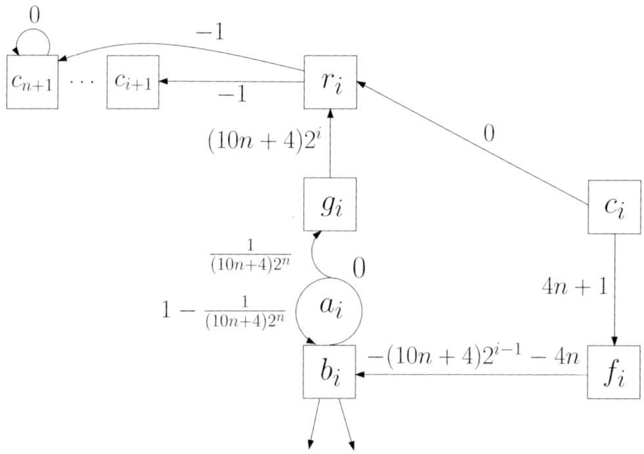

Fig. 4. The structure associated with the state b_i

Figure 4 shows the structure that is associated with each state b_i. We complete the example by specifying the outgoing actions from x and y: there is an action (y, c_i) with reward 0 for every i in the range $1 \leq i \leq n+1$, there is an action (x, f_i) with reward 0 for every i in the range $1 \leq i \leq n$, and there is an action (x, c_{n+1}) with reward -1.

The idea is that the state c_i should use the action (c_i, f_i) only when the index i is a member of B. Moreover, the state r_i should use the action (r_i, c_j) where $j \in B$ is the smallest bit that is both larger than i and a member of B. The state x should use the action (x, f_j) and the state y should use the action (y, c_j) where j is the smallest index that is a member of B.

Formally, for each configuration B we define a partial policy π^B for these states. We define $\pi^B(c_i) = (c_i, f_i)$ if $i \in B$ and $\pi^B(c_i) = (c_i, r_i)$ if $i \notin B$. We define $\pi^B(r_i) = (r_i, c_j)$ where $j = \min(B^{>i} \cup \{n+1\})$. We define $\pi^B(y) = (y, c_j)$ where $j = \min(B \cup \{n+1\})$. We define $\pi^B(x) = (x, f_j)$ where $j = \min(B)$ if $B \neq \emptyset$, and we define $\pi^B(x) = (x, c_{n+1})$ if $B = \emptyset$.

We can now define the sequence of policies that policy iteration will pass through for each configuration B. This definition combines the partial policies π_j, π_j^o, π_j^c, and π^B to give a complete policy π_j^B. If $i = \min(\{i \notin B \;:\; 1 \leq i \leq n\})$ then we define Sequence$(B) = \langle \pi_1^B, \pi_2^B, \ldots \pi_{2i+1}^B \rangle$, where:

$$\pi_j^B(s) = \begin{cases} \pi_j(s) & \text{if } s = d_k \text{ for some } k, \\ \pi_j^c(s) & \text{if } s = b_i \text{ where } i \in B, \\ \pi_j^o(s) & \text{if } s = b_i \text{ where } i \notin B. \\ \pi^B(s) & \text{otherwise.} \end{cases}$$

We can now see why the assumptions that we have made are true in the full example. For example, in Assumption 3 we asserted that $\text{Val}^\pi(g_i) \leq (10n+4)2^n$. This holds for every policy π_j^B because by following this policy from the state g_i

we pass through r_i followed by c_j, f_j, b_j, g_j, and r_j for every index $j \in B^{>i}$, before arriving at the sink state c_{n+1}. Therefore, the value of the state g_i under the policy π_j^B can be at most $\sum_{l=i+1}^{n}(10n+4)(2^l - 2^{l-1}) + (10n+4)2^i = (10n+4)2^n$. The other assumptions that we have made can be also be shown to be true for every policy π_j^B.

Proposition 11. *For every configuration B we have that Assumptions 3, 5, 7, and 9 hold for every policy π in* Sequence(B).

Our previous propositions have done most of the work in showing that if policy iteration is applied π_0^B, then it will pass through Sequence(B). To complete the proof it is sufficient to note that policy iteration never switches away from the policy π^B at the states c_i, r_i, x, and y.

Proposition 12. *When policy iteration is applied to π_0^B policy iteration will pass through the sequence of policies given by* Sequence(B).

4.3 Moving between Configurations

In this section we will describe the behaviour of policy iteration after the final policy in Sequence(B) has been reached. Throughout this section we define $i = \min(\{j \notin B : 1 \leq j \leq n\})$ to be the smallest index that is not in the configuration B, and we define $B' = B \cup \{i\} \setminus \{1, 2, \ldots i-1\}$. Our goal is to show that policy iteration moves from the policy π_{2i+1}^B to the policy $\pi_0^{B'}$.

The first policy that policy iteration will move to is identical to the policy π_{2i+2}^B, with the exception that the state b_i is switched to the action a_i. We define:

$$\pi_{\text{R1}}^B(s) = \begin{cases} a_i & \text{if } s = b_i, \\ \pi_{2i+2}^B(s) & \text{otherwise.} \end{cases}$$

This occurs because the state b_i only has $2i$ actions of the form (b_i, d_k). Therefore, once the policy π_{2i+1}^B is reached there will be no action of the form (b_i, d_k) to distract policy iteration from switching the action a_i. Since every other state b_j with $j \notin B$ has at least two actions (b_j, d_k) with $k > 2i$, they move to the policy π_{2i+2}^B.

Proposition 13. *Policy iteration moves from the policy π_{2i+1}^B to the policy π_{R1}^B.*

Since the action a_i has been switched the value of the state f_i is raised to $\text{Val}^{\pi_{\text{R1}}^B}(r_i) + (10n+4)(2^i - 2^{i-1}) - 4n$. The reward of $(10n+4)2^i$ is sufficiently large to cause policy iteration to switch the actions (c_i, f_i) and (x, f_i). It will also switch the actions (b_j, f_i) where for every index $j < i$. Since every index $j \notin B$ other than i has at least one action (b_j, d_k), these states can be switched to the policy $\pi_{2i+3}^B(s)$. Therefore, we define:

$$\pi_{\text{R2}}^B(s) = \begin{cases} \pi_0^B(s) & \text{if } s = b_i \text{ or } s = r_i \text{ or } s \in \{c_j, b_j, r_j \ : \ j > i\}, \\ f_i & \text{if } s = x \text{ or } s = c_i \text{ or } s = b_j \text{ with } j < i, \\ \pi_{2i+3}^B(s) & \text{otherwise.} \end{cases}$$

The most important thing in this iteration is that every state b_j with index $j < i$ is switched away from the action a_j. This provides the critical property of reseting every bit that has a smaller index than i. Another important property is that, while the action (x, f_i) can be switched in this iteration, the action (y, c_i) cannot be switched until after the action (c_i, f_i) has been switched. This will provide a single iteration in which the value of x will exceed the value of y, which is the first of the two conditions necessary to reset the deceleration lane.

Proposition 14. *Policy iteration moves from the policy π^B_{R1} to the policy π^B_{R2}.*

In the next iteration the deceleration lane begins to reset as policy iteration switches (d_k, x) for all k and (b_j, x) where $j > i$ and $j \notin B$. Policy iteration also switches (y, c_i) and (r_j, c_i) with $j < i$. We define:

$$\pi^B_{\mathrm{R3}}(s) = \begin{cases} \pi^B_0(s) & \text{if } s \in \{c_j, b_j, r_j \,:\, j \geq i\} \cup \{x\}, \\ c_i & s = y \text{ or } s = r_j \text{ with } j < i, \\ x & s = d_k \text{ for some } k \text{ or } s = b_j \text{ with } j \notin B \setminus \{x\}, \\ \pi^B_{2i+3}(s) & \text{if } s = c_j \text{ with } j < i. \end{cases}$$

The switching of (y, c_i) provides the second condition for the reset of the deceleration lane. After the action is switched the value of y will be $\mathrm{Val}^{\pi^B_{\mathrm{R2}}}(f_i) + 4n + 1$ whereas the value of x will be $\mathrm{Val}^{\pi^B_{\mathrm{R2}}}(f_i)$. Therefore, policy iteration will reset the deceleration lane in the next iteration. It is also important that the action (b_j, x) for $j \notin B$ is switchable in this iteration, since if $i + 1 \notin B$ then b_{i+1} will have run out of actions (b_{i+1}, d_k) to distract it from switching a_{i+1}. The is the reason why each state b_i must have $2i$ actions to the deceleration lane.

Proposition 15. *Policy iteration moves from the policy π^B_{R2} to the policy π^B_{R3}.*

Finally, once policy iteration has reached the policy π^B_{R3} it will move to the policy $\pi^{B'}_0$. This involves completing the reset of the deceleration lane by switching (d_k, y) for all k, and switching the actions (b_j, y) for every state b_j with index $j \notin B'$. It also makes the final step in transforming the policy π^B to the policy $\pi^{B'}$ by switching the actions (c_j, r_j) at every state c_j with $j < i$.

Proposition 16. *Policy iteration moves from the policy π^B_{R3} to the policy $\pi^{B'}_0$.*

When combined with Proposition 12, the propositions in this section imply that policy iteration will move from the policy π^B_0 to the policy $\pi^{B'}_0$. The optimal policy for the example is π^B_{2n+1} where $B = \{1, 2, \dots n\}$. This is the policy that selects a_i at b_i for all i, and in which the deceleration lane has reached its optimal policy. Our results so far indicate that if we begin policy iteration at the policy $\pi^{\emptyset}_0$, then policy iteration must pass through a policy π^B_0 for every $B \subseteq \{1, 2, \dots n\}$. Therefore, it will take at least 2^n iterations to terminate.

Theorem 17. *When policy iteration for the total reward criterion is applied to the policy $\pi^{\emptyset}_0$ it will take at least 2^n iterations to find the optimal policy.*

Finally, we can also argue that the example also provides an exponential lower bound for policy iteration for the average-reward criterion. The first thing to note that $G^\pi(s) = 0$ for every policy that we have specified. This is because all runs eventually reach the sink state c_{n+1}. Since the reward of the action (c_{n+1}, c_{n+1}) is 0, the long term average-reward of every policy will be 0. Note that when $G^\pi(s) = 0$, the bias optimality equation (3) becomes identical to the total reward optimality equation (1). This causes policy iteration for the average-reward criterion to behave identically to policy iteration for the total reward criterion on this example.

Theorem 18. *When policy iteration for the average-reward criterion is applied to the policy $\pi_0^\emptyset$ it will take at least 2^n iterations to find the optimal policy.*

Acknowledgements. I am indebted to Marcin Jurdziński for his guidance, support, and encouragement while preparing this paper.

References

1. Andersson, D.: Extending Friedmann's lower bound to the Hoffman-Karp algorithm. Preprint (June 2009)
2. Andersson, D., Hansen, T.D., Miltersen, P.B.: Toward better bounds on policy iteration. Preprint (June 2009)
3. Ash, R.B., Doléans-Dade, C.A.: Probability and Measure Theory. Academic Press, London (2000)
4. Friedmann, O.: A super-polynomial lower bound for the parity game strategy improvement algorithm as we know it. In: Logic in Computer Science (LICS). IEEE, Los Alamitos (2009)
5. Howard, R.: Dynamic Programming and Markov Processes. Technology Press and Wiley (1960)
6. Mansour, Y., Singh, S.P.: On the complexity of policy iteration. In: Laskey, K.B., Prade, H. (eds.) UAI 1999: Proceedings of the Fifteenth Conference on Uncertainty in Artificial Intelligence, pp. 401–408. Morgan Kaufmann, San Francisco (1999)
7. Melekopoglou, M., Condon, A.: On the complexity of the policy improvement algorithm for Markov decision processes. ORSA Journal on Computing 6, 188–192 (1994)
8. Puterman, M.L.: Markov Decision Processes: Discrete Stochastic Dynamic Programming. John Wiley & Sons, Inc., New York (1994)
9. Vöge, J., Jurdziński, M.: A discrete strategy improvement algorithm for solving parity games (Extended abstract). In: Emerson, E.A., Sistla, A.P. (eds.) CAV 2000. LNCS, vol. 1855, pp. 202–215. Springer, Heidelberg (2000)

Regular Temporal Cost Functions

Thomas Colcombet[1], Denis Kuperberg[1], and Sylvain Lombardy[2]

[1] Liafa/CNRS/Université Paris 7, Denis Diderot, France
[2] Ligm - Université Paris-Est Marne-la-Vallée, France

Abstract. Regular cost functions have been introduced recently as an extension to the notion of regular languages with counting capabilities. The specificity of cost functions is that exact values are not considered, but only estimated.

In this paper, we study the strict subclass of *regular temporal cost functions*. In such cost functions, it is only allowed to count the number of occurrences of consecutive events. For this reason, this model intends to measure the length of intervals, i.e., a discrete notion of time. We provide various equivalent representations for functions in this class, using automata, and 'clock based' reduction to regular languages. We show that the conversions are much simpler to obtain, and much more efficient than in the general case of regular cost functions.

Our second aim in this paper is to use temporal cost function as a test-case for exploring the algebraic nature of regular cost functions. Following the seminal ideas of Schützenberger, this results in a decidable algebraic characterization of regular temporal cost functions inside the class of regular cost functions.

1 Introduction

Since the seminal works of Kleene and Rabin and Scott, regularity languages appear as major concept in computer science thanks to their closure properties, their various equivalent characterizations, and the decidability results concerning them.

Recently, the notion of regular cost function for words has been presented as a candidate for being a quantitative extension to the notion of regular languages [7]. A cost function is an equivalence class of the functions from the domain (words in our case) to $\mathbb{N}_\infty$, modulo an equivalence relation $\approx$ which allows some distortion, but preserves the boundedness property over each subset of the domain.

1.1 Related Works and Motivating Examples

Regular cost functions are the continuation of a sequence of works that have intended to solve difficult questions in language theory. The prominent example is the star-height problem raised by Eggan in 1963 [8], but solved only 25 years later by Hashigushi using a very intricate proof [10]. An improved and self-contained proof has been more recently proposed by Kirsten [12]. The two proofs work along the same lines: show that the original problem can be reduced to the existence of a bound over some function from words to integers. This function can be represented

S. Abramsky et al. (Eds.): ICALP 2010, Part II, LNCS 6199, pp. 563–574, 2010.

using an automaton that have counting features. The proof is concluded by showing that such boundedness problems are decidable. Other decision problems can be reduced to boundedness questions over words: in language theory the *finite power property* [14,9] and the *finite substitution problem* [2,11], and in model theory the *boundedness problem* of monadic formulas over words [3]. Distance automata are also used in the context of databases and image compression. Automata similar to the ones of Kirsten have also been introduced independently in the context of verification [1].

Finally, using also ideas inspired from [4], the theory of those automata over words has been unified in [7], in which cost functions are introduced, and suitable models of automata, algebra, and logic for defining them are presented and shown equivalent. Corresponding decidability results are provided. The resulting theory is a neat extension of the standard theory of regular languages to a quantitative setting. All the limitedness problems from the literature appear as special instances of those results, as well as all the central results known for regular languages.

1.2 Contributions

We introduce the subclass of regular temporal cost functions. Regular temporal cost functions are regular cost functions in which one can only count consecutive events: for instance, over the alphabet $\{a, b\}$, the maximal length of a sequence of consecutive letter a's is temporal, while the number of occurrences of letter a is not. This corresponds to the model of *desert automata* introduced by Kirsten [11]. We believe that the notion of regular temporal cost function is of interest in the context of modelization of time.

We show that regular temporal cost functions admit various equivalent presentations. The first such representation is obtained in Section 3 as a syntactic restriction of B-automata and S-automata (the automata used for describing regular cost functions [7]). Second, in Section 4, we provide an equivalent *clock-based* presentation, in which the regular temporal cost functions is represented as a regular language over words labeled with the ticks of a clock as an extra information. We show all the closure results for regular temporal cost functions (e.g., min, max, etc...) using this presentation.This results in constructions of better complexity, both in terms of number of states of automata, and in terms of technicality of the constructions themselves. Last but not least, while in the general theory of regular cost functions the error committed during the construction is bounded by a polynomial, it is linear for regular temporal cost functions.

Our second contribution, in Section 5, is an algebraic characterization of this class. It is known from [7] that regular cost functions are the one recognizable by stabilization monoids. This model of monoids extends the standard approach for languages. One of our objectives in studying regular temporal cost function was to validate the interest of this algebraic approach, and show that results similar to the famous Schützenberger theorem on star-free languages [13] were possible. We believe that we succeeded in this direction, since we are able to algebraically characterize the class of regular temporal cost functions, and furthermore that this characterization is effective.

2 Notations

We will note $\mathbb{N}$ the set of non-negative integers and $\mathbb{N}_\infty$ the set $\mathbb{N}\cup\{\infty\}$, ordered by $0 < 1 < \cdots < \infty$. If E is a set, $E^{\mathbb{N}}$ is the set of infinite sequences of elements of E (we will not use here the notion of infinite words). Such sequences will be denoted by bold letters ($\boldsymbol{a}$, $\boldsymbol{b}$,...). We will work with a fixed finite alphabet $\mathbb{A}$. The set of words over $\mathbb{A}$ is $\mathbb{A}^*$. The empty word is ε, and $\mathbb{A}^+ = \mathbb{A}^* \setminus \{\varepsilon\}$. The concatenation of words u and v is uv.The length of u is $|u|$. The number of occurrences of letter a in u is $|u|_a$. If $L \subseteq \mathbb{A}^*$ is a language, $\complement L$ is its complement $\mathbb{A}^* \setminus L$. We will note $\inf E$ and $\sup E$ the lower and upper bounds of a set $E \subseteq \mathbb{N}_\infty$, in particular $\inf \emptyset = \infty$ and $\sup \emptyset = 0$.

3 Regular Cost Functions

The theory of regular cost functions has been proposed in [7]. In this section, we review some of the definitions useful for the present paper.

3.1 Basics on Cost Functions

The principle of cost functions is to consider functions modulo an equivalence relation $\approx$ allowing some distortions of the values. This distortion is controlled using a parameter $(\alpha, \alpha', \alpha_1 \ldots)$ which is a mapping from $\mathbb{N}$ to $\mathbb{N}$ such that $\alpha(n) \geq n$ for all n, called the *correction function*. For $x, y \in \mathbb{N}_\infty$, $x \preccurlyeq_\alpha y$ means that either x and y are in $\mathbb{N}$ and $x \leq \alpha(y)$, or $y = \infty$. It is equivalent to write that $x \leq \alpha(y)$ in which we implicitly extend α to $\mathbb{N}_\infty$ by $\alpha(\infty) = \infty$. For all sets E, $\preccurlyeq_\alpha$ is naturally extended to mappings from E to $\mathbb{N}_\infty$ by $f \preccurlyeq_\alpha g$ if $f(x) \preccurlyeq_\alpha g(x)$ for all $x \in E$, or equivalently if $f \leq \alpha \circ g$ (using the same implicit extension of α). The intuition here is to consider that g dominates f up to a 'stretching factor' α. We note $f \approx_\alpha g$ if $f \preccurlyeq_\alpha g$ and $g \preccurlyeq_\alpha f$. Finally, we note $f \preccurlyeq g$ (resp. $f \approx g$) if $f \preccurlyeq_\alpha g$ (resp. $f \approx_\alpha g$) for some α. A *cost function* (over a set E) is an equivalence class of $\approx$ among the set of functions from E to $\mathbb{N}_\infty$.

Proposition 1. *For all functions $f, g : E \to \mathbb{N}_\infty$, $f \preccurlyeq g$ if and only if for all $X \subseteq E$, g bounded over X implies f bounded over X.*

To each subset $X \subseteq E$, one associates its characteristic mapping χ_X from E to $\mathbb{N}_\infty$ which to x associates 0 if $x \in X$, and ∞ otherwise. It is easy to see that $X \subseteq Y$ iff $\chi_X \preccurlyeq \chi_Y$. In this way, the notion of cost functions can be seen as an extension to the notion of language.

3.2 Cost-Automata

A *cost automaton* is a tuple $\langle Q, \mathbb{A}, In, Fin, \Gamma, \Delta \rangle$ where Q is a finite set of *states*, $\mathbb{A}$ is a finite *alphabet*, In and Fin are the set of *initial* and *final* states respectively, Γ is a finite set of *counters*, and $\Delta \subseteq Q \times \mathbb{A} \times (\{\mathrm{i}, \mathrm{r}, \mathrm{c}\}^*)^\Gamma \times Q$ is the set of *transitions*.

The value of each counter ranges over $\mathbb{N}$, and evolves according to *atomic actions* in $\{\mathrm{i}, \mathrm{r}, \mathrm{c}\}$: i *increments* the value by 1, r *resets* the value to 0, and c *checks* the value (but does not change it). Each action in $(\{\mathrm{i}, \mathrm{r}, \mathrm{c}\}^*)^\Gamma$ tells for each counter which sequence of atomic actions has to be performed. When a transition is taken, each counter evolves according to the action of the transition.

A *run* σ of a cost automaton over a word $u = a_1 \dots a_n$ is a sequence in Δ^* of the form $(q_0, a_1, t_1, q_1)(q_1, a_2, t_2, q_2) \dots (q_{n-1}, a_n, t_n, q_n)$ such that q_0 is initial, q_n is final (the run ε is also valid iff there exists q_0, both initial and final). At the begining of the run, all counters share the value 0. The set $C(\sigma) = C(t_1 \dots t_n)$ collects the checked values of all counters during the run; there is no distinction concerning the counter the value originates from, or the moment of the check.

At this point, cost automata are instantiated in two versions, namely *B-automata* and *S-automata* that differ by their dual semantics, $[\![\cdot]\!]_B$ and $[\![\cdot]\!]_S$ respectively. These semantics are defined for all $u \in \mathbb{A}^*$ by:

$$[\![\mathcal{A}]\!]_B(u) = \inf\{\sup C(\sigma) \ : \ \sigma \text{ run over } u\} \ ,$$
$$\text{and} \quad [\![\mathcal{A}]\!]_S(u) = \sup\{\inf C(\sigma) \ : \ \sigma \text{ run over } u\} \ .$$

(Recall that $\sup \emptyset = 0$ and $\inf \emptyset = \infty$) One says that a B-automaton (resp. an S-automaton) *accepts* $[\![\mathcal{A}]\!]_B$ (resp. $[\![\mathcal{A}]\!]_S$).

Example 1. We describe the one counter cost automata $\mathcal{A}$ and $\mathcal{A}'$ by drawings:

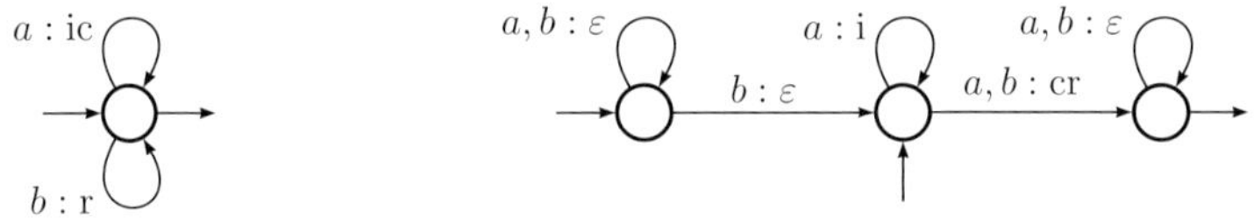

Circles represent states, and a transition (p, a, t, q) is denoted by an edge from p to q labeled $a : t$ (the notation $a, b : t$ abbreviates multiple transitions). Initial states are identified by unlabeled ingoing arrows, while final states use unlabeled outgoing arrows. One checks that $[\![\mathcal{A}]\!]_B \approx [\![\mathcal{A}']\!]_S \approx f_a$ where $f_a(u) = \max\{n \in \mathbb{N} \ / \ u = va^n w\}$.

The following theorem is central in the theory:

Theorem 2 (duality [7,5]). *It is equivalent for a cost function (i.e. always up to $\approx$), to be accepted by a B-automaton or to be accepted by a S-automaton.*

Such cost functions are called *regular*. This comes with a decision procedure:

Theorem 3 ([7,5]). *The relations $\preccurlyeq$ and $\approx$ are decidable for regular cost functions. (i.e. these relations are computed by algorithms taking f and g as input and deciding if $f \preccurlyeq g$ or $f \approx g$)*

3.3 Regular Temporal Cost Functions

The subject of the paper is to study the regular temporal cost functions, a subclass of regular cost functions. We give here a first definition of this class.

A B-automaton (resp. S-automaton) is *temporal* if it uses only actions in $\{\mathrm{ic}, \mathrm{r}\}^{\Gamma}$ (resp. $\{\mathrm{i}, \mathrm{cr}\}^{\Gamma}$). Hence temporal automata are restricted form of automata in which it is disallowed in an action to leave counters unchanged. Intuitively, such automata can only measure consecutive events. We define $temp_B$ (resp. $temp_S$) to map sequences in $\{\mathrm{ic}, \mathrm{r}\}^*$ to $\mathbb{N}$ (resp. $\{\mathrm{i}, \mathrm{cr}\}^*$ to $\mathbb{N}_\infty$) which to u associates $(\sup C(u))$ (resp. $(\inf C(u))$). Those functions are extended to sets of counters and runs as in the general case of cost automata. We say that a cost function is B-temporal (resp. S-temporal) if it is accepted by a temporal B-automaton (resp. a temporal S-automaton). We will see below that these two notions coincide, up to $\approx$ (Theorem 7).

Example 2. Over the alphabet $\{a, b\}$, the cost function f_a from Example 1 is B-temporal (as witnessed by the example automaton).

However, the function $u \mapsto |u|_a$ is not B-temporal, even modulo $\approx$. It can be proved by considering words of the form $(b^N a)^K$.

4 Clock-Form of Temporal Cost Functions

In this section, we give another characterization to B-temporal and S-temporal regular cost functions. This presentation makes use of clocks (the notion of clock should not be confused with the notion of clock used for timed automata).

A *clock* c is a word over the alphabet $\{\llcorner, \downarrow\}$. It should be seen as describing the *ticks* of a clock: the letter is $\llcorner$ if there is no tick at this moment, and it is $\downarrow$ when there is a tick. A clock naturally determines a factorization of time into intervals (we say segments). Here, one factorizes c as:

$$c = (\llcorner^{n_1-1}\downarrow)(\llcorner^{n_2-1}\downarrow)\dots(\llcorner^{n_k-1}\downarrow)\llcorner^{m-1}\ .$$

Let $\max\text{-seg}(c) = \max\{n_1, \dots, n_k, m\} \in \mathbb{N}$ and $\min\text{-seg} = \inf\{n_1, \dots, n_k\} \in \mathbb{N}_\infty$ (remark the asymmetry). A clock c *has period* $P \in \mathbb{N}$ if $n_1 = \dots = n_k = P$, and $m \leq P$. This is equivalent to stating $\max\text{-seg}(c) \leq P \leq \min\text{-seg}(c)$. Remark that given n and P, there exists one and only one clock of length n and period P. Moreover, $\max\text{-seg}(c) = temp_B(h_B(c)) + 1$ in which h_B maps $\llcorner$ to ic and $\downarrow$ to r. Similarly, $\min\text{-seg}(c) = temp_S(h_S(c)) + 1$ in which h_S maps $\llcorner$ to i and $\downarrow$ to cr.

A *clock on* $u \in \mathbb{A}^*$ is a clock c of length $|u|$. One denotes by $\langle u, c\rangle$ the word over $\mathbb{A} \times \{\llcorner, \downarrow\}$ obtained by pairing the letters in u and in c of same index. For L a language in $(\mathbb{A} \times \{\llcorner, \downarrow\})^*$, we define the following functions from $\mathbb{A}^*$ to $\mathbb{N}_\infty$:

$$\langle\!\langle L\rangle\!\rangle_B : u \mapsto \inf\{\max\text{-seg}(c)\ :\ c \text{ clock on } u,\ \langle u, c\rangle \in L\}$$
$$\langle\!\langle L\rangle\!\rangle_S : u \mapsto \sup\{\min\text{-seg}(c)\ :\ c \text{ clock on } u,\ \langle u, c\rangle \notin L\} + 1$$

Lemma 1. *For all languages* $L \subseteq (\mathbb{A} \times \{\llcorner, \downarrow\})^*$, $\langle\!\langle L\rangle\!\rangle_B \leq \langle\!\langle L\rangle\!\rangle_S$.

Proof. Fix u. First case, there is no P such that the clock c over u of period P verifies $\langle u, c\rangle \in L$. In this case, $\langle u, \llcorner^{|u|}\rangle \notin L$, and $\langle\!\langle L\rangle\!\rangle_S(u) = \infty$, so the lemma is verified. Otherwise, we consider the minimal P such that the clock c over u of period P is such that $\langle u, c\rangle \in L$. We clearly have $\langle\!\langle L\rangle\!\rangle_B(u) \leq P$. On the other hand, $\langle u, c'\rangle \notin L$, where c' is the clock over u of period $P-1$. Hence $\langle\!\langle L\rangle\!\rangle_B(u) \leq P \leq \langle\!\langle L\rangle\!\rangle_S(u)$. □

The notations $\langle\!\langle\cdot\rangle\!\rangle_B$ and $\langle\!\langle\cdot\rangle\!\rangle_S$ are easily convertible into temporal cost automata as shown by Fact 4.

Fact 4. *If L is regular and L (resp. $\complement L$) is accepted by a non-deterministic automaton with n states, then $\langle\!\langle L\rangle\!\rangle_B - 1$ (resp. $\langle\!\langle L\rangle\!\rangle_S - 1$) is accepted by a temporal B-automaton (resp. a temporal S-automaton) with n states and one counter.*

Proof. In the automaton for L, each transition of the form $(p, (a, c), q)$ is replaced by a transition $(p, a, h_B(c), q)$; it gives immediately the desired temporal B-automaton. The construction for temporal S-automata is identical, starting from the complement automaton, and using h_S. □

Definition 5. *An* α-clock-language *(or simply a* clock-language *if there exists such an α) is a language $L \subseteq (\mathbb{A} \times \{\lrcorner, \downarrow\})^*$ such that $\langle\!\langle L\rangle\!\rangle_B \approx_\alpha \langle\!\langle L\rangle\!\rangle_S$. A function f* has an α-clock-form *if there exists an α-clock-language L such that $\langle\!\langle L\rangle\!\rangle_S \leq f \preccurlyeq_\alpha \langle\!\langle L\rangle\!\rangle_B$. A cost function* has a clock-form *if it contains a function that has an α-clock-form for some α. We denote by $\mathcal{CF}$ the set of cost functions that have a clock-form.*

One can remark that it is sufficient to prove $\langle\!\langle L\rangle\!\rangle_S \preccurlyeq_\alpha \langle\!\langle L\rangle\!\rangle_B$ for proving that L is an α-clock-language: Lemma 1 provides indeed the other direction.

Example 3. For $L \subseteq \mathbb{A}^*$, $K = (L \times \{\lrcorner, \downarrow\}^*) \cap (\mathbb{A} \times \{\lrcorner, \downarrow\})^*$ is a clock-language, which witnesses that $\chi_L + 1$ has an *identity*-clock-form.

Example 4. Consider the function f_a of Example 1, computing the maximal number of consecutive a's. $M = ((a, \lrcorner) + (b, \downarrow))^*$ verifies $\langle\!\langle M\rangle\!\rangle_B \approx f_a$ (in fact $\langle\!\langle M\rangle\!\rangle_B = f_a$) , but it is not a clock-language: for instance the word ba^m is such that $f_a(ba^m) = m$, but $\langle\!\langle M\rangle\!\rangle_S(ba^m) = 0$. This contradicts $\langle\!\langle M\rangle\!\rangle_S \approx f_a$ according to Proposition 1. Actually, the important intuition behind being in clock-form is that the clock can be chosen independently from the word.

However, we can construct a rational clock-language L for f_a. It checks that each segment of consecutive a's contains at most one tick of the clock, i.e.:

$$L = K[((b, \lrcorner) + (b, \downarrow))K]^* \quad \text{in which} \quad K = (a, \lrcorner)^* + (a, \lrcorner)^*(a, \downarrow)(a, \lrcorner)^* .$$

Let u be a word, and c be a clock such that $\min\text{-seg}(c) = n$ and $\langle u, c\rangle \notin L$. Since $\langle u, c\rangle \notin L$, there exists a factor of u of the form a^k in which there are two ticks of the clock. Hence, $k \geq n + 1$. From which we obtain $\langle\!\langle L\rangle\!\rangle_S \leq f_a$. Conversely, let u be a word, and c be a clock such that $\max\text{-seg}(c) = n$ and $\langle u, c\rangle \in L$. Let $k = f_a(u)$. This means that there is a factor of the form a^k in u. Since $\langle u, c\rangle \in L$, there is at most one tick of the clock in this factor a^k. Hence, $k \leq 2n-1$. We obtain that $f_a < 2\langle\!\langle L\rangle\!\rangle_B$. Hence, L is an α-clock-language for f_a, with $\alpha : n \mapsto 2n$.

Let us turn ourselves to closure properties for languages in clock-form. Consider a mapping f from $\mathbb{A}^*$ to $\mathbb{N}_\infty$ and a mapping h from $\mathbb{A}$ to $\mathbb{B}$ ($\mathbb{B}$ being another alphabet) that we extend into a monoid morphism from $\mathbb{A}^*$ to $\mathbb{B}^*$, the inf-projection of f (resp. sup-projection) with respect to h is the mapping $f_{\inf,h}$ (resp. $f_{\sup,h}$) from $\mathbb{B}^*$ to $\mathbb{N}_\infty$ defined for all $v \in \mathbb{B}^*$ by:

$$f_{\inf,h}(v) = \inf\{f(u) : h(u) = v\} \quad (\text{resp. } f_{\sup,h}(v) = \sup\{f(u) : h(u) = v\})$$

The following theorem shows closure properties of cost functions in clock-form that are obtained by translation to a direct counterpart in language theory:

Theorem 6. *Given L, M α-clock-languages over $\mathbb{A}$, h from $\mathbb{A}$ to $\mathbb{B}$ and g from $\mathbb{B}$ to $\mathbb{A}$, we have:*
- *$L \cup M$ is an α-clock-language and $\langle\langle L \cup M\rangle\rangle_B = \min(\langle\langle L\rangle\rangle_B, \langle\langle M\rangle\rangle_B)$*
- *$L \cap M$ is an α-clock-language and $\langle\langle L \cap M\rangle\rangle_S = \max(\langle\langle L\rangle\rangle_S, \langle\langle M\rangle\rangle_S)$*
- *$L_{\circ g} = \{\langle u, c\rangle : \langle g(u), c\rangle \in L\}$ is an α-clock-language and $\langle\langle L_{\circ g}\rangle\rangle_B = \langle\langle L\rangle\rangle_B \circ g$*
- *$L_{\inf,h} = \{\langle h(u), c\rangle : \langle u, c\rangle \in L\}$ is an α-clock-language and $\langle\langle L_{\inf,h}\rangle\rangle_B = (\langle\langle L\rangle\rangle_B)_{\inf,h}$*
- *$L_{\sup,h} = \complement\{\langle h(u), c\rangle : \langle u, c\rangle \notin L\}$ is an α-clock-language and $\langle\langle L_{\sup,h}\rangle\rangle_S = (\langle\langle L\rangle\rangle_S)_{\sup,h}$*

Proof. Each item follows the same proof principle. For instance,

$$\begin{aligned}(\langle\langle L_{\inf,h}\rangle\rangle_B)(v) &= \inf\{\text{max-seg}(c) : \langle v, c\rangle \in L_{\inf,h}\} = \inf\{\text{max-seg}(c) : \langle u, c\rangle \in L,\ h(u) = v\} \\ &= \inf\{\inf\{\text{max-seg}(c) : \langle u, c\rangle \in L\} : h(u) = v\} = (\langle\langle L\rangle\rangle_B)_{\inf,h}(v)\end{aligned}$$

Assume L is an α-clock-language, and let v be a word and c be the clock witnessing $\langle\langle L\rangle\rangle_B(v) = n$, i.e., such that $\langle v, c\rangle \in L_{\inf,h}$ and $\text{max-seg}(c) = n$. Let c' be a clock over v such that $\text{min-seg}(c') > \alpha(n)$, we have to show $\langle v, c'\rangle \in L_{\inf,h}$. Since $\langle v, c\rangle \in L_{\inf,h}$, there exists u such that $v = h(u)$ and $\langle u, c\rangle \in L$. Hence, since L is an α-clock-language, $\langle u, c'\rangle \in L$. It follows that $\langle v, c'\rangle \in L_{\inf,h}$. □

Lemma 2. *$temp_B$ and $temp_S$ have $\times 2$-clock-forms with $\times 2(n) = 2n$.*

Proof. The proof for $temp_B$ is the same as in Example 4, in which one replaces the letter a by ic and the letter b by r. The $temp_S$ side is similar. □

Theorem 7. *If f is a regular cost function, the following assertions are equivalent :*
1. *f has a clock-form,*
2. *f is B-temporal,*
3. *f is computed by a temporal B-automaton with only one counter,*
4. *f is S-temporal,*
5. *f is computed by a temporal S-automaton with only one counter.*

Proof. (1)⇒(3) follows from Fact 4. (3)⇒(2) is trivial.

(2)⇒(1): Consider a temporal B-automaton $\mathcal{A} = \langle Q, \mathbb{A}, In, Fin, \Gamma, \Delta\rangle$ using counters $\Gamma = \{\gamma_1, \ldots, \gamma_k\}$. A run of $\mathcal{A}$ is a word on the alphabet $\mathbb{B} = Q \times \mathbb{A} \times \{\text{ic}, \text{r}\}^\Gamma \times Q$. It follows from the definition of $[\![\cdot]\!]_B$ that for all $u \in \mathbb{A}^*$:

$$[\![\mathcal{A}]\!]_B(u) = \inf_{\sigma \in \mathbb{B}^*} \{\max(\chi_R(\sigma), \mathit{temp}_B \circ \pi_1(\sigma), \cdots, \mathit{temp}_B \circ \pi_k(\sigma)) \ : \ \pi_{\mathbb{A}}(\sigma) = u\}$$

in which $R \subseteq \Delta^*$ is the (regular) set of valid runs; for all $i \in [\![1,k]\!]$, π_i projects each transition (p, a, t, q) to the its γ_i^{th} component of t (and is extended to words). Finally $\pi_{\mathbb{A}}$ projects each transition (p, a, t, q) to a (and is also extended to words). By Example 3, $\chi_R \in \mathcal{CF}$. By Lemma 2, $\mathit{temp}_B \in \mathcal{CF}$, and by Theorem 6, $\mathcal{CF}$ is stable under composition, max and inf-projection. Hence $[\![\mathcal{A}]\!]_B \in \mathcal{CF}$.

The equivalences (2)⇔(4)⇔(5) are proved in a similar way. □

Actually, Theorem 6 and Lemma 2 allow to state that if a function f is given by one of the five descriptions of Theorem 7, then for any other among these descriptions, there exists a function g which is $\approx_{\times 2}$-equivalent to f.

In the following, we will simply say that f is a *temporal* cost function instead of B-temporal or S-temporal.

4.1 Conclusion on Clock-Forms, and Perspectives

Independently from the second part of the paper, we believe that some extra comments on the clock-form approach are interesting.

First of all, let us stress the remarkable property of the clock-form presentation of temporal cost functions: those can be seen either as defining a function as an infimum ($\langle\!\langle\cdot\rangle\!\rangle_B$) or as a supremum ($\langle\!\langle\cdot\rangle\!\rangle_S$). Hence, regular cost function in clock-forms can be seen either as B-automata or as S-automata. This presentation is in some sense 'self-dual'. Nothing similar is known for general regular cost functions.

Another difference with the general case is that all constructions are in fact reduction to constructions for languages, and any suitable representation can be used to optimize them. However, since two different languages L, L' can be such that $\langle\!\langle L\rangle\!\rangle_B \approx \langle\!\langle L'\rangle\!\rangle_B$ (even $\langle\!\langle L\rangle\!\rangle_B = \langle\!\langle L'\rangle\!\rangle_B$), one must keep aware that optimal operations performed at the level of languages – such as minimization – will not be optimal anymore when used for describing temporal cost functions. It is a perspective of research to develop dedicated algorithmic for regular temporal cost functions.

A third difference is that the error committed, which is measured by the stretching factor α, is linear. This is much better than the general case of cost functions, in which, e.g., the equivalence between B-automata and S-automata requires a polynomial stretching factor. There are also researches to be conducted to take full advantage of this.

In fact, the argument underlying temporal cost functions in clock-forms is interesting per se: it consists in approximating some quantitative notion, here the notion of length of intervals, using some extra unary information, here the ticks of the clock. Since unary information can be handled by automata, the approximation of the quantitative notion becomes also available to the automaton. This is a very robust principle that clearly can be reused in several other ways: infinite word or trees – finite or infinite. Keeping on the same track, a clock is even not required to count the time, it could count some events already written on the input, such as the number of a's, etc. These examples show the versatility of the approach.

5 Algebraic Approach

We first recall the definitions of stabilization semigroups and use them in a decidable algebraic characterization of temporal cost functions.

5.1 Standard Semigroups

Definition. An *ordered semigroup* $\mathbf{S} = \langle S, \cdot, \leq \rangle$ is a set S endowed with an associative product and a partial order $\leq$ over S compatible with the product.

An *idempotent* element of $\mathbf{S}$ is an element $e \in S$ such that $e \cdot e = e$. We note $E(\mathbf{S})$ the set of idempotent elements of $\mathbf{S}$.

Recognizing languages. In the standard theory, the recognition of a language by a finite semigroup is made through a morphism from words into the semigroup which can be decomposed into two steps: first, a length-preserving morphism $h : \mathbb{A}^+ \to S^+$, where S^+ is the set of words whose letters are in S, and second the function π: $S^+ \to S$ which maps every word on S onto the product of its letters. A word u is in the language recognized by the triple (S, h, P), where P is a subset of S, if and only if $\pi(h(u)) \in P$.

It is standard that languages recognized by finite semigroups are exactly the regular languages. It is also by now well known that families of regular languages can be characterized by restrictions on the semigroups which recognize them.

5.2 Stabilization Semigroup

The notion of stabilization monoid has been introduced in [7] as a quantitative extension of standard monoids, for the recognition of cost functions. For simplicity, we consider from now regular cost functions over non-empty words and stabilization semigroups instead of stabilization monoids. The relationship between these objects is made explicit in [6].

Definition 8. *A* stabilization semigroup $\langle S, \cdot, \leq, \sharp \rangle$ *is an ordered semigroup endowed with an operator* $\sharp$: $E(\mathbf{S}) \to E(\mathbf{S})$ *(called* stabilization*) such that:*

$$\forall a, b \in S,\ a \cdot b \in E(\mathbf{S}) \text{ and } b \cdot a \in E(\mathbf{S}) \Longrightarrow (a \cdot b)^\sharp = a \cdot (b \cdot a)^\sharp \cdot b;$$
$$\forall e \in E(\mathbf{S}),\ (e^\sharp)^\sharp = e^\sharp \leq e; \qquad \forall e, f \in E(\mathbf{S}), e \leq f \Longrightarrow e^\sharp \leq f^\sharp.$$

The intuition of the $\sharp$ operator is that $e^\sharp$ represents the value that gets e 'when repeated many times'. This may be different from e if one is interested in counting the number of occurrences of e.

5.3 Recognizing Cost Functions

The first step for recognizing cost function is to provide a 'quantitative semantic' to the stabilization semigroup $\mathbf{S} = \langle S, \cdot, \leq, \sharp \rangle$. This is done by a mapping ρ named a *compatible mapping*, which maps every word of S^+ to an infinite non-decreasing sequence of $S^{\mathbb{N}}$ (see e.g., [7]). The principle is that the ith position in the sequence $\rho(u)$ tells the value of the word u for a threshold i separating what is considered as few and as lot. This is better seen on an example.

Example 5. Consider the following stabilization semigroup:

	b	a	0	$\sharp$
b	b	a	0	b
a	a	a	0	0
0	0	0	0	0

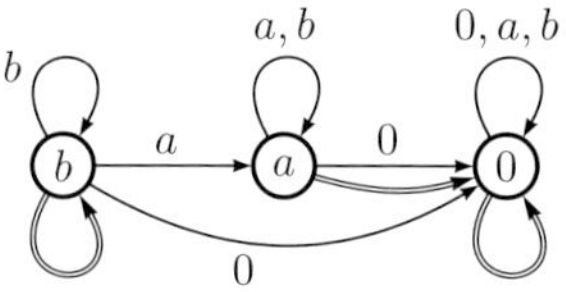

It is given both by its table of product augmented by a column for the stabilization and by its Cayley graph. In the Cayley graph there is an edge labelled by y linking element x to element $x \cdot y$. There is furthermore a double arrow going from each idempotent to its stabilized version.

The intention is to count the number of a's. Words with no a's correspond to element b. Words with a few a's correspond to element a. Finally, words that contain a lot of a's should have value 0: for instance, $a^\sharp = 0$ witnesses that iterating a lot of time a word with at least one a yields a word with a lot of a's.

A possible compatible mapping ρ for this stabilization semigroup attaches to each word over $\{b, a, 0\}^+$ an infinite sequence of values in $\{b, a, 0\}$ as follows: every word in b^+ is mapped to the constant sequence b; every word containing 0 is mapped to the constant sequence 0; every word $u \in b^*(ab^*)^+$ is mapped to 0 for indices up to $|u|_a - 1$ and a for indice $|u|_a$ and beyond. The idea is that for a threshold $i < |u|_a$, the word is considered as having a lot of a's in front of i (hence value 0), while it has few a's in front of i for $i \geq |u|_a$ (hence the value a). One can see that this sequence 'codes' the number of a's in the position in which it switches from value 0 to value a.

A formal definition of a compatible mapping requires to state the properties it has to satisfy, and which relate it to the stabilization monoid. This would require much more material, and we have to stay at this informal level in this short abstract. The important result here is that given a finite stabilization monoid, there exists a mapping compatible with it, and furthermore that it is unique up to an equivalence $\sim$ (which essentially corresponds to $\approx$) [7,6].

The quantitative recognition consists in considering the infinite sequence obtained by the compatible mapping and observing the first moment it leaves a fixed ideal I of the semigroup (an ideal is a downward $\leq$-closed subset). Formally, the cost function f over $\mathbb{A}^+$ recognized by $(\mathbf{S}, h, I)$ is $f : u \mapsto \inf\{n \in \mathbb{N}, \rho(h(u))(n) \notin I\}$, where $h : \mathbb{A}^+ \to S^+$ is a length-preserving morphism, and ρ is a mapping compatible with $\mathbf{S}$.

Typically, on the above example, the ideal is $\{0\}$, and h maps each letter in $\{a, b\}$ to the element of same name. For all words $u \in \{a + b\}^+$, the value computed is exactly $|u|_a$.

Theorem 9. *[7] A cost function is regular iff it is recognized by a stabilization semigroup.*

Like for regular languages, this algebraic presentation can be minimized.

Theorem 10. *If f is a regular cost function, there exists effectively a (quotient-wise) minimal stabilization semigroup recognizing f.*

This minimal stabilization semigroup can be obtained from $(\mathbf{S}, h, I)$ by a kind of Moore algorithm. This procedure is polynomial in the size of $\mathbf{S}$.

5.4 Temporal Stabilization Semigroups

Let us now characterize the regular temporal cost functions.

An idempotent e is *stable* if $e^\sharp = e$. Otherwise it is *unstable*: stable idempotents are not counted by the stabilization semigroup (b in the example), while the iteration of unstable idempotents matters (a in the example).

Definition 11. *Let* $\mathbf{S} = \langle S, \cdot, \leq, \sharp \rangle$ *be a stabilization semigroup.* $\mathbf{S}$ *is* temporal *if for all idempotent s and e, if s is stable and there exists $x, y \in S \cup \{1\}$ such that $e = x \cdot s \cdot y$, then e is also stable.*

For instance, the example stabilization semigroup is not temporal since b is stable but $a = a \cdot b \cdot a$ is unstable. This is related to temporal cost functions as follows:

Theorem 12. *Let f be a regular cost function, the following assertions are equivalent:*
- *f is temporal*
- *f is recognized by a temporal stabilization semigroup*
- *the minimal stabilization semigroup recognizing f is temporal*

We will briefly give an idea on how the definition of temporal semigroups is related to the intuition of consecutive events. Indeed, an unstable idempotent must be seen as an event we want to 'measure', whereas we are not interested in the number of occurrences of a stable idempotent. But if we have $e = x \cdot s \cdot y$ with e unstable and s stable, it means that we want to 'count' the number of occurrences of e without counting the number of s within e. In other words, we want to increment a counter when e is seen, but s can be repeated a lot inside a single occurrence of e. To accomplish this, we have no other choice but doing action ϵ on the counter measuring e while reading all the s's, however, this kind of behaviour is disallowed for temporal automata.

The two last assertions are equivalent, since temporality is preserved by quotient of stabilization semigroups. On our example, the stabilization semigroup is already the minimal one recognizing the number of occurrences of a, and hence, this cost function is not temporal. We gave a direct proof for this fact in Example 2.

Corollary 1. *The class of temporal cost functions is decidable.*

The corollary is obvious since the property can be decided on the minimal stabilization semigroup, which can be computed either from a cost automaton or a stabilization semigroup defining the cost function.

6 Conclusion

We defined a subclass of regular cost functions called the temporal class. Our first definition used cost automata. We then characterized these cost functions as the ones describable by clock-languages. This presentation allows to reuse all standard constructions from classic language theory. We then characterized the class in the algebraic framework of stabilization semigroups. This together with the construction of minimal stabilization semigroups gave a decision procedure for the temporal class, and hopefully for more classes in future works.

The later decidable characterization result calls for continuations. Temporal cost functions correspond to desert automata of Kirsten [11], but other subclasses of automata are present in the literature such as distance automata (which correspond to one-counter no-reset B-automata) or distance desert automata (a special case of two counters B-automata). Is there decidable characterizations for the regular cost functions described by those automata? More generally, what is the nature of the hierarchy of counters?

References

1. Abdulla, P.A., Krcal, P., Yi, W.: R-automata. In: van Breugel, F., Chechik, M. (eds.) CONCUR 2008. LNCS, vol. 5201, pp. 67–81. Springer, Heidelberg (2008)
2. Bala, S.: Regular language matching and other decidable cases of the satisfiability problem for constraints between regular open terms. In: Diekert, V., Habib, M. (eds.) STACS 2004. LNCS, vol. 2996, pp. 596–607. Springer, Heidelberg (2004)
3. Blumensath, A., Otto, M., Weyer, M.: Boundedness of monadic second-order formulae over finite words. In: Albers, S., Marchetti-Spaccamela, A., Matias, Y., Nikoletseas, S., Thomas, W. (eds.) ICALP 2009. LNCS, vol. 5556, pp. 67–78. Springer, Heidelberg (2009)
4. Bojańczyk, M., Colcombet, T.: Bounds in ω-regularity. In: LICS, pp. 285–296. IEEE Computer Society Press, Los Alamitos (2006)
5. Colcombet, T.: Regular cost functions over words. Manuscript available online (2009)
6. Colcombet, T.: Regular cost functions, part i: logic and algebra over words (2009) (Submitted)
7. Colcombet, T.: The theory of stabilization monoids and regular cost functions. In: Albers, S., Marchetti-Spaccamela, A., Matias, Y., Nikoletseas, S., Thomas, W. (eds.) ICALP 2009. LNCS, vol. 5556, pp. 139–150. Springer, Heidelberg (2009)
8. Eggan, L.C.: Transition graphs and the star-height of regular events. Michigan Math. J. 10, 385–397 (1963)
9. Hashiguchi, K.: A decision procedure for the order of regular events. Theor. Comput. Sci. 8, 69–72 (1979)
10. Hashiguchi, K.: Relative star height, star height and finite automata with distance functions. In: Pin, J.E. (ed.) LITP 1988. LNCS, vol. 386, pp. 74–88. Springer, Heidelberg (1989)
11. Kirsten, D.: Desert automata and the finite substitution problem. In: Diekert, V., Habib, M. (eds.) STACS 2004. LNCS, vol. 2996, pp. 305–316. Springer, Heidelberg (2004)
12. Kirsten, D.: Distance desert automata and the star height problem. ITA - RAIRO 3(39), 455–509 (2005)
13. Schützenberger, M.-P.: On finite monoids having only trivial subgroups. Information and Control 8, 190–194 (1965)
14. Simon, I.: Limited subsets of a free monoid. In: FOCS, pp. 143–150 (1978)

Model Checking Succinct and Parametric One-Counter Automata

Stefan Göller[1], Christoph Haase[2], Joël Ouaknine[2], and James Worrell[2]

[1] Universität Bremen, Institut für Informatik, Germany
[2] Oxford University Computing Laboratory, UK

Abstract. We investigate the decidability and complexity of various model checking problems over one-counter automata. More specifically, we consider *succinct* one-counter automata, in which additive updates are encoded in binary, as well as *parametric* one-counter automata, in which additive updates may be given as unspecified parameters. We fully determine the complexity of model checking these automata against CTL, LTL, and modal μ-calculus specifications.

1 Introduction

Counter automata, which comprise a finite-state controller together with a number of counter variables, are a fundamental and widely-studied computational model. One of the earliest results about counter automata, which appeared in a seminal paper of Minsky's five decades ago, is the fact that two counters suffice to achieve Turing completeness [19].

Following Minsky's work, much research has been directed towards studying restricted classes of counter automata and related formalisms. Among others, we note the use of restrictions to a single counter, on the kinds of allowable tests on the counters, on the underlying topology of the finite controller (such as flatness [8,18]), and on the types of computations considered (such as reversal-boundedness [16]). Counter automata are also closely related to Petri nets and pushdown automata.

In Minsky's original formulation, counters were represented as integer variables that could be incremented, decremented, or tested for equality with zero by the finite-state controller. More recently, driven by complexity-theoretic considerations on the one hand, and potential applications on the other, researchers have investigated additional primitive operations on counters, such as additive updates encoded in binary [2,18] or even in *parametric* form, i.e., whose precise values depend on parameters [3,15]. We refer to such counter automata as *succinct* and *parametric* resp., the former being viewed as a subclass of the latter. Natural applications of such counter machines include the modelling of resource-bounded processes, programs with lists, recursive or multi-threaded programs, and XML query evaluation; see, e.g., [2,6,16].

In most cases, investigations have centered around the decidability and complexity of the *reachability* problem, i.e., whether a given control state can be reached starting from the initial configuration of the counter automaton. Various instances of the reachability problem for succinct and parametric counter automata are examined, for example, in [9,13,15].

S. Abramsky et al. (Eds.): ICALP 2010, Part II, LNCS 6199, pp. 575–586, 2010.

Table 1. The complexity of CTL, the modal μ-calculus, and LTL on SOCA and POCA

<table>
<tr><th></th><th></th><th>SOCA</th><th>POCA</th></tr>
<tr><td rowspan="2">CTL, μ-calculus</td><td>data</td><td rowspan="2">EXPSPACE-complete</td><td rowspan="2">Π^0_1-complete</td></tr>
<tr><td>combined</td></tr>
<tr><td rowspan="2">LTL</td><td>data</td><td colspan="2">coNP-complete</td></tr>
<tr><td>combined</td><td>PSPACE-complete</td><td>coNEXP-complete</td></tr>
</table>

The aim of the present paper is to study the decidability and complexity of *model checking* for succinct and parametric one-counter automata. In view of Minsky's result, we restrict our attention to *succinct one-counter automata (SOCA)* and *parametric one-counter automata (POCA)*. On the specification side, we focus on the three most prominent formalisms in the literature, namely the temporal logics CTL and LTL, as well as the modal μ-calculus. For a counter automaton $\mathbb{A}$ and a specification φ, we therefore consider the question of deciding whether $\mathbb{A} \models \varphi$, in case of POCA for all values of the parameters, and investigate both the *data* complexity (in which the formula φ is fixed) as well as the *combined* complexity of this problem. Our main results are summarized in Table 1.

One of the motivations for our work was the recent discovery that reachability is decidable and in fact NP-complete for both SOCA and POCA [13]. We were also influenced by the work of Demri and Gascon on model checking extensions of LTL over non-succinct, non-parametric one-counter automata [9], as well as the recent result of Göller and Lohrey establishing that model checking CTL on such counter automata is PSPACE-complete [12].

On a technical level, the most intricate result is the EXPSPACE-hardness of CTL model checking for SOCA, which requires several steps. We first show that EXPSPACE is 'exponentially LOGSPACE-serializable', adapting the known proof that PSPACE is LOGSPACE-serializable. Unfortunately, and in contrast to [12], this does not immediately provide an EXPSPACE lower bound. In a subsequent delicate stage of the proof, we show how to partition the counter in order simultaneously to perform PSPACE computations in the counter and manipulate numbers of exponential size in a SOCA of polynomial size.

For reasons of space, we have had to abbreviate or omit a number of proofs; full details can however be found in the technical report [10].

2 Preliminaries

By $\mathbb{Z}$ we denote the *integers* and by $\mathbb{N} = \{0, 1, 2, \ldots\}$ the *naturals*. For each $i, j \in \mathbb{Z}$ we define $[i, j] = \{k \in \mathbb{Z} \mid i \leq k \leq j\}$ and $[j] = [1, j]$. For each $i, n \in \mathbb{N}$, let $\mathrm{bit}_i(n)$ denote the ith least significant bit of the binary representation of n. Hence $n = \sum_{i \in \mathbb{N}} 2^i \cdot \mathrm{bit}_i(n)$. By $\mathrm{bin}_m(n) = \mathrm{bit}_0(n) \cdots \mathrm{bit}_{m-1}(n)$ we denote the first m least significant bits written from *left to right*. Let p_i denote the ith prime number for each

$i \geq 1$. We define $\log(n) = \min\{i \geq 1 \mid 2^i > n\}$, i.e. $\log(n)$ denotes the number of bits that are needed to represent n in binary. For each word $v = a_1 \cdots a_n \in \Sigma^n$ over some finite alphabet Σ and each $i, j \in [n]$ define $v[i,j] = a_i \cdots a_j$ and $v(i) = v[i,i]$. For the rest of the paper, we fix a countable set of *atomic propositions* $\mathcal{P}$. A *transition system* is a tuple $T = (S, \{S_\rho \mid \rho \in \mathcal{P}\}, \rightarrow)$, where S is a set of *states*, $S_\rho \subseteq S$ for each $\rho \in \mathcal{P}$ and S_ρ is non-empty for finitely many $\rho \in \mathcal{P}$, and finally $\rightarrow \subseteq S \times S$ is a set of *transitions*. We prefer to use the infix notation $s_1 \rightarrow s_2$ instead of $(s_1, s_2) \in \rightarrow$. An *infinite path* is an infinite sequence $\pi = s_0 \rightarrow s_1 \rightarrow \cdots$. For each infinite path $\pi = s_0 \rightarrow s_1 \rightarrow \cdots$ and each $i \in \mathbb{N}$, we denote by π^i the suffix $s_i \rightarrow s_{i+1} \rightarrow \cdots$ and by $\pi(i)$ the state s_i. A *SOCA* is a tuple $\mathbb{S} = (Q, \{Q_\rho \mid \rho \in \mathcal{P}\}, E, \lambda)$, where Q is a finite set of *control states*, $Q_\rho \subseteq Q$ for each $\rho \in \mathcal{P}$ and Q_ρ is non-empty for finitely many $\rho \in \mathcal{P}$, $E \subseteq Q \times Q$ is a finite set of *transitions*, and $\lambda : E \rightarrow \mathbb{Z} \cup \{\mathsf{zero}\}$. We call a SOCA $\mathbb{S}$ with $\lambda : E \rightarrow \{-1, 0, 1\} \cup \{\mathsf{zero}\}$ a *unary one-counter automaton (OCA)*. A *POCA* is a tuple $\mathbb{P}(X) = (Q, \{Q_\rho \mid \rho \in \mathcal{P}\}, E, \lambda)$, where the first three components are same as for a SOCA, X is a finite set of *parameters over the naturals*, and $\lambda : E \rightarrow (\mathbb{Z} \cup \{\mathsf{zero}\} \cup \{-x, +x \mid x \in X\})$. For each assignment $\sigma : X \rightarrow \mathbb{N}$ the induced SOCA is defined as $\mathbb{P}^\sigma = (Q, E, \lambda')$ where $\lambda'(e) = \sigma(x)$ if $\lambda(e) = x$, $\lambda'(e) = -\sigma(x)$ if $\lambda(e) = -x$, and $\lambda'(e) = \lambda(e)$ otherwise. If $X = \{x\}$ we also write $\mathbb{P}(x)$ instead of $\mathbb{P}(X)$. The *size* of a POCA is defined as $|\mathbb{P}| = |Q| + |X| + |E| \cdot \max\{\log(|a|) \mid a \in \lambda(E) \cap \mathbb{Z}\}$. Hence, we represent each appearing integer in binary. The size of a SOCA is defined analogously. A SOCA $\mathbb{S} = (Q, \{Q_\rho \mid \rho \in \mathcal{P}\}, E, \lambda)$ describes a transition system $T(\mathbb{S}) = (Q \times \mathbb{N}, \{Q_\rho \times \mathbb{N} \mid \rho \in \mathcal{P}\}, \rightarrow)$, where for each $q_1, q_2 \in Q$ and each $n_1, n_2 \in \mathbb{N}$ we have $q_1(n_1) \rightarrow q_2(n_2)$ iff either $\lambda(q_1, q_2) = n_2 - n_1$, or both $n_1 = n_2 = 0$ and $\lambda(q_1, q_2) = \mathsf{zero}$.

3 CTL Model Checking

Formulas φ of CTL are given by the following grammar, where ρ ranges over $\mathcal{P}$:

$$\varphi \quad ::= \quad \rho \mid \neg\varphi \mid \varphi \wedge \varphi \mid \mathsf{EX}\varphi \mid \mathsf{E}(\varphi \mathsf{U} \varphi) \mid \mathsf{E}(\varphi \mathsf{WU} \varphi)$$

Given a transition system $T = (S, \{S_\rho \mid \rho \in \mathcal{P}\}, \rightarrow)$, a state $s \in S$, and some CTL formula φ, define $(T, s) \models \varphi$ by induction on the structure of φ as follows:

$$\begin{aligned}
(T,s) \models \rho &\iff s \in S_\rho \quad \text{for each } \rho \in \mathcal{P} \\
(T,s) \models \varphi_1 \wedge \varphi_2 &\iff (T,s) \models \varphi_1 \text{ and } (T,s) \models \varphi_2 \\
(T,s) \models \neg\varphi &\iff (T,s) \not\models \varphi \\
(T,s) \models \mathsf{EX}\varphi &\iff (T,t) \models \varphi \text{ for some } t \in S \text{ with } s \rightarrow t \\
(T,s) \models \mathsf{E}(\varphi_1 \mathsf{U} \varphi_2) &\iff \exists s_0, \ldots, s_n \in S, n \geq 0 : s_0 = s, (T, s_n) \models \varphi_2, \\
& \forall i \in [0, n-1] : (T, s_i) \models \varphi_1 \text{ and } s_i \rightarrow s_{i+1} \\
(T,s) \models \mathsf{E}(\varphi_1 \mathsf{WU} \varphi_2) &\iff (T,s) \models \mathsf{E}(\varphi_1 \mathsf{U} \varphi_2) \text{ or } \exists s_0, s_1, \ldots \in S. \forall i \geq 0 : \\
& s = s_0, (T, s_i) \models \varphi_1 \text{ and } s_i \rightarrow s_{i+1}
\end{aligned}$$

Subsequently we use the standard abbreviations for disjunction, and implication. Moreover, we define $\mathtt{tt} = \rho \vee \neg\rho$ for some $\rho \in \mathcal{P}$ and $\mathsf{EF}\varphi = \mathsf{E}(\mathtt{tt}\ \mathsf{U}\varphi)$. Let us define the

CTL model checking problem on SOCA and POCA resp.

CTL MODEL CHECKING ON SOCA

INPUT: SOCA $\mathbb{S} = (Q, E, \lambda)$, $q \in Q$, $n \in \mathbb{N}$ in binary, a CTL formula φ.
QUESTION: Does $(T(\mathbb{S}), q(n)) \models \varphi$?

CTL MODEL CHECKING ON POCA

INPUT: POCA $\mathbb{P}(X) = (Q, E, \lambda)$, $q \in Q$, $n \in \mathbb{N}$ in binary, a CTL formula φ.
QUESTION: Does $(T(\mathbb{P}^\sigma), q(n)) \models \varphi$ for every $\sigma : X \to \mathbb{N}$?

3.1 Upper Bounds

Due to space restrictions we do not formally introduce the modal μ-calculus and refer to [1] for more details instead. In [21] Serre showed that the combined complexity of the modal μ-calculus on OCA is in PSPACE. Since every SOCA can be transformed into an OCA of exponential size, and since each CTL formula can be translated into an alternation-free μ-calculus formula with a linear blowup, the following proposition is immediate by adjusting the resulting μ-calculus formula appropriately. Moreover, this immediately implies the containment in the arithmetic hierarchy of the combined complexity of the modal μ-calculus and CTL on POCA.

Proposition 1. *For the modal μ-calculus and CTL the combined complexity on SOCA is in* EXPSPACE*, whereas it is in Π^0_1 on POCA.*

3.2 Hardness of the Data Complexity of CTL on SOCA

Before we prove EXPSPACE-hardness of the data complexity of CTL on SOCA, we introduce some notions and results from complexity theory. Given a language $L \subseteq \Sigma^*$, let $\chi_L : \Sigma^* \to \{0,1\}$ denote the *characteristic function of L*. We define the *lexicographic order on n-bit strings* by $x \preceq_n y$ if and only if $\mathrm{bin}_n(x) \leq \mathrm{bin}_n(y)$, e.g. $011 \preceq_3 101$. We say a language L is *exponentially $\mathcal{C}$-serializable via some language $R \subseteq \{0,1\}^*$* if there is some polynomial $p(n)$ and some language $U \in \mathcal{C}$ s.t. for all $x \in \{0,1\}^n$

$$x \in L \iff \chi_U\left(x \cdot 0^{2^{p(n)}}\right) \cdots \chi_U\left(x \cdot 1^{2^{p(n)}}\right) \in R,$$

where the bit strings on the right-hand side of the concatenation symbol are enumerated in lexicographic order. This definition is a padded variant of the serializability notion used in [11], which in turn is a variant of the serializability notion from [5,14,22]. Some subtle technical padding arguments are required to lift AC^0-serializability of PSPACE, proven in Theorem 22 in [11], to exponential LOGSPACE-serializability of EXPSPACE.

Theorem 2. *For every language L in* EXPSPACE *there is some regular language R such that L is exponentially* LOGSPACE*-serializable via R.*

A further concept we use is the Chinese remainder representation of a natural number. For every $m, M \in \mathbb{N}$ we denote by $\mathrm{CRR}_m(M)$ *the Chinese remainder representation* of M as the Boolean tuple $(b_{i,c})_{i\in[m],0\leq c<p_i}$, where $b_{i,c} = 1$ if $M \bmod p_i = c$ and $b_{i,c} = 0$ otherwise. The following theorem tells us that in logarithmic space we can compute the binary representation of a natural number from its Chinese remainder representation. This result is a consequence of [7], where it is shown that division is in logspace-uniform NC^1.

Theorem 3 ([7] Theorem 3.3). *The following problem is in* LOGSPACE*:*
INPUT: $\mathrm{CRR}_m(M), j \in [m], b \in \{0,1\}$.
QUESTION: Is $bit_j(M \bmod 2^m) = b$?

In the rest of this section, we sketch the proof of EXPSPACE-hardness of the data complexity of CTL on SOCA. Let $L \subseteq \{0,1\}^*$ be an arbitrary language in EXPSPACE. Then by Theorem 2, there is some regular language $R \subseteq \{0,1\}^*$ s.t. L is exponentially LOGSPACE-serializable via R. Hence there is some language $U \in$ LOGSPACE s.t. for all $x \in \{0,1\}^n$ we have

$$x \in L \qquad \Longleftrightarrow \qquad \chi_U\left(x \cdot 0^{2^{p(n)}}\right) \quad \cdots \quad \chi_U\left(x \cdot 1^{2^{p(n)}}\right) \in R, \tag{1}$$

where the bit strings on the right-hand side of the concatenation symbol are enumerated in lexicographic order. For the rest of this section, let us fix an input $x_0 \in \{0,1\}^n$. Let $N = p(n)$ and $A = (Q, \{0,1\}, q_0, \delta, F)$ be some deterministic finite automaton with $L(A) = R$. Let us describe equivalence (1) differently: We have $x_0 \in L$ iff the program in Fig. 1 returns `true`. We are going to mimic the execution of the program by a fixed CTL formula and a SOCA that can be computed from x_0 in logarithmic space. Before we start with the reduction, let us discuss the obstacles that arise:

(A) We need some way of storing d on the counter. Of course there are a lot of ways to do this, but since we want to access all bits of d in the assignment $b := \chi_U(x_0 \cdot \mathrm{bin}_{2^N}(d))$, the most natural way is probably to represent d in binary. However, for this 2^N bits are required. More problematically, we need to be able to check if d is equal to 2^{2^N}. This cannot be achieved by a transition in a SOCA that subtracts 2^{2^N}, since the representation of this number requires exponentially many bits in n. **(B)** As in [12], a solution to obstacle (A) is to store d in Chinese remainder representation with the first 2^N prime numbers. A polynomial number of bits (in n) suffice to represent each of the occurring prime numbers, but we need exponentially many of them. Thus, we cannot equip a polynomial size SOCA with transitions for each prime number, simply because there are too many of them. **(C)** The assignment $b := \chi_U(x_0 \cdot \mathrm{bin}_{2^N}(d))$ implies that we need to simulate on the counter a logarithmically space bounded DTM for the language U on an exponentially large input (in n). Speaking in terms of the input size n, this means that we need to provide polynomially many bits on the counter that can be used to describe the working tape for this DTM. However, we need to provide some on-the-fly mechanism for reading the input.

$q \in Q; q := q_0;$
$d \in \mathbb{N}; d := 0;$
$b \in \{0,1\};$
`while` $d \neq 2^{2^N}$ `loop`
  $b := \chi_U(x_0 \cdot \mathrm{bin}_{2^N}(d));$
  $q := \delta(q, b);$
  $d := d + 1;$
`endloop`
`return` $q \in F$;

Fig. 1. A program that returns `true` iff $x_0 \in L$

Let us give a high-level description of the EXPSPACE-hardness proof. In the first step, we carefully design a data structure on the counter and explain the intuition behind it. In the second step, we list five queries which we aim at implementing via fixed CTL formulas and by SOCA that can be computed from the input x_0 in logarithmic space.

The data structure and how to access it: Let $K = n + 2^N + 1$ denote the number of bits that are required to store an input for U. Let $\alpha = \log K$ denote the number of bits that we require for storing a pointer to an input for U and let β be the number of bits that suffice for storing the Kth prime. Hence $\alpha = O(N)$ and by the Prime Number Theorem, it follows that $\beta = O(\log(K \log(K))) = O(N)$. The number α and such a sufficiently large number β can be computed from x_0 in logarithmic space.

Let us describe the data structure on the counter in our reduction. Assume that the counter value is $v \in \mathbb{N}$. We are interested only in the l least significant bits of the binary representation of v, where l is some number that is exponentially bounded in n; the value of l will be made clear below. Assume $V = \text{bit}_0(v) \cdots \text{bit}_{l-1}(v)$. We imagine V to be factorized into blocks of bits

$$V = I\ M\ C\ J\ X\ Y\ Z\ B \qquad (*)$$

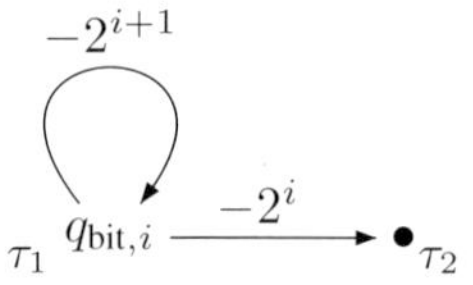

$$\varphi_{\text{bit},1} = \tau_1 \wedge \mathsf{EF}(\tau_1 \wedge \neg\mathsf{EX}\tau_1 \wedge \mathsf{EX}\tau_2)$$
$$\varphi_{\text{bit},0} = \tau_1 \wedge \mathsf{EF}(\tau_1 \wedge \neg\mathsf{EX}\tau_1 \wedge \neg\mathsf{EX}\tau_2)$$

Fig. 2. SOCA $\mathbb{S}_{\text{bit},i}$ and CTL formulas $\varphi_{\text{bit},b}$ for checking if $\text{bit}_i(v) = b$

where $I \in \{0,1\}^\alpha$ is a prime number index; $M \in \{0,1\}^\beta$ is intended to represent the Ith prime number p_I; $C \in \{0,1\}^\beta$ is some residue class modulo M; $J \in \{0,1\}^\alpha$ represents a pointer to some bit of B; X, Y and Z consist of polynomially many bits (in n) and are intended to represent the working tape of three space-bounded DTMs that we will comment on later in more detail; and $B \in \{0,1\}^{n+2^N}$ with $B = x_0 B'$ for some $B' \in \{0,1\}^{2^N}$. Our intention is that B represents the current input for U, and in particular B' represents the counting variable d from Fig. 1. Throughout the rest of this section, v will denote an arbitrary natural number. Moreover I, M, C, J, X, Y, Z and B will implicitly be coupled with v via the factorization $(*)$. Note that all of the bit strings have polynomial length in n except for B. Subsequently, we identify each of the blocks with the natural number they represent. A simple but powerful gadget, which will subsequently be used to check for each $b \in \{0,1\}$ if the ith bit of the counter is b, is shown in Fig. 2. We have that $q_{\text{bit},i}(v)$ satisfies $\varphi_{\text{bit},b}$ iff $\text{bit}_i(v) = b$, for each $b \in \{0,1\}$.

Queries that we need to implement: Next, we list five queries that we aim at answering by instances of the model checking problem. Each query is based on its preceding queries.

(Q1) Assuming $C < M$, does $C \equiv B \bmod M$ hold?
(Q2) Is M the Ith prime number, i.e. $M = p_I$?
(Q3) What is $\text{bit}_J(B)$?
(Q4) Does $(B[1,n] \cdot B[n+1, n+2^N]) \in U$ hold?
(Q5) Does $x_0 \in L$ hold?

EXPSPACE-hardness of data complexity of CTL on SOCA will hence follow from the implementation of query Q5. Let $\gamma = O(N)$ denote the absolute value of the leftmost bit position of B in V. Hence, when the γth bit of V is set to 1 and we subtract 2^γ from the counter, then the leftmost bit of B is set to 0. Similarly, let μ denote the leftmost bit position of M in V. Q1 can now be realized as follows.

Lemma 4. *There is a CTL formula* φ_{mod} *s.t. we can compute from* x_0 *in logarithmic space a SOCA* $\mathbb{S}_{mod}$ *and a control state* q_{mod} *s.t.* $(T(\mathbb{S}_{mod}), q_{mod}(v)) \models \varphi_{mod}$ *iff* $C \equiv B \bmod M$.

Proof. For brevity, we illustrate the special case $C = 0$, i.e. $(T(\mathbb{S}_{\text{mod}}), q_{\text{mod}}(v)) \models \varphi_{\text{mod}}$ iff $B \equiv 0 \bmod M$. The SOCA $\mathbb{S}_{\text{mod}}$ contains four atomic propositions ρ_0, ρ_1, y, z and is depicted below. The CTL formula φ_{mod} expresses that we traverse the sequence of diamonds and thereby repeatedly subtract M from B. The number of diamonds equals β, the number of bits of M. One diamond corresponds to one bit of M. In case bit β of M is 1, which we can verify by a transition to the initial control state of the SOCA $\mathbb{S}_{\text{bit},\mu+\beta}$ (see Fig. 2), we subtract $2^{\gamma+\beta}$ from B, otherwise we do not modify the counter value. This process is repeated until we reach the last diamond in which we consider the first bit of M. Finally, the transition from q_{mod} to the control state satisfying z serves for checking if $B = 0$ by trying to subtract 2^γ.

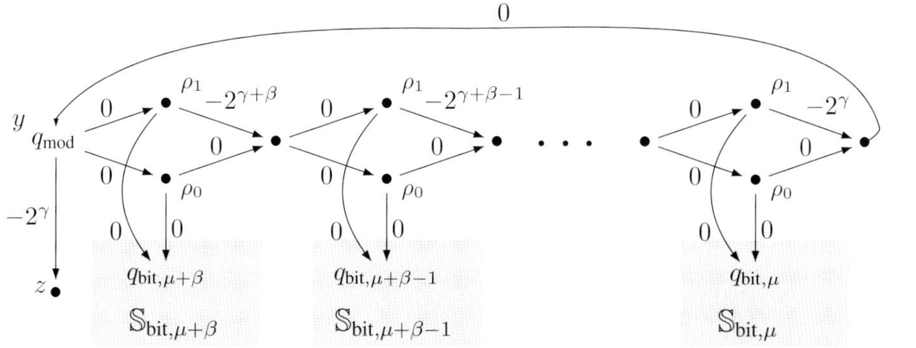

We put $\varphi_{\text{mod}} = \mathsf{E}\left(\bigwedge_{b\in\{0,1\}} \rho_b \to \mathsf{EX}\varphi_{\text{bit},b}\right) \mathsf{U}(y \wedge \neg\mathsf{EX}z)$. □

Let us give some informal ideas on how to implement the queries Q2 to Q5. We strongly recommend the reader to consult the technical report [10] to understand the technical subtleties.

For implementing Q2 we simulate with a SOCA $\mathbb{S}_{\text{prime}}$ some polynomially space-bounded DTM that decides, on the input $\langle I, M\rangle$, whether $M = p_I$. We use the bit string X from $(*)$ for storing the working tape of this DTM on the counter. The current input and working tape symbol and the position of the input and working tape in the counter can directly be hard-wired into the control states of $\mathbb{S}_{\text{prime}}$. We can construct a fixed CTL formula that simulates the computation of this DTM.

Implementing Q3, i.e. deciding the Jth bit of B, is more involved. Recall that B consists of $n+2^N$ bits and J consists of $\alpha = O(N)$ bits. Hence checking if $\text{bit}_J(B) = 1$ cannot be done in a similar fashion as in Fig. 2, since J is too big. The solution is the following: By making use of $\mathbb{S}_{\text{prime}}$, one can initialize M with p_I and after that decide if $C \equiv B \bmod p_I$ by making use of $\mathbb{S}_{\text{mod}}$ and φ_{mod} from Lemma 4. Hence, we can access bits of the Chinese remainder representation of B. Let us assume that $\mathcal{R} = \mathrm{CRR}_K(B) = (b_{i,c})_{1\leq i\leq K, 0\leq c<p_i}$ is the Chinese remainder representation of B. Observe that $|\mathcal{R}|$ is exponential in n and $\mathcal{R}$ is not stored anywhere on the counter. However we can use the bit strings I and C as pointers to access the bit $b_{I,C}$ of $\mathcal{R}$. By Theorem 3, given $\mathcal{R}$ (in our case on-the-fly by the pointers I and C), the bit string J and $b \in \{0,1\}$, we can decide if $\mathrm{bit}_J(B) = b$ by simulating a logarithmically space-bounded DTM on the input $\langle \mathcal{R}, J, b\rangle$ of exponential size. In the block Y of $(*)$ we reserve the space that this DTM requires. Q4 can be implemented similarly as Q3 by simulating a logarithmically space-bounded DTM that decides U on input $B[1,n] \cdot B[n+1, n+2^N]$ of exponential size. We use Z for simulating the working tape and the bit sequence J as a pointer to access the bits of B.

For implementing Q5 we simulate the program from in Fig. 1. Recall that our bit sequence B is of length $n + 2^N$. We initialize the first n bits of B with x_0. The remaining bit sequence B' stores the variable d of the program, initialized with 0 and being repeatedly incremented by adding $2^{\gamma+n}$. Thus, checking when d becomes 2^{2^N} for the first time boils down to checking when B' overflows for the first time. This can be checked by initializing J appropriately and being able to access the Jth bit via query Q3. The states of the automaton A can directly be handled by the control states of the SOCA. To obtain $\chi_U(x_0, \mathrm{bin}_{2^N}(d))$, we invoke the query Q4 and store this bit in the control state of the SOCA. This concludes our EXPSPACE-hardness proof.

Theorem 5. *The data complexity and the combined complexity of CTL and the modal μ-calculus on SOCA is* EXPSPACE*-complete.*

3.3 Hardness of the Data Complexity of CTL on POCA

We now show that there exists a fixed CTL formula for which model checking of POCA is Π^0_1-hard by a reduction from the emptiness problem for *two-counter automata*, which is Π^0_1-complete [19]. Similar to a SOCA, a two-counter automaton $\mathbb{A}$ consists of a finite set of control states and transitions between them. However, each transition of $\mathbb{A}$ acts on two counters, which it can in- and decrement and test for zero.

The idea of our reduction is as follows: Given a two-counter automaton $\mathbb{A}$, we construct a POCA $\mathbb{P}(x)$ with one parameter in such a way that the two counters from $\mathbb{A}$ are encoded into the single counter from $\mathbb{P}(x)$. Given a counter value n of $\mathbb{P}(x)$, $n \bmod x$ encodes the value of the first, and $n \operatorname{div} x$ encodes the value of the second counter of $\mathbb{A}$. Hence, testing whether the first equals 0 corresponds to checking whether $n \equiv 0 \bmod x$, while testing whether the second counter equals 0 corresponds to checking whether $n \geq x$. Incrementing (resp. decrementing) the first counter of $\mathbb{A}$ can be mimicked by adding (resp. subtracting) 1, whereas on counter two this corresponds to adding (resp. subtracting) x. Of course, we need CTL formulas to ensure that we do not overflow when simulating an increment of the first counter of $\mathbb{A}$. For instance, if $n \equiv -1 \bmod x$ and we want to simulate an increment of the first counter of $\mathbb{A}$ in that way, we would actually set the first counter to 0 and simultaneously increment the second counter. However, if $\mathbb{A}$ is not empty, then x can be instantiated with a large enough value such that such an overflow does not occur. Conversely, if $\mathbb{A}$ is empty then there is no such instantiation.

Theorem 6. *The data and combined complexity of CTL on POCA is Π^0_1-complete.*

4 LTL Model Checking

Formulas of LTL are given by the following grammar, where ρ ranges over $\mathcal{P}$:

$$\varphi \quad ::= \quad \rho \mid \neg\varphi \mid \varphi \wedge \varphi \mid \mathsf{X}\varphi \mid \varphi \mathsf{U} \varphi$$

The semantics of LTL is given in terms of infinite paths in a transition system. Let $T = (S, \{S_\rho \mid \rho \in \mathcal{P}\}, \rightarrow)$ be a transition system, $\pi = s_0 \rightarrow s_1 \rightarrow \cdots$ an infinite path in T and φ an LTL formula, we define $(T, \pi) \models \varphi$ by induction on the structure φ.

$$(T,\pi) \models \rho \iff \pi(0) \in S_\rho, \rho \in \mathcal{P} \qquad (T,\pi) \models \neg\varphi \iff \pi \not\models \varphi$$

$$(T,\pi) \models \varphi_1 \wedge \varphi_2 \iff \forall i \in \{1,2\} : (T,\pi) \models \varphi_i \qquad (T,\pi) \models \mathsf{X}\varphi \iff (T,\pi^1) \models \varphi$$

$$(T,\pi) \models \varphi_1 \mathsf{U} \varphi_2 \iff \exists j \geq 0 : (T,\pi^j) \models \varphi_2 \text{ and } \forall 0 \leq i < j : (T,\pi^i) \models \varphi_1$$

LTL MODEL CHECKING ON SOCA

INPUT: SOCA $\mathbb{S} = (Q, E, \lambda)$, $q \in Q$, $n \in \mathbb{N}$ in binary, an LTL formula φ.
QUESTION: Does $(T(\mathbb{S}), \pi) \models \varphi$ for all infinite paths π with $\pi(0) = q(n)$?

LTL MODEL CHECKING ON POCA

INPUT: POCA $\mathbb{P}(X) = (Q, E, \lambda)$, $q \in Q$, $n \in \mathbb{N}$ in binary, an LTL formula φ.
QUESTION: Does $(T(\mathbb{P}^\sigma), \pi) \models \varphi$ for all $\sigma : X \rightarrow \mathbb{N}$ and for all infinite paths π with $\pi(0) = q(n)$?

4.1 Upper Bounds

A standard approach to LTL model checking is the automata-based approach, in which behaviours of *systems* are modelled as non-deterministic Büchi automata (NBA). Given an NBA A modelling a system and an LTL formula φ, the idea is to translate φ into an NBA $A_{\neg\varphi}$ of size $2^{O(|\varphi|)}$ such that the language of $A \times A_{\neg\varphi}$ is empty iff φ holds on all infinite traces of A. The concept of Büchi automata can easily be adopted to the setting of counter automata. Then a *Büchi-SOCA* is not empty if there is an infinite path on which some designated control states occurs infinitely often. The latter boils down to just checking for recurrent reachability. Moreover, the Büchi-SOCA obtained from the product of a SOCA and an NBA can be defined and constructed in a straightforward way. We omit details for brevity.

It was shown in [13] that checking emptiness is coNP-complete for both Büchi-SOCA and Büchi-POCA, and in [9] that it is NL-complete for Büchi-OCA. We use these results for establishing upper bounds for the LTL model checking problems.

For every fixed LTL formula φ, and every POCA $\mathbb{P}$, the size of $\mathbb{P} \times A_{\neg\varphi}$ is $O(|\mathbb{P}|)$, hence the data complexity of LTL on SOCA and POCA is in coNP. Hardness for coNP follows from NP-hardness of reachability using a fixed formula $\mathtt{tt}\mathsf{U}\rho$ for some $\rho \in \mathcal{P}$.

If both $\mathbb{P}$ and φ are part of the input then $|\mathbb{P} \times A_{\neg\varphi}| = |\mathbb{P}| \cdot 2^{O(|\varphi|)}$, and hence [13] gives a coNEXP upper bound for the combined complexity of LTL model checking on both SOCA and POCA. This upper bound can however be improved for SOCA. Given a SOCA $\mathbb{S}$, let m be the absolute value of the maximum increment or decrement on the transitions in $\mathbb{S}$. Let $\mathbb{S}'$ be the Büchi-SOCA obtained from the product $\mathbb{S} \times A_{\neg\varphi}$ by replacing every transition labeled with z with a sequence of fresh transitions and control states of length z, where, depending on the sign of z, each transition is labeled with $+1$ resp. -1. We have $|\mathbb{S}'| = m \cdot |\mathbb{S}| \cdot 2^{O(|\varphi|)}$, and hence the NL upper bound for emptiness of Büchi-OCA from [9] yields a PSPACE upper bound.

Proposition 7. *The data complexity of LTL model checking on SOCA and POCA is* coNP*-complete, the combined complexity of LTL model checking on SOCA is* PSPACE*-complete, and the combined complexity of LTL model checking on POCA is in* coNEXP.

4.2 Hardness of the Combined Complexity of LTL on POCA

We are now going to sketch a proof of coNEXP-hardness of LTL model checking on POCA via a reduction from the complement of the NEXP-complete Succinct 3-SAT problem [20]. An input of Succinct 3-SAT is given by a Boolean circuit $\mathbb{C}$ that encodes a Boolean formula ψ in 3-CNF, i.e. $\psi = \bigwedge_{0 \le j < M}(\ell_1^j \vee \ell_2^j \vee \ell_3^j)$. Let $j \in [M]$ be the index of a clause encoded in *binary* and $k \in \{1, 2, 3\}$. Assume that ψ uses N different variables $y_1, \ldots, y_N$. On input $(j \cdot k)$, the output of $\mathbb{C}$ is $(i \cdot b)$, where $i \in [N]$ is the index of the Boolean variable that appears in literal ℓ_k^j, and where $b = 0$ when ℓ_k^j is negative and $b = 1$ when ℓ_k^j is positive. Succinct 3-SAT is to decide whether ψ is satisfiable. Fig. 3 depicts on a high-level the POCA $\mathbb{P}(x)$ derived from $\mathbb{C}$ that we are using in our reduction.

As a first step, let us provide a suitable encoding of truth assignments by natural numbers. The encoding we use has also been employed for establishing lower bounds for model checking OCA [17]. Recall that p_i denotes the ith prime number. Every natural number n defines a truth assignment $\nu_n : \{y_1, \ldots, y_N\} \to \{0, 1\}$ such that $\nu_n(y_i) = 1$ iff p_i divides n. By the Prime Number Theorem, $p_N = O(N \log N)$ and hence $O(|\mathbb{C}|)$ bits are sufficient to represent p_N. Of course, since we need exponentially many prime numbers they cannot be hard-wired into $\mathbb{P}(x)$.

Let us now take a look at $\mathbb{P}(x)$. It uses one parameter x and employs several gadgets. Only the gadgets $\mathbb{S}_{\mathsf{divides}}$ and $\mathbb{S}_{\mathsf{not\_divides}}$ manipulate the counter. All gadgets are designed so that they communicate via designated propositional variables, and not as in Section 3.2 with the help of the counter. Starting in q_{start}, $\mathbb{P}(x)$ first loads the value of the parameter x on the counter. Think of x encoding a truth assignment of ψ. Next, $\mathbb{P}(x)$ traverses through $\mathbb{S}_{\mathsf{inc}}$, which initially chooses an arbitrary index j identifying a clause of ψ. Every time $\mathbb{S}_{\mathsf{inc}}$ is traversed afterwards, it increments j modulo N and hereby moves on to the next clause. Now $\mathbb{P}(x)$ branches non-deterministically into a gadget $\mathbb{S}_{\mathbb{C}}$ in order to compute $(i \cdot b)$ from $\mathbb{C}$ on input $(j \cdot 1)$, $(j \cdot 2)$, resp. $(j \cdot 3)$. The index i is then used as input to a gadget $\mathbb{S}_{\mathsf{prime}}$, which computes p_i. Then if $b = 0$, it is checked that p_i does not divide x, and likewise that p_i divides x if $b = 1$. Those checks need to modify the counter. After they have finished, we restore the value x on the counter and the process continues with clause $j + 1 \bmod N$. We can construct an LTL formula φ that ensures that all gadgets work and communicate correctly, and prove that ψ is satisfiable iff there is an assignment σ and an infinite path $\pi = q_{\mathsf{start}}(0) \to \cdots$ such that $(T(\mathbb{P}^\sigma), \pi) \not\models \varphi$. The gadgets $\mathbb{S}_{\mathsf{inc}}$, $\mathbb{S}_{\mathsf{circuit}}$ and $\mathbb{S}_{\mathsf{inc}}$ can be realized by simulating

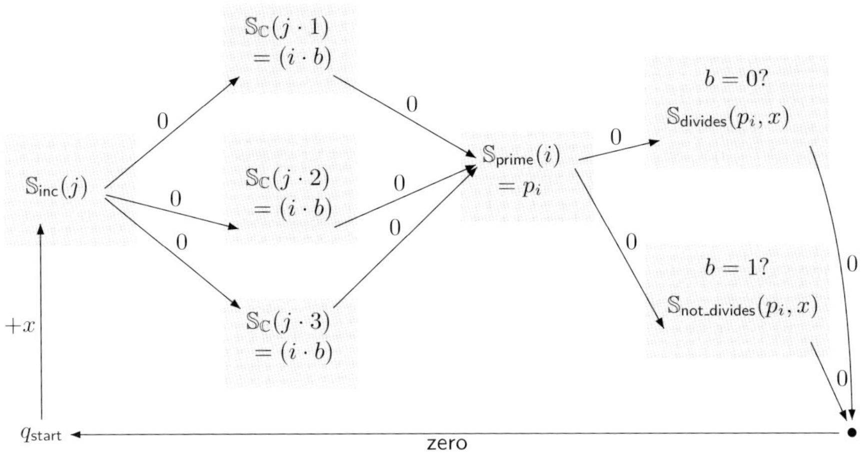

Fig. 3. High-level description of the POCA $\mathbb{P}(x)$ used for the reduction from Succinct 3-SAT

space-bounded Turing machines with SOCA and some appropriate LTL formulas. Here it is important that our LTL formula φ is not fixed. Divisibility resp. non-divisibility is checked similar as in the CTL case, cf. Lemma 4. We refer the reader to the technical report for further details [10].

Theorem 8. *The combined complexity of LTL model checking on POCA is* coNEXP-*complete.*

5 Conclusion

In this paper, we have settled the computational complexity of model checking CTL, the modal μ-calculus and LTL on SOCA and POCA with respect to data and combined complexity. Our proofs for providing lower bounds have introduced some non-trivial concepts and techniques, which we believe may be of independent interest for providing lower bounds for decision problems in the verification of infinite state systems.

An interesting aspect of future work could be to consider *synthesis problems* for POCA. Given a POCA $\mathbb{P}(X)$ and a formula φ, a natural question to ask is whether there *exists an assignment* σ such that $(T(\mathbb{P}^\sigma), \pi) \models \varphi$ on all infinite paths π starting in some state of $T(\mathbb{P}^\sigma)$. For CTL resp. the modal μ-calculus, such a problem is undecidable by Theorem 6. However for LTL it seems conceivable that this problem can be translated into a sentence of a decidable fragment of Presburger arithmetic with divisibility, similar to those studied in [4].

References

1. Arnold, A., Niwiński, D.: Rudiments of μ-calculus. Studies in Logic and the Foundations of Mathematics, vol. 146. North-Holland, Amsterdam (2001)
2. Bouajjani, A., Bozga, M., Habermehl, P., Iosif, R., Moro, P., Vojnar, T.: Programs with lists are counter automata. In: Ball, T., Jones, R.B. (eds.) CAV 2006. LNCS, vol. 4144, pp. 517–531. Springer, Heidelberg (2006)

3. Bozga, M., Iosif, R., Lakhnech, Y.: Flat parametric counter automata. In: Bugliesi, M., Preneel, B., Sassone, V., Wegener, I. (eds.) ICALP 2006. LNCS, vol. 4052, pp. 577–588. Springer, Heidelberg (2006)
4. Bozga, M., Iosif, R.: On decidability within the arithmetic of addition and divisibility. In: Sassone, V. (ed.) FOSSACS 2005. LNCS, vol. 3441, pp. 425–439. Springer, Heidelberg (2005)
5. Cai, J.-Y., Furst, M.: PSPACE survives constant-width bottlenecks. International Journal of Foundations of Computer Science 2(1), 67–76 (1991)
6. Chitic, C., Rosu, D.: On validation of xml streams using finite state machines. In: Proc. of WebDB, pp. 85–90. ACM, New York (2004)
7. Chiu, A., Davida, G., Litow, B.: Division in logspace-uniform NC^1. Theoretical Informatics and Applications. Informatique Théorique et Applications 35(3), 259–275 (2001)
8. Comon, H., Jurski, Y.: Multiple counters automata, safety analysis and presburger arithmetic. In: Y. Vardi, M. (ed.) CAV 1998. LNCS, vol. 1427, Springer, Heidelberg (1998)
9. Demri, S., Gascon, R.: The effects of bounding syntactic resources on Presburger LTL. Journal of Logic and Computation 19(6), 1541–1575 (2009)
10. Göller, S., Haase, C., Ouaknine, J., Worrel, J.: Model checking succinct and parametric one-counter automata. Technical report, University of Bremen (2010), `http://www.informatik.uni-bremen.de/tdki/research/papers/succ.pdf`
11. Göller, S., Lohrey, M.: Branchning-time model checking of one-counter processes. Technical report, arXiv.org (2009), `http://arxiv.org/abs/0909.1102`
12. Göller, S., Lohrey, M.: Branchning-time model checking of one-counter processes. In: Proc. of STACS, IFIB Schloss Dagstuhl (2010)
13. Haase, C., Kreutzer, S., Ouaknine, J., Worrell, J.: Reachability in parametric one-counter automata (2010) (submitted), `http://www.comlab.ox.ac.uk/files/2833/iandc.pdf`
14. Hertrampf, U., Lautemann, C., Schwentick, T., Vollmer, H., Wagner, K.W.: On the power of polynomial time bit-reductions. In: Proc. of CoCo, pp. 200–207. IEEE Computer Society Press, Los Alamitos (1993)
15. Ibarra, O.H., Jiang, T., Trân, N., Wang, H.: New decidability results concerning two-way counter machines and applications. In: Lingas, A., Carlsson, S., Karlsson, R. (eds.) ICALP 1993. LNCS, vol. 700, pp. 313–324. Springer, Heidelberg (1993)
16. Ibarra, O.H., Dang, Z.: On the solvability of a class of diophantine equations and applications. Theor. Comput. Sci. 352(1), 342–346 (2006)
17. Jančar, P., Kučera, A., Moller, F., Sawa, Z.: DP lower bounds for equivalence-checking and model-checking of one-counter automata. Information Computation 188(1), 1–19 (2004)
18. Leroux, J., Sutre, G.: Flat counter automata almost everywhere! In: Peled, D.A., Tsay, Y.-K. (eds.) ATVA 2005. LNCS, vol. 3707, pp. 489–503. Springer, Heidelberg (2005)
19. Minsky, M.L.: Recursive unsolvability of Post's problem of "tag" and other topics in theory of Turing machines. Annals of Mathematics. Second Series 74, 437–455 (1961)
20. Papadimitriou, C.H.: Computational Complexity. Addison-Wesley, Reading (1994)
21. Serre, O.: Parity games played on transition graphs of one-counter processes. In: Aceto, L., Ingólfsdóttir, A. (eds.) FOSSACS 2006. LNCS, vol. 3921, pp. 337–351. Springer, Heidelberg (2006)
22. Vollmer, H.: A generalized quantifier concept in computational complexity theory. Technical report, arXiv.org (1998), `http://arxiv.org/abs/cs.CC/9809115`

Pebble Weighted Automata and Transitive Closure Logics*

Benedikt Bollig[1], Paul Gastin[1], Benjamin Monmege[1], and Marc Zeitoun[1,2]

[1] LSV, ENS Cachan, CNRS & INRIA, France
firstname.lastname@lsv.ens-cachan.fr
[2] LaBRI, Univ. Bordeaux & CNRS, France

Abstract. We introduce new classes of weighted automata on words. Equipped with pebbles and a two-way mechanism, they go beyond the class of recognizable formal power series, but capture a weighted version of first-order logic with bounded transitive closure. In contrast to previous work, this logic allows for unrestricted use of universal quantification. Our main result states that pebble weighted automata, nested weighted automata, and this weighted logic are expressively equivalent. We also give new logical characterizations of the recognizable series.

1 Introduction

Connections between logical and state-based formalisms have always been a fascinating research area in theoretical computer science, which produced some fundamental theorems. The line of classical results started with the equivalence of MSO logic and finite automata [5,8,18].

Some extensions of finite automata are of quantitative nature and include timed automata, probabilistic systems, and transducers, which all come with more or less natural, specialized logical characterizations. A generic concept of adding weights to qualitative systems is provided by the theory of weighted automata [7], first introduced by Schützenberger [15]. The output of a weighted automaton running on a word is no longer a Boolean value discriminating between accepted and rejected behaviors. A word is rather mapped to a weight from a semiring, summing over all possible run weights, each calculated as the product of its transition outcomes. Indeed, probabilistic automata and word transducers appear as instances of that framework (see [7, Part IV]).

A logical characterization of weighted automata, however, was established only recently [6], in terms of a (restricted) weighted MSO logic capturing the recognizable formal power series (*i.e.*, the behaviors of finite weighted automata). The key idea is to interpret existential and universal quantification as sum and product from a semiring. To make this definition work, however, one has to restrict the universal first-order quantification, which, otherwise, appears to be too powerful and goes beyond the class of recognizable series. In this paper, we follow a different approach. Instead of restricting the logic, we define an extended

* Supported by FP7 Quasimodo, ANR-06-SETI-003 DOTS, ARCUS Île de France-Inde.

S. Abramsky et al. (Eds.): ICALP 2010, Part II, LNCS 6199, pp. 587–598, 2010.

automata model that naturally *reflects* it. Indeed, it turns out that universal quantification is essentially captured by a pebble (two-way) mechanism in the automata-theoretic counterpart. Inspired by the theory of two-way and pebble automata on words and trees [12,9,2], we actually define weighted generalizations that preserve their natural connections with logic.

More precisely, we introduce pebble weighted automata on words and establish expressive equivalence to weighted first-order logic with bounded transitive closure and unrestricted use of quantification, extending the classical Boolean case for words [10]. Our equivalence proof makes a detour via another natural concept, named nested weighted automata, which resembles the nested tree-walking automata of [16]. The transitive closure logic also yields alternative characterizations of the recognizable formal power series.

Proofs omitted due to lack of space are available in [4].

2 Notation and Background

In this section we set up the notation and we recall some basic results on weighted automata and weighted logics. We refer the reader to [6,7] for details.

Throughout the paper, Σ denotes a finite alphabet and Σ^+ is the free semigroup over Σ, *i.e.*, the set of nonempty words. The length of $u \in \Sigma^+$ is denoted $|u|$. If $|u| = n \geq 1$, we usually write $u = u_1 \cdots u_n$ with $u_i \in \Sigma$ and we let $\mathrm{Pos}(u) = \{1, \ldots, n\}$. For $1 \leq i \leq j \leq n$, we denote by $u[i..j]$ the factor $u_i u_{i+1} \cdots u_j$ of u. Finally, we let $\Sigma^{\leq k} = \bigcup_{1 \leq i \leq k} \Sigma^i$.

Formal power series. A *semiring* is a structure $\mathbb{K} = (K, +, \cdot, \mathbf{0}, \mathbf{1})$ where $(K, +, \mathbf{0})$ is a commutative monoid, $(K, \cdot, \mathbf{1})$ is a monoid, $\cdot$ distributes over $+$, and $\mathbf{0}$ is absorbing for $\cdot$. We say that $\mathbb{K}$ is *commutative* if so is $(K, \cdot, \mathbf{1})$. We shall refer in the examples to the usual Boolean semiring $\mathbb{B} = (\{\mathbf{0}, \mathbf{1}\}, \vee, \wedge, \mathbf{0}, \mathbf{1})$ and to the semiring $(\mathbb{N}, +, \cdot, 0, 1)$ of natural numbers, denoted $\mathbb{N}$. A *formal power series* (or *series*, for short) is a mapping $f : \Sigma^+ \to \mathbb{K}$. The set of series is denoted $\mathbb{K}\langle\langle\Sigma^+\rangle\rangle$. We denote again by $+$ and $\cdot$ the pointwise addition and multiplication (called the *Hadamard product*) on $\mathbb{K}\langle\langle\Sigma^+\rangle\rangle$, and by $\mathbf{0}$ and $\mathbf{1}$ the constant series with values $\mathbf{0}$ and $\mathbf{1}$, respectively. Then $(\mathbb{K}\langle\langle\Sigma^+\rangle\rangle, +, \cdot, \mathbf{0}, \mathbf{1})$ is itself a semiring.

Weighted automata. All automata we consider are finite. A *weighted automaton* (wA) over $\mathbb{K} = (K, +, \cdot, \mathbf{0}, \mathbf{1})$ and Σ is a tuple $\mathcal{A} = (Q, \mu, \lambda, \gamma)$, where Q is the set of states, $\mu : \Sigma \to K^{Q \times Q}$ is the transition weight function and $\lambda, \gamma : Q \to K$ are weight functions for entering and leaving a state. The function μ gives, for each $a \in \Sigma$ and $p, q \in Q$, the weight $\mu(a)_{p,q}$ of the transition $p \xrightarrow{a} q$. It extends uniquely to a homomorphism $\mu : \Sigma^+ \to K^{Q \times Q}$. Viewing μ as a mapping $\mu : Q \times \Sigma^+ \times Q \to K$, we sometimes write $\mu(p, u, q)$ instead of $\mu(u)_{p,q}$. A *run* on a word $u = u_1 \cdots u_n$ is a sequence of transitions $\rho = p_0 \xrightarrow{u_1} p_1 \xrightarrow{u_2} \cdots \xrightarrow{u_n} p_n$. The *weight* of the run ρ is $\mathrm{weight}(\rho) \stackrel{\mathrm{def}}{=} \lambda(p_0) \cdot [\prod_{i=1}^{n} \mu(p_{i-1}, u_i, p_i)] \cdot \gamma(p_n)$, and the *weight* $[\![\mathcal{A}]\!](u)$ of u is the sum of all weights of runs on u, which can also be computed as $[\![\mathcal{A}]\!](u) = \lambda \cdot \mu(u) \cdot \gamma$, viewing λ, $\mu(u)$, γ as matrices of dimension $1 \times |Q|$, $|Q| \times |Q|$ and $|Q| \times 1$, respectively. We call $[\![\mathcal{A}]\!] \in \mathbb{K}\langle\langle\Sigma^+\rangle\rangle$ the *behavior*, or *semantics* of $\mathcal{A}$. A series $f \in \mathbb{K}\langle\langle \Sigma^+ \rangle\rangle$ is *recognizable* if it is the behavior of some wA. We let $\mathbb{K}^{\text{rec}}\langle\langle \Sigma^+ \rangle\rangle$ be the collection of all recognizable series.

Example 1. Consider $(\mathbb{N}, +, \cdot, 0, 1)$ and let $\mathcal{A}$ be the automaton with a single state, $\mu(a) = 2$ for all $a \in \Sigma$, and $\lambda = \gamma = 1$. Then, $[\![\mathcal{A}]\!](u) = 2^{|u|}$ for all $u \in \Sigma^+$.

It is well-known that $\mathbb{K}^{\text{rec}}\langle\langle \Sigma^+ \rangle\rangle$ is stable under $+$ and, if $\mathbb{K}$ is commutative, also under $\cdot$, making $(\mathbb{K}^{\text{rec}}\langle\langle \Sigma^+ \rangle\rangle, +, \cdot, \mathbf{0}, \mathbf{1})$ a subsemiring of $(\mathbb{K}\langle\langle \Sigma^+ \rangle\rangle, +, \cdot, \mathbf{0}, \mathbf{1})$.

Weighted logics. We fix infinite supplies $\text{Var} = \{x, y, z, t, \ldots\}$ of first-order variables, and $\text{VAR} = \{X, Y, \ldots\}$ of second-order variables. The class of *weighted monadic second-order* formulas over $\mathbb{K}$ and Σ, denoted $\text{MSO}(\mathbb{K}, \Sigma)$ (shortly MSO), is given by the following grammar, with $k \in K$, $a \in \Sigma$, $x, y \in \text{Var}$ and $X \in \text{VAR}$:

$$\varphi ::= k \mid P_a(x) \mid x \leq y \mid x \in X \mid \neg\varphi \mid \varphi \vee \varphi \mid \varphi \wedge \varphi \mid \exists x\varphi \mid \forall x\varphi \mid \exists X\varphi \mid \forall X\varphi\,.$$

For $\varphi \in \text{MSO}(\mathbb{K}, \Sigma)$, let $\text{Free}(\varphi)$ denote the set of free variables of φ. If $\text{Free}(\varphi) = \emptyset$, then φ is called a *sentence*. For a finite set $\mathcal{V} \subseteq \text{Var} \cup \text{VAR}$ and a word $u \in \Sigma^+$, a $(\mathcal{V}, u)$*-assignment* is a function σ that maps a first-order variable in $\mathcal{V}$ to an element of $\text{Pos}(u)$ and a second-order variable in $\mathcal{V}$ to a subset of $\text{Pos}(u)$. For $x \in \text{Var}$ and $i \in \text{Pos}(u)$, $\sigma[x \mapsto i]$ denotes the $(\mathcal{V} \cup \{x\}, u)$-assignment that maps x to i and, otherwise, coincides with σ. For $X \in \text{VAR}$ and $I \subseteq \text{Pos}(u)$, the $(\mathcal{V} \cup \{X\}, u)$-assignment $\sigma[X \mapsto I]$ is defined similarly.

A pair (u, σ), where σ is a $(\mathcal{V}, u)$-assignment, can be encoded as a word over the extended alphabet $\Sigma_{\mathcal{V}} \stackrel{\text{def}}{=} \Sigma \times \{0,1\}^{\mathcal{V}}$. We write a word $(u_1, \sigma_1) \cdots (u_n, \sigma_n) \in \Sigma_{\mathcal{V}}^+$ as (u, σ) where $u = u_1 \cdots u_n$ and $\sigma = \sigma_1 \cdots \sigma_n$. We call (u, σ) *valid* if, for each first-order variable $x \in \mathcal{V}$, the x-row of σ contains exactly one 1. If (u, σ) is valid, then σ can be considered as the $(\mathcal{V}, u)$-assignment that maps a first-order variable $x \in \mathcal{V}$ to the unique position carrying 1 in the x-row, and a second-order variable $X \in \mathcal{V}$ to the set of positions carrying 1 in the X-row.

Fix a finite set $\mathcal{V}$ of variables such that $\text{Free}(\varphi) \subseteq \mathcal{V}$. The semantics $[\![\varphi]\!]_{\mathcal{V}} \in \mathbb{K}\langle\langle \Sigma_{\mathcal{V}}^+ \rangle\rangle$ of φ wrt. $\mathcal{V}$ is given as follows: if (u, σ) is not valid, we set $[\![\varphi]\!]_{\mathcal{V}}(u, \sigma) = \mathbf{0}$, otherwise $[\![\varphi]\!]_{\mathcal{V}}$ is given by Figure 1. Hereby, the product follows the natural order on $\text{Pos}(u)$ and some fixed order on the power set of $\text{Pos}(u)$. We simply write $[\![\varphi]\!]$ for $[\![\varphi]\!]_{\text{Free}(\varphi)}$ and say that φ is recognizable if so is $[\![\varphi]\!]$. We note $\mathbb{K}^{\text{MSO}}\langle\langle \Sigma^+ \rangle\rangle$ the class of all series definable by a sentence of $\text{MSO}(\mathbb{K}, \Sigma)$.

Example 2. For $\mathbb{K} = \mathbb{B}$, recognizable and $\text{MSO}(\mathbb{K}, \Sigma)$-definable languages coincide. In contrast, for $\mathbb{K} = (\mathbb{N}, +, \cdot, 0, 1)$, the very definition yields $[\![\forall x \forall y\, 2]\!](u) = 2^{|u|^2}$, which is not recognizable [6]. Indeed, the function computed by a wA $\mathcal{A}$ satisfies $[\![\mathcal{A}]\!](u) = 2^{\mathcal{O}(|u|)}$. Also observe that the behavior of the automaton of Example 1 is $[\![\forall y\, 2]\!]$. Therefore, recognizable series are not stable under universal first-order quantification.

Let $\text{bMSO}(\mathbb{K}, \Sigma)$ be the syntactic Boolean fragment of $\text{MSO}(\mathbb{K}, \Sigma)$ given by

$$\varphi ::= \mathbf{0} \mid \mathbf{1} \mid P_a(x) \mid x \leq y \mid x \in X \mid \neg\varphi \mid \varphi \wedge \varphi \mid \forall x\varphi \mid \forall X\varphi\,,$$

$$[\![k]\!]_{\mathcal{V}}(u,\sigma) = k, \quad \text{for } k \in K$$

$$[\![P_a(x)]\!]_{\mathcal{V}}(u,\sigma) = \begin{cases} \mathbf{1} \text{ if } u_{\sigma(x)} = a \\ \mathbf{0} \text{ otherwise} \end{cases}$$

$$[\![x \in X]\!]_{\mathcal{V}}(u,\sigma) = \begin{cases} \mathbf{1} \text{ if } \sigma(x) \in \sigma(X) \\ \mathbf{0} \text{ otherwise} \end{cases}$$

$$[\![x \leq y]\!]_{\mathcal{V}}(u,\sigma) = \begin{cases} \mathbf{1} \text{ if } \sigma(x) \leq \sigma(y) \\ \mathbf{0} \text{ otherwise} \end{cases}$$

$$[\![\neg\varphi]\!]_{\mathcal{V}}(u,\sigma) = \begin{cases} \mathbf{1} \text{ if } [\![\varphi]\!]_{\mathcal{V}}(u,\sigma) = \mathbf{0} \\ \mathbf{0} \text{ otherwise} \end{cases}$$

$$[\![\varphi_1 \vee \varphi_2]\!]_{\mathcal{V}}(u,\sigma) = [\![\varphi_1]\!]_{\mathcal{V}}(u,\sigma) + [\![\varphi_2]\!]_{\mathcal{V}}(u,\sigma)$$

$$[\![\varphi_1 \wedge \varphi_2]\!]_{\mathcal{V}}(u,\sigma) = [\![\varphi_1]\!]_{\mathcal{V}}(u,\sigma) \cdot [\![\varphi_2]\!]_{\mathcal{V}}(u,\sigma)$$

$$[\![\exists x\varphi]\!]_{\mathcal{V}}(u,\sigma) = \sum_{i \in \mathrm{Pos}(u)} [\![\varphi]\!]_{\mathcal{V}\cup\{x\}}(u,\sigma[x \mapsto i])$$

$$[\![\exists X\varphi]\!]_{\mathcal{V}}(u,\sigma) = \sum_{I \subseteq \mathrm{Pos}(u)} [\![\varphi]\!]_{\mathcal{V}\cup\{X\}}(u,\sigma[X \mapsto I])$$

$$[\![\forall x\varphi]\!]_{\mathcal{V}}(u,\sigma) = \prod_{i \in \mathrm{Pos}(u)} [\![\varphi]\!]_{\mathcal{V}\cup\{x\}}(u,\sigma[x \mapsto i])$$

$$[\![\forall X\varphi]\!]_{\mathcal{V}}(u,\sigma) = \prod_{I \subseteq \mathrm{Pos}(u)} [\![\varphi]\!]_{\mathcal{V}\cup\{X\}}(u,\sigma[X \mapsto I])$$

Fig. 1. Semantics of weighted MSO

where $a \in \Sigma$, $x, y \in \mathrm{Var}$ and $X \in \mathrm{VAR}$. One can check, by induction, that the semantics of any bMSO formula over an arbitrary semiring $\mathbb{K}$ assumes values in $\{\mathbf{0},\mathbf{1}\}$ and coincides with the classical semantics in $\mathbb{B}$.

We use macros for Boolean disjunction $\varphi \veebar \psi \stackrel{\text{def}}{=} \neg(\neg\varphi \wedge \neg\psi)$ and Boolean existential quantifications $\underline{\exists} x\varphi \stackrel{\text{def}}{=} \neg\forall x\neg\varphi$, and $\underline{\exists} X\varphi \stackrel{\text{def}}{=} \neg\forall X\neg\varphi$. The semantics of $\veebar$ and $\underline{\exists}$ coincide with the classical semantics of disjunction and existential quantification in the Boolean semiring $\mathbb{B}$. Finally, we define $\varphi \xrightarrow{+} \psi \stackrel{\text{def}}{=} \neg\varphi \vee (\varphi \wedge \psi)$ so that, if φ is a Boolean formula (*i.e.*, $[\![\varphi]\!](\Sigma^+) \subseteq \{\mathbf{0},\mathbf{1}\}$), $[\![\varphi \xrightarrow{+} \psi]\!](u,\sigma) = [\![\psi]\!](u,\sigma)$ if $[\![\varphi]\!](u,\sigma) = \mathbf{1}$, and $[\![\varphi \xrightarrow{+} \psi]\!](u,\sigma) = \mathbf{1}$ if $[\![\varphi]\!](u,\sigma) = \mathbf{0}$.

A common fragment of $\mathrm{MSO}(\mathbb{K},\Sigma)$ is the weighted first-order logic $\mathrm{FO}(\mathbb{K},\Sigma)$, where no second-order quantifier appears (note that second order variables may still appear free): $\varphi ::= k \mid P_a(x) \mid x \leq y \mid x \in X \mid \neg\varphi \mid \varphi\vee\varphi \mid \varphi\wedge\varphi \mid \exists x\varphi \mid \forall x\varphi$.

We define similarly $\mathrm{bFO}(\mathbb{K},\Sigma)$ as the fragment of $\mathrm{bMSO}(\mathbb{K},\Sigma)$ with no second-order quantifiers. We also let bFO+mod be the fragment of bMSO consisting of bFO augmented with modulo constraints $x \equiv_\ell m$ for constants $1 \leq m \leq \ell$ (since the positions of words start with 1, it is more convenient to compute modulo as a value between 1 and ℓ). The semantics is given by $[\![x \equiv_\ell m]\!](u,\sigma) = \mathbf{1}$ if $\sigma(x) \equiv m \bmod \ell$ and $\mathbf{0}$ otherwise: it can be defined in bMSO by

$$x \equiv_\ell m \stackrel{\text{def}}{=} \forall X\Big(\big[(x \in X) \wedge \big(\forall y(y \in X \wedge y > \ell) \xrightarrow{+} y - \ell \in X\big)\big] \xrightarrow{+} m \in X\Big).$$

For $\mathcal{L} \subseteq$ bMSO closed under $\vee$, $\wedge$ and $\neg$, an *$\mathcal{L}$-step formula* is a formula obtained from the grammar $\varphi ::= k \mid \alpha \mid \neg\varphi \mid \varphi \vee \varphi \mid \varphi \wedge \varphi$, with $k \in K$ and $\alpha \in \mathcal{L}$. In particular, quantifications are only allowed in formulas $\alpha \in \mathcal{L}$. The following lemma shows in particular that an $\mathcal{L}$-step formula assumes a finite number of values, each of which corresponds to an $\mathcal{L}$-definable language.

Lemma 3. *For every $\mathcal{L}$-step formula φ, one can construct an equivalent formula $\psi = \bigvee_i(\varphi_i \wedge k_i)$ with $\varphi_i \in \mathcal{L}$ and $k_i \in K$, with the same set of free variables.*

From now on, we freely use Lemma 3, using the special form it provides for $\mathcal{L}$-step formulas. All bMSO-step formulas are clearly recognizable. By [6], $\forall x\,\varphi$ is recognizable for any bMSO-step formula φ. The fragment $\mathrm{RMSO}(\mathbb{K},\Sigma)$ of MSO is defined by restricting universal second-order quantification to bMSO formulas and universal first-order quantification to bMSO-step formulas.

Theorem 4 ([6]). *A series is recognizable iff it is definable in* $\mathrm{RMSO}(\mathbb{K},\Sigma)$.

3 Transitive Closure Logic and Weighted Automata

To ease notation, we write $[\![\varphi(x,y)]\!](u,i,j)$ instead of $[\![\varphi(x,y)]\!](u,[x\mapsto i, y\mapsto j])$. We allow constants, modulo constraints and comparisons, like *e.g.* $x \le y+2$. We use first and last as abbreviations for the first and last positions of a word. All of these shortcuts can be replaced by suitable bFO-formulas, except "$x =_\ell m$" with $1 \le m \le \ell$, which is bMSO-definable.

Bounded transitive closure. For a formula $\varphi(x,y)$ with at least two free variables x and y, and an integer $N>0$, we let $\varphi^{1,N}(x,y) \stackrel{\text{def}}{=} (x \le y \le x+N) \wedge \varphi(x,y)$ and for $n\ge 2$, we define the formula $\varphi^{n,N}(x,y)$ as

$$\exists z_0 \cdots \exists z_n \big[x = z_0 \wedge y = z_n \wedge \bigwedge_{1\le \ell\le n} (z_{\ell-1} < z_\ell \le z_{\ell-1}+N) \wedge \varphi(z_{\ell-1}, z_\ell)\big]\,. \quad (1)$$

We define for each $N>0$ the $N\text{-}\mathrm{TC}^<_{xy}$ operator by $N\text{-}\mathrm{TC}^<_{xy}\varphi = \bigvee_{n\ge 1}\varphi^{n,N}$. This infinite disjunction is well-defined: $[\![\varphi^{n,N}(x,y)]\!](u,\sigma)=0$ if $n \ge \max(2,|u|)$, *i.e.*, on each pair (u,σ), only finitely many disjuncts assume a nonzero value. Intuitively, the $N\text{-}\mathrm{TC}^<_{xy}$ operator generalizes the forward transitive closure operator from the Boolean case, but limiting it to *intermediate* forward steps of length $\le N$. The fragment $\mathrm{FO{+}BTC}^<(\mathbb{K},\Sigma)$ is then defined by the grammar

$$\varphi ::= k \mid P_a(x) \mid x \le y \mid \neg\varphi \mid \varphi \vee \varphi \mid \varphi\wedge\varphi \mid \exists x\varphi \mid \forall x\varphi \mid N\text{-}\mathrm{TC}^<_{xy}\varphi\,,$$

with $N \ge 1$ and the restriction that one can apply negation only over bFO-formulas. We denote by $\mathbb{K}^{\mathrm{FO+BTC}^<}\langle\!\langle \Sigma^+\rangle\!\rangle$ the class of all $\mathrm{FO{+}BTC}^<(\mathbb{K},\Sigma)$-definable series.

Example 5. Let $\varphi(x,y) \stackrel{\text{def}}{=} (y=x+1)\wedge\forall z\, 2\wedge(x=1 \stackrel{+}{\to} \forall z\, 2)$ over $\mathbb{K}=\mathbb{N}$. Let $u = u_1\cdots u_n$. For any $N\ge 1$, we have $[\![N\text{-}\mathrm{TC}^<_{xy}\varphi]\!](u,\mathsf{first},\mathsf{last}) = \prod_{i=1}^{n-1}[\![\varphi]\!](u,i,i+1)$ due to the constraint $y=x+1$ in φ. Now, $[\![\varphi]\!](u,1,2)=2^{2|u|}$ and $[\![\varphi]\!](u,i,i+1) = 2^{|u|}$ if $i>1$, so $[\![N\text{-}\mathrm{TC}^<_{xy}\varphi]\!](u,\mathsf{first},\mathsf{last}) = 2^{|u|^2}$. This example shows in particular that the class of recognizable series is not closed under $\mathrm{BTC}^<$.

Example 6. It is well-known that *modulo* can be expressed in $\mathrm{bFO{+}BTC}^<$ by

$$x \equiv_\ell m \stackrel{\text{def}}{=} (x=m) \vee [\ell\text{-}\mathrm{TC}^<_{yz}(z=y+\ell)](m,x)\,.$$

We now consider syntactical restrictions of FO+BTC$^<$, inspired by normal form formulas of [13] where only one "external" transitive closure is allowed.

For $\mathcal{L} \subseteq$ bMSO, $\mathrm{BTC}^<_{\mathrm{step}}(\mathcal{L})$ consists of formulas of the form $N\text{-}\mathrm{TC}^<_{xy}\varphi$, where $\varphi(x,y)$ is an $\mathcal{L}$-step formula with two free variables x, y. We say that $f \in \mathbb{K}\langle\langle \Sigma^+ \rangle\rangle$ is $\mathrm{BTC}^<_{\mathrm{step}}(\mathcal{L})$*-definable* if there exists an $\mathcal{L}$-step formula $\varphi(x,y)$ such that, for all $u \in \Sigma^+$, $f(u) = [\![N\text{-}\mathrm{TC}^<_{xy}\varphi]\!](u, \mathsf{first}, \mathsf{last})$.

For $\mathcal{L} \subseteq$ bMSO, let $\exists\forall_{\mathrm{step}}(\mathcal{L})$ consists of all MSO-formulas of the form $\exists X \forall x\, \varphi(x, X)$ with φ an $\mathcal{L}$-step formula: this defines a fragment of the logic RMSO($\mathbb{K}, \Sigma$) introduced in [6]. The following result characterizes the expressive power of weighted automata.

Theorem 7. *Let* $\mathbb{K}$ *be a (possibly noncommutative) semiring and* $f \in \mathbb{K}\langle\langle \Sigma^+ \rangle\rangle$. *The following assertions are equivalent over* $\mathbb{K}$ *and* Σ*:*

(1) f *is recognizable.*
(2) f *is* $\mathrm{BTC}^<_{\mathrm{step}}(\mathrm{bFO{+}mod})$*-definable.*
(3) f *is* $\mathrm{BTC}^<_{\mathrm{step}}(\mathrm{bMSO})$*-definable.*
(4) f *is* $\exists\forall_{\mathrm{step}}(\mathrm{bFO})$*-definable.*
(5) f *is* $\exists\forall_{\mathrm{step}}(\mathrm{bMSO})$*-definable.*

Proof. Fix a weighted automaton $\mathcal{A} = (Q, \mu, \lambda, \gamma)$ with $Q = \{1, \ldots, n\}$. For $d \geq 1$ and $p, q \in Q$, we use a formula $\psi^d_{p,q}(x,y)$ to compute the weight of the factor of length d located between positions x and y, when $\mathcal{A}$ goes from p to q:

$$\psi^d_{p,q}(x,y) \stackrel{\mathrm{def}}{=} (y = x + d - 1) \wedge \bigvee_{v = v_1 \cdots v_d} \Big(\mu(v)_{p,q} \wedge \bigwedge_{1 \leq i \leq d} P_{v_i}(x + i - 1) \Big) .$$

We construct a formula $\varphi(x,y)$ of bFO+mod allowing to define the semantics of $\mathcal{A}$ using a BTC$^<$: $[\![\mathcal{A}]\!](u) = [\![2n\text{-}\mathrm{TC}^<_{xy}\varphi]\!](u, \mathsf{first}, \mathsf{last})$. The idea, inspired by [17], consists in making the transitive closure pick positions $z_\ell = \ell n + q_\ell$, with $1 \leq q_\ell \leq n$, for successive values of ℓ, to encode runs of $\mathcal{A}$ going through state q_ℓ just before reading the letter at position $\ell n + 1$. To make this still work for $\ell = 0$, one can assume wlog. that $\lambda(1) = \mathbf{1}$ and $\lambda(q) = \mathbf{0}$ for $q \neq 1$, *i.e.*, the only initial state yielding a nonzero value is $q_0 = 1$. Consider slices $[\ell n + 1, (\ell + 1)n]$ of positions in the word where we evaluate the formula (the last slice might be incomplete). Each position y is located in exactly one such slice. We write $\langle y \rangle = \ell n + 1$ for the first position of that slice, as well as $[y] \stackrel{\mathrm{def}}{=} y + 1 - \langle y \rangle \in Q$ for the corresponding "offset". Notice that, for $q \in Q$, $[y] = q$ can be expressed in bFO+mod simply by $y \equiv_n q$. Hence, we will freely use $[y]$ as well as $\langle y \rangle = y + 1 - [y]$ as macros in formulas. Our BTC$^<$-formula picks positions x and y marked $\bullet$ in Figure 2, and computes the weight of the factor of length n between the positions $\langle x \rangle$ and $\langle y \rangle - 1$, assuming states $[x]$ and $[y]$ just before and after these positions.

The formula φ distinguishes the cases where x is far or near from the last position:

$$\begin{aligned} \varphi(x,y) = {} & \Big((\langle x \rangle + 2n \leq \mathsf{last}) \wedge (\langle y \rangle = \langle x \rangle + n) \wedge \psi^n_{[x],[y]}(\langle x \rangle, \langle y \rangle - 1) \Big) \\ & \vee \Big((\langle x \rangle + 2n > \mathsf{last}) \wedge (y = \mathsf{last}) \wedge \bigvee_{q \in Q} \psi^{y - \langle x \rangle + 1}_{[x],q}(\langle x \rangle, y) \wedge \gamma(q) \Big) . \end{aligned}$$

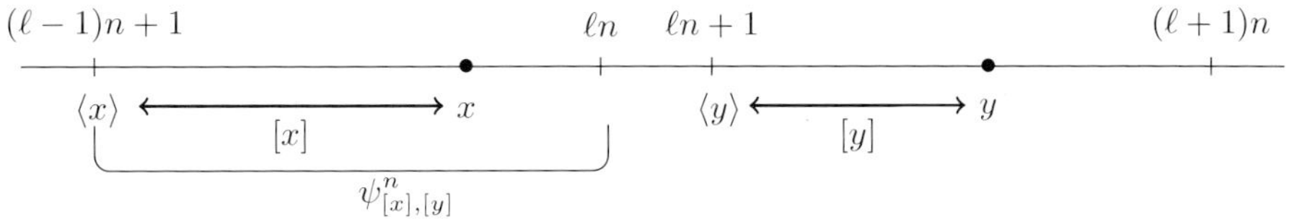

Fig. 2. Positions picked by the BTC$^<$-formula

4 Weighted Nested Automata

Example 2 shows that weighted automata lack closure properties to capture FO+BTC$^<$. We introduce a notion of nested automata making up for this gap.

For $r \geq 0$, the class r-nwA(Σ) (r-nwA if Σ is understood) of *r-nested weighted automata* over Σ (and $\mathbb{K}$) consists of all tuples $(Q, \mu, \lambda, \gamma)$ where Q is the set of states, $\lambda, \gamma : Q \to K$, and $\mu : Q \times \Sigma \times Q \to (r-1)$-nwA$(\Sigma \times \{0,1\})$. Here, we agree that (-1)-nwA $= K$. In particular, a 0-nwA(Σ) is a weighted automaton over Σ. Intuitively, the weight of a transition is computed by an automaton of the preceding level running on the whole word, where the additional $\{0,1\}$ component marks the letter of the transition whose weight is to be computed.

Let us formally define the behavior $[\![\mathcal{A}]\!] \in \mathbb{K}\langle\langle\Sigma^+\rangle\rangle$ of $\mathcal{A} = (Q, \mu, \lambda, \gamma) \in r$-nwA$(\Sigma)$. If $r = 0$, then $[\![\mathcal{A}]\!]$ is the behavior of $\mathcal{A}$ considered as wA over Σ. For $r \geq 1$, the weight of a *run* $\rho = q_0 \xrightarrow{u_1} q_1 \xrightarrow{u_2} \cdots \xrightarrow{u_n} q_n$ of $\mathcal{A}$ on $u = u_1 \cdots u_n$ is

$$\text{weight}(\rho) \stackrel{\text{def}}{=} \lambda(q_0) \cdot \left[\prod_{i=1}^{n} [\![\mu(q_{i-1}, u_i, q_i)]\!](u, i)\right] \cdot \gamma(q_n)\,,$$

where $(u, i) \in (\Sigma \times \{0,1\})^+$ is the word $v = v_1 \cdots v_n$ with $v_i = (u_i, 1)$ and $v_j = (u_j, 0)$ if $j \neq i$. As usual, $[\![\mathcal{A}]\!](u)$ is the sum of the weights of all runs of $\mathcal{A}$ on u. Note that, unlike the nested automata of [16], the values given by lower automata do not explicitly influence the possible transitions.

A series $f \in \mathbb{K}\langle\langle\Sigma^+\rangle\rangle$ is r-nwA-*recognizable* if $f = [\![\mathcal{A}]\!]$ for some r-nwA $\mathcal{A}$. It is nwA-*recognizable* if it is r-nwA-recognizable for some r. We let $\mathbb{K}^{r\text{-nwA}}\langle\langle\Sigma^+\rangle\rangle$ (resp., $\mathbb{K}^{\text{nwA}}\langle\langle\Sigma^+\rangle\rangle$) be the class of r-nwA-recognizable (resp., nwA-recognizable) series over $\mathbb{K}$ and Σ.

Example 8. A 1-nwA recognizing the series $u \mapsto 2^{|u|^2}$ over $\mathbb{N}$ is $\mathcal{A} = (\{p\}, \mu, \mathbf{1}, \mathbf{1})$ where, for every $a \in \Sigma$, $\mu(p, a, p)$ is the weighted automaton of Example 1.

We can generalize the proof of (1) $\Rightarrow$ (2) in Theorem 7 in order to get the following result. The converse will be obtained in Section 5.

Proposition 9. *Every* nwA-*recognizable series is* FO+BTC$^<$-*definable.*

5 Pebble Weighted Automata

We now consider *pebble weighted automata* (pwA). A pwA has a read-only tape. At each step, it can move its head one position to the left or to the right (within the boundaries of the input tape), or either drop or lift a pebble at the current head position. Applicable transitions and weights depend on the current letter, current state, and the pebbles carried by the current position. Pebbles are handled using a stack policy: if the automaton has r pebbles and pebbles $\ell, \ldots, r$ have already been dropped, it can either lift pebble ℓ (if $\ell \leq r$), drop pebble $\ell - 1$ (if $\ell \geq 2$), or move. As these automata can go in either direction, we add two fresh symbols $\rhd$ and $\lhd$ to mark the beginning and the end of an input word. Let $\tilde{\Sigma} = \Sigma \uplus \{\rhd, \lhd\}$. To compute the value of $w = w_1 \cdots w_n \in \Sigma^+$, a pwA will work on a tape holding $\widetilde{w} = \rhd w \lhd$. For convenience, we number the letters of $\widetilde{w}$ from 0, setting $\widetilde{w}_0 = \rhd$, $\widetilde{w}_{n+1} = \lhd$, and $\widetilde{w}_i = w_i$ for $1 \leq i \leq n$.

Let $r \geq 0$. Formally, an *r-pebble weighted automaton (r-pwA)* over $\mathbb{K}$ and Σ is a pair $\mathcal{A} = (Q, \mu)$ where Q is a finite set of states and $\mu : Q \times \tilde{\Sigma} \times 2^r \times D \times Q \to K$ is the transition weight function, with $D = \{\leftarrow, \rightarrow, \text{drop}, \text{lift}\}$.

A *configuration* of a r-pwA $\mathcal{A}$ on a word $w \in \Sigma^+$ of length n is a triple $(p, i, \zeta) \in Q \times \{0, \ldots, n+2\} \times \{1, \ldots, n\}^{\leq r}$. The word w itself will be understood. Informally, p denotes the current state of $\mathcal{A}$ and i is the head position in $\widetilde{w}$, *i.e* positions 0 and $n+1$ point to $\rhd$ and $\lhd$, respectively, position $1 \leq i \leq n$ points to $\widetilde{w}_i \in \Sigma$, and position $n+2$ is outside $\widetilde{w}$. Finally, $\zeta = \zeta_\ell \cdots \zeta_r$ with $1 \leq \ell \leq r+1$ encodes the locations of pebbles $\ell, \ldots, r$ ($\zeta_m \in \{1, \ldots, n\}$ is the position of pebble m) while pebbles $1, \ldots, \ell-1$ are currently not on the tape. For $i \in \{0, \ldots, n+1\}$, we set $\zeta^{-1}(i) = \{m \in \{\ell, \ldots, r\} \mid \zeta_m = i\}$ (viewing ζ as a partial function from $\{1, \ldots, r\}$ to $\{0, \ldots, n+1\}$). Note that $\zeta^{-1}(0) = \zeta^{-1}(n+1) = \emptyset$.

There is a *step* of weight k from configuration (p, i, ζ) to configuration (q, j, η) if $i \leq n+1$, $k = \mu(p, \widetilde{w}_i, \zeta^{-1}(i), d, q)$, and

$$\begin{cases} j = i - 1 & \text{if } d = \leftarrow \\ j = i + 1 & \text{if } d = \rightarrow \\ j = i & \text{otherwise} \end{cases} \quad \text{and} \quad \begin{cases} \eta = i\zeta & \text{if } d = \text{drop} \\ \zeta = i\eta & \text{if } d = \text{lift} \\ \eta = \zeta & \text{otherwise.} \end{cases}$$

A *run* ρ of $\mathcal{A}$ is a sequence of steps from a configuration $(p, 0, \varepsilon)$ to a configuration $(q, n+2, \varepsilon)$ (at the end, no pebble is left on the tape). We denote by weight(ρ) the product of weights of the steps of run ρ (from left to right, but we will mainly work with a commutative semiring in this section). The run ρ is *simple* if whenever two configurations α and β appear in ρ, we have $\alpha \neq \beta$.

The series $[\![\mathcal{A}]\!] \in \mathbb{K}\langle\langle \Sigma^+ \rangle\rangle$ is defined by $[\![\mathcal{A}]\!](w) = \sum_{\rho \text{ simple run on } w} \text{weight}(\rho)$. We denote by $\mathbb{K}^{r\text{-pwA}}\langle\langle \Sigma^+ \rangle\rangle$ the collection of formal power series definable by a r-pwA, and we let $\mathbb{K}^{\text{pwA}}\langle\langle \Sigma^+ \rangle\rangle = \bigcup_{r \geq 0} \mathbb{K}^{r\text{-pwA}}\langle\langle \Sigma^+ \rangle\rangle$. Note that a 0-pwA is in fact a 2-way weighted automaton. It follows from Theorem 11 that 2-way wA have the same expressive power as classical (1-way) wA.

Example 10. Let us sketch a 1-pwA $\mathcal{A}$ recognizing the series $u \mapsto 2^{|u|^2}$ over $\mathbb{N}$. The idea is that $\mathcal{A}$ drops its pebble successively on every position of the input word. Transitions for reallocating the pebble have weight **1**. When a pebble is dropped, $\mathcal{A}$ scans the whole word from left to right where every transition has weight 2. As this scan happens $|u|$ times, we obtain $[\![\mathcal{A}]\!](u) = 2^{|u|^2}$.

Theorem 11. *For every commutative semiring* $\mathbb{K}$*, and every* $r \geq 0$*, we have*
(1) $\mathbb{K}^{r\text{-pwA}}\langle\langle\Sigma^+\rangle\rangle \subseteq \mathbb{K}^{r\text{-nwA}}\langle\langle\Sigma^+\rangle\rangle$
(2) $\mathbb{K}^{\mathrm{FO+BTC}^<}\langle\langle\Sigma^+\rangle\rangle = \mathbb{K}^{\mathrm{pwA}}\langle\langle\Sigma^+\rangle\rangle = \mathbb{K}^{\mathrm{nwA}}\langle\langle\Sigma^+\rangle\rangle$.
(3) $\mathbb{K}^{\mathrm{FO+BTC}^<}\langle\langle\Sigma^+\rangle\rangle \subseteq \mathbb{K}^{\mathrm{pwA}}\langle\langle\Sigma^+\rangle\rangle$ *holds even for noncommutative semirings.*

Proof. (1) We provide a translation of a generalized version of r-pwA to r-nwA. That generalized notion equips an r-pwA $\mathcal{A} = (P, \mu)$ with an equivalence relation $\sim \subseteq P \times P$, which is canonically extended to configurations of $\mathcal{A}$: we write $(p, i, u) \sim (p', i', u')$ if $p \sim p'$, $i = i'$, and $u = u'$.

The semantics $[\![\mathcal{A}]\!]_\sim$ is then defined by replacing equality of configurations with $\sim$ in the definition of simple run. To stress this fact, we henceforth say that a run is $\sim$-*simple*. So let $r \geq 0$, $\mathcal{A} = (P, \mu)$ be an r-pwA over $\mathbb{K}$ and Σ, and $\sim \subseteq P \times P$ be an equivalence relation. We assume wlog. that all runs in which a pebble is dropped and immediately lifted have weight $\mathbf{0}$. We build an r-nwA $\langle\mathcal{A}\rangle_\sim = (Q, \nu, \lambda, \gamma)$ over Σ such that $[\![\langle\mathcal{A}\rangle_\sim]\!] = [\![\mathcal{A}]\!]_\sim$.

The construction of $\langle\mathcal{A}\rangle_\sim$ proceeds inductively on the number of pebbles r. It involves two alternating transformations, as illustrated in Figure 3. The left-hand side depicts a $\sim$-simple run of $\mathcal{A}$ on some word w with factor ab. To simulate such a run, $\langle\mathcal{A}\rangle_\sim$ scans w from left to right and guesses, at each position i, the sequence of those states and directions that are encountered at i while pebble r has not, or just, been dropped. The state of $\langle\mathcal{A}\rangle_\sim$ taken before reading the a at position i is $q = p_0 \rightarrow p_3 \leftarrow p_4\, \mathrm{drop}\, p_5\, \hat{p}_5\, \mathrm{lift}\, p_6 \leftarrow p_7\, \mathrm{drop}\, p_8\, \hat{p}_8\, \mathrm{lift}\, p_9 \rightarrow$ (which is enriched by the input letter a, as will be explained below). As the micro-states $p_0, p_3, \ldots$ form a segment of a $\sim$-simple run, $p_0, p_3, p_4, p_6, p_7, p_9$ are pairwise distinct (wrt. $\sim$) and so are $p_5, \hat{p}_5, p_8, \hat{p}_8$. Segments when pebble r is dropped on position i are defered to a $(r-1)$-nwA $\mathcal{B}_q$, which is called at position i and computes the run segments from p_5 to $\hat{p}_5$ and from p_8 to $\hat{p}_8$ that both start in i. To this aim, $\mathcal{B}_q$ works on an extension of w where position i is marked, indicating that pebble r is considered to be at i.

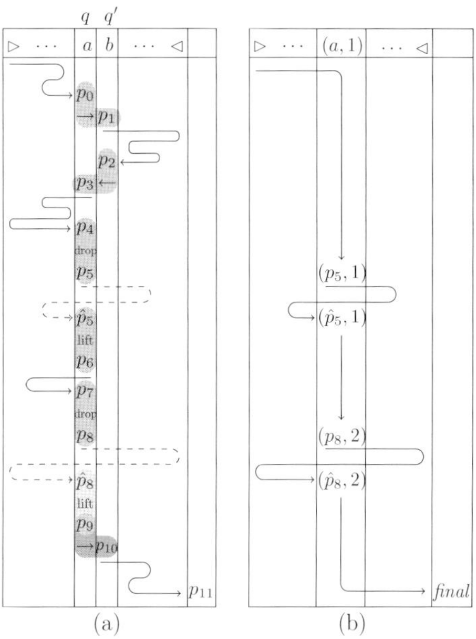

Fig. 3. (a) Runs of r-pwA $\mathcal{A}$ and r-nwA $\langle\mathcal{A}\rangle_\sim$; (b) run of $(r-1)$-pwA $\mathcal{A}_q$

We define the r-nwA $\langle\mathcal{A}\rangle_\sim$. Let $\Pi = (P\{\rightarrow, \leftarrow\} \cup P\{\mathrm{drop}\}PP\{\mathrm{lift}\})^* P\{\rightarrow\}$. Sequences from Π keep track of states and directions that are taken at one given position. As aforementioned, they must meet the requirements of $\sim$-simple runs so that only some of them can be considered as states. Formally, given $\pi \in \Pi$, we define projections $\mathrm{pr}_1(\pi) \in P^+$ and $\mathrm{pr}_2(\pi) \in (PP)^*$ inductively by $\mathrm{pr}_1(\varepsilon) = \mathrm{pr}_2(\varepsilon) = \varepsilon$ and

$$\begin{array}{ll} \mathrm{pr}_1(p \rightarrow \pi) = \mathrm{pr}_1(p \leftarrow \pi) = p\,\mathrm{pr}_1(\pi) & \mathrm{pr}_1(p\,\mathrm{drop}\,p_1\,\hat{p}_1\,\mathrm{lift}\,\pi) = p\,\mathrm{pr}_1(\pi) \\ \mathrm{pr}_2(p \rightarrow \pi) = \mathrm{pr}_2(p \leftarrow \pi) = \mathrm{pr}_2(\pi) & \mathrm{pr}_2(p\,\mathrm{drop}\,p_1\,\hat{p}_1\,\mathrm{lift}\,\pi) = p_1\,\hat{p}_1\,\mathrm{pr}_2(\pi). \end{array}$$

Let $\Pi_\sim$ denote the set of sequences $\pi \in \Pi$ such that $\mathrm{pr}_1(\pi)$ consists of pairwise distinct states wrt. $\sim$ and so does $\mathrm{pr}_2(\pi)$ (there might be states that occur in both $\mathrm{pr}_1(\pi)$ and $\mathrm{pr}_2(\pi)$). With this, we set $Q = (\tilde{\Sigma} \uplus \{\square\}) \times \Pi_\sim$. The letter $a \in \tilde{\Sigma} \uplus \{\square\}$ of a state $(a, \pi) \in Q$ will denote the symbol that is to be read next. Symbol $\square$ means that there is no letter left so that the automaton is beyond the scope of $\rhd w \lhd$ when w is the input word.

Next, we explain how the weight of the run segments of $\mathcal{A}$ with lifted pebble r is computed in $\langle\mathcal{A}\rangle_\sim$. Two neighboring states of $\langle\mathcal{A}\rangle_\sim$ need to match each other, which can be checked locally by means of transitions. To determine a corresponding weight, we first count weights of those transitions that move from the current position i to $i+1$ or from $i+1$ to i. This is the reason why a state of $\langle\mathcal{A}\rangle_\sim$ also maintains the letter that is to be read next. In Figure 3(a), the 7 micro-transitions that we count in the step from q to q' are highlighted in gray. Assuming $q = (a, \pi_0)$ and $q' = (b, \pi_1)$, we obtain a value $\mathrm{weight}_{a,b}(\pi_0 \mid \pi_1)$ as the product $\mu(p_0, a, \emptyset, \rightarrow, p_1) \cdot \mu(p_2, b, \emptyset, \leftarrow, p_3) \cdot \cdots \cdot \mu(\hat{p}_8, a, \{r\}, \mathrm{lift}, p_9) \cdot \mu(p_9, a, \emptyset, \rightarrow, p_{10})$. The formal definition of $\mathrm{weight}_{a,b}(\pi_0 \mid \pi_1) \in K$ is omitted.

We are now prepared to define the components ν, λ, γ of $\langle\mathcal{A}\rangle_\sim$. For $q_0 = (a_0, \pi_0)$ and $q_1 = (a_1, \pi_1)$ states in Q, we set

$$\begin{aligned} \lambda(q_0) &= \textstyle\sum_{(\rhd,\pi)\in Q} \mathrm{weight}_{\rhd,a_0}(\pi \mid \pi_0) \\ \gamma(q_0) &= \textstyle\sum_{(\square,\pi)\in Q} \mathrm{weight}_{\lhd,\square}(\pi_0 \mid \pi) \qquad\qquad \text{if } a_0 = \lhd \\ \nu(a_0)_{q_0,q_1} &= \mathrm{weight}_{a_0,a_1}(\pi_0 \mid \pi_1) \cdot \mathcal{B}_{q_0}\,. \end{aligned}$$

Here, $\mathcal{B}_q$ is the constant $\mathbf{1}$ if $r = 0$. Otherwise, $\mathcal{B}_q = \langle\mathcal{A}_q\rangle_{\sim_q}$ is an $(r-1)$-nwA over $\Delta = \Sigma \times \{0,1\}$ obtained inductively from the $(r-1)$-pwA $\mathcal{A}_q$ which is defined below together with its equivalence relation $\sim_q$. Notice that $k \cdot \mathcal{B}_q$ is obtained from $\mathcal{B}_q$ by multiplying its input weights by k.

Let us define the $(r-1)$-pwA $\mathcal{A}_q = (P', \mu')$ over Δ as well as $\sim_q \subseteq P' \times P'$. Suppose $q = (a, \pi)$ and $\mathrm{pr}_2(\pi) = p_1\,\hat{p}_1 \cdots p_N\,\hat{p}_N$. The behavior of $\mathcal{A}_q$ is split into $N+2$ phases. In phase 0, it scans the input word from left to right until it finds the (unique) letter of the form $(a, 1)$ with $a \in \Sigma$. At that position, call it i, $\mathcal{A}_q$ enters state $(p_1, 1)$ (the second component indicating the current phase). All these transitions are performed with weight $\mathbf{1}$. Then, $\mathcal{A}_q$ starts simulating $\mathcal{A}$, considering pebble r at position i. Back at position i in state $(\hat{p}_1, 1)$, weight-$\mathbf{1}$ transitions will allow $\mathcal{A}_q$ to enter the next phase, starting in $(p_2, 2)$ and again considering pebble r at position i. The simulation of $\mathcal{A}$ ends when $(\hat{p}_N, N)$ is reached in position i. In the final phase $(N+1)$ weight-$\mathbf{1}$ transitions guides $\mathcal{A}_q$ to the end of the tape where it stops. The relation $\sim_q$ will consider states (p, j) and (p', j') equivalent iff $p \sim p'$, *i.e.*, it ignores the phase number. This explains the purpose of the equivalence relation: in order for the automaton $\mathcal{A}_q$ to simulate the dashed part of the run of $\mathcal{A}$, we use phase numbers, so that, during the simulation two different states (p, j) and (p, j') of $\mathcal{A}_q$ may correspond to the same original state p of $\mathcal{A}$. Now, only simple runs are considered to compute $[\![\mathcal{A}]\!]$. Therefore, for the simulation to be faithful, we want to rule out runs of $\mathcal{A}_q$ containing two configurations which only differ by the phase number, that is, containing two $\sim_q$-equivalent configurations, which is done by keeping only $\sim_q$-simple runs. A run of $\mathcal{A}_q$ is illustrated in Figure 3(b) (with $N = 2$). Note that, if $N = 0$, then $\mathcal{A}_q$ simply scans the word from left to right, outputting weight $\mathbf{1}$. Finally, we sketch the proof of (3).

We proceed by induction on the structure of the formula and suppose that a valuation of free variables is given in terms of pebbles that are already placed on the word and cannot be lifted. Disjunction, conjunction, and first-order quantifications are easy to simulate. To evaluate $[N\text{-TC}^{<}_{xy}\varphi](z, t)$ for some formula $\varphi(x, y)$, we either evaluate $\varphi(x, y)$, with pebbles being placed on z and t such that $z \leq t \leq z + N$, or choose non-deterministically (and with weight $\mathbf{1}$) positions $z = z_0 < z_1 < \cdots < z_{n-1} < z_n = t$ with $n \geq 2$, using two additional pebbles, 2 and 1. We drop pebble 2 on position z_0 and pebble 1 on some guessed position z_1 with $z_0 < z_1 \leq \min(t, z_0 + N)$. We then run the subroutine to evaluate $\varphi(z_0, z_1)$. Next we move to position z_1 and lift pebble 1. We move left to position z_0 remembering the distance $z_1 - z_0$. We lift pebble 2 and move right to z_1 using the stored distance $z_1 - z_0$. We drop pebble 2 on z_1 and iterate this procedure until t is reached. □

6 Conclusion and Perspectives

We have introduced pebble weighted automata and characterized their expressive power in terms of first-order logic with a bounded transitive closure operator. It follows that satisfiability is decidable over commutative positive semirings. Here, a sentence $\varphi \in \text{FO+BTC}^{<}$ is said *satisfiable* if there is a word $w \in \Sigma^+$ such that $[\![\varphi]\!](w) \neq \mathbf{0}$. From Theorem 11, satisfiability reduces to non-emptiness of the support of a series recognized by a pwA. For positive semirings, the latter problem, in turn, can be reduced to the decidable emptiness problem for classical pebble automata over the Boolean semiring. We leave it as an open problem to determine for which semirings the satisfiability problem is decidable.

Unbounded transitive closure. We do not know if allowing unbounded steps in the transitive closure leads beyond the power of (weak) pebble automata. We already know that allowing unbounded steps is harmless for bMSO-step formulas. It is also easy to show that such an unbounded transitive closure can be captured with *strong* pebble automata, *i.e.*, that can lift the last dropped pebble even when not scanning its position. Therefore, we aim at studying the expressive power of strong pebble automata and unbounded transitive closure.

Tree-walking automata. Our results are not only of theoretical interest. They also lay the basis for quantitative extensions of database query languages such as XPath, and may provide tracks to evaluate quantitative aspects of the structure of XML documents. The framework of weighted tree (walking) automata [1,11] is natural for answering questions such as "How many nodes are selected by a request?", or "How difficult is it to answer a query?". The navigational mechanism of pebble tree-walking automata [3,14,2] is also well-suited in this context. For these reasons, we would like to adapt our results to tree languages.

We thank the anonymous referees for their valuable comments.

References

1. Berstel, J., Reutenauer, C.: Recognizable formal power series on trees. TCS 18(2), 115–148 (1982)
2. Bojańczyk, M.: Tree-walking automata. In: Martín-Vide, C., Otto, F., Fernau, H. (eds.) LATA 2008. LNCS, vol. 5196, pp. 1–17. Springer, Heidelberg (2008)
3. Bojańczyk, M., Samuelides, M., Schwentick, T., Segoufin, L.: Expressive power of pebble automata. In: Bugliesi, M., Preneel, B., Sassone, V., Wegener, I. (eds.) ICALP 2006. LNCS, vol. 4051, pp. 157–168. Springer, Heidelberg (2006)
4. Bollig, B., Gastin, P., Monmege, B., Zeitoun, M.: Pebble weighted automata and transitive closure logics, `http://www.lsv.ens-cachan.fr/Publis/RAPPORTS_LSV/rapports`
5. Büchi, J.R.: Weak second-order arithmetic and finite automata. Z. Math. Logik Grundlagen Math. 6, 66–92 (1960)
6. Droste, M., Gastin, P.: Weighted automata and weighted logics. Theoretical Computer Science 380(1-2), 69–86 (2007); Caires, L., Italiano, G.F., Monteiro, L., Palamidessi, C., Yung, M. (eds.): ICALP 2005. LNCS, vol. 3580, pp. 513–525. Springer, Heidelberg (2005)
7. Droste, M., Kuich, W., Vogler, H. (eds.): Handbook of Weighted Automata. EATCS Monographs in Theoret. Comput. Sci. Springer, Heidelberg (2009)
8. Elgot, C.C.: Decision problems of finite automata design and related arithmetics. Trans. Amer. Math. Soc. 98, 21–52 (1961)
9. Engelfriet, J., Hoogeboom, H.J.: Tree-walking pebble automata. In: Jewels Are Forever, Contributions to Theoretical Computer Science in Honor of Arto Salomaa, pp. 72–83. Springer, Heidelberg (1999)
10. Engelfriet, J., Hoogeboom, H.J.: Automata with nested pebbles capture first-order logic with transitive closure. Log. Meth. in Comput. Sci. 3 (2007)
11. Fülöp, Z., Muzamel, L.: Weighted Tree-Walking Automata. Acta Cybernetica 19(2), 275–293 (2009)
12. Globerman, N., Harel, D.: Complexity results for two-way and multi-pebble automata and their logics. Theoretical Computer Science 169(2), 161–184 (1996)
13. Neven, F., Schwentick, T.: On the power of tree-walking automata. In: Welzl, E., Montanari, U., Rolim, J.D.P. (eds.) ICALP 2000. LNCS, vol. 1853, pp. 547–560. Springer, Heidelberg (2000)
14. Samuelides, M., Segoufin, L.: Complexity of pebble tree-walking automata. In: Csuhaj-Varjú, E., Ésik, Z. (eds.) FCT 2007. LNCS, vol. 4639, pp. 458–469. Springer, Heidelberg (2007)
15. Schützenberger, M.P.: On the definition of a family of automata. Information and Control 4, 245–270 (1961)
16. ten Cate, B., Segoufin, L.: Transitive closure logic, nested tree walking automata, and XPath. J. ACM (to appear, 2010); Short version in PODS 2008 (2008)
17. Thomas, W.: Classifying regular events in symbolic logic. Journal of Computer and System Sciences 25(3), 360–376 (1982)
18. Trakhtenbrot, B.A.: Finite automata and logic of monadic predicates. Doklady Akademii Nauk SSSR 149, 326–329 (1961) (in Russian)

Energy Parity Games

Krishnendu Chatterjee[1] and Laurent Doyen[2]

[1] IST Austria, Institute of Science and Technology, Austria
[2] LSV, ENS Cachan & CNRS, France

Abstract. Energy parity games are infinite two-player turn-based games played on weighted graphs. The objective of the game combines a (qualitative) parity condition with the (quantitative) requirement that the sum of the weights (i.e., the level of energy in the game) must remain positive. Beside their own interest in the design and synthesis of resource-constrained omega-regular specifications, energy parity games provide one of the simplest model of games with combined qualitative and quantitative objective. Our main results are as follows: (a) exponential memory is sufficient and may be necessary for winning strategies in energy parity games; (b) the problem of deciding the winner in energy parity games can be solved in NP $\cap$ coNP; and (c) we give an algorithm to solve energy parity by reduction to energy games. We also show that the problem of deciding the winner in energy parity games is polynomially equivalent to the problem of deciding the winner in mean-payoff parity games, which can thus be solved in NP $\cap$ coNP. As a consequence we also obtain a conceptually simple algorithm to solve mean-payoff parity games.

1 Introduction

Two-player games on graphs are central in many applications of computer science. For example, in the synthesis problem implementations are obtained from winning strategies in games with a qualitative objective such as ω-regular specifications [17,16,1]. Games also provide a theoretical instrument to deal with logics and automata [5,14,12,13]. In all these applications, the games have a qualitative (boolean) objective that determines which player wins. On the other hand, games with quantitative objective which are natural models in economics (where players have to optimize a real-valued payoff) have also been studied in the context of automated design and synthesis [18,9,21]. In the recent past, there has been considerable interest in the design of reactive systems that work in resource-constrained environments (such as embedded systems). The specifications for such reactive systems have both a quantitative component (specifying the resource constraint such as power consumption) and a qualitative component (specifying the functional requirement). The desired reactive system must respect both the qualitative and quantitative specifications. Only recently objectives combining both qualitative and quantitative specifications have been considered [6,8,3].

S. Abramsky et al. (Eds.): ICALP 2010, Part II, LNCS 6199, pp. 599–610, 2010.

In this paper, we consider two-player turn-based games played for infinitely many rounds on a weighted graph where a *priority* is associated to each state and a *weight* is associated to each edge. In each round, the player owning the current state chooses an outgoing edge to a successor state, thus the game results in an infinite play. The qualitative specification is a parity condition, a canonical way to express the ω-regular objectives [19]: a play satisfies the parity condition if the least priority occurring infinitely often in the play is even; the quantitative specification requires that the sum of the weights along the play (that we interpret as the level of energy, or resource usage) remains always positive. The main algorithmic question about such *energy parity games* is to decide if there exists an initial credit (or initial energy level) such that one player has a strategy to maintain the level of energy positive while satisfying the parity condition, and if the answer is yes, to compute the minimum such initial credit.

Energy parity games generalize both parity games and energy games. It is known that memoryless strategies are sufficient to win parity games [11] and energy games [6,4], and therefore the problem of deciding the winner of a parity game, and the problem of deciding the existence of an initial credit sufficient to win an energy game are both in NP $\cap$ coNP. It is a long standing open question to know if these problems can be solved in polynomial time. In this paper, we present the following results about energy parity games: (a) we study the complexity of winning strategies and we give bounds on the amount of memory needed to win; (b) establish the computational complexity of the problem of deciding the winner; (c) present an algorithmic solution to compute the minimum initial credit; and (d) show polynomial equivalence with mean-payoff parity games. The details of our contributions are as follows, some proofs are omitted by lack of space.

Strategy complexity. First, we show that finite-memory strategies are sufficient to win energy parity games, but memory of exponential may be required even in the special case of one-player games. We present an exponential memory upper bound for the winning strategies, and we show that the spoiling strategies of the opponent need no memory at all (memoryless spoiling strategies exist).

Computational complexity. Second, we show that the decision problem for energy parity games lie in NP $\cap$ coNP, matching the bounds known for the simpler case of parity and energy games. The classical NP $\cap$ coNP result for parity and energy games crucially relies on the existence of memoryless winning strategies. In the case of energy parity games, the existence of memoryless spoiling strategies gives the coNP upper bound. However, and in contrast with parity games and energy games, winning strategies may require exponential memory in energy parity games. Therefore, more subtle arguments are needed to obtain the NP upper bound: we show that the winning strategies (that require exponential memory) can be characterized with certain special structures and decomposed into two memoryless strategies (roughly, one to ensure the parity condition, and the other to maintain the energy level positive). This insight allows us to derive a nondeterministic polynomial-time algorithm to solve energy parity games. Thus the problem of deciding the existence of an initial credit which is sufficient to win an energy parity game is (perhaps surprisingly) in NP ∩ coNP. Finding a deterministic polynomial algorithm for this problem is obviously open.

Algorithm. Third, we present an algorithm to solve energy parity games with complexity exponential in the number of states (as for parity games), and linear in the largest weight (as for energy games). This algorithm relies on our analysis of the structure of winning strategies, and reduces to iteratively solving reachability games and energy games.

Equivalence with mean-payoff parity games. Finally, we show that energy parity games are polynomially equivalent to mean-payoff parity games [8], where the parity condition is combined with the quantitative requirement that the limit-average (or mean-payoff) of the weights remains positive. Again, this result is surprising because in mean-payoff parity games, optimal strategies (that realize the largest possible mean-payoff value while satisfying the parity condition) may require infinite memory. Moreover, we get as a corollary of our results that that the problem of deciding the winner in mean-payoff parity games is also in NP ∩ coNP. Our algorithm for energy parity games also solves mean-payoff parity games with essentially the same complexity as in [8], but with a conceptually simpler approach.

2 Definitions

Game graphs. A *game graph* $G = \langle Q, E \rangle$ consists of a finite set Q of states partitioned into player-1 states Q_1 and player-2 states Q_2 (i.e., $Q = Q_1 \cup Q_2$), and a set $E \subseteq Q \times Q$ of edges such that for all $q \in Q$, there exists (at least one) $q' \in Q$ such that $(q, q') \in E$. A *player-1 game* is a game graph where $Q_1 = Q$ and $Q_2 = \emptyset$. The subgraph of G induced by $S \subseteq Q$ is the graph $\langle S, E \cap (S \times S) \rangle$ (which is not a game graph in general); the subgraph induced by S is a game graph if for all $s \in S$ there exist $s' \in S$ such that $(s, s') \in E$.

Plays and strategies. A game on G starting from a state $q_0 \in Q$ is played in rounds as follows. If the game is in a player-1 state, then player 1 chooses the successor state from the set of outgoing edges; otherwise the game is in a player-2 state, and player 2 chooses the successor state. The game results in a *play* from q_0, i.e., an infinite path $\rho = q_0 q_1 \dots$ such that $(q_i, q_{i+1}) \in E$ for all $i \geq 0$. The prefix of length n of ρ is denoted by $\rho(n) = q_0 \dots q_n$. A *strategy* for player 1 is a function $\sigma : Q^* Q_1 \to Q$ such that $(q, \sigma(\rho \cdot q)) \in E$ for all $\rho \in Q^*$ and $q \in Q_1$. An *outcome* of σ from q_0 is a play $q_0 q_1 \dots$ such that $\sigma(q_0 \dots q_i) = q_{i+1}$ for all $i \geq 0$ such that $q_i \in Q_1$. Strategy and outcome for player 2 are defined analogously.

Finite-memory strategies. A strategy uses *finite-memory* if it can be encoded by a deterministic transducer $\langle M, m_0, \alpha_u, \alpha_n \rangle$ where M is a finite set (the memory of the strategy), $m_0 \in M$ is the initial memory value, $\alpha_u : M \times Q \to M$ is an update function, and $\alpha_n : M \times Q_1 \to Q$ is a next-move function. The *size* of the strategy is the number $|M|$ of memory values. If the game is in a player-1 state q and m is the current memory value, then the strategy chooses

$q' = \alpha_n(m, q)$ as the next state and the memory is updated to $\alpha_u(m, q)$. Formally, $\langle M, m_0, \alpha_u, \alpha_n \rangle$ defines the strategy α such that $\alpha(\rho \cdot q) = \alpha_n(\hat{\alpha}_u(m_0, \rho), q)$ for all $\rho \in Q^*$ and $q \in Q_1$, where $\hat{\alpha}_u$ extends α_u to sequences of states as expected. A strategy is *memoryless* if $|M| = 1$. For a finite-memory strategy σ, let G_σ be the graph obtained as the product of G with the transducer defining σ, where $(\langle m, q \rangle, \langle m', q' \rangle)$ is a transition in G_σ if $m' = \alpha_u(m, q)$ and either $q \in Q_1$ and $q' = \alpha_n(m, q)$, or $q \in Q_2$ and $(q, q') \in E$. In G_σ, the expression *reachable from* q stands for *reachable from* $\langle q, m_0 \rangle$.

Objectives. An *objective* for G is a set $\phi \subseteq Q^\omega$. Let $p : Q \to \mathbb{N}$ be a *priority function* and $w : E \to \mathbb{Z}$ be a *weight function*[1] where positive numbers represent rewards. We denote by W the largest weight (in absolute value) according to w. The *energy level* of a prefix $\gamma = q_0 q_1 \dots q_n$ of a play is $\mathsf{EL}(w, \gamma) = \sum_{i=0}^{n-1} w(q_i, q_{i+1})$, and the *mean-payoff value* of a play $\rho = q_0 q_1 \dots$ is $\mathsf{MP}(w, \rho) = \liminf_{n \to \infty} \frac{1}{n} \cdot \mathsf{EL}(w, \rho(n))$. In the sequel, when the weight function w is clear from context we will omit it and simply write $\mathsf{EL}(\gamma)$ and $\mathsf{MP}(\rho)$. We denote by $\mathsf{Inf}(\rho)$ the set of states that occur infinitely often in ρ. We consider the following objectives:

- *Parity objectives.* The *parity* objective $\mathsf{Parity}_G(p) = \{\pi \in \mathsf{Plays}(G) \mid \min\{p(q) \mid q \in \mathsf{Inf}(\pi)\}$ is even $\}$ requires that the minimum priority visited infinitely often be even. The special cases of *Büchi* and *coBüchi* objectives correspond to the case with two priorities, $p : Q \to \{0, 1\}$ and $p : Q \to \{1, 2\}$ respectively.
- *Energy objectives.* Given an initial credit $c_0 \in \mathbb{N} \cup \{\infty\}$, the *energy* objective $\mathsf{PosEnergy}_G(c_0) = \{\pi \in \mathsf{Plays}(G) \mid \forall n \geq 0 : c_0 + \mathsf{EL}(\pi(n)) \geq 0\}$ requires that the energy level be always positive.
- *Mean-payoff objectives.* Given a threshold $\nu \in \mathbb{Q}$, the *mean-payoff* objective $\mathsf{MeanPayoff}_G(\nu) = \{\pi \in \mathsf{Plays}(G) \mid \mathsf{MP}(\pi) \geq \nu\}$ requires that the mean-payoff value be at least ν.
- *Combined objectives.* The *energy parity* objective $\mathsf{Parity}_G(p) \cap \mathsf{PosEnergy}_G(c_0)$ and the *mean-payoff parity* objective $\mathsf{Parity}_G(p) \cap \mathsf{MeanPayoff}_G(\nu)$ combine the requirements of parity and energy (resp., mean-payoff) objectives.

When the game G is clear form the context, we omit the subscript in objective names.

Winning strategies. A player-1 strategy σ is *winning*[2] in a state q for an objective ϕ if $\rho \in \phi$ for all outcomes ρ of σ from q. For energy and energy parity objectives with unspecified initial credit, we also say that a strategy is winning if it is winning for some finite initial credit.

Finite and minimum initial credit problems. We are interested in the following decision problem. The *finite initial credit problem* (initial credit problem for short) asks, given an energy parity game $\langle G, p, w \rangle$ and a state q, whether

[1] In some proofs, we take the freedom to use rational weights (i.e., $w : E \to \mathbb{Q}$), while we always assume that weights are integers encoded in binary for complexity results.

[2] We also say that player-1 is winning, or that q is a winning state.

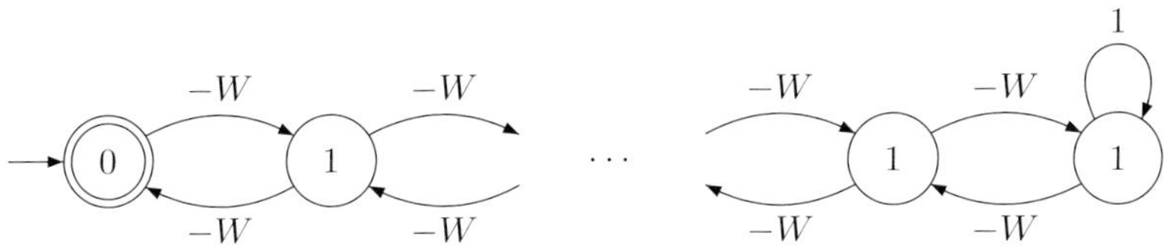

Fig. 1. A family of 1-player energy parity games where Player 1 needs memory of size $2 \cdot (n-1) \cdot W$ and initial credit $(n-1) \cdot W$. Edges are labeled by weights, states by priorities.

there exists a finite initial credit $c_0 \in \mathbb{N}$ and a winning strategy for player 1 from q with initial credit c_0. The *minimum initial credit* in a state $q_0 \in Q$ is the least value of initial credit for which there exists a winning strategy for player 1 in q_0. A strategy for player 1 is *optimal* in a state q_0 if it is winning from q_0 with the minimum initial credit.

It is known that the initial credit problem for simple energy games can be solved in NP $\cap$ coNP because memoryless strategies are sufficient to win such games [6,4]. For winning states of energy games, an initial credit of $(|Q|-1) \cdot W$ is always sufficient to win. For parity games, memoryless strategies are also sufficient to win and the associated decision problem also lies in NP $\cap$ coNP [11]. Moreover, energy games and parity games are determined, which implies that from states that are not winning for player 1, there exists a (memoryless) spoiling strategy for player 2 which is winning for the complementary objective (note that the complement of a parity objective is again a parity objective). Moreover, for energy games, the same spoiling strategy can be used against all initial credit values.

3 Strategy Complexity of Energy Parity Games

In this section we show that in energy parity games with n states and d priorities, memory of size $4 \cdot n \cdot d \cdot W$ is sufficient for a winning strategy of player 1 . This amount of memory is exponential (because weights are encoded in binary) and we show that exponential memory is already necessary in the special case of player-1 games where memory of size $2 \cdot (n-1) \cdot W + 1$ may be necessary (and is always sufficient). For player 2, we show that memoryless winning strategies exist. Moreover, if player 1 wins, then the minimum initial credit is at most $(n-1) \cdot W$.

Lemma 1. *Let G be a player-1 energy parity game with n states. If player 1 wins in G from a state q_0, then player 1 has a winning strategy from q_0 with memory of size $2 \cdot (n-1) \cdot W + 1$ and initial credit $(n-1) \cdot W$.*

Example 1 (Memory requirement). We present a family of player-1 games where memory of size $2 \cdot (n-1) \cdot W + 1$ may be necessary. The example is shown in

Fig. 1, and the example also shows that initial credit of $(n-1) \cdot W$ may be necessary. To satisfy the parity condition, the play has to visit the initial state infinitely often, and to maintain the energy positive, the play has to visit the state with the positive-weighted self-loop. Since the paths between these two state have weight $-(n-1) \cdot W$, it is easy to see that initial credit $(n-1) \cdot W$ is necessary, and the self-loop has to be taken $M = 2 \cdot (n-1) \cdot W$ times requiring memory of size $M + 1$. □

We state the next lemma because it is useful in several proofs, though its argument is fairly easy.

Lemma 2. *Let G be an energy parity game, and for each winning state q let $v(q) \in \mathbb{N}$ be the minimum initial credit in q. For all outcomes ρ of an optimal strategy σ in G from a winning state q_0, if the initial credit is $v(q_0) + \Delta$ for $\Delta \geq 0$, then the energy level at all positions of ρ where a state q occurs is at least $v(q) + \Delta$.*

We show that player 2 needs no memory at all in energy parity games. This result is useful to show that energy parity games are in coNP.

Lemma 3. *For all energy parity games G, memoryless strategies are sufficient for player 2 (i.e., the minimum initial credit for player 1 does not change if player 2 is restricted to play memoryless).*

Finally, we give upper bounds on the memory and initial credit necessary for player 1 in energy parity games. The bounds are established using strategies of a special form that alternate between *good-for-energy* strategies and *attractor* strategies, defined as follows.

Good-for-energy strategy. A strategy σ for player 1 is *good-for-energy* in state q if for all outcomes $\rho = q_0 q_1 \dots$ of σ such that $q_0 = q$, for all cycles $\gamma = q_i \dots q_{i+k}$ in ρ (where $k > 0$ and $q_i = q_{i+k}$), either $\mathsf{EL}(\gamma) > 0$, or $\mathsf{EL}(\gamma) = 0$ and γ is even (i.e., $\min\{p(q) \mid q \in \gamma\}$ is even). A key result is to show the existence of good-for-energy strategies that are *memoryless*.

Lemma 4. *Let* Win *be the set of winning states for player 1 in an energy parity game. Then, there exists a memoryless strategy for player 1 which is good-for-energy in every state $q \in \mathsf{Win}$.*

Proof. First, the definition of good-for-energy strategy in a state q can be viewed as a winning strategy in a finite cycle-forming game from q where the game stops when a cycle C is formed, and the winner is determined by the sequence of states in C (and is independent of cyclic permutations). By the results of [2], both players have memoryless optimal strategies in this finite cycle-forming game.

Now, assume that player 1 wins an energy parity game from a state q. Towards contradiction, assume that player 1 has no good-for-energy strategy from q_0. Then, player 2 would have a memoryless winning strategy in the finite cycle-forming game. Fix this strategy in the original energy parity game and then all cycles have either negative weight, or weight is zero and the least priority is odd.

It follows that player 1 looses the energy parity game from q (no matter the value of the initial credit), a contradiction. Hence, player 1 has a memoryless good-for-energy strategy σ_q from q. Finally, to obtain a uniform good-for-energy strategy σ_{gfe}, fix a (total) order on the states: $q_1 < q_2 < \cdots < q_n$, and let $R(q_i)$ be the set of all states occurring in the outcomes of σ_{q_i}. Then $\sigma_{gfe}(q_i) = \sigma_{q_j}(q_i)$ where $j = \min\{k \mid q_i \in R(q_k)\}$. □

Attractor. The player-1 *attractor* of a given set $S \subseteq Q$ is the set of states from which player 1 can force to reach a state in S. It is defined as the limit $Attr_1(S)$ of the sequence $A_0 = S$, $A_{i+1} = A_i \cup \{q \in Q_1 \mid \exists (q, q') \in E : q' \in A_i\} \cup \{q \in Q_2 \mid \forall (q, q') \in E : q' \in A_i\}$ for all $i \geq 0$. The player-2 *attractor* $Attr_2(S)$ is defined symmetrically. Note that for $i = 1, 2$, the subgraph of G induced by $Q \setminus Attr_i(S)$ is again a game graph (i.e., every state has an outgoing edge). It is well known that attractors can be computed in polynomial time.

Lemma 5. *For all energy parity games G with n states and d priorities, if player 1 wins from a state q_0, then player 1 has a winning strategy from q_0 with memory of size $4 \cdot n \cdot d \cdot W$ and initial credit $(n-1) \cdot W$.*

The following theorem summarizes the upper bounds on memory requirement in energy parity games. Note that player 1 may need exponential memory as illustrated in Example 1.

Theorem 1 (Strategy Complexity). *For all energy parity games, the following assertions hold: (1) winning strategies with memory of size $4 \cdot n \cdot d \cdot W$ exist for player 1; (2) memoryless winning strategies exist for player 2.*

4 Computational Complexity of Energy Parity Games

We show that the initial credit problem for energy parity games is in NP ∩ coNP. This may be surprising since exponential memory may be necessary for player 1 to win. However, winning strategies with a special structure (that alternate between good-for-energy strategies and attractor strategies) can be constructed and this entails the NP upper bound.

Lemma 6. *Let G be an energy parity game. The problem of deciding, given a state q_0 and a memoryless strategy σ, whether σ is good-for-energy in q_0, can be solved in polynomial time.*

We first establish the NP membership of the initial credit problem for the case of energy parity games with two priorities. For energy coBüchi games, the result is obtained by showing that memoryless strategies are sufficient, and for energy Büchi games, the proof gives a good flavor of the argument in the general case.

Lemma 7. *Memoryless strategies are sufficient for player 1 to win energy coBüchi games (i.e., the minimum initial credit for player 1 does not change if player 1 is restricted to play memoryless).*

Lemma 8. *The problem of deciding, given a state q in an energy Büchi (resp. coBüchi) game G, if there exists a finite initial credit such that player 1 wins in G from q is in NP.*

Proof. By Lemma 7, an NP-algorithm for energy coBüchi games $\langle G, p, w\rangle$ guesses a memoryless strategy σ and checks in polynomial time that σ is winning for both the energy game $\langle G, w\rangle$ and the coBüchi game $\langle G, p\rangle$. This ensures that all cycles in G_σ are positive (for energy) and visit only priority-2 states, and thus σ is winning in the energy coBüchi game.

For energy Büchi games, let Win be the set of winning states for player 1 in $\langle G, p, w\rangle$, and let G_{Win} be the subgraph of G induced by Win. Clearly there exists a memoryless strategy σ_b in G_{Win} that enforces a visit to a priority-0 state from every state in Win, and there exists a memoryless good-for-energy strategy σ_{gfe} in G_{Win} (by Lemma 4). We show that the converse holds: if such strategies σ_b and σ_{gfe} exist, then player 1 wins in the energy Büchi game $\langle G, p, w\rangle$. Let $n = |Q|$ be the number of states. To prove this, we give an informal description of a winning strategy for player 1 (with initial credit $(n-1)\cdot W$) as follows: (1) play strategy σ_{gfe} as long as the energy level is below $2\cdot(n-1)\cdot W$; (2) if the energy level gets higher than $2\cdot(n-1)\cdot W$, then play σ_b until a priority-0 state is visited (thus σ_b is played during at most $n-1$ steps), and proceed to step (1) with energy level at least $(n-1)\cdot W$.

Let ρ be an outcome of this strategy with initial credit $(n-1)\cdot W$. First, we show that the energy level is nonnegative in every position of ρ. By definition of good-for-energy strategies, in every cycle of $G_{\sigma_{gfe}}$ the sum of the weights is nonnegative. Therefore in the prefixes of ρ corresponding to part (1) of the strategy, the energy level is always nonnegative. Whenever, part (2) of the strategy is played, the energy level is at least $2\cdot(n-1)\cdot W$ and thus after (at most) $n-1$ steps of playing σ_b, the energy level is still at least $(n-1)\cdot W$, and the argument can be repeated. Second, we show that priority-0 states are visited infinitely often in ρ. This is obvious if part (2) of the strategy is played infinitely often; otherwise, from some point in ρ, part (1) of the strategy is played forever which implies that in the cycle decomposition[3] of ρ, ultimately all cycles have sum of weights equal to zero. By definition of good-for-energy strategies, every such cycle is even, i.e., visits a priority-0 state.

Therefore, an NP-algorithm for energy Büchi games guesses the set $\mathsf{Win} \subseteq Q$ and the memoryless strategies σ_b and σ_{gfe} on Win, and checks in polynomial time using standard graph algorithms that σ_b enforces a visit to a priority-0 state in Win, that σ_{gfe} is good-for-energy (see Lemma 6), and that $q \in \mathsf{Win}$. □

Lemma 9. *The problem of deciding, given a state q in an energy parity game G, if there exists a finite initial credit such that player 1 wins in G from q is in NP.*

Theorem 2 (Computational Complexity). *The problem of deciding the existence of a finite initial credit for energy parity games is in NP $\cap$ coNP.*

[3] To obtain the cycle decomposition of a path ρ, we push the states of ρ onto a stack. Whenever we push a state already in the stack, a cycle is formed and we remove it from the stack. We call $C_1, C_2, \ldots$ the sequence of cycles so obtained.

5 Algorithm for Energy Parity Games

We present an algorithm to decide the winner in energy parity games with complexity exponential in the number of states (as for parity games), but linear in the largest weight (as for energy games). Our algorithm is based on a procedure to construct memoryless good-for-energy strategies. To obtain a good-for-energy strategy, we modify the weights in the game so that every simple cycle with (original) sum of weight 0 gets a strictly positive weight if it is even, and a strictly negative weight if it is odd. Formally, the new weight function w' is defined by $w'(q, q') = w(q, q') + \Delta(q)$ where $\Delta(q) = (-1)^k \cdot \left(\frac{1}{n^{k+1}} - \frac{1}{n^{k+2}}\right)$ for all $q, q' \in Q$ with $k = p(q)$ is the priority of q, and $n = |Q|$. Winning strategies in the energy game with modified weights w' correspond to good-for-energy strategies in the original game.

Lemma 10. *The problem of deciding the existence of a memoryless good-for-energy strategy in energy parity games can be solved in time* $O(|E| \cdot |Q|^{d+2} \cdot W)$.

We present a recursive fixpoint algorithm for solving energy parity games, using the result of Lemma 10. Our algorithm is a generalization of the classical algorithm of McNaughton [15] and Zielonka [20] for solving parity games. The formal description of the algorithm is shown as Algorithm 1.

Informal description and correctness of Algorithm 1. We assume without loss of generality that the least priority in the input game graph is either 0 or 1; if not, then we can reduce the priority in every state by 2. The algorithm considers two cases: (a) when the minimum priority is 0, and (b) when the minimum priority is 1. The details of the two cases are as follows:

(a) If the least priority in the game is 0, then we compute the winning states of Player 1 as the limit of a decreasing sequence $A_0, A_1, \ldots$ of sets. Each iteration removes from A_i some states that are winning for Player 2. The set $A'_i \subseteq A_i$ contains the states having a good-for-energy strategy (line 8) which is a necessary condition to win, according to Lemma 4. We decompose A'_i into X_i and $A'_i \setminus X_i$, where X_i is the set of states from which Player 1 can force a visit to priority-0 states, and $A'_i \setminus X_i$ has less priorities than A'_i. The winning states Z_i in $A'_i \setminus X_i$ for Player 2 are also winning in the original game (as in $A'_i \setminus X_i$ Player 1 has no edge going out of $A'_i \setminus X_i$). Therefore we remove Z_i and Player-2 attractor to Z_i in A_{i+1}. The correctness argument for this case is similar to the proof of Lemma 9, namely that when $A_i = A'_i = A_{i-1}$, Player 1 wins by playing a winning strategy in $A'_i \setminus X_i$ (which exists by an inductive argument on the number of recursive calls of the algorithm), and whenever the game enters X_i, then Player 1 can survive while forcing a visit to a priority-0 state, and then uses a good-for-energy strategy to recover enough energy to proceed.

(b) The second part of the algorithm (when the least priority in the game is 1) computes a decreasing sequence $B_0, B_1, \ldots$ of sets containing the winning states of Player 2. The correctness is proven in a symmetric way using the same argument as in the second part of the proof of Lemma 9.

Algorithm 1. SolveEnergyParityGame

Input : An energy parity game $\langle G, p, w\rangle$ with state space Q.
Output : The set of winning states in $\langle G, p, w\rangle$ for player 1.
begin

1 **if** $Q = \emptyset$ **then return** $\emptyset$
2 Let k^* be the minimal priority in G. Assume w.l.o.g. that $k^* \in \{0, 1\}$
3 Let G_0 be the game G
4 $i \leftarrow 0$
5 **if** $k^* = 0$ **then**
6     $A_0 \leftarrow Q$ `/* over-approximation of Player-1 winning states */`
7   **repeat**
8         $A'_i \leftarrow$ SolveEnergyGame(G_i, w') (where w' is defined in Lemma 10)
9         $X_i \leftarrow Attr_1(A'_i \cap p^{-1}(0))$
10   Let G'_i be the subgraph of G_i induced by $A'_i \setminus X_i$
11         $Z_i \leftarrow (A'_i \setminus X_i) \setminus$ SolveEnergyParityGame(G'_i, p, w)
12         $A_{i+1} \leftarrow A'_i \setminus Attr_2(Z_i)$
13   Let G_{i+1} be the subgraph of G_i induced by A_{i+1}
14         $i \leftarrow i + 1$
    until $A_i = A_{i-1}$
15   **return** A_i
16 **if** $k^* = 1$ **then**
17     $B_0 \leftarrow Q$ `/* over-approximation of Player-2 winning states */`
18   **repeat**
19         $Y_i \leftarrow Attr_2(B_i \cap p^{-1}(1))$
20   Let G_{i+1} be the subgraph of G_i induced by $B_i \setminus Y_i$
21         $B_{i+1} \leftarrow B_i \setminus Attr_1($SolveEnergyParityGame$(G_{i+1}, p, w))$
22         $i \leftarrow i + 1$
    until $B_i = B_{i-1}$
23   **return** $Q \setminus B_i$

end

We obtain the following result, where d is the number of priorities in the game, and W is the largest weight.

Theorem 3 (Algorithmic Complexity). *The problem of deciding the existence of a finite initial credit for energy parity games can be solved in time* $O(|E| \cdot d \cdot |Q|^{d+3} \cdot W)$.

Energy Büchi and coBüchi games. In the special case of energy Büchi objectives, since d is constant ($d = 2$), the analysis in the proof of Theorem 3 gives time complexity $O(|E| \cdot |Q|^5 \cdot W)$. In the case of energy coBüchi objectives, the smallest priority is 1 and there is only one other priority. In this case, line 21 of Algorithm 1 requires to solve an energy parity game with one priority which can be solved as simple energy games in $O(|E| \cdot |Q| \cdot W)$. Thus in the special case of energy coBüchi objectives Algorithm 1 has $O(|E| \cdot |Q|^2 \cdot W)$ running time.

Table 1. Strategy, computational and algorithmic complexity of energy parity games

Objective	Player 1 Strategy	Player 2 Strategy	Computational Complexity	Algorithmic Complexity
Energy coBüchi	Memoryless	Memoryless	NP $\cap$ coNP	$O(\|E\| \cdot \|Q\|^2 \cdot W)$
Energy Büchi	Optimal memory: $2 \cdot (\|Q\| - 1) \cdot W + 1$	Memoryless	NP $\cap$ coNP	$O(\|E\| \cdot \|Q\|^5 \cdot W)$
Energy parity	Memory at most: $4 \cdot \|Q\| \cdot d \cdot W$	Memoryless	NP $\cap$ coNP	$O(\|E\| \cdot d \cdot \|Q\|^{d+3} \cdot W)$

Computing the minimum initial credit. Note that if the procedure SolveEnergyGame used in Algorithm 1 also computes the minimum initial credit $v(q)$ in each winning state q of the energy game $\langle G_i, w' \rangle$ (and it is the case of the algorithm in [7,10]), then we can also obtain the minimum initial credit in the energy parity game $\langle G, p, w \rangle$ by rounding $v(q)$ to an integer, either up or down. Therefore, computing the minimum initial credit in energy parity games can be done in time $O(|E| \cdot d \cdot |Q|^{d+3} \cdot W)$.

Our results about the memory requirement of strategies, and the computational and algorithmic complexity of energy parity games are summarized in Table 1.

6 Relationship with Mean-Payoff Parity Games

We show that there is a tight relationship between energy parity games and mean-payoff parity games. The work in [8] shows that optimal[4] strategies in mean-payoff parity games may require infinite memory, though they can be decomposed into several memoryless strategies. We show that energy parity games are polynomially equivalent to mean-payoff parity games, leading to NP $\cap$ coNP membership of the problem of deciding the winner in mean-payoff parity games, and leading to an algorithm for solving such games which is conceptually much simpler than the algorithm of [8], with essentially the same complexity (linear in the largest weight, and exponential in the number of states only).

Theorem 4. *Let $\langle G, p, w \rangle$ be a game, and let $\epsilon = \frac{1}{|Q|+1}$. Player 1 has a winning strategy in the mean-payoff parity game $\langle G, p, w \rangle$ if and only if player 1 has a winning strategy in the energy parity game $\langle G, p, w + \epsilon \rangle$.*

Corollary 1. *Given a mean-payoff parity game, whether player 1 has a winning strategy from a state q_0 can be decided in NP $\cap$ coNP.*

Corollary 2. *The problem of deciding the winner in mean-payoff parity games can be solved in time $O(|E| \cdot d \cdot |Q|^{d+3} \cdot W \cdot (|Q| + 1))$.*

Acknowledgements. We thank Thomas A. Henzinger and Barbara Jobstmann for inspiring discussions, and Patricia Bouyer, Nicolas Markey, Jörg Olschewski, and Michael Ummels for helpful comments on a preliminary draft.

[4] A strategy is optimal if it is winning for $\mathsf{Parity}_G(p) \cap \mathsf{MeanPayoff}_G(\nu)$ with the largest threshold ν. It is known that the largest threshold is rational [8].

References

1. Abadi, M., Lamport, L., Wolper, P.: Realizable and unrealizable specifications of reactive systems. In: Ronchi Della Rocca, S., Ausiello, G., Dezani-Ciancaglini, M. (eds.) ICALP 1989. LNCS, vol. 372, pp. 1–17. Springer, Heidelberg (1989)
2. Björklund, H., Sandberg, S., Vorobyov, S.G.: Memoryless determinacy of parity and mean payoff games: a simple proof. Theor. Comput. Sci. 310(1-3), 365–378 (2004)
3. Bloem, R., Chatterjee, K., Henzinger, T.A., Jobstmann, B.: Better quality in synthesis through quantitative objectives. In: Bouajjani, A., Maler, O. (eds.) CAV 2009. LNCS, vol. 5643, pp. 140–156. Springer, Heidelberg (2009)
4. Bouyer, P., Fahrenberg, U., Larsen, K.G., Markey, N., Srba, J.: Infinite runs in weighted timed automata with energy constraints. In: Cassez, F., Jard, C. (eds.) FORMATS 2008. LNCS, vol. 5215, pp. 33–47. Springer, Heidelberg (2008)
5. Büchi, J.R., Landweber, L.H.: Solving sequential conditions by finite-state strategies. SIAM Journal on Control and Optimization 25(1), 206–230 (1987)
6. Chakrabarti, A., de Alfaro, L., Henzinger, T.A., Stoelinga, M.: Resource interfaces. In: Alur, R., Lee, I. (eds.) EMSOFT 2003. LNCS, vol. 2855, pp. 117–133. Springer, Heidelberg (2003)
7. Chaloupka, J., Brim, L.: Faster algorithm for mean-payoff games. In: Proc. of MEMICS, pp. 45–53. Nov. Press (2009)
8. Chatterjee, K., Henzinger, T.A., Jurdzinski, M.: Mean-payoff parity games. In: Proc. of LICS, pp. 178–187. IEEE Computer Society, Los Alamitos (2005)
9. Condon, A.: The complexity of stochastic games. Inf. Comput. 96(2), 203–224 (1992)
10. Doyen, L., Gentilini, R., Raskin, J.-F.: Faster pseudopolynomial algorithms for mean-payoff games. Technical Report 2009.120, Université Libre de Bruxelles (ULB), Bruxelles, Belgium (2009)
11. Emerson, E.A., Jutla, C.: Tree automata, mu-calculus and determinacy. In: Proc. of FOCS, pp. 368–377. IEEE, Los Alamitos (1991)
12. Emerson, E.A., Jutla, C.S., Sistla, A.P.: On model-checking for fragments of μ-calculus. In: Courcoubetis, C. (ed.) CAV 1993. LNCS, vol. 697, pp. 385–396. Springer, Heidelberg (1993)
13. Grädel, E., Thomas, W., Wilke, T. (eds.): Automata, Logics, and Infinite Games. LNCS, vol. 2500. Springer, Heidelberg (2002)
14. Gurevich, Y., Harrington, L.: Trees, automata, and games. In: Proc. of STOC, pp. 60–65. ACM Press, New York (1982)
15. McNaughton, R.: Infinite games played on finite graphs. Annals of Pure and Applied Logic 65(2), 149–184 (1993)
16. Pnueli, A., Rosner, R.: On the synthesis of a reactive module. In: Proc. of POPL, pp. 179–190 (1989)
17. Ramadge, P.J., Wonham, W.M.: Supervisory control of a class of discrete event processes. SIAM Journal on Control and Optimization 25(1), 206–230 (1987)
18. Shapley, L.S.: Stochastic games. Proc. of the National Acadamy of Science USA 39, 1095–1100 (1953)
19. Thomas, W.: Languages, automata, and logic. In: Handbook of Formal Languages, Beyond Words, ch.7, vol. 3, pp. 389–455. Springer, Heidelberg (1997)
20. Zielonka, W.: Infinite games on finitely coloured graphs with applications to automata on infinite trees. Theor. Comput. Sci. 200, 135–183 (1998)
21. Zwick, U., Paterson, M.: The complexity of mean payoff games on graphs. Theor. Comput. Sci. 158(1&2), 343–359 (1996)

Author Index

Printing: Mercedes-Druck, Berlin
Binding: Stein + Lehmann, Berlin